Lecture Notes in Computer Science   8282

Commenced Publication in 1973
Founding and Former Series Editors:
Gerhard Goos, Juris Hartmanis, and Jan van Leeuwen

For further volumes:
http://www.springer.com/series/7410

tical and Computational Sciences Centre (IRMACS) at Simon Fraser Uni-
The conference was held in co-operation with the International Association
tologic Research (IACR). Hugh Williams from the Tutte Institute delivered
ed lecture "The Tutte Institute for Mathematics and Computing."
al thanks go to Carlisle Adams, Huapeng Wu, and Ali Miri for generously
their experience in organizing SAC conferences with us. We would also like
Springer for publishing the SAC proceedings series since 1998 in the *Lecture*
Computer Science series.
would like to thank Pam Borghardt, Zena Bruneau, and Kelly Gardiner for their
tireless work in taking care of the local arrangements.

ber 2013

Tanja Lange
Kristin Lauter
Petr Lisoněk

Tanja Lange · Kristin Lauter
Petr Lisoněk (Eds.)

Selected Areas in Cryptography – SAC 2013

20th International Conference
Burnaby, BC, Canada, August 14–16, 2013
Revised Selected Papers

 Springer

Editors
Tanja Lange
Technische Universiteit Eindhoven
Eindhoven
The Netherlands

Kristin Lauter
Microsoft Research
Redmond, WA
USA

Petr Lisoněk
Simon Fraser University
Burnaby, BC
Canada

ISSN 0302-9743   ISSN 1611-3349 (electronic)
ISBN 978-3-662-43413-0   ISBN 978-3-662-43414-7 (eBook)
DOI 10.1007/978-3-662-43414-7
Springer Heidelberg New York Dordrecht London

Library of Congress Control Number: 2014939415

LNCS Sublibrary: SL4 – Security and Cryptology

Preface

Previously called the Workshop on Selected Areas in Crypt... on Selected Areas in Cryptography (SAC) series was initiate... workshop was held at Queen's University in Kingston. The S... held annually since 1994 in various Canadian locations, inclu... Montreal, Ottawa, Sackville, St. John's, Toronto, Waterlo... information on SAC conferences can be found at the main SA... at http://sacconference.org/.

SAC 2013 was the 20th conference in this series, and for t... was extended to a two-and-half day conference, which... participants.

This volume contains revised versions of papers presentec... during August 14–16, 2013, at Simon Fraser University in B... objective of the conference is to present cutting-edge research in... of cryptography and to facilitate future research through an in... conference setting.

The themes for the SAC 2013 conference were:

- Design and analysis of symmetric key primitives and crypto... block and stream ciphers, hash functions and MAC algorithms
- Efficient implementations of symmetric and public key algorith...
- Mathematical and algorithmic aspects of applied cryptology
- Elliptic and hyperelliptic curve cryptography, including theory a... pairings

There were 105 paper submissions, of which seven were withd... submission deadline, and 98 submissions were refereed. Each... reviewed by at least three Program Committee members. Submissic... by a Program Committee member were reviewed by at least five Pro... members. Upon recommendations of the Program Committee, ... accepted making the acceptance rate $26/98 = 26.5$ %. The program al... invited lectures, which were given by Paulo Barreto, Anne Canteaut... and Douglas Stinson. The speakers were invited to submit papers to th... these invited papers underwent a thorough reviewing process.

We greatly appreciate the hard work of the SAC 2013 Program Com... also very grateful to the many others who participated in the review... reviewing process was run using the iChair software, written by Thon... from CryptoExperts, France, and Matthieu Finiasz from EPFL, LASEC... We are grateful to them for letting us use their software.

SAC 2013 was generously supported by its sponsors and partner... Research, Tutte Institute for Mathematics and Computing, Simon Frase... Pacific Institute for the Mathematical Sciences, and Interdisciplinary Res...

SAC 2013
Conference on Selected Areas in Cryptography

Burnaby, Canada
August 14–16, 2013

Program Chairs

Tanja Lange	Technische Universiteit Eindhoven, The Netherlands
Kristin Lauter	Microsoft Research, USA
Petr Lisoněk	Simon Fraser University, Canada

Program Committee

Carlisle Adams	University of Ottawa, Canada
Jean-Philippe Aumasson	Kudelski Security, Switzerland
Paulo S.L.M. Barreto	University of São Paulo, Brazil
Lejla Batina	Radboud University Nijmegen, The Netherlands and KU Leuven, Belgium
Daniel J. Bernstein	University of Illinois at Chicago, USA and Technische Universiteit Eindhoven, The Netherlands
Andrey Bogdanov	Technical University of Denmark, Denmark
Joppe Bos	Microsoft Research, USA
Christophe De Cannière	Google Switzerland, Switzerland
Anne Canteaut	Inria Paris-Rocquencourt, France
Sanjit Chatterjee	Indian Institute of Science, India
Carlos Cid	Royal Holloway, University of London, UK
Craig Costello	Microsoft Research, USA
Joan Daemen	ST Microelectronics, Belgium
Vassil Dimitrov	University of Calgary, Canada
Orr Dunkelman	University of Haifa, Israel
Andreas Enge	Inria Bordeaux-Sud-Ouest and University of Bordeaux, France
Matthieu Finiasz	CryptoExperts, France
Guang Gong	University of Waterloo, Canada
Tim Güneysu	Ruhr University Bochum, Germany
Huseyin Hisil	Yasar University, Turkey
Sorina Ionica	ENS Paris, France
Mike Jacobson	University of Calgary, Canada
Dmitry Khovratovich	University of Luxembourg, Luxembourg

Tanja Lange (co-chair)	Technische Universiteit Eindhoven, The Netherlands
Kristin Lauter (co-chair)	Microsoft Research, USA
Gregor Leander	Ruhr University Bochum, Germany
Hyang-Sook Lee	Ewha Womans University, Republic of Korea
Jooyoung Lee	Sejong University, Seoul, Republic of Korea
Gaëtan Leurent	UCL Crypto Group, Belgium
Petr Lisoněk (co-chair)	Simon Fraser University, Canada
Stefan Lucks	University Weimar, Germany
Alfred Menezes	University of Waterloo, Canada
Michael Naehrig	Microsoft Research, USA
María Naya-Plasencia	Inria Paris-Rocquencourt, France
Kaisa Nyberg	Aalto University, Finland
Roger Oyono	Université de la Polynésie Française, French Polynesia
Daniel Page	University of Bristol, UK
Christiane Peters	Technical University of Denmark, Denmark
Bart Preneel	KU Leuven, Belgium
Christian Rechberger	Technical University of Denmark, Denmark
Christophe Ritzenthaler	Institut de Mathématiques de Luminy, France
Damien Robert	Inria Bordeaux Sud-Ouest, France
Francisco Rodríguez-Henríquez	CINVESTAV-IPN, Mexico
Yu Sasaki	NTT Secure Platform Laboratories, Japan
Renate Scheidler	University of Calgary, Canada
Martin Schläffer	Graz University of Technology, Austria
Peter Schwabe	Radboud University Nijmegen, The Netherlands
Douglas R. Stinson	University of Waterloo, Canada
Andrew Sutherland	MIT, USA
Vanessa Vitse	Université Joseph Fourier, France
Michael J. Wiener	Irdeto, Canada

External Reviewers

Hoda A. Alkhzaimi	Céline Blondeau	Sebastian Faust
Farzaneh Abed	Andrey Bogdanov	Robert Fitzpatrick
Jithra Adikari	Charles Bouillaguet	Christian Forler
Gora Adj	Christina Boura	Steven Galbraith
Elena Andreeva	Donghoon Chang	Nadia Heninger
Kazumaro Aoki	Jung Hee Cheon	Andreas Hülsing
Thomas Baignères	Itai Dinur	Fei Huo
Guido Bertoni	Christophe Doche	Kimmo Järvinen
Rishiraj Bhattacharyya	Baris Ege	Koray Karabina
Begul Bilgin	Maria Eichlseder	Elif Bilge Kavun
Gaetan Bisson	Xinxin Fan	Nathan Keller

Taechan Kim
Thomas Korak
Soonhak Kwon
Pascal Lafourcade
Martin Gagné
Cédric Lauradoux
Martin M. Lauridsen
Tancréde Lepoint
Yang Li
Seongan Lim
Eik List
Jake Loftus
Adriana Lopez-Alt
Cuauhtemoc Mancillas
Ingo von Maurich
Florian Mendel
Oliver Mischke
Amir Moradi
Sayantan Mukherjee

Sean Murphy
Samuel Neves
Thomaz Oliveira
Cheol-Min Park
Souradyuti Paul
Thomas Pöppelmann
Gordon Procter
Francesco Regazzoni
Matthieu Rivain
Joern-Marc Schmidt
Michael Schneider
Kyoji Shibutani
Boris Skoric
Hadi Soleimany
Raphael Spreitzer
Damien Stehle
Valentin Suder
Yin Tan
Enrico Thomae

Nicolas Thériault
Mehdi Tibouchi
Elmar Tischhauser
Deniz Toz
Michael Tunstall
Gilles Van Assche
Kerem Varici
Damien Vergnaud
Vincent Verneuil
Vanessa Vitse
Jakob Wenzel
Carolyn Whitnall
Brecht Wyseur
Tolga Yalcin
Bo-Yin Yang
Masaya Yasuda
Yongjin Yeom
Bo Zhu
Ralf Zimmermann

Tanja Lange · Kristin Lauter
Petr Lisoněk (Eds.)

Selected Areas in Cryptography – SAC 2013

20th International Conference
Burnaby, BC, Canada, August 14–16, 2013
Revised Selected Papers

 Springer

Editors

Tanja Lange
Technische Universiteit Eindhoven
Eindhoven
The Netherlands

Petr Lisoněk
Simon Fraser University
Burnaby, BC
Canada

Kristin Lauter
Microsoft Research
Redmond, WA
USA

ISSN 0302-9743   ISSN 1611-3349   (electronic)
ISBN 978-3-662-43413-0   ISBN 978-3-662-43414-7   (eBook)
DOI 10.1007/978-3-662-43414-7
Springer Heidelberg New York Dordrecht London

Library of Congress Control Number: 2014939415

LNCS Sublibrary: SL4 – Security and Cryptology

Printed on acid-free paper

Springer is part of Springer Science+Business Media (www.springer.com)

Preface

Previously called the Workshop on Selected Areas in Cryptography, the Conference on Selected Areas in Cryptography (SAC) series was initiated in 1994, when the first workshop was held at Queen's University in Kingston. The SAC conference has been held annually since 1994 in various Canadian locations, including Calgary, Kingston, Montreal, Ottawa, Sackville, St. John's, Toronto, Waterloo, and Windsor. More information on SAC conferences can be found at the main SAC conferences website at http://sacconference.org/.

SAC 2013 was the 20th conference in this series, and for this special occasion it was extended to a two-and-half day conference, which was attended by 65 participants.

This volume contains revised versions of papers presented at SAC 2013, held during August 14–16, 2013, at Simon Fraser University in Burnaby, Canada. The objective of the conference is to present cutting-edge research in the designated areas of cryptography and to facilitate future research through an informal and friendly conference setting.

The themes for the SAC 2013 conference were:

- Design and analysis of symmetric key primitives and cryptosystems, including block and stream ciphers, hash functions and MAC algorithms
- Efficient implementations of symmetric and public key algorithms
- Mathematical and algorithmic aspects of applied cryptology
- Elliptic and hyperelliptic curve cryptography, including theory and applications of pairings

There were 105 paper submissions, of which seven were withdrawn prior to the submission deadline, and 98 submissions were refereed. Each submission was reviewed by at least three Program Committee members. Submissions (co-)authored by a Program Committee member were reviewed by at least five Program Committee members. Upon recommendations of the Program Committee, 26 papers were accepted making the acceptance rate $26/98 = 26.5$ %. The program also included four invited lectures, which were given by Paulo Barreto, Anne Canteaut, Antoine Joux, and Douglas Stinson. The speakers were invited to submit papers to the proceedings; these invited papers underwent a thorough reviewing process.

We greatly appreciate the hard work of the SAC 2013 Program Committee. We are also very grateful to the many others who participated in the review process. The reviewing process was run using the iChair software, written by Thomas Baignères from CryptoExperts, France, and Matthieu Finiasz from EPFL, LASEC, Switzerland. We are grateful to them for letting us use their software.

SAC 2013 was generously supported by its sponsors and partners: Microsoft Research, Tutte Institute for Mathematics and Computing, Simon Fraser University, Pacific Institute for the Mathematical Sciences, and Interdisciplinary Research in the

Mathematical and Computational Sciences Centre (IRMACS) at Simon Fraser University. The conference was held in co-operation with the International Association for Cryptologic Research (IACR). Hugh Williams from the Tutte Institute delivered the invited lecture "The Tutte Institute for Mathematics and Computing."

Special thanks go to Carlisle Adams, Huapeng Wu, and Ali Miri for generously sharing their experience in organizing SAC conferences with us. We would also like to thank Springer for publishing the SAC proceedings series since 1998 in the *Lecture Notes in Computer Science* series.

We would like to thank Pam Borghardt, Zena Bruneau, and Kelly Gardiner for their hard and tireless work in taking care of the local arrangements.

November 2013

Tanja Lange
Kristin Lauter
Petr Lisoněk

SAC 2013
Conference on Selected Areas in Cryptography

Burnaby, Canada
August 14–16, 2013

Program Chairs

Tanja Lange	Technische Universiteit Eindhoven, The Netherlands
Kristin Lauter	Microsoft Research, USA
Petr Lisoněk	Simon Fraser University, Canada

Program Committee

Carlisle Adams	University of Ottawa, Canada
Jean-Philippe Aumasson	Kudelski Security, Switzerland
Paulo S.L.M. Barreto	University of São Paulo, Brazil
Lejla Batina	Radboud University Nijmegen, The Netherlands and KU Leuven, Belgium
Daniel J. Bernstein	University of Illinois at Chicago, USA and Technische Universiteit Eindhoven, The Netherlands
Andrey Bogdanov	Technical University of Denmark, Denmark
Joppe Bos	Microsoft Research, USA
Christophe De Cannière	Google Switzerland, Switzerland
Anne Canteaut	Inria Paris-Rocquencourt, France
Sanjit Chatterjee	Indian Institute of Science, India
Carlos Cid	Royal Holloway, University of London, UK
Craig Costello	Microsoft Research, USA
Joan Daemen	ST Microelectronics, Belgium
Vassil Dimitrov	University of Calgary, Canada
Orr Dunkelman	University of Haifa, Israel
Andreas Enge	Inria Bordeaux-Sud-Ouest and University of Bordeaux, France
Matthieu Finiasz	CryptoExperts, France
Guang Gong	University of Waterloo, Canada
Tim Güneysu	Ruhr University Bochum, Germany
Huseyin Hisil	Yasar University, Turkey
Sorina Ionica	ENS Paris, France
Mike Jacobson	University of Calgary, Canada
Dmitry Khovratovich	University of Luxembourg, Luxembourg

Tanja Lange (co-chair)	Technische Universiteit Eindhoven, The Netherlands
Kristin Lauter (co-chair)	Microsoft Research, USA
Gregor Leander	Ruhr University Bochum, Germany
Hyang-Sook Lee	Ewha Womans University, Republic of Korea
Jooyoung Lee	Sejong University, Seoul, Republic of Korea
Gaëtan Leurent	UCL Crypto Group, Belgium
Petr Lisoněk (co-chair)	Simon Fraser University, Canada
Stefan Lucks	University Weimar, Germany
Alfred Menezes	University of Waterloo, Canada
Michael Naehrig	Microsoft Research, USA
María Naya-Plasencia	Inria Paris-Rocquencourt, France
Kaisa Nyberg	Aalto University, Finland
Roger Oyono	Université de la Polynésie Française, French Polynesia
Daniel Page	University of Bristol, UK
Christiane Peters	Technical University of Denmark, Denmark
Bart Preneel	KU Leuven, Belgium
Christian Rechberger	Technical University of Denmark, Denmark
Christophe Ritzenthaler	Institut de Mathématiques de Luminy, France
Damien Robert	Inria Bordeaux Sud-Ouest, France
Francisco Rodríguez-Henríquez	CINVESTAV-IPN, Mexico
Yu Sasaki	NTT Secure Platform Laboratories, Japan
Renate Scheidler	University of Calgary, Canada
Martin Schläffer	Graz University of Technology, Austria
Peter Schwabe	Radboud University Nijmegen, The Netherlands
Douglas R. Stinson	University of Waterloo, Canada
Andrew Sutherland	MIT, USA
Vanessa Vitse	Université Joseph Fourier, France
Michael J. Wiener	Irdeto, Canada

External Reviewers

Hoda A. Alkhzaimi	Céline Blondeau	Sebastian Faust
Farzaneh Abed	Andrey Bogdanov	Robert Fitzpatrick
Jithra Adikari	Charles Bouillaguet	Christian Forler
Gora Adj	Christina Boura	Steven Galbraith
Elena Andreeva	Donghoon Chang	Nadia Heninger
Kazumaro Aoki	Jung Hee Cheon	Andreas Hülsing
Thomas Baignères	Itai Dinur	Fei Huo
Guido Bertoni	Christophe Doche	Kimmo Järvinen
Rishiraj Bhattacharyya	Baris Ege	Koray Karabina
Begul Bilgin	Maria Eichlseder	Elif Bilge Kavun
Gaetan Bisson	Xinxin Fan	Nathan Keller

Taechan Kim
Thomas Korak
Soonhak Kwon
Pascal Lafourcade
Martin Gagné
Cédric Lauradoux
Martin M. Lauridsen
Tancréde Lepoint
Yang Li
Seongan Lim
Eik List
Jake Loftus
Adriana Lopez-Alt
Cuauhtemoc Mancillas
Ingo von Maurich
Florian Mendel
Oliver Mischke
Amir Moradi
Sayantan Mukherjee

Sean Murphy
Samuel Neves
Thomaz Oliveira
Cheol-Min Park
Souradyuti Paul
Thomas Pöppelmann
Gordon Procter
Francesco Regazzoni
Matthieu Rivain
Joern-Marc Schmidt
Michael Schneider
Kyoji Shibutani
Boris Skoric
Hadi Soleimany
Raphael Spreitzer
Damien Stehle
Valentin Suder
Yin Tan
Enrico Thomae

Nicolas Thériault
Mehdi Tibouchi
Elmar Tischhauser
Deniz Toz
Michael Tunstall
Gilles Van Assche
Kerem Varici
Damien Vergnaud
Vincent Verneuil
Vanessa Vitse
Jakob Wenzel
Carolyn Whitnall
Brecht Wyseur
Tolga Yalcin
Bo-Yin Yang
Masaya Yasuda
Yongjin Yeom
Bo Zhu
Ralf Zimmermann

Abstract of Invited Talk

Similarities Between Encryption and Decryption: How Far Can We Go?

Anne Canteaut

INRIA Paris-Rocquencourt, France
anne.canteaut@inria.fr

Abstract. In this talk, I will investigate some approaches for reducing the hardware footprint of a block cipher for different constraints of the targeted applications. In this context, I will focus on the strategies which can be used for minimizing the overhead for decryption on top of encryption. These strategies include involutive ciphers and the construction used in PRINCE. In particular, I will discuss the potential weaknesses which might be introduced by this type of constructions.

Contents

Invited Talk

The Realm of the Pairings 3
    Diego F. Aranha, Paulo S.L.M. Barreto, Patrick Longa,
    and Jefferson E. Ricardini

Lattices Part I

A Three-Level Sieve Algorithm for the Shortest Vector Problem 29
    Feng Zhang, Yanbin Pan, and Gengran Hu

Improvement and Efficient Implementation of a Lattice-Based
Signature Scheme 48
    Rachid El Bansarkhani and Johannes Buchmann

Towards Practical Lattice-Based Public-Key Encryption on Reconfigurable
Hardware 68
    Thomas Pöppelmann and Tim Güneysu

Invited Talk

Practical Approaches to Varying Network Size in Combinatorial Key
Predistribution Schemes 89
    Kevin Henry, Maura B. Paterson, and Douglas R. Stinson

Discrete Logarithms

A Group Action on $\mathbb{Z}_p^\times$ and the Generalized DLP with Auxiliary Inputs 121
    Jung Hee Cheon, Taechan Kim, and Yong Soo Song

Solving a 6120-bit DLP on a Desktop Computer 136
    Faruk Göloğlu, Robert Granger, Gary McGuire, and Jens Zumbrägel

Stream Ciphers and Authenticated Encryption

How to Recover Any Byte of Plaintext on RC4 155
    Toshihiro Ohigashi, Takanori Isobe, Yuhei Watanabe, and Masakatu Morii

The LOCAL Attack: Cryptanalysis of the Authenticated Encryption
Scheme ALE 174
    Dmitry Khovratovich and Christian Rechberger

AEGIS: A Fast Authenticated Encryption Algorithm................. 185
  Hongjun Wu and Bart Preneel

Post–quantum (Hash-Based and System Solving)

Fast Exhaustive Search for Quadratic Systems in $\mathbb{F}_2$ on FPGAs.......... 205
  Charles Bouillaguet, Chen-Mou Cheng, Tung Chou, Ruben Niederhagen, and Bo-Yin Yang

Faster Hash-Based Signatures with Bounded Leakage................. 223
  Thomas Eisenbarth, Ingo von Maurich, and Xin Ye

White Box Crypto

White-Box Security Notions for Symmetric Encryption Schemes......... 247
  Cécile Delerablée, Tancrède Lepoint, Pascal Paillier, and Matthieu Rivain

Two Attacks on a White-Box AES Implementation 265
  Tancrède Lepoint, Matthieu Rivain, Yoni De Mulder, Peter Roelse, and Bart Preneel

Block Ciphers

Extended Generalized Feistel Networks Using Matrix Representation...... 289
  Thierry P. Berger, Marine Minier, and Gaël Thomas

Zero-Correlation Linear Cryptanalysis with FFT and Improved Attacks
on ISO Standards Camellia and CLEFIA......................... 306
  Andrey Bogdanov, Huizheng Geng, Meiqin Wang, Long Wen, and Baudoin Collard

Implementing Lightweight Block Ciphers on x86 Architectures 324
  Ryad Benadjila, Jian Guo, Victor Lomné, and Thomas Peyrin

Invited Talk

A New Index Calculus Algorithm with Complexity $L(1/4 + o(1))$
in Small Characteristic 355
  Antoine Joux

Lattices Part II

High Precision Discrete Gaussian Sampling on FPGAs............... 383
  Sujoy Sinha Roy, Frederik Vercauteren, and Ingrid Verbauwhede

Discrete Ziggurat: A Time-Memory Trade-Off for Sampling
from a Gaussian Distribution over the Integers...................   402
    Johannes Buchmann, Daniel Cabarcas, Florian Göpfert,
    Andreas Hülsing, and Patrick Weiden

Elliptic Curves, Pairings and RSA

A High-Speed Elliptic Curve Cryptographic Processor for Generic Curves
over GF(p)..   421
    Yuan Ma, Zongbin Liu, Wuqiong Pan, and Jiwu Jing

Exponentiating in Pairing Groups..............................   438
    Joppe W. Bos, Craig Costello, and Michael Naehrig

Faster Repeated Doublings on Binary Elliptic Curves.................   456
    Christophe Doche and Daniel Sutantyo

Montgomery Multiplication Using Vector Instructions   471
    Joppe W. Bos, Peter L. Montgomery, Daniel Shumow,
    and Gregory M. Zaverucha

Hash Functions and MACs

Improved Single-Key Distinguisher on HMAC-MD5 and Key Recovery
Attacks on Sandwich-MAC-MD5..............................   493
    Yu Sasaki and Lei Wang

Provable Second Preimage Resistance Revisited....................   513
    Charles Bouillaguet and Bastien Vayssière

Multiple Limited-Birthday Distinguishers and Applications   533
    Jérémy Jean, María Naya-Plasencia, and Thomas Peyrin

Side-Channel Attacks

Horizontal Collision Correlation Attack on Elliptic Curves   553
    Aurélie Bauer, Eliane Jaulmes, Emmanuel Prouff, and Justine Wild

When Reverse-Engineering Meets Side-Channel Analysis –
Digital Lockpicking in Practice   571
    David Oswald, Daehyun Strobel, Falk Schellenberg, Timo Kasper,
    and Christof Paar

Author Index   589

Invited Talk

The Realm of the Pairings

Diego F. Aranha[1], Paulo S.L.M. Barreto[2]([⊠]), Patrick Longa[3],
and Jefferson E. Ricardini[2]

[1] Department of Computer Science, University of Brasília, Brasília, Brazil
dfaranha@unb.br
[2] Departamento de Engenharia de Computação e Sistemas Digitais,
Escola Politécnica, University of São Paulo, São Paulo, Brazil
{pbarreto,jricardini}@larc.usp.br
[3] Microsoft Research, One Microsoft Way, Redmond, USA
plonga@microsoft.com

Abstract. Bilinear maps, or pairings, initially proposed in a cryptologic
context for cryptanalytic purposes, proved afterward to be an amazingly
flexible and useful tool for the construction of cryptosystems with unique
features. Yet, they are notoriously hard to implement efficiently, so that
their effective deployment requires a careful choice of parameters and
algorithms. In this paper we review the evolution of pairing-based cryptosystems, the development of efficient algorithms and the state of the
art in pairing computation, and the challenges yet to be addressed on the
subject, while also presenting some new algorithmic and implementation
refinements in affine and projective coordinates.

Keywords: Pairing-based cryptosystems · Efficient algorithms

1 Introduction

Bilinear maps, or *pairings*, between the (divisors on the) groups of points
of certain algebraic curves over a finite field, particularly the Weil pairing [94]
and the Tate (or Tate-Lichtenbaum) pairing [45], have been introduced in a
cryptological scope for destructive cryptanalytic purposes, namely, mapping the
discrete logarithm problem on those groups to the discrete logarithm problem
on the multiplicative group of a certain extension of the base field [46,66]: while
the best generic classical (non-quantum) algorithm for the discrete logarithm
problem on the former groups may be exponential, in the latter case subexponential algorithms are known, so that such a mapping may yield a problem that
is asymptotically easier to solve.

It turned out, perhaps surprisingly, that these same tools have a much more
relevant role in a constructive cryptographic context, as the basis for the definition of cryptosystems with unique properties. This has been shown in the

---

Supported by CNPq research productivity grant 306935/2012-0.

T. Lange, K. Lauter, and P. Lisoněk (Eds.): SAC 2013, LNCS 8282, pp. 3–25, 2014.
DOI: 10.1007/978-3-662-43414-7_1, © Springer-Verlag Berlin Heidelberg 2014

seminal works on identity-based non-interactive authenticated key agreement by Sakai, Ohgishi and Kasahara [84], and on one-round tripartite key agreement by Joux [56], which then led to an explosion of protocols exploring the possibilities of *identity-based cryptography* and many other schemes, with ever more complex features.

All this flexibility comes at a price: pairings are notoriously expensive in implementation complexity and processing time (and/or storage occupation, in a trade-off between time and space requirements). This imposes a very careful choice of algorithms and curves to make them really practical. The pioneering approach by Miller [67,68] showed that pairings could be computed in polynomial time, but there is a large gap from there to a truly efficient implementation approach.

Indeed, progress in this line of research has not only revealed theoretical bounds on how efficiently a pairing can be computed in the sense of its overall order of complexity [93], but actually the literature has now very detailed approaches on how to attain truly practical, extremely optimized implementations that cover all operations typically found in a pairing-based cryptosystem, rather than just the pairing itself [4,80]. One can therefore reasonably ask how far this trend can be pushed, and how "notoriously expensive" pairings really are (or even whether they really are as expensive as the folklore pictures them).

Our Contribution. In this paper we review the evolution of pairing-based cryptosystems, the development of efficient algorithms for the computation of pairings and the state of the art in the area, and the challenges yet to be addressed on the subject.

Furthermore, we provide some new refinements to the pairing computation in affine and projective coordinates over ordinary curves, perform an up-to-date analysis of the best algorithms for the realization of pairings with special focus on the 128-bit security level and present a very efficient implementation for x64 platforms.

Organization. The remainder of this paper is organized as follows. Section 2 introduces essential notions on elliptic curves and bilinear maps for cryptographic applications, including some of the main pairing-based cryptographic protocols and their underlying security assumptions. Section 3 reviews the main proposals for pairing-friendly curves and the fundamental algorithms for their construction and manipulation. In Sect. 4, we describe some optimizations to formulas in affine and projective coordinates, carry out a performance analysis of the best available algorithms and discuss benchmarking results of our high-speed implementation targeting the 128-bit security level on various x64 platforms. We conclude in Sect. 5.

2 Preliminary Concepts

Let $q = p^m$. An *elliptic curve* $E/\mathbb{F}_q$ is a smooth projective algebraic curve of genus one with at least one point. The affine part satisfies an equation of the form $E : y^2 + a_1xy + a_3y = x^3 + a_2x^2 + a_4x + a_6$ where $a_i \in \mathbb{F}_q$. Points on E are affine points $(x, y) \in \mathbb{F}_q^2$ satisfying the curve equation, together with an additional point at infinity, denoted ∞. The set of curve points whose coordinates lie in a particular extension field $\mathbb{F}_{q^k}$ is denoted $E(\mathbb{F}_{q^k})$ for $k > 0$ (note that the a_i remain in $\mathbb{F}_q$). Let $\#E(\mathbb{F}_q) = n$ and write n as $n = p+1-t$; t is called the *trace* of the Frobenius endomorphism. By Hasse's theorem, $|t| \leqslant 2\sqrt{q}$.

An (additive) Abelian group structure is defined on E by the well known chord-and-tangent method [91]. The order of a point $P \in E$ is the least nonzero integer r such that $[r]P = \infty$, where $[r]P$ is the sum of r terms equal to P. The order r of a point divides the curve order n. For a given integer r, the set of all points $P \in E$ such that $[r]P = \infty$ is denoted $E[r]$. We say that $E[r]$ has *embedding degree* k if $r \mid q^k - 1$ and $r \nmid q^s - 1$ for any $0 < s < k$.

The *complex multiplication* (CM) method [37] constructs an elliptic curve with a given number of points n over a given finite field $\mathbb{F}_q$ as long as $n = q+1-t$ as required by the Hasse bound, and the norm equation $DV^2 = 4q - t^2$ can be solved for "small" values of the discriminant D, from which the j-invariant of the curve (which is a function of the coefficients of the curve equation) can be computed, and the curve equation is finally given by $y^2 = x^3 + b$ (for certain values of b) when $j = 0$, by $y^2 = x^3 + ax$ (for certain values of a) when $j = 1728$, and by $y^2 = x^3 - 3cx + 2c$ with $c := j/(j-1728)$ when $j \notin \{0, 1728\}$.

A *divisor* is a finite formal sum $\mathcal{A} = \sum_P a_P(P)$ of points on the curve $E(\mathbb{F}_{q^k})$. An Abelian group structure is defined on the set of divisors by the addition of corresponding coefficients in their formal sums; in particular, $n\mathcal{A} = \sum_P (n\,a_P)(P)$. The *degree* of a divisor $\mathcal{A}$ is the sum $\deg(\mathcal{A}) = \sum_P a_P$. Let $f : E(\mathbb{F}_{q^k}) \to \mathbb{F}_{q^k}$ be a function on the curve. We define $f(\mathcal{A}) \equiv \prod_P f(P)^{a_P}$. Let $\mathrm{ord}_P(f)$ denote the multiplicity of the zero or pole of f at P (if f has no zero or pole at P, then $\mathrm{ord}_P(f) = 0$). The divisor of f is $(f) := \sum_P \mathrm{ord}_P(f)(P)$. A divisor $\mathcal{A}$ is called *principal* if $\mathcal{A} = (f)$ for some function (f). A divisor $\mathcal{A}$ is principal if and only if $\deg(\mathcal{A}) = 0$ and $\sum_P a_P P = \infty$ [65, theorem 2.25]. Two divisors $\mathcal{A}$ and $\mathcal{B}$ are *equivalent*, $\mathcal{A} \sim \mathcal{B}$, if their difference $\mathcal{A} - \mathcal{B}$ is a principal divisor. Let $P \in E(\mathbb{F}_q)[r]$ where r is coprime to q, and let $\mathcal{A}_P$ be a divisor equivalent to $(P) - (\infty)$; under these circumstances the divisor $r\mathcal{A}_P$ is principal, and hence there is a function f_P such that $(f_P) = r\mathcal{A}_P = r(P) - r(\infty)$.

Given three groups $\mathbb{G}_1$, $\mathbb{G}_2$, and $\mathbb{G}_T$ of the same prime order n, a *pairing* is a feasibly computable, non-degenerate bilinear map $e : \mathbb{G}_1 \times \mathbb{G}_2 \to \mathbb{G}_T$. The groups $\mathbb{G}_1$ and $\mathbb{G}_2$ are commonly (in the so-called *Type III* pairing setting) determined by the eigenspaces of the Frobenius endomorphism ϕ_q on some elliptic curve $E/\mathbb{F}_q$ of embedding degree $k > 1$. More precisely, $\mathbb{G}_1$ is taken to be the 1-eigenspace $E[n] \cap \ker(\phi_q - [1]) = E(\mathbb{F}_q)[n]$. The group $\mathbb{G}_2$ is usually taken to be the preimage $E'(\mathbb{F}_{q^g})[n]$ of the q-eigenspace $E[n] \cap \ker(\phi_q - [q]) \subseteq E(\mathbb{F}_{q^k})[n]$ under a twisting isomorphism $\psi : E' \to E$, $(x, y) \mapsto (\mu^2 x, \mu^3 y)$ for some $\mu \in \mathbb{F}_{q^k}^*$. In particular, $g = k/d$ where the curve $E'/\mathbb{F}_{q^g}$ is the unique twist of E with largest possible twist degree $d \mid k$ for which n divides $\#E'(\mathbb{F}_{q^g})$ (see [55] for details). This means that g is as small as possible.

A Miller function $f_{i,P}$ is a function with divisor $(f_{i,P}) = i(P) - ([i]P) - (i-1)(\infty)$. Miller functions are at the root of most if not all pairings proposed for cryptographic purposes, which in turn induce efficient algorithms derived from Miller's algorithm [67,68]. A Miller function satisfies $f_{a+b,P}(Q) = f_{a,P}(Q) \cdot f_{b,P}(Q) \cdot g_{[a]P,[b]P}(Q)/g_{[a+b]P}(Q)$ up to a constant nonzero factor in $\mathbb{F}_q$, for all $a, b \in \mathbb{Z}$, where the so-called line functions $g_{[a]P,[b]P}$ and $g_{[a+b]P}$ satisfy $(g_{[a]P,[b]P}) = ([a]P) + ([b]P) + (-[a+b]P) - 3(\infty)$, $(g_{[a+b]P}) = ([a+b]P) + (-[a+b]P) - 2(\infty)$. The advantage of Miller functions with respect to elliptic curve arithmetic is now clear, since with these relations the line functions, and hence the Miller functions themselves, can be efficiently computed as a side result during the computation of $[n]P$ by means of the usual chord-and-tangent method.

2.1 Protocols and Assumptions

As an illustration of the enormous flexibility that pairings bring to the construction of cryptographic protocols, we present a (necessarily incomplete) list of known schemes according to their overall category.

Foremost among pairing-based schemes are the identity-based cryptosystems. These include plain encryption [17], digital signatures [24,83], (authenticated) key agreement [25], chameleon hashing [27], and hierarchical extensions thereof with or without random oracles [22,51].

Other pairing-based schemes are not identity-based but feature special functionalities like secret handshakes [5], short/aggregate/verifiably encrypted/group/ring/blind signatures [19,20,26,97,98] and signcryption [9,21,61].

Together with the abundance of protocols came a matching abundance of security assumptions, often tailored to the nature of each particular protocol although some assumptions found a more general use and became classical. Some of the most popular and useful security assumptions occurring in security proofs of pairing-based protocols are the following, with groups $\mathbb{G}_1$ and $\mathbb{G}_2$ of order n in multiplicative notation (and $\mathbb{G}$ denotes either group):

- q-Strong Diffie-Hellman (q-SDH) [16] and many related assumptions (like the Inverse Computational Diffie-Hellman (Inv-CDH), the Square Computational Diffie-Hellman (Squ-CDH), the Bilinear Inverse Diffie-Hellman (BIDH), and the Bilinear Square Diffie-Hellman (BSDH) assumptions [98]): *Given a* (q+2)-*tuple* $(g_1, g_2, g_2^x, \ldots, g_2^{x^q}) \in \mathbb{G}_1 \times \mathbb{G}_2^{q+1}$ *as input, compute a pair* $(c, g_1^{1/(x+c)}) \in \mathbb{Z}/n\mathbb{Z} \times \mathbb{G}_1$.

- Decision Bilinear Diffie-Hellman (DBDH) [18] and related assumptions (like the k-BDH assumption [14]): *Given generators* g_1 *and* g_2 *of* $\mathbb{G}_1$ *and* $\mathbb{G}_2$ *respectively, and given* g_1^a, g_1^b, g_1^c, g_2^a, g_2^b, g_2^c, $e(g_1,g_2)^z$ *determine whether* $e(g_1,g_2)^{abc} = e(g_1,g_2)^z$.

- Gap Diffie-Hellman (GDH) assumption [77]: *Given* $(g, g^a, g^b) \in \mathbb{G}^3$ *for a group* $\mathbb{G}$ *equipped with an oracle for deciding whether* $g^{ab} = g^c$ *for any given* $g^c \in \mathbb{G}$, *find* g^{ab}.

– $(k+1)$ Exponent Function meta-assumption: *Given a function $f : \mathbb{Z}/n\mathbb{Z} \to \mathbb{Z}/n\mathbb{Z}$ and a sequence $(g, g^a, g^{f(h_1+a)}, \ldots, g^{f(h_k+a)}) \in \mathbb{G}_1^{k+2}$ for some $a, h_1, \ldots, h_k \in \mathbb{Z}/n\mathbb{Z}$, compute $g^{f(h+a)}$ for some $h \notin \{h_1, \ldots, h_k\}$.*

The last of these is actually a meta-assumption, since it is parameterized by a function f on the exponents. This meta-assumption includes the Collusion attack with k traitors (k-CAA) assumption [70], where $f(x) := 1/x$, and the $(k+1)$ Square Roots (($k+1$)-SR) assumption [96], where $f(x) := \sqrt{x}$, among others. Of course, not all choices of f may lead to a consistent security assumption (for instance, the constant function is certainly a bad choice), so the instantiation of this meta-assumption must be done in a case-by-case basis.

Also, not all of these assumptions are entirely satisfactory from the point of view of their relation to the computational complexity of the more fundamental discrete logarithm problem. In particular, the Cheon attack [28, 29] showed that, contrary to most discrete-logarithm style assumptions, which usually claim a practical security level of 2^λ for 2λ-bit keys due to e.g. the Pollard-ρ attack [81], the q-SDH assumption may need 3λ-bit keys to attain that security level, according to the choice of q.

3   Curves and Algorithms

3.1   Supersingular Curves

Early proposals to obtain efficient pairings invoked the adoption of supersingular curves [40, 49, 82], which led to the highly efficient concept of η pairings [7] over fields of small characteristic. This setting enables the so called Type I pairings, which are defined with both arguments from the same group [50] and facilitates the description of many protocols and the construction of formal security proofs. Unfortunately, recent developments bring that approach into question, since discrete logarithms in the multiplicative groups of the associated extension fields have proven far easier to compute than anticipated [6].

Certain ordinary curves, on the other hand, are not known to be susceptible to that line of attack, and also yield very efficient algorithms, as we will see next.

3.2   Generic Constructions

Generic construction methods enable choosing the embedding degree at will, limited only by efficiency requirements. Two such constructions are known:

– The Cocks-Pinch construction [32] enables the construction of elliptic curves over $\mathbb{F}_q$ containing a pairing-friendly group of order n with $\lg(q)/\lg(n) \approx 2$.
– The Dupont-Enge-Morain strategy [39] is similarly generic in the sense of its embedding degree flexibility by maximizing the trace of the Frobenius endomorphism. Like the Cocks-Pinch method, it only attains $\lg(q)/\lg(n) \approx 2$.

Because the smallest attainable ratio $\lg(q)/\lg(n)$ is relatively large, these methods do not yield curves of prime order, which are necessary for certain applications like short signatures, and also tend to improve the overall processing efficiency.

3.3 Sparse Families of Curves

Certain families of curves may be obtained by parameterizing the norm equation $4q - t^2 = 4hn - (t - 2)^2 = DV^2$ with polynomials $q(u)$, $t(u)$, $h(u)$, $n(u)$, then choosing $t(u)$ and $h(u)$ according to some criteria (for instance, setting $h(u)$ to be some small constant polynomial yields near-prime order curves), and directly finding integer solutions (in u and V) to the result. In practice this involves a clever mapping of the norm equation into a Pell-like equation, whose solutions lead to actual curve equations via complex multiplication (CM).

The only drawback they present is the relative rarity of suitable curves (the only embedding degrees that are known to yield solutions are $k \in \{3, 4, 6, 10\}$, and the size of the integer solutions u grows exponentially), especially those with prime order. Historically, sparse families are divided into Miyaji-Nakabayashi-Takano (MNT) curves and Freeman curves.

MNT curves were the first publicly known construction of ordinary pairing-friendly curves [71]. Given their limited range of admissible embedding degrees (namely, $k \in \{3, 4, 6\}$), the apparent finiteness of MNT curves of prime order [58,63,92], and efficiency considerations (see e.g. [44]), MNT curves are less useful for higher security levels (say, from about 2^{112} onward).

Freeman curves [43], with embedding degree $k = 10$, are far rarer and suffer more acutely from the fact that the nonexistence of a twist of degree higher than quadratic forces its $\mathbb{G}_2$ group to be defined over $\mathbb{F}_{q^5}$. Besides, this quintic extension cannot be constructed using a binomial representation.

3.4 Complete Families of Curves

Instead of trying to solve the partially parameterized norm equation $4h(u)n(u) - (t(u)-2)^2 = DV^2$ for u and V directly as for the sparse families of curves, one can also parameterize $V = V(u)$ as well. Solutions may exist if the parameters can be further constrained, which is usually done by considering the properties of the number field $\mathbb{Q}[u]/n(u)$, specifically by requiring that it contains a k-th root of unity where k is the desired embedding degree. Choosing $n(u)$ to be a cyclotomic polynomial $\Phi_\ell(u)$ with $k \mid \ell$ yields the suitably named cyclotomic family of curves [10,11,23,44], which enable a reasonably small ratio $\rho := \lg(q)/\lg(n)$ (e.g. $\rho = (k + 1)/(k - 1)$ for prime $k \equiv 3 \pmod 4$).

Yet, there is one other family of curves that attain $\rho \approx 1$, namely, the Barreto-Naehrig (BN) curves [12]. BN curves arguably constitute one of the most versatile classes of pairing-friendly elliptic curves. A BN curve is an elliptic curve $E_u : y^2 = x^3 + b$ defined over a finite prime[1] field $\mathbb{F}_p$ of (typically prime) order n, where p and n are given by $p = p(u) = 36u^4 + 36u^3 + 24u^2 + 6u + 1$ and $n = n(u) = 36u^4 + 36u^3 + 18u^2 + 6u + 1$ (hence $t = t(u) = 6u^2 + 1$) for $u \in \mathbb{Z}$. One can check by straightforward inspection that $\Phi_{12}(t(u) - 1) = n(u)n(-u)$,

---

[1] Although there is no theoretical reason not to choose p to be a higher prime power, in practice such parameters are exceedingly rare and anyway unnecessary, so usually p is taken to be simply a prime.

hence $\Phi_{12}(p(u)) \equiv \Phi_{12}(t(u) - 1) \equiv 0 \pmod{n(u)}$, so the group of order $n(u)$ has embedding degree $k = 12$.

BN curves also have j-invariant 0, so there is no need to resort explicitly to the CM curve construction method: all one has to do is choose an integer u of suitable size such that p and n as given by the above polynomials are prime. To find a corresponding curve, one chooses $b \in \mathbb{F}_p$ among the six possible classes so that the curve $E : y^2 = x^3 + b$ has order n.

Furthermore, BN curves admit a sextic twist ($d = 6$), so that one can set $\mathbb{G}_2 = E'(\mathbb{F}_{p^2})[n]$. This twist $E'/\mathbb{F}_{p^2}$ may be selected by finding a non-square and non-cube $\xi \in \mathbb{F}_{p^2}$ and then checking via scalar multiplication whether the curve $E' : y^2 = x^3 + b'$ given by $b' = b/\xi$ or by $b' = b/\xi^5$ has order divisible by n. However, construction methods are known that dispense with such procedure, yielding the correct curve and its twist directly [80]. For convenience, following [85] we call the twist $E' : y^2 = x^3 + b/\xi$ a D-type twist, and we call the twist $E' : y^2 = x^3 + b\xi$ an M-type twist.

3.5   Holistic Families

Early works targeting specifically curves that have some efficiency advantage have focused on only one or a few implementation aspects, notably the pairing computation itself [13, 15, 38, 90].

More modern approaches tend to consider most if not all efficiency aspects that arise in pairing-based schemes [34, 36, 80]. This means that curves of those families tend to support not only fast pairing computation, but efficient finite field arithmetic for all fields involved, curve construction, generator construction for both $\mathbb{G}_1$ and $\mathbb{G}_2$, multiplication by a scalar in both $\mathbb{G}_1$ and $\mathbb{G}_2$, point sampling, hashing to the curve [42], and potentially other operations as well.

Curiously enough, there is not a great deal of diversity among the most promising such families, which comprise essentially only BN curves, BLS curves [10], and KSS curves [57].

3.6   Efficient Algorithms

Ordinary curves with small embedding degree also come equipped with efficient pairing algorithms, which tend to be variants of the Tate pairing [8, 48, 55, 60, 76] (although some fall back to the Weil pairing while remaining fairly efficient [94]). In particular, one now knows concrete practical limits to how efficient a pairing can be, in the form of the so-called optimal pairings [93].

As we pointed out, Miller functions are essential to the definition of most cryptographic pairings. Although all pairings can be defined individually in formal terms, it is perhaps more instructive to give the following constructive definitions, assuming an underlying curve $E/\mathbb{F}_q$ containing a group $E(\mathbb{F}_q)[n]$ of prime order n with embedding degree k and letting $z := (q^k - 1)/n$:

– Weil pairing: $w(P, Q) := (-1)^n f_{n,P}(Q)/f_{n,Q}(P)$.
– Tate pairing: $\tau(P, Q) := f_{n,P}(Q)^z$.

- Eta pairing [7] (called the twisted Ate pairing when defined over an ordinary curve): $\eta(P, Q) := f_{\lambda, P}(Q)^z$ where $\lambda^d \equiv 1 \pmod{n}$.
- Ate pairing [55]: $a(P, Q) := f_{t-1, Q}(P)^z$, where t is the trace of the Frobenius.
- Optimized Ate and twisted Ate pairings [64]: $a_c(P, Q) := f_{(t-1)^c \bmod n, Q}(P)^z$, $\eta_c(P, Q) := f_{\lambda^c \bmod n, P}(Q)^z$, for some $0 < c < k$.
- Optimal Ate pairing [93]: $a_{\mathrm{opt}}(P, Q) := f_{\ell, Q}(P)^z$ for a certain ℓ such that $\lg \ell \approx (\lg n)/\varphi(k)$.

Optimal pairings achieve the shortest loop length among all of these pairings. To obtain unique values, most of these pairings (the Weil pairing is an exception) are reduced via the final exponentiation by z. The very computation of z is the subject of research *per se* [89]. In particular, for a BN curve with parameter u there exists an optimal Ate pairing with loop length $\ell = |6u + 2|$.

A clear trend in recent works has been to attain exceptional performance gains by limiting the allowed curves to a certain subset, sometimes to a single curve at a useful security level [4,15,75,80]. In the next section, we discuss aspects pertaining such implementations.

4   Implementation Aspects

The optimal Ate pairing on BN curves has been the focus of intense implementation research in the last few years. Most remarkably, beginning in 2008, a series of works improved, each one on top of the preceding one, the practical performance on Intel 64-bit platforms [15,54,75]. This effort reached its pinnacle in 2011, when Aranha et al. [4] reported an implementation running in about half a millisecond (see also [62]). Since then, performance of efficient software implementations has mostly stabilized, but some aspects of pairing computation continuously improved through the availability of new techniques [47], processor architecture revisions and instruction set refinements [79]. In this section, we revisit the problem of efficient pairing computation working on top of the implementation presented in [4], to explore these latest advances and provide new performance figures. Our updated implementation achieves high performance on a variety of modern 64-bit computing platforms, including both relatively old processors and latest microarchitectures.

4.1   Pairing Algorithm

The BN family of curves is ideal from an implementation point of view. Having embedding degree $k = 12$, it is perfectly suited to the 128-bit security level and a competitive candidate at the 192-bit security level for protocols involving a small number of pairing computations [2]. Additionally, the size of the family facilitates generation [80] and supports many different parameter choices, allowing for customization of software implementations to radically different computing architectures [4,52,53]. The optimal Ate pairing construction applied to general BN curves further provides a rather simple formulation among the potential candidates [60,76]:

$$a_{\mathrm{opt}} : \mathbb{G}_2 \times \mathbb{G}_1 \to \mathbb{G}_T$$

$$(Q,P) \mapsto \left(f_{\ell,Q}(P) \cdot g_{[\ell]Q,\phi_p(Q)}(P) \cdot g_{[\ell]Q+\phi_p(Q),-\phi_p^2(Q)}(P) \right)^{\frac{p^{12}-1}{n}},$$

with $\ell = 6u + 2$, map ϕ_p and groups $\mathbb{G}_1, \mathbb{G}_2, \mathbb{G}_T$ as previously defined; and an especially efficient modification of Miller's Algorithm for accumulating all the required line evaluations in the Miller variable f (Algorithm 1).

The extension field arithmetic involving f is in fact the main building block of the pairing computation, including Miller's algorithm and final exponentiation. Hence, its efficient implementation is crucial. To that end, it has been recommended to implement the extension field through a tower of extensions built with appropriate choices of irreducible polynomials [15,38,54,80]:

$$\mathbb{F}_{p^2} = \mathbb{F}_p[i]/(i^2 - \beta), \text{with } \beta \text{ a non-square,} \tag{1}$$

$$\mathbb{F}_{p^4} = \mathbb{F}_{p^2}[s]/(s^2 - \xi), \text{with } \xi \text{ a non-square,} \tag{2}$$

$$\mathbb{F}_{p^6} = \mathbb{F}_{p^2}[v]/(v^3 - \xi), \text{with } \xi \text{ a non-cube,} \tag{3}$$

$$\mathbb{F}_{p^{12}} = \mathbb{F}_{p^4}[t]/(t^3 - s) \tag{4}$$

$$\text{or } \mathbb{F}_{p^6}[w]/(w^2 - v) \tag{5}$$

$$\text{or } \mathbb{F}_{p^2}[w]/(w^6 - \xi), \text{with } \xi \text{ a non-square and non-cube.} \tag{6}$$

Note that ξ is the same non-residue used to define the twist equations in Sect. 3.4 and that converting from one towering scheme to another is possible by simply reordering coefficients. By allowing intermediate values to grow to double precision and choosing p to be a prime number slightly smaller than a multiple of the processor word, lazy reduction can be efficiently employed in all levels of the towering arithmetic [4]. A remarkably efficient set of parameters arising from the curve choice $E(\mathbb{F}_p) : y^2 = x^3 + 2$, with $p \equiv 3 \pmod 4$, is $\beta = -1$, $\xi = (1+i)$ [80], simultaneously optimizing finite field and curve arithmetic.

4.2   Field Arithmetic

Prime fields involved in pairing computation in the asymmetric setting are commonly represented with dense moduli, resulting from the parameterized curve constructions. While the particular structure of the prime modulus has been successfully exploited for performance optimization in both software [75] and hardware [41], current software implementations rely on the standard Montgomery reduction [72] and state-of-the-art hardware implementations on the parallelization capabilities of the Residue Number System [30].

Arithmetic in the base field is usually implemented in carefully scheduled Assembly code, but the small number of words required to represent a 256-bit prime field element in a 64-bit processor encourages the use of Assembly directly in the quadratic extension field, to avoid penalties related to frequent function calls [15]. Multiplication and reduction in $\mathbb{F}_p$ are implemented through a Comba strategy [33], but a Schoolbook approach is favored in recent Intel processors, due to the availability of the carry-preserving multiplication instruction mulx,

Algorithm 1. Optimal Ate pairing on general BN curves [4]

Input: $P \in \mathbb{G}_1, Q \in \mathbb{G}_2, \ell = |6u + 2| = \sum_{i=0}^{\log_2(\ell)} \ell_i 2^i$
Output: $a_{\mathrm{opt}}(Q, P)$

1: $d \leftarrow g_{Q,Q}(P), T \leftarrow 2Q, e \leftarrow 1$
2: **if** $\ell_{\lfloor \log_2(\ell) \rfloor - 1} = 1$ **then** $e \leftarrow g_{T,Q}(P), T \leftarrow T + Q$
3: $f \leftarrow d \cdot e$
4: **for** $i = \lfloor \log_2(\ell) \rfloor - 2$ **downto** 0 **do**
5: $\quad f \leftarrow f^2 \cdot g_{T,T}(P), T \leftarrow 2T$
6: $\quad$ **if** $\ell_i = 1$ **then** $f \leftarrow f \cdot g_{T,Q}(P), T \leftarrow T + Q$
7: **end for**
8: $Q_1 \leftarrow \phi_p(Q), Q_2 \leftarrow \phi_p^2(Q)$
9: **if** $u < 0$ **then** $T \leftarrow -T, f \leftarrow f^{p^6}$
10: $d \leftarrow g_{T,Q_1}(P), T \leftarrow T + Q_1, e \leftarrow g_{T,-Q_2}(P), T \leftarrow T - Q_2, f \leftarrow f \cdot (d \cdot e)$
11: $f \leftarrow f^{(p^6-1)(p^2+1)(p^4-p^2+1)/n}$
12: **return** f

---

allowing delayed handling of carries [79]. Future processors will allow similar speedups on the Comba-based multiplication and Montgomery reduction routines by carry-preserving addition instructions [78].

Divide-and-conquer approaches are used only for multiplication in $\mathbb{F}_{p^2}$, $\mathbb{F}_{p^6}$ and $\mathbb{F}_{p^{12}}$, because Karatsuba is typically more efficient over extension fields, since additions are relatively inexpensive in comparison with multiplication. The full details of the formulas that we use in our implementation of extension field arithmetic can be found in [4], including the opportunities for reducing the number of Montgomery reductions via lazy reduction. The case of squaring is relatively more complex. We use the complex squaring in $\mathbb{F}_{p^2}$ and, for $\mathbb{F}_{p^6}$ and $\mathbb{F}_{p^{12}}$, we employ the faster Chung-Hasan asymmetric SQR3 formula [31]. The sparseness of the line functions motivates the implementation of specialized multiplication routines for accumulating the line function into the Miller variable f (*sparse* multiplication) or for multiplying line functions together (*sparser* multiplication). For sparse multiplication over $\mathbb{F}_{p^6}$ and $\mathbb{F}_{p^{12}}$, we use the formulas proposed by Grewal et al. (see Algorithms 5 and 6 in [53]). Faster formulas for sparser multiplication can be trivially obtained by adapting the sparse multiplication formula to remove operations involving the missing subfield elements.

In the following, we closely follow notation for operation costs from [4]. Let m, s, a, i denote the cost of multiplication, squaring, addition and inversion in $\mathbb{F}_p$, respectively; $\tilde{m}, \tilde{s}, \tilde{a}, \tilde{\imath}$ denote the cost of multiplication, squaring, addition and inversion in $\mathbb{F}_{p^2}$, respectively; m_u, s_u, r denote the cost of unreduced multiplication and squaring producing double-precision results, and modular reduction of double-precision integers, respectively; $\tilde{m}_u, \tilde{s}_u, \tilde{r}$ denote the cost of unreduced multiplication and squaring, and modular reduction of double-precision elements in $\mathbb{F}_{p^2}$, respectively. To simplify the operation count, we consider the cost of field subtraction, negation and division by two equivalent to that of field addition.

Also, one double-precision addition is considered equivalent to the cost of two single-precision additions.

4.3 Curve Arithmetic

Pairings can be computed over elliptic curves represented in any coordinate system, but popular choices have been homogeneous projective and affine coordinates, depending on the ratio between inversion and multiplication. Jacobian coordinates were initially explored in a few implementations [15,75], but ended superseded by homogeneous coordinates because of their superior efficiency [35]. Point doublings and their corresponding line evaluations usually dominate the cost of the Miller loop, since efficient parameters tend to minimize the Hamming weight of the Miller variable ℓ and the resulting number of points additions. Below, we review and slightly refine the best formulas available for the curve arithmetic involved in pairing computation on affine and homogeneous projective coordinates.

Affine Coordinates. The choice of affine coordinates has proven more useful at higher security levels and embedding degrees, due to the action of the norm map on simplifying the computation of inverses at higher extensions [59,86]. The main advantages of affine coordinates are the simplicity of implementation and format of the line functions, allowing faster accumulation inside the Miller loop if the additional sparsity is exploited. If $T = (x_1, y_1)$ is a point in $E'(\mathbb{F}_{p^2})$, one can compute the point $2T := T + T$ with the following formula [53]:

$$\lambda = \frac{3x_1^2}{2y_1}, \quad x_3 = \lambda^2 - 2x_1, \quad y_3 = (\lambda x_1 - y_1) - \lambda x_3. \tag{7}$$

When E' is a D-type twist given by the twisting isomorphism ψ, the tangent line evaluated at $P = (x_P, y_P)$ has the format $g_{2\psi(T)}(P) = y_P - \lambda x_P w + (\lambda x_1 - y_1)w^3$ according to the tower representation given by Eq. (6). This function can be evaluated at a cost of $3\tilde{m} + 2\tilde{s} + 7\tilde{a} + \tilde{\imath} + 2m$ with the precomputation cost of $1a$ to compute $\bar{x}_P = -x_P$ [53]. By performing more precomputation as $y_P' = 1/y_P$ and $x_P' = \bar{x}_P/y_P$, we can simplify the tangent line further:

$$y_P' \cdot g_{2\psi(T)}(P) = 1 + \lambda x_P' w + y_P'(\lambda x_1 - y_1)w^3.$$

Since the final exponentiation eliminates any subfield element multiplying the pairing value, this modification does not change the pairing result. Computing the simpler line function now requires $3\tilde{m} + 2\tilde{s} + 7\tilde{a} + \tilde{\imath} + 4m$ with an additional precomputation cost of $(i + m)$:

$$A = \frac{1}{2y_1}, \quad B = 3x_1^2, \quad C = AB, \quad D = 2x_1, \quad x_3 = C^2 - D,$$
$$E = Cx_1 - y_1, \quad y_3 = E - Cx_3, \quad F = Cx_P', \quad G = Ey_P',$$
$$y_P' \cdot g_{2\psi(T)}(P) = 1 + Fw + Gw^3.$$

This clearly does not save any operations compared to Eq. (7) and increases the cost by $2m$. However, the simpler format allows the faster accumulation $f^2 \cdot g_{2\psi(T)}(P) = (f_0 + f_1 w)(1 + g_1 w)$, where $f_0, f_1, g_1 \in \mathbb{F}_{p^6}$, by saving $6m$ corresponding to the multiplication between y_P and each subfield element of f_0. The performance trade-off compared to [53] is thus $4m$ per Miller doubling step.

When different points $T = (x_1, y_1)$ and $Q = (x_2, y_2)$ are considered, the point $T + Q$ can be computed with the following formula:

$$\lambda = \frac{y_2 - y_1}{x_2 - x_1}, \quad x_3 = \lambda^2 - x_2 - x_1, \quad y_3 = \lambda(x_1 - x_3) - y_1. \tag{8}$$

Applying the same trick described above gives the same performance trade-off, with a cost of $3\tilde{m} + \tilde{s} + 6\tilde{a} + \tilde{i} + 4m$ [53]:

$$A = \frac{1}{x_2 - x_1}, \quad B = y_2 - y_1, \quad C = AB, \quad D = x_1 + x_2, \quad x_3 = C^2 - D,$$
$$E = Cx_1 - y_1, \quad y_3 = E - Cx_3, \quad F = Cx'_P, \quad G = Ey'_P,$$
$$y'_P \cdot g_{\psi(T),\psi(Q)}(P) = 1 + Fw + Gw^3.$$

The technique can be further employed in M-type twists, conserving their equivalent performance to D-type twists [53], with some slight changes in the formula format and accumulation multiplier. A generalization for other pairing-friendly curves with degree-d twists and even embedding degree k would provide a performance trade-off of $(k/2 - k/d)$ multiplications per step in Miller's Algorithm. The same idea was independently proposed and slightly improved in [73].

Homogeneous Projective Coordinates. The choice of projective coordinates has proven especially advantageous at the 128-bit security level for single pairing computation, due to the typically large inversion/multiplication ratio in this setting. If $T = (X_1, Y_1, Z_1) \in E'(\mathbb{F}_{p^2})$ is a point in homogeneous coordinates, one can compute the point $2T = (X_3, Y_3, Z_3)$ with the following formula [4]:

$$X_3 = \frac{X_1 Y_1}{2}(Y_1^2 - 9b' Z_1^2),$$
$$Y_3 = \left[\frac{1}{2}(Y_1^2 + 9b' Z_1^2)\right]^2 - 27b'^2 Z_1^4, \quad Z_3 = 2Y_1^3 Z_1. \tag{9}$$

The twisting point P can be represented by $(x_P w, y_P)$. When E' is a D-type twist given by the twisting isomorphism ψ, the tangent line evaluated at $P = (x_P, y_P)$ can be computed with the following formula [53]:

$$g_{2\psi(T)}(P) = -2YZy_P + 3X^2 x_P w + (3b'Z^2 - Y^2)w^3 \tag{10}$$

Equation (10) is basically the same line evaluation formula presented in [35] plus an efficient selection of the positioning of terms (obtained by multiplying the line evaluation by w^3), which was suggested in [53] to obtain a fast sparse multiplication in the Miller loop (in particular, the use of terms $1, w$ and w^3 [53] induces a sparse multiplication that saves $13\tilde{a}$ in comparison to the use of terms

$1, v^2$ and wv in [4]). The full doubling/line function formulae in [35] costs $2\tilde{m} + 7\tilde{s} + 23\tilde{a} + 4m + m_{b'}$. Based on Eqs. (9) and (10), [53] reports a cost of $2\tilde{m} + 7\tilde{s} + 21\tilde{a} + 4m + m_{b'}$. We observe that the same formulae can be evaluated at a cost of only $2\tilde{m} + 7\tilde{s} + 19\tilde{a} + 4m + m_{b'}$ with the precomputation cost of $3a$ to compute $\bar{y}_P = -y_P$ and $x'_P = 3x_P$. Note that all these costs consider the computation of $X_1 \cdot Y_1$ using the equivalence $2XY = (X + Y)^2 - X^2 - Y^2$. We remark that, as in Aranha et al. [4], on x64 platforms it is more efficient to compute such term with a direct multiplication since $\tilde{m} - \tilde{s} < 3\tilde{a}$. Considering this scenario, the cost applying our precomputations is then given by $3\tilde{m} + 6\tilde{s} + 15\tilde{a} + 4m + m_{b'}$. Finally, further improvements are possible if b is cleverly selected [80]. For instance, if $b = 2$ then $b' = 2/(1 + i) = 1 - i$, which minimizes the number of additions and subtractions. Computing the simpler doubling/line function now requires $3\tilde{m} + 6\tilde{s} + 16\tilde{a} + 4m$ with the precomputation cost of $3a$ (in comparison to the computation proposed in [4,35,53], we save $2\tilde{a}, 3\tilde{a}$ and $5\tilde{a}$, respectively, when $\tilde{m} - \tilde{s} < 3\tilde{a}$):

$$
\begin{aligned}
&A = X_1 \cdot Y_1/2, \;\; B = Y_1^2, \;\; C = Z_1^2, \;\; D = 3C, \;\; E_0 = D_0 + D_1, \\
&E_1 = D_1 - D_0, \;\; F = 3E, \;\; X_3 = A \cdot (B - F), \;\; G = (B + F)/2, \\
&Y_3 = G^2 - 3E^2, \;\; H = (Y_1 + Z_1)^2 - (B + C), \;\; Z_3 = B \cdot H, \\
&g_{2\psi(T)}(P) = H\bar{y}_P + X_1^2 x'_P w + (E - B)w^3.
\end{aligned}
\tag{11}
$$

Similarly, if $T = (X_1, Y_1, Z_1)$ and $Q = (x_2, y_2) \in E'(\mathbb{F}_{p^2})$ are points in homogeneous and affine coordinates, respectively, one can compute the point $T + Q = (X_3, Y_3, Z_3)$ with the following formula:

$$
\begin{aligned}
&X_3 = \lambda(\lambda^3 + Z_1\theta^2 - 2X_1\lambda^2), \\
&Y_3 = \theta(3X_1\lambda^2 - \lambda^3 - Z_1\theta^2) - Y_1\lambda^3, \;\; Z_3 = Z_1\lambda^3,
\end{aligned}
\tag{12}
$$

where $\theta = Y_1 - y_2 Z_1$ and $\lambda = X_1 - x_2 Z_1$. In the case of a D-type twist, the line evaluated at $P = (x_P, y_P)$ can be computed with the following formula [53]:

$$
g_{\psi(T+Q)}(P) = -\lambda y_P - \theta x_P w + (\theta X_2 - \lambda Y_2)w^3.
\tag{13}
$$

Similar to the case of doubling, Eq. (13) is basically the same line evaluation formula presented in [35] plus an efficient selection of the positioning of terms suggested in [53] to obtain a fast sparse multiplication inside the Miller loop. The full mixed addition/line function formulae can be evaluated at a cost of $11\tilde{m} + 2\tilde{s} + 8\tilde{a} + 4m$ with the precomputation cost of $2a$ to compute $\bar{x}_P = -x_P$ and $\bar{y}_P = -y_P$ [53]:

$$
\begin{aligned}
&A = Y_2 Z_1, \;\; B = X_2 Z_1, \;\; \theta = Y_1 - A, \;\; \lambda = X_1 - B, \;\; C = \theta^2, \\
&D = \lambda^2, \;\; E = \lambda^3, \;\; F = Z_1 C, \;\; G = X_1 D, \;\; H = E + F - 2G, \\
&X_3 = \lambda H, \;\; I = Y_1 E, \;\; Y_3 = \theta(G - H) - I, \;\; Z_3 = Z_1 E, \;\; J = \theta X_2 - \lambda Y_2, \\
&g_{2\psi(T)}(P) = \lambda \bar{y}_P + \theta \bar{x}_P w + J w^3.
\end{aligned}
$$

In the case of an M-type twist, the line function evaluated at $\psi(P) = (x_P w^2, y_P w^3)$ can be computed with the same sequence of operations shown above.

4.4 Operation Count

Table 1 presents a detailed operation count for each operation relevant in the computation of a pairing over a BN curve, considering all the improvements described in the previous section. Using these partial numbers, we obtain an operation count for the full pairing computation on a fixed BN curve.

Table 1. Computational cost for arithmetic required by Miller's Algorithm.

$E'(\mathbb{F}_{p^2})$-Arithmetic	Operation count
Precomp. (Affine)	$i + m + a$
Precomp. (Proj)	$4a$
Dbl./Eval. (Affine)	$3\tilde{m} + 2\tilde{s} + 7\tilde{a} + \tilde{\imath} + 4m$
Add./Eval. (Affine)	$3\tilde{m} + \tilde{s} + 6\tilde{a} + \tilde{\imath} + 4m$
Dbl./Eval. (Proj)	$3\tilde{m}_u + 6\tilde{s}_u + 8\tilde{r} + 19\tilde{a} + 4m$
Add./Eval. (Proj)	$11\tilde{m}_u + 2\tilde{s}_u + 11\tilde{r} + 10\tilde{a} + 4m$
p-power Frobenius	$2\tilde{m} + 2a$
p^2-power Frobenius	$2m + \tilde{a}$
Negation	$\tilde{a}$

$\mathbb{F}_{p^2}$-Arithmetic	Operation count
Add./Sub./Neg.	$\tilde{a} = 2a$
Conjugation	a
Multiplication	$\tilde{m} = \tilde{m}_u + \tilde{r} = 3m_u + 2r + 8a$
Squaring	$\tilde{s} = \tilde{s}_u + \tilde{r} = 2m_u + 2r + 3a$
Multiplication by β	a
Multiplication by ξ	$2a$
Inversion	$\tilde{\imath} = i + 2s_u + 2m_u + 2r + 3a$

$\mathbb{F}_{p^{12}}$-Arithmetic	Operation count
Add./Sub.	$6\tilde{a}$
Conjugation	$3\tilde{a}$
Multiplication	$18\tilde{m}_u + 6\tilde{r} + 110\tilde{a}$
Sparse Mult. (Affine)	$10\tilde{m}_u + 6\tilde{r} + 31\tilde{a}$
Sparser Mult. (Affine)	$5\tilde{m}_u + 3\tilde{r} + 13\tilde{a}$
Sparse Mult. (Proj)	$13\tilde{m}_u + 6\tilde{r} + 48\tilde{a}$
Sparser Mult. (Proj)	$6\tilde{m}_u + 5\tilde{r} + 22\tilde{a}$
Squaring	$3\tilde{m}_u + 12\tilde{s}_u + 6\tilde{r} + 93\tilde{a}$
Cyc. Squaring	$9\tilde{s}_u + 6\tilde{r} + 46\tilde{a}$
Comp. Squaring	$6\tilde{s}_u + 4\tilde{r} + 31\tilde{a}$
Simult. Decomp.	$9\tilde{m} + 6\tilde{s} + 22\tilde{a} + \tilde{\imath}$
p-power Frobenius	$5\tilde{m} + 6a$
p^2-power Frobenius	$10m + 2\tilde{a}$
p^3-power Frobenius	$5\tilde{m} + 2\tilde{a} + 6a$
Inversion	$23\tilde{m}_u + 11\tilde{s}_u + 16\tilde{r} + 129\tilde{a} + \tilde{\imath}$

Miller Loop. Sophisticated pairing-based protocols may impose additional restrictions on the parameter choice along with some performance penalty, for example requiring the cofactor of the $\mathbb{G}_T$ group to be a large prime number [87]. For efficiency and a fair comparison with related works, we adopt the parameters β, ξ, $b = 2$, $u = -(2^{62} + 2^{55} + 1)$ from [80]. For this set of parameters, the Miller loop in Algorithm 1 and the final line evaluations execute some amount of precomputation for accelerating the curve arithmetic formulas, 64 points doublings with line evaluations and 6 point additions with line evaluations; a single p-power Frobenius, a single p^2-power Frobenius and 2 negations in $E'(\mathbb{F}_{p^2})$; and 66 sparse accumulations in the Miller variable, 2 sparser multiplications, 1 multiplication, 1 conjugation and 63 squarings in $\mathbb{F}_{p^{12}}$. The corresponding costs in affine and homogeneous projective coordinates are, respectively:

$$
\begin{aligned}
\text{MLA} = {} & (i + m + a) + 64 \cdot (3\tilde{m} + 2\tilde{s} + 7\tilde{a} + \tilde{i} + 4m) \\
& + \; 6 \cdot (3\tilde{m} + \tilde{s} + 6\tilde{a} + \tilde{i} + 4m) + 2\tilde{m} + 2a + 2m + 2\tilde{a} \\
& + \; 66 \cdot (10\tilde{m}_u + 6\tilde{r} + 31\tilde{a}) + 2 \cdot (5\tilde{m}_u + 3\tilde{r} + 13\tilde{a}) \\
& + \; 3\tilde{a} + (18\tilde{m}_u + 6\tilde{r} + 110\tilde{a}) + 63 \cdot (3\tilde{m}_u + 12\tilde{s}_u + 6\tilde{r} + 93\tilde{a}) \\
= {} & 1089\tilde{m}_u + 890\tilde{s}_u + 1132\tilde{r} + 8530\tilde{a} + 70\tilde{i} + i + 283m + 3a.
\end{aligned}
$$

$$
\begin{aligned}
\text{MLP} = {} & (4a) + 64 \cdot (3\tilde{m}_u + 6\tilde{s}_u + 8\tilde{r} + 19\tilde{a} + 4m) \\
& + \; 6 \cdot (11\tilde{m}_u + 2\tilde{s}_u + 11\tilde{r} + 10\tilde{a} + 4m) + 2\tilde{m} + 2a + 2m + 2\tilde{a} \\
& + \; 66 \cdot (13\tilde{m}_u + 6\tilde{r} + 48\tilde{a}) + 2 \cdot (6\tilde{m}_u + 5\tilde{r} + 22\tilde{a}) \\
& + \; 3\tilde{a} + (18\tilde{m}_u + 6\tilde{r} + 110\tilde{a}) + 63 \cdot (3\tilde{m}_u + 12\tilde{s}_u + 6\tilde{r} + 93\tilde{a}) \\
= {} & 1337\tilde{m}_u + 1152\tilde{s}_u + 1388\tilde{r} + 10462\tilde{a} + 282m + 6a.
\end{aligned}
$$

Final Exponentiation. For computing the final exponentiation, we employ the state-of-the-art approach by [47] in the context of BN curves. As initially proposed by [89], power $\frac{p^{12}-1}{r}$ is factored into the easy exponent $(p^6 - 1)(p^2 + 1)$ and the hard exponent $\frac{p^4 - p^2 + 1}{n}$. The easy power is computed by a short sequence of multiplications, conjugations, fast applications of the Frobenius map [15] and a single inversion in $\mathbb{F}_{p^{12}}$. The hard power is computed in the cyclotomic subgroup, where additional algebraic structure allows elements to be compressed and squared consecutively in their compressed form, with decompression required only when performing multiplications [4,74,88].

Moreover, lattice reduction is able to obtain parameterized multiples of the hard exponent and significantly reduce the length of the addition chain involved in that exponentiation [47]. In total, the hard part of the final exponentiation requires 3 exponentiations by parameter u, 3 squarings in the cyclotomic subgroup, 10 full extension field multiplications and 3 applications of the Frobenius maps with increasing pth-powers. We refer to [4] for the cost of an exponentiation by our choice of u and compute the exact operation count of the final exponentiation:

$$FE = (23\tilde{m}_u + 11\tilde{s}_u + 16\tilde{r} + 129\tilde{a} + \tilde{\imath}) + 3\tilde{a} + 12 \cdot (18\tilde{m}_u + 6\tilde{r} + 110\tilde{a})$$
$$+ \; 3 \cdot (45\tilde{m}_u + 378\tilde{s}_u + 275\tilde{r} + 2164\tilde{a} + \tilde{\imath}) + 3 \cdot (9\tilde{s}_u + 6\tilde{r} + 46\tilde{a})$$
$$+ \; (5\tilde{m} + 6a) + 2 \cdot (10m + 2\tilde{a}) + (5\tilde{m} + 2\tilde{a} + 6a)$$
$$= \; 384\tilde{m}_u + 1172\tilde{s}_u + 941\tilde{r} + 8085\tilde{a} + 4\tilde{\imath} + 20m + 12a.$$

4.5   Results and Discussion

The combined cost for a pairing computation in homogeneous projective coordinates can then be expressed as:

$$MLP + FE = 1721\tilde{m}_u + 2324\tilde{s}_u + 2329\tilde{r} + 18547\tilde{a} + 4\tilde{\imath} + i + 302m + 18a$$
$$= 9811m_u + 4658r + 57384a + 4\tilde{\imath} + i + 302m + 18a$$
$$= 10113m_u + 4960r + 57852a + 4\tilde{\imath} + i.$$

A direct comparison with a previous record-setting implementation [4], considering only the number of multiplications in $\mathbb{F}_p$ generated by arithmetic in $\mathbb{F}_{p^2}$ as the performance metric, shows that our updated implementation in projective coordinates saves 3.4 % of the base field multiplications. This reflects the faster final exponentiation adopted from [47] and the more efficient formulas for inversion and squaring in $\mathbb{F}_{p^{12}}$. These formulas were not the most efficient in [4] due to higher number of additions, but this additional cost is now offset by improved addition handling and faster division by 2. Now comparing the total number of multiplications with more recent implementations [69,95], our updated implementation saves 1.9 %, or 198 multiplications.

The pairing code was implemented in the C programming language, with the performance-critical code implemented in Assembly. The compiler used was GCC version 4.7.0, with switches turned on for loop unrolling, inlining of small functions to reduce function call overhead and optimization level −03. Performance experiments were executed in a broad set of 64-bit Intel-compatible platforms: older Nehalem Core i5 540M 2.53 GHz and AMD Phenom II 3.0 GHz processors, and modern Sandy Bridge Xeon E31270 3.4 GHz and Ivy Bridge Core i5 3570 3.4 GHz processors, including a recent Haswell Core i7 4750 HQ 2.0 GHz processor. All machines had automatic overclocking capabilities disabled to reduce randomness in the results. Table 2 presents the timings split in the Miller loop and final exponentiation. This is not only useful for more fine-grained comparisons, but also to allow more accurate estimates of the latency of multi-pairings or precomputed pairings. The complete implementation will be made available in the next release of the RELIC toolkit [3].

We obtain several performance improvements in comparison with current literature. Our implementation based on projective coordinates improves results from [4] by 6 % and 9 % in the Nehalem and Phenom II machines, respectively. Comparing to an updated version [95] of a previous record setting implementation [15], our Sandy Bridge timings are faster by 82,000 cycles, or 5 %. When independently benchmarking their available software in the Ivy Bridge machine, we observe a latency of 1,403 K cycles, thus an improvement by our software of

Table 2. Comparison between implementations based on affine and projective coordinates on 64-bit architectures. Timings are presented in 10^3 clock cycles and were collected as the average of 10^4 repetitions of the same operation. Target platforms are AMD Phenom II (P II) and Intel Nehalem (N), Sandy Bridge (SB), Ivy Bridge (IB), Haswell (H) with or without support to the `mulx` instruction.

Operation	Platform					
	N	P II	SB	IB	H	H+`mulx`
Affine Miller loop	1,680	1,341	1,365	1,315	1,259	1,212
Projective Miller loop	1,170	862	856	798	721	704
Final exponentiation	745	557	572	537	492	473
Affine pairing	2,425	1,898	1,937	1,852	1,751	1,685
Projective pairing	1,915	1,419	1,428	1,335	1,213	1,177

5 %. Now considering the Haswell results from the same software available at [69], we obtain a speedup of 8 % without taking into account the `mulx` instruction and comparable performance when `mulx` is employed. It is also interesting to note that the use of `mulx` injects a relatively small speedup of 3 %. When exploiting such an instruction, the lack of carry-preserving addition instructions in the first generation of Haswell processors makes an efficient implementation of Comba-based multiplication and Montgomery reduction difficult, favoring the use of the typically slower Schoolbook versions. We anticipate a better support for Comba variants with the upcoming addition instructions [78].

In the implementation based on affine coordinates, the state-of-the-art results at the 128-bit security level is the one described by Acar *et al.* [1]. Unfortunately, only the latency of 15,6 million cycles on a Core 2 Duo is provided for 64-bit Intel architectures. While this does not allow a direct comparison, observing the small performance improvement between the Core 2 Duo and Nehalem reported in [4] implies that our affine implementation should be around 6 times faster than [1] when executed in the same machine.

Despite being slower than our own projective version, our affine implementation is still considerably faster than some previous speed records on projective coordinates [15,54,75]. This hints at the possibility that affine pairings could be improved even further, contrary to the naive intuition that the affine representation is exceedingly worse than a projective approach.

5 Conclusion

Pairings are amazingly flexible tools that enable the design of innovative cryptographic protocols. Their complex implementation has been the focus of intense research since the beginning of the millennium in what became a formidable race to make it efficient and practical.

We have reviewed the theory behind pairings and covered state-of-the-art algorithms, and also presented some further optimizations to the pairing computation in affine and projective coordinates, and analyzed the performance of the most efficient algorithmic options for pairing computation over ordinary curves at the 128-bit security level. In particular, our implementations of affine and projective pairings using Barreto-Naehrig curves shows that the efficiency of these two approaches are not as contrasting as it might seem, and hints that further optimizations might be possible. Remarkably, the combination of advances in processor technology and carefully crafted algorithms brings the computation of pairings close to the one million cycle mark.

Acknowledgements. The authors would like to thank Tanja Lange for the many suggestions to improve the quality of this paper.

References

1. Acar, T., Lauter, K., Naehrig, M., Shumow, D.: Affine pairings on ARM. In: Abdalla, M., Lange, T. (eds.) Pairing 2012. LNCS, vol. 7708, pp. 203–209. Springer, Heidelberg (2013)
2. Aranha, D.F., Fuentes-Castañeda, L., Knapp, E., Menezes, A., Rodríguez-Henríquez, F.: Implementing pairings at the 192-bit security level. In: Abdalla, M., Lange, T. (eds.) Pairing 2012. LNCS, vol. 7708, pp. 177–195. Springer, Heidelberg (2013)
3. Aranha, D.F., Gouvêa, C.P.L.: RELIC is an Efficient LIbrary for Cryptography. http://code.google.com/p/relic-toolkit/
4. Aranha, D.F., Karabina, K., Longa, P., Gebotys, C.H., López, J.: Faster explicit formulas for computing pairings over ordinary curves. In: Paterson, K.G. (ed.) EUROCRYPT 2011. LNCS, vol. 6632, pp. 48–68. Springer, Heidelberg (2011)
5. Balfanz, D., Durfee, G., Shankar, N., Smetters, D.K., Staddon, J., Wong, H.C.: Secret handshakes from pairing-based key agreements. In: IEEE Symposium on Security and Privacy - S&P 2003, Berkeley, USA, pp. 180–196. IEEE Computer Society (2003)
6. Barbulescu, R., Gaudry, P., Joux, A., Thomé, E.: A quasi-polynomial algorithm for discrete logarithm in finite fields of small characteristic. Cryptology ePrint Archive, Report 2013/400 (2013). http://eprint.iacr.org/2013/400
7. Barreto, P.S.L.M., Galbraith, S.D., ÓhÉigeartaigh, C., Scott, M.: Efficient pairing computation on supersingular abelian varieties. Des. Codes Crypt. **42**(3), 239–271 (2007)
8. Barreto, P.S.L.M., Kim, H.Y., Lynn, B., Scott, M.: Efficient algorithms for pairing-based cryptosystems. In: Yung, M. (ed.) CRYPTO 2002. LNCS, vol. 2442, pp. 354–369. Springer, Heidelberg (2002)
9. Barreto, P.S.L.M., Libert, B., McCullagh, N., Quisquater, J.-J.: Efficient and provably-secure identity-based signatures and signcryption from bilinear maps. In: Roy, B. (ed.) ASIACRYPT 2005. LNCS, vol. 3788, pp. 515–532. Springer, Heidelberg (2005)
10. Barreto, P.S.L.M., Lynn, B., Scott, M.: Constructing elliptic curves with prescribed embedding degrees. In: Cimato, S., Galdi, C., Persiano, G. (eds.) SCN 2002. LNCS, vol. 2576, pp. 257–267. Springer, Heidelberg (2003)
11. Barreto, P.S.L.M., Lynn, B., Scott, M.: On the selection of pairing-friendly groups. In: Matsui, M., Zuccherato, R.J. (eds.) SAC 2003. LNCS, vol. 3006, pp. 17–25. Springer, Heidelberg (2004)

12. Barreto, P.S.L.M., Naehrig, M.: Pairing-friendly elliptic curves of prime order. In: Preneel, B., Tavares, S. (eds.) SAC 2005. LNCS, vol. 3897, pp. 319–331. Springer, Heidelberg (2006)

13. Benger, N., Scott, M.: Constructing tower extensions of finite fields for implementation of pairing-based cryptography. In: Hasan, M.A., Helleseth, T. (eds.) WAIFI 2010. LNCS, vol. 6087, pp. 180–195. Springer, Heidelberg (2010)

14. Benson, K., Shacham, H., Waters, B.: The k-BDH assumption family: bilinear map cryptography from progressively weaker assumptions. In: Dawson, E. (ed.) CT-RSA 2013. LNCS, vol. 7779, pp. 310–325. Springer, Heidelberg (2013)

15. Beuchat, J.-L., González-Díaz, J.E., Mitsunari, S., Okamoto, E., Rodríguez-Henríquez, F., Teruya, T.: High-speed software implementation of the optimal ate pairing over Barreto–Naehrig curves. In: Joye, M., Miyaji, A., Otsuka, A. (eds.) Pairing 2010. LNCS, vol. 6487, pp. 21–39. Springer, Heidelberg (2010)

16. Boneh, D., Boyen, X.: Short signatures without random oracles. In: Cachin, C., Camenisch, J.L. (eds.) EUROCRYPT 2004. LNCS, vol. 3027, pp. 56–73. Springer, Heidelberg (2004)

17. Boneh, D., Franklin, M.: Identity-based encryption from the Weil pairing. In: Kilian, J. (ed.) CRYPTO 2001. LNCS, vol. 2139, pp. 213–229. Springer, Heidelberg (2001)

18. Boneh, D., Franklin, M.: Identity-based encryption from the Weil pairing. SIAM J. Comput. **32**(3), 586–615 (2003)

19. Boneh, D., Gentry, C., Lynn, B., Shacham, H.: Aggregate and verifiably encrypted signatures from bilinear maps. In: Biham, E. (ed.) EUROCRYPT 2003. LNCS, vol. 2656, pp. 416–432. Springer, Heidelberg (2003)

20. Boneh, D., Lynn, B., Shacham, H.: Short signatures from the Weil pairing. In: Boyd, C. (ed.) ASIACRYPT 2001. LNCS, vol. 2248, pp. 514–532. Springer, Heidelberg (2001)

21. Boyen, X.: Multipurpose identity-based signcryption: A swiss army knife for identity-based cryptography. In: Boneh, D. (ed.) CRYPTO 2003. LNCS, vol. 2729, pp. 383–399. Springer, Heidelberg (2003)

22. Boyen, X., Waters, B.: Anonymous hierarchical identity-based encryption (without random oracles). In: Dwork, C. (ed.) CRYPTO 2006. LNCS, vol. 4117, pp. 290–307. Springer, Heidelberg (2006)

23. Brezing, F., Weng, A.: Elliptic curves suitable for pairing based cryptography. Des. Codes Crypt. **37**(1), 133–141 (2005)

24. Cha, J.C., Cheon, J.H.: An identity-based signature from gap Diffie-Hellman groups. In: Desmedt, Y.G. (ed.) PKC 2003. LNCS, vol. 2567, pp. 18–30. Springer, Heidelberg (2002)

25. Chen, L., Cheng, Z., Smart, N.P.: Identity-based key agreement protocols from pairings. Int. J. Inf. Secur. **6**(4), 213–241 (2007)

26. Chen, X., Zhang, F., Kim, K.: New ID-based group signature from pairings. J. Electron. (China) **23**(6), 892–900 (2006)

27. Chen, X., Zhang, F., Susilo, W., Tian, H., Li, J., Kim, K.: Identity-based chameleon hash scheme without key exposure. In: Steinfeld, R., Hawkes, P. (eds.) ACISP 2010. LNCS, vol. 6168, pp. 200–215. Springer, Heidelberg (2010)

28. Cheon, J.H.: Security analysis of the strong Diffie-Hellman problem. In: Vaudenay, S. (ed.) EUROCRYPT 2006. LNCS, vol. 4004, pp. 1–11. Springer, Heidelberg (2006)

29. Cheon, J.H.: Discrete logarithm problems with auxiliary inputs. J. Cryptology **23**(3), 457–476 (2010)

30. Cheung, R.C.C., Duquesne, S., Fan, J., Guillermin, N., Verbauwhede, I., Yao, G.X.: FPGA implementation of pairings using residue number system and lazy reduction. In: Preneel, B., Takagi, T. (eds.) CHES 2011. LNCS, vol. 6917, pp. 421–441. Springer, Heidelberg (2011)

31. Chung, J., Hasan, M.: Asymmetric squaring formulae. In: 18th IEEE Symposium on Computer Arithmetic - ARITH-18 2007, pp. 113–122 (2007)

32. Cocks, C., Pinch, R.G.E.: Identity-based cryptosystems based on the Weil pairing (2001) (unpublished manuscript)

33. Comba, P.G.: Exponentiation cryptosystems on the IBM PC. IBM Syst. J. **29**(4), 526–538 (1990)

34. Costello, C.: Particularly friendly members of family trees. Cryptology ePrint Archive, Report 2012/072 (2012). http://eprint.iacr.org/

35. Costello, C., Lange, T., Naehrig, M.: Faster pairing computations on curves with high-degree twists. In: Nguyen, P.Q., Pointcheval, D. (eds.) PKC 2010. LNCS, vol. 6056, pp. 224–242. Springer, Heidelberg (2010)

36. Costello, C., Lauter, K., Naehrig, M.: Attractive subfamilies of BLS curves for implementing high-security pairings. In: Bernstein, D.J., Chatterjee, S. (eds.) INDOCRYPT 2011. LNCS, vol. 7107, pp. 320–342. Springer, Heidelberg (2011)

37. Crandall, R., Pomerance, C.: Prime Numbers: A Computational Perspective. Springer, Berlin (2001)

38. Devegili, A.J., Scott, M., Dahab, R.: Implementing cryptographic pairings over Barreto-Naehrig curves. In: Takagi, T., Okamoto, E., Okamoto, T., Okamoto, T. (eds.) Pairing 2007. LNCS, vol. 4575, pp. 197–207. Springer, Heidelberg (2007)

39. Dupont, R., Enge, A., Morain, F.: Building curves with arbitrary small MOV degree over finite prime fields. J. Cryptology **18**(2), 79–89 (2005)

40. Duursma, I., Lee, H.-S.: Tate pairing implementation for hyperelliptic curves $y^2 = x^p - x + d$. In: Laih, C.S. (ed.) ASIACRYPT 2003. LNCS, vol. 2894, pp. 111–123. Springer, Heidelberg (2003)

41. Fan, J., Vercauteren, F., Verbauwhede, I.: Efficient hardware implementation of $\mathbb{F}_p$-arithmetic for pairing-friendly curves. IEEE Trans. Comput. **61**(5), 676–685 (2012)

42. Fouque, P.-A., Tibouchi, M.: Indifferentiable hashing to Barreto-Naehrig curves. In: Hevia, A., Neven, G. (eds.) LatinCrypt 2012. LNCS, vol. 7533, pp. 1–17. Springer, Heidelberg (2012)

43. Freeman, D.: Constructing pairing-friendly elliptic curves with embedding degree 10. In: Hess, F., Pauli, S., Pohst, M. (eds.) ANTS 2006. LNCS, vol. 4076, pp. 452–465. Springer, Heidelberg (2006)

44. Freeman, D., Scott, M., Teske, E.: A taxonomy of pairing-friendly elliptic curves. J. Cryptology **23**(2), 224–280 (2010)

45. Frey, G., Müller, M., Rück, H.: The Tate pairing and the discrete logarithm applied to elliptic curve cryptosystems. IEEE Trans. Inf. Theory **45**(5), 1717–1719 (1999)

46. Frey, G., Rück, H.G.: A remark concerning m-divisibility and the discrete logarithm problem in the divisor class group of curves. Math. Comput. **62**, 865–874 (1994)

47. Fuentes-Castañeda, L., Knapp, E., Rodríguez-Henríquez, F.: Faster hashing to $\mathbb{G}_2$. In: Miri, A., Vaudenay, S. (eds.) SAC 2011. LNCS, vol. 7118, pp. 412–430. Springer, Heidelberg (2012)

48. Galbraith, S.D., Harrison, K., Soldera, D.: Implementing the Tate pairing. In: Fieker, C., Kohel, D.R. (eds.) ANTS 2002. LNCS, vol. 2369, pp. 324–337. Springer, Heidelberg (2002)

49. Galbraith, S.D.: Supersingular curves in cryptography. In: Boyd, C. (ed.) ASIACRYPT 2001. LNCS, vol. 2248, pp. 495–513. Springer, Heidelberg (2001)

50. Galbraith, S.D., Paterson, K.G., Smart, N.P.: Pairings for cryptographers. Discrete Appl. Math. **156**(16), 3113–3121 (2008)

51. Gentry, C., Silverberg, A.: Hierarchical ID-based cryptography. In: Zheng, Y. (ed.) ASIACRYPT 2002. LNCS, vol. 2501, pp. 548–566. Springer, Heidelberg (2002)

52. Gouvêa, C.P.L., López, J.: Software implementation of pairing-based cryptography on sensor networks using the MSP430 microcontroller. In: Roy, B., Sendrier, N. (eds.) INDOCRYPT 2009. LNCS, vol. 5922, pp. 248–262. Springer, Heidelberg (2009)

53. Grewal, G., Azarderakhsh, R., Longa, P., Hu, S., Jao, D.: Efficient implementation of bilinear pairings on ARM processors. In: Knudsen, L.R., Wu, H. (eds.) SAC 2012. LNCS, vol. 7707, pp. 149–165. Springer, Heidelberg (2013)

54. Hankerson, D., Menezes, A., Scott, M.: Software implementation of pairings. In: Identity-Based Cryptography, ch. 12, pp. 188–206. IOS Press, Amsterdam (2008)

55. Hess, F., Smart, N., Vercauteren, F.: The eta pairing revisited. IEEE Trans. Inf. Theory **52**, 4595–4602 (2006)

56. Joux, A.: A one-round protocol for tripartite Diffie-Hellman. In: Bosma, W. (ed.) ANTS 2000. LNCS, vol. 1838, pp. 385–394. Springer, Heidelberg (2000)

57. Kachisa, E.J., Schaefer, E.F., Scott, M.: Constructing Brezing-Weng pairing-friendly elliptic curves using elements in the cyclotomic field. In: Galbraith, S.D., Paterson, K.G. (eds.) Pairing 2008. LNCS, vol. 5209, pp. 126–135. Springer, Heidelberg (2008)

58. Karabina, K., Teske, E.: On prime-order elliptic curves with embedding degrees $k = 3, 4$, and 6. In: van der Poorten, A.J., Stein, A. (eds.) ANTS-VIII 2008. LNCS, vol. 5011, pp. 102–117. Springer, Heidelberg (2008)

59. Lauter, K., Montgomery, P.L., Naehrig, M.: An analysis of affine coordinates for pairing computation. In: Joye, M., Miyaji, A., Otsuka, A. (eds.) Pairing 2010. LNCS, vol. 6487, pp. 1–20. Springer, Heidelberg (2010)

60. Lee, E., Lee, H.-S., Park, C.-M.: Efficient and generalized pairing computation on abelian varieties. IEEE Trans. Inf. Theory **55**(4), 1793–1803 (2009)

61. Libert, B., Quisquater. J.-J.: New identity based signcryption schemes from pairings. In: Information Theory Workshop - ITW 2003, pp. 155–158. IEEE (2003)

62. Longa, P.: High-speed elliptic curve and pairing-based cryptography. Ph.D. thesis, University of Waterloo, April 2011

63. Luca, F., Shparlinski, I.E.: Elliptic curves with low embedding degree. J. Cryptology **19**(4), 553–562 (2006)

64. Matsuda, S., Kanayama, N., Hess, F., Okamoto, E.: Optimised versions of the ate and twisted ate pairings. In: Galbraith, S.D. (ed.) Cryptography and Coding 2007. LNCS, vol. 4887, pp. 302–312. Springer, Heidelberg (2007)

65. Menezes, A.J.: Elliptic Curve Public Key Cryptosystems. Kluwer Academic Publishers, Boston (1993)

66. Menezes, A.J., Okamoto, T., Vanstone, S.A.: Reducing elliptic curve logarithms to logarithms in a finite field. IEEE Trans. Inf. Theory **39**, 1639–1646 (1993)

67. Miller, V.S.: Short programs for functions on curves. IBM Thomas J. Watson Research Center Report (1986). http://crypto.stanford.edu/miller/miller.pdf

68. Miller, V.S.: The Weil pairing, and its efficient calculation. J. Cryptology **17**(4), 235–261 (2004)

69. Mitsunari, S.: A fast implementation of the optimal ate pairing over BN curve on Intel Haswell processor. Cryptology ePrint Archive, Report 2013/362 (2013). http://eprint.iacr.org/

70. Mitsunari, S., Sakai, R., Kasahara, M.: A new traitor tracing. IEICE Trans. Fundam. **E85–A**(2), 481–484 (2002)

71. Miyaji, A., Nakabayashi, M., Takano, S.: New explicit conditions of elliptic curve traces for FR-reduction. IEICE Trans. Fundam. **E84–A**(5), 1234–1243 (2001)
72. Montgomery, P.L.: Modular multiplication without trial division. Math. Comput. **44**(170), 519–521 (1985)
73. Mori, Y., Akagi, S., Nogami, Y., Shirase, M.: Pseudo 8-sparse multiplication for efficient ate-based pairing on Barreto-Naehrig curve. In: Cao, Z., Zhang, F. (eds.) Pairing 2013. LNCS, vol. 8365, pp. 186–198. Springer, Heidelberg (2014)
74. Naehrig, M., Barreto, P.S.L.M., Schwabe, P.: On compressible pairings and their computation. In: Vaudenay, S. (ed.) AFRICACRYPT 2008. LNCS, vol. 5023, pp. 371–388. Springer, Heidelberg (2008)
75. Naehrig, M., Niederhagen, R., Schwabe, P.: New software speed records for cryptographic pairings. In: Abdalla, M., Barreto, P.S.L.M. (eds.) LATINCRYPT 2010. LNCS, vol. 6212, pp. 109–123. Springer, Heidelberg (2010)
76. Nogami, Y., Akane, M., Sakemi, Y., Kato, H., Morikawa, Y.: Integer variable $\chi-$ based ate pairing. In: Galbraith, S.D., Paterson, K.G. (eds.) Pairing 2008. LNCS, vol. 5209, pp. 178–191. Springer, Heidelberg (2008)
77. Okamoto, T., Pointcheval, D.: The gap-problems: a new class of problems for the security of cryptographic schemes. In: Kim, K. (ed.) PKC 2001. LNCS, vol. 1992, pp. 104–118. Springer, Heidelberg (2001)
78. Ozturk, E., Guilford, J., Gopal, V.: Large integer squaring on intel architecture processors. Intel white paper (2013)
79. Ozturk, E., Guilford, J., Gopal, V., Feghali, W.: New instructions supporting large integer arithmetic on intel architecture processors. Intel white paper (2012)
80. Pereira, G.C.C.F., Simplício Jr, M.A., Naehrig, M., Barreto, P.S.L.M.: A family of implementation-friendly BN elliptic curves. J. Syst. Softw. **84**(8), 1319–1326 (2011)
81. Pollard, J.M.: Monte Carlo methods for index computation (mod p). Math. Comput. **32**, 918–924 (1978)
82. Rubin, K., Silverberg, A.: Supersingular abelian varieties in cryptology. In: Yung, M. (ed.) CRYPTO 2002. LNCS, vol. 2442, pp. 336–353. Springer, Heidelberg (2002)
83. Sakai, R., Kasahara, M.: Cryptosystems based on pairing over elliptic curve. In: Symposium on Cryptography and Information Security - SCIS 2003, pp. 8C-1, January 2003
84. Sakai, R., Ohgishi, K., Kasahara, M.: Cryptosystems based on pairing. In: Symposium on Cryptography and Information Security - SCIS 2000, Okinawa, Japan, January 2000
85. Scott, M.: A note on twists for pairing friendly curves (2009). ftp://ftp.computing. dcu.ie/pub/resources/crypto/twists.pdf
86. Scott, M.: On the efficient implementation of pairing-based protocols. In: Chen, L. (ed.) IMACC 2011. LNCS, vol. 7089, pp. 296–308. Springer, Heidelberg (2011)
87. Scott, M.: Unbalancing pairing-based key exchange protocols. Cryptology ePrint Archive, Report 2013/688 (2013). http://eprint.iacr.org/2013/688
88. Scott, M., Barreto, P.S.L.M.: Compressed pairings. In: Franklin, M. (ed.) CRYPTO 2004. LNCS, vol. 3152, pp. 140–156. Springer, Heidelberg (2004)
89. Scott, M., Benger, N., Charlemagne, M., Dominguez Perez, L.J., Kachisa, E.J.: On the final exponentiation for calculating pairings on ordinary elliptic curves. In: Shacham, H., Waters, B. (eds.) Pairing 2009. LNCS, vol. 5671, pp. 78–88. Springer, Heidelberg (2009)
90. Shirase, M.: Barreto-Naehrig curve with fixed coefficient. IACR ePrint Archive, report 2010/134 (2010). http://eprint.iacr.org/2010/134

91. Silverman, J.H.: The Arithmetic of Elliptic Curves. Graduate Texts in Mathematics, vol. 106. Springer, Berlin (1986)
92. Urroz, J.J., Luca, F., Shparlinski, I.: On the number of isogeny classes of pairing-friendly elliptic curves and statistics of MNT curves. Math. Comput. **81**(278), 1093–1110 (2012)
93. Vercauteren, F.: Optimal pairings. IEEE Trans. Inf. Theory **56**(1), 455–461 (2010)
94. Weil, A.: Sur les fonctions algébriques à corps de constantes fini. Comptes Rendus de l'Académie des Sciences **210**, 592–594 (1940)
95. Zavattoni, E., Domínguez-Pérez, L.J., Mitsunari, S., Sánchez, A.H., Teruya, T., Rodríguez-Henríquez, F.: Software implementation of attribute-based encryption (2013). http://sandia.cs.cinvestav.mx/index.php?n=Site.CPABE
96. Zhang, F., Chen, X.: Yet another short signatures without random oracles from bilinear pairings. IACR Cryptology ePrint Archive, report 2005/230 (2005)
97. Zhang, F., Kim, K.: ID-based blind signature and ring signature from pairings. In: Zheng, Y. (ed.) ASIACRYPT 2002. LNCS, vol. 2501, pp. 533–547. Springer, Heidelberg (2002)
98. Zhang, F., Safavi-Naini, R., Susilo, W.: An efficient signature scheme from bilinear pairings and its applications. In: Bao, F., Deng, R., Zhou, J. (eds.) PKC 2004. LNCS, vol. 2947, pp. 277–290. Springer, Heidelberg (2004)

Lattices Part I

A Three-Level Sieve Algorithm for the Shortest Vector Problem

Feng Zhang[✉], Yanbin Pan[✉], and Gengran Hu

Key Laboratory of Mathematics Mechanization,
Academy of Mathematics & NCMIS,
Chinese Academy of Sciences, 100190 Beijing, China
{zhangfeng,panyanbin}@amss.ac.cn, hudiran10@mails.ucas.ac.cn

Abstract. In AsiaCCS 2011, Wang *et al.* proposed a two-level heuristic sieve algorithm for the shortest vector problem in lattices, which improves the Nguyen-Vidick sieve algorithm. Inspired by their idea, we present a three-level sieve algorithm in this paper, which is shown to have better time complexity. More precisely, the time complexity of our algorithm is $2^{0.3778n+o(n)}$ polynomial-time operations and the corresponding space complexity is $2^{0.2833n+o(n)}$ polynomially many bits.

Keywords: Lattice · Shortest vector problem · Sieve algorithm · Sphere covering

1 Introduction

Lattices are discrete subgroups of $\mathbb{R}^n$ and have been widely used in cryptology. The *shortest vector problem*(SVP) refers the question to find a shortest non-zero vector in a given lattice, which is one of the most famous and widely studied computational problems on lattices.

It is well known that SVP is NP-hard under random reductions [2], so no polynomial time exact algorithms for it are expected to exist. Up to now, only approximation algorithms, such as [7,8,13,25], are efficient and all known exact algorithms are proven to cost exponential time. However, almost all known approximation algorithms (such as [8,25]) invoke some exact algorithm for solving SVP on some low dimensional lattices to improve the quantity of their outputs. Therefore, it is important to know how fast the best exact algorithm can be. What's more, algorithms for SVP play a very important role in cryptanalysis (see [19] for a survey). For example, nearly all knapsack-based public-key cryptosystems have been broken with a lattice algorithm (see [1,14,27]) and many lattice-based public-key cryptosystems can be broken by solving some

This work was supported in part by the NNSF of China (No.11071285, No.11201458, and No.61121062), in part by 973 Project (No. 2011CB302401) and in part by the National Center for Mathematics and Interdisciplinary Sciences, CAS.

T. Lange, K. Lauter, and P. Lisoněk (Eds.): SAC 2013, LNCS 8282, pp. 29–47, 2014.
DOI: 10.1007/978-3-662-43414-7_2, © Springer-Verlag Berlin Heidelberg 2014

SVP, including the famous NTRU [10]. Hence, better exact algorithm for SVP can also help us to know the security of these lattice-based public-key cryptosystems better, and choose more appropriate parameters for these cryptosystems.

The exact algorithms for SVP can be classified into two classes by now: deterministic algorithms and randomized sieve algorithms.

The first deterministic algorithm to find the shortest vector in a given lattice was proposed by Fincke, Pohst [5,6] and Kannan [11], by enumerating all lattice vectors shorter than a prescribed bound. If the input is an LLL-reduced basis, the running time is $2^{O(n^2)}$ polynomial-time operations. Kannan [11] also showed the running time can reach $2^{O(n \log n)}$ polynomial-time operations by choosing a suitable preprocessing algorithm. Schnorr and Euchner [26] presented a zig-zag strategy for enumerating the lattice vectors to make the algorithm have a better performance in practice. In 2010, Gama, Nguyen and Regev [9] introduced an extreme pruning technique and improved the running time in both theory and practice. All enumeration algorithms above require a polynomial space complexity. Another deterministic algorithm for SVP was proposed by Micciancio and Voulgaris [15] in 2010. Different from the previous algorithms, it is based on Voronoi cell computation and is the first deterministic single exponential time exact algorithm for SVP. The time complexity is $2^{2n+o(n)}$ polynomial-time operations. One drawback of the algorithm is that its space requirement is not polynomial but $2^{O(n)}$.

The randomized sieve algorithm was discovered by Ajtai, Kumar and Sivakumar (AKS) [3] in 2001. The running time and space requirement were proven to be $2^{O(n)}$. Regev's alternative analysis [22] showed that the hidden constant in $O(n)$ was at most 16, and it was further decreased to 5.9 by Nguyen and Vidick [20]. Blömer and Naewe [4] generalized the results of AKS to l_p norms. Micciancio and Voulgaris [16] presented a provable sieving variant called the ListSieve algorithm, whose running time is $2^{3.199n+o(n)}$ polynomial-time operations and space requirement is $2^{1.325n+o(n)}$ polynomially many bits. Subsequently, Pujol and Stehlé [21] improved the theoretical bound of the ListSieve algorithm to running time $2^{2.465n+o(n)}$ and space $2^{1.233n+o(n)}$ by introducing the birthday attack strategy. In the same work [16], Micciancio and Voulgaris also presented a heuristic variant of the ListSieve algorithm, called the GaussSieve algorithm. However, no upper bound on the running time of the GaussSieve Algorithm is currently known and the space requirement is provably bounded by $2^{0.41n}$. In [23], Schneider analyzed the GaussSieve algorithm and showed its strengths and weakness. What's more, a parallel implementation of the GaussSieve algorithm was presented by Milde and Schneider [17]. Recently, Schneider [24] presented an IdealListSieve algorithm to improve the ListSieve algorithm for the shortest vector problem in ideal lattices and the practical speed up is linear in the degree of the field polynomial. He also proposed a variant of the heuristic GaussSieve algorithm for ideal lattice with the same speedup.

To give a correct analysis of its complexity, the AKS algorithm involves some perturbations. However, getting rid of the perturbations, Nguyen and Vidick [20] proposed the first heuristic variant of the AKS algorithm, which in practice performs better and can solve SVP up to dimension 50. Its running time was proven to be $2^{0.415n+o(n)}$ polynomial-time operations under some nature heuristic assumption of uniform distribution of the sieved lattice vectors. By introducing a two-level technique, Wang *et al.* [30] gave an algorithm (WLTB) to improve the Nguyen-Vidick algorithm. Under a similar assumption of the distribution of sieved lattice vectors, the WLTB algorithm has the best theoretical time complexity so far, that is, $2^{0.3836n+o(n)}$. Both the heuristic assumptions can be supported by the experimental results on low dimensional lattices.

Our Contribution. Observing that the WLTB algorithm involves some data structure like skip list to reduce the time complexity, we present a three-level sieve algorithm in this paper. To estimate the complexity of the algorithm, it needs to compute the volume of some irregular spherical cap, which is a very complicated and tough work. By involving a smart technique, we simplify the complicated computation and prove that the optimal time complexity is $2^{0.3778n+o(n)}$ polynomial-time operations and the corresponding space complexity is $2^{0.2833n+o(n)}$ polynomially many bits under a similar natural heuristic assumption.

Table 1 summarizes the complexities of the heuristic variants of AKS algorithm and the GaussSieve algorithm. It can be seen that the latter two algorithms employ the time-memory tradeoffs that decrease the running time complexity at the cost of space complexity.

Table 1. Complexities of some heuristic algorithms for SVP

Algorithm	Time complexity	Space complexity
GaussSieve algorithm	-	$2^{0.41n+o(n)}$
Nguyen-Vidick algorithm	$2^{0.415n+o(n)}$	$2^{0.2075n+o(n)}$
WLTB algorithm	$2^{0.3836n+o(n)}$	$2^{0.2557n+o(n)}$
Our three-level algorithm	$2^{0.3778n+o(n)}$	$2^{0.2883n+o(n)}$

A natural question is whether we can improve the time complexity by four-level or higher-level algorithm. It may have a positive answer. However, by our work, it seems that the improvements get smaller and smaller, whereas the analysis of the complexity becomes more and more difficult when the number of levels increases.

Road Map. The rest of the paper is organized as follows. In Sect. 2 we provide some notations and preliminaries. We present our three-level sieve algorithm and the detailed analysis of its complexity in Sect. 3. Some experimental results are described in Sect. 4. Finally, Sect. 5 gives a short conclusion.

2 Notations and Preliminaries

Notations. Bold lower-case letters are used to denote vectors in $\mathbb{R}^n$. Denote by v_i the i-th entry of a vector v. Let $\|\cdot\|$ and $\langle\cdot,\cdot\rangle$ be the Euclidean norm and inner product of $\mathbb{R}^n$. Matrices are written as bold capital letters and the i-th column vector of a matrix $\boldsymbol{B}$ is denoted by $\boldsymbol{b}_i$.

Let $B_n(\boldsymbol{x}, R) = \{\boldsymbol{y} \in \mathbb{R}^n \mid \|\boldsymbol{y} - \boldsymbol{x}\| \le R\}$ be the n-dimensional ball centered at $\boldsymbol{x}$ with radius R. Let $B_n(R) = B_n(\boldsymbol{O}, R)$. Let $C_n(\gamma, R) = \{\boldsymbol{x} \in \mathbb{R}^n \mid \gamma R \le \|\boldsymbol{x}\| \le R\}$ be a spherical shell in $B_n(R)$, and $S^n = \{\boldsymbol{x} \in \mathbb{R}^n \mid \|\boldsymbol{x}\| = 1\}$ be the unit sphere in $\mathbb{R}^n$. Denote by $|S^n|$ the area of S^n.

2.1   Lattices

Let $\boldsymbol{B} = \{\boldsymbol{b}_1, \boldsymbol{b}_2, \dots, \boldsymbol{b}_n\} \subset \mathbb{R}^m$ be a set of n linearly independent vectors. The lattice $\mathcal{L}$ generated by the basis $\boldsymbol{B}$ is defined as $\mathcal{L}(\boldsymbol{B}) = \{\sum_{i=1}^{n} x_i \mathbf{b}_i : x_i \in \mathbb{Z}\}$. n is called the rank of the lattice. Denote by $\lambda_1(\mathcal{L})$ the norm of a shortest non-zero vector of $\mathcal{L}$.

2.2   The Basic Framework of Some Heuristic Sieve Algorithms

The Nguyen-Vidick algorithm and the WLTB algorithm have a common basic framework, which can be described as Algorithm 1 [30].

Algorithm 1. Finding short lattice vectors based on sieving

Input: An LLL-reduced basis $\boldsymbol{B} = [\boldsymbol{b}_1, \dots, \boldsymbol{b}_n]$ of a lattice $\mathcal{L}$, sieve factors
                and a number N.
Output: A short non-zero vector of $\mathcal{L}$.
1: $S' \leftarrow \emptyset$
2: **for** $j = 1$ to N **do**
3: $\quad$ $S' \leftarrow S' \cup$ sampling($\boldsymbol{B}$) using Klein's algorithm [12]
4: **end for**
5: Remove all zero vectors from S'
6: **Repeat**
7: $\quad$ $S \leftarrow S'$
8: $\quad$ $S' \leftarrow$ sieve(S, sieve factors) using **Sieve Algorithm**
9: $\quad$ Remove all zero vectors from S'
10: **until** $S' = \emptyset$
11: Compute $\boldsymbol{v}_0 \in S$ such that $\|\boldsymbol{v}_0\| = \min\{\|\boldsymbol{v}\|, \boldsymbol{v} \in S\}$
12: **Return** $\boldsymbol{v}_0$

In general the **Sieve Algorithm** in Line 8 will output a set S' of shorter lattice vectors than those in S. When we repeat the sieve process enough times, a shortest vector is expected to be found.

Denote by R' (*resp.* R) the maximum length of those vectors in S' (*resp.* S). To find S', the sieve algorithm usually tries to find a set C of lattice vectors in S such that the balls centered at these vectors with radius R' can cover all the lattice points in some spherical shell $C_n(\gamma, R)$. By subtracting the corresponding center from every lattice point in every ball, shorter lattice vectors will be obtained, which form the set S'.

Different ways to find C lead to different algorithms. Roughly speaking,

- The Nguyen-Vidick algorithm checks every lattice point in S' sequentially to decide whether it is also in some existing ball or it is a new vector in C (see Fig. 1 for a geometric description).
- The WLTB algorithm involves a two-level strategy, that is, the big-ball-level and the small-ball-level. It first covers the spherical shell with big balls centered at some lattice vectors, then covers the intersection of every big ball and $C_n(\gamma, R)$ with small balls centered at some lattice points in the intersection. The centers of the small balls form C. It can be shown that it is faster to decide whether a lattice vector is in C or not. We first check whether it is in some big ball or not. If not, it must be a new point in C. If so, we just check whether it is in some small ball in the big ball it belongs to, regardless of those small balls of the other big balls (see Fig. 2 for a geometric description).

For either the Nguyen-Vidick algorithm or the WLTB algorithm, to analyze its complexity needs a natural assumption below.

Heuristic Assumption 1: At any stage in Algorithm 1, the lattice vectors in $S' \cap C_n(\gamma, R)$ are uniformly distributed in $C_n(\gamma, R)$.

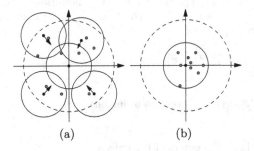

(a)   (b)

Fig. 1. Geometric description of Nguyen-Vidick's sieve algorithm

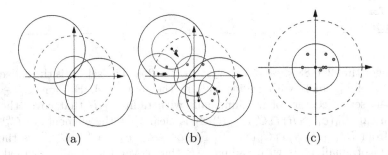

(a)   (b)   (c)

Fig. 2. Geometric description of WLTB's sieve algorithm

3 A Three-Level Sieve Algorithm

3.1 Description of the Three-Level Sieve Algorithm

Different from the two-level algorithm, our algorithm involves a medium-ball-level. Simply speaking, the algorithm first covers the spherical shell with big balls, then covers every big ball with medium balls, and at last covers every medium ball with small balls. Algorithm 2 gives a detailed description of the three-level sieve algorithm.

Algorithm 2. A three-level sieve algorithm

Input: A subset $S \subseteq B_n(R)$ of vectors in a lattice $\mathcal{L}$ where $R \leftarrow \max_{v \in S} \|v\|$
      and sieve factors $0.88 < \gamma_3 < 1 < \gamma_2 < \gamma_1 < \sqrt{2}\gamma_3$.
Output: A subset $S' \subseteq B_n(\gamma_3 R) \cap \mathcal{L}$.
1: $S' \leftarrow \emptyset, C_1 \leftarrow \emptyset$.
2: **for** $v \in S$ **do**
3:    **if** $\|v\| \leq \gamma_3 R$ **then**
4:       $S' \leftarrow S' \cup \{v\}$
5:    **else**
6:       **if** $\exists\, c_1 \in C_1, \|v - c_1\| \leq \gamma_1 R$ **then**
7:          **if** $\exists\, c_2 \in C_2^{c_1}, \|v - c_2\| \leq \gamma_2 R$ **then**   \\$C_2^{c_1}$ is initialized as $\emptyset$\\
8:             **if** $\exists\, c_3 \in C_3^{c_1,c_2}, \|v - c_3\| \leq \gamma_3 R$ **then**   \\$C_3^{c_1,c_2}$ is initialized as $\emptyset$\\
9:                $S' \leftarrow S' \cup \{v - c_3\}$
10:             **else**
11:                $C_3^{c_1,c_2} \leftarrow C_3^{c_1,c_2} \cup \{v\}$ \ centers of small balls \
12:             **end if**
13:          **else**
14:             $C_2^{c_1} \leftarrow C_2^{c_1} \cup \{v\}$ \ centers of medius balls \
15:          **end if**
16:       **else**
17:          $C_1 \leftarrow C_1 \cup \{v\}$ \ centers of big balls \
18:       **end if**
19:    **end if**
20: **end for**
21: **return** S'

In Algorithm 2, $0.88 < \gamma_3 < 1 < \gamma_2 < \gamma_1 < \sqrt{2}\gamma_3$. The set C_1 is the collection of centers of big balls with radius $\gamma_1 R$ in the first level. For any $c_1 \in C_1$, $C_2^{c_1}$ is the set of centers of medium balls with radius $\gamma_2 R$ that cover the big spherical cap $B_n(c_1, \gamma_1 R) \cap C_n(\gamma_3, R)$. It is clear that the elements of $C_2^{c_1}$ are chosen from $B_n(c_1, \gamma_1 R) \cap C_n(\gamma_3, R)$. For $c_1 \in C_1, c_2 \in C_2^{c_1}$, $C_3^{c_1,c_2}$ is the set of centers of small balls with radius $\gamma_3 R$ that cover the small spherical cap $B_n(c_2, \gamma_2 R) \cap B_n(c_1, \gamma_1 R) \cap C_n(\gamma_3, R)$. Also the elements of $C_3^{c_1,c_2}$ are chosen from the small spherical cap.

3.2   Complexity of the Algorithm

Denote by N_1, N_2 and N_3 the corresponding upper bound on the expected number of lattice points in C_1, $C_2^{c_1}$ (for any $c_1 \in C_1$) and $C_3^{c_1,c_2}$ (for any $c_1 \in C_1, c_2 \in C_2^{c_1}$).

The Space Complexity. Notice that the total number of big, medium and small balls can be bounded by N_1, $N_1 N_2$ and $N_1 N_2 N_3$ respectively. As in [20] and [30], if we sample $\text{poly}(n)N_1 N_2 N_3$ vectors, after a polynomial number of iterations in Algorithm 1, it is expected that a shortest non-zero lattice vector can be obtained with the left vectors. So the space complexity is bounded by $O(N_1 N_2 N_3)$.

The Time Complexity. The initial size of S is $\text{poly}(n)N_1 N_2 N_3$. In each iteration in Algorithm 1, steps 3–19 in Algorithm 2 repeat $\text{poly}(n)N_1 N_2 N_3$ times, and in each repeat, at most $N_1 + N_2 + N_3$ comparisons are needed. Therefore, the total time complexity can be bounded by $O(N_1 N_2 N_3(N_1 + N_2 + N_3))$ polynomial-time operations.

We next give the estimation of N_1, N_2 and N_3. Without loss of generality, we restrict $R = 1$ and let $C_n(\gamma) = C_n(\gamma, 1) = \{\boldsymbol{x} \in \mathbb{R}^n \mid \gamma R \le \|\boldsymbol{x}\| \le 1\}$ through our proofs for simplicity.

The Upper Bound of N_1. Nguyen and Vidick [20] first gave a proof of the upper bound N_1, and a more refined proof was given by Wang et al. [30].

Theorem 1. (Wang et al. [30]) *Let n be a non-negative integer, N be an integer and $0.88 < \gamma_3 < 1 < \gamma_1 < \sqrt{2}\gamma_3$. Let*

$$N_1 = c_{\mathcal{H}_1}^n \lceil 3\sqrt{2\pi}n^{\frac{3}{2}} \rceil,$$

where $c_{\mathcal{H}_1} = 1/(\gamma_1 \sqrt{1 - \frac{\gamma_1^2}{4}})$ and S a subset of $C_n(\gamma_3 R)$ of cardinality N whose points are picked independently at random with uniform distribution. If $N_1 < N < 2^n$, then for any subset $C \subseteq S$ of size at least N_1 whose points are picked independently at random with uniform distribution, with overwhelming probability, for all $\boldsymbol{v} \in S$, there exists a $\boldsymbol{c} \in C$ such that $\|\boldsymbol{v} - \boldsymbol{c}\| \le \gamma_1 R$.

The Upper Bound of N_2. Let

- $\Omega_n(\gamma_1)$ be the fraction of $C_n(\gamma_3)$ that is covered by a ball of radius γ_1 centered at a point of $C_n(\gamma_3)$,
- $\Gamma_n(\gamma_1, \gamma_2)$ be the fraction of $C_n(\gamma_3)$ covered by a big spherical cap $B_n(\boldsymbol{c}_2, \gamma_2) \cap B_n(\boldsymbol{c}_1, \gamma_1) \cap C_n(\gamma_3)$,
- $\Omega_n(\gamma_1, \gamma_2)$ be the fraction of $B_n(\boldsymbol{c}_1, \gamma_1) \cap C_n(\gamma_3)$ covered by $B_n(\boldsymbol{c}_2, \gamma_2) \cap B_n(\boldsymbol{c}_1, \gamma_1) \cap C_n(\gamma_3)$, where $\boldsymbol{c}_2 \in C_2^{c_1}, \boldsymbol{c}_1 \in C_1$.

Clearly, $\Omega_n(\gamma_1, \gamma_2) = \frac{\Gamma_n(\gamma_1,\gamma_2)}{\Omega_n(\gamma_1)}$. To compute N_2, we need the minimal value of $\Omega_n(\gamma_1, \gamma_2)$. We estimate $\Omega_n(\gamma_1)$ and $\Gamma_n(\gamma_1, \gamma_2)$ respectively.

Lemma 1. (Wang *et al.* [30]) *Let* $0.88 < \gamma_3 < 1 < \gamma_1 < \sqrt{2}\gamma_3$, *then*

$$\frac{1}{3\sqrt{2\pi n}}\frac{(\sin\theta_2)^{n-1}}{\cos\theta_2} < \Omega_n(\gamma_1) < \frac{1}{\sqrt{2\pi(n-1)}}\frac{(\sin\theta_1)^{n-1}}{\cos\theta_1},$$

where $\theta_1 = \arccos(1 - \frac{\gamma_1^2}{2\gamma_3^2}), \theta_2 = \arccos(1 - \frac{\gamma_1^2}{2})$.

Note that the proportion $\Gamma_n(\gamma_1, \gamma_2)$ is different from that of Lemma 4 in [30], as the radius of $B_n(c_2, \gamma_2)$ is larger than the inside radius of the shell $C_n(\gamma_3)$. Thus, it leads to the slightly different bounds of $\Gamma_n(\gamma_1, \gamma_2)$ from that of Lemma 4 in [30]. If c_2 lies on the sphere of a big ball $B_n(c_1, \gamma_1)$, the fraction $\Gamma_n(\gamma_1, \gamma_2)$ is minimal. Lemma 2 gives the minimal and maximal value of $\Gamma_n(\gamma_1, \gamma_2)$ when c_2 lies on the sphere of a big ball $B_n(c_1, \gamma_1)$.

Lemma 2. *Let* $0.88 < \gamma_3 < 1 < \gamma_2 < \gamma_1 < \sqrt{2}\gamma_3$, *where* γ_3 *is very close to* 1. *Then*

$$\frac{cd_{\min}^{n-2}}{2\pi n} \le \Gamma_n(\gamma_1, \gamma_2) \le \frac{c'd_{\max}^{n-2}}{2\pi},$$

where $d_{\max} = \sqrt{1 - \left(\frac{\gamma_3^2 - \gamma_1^2 + 1}{2\gamma_3}\right)^2 - \left(\frac{1}{c_{\mathcal{H}_2}}\left(\frac{\gamma_3^2 + 1 - \gamma_2^2}{2} - \frac{(2\gamma_3^2 - \gamma_1^2)(\gamma_3^2 - \gamma_1^2 + 1)}{4\gamma_3^2}\right)\right)^2}$, $d_{\min}$

$= \gamma_2\sqrt{1 - \frac{\gamma_2^2 c_{\mathcal{H}_1}^2}{4}}$, $c_{\mathcal{H}_1} = 1/(\gamma_1\sqrt{1 - \frac{\gamma_1^2}{4}})$, $c_{\mathcal{H}_2} = \frac{\gamma_1}{\gamma_3}\sqrt{1 - \frac{\gamma_1^2}{4\gamma_3^2}}$, c *and* c' *are constants unrelated to* n.

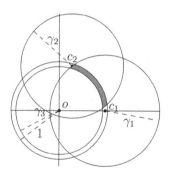

Fig. 3. The region of $B_n(c_2, \gamma_2) \cap B_n(c_1, \gamma_1) \cap C_n(\gamma_3)$.

Proof. Note that γ_3 is very close to 1. We just consider the proportion on the sphere covering as in [30].

Without loss of generality, we assume the center of $B_n(c_1, \gamma_1)$ is $c_1 = (\alpha_1, 0, \ldots, 0)$, and the center of $B_n(c_2, \gamma_2)$ is $c_2 = (\beta_1, \beta_2, 0 \ldots, 0)$, where $\alpha, \beta_1, \beta_2 > 0$. The spherical cap $B_n(c_2, \gamma_2) \cap B_n(c_1, \gamma_1) \cap C_n(\gamma_3)$ is

$$\begin{cases} x_1^2 + x_2^2 + \ldots + x_n^2 = 1 \\ (x_1 - \alpha_1)^2 + x_2^2 + \ldots + x_n^2 < \gamma_1^2 \\ (x_1 - \beta_1)^2 + (x_2 - \beta_2)^2 + \ldots + x_n^2 < \gamma_2^2 \end{cases}$$

where $\gamma_3 \leq \alpha_1 \leq 1, (\beta_1 - \alpha_1)^2 + \beta_2^2 = \gamma_1^2$ and $\gamma_3^2 \leq \beta_1^2 + \beta_2^2 \leq 1$. The region is as the shadow of the Fig. 3. Denote by Q the volume of the region. By projecting the target region to the hyperplane orthogonal to x_1 and by sphere coordinate transformation (for details see the proof of Lemma 4 in [30]), we get

$$\frac{cd^{n-2}}{2\pi n} \leq \Gamma_n(\gamma_1, \gamma_2) = \frac{Q}{|S^n|} \leq \frac{c'd^{n-2}}{2\pi}$$

where $d = \sqrt{1 - \left(\frac{\alpha_1^2 - \gamma_1^2 + 1}{2\alpha_1}\right)^2 - \left(\frac{1}{\beta_2}\left(\frac{\beta_1^2 + \beta_2^2 + 1 - \gamma_2^2}{2} - \beta_1 \frac{\alpha_1^2 - \gamma_1^2 + 1}{2\alpha_1}\right)\right)^2}$ and c, c' are constants unrelated to n. Let $\alpha_2 = \sqrt{\beta_1^2 + \beta_2^2}$. From the equation $(\beta_1 - \alpha_1)^2 + \beta_2^2 = \gamma_1^2$, we obtain

$$\beta_1 = \frac{\alpha_2^2 + \alpha_1^2 - \gamma_1^2}{2\alpha_1}, \beta_2 = \sqrt{\alpha_2^2 - \left(\frac{\alpha_2^2 + \alpha_1^2 - \gamma_1^2}{2\alpha_1}\right)^2}.$$

Therefore, d can be regarded as a function with respect to α_1, α_2, where $\gamma_3 \leq \alpha_1 \leq 1, \gamma_3 \leq \alpha_2 \leq 1$. Since $0.88 < \gamma_3 < 1 < \gamma_2 < \gamma_1 < \sqrt{2}\gamma_3$, it can be proven that d decreases with α_1, α_2 increasing. Then $d_{\min}$ can be obtained by letting $\alpha_1 = 1, \alpha_2 = 1$ and $d_{\max}$ can be obtained by letting $\alpha_1 = \gamma_3, \alpha_2 = \gamma_3$. Hence, the lemma follows.

Theorem 2. *Let n be a non-negative integer, N be an integer and $0.88 < \gamma_3 < 1 < \gamma_2 < \gamma_1 < \sqrt{2}\gamma_3$, where γ_3 is very close to 1. Let*

$$N_2 = c_2 \left(\frac{c_{\mathcal{H}_2}}{d_{\min}}\right)^n \lceil n^{\frac{3}{2}} \rceil,$$

where $c_{\mathcal{H}_2} = \frac{\gamma_1}{\gamma_3}\sqrt{1 - \frac{\gamma_1^2}{4\gamma_3^2}}, d_{\min} = \gamma_2\sqrt{1 - \frac{\gamma_2^2 c_{\mathcal{H}_1}^2}{4}}, c_{\mathcal{H}_1} = 1/(\gamma_1\sqrt{1 - \frac{\gamma_1^2}{4}})$, and c_2 is a positive constant unrelated to n. Let S be a subset of $C_n(\gamma_3 R) \cap B_n(c_1, \gamma_1 R) \cap B_n(c_2, \gamma_2 R)$ of cardinality N whose points are picked independently at random with uniform distribution. If $N_2 < N < 2^n$, then for any subset $C \subseteq S$ of size at least N_2 whose points are picked independently at random with uniform distribution, with overwhelming probability, for all $v \in S$, there exists a $c \in C$ such that $\|v - c\| \leq \gamma_2 R$.

Proof. Combining Lemmas 1 and 2, we have $\Omega_n(\gamma_1, \gamma_2) = \frac{\Gamma_n(\gamma_1, \gamma_2)}{\Omega_n(\gamma_1)} \geq \frac{c}{\sqrt{2\pi n}} \cdot \left(1 - \frac{\gamma_2^2}{2\gamma_2^2}\right)\left(\frac{d_{\min}}{c_{\mathcal{H}_2}}\right)^n$. The expected fraction of $B_n(c_1, \gamma_1) \cap C_n(\gamma_3)$ that is not covered by N_2 balls of radius γ_2 centered at randomly chosen points of $B_n(c_1, \gamma_1) \cap C_n(\gamma_3)$ is $(1 - \Omega_n(\gamma_1, \gamma_2))^{N_2}$. So,

$$N_2 \log(1 - \Omega_n(\gamma_1, \gamma_2)) \leq N_2(-\Omega_n(\gamma_1, \gamma_2))$$
$$< c_2 n^{3/2} \left(\frac{c_{\mathcal{H}_2}}{d_{\min}}\right)^n \cdot \frac{1}{c_2\sqrt{n}} \left(\frac{d_{\min}}{c_{\mathcal{H}_2}}\right)^n \leq -n < -\log N.$$

which implies $(1 - \Omega_n(\gamma_1, \gamma_2))^{N_2} < e^{-n} < \frac{1}{N}$. The expected number of uncovered points is smaller than 1. It means that any point in $B_n(c_1, \gamma_1) \cap C_n(\gamma_3)$ is covered by a ball centered at a vector in $B_n(c_1, \gamma_1) \cap C_n(\gamma_3)$ with radius γ_2 with probability $1 - e^{-n}$.

The Upper Bound of N_3. Let

- $\Gamma_n(\gamma_1, \gamma_2, \gamma_3)$ be the fraction of $C_n(\gamma_3)$ that is covered by a small spherical cap $B_n(c_3, \gamma_3) \cap B_n(c_2, \gamma_2) \cap B_n(c_1, \gamma_1) \cap C_n(\gamma_3)$,
- $\Omega_n(\gamma_1, \gamma_2, \gamma_3)$ the fraction of $B_n(c_2, \gamma_2) \cap B_n(c_1, \gamma_1) \cap C_n(\gamma_3)$ covered by $B_n(c_3, \gamma_3) \cap B_n(c_2, \gamma_2) \cap B_n(c_1, \gamma_1) \cap C_n(\gamma_3)$, where $c_3 \in C_3^{c_1, c_2}, c_2 \in C_2^{c_1}$, $c_1 \in C_1$.

Clearly, $\Omega_n(\gamma_1, \gamma_2, \gamma_3) = \frac{\Gamma_n(\gamma_1, \gamma_2, \gamma_3)}{\Gamma_n(\gamma_1, \gamma_2)}$. To estimate N_3, we need to compute the lower bound of $\Omega_n(\gamma_1, \gamma_2, \gamma_3)$. To obtain the lower bound of $\Gamma_n(\gamma_1, \gamma_2, \gamma_3)$, we need to compute the volume of some irregular convex region, which is very complicated. However, using the inscribed triangle of the region, we get a reasonable lower bound of the volume successfully.

Lemma 3. *Let $0.88 < \gamma_3 < 1 < \gamma_2 < \gamma_1 < \sqrt{2}\gamma_3$, where γ_3 is very close to 1. We have*

$$\Gamma_n(\gamma_1, \gamma_2, \gamma_3) \geq \frac{c'' r_{\min}^{n-3}}{2\pi^{3/2} n^2},$$

where $r_{\min} = \sqrt{c_{\mathcal{H}_3} - \left(1 - \frac{\gamma_3^2}{2c_{\mathcal{H}_3}}\right)^2}$, $c_{\mathcal{H}_3} = \gamma_2^2 \left(1 - \frac{\gamma_2^2 c_{\mathcal{H}_1}^2}{4}\right), c''$ *is a constant unrelated to n.*

Proof. We consider the proportion on the sphere covering. W.l.o.g., we assume the centers of $B_n(c_1, \gamma_1), B_n(c_2, \gamma_2), B_n(c_3, \gamma_3)$ are, respectively,

$$c_1 = (\alpha_1, 0, \ldots, 0), \ \alpha_1 > 0,$$
$$c_2 = (\beta_1, \beta_2, 0 \ldots, 0), \ \beta_1, \beta_2 > 0,$$
$$c_3 = (\delta_1, \delta_2, \delta_3, 0 \ldots, 0), \ \delta_1, \delta_2, \delta_3 > 0.$$

The spherical cap $B_n(c_3, \gamma_3) \cap B_n(c_2, \gamma_2) \cap B_n(c_1, \gamma_1) \cap C_n(\gamma_3)$ is

$$\begin{cases} x_1^2 + x_2^2 + \ldots + x_n^2 = 1 & (E_1) \\ (x_1 - \alpha_1)^2 + x_2^2 + \ldots + x_n^2 < \gamma_1^2 & (E_2) \\ (x_1 - \beta_1)^2 + (x_2 - \beta_2)^2 + x_3^2 + \ldots + x_n^2 < \gamma_2^2 & (E_3) \\ (x_1 - \delta_1)^2 + (x_2 - \delta_2)^2 + (x_3 - \delta_3)^2 + \ldots + x_n^2 < \gamma_3^2 & (E_4) \end{cases}$$

where $\gamma_3 \leq \alpha_1 \leq 1, \gamma_3^2 \leq \beta_1^2 + \beta_2^2 \leq 1, (\beta_1 - \alpha_1)^2 + \beta_2^2 = \gamma_1^2, \gamma_3^2 \leq \delta_1^2 + \delta_2^2 + \delta_3^2 \leq 1, (\delta_1 - \alpha_1)^2 + \delta_2^2 + \delta_3^2 = \gamma_1^2, (\delta_1 - \beta_1)^2 + (\delta_2 - \beta_2)^2 + \delta_3^2 = \gamma_2^2$.

Denote by Q the volume of the region, and project the target region to the hyperplane orthogonal to x_1. Denote by D the projection region. Therefore, the volume of the target region is

$$Q = \iint \cdots \int_D \sqrt{1 + \sum_{i=2}^n \left(\frac{\partial x_1}{\partial x_i}\right)^2} \, dx_2 dx_3 \cdots dx_n = \iint \cdots \int_D \frac{dx_2 dx_3 \cdots dx_n}{\sqrt{1 - \sum_{i=2}^n x_i^2}}.$$

Now we determine the projection region D. To simplify the expression, we let
$\alpha_2 = \sqrt{\beta_1^2 + \beta_2^2}, \alpha_3 = \sqrt{\delta_1^2 + \delta_2^2 + \delta_3^2}, a = \frac{\alpha_1^2 + 1 - \gamma_1^2}{2\alpha_1}, b = \frac{\alpha_2^2 + 1 - \gamma_2^2}{2}, f = \frac{\alpha_3^2 + 1 - \gamma_3^2}{2}.$
From the equations $(\beta_1 - \alpha_1)^2 + \beta_2^2 = \gamma_1^2, (\delta_1 - \alpha_1)^2 + \delta_2^2 + \delta_3^2 = \gamma_1^2, (\delta_1 - \beta_1)^2 +$
$(\delta_2 - \beta_2)^2 + \delta_3^2 = \gamma_2^2,$ it is easy to write $\beta_1, \beta_2, \delta_1, \delta_2, \delta_3$ as the expressions of
$\alpha_i, \gamma_i, i = 1, 2, 3,$ i.e.,

$$\beta_1 = \frac{\alpha_1^2 + \alpha_2^2 - \gamma_1^2}{2\alpha_1}, \quad \beta_2 = \sqrt{\alpha_2^2 - \left(\frac{\alpha_2^2 + \alpha_1^2 - \gamma_1^2}{2\alpha_1}\right)^2},$$

$$\delta_1 = \frac{\alpha_1^2 + \alpha_3^2 - \gamma_1^2}{2\alpha_1}, \quad \delta_2 = \frac{\alpha_2^2 + \alpha_3^2 - \gamma_2^2 - \frac{(\alpha_1^2 + \alpha_2^2 - \gamma_1^2)(\alpha_1^2 + \alpha_3^2 - \gamma_1^2)}{2\alpha_1^2}}{2\sqrt{\alpha_2^2 - \left(\frac{\alpha_1^2 + \alpha_2^2 - \gamma_1^2}{2\alpha_1}\right)^2}},$$

$$\delta_3 = \left(\alpha_3^2 - \left(\frac{\alpha_1^2 + \alpha_3^2 - \gamma_1^2}{2\alpha_1}\right)^2 - \frac{\left(\alpha_2^2 + \alpha_3^2 - \gamma_2^2 - \frac{(\alpha_1^2 + \alpha_2^2 - \gamma_1^2)(\alpha_1^2 + \alpha_3^2 - \gamma_1^2)}{2\alpha_1^2}\right)^2}{4\left(\alpha_2^2 - \left(\frac{\alpha_1^2 + \alpha_2^2 - \gamma_1^2}{2\alpha_1}\right)^2\right)}\right)^{\frac{1}{2}}.$$

We project the intersection of equation (E_1) and (E_i) to the hyperplane orthogonal to x_1 and suppose the projection region is $D_{i-1}, i = 2, 3, 4.$ Then $D = D_1 \cap D_2 \cap D_3$, where

$$D_1 = \{(x_2, x_3, \ldots, x_n) \in \mathbb{R}^{n-1} | x_2^2 + x_3^2 + \cdots + x_n^2 < 1 - a^2\}.$$

$$D_2^1 = \left\{(x_2, x_3, \ldots, x_n) \in \mathbb{R}^{n-1} | x_2^2 + x_3^2 + \cdots + x_n^2 < 1 - \left(\frac{b - \beta_2 x_2}{\beta_1}\right)^2, x_2 < \frac{b}{\beta_2}\right\},$$

$$D_2^2 = \left\{(x_2, x_3, \ldots, x_n) \in \mathbb{R}^{n-1} | x_2^2 + x_3^2 + \cdots + x_n^2 < 1, x_2 \geq \frac{b}{\beta_2}\right\},$$

$$D_2 = D_2^1 \cup D_2^2.$$

$$D_3^1 = \left\{(x_2, x_3, \ldots, x_n) \in \mathbb{R}^{n-1} | x_2^2 + x_3^2 + \cdots + x_n^2 < 1 - \left(\frac{f - \delta_2 x_2 - \delta_2 x_3}{\delta_1}\right)^2,\right.$$
$$\left. f - \delta_2 x_2 - \delta_2 x_3 > 0\right\},$$

$$D_3^2 = \{(x_2, x_3, \ldots, x_n) \in \mathbb{R}^{n-1} | x_2^2 + x_3^2 + \cdots + x_n^2 < 1, f - \delta_2 x_2 - \delta_2 x_3 \leq 0\},$$
$$D_3 = D_3^1 \cup D_3^2.$$

The region of (x_2, x_3) for D is the shadow of Fig. 4, and that of $(x_4, \ldots, x_n)$ is an

$(n-3)$-dimensional ball with radius $r = \sqrt{1 - a^2 - \left(\frac{b - a\beta_1}{\beta_2}\right)^2 - \left(\frac{f - \delta_1 a - \delta_2 \frac{b - a\beta_1}{\beta_2}}{\delta_3}\right)^2}.$

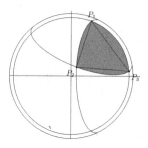

Fig. 4. The region of (x_2, x_3) for D.

For $(x_4, \ldots, x_n)$, we adopt hyper sphere coordinate transformation. Let

$$
\begin{cases}
x_4 = t \cos \varphi_1 \\
x_5 = t \sin \varphi_1 \cos \varphi_2 \\
\quad \vdots \\
x_{n-1} = t \sin \varphi_1 \cdots \sin \varphi_{n-5} \cos \varphi_{n-4} \\
x_n = t \sin \varphi_1 \cdots \sin \varphi_{n-5} \sin \varphi_{n-4}
\end{cases}
$$

where $0 \le t \le r, 0 \le \varphi_k \le \pi, k = 1, \ldots, n-5, 0 \le \varphi_{n-4} \le 2\pi$.

For a fixed t, denote by $D(t)$ the corresponding region of (x_2, x_3) and by $s(t)$ the area of $D(t)$. Let $f(t)$ be the area of triangular $\triangle_{P_1 P_2 P_3}$, then $s(t) \ge f(t)$. Thus,

$$
Q = \int_0^r \int_0^{2\pi} \int_0^{\pi} \cdots \int_0^{\pi} t^{n-4} \sin \varphi_{n-5} \cdots \sin^{n-4} \varphi_1 \iint_{D(t)} \frac{dx_2 dx_3}{\sqrt{1 - \sum_{i=2}^n x_i^2}} d\varphi_1 \cdots dt
$$

$$
\ge \int_0^r \int_0^{2\pi} \int_0^{\pi} \cdots \int_0^{\pi} t^{n-4} \sin \varphi_{n-5} \cdots \sin^{n-4} \varphi_1 \iint_{D(t)} dx_2 dx_3 d\varphi_1 \cdots d\varphi_{n-4} dt
$$

$$
= 2\pi \int_0^r t^{n-4} s(t) dt \prod_{k=1}^{n-5} \int_0^{\pi} \sin^k \varphi d\varphi \ge 2\pi \int_0^r t^{n-4} f(t) dt \prod_{k=1}^{n-5} \int_0^{\pi} \sin^k \varphi d\varphi,
$$

and

$$
\Gamma_n(\gamma_1, \gamma_2, \gamma_3) = \frac{Q}{|S^n|} \ge \frac{2\Gamma(\frac{n+2}{2}) \prod_{k=1}^{n-5} \int_0^{\pi} \sin^k \varphi d\varphi}{n \pi^{n/2-1}} \int_0^r t^{n-4} f(t) dt. \tag{1}
$$

We next give the lower bounds of $\dfrac{2\Gamma(\frac{n+2}{2}) \prod_{k=1}^{n-5} \int_0^{\pi} \sin^k \varphi d\varphi}{n \pi^{n/2-1}}$ and $\int_0^r t^{n-4} f(t) dt$.

Since $\int_0^\pi \sin^k \varphi d\varphi = \sqrt{\pi} \frac{\Gamma((k+1)/2)}{\Gamma(k/2+1)}$ and $\Gamma(x)$ is increasing when $x > 2$, we obtain

$$\frac{2\Gamma(\frac{n+2}{2})\prod_{k=1}^{n-5}\int_0^\pi \sin^k \varphi d\varphi}{n\pi^{n/2-1}} \geq \frac{2\Gamma(\frac{n+2}{2})}{\pi^{3/2}n\Gamma(\frac{n-3}{2})} \geq \frac{n-3}{2\pi^{3/2}}. \tag{2}$$

For the lower bound of $\int_0^r t^{n-4} f(t)dt$, we first have the coordinate of P_1, P_2, P_3:

$$P_1 = \left(\frac{b-a\beta_1}{\beta_2}, \sqrt{1-a^2-\left(\frac{b-a\beta_1}{\beta_2}\right)^2 - t^2}\right) \triangleq (a_1, b_1),$$

$$P_2 = \left(k_1(s_1 - \sqrt{t_1 - q_1 t^2}) + k_2, s_1 - \sqrt{t_1 - q_1 t^2}\right) \triangleq (a_2, b_2),$$

$$P_3 = \left(\frac{f - a\delta_1 - \delta_3(s_2 - \sqrt{t_2 - q_2 t^2})}{\delta_2}, s_2 - \sqrt{t_2 - q_2 t^2}\right) \triangleq (a_3, b_3).$$

where

$$h_1 = -\frac{\delta_3\beta_2}{\delta_1\beta_2 - \delta_2\beta_1}, \quad h_2 = \frac{f\beta_2 - b\delta_2}{\delta_1\beta_2 - \delta_2\beta_1}, \quad k_1 = \frac{\delta_3\beta_1}{\delta_1\beta_2 - \delta_2\beta_1}, \quad k_2 = \frac{b\delta_1 - f\beta_1}{\delta_1\beta_2 - \delta_2\beta_1},$$

$$s_1 = -\frac{h_1 h_2 + k_1 k_2}{1 + k_1^2 + h_1^2}, \quad q_1 = \frac{1}{1 + k_1^2 + h_1^2}, \quad t_1 = \frac{1 - h_2^2 - k_2^2}{1 + k_1^2 + h_1^2} + \left(\frac{h_1 h_2 + k_1 k_2}{1 + k_1^2 + h_1^2}\right)^2,$$

$$s_2 = \frac{(f - \delta_1 a)\delta_3}{\delta_2^2 + \delta_3^2}, \quad q_2 = \frac{\delta_2^2}{\delta_2^2 + \delta_3^2}, \quad t_2 = \left(1 - a^2 - \frac{(f - \delta_1 a)^2}{\delta_2^2 + \delta_3^2}\right)\frac{\delta_2^2}{\delta_2^2 + \delta_3^2}.$$

The area of $\triangle_{P_1 P_2 P_3}$ is $f(t) = \frac{1}{2}(a_1 b_2 + a_2 b_3 + a_3 b_1 - a_3 b_2 - a_2 b_1 - a_1 b_3)$. It can be verified that $f(t)$ is decreasing when $t \in [0, r]$ and $f(r) = f'(r) = 0, f''(r) > 0$. We have

$$\int_0^r t^{n-4} f(t)dt \geq \int_0^{r-\frac{r}{n}} t^{n-4} f(t)dt \geq \frac{r^{n-3}}{n-3}(1 - \frac{1}{n})^{n-3} f(r - \frac{r}{n}).$$

Notice that $\left(1 - \frac{1}{n}\right)^{n-3} \geq \left(1 - \frac{1}{n}\right)^n \approx e^{-1}$ when n is sufficiently large, and by Taylor series for $f(r - \frac{r}{n})$, $f(r - \frac{r}{n}) = \Theta(\frac{1}{n^2})$. We have for some constant c'' unrelated to n,

$$\int_0^r t^{n-4} f(t)dt \geq \frac{c'' r^{n-3}}{n^2(n-3)}. \tag{3}$$

Combining (1), (2) and (3), we have $\Gamma_n(\gamma_1, \gamma_2, \gamma_3) \geq \frac{c'' r^{n-3}}{2\pi^{3/2} n^2}$. Now r can be regarded as a function with respect to $\alpha_1, \alpha_2, \alpha_3$, where $\gamma_3 \leq \alpha_1, \alpha_2, \alpha_3 \leq 1$. It can be verified that r decreases with $\alpha_1, \alpha_2, \alpha_3$ increasing. Let $\alpha_1 = 1, \alpha_2 = 1, \alpha_3 = 1$, we get the minimal value of r. $r_{min} = \sqrt{c_{\mathcal{H}_3} - \left(1 - \frac{\gamma_3^2}{2c_{\mathcal{H}_3}}\right)^2}$, $c_{\mathcal{H}_3} = \gamma_2^2\left(1 - \frac{\gamma_2^2 c_{\mathcal{H}_1}}{4}\right)$. So, $\Gamma_n(\gamma_1, \gamma_2, \gamma_3) \geq \frac{c'' r_{min}^{n-3}}{2\pi^{3/2} n^2}$.

Theorem 3. *Let n be a non-negative integer, N be an integer and $0.88 < \gamma_3 < 1 < \gamma_2 < \gamma_1 < \sqrt{2}\gamma_3$, where γ_3 is very close to 1. Let*

$$N_3 = c_3 n^3 (\frac{d_{\max}}{r_{\min}})^n,$$

*where $d_{\max} = \sqrt{1 - \left(\frac{\gamma_3^2 - \gamma_1^2 + 1}{2\gamma_3}\right)^2 - \left(\frac{1}{c_{\mathcal{H}_2}}\left(\frac{\gamma_3^2 + 1 - \gamma_2^2}{2} - \frac{2\gamma_3^2 - \gamma_1^2}{2\gamma_3}\frac{\gamma_3^2 - \gamma_1^2 + 1}{2\gamma_3}\right)\right)^2}, r_{\min} = $
$\sqrt{c_{\mathcal{H}_3} - \left(1 - \frac{\gamma_3^2}{2c_{\mathcal{H}_3}}\right)^2}, c_{\mathcal{H}_1} = \frac{1}{\gamma_1\sqrt{1 - \frac{\gamma_1^2}{4}}}, c_{\mathcal{H}_2} = \frac{\gamma_1}{\gamma_3}\sqrt{1 - \frac{\gamma_1^2}{4\gamma_3^2}}, c_{\mathcal{H}_3} = \gamma_2^2\left(1 - \frac{\gamma_2^2 c_{\mathcal{H}_1}^2}{4}\right),$*

and c_3 is a positive constant unrelated to n. Let S be a subset of $C_n(\gamma_3 R) \cap B_n(\mathbf{c}_1, \gamma_1 R) \cap B_n(\mathbf{c}_2, \gamma_2 R) \cap B_n(\mathbf{c}_3, \gamma_3 R)$ of cardinality N whose points are picked independently at random with uniform distribution. If $N_3 < N < 2^n$, then for any subset $C \subseteq S$ of size at least N_3 whose points are picked independently at random with uniform distribution, with overwhelming probability, for all $\mathbf{v} \in S$, there exists a $\mathbf{c} \in C$ such that $\|\mathbf{v} - \mathbf{c}\| \leq \gamma_3 R$.

Proof. Combining Lemmas 2 and 3, we have

$$\Omega_n(\gamma_1, \gamma_2, \gamma_3) = \frac{\Gamma_n(\gamma_1, \gamma_2, \gamma_3)}{\Gamma_n(\gamma_1, \gamma_2)} \geq \frac{c''}{\sqrt{\pi}n^2}\left(\frac{r_{\min}}{d_{\max}}\right)^n.$$

Let $N_3 = c_3 n^3 (\frac{d_{\max}}{r_{\min}})^n$, the remaining proof is similar to that of Theorem 2.

The Optimal Time Complexity. It can be proved that $N_1 N_2 N_3 (N_1 + N_2 + N_3)$ decreases with γ_3. In fact,

- $N_1 = (\frac{1}{\gamma_1\sqrt{1 - \gamma_1^2/4}})^n \lceil 3\sqrt{2\pi}n^{3/2}\rceil$ is unrelated to γ_3.

- $N_2 = c_2(\frac{c_{\mathcal{H}_2}}{d_{\min}})^n \lceil n^{\frac{3}{2}}\rceil$. Only $c_{\mathcal{H}_2} = \frac{\gamma_1}{\gamma_3}\sqrt{1 - \frac{\gamma_1^2}{4\gamma_3^2}} = \sqrt{1 - (1 - \frac{\gamma_1^2}{2\gamma_3^2})^2}$ is related to γ_3, and it is easy to see that $c_{\mathcal{H}_2}$ decreases with respect to γ_3, which implies that N_2 is a monotonically decreasing function of γ_3.

- $N_3 = c_3 n^3 \left(\frac{\sqrt{1 - \left(\frac{\gamma_3^2 - \gamma_1^2 + 1}{2\gamma_3}\right)^2 - \left(\frac{1}{c_{\mathcal{H}_2}}\left(\frac{\gamma_3^2 + 1 - \gamma_2^2}{2} - \frac{2\gamma_3^2 - \gamma_1^2}{2\gamma_3}\frac{\gamma_3^2 - \gamma_1^2 + 1}{2\gamma_3}\right)\right)^2}}{\sqrt{c_{\mathcal{H}_3} - \left(1 - \frac{\gamma_3^2}{2c_{\mathcal{H}_3}}\right)^2}}\right)^n$. First, the

denominator of N_3 increases with γ_3, since $c_{\mathcal{H}_3}$ is unrelated to γ_3. By $\gamma_1 > 1$,
we have $\left(\frac{\gamma_3^2 - \gamma_1^2 + 1}{2\gamma_3}\right)' = \frac{\gamma_3^2 + \gamma_1^2 - 1}{2\gamma_3^2} > 0$, and $\left(\frac{\gamma_3^2 + 1 - \gamma_2^2}{2} - \frac{2\gamma_3^2 - \gamma_1^2}{2\gamma_3}\frac{\gamma_3^2 - \gamma_1^2 + 1}{2\gamma_3}\right)' = $
$\gamma_3 - \frac{2\gamma_3^2 + \gamma_1^2}{2\gamma_3^2}\frac{\gamma_3^2 - \gamma_1^2 + 1}{2\gamma_3} - \frac{2\gamma_3^2 - \gamma_1^2}{2\gamma_3}\frac{\gamma_3^2 + \gamma_1^2 - 1}{2\gamma_3^2} = \frac{\gamma_1^2(\gamma_1^2 - 1)}{2\gamma_3^3} > 0$. Together with $\frac{1}{c_{\mathcal{H}_2}}$
increases with γ_3, then we have the numerator of N_3 decreases with γ_3. Thus,
N_3 decreases with respect to γ_3.

Therefore, $N_1 N_2 N_3 (N_1 + N_2 + N_3)$ decreases with γ_3.

Since the expression of the time complexity is complicated, we solve a numerical optimal solution. Take $\gamma_3 = 1$. Let γ_1 go through from 1 to 1.414 by 0.0001 and for a fixed γ_1, let γ_2 go through from 1 to γ_1 by 0.0001, then we can easily find the minimal value of the exponential constant for the running time. Thus, we obtain the numerical optimal time complexity of our three-level sieve algorithm.

Theorem 4. *The optimal time complexity of the algorithm is* $2^{0.3778n+o(n)}$ *poly-nomial-time operations with* $\gamma_3 \to 1, \gamma_1 = 1.1399, \gamma_2 = 1.0677$, *and the corresponding space complexity is* $2^{0.2833n+o(n)}$ *polynomially many bits under Heuristic Assumption 1.*

Remark 1. As in [20], the number of iterations is usually linear in the dimension of lattices. Regardless of the number of iterations, the polynomial factors hidden in the time complexity in NV algorithm and WLTB algorithm are respectively n^3 and $n^{4.5}$. In our three level sieve algorithm, the polynomial parts of N_1, N_2 and N_3 given by Theorem 1, 2, and 3 are $n^{3/2}, n^{3/2}$ and n^3 respectively. So the hidden polynomial factor in our algorithm is n^9 without the number of iterations.

Remark 2. It is natural to extend the three-level sieve algorithm to multiple-level, such as four-level algorithm. However, the number of small balls will increase as the number of the levels increases. Therefore, we conjecture that the time complexity may be decreased with small number levels, but will increase if the number of levels is greater than some positive integer.

4   Experimental Results

4.1   Comparison with the Other Heuristic Sieve Algorithms

We implemented the NV algorithm, the WLTB algorithm and our three-level sieve algorithm on a PC with Windows 7 system, 3.00 GHz Intel 4 processor and 2 GByte RAM using Shoup's NTL library version 5.4.1 [28]. Instead of implementing the GaussSieve algorithm, we directly applied the GaussSieve Alpha V.01 published by Voulgaris [29] on a PC with Fedora 15 system, 3.00 GHz Intel 4 processor and 2 GByte RAM.

We performed experiments to compare our three-level sieve algorithm with the other three algorithms. For every dimension n, we first used the method in [18] to pick some random n-dimensional lattice and computed the LLL-reduced basis, then we sampled the same number of lattice vectors, and performed the NV algorithm with $\gamma = 0.97$, the WLTB algorithm with $\gamma_1 = 1.0927, \gamma_2 = 0.97$ and our three-level sieve algorithm with $\gamma_1 = 1.1399, \gamma_2 = 1.0667, \gamma_3 = 0.97$ using these samples. We performed one experiments on lattices with dimension 10, 20 with more than 100000 samples, but about fifty experiments with fewer samples, and two experiments on dimension 25, 30, 40, 50. Instead of using our samples, we just performed the GaussSieve Alpha V.01 with the selected lattices as its inputs. The experimental results of the four algorithms are shown in Table 2, where v is the output vector of the corresponding algorithm.

In our experiments, the GaussSieve algorithm is much faster than the others and succeeds to find the shortest vectors for all the lattices we picked. Besides of the major reason that the GaussSieve algorithm performs better in practice (it has been reported that the GaussSieve algorithm is more efficient than the NV algorithm), another possible reason is that our implementation is a little poor.

Table 2. Experimental results.

Dimension		10	20	25	30	40	50	60
Number of sample		150000	100000	8000	5000	5000	3000	2000
Time of sample (s)		301	810	87833	73375	147445	120607	167916
Time (s)	NV algorithm	25005	64351	120	220	625	254	187
	WLTB algorithm	23760	18034	35	42	93	46	47
	Our algorithm	20942	13947	27	27	57	29	30
	GaussSieve algorithm	0.003	0.013	0.068	0.098	0.421	3.181	42.696
$\frac{\|v\|}{\lambda_1}$	NV algorithm	1	1	23.8	38.3	170.1	323	347.7
	WLTB algorithm	1	1	25.9	35.1	170.1	323	347.7
	Our three-level algorithm	1	1	21.2	38.3	170.1	323	347.7
	GaussSieve algorithm	1	1	1	1	1	1	1

Compared with the NV and WLTB algorithms, it seems that our algorithm may be slower for low dimensional lattices due to the larger hidden polynomial factor. However, on one hand, the number of sieved vectors in each iteration of our algorithm decreases faster because the number of small balls is larger, which implies that the number of iterations is smaller and the number of the vectors to be sieved in the next iteration is smaller as well. On the other hand, the time complexity is for the worst case. In practice, we need not to check all the big balls, medium balls and small balls to decide which small ball the sieved vector belongs to. Thus, with the same number of samples in our experiments, our algorithm runs faster than the NV and WLTB algorithms. Since the sample procedure is very fast when the dimension n is not greater than twenty, we can sample enough lattice vectors to ensure that the three algorithms can find a shortest nonzero lattice vector. In such case, the time of sieving overwhelms the time of sampling, so our algorithm usually costs the least total time.

4.2   On Heuristic Assumption 1

To test the validity of the Heuristic Assumption 1 that the distribution of the sieved vectors remains uniform, we picked four random lattices of dimension 10, 25, 40 and 50, sampled 150000, 8000, 5000, 3000 lattice vectors and then sieved them respectively. As in [20], we plotted the number of sieved vectors in each iteration (see Fig. 5). It can be seen that the head and the tail of the curve change slightly, but most of the curve, the middle part, decreases *regularly*. The lost vectors in each iteration are those used as centers or reduced to zero which means collisions occur. So the curve shows that the numbers of centers and collisions in most of the iterations are nearly the same, which partially suggests that the distribution of the sieved vectors is close to uniform throughout the iterations.

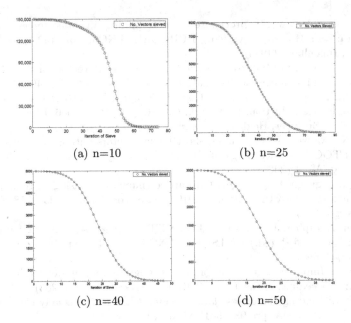

(a) n=10   (b) n=25

(c) n=40   (d) n=50

Fig. 5. Cardinality of the set of sieved vectors.

5   Conclusion

In this paper, we propose a three-level heuristic sieve algorithm to solve SVP and prove that the optimal running time is $2^{0.3778n+o(n)}$ polynomial-time operations and the space requirement is $2^{0.2833n+o(n)}$ polynomially many bits under Heuristic Assumption 1.

Acknowledgement. We like to thank Michael Schneider very much for his valuable suggestions on how to improve this paper. We also thank the anonymous referees for their helpful comments. We are grateful to Panagiotis Voulgaris for the publication of his implementation of the GaussSieve algorithm. Pan would like to thank Hai Long for his help on the programming.

References

1. Adleman, L.M.: On breaking generalized knapsack public key cryptosystems. In: The 15th Annual ACM Symposium on Theory of Computing Proceedings, pp. 402–412. ACM, April 1983
2. Ajtai, M.: The shortest vector problem in l_2 is NP-hard for randomized reductions. In: Proceedings of the 30th STOC. ACM (1998)
3. Ajtai, M., Kumar, R., Sivakumar, D.: A sieve algorithm for the shortest lattice vector problem. In: Proceedings of the 33rd STOC, pp. 601–610. ACM (2001)
4. Blömer, J., Naewe, S.: Sampling methods for shortest vectors, closest vectors and successive minima. Theor. Comput. Sci. **410**(18), 1648–1665 (2009)

5. Fincke, U., Pohst, M.: A procedure for determining algebraic integers of given norm. In: van Hulzen, J.A. (ed.) EUROCAL. LNCS, vol. 162, pp. 194–202. Springer, Heidelberg (1983)

6. Fincke, U., Pohst, M.: Improved methods for calculating vectors of short length in a lattice, including a complexity analysis. Math. Comp. **44**(170), 463–471 (1985)

7. Gama, N., Howgrave-Graham, N., Koy, H., Nguyên, P.Q.: Rankin's constant and blockwise lattice reduction. In: Dwork, C. (ed.) CRYPTO 2006. LNCS, vol. 4117, pp. 112–130. Springer, Heidelberg (2006)

8. Gama, N., Nguyen, P.Q.: Finding short lattice vectors within Mordell's inequality. In: STOC '08-Proceedings of the 40th ACM Symposium on the Theory of Computing. ACM (2008)

9. Gama, N., Nguyen, P.Q., Regev, O.: Lattice enumeration using extreme pruning. In: Gilbert, H. (ed.) EUROCRYPT 2010. LNCS, vol. 6110, pp. 257–278. Springer, Heidelberg (2010)

10. Hoffstein, J., Pipher, J., Silverman, J.H.: NTRU: a ring-based public key cryptosystem. In: Buhler, J.P. (ed.) ANTS 1998. LNCS, vol. 1423, pp. 267–288. Springer, Heidelberg (1998)

11. Kannan, R.: Improved algorithms for integer programming and related lattice problems. In: Proceedings of the 15th STOC, pp. 193–206. ACM (1983)

12. Klein, P.N.: Finding the closest lattice vector when it's unusually close. In: Proceedings of the SODA, pp. 937–941. ACM (2000)

13. Lenstra, A.K., Lenstra Jr, H.W., Lovász, L.: Factoring polynomials with rational coefficients. Math. Ann. **261**, 513–534 (1982)

14. Lagarias, J.C., Odlyzko, A.M.: Solving low-density subset sum problems. J. ACM **32**(1), 229–246 (1985)

15. Micciancio, D., Voulgaris, P.: A deterministic single exponential time algorithm for most lattice problems based on Voronoi cell computations. In: Proceedings of the STOC, pp. 351–358. ACM (2010)

16. Micciancio, D., Voulgaris, P.; Faster exponential time algorithms for the shortest vector problem. In: The 21st Annual ACM-SIAM Symposium on Discrete Algorithms Proceedings, pp. 1468–1480. SIAM, January 2010

17. Milde, B., Schneider, M.: A parallel implementation of GaussSieve for the shortest vector problem in lattices. In: Malyshkin, V. (ed.) PaCT 2011. LNCS, vol. 6873, pp. 452–458. Springer, Heidelberg (2011)

18. Nguyên, P.Q., Stehlé, D.: LLL on the average. In: Hess, F., Pauli, S., Pohst, M. (eds.) ANTS 2006. LNCS, vol. 4076, pp. 238–256. Springer, Heidelberg (2006)

19. Nguyên, P.Q., Stern, J.: The two faces of lattices in cryptology. In: Silverman, J.H. (ed.) CaLC 2001. LNCS, vol. 2146, pp. 146–180. Springer, Heidelberg (2001)

20. Nguyen, P.Q., Vidick, T.: Sieve algorithms for the shortest vector problem are practical. J. Math. Cryptology **2**(2), 181–207 (2008)

21. Pujol, X., Stehlé, D.: Solving the shortest lattice vector problem in time $2^{2.465n}$. Cryptology ePrint Archive, Report 2009/605 (2009)

22. Regev, O.: Lecture notes on lattices in computer science. http://www.cs.tau.ac.il/odedr/teaching/latticesfall2004/index.html (2004)

23. Schneider, M.: Analysis of Gauss-sieve for solving the shortest vector problem in lattices. In: Katoh, N., Kumar, A. (eds.) WALCOM 2011. LNCS, vol. 6552, pp. 89–97. Springer, Heidelberg (2011)

24. Schneider, M.: Sieving for shortest vectors in ideal lattices. In: Youssef, A., Nitaj, A., Hassanien, A.E. (eds.) AFRICACRYPT 2013. LNCS, vol. 7918, pp. 375–391. Springer, Heidelberg (2013)

25. Schnorr, C.P.: A hierarchy of polynomial lattice basis reduction algorithms. Theoret. Comput. Sci. **53**, 201–224 (1987)
26. Schnorr, C.P., Euchner, M.: Lattice basis reduction: improved practical algorithms and solving subset sum problems. Math. Program. **66**, 181–199 (1994)
27. Shamir, A.: A polynomial time algorithm for breading the basic Merkel-Hellman cryptosystem. In: The 23rd IEEE Symposium on Foundations of Computer Science Proceedings, pp. 145–152. IEEE (1982)
28. Shoup, V.: NTL: a library for doing number theory. http://www.shoup.net/ntl/
29. Voulgaris, P.: Gauss Sieve alpha V. 0.1 (2010). http://cseweb.ucsd.edu/pvoulgar/impl.html
30. Wang, X., Liu, M., Tian, C., Bi, J.: Improved Nguyen-Vidick Heuristic sieve algorithm for shortest vector problem. In: The 6th ACM Symposium on Information, Computer and Communications Security Proceedings, pp. 1–9. ACM (2011)

Improvement and Efficient Implementation of a Lattice-Based Signature Scheme

Rachid El Bansarkhani[✉] and Johannes Buchmann

Fachbereich Informatik Kryptographie und Computeralgebra,
Technische Universität Darmstadt, Hochschulstraße 10,
64289 Darmstadt, Germany
{elbansarkhani,buchmann}@cdc.informatik.tu-darmstadt.de

Abstract. Lattice-based signature schemes constitute an interesting alternative to RSA and discrete logarithm based systems which may become insecure in the future, for example due to the possibility of quantum attacks. A particularly interesting scheme in this context is the GPV signature scheme [GPV08] combined with the trapdoor construction from Micciancio and Peikert [MP12] as it admits strong security proofs and is believed to be very efficient in practice. This paper confirms this belief and shows how to improve the GPV scheme in terms of space and running time and presents an implementation of the optimized scheme. A ring variant of this scheme is also introduced which leads to a more efficient construction. Experimental results show that GPV with the new trapdoor construction is competitive to the signature schemes that are currently used in practice.

Keywords: Lattice-based cryptography · Practicality · Implementations

1 Introduction

The security notion of most cryptographic applications changes in the presence of quantum computers. In the breakthrough work [Sho97] in 1994, Shor pointed out that cryptographic schemes with security based on the hardness of number theoretic assumptions can efficiently be attacked by quantum computers. Since then, many efforts have been spent on the search for alternatives in order to face this challenge. Lattice-based cryptography is a promising candidate that has the potential to meet the security needs of future cryptographic applications. This is mainly due to Ajtai's worst-case to average-case reductions [Ajt96], which attracted a lot of researchers into the field of lattice-based cryptography. Specifically, it states that attacking random instances of a cryptosystem is at least as hard as solving all instances of the underlying lattice problem. As opposed to the discrete log problem and factoring, lattice problems are conjectured to withstand quantum attacks. In the last couples of years, a number of efficient cryptosystems emerged that base the security on the hardness of well-studied lattice problems.

T. Lange, K. Lauter, and P. Lisoněk (Eds.): SAC 2013, LNCS 8282, pp. 48–67, 2014.
DOI: 10.1007/978-3-662-43414-7_3, © Springer-Verlag Berlin Heidelberg 2014

Unlike number theoretic constructions such as RSA, there exists no subexponential time attack on lattice problems up to date. All known attacks have exponential time complexity and thus serve as a further supporting argument for a replacement by lattice-based cryptosystems. Based on this observation, one realizes an inherent need to develop new cryptographic primitives that can be based on worst-case lattice problems.

1.1   Our Contribution

In this paper we give the first software implementation of the GPV signature [GPV08] scheme using the newest trapdoor construction from Micciancio and Peikert [MP12]. Moreover, we present an efficient ring variant of the scheme based on the ring-LWE problem. In addition, we propose improvements that lower the memory claims for the perturbation matrix by a factor of about 240 compared to the proposal in [MP12]. When generating signatures the perturbation matrix is required to sample integer vectors with a given covariance. In both variants the matrix and ring variant we considerably improved the running times of key and signature generation. For instance, the running times of key and signature generation are lowered by a factor of 30–190 respectively 2–6 in the ring variant. By providing running times, storage sizes and security levels for different parameter sets we show that the ring variant has a 3–6 times faster signature generation engine compared to the matrix variant. At the same time verification is about 3–9 times faster. Thus, we show that the proposed constructions are quite efficient and hence competitive regarding the performance.

1.2   Related Work

The construction of lattice based signature schemes appeared to be a big challenge up to the last couples of years. This is due to the absence of practical constructions enjoying provable security. First constructions, however, such as GGH [GGH97] and NTRU Sign [HHGP+03] were completely broken. This fundamentally changed in 2008 by introducing the GPV signature scheme by Gentry et al. [GPV08] and the one time signature LM-OTS by Micciancio and Lyubashevsky [LM08]. The latter one operates in ideal lattices which allows for faster computations and smaller key sizes while providing provable security. When using Merkle Trees one can transform LM-OTS into a full signature scheme. The subsequent works [Lyu08, Lyu09] build upon the one time signature scheme using the Fiat-Shamir transform [FS87]. Recently, Lyubashevsky proposed an efficient construction [Lyu12] that performs very well on hardware [GLP12].

The hash-and-sign approach in turn was reconsidered in [GPV08] leading to constructions that admit security based on the hardness of the SIS Problem. Specifically, they aim at building a uniform random matrix $\mathbf{A} \in \mathbb{Z}^{n \times m}$ endowed with a trapdoor $\mathbf{S} \in \mathbb{Z}^{m \times m}$ in such a way that $\mathbf{S}$ has small entries and $\mathbf{A} \cdot \mathbf{S} \equiv 0 \bmod q$ holds. By means of the secret matrix $\mathbf{S}$ a signer can produce short preimages $\mathbf{x}$ for the hash value $H(\mu)$ of a message μ to be signed such that $\mathbf{A}\mathbf{x} \equiv H(\mu)$. The quality of the secret matrix immediately transfers to the quality of the signatures and hence plays a major role for assessing the security. Therefore, improving the algorithms for key generation is an ongoing research objective. Such constructions were considered for the first time in [Ajt99] and later on improved by [AP09, Pei10], but unfortunately they are inefficient and thus not suitable for practice. This is because the involved algorithms are complex and expensive in terms of space and runtime. However, Micciancio and Peikert recently proposed in [MP12] an elegant trapdoor construction which allows for fast signature generation while providing an improved output quality.

1.3   Organization

This paper is structured as follows. In Sect. 3 we introduce the GPV signature scheme together with the most recent trapdoor construction [MP12]. Furthermore, we provide a ring variant for this construction in Sect. 3.2. Section 4 contains a detailed description of our implementation and optimizations. In Sect. 5 we present the experimental results and their analysis.

2   Preliminaries

2.1   Notation

We will use the polynomial rings $R = \mathbb{Z}[x]/\langle f(x)\rangle$ and $R_q = \mathbb{Z}_q[x]/\langle f(x)\rangle$ such that $f(x)$ is a monic and irreducible polynomial over $\mathbb{Z}$ and q denotes the modulus. Throughout this paper we will mainly consider the case $q = 2^k$, $k > \mathbb{N}$. For the ring-LWE problem we consider the cyclotomic polynomials, such as $f(x) = x^n + 1$ for n being a power of 2. The m-th cyclotomic polynomial with integer coefficients is the polynomial of degree $n = \phi(m)$ whose roots are the primitive m-th roots of unity.

We denote ring elements by boldface lower case letters e.g. $\mathbf{p}$, whereas for vectors of ring elements we use $\hat{\mathbf{p}}$. For a vector $\mathbf{v} \in \mathbb{R}^n$, a positive real s, and a lattice $\Lambda \subset \mathbb{R}^n$, let $D_{\Lambda,\mathbf{v},s}$ denote the n-dimensional discrete Gaussian distribution over Λ, centered at $\mathbf{v}$, with parameter s. For $x \in \Lambda$, the distribution $D_{\Lambda,\mathbf{v},s}$ assigns the probability $D_{\Lambda,\mathbf{v},s}(\mathbf{x}) := \rho_{\mathbf{v},s}(\mathbf{x})/\sum_{\mathbf{z}\in\Lambda} \rho_{\mathbf{v},s}(\mathbf{z})$ with $\rho_{\mathbf{v},s}(\mathbf{x}) = \exp\left(-\pi \|\mathbf{x} - \mathbf{v}\|^2 /s^2\right)$. For brevity we write $D_{\Lambda,s}$ for $D_{\Lambda,\mathbf{0},s}$ and ρ_s for $\rho_{\mathbf{0},s}$. Micciancio and Regev introduced the smoothing parameter in [MR04]:

Definition 1. *For any n-dimensional lattice Λ and positive real $\epsilon > 0$, the smoothing parameter $\eta_\epsilon(\Lambda)$ is the smallest real $s > 0$ such that $\rho_{1/s}(\Lambda^*\backslash\{0\}) \leq \epsilon$*

The matrix $\tilde{\mathbf{B}}$ stands for the Gram-Schmidt orthogonalized basis of the basis matrix $\mathbf{B}$. And $\|\mathbf{B}\|$ denotes the matrix norm of matrix $\mathbf{B}$. By $[\mathbf{A}|\mathbf{B}]$ we define the matrix obtained by the concatenation of the matrices $\mathbf{A}$ and $\mathbf{B}$.

3 Trapdoor Signatures

The signature scheme due to Gentry, Peikert and Vaikuntanathan [GPV08] consists mainly of sampling a preimage from a hash function featured with a trapdoor. The security of this construction is based on the hardness of ℓ_2-SIS. In [MP12] Micciancio and Peikert provide a new trapdoor notion that improved all relevant bounds of the previous proposals [Ajt99, AP09].

3.1 Description of the Matrix Version

Similar to the constructions of [Ajt99, AP09], the authors of [MP12] start with a uniform random matrix $\bar{\mathbf{A}} \in \mathbb{Z}^{n \times \bar{m}}$ and extend it to a matrix $\mathbf{A} = [\bar{\mathbf{A}} | \mathbf{G} - \bar{\mathbf{A}}\mathbf{R}] \in \mathbb{Z}^{n \times m}$ via deterministic transformations [GPV08, MP12]. The main idea behind this proposal is to use a primitive matrix $\mathbf{G} \in \mathbb{Z}^{n \times \omega}$, which has the property of generating $\mathbb{Z}_q^n$ and for which one can easily sample preimages. Due to the nice structure of this matrix one can find a basis $\mathbf{S} \in \mathbb{Z}^{\omega \times \omega}$ satisfying the congruence relation $\mathbf{G} \cdot \mathbf{S} \equiv \mathbf{0} \bmod q$.

Below we provide the main algorithms of the GPV signature scheme in conjunction with the trapdoor construction from [MP12]:

KeyGen$(1^n) \to (\mathbf{A}, \mathbf{R})$: Sample $\bar{\mathbf{A}} \xleftarrow{\$} \mathbb{Z}_q^{n \times \bar{m}}$ and $\mathbf{R} \xleftarrow{\$} D$ such that $\mathbf{R} \in \mathbb{Z}^{\bar{m} \times \lceil \log_2(q) \rceil \cdot n}$ and D (typically $D_{\mathbb{Z}^{\bar{m} \times \lceil \log_2(q) \rceil \cdot n}, \alpha q}$) is a distribution which depends on the instantiation [MP12]. Output the signing key $\mathbf{R}$ and the verification key $\mathbf{A} = [\bar{\mathbf{A}} | \mathbf{G} - \bar{\mathbf{A}}\mathbf{R}] \in \mathbb{Z}_q^{n \times m}$ where $\mathbf{G}$ is a primitive matrix.

Sign$(\mu, \mathbf{R}) \to \mathbf{x} \in \mathbb{Z}^m$: Compute the syndrome $\mathbf{u} = H(\mu)$, sample $\mathbf{p} \leftarrow D_{\mathbb{Z}^m, \sqrt{\Sigma_\mathbf{p}}}$ and determine the perturbed syndrome $\mathbf{v} = \mathbf{u} - \mathbf{A} \cdot \mathbf{p}$. Then sample $\mathbf{z} \leftarrow D_{\Lambda_\mathbf{v}^\perp(\mathbf{G}), r}$ with $r \geq 2 \cdot \sqrt{\ln(2n(1 + \frac{1}{\epsilon}))/\pi}$. Compute $\mathbf{x} = \mathbf{p} + \begin{bmatrix} \mathbf{R} \\ \mathbf{I} \end{bmatrix} \mathbf{z}$ and output the signature $\mathbf{x}$.

Verify$(\mu, \mathbf{x}, (H, \mathbf{A})) \to \{0, 1\}$: Check whether $\mathbf{A} \cdot \mathbf{x} \equiv H(\mu)$ and $\|\mathbf{x}\|_2 \leq s\sqrt{m}$. If so, output 1 (accept), otherwise 0 (reject).

Throughout this paper fix the modulus q to be 2^k for some $k \in \mathbb{N}$ and use the primitive matrix $\mathbf{G}$ as defined in [MP12]. To this end, we start defining the primitive vector $\mathbf{g}^T := (1, 2, 4, \ldots, 2^{k-1}) \in \mathbb{Z}_q^k$ since $\mathbf{G} = \mathbf{I}_n \otimes \mathbf{g}^T$. Due to its simple structure one can find an associated basis $\mathbf{S}_k$ for the lattice $\Lambda_q^\perp(\mathbf{g}^T)$ which has the following shape

$$\mathbf{S}_k = \begin{bmatrix} 2 & & & 0 \\ -1 & 2 & & \\ & \ddots & \ddots & \\ 0 & & -1 & 2 \end{bmatrix} \in \mathbb{Z}_q^{k \times k}.$$

By means of the vector $\mathbf{g}^T$ and the associated basis $\mathbf{S}_k$ one can easily create $\mathbf{S} \in \mathbb{Z}_q^{nk \times nk}$ and the primitive matrix $\mathbf{G} \in \mathbb{Z}_q^{n \times nk}$, respectively:

$$\mathbf{G} = \begin{bmatrix} \mathbf{g}^T & & 0 \\ & \ddots & \\ 0 & & \mathbf{g}^T \end{bmatrix}, \qquad \mathbf{S} = \begin{bmatrix} \mathbf{S}_k & & 0 \\ & \ddots & \\ 0 & & \mathbf{S}_k \end{bmatrix}.$$

An optimal bound for the smoothing parameter of the lattice $\Lambda_q^\perp(\mathbf{g}^T)$ is easily obtained using the orthogonalized basis $\tilde{\mathbf{S}}_{\mathbf{k}} = 2 \cdot \mathbf{I}_k$. Since $\|\tilde{\mathbf{S}}\| = \|\tilde{\mathbf{S}}_{\mathbf{k}}\| = 2$, we have $\eta_\epsilon(\Lambda_q^\perp(\mathbf{G})) \leq r = 2 \cdot \sqrt{\ln\left(2n\left(1 + \frac{1}{\epsilon}\right)\right)/\pi}$ according to [GPV08, Theorem 3.1]. Using this parameter we can bound the preimage length. Due to [Ban93, Lemma 1.5] the probability of the preimage to be greater or equal to $r \cdot \sqrt{n \cdot k}$ is bounded by $2^{-n \cdot k} \cdot \frac{1+\epsilon}{1-\epsilon}$.

Sampling Algorithms for Preimages and Perturbations. In what follows we describe the preimage sampling algorithm for a syndrome $t \in \mathbb{Z}_q$ from the coset $\Lambda_t^\perp(\mathbf{g}^T) = \{\mathbf{x} \mid \mathbf{g}^T \cdot \mathbf{x} \equiv t \bmod q\}$ using the randomized nearest plane algorithm [MP12]. Due to the nice properties of the orthogonalized basis, the algorithm reduces to a few steps with $a_0 = t$:

for $i = 0, \ldots, k - 1$ do:

1. $v_i \leftarrow D_{2\mathbb{Z}+a_i, r}$
2. $a_{i+1} = (a_i - v_i)/2$

Output: $\mathbf{v} = (v_0, \ldots, v_{k-1})^T$

The resulting vector is $\mathbf{v} \in \Lambda_t^\perp(\mathbf{g}^T)$ distributed as $D_{\Lambda_t^\perp(\mathbf{g}^T), r}$. Of course, similarly one can sample preimages from $\Lambda_{\mathbf{u}}^\perp(\mathbf{G})$ for a syndrome vector $\mathbf{u} \in \mathbb{Z}_q^n$ by independently running n instances of the algorithm on each component of $\mathbf{u}$.

The authors provide two different types of instantiations for the trapdoor generation algorithm, namely the statistical and computational instantiation. Regarding the GPV signature scheme we used the latter one in our implementation because the dimension of $\mathbf{A}$ is much smaller. Therefore, we will always refer to the computational instantiation in the rest of this work. Such a representation can easily be achieved by generating a uniform random matrix $\bar{\mathbf{A}} \in \mathbb{Z}^{n \times n}$ and sampling a trapdoor $\mathbf{R} = \begin{bmatrix} \mathbf{R_1} \\ \mathbf{R_2} \end{bmatrix}$ from the discrete Gaussian distribution $D_{\mathbb{Z}^{2n \times nk}, \alpha q}$ where $\alpha \in \mathbb{R}_{>0}$ satisfies $\alpha q > \sqrt{n}$. The resulting matrix $[\bar{\mathbf{A}}|\mathbf{G} - (\bar{\mathbf{A}}\mathbf{R_2} + \mathbf{R_1})]$ with $\bar{\mathbf{A}} = [\mathbf{I}_n|\tilde{\mathbf{A}}]$ is an instance of decision-$LWE_{n,\alpha,q}$ and hence pseudorandom when ignoring the identity submatrix.

Applying the framework of [GPV08] requires to sample a spherically distributed preimage for a given syndrome $\mathbf{u} \in \mathbb{Z}_q^n$ using Gaussian sampling algorithms and the trapdoor $\mathbf{R}$. In fact, the spherical distribution is a common tool to make the distribution of the signature independent from the secret key. The Gaussian sampling algorithm mainly consists of two parts. The first part involves the trapdoor $\mathbf{R}$ which is used to transform a sample $\mathbf{x}$ from the set $\Lambda_{\mathbf{u}}^\perp(\mathbf{G})$ with parameter $r \geq \|\tilde{\mathbf{S}}\| \cdot \sqrt{\ln(2n(1 + \frac{1}{\epsilon}))/\pi}$ to a sample $\mathbf{y} = \begin{bmatrix} \mathbf{R} \\ \mathbf{I} \end{bmatrix} \cdot \mathbf{x}$ of the set $\Lambda_{\mathbf{u}}^\perp(\mathbf{A})$. Due to the fact that $\begin{bmatrix} \mathbf{R} \\ \mathbf{I} \end{bmatrix}$ is not a square matrix and the non-spherical covariance $\mathbf{COV} = r^2 \begin{bmatrix} \mathbf{R} \\ \mathbf{I} \end{bmatrix} [\mathbf{R}^T\ \mathbf{I}]$ is not of full-rank, the distribution of $\mathbf{y}$ is skewed and hence leaks information about the trapdoor. An attacker could collect samples and reconstruct the covariance matrix. Therefore, we need the second part to correct this flaw. This can be done by adding perturbations from a properly chosen distribution. Using the convolution technique from [Pei10], we can choose a parameter s in such a way that s^2 is slightly larger than the largest absolute eigenvalue of the covariance $\mathbf{COV}$ and generate Gaussian perturbations $\mathbf{p} \in \mathbb{Z}^m$ having covariance $\mathbf{\Sigma_p} = s^2\mathbf{I} - \mathbf{COV}$. In order to obtain a vector $\mathbf{b}$ that is from a spherical Gaussian distribution with parameter s, one samples a preimage $\mathbf{y}$ for an adjusted syndrome $\mathbf{v} = \mathbf{u} - \mathbf{Ap}$ from $\Lambda_{\mathbf{v}}^{\perp}(\mathbf{A})$. The vector $\mathbf{b} = \mathbf{p} + \mathbf{y}$ provides a spherical distributed sample satisfying $\mathbf{Ab} \equiv \mathbf{u} \bmod q$.

Parameters. When applying the framework of [RS10] we get Table 1 which contains different parameter sets with their corresponding estimated sub-lattice attack dimension d and the more relevant estimated Hermite factor δ. The SIS norm bound is denoted by ν. Columns marked with $\star$ provide according to [GPV08, Proposition 5.7] additional worst-case to average-case hardness satisfying $q \geq \nu \cdot \omega(\sqrt{n \log_2(n)})$. The parameters of the scheme should be set in such a way that $\delta \approx 1.0064$ in order to ensure about 100 bits of security [RS10]. In Table 4 (see Appendix A.1) we provide a guideline of how to select parameters in the matrix and ring variant (Construction 1).

Table 1. Parameter sets with the corresponding estimated sublattice attack dimensions d and Hermite factors δ according to [RS10].

n	128	128*	256	256*	284	284*	384	384*	484	484*	512	512*	1024	1024
k	24	27	24	27	24	28	24	29	24	29	24	30	27	30
m	3328	3712	6656	7424	7384	8520	9984	11136	12584	15004	13312	16384	29696	32768
q	2^{24}	2^{27}	2^{24}	2^{27}	2^{24}	2^{29}	2^{24}	2^{29}	2^{24}	2^{29}	2^{24}	2^{30}	2^{27}	2^{30}
d	324	346	586	659	650	758	838	1013	1057	1221	1118	1336	2305	2561
ν	4.8e5	5.4e5	1.3e6	1.5e6	1.6e6	1.8e6	2.5e6	3.0e6	3.5e6	4.3e6	3.9e6	4.8e6	1.2e7	1.3e7
δ	1.0203	1.0183	1.0117	1.0106	1.0108	1.0095	1.0085	1.0072	1.0070	1.0060	1.0067	1.0055	1.0034	1.0031
λ bits	<75	<75	75	78	78	82	86	94	95	103	97	108	148	158

Different to [MR08] the approach taken in [RS10] requires to determine the optimal sub-dimension $d = \{x \in \mathbb{Z} \mid q^{2n/x} \leq \nu\}$ of the matrix $\mathbf{A}$ consisting of m columns and n rows. The lattice $\Lambda_q^{\perp}(\mathbf{A'})$ generated by $\mathbf{A'}$ when leaving out $m - d$ columns from $\mathbf{A}$ has still determinant q^n with very high probability. This means that a solution $\mathbf{v} \in \Lambda_q^{\perp}(\mathbf{A'})$ with $\|\mathbf{v}\| \leq \nu$ can easily be transformed to the vector $(\mathbf{v}, \mathbf{0})$ such that $\mathbf{A} \cdot (\mathbf{v}, \mathbf{0}) \equiv 0 \bmod q$ holds. For a given d we obtain the Hermite factor $\delta = 2^{n \cdot \log_2(q)/d^2}$ implying that a sufficiently good HSVP solver can find vectors $\mathbf{v} \in \Lambda_q^{\perp}(\mathbf{A'})$ bounded by $q^{2n/d}$. From the Hermite factor one can compute the effort $T(\delta)$ required to solve $\delta - $ HSVP according to [RS10, Conjecture 3]. Subsequently, one maps the result to the corresponding security levels (e.g. see [RS10, Table 2]).

3.2 The Ring Setting

In [MP12] the authors state that the construction can be adapted to the ring setting in such a way that the elements of the primitive vector $\mathbf{g}^{\top}$ are considered as ring elements of $R_q = \mathbb{Z}_q[X]/\phi_m(X)$ rather than $\mathbb{Z}_q$, where $\phi_m(X)$ is the m-th cyclotomic polynomial. In the following section we present our construction of this idea and show that a polynomial matrix $\hat{\mathbf{G}}$ as in the matrix case is indeed not needed. This results in a more efficient instantiation.

Construction 1. The public key is generated by drawing k samples $(\bar{\mathbf{a}}_i, \bar{\mathbf{a}}_i\mathbf{r}_i + \mathbf{e}_i)$ from the ring-LWE distribution. By this, we obtain a public key that is pseudorandom and enjoys the hardness of ring-LWE. Following [ACPS09] one can use the error distribution in order to sample the trapdoor polynomials $\hat{\mathbf{r}} \in R_q^k$ and $\hat{\mathbf{e}} \in R_q^k$. This does not incur any security flaws. Indeed, this property is essential for the signature scheme to work due to the need for smaller secret keys. As in the matrix variant one can use only one uniformly distributed sample $\bar{\mathbf{a}}_1$ rather than a set in $\mathbf{A}$. By a standard hybrid argument the hardness of distinguishing $\bar{\mathbf{a}}_1\mathbf{r}_i + \mathbf{e}_i$ from uniformly distributed samples can be reduced to decision ring-LWE [BPR12]. Thus, we obtain a public key of the following shape:

$$\mathbf{A} = [1, \ \bar{\mathbf{a}}_1, \ \mathbf{g}_1 - (\bar{\mathbf{a}}_1\mathbf{r}_1 + \mathbf{e}_1), \ \dots, \ \mathbf{g}_k - (\bar{\mathbf{a}}_1\mathbf{r}_k + \mathbf{e}_k)]$$

Similar to the matrix version $\hat{\mathbf{g}}^\top = [1, \cdots, 2^{k-1}]$ defines the primitive vector of polynomials where each component is considered as a constant polynomial. Sampling from $\Lambda_{\mathbf{u}}^\perp(\hat{\mathbf{g}}^\top) = \{\hat{\mathbf{x}} \in R_q^k \mid \mathbf{g}_1\mathbf{x}_1 + \cdots + \mathbf{g}_k\mathbf{x}_k = \mathbf{u}\ \}$ is performed as in the matrix case with $\mathbf{y}^\top = [\mathbf{x}_1^{(0)}, \ \dots, \mathbf{x}_k^{(0)}, \ \dots, \mathbf{x}_1^{(n)}, \ \dots, \mathbf{x}_k^{(n)}]$ satisfying $\mathbf{G}\mathbf{y} \equiv \mathbf{u} \bmod q$, where $\mathbf{x}_j^{(i)}$ is the i-th coefficient of the j-th polynomial. The resulting vector $\mathbf{y}$ is from a spherical Gaussian distribution having covariance matrix $r^2\mathbf{I}$. Sampling a preimage for a syndrome $\mathbf{u} \in R_q$ requires to sample polynomials $\hat{\mathbf{x}} = (\mathbf{x}_1, \dots, \mathbf{x}_k)$ from $\Lambda_{\mathbf{u}}^\perp(\hat{\mathbf{g}}^\top)$. These are then used to construct the preimage $\hat{\mathbf{z}} = [\sum_{i=1}^{k} \mathbf{e}_i\mathbf{x}_i, \ \sum_{i=1}^{k} \mathbf{r}_i\mathbf{x}_i, \ \mathbf{x}_1, \ \dots, \ \mathbf{x}_k] \in R_q^{k+2}$. It can easily be verified, that $\mathbf{A}\hat{\mathbf{z}} \equiv \mathbf{u}$ holds. With the same arguments as in the matrix case we need to add some perturbation to transform the skewed distribution into a spherical one. Since we mainly operate on rings modulo $x^n + 1$ with n a power of two, multiplication of polynomials $\mathbf{r}_i\mathbf{x}_i$ corresponds to matrix multiplication $\mathbf{Rot}(\mathbf{r}_i)\mathbf{x}_i$. The matrix $\mathbf{Rot}(\mathbf{r}_i)$ consists of n columns $[\mathbf{r}_i, \mathrm{rot}(\mathbf{r}_i), \cdots, \mathrm{rot}^{n-1}(\mathbf{r}_i)]$ with $\mathrm{rot}(\mathbf{y}) = [-y_{n-1}, y_0, \ \dots, y_{n-2}]$ defining the rotation in anti-cyclic integer lattices. Of course, other irreducible polynomials are also possible, but have the drawback of larger expansion factors which imply increased preimage lengths. The covariance matrix of the preimage has the following shape:

$$\mathbf{COV} = r^2 \begin{bmatrix} \mathbf{R}_1 \\ \mathbf{R}_2 \\ \mathbf{I} \end{bmatrix} [\mathbf{R}_1^\top \ \mathbf{R}_2^\top \ \mathbf{I}]$$

with $\mathbf{R}_1 = [\mathbf{Rot}(\mathbf{e}_1) \mid \dots \mid \mathbf{Rot}(\mathbf{e}_k)]$ and $\mathbf{R}_2 = [\mathbf{Rot}(\mathbf{r}_1) \mid \dots \mid \mathbf{Rot}(\mathbf{r}_k)]$ respectively. One observes, that the computation of this matrix is very simple since matrix multiplication corresponds to polynomial multiplication with

$\beta(\mathbf{x}) = [x_1, -x_n, -x_{n-1}, \ldots, -x_2]$ which is the first row of $\mathbf{Rot}(\mathbf{x})$:

$$\mathbf{COV} = r^2 \begin{bmatrix} \mathbf{Rot}(\sum\limits_{i=1}^{k} \mathbf{e}_i \beta(\mathbf{e}_i)) & \mathbf{Rot}(\sum\limits_{i=1}^{k} \mathbf{e}_i \beta(\mathbf{r}_i)) & \mathbf{R_1} \\ \mathbf{Rot}(\sum\limits_{i=1}^{k} \mathbf{r}_i \beta(\mathbf{e}_i)) & \mathbf{Rot}(\sum\limits_{i=1}^{k} \mathbf{r}_i \beta(\mathbf{r}_i)) & \mathbf{R_2} \\ \mathbf{R_1^\top} & \mathbf{R_2^\top} & \mathbf{I} \end{bmatrix} .$$

Now one can use the techniques from the previous section in order to generate perturbations. A perturbation vector $\mathbf{p} \in \mathbb{Z}^{n(k+2)}$ is then split into $k+2$ parts of length n. Each part corresponds to a perturbation polynomial $\mathbf{p}_i \in R_q$. In order to provide a preimage for a syndrome polynomial $\mathbf{u}$ one samples perturbations $\mathbf{p}_1, \ldots, \mathbf{p}_{k+2} \in R_q$ as shown before. Then we create sample polynomials $\hat{\mathbf{x}}$ from $\Lambda_{\mathbf{u} - \mathbf{Ap}}^\perp(\hat{\mathbf{g}}^\top)$. The resulting preimage $\hat{\mathbf{z}}$ is then spherically distributed:

$$\hat{\mathbf{z}} = \left[\mathbf{p}_1 + \hat{\mathbf{e}} \cdot \hat{\mathbf{x}}, \ \mathbf{p}_2 + \hat{\mathbf{r}} \cdot \hat{\mathbf{x}}, \ \mathbf{p}_3 + \mathbf{x}_1, \ \ldots \ , \ \mathbf{p}_{k+2} + \mathbf{x}_k\right] .$$

Now we give a short description of how to instantiate the ring-LWE problem and how to sample the secret keys $\mathbf{r}_i$ and $\mathbf{e}_i$ for $1 \le i \le k$ according to [DD12]. The authors provide different from the work [LPR10] a relatively simple ring-LWE setting avoiding the work in the dual ring $R_q^\vee$ or the H-Space [LPR10] which turns out to be more convenient in certain applications. Following the paper of [BLP+13] we can take q to be a power of two as in the matrix variant. Such choices are more suitable for practice since the nice sampling algorithms introduced in the previous section are applicable. A prime number would involve costly sampling procedures which lead to a slower signature generation engine. As stated in [ACPS09] it is possible to generate both the secret key $\mathbf{r}_i$ and $\mathbf{e}_i$ from the same error distribution without affecting the security. Indeed, this property is important in order to make the trapdoor construction work based on the ring-LWE assumption. Specifically, we need small keys to provide short preimages. If one operates in the ring $\mathbb{Z}_q[X]/(X^n + 1)$ with n a power of two, the coefficients of both $\mathbf{r}_i$ and $\mathbf{e}_i$ are chosen from the Gaussian distribution on the rationals and then rounded to the nearest integers. In particular, the polynomials $\mathbf{r}_i$ and $\mathbf{e}_i$ are distributed as $\lceil D_{\mathbb{Q}^n, c} \rfloor$ for $c = \sqrt{n}\alpha q(\frac{nl}{2\log(nl/2)})^{1/4}$ where l is the number of samples and $\alpha q > \omega(\sqrt{\log 2n})$. In practical applications one can omit the last term [DD12] or set $l = 1$ due to the fact that a possible adversary can always create own samples by using $\bar{\mathbf{a}}_1$. For other choice of cyclotomic polynomials Φ_m it is possible to sample the trapdoor polynomials in extension rings according to [DD12, Theorem 2]. But a better approach is to use the framework presented in [LPR13] since it allows to work in arbitrary cyclotomic rings without incurring any ring-dependent expansion factor. We will provide such a construction in the full version of this paper.

Construction 2. We briefly explain another ring construction that is derived from [Mic07]. Take $k = \lceil \log_2 q \rceil$ and $\bar{m} = O(\log_2(n))$. Then select $\bar{m}$ uniformly random polynomials $\hat{\mathbf{a}} = [\mathbf{a}_1, \ldots, \mathbf{a}_{\bar{m}}] \in R_q^{\bar{m}}$. Define by $h_{\hat{\mathbf{a}}}(\hat{\mathbf{x}}) = \sum\limits_{i=1}^{\bar{m}} \mathbf{a}_i \mathbf{x}_i$ a generalized compact knapsack. Furthermore choose k vectors $\hat{\mathbf{r}}_i$ for $1 \le i \le k$, each consisting of $\bar{m}$ random polynomials $\mathbf{r}_{i1}$, ... , $\mathbf{r}_{i\bar{m}}$ of degree $n-1$ with small coefficients. By [SSTX09, Lemma 6], which is an adapted variant of the regularity lemma of [Mic07], the function values $\mathbf{a}_{\bar{m}+i} = h_a(\hat{\mathbf{r}}_i)$ with $1 \le i \le k$ are essentially uniformly distributed. Thus, we can create an almost uniformly random vector of polynomials $\mathbf{A}$ endowed with the trapdoor $\hat{\mathbf{r}}_i \in R_q^{\bar{m}}$ where $1 \le i \le k$:

$$\mathbf{A} = [\mathbf{a}_1, \ \ldots \ , \ \mathbf{a}_{\bar{m}}, \ \mathbf{g}_1 - \mathbf{a}_{\bar{m}+1}, \ \ldots \ , \ \mathbf{g}_k - \mathbf{a}_{\bar{m}+k}] .$$

To generate a preimage of a given syndrome polynomial $\mathbf{u} \in R_q$, one has to sample a vector $\hat{\mathbf{x}} \in \Lambda_{\mathbf{u}}^{\perp}(\hat{\mathbf{g}}^{\top})$ using the methods from above. As one can easily verify, the vector $\hat{\mathbf{y}} = [\hat{\mathbf{r}}_1 \mathbf{x}_1, \ \ldots \ , \ \hat{\mathbf{r}}_k \mathbf{x}_k , \ \mathbf{x}_1, \ \ldots \ , \mathbf{x}_k]$ is a preimage of the syndrome $\mathbf{u}$ for $\mathbf{A}$. Using the techniques from the descriptions before, one can produce spherically distributed samples.

4   Improvements and Implementation Details

In our implementation we have to face several challenges that affect the performance of the signature scheme both in the matrix and ring variant. In the following sections we give a detailed description of our improvements and implementation results.

4.1   Computation of the Covariance matrix

Firstly, we observed that the computation of the covariance matrix $\mathbf{COV}$ is too expensive in terms of running time. Since the basis matrix $\mathbf{COV}$ is sparse, we were able to significantly reduce the computational efforts. It can be split into four parts as below. The only block to be computed is the symmetric matrix $\mathbf{RR}^T$.

$$\mathbf{COV} = r^2 \begin{bmatrix} \mathbf{RR}^T & \mathbf{R} \\ \mathbf{R}^T & \mathbf{I} \end{bmatrix}$$

In the ring variant the computation of the covariance matrix is much faster because multiplication is performed in polynomial rings as explained in the description. Running these parts in parallel offers another source of optimization.

4.2   Estimating the Parameter s

As in [MP12] one sets the parameter s large enough such that it is independent from a specific trapdoor. In particular, s is chosen to be not smaller than $\sqrt{s_1(\mathbf{R})^2 + 1} \cdot \sqrt{6} \cdot a$, where $s_1(\mathbf{R})$ denotes the largest singular value of the secret key $\mathbf{R}$ and a is selected as above. The perturbation covariance matrix $\Sigma_{\mathbf{p}} = s^2 \mathbf{I}_m - \mathbf{COV}$ is well-defined, if one selects s such that $s > s_1\left(\begin{bmatrix} \mathbf{R} \\ \mathbf{I} \end{bmatrix}\right) \cdot r$ is satisfied. Since $\mathbf{R}$ is a subgaussian random variable, the matrix $\mathbf{R}$ satisfies $s_1(\mathbf{R}) \le C \cdot (\sqrt{2n} + \sqrt{n \cdot k} + 4.7) \cdot \alpha q$ except with probability $\approx 2^{-100}$ according to [MP12, Lemma 2.9]. The universal constant C is very close to $1/\sqrt{2\pi}$.

4.3 Generation of Perturbation Vectors

One of the main ingredients of the signature scheme is the idea of creating perturbations [MP12] in order to get spherically distributed preimages that do not carry any information about the secret key. A perturbation vector is generated by means of the distribution $D_{\mathbb{Z}^m, \sqrt{\Sigma_\mathbf{p}}}$ which outputs random vectors from $\mathbb{Z}^m$ with covariance matrix $\Sigma_\mathbf{p}$. By [Pei10] this can be achieved by sampling a vector $\mathbf{p}$ according to $\lceil \sqrt{\Sigma_\mathbf{p} - a^2\mathbf{I}} \cdot D_1^m \rceil_a$, where D_1^m denotes the m-dimensional Gaussian distribution. Each vector sampled from D_1^m has entries coming from the standard continuous Gaussian distribution with parameter 1. $\lceil \cdot \rceil_a$ denotes the randomized rounding operation from [Pei10] with parameter $a = r/2 \geq \sqrt{\ln(2n(1 + \frac{1}{\epsilon}))/\pi}$, which rounds each coordinate of the vector independently to a nearby integer using the discrete Gaussian distribution. The generation of perturbation vectors requires the square root computation $\sqrt{\Sigma_\mathbf{p} - a^2\mathbf{I}}$. Below we discuss one method for this purpose and provide improvements through a better analysis.

4.4 Square Root Computation

The Cholesky decomposition splits any positive definite matrix $\mathbf{M}$ into the product of a lower triangular matrix and its conjugate transpose, i.e. $\mathbf{M} = \mathbf{L} \cdot \mathbf{L}^T$, and runs in time $O(m^3) = O((k+2)^3 n^3)$. If one selects $k = 19$, then the constant factor grows by 9261, which is very high compared to $n = 256$. The Cholesky decomposition is needed to generate perturbations that have covariance matrix $\Sigma_\mathbf{p}$, where $\sqrt{\Sigma_\mathbf{p}}$ is the Cholesky matrix. An algorithm for the Cholesky decomposition is shown in the Appendix A.2 (Algorithm 1). When decomposing the matrix $\Sigma_\mathbf{p} - a^2\mathbf{I}$ into its roots, one can improve the running time by our modified Cholesky decomposition taking into account the $n^2 k^2 - n \cdot k$ zero entries, meaning that one can skip line 8 in Algorithm 1 whenever l_{ik} or l_{jk} is known to be zero. Due to the sparsity of $\Sigma_\mathbf{p} - a^2\mathbf{I}$ this occurs very often. We call this optimized algorithm variant 1.

Although this optimization in variant 1 noticeably improves the timings of key generation, the algorithm is still inefficient and is the main source of slow key generation. Moreover, the resulting perturbation matrix is dense and has no structure, which leads to high memory claims in order to store the matrix of floating entries and to worse signature generation running times. This is due to the fact that each generation of a perturbation vector requires to multiply a huge triangular matrix consisting of multi-precision floating point entries with a floating point vector. To circumvent this problem we applied a pivoting strategy followed by the Block Cholesky decomposition, meaning that we permute the covariance matrix such that $\mathbf{P}\Sigma_\mathbf{p}\mathbf{P}^\top = \Sigma_\mathbf{p}'$.

This corresponds to left multiplication of the permutation matrix $\mathbf{P} = \begin{bmatrix} 0 & \mathbf{I}_{nk} \\ \mathbf{I}_{2n} & 0 \end{bmatrix}$ to the public key $\mathbf{A}$. It is obvious that this transformation does not cause any security flaws because it is a simple reordering. The advantage of using $\mathbf{P}$ is a perturbation covariance matrix $\Sigma_\mathbf{p}'$ with a nice structure which enables us to work with

Schur complements [Zha10] in a very efficient way:

$$\Sigma_{\mathbf{p}}' = s^2 \mathbf{I}_m - r^2 \begin{bmatrix} \mathbf{I}_{nk} & \mathbf{R}^\top \\ \mathbf{R} & \mathbf{R}\mathbf{R}^\top \end{bmatrix} = \begin{bmatrix} 0 & \mathbf{I}_{nk} \\ \mathbf{I}_{2n} & 0 \end{bmatrix} \Sigma_{\mathbf{p}} \begin{bmatrix} 0 & \mathbf{I}_{nk} \\ \mathbf{I}_{2n} & 0 \end{bmatrix}^\top.$$

Therefore we get an algorithm which outperforms the optimized Cholesky decomposition applied on the non-permuted matrix by a factor of 30–190. Furthermore, we obtain a signature generation engine which yields a factor improvement of 2–6 in the ring variant. This is due to the sparse matrix and its nice structure. In both the key and signature generation steps the factor grows as n increases. In general the Schur complement is defined as follows:

Lemma 1. *Let the matrix* $\mathbf{S_i} = \begin{bmatrix} b_i & \mathbf{h}_i^\top \\ \mathbf{h}_i & \mathbf{C}_i \end{bmatrix} \in \mathbb{R}^{m-i \times m-i}$ *be symmetric positive definite with* $b_i > 0$. *Then the Schur complement* $\mathbf{S}_{i+1} := \mathbf{C}_i - \frac{1}{b_i}\mathbf{h}_i\mathbf{h}_i^\top \in \mathbb{R}^{m-i-1 \times m-i-1}$ *is well-defined and also symmetric positive definite.*

This decomposition is successively applied on the submatrices $\mathbf{S_i} \in \mathbb{R}^{m-i \times m-i}$. Doing this, one obtains an efficient method to construct the columns of the matrix $\sqrt{\Sigma_{\mathbf{p}}' - a^2\mathbf{I}}$. The first nk colums $\frac{1}{\sqrt{b}} \cdot \begin{bmatrix} b \cdot \mathbf{I} \\ \mathbf{R} \end{bmatrix} \in \mathbb{R}^{m \times nk}$ for $b = s^2 - r^2 - a^2 = s^2 - 5a^2$ involve only a simple scaling operation. Therefore, we need no additional memory in order to store these columns. Due to the sparse columns multiplication involves only the non-zero columns $(\mathbf{R})_i$ of the matrix $\mathbf{R} = \begin{bmatrix} \mathbf{R_1} \\ \mathbf{R_2} \end{bmatrix}$. Thus, transformations are focused only on the $(2n \times 2n)$ matrix:

$$\mathbf{S}_{nk} = (s^2 - a^2)\mathbf{I} - r^2\mathbf{R}\mathbf{R}^\top - \frac{1}{b}\sum_{i=1}^{nk}(\mathbf{R})_i(\mathbf{R})_i^\top = (s^2 - a^2)\mathbf{I} - (r^2 + \frac{1}{b})\mathbf{R}\mathbf{R}^\top \in \mathbb{R}^{2n \times 2n}.$$

The last sum of vector products reduces to the simple scaling operation $\frac{1}{b}\mathbf{R}\mathbf{R}^\top$. Thus, one can save the costly vector product computations. When continuing the decomposition on the remaining matrix $\mathbf{S}_{nk}$ one obtains the Cholesky decomposition. One can easily verify that

$$\mathbf{X}\mathbf{X}^\top = \Sigma_{\mathbf{p}}' - a^2\mathbf{I}, \quad \mathbf{X} = \begin{bmatrix} \sqrt{b}\mathbf{I}_{nk} & 0 \\ \frac{\mathbf{R}}{\sqrt{b}} & \mathbf{L} \end{bmatrix}$$

holds. Consequently one needs only to store $n(2n+1)$ floating point entries of the last part $\mathbf{L} = Decomp(\mathbf{S}_{nk})$ instead of $m(m+1)/2$ in the case without permutation. For instance, this induces an improvement factor of $m(m+1)/2n(2n+1) \approx 240$ for $n = 512$ and $k = 29$. A nice sideeffect of this transformation is a much faster algorithm for generating perturbations since the number of operations drastically decreases as the factor grows. In the matrix version, one makes use of the sparse decomposition matrix. In particular $\sqrt{\Sigma_{\mathbf{p}} - a^2\mathbf{I}} \cdot D_1^m$ is reduced to the simple scaling operation of $\sqrt{b} \cdot D_1^{nk}$ and the computation $\begin{bmatrix} \frac{1}{\sqrt{b}}\mathbf{R} & \mathbf{L} \end{bmatrix} \cdot D_1^m$. Especially in the ring version we preserve the nice properties of polynomial multiplication and therefore use only the scaled set of trapdoor polynomials $\frac{1}{\sqrt{b}}e_i, \frac{1}{\sqrt{b}}r_i$

and the lower triangular matrix $\mathbf{L} = \begin{bmatrix} \mathbf{L_1} \\ \mathbf{L_2} \end{bmatrix}$ in order to generate perturbations. Specifically, one obtains the perturbation vector $\mathbf{p} = [\mathbf{p_1}|\mathbf{p_2}|\mathbf{p_3}] \in \mathbb{Q}^{(k+2)n}$ with $\mathbf{p_1} = \sqrt{b} \cdot D_1^{nk}$, $\mathbf{p_2} = \frac{1}{\sqrt{b}} \sum_{i=1}^{k} \mathbf{r}_i D_1^n + \mathbf{L_1} \cdot D_1^n$ and $\mathbf{p_3} = \frac{1}{\sqrt{b}} \sum_{i=1}^{k} \mathbf{r}_i D_1^n + \mathbf{L_2} \cdot D_1^n$. Thus, we get a fast signature generation algorithm which is about three times faster than its matrix analogue. It is also worth to mention that these operations can also be executed in parallel.

4.5 Sampling

For sampling discrete Gaussian distributed integers in the key generation step we used the inversion transform method rather than rejection sampling because the number of stored entries is small and can be deleted afterwards. This improves the running times of the sampling step significantly. In particular, suppose the underlying parameter is denoted by s. We precompute a table of cumulative probabilities p_t from the discrete Gaussian distribution with $t \in \mathbb{Z}$ in the range $[-\omega(\sqrt{\log n}) \cdot s, \omega(\sqrt{\log n}) \cdot s]$. We then choose a uniformly random $x \in [0,1)$ and find t such that $x \in [p_{t-1}, p_t]$. This can be done using binary search. The same method is applied when sampling preimages from the set $\Lambda_{\mathbf{u}}^{\perp}(\mathbf{G})$ with parameter r. This parameter is always fixed and relatively small. Storing this table takes about 150 Bytes of memory. In this case signature generation is much faster than with simple rejection sampling. But, unfortunately, this does not apply in the randomized rounding step because the center always changes and thus involves a costly recomputation of tables after each sample. Therefore we used rejection sampling from [GPV08] instead. As for sampling continuous Gaussians with parameter $t = 1$, we used the Ziggurat algorithm [MT84] which is one of the fastest algorithms to produce continuous Gaussians. It belongs to the class of rejection sampling algorithms and uses precomputed tables. When operating with multiprecision vectors such as sampling continuous random vectors one should use at least λ bits of precision for a cryptographic scheme ensuring λ bits of security (e.g. 16 bytes floating points for $\lambda = 100$).

4.6 Random Oracle Instantiation

For the GPV signature scheme a random oracle $H(\cdot)$ is required which on an input message x outputs a uniformly random response $H(x)$ from its image space. In most practical applications this is achieved by a cryptographic hash function together with a pseudorandom generator which provides additional random strings in order to extend the output length. In our implementation we used SHA256 together with the GMSS-PRNG [BDK+07] because strings of arbitrary size are mapped to vectors from $\mathbb{Z}_q^n$. Each component of the vector has at most $\lfloor \log q \rfloor$ bits.

$$Rand \leftarrow H(Seed_{in}), Seed_{out} \leftarrow (1 + Seed_{in} + Rand) \bmod 2^n. \tag{1}$$

The first $Seed_{in}$ is the input message, and the function is repeated until enough random output $Rand$ is generated.

We implemented the GPV signature scheme, the trapdoor generation and sampling algorithms in C using the Fast Library for Number Theory (FLINT 2.3) and the GNU Scientific Library (GSL 1.15). FLINT comprises different data types for matrices and vectors operating in residue classes such as $\mathbb{Z}_q$ and $\mathbb{Z}_q[X]$ whereas the GSL library provides a huge variety of mathematical tools from linear algebra, that can be applied on different primitive data types. We also included the Automatically Tuned Linear Algebra Software Library (ATLAS) which is an empirical tuning system that creates an individual BLAS (Basic Linear Algebra Subprograms) library on the target platform on which the library is installed on. Specifically, this library provides optimized BLAS routines which have a significant impact on the running times of the used mathematical operations in the key and signature generation steps. So it is always recommended to include this library whenever one has to work with GSL. For the representation of matrices in $\mathbb{Z}_q^{n \times m}$ FLINT provides the data structure nmod_mat_t which comes into use in our implementation of the matrix version. Regarding the ring version, working with polynomials is performed by using the data structure nmod_poly_t. FLINT makes use of a highly optimised Fast Fourier Transform routine for polynomial multiplication and some integer multiplication operations.

5 Experimental Results

In this section we present our experimental results and compare the matrix version with the ring variant. Regarding the GPV signature scheme we used Construction 1 operating with a smaller number of polynomials compared to Construction 2. Hence, we obtain faster signature generation algorithms with a view to polynomial multiplication, generation of perturbations and sampling algorithms. We provide running times and file sizes of keys and signatures. The experiments were performed on a Sun XFire 4400 server with 16 Quad-Core AMD Opteron(tm) Processor 8356 CPUs running at 2.3 GHz, having 64 GB of memory and running 64 bit Debian 6.0.6. We used only one core in our experiments. In most works private keys and signature sizes are estimated based on the underlying distributions ignoring the norm bound of the sampled vectors and thus lead to overestimations of signature sizes. By Lemma 2 we show that we can ignore the underlying distributions and focus solely on the norm bound. This allows us to give tighter bounds compared to previous proposals. For instance, in [Lyu12] signatures $\mathbf{y} \in \mathbb{Z}^m$ are distributed as discrete Gaussians with standard deviation σ. The estimated signature size is $m \cdot \lceil \log_2(12 \cdot \sigma) \rceil$ bits (ignoring the norm bound). In our case signatures are distributed as discrete Gaussians with parameter s such that $\|\mathbf{y}\|_2 < s \cdot \sqrt{m}$. Using Lemma 2 the bit size needed to represent $\mathbf{y}$ is bounded by $m \cdot (1 + \lceil \log_2(s) \rceil)$ bits. The private key $\mathbf{R} \in \mathbb{Z}^{2n \times n \cdot k}$ from Sect. 3.1 can be viewed as a vector $\mathbf{r}$ with $2n^2 k$ entries such that $\|\mathbf{r}\|_2 < \alpha q \cdot \sqrt{2n^2 k}$ by [Ban93, Lemma 1.5].

Lemma 2. *Let* $\mathbf{v} \in \mathbb{Z}^n$ *be a vector with* $\|\mathbf{v}\|_2 < b \cdot \sqrt{n}$. *Then, the maximum number of bits required to store this vector is bounded by* $n \cdot (1 + \lceil \log_2(b) \rceil)$.

The proof of Lemma 2 is in the Appendix (see A.3). Below we provide two tables comparing the ring variant with the matrix variant. They contain the filesizes of the private key, public key, perturbation matrix and the signature (Table 2 bottom) as well as the running times of key generation, signature generation and verification (Table 2 top). The last line of the table reflects the improvement induced by the modification of the public key $\mathbf{A}$ and hence the covariance matrix. The improvement factor is related to the optimized Cholesky decomposition (variant 1) which makes use of the sparsity of $\mathbf{\Sigma_p}$. Indeed, the improvement factor is much higher when comparing to the original Cholesky decomposition. The impact of the discrete Gaussian samplers and the ATLAS library used in our implementation are notably but not addressed in this work.

Table 2. Experimental results for the matrix and ring variant. By ↑ we mean that the factor grows as n increases.

		Running times [ms]								
		Keygen			Signing			Verification		
n	k	Ring	Mat	M/R	Ring	Mat	M/R	Ring	Mat	M/R
128	24	277	984	3.6	5	9	1.8	0.6	1.4	2.3
128	27	317	1,108	3.5	6	11	1.8	0.7	1.7	2.4
256	24	1,070	5,148	4.3	12	30	2.5	1.5	5	3.3
256	27	1,144	5,728	4.1	14	36	2.5	1.7	6	3.5
512	24	4,562	28,449	5.0	27	103	3.8	3	18	6
512	27	5,354	30,458	5.1	31	125	4.0	4	21	5.3
512	29	5,732	34,607	5.4	35	136	3.8	5	22	4.4
1024	27	28,074	172,570	6.0	74	478	6.4	10	97	9.7
1024	29	30,881	198,620	6.3	81	518	6.4	11	102	9.3
Improvement factor		30-190 ↑	10 -40 ↑	-	2-6 ↑	1.4 - 2 ↑	-	-	-	-

		Sizes [kB]									
		Public Key			Secret Key			Pert. Matrix	Signature		
n	k	Ring	Mat	M/R	Ring	Mat	M/R	R and M	Ring	Mat	M/R
128	24	9.4	1200	128	4.4	528	163	257	5.8	5.3	0.9
128	27	11.8	1512	128	5.0	594	163	257	6.5	5.9	0.9
256	24	18.8	4800	256	9.8	2304	236	1026	12.5	11.4	0.9
256	27	23.6	6048	256	11.0	2592	236	1026	14.1	12.8	0.9
512	24	37.5	19,200	512	21.3	9984	469	4100	26.8	24.5	0.9
512	27	47.3	24,192	512	23.9	11232	470	4100	30.1	27.4	0.9
512	29	54.4	27,840	512	25.7	12064	470	4100	32.2	29.4	0.9
1024	27	94.5	96,768	1024	51.7	48384	936	16392	63.8	58.5	0.9
1024	29	108.8	111,360	1024	55.5	51968	936	16392	68.4	62.7	0.9
Improvement factor		-	-	-	-			170 - 260	-	-	-

By the modification we obtain a key generation engine that is about 30–190 times faster in the ring variant. For $n = 512$ and $n = 1024$ signature generation is about 3 and respectively 6 times faster. It is also worth to mention that the authors of [MP12] explain the possibility of splitting the signing algorithm into an offline and online phase. The task of generating perturbations is independent from the message to be signed, hence it is possible to generate them in advance

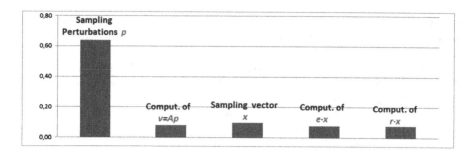

Fig. 1. Breakdown of signing running time into the major parts

or create many samples and store them. This obviously requires to periodically create the perturbation matrix or storing it. From a practical point of view we do not consider such a breakdown in our implementations. But indeed, generating perturbations amounts after the optimizations to more than 60 % (see Fig. 1) of the running time in the ring variant and 13–30 % in the matrix variant. In Fig. 1 we present a breakdown of the signing running time into four major parts which are the most time consuming. In particular, we differentiate the generation of perturbations $\hat{\mathbf{p}}$, sampling of $\hat{\mathbf{x}}$, computation of the syndrome polynomial $\mathbf{v} = \mathbf{A}\hat{\mathbf{p}}$, polynomial multiplications $\hat{\mathbf{e}} \cdot \hat{\mathbf{x}}$ and $\hat{\mathbf{r}} \cdot \hat{\mathbf{x}}$. By our experiments for different parameter sets we obtain Fig. 1 illustrating the average measurements.

In Table 3 we compare our implementation with classical signature schemes such as ECDSA, DSA and RSA for the same machine (AMD Opteron at 2.3 GHz). The experiments were performed based on `openssl` implementations of the corresponding schemes. In addition, we provide implementation results of current post quantum schemes, such as the code-based signature schemes [V97, Ste94] using the Fiat-Shamir transform [FS87, ADV+12]. As one observes, all classical schemes have faster signing algorithms compared to our implementation except for RSA 4096. However, our implementation has a faster signature verification engine than ECDSA and outperforms the code-based Véron und Stern signature schemes as well as the software implementations [WHCB13] of the lattice-based signature scheme [Lyu12]. Newer variants and implementations [GOPS13] are highly optimized and testify the superiority of lattice-based signature schemes over number theoretic ones.

Table 5 in the Appendix A.4 depicts the sizes of signatures, secret and public keys of the most recent lattice-based signature schemes at a glance. A look to this table reveals that the storage sizes of the GPV signature scheme are still large compared to [Lyu12, GLP12]. When comparing our scheme with the ring equivalent of l_2-SIS, one observes that the public key and signature sizes are about 30% higher. The secret key sizes of our implementation are even higher if one stores the perturbation matrix and does not create it for each signature (see Table 2). The optimizations due to [GLP12] furtherly improve the sizes of [Lyu12] by using more aggressive parameters. In [DDLL13] Ducas et al. present a novel signature scheme that benefits from a highly efficient bimodal discrete

Table 3. Comparison of different signature schemes.

Scheme	Security level	Sizes [kB]			Running times [ms]	
		Public key	Secret key	Signature	Signing	Verification
GPV Ring (n=512, k=24)	≈90	37.5	21.3	26.8	27	3
GPV Ring (n=512, k=27)	≈100	47.3	23.9	30.1	31	4
TSS [WHCB13, Lyu12] (n=512)	80	12.8	12.9	8.1	40.7	5.6
LyuSig [GOPS13] (n=512)	100	1.5	0.3	1.2	0.3	0.02
Stern Sign. [Ste94, ADV+12] (rounds=140)	80	36	0.05	25	32	23
Veron Sign. [V97, ADV+12] (rounds=140)	80	36	0.05	25	31	24
RSA 2048	112	0.3	2	0.3	5.0	0.05
RSA 4096	≥ 128	0.5	4	0.5	27.5	0.14
DSA 2048	112	0.3	0.02	0.04	0.7	0.8
ECDSA 233	112	0.06	0.09	0.06	7	3.5
ECDSA 283	128	0.07	0.11	0.07	11.5	6.5

Gaussian sampler and a modified scheme instantiation compared to [Lyu12, GLP12]. Furthermore, they provide a scheme variant that allows key generation to be performed in a NTRU-like manner. The corresponding sizes of keys and signatures for BLISS providing 128 bits of security are also depicted in Table 5.

Acknowledgements. We would like to thank Chris Peikert and Özgür Dagdelen for the fruitful discussions as well as the reviewers of SAC. The work presented in this paper was performed within the context of the Software Campus project *IT-GiKo*. It was funded by the German Federal Ministry of Education and Research (BMBF).

A Appendix

A.1 Parameter Choices for the Matrix and Ring Variant

	Matrix	Ring
n	e.g. $n \geq 384$ (cf. Table 1)	$n = 2^l$, $n \geq 512$
q	e.g. power of 2 with $q \geq 2^{19}$	
k	$\lceil \log_2(q) \rceil$	
m	$n(2 + k)$	
c	$c = \alpha q > \sqrt{n}$	$c > \sqrt{n}\omega(\sqrt{\log(2n)})$
r	$r \geq 2 \cdot \sqrt{\ln(2n(1 + \frac{1}{\epsilon}))/\pi}$	
a	$a \geq \sqrt{\ln(2(1 + \frac{1}{\epsilon}))/\pi}$, e.g. a=r/2	
s	$\approx C \cdot (\sqrt{n \cdot k} + \sqrt{2n}) \cdot c \cdot r$	

A.2 Cholesky Decomposition

Algorithm 1: Cholesky decomposition
Data: Matrix $\mathbf{L} \in \mathbb{Z}^{m \times m}$
Result: Lower triangular part of $\mathbf{L}$
1   **for** $k = 1 \to m$ **do**
2      $l_{kk} = \sqrt{l_{kk}}$;
3   **for** $i = k + 1 \to m$ **do**
4         $l_{ik} = l_{ik}/l_{kk}$;
5   **end**
6   **for** $j = k + 1 \to m$ **do**
7   **for** $i = j \to m$ **do**
8            $l_{ij} = l_{ij} - l_{ik}l_{jk}$;
9   **end**
10   **end**
11 **end**

A.3 Proof of Lemma 2

Proof. We determine the maximum number of bits needed to store a vector $\mathbf{v}$ bounded by $\|\mathbf{v}\|_2 < b \cdot \sqrt{n}$ by means of Lagrange multipliers [Lar12]. The general form of Lagrange multipliers is defined by $L(v_1, \ldots, v_n) = f(v_1, \ldots, v_n) + \lambda \cdot g(v_1, \ldots, v_n)$, where $g(\cdot)$ takes into account the constraints and $f(\cdot)$ is the function to be maximized. Obviously, the maximum number of bits grows with increasing norm bound. Therefore, let $\mathbf{v} \in \mathbb{N}^n$ (ignoring the signs) be a vector such that $\|\mathbf{v}\|_2^2 = \sum_{i=1}^{n} v_i^2 = nb^2$. Now, consider the log entries of the vector $\mathbf{v}$, which are needed to determine the bit size of any vector. Applying simple logarithm rules we have $\sum_{i=1}^{n} \log_2(v_i) = \log_2(\prod_{i=1}^{n} v_i)$. Since log is monotone increasing, maximizing of log is equivalent to maximizing the product. The function giving the constraint is $g(v_1, \ldots, v_n) = nb^2 - \sum_{i=1}^{n} v_i^2$. We then maximize the function

$$L(v_1, \ldots, v_n, \lambda) = f(v_1, \ldots, v_n) + \lambda \cdot g(v_1, \ldots, v_n), \text{ where } f(v_1, \ldots, v_n) = \prod_{i=1}^{n} v_i.$$

Taking the partial derivatives we get $n + 1$ equations:

$$\frac{\Delta L}{\Delta v_i} = \frac{\Delta f}{\Delta v_i} + \frac{\lambda \cdot \Delta g}{\Delta v_i} = \prod_{j=1, j \neq i}^{n} v_j - 2\lambda v_i = 0, \qquad \forall 1 \leq i \leq n$$

$$\frac{\Delta L}{\Delta \lambda} = nb^2 - \sum_{i=1}^{n} v_i^2 = 0.$$

By reordering the first n equations, we get $\lambda = \frac{v_1 \cdot \ldots \cdot v_{i-1} \cdot v_{i+1} \cdot \ldots \cdot v_n}{2v_i}$, $\forall 1 \leq i \leq n$. It is easy to see that the only solution is $v_i = b$, $\forall 1 \leq i \leq n$ that satisfies all equations, because from any two out of the first n equations it follows $v_i = v_j$, $i \neq j$. By the last equation we then obtain $v_i = b$. The only extremum we obtain is $\mathbf{v} = (v_1, \ldots, v_n) = (b, \ldots, b)$ with $f(\mathbf{v}) = b^n$. Since we have $0 = f(\mathbf{v}') < b^n$ for the boundary points $v_i' = b \cdot \sqrt{n}$ with $v_j' = 0$ and $j \neq i$, the extremum $\mathbf{v}$ is a maximum. Therefore the maximum possible bit size required to store such a vector is bounded by $n \cdot \lceil \log_2(b) \rceil$. We need an additional bit for the sign of each entry. This concludes the proof. The proof can be extended to any p-norm $1 \leq p < \infty$. $\qquad\square$

A.4 Sizes

This scheme has the following efficiency measures.

Table 4. GPV-Trapdoor storage requirements

	Public key (bits)	Private key (bits)	Signature (bits)
Trapdoor [GPV08, MP12]	nmk	$2n^2k(1 + \lceil \log_2(c) \rceil)$	$m \cdot (1 + \lceil \log_2(s) \rceil)$

Table 5. Comparison of our implementation with other lattice-based schemes with regard to storage sizes (in kilobytes).

Scheme	(n,q)	Sizes [kB]		
		Public key	Secret key	Signature
GPV ring	$(512, 2^{24})$	37.5	21.3	26.8
GPV ring	$(512, 2^{27})$	47.3	23.9	30.1
TSS12 [Lyu12, Table 2]	$(512, 2^{26})$	4.9	0.8	2.4
(based on decisional ring-LWE, m=2)				
TSS12 [Lyu12, Table 2]	$(512, 2^{27})$	30.4	2.1	19.9
(ring equivalent of l_2-SIS, m=17)				
LyubSig [GLP12]	$(512, 2^{23})$	1.4	0.2	1.1
(based on decisional ring-LWE, m=2)				
BLISS I [DDLL13]	$(512, 2^{14})$	0.9	0.3	0.7
BLISS II [DDLL13]	$(512, 2^{14})$	0.9	0.3	0.6

References

[ACPS09] Applebaum, B., Cash, D., Peikert, Ch., Sahai, A.: Fast cryptographic primitives and circular-secure encryption based on hard learning problems. In: Halevi, S. (ed.) CRYPTO 2009. LNCS, vol. 5677, pp. 595–618. Springer, Heidelberg (2009)

[ADV+12] El Yousfi Alaoui, S.M., Dagdelen, Ö., Véron, P., Galindo, D., Cayrel, P.-L.: Extended security arguments for signature schemes. In: Mitrokotsa, A., Vaudenay, S. (eds.) AFRICACRYPT 2012. LNCS, vol. 7374, pp. 19–34. Springer, Heidelberg (2012)

[Ajt96] Ajtai, M.: Generating hard instances of lattice problems (extended abstract). In: 28th Annual ACM Symposium on Theory of Computing, pp. 99–108. ACM, May 1996

[Ajt99] Ajtai, M.: Generating hard instances of the short basis problem. In: Wiedermann, J., Van Emde Boas, P., Nielsen, M. (eds.) ICALP 1999. LNCS, vol. 1644, pp. 1–9. Springer, Heidelberg (1999)

[AP09] Alwen, J., Peikert, C.: Generating shorter bases for hard random lattices. In: STACS, vol. 3 of LIPIcs, pp. 75–86. Schloss Dagstuhl - Leibniz-Zentrum fuer Informatik, Germany (2009)

[Ban93] Banaszczyk, W.: New bounds in some transference theorems in the geometry of numbers. Math. Ann. **296**(4), 625–635 (1993)

[BDK+07] Buchmann, J., Dahmen, E., Klintsevich, E., Okeya, K., Vuillaume, C.: Merkle signatures with virtually unlimited signature capacity. In: Katz, J., Yung, M. (eds.) ACNS 2007. LNCS, vol. 4521, pp. 31–45. Springer, Heidelberg (2007)

[BLP+13] Brakerski, Z., Langlois, A., Peikert, C., Regev, O., Stehlé, D.: Classical hardness of learning with errors. In: STOC (2013)

[BPR12] Banerjee, A., Peikert, Ch., Rosen, A.: Pseudorandom functions and lattices. In: Pointcheval, D., Johansson, T. (eds.) EUROCRYPT 2012. LNCS, vol. 7237, pp. 719–737. Springer, Heidelberg (2012)

[DD12] Ducas, L., Durmus, A.: Ring-LWE in polynomial rings. In: Fischlin, M., Buchmann, J., Manulis, M. (eds.) PKC 2012. LNCS, vol. 7293, pp. 34–51. Springer, Heidelberg (2012)

[DDLL13] Ducas, L., Durmus, A., Lepoint, T., Lyubashevsky, V.: Lattice signatures and bimodal Gaussians. Cryptology ePrint Archive, Report 2013/383. http://eprint.iacr.org/2013/383 (2013)

[FS87] Fiat, A., Shamir, A.: How to prove yourself: practical solutions to identification and signature problems. In: Odlyzko, A.M. (ed.) CRYPTO 1986. LNCS, vol. 263, pp. 186–194. Springer, Heidelberg (1987)

[GGH97] Goldreich, O., Goldwasser, S., Halevi, S.: Public-key cryptosystems from lattice reduction problems. In: Kaliski Jr, B.S. (ed.) CRYPTO 1997. LNCS, vol. 1294, pp. 112–131. Springer, Heidelberg (1997)

[GLP12] Güneysu, T., Lyubashevsky, V., Pöppelmann, T.: Practical lattice-based cryptography: a signature scheme for embedded systems. In: Prouff, E., Schaumont, P. (eds.) CHES 2012. LNCS, vol. 7428, pp. 530–547. Springer, Heidelberg (2012)

[GOPS13] Güneysu, T., Oder, T., Pöppelmann, T., Schwabe, P.: Software speed records for lattice-based signatures. In: Gaborit, P. (ed.) PQCrypto 2013. LNCS, vol. 7932, pp. 67–82. Springer, Heidelberg (2013)

[GPV08] Gentry, C., Peikert, C., Vaikuntanathan, V.: Trapdoors for hard lattices and new cryptographic constructions. In: Ladner, R.E., Dwork, C. (eds.) 40th Annual ACM Symposium on Theory of Computing, pp. 197–206. ACM, May 2008

[HHGP+03] Hoffstein, J., Howgrave-Graham, N., Pipher, J., Silverman, J.H., Whyte, W.: NTRUsign: digital signatures using the NTRU lattice. In: Joye, M. (ed.) CT-RSA 2003. LNCS, vol. 2612, pp. 122–140. Springer, Heidelberg (2003)

[Lar12] Larson, R.: Brief Calculus: An Applied Approach, vol. 9. (2012)

[LM08] Lyubashevsky, V., Micciancio, D.: Asymptotically efficient lattice-based digital signatures. In: Canetti, R. (ed.) TCC 2008. LNCS, vol. 4948, pp. 37–54. Springer, Heidelberg (2008)

[LPR10] Lyubashevsky, V., Peikert, Ch., Regev, O.: On ideal lattices and learning with errors over rings. In: Gilbert, H. (ed.) EUROCRYPT 2010. LNCS, vol. 6110, pp. 1–23. Springer, Heidelberg (2010)

[LPR13] Lyubashevsky, V., Peikert, Ch., Regev, O.: A toolkit for ring-LWE cryptography. In: Johansson, T., Nguyen, P.Q. (eds.) EUROCRYPT 2013. LNCS, vol. 7881, pp. 35–54. Springer, Heidelberg (2013)

[Lyu08] Lyubashevsky, V.: Towards practical lattice-based cryptography (2008)

[Lyu09] Lyubashevsky, V.: Fiat-shamir with aborts: applications to lattice and factoring-based signatures. In: Matsui, M. (ed.) ASIACRYPT 2009. LNCS, vol. 5912, pp. 598–616. Springer, Heidelberg (2009)

[Lyu12] Lyubashevsky, V.: Lattice signatures without trapdoors. In: Pointcheval, D., Johansson, T. (eds.) EUROCRYPT 2012. LNCS, vol. 7237, pp. 738–755. Springer, Heidelberg (2012)

[Mic07] Micciancio, D.: Generalized compact knapsacks, cyclic lattices, and efficient one-way functions. Comput. Complex. **16**(4), 365–411 (2007)

[MP12] Micciancio, D., Peikert, Ch.: Trapdoors for lattices: simpler, tighter, faster, smaller. In: Pointcheval, D., Johansson, T. (eds.) EUROCRYPT 2012. LNCS, vol. 7237, pp. 700–718. Springer, Heidelberg (2012)

[MR04] Micciancio, D., Regev, O.: Worst-case to average-case reductions based on Gaussian measures. In: 45th Annual Symposium on Foundations of Computer Science, pp. 372–381. IEEE Computer Society, October 2004

[MR08] Micciancio, D., Regev, O.: Lattice-based cryptography. In: Bernstein, D.J., Buchmann, J., Dahmen, E. (eds.) Post-Quantum Cryptography, pp. 147–191. Springer, Heidelberg (2008)

[MT84] Marsaglia, G., Tsang, W.: A fast, easily implemented method for sampling from decreasing or symmetric unimodal density functions. SIAM J. Sci. Stat. Comput. **5**(2), 349–359 (1984)

[Pei10] Peikert, Ch.: An efficient and parallel Gaussian sampler for lattices. In: Rabin, T. (ed.) CRYPTO 2010. LNCS, vol. 6223, pp. 80–97. Springer, Heidelberg (2010)

[RS10] Rückert, M., Schneider, M.: Estimating the security of lattice-based cryptosystems. http://eprint.iacr.org/2010/137 (2010)

[Sho97] Shor, P.W.: Polynomial-time algorithms for prime factorization and discrete logarithms on a quantum computer. SIAM J. Comput. **26**(5), 1484–1509 (1997)

[SSTX09] Stehlé, D., Steinfeld, R., Tanaka, K., Xagawa, K.: Efficient public key encryption based on ideal lattices. In: Matsui, M. (ed.) ASIACRYPT 2009. LNCS, vol. 5912, pp. 617–635. Springer, Heidelberg (2009)

[Ste94] Stern, J.: A new identification scheme based on syndrome decoding. In: Stinson, D.R. (ed.) CRYPTO 1993. LNCS, vol. 773, pp. 13–21. Springer, Heidelberg (1994)

[V97] Vron, P.: Improved identification schemes based on error-correcting codes. Appl. Algebra Eng. Commun. Comput. **8**, 57–69 (1997)

[WHCB13] Weiden, P., Hülsing, A., Cabarcas, D., Buchmann, J.: Instantiating treeless signature schemes. IACR Cryptology ePrint Archive (2013)

[Zha10] Zhang, F.: The Schur Complement and its Applications, vol. 4. Springer, New York (2010)

Towards Practical Lattice-Based Public-Key Encryption on Reconfigurable Hardware

Thomas Pöppelmann$^{(\boxtimes)}$ and Tim Güneysu

Horst Görtz Institute for IT-Security, Ruhr University Bochum, Bochum, Germany
thomas.poeppelmann@rub.de

Abstract. With this work we provide further evidence that lattice-based cryptography is a promising and efficient alternative to secure embedded applications. So far it is known for solid security reductions but implementations of specific instances have often been reported to be too complex beyond any practicability. In this work, we present an efficient and scalable micro-code engine for Ring-LWE encryption that combines polynomial multiplication based on the Number Theoretic Transform (NTT), polynomial addition, subtraction, and Gaussian sampling in a single unit. This unit can encrypt and decrypt a block in 26.19 µs and 16.80 µs on a Virtex-6 LX75T FPGA, respectively – at moderate resource requirements of about 1506 slices and a few block RAMs. Additionally, we provide solutions for several practical issues with Ring-LWE encryption, including the reduction of ciphertext expansion, error rate and constant-time operation. We hope that this contribution helps to pave the way for the deployment of ideal lattice-based encryption in future real-world systems.

Keywords: Ideal lattices · Ring-LWE · FPGA implementation

1 Introduction and Motivation

Resistance against quantum computers and long term security has been an issue that cryptographers are trying so solve for some time [12]. However, while quite a few alternative schemes and problem classes are available, not many of them received the attention both from cryptanalysts and implementers that would be needed to establish the confidence and efficiency for their deployment in real-world systems. In the field of patent-free lattice-based public-key encryption there are a few promising proposals such as a provably secure NTRU variant [49] or the cryptosystem based on the (Ring) LWE problem [32,36]. For the latter scheme Göttert et al. presented a proof-of-concept implementation in [22] demonstrating that LWE encryption is feasible in software. However, their corresponding hardware implementation is quite large and can only be placed fully on a Virtex-7 2000T and does not even fit onto the largest Xilinx Virtex-6 FPGA

T. Lange, K. Lauter, and P. Lisoněk (Eds.): SAC 2013, LNCS 8282, pp. 68–85, 2014.
DOI: 10.1007/978-3-662-43414-7_4, © Springer-Verlag Berlin Heidelberg 2014

for secure parameters.[1] Several other important aspects for Ring-LWE encryption have also not been regarded yet, such as the reduction of the extensive ciphertext expansion and constant-time operation to withstand timing attacks.

Contribution. In this work we aim to resolve the aforementioned deficiencies and present an efficient hardware implementation of Ring-LWE encryption that can be placed even on a low-cost Xilinx Spartan-6 FPGA. Our implementation of Ring-LWE encryption achieves significant performance, namely 42.88 μs to encrypt and 27.51 μs to decrypt a block, even with very moderate resource requirements on the low-cost Spartan-6 family. Providing the evidence that Ring-LWE encryption can be both fast and cheap in hardware, we hope to complement the work by Göttert et al. [22] and demonstrate that lattice-based cryptography is indeed a promising and practical alternative for asymmetric encryption in future real-world systems. In summary, the contributions of this work are as follows:

1. *Efficient hardware implementation of Ring-LWE encryption.* We present a micro-code processor implementing Ring-LWE encryption as proposed by [32,36] in hardware, capable to perform the Number Theoretic Transform (NTT), polynomial additions and subtractions as well as Gaussian sampling. For a fair comparison of our implementation with previous work, we use the same parameters as in [22] and improve their results by at least an order of magnitude considering throughput/area on a similar reconfigurable platform. Moreover, our processor is designed as a versatile building block for the implementation of future ideal lattice-based schemes and is not solely limited to Ring-LWE encryption. All parts of our implementation have constant runtime and inherently provide resistance against timing attacks.
2. *Efficient Gaussian sampling.* We present a constant-time Gaussian sampler implementing the inverse transform method. The sampler is optimized for sampling from narrow Gaussian distributions and is the first hardware implementation of this method in the context of lattice-based cryptography.
3. *Reducing ciphertext expansion and decryption failure rates.* A major drawback of Ring-LWE encryption is the large expansion of the ciphertext[2] and the occurrence of (rare) decryption errors. We analyze different approaches to reduce the impact of both problems and harden Ring-LWE encryption for deployment in real-world systems.

In order to allow third-party evaluation of our results we will make source code files, test-benches and documentation available on our website.[3]

---

[1] The authors report that the utilization of LUTs required for LWE encryption exceeds the number of available LUTs on a Virtex-6 LX240T by 197 % and 410 % for parameters $n = 256$ and $n = 512$, respectively. Note that the Virtex-6 LX240T is a very expensive (above €1000 as of August 2013) and large FPGA.

[2] For example, the parameters used for implementation in [22] result in a ciphertext expansion by a factor of 26.

[3] See our web page at http://www.sha.rub.de/research/projects/lattice/

Outline. In Sect. 2 we introduce the implemented ring-based encryption scheme. The implementation of our processor, the Gaussian sampler and the cryptosystem are discussed in Sect. 3. In Sect. 4 we give detailed results including a comparison with previous and related works and conclude with Sect. 5.

2   The Ring-LWEEncryptCryptosystem

In this section we briefly introduce the original definition of the implemented Ring-LWE public key encryption system (RING-LWEENCRYPT) and propose modifications in order to decrease ciphertext expansion and error rate without affecting the security properties of the scheme.

2.1   Background on LWE

Since the seminal result by Ajtai [2] who proved a worst-case to average-case reduction between several lattice problems, the whole field of lattice-based cryptography has received significant attention. The reasons for this seems to be that the underlying lattice problems are very versatile and allow the construction of hierarchical identity based encryption (HIBE) [1] or homomorphic encryption [19,42] but have also led to the introduction of reasonably efficient public-key encryption systems [22,32,36], signature schemes [14,23,34], and even hash functions [35]. A significant long-term advantage of such schemes is that quantum algorithms do not seem to yield significant improvements over classical ones and that some schemes exhibit a security reduction that relates the hardness of breaking the scheme to the presumably intractable problem of solving a worst-case (ideal) lattice problem. This is a huge advantage to heuristic and patent-protected schemes like NTRU [29], which are just related to lattice problems but might suffer from yet not known weaknesses and had to repeatedly raise their parameters as immediate reaction to attacks [28]. A particular example is the NTRU signature scheme NTRUSign which has been completely broken [17,43]. As a consequence, while NTRU with larger parameters can be considered secure, it seems to be worthwhile to investigate possible alternatives.

However, the biggest practical problem of lattice-based cryptography are huge key sizes and also quite inefficient matrix-vector and matrix-matrix arithmetic. This led to the definition of cyclic [40] and more generalized ideal lattices [33] which correspond to ideals in the ring $\mathbb{Z}[x]/\langle f \rangle$ for some irreducible polynomial f of degree n. While certain properties can be established for various rings, in most cases the ring $R = \mathbb{Z}_q[\mathbf{x}]/\langle x^n + 1 \rangle$ is used. Some papers proposing parameters then also follow the methodology to choose n as a power of two and q a prime such that $q \equiv 1 \bmod 2n$ and thus support asymptotic quasi-linear runtime by direct usage of FFT techniques. Recent work also suggests that q does not have to be prime in order to allow security reductions [11].

Nowadays, the most popular average-case problem to base lattice-based cryptography on is presumably the learning with errors (LWE) problem [48]. In order to solve the decisional Ring-LWE problem in the ring $R = \mathbb{Z}_q[\mathbf{x}]/\langle x^n + 1 \rangle$, an attacker has to decide whether the samples $(a_1, t_1), \ldots, (a_m, t_m) \in R \times R$ are chosen uniformly random or whether each $t_i = a_i s + e_i$ with $s, e_1, \ldots, e_m$ has small coefficients from a Gaussian distribution D_σ [36].[4] This distribution D_σ is defined as the (one-dimensional) discrete Gaussian distribution on $\mathbb{Z}$ with standard deviation σ and mean 0. The probability of sampling $x \in \mathbb{Z}$ is $\rho_\sigma(x)/\rho_\sigma(\mathbb{Z})$ where $\rho_\sigma(x) = \exp\left(\frac{-x^2}{2\sigma^2}\right)$ and $\rho_\sigma(\mathbb{Z}) = \sum_{k=-\infty}^{\infty} \rho_\sigma(k)$. In this simple case the standard deviation σ completely describes the Gaussian distribution. Note that some works, e.g., [22, 32] use the parameter $s = \sqrt{2\pi}\sigma$ to describe the Gaussian.

2.2   Ring-LWEEncrypt

The properties of the Ring-LWE problem can be used to realize a semantically secure public key encryption scheme with a reduction to decisional Ring-LWE. The scheme has been introduced in the full version [37] of Lyubashevsky et al. [36] and parameters have been proposed by Lindner and Peikert [32] as well as Göttert et al. [22]. The scheme (Gen, Enc, Dec) is defined as follows and will from now on be referred to as RING-LWEENCRYPT:

- Gen(a): Choose $r_1, r_2 \leftarrow D_\sigma$ and let $p = r_1 - a \cdot r_2 \in R$. The public key is p and the secret key is r_2 while r_1 is just noise and not needed anymore after key generation. The value $a \in R$ can be defined as global constant or chosen uniformly random during key generation.
- Enc($a, p, m \in \{0,1\}^n$): Choose the noise terms $e_1, e_2, e_3 \leftarrow D_\sigma$. Let $\bar{m} = \text{encode}(m) \in R$, and compute the ciphertext $[c_1 = a \cdot e_1 + e_2, c_2 = p \cdot e_1 + e_3 + \bar{m}] \in R^2$
- Dec($c = [c_1, c_2], r_2$): Output $\text{decode}(c_1 \cdot r_2 + c_2) \in \{0,1\}^n$.

During encryption the encoded message $\bar{m}$ is added to $pe_1 + e_3$ which is uniformly random and thus hides the message. Decryption is only possible with knowledge of r_2 since otherwise the large term $ae_1 r_2$ cannot be eliminated when computing $c_1 r_2 + c_2$. According to [32] the polynomial a can be chosen during key generation (as part of each public key) or regarded as a global constant and should then be generated from a public verifiable random generator (e.g., using a binary interpretation of π). The encoding of the message of length n is necessary as the noise given by $e_1 r_1 + e_2 r_2 + e_3$ is still present after calculating $c_1 r_2 + c_2$ and would prohibit the retrieval of the binary message after decryption. Note that the noise is relatively small as all noise terms are sampled from a narrow Gaussian distribution. With the simple threshold encoding $\text{encode}(m) = \frac{q-1}{2}m$ the value $\frac{q-1}{2}$ is assigned only to each binary one of the string m. The corresponding decoding function needs to test whether a received coefficient $z \in [0..q-1]$ is in the interval $\frac{q-1}{4} \leq z < 3\frac{q-1}{4}$ which is interpreted as one and zero otherwise. As a consequence, the maximum error added to each coefficient must not be larger that $\lfloor \frac{q}{4} \rfloor$ in order to decrypt correctly. The probability of an decryption error

---

[4] Note that this is the definition of Ring-LWE in **Hermite normal form** where the secret s is sampled from the noise distribution D_σ instead of uniformly random [37].

is mainly dominated by the tailcut and the standard deviation of the Gaussian $\sigma = \frac{s}{\sqrt{2\pi}}$. Decreasing s decreases the error probability but also negatively affects the security of the scheme.

Parameter Selection. For details regarding parameter selection we refer to the work by Lindner and Peikert [32] who propose the parameter sets (n, q, s) with (192, 4093, 8.87), (256, 4093, 8.35), and (320, 4093, 8.00) for low, medium, and high security levels, respectively. In this context, Lindner and Peikert [32] state that medium security should be roughly considered equivalent to the security of the symmetric AES-128 block cipher as the decoding attack requires an estimated runtime of approximately 2^{120} s for the best runtime/advantage ratio. However, they did not provide bit-security results due to the new nature of the problem and several trade-offs in their attack.

In this context, the authors of [22] introduced hardware-friendly parameter sets for medium (256, 7681, 11.31) and high security (512, 12289, 12.18). With n being a power of two and q a prime such that $q = 1 \bmod 2n$, the Fast Fourier Transform (FFT) in $\mathbb{Z}_q$ (namely the Number Theoretic Transform (NTT)) can be directly applied for polynomial multiplication with a quasi-linear runtime of $\mathcal{O}(n \log n)$. Increased security parameters (e.g., a larger n) have therefore much less impact on the efficiency compared to other schemes [36].

Security Implications of Gaussian Sampling. For practical and efficiency reasons it is common to bound the tail of the Gaussian. As an example, the authors of the first proof-of-concept implementation of RING-LWEENCRYPT [22] have chosen to bound their sampler to $[-\lceil 2s \rceil, \lceil 2s \rceil]$. Unfortunately, they do not provide either a security analysis or justification for this specific value. In this context, the probability of sampling ± 24 which is out of this bound (recall that $\lceil 2s \rceil = \lceil 2 \cdot 11.32 \rceil = 23$) is $6.505 \cdot 10^{-8}$ and thus not negligible. However, when increasing the tail-cut up to a certain level it can be ensured that certain values will only occur with a negligible probability. For $[-48, 48]$, the probability of sampling an $x = \pm 49$ is $2.4092 \cdot 10^{-27} < 2^{-80}$ which is unlikely to happen in a real world scenario. The overall quality of a Gaussian random number generator (GRNG) can be measured by computing the statistical distance $\Delta(X, Y) = \frac{1}{2} \sum_{\omega \in \Omega} |X(\omega) - Y(\omega)|$ over a finite domain Ω between the probability of sampling a value x by the GRNG and the probability given by $\rho_\sigma(x)/\rho_\sigma(\mathbb{Z})$.

Since in general attacks on LWE work better for smaller secrets (see [3,4] for a survey on current attacks) the tail-cut will certainly influence the security level of the scheme. However, we are not aware of any detailed analysis whether short tails or certain statistical distances lead to better attacks. Moreover, a recent trend in lattice-based cryptography is to move away from Gaussian to very small uniform distributions (e.g., $-1/0/1$) [23,41]. It is therefore not clear whether a sampler has to have a statistical distance of 2^{-80} or 2^{-100} (which is required for a worst-case to average-case reductions) in order to withstand practical attacks. Moreover the parameter choices for the RING-LWEENCRYPT scheme and for most other practical lattice-based schemes already sacrifice the worstcase to average-case reduction in order to obtain practical parameters (i.e., small keys). As a consequence, we primarily implemented a $\pm\lceil 2s\rceil$ bound sampler for straightforward comparison with the work by Göttert et al. [22] but also provide details and implementation results for larger sampler instantiations that support a much larger tail.

2.3 Improving Efficiency

In this section we propose efficient modifications to RING-LWEENCRYPT to decrease the undesirable ciphertext expansion and the error rate at the same level of security.

Reducing the Ciphertext Expansion. Threshold encoding was proposed in [22,32] to transfer n bits resulting in an inflated ciphertext of size $2n\log_2 q$. Efficiency is further reduced if only a part of the n bits is used, for example to transfer a 128-bit AES key. Moreover, the RING-LWEENCRYPT scheme suffers from random decryption errors so that redundancy in the message m is required to correct those errors. In the following we analyze a simple but effective way to reduce the ciphertext expansion without significantly affecting the error rate. This approach has been previously applied to homomorphic encryption schemes [9, Sect. 6.4], [10, Sect. 4.2] and the idea is basically to cut-off a certain number of least significant bits of c_2 since they mostly carry noise but only few information supporting the threshold decoding. We experimentally verified the applicability of this approach in practice with regard to concrete parameters by measuring the error rates for reduced versions of c_2 as shown in Table 1 ($u = 1$).

Table 1. Bit-error rate for the encryption and decryption of 160,000,000 bytes of plaintext when cutting off a certain number x of least significant bits of every coefficient of c_2 for the parameter set ($n = 256, q = 7681, s = 11.31$) where u is the parameter of the additive threshold encoding (see Algorithm 1) and $\pm\lceil 2s\rceil$ the tailcut bound. For a cutoff of 12 or 13 bits almost no message can be recovered.

u Cut-off x bits	0	1	2	3	4	5	6	7	8	9	10	11
1 Errors (10^3)	46	46	45.5	45.6	46	46.5	48.6	56.1	94.4	381	5359	135771
Error rate (10^{-5})	3.59	3.59	3.56	3.57	3.59	3.63	3.80	4.38	7.38	29.81	418.7	10610
2 Errors	26	20	26	27	23	21	21	32	71	957	125796	$44\cdot10^6$
Error rate (10^{-8})	2.03	1.56	2.03	2.11	1.80	1.64	1.64	2.5	5.55	74.7	9830	$34\cdot10^5$

As it turns out the error rate does not significantly increase – even if we remove 7 least significant bits of every coefficient and thus have halved the size of c_2. It would also be possible to cut-off very few bits (e.g., 1 to 3) of c_1 at the cost of an higher error rate. A further extreme option to reduce ciphertext expansion is to omit whole coefficients of c_2 in case they are not used to transfer message bits (e.g., to securely transport a symmetric key). Note that this approach does not affect the concrete security level of the scheme as the modification does not involve any knowledge of the secret key or message and thus does not leak any further information. When compared with much more complicated and hardware consuming methods, e.g., the compression function for the Lyubashevsky signature scheme presented in [23], this straightforward approach is much more practical.

Decreasing the Error Rate. As noted above decryption of RING-LWEENCRYPT is prone to undesired message bit-flips with some small probability. Such a faulty decryption is certainly highly undesirable and can also negatively affect security properties. One solution can be the subsequent application of forward error correcting codes but such methods obviously introduce additional complexity in hardware or software. As another approach, the error probability can be lowered by modifying the threshold encoding scheme, i.e., instead of encoding one bit into each coefficient of c_2, a plaintext bit is now encoded into u coefficients of c_2. This additive threshold encoding algorithm is shown in Fig. 1 where encode takes as input a plaintext bit-vector m of length $\lfloor \frac{n}{u} \rfloor$ and outputs the threshold encoded vector $\bar{m}$ of size m. The decoding algorithm is given the encoded message vector $\tilde{m}$ affected by an unknown error vector. The impact on the error rate by using additive threshold encoding ($u = 2$) jointly with the removal of least significant bits is shown in Table 1. Note that this significantly lowers the error rate without any expensive encoding or decoding operations and is much more efficient than, e.g., a simple repetition code [38].

Algorithm Encode($m = \{0,1\}^{\lfloor \frac{n}{u} \rfloor}, u$)

1: **for** i=0 to $\lfloor \frac{n}{u} \rfloor - 1$ **do**
2:     **for** j=0 to u-1 **do**
3:         $\bar{m}[u \cdot i + j] = m[i] \cdot \frac{q-1}{2}$
4:     **end for**
5: **end for**
6: **return** $\bar{m}$

Algorithm Decode($\tilde{m} = \{-\frac{q-1}{2}, \frac{q-1}{2}\}^n, u$)

1: **for** i=0 to $\lfloor \frac{n}{u} \rfloor$ **do**
2:     $s = 0$
3:     **for** j=0 to u-1 **do**
4:         $s = s + |\tilde{m}[u \cdot i + j]|$
5:     **end for**
6:     **if** $s < \frac{u \cdot q}{4}$ **then**
7:         $m[i] = 0$
8:     **else**
9:         $m[i] = 1$
10:     **end if**
11: **end for**
12: **return** m

Fig. 1. Additive threshold encoding.

3   Implementation of Ring-LWEEncrypt

In this section we describe the design and implementation of our processor with special focus on the efficient and flexible implementation of Gaussian sampling.

3.1 Gaussian Sampling

Beside its versatile applicability in lattice-based cryptography, sampling of Gaussian distributed numbers is also crucial in electrical engineering and information technology, e.g., for the simulation of complex communication systems (see [51] for a survey from this perspective). However, it is not clear how to adapt continuous Gaussian samplers, like the ones presented in [25,31,54], for the requirements of lattice-based cryptography. In the context of discrete Gaussian sampling for lattice-based cryptography the most straightforward method is rejection sampling. In this case an uniform integer $x \in \{-\tau\sigma, ..., \tau\sigma\}$, where τ is the "tail-cut" factor, is chosen from a certain range depending on the security parameter and then accepted with probability proportional to $e^{-x^2/2\sigma^2}$ [20]. This method has been implemented in software in [22] but the success rate is only approximately 20 % and requires costly floating point arithmetic (cf. to the laziness approach in [16]). Another method is a table-based approach where a memory array is filled with Gaussian distributed values and selected by a randomly generated address. Unfortunately, a large resolution – resulting in a very large table – is required for accurate sampling. It is not explicitly addressed in [22] how larger values such as $x = \lceil 2s \rceil$ for $s = 6.67$ with a probability of $\Pr[x = 14] = 1.46 \cdot 10^{-7}$ are accurately sampled from a table with a total resolution of only 1024 entries. We further refer to [15, Table 2] for a comparison of different methods to sample from a Gaussian distribution and a new approach.

Hardware Implementation Using the Inverse Transform Method. Since the aforementioned methods seem to be unsuitable for an efficient hardware implementation we decided to use the inverse transform method. When applying this method in general a table of cumulative probabilities $p_z = \Pr(x \leqslant z : x \leftarrow D_\sigma)$ for integers $z \in [-\tau\sigma, ..., \tau\sigma]$ is computed with a precision of λ bits. For a uniformly random chosen value x from the interval $[0, 1)$ the integer $y \in \mathbb{Z}$ is then returned (still requiring costly floating point arithmetic) for which it holds that $p_{z-1} \leq x < p_z$ [15,18,44].

In hardware we operate with integers instead of floats by feeding a uniformly random value into a parallel array of comparators. Each comparator c_i compares its input to the commutative distribution function scaled to the range of the PRNG outputting r bits. As we have to cut the tail at a certain point, we compute the accumulated probability over the positive half (as it is slightly smaller than 0.5) until we reach the maximum value j (e.g., $j = \lceil 2s \rceil$) so that $w = \sum_{k=0}^{j} \rho_\sigma(x)/\rho_\sigma(\mathbb{Z})$. We then compute the values fed into the comparators as $v_k = \frac{2^{r-1}-1}{w}(v_{k-1} + \sum_{k=0}^{j} \rho_\sigma(x)/\rho_\sigma(\mathbb{Z}))$ for $0 < k \leq j$ and with $v_0 = \frac{2^{r-1}-1}{2w}\rho_\sigma(0)/\rho_\sigma(\mathbb{Z})$. Each comparator c_i is preloaded with the rounded value v_i and outputs a one bit if the input was smaller or equal to v_i. A subsequent circuit then identifies the first comparator c_l which returned a one bit and outputs either l or $-l$.

The block diagram of the sampler is shown in Fig. 2 for the concrete parameter set $(n = 256, q = 7681, s = 11.32)$ where the output of the sampler is bound to $[-\lceil 2s \rceil, \lceil 2s \rceil] = [-5.09\sigma, 5.09\sigma]$ and the amount of required randomness is

25 bits per sample. These random bits are supplied by a PRNG for which we used the output of an AES block cipher operating in counter mode. Each 128-bit output block of our AES-based PRNG allows sampling of 5 coefficients. One random bit is used for sign determination while the other 24 bits form a uniformly random value. Finally, the output of the sampler is buffered in a FIFO. When leaving the FIFO, the values are lifted to the target domain $[0, q-1)$. Although it is possible to generate a sampler directly in VHDL by computing the cumulative distribution function on-the-fly during synthesis, we have implemented a Python script for this purpose. The reason is that the VHDL floating point implementation only provides double accuracy while the `Decimal`[5] data type supports arbitrary precision. The Python script also performs a direct evaluation of the properties of the sampler (e.g., statistical distance).

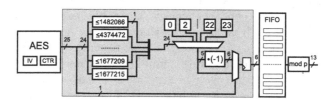

Fig. 2. Gaussian sampler using the inverse transform sampling method.

3.2   Ring-LWE Processor Architecture

The core of our processor is built around an NTT-based polynomial multiplier which is described in [45]. The freely available implementation has been further optimized and the architecture has been extended from a simple polynomial multiplier into a full-blown and highly configurable micro-code engine. Note that Aysu et al. [6] recently proposed some improvements to the architecture of [45] in order to increase the efficiency and area usage of the polynomial multiplier. While some improvements rely on their decision to fix the modulus q to $2^{16} + 1$ other ideas are clearly applicable in future work and revisions of our implementations. However, we do not fix q as the design goal of our hardware processor is the native support for a large variety of ideal lattice-based schemes, including the most common operations on polynomials like addition, subtraction, multiplication by the NTT as well as sampling of Gaussian distributed polynomials. By supporting an arbitrary number of internal registers (each can store one polynomial) realized in block RAMs and by reusing the data path of the NTT multiplier for other arithmetic operations we achieve high performance at low resource consumption.

General Description and Instruction Set. The datapath of our engine depicted in Fig. 3 depends on the size of the reduction prime q and is thus $\log_2 q$ as polynomial coefficients are processed serially in a pipeline. Four registers are

---

[5] http://docs.python.org/2/library/decimal.html

fixed where register R0 and R1 are part of the NTT block, while the Gaussian sampler is connected to register R2. Register R3 is exported to upper layers and operates as I/O port. More registers R4 to Rx can be flexibly enabled during synthesis where each additional register can hold a polynomial with n elements of size $\log_2 q$. The `Switch matrix` is a dynamic multiplexer that connects registers to the `ALU` and the external interface and is designed to process statements in two-operand form like $R1 \leftarrow R1 + R2$. All additional registers Rx for $x > 4$ are placed inside of the `Register array` component. The `Decoder` unit is responsible for interpreting instructions that configure the switch matrix, determines whether the `ALU` has to be used (SUB, ADD, MOV) or if NTT specific commands need to invoke the `NTT multiplier`. To improve resource utilization of the overall system, the butterfly unit of the NTT core is shared between the NTT multiplier and the ALU.

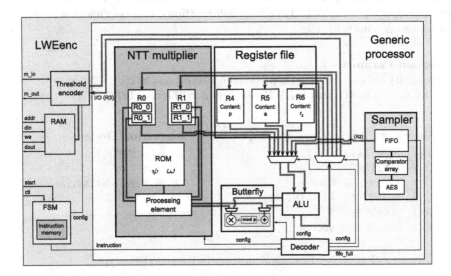

Fig. 3. Architecture of our implementation of the RING-LWEENCRYPTengine with a particular instance of our generic lattice processor with three additional registers R4-6.

The most important instructions supported by the processor are the iterative forward (NTT_NTT) as well as the backward transform (NTT_INTT) which take $\approx \frac{n}{2} \log_2 n$ cycles. Other instructions are for example used for the bit-reversal step (NTT_REV), point-wise multiplication (NTT_PW_MUL), addition (ADD), or subtraction (SUB) – each consuming $\approx n$ cycles. Note that the sampler and the I/O port are just treated as general purpose registers. Thus no specific I/O or sampling instructions are necessary and for example the MOV command can be used. Note also that the implementation of the NTT is performed in place and commands for the backward transformation (e.g., NTT_PW_MUL, or NTT_INTT) modify only register R1. Therefore, after a backward transform a value in R0 is still available.

Implementation of Ring-LWEEncrypt. For our implementation we used the medium and high security parameter sets as proposed in [22] which are specifically optimized for hardware. We further exploit the general characteristic of the NTT which allows it to "decompose" a multiplication into two forward transforms and one backward transform. If one coefficient is fixed or needed twice it is wise to directly store it in NTT representation to save subsequent transformations. In Fig. 4 the modified algorithm is given which is more efficient since the public constant a as well as the public and private keys p and r_2 are stored in NTT representation.

As a consequence, an encryption operation consists of a certain overhead, one forward NTT transformation ($n + \frac{1}{2}n \log_2 n$ cycles), two backward transforms ($2 \cdot (2n + \frac{1}{2}n \log_2 n)$) cycles), two coefficient-wise multiplications ($2n$ cycles), three calls to the Gaussian sampling routine ($3n$ cycles) and some additions as well as data movement operations ($3n$ cycles) which return the error vectors. For decryption, we just need two NTT transformations, one coefficient-wise multiplications and one addition.

Domain Parameters
Temporary value: $r_1 = $ `sample()`, Global constant: $\tilde{a} = $ `NTT`(a)
Secret key: $\tilde{r}_2 = $ `NTT(sample())`, Public key: $\tilde{p} = $ `NTT`$(r_1 - $ `INTT`$(\tilde{a} \circ \tilde{r}_2))$

Algorithm Enc$(\tilde{a}, \tilde{p}, m \in \{0,1\}^n)$
1: $e_1, e_2, e_3 = $ `sample()`
2: $\tilde{e}_1 = $ `NTT`(e_1)
3: $\tilde{h}_1 = \tilde{a} \circ \tilde{e}_1, \tilde{h}_2 = \tilde{p} \circ \tilde{e}_1$
4: $h_1 = $ `INTT`$(\tilde{h}_1), h_2 = $ `INTT`$(\tilde{h}_2)$
5: $c_1 = h_1 + e_2$
6: $c_2 = h_2 + e_3 + $ `encode`(m)

Algorithm Dec$(c_1, c_2, \tilde{r}_2)$
1: $\tilde{h}_1 = $ `NTT`(c_1)
2: $\tilde{h}_2 = \tilde{c}_1 \circ \tilde{r}_2$
3: $m = $ `decode`(`INTT`$(\tilde{h}_2) + c_2)$

Fig. 4. NTT-aware algorithms forRing-LWEEncrypt.

The top-level module (`LWEenc`) in Fig. 3 instantiates the ideal lattice processor and uses a block RAM as external interface to export or import ciphertexts c_1, c_2, keys r_2, p or messages m with straightforward clock domain separation (see again Fig. 3). The processor is controlled by a finite state machine (`FSM`) issuing commands to the lattice processor to perform encryption, decryption, key import or key generation. It is configured with three general purpose registers R4-R6 in order to permanently store the public key p, the global constant a and the private key r_2. More registers for several key-pairs are also supported but optional. The implementation supports pre-initialization of registers so that all constant values and keys can be directly included in the (encrypted) bitstream. Note that, for encryption, the core is run similar to a stream cipher as c_1 and c_2 can be computed independently from the message which is then only added in the last step (e.g., comparable to the XOR operation used within stream ciphers).

4   Results and Performance

For performance analysis we primarily focus on Virtex-6 platforms (speed grade -2) but would also like to emphasize that our solution can be efficiently implemented even on a small and low-cost Spartan-6 FPGA. All results were obtained after post-place and route (Post-PAR) with Xilinx ISE 14.2.

4.1   Gaussian Sampling

In Table 2 we summarize resource requirements of six setups of the implemented comparator-based Gaussian sampler for different tail cuts and statistical distances. Our random number generator is a round based AES in counter mode that computes a 128-bit AES block in 13 cycles and comprises 349 slices, 1181/ 350 LUT/FF, two 18K block RAMs and runs with a maximum frequency of about 265 MHz. Combined with this PRNG[6], Gaussian sampling based on the inverse transform method is efficient for small values of s (as typically used for RING-LWEENCRYPT) but would not be suitable for larger Gaussian parameters like, e.g., $s = \sqrt{2\pi}2688 = 6737.8$ for the treeless signature scheme presented in [34]. While our sampler needs a huge number of random inputs, the AES engine is still able to generate these numbers (for each encryption we need $3n$ samples). Table 2 also shows that it is possible to realize an efficient sampler even for a small statistical distance $<2^{-80}$ since its resource consumption of roughly 250 slices is quite moderate (setup III/IV). With additional register levels and pipelining for versions I/II we achieved the overall clock frequency for the whole core reported in Table 3 in this section. As the PRNG does not provide enough randomness to sample a value in every clock cycle it is not required to evaluate the comparator array in every single cycle so that in particular setups III-VI can use several clock cycles until output is provided. This lowers the critical path and thus allows higher clock frequencies without costs for pipelining registers. Setups V/VI are even more accurate and support (theoretical) requirements of a statistical distance smaller than 2^{-100} [18]. However, then a faster PRNG would be required as for $n = 256$ we would need $105 \cdot 3n = 80640$ bits of random input.

4.2   Performance of Ring-LWEEncrypt

Table 3 lists the resource consumption and performance of our implementation of RING-LWEENCRYPT. As stated in Sect. 3.2 our implementation combines key generation, encryption and decryption in a holistic design and would not significantly benefit from removing any one of these functional units. The only exception might be a decryption-only core in which no Gaussian sampling is needed.

Table 4 compares the results achieved in this work with the implementation by Göttert et al. [22] as well as other relevant asymmetric schemes and also adds performance figures for a Spartan-6 instantiation. Note that a detailed

---

[6] Generation of true random numbers is not in the scope of this work; we refer to the survey by Varchola [52] how to achieve this.

Table 2. Performance, resource consumption, and quality of the core part (shaded grey in Fig. 2) of the Gaussian sampler on a Virtex-6 LX75T (Post-PAR). The entry rnd denotes the number of used random bits to sample one value.

Setup	s	Max s	rnd	Slices	LUT/FF	MHz	Stat. distance
I	11.32	23	25	42	136/5	115	$<2^{-22}$
II	12.18	25	25	46	149/5	118	$<2^{-22}$
III	11.32	48	85	231	863/6	61	$<2^{-80}$
IV	12.18	51	85	255	911/6	61	$<2^{-80}$
V	11.32	53	105	314	1157/6	58	$<2^{-100}$
VI	12.18	57	105	342	1248/6	50	$<2^{-100}$

Table 3. Resource consumption and performance of the combined key generation, encryption and decryption engine for the two different security levels on a Virtex-6 LX75T (Post-PAR). The public key requires $n \log_2 q$ bits (when stored in NTT representation), the private key $n \log_2 q$ bits and the ciphertext $2n \log_2 q$ bits.

Aspect		Medium Security (n=256,q=7681,s=11.32)	High Security (n=512,q=12289,s=12.18)
Resources	Slices	1506	1887
	LUT/FF	4549/3624	5595/4760
	18K BRAM	12	14
	DSP48E1	1	1
Performance	MHz	262	251
	Key generation (cycles/time)	7235/27.61 µs	14532/57.90 µs
	Encryption (cycles/time)	6861/26.19 µs	13769/54.86 µs
	Decryption (cycles/time)	4404/16.80 µs	8883/35.39 µs

comparison with [22] is unfair due to inaccuracies of synthesis results (the Virtex-6 LX240T FPGA used in [22] was overmapped so that the subsequent place-and-route (PAR) step providing final results could not be performed). Figures for clock frequency, overall slice consumption, and cycles counts for individual operations or the whole encryption block are thus not given in [22]. We therefore can only refer to numbers providing the resource consumption of registers and LUT usage. For a rough comparison we apply the throughput to area (T/A) metric and define area equivalent to the usage of LUTs due to the restriction mentioned above. It turns out that our implementation for $n = 256$ is 32 times smaller regarding key generation, 65 times smaller for encryption and 27 times smaller for decryption, at a loss of a factor of about 2 and 3.3 in performance. When employing the $\frac{Bit/s}{LUT}$ metric for medium security encryption we achieve $\frac{9.77 \cdot 10^6 \text{Bits}}{4549 \text{LUTs}} = 2147$ while the work presented in [22] gives $\frac{31.8 \cdot 10^6 \text{Bits}}{298016 \text{LUTs}} = 106$. This results in an improvement of a factor of roughly 20.[7]

---

[7] For this comparison we assumed that for each encryption 256 bits are transmitted.

In comparison with a recent implementations of the code-based Niederreiter scheme [27] we are faster for decryption and we also use fewer resources on the same platform. Another natural target for comparison is the patent-protected NTRU scheme which has been implemented on a large number of architectures [5,7,26]. The implementation in [30] is clearly faster than ours. However, the implemented NTRU(251,3,12) variant in [30] seems to be less secure than our scheme [28]. Unfortunately, we are not aware of any newer NTRU FPGA implementations in order to determine the impact of increased security parameters on runtime and area consumption. In software, NTRU even seems to be rather slow for higher security levels what can be obtained from the 256-bit secure NTRU software implementation (`ntruees787ep1`) benchmarked using the eBACS framework [8] with secret/public key sizes of 1854/1574 bytes and a ciphertext of 1574 bytes. For the ideal lattice-based NTRU version presented in [49], no implementation and concrete parameters have been published yet. In comparison with ECC over prime curves (i.e., a single point multiplication [24]) and RSA (random-exponent 1024-bit exponentiation [50]) our implementation is by an order of magnitude faster, scales better for higher security levels, and also consumes less resources. However, we are not able to beat the recent binary curve implementation of Rebeiro et al. [47] in terms of throughput and performance.

Table 4. Performance comparison of our proposal with other public key encryption schemes ($\approx$80..128 bit) comparable to the medium security ($n = 256, q = 7681, s = 11.31$) parameter set which is capable of transferring 256-bit messages. Our implementation is versatile enough to perform encryption, decryption and key generation in a single core. Figures denoted with an asterisk (*) are less accurate results obtained from synthesis due to extensive overmapping of resources.

Scheme	Device	Resources	Speed
Our work [Gen/Enc/Dec] (n=256)	S6LX16 @160 MHz	4121 LUT/3513 FF/ 14 BRAM(8K)/1 DSP48	45.22 µs 42.88 µs 27.51 µs
Our work [Gen/Enc/Dec] (n=256)	V6LX75T @262 MHz	4549 LUT/3624 FF/ 12 BRAM(18K)/1 DSP48	27.61 µs 26.19 µs 16.80 µs
RING-LWEENCRYPT [Gen/Enc/Dec] (n=256) [22]	V6LX240T V6LX240T V6LX240T	146718 LUT/82463 FF 298016 LUT/143396 FF 124158 LUT/65174 FF	- 8.05 µs* 8.10 µs
Niederreiter [Enc/Dec] [27]	V6LX240T V6LX240T	888 LUT/875 FF/17 BRAM 9409 LUT/12861 FF/ 12 BRAM	0.66 µs 57.78 µs
NTRU [Enc/Dec] [30]	XCV1600E	27292 LUT/5160 FF	1.54 µs 1.41 µs
1024-bit mod. Exp. [50]	XC4VFX12	3937 SLICE/17 DSP48	1.71 ms
ECC-P224 [24]	XC4VFX12	1825 LUT/1892 FF/ 26 DSP48/ 11 BRAM	365.1 µs
ECC-B233 [47]	XC5VLX85T	18097 LUT/5644 SLICE	12.3 µs

4.3 Constant Time Operation

Side-channel attacks are a problem for all physical implementations [39]. A simple target for a side-channel attack is the use of timing information of the security algorithm by measuring execution time or cycles. Our implementation of RING-LWEENCRYPT is fully pipelined and has no data-dependent operations. The processor core does not support any branches and Gaussian sampling based on the inverse transform operates in constant time. Summarizing, all cryptographic operations of our core are timing-invariant.

5 Conclusions and Future Work

In this work we presented a novel implementation of the ideal lattice-based Ring-LWE encryption scheme that fits even on a low-cost Spartan-6 FPGA. According to our findings, we improved the results obtained in the previous work of [22] by at least an order of magnitude using the same FPGA platform and much less resources.

Future work can combine our hardware engine with error correction facilities and CCA2 conversion. Additionally, countermeasures against further side-channel and fault-injection attacks need to be considered. As we intend to make our implementation publicly available, our work also offers the chance for third-party side-channel evaluation and cryptanalysis (e.g., exploiting the concrete implementation of the Gaussian sampler). Since our processor could also be utilized by other lattice-based cryptosystems, the provably secure NTRU variant presented in [49] can be another target for implementation. Moreover, a recent proposal of a lattice-based signature scheme by Ducas et al. [14] uses exactly the same parameters ($n = 512, q = 12289$) as RING-LWEENCRYPT and is thus a natural target for implementation based on our micro-code engine.

References

1. Agrawal, S., Boneh, D., Boyen, X.: Efficient lattice (H)IBE in the standard model. In: Gilbert [21], pp. 553–572
2. Ajtai, M.: Generating hard instances of lattice problems. In: Proceedings of the Twenty-Eighth Annual ACM Symposium on Theory of Computing, pp. 99–108. ACM (1996)
3. Albrecht, M., Cid, C., Faugère, J.-C., Fitzpatrick, R., Perret, L.: On the complexity of BKW algorithm against LWE. In: SCC'12: Proceedings of the 3nd International Conference on Symbolic Computation and Cryptography, Castro-Urdiales, July 2012, pp. 100–107 (2012)
4. Albrecht, M., Cid, C., Faugère, J.-C., Fitzpatrick, R., Perret, L.: On the complexity of the Arora-Ge algorithm against LWE. In: SCC'12: Proceedings of the 3nd International Conference on Symbolic Computation and Cryptography, Castro-Urdiales, July 2012, pp. 93–99 (2012)
5. Atici, A.C., Batina, L., Fan, J., Verbauwhede, I., Örs, S.B.: Low-cost implementations of NTRU for pervasive security. In: ASAP, pp. 79–84. IEEE Computer Society (2008)

6. Aysu, A., Patterson, C., Schaumont, P.: Low-cost and area-efficient FPGA implementations of lattice-based cryptography. In: IEEE International Symposium on Hardware-Oriented Security and Trust (HOST), 2013. IEEE (2013, to appear)
7. Bailey, D.V., Coffin, D., Elbirt, A., Silverman, J.H., Woodbury, A.D.: NTRU in constrained devices. In: Koç, Ç.K., Naccache, D., Paar, C. (eds.) CHES 2001. LNCS, vol. 2162, pp. 262–272. Springer, Heidelberg (2001)
8. Bernstein, D.J., Lange, T.: eBACS: ECRYPT benchmarking of cryptographic systems. http://bench.cr.yp.to. Accessed 10 May 2013
9. Bos, J.W., Lauter, K., Loftus, J., Naehrig, M.: Improved security for a ring-based fully homomorphic encryption scheme. IACR Cryptol. ePrint Arch. **2013**, 75 (2013)
10. Brakerski, Z.: Fully homomorphic encryption without modulus switching from classical GapSVP. In: Safavi-Naini, R., Canetti, R. (eds.) CRYPTO 2012. LNCS, vol. 7417, pp. 868–886. Springer, Heidelberg (2012)
11. Brakerski, Z., Langlois, A., Peikert, C., Regev, O., Stehlé, D.: Classical hardness of learning with errors. In: Boneh, D., Roughgarden, T., Feigenbaum, J. (eds.) STOC, pp. 575–584. ACM (2013)
12. Buchmann, J., May, A., Vollmer, U.: Perspectives for cryptographic long-term security. Commun. ACM **49**(9), 50–55 (2006)
13. Canetti, R., Garay, J.A. (eds.): CRYPTO 2013, Part I. LNCS, vol. 8042. Springer, Heidelberg (2013)
14. Ducas, L., Durmus, A., Lepoint, T., Lyubashevsky, V.: Lattice signatures and bimodal Gaussians. In: Canetti and Garay [13], pp. 40–56. Proceedings version of [15]
15. Ducas, L., Durmus, A., Lepoint, T., Lyubashevsky, V.: Lattice signatures and bimodal Gaussians. IACR Cryptol. ePrint Arch. **2013**, 383 (2013). (Full version of [14])
16. Ducas, L., Nguyen, P.Q.: Faster Gaussian lattice sampling using lazy floating-point arithmetic. In: Wang and Sako [53], pp. 415–432
17. Ducas, L., Nguyen, P.Q.: Learning a zonotope and more: cryptanalysis of NTRUSign countermeasures. In: Wang and Sako [53], pp. 433–450
18. Galbraith, S.D., Dwarakanath, N.C.: Efficient sampling from discrete gaussians for lattice-based cryptography on a constrained device
19. Gentry, C.: Fully homomorphic encryption using ideal lattices. In: Proceedings of the 41st Annual ACM Symposium on Theory of Computing, pp. 169–178. ACM (2009)
20. Gentry, C., Peikert, C., Vaikuntanathan, V.: Trapdoors for hard lattices and new cryptographic constructions. In: Dwork, C. (ed.) STOC, pp. 197–206. ACM (2008)
21. Gilbert, H. (ed.): EUROCRYPT 2010. LNCS, vol. 6110. Springer, Heidelberg (2010)
22. Göttert, N., Feller, T., Schneider, M., Buchmann, J., Huss, S.: On the design of hardware building blocks for modern lattice-based encryption schemes. In: Prouff and Schaumont [46], pp. 512–529
23. Güneysu, T., Lyubashevsky, V., Pöppelmann, T.: Practical lattice-based cryptography: a signature scheme for embedded systems. In: Prouff and Schaumont [46], pp. 530–547
24. Güneysu, T., Paar, C.: Ultra high performance ECC over NIST primes on commercial FPGAs. In: Oswald, E., Rohatgi, P. (eds.) CHES 2008. LNCS, vol. 5154, pp. 62–78. Springer, Heidelberg (2008)

25. Gutierrez, R., Torres, V., Valls, J.: Hardware architecture of a Gaussian noise generator based on the inversion method. IEEE Trans. Circ. Syst. **59-II**(8), 501–505 (2012)
26. Hermans, J., Vercauteren, F., Preneel, B.: Speed records for NTRU. In: Pieprzyk, J. (ed.) CT-RSA 2010. LNCS, vol. 5985, pp. 73–88. Springer, Heidelberg (2010)
27. Heyse, S., Güneysu, T.: Towards one cycle per bit asymmetric encryption: code-based cryptography on reconfigurable hardware. In: Prouff and Schaumont [46], pp. 340–355
28. Hirschhorn, P.S., Hoffstein, J., Howgrave-Graham, N., Whyte, W.: Choosing NTRUEncrypt parameters in light of combined lattice reduction and MITM approaches. In: Abdalla, M., Pointcheval, D., Fouque, P.-A., Vergnaud, D. (eds.) ACNS 2009. LNCS, vol. 5536, pp. 437–455. Springer, Heidelberg (2009)
29. Hoffstein, J., Pipher, J., Silverman, J.H.: NTRU: a ring-based public key cryptosystem. In: Buhler, J.P. (ed.) ANTS 1998. LNCS, vol. 1423, pp. 267–288. Springer, Heidelberg (1998)
30. Kamal, A.A., Youssef, A.M.: An FPGA implementation of the NTRUEncrypt cryptosystem. In: 2009 International Conference on Microelectronics (ICM), pp. 209–212. IEEE (2009)
31. Lee, D.-U., Luk, W., Villasenor, J.D., Zhang, G., Leong, P.H.-W.: A hardware Gaussian noise generator using the Wallace method. IEEE Trans. Very Large Scale Integr. VLSI Syst. **13**(8), 911–920 (2005)
32. Lindner, R., Peikert, C.: Better key sizes (and Attacks) for LWE-based encryption. In: Kiayias, A. (ed.) CT-RSA 2011. LNCS, vol. 6558, pp. 319–339. Springer, Heidelberg (2011)
33. Lyubashevsky, V., Micciancio, D.: Generalized compact knapsacks are collision resistant. In: Bugliesi, M., Preneel, B., Sassone, V., Wegener, I. (eds.) ICALP 2006. LNCS, vol. 4052, pp. 144–155. Springer, Heidelberg (2006)
34. Lyubashevsky, V.: Lattice signatures without trapdoors. In: Pointcheval, D., Johansson, T. (eds.) EUROCRYPT 2012. LNCS, vol. 7237, pp. 738–755. Springer, Heidelberg (2012)
35. Lyubashevsky, V., Micciancio, D., Peikert, C., Rosen, A.: SWIFFT: a modest proposal for FFT hashing. In: Nyberg, K. (ed.) FSE 2008. LNCS, vol. 5086, pp. 54–72. Springer, Heidelberg (2008)
36. Lyubashevsky, V., Peikert, C., Regev, O.: On ideal lattices and learning with errors over rings. In: Gilbert [21], pp. 1–23. Proceedings version of [37]
37. Lyubashevsky, V., Peikert, C., Regev, O.: On ideal lattices and learning with errors over rings. IACR Cryptol. ePrint Arch. **2012**, 230 (2012). (Full version of [36])
38. MacWilliams, F.J., Sloane, N.J.A.: The Theory of Error-Correcting Codes. vol. 16, 762 pp, Elsevier Science Publishers B. V., North-Holland (2006). ISBN: 0-444-85193-3
39. Mangard, S., Oswald, E., Popp, T.: Power Analysis Attacks: Revealing the Secrets of Smart Cards (Advances in Information Security), 3rd edn. Springer, New York (2007)
40. Micciancio, D.: Generalized compact knapsacks, cyclic lattices, and efficient one-way functions. Comput. Complex. **16**(4), 365–411 (2007)
41. Micciancio, D., Peikert, C.: Hardness of SIS and LWE with small parameters. In: Canetti and Garay [13], pp. 21–39
42. Naehrig, M., Lauter, K., Vaikuntanathan, V.: Can homomorphic encryption be practical? In: Proceedings of the 3rd ACM Workshop on Cloud Computing Security Workshop, CCSW '11, pp. 113–124. ACM, New York (2011)

43. Nguyên, P.Q., Regev, O.: Learning a parallelepiped: cryptanalysis of GGH and NTRU signatures. In: Vaudenay, S. (ed.) EUROCRYPT 2006. LNCS, vol. 4004, pp. 271–288. Springer, Heidelberg (2006)
44. Peikert, C.: An efficient and parallel Gaussian sampler for lattices. In: Rabin, T. (ed.) CRYPTO 2010. LNCS, vol. 6223, pp. 80–97. Springer, Heidelberg (2010)
45. Pöppelmann, T., Güneysu, T.: Towards efficient arithmetic for lattice-based cryptography on reconfigurable hardware. In: Hevia, A., Neven, G. (eds.) LatinCrypt 2012. LNCS, vol. 7533, pp. 139–158. Springer, Heidelberg (2012)
46. Prouff, E., Schaumont, P. (eds.): CHES 2012. LNCS, vol. 7428. Springer, Heidelberg (2012)
47. Rebeiro, C., Roy, S.S., Mukhopadhyay, D.: Pushing the limits of high-speed $GF(2^m)$ elliptic curve scalar multiplication on FPGAs. In: Prouff and Schaumont [46], pp. 494–511
48. Regev, O.: On lattices, learning with errors, random linear codes, and cryptography. In: Gabow, H.N., Fagin, R. (eds.) STOC, pp. 84–93. ACM (2005)
49. Stehlé, D., Steinfeld, R.: Making NTRU as secure as worst-case problems over ideal lattices. In: Paterson, K.G. (ed.) EUROCRYPT 2011. LNCS, vol. 6632, pp. 27–47. Springer, Heidelberg (2011)
50. Suzuki, D.: How to maximize the potential of FPGA resources for modular exponentiation. In: Paillier, P., Verbauwhede, I. (eds.) CHES 2007. LNCS, vol. 4727, pp. 272–288. Springer, Heidelberg (2007)
51. Thomas, D.B., Luk, W., Leong, P.H.W., Villasenor, J.D.: Gaussian random number generators. ACM Comput. Surv. **39**(4), 11:1–11:38 (2007)
52. Varchola, M.: FPGA based true random number generators for embedded cryptographic applications. Ph.D. thesis, Technical University of Kosice (2008)
53. Wang, X., Sako, K. (eds.): ASIACRYPT 2012. LNCS, vol. 7658. Springer, Heidelberg (2012)
54. Zhang, G., Leong, P.H.-W., Lee, D.-U., Villasenor, J.D., Cheung, R.C.C., Luk, W.: Ziggurat-based hardware Gaussian random number generator. In: International Conference on Field Programmable Logic and Applications, 2005, pp. 275–280 (2005)

Invited Talk

Practical Approaches to Varying Network Size in Combinatorial Key Predistribution Schemes

Kevin Henry[1], Maura B. Paterson[2], and Douglas R. Stinson[1(✉)]

[1] David R. Cheriton School of Computer Science, University of Waterloo,
Waterloo, ON N2L 3G1, Canada
k2henry@cs.uwaterloo.ca, dstinson@math.uwaterloo.ca
[2] Department of Economics, Mathematics and Statistics,
Birkbeck, University of London, Malet Street, London WC1E 7HX, UK
m.paterson@bbk.ac.uk

Abstract. Combinatorial key predistribution schemes can provide a practical solution to the problem of distributing symmetric keys to the nodes of a wireless sensor network. Such schemes often inherently suit networks in which the number of nodes belongs to some restricted set of values (such as powers of primes). In a recent paper, Bose, Dey and Mukerjee have suggested that this might pose a problem, since discarding keyrings to suit a smaller network might adversely affect the properties of the scheme.

In this paper we explore this issue, with specific reference to classes of key predistribution schemes based on transversal designs. We demonstrate through experiments that, for a wide range of parameters, randomly removing keyrings in fact has a negligible and largely predictable effect on the parameters of the scheme. In order to facilitate these computations, we provide a new, efficient, generally applicable approach to computing important properties of combinatorial key predistribution schemes.

We also show that the structure of a resolvable transversal design can be exploited to give a deterministic method of removing keyrings to adjust the network size, in such a way that the properties of the resulting scheme are easy to analyse. We show that these schemes have the same asymptotic properties as the transversal design schemes on which they are based, and that for most parameter choices their behaviour is very similar.

Keywords: Wireless sensor network · Key predistribution scheme · Combinatorial design

1 Introduction

In this paper, we consider *wireless sensor networks* (WSNs) consisting of a large number m of identical sensor nodes that are randomly deployed over a

D. Stinson's research is supported by NSERC discovery grant 203114-11.

T. Lange, K. Lauter, and P. Lisoněk (Eds.): SAC 2013, LNCS 8282, pp. 89–117, 2014.
DOI: 10.1007/978-3-662-43414-7_5, © Springer-Verlag Berlin Heidelberg 2014

target area. After deployment, each node communicates in a wireless manner with other nodes that are within communication range, thus forming an ad hoc network. Due to the wireless nature of the communication, it is desirable for cryptographic tools to be used for provision of secrecy, data integrity, and/or authentication. The nodes' restricted computational ability and battery power mean that, in many situations, it is preferable to use symmetric algorithms rather than relying on more computationally-intensive public key techniques. This requires nodes to share keys; one standard approach to providing such keys is the use of a *key predistribution scheme* (KPS), in which keys are stored in the nodes' keyrings prior to deployment. For example, in the seminal scheme of Eschenauer and Gligor [4], the keys are randomly drawn from a common keypool.

After the nodes have been deployed, nodes that are within communication range execute a *shared key discovery* protocol to determine which keys they have in common. Two nodes that share at least η keys (for some predetermined *intersection threshold* $\eta \geq 1$) use all their common keys to derive a new key that is used to secure communication between them. This is referred to as a secure *link* between these nodes. There exists a large quantity of literature relating to the construction of KPSs for WSNs; surveys include [2,7,10].

KPSs based on combinatorial structures such as designs or codes have been studied as an alternative to random schemes (see [6,9] for surveys of combinatorial schemes). Such schemes have several advantages over the random schemes: for instance, they make it possible to prove the scheme has desirable properties relating to connectivity and resilience, they enable more efficient discovery of shared keys, and they reduce the amount of randomness required when instantiating the schemes [5].

Key predistribution schemes for WSNs are typically evaluated using certain metrics that relate to the performance of the resulting networks. Firstly, it is desirable to restrict the total amount of memory each node must use for storing keys/keying material. Secondly, after the nodes have been deployed, it is desirable for there to be as many secure links as possible between neighbouring nodes, so as to increase the (secure) *connectivity* of the resulting network. The extent to which a KPS facilitates achieving this objective is frequently measured in terms of the quantity Pr_1, which denotes the probability that any two given nodes share at least η common keys.

Finally, we wish to measure the scheme's ability to withstand adversarial attack. A widely studied attack model, which we follow in this paper, is that of *random node capture* [4], where the adversary can eavesdrop on all communication in the network, and can also comprise random nodes in order to extract any keys/keying material they contain. The *resilience* of a KPS in the face of an attacker is expressed in terms of the quantity $\mathsf{fail}(s)$, which is defined to be the probability that a randomly chosen link is broken when an attacker compromises s nodes uniformly at random, and then extracts their keys.

For simplicity, we focus particularly on $\mathsf{fail}(1)$ in this work. In this case, a link $\{A, B\}$ is broken by another node C when $A \cap B \subseteq C$, where A, B and C denote the sets of keys held by the three corresponding nodes.

There is an inherent tension between the need to provide good connectivity and the need to maintain a high level of resilience without requiring an excessive number of keys to be stored. Designing a KPS involves finding a scheme that delivers a good tradeoff between these properties, and which is sufficiently flexible to be useful for a range of practical choices of parameters such as network size, available storage and desired level of security.

One feature of combinatorial schemes that could be viewed as a drawback is the fact that, due to the structure of the combinatorial object used, the number of nodes in the scheme may be required to be of a particular form, such as a power of a prime, for example. If the number n of nodes in the network in which we wish to employ such a scheme is not of this form, then the most commonly suggested remedy is to take the smallest number of that form that is larger than n, and simply select some (randomly chosen) subset of n keyrings from the resulting scheme (e.g., see [5]). In a recent paper [1], Bose, Dey and Mukerjee have suggested that removing keyrings in this manner from a combinatorial scheme may adversely affect its properties, thus negating some of the main benefits of such schemes. Instead, they propose a deterministic KPS in which various block designs are combined to give a scheme in which the number of keyrings can be varied directly in a more flexible manner.

In this paper, we examine more closely the actual effects of removing keyrings from a combinatorial KPS. We focus specifically on the family of schemes proposed by Lee and Stinson based on transversal designs [5], since they have been shown to behave well for a wide range of parameters [9]. In Sect. 2, we exploit the structure of resolvable transversal designs to propose a deterministic method for selecting keyrings to remove from the schemes of Lee and Stinson without unduly affecting their performance. The properties of these modified schemes are easy to analyse using the framework established in [9], and we exploit this feature to compare their performance directly with the combinatorial schemes from which they were derived, demonstrating that they yield a family of schemes with a flexible choice of parameters whose properties compare favourably with those of existing schemes.

In addition, for a broad range of parameter choices, we consider networks consisting of various numbers of nodes with keyrings chosen uniformly at random from transversal design KPSs, and we compute the mean and standard deviation of the resulting values of the security and performance metrics for these schemes. The results, given in Sect. 3.2, demonstrate that the change in these metrics as keyrings are removed is in fact very limited, and largely predictable.

Computing properties of schemes obtained by randomly deleting some number of keyrings from a combinatorial scheme can be time-consuming. Therefore, in Sect. 4 we describe a new approach to facilitate the efficient evaluation of metrics for connectivity and resilience in general KPSs. This approach is based on some new formulas for these metrics that are of independent interest.

1.1   Overview of the Construction and Analysis of Combinatorial Key Predistribution Schemes

A *set system* $(X, \mathcal{A})$ consists of a finite set X of *points*, together with a finite set $\mathcal{A}$ of subsets of X, which are known as *blocks*. A set system can be used to construct a KPS by associating each key in a certain keyspace with an element of X and each node with an element of $\mathcal{A}$, so that a node is preloaded with the keys that correspond to points lying in its corresponding block. The point x acts as a *key identifier* for the corresponding secret key. Key identifiers (and which nodes hold which key identifiers) are public information, whereas the values of the keys are secret (known only to the nodes that hold them).

Example 1. Let

$$X = \{1, 2, 3, 4, 5, 6, 7, 8, 9\}, \quad \text{and}$$
$$\mathcal{A} = \{123, 456, 789, 147, 258, 369,$$
$$159, 267, 348, 168, 249, 357\}.$$

Then $(X, \mathcal{A})$ is a set system in which there are nine points and twelve blocks. Each block contains three points. The associated KPS will have 12 nodes, each of which possesses three of the nine secret keys.

It is easy to see that, in this model, the Eschenauer-Gligor scheme [4] is obtained when the underlying set system consists of n random k-subsets of the v-set X. On the other hand, combinatorial key predistribution schemes are typically based on set systems arising from combinatorial objects with nice properties that ensure the resulting schemes perform well and are amenable to analysis. Particular examples of combinatorial objects that have been proposed for use in key distribution in this way include projective planes, generalised quadrangles, configurations, common intersection designs, transversal designs of strength 2 or 3, partially balanced incomplete block designs, inversive planes [3], orthogonal arrays, Reed-Solomon codes, mutually-orthogonal Latin squares, and rational normal curves in projective spaces (see [9] for a survey and analysis of such schemes).

In this paper, we focus mainly on transversal designs, which we define now.

Definition 1. *Let t, n and k be positive integers such that $t \leq k \leq n$. A transversal design TD(t,k,n) is a triple $(X, \mathcal{H}, \mathcal{A})$, where X is a finite set of cardinality kn, $\mathcal{H}$ is a partition of X into k parts (called groups) of size n and $\mathcal{A}$ is a set of k-subsets of X (called blocks), which satisfy the following properties:*

1. *$|H \cap A| = 1$ for every $H \in \mathcal{H}$ and every $A \in \mathcal{A}$, and*
2. *every subset of t elements of X from t different groups occurs in exactly one block in $\mathcal{A}$.*

The parameter t is called the strength of the transversal design.

We note that transversal designs are equivalent to other familiar combinatorial objects such as orthogonal arrays and maximum distance separable (MDS) codes; see [9, Sect. 2.7] for further discussion on these equivalences.

Example 2. Lee and Stinson [5] proposed a family of combinatorial KPSs based on transversal designs $TD(2, k, p)$. The set systems they use can be constructed explicitly as follows:

For p a prime and k an integer with $2 \leq k \leq p$ we construct a $TD(2, k, p)$ by letting the points be all elements of the form (a, b) where $a \in \{0, 1, \ldots, k-1\}$ and $b \in \mathbb{Z}_p$. The transversal design has p^2 blocks, which are given by the sets of the form

$$A_{i,j} = \{(x, ix + j \pmod{p}) | 0 \leq x \leq k - 1\}.$$

This construction can be generalised in an obvious way by replacing $\mathbb{Z}_p$ by the finite field $GF(n)$. Hence, we can obtain a transversal design $TD(2, k, n)$ with n^2 blocks for any prime power n. It is straightforward to show that in this scheme any two nodes share either 1 key or 0 keys; as such we specify that $\eta = 1$ and hence two neighbouring nodes form a secure link if they share one common key.

To construct a transversal design of strength 3 (a $TD(3, k, p)$) the points are taken to be all elements of the form (a, b) where $a \in \{0, 1, \ldots, k-1\}$ and $b \in \mathbb{Z}_p$, as before. For each of the p^3 polynomials f in $\mathbb{Z}_p[x]$ of degree at most 2 we obtain a block by taking the set of points of the form

$$A_f = \{(x, f(x) \pmod{p}) | 0 \leq x \leq k - 1\}.$$

Once again, we can replace $\mathbb{Z}_p$ by the finite field $GF(n)$ in this construction and obtain a $TD(3, k, n)$ for any prime power n. Two nodes in this scheme share either 0, 1 or 2 keys. Hence we can choose to use an intersection threshold of either $\eta = 1$ or $\eta = 2$ for specifying the minimum number of keys that must be shared by two nodes before they can form a secure link.

The values of $\mathsf{fail}(1)$ and Pr_1 for these schemes, in the case of strength 2 with $\eta = 1$ and strength 3 with $\eta = 1$ or $\eta = 2$, are given in Table 1.

For the transversal designs $TD(t, k, n)$ for both $t = 2$ and $t = 3$ described above, the points of the design can be partitioned into k subsets H_i, for $0 \leq i \leq k - 1$, by setting

$$H_i = \{(i, b) | b \in GF(n)\}.$$

These sets H_i are known as the *groups* of the transversal design. It is straightforward to show that each subset of t points of the transversal design from t different groups occur together in exactly one block of the transversal design.

Example 3. Bose et al. [1] proposed a family of KPSs obtained by combining η designs that are the duals of designs derived from association schemes. For the sake of clarity, we will restrict ourselves to the specific instantiation in which the designs are all copies of a $TD(2, k, n)$.

In the case of $\eta = 1$, the Bose et al. scheme instantiated with a $TD(2, k, n)$ coincides exactly with Lee and Stinson's transversal design scheme.

For $\eta = 2$, they take two copies of a $TD(2, k, n)$ and construct a new set system by letting the set of points be the union of the sets of points of each of the designs, and by letting the blocks be given by all possible unions of the form $B_1 \cup B_2$ where B_1 is a block of the first $TD(2, k, n)$ and B_2 is a block of the second $TD(2, k, n)$. This scheme has $2kn$ points, and n^4 blocks. Each block contains $2k$ points, and two blocks intersect in either 0, 1, 2, k, or $k + 1$ points.

As observed in [5], combinatorial schemes possess several distinct advantages as compared to random schemes such as Eschenauer-Gligor:

- the deterministic nature and regular structure of combinatorial schemes ensure that the precise values of metrics of the scheme such as $\mathsf{fail}(1)$ and Pr_1 can be computed exactly, rather than simply the expected value of these quantities;
- combinatorial schemes reduce the quantity of random numbers that must be generated in setting up the scheme;
- most importantly, for many combinatorial schemes, their regular structure leads to very efficient algorithms for performing tasks such as shared key discovery once the nodes are deployed.

As such, combinatorial schemes can represent an efficient and effective way of establishing keys in many WSN scenarios.

A survey and analysis of many existing combinatorial schemes was carried out in [9]. The concept of a *partially balanced t-design* (PBtD) was introduced, and explicit formulas for evaluating $\mathsf{fail}(1)$ and Pr_1 were given for any combinatorial scheme that can be constructed from a PBtD.

Definition 2. *For positive integers v, k, t and λ_i with $0 \leq i \leq t - 1$, a $t - (v, k, \lambda_0, \lambda_1, \ldots, \lambda_{t-i})$-partially balanced t-design is a pair $(X, \mathcal{A})$ with the following properties:*

1. *X is a finite set whose elements are referred to as points, and $\mathcal{A}$ is a finite set of k-subsets of X; its elements are referred to as blocks.*
2. *There are λ_0 blocks in $\mathcal{A}$.*
3. *For $1 \leq i \leq t - 1$, each subset of i points of X occurs in either no blocks, or in exactly λ_i blocks.*
4. *For $t \leq i \leq k$, each subset of i points occurs in either 0 or 1 blocks.*

Paterson and Stinson [9] showed that a wide range of existing combinatorial KPSs (including KPSs constructed from transversal designs) could be modelled as PBtDs. The advantage of doing so is that the properties of these schemes can easily be evaluated and compared with the aid of the formulas given in [9]. The resulting values for a range of schemes are given in Table 1. The transversal-design based schemes described in Example 2 were shown to provide a good degree of flexibility for the construction of KPSs relative to other PBtDs, since they are easily constructed for a wide range of useful parameters, the block size can be chosen independently of the network size, and the values of t and η can also be varied independently.

The KPSs of Bose et al. [1] are not PBtDs, and hence they cannot be analysed directly using the approach of [9]. One of the motivations behind their schemes is to provide constructions that can yield KPSs for a flexible choice of network size; in [1], they note that "the number of nodes need not be of the particular forms p^2 or p^3, with p prime or prime power". The traditional view of combinatorial construction of KPSs is that, provided a range of parameters is available, then if a specific network size n is desired it suffices to choose parameters to give a scheme that suits a network of size greater than n and simply discard the unneeded keyrings. Bose et al. [1] object (with particular reference to [5]) that "if we then discard the unnecessary node allocations to get the final scheme for use, this final scheme will not preserve the Pr_1 and $\mathsf{fail}(s)$ values of the original scheme and hence the properties of the final scheme in this regard can become quite erratic" [1]. One main goal of our paper is to refute this statement.

1.2   Outline of the Paper

In Sect. 2, we present two approaches to increasing the flexibility of combinatorial predistribution schemes based on transversal designs. One approach is randomized and the other is deterministic. In Sect. 3, we perform extensive comparisons of our generalized constructions to the original transversal design schemes. In Sect. 4, we derive new formulas that facilitate the computation of metrics for connectivity and resilience for arbitrary key predistribution schemes based on set systems. Finally, Sect. 5 is a short conclusion.

2   Two Approaches to Varying the Network Size in KPSs based on Transversal Designs

In this section we consider two distinct approaches to varying the network size in the transversal design-based KPSs of Lee and Stinson. One option is to use the standard approach of randomly removing blocks from the design.

Scheme 1 (Random scheme). *Suppose a KPS is desired for a network containing m nodes. Let n be the smallest prime power satisfying $n^2 \geq m$. Then by constructing a* TD$(2, k, n)$ *and selecting a subset of m blocks uniformly at random we obtain a set system that can be used to provide a KPS for the network.*

Similarly, we can construct a KPS for this network based on a transversal design of strength 2 by taking n to be the smallest prime power with $n^3 \geq m$, and then selecting m blocks uniformly at random from the set of blocks of a TD$(3, k, n)$.

The benefits of such an approach include its simplicity and the fact that it can be applied for any value of m. It is a very natural approach, given that it mirrors precisely the commonly anticipated situation in which a small number of nodes may fail or run out of power after deployment. We will see that this scheme performs well in practice: in Sect. 3.2 we demonstrate that for a wide range of parameter choices, restricting to a random subset of blocks of a $TD(2, k, n)$ does not adversely affect the expected performance of schemes based on these designs. Furthermore, we still retain some desirable properties of combinatorial schemes such as efficient shared key discovery.

One of the other underlying motivations of using combinatorial designs to construct KPSs is the fact that their deterministic and highly structured nature allows us to guarantee the values they attain for metrics such as $\mathsf{fail}(1)$ and Pr_1. If blocks are deleted at random, we lose these guarantees, even though diminished performance is very unlikely. In this section we propose a second technique, to overcome this possible drawback. We demonstrate how to exploit the structure of transversal designs in order to select subsets of the blocks *deterministically* in such a way that the precise performance of the resulting structure is straightforward to evaluate. Specifically, we will make use of *resolvable transversal designs* to accomplish this objective.

2.1   Resolvable Transversal Designs of Strength 2

Definition 3. *A transversal design* $TD(2, k, n)$ *is said to be* resolvable *if it is possible to partition the blocks of the design into sets* $\mathcal{B}_1, \mathcal{B}_2, \ldots, \mathcal{B}_n$, *such that each point of the design belongs to precisely one block in each set. The sets* $\mathcal{B}_i$ *are known as* parallel classes *of the design.*

Resolvable transversal designs have previously been exploited for constructing KPSs suited for networks where there is group deployment of nodes; see [8]. The transversal design KPSs proposed by Lee and Stinson do not require the resolvability property; however, the transversal designs $TD(2, k, n)$ used in [5] are in fact resolvable.

Example 4. For the $TD(2, k, n)$ described in Example 2, the parallel classes of blocks are given by

$$\mathcal{B}_i = \{\mathcal{A}_{i,j} | j \in \mathrm{GF}(n)\}, i \in \mathrm{GF}(n).$$

It is straightforward to see that no point lies in two distinct blocks of a given parallel class, since if a point (x, y) were in blocks $\mathcal{A}_{i,j}$ and $\mathcal{A}_{i,h}$, this would imply that $y = ix + j$ and also $y = ix + h$, whence $j = h$.

A resolvable transversal design $TD(2, k, n)$ has n parallel classes with n blocks in each class. We propose using such designs for key predistribution as follows:

Scheme 2 (Linear scheme). *We construct a set system for use in a KPS by starting with a resolvable* $TD(2, k, n)$, *where* n *is a prime power. Let* ℓ *be an integer between 1 and* n. *Select* ℓ *parallel classes of blocks of the design, and let the blocks in these parallel classes be the blocks of the set system. We refer to the resulting set system as a* $\overline{TD}(2, k, n, \ell)$.

As each parallel class contains n blocks, this means that Scheme 2 yields a KPS with ℓn keyrings. This number can be varied as required by choosing an appropriate value of ℓ: roughly speaking, we require that $n \geq \sqrt{m}$ and $\ell \approx m/n$. One nice feature of this method of choosing blocks is that the resulting incidence structure is in fact a PBtD, and hence its properties can be determined in a straightforward manner simply by using the formulas given in [9]. We now perform this analysis to show that Scheme 2 performs well even for comparatively small values of ℓ.

Theorem 1. *A* $\overline{\mathrm{TD}}(2, k, n, \ell)$ *is a* 2-$(kn, k, \ell n, \ell)$-*PBtD*

Proof. Take ℓ parallel classes of blocks from a resolvable $\mathrm{TD}(2, k, n)$, and let $\mathcal{A}$ be the set of blocks in these parallel classes. Let X be the set of points in the $\mathrm{TD}(2, k, n)$; we note that X contains kn points. Now, $\mathcal{A}$ contains $\lambda_0 = \ell n$ blocks, each containing k points. Every point of X is contained in precisely one block in each parallel class, and hence is contained in precisely $\lambda_1 = \ell$ blocks of $\mathcal{A}$. Furthermore, since each pair of points in X is contained in either 0 or 1 blocks of the $\mathrm{TD}(2, k, n)$, it follows that any pair of points is contained in either 0 or 1 blocks of $\mathcal{A}$. Thus $(X, \mathcal{A})$ satisfies all the properties of a 2-$(kn, k, \ell n, \ell)$-PBtD. $\square$

The values of fail(1) and Pr_1 for a PBtD are easy to compute systematically using the explicit formulas given in [9]. For a given block B of a PBtD and a point C on that block, denote by $\mu'(1)$ the number of blocks A of the PBtD such that $A \cap B = \{C\}$ (it was shown in [9] that this value is independent of the choice of point and block.) Define a *link* to be a pair of blocks with nonempty intersection. We let L denote the total number of links in a PBtD, we let α denote the number of links in which a given block B is contained, and we let β denote the number of links $\{A, C\}$ with $B \neq A, C$ such that $A \cap C \subset B$ (again, these values do not depend on the specific choice of B). Then, applying the formulas of [9] to a 2-$(kn, k, \ell n, \ell)$-PBtD, we have:

$$\mu'(1) = \lambda_1 - 1 = \ell - 1,$$

$$\alpha = k\mu'(1) = k(\ell - 1),$$

$$\beta = \mu'(1)\left(\frac{\lambda_1}{2} - 1\right)k = (\ell - 1)\left(\frac{\ell}{2} - 1\right)k,$$

$$L = \frac{b\alpha}{2} = \frac{\ell n k(\ell - 1)}{2},$$

$$\mathsf{fail}(1) = \frac{\beta}{L - \alpha} = \frac{\ell - 2}{\ell n - 2},$$

$$\mathsf{Pr}_1 = \frac{\alpha}{b - 1} = \frac{k(\ell - 1)}{\ell n - 1}.$$

In the case where $\ell = n$, a $\overline{\mathrm{TD}}(2, k, n, \ell)$ is simply a $\mathrm{TD}(2, k, n)$, and hence Scheme 2 is a generalisation of the corresponding scheme of Lee and Stinson. The formulas computed above for fail(1) and Pr_1 can be seen to agree with the corresponding formulas for Lee and Stinson's scheme in the case where $\ell = n$.

2.2   Transversal Designs of Higher Strength

Just as in the case of transversal designs of strength 2, it is possible to determin-istically select subsets of blocks from transversal designs of higher strength, such as the $TD(3, k, n)$ suggested for use in key predistribution by Lee and Stinson, in a way that allows flexibility in the number of keyrings of the resulting scheme, while still maintaining good performance. We begin by illustrating a useful app-roach to partitioning the blocks of the $TD(3, k, n)$ described in Example 2.

Example 5. Let n be a prime power and let X be the set of points of one of the $TD(3, k, n)$ whose construction is described in Example 2. We can partition the blocks of this design into sets $\mathcal{B}_1, \mathcal{B}_2, \ldots, \mathcal{B}_n$ by defining

$$\mathcal{B}_i = \{A_f | f(x) = ix^2 + ax + b \text{ for some } a, b \in GF(n)\}, i \in GF(n).$$

We show, for each i, that the incidence structure $(X, \mathcal{B}_i)$ is a $TD(2, k, n)$, with the same groups as the original $TD(3, k, n)$. Suppose this is not the case. Then there is a pair $\{(x, A), (y, B)\}$ (where $x \neq y$) that appears in two blocks of the same $\mathcal{B}_i$. So we have

$$ix^2 + ax + b = A = ix^2 + cx + d \quad \text{and} \quad iy^2 + ay + b = B = iy^2 + cy + d.$$

From this, we get

$$ax + b = cx + d \quad \text{and} \quad ay + b = cy + d.$$

Since $x \neq y$, we have $a = c$, which implies $b = d$. Therefore the two blocks coincide and we have a contradiction.

Scheme 3 (Quadratic scheme). *Let n be a prime power. Starting with a $TD(3, k, n)$, we define a set system by letting ℓ be an integer between 1 and n, selecting ℓ of the sets $\mathcal{B}_i$, and letting $\mathcal{A}$ be the set of blocks in these ℓ sets. We refer to the incidence structure $(X, \mathcal{A})$ as a $\overline{TD}(3, k, n, \ell)$. Using a $\overline{TD}(3, k, n, \ell)$ for constructing a KPS in the standard way yields a scheme with ℓn^2 keyrings, for which we can choose an intersection threshold of either $\eta = 1$ or $\eta = 2$.*

As before, this method of selecting blocks yields a structure that is easy to analyse:

Theorem 2. *A $\overline{TD}(3, k, n, \ell)$ is a 3-$(kn, k, \ell n^2, \ell n, \ell)$-PBtD.*

Proof. A $\overline{TD}(3, k, n, \ell)$ consists of a set of kn points, together with ℓ disjoint sets of n^2 blocks of k points, and thus has ℓn^2 blocks in total. Every point of the $\overline{TD}(3, k, n, \ell)$ is contained in n blocks in each of these sets, and therefore is con-tained in ℓn blocks in total. If a pair of points belong to a group of the underlying $TD(3, k, n)$ then they do not occur together in any block of the $\overline{TD}(3, k, n, \ell)$. If two points lie in different groups, then in each of the ℓ sets $\mathcal{B}_i$ there is precisely one block that contains them. Thus any pair of points occurs together in either 0 or ℓ blocks of the $\overline{TD}(3, k, n, \ell)$. Finally, any set of three points occur together in either 0 or 1 blocks of the $TD(3, k, n)$ and thus also occur together in 0 or 1 blocks of the $\overline{TD}(3, k, n, \ell)$.

This allows us to use the formulas of [9] to compute $\mathsf{fail}(1)$ and Pr_1. Defining $\mu'(2)$ to be the number of blocks C whose intersection with a given block B is a given set $S \subset B$ of two points, we have

$$\mu'(2) = \lambda_2 - 1 = \ell - 1,$$
$$\mu'(1) = \lambda_1 - 1 - (k-1)\mu'(2) = \ell n - 1 - (k-1)(\ell-1).$$

For a KPS with intersection threshold $\eta = 2$ we have

$$\alpha = \binom{k}{2}\mu'(2) = \binom{k}{2}(\ell-1),$$
$$\beta = \mu'(2)\left(\frac{\lambda_2}{2} - 1\right)\binom{k}{2} = (\ell-1)\left(\frac{\ell}{2} - 1\right)\binom{k}{2},$$
$$L = \frac{b\alpha}{2} = \frac{\ell n^2(\ell-1)}{2}\binom{k}{2},$$
$$\mathsf{fail}(1) = \frac{\beta}{L-\alpha} = \frac{\ell-2}{\ell n^2 - 2},$$
$$\mathsf{Pr}_1 = \frac{\alpha}{b-1} = \frac{k(k-1)(\ell-1)}{2(\ell n^2-1)}.$$

Using intersection threshold $\eta = 1$ gives

$$\alpha = k\mu'(1) + \binom{k}{2}\mu'(2) = k(\ell n - 1) - \binom{k}{2}(\ell-1),$$
$$\beta = \mu'(1)\left(\frac{\lambda_1}{2} - 1\right)k + \mu'(2)\left(\frac{\lambda_2}{2} - 1\right)\binom{k}{2},$$
$$= (\ell n - 1 - (k-1)(\ell-1))\,k\left(\frac{\ell n}{2} - 1\right) + (\ell-1)\left(\frac{\ell}{2} - 1\right)\binom{k}{2},$$
$$L = \frac{b\alpha}{2} = \frac{\ell n^2\left(k(\ell n-1) - \binom{k}{2}(\ell-1)\right)}{2},$$
$$\mathsf{fail}(1) = \frac{\beta}{L-\alpha} = \frac{2(\ell n - 1)(\ell n - 2) - (k-1)(\ell-1)(2\ell n - \ell - 2)}{(\ell n^2 - 2)(2\ell n - 2 - (k-1)(\ell-1))},$$
$$\mathsf{Pr}_1 = \frac{\alpha}{b-1} = \frac{k(2\ell n - 2 - (k-1)(\ell-1))}{2(\ell n^2 - 1)}.$$

In the case where $\ell = n$, a $\overline{\mathrm{TD}}(3, k, n, \ell)$ is simply a $\mathrm{TD}(3, k, n)$ and Scheme 2 is a generalisation of the corresponding scheme of Lee and Stinson. When $\ell = n$, the formulas computed above for $\mathsf{fail}(1)$ and Pr_1 agree with the corresponding formulas for Lee and Stinson's scheme.

2.3   Finer Control Over the Number of Blocks

Scheme 3 provides KPSs with ℓn^2 keyrings by selecting ℓ disjoint sets of n^2 blocks from a $\mathrm{TD}(3, k, n)$. Each of these sets of blocks is in fact a resolvable

$TD(2, k, n)$. Thus, if a more fine-grained choice of network size is required, it would be possible to choose ℓ sets of blocks, together with m parallel classes of blocks from an $(\ell + 1)^{\text{th}}$ copy of a $TD(2, k, n)$. This would yield a network with $\ell n^2 + mn$ keyrings; appropriate choices of ℓ and m thus allow the network size to be adjusted to the nearest multiple of n. The resulting combinatorial structure would be a $3\text{-}(kn, k, \ell n^2 + mn, \ell n + m, \ell + 1)\text{-PBtD}$, and hence could be analysed in a similar manner to the schemes based on a $\overline{TD}(3, k, n, \ell)$.

3 Analysis and Comparisons of the New Constructions with Previous Schemes

In this section, we compare the new schemes (Scheme 1, 2 and 3) with the transversal design schemes from which they were derived. Recall that Scheme 1 consists of random blocks chosen from a transversal design, while Scheme 2 and Scheme 3 are deterministic schemes consisting of specified blocks from transversal designs of strength 2 and 3, respectively.

First, Table 1 summarizes the formulas for six deterministic schemes. The six schemes considered in Table 1 (denoted A–F) are the following:

A: Scheme 2, based on a $\overline{TD}(2, k, n, \ell)$
B: Scheme 3, based on a $\overline{TD}(3, k, n, \ell), \eta = 2$
C: Scheme 3, based on a $\overline{TD}(3, k, n, \ell), \eta = 1$
D: Scheme 2, based on a $TD(2, k, n)$ (i.e., Scheme 2 with $\ell = n$)
E: Scheme 3, based on a $TD(3, k, n), \eta = 2$ (i.e., Scheme 3 with $\ell = n$)
F: Scheme 3, based on a $TD(3, k, n), \eta = 1$ (i.e., Scheme 3 with $\ell = n$)

Table 1. Metrics for some transversal design based schemes

Scheme	$\Pr_1$	$\text{fail}(1)$
A.	$\dfrac{k(\ell - 1)}{\ell n - 1}$	$\dfrac{\ell - 2}{\ell n - 2}$
B.	$\dfrac{k(k - 1)(\ell - 1)}{2(\ell n^2 - 1)}$	$\dfrac{\ell - 2}{\ell n^2 - 2}$
C.	$\dfrac{k(2\ell n - 2 - (k - 1)(\ell - 1))}{2(\ell n^2 - 1)}$	$\dfrac{2(\ell n - 1)(\ell n - 2) - (k - 1)(\ell - 1)(2\ell n - \ell - 2)}{(\ell n^2 - 2)(2\ell n - 2 - (k - 1)(\ell - 1))}$
D.	$\dfrac{k}{n + 1}$	$\dfrac{n - 2}{n^2 - 2}$
E.	$\dfrac{k(k - 1)}{2(n^2 + n + 1)}$	$\dfrac{n - 2}{n^3 - 2}$
F.	$\dfrac{k(2n - k + 3)}{2(n^2 + n + 1)}$	$\dfrac{2n^3 + (4 - 2k)n^2 + (k - 5)n + 2k - 6}{(2n - k + 3)(n^3 - 2)}$

In Sect. 3.1, we briefly discuss asymptotic comparisons between the deterministic schemes A–F, using the formulas in Table 1. In Sect. 3.2, these formulas are evaluated for a range of parameter choices to provide a direct comparison with the corresponding values for equivalent parameter choices in Scheme 1 (the Random Scheme).

3.1 Asymptotic Comparisons

It is interesting to compare Scheme 2 and Scheme 3 to the transversal design schemes on which they are based. In Scheme 2 and Scheme 3, we have an additional parameter $\ell \leq n$ (the original schemes correspond to $\ell = n$). Suppose $c < 1$ is a positive real number and we take $\ell = cn$. We compute the ratio of the values of Pr_1 for schemes labelled A and D in Table 1 using the formulas given there:

$$\frac{\mathrm{Pr}_1(\text{scheme } A)}{\mathrm{Pr}_1(\text{scheme } D)} = \frac{\frac{k(cn-1)}{cn^2-1}}{\frac{k}{n+1}} = \frac{(cn-1)(n+1)}{cn^2-1}.$$

As $n \to \infty$, it is easy to see that this ratio approaches 1.

Thus, for example, if we use only $n/1000$ of the n parallel classes, the connectivity of the partial scheme is asymptotically the same as the transversal design scheme on which it is based. A similar result holds for resilience, as can be seen by computing the ratios of the relevant fail(1) values. Furthermore, a similar phenomenon is observed for Scheme 3, for both $\eta = 1$ and $\eta = 2$, i.e., when we use the formulas for the schemes labelled B and E, as well as for the schemes labelled C and F. We summarize this as follows.

Theorem 3. *Let $0 < c < 1$ and let $\ell = cn$ in scheme A, B or C from Table 1. Then*

$$\lim_{n\to\infty} \frac{\mathrm{Pr}_1(\text{scheme } A)}{\mathrm{Pr}_1(\text{scheme } D)} = \lim_{n\to\infty} \frac{\mathsf{fail}(1)(\text{scheme } A)}{\mathsf{fail}(1)(\text{scheme } D)} = 1,$$

$$\lim_{n\to\infty} \frac{\mathrm{Pr}_1(\text{scheme } B)}{\mathrm{Pr}_1(\text{scheme } E)} = \lim_{n\to\infty} \frac{\mathsf{fail}(1)(\text{scheme } B)}{\mathsf{fail}(1)(\text{scheme } E)} = 1,$$

and

$$\lim_{n\to\infty} \frac{\mathrm{Pr}_1(\text{scheme } C)}{\mathrm{Pr}_1(\text{scheme } F)} = \lim_{n\to\infty} \frac{\mathsf{fail}(1)(\text{scheme } C)}{\mathsf{fail}(1)(\text{scheme } F)} = 1.$$

3.2 Comparisons for Explicit Parameter Choices

In this section, we compare the random and deterministic schemes we have presented. We consider transversal designs of strengths 2 and 3 that are appropriate for maximum network sizes of (approximately) 5000 nodes and 24000 nodes:

- The transversal designs yielding maximum network size 5000 (approximately) are TD(2,15,71) and TD(3,15,17); note that $71^2 = 5041$ and $17^3 = 4913$. Here the block size is 15, which means that nodes will each store 15 keys.
- The transversal designs for maximum network size 24000 (approximately) are TD(2,25,157) and TD(3,25,29); note that $157^2 = 24649$ and $29^3 = 24387$. Here the block size is 25, which means that nodes will each store 25 keys.

We analyse and compare the behaviour of Scheme 1, Scheme 2 and Scheme 3 for the parameters listed above; in particular, we evaluate fail(1) and Pr_1 for these schemes. In the case of Scheme 2 and Scheme 3, we have used the formulas from Table 1 to obtain these values. For each choice of n and k, we evaluated fail(1) and Pr_1 for the schemes based on a $\overline{\mathrm{TD}}(2, k, n, \ell)$ or $\overline{\mathrm{TD}}(3, k, n, \ell)$ with $\eta = 1, 2$, for every ℓ between 2 and n inclusive. In the case of Scheme 1, for each network size m, we constructed 100 random instances of the KPS and we computed the exact values of fail(1) and Pr_1 for each of these 100 instances.

The results of these calculations are presented in graphical form in Figs. 1, 2, 3, 4, 5 and 6. In these figures, we plot the connectivity or resilience of a random scheme and a corresponding deterministic scheme. The solid lines, labelled "random", refer to Scheme 1; the dashed lines, labelled "parallel", refer to Scheme 2 or Scheme 3. The dotted lines, labelled "σ", indicate the standard deviation of the values computed for Scheme 1 over the 100 trials (since the standard deviations are quite small, these lines are very close to the bottom of the graphs). The value m is the number of blocks in the associated set system (i.e., the number of nodes in the network).

In the case of Scheme 1, we also computed the maximum and minimum values of fail(1) and Pr_1 obtained over the 100 trials, for each value of m. As well, we

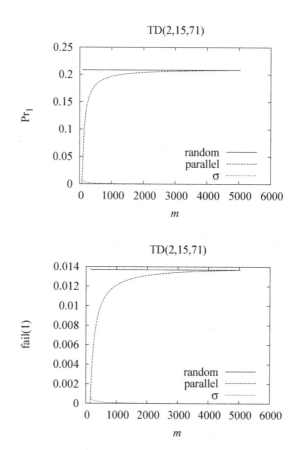

Fig. 1. Connectivity and resilience of KPSs derived from TD(2,15,71)

have tabulated the mean and standard deviation over the 100 samples. In these two tables, the network size is $m = \ell n = 71\ell$. This data is presented, for the schemes derived from a TD(2,15,71), in Tables 3 and 4 in the Appendix.

Some of the main observations we can draw from these results are as follows:

- In Figs. 1–6, the plots of the values of fail(1) or Pr_1 as blocks are selected uniformly from a $TD(2, k, n)$ or $TD(3, k, n)$ (Scheme 1) are all essentially a horizontal line, indicating that on average the values of fail(1) and Pr_1 do not change greatly, even if the number of blocks selected is quite small. This is entirely to be expected: fail(1) and Pr_1 by definition are quantities that represent an average over all the keyrings in the network, so taking the average over smaller, uniformly selected subsets of keyings should not affect these values too much. The average values computed in our experiments are in fact very close to the exact average values that are computed theoretically.
- One quantity of particular interest here is the standard deviation of fail(1) and Pr_1 for Scheme 1, since this determines the extent to which a particu-

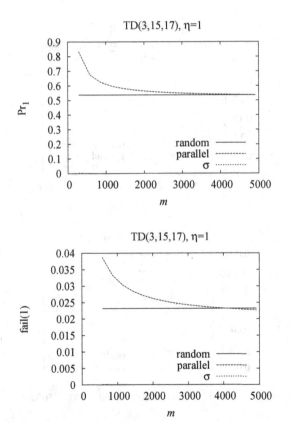

Fig. 2. Connectivity and resilience of KPSs derived from TD(3,15,17) with $\eta = 1$

lar random choice of subnetwork may have fail(1) or Pr_1 values that differ from the average values for the scheme as a whole. Naturally, the standard deviation of these values increases slightly when the number blocks is very small. However, we can see from Figs. 1–6 that these standard deviations are still extremely low, especially in the case of schemes obtained from the larger designs. Moreover, there is a very low range of values of fail(1) and Pr_1 encountered in our experiments. This is evident from Tables 3 and 4 in the Appendix, for the schemes derived from a TD(2,15,71). Schemes derived from other transversal designs exhibit similar behaviour in terms of the variability of these metrics. Thus we see that in practice, selecting random subsets of the keyrings is unlikely to have much of an effect on the values of fail(1) and Pr_1 for the scheme.

– In Scheme 2, when the number ℓ of parallel classes is very small, the value of Pr_1 is low, due to the fact that no two blocks within a given parallel class have any points in common. Nevertheless, Figs. 1 and 4 demonstrate that this value grows rapidly as ℓ increases, and soon approaches the Pr_1 value

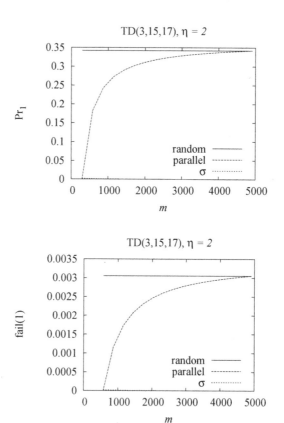

Fig. 3. Connectivity and resilience of KPSs derived from TD(3,15,17) with $\eta = 2$

attained by Scheme 1. On the other hand, for Scheme 2, the value of fail(1) is also low initially, and similarly becomes closer to that of Scheme 1 as ℓ increases. Thus we see that the properties of Scheme 2 and Scheme 1 are very similar in practice, for even moderately large values of ℓ.

- Figures 3 and 6 show that Scheme 3 with intersection threshold $\eta = 2$ exhibits a similar behaviour to that of Scheme 2: the Pr_1 and fail(1) values are low when ℓ is small, but increase rapidly as ℓ becomes larger. The reason for this is entirely analogous: for any given set $\mathcal{B}_i$ of blocks, no two of the blocks in that set intersect in two points, and hence for $\eta = 2$ there are no secure links formed between nodes whose keyrings are derived from such blocks.
- Figures 2 and 5 are interesting, as they show a slightly different behaviour pattern for Scheme 3 in the case of intersection threshold $\eta = 1$. Here the Pr_1 and fail(1) values are in fact higher when ℓ is small, and then decrease for larger values of ℓ, eventually approaching the properties of Scheme 1. This is explained by the fact that two blocks within the same set $\mathcal{B}_i$ have probability $\frac{k}{n+1}$ of sharing a common key (cf. Table 2), which is higher (for the parameters under consideration) than the average probability $\frac{k(2n-k+3)}{2(n^2+n+1)}$ that two blocks chosen uniformly from a $TD(3, k, n)$ share at least one key. As in previous cases, it is clear from these graphs that once a reasonable number of the sets $\mathcal{B}_i$ are chosen, the properties of Scheme 3 are very close to those of Scheme 1.

We conclude that removal of keyrings from a KPS based on transversal designs, whether randomly or deterministically as in Scheme 2 or 3, causes no undue disruption to the behaviour of the scheme.

4 An Efficient New Approach to Calculating Connectivity and Resilience for Arbitrary Set Systems

In this section, we describe a new approach to facilitate the efficient evaluation of metrics for connectivity and resilience in general KPSs. We were motivated to do this in order to compute the metrics of our random scheme that consists of random subsets of blocks of a transversal design. Suppose we start with any set system $(X, \mathcal{A})$ having blocks of size k. Denote $b = |\mathcal{A}|$. Suppose the maximum intersection of any two blocks in $\mathcal{A}$ is $t - 1$. (In a given application, the value of t may already be known beforehand. However, if it were not already known, it could be computed as the first step of the process we are about to describe.)

For $|C| = i$ where $\eta \leq i \leq t - 1$, define λ_C to be the number of blocks $A \in \mathcal{A}$ containing all the points in C. It will turn out that we can compute Pr_1 and fail(1) fairly easily if we know all the λ_C values. This has at least two desirable consequences:

1. For various types of "structured" set systems (for example, a partially balanced t-design) we know the relevant λ_C's and so we can compute formulas for Pr_1 and fail(1) in a straightforward manner.

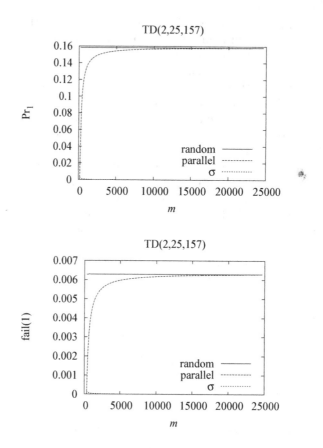

Fig. 4. Connectivity and resilience of KPSs derived from TD(2,25,157)

2. For an arbitrary "unstructured" set system, we can use this approach to compute Pr_1 efficiently. In a "naive" approach, we would probably examine all pairs of blocks to see which pairs form links, which would already require time $\Theta(b^2)$. However, it is straightforward to tabulate all the relevant λ_C values in time $\Theta(b)$, and then apply the formulas we derive, in order to compute Pr_1. This will be discussed further in Sect. 4.3.

4.1 Formulas for Connectivity

For a set of points C with $|C| \geq \eta$, define a C-link to be a set of two nodes $\{A, B\}$ such that $A \cap B = C$. The number of C-links is denoted by $\lambda'(C)$; therefore,

$$\lambda'(C) = |\{\{A, B\} : A, B \in \mathcal{A}, A \cap B = C\}|.$$

The next lemma follows easily from the principle of inclusion-exclusion.

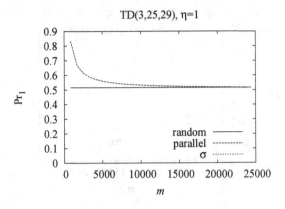

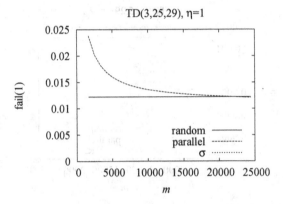

Fig. 5. Connectivity and resilience of KPSs derived from TD(3,25,29) with $\eta = 1$

Lemma 1. *If $|C| = i \leq t - 1$, then*

$$\lambda'(C) = \sum_{D \subseteq X \setminus C, |D| \leq t-1-i} (-1)^{|D|} \binom{\lambda_{C \cup D}}{2}. \tag{1}$$

In particular, $\lambda'(C) = \binom{\lambda_C}{2}$ if $|C| = t - 1$.

Define an *i-link* to be any C-link where $|C| = i$. For $\eta \leq i \leq t - 1$, let L_i denote the number of *i*-links (or course, there are no *i*-links with $i \geq t$). For $\eta \leq i \leq t - 1$, it is clear that

$$L_i = \sum_{|C|=i} \lambda'(C). \tag{2}$$

The quantity

$$L = \sum_{i=\eta}^{t-1} L_i \tag{3}$$

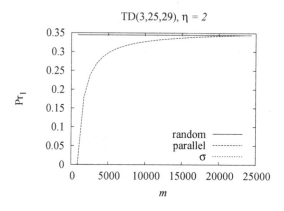

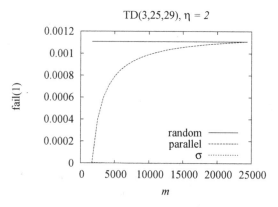

Fig. 6. Connectivity and resilience of KPSs derived from TD(3,25,29) with $\eta = 2$

is the total number of links. From this, it immediately follows that

$$\mathsf{Pr}_1 = \frac{L}{\binom{b}{2}}. \tag{4}$$

Define

$$q_i = \sum_{|C|=i} \binom{\lambda_C}{2}. \tag{5}$$

We now provide a useful formula for L_i.

Lemma 2. *For $\eta \leq i \leq t - 1$, we have that*

$$L_i = \sum_{j=i}^{t-1} (-1)^{j-i} \binom{j}{i} q_j. \tag{6}$$

Proof. In view of (2), we need to sum (1) over all C with $|C| = i$. When we do this, each possible term $(-1)^{|D|}\binom{\wedge_C \cup D}{2}$ is included in the sum $\binom{|C \cup D|}{|C|} = \binom{|D|+i}{i}$ times.

For $\eta \leq i \leq t-1$, let

$$a_i = \sum_{j=\eta}^{i} (-1)^{i-j} \binom{i}{j}. \tag{7}$$

Then we have the following.

Theorem 4.

$$L = \sum_{i=\eta}^{t-1} a_i q_i, \tag{8}$$

where the q_i's and a_i's are defined in (5) and (7), respectively.

Proof. We sum the formula (6) as i ranges from η to $t-1$. The number of times q_i is included in the sum is easily seen to be equal to a_i.

We present some applications of the formula (8) for small values of t and η in Table 2.

Table 2. Applications of Theorem 4

t	η	L
2	1	q_1
3	2	q_2
3	1	$q_1 - q_2$
4	3	q_3
4	2	$q_2 - 2q_3$
4	1	$q_1 - q_2 + q_3$
5	4	q_4
5	3	$q_3 - 3q_4$
5	2	$q_2 - 2q_3 + 3q_4$
5	1	$q_1 - q_2 + q_3 - q_4$

Now, applying (8) and (4), we have the following formula for Pr_1.

Corollary 1.

$$\mathsf{Pr}_1 = \frac{\sum_{i=\eta}^{t-1} a_i q_i}{\binom{b}{2}}. \tag{9}$$

4.2   Formulas for Resilience

Recall that a C-link is a set of two nodes $\{A, B\}$ such that $A \cap B = C$. The number of C-links is $\lambda'(C)$ and the number of nodes that break the C-link $\{A, B\}$ is $\lambda_C - 2$. The probability that the C-link $\{A, B\}$ is broken by the compromise of a random node not in the link is $(\lambda_C - 2)/(b - 2)$. Averaging over all L links, we obtain the following formula for $\mathsf{fail}(1)$, which can be viewed as a generalisation of [9, Corollary 4.6]:

$$\mathsf{fail}(1) = \frac{1}{L} \sum_{\{C:\eta \leq |C| \leq t-1\}} \frac{(\lambda_C - 2)\lambda'(C)}{b - 2}. \tag{10}$$

In order to compute $\mathsf{fail}(1)$ using (10), we first need to evaluate the expression $\sum \lambda_C \lambda'(C)$. Substituting (1) into this sum, we have

$$\sum_{\{C:\eta \leq |C| \leq t-1\}} \lambda_C \lambda'(C) = \sum_{\{C:\eta \leq |C| \leq t-1\}} \left(\lambda_C \sum_{D \subseteq X \setminus C, |D| \leq t-1-i} (-1)^{|D|} \binom{\lambda_{C \cup D}}{2} \right)$$

$$= \sum_{\{E:\eta \leq |E| \leq t-1\}} \left(\binom{\lambda_E}{2} \sum_{\{C:\eta \leq |C|, C \subseteq E\}} (-1)^{|E|-|C|} \lambda_C \right),$$

letting $E = C \cup D$. As a result, we obtain the following.

Lemma 3.

$$\sum_{\{C:\eta \leq |C| \leq t-1\}} \lambda_C \lambda'(C) = \sum_{\{E:\eta \leq |E| \leq t-1\}} \mu_E \binom{\lambda_E}{2}, \tag{11}$$

where

$$\mu_E = \sum_{\{C:\eta \leq |C|, C \subseteq E\}} (-1)^{|E|-|C|} \lambda_C. \tag{12}$$

For future use, we mention a couple of special cases of (12):

$$\mu_E = \begin{cases} \lambda_E & \text{if} |E| = \eta \\ \lambda_E - \sum_{x \in E} \lambda_{E \setminus \{x\}} & \text{if} |E| = \eta + 1. \end{cases} \tag{13}$$

Next, applying (3) and (2) we have that

$$\sum_{\{C:\eta \leq |C| \leq t-1\}} 2\lambda'(C) = 2L. \tag{14}$$

Now we can state our main formula.

Theorem 5.

$$\mathsf{fail}(1) = \frac{1}{L(b-2)} \left(\sum_{\{E:\eta \leq |E| \leq t-1\}} \mu_E \binom{\lambda_E}{2} \right) - \frac{2}{b-2}. \tag{15}$$

Proof. The result follows immediately from (10), (11) and (14).

4.3   Computing Connectivity and Resilience

Suppose we are given a set system $(X, \mathcal{A})$, where $b = |\mathcal{A}|$. As previously mentioned, we assume that value of the parameter t is already known. Here are the steps that would be followed to compute Pr_1 and $\mathsf{fail}(1)$.

1. Compute all the values λ_C for $\eta \leq |C| \leq t-1$. This can be done efficiently as follows:
   (a) Initialise $\lambda_C \leftarrow 0$ for all relevant C.
   (b) For every block $A \in \mathcal{A}$ and for every $C \subseteq A$ such that $\eta \leq |C| \leq t-1$, set $\lambda_C \leftarrow \lambda_C + 1$.
   (For fixed values of η and t, we observe that the λ_C's can be computed in time $\Theta(b)$ by this method.)
2. Compute all the values μ_C for $\eta \leq |C| \leq t-1$, using the formula (12).
3. Compute the values q_i for $\eta \leq i \leq t-1$, using the formula (5).
4. Compute L using the formula (8).
5. Compute $\mathsf{Pr}_1 = L/\binom{b}{2}$ and compute $\mathsf{fail}(1)$ using the formula (15).

Remark. If we only wanted to compute Pr_1, then step 2 could be omitted.

4.4   Examples

Here are some small examples to illustrate the application of the formulas we have developed.

Example 6. Suppose $X = \{1, \ldots, 6\}$ and

$$\mathcal{A} = \{\{123\}, \{124\}, \{125\}, \{456\}, \{136\}\}.$$

It easy to check that $t = 3$ in this design. Then we have

$$\lambda_{12} = 3 \ \lambda_{13} = 2 \ \lambda_{14} = 1 \ \lambda_{15} = 1 \ \lambda_{16} = 1 \ \lambda_{23} = 1$$
$$\lambda_{24} = 1 \ \lambda_{25} = 1 \ \lambda_{26} = 0 \ \lambda_{34} = 0 \ \lambda_{35} = 0 \ \lambda_{36} = 1$$
$$\lambda_{45} = 1 \ \lambda_{46} = 1 \ \lambda_{56} = 1$$
$$\overline{\lambda_1 = 4 \ \lambda_2 = 3 \ \lambda_3 = 2 \ \lambda_4 = 2 \ \lambda_5 = 2 \ \lambda_6 = 2}$$

It is easy to compute $q_1 = 13$ and $q_2 = 4$. When $\eta = 1$, we have $L = q_1 - q_2 = 9$ and $\mathsf{Pr}_1 = 9/10$; when $\eta = 2$, we have $L = q_2 = 4$ and $\mathsf{Pr}_1 = 4/10$.

In order to compute fail(1), we also need to compute the μ_C's. First, suppose $\eta = 2$. Then $\mu_C = \lambda_C$ for $|C| = 2$, and

$$\text{fail}(1) = \frac{1}{4 \times 3} \left(3 \binom{3}{2} + 2 \binom{2}{2} \right) - \frac{2}{3} = \frac{1}{4}.$$

When $\eta = 1$, we need to compute λ_C when $|C| = 1, 2$. When $|C| = 1$, we have $\mu_C = \lambda_C$. When $|C| = 2$, we use (13) to compute μ_C:

$$\mu_{12} = -4 \; \mu_{13} = -4 \; \mu_{14} = -5 \; \mu_{15} = -5 \; \mu_{16} = -5 \; \mu_{23} = -4$$
$$\mu_{24} = -4 \; \mu_{25} = -4 \; \mu_{26} = -5 \; \mu_{34} = -4 \; \mu_{35} = -4 \; \mu_{36} = -3$$
$$\mu_{45} = -3 \; \mu_{46} = -3 \; \mu_{56} = -3$$

$$\text{fail}(1) = \frac{1}{9 \times 3} \left(4 \binom{4}{2} + 3 \binom{3}{2} + 4 \times 2 \binom{2}{2} - 4 \binom{3}{2} - 4 \binom{2}{2} \right) - \frac{2}{3} = \frac{7}{27}.$$

Here is an example with $t = 4$. We just compute Pr_1 for this example.

Example 7. Suppose $X = \{1, \ldots, 9\}$ and

$$\mathcal{A} = \{\{1234\}, \{1235\}, \{1367\}, \{5678\}, \{4789\}\}.$$

Here $t = 4$ and we compute $q_1 = 14$, $q_2 = 7$ and $q_3 = 1$. When $\eta = 1$, we have $L = q_1 - q_2 + q_3 = 8$ and $\text{Pr}_1 = 4/5$; when $\eta = 2$, we have $L = q_2 - 2q_3 = 5$ and $\text{Pr}_1 = 1/2$; and when $\eta = 3$, we have $L = q_3 = 1$ and $\text{Pr}_1 = 1/10$.

5 Conclusion

We have provided two methods of increasing the flexibility of combinatorial key predistribution schemes. These methods are discussed and evaluated in reference to the transversal design schemes introduced in [5]. The first method is to exploit the underlying structure of transversal designs to explicitly describe a wide range of "partial" designs whose properties can easily be analysed using existing formulas [9]. The schemes based on these partial designs have properties very similar to the transversal design schemes from which they are derived. The second method (e.g., see [5]) is to randomly delete blocks from a specified set system. We show by running extensive experiments that this method also does not affect performance adversely, which contradicts assertions made in [1]. Finally, we develop some new formulas that facilitate the efficient computation of metrics of KPS derived from arbitrary set systems. These formulas were useful in the experiments we carried out, but they may have additional applications in the theoretical study of combinatorial KPS for wireless sensor networks.

Appendix

Table 3. Resilience of random KPSs derived from TD(2,15,71)

ℓ	fail(1) (mean)	fail(1) (std. dev.)	fail(1) (min)	fail(1) (max)
2	0.013749	0.000642	0.011989	0.015357
3	0.013660	0.000381	0.012879	0.014684
4	0.013687	0.000278	0.013134	0.014481
5	0.013702	0.000234	0.013158	0.014362
6	0.013704	0.000179	0.013294	0.014108
7	0.013676	0.000140	0.013338	0.014077
8	0.013687	0.000136	0.013356	0.014063
9	0.013707	0.000109	0.013418	0.013950
10	0.013690	0.000094	0.013476	0.013964
11	0.013682	0.000077	0.013505	0.013850
12	0.013698	0.000071	0.013552	0.013897
13	0.013696	0.000068	0.013517	0.013836
14	0.013685	0.000058	0.013558	0.013820
15	0.013691	0.000055	0.013528	0.013841
16	0.013685	0.000055	0.013586	0.013830
17	0.013694	0.000053	0.013583	0.013862
18	0.013692	0.000044	0.013579	0.013800
19	0.013694	0.000042	0.013602	0.013808
20	0.013694	0.000042	0.013582	0.013812
21	0.013693	0.000037	0.013588	0.013780
22	0.013694	0.000033	0.013602	0.013792
23	0.013687	0.000034	0.013603	0.013760
24	0.013693	0.000031	0.013632	0.013780
25	0.013692	0.000025	0.013614	0.013746
26	0.013690	0.000026	0.013592	0.013749
27	0.013690	0.000025	0.013631	0.013743
28	0.013692	0.000021	0.013630	0.013737
29	0.013691	0.000019	0.013633	0.013730
30	0.013688	0.000019	0.013639	0.013729
31	0.013693	0.000020	0.013655	0.013749
32	0.013693	0.000018	0.013645	0.013732
33	0.013693	0.000016	0.013661	0.013752
34	0.013693	0.000016	0.013659	0.013737
35	0.013695	0.000014	0.013667	0.013724
36	0.013691	0.000014	0.013655	0.013727
37	0.013694	0.000012	0.013664	0.013725
38	0.013694	0.000015	0.013664	0.013735
39	0.013693	0.000012	0.013662	0.013726
40	0.013691	0.000012	0.013668	0.013720
41	0.013693	0.000011	0.013668	0.013726
42	0.013695	0.000013	0.013664	0.013726

Table 3. (*Continued*)

ℓ	fail(1) (mean)	fail(1) (std. dev.)	fail(1) (min)	fail(1) (max)
43	0.013693	0.000010	0.013674	0.013725
44	0.013693	0.000009	0.013664	0.013712
45	0.013692	0.000008	0.013673	0.013715
46	0.013694	0.000007	0.013679	0.013715
47	0.013693	0.000007	0.013679	0.013709
48	0.013693	0.000008	0.013676	0.013715
49	0.013693	0.000007	0.013676	0.013710
50	0.013693	0.000007	0.013673	0.013710
51	0.013694	0.000005	0.013682	0.013709
52	0.013693	0.000006	0.013679	0.013705
53	0.013694	0.000005	0.013683	0.013707
54	0.013694	0.000005	0.013681	0.013704
55	0.013694	0.000004	0.013683	0.013707
56	0.013693	0.000004	0.013683	0.013703
57	0.013693	0.000004	0.013681	0.013706
58	0.013693	0.000003	0.013683	0.013704
59	0.013693	0.000003	0.013684	0.013698
60	0.013693	0.000003	0.013685	0.013700
61	0.013693	0.000002	0.013688	0.013698
62	0.013693	0.000002	0.013688	0.013700
63	0.013693	0.000002	0.013687	0.013702
64	0.013693	0.000002	0.013689	0.013697
65	0.013693	0.000001	0.013689	0.013697
66	0.013693	0.000001	0.013690	0.013697
67	0.013693	0.000001	0.013691	0.013696
68	0.013693	0.000001	0.013692	0.013695
69	0.013693	0.000000	0.013692	0.013694
70	0.013693	0.000000	0.013693	0.013694
71	0.013693	0.000000	0.013693	0.013693

Table 4. Connectivity of random KPSs derived from TD(2,15,71)

ℓ	Pr_1 (mean)	Pr_1 (std. dev.)	Pr_1 (min)	Pr_1 (max)
1	0.208129	0.008217	0.185111	0.228169
2	0.208647	0.003964	0.197283	0.218659
3	0.208178	0.002706	0.202719	0.215121
4	0.208296	0.001944	0.204200	0.213159
5	0.208403	0.001608	0.204138	0.212795
6	0.208455	0.001297	0.204861	0.211721
7	0.208241	0.001010	0.205467	0.210976
8	0.208214	0.000963	0.205741	0.210926
9	0.208424	0.000790	0.206175	0.210355
10	0.208313	0.000695	0.206834	0.210374

Table 4. (*Continued*)

ℓ	Pr_1 (mean)	Pr_1 (std. dev.)	Pr_1 (min)	Pr_1 (max)
11	0.208234	0.000541	0.206914	0.209409
12	0.208359	0.000501	0.207433	0.209764
13	0.208359	0.000477	0.207073	0.209418
14	0.208284	0.000427	0.207436	0.209333
15	0.208332	0.000422	0.207219	0.209515
16	0.208267	0.000397	0.207473	0.209335
17	0.208340	0.000391	0.207518	0.209341
18	0.208324	0.000329	0.207455	0.209105
19	0.208339	0.000311	0.207681	0.209109
20	0.208333	0.000309	0.207523	0.209267
21	0.208333	0.000277	0.207566	0.209007
22	0.208340	0.000243	0.207638	0.209064
23	0.208282	0.000248	0.207686	0.208775
24	0.208336	0.000230	0.207860	0.208999
25	0.208327	0.000184	0.207737	0.208744
26	0.208307	0.000198	0.207572	0.208763
27	0.208309	0.000186	0.207903	0.208706
28	0.208322	0.000160	0.207863	0.208648
29	0.208314	0.000145	0.207887	0.208595
30	0.208295	0.000146	0.207896	0.208618
31	0.208337	0.000148	0.208046	0.208760
32	0.208330	0.000136	0.207953	0.208620
33	0.208334	0.000125	0.208096	0.208799
34	0.208331	0.000122	0.208052	0.208685
35	0.208344	0.000109	0.208120	0.208560
36	0.208318	0.000109	0.208046	0.208621
37	0.208338	0.000094	0.208113	0.208588
38	0.208338	0.000114	0.208114	0.208655
39	0.208330	0.000089	0.208108	0.208568
40	0.208316	0.000091	0.208140	0.208556
41	0.208336	0.000086	0.208144	0.208569
42	0.208345	0.000098	0.208104	0.208569
43	0.208331	0.000074	0.208187	0.208585
44	0.208334	0.000065	0.208109	0.208480
45	0.208328	0.000060	0.208179	0.208492
46	0.208335	0.000053	0.208232	0.208499
47	0.208334	0.000053	0.208223	0.208458
48	0.208331	0.000058	0.208205	0.208499
49	0.208330	0.000050	0.208211	0.208460
50	0.208332	0.000051	0.208178	0.208459
51	0.208339	0.000041	0.208246	0.208457
52	0.208332	0.000042	0.208226	0.208426

Table 4. (*Continued*)

ℓ	Pr_1 (mean)	Pr_1 (std. dev.)	Pr_1 (min)	Pr_1 (max)
53	0.208338	0.000034	0.208256	0.208440
54	0.208339	0.000036	0.208245	0.208418
55	0.208336	0.000033	0.208255	0.208437
56	0.208333	0.000030	0.208256	0.208410
57	0.208334	0.000028	0.208241	0.208427
58	0.208329	0.000026	0.208255	0.208417
59	0.208331	0.000023	0.208262	0.208371
60	0.208332	0.000021	0.208273	0.208386
61	0.208333	0.000017	0.208295	0.208371
62	0.208335	0.000017	0.208291	0.208387
63	0.208334	0.000016	0.208285	0.208397
64	0.208332	0.000012	0.208301	0.208361
65	0.208332	0.000010	0.208305	0.208360
66	0.208332	0.000009	0.208312	0.208360
67	0.208333	0.000007	0.208316	0.208358
68	0.208334	0.000005	0.208321	0.208347
69	0.208333	0.000003	0.208324	0.208343
70	0.208333	0.000002	0.208329	0.208339
71	0.208333	0.000000	0.208333	0.208333

References

1. Bose, M., Dey, A., Mukerjee, R.: Key predistribution schemes for distributed sensor networks via block designs. Des. Codes Crypt. **67**(1), 111–136 (2013)
2. Çamtepe, S.A., Yener, B.: Key distribution mechanisms for wireless sensor networks: a survey. Technical Report TR-05-07, Rensselaer Polytechnic Institute (2005)
3. Dong, J., Pei, D., Wang, X.: A key predistribution scheme based on 3-designs. In: Pei, D., Yung, M., Lin, D., Wu, C. (eds.) Inscrypt 2007. LNCS, vol. 4990, pp. 81–92. Springer, Heidelberg (2008)
4. Eschenauer, L., Gligor, V.: A key-management scheme for distributed sensor networks. In Proceedings of the 9th ACM Conference on Computer and Communications Security, pp. 41–47. ACM (2002)
5. Lee, J., Stinson, D.R.: On the construction of practical key predistribution schemes for distributed sensor networks using combinatorial designs. ACM Trans. Inf.Syst. Secur. **11**(2), 1–35 (2008). (Article No. 1)
6. Martin, K.M.: On the applicability of combinatorial designs to key predistribution for wireless sensor networks. In: Chee, Y.M., Li, Ch., Ling, S., Wang, H., Xing, Ch. (eds.) IWCC 2009. LNCS, vol. 5557, pp. 124–145. Springer, Heidelberg (2009)
7. Martin, K.M., Paterson, M.B.: An application-oriented framework for wireless sensor network key establishment. Electron. Notes Theor. Comput. Sci. **192**(2), 31–41 (2008)
8. Martin, K.M., Paterson, M.B., Stinson, D.R.: Key predistribution for homogeneous wireless sensor networks with group deployment of nodes. ACM Trans. Sens. Netw. **7**(2), 1–27 (2010). (Article No. 11)

9. Paterson, M.B., Stinson, D.R.: A unified approach to combinatorial key predistribution schemes for sensor networks. Des. Codes Crypt. **71**, 433–457 (2014)
10. Xiao, Y., Rayi, V.K., Sun, B., Du, X., Hu, F., Galloway, M.: A survey of key management schemes in wireless sensor networks. Comput. Commun. **30**(11–12), 2314–2341 (2007)

Discrete Logarithms

A Group Action on $\mathbb{Z}_p^\times$ and the Generalized DLP with Auxiliary Inputs

Jung Hee Cheon$^{(\boxtimes)}$, Taechan Kim, and Yong Soo Song

Department of Mathematical Sciences and ISaC-RIM,
Seoul National University, Seoul, South Korea
{jhcheon,yoshiki1,lucius05}@snu.ac.kr

Abstract. The Discrete Logarithm Problem with Auxiliary Inputs (DLPwAI) is an important cryptographic hard problem to compute $\alpha \in \mathbb{Z}_p$ for given $g, g^\alpha, \cdots, g^{\alpha^d}$ where g is a generator of a group of order p. In this paper, we introduce a generalized version of this problem, so called the generalized DLPwAI (GDLPwAI) problem which is asked to compute α for given $g, g^{\alpha^{e_1}}, \cdots, g^{\alpha^{e_d}}$, and propose an efficient algorithm when $K := \{e_1, \cdots, e_d\}$ is a multiplicative subgroup of $\mathbb{Z}_{p-1}^\times$. Although the previous algorithms can only compute α when $p \pm 1$ has a small divisor d, our algorithm resolves the problem when neither $p + 1$ or $p - 1$ has an appropriate small divisor. Our method exploits a group action of K on $\mathbb{Z}_p^\times$ to partition $\mathbb{Z}_p^\times$ efficiently.

Keywords: The discrete logarithm problem · The discrete logarithm problem with auxiliary inputs · Cheon's algorithm

1 Introduction

The Discrete Logarithm Problem (DLP) is a cryptographic hard problem which is asked to find $\alpha \in \mathbb{Z}_p$ for given g and g^α where g is a generator of a group G of prime order p. In recent decades, many variants of this hard problem such as the Bilinear Diffie-Hellman Problem (BDHP) [6], the ℓ-Strong Diffie-Hellman Problem (ℓ-SDHP) [2], the Bilinear Diffie-Hellman Exponent Problem [7], and the Bilinear Diffie-Hellman Inverse Problem [1] have been introduced to support the security of many cryptographic applications using pairing groups such as ID-based encryption (IBE) [1,6], the short signatures [2], the broadcast encryption [7], and so on [3–5,8]. In spite of the importance of these computational problems, there have been only few researches on these assumptions to the best of our knowledge. The first realization of this importance was done by Brown and Gallant [9] and Cheon [10,11]. Brown and Gallant presented an algorithm to compute α for given $g, g^\alpha, g^{\alpha^d}$ when d divides $p - 1$. Cheon generalized this problem into the Discrete Logarithm Problem with Auxiliary Inputs (DLPwAI), which finds the value α for given $g, g^\alpha, \cdots, g^{\alpha^d}$, and solved it when either $p - 1$ or $p + 1$ has a small divisor d. Jao and Yoshida [14] gave an algorithm to forge the Boneh-Boyen signatures using the Cheon's algorithm.

T. Lange, K. Lauter, and P. Lisoněk (Eds.): SAC 2013, LNCS 8282, pp. 121–135, 2014.
DOI: 10.1007/978-3-662-43414-7_6, © Springer-Verlag Berlin Heidelberg 2014

The idea of Cheon is to utilize the embedding to an auxiliary group such as $\mathbf{F}_p$ or $\mathbf{F}_{p^2}$. The similar technique to embed into auxiliary groups such as an elliptic curve group or a finite field can also be found in the famous reduction algorithms from the DL problem to the DH problem [13,18,19]. After the Cheon's algorithm, Satoh [21] tried to generalize the attack using an embedding $\mathbf{F}_p$ into a subgroup of order $\Phi_k(p)$ in $GL(n, \mathbf{F}_p)$, where $\Phi_k(x)$ is the k-th cyclotomic polynomial for $k \geq 3$, but the efficiency of the algorithm was not clear. Finally, Kim [15] realized that the Satoh's algorithm essentially uses an embedding from $\mathbf{F}_p$ into $\mathbf{F}_{p^n}$ and proved that the algorithm can never be faster than the ordinary algorithm for the DLP when $d|\Phi_k(p)$ for $k \geq 3$. All these algorithms are developed by embedding an element in $\mathbf{F}_p$ into a certain auxiliary group. More recently, Kim and Cheon [16] suggested rather different approach. Their result reduced the problem to find a polynomial with small value sets. However, finding a good polynomial with small value sets is not easy and still open.

In this paper, we introduce the generalized version of the DLPwAI called the GDLPwAI. The GDLPwAI is a problem to compute $\alpha \in \mathbb{Z}_p$ for given $g, g^{\alpha^{e_1}}, \cdots g^{\alpha^{e_d}}$. The rest of the paper is devoted to recover α efficiently but heuristically when $K := \{e_i : 1 \leq i \leq d\}$ is a multiplicative subgroup of $\mathbb{Z}_{p-1}^{\times}$ (Theorem 2). Note that in our algorithm e_i's do not divide $p-1$ while the Cheon's algorithm requires g^{α^d} as an instance for a small divisor d of $p \pm 1$.

The outline of the proof is as follows: (1) For a multiplicative subgroup $K \leq \mathbb{Z}_{p-1}^{\times}$, we define the K-group action on $\mathbb{Z}_p^{\times}$ to partition $\mathbb{Z}_p^{\times}$ into orbits generated by group action. (2) Then we define a polynomial $f(x)$ over $\mathbb{Z}_p$ which takes the same value for all elements in an orbit but takes different values for those elements in different orbits. (3) Finally, for randomly chosen β from $\mathbb{Z}_p^{\times}$, we find an orbit containing β by computing $g^{f(\beta)}$ and finding a collision with $g^{f(\alpha_j)}$ where $\alpha_j = \zeta^{-j}\alpha$'s are the representatives of distinct orbits. By solving the equation $f(\beta) = f(\alpha_j)$, we can find the desired value α.

For a multiplicative subgroup K of $\mathbb{Z}_p^{\times}$ we define a K-group action on $\mathbb{Z}_p^{\times}$ by $(k, x) \mapsto x^k$ for $x \in \mathbb{Z}_p^{\times}$ and $k \in K$. Then the orbit generated by x is a set $\{x^k : k \in K\}$. In particular, an orbit containing just one element is called a fixed point. We show that the set of fixed points is generated by an element ζ, a primitive λ-th root of unity for $\lambda := \gcd(K - 1)$, which is defined to be the greatest common divisor of $(k-1)$'s for all integers k such that $k \mod (p-1)$ belongs to K. Moreover, the collection of orbits $(\zeta^i\alpha)^K$ is pairwise disjoint for $0 \leq i < \lambda$ and each orbit contains exactly $|K|$ elements, if α^k are distinct for all $k \in K$. Hence $\lambda|K|$ elements of $\mathbb{Z}_p^{\times}$ belong to one of orbits $(\zeta^i\alpha)^K$ for some i.

Now define a polynomial $f_K(x)$ by $\sum_{k \in K} x^k$ for K. Then f_K takes the same value for the elements in the same orbit and $f_K(\zeta^i x) = \zeta^i f_K(x)$ for a fixed point ζ. For given g^{α^k} for all $k \in K$, we compute $g^{f(\alpha)}$ in $|K|$ group multiplications and compute $g^{f(\beta)}$ for randomly chosen $\beta \in \mathbb{Z}_p^{\times}$. If β belongs one of orbits $(\zeta^i\alpha)^K$, then we can find $t \in [0, \lambda)$ such that $g^{f(\alpha)} = g^{\zeta^t f(\beta)}$ in $O(\sqrt{\lambda})$ exponentiations using the baby-step giant-step technique. Finally by finding $k \in K$ satisfying $\alpha^k = \zeta^t \beta$, we can recover the value α. Since the probability that a random $\beta \in \mathbb{Z}_p^\times$ belongs to one of the orbits is $\lambda|K|/(p-1)$, the total complexity is $O\left(\frac{p}{\lambda|K|}(\sqrt{\lambda} + |K|)\right)$ exponentiations in $\mathbb{Z}_p$ and G. Under the assumption that the cost of a group operation in G is a constant times of the cost of a multiplication in $\mathbb{Z}_p$, the total complexity can be lowered down $O(p^{1/3} \log p)$ multiplications in $\mathbb{Z}_p$ when $\sqrt{\lambda} \approx |K| \approx p^{1/3}$.

It also remains an open question to solve the usual DLPwAI by using our algorithm to solve the GDLPwAI.

Organization. In Sect. 2, we introduce a new representation for multiplicative subgroup of $\mathbb{Z}_{p-1}^\times$. In Sect. 3, we define a group action on $\mathbb{Z}_p^\times$ and develop how all elements in $\mathbb{Z}_p^\times$ can be represented with only a few elements. In Sect. 4, we construct a polynomial over $\mathbb{Z}_p$ which takes the same value on the same orbit. Finally, we prove our theorem in Sect. 5 and conclude in Sect. 6.

2   Multiplicative Subgroups of $\mathbb{Z}_n^\times$

Before the state of our main theorem, we first introduce somewhat new representation for multiplicative subgroup K of $\mathbb{Z}_n^\times$. From our observation, elements of a multiplicative subgroup $K \leq \mathbb{Z}_n^\times$ seem to form an arithmetic sequence in many cases.

2.1   Representation of a Multiplicative Subgroup of $\mathbb{Z}_n^\times$

Definition 1. *For any positive integer n, let S be a subset of $\mathbb{Z}_n$. We define $\gcd(S; \mathbb{Z}_n)$ or $\gcd(S)$ unless confused, to be the greatest common divisor of all integers x such that $x \bmod n$ belongs to S. Given a divisor λ of n, we define a subset K_λ of $\mathbb{Z}_n^\times$ by $K_\lambda := (1 + \lambda \mathbb{Z}_n) \cap \mathbb{Z}_n^\times$, where $1 + \lambda \mathbb{Z}_n := \{1 + \lambda m : m \in \mathbb{Z}_n\}$.*

We can see that K_λ is a multiplicative subgroup of $\mathbb{Z}_n^\times$ because it is closed under the multiplication and inverse. If K is a multiplicative subgroup of $\mathbb{Z}_n^\times$, then K is a subgroup of K_λ for $\lambda = \gcd(K-1)$ where $K - 1 = \{k - 1 : k \in K\} \subseteq \mathbb{Z}_n$.

Remark 1. For an even integer n and any multiplicative subgroup $K \leq \mathbb{Z}_n^\times$, every element of K is an odd integer so that $\gcd(K-1)$ is even. It shows that

$$K_\lambda = (1 + \lambda \mathbb{Z}_n) \cap \mathbb{Z}_n^\times = (1 + 2\lambda \mathbb{Z}_n) \cap \mathbb{Z}_n^\times = K_{2\lambda}$$

for odd λ. For this reason, we only treat the case that λ is even.

From now on, we restrict the case to $n = p - 1$ for odd prime p. The next proposition determines the size of K_λ in $\mathbb{Z}_{p-1}^\times$ for given divisor λ of $p - 1$.

Proposition 1. *Let λ be a divisor of $p - 1$. Then $|K_\lambda| = \frac{p-1}{\lambda} \cdot \prod_{q \in Q}\left(1 - \frac{1}{q}\right)$, where Q is the set of prime divisors of $p-1$ which do not divide λ. In particular, if $\gcd(\lambda, \frac{p-1}{\lambda}) = 1$, then $|K_\lambda| = \phi(\frac{p-1}{\lambda})$, where ϕ denotes the Euler-totient function.*

Proof. Note that $1 + \lambda m \in K_\lambda$ if and only if $\gcd(1 + \lambda m, p - 1) = 1$, which is equivalent to $\gcd(1 + \lambda m, q) = 1$ for all $q \in Q$. Consider a surjective homomorphism

$$\pi : \mathbb{Z}_{p-1} \longrightarrow \mathbb{Z}_\lambda \times \mathbb{Z}_{q_1} \times \cdots \times \mathbb{Z}_{q_\ell}$$
$$x \longmapsto (x \bmod \lambda, x \bmod q_1, \cdots, x \bmod q_\ell),$$

where $Q = \{q_1, \cdots, q_\ell\}$. Then each element λm is in the set $K_\lambda - 1 \subseteq \mathbb{Z}_{p-1}$ if and only if $\pi(\lambda m)$ is contained in $\{0\} \times T$, where $T = (\mathbb{Z}_{q_1} \backslash \{-1\}) \times (\mathbb{Z}_{q_2} \backslash \{-1\}) \times \cdots \times (\mathbb{Z}_{q_\ell} \backslash \{-1\})$. Hence

$$
\begin{aligned}
|K_\lambda| = |K_\lambda - 1| &= |\pi^{-1}(\{0\} \times T)| \\
&= |T| \cdot |\ker(\pi)| \\
&= \textstyle\prod_{i=1}^\ell (q_i - 1) \cdot \left(\frac{p-1}{\lambda \cdot \prod_{i=1}^\ell q_i} \right) \\
&= \frac{p-1}{\lambda} \cdot \prod_{i=1}^\ell \left(1 - \frac{1}{q_i} \right).
\end{aligned}
$$

Moreover, if $\gcd\left(\lambda, \frac{p-1}{\lambda}\right) = 1$, then Q is the set of all prime divisors of $\frac{p-1}{\lambda}$. Thus, we have $|K_\lambda| = \phi\left(\frac{p-1}{\lambda}\right)$. □

Proposition 2. *If λ is an even divisor of $p - 1$, then $\gcd(K_\lambda - 1; \mathbb{Z}_{p-1}) = \lambda$.*

Proof. Let us use the same notations in the proof of Proposition 1. First, we note that an integer x such that $x \pmod{p-1} \in K_\lambda - 1 = \pi^{-1}(\{0\} \times T)$ is a multiple of λ, and $\gcd(K_\lambda - 1; \mathbb{Z}_{p-1})$ is a multiple of λ by definition.

Let $P = \{p_j : 1 \le j \le k\}$ be the set of common prime divisors of λ and $\frac{p-1}{\lambda}$. Then $P \cup Q$ is the set of prime divisors of $\frac{p-1}{\lambda}$. Every element q of Q is greater than 2, and there exist integers m_i for $1 \le i \le \ell$ satisfying $\lambda m_i \pmod{q_i}$ is not equal to 0 or -1. Using the Chinese Remainder Theorem, we can find an integer m such that $m \equiv m_i \pmod{q_i}$ for all $1 \le i \le \ell$ and $m \equiv 1 \pmod{p_j}$ for all $1 \le k \le j$.

We can check that $1 + \lambda m$ is not divisible by $q \in Q$ and $1 + \lambda m \pmod{p-1}$ is contained in K_λ. In addition, $\gcd(\lambda m; \mathbb{Z}_{p-1}) = \lambda \gcd(m; \mathbb{Z}_{\frac{p-1}{\lambda}}) = \lambda$ since m is not divisible by every prime divisor of $\frac{p-1}{\lambda}$. Hence, $\gcd(K_\lambda - 1; \mathbb{Z}_{p-1})$ is equal to λ. □

Example 1. Consider a prime $p = 29$ and $\lambda = 4$ be an even divisor of $p - 1$. Then, we have

$$K_\lambda = K_4 = \{1, 5, 9, 13, 17, 21, 25\} \cap \mathbb{Z}_{28}^\times,$$

and 21 is the only element which is not in $\mathbb{Z}_{28}^\times$. Since $\frac{p-1}{\lambda} = 7$, we can see that the cardinality of K_4 is $\phi(7) = 6$ as shown in Proposition 1. Also we can check that $\gcd(K_4 - 1) = 4$.

3   A Group Action on $\mathbb{Z}_p^\times$

In this section, we consider a K-group action on $\mathbb{Z}_p^\times$ and partition $\mathbb{Z}_p^\times$ into disjoint orbits generated by group action. A group action on a set clearly induces a partition of the set with orbits. However, what we are dealing here is to partition $\mathbb{Z}_p^\times$ with only a few information. Namely, for a certain case, we can represent almost all elements of $\mathbb{Z}_p^\times$ with only two elements, one fixed point (*i.e.* an orbit with just one element) and the other point not a fixed point. We begin with defining the group action on $\mathbb{Z}_p^\times$. For more information on group theory, refer to [12, 17].

Definition 2. Let K be a multiplicative subgroup of $\mathbb{Z}_{p-1}^\times$. Define a <u>K-action</u> on $\mathbb{Z}_p^\times$ by $(k, x) \mapsto x^k$ for $k \in K$ and $x \in \mathbb{Z}_p^\times$. The <u>$K$-orbit of x</u> is a set $x^K := \{x^k : k \in K\}$. The <u>set of fixed point $(\mathbb{Z}_p^\times)_K$</u> is a set $\{x \in \mathbb{Z}_p^\times : x^k = x \text{ for all } k \in K\}$

We can easily check that Definition 2 satisfies the definition of group action. Note that we have $|x^K| = |K|/|K_x|$ where K_x is a stabilizer of x which is a set defined by $K_x := \{k \in K : x^k = x\}$, thus $|x^K| = |K|$ if and only if $|K_x| = 1$. The next proposition states that if two multiplicative subgroups H and K of $\mathbb{Z}_{p-1}^\times$ satisfies $\gcd(H - 1) = \gcd(K - 1)$, then the two sets of fixed points by H-action and K-action respectively are the same. Furthermore, the set of fixed points forms a cyclic group of order $\lambda = \gcd(H - 1) = \gcd(K - 1)$.

Proposition 3. Let K be a multiplicative subgroup of $\mathbb{Z}_{p-1}^\times$ and $\lambda = \gcd(K-1)$. Then, $(\mathbb{Z}_p^\times)_K = (\mathbb{Z}_p^\times)_{K_\lambda} = \{z \in \mathbb{Z}_p^\times : z^\lambda = 1\}$.

Proof. The set of fixed point by K-action is denoted by $(\mathbb{Z}_p^\times)_K = \{z \in \mathbb{Z}_p^\times : z^{k-1} = 1 \text{ for all } k \in K\}$. Now it is easy to see that $z^{k-1} = 1$ for all $k \in K$ if and only if $z^\lambda = 1$ where $\lambda = \gcd\{k-1 : k \in K\}$. Since $\lambda = \gcd(K-1) = \gcd(K_\lambda-1)$, we have $(\mathbb{Z}_p^\times)_K = (\mathbb{Z}_p^\times)_{K_\lambda}$ by the same argument. $\square$

Let ξ be a primitive element in $\mathbb{Z}_p$, then $\zeta = \xi^{\frac{p-1}{\lambda}}$ is a generator of a cyclic group of fixed points $(\mathbb{Z}_p^\times)_K = \langle\zeta\rangle = \{z \in \mathbb{Z}_p^\times : z^\lambda = 1\}$. Note that the orbit generated by $\zeta^i x$ satisfies $(\zeta^i x)^K = \zeta^i x^K$ for all $1 \le i \le \lambda$, since $\zeta^k = \zeta$ for all $k \in K$. The following proposition considers two orbits generated by $\zeta^i x$ and $\zeta^j x$ are disjoint for $0 \le i, j < \lambda$ and $i \ne j$.

Proposition 4. *(Disjoint Orbit Condition)* Let K be a multiplicative subgroup of $\mathbb{Z}_{p-1}^\times$, ζ a generator of a cyclic group of fixed points $\{z \in \mathbb{Z}_p^\times : z^\lambda = 1\}$ for $\lambda = \gcd(K - 1)$. If $\gcd(\lambda, \frac{p-1}{\lambda}) = 1$, then two orbits $\zeta^i x^K$ and $\zeta^j x^K$ are disjoint i.e. $(\zeta^i x^K) \cap (\zeta^j x^K) = \emptyset$ for $0 \le i, j < \lambda, i \ne j$, and $x \in \mathbb{Z}_p^\times$.

Proof. Note that two orbits are identical or disjoint. Suppose that $(\zeta^i x^K) \cap (\zeta^j x^K) \ne \emptyset$ for some i, j. Then, $\zeta^i x^K = \zeta^j x^K$ and $y := \zeta^{i-j} = x^{k_1-k_2}$ for some $k := k_1 - k_2 \in K$. Since $(\zeta^{i-j})^\lambda = 1$ and $(x^{k_1-k_2})^{\frac{p-1}{\lambda}} = 1$ for a non-fixed point $x \in \mathbb{Z}_p^\times$, the order of y divides both λ and $\frac{p-1}{\lambda}$. In other words, it divides $\gcd(\lambda, \frac{p-1}{\lambda})$ which equals to 1, following that y must be equal to 1. $\square$

Example 2. Let $K := K_4 = \{1, 5, 9, 13, 17, 25\} \leq \mathbb{Z}_{28}^\times$ and consider the K-action on $\mathbb{Z}_{29}^\times$. Then we have 4 disjoint orbits of length 6,

$$2^K = \{2, 2^5, 2^9, 2^{13}, 2^{17}, 2^{25}\} = \{2, 3, 19, 14, 21, 11\}$$
$$4^K = \{4, 9, 13, 22, 6, 5\}$$
$$7^K = \{7, 16, 20, 25, 24, 23\}$$
$$8^K = \{8, 27, 15, 18, 10, 26\},$$

and 4 fixed points $\{1, 12, 17, 28\}$. Note that $1^4 \equiv 12^4 \equiv 17^4 \equiv 28^4 \equiv 1 \bmod 29$.

Since there is an one-to-one correspondence between $\zeta^i x^K$ and $\zeta^j x^K$ for all i, j, they have the same number of elements. If we define

$$\mathcal{O}_{x,K} := x^K \,\dot{\cup}\, \zeta x^K \,\dot{\cup}\, \cdots \,\dot{\cup}\, \zeta^{\lambda-1} x^K,$$

where $\dot{\cup}$ denotes the disjoint union, we have $|\mathcal{O}_{x,K}| = |x^K|\lambda$ for $x \in \mathbb{Z}_p^\times$. Along with the set of fixed points, we have $|\mathcal{O}_{x,K} \cup \langle \zeta \rangle| = (|x^K| + 1)\lambda$ number of elements in $\mathbb{Z}_p^\times$ for a non-fixed point $x \in \mathbb{Z}_p^\times$. From now on, $\mathrm{ord}_p(x)$ denotes the order of x modulo p.

Remark 2. The set $\mathcal{O}_{x,K}$ behaves just like an extended orbit, which means that for $x, y \in \mathbb{Z}_p^\times$, $\mathcal{O}_{x,K}$ and $\mathcal{O}_{y,K}$ are disjoint or identical. In other words, $\mathcal{O}_{x,K} \cap \mathcal{O}_{y,K} \neq \emptyset$ implies $y = \zeta^i x^k$ and $\mathcal{O}_{x,K} = \mathcal{O}_{y,K}$. Therefore, $\mathbb{Z}_p^\times$ can be expressed by the disjoint union of distinct $\mathcal{O}_{x,K}$'s. Moreover, if $\mathcal{O}_{x,K} = \mathcal{O}_{y,K}$, then $y = \zeta^i x^k$ for some $0 \leq i < \lambda, k \in K$ and $y^\lambda = x^{\lambda k}$. It implies that $\mathrm{ord}_p(x^\lambda) = \mathrm{ord}_p(y^\lambda)$.

The next proposition gives a condition to satisfy $|x^K| = |K|$.

Proposition 5. *Let K be a multiplicative subgroup of $\mathbb{Z}_{p-1}^\times$, $\lambda = \gcd(K-1)$ and $x \in \mathbb{Z}_p$. If $\gcd(\lambda, \frac{p-1}{\lambda}) = 1$, then $|x^K| = |K|$ for x satisfying $\mathrm{ord}_p(x^\lambda) = \frac{p-1}{\lambda}$. In particular, if $\frac{p-1}{\lambda}$ is prime, then $|x^K| = |K|$ for $x \notin (\mathbb{Z}_p^\times)^K$.*

Proof. Note that $|x^K| = |K|$ if and only if $|K_x| = |\{k \in K : x^k = x\}| = 1$. Suppose that $x^k = x$ for some $k = 1 + \lambda n \in K$ and $0 \leq n < \frac{p-1}{\lambda}$. It implies that $(x^\lambda)^n = 1$ for some $0 \leq n < \frac{p-1}{\lambda}$. However, since $\mathrm{ord}_p(x^\lambda) = \frac{p-1}{\lambda}$, n must be zero. It follows that K_x contains only one element, $k = 1$.

Since $(x^\lambda)^{\frac{p-1}{\lambda}} \equiv 1 \pmod{p}$ for all $x \in \mathbb{Z}_p$, we have $\mathrm{ord}_p(x^\lambda)$ divides $\frac{p-1}{\lambda}$. In addition, $\mathrm{ord}_p(x^\lambda) = 1$ if and only if $x \in (\mathbb{Z}_p^\times)^K$. Thus, if $\frac{p-1}{\lambda}$ is a prime, it follows that $\mathrm{ord}_p(x^\lambda) = \frac{p-1}{\lambda}$ if and only if $x \notin (\mathbb{Z}_p^\times)^K$. $\qquad\square$

Example 3. Note that for $p = 29$ and $\lambda = 4$, we have $|K| = |2^K| = |4^K| = |7^K| = |8^K| = 6$ for $K = K_4$, and $\langle 17 \rangle = \{17, 28, 12, 1\}$ forms a cyclic group of fixed points. It is easily verified that $17 \cdot 2^K = 4^K$, $28 \cdot 2^K = 8^K$ and $12 \cdot 2^K = 7^K$, thus $\mathcal{O}_{2,K} = 2^K \,\dot{\cup}\, 4^K \,\dot{\cup}\, 8^K \,\dot{\cup}\, 7^K = \mathbb{Z}_{29}^\times \backslash \langle 17 \rangle$.

The following proposition shows how many x's in $\mathbb{Z}_p^\times$ satisfy $\mathrm{ord}_p(x^\lambda) = \frac{p-1}{\lambda}$.

Proposition 6. *Assume that λ is a divisor of $p-1$. Then there are exactly $\lambda\phi(\frac{p-1}{\lambda})$ elements x in $\mathbb{Z}_p^\times$ such that $\mathrm{ord}_p(x^\lambda) = \frac{p-1}{\lambda}$.*

Proof. Let ξ be a primitive element of $\mathbb{Z}_p$. There exists a unique $0 \le j < p$ satisfying $x = \xi^j$ for any $x \in \mathbb{Z}_p^\times$. We will use the fact that $\mathrm{ord}_p(\xi^i) = \frac{p-1}{\gcd(i,p-1)}$ for all i.

From $\mathrm{ord}_p(x^\lambda) = \mathrm{ord}_p(\xi^{\lambda j}) = \frac{p-1}{\gcd(\lambda j, p-1)} = \frac{p-1}{\lambda} \frac{1}{\gcd(j, \frac{p-1}{\lambda})}$, we show that $\mathrm{ord}_p(x^\lambda) = \frac{p-1}{\lambda}$ if and only if $\gcd(j, \frac{p-1}{\lambda}) = 1$. Therefore, there are exactly $\phi(\frac{p-1}{\lambda})$-number of j's modulo $\frac{p-1}{\lambda}$ satisfying $\gcd(j, \frac{p-1}{\lambda}) = 1$, thus $\lambda\phi(\frac{p-1}{\lambda})$-number of x's in $\mathbb{Z}_p^\times$ satisfying $\mathrm{ord}_p(x^\lambda) = \frac{p-1}{\lambda}$. $\qquad\square$

Note that $\lambda\phi(\frac{p-1}{\lambda}) = \lambda\frac{p-1}{\lambda}\prod_{q\in Q}(1 - \frac{1}{q}) = (p-1)\prod_{q\in Q}(1 - \frac{1}{q})$ where Q is the set of prime divisors of $\frac{p-1}{\lambda}$. Hence, if we randomly take x in $\mathbb{Z}_p^\times$, then the probability that $\mathrm{ord}_p(x^\lambda) = \frac{p-1}{\lambda}$ is $\prod_{q\in Q}(1 - \frac{1}{q})$. Moreover, if $\frac{p-1}{\lambda}$ has only large prime divisors, then the probability $\prod_{q\in Q}(1 - \frac{1}{q})$ will be almost equal to 1.

Combining these results with Proposition 1, we surprisingly obtain an immediate partition of $\mathbb{Z}_p^\times$. Recall that for an even divisor λ of $p-1$, we defined a multiplicative subgroup $K_\lambda = \{1 + \lambda n : n \in [0, \frac{p-1}{\lambda}) \cap \mathbb{Z}\} \cap \mathbb{Z}_{p-1}^\times$.

Theorem 1. *Let λ be an even divisor of $p-1$ satisfying $\gcd(\lambda, \frac{p-1}{\lambda}) = 1$ and K_λ be a multiplicative subgroup of $\mathbb{Z}_{p-1}^\times$ defined as above. Consider the K_λ-action on $\mathbb{Z}_p^\times$. Let ζ be a generator of a cyclic group of fixed points by the K_λ-action, $\{z \in \mathbb{Z}_p^\times : z^\lambda = 1\}$. Then the followings hold:*

1. *If $\frac{p-1}{\lambda} = \mu$ is prime, then $\mathbb{Z}_p^\times = \mathcal{O}_{x,K_\lambda} \,\dot\cup\, (\mathbb{Z}_p^\times)_{K_\lambda}$ for $x \notin (\mathbb{Z}_p^\times)_{K_\lambda}$.*

2. *If $\frac{p-1}{\lambda} = \mu_1 \cdots \mu_\ell$ is square-free for prime $\mu_1, \cdots, \mu_\ell$, then $\mathbb{Z}_p^\times = \dot\cup_{J \subseteq I}\, \mathcal{O}_{x^{\mu_J}, K_\lambda}$ for $x \in \mathbb{Z}_p^\times$ such that $\mathrm{ord}_p(x^\lambda) = \frac{p-1}{\lambda}$, where $I = \{1, 2, \cdots, \ell\}$ is an index set and $\mu_J = \prod_{j \in J} \mu_j$ for $J \subseteq I$ (For the convenience, define $\mu_\emptyset = 1$ for the empty subset $\emptyset \subseteq I$). In particular, $\mathcal{O}_{x^{\mu_I}, K_\lambda} = (\mathbb{Z}_p^\times)_{K_\lambda}$.*

Proof. If $\frac{p-1}{\lambda} = \mu$ is prime, then $|K_\lambda| = \phi(\frac{p-1}{\lambda}) = \phi(\mu) = \mu - 1$ by Proposition 1. Note that $\mathcal{O}_{x,K_\lambda}$ and $(\mathbb{Z}_p^\times)_{K_\lambda}$ are disjoint subsets of $\mathbb{Z}_p^\times$ for $x \notin (\mathbb{Z}_p^\times)_{K_\lambda}$. Thus we have $|\mathcal{O}_{x,K_\lambda} \,\dot\cup\, (\mathbb{Z}_p^\times)_{K_\lambda}| = |\mathcal{O}_{x,K_\lambda}| + |(\mathbb{Z}_p^\times)_{K_\lambda}|$. By Proposition 5, we obtain $|\mathcal{O}_{x,K_\lambda}| = |x^{K_\lambda}|\lambda = |K_\lambda|\lambda = (\mu - 1)\lambda$ and $|(\mathbb{Z}_p^\times)_{K_\lambda}| = \lambda$. Therefore, $|\mathcal{O}_{x,K_\lambda} \,\dot\cup\, (\mathbb{Z}_p^\times)_{K_\lambda}| = p - 1$ deduces that $\mathcal{O}_{x,K_\lambda} \,\dot\cup\, (\mathbb{Z}_p^\times)_{K_\lambda} = \mathbb{Z}_p^\times$.

In the case that $\frac{p-1}{\lambda} = \mu_1 \cdots \mu_\ell$ is square-free and $\mathrm{ord}_p(x^\lambda) = \frac{p-1}{\lambda}$, we have $|x^{K_\lambda}| = |K_\lambda| = \phi(\frac{p-1}{\lambda}) = \phi(\mu_I) = \prod_{1 \le j \le \ell}(\mu_j - 1)$ by Proposition 1. For a subset J of I and $y = x^{\mu_J}$, we first calculate $|y^{K_\lambda}|$ and $|\mathcal{O}_{y,K_\lambda}|$ by using the fact that $|y^{K_\lambda}| = |K_\lambda|/|(K_\lambda)_y|$, where $(K_\lambda)_y = \{k \in K_\lambda : y^k = y\}$. Since $k = 1 + \lambda n \in (K_\lambda)_y$ if and only if $y^{k-1} = (x^{\mu_J})^{\lambda \cdot n} = 1$ if and only if $\mu_{I\setminus J} = \mu_I/\mu_J$ divides n, the size of $(K_\lambda)_y$ is equal to the number of n satisfying that $1 + \lambda n \in \mathbb{Z}_{p-1}^\times$, $0 \le n < \mu_I$ and $\mu_{I\setminus J}$ divides n. Therefore, by the similar argument in Proposition 1, we get

$$|(K_\lambda)_y| = \left|\{n \in [0, \mu_I) \cap \mathbb{Z} : 1 + \lambda n \in \mathbb{Z}_{p-1}^\times \text{ and } \mu_{I\backslash J}|(\lambda n)\}\right|$$

$$= \left|\{n \in [0, \mu_I) \cap \mathbb{Z} : \mu_j \nmid (1 + \lambda n) \text{ for each } j \text{ and } \mu_{I\backslash J}|n\}\right|$$

$$= \frac{\mu_I}{\mu_{I\backslash J}} \cdot \prod_{j \in J} \left(1 - \frac{1}{\mu_j}\right)$$

$$= \mu_J \cdot \prod_{j \in J} \left(1 - \frac{1}{\mu_j}\right) = \phi(\mu_J),$$

resulting $|y^{K_\lambda}| = \frac{|K_\lambda|}{|(K_\lambda)_y|} = \frac{\phi(\mu_I)}{\phi(\mu_J)} = \phi(\mu_{I\backslash J})$ and $|\mathcal{O}_{y,K_\lambda}| = \lambda|y^{K_\lambda}| = \lambda\phi(\mu_{I\backslash J})$.

Since $\mathcal{O}_{x^{\mu_J},K_\lambda}$'s are pairwise disjoint for all $J \subseteq I$, we have $\left|\dot{\bigcup}_{J \subseteq I} \mathcal{O}_{x^{\mu_J},K_\lambda}\right| = \sum_{J \subseteq I} |\mathcal{O}_{x^{\mu_J},K_\lambda}| = \lambda \sum_{J \subseteq I} \phi(\mu_{I\backslash J})$. Finally, using elementary number theory, we have $\sum_{J \subseteq I} \phi(\mu_{I\backslash J}) = \sum_{d|\mu_I} \phi(d) = \mu_I$ and $\left|\dot{\bigcup}_{J \subseteq I} \mathcal{O}_{x^{\mu_J},K_\lambda}\right| = \lambda \cdot \mu_I = p - 1$ deducing that $\mathbb{Z}_p^\times = \dot{\bigcup}_{J \subseteq I} (\mathcal{O}_{x^{\mu_J},K_\lambda})$. $\square$

Note that for any given $x \in \mathcal{O}_{y,K_\lambda}$, there exist $0 \le i < \lambda$ and $k \in K_\lambda$ satisfying $x = \zeta^i y^k$. By virtue of Theorem 1, all elements in $\mathbb{Z}_p^\times$ can be expressed with only a few information. For example, we can simply partition $\mathbb{Z}_p^\times$ with only two elements $x \in \mathbb{Z}_p^\times - (\mathbb{Z}_p^\times)_{K_\lambda}$ and $\zeta \in (\mathbb{Z}_p^\times)_{K_\lambda}$, when $\gcd(\lambda, \frac{p-1}{\lambda}) = 1$ and $q = \frac{p-1}{\lambda}$ is prime, so that any of element in $\mathbb{Z}_p^\times$ is of form $\zeta^i x^k$ for $0 \le i < \lambda$ and $k \in K$. In our example, with only $x = 2$ and $\zeta = 17$, we can express all elements in $\mathbb{Z}_{29}^\times$.

In the case of $\frac{p-1}{\lambda} = \mu_1 \cdots \mu_\ell$ is square-free and $\text{ord}_p(x^\lambda) = \frac{p-1}{\lambda}$, Remark 2 says that $\text{ord}_p(y^\lambda) = \mu_{I\backslash J}$ if $y \in \mathcal{O}_{x^{\mu_J},K_\lambda}$. The converse is also true because $\mathbb{Z}_p^\times = \dot{\bigcup}_{J \subseteq I} \mathcal{O}_{x^{\mu_J},K_\lambda}$ and y cannot be contained in $\mathcal{O}_{x^{\mu_{J'}},K_\lambda}$ for $J \ne J' \subseteq I$.

4   Polynomial Construction

In this section, we will define a polynomial $f(x) \in \mathbb{Z}_p[x]$ of degree d having small value sets. Recently, the similar idea was developed by Kim and Cheon [16] to solve the DLPwAI. Their approach exploited the fast multipoint evaluation method, so the degree of their polynomial was restricted to at most $d \approx p^{1/3}$ due to the efficiency issue.

The polynomial we will use in this paper is of very large degree which might be greater than $p^{1/3}$ but is sparse (all but d coefficients are zero) and have small value sets. Thus the fast multipoint evaluation method as in [16] seems hardly to be applied in our case. Instead, we take somewhat different approach with the idea developed in Sect. 3. We will define a polynomial so that it takes the same value for all elements in an orbit. In the proof of our main theorem, we will make some lists of $f(\alpha_1), \cdots, f(\alpha_\ell)$ from $f(\alpha)$ where α_i's are the representatives of distinct orbits and α is a discrete log to find. Then we find an index j such that $f(\alpha_j) = f(\beta)$ for randomly chosen $\beta \in \mathbb{Z}_p^\times$ i.e. we find an orbit in which β is contained. For this process, $f(\alpha)$ should be nonzero.

Definition 3. *Let K be a multiplicative subgroup of $\mathbb{Z}_{p-1}^\times$. Define a polynomial $f_K(x)$ over $\mathbb{Z}_p$ by $f_K(x) := \sum_{k \in K} x^k$. We will simply write $f_K = f$ if there is no ambiguity in the meaning.*

By the definition, it is clear that f_K takes the same value for the elements in the same orbit defined by K-action.

Proposition 7. *For any $k \in K$ and $x \in \mathbb{Z}_p^\times$, we have $f(x^k) = f(x)$. If $\zeta^i \in (\mathbb{Z}_p^\times)_K$ is a fixed point, then $f(\zeta^i x) = \zeta^i f(x)$.*

Since the degree of $f = f_K$ might be large (approximately p), it looks hard to evaluate $f(\alpha_1), \cdots, f(\alpha_\ell)$ in $O(\ell)$ time complexity for random α_i's with fast multipoint evaluation method. However, for a non-fixed point $\alpha \in \mathbb{Z}_p^\times$ and a fixed point (not necessarily generator) $\zeta \in (\mathbb{Z}_p)_K$, we can compute $f(\alpha), f(\zeta\alpha) = \zeta f(\alpha), \cdots, f(\zeta^\ell\alpha) = \zeta^\ell f(\alpha)$ in ℓ multiplications by ζ with $O(|K|)$ exponentiations for computing $f(\alpha)$. Furthermore, if $f(\alpha)$ is nonzero, then we can deduce that all $\alpha, \zeta\alpha, \cdots, \zeta^\ell\alpha$ are the different representatives for distinct orbits. The following proposition calculates $f(x)$ explicitly in special cases.

Proposition 8. *Assume that λ is an even divisor of $p-1$ satisfying $\gcd(\lambda, \frac{p-1}{\lambda}) = 1$. Let $K = K_\lambda$ and $f = f_K$ be defined as aforementioned. Then the followings hold:*

1. *If $\frac{p-1}{\lambda} = \mu$ is prime, then $f(x) \neq 0$ for $x \in \mathbb{Z}_p^\times$.*
2. *If $\frac{p-1}{\lambda} = \mu_1 \cdots \mu_\ell$ is square-free for prime $\mu_1, \ldots, \mu_\ell$, then $f(x) \neq 0$ for $x \in \mathbb{Z}_p^\times$.*

Proof. If $\frac{p-1}{\lambda} = \mu$ is prime, then $|K| = \mu - 1$ by Proposition 1. Consider a map from $\mathbb{Z}_\mu$ to itself defined by $n \mapsto (1 + \lambda n)$. Since λ and μ are relatively prime, this map is bijective. In other words, $1 + \lambda n$ for $0 \leq n < \mu$ induces complete residue modulo μ. Thus, there exists a unique $0 \leq n_0 < \mu$ such that $1 + \lambda n_0$ is divisible by μ. Therefore,

$$f(x) = \sum_{k \in K} x^k = \sum_{0 \leq n < \mu} x^{1+\lambda n} - x^{1+\lambda n_0} = x \cdot \frac{x^{p-1} - 1}{x^\lambda - 1} - x^{1+\lambda n_0} = -x^{1+\lambda n_0}$$

for $x \notin (\mathbb{Z}_p^\times)_K$. Otherwise, if $x^\lambda = 1$ then $x^k = x$ for all $k \in K$ and $f(x) = (\mu - 1)x \neq 0$.

In the case of $\frac{p-1}{\lambda} = \mu_1 \cdots \mu_\ell$ is square-free, $|K| = \phi(\mu_1 \cdots \mu_\ell)$ by Proposition 1. By similar argument as above, for a subset J of an index set $I = \{1, 2, \cdots \ell\}$, let $\mu_J = \prod_{j \in J} \mu_j$, and define a map from $\mathbb{Z}_{\mu_J}$ to itself by $n \mapsto (1 + \lambda n)$. Since λ and μ_J are relatively prime, it also induces the complete residue modulo μ_J. Thus, there exists a unique $0 \leq n_J < \mu_J$ such that $1 + \lambda n_J$ is divisible by μ_J (For convenience, define $\mu_J = 1$ and $n_J = 0$ for empty set $J = \emptyset$). We easily check that $n_J \equiv n_I \pmod{\mu_J}$ for all $J \subseteq I$. Now, $\text{ord}_p(x^\lambda) = \mu_{I_0}$ for some $I_0 \subseteq I$ since $\text{ord}_p(x^\lambda)$ is a divisor of $\frac{p-1}{\lambda} = \mu_I$. For $J \subseteq I$, $x^{\lambda \mu_J} = 1$ if and only if $I_0 \subseteq J$.

Using the inclusion–exclusion principle, we have

$$f(x) = \sum_{k \in K} x^k = \sum_{J \subseteq I} (-1)^{|J|} \sum_n x^{1+\lambda n},$$

where n in summation runs through $0 \le n < \mu_I$ satisfying $n \equiv n_J \pmod{\mu_J}$.

If $I_0 \not\subseteq J \subseteq I$, then $x^{\lambda \mu_J} \ne 1$ and $\sum_n x^{1+\lambda n} = x^{1+\lambda n_J} \frac{x^{\mu_J} - 1}{x^{\lambda \mu_J} - 1} = 0$. Otherwise $I_0 \subseteq J \subseteq I$, then $x^{\lambda \mu_J} = 1$ and $\sum_n x^{1+\lambda n} = \sum_n x^{1+\lambda n_J} = \frac{\mu_I}{\mu_J} x^{1+\lambda n_J} = \mu_{I \setminus J} x^{1+\lambda n_I}$ since n in summation is equivalent to n_J modulo μ_J, and $n_J \equiv n_I \pmod{\mu_J}$.

Finally, we have

$$f(x) = \sum_{J \subseteq I} (-1)^{|J|} \sum_n x^{1+\lambda n} = \sum_{I_0 \subseteq J \subseteq I} (-1)^{|J|} \sum_n x^{1+\lambda n}$$

$$= x^{1+\lambda n_I} \sum_{I_0 \subseteq J \subseteq I} (-1)^{|J|} \mu_{I \setminus J} = x^{1+\lambda n_I} \sum_{J \subseteq I \setminus I_0} (-1)^{|I \setminus J|} \mu_J$$

$$= x^{1+\lambda n_I} (-1)^{\ell} \prod_{j \in I \setminus I_0} (1 - \mu_j) \ne 0.$$

In particular, if $\mathrm{ord}_p(x^\lambda) = \mu_I$, then $f(x) = (-1)^\ell x^{1+\lambda n_I}$.   □

The above proposition says that $f_K(x)$ is not identically zero for $K_\lambda = K$ for even divisor λ of $p - 1$. Actually, it appears to be of form $f_K(x) = -x^d$ where $\gcd(d, p - 1)$ is large, however in our application, it is desirable that $f_K(x) \ne 0$ but is not of simple form such as x^d, where d has large common divisor with $p-1$, since this simple form leads us to the already known Cheon's $p - 1$ algorithm. In many cases, for a non proper subgroup K of K_λ, $f_K(x)$ also tends to not to be identically zero, although it seems hard to show it.

Example 4. For $K = K_4 = \{1, 5, 9, 13, 17, 25\} \le \mathbb{Z}_{28}^\times$, define $f_K(x) = x + x^5 + x^9 + x^{13} + x^{17} + x^{25} = -x^{21} \in \mathbb{Z}_{29}[x]$, where 21 and 28 have common divisor 7. For a subgroup $K' = \langle 9 \rangle = \{9, 25, 1\}$ of K, we have $K/\langle 9 \rangle = \{1, 5\}$. Now consider $f_{K'}(x) = x + x^9 + x^{25}$. Then $f_{K'}(x)$ takes same value for x in the same orbit. We have 8 disjoint orbits of length 3 and 4 fixed points. Note that the fixed points for K and K' are same as shown in Proposition 3.

$$2^{K'} = \{2, 19, 11\}, \quad 2^5 K' = 3^{K'} = \{3, 14, 21\}$$
$$4^{K'} = \{4, 13, 5\}, \quad 4^5 K' = 9^{K'} = \{9, 22, 6\}$$
$$7^{K'} = \{7, 20, 23\}, \quad 7^5 K' = 16^{K'} = \{16, 25, 24\}$$
$$8^{K'} = \{8, 15, 26\}, \quad 8^5 K' = 27^{K'} = \{27, 18, 10\}.$$

The polynomial $f_{K'}(x)$ takes nonzero value $2 + 19 + 11 \equiv 3 \bmod 29$ for all $x \in 2^{K'}$, and we can check that $f_{K'}(x)$ take distinct values for disjoint orbits.

Proposition 9. *Assume that λ is an even divisor of $p-1$ satisfying $\gcd(\lambda, \frac{p-1}{\lambda}) = 1$. Let $K = K_\lambda$ and $f = f_K$. If $\frac{p-1}{\lambda} = q^e$ for some prime q and $e \ge 2$, then $f(x) = 0$ unless $x^{\lambda q} = 1$ in $\mathbb{Z}_p^\times$.*

Proof. Since $\frac{p-1}{\lambda}$ has only one prime divisor q, we can efficiently express elements of K and compute $f(x)$. For $n \in \mathbb{Z}_\mu$, $1 + \lambda n$ is contained in K if and only if $\gcd(1+\lambda n, q) = 1$. Since $1 + \lambda n \equiv 0 \pmod{q}$ has exactly one solution $n_0 \equiv -\lambda^{-1}$ in modulo q, there exist q^{e-1}-number of solutions $\{n_0 + qm : 0 \leq m < q^{e-1}\}$ in $\mathbb{Z}_\mu$. Therefore, $f(x)$ is computed by

$$f(x) = \sum_{n \in [0, \frac{p-1}{\lambda}) \cap \mathbb{Z}, 1+\lambda n \in K} x^{1+\lambda n} = \sum_{0 \leq n < q^e} x^{1+\lambda n} - \sum_{0 \leq m < q^{e-1}} x^{1+\lambda(n_0 + qm)}$$

$$= x \left(\sum_{0 \leq n < q^e} x^{\lambda n} \right) - x^{1+\lambda n_0} \left(\sum_{0 \leq m < q^{e-1}} x^{\lambda q m} \right),$$

and it is equal to zero unless $x^{\lambda q} = 1$. However, there are only $\lambda q = \frac{p-1}{q^{e-1}}$-number of such elements x in $\mathbb{Z}_{p-1}^\times$. $\qquad\square$

In general, if $\frac{p-1}{\lambda}$ is not square-free, then $f_{K_\lambda}(x) = 0$ for most of the elements in $\mathbb{Z}_{p-1}^\times$. Modifying the proofs of Propositions 8 and 9 easily show it. We will omit details here.

5   Main Theorem

By using a group action on $\mathbb{Z}_p^\times$, we can efficiently partition $\mathbb{Z}_p^\times$ with only a few elements. This leads us to a new algorithm that solves the GDLPwAI efficiently. Now we can state our main theorem as follows.

Theorem 2. *Let K be a multiplicative subgroup of $\mathbb{Z}_{p-1}^\times$ with $\lambda = \gcd(K-1)$. Assume that we are given $\left\{ \left(k, g^{\alpha^k} \right) : k \in K \right\}$ and $|\alpha^K| = |K|$. Then, we can solve $\alpha \in \mathbb{Z}_p$ in $O\left(\frac{p}{\lambda}\right)$ exponentiations in $\mathbb{Z}_p$ and $O\left(\frac{p}{|K|\sqrt{\lambda}} + |K|\right)$ exponentiations in G unless $\sum_{k \in K} \alpha^k = 0$.*

Proof. We give a sketch of the proof following the next steps.

1. For given g^{α^k} for all $k \in K$, one computes $g^{f(\alpha)} = \prod_{k \in K} g^{\alpha^k} \in G$ in $|K|$ multiplications in G. Note that $g^{f(\alpha)} \neq 1$, since $f(\alpha) \neq 0$.
2. Take a random element β from $\mathbb{Z}_p^\times$ and compute $f(\beta) = \sum_{k \in K} \beta^k \in \mathbb{Z}_p$ in $|K|$ exponentiations in $\mathbb{Z}_p$. If $\beta \in \mathcal{O}_{\alpha,K}$, then there exists a unique $0 \leq t < \lambda$ satisfying $\alpha^K = \zeta^t \beta^K$ and $f(\alpha) = \zeta^t f(\beta)$.
3. To find such t, we use Baby-Step Giant-Step method. Let $L := \lceil \sqrt{\lambda} \rceil$. Make two lists $\{g^{f(\zeta^{L \cdot i}\beta)} = (g^{f(\beta)})^{\zeta^{L \cdot i}} \in G : 0 \leq i < L\}$ and $\{g^{f(\zeta^{-j}\alpha)} = (g^{f(\alpha)})^{\zeta^{-j}} \in G : 0 \leq j < L\}$ in $2\sqrt{\lambda}$ exponentiations in G. If $\beta \in \mathcal{O}_{\alpha,K}$, these two lists must have a collision since there exist $0 \leq i, j < L$ satisfying $t = Li + j$.
4. Repeat the steps 2 and 3 until finding a collision. The expected number of repetitions is $\frac{p}{|K|\lambda}$, since the probability that $\beta \in \mathcal{O}_{\alpha,K}$ is $\frac{|\mathcal{O}_{\alpha,K}|}{p} = \frac{|\alpha^K|\lambda}{p} = \frac{|K|\lambda}{p}$.

5. Locate $g^{\zeta^t \beta}$ from the set $\left\{ g^{\alpha^k} : k \in K \right\}$ to find $k_0 \in K$ such that $g^{\alpha^{k_0}} = g^{\zeta^t \beta}$. This gives $\alpha = (\zeta^t \beta)^{k_0^{-1}}$ in $|K|$ comparisons in G.

We carry out the above process in

$|K|$ multiplications in G in Step 1, $O\left(\frac{p}{|K|\lambda} \cdot |K|\right) = O\left(\frac{p}{\lambda}\right)$ exponentiations in $\mathbb{Z}_p$ in Steps 2 and $O\left(\frac{p}{|K|\sqrt{\lambda}}\right)$ exponentiations in G in Step 3 and 4, and $|K|$ comparisons in G in Step 5. The overall complexity is as in the theorem. □

Remark 3. In the proof of Theorem 2, we may find a fake collision. That is, some element $\beta \in \mathbb{Z}_p$ could satisfy $f(\alpha) = \zeta^t f(\beta)$ but $\zeta^t \beta \notin \alpha^K$. If a fake collision occurs in Step 3 and 4, there would be no element $k_0 \in K$ such that $\alpha^{k_0} = \zeta^t \beta$ and we can check it in Step 5. They do not affect the total complexity.

For any multiplicative subgroup K of $\mathbb{Z}_{p-1}^\times$, K is a multiplicative subgroup of K_λ where $\lambda = \gcd(K - 1)$. Hence we can define $\kappa = [K_\lambda : K]$.

Corollary 1. *For a multiplicative subgroup K of $\mathbb{Z}_p^\times$, set $\lambda = \gcd(K - 1)$ and define $\kappa = [K : K_\lambda]$. Assume that the computational cost for the multiplications in G is a constant times of the cost for the multiplications in $\mathbb{Z}_p$. Then we can solve the GDLPwAI in $O\left(\left(\kappa\sqrt{\lambda} + \frac{p}{\lambda}\right)\log p\right)$ multiplications in $\mathbb{Z}_p$.*

Proof. In Proposition 1, we showed that $|K_\lambda| = \frac{p-1}{\lambda}\prod_{q \in Q}(1 - \frac{1}{q})$ where Q is the set of prime divisors of $p - 1$ not dividing λ. We may assume that $\prod_{q \in Q}(1 - \frac{1}{q})$ is a constant greater than zero since $\prod_{q \in Q}(1 - \frac{1}{q}) \geq \frac{\phi(\frac{p-1}{\lambda})}{\frac{p-1}{\lambda}} \geq \frac{1}{6\log\log\frac{p-1}{\lambda}}$ and $\log\log\frac{p-1}{\lambda}$ is not so large for usual size of p. In fact, $\prod_{q \in Q}(1 - \frac{1}{q})$ is much greater than this lower bound in almost cases. Then we have $|K| = \frac{|K_\lambda|}{\kappa} = O\left(\frac{p}{\lambda\kappa}\right)$ and $\frac{p}{|K|\sqrt{\lambda}} = O\left(\kappa\sqrt{\lambda}\right)$.

By Theorem 2, the overall complexity is $O(|K|\log p) = O\left(\frac{p}{\lambda}\log p\right)$ multiplications in $\mathbb{Z}_p$ and $O\left(\left(|K| + \frac{p}{|K|\sqrt{\lambda}}\right)\log p\right) = O\left(\left(\kappa\sqrt{\lambda} + \frac{p}{\lambda}\right)\log p\right)$ multiplications in G. By the assumption, we can put them together in one notation. □

Example 5. Consider a multiplicative group $\mathbb{Z}_q^\times$ for prime $q = 1984044749$. The element $g = 268435456 \in \mathbb{Z}_q^\times$ generates the multiplicative subgroup $G = \langle g \rangle$ of 20-bit prime order $p = 70858741$. Suppose that we are given $\left\{ \left(k, g^{\alpha^k}\right) : k \in K \right\}$ $= \{(1, 368141755), (9447833, 908277040), (14171749, 1018628336), (51963077, 651549246)\}$ for the multiplicative subgroup K of $\mathbb{Z}_{p-1}^\times$ with $\lambda = \gcd(K; \mathbb{Z}_{p-1}) = 4723916$. Following Theorem 2, we have $g^{f(\alpha)} = 104646375$ and $f(\beta) = 29994755$ for randomly chosen $\beta = 27015355$ in G. Using the BSGS technique, we find $t = 993142$ satisfying $g^{f(\alpha)} = g^{\zeta^t f(\beta)}$ for a primitive element ξ and a fixed point $\zeta = \xi^{\frac{p-1}{\lambda}}$. Then we find out that $\alpha^{k_0} = \zeta^t \beta$ for $k_0 = 51963077$ by comparing $g^{\zeta^t \beta}$ with $\{g^{\alpha^k} : k \in K\}$. Finally, we have $\alpha = (\zeta^t \beta)^{k_0^{-1}} = 37217684$.

Example 6. We use the same notations with Example 5. Set $q = 8307519720650407$, $g = 3814697265625 \in \mathbb{Z}_q^\times$. The element g has the order $p = 461528873369467$ of 50-bit prime. We are given our instance for a multiplicative subgroup K of K_λ such that $\lambda = 4742043558$, $|K_\lambda| = 97326$, $|K| = 16221$. Our algorithm finds that

$$\alpha = \zeta^t \beta = 55526261320836$$

for $\zeta = 265871590696697$, $\beta = 257387303120427$ and $t = 275438533$.

In summary, if we are given g^{α^k} for all $k \in K_\lambda$, then $\kappa = 1$ and we can solve the GSDL problem in $O\left(\left(\sqrt{\lambda} + \frac{p}{\lambda}\right)\log p\right)$. However, in this case, $g^{f_{K_\lambda}(\alpha)} = g^{-d}$ with nontrivial $\gcd(d, p-1)$, which falls into the Cheon's $p-1$ algorithm. When we are working with $|K| < |K_\lambda|$, then we need to carry out $O\left(\left(\kappa\sqrt{\lambda} + \frac{p}{\lambda}\right)\log p\right)$ multiplications, so we want $\kappa > 1$ to be sufficiently small. The computation amount can be reduced to $O\left(p^{1/3}\log p\right)$, when κ is small enough and $\lambda \approx p^{2/3}$.

Remark 4. If we assume that α is chosen randomly in $\mathbb{Z}_p^\times$, the condition $|\alpha^K| = |K|$ is satisfied with high probability. As we mentioned in Proposition 5 and Proposition 6, there are $\lambda\phi(\frac{p-1}{\lambda})$-number of x's in $\mathbb{Z}_p^\times$ such that $\mathrm{ord}_p(x^\lambda) = \frac{p-1}{\lambda}$, and they satisfy $|x^K| = |K|$. Therefore, the probability is greater than $\frac{1}{6\log\log(p-1)}$, since $\frac{\lambda\phi(\frac{p-1}{\lambda})}{p-1} \geq \frac{\phi(p-1)}{p-1}$ and $\frac{\phi(n)}{n} \geq \frac{1}{6\log\log n}$ for all $n \geq 5$ [20].

Remark 5. It is hard to compute the probability of $\sum_{k \in K}\alpha^k = 0$ in general, but we can predict that $f_K(x) = 0$ has not so many roots in $\mathbb{Z}_p$ if $\frac{p-1}{\lambda}$ is a square-free which is relatively prime to λ. Let $\kappa = [K_\lambda : K]$ and $\{k_1, \cdots k_\kappa\}$ be elements of distinct left cosets of K in K_λ. Then we have $f_{K_\lambda}(x) = \sum_{i=1}^\kappa f_K(x^{k_i})$. We saw in Proposition 8 that if $\frac{p-1}{\lambda}$ is a square-free which is relatively prime to λ, then f_{K_λ} is a monomial and hence it is never zero on $\mathbb{Z}_p$. Therefore, we can say that the condition $f_K(\alpha) \neq 0$ in Theorem 2 is not so unnatural in this case. In the contrary, it may be harder to satisfy the condition $f_K(\alpha) \neq 0$ if $\frac{p-1}{\lambda}$ has prime powers. The case of Proposition 9 is a typical example.

We have another strategy to avoid 'bad cases' aforementioned by randomizing α. In the case of $|\alpha^K| \neq |K|$, take a random element γ in $\mathbb{Z}_p^\times$ and compute new parameters $\{(g^{\alpha^k})^{\gamma^k} : k \in K\}$, which can be done in $|K|$ exponentiations in $\mathbb{Z}_p$ and G. We repeat this process until finding γ which satisfies $|(\alpha\gamma)^K| = |K|$, and the expected number of repetition is less than $6\log\log(p-1)$. Finally, we can compute $\alpha\gamma$ in $O\left(\frac{p}{\lambda|K|}(\sqrt{\lambda} + |K|)\right)$ exponentiations by Theorem 2, and get $\alpha = (\alpha\gamma) \cdot \gamma^{-1}$. The total number of computations is $O\left(|K|\log\log p + \frac{p}{\lambda|K|}(\sqrt{\lambda} + |K|)\right)$, which does not have significant difference with $O\left(\frac{p}{\lambda|K|}(\sqrt{\lambda} + |K|)\right)$.

This strategy can be also used in the case of $f_K(\alpha) = 0$. We can compute new parameters $\{(g^{\alpha^k})^{\gamma^k} : k \in K\}$ in $|K|$ exponentiations in $\mathbb{Z}_p$, and check whether $f_K(\alpha\gamma)$ is equal to zero or not in $|K|$ multiplications in G. The expected number of repetition depends on the number of roots of $f_K(x) = 0$ in $\mathbb{Z}_{p-1}$. This algorithm must be more efficient than the above, but the exact complexity is not resolved yet.

6   Conclusion

In this paper, we generalized the discrete logarithm problem with auxiliary inputs and proposed an algorithm to solve this problem efficiently. Precisely, our algorithm takes $g, g^\alpha, g^{\alpha^{e_1}}, \cdots, g^{\alpha^{e_{d-1}}}$ as an instance where e_i's form a multiplicative subgroup in $\mathbb{Z}_{p-1}^\times$. If $d \approx p^{1/3}$ is a prime (or square-free) divisor of $p - 1$ and $e_i = 1 + \frac{p-1}{d} \cdot n_i \in \mathbb{Z}_{p-1}^\times$ for some $0 \le n_i < d$, then our algorithm solves $\alpha \in \mathbb{Z}_p$ in $O(p^{1/3})$ group operations.

The main part of our technique is to partition the set $\mathbb{Z}_p^\times$ using a group action. In particular, if d is square-free with ℓ prime factors, then all elements in $\mathbb{Z}_p^\times$ can be represented by using only 2^ℓ elements.

It would be of interest to find an algorithm to solve the DLPwAI using our algorithm, that is, to convert an instance of the form $g, g^\alpha, \cdots, g^{\alpha^d}$ for $d < p^{1/3}$ into g^{α^k}'s with $k \in K$ for a multiplicative subgroup K of $\mathbb{Z}_{p-1}^\times$.

Acknowledgement. This work was supported by the National Research Foundation of Korea (NRF) grant funded by the Korea government (MSIP) (No. 2011-0018345). Yongsoo Song was partially supported by NRF-12-Global Ph.D. Fellowship Program.

References

1. Boneh, D., Boyen, X.: Efficient selective-ID secure identity-based encryption without random oracles. In: Cachin, Ch., Camenisch, J.L. (eds.) EUROCRYPT 2004. LNCS, vol. 3027, pp. 223–238. Springer, Heidelberg (2004)
2. Boneh, D., Boyen, X.: Short signatures without random oracles. In: Cachin, Ch., Camenisch, J.L. (eds.) EUROCRYPT 2004. LNCS, vol. 3027, pp. 56–73. Springer, Heidelberg (2004)
3. Boneh, D., Boyen, X.: Short signatures without random oracles and the SDH assumption in bilinear groups. J. Cryptol. **21**(2), 149–177 (2008)
4. Boneh, D., Boyen, X., Goh, E.-J.: Hierarchical identity based encryption with constant size ciphertext. In: Cramer, R. (ed.) EUROCRYPT 2005. LNCS, vol. 3494, pp. 440–456. Springer, Heidelberg (2005)
5. Boneh, D., Boyen, X., Shacham, H.: Short group signatures. In: Franklin, M. (ed.) CRYPTO 2004. LNCS, vol. 3152, pp. 41–55. Springer, Heidelberg (2004)
6. Boneh, D., Franklin, M.: Identity-based encryption from the Weil pairing. In: Kilian, J. (ed.) CRYPTO 2001. LNCS, vol. 2139, pp. 213–229. Springer, Heidelberg (2001)
7. Boneh, D., Gentry, C., Waters, B.: Collusion resistant broadcast encryption with short ciphertexts and private keys. In: Shoup, V. (ed.) CRYPTO 2005. LNCS, vol. 3621, pp. 258–275. Springer, Heidelberg (2005)

8. Boneh, D., Lynn, B., Shacham, H.: Short signatures from the Weil pairing. J. Cryptol. **17**(4), 297–319 (2004)
9. Brown, D.R.L., Gallant, R.P.: The static Diffie-Hellman problem. IACR Cryptology ePrint Archive. http://eprint.iacr.org/2004/306 (2004)
10. Cheon, J.H.: Security analysis of the strong Diffie-Hellman problem. In: Vaudenay, S. (ed.) EUROCRYPT 2006. LNCS, vol. 4004, pp. 1–11. Springer, Heidelberg (2006)
11. Cheon, J.H.: Discrete logarithm problems with auxiliary inputs. J. Cryptol. **23**(3), 457–476 (2010)
12. Conrad, K.: Group theory. http://www.math.uconn.edu/~kconrad/blurbs/
13. den Boer, B.: Diffie-Hellman is as strong as discrete log for certain primes. In: Goldwasser, S. (ed.) CRYPTO 1988. LNCS, vol. 403, pp. 530–539. Springer, Heidelberg (1990)
14. Jao, D., Yoshida, K.: Boneh-Boyen signatures and the strong Diffie-Hellman problem. In: Shacham, H., Waters, B. (eds.) Pairing 2009. LNCS, vol. 5671, pp. 1–16. Springer, Heidelberg (2009)
15. Kim, M.: Integer factorization and discrete logarithm with additional information. Ph.D. dissertation, Seoul National University (2011)
16. Kim, T., Cheon, J.H.: A new approach to discrete logarithm problem with auxiliary inputs. IACR Cryptology ePrint Archive. http://eprint.iacr.org/2012/609 (2012)
17. Lang, S.: Algebra, 3rd edn. Springer, New York (2002)
18. Maurer, U.M.: Towards the equivalence of breaking the Diffie-Hellman protocol and computing discrete logarithms. In: Desmedt, Y.G. (ed.) CRYPTO 1994. LNCS, vol. 839, pp. 271–281. Springer, Heidelberg (1994)
19. Maurer, U.M., Wolf, S.: The relationship between breaking the Diffie-Hellman protocol and computing discrete logarithms. SIAM J. Comput. **28**(5), 1689–1721 (1999)
20. Menezes, A., van Oorschot, P., Vanstone, S.: Handbook of Applied Cryptography. CRC Press, Boca Raton (1996)
21. Satoh, T.: On generalization of Cheon's algorithm. IACR Cryptology ePrint Archive. http://eprint.iacr.org/2009/058 (2009)

Solving a 6120-bit DLP on a Desktop Computer

Faruk Göloğlu, Robert Granger, Gary McGuire, and Jens Zumbrägel[✉]

Complex and Adaptive Systems Laboratory, School of Mathematical Sciences,
University College Dublin, Dublin, Ireland
{farukgologlu,robbiegranger}@gmail.com,
{gary.mcguire,jens.zumbragel}@ucd.ie

Abstract. In this paper we show how some recent ideas regarding the discrete logarithm problem (DLP) in finite fields of small characteristic may be applied to compute logarithms in some very large fields extremely efficiently. By combining the polynomial time relation generation from the authors' CRYPTO 2013 paper, an improved degree two elimination technique, and an analogue of Joux's recent small-degree elimination method, we solved a DLP in the record-sized finite field of 2^{6120} elements, using just a single core-month. Relative to the previous record set by Joux in the field of 2^{4080} elements, this represents a 50 % increase in the bitlength, using just 5 % of the core-hours. We also show that for the fields considered, the parameters for Joux's $L_Q(1/4 + o(1))$ algorithm may be optimised to produce an $L_Q(1/4)$ algorithm.

Keywords: Discrete logarithm problem · Binary finite fields

1 Introduction

The understanding of the hardness of the DLP in the multiplicative group of finite extension fields could be said to be undergoing a mini-revolution. It began with Joux's 2012 paper in which he introduced a method of relation generation dubbed 'pinpointing', which reduces the time required to obtain the logarithms of the elements of the factor base [11]. For medium-sized base fields, this technique has heuristic complexity as low as $L_Q(1/3, 2/3^{2/3}) \approx L_Q(1/3, 0.961)^1$, where

$$L_Q(a, c) = \exp\left((c + o(1)) (\log Q)^a (\log \log Q)^{1-a}\right),$$

and Q is the cardinality of the finite field. This improves upon the previous best by Joux and Lercier [17] of $L_Q(1/3, 3^{1/3}) \approx L_Q(1/3, 1.442)$. To demonstrate the practicality of this approach, Joux solved two example DLPs in fields of bitlength 1175 and 1425 respectively, both with prime base fields.

Research supported by the Claude Shannon Institute, Science Foundation Ireland Grant 06/MI/006. The fourth author was in addition supported by SFI Grant 08/IN.1/I1950.

[1] On foot of recent communications [13], the complexity may in fact be $L_Q(1/3, 2^{1/3})$.

T. Lange, K. Lauter, and P. Lisoněk (Eds.): SAC 2013, LNCS 8282, pp. 136–152, 2014.
DOI: 10.1007/978-3-662-43414-7_7, © Springer-Verlag Berlin Heidelberg 2014

Soon afterwards the present authors showed that in the context of binary fields (and more generally small characteristic fields), finding relations for the factor base can be *polynomial time* in the size of the field [6]. By extending the basic idea to eliminate degree two elements during the descent phase, for medium-sized base fields a heuristic complexity as low as $L_Q(1/3, (4/9)^{1/3}) \approx L_Q(1/3, 0.763)$ was achieved; this approach was demonstrated via the solution of a DLP in the field $\mathbb{F}_{2^{1971}}$ [7], and in the field $\mathbb{F}_{2^{3164}}$.

After the initial publication of [6], Joux released a preprint [12] detailing an algorithm for solving the discrete logarithm problem for fields of the form $\mathbb{F}_{q^{2n}}$, with $q = p^\ell$ and $n \approx q$, which was used in the solving of a DLP in $\mathbb{F}_{2^{1778}}$ [14], and later in $\mathbb{F}_{2^{4080}}$ [15]. This algorithm has heuristic complexity $L_Q(1/4 + o(1))$, and also has a heuristic polynomial time relation generation method, similar in principle to that in [6]. While the degree two element elimination in [6] is arguably superior, for other small degrees, Joux's elimination method is faster, resulting in the stated complexity. Joux's discrete logarithm computation in $\mathbb{F}_{2^{4080}}$ [15] required about 14,100 core-hours: 9,300 core-hours for the computation of the logarithms of all degree one and two elements; and 4,800 core-hours for the descent step, i.e., for computing the logarithm of an arbitrary element. For this computation, the field $\mathbb{F}_{2^{4080}}$ was represented as a degree 255 Kummer extension of $\mathbb{F}_{2^{16}}$, i.e., $\mathbb{F}_{(q^2)^{q-1}}$ with $q = 2^8$, as per [12]. The use of Kummer extensions (with extension degree either $q - 1$ or $q + 1$) gives a reduction in the size of the degree one and two factor base [11,12,17]; they are therefore preferable when it comes to setting record DLP computations.

The relation generation method in [6, Sect. 3.3] applies to larger base fields of the form $\mathbb{F}_{q^k}$ with $k \geq 3$ (rather than $k = 2$) and extension degrees up to $n \approx q\delta_1$ with $\delta_1 \geq 1$ a small integer. Hence the methods in this paper naturally apply to any extension degree. Note that this representation offers greater flexibility than Joux's (which can represent extension degrees up to $q + \delta_1'$) for essentially the same algorithmic cost, and may therefore provide a more practical DLP break when small base fields need to be embedded into larger ones in order to apply the attacks. However, here we choose to focus on Kummer extensions of degree $q \pm 1$, as these optimise the relation generation efficiency [6, Sect. 3.4], and linear algebra step. While the two DLP breaks in the fields $\mathbb{F}_{2^{1971}}$ and $\mathbb{F}_{2^{3164}}$ contained therein did not fully exploit the above 'extreme' fields in which the extension degree is polynomially related to the size of the base field, thanks to Joux's fast small-degree elimination method, one can now do this more efficiently. Hence, with a view to solving the DLP in larger fields than before and in as short a time as possible, in this work we identify a family of fields for which the DLP is very easily solved, relative to other fields of a similar size. While this does not mean other fields of a similar size are infeasible to break, it requires more time in practice to find the logarithms of the factor base elements, with the complexities remaining the same.

One benefit of using base fields with $k \geq 3$ is that there is an efficient probabilistic elimination technique for degree two elements [6, Sect. 4.1]. For any fixed $k \geq 4$ the elimination probability very quickly tends to 1 for increasing q. In this paper we present an improved technique which allows one to find the logarithm of degree two elements extremely fast, once the logarithms of all degree one elements are known. However, for $k = 3$ the elimination probability is $1/(2(\delta_1 - 1)!)$, or exactly $1/2$ for $\mathbb{F}_{2^{6120}} = \mathbb{F}_{(q^3)^{q-1}}$ with $q = 2^8$. Therefore the natural next choice is to set $k = 4$ and solve a DLP in $\mathbb{F}_{2^{8160}} = \mathbb{F}_{(q^4)^{q-1}}$. This would require solving a sparse linear system in $\approx 4.2 \cdot 10^6$ variables, and a slightly more costly descent step. Instead of carrying out this computation, we devised a technique for the 6120 bit case for which the elimination of each degree two element took only 0.03 s, and which required solving a much smaller linear system in 21,932 variables. This culminated in the resolution of a DLP in $\mathbb{F}_{2^{6120}}$ in under 750 core-hours [8], which represents a 50 % increase in bitlength over the previous record, whilst requiring just 5 % of the computation time.

We note that the solving of DLPs in $\mathbb{F}_{2^{6120}} = \mathbb{F}_{2^{24 \cdot 255}}$ renders insecure all pairing-based protocols based on supersingular curves of genus one and two over $\mathbb{F}_{2^{255}}$, since the corresponding embedding degrees are 4 and 12 (in the best cases), respectively [1]. However, since 255 is not prime, such curves would not be recommended due to possible Weil descent attacks [5]. In any case, the Jacobians of the curves do not have prime or nearly prime order and so are not cryptographically interesting. As stated above, we could just as easily have solved the corresponding DLP with extension degree $q+1$ rather than $q-1$, i.e., with extension degree 257 rather than 255. However, since the full factorisation of $2^{6120} - 1$ is known, we were able to use a proven generator and so for completeness we chose to solve this case[2].

Since our break of the DLP in $\mathbb{F}_{2^{6120}}$ may be considered as a proof-of-concept implementation for our approach, at the time we were not overly concerned with the issue of complexity. Indeed, as the elimination times are reasonable and as just noted, comparable to Joux's elimination timings, further experimentation is needed to ascertain if the performance is comparable for larger systems. However, one basic difference between the two approaches is that the quadratic systems which arise when using our analogue of Joux's small-degree elimination method are not bilinear, and hence are not guaranteed to enjoy the same resolution complexity, as given in Spaenlehauer's thesis [25, Corollary 6.30]. Therefore, we can not currently argue that the heuristic complexity is the same. Nevertheless, we show that with a better choice of parameter and a tighter analysis, the final part of the descent in Joux's $L_Q(1/4 + o(1))$ algorithm may be improved to an $L_Q(1/4)$ algorithm, for the fields we consider, i.e., those for which the extension degree is polynomially related to the size of the basefield. Since the other phases of the algorithm have complexity $L_Q(1/4)$, or lower, the overall complexity for solving the DLP is $L_Q(1/4)$ as well.

---

[2] Forty days after the announcement of our full DLP break in $\mathbb{F}_{2^{6120}} = \mathbb{F}_{2^{24 \cdot 255}}$ [8] – and after the submission of this paper – Joux announced a break of the DLP in a 1843-bit subgroup of $\mathbb{F}_{2^{6168}}^{\times} = \mathbb{F}_{2^{24 \cdot 257}}^{\times}$, using a nearly identical degree two elimination technique and the same descent parameters, in under 550 core-hours [16]. Noting that the logarithms were not computed in the full multiplicative group and that this computation was performed on faster processors, it is clear that the number of our core-hours and Joux's are comparable. In this case too the corresponding Jacobians do not have prime or nearly prime order.

The remainder of the paper is organised as follows. Section 2 explains our field setup and algorithm in detail. Section 3 covers the other essential algorithms and issues regarding the computation. Section 4 gives the details of a discrete logarithm computation in $\mathbb{F}_{2^{6120}}$, while finally in Sect. 5 we briefly address the issue of complexity.

2   The Algorithm

The following describes the field setup and index calculus method that we use for our discrete logarithm computation.

2.1   Setup

We consider here Kummer extensions, which are our focus for efficiency reasons; the general case can be found in [6, Sect. 3.3] and is recalled in Sect. 5.

Let ℓ, k be positive integers, $q := 2^\ell$, and $n := q - 1$. We construct the finite field $\mathbb{F}_{(q^k)^n}$ of bit length $\ell k n = \ell k(q-1)$ in which we solve the DLP, as follows[3]. As stated in the introduction, the case $n := q + 1$ follows *mutatis mutandis*.

We express our base field $\mathbb{F}_{q^k}$ as a degree k extension of $\mathbb{F}_q$. Then we choose $\gamma \in \mathbb{F}_{q^k}$ such that the polynomial $X^n + \gamma$ is irreducible in $\mathbb{F}_{q^k}[X]$ and define $\mathbb{F}_{(q^k)^n}$ as the Kummer extension

$$\mathbb{F}_{q^k}(x) \cong \mathbb{F}_{q^k}[X]/\big((X^n + \gamma)\,\mathbb{F}_{q^k}[X]\big)\,,$$

where x is a root of the polynomial $X^n + \gamma$ in $\mathbb{F}_{(q^k)^n}$. Note that a Kummer extension of degree n over $\mathbb{F}_{q^k}$ exists if and only if $n \mid q^k - 1$. Throughout the paper, the upper case letters $X, W, \ldots$ are used for indeterminates and the lower case letters $x, w, \ldots$ are reserved for finite fields elements that are roots of polynomials.

The following table displays the bit length $\ell k n$ of the finite field $\mathbb{F}_{(q^k)^n}$ for various choices of the numbers ℓ and k.

$k \setminus \ell$	6	7	8	9
3	1134	2667	6120	13797
4	1512	3556	8160	18396
5	1890	4445	10200	22995
6	2268	5334	12240	27594

In Sect. 4, we will give the details of the discrete logarithm computation when $\ell k n = 6120$. The algorithm we explain in this section may be successfully applied to any of the above parameters with $k \geq 4$, whereas for $k = 3$ one would normally be required to precompute the logarithms of all degree two elements using a method analogous to Joux's [12]. However, for $k = 3$ and $\ell = 8$, precomputation can be avoided entirely; see Sect. 4.4.

---

[3] Our choice of representation of the finite field $\mathbb{F}_{(q^k)^n}$ will be advantageous for our method to solve the DLP. Note that it is a computationally easy problem to switch between two different representations of a finite field [22].

2.2   Factor Base and Automorphisms

The factor base we use consists of the elements in $\mathbb{F}_{(q^k)^n}$ which have degree one in the polynomial representation over $\mathbb{F}_{q^k}$, i.e., we consider the set $\{x + a \mid a \in \mathbb{F}_{q^k}\}$. As noted in [6,11,17], factor base preserving automorphisms of $\mathbb{F}_{(q^k)^n}$, which are provided by Kummer extensions, can be used to significantly reduce the number of variables involved in the linear algebra step. Indeed, the map $\sigma := \mathrm{Frob}^\ell : \alpha \to \alpha^q$ satisfies $\sigma(x) = \gamma x$ with $\gamma \in \mathbb{F}_{q^k}$, and thus preserves the factor base. Furthermore, for $\varphi := \sigma^k = \mathrm{Frob}^{\ell k} : \alpha \to \alpha^{q^k}$ we have $\varphi(x) = \mu x$ with $\mu \in \mathbb{F}_q$ a primitive n-th root of unity, and thus we find

$$(x + a)^{q^{kj+i}} = \sigma^{kj+i}(x + a) = \sigma^i(\varphi^j(x + a)) = \sigma^i(\mu^j x + a) = \mu^j \gamma^{e_i} x + a^{q^i} ,$$

where $e_0 = 0$ and $e_i = qe_{i-1} + 1$ for $1 \le i < k$; thus it follows that

$$\log\left(x + \frac{a^{q^i}}{\mu^j \gamma^{e_i}}\right) = q^{kj+i} \log(x + a)$$

for all $0 \le j < n$ and $0 \le i < k$.

The automorphism σ generates a group of order kn, which acts on the set of q^k factor base elements, thus dividing the factor base into about N orbits, where $N \approx \frac{q^k}{kn} \approx \frac{1}{k}q^{k-1}$ is the number of variables to consider.

2.3   Relation Generation

In order to generate relations between the factor base elements we use the method from [6, Sect. 3.1–4]. We exploit properties of polynomials of the form

$$F_B(X) := X^{q+1} + BX + B ,$$

which have been studied by Bluher [2] and Helleseth/Kholosha [10]. We recall in particular the following result of Bluher [2] (see also [6,10]):

Theorem 1. *The number of elements $B \in \mathbb{F}_{q^k}^\times$ such that the polynomial $F_B(X)$ splits completely over $\mathbb{F}_{q^k}$ equals*

$$\frac{q^{k-1} - 1}{q^2 - 1} \quad \textit{if } k \textit{ odd}, \qquad \frac{q^{k-1} - q}{q^2 - 1} \quad \textit{if } k \textit{ even}.$$

Let $B \in \mathbb{F}_{q^k}^\times$ be an element such that $F_B(X)$ splits and denote its roots by μ_i, for $i = 1, \ldots, q + 1$. For arbitrary $a, b \in \mathbb{F}_{q^k}$ (with $a^q \ne b$) there exists $c \in \mathbb{F}_{q^k}$ with $(a^q + b)^{q+1} = B(ab + c)^q$ and we then find that

$$f(X) := F_B\left(\frac{ab + c}{a^q + b} X + a\right) = X^{q+1} + aX^q + bX + c$$

and that $f(X)$ also splits over $\mathbb{F}_{q^k}$, with roots $\nu_i := \frac{ab+c}{a^q+b} \mu_i + a$.

Now by the definition of $\mathbb{F}_{(q^k)^n}$ we have $x^n = \gamma$ and thus $x^q = \gamma x$, with $\gamma \in \mathbb{F}_{q^k}$. Hence in $\mathbb{F}_{(q^k)^n}$ we have

$$f(x) = \gamma x^2 + a\gamma x + bx + c = \gamma(x^2 + (a + \tfrac{b}{\gamma})x + \tfrac{c}{\gamma}) = \gamma g(x) \,,$$

where $g(X) := X^2 + (a + \tfrac{b}{\gamma})X + \tfrac{c}{\gamma}$. Hence, if the polynomial $g(X)$ splits, i.e., if $g(X) = (X + \xi_1)(X + \xi_2)$, which heuristically occurs with probability $1/2$, then we find a relation of factor base elements, namely

$$\prod_{i=1}^{q+1}(x + \nu_i) = \gamma(x + \xi_1)(x + \xi_2) \,.$$

Such a relation corresponds to a linear relation between the logarithms of the factor base elements. Once we have found more than N relations we can solve the discrete logarithms of the factor base elements by means of linear algebra; see Sect. 3.3.

2.4   Individual Logarithms

After the logarithms of the factor base elements have been found, a general individual discrete logarithm can be computed, as is common, by a descent strategy. The basic idea of this method is trying to write an element, given by its polynomial representation over $\mathbb{F}_{q^k}$, as a product in $\mathbb{F}_{(q^k)^n}$ of factors represented by lower degree polynomials. By applying this principle recursively a descent tree is constructed, and one can eventually express a given target element by a product of factor base elements, thus solving the DLP.

While for large degree polynomials it is relatively easy to find an expression involving lower degree polynomials by a standard approach, this method becomes increasingly less efficient as the degree becomes smaller. In addition, the number of small degree polynomials in the descent tree grows significantly with lower degree. We therefore propose new methods for degree 2 elimination and small degree descent, which are inspired by the recent works [6] and [12] respectively.

Degree 2 Elimination. Given a polynomial $Q(X) := X^2 + q_1 X + q_0 \in \mathbb{F}_{q^k}[X]$ we aim at expressing the corresponding finite field element $Q(x) \in \mathbb{F}_{(q^k)^n}$ as a product of factor base elements. In essence, what we do is just the reverse of the degree one relation generation, with the polynomial $g(X)$ set to be $Q(X)$.

In particular, we compute – when possible – $a, b, c \in \mathbb{F}_{q^k}$ such that, up to a multiplicative constant in $\mathbb{F}_{q^k}^{\times}$, $Q(x) = x^2 + q_1 x + q_0$ equals $x^{q+1} + ax^q + bx + c$ where the polynomial $X^{q+1} + aX^q + bX + c$ splits into linear factors (cf. [6, Sect. 4.1]).

As $x^n = \gamma$ holds, we have $x^{q+1} + ax^q + bx + c = \gamma(x^2 + (a + \tfrac{b}{\gamma})x + \tfrac{c}{\gamma})$ and comparing coefficients we find $\gamma q_0 = c$ and $\gamma q_1 = \gamma a + b$. Now letting $B \in \mathbb{F}_{q^k}^{\times}$

be an element satisfying the splitting property of Theorem 1 and combining the previous equations with $(a^q + b)^{q+1} = B(ab + c)^q$ we arrive at the condition

$$(a^q + \gamma a + \gamma q_1)^{q+1} + B(\gamma a^2 + \gamma q_1 a + \gamma q_0)^q = 0.$$

Considering $\mathbb{F}_{q^k}$ as a degree k extension over $\mathbb{F}_q$ this equation gives a quadratic system in the k $\mathbb{F}_q$-components of a, which can be solved very fast by a Gröbner basis method.

Heuristically, for each of the above B's the probability of success of this method, i.e., when an $a \in \mathbb{F}_{q^k}$ as above exists, is $1/2$. Note that if $k = 3$ there is just one single B in the context of Theorem 1, and so this direct method fails in half of the cases. However, as noted earlier, this issue can be resolved under certain circumstances, e.g., for $\ell = 8$; see Sect. 4.4.

Small Degree Descent. The following describes the Gröbner basis descent of Joux [12] applied in the context of the polynomials $F_B(X) = X^{q+1} + BX + B$ of Theorem 1. Let $f(X)$ and $g(X)$ be polynomials over $\mathbb{F}_{q^k}$ of degree δ_f and δ_g respectively. We substitute X by the rational function $\frac{f(X)}{g(X)}$ and thus find that the polynomial

$$P(X) := f(X)^{q+1} + Bf(X)g(X)^q + Bg(X)^{q+1}$$

factors into polynomials of degree at most $\delta = \max\{\delta_f, \delta_g\}$. Since $x^q = \gamma x$ holds in $\mathbb{F}_{(q^k)^n}$ the element $P(x)$ can also be represented by a polynomial of degree 2δ.

Now given a monic polynomial $Q(X) \in \mathbb{F}_{q^k}[X]$ of degree 2δ (resp. $2\delta - 1$) to be eliminated we consider the equation $P(x) = Q(x)$ (resp. $P(x) = (x + a)Q(x)$ with some random fixed $a \in \mathbb{F}_{q^k}$). It results as above in a quadratic system of $\mathbb{F}_q$-variables representing the coefficients of $f(X)$ and $g(X)$ in $\mathbb{F}_{q^k}$, and can be solved by a Gröbner basis algorithm. In order to minimise the number of variables involved we set $f(X)$ to be monic of degree $\delta_f = \delta$ and $g(X)$ of degree $\delta_g = \delta - 1$, resulting in $k\delta + k\delta = 2k\delta$ variables in $\mathbb{F}_q$. Since the number of equations to be satisfied equals $2k\delta$ as well, we find a solution of this system with good probability.

Large Degree Descent. This part of the descent is somewhat classical (see [17] for example), but includes the degree balancing technique described in [6, Sect. 4], which makes the descent far more rapid when the base field $\mathbb{F}_{q^k}$ is a degree k extension of a non-prime field. In the finite field $\mathbb{F}_{(q^k)^n}$ we let $y := x^q$ and $\bar{x} := x^{2^{\ell-a}}$ for some suitably chosen integer $1 < a < k$. Then $y = \bar{x}^{2^a}$ and $\bar{x} = (\frac{y}{\gamma})^{2^{\ell-a}}$ holds. Now for given $Q(X) \in \mathbb{F}_{q^k}[X]$ of degree d representing $Q(y)$ we consider the lattice

$$L := \left\{(w_0, w_1) : Q(X) \mid (\tfrac{X}{\gamma})^{2^{\ell-a}} w_0(X) + w_1(X)\right\} \subseteq \mathbb{F}_{q^k}[X]^2.$$

By Gaussian lattice reduction we find a basis (u_0, u_1), (v_0, v_1) of L of degree $\approx d/2$ and can thus generate lattice elements $(w_0, w_1) = r(u_0, u_1) + s(v_0, v_1)$ of low degree. In $\mathbb{F}_{(q^k)^n}$ we then consider the equation

$$\bar{x}w_0(\bar{x}^{2^a}) + w_1(\bar{x}^{2^a}) = \bar{x}w_0(y) + w_1(y) = \left(\tfrac{y}{\gamma}\right)^{2^{\ell-a}} w_0(y) + w_1(y),$$

where the right-hand side is divisible by $Q(y)$ by construction, and a is chosen so as to make the degrees of both sides as close as possible. The descent is successful whenever a lattice element (w_0, w_1) is found such that the involved polynomials $Xw_0(X^{2^a}) + w_1(X^{2^a})$ and $\frac{1}{Q(x)}(X^{2^{\ell-a}}w_0(X) + \gamma^{2^{\ell-a}}w_1(X))$ are $(d-1)$-smooth, i.e., have only factors of degree less than d.

3 Other Essentials

In this section we give an explicit account of further basics required for a discrete logarithm computation.

3.1 Factorisation of the Group Order

The factorisation of the group order $|\mathbb{F}_{(q^k)^n}^{\times}| = 2^{\ell k n} - 1$ is of interest for several reasons. Firstly it indicates the difficulty of solving the associated DLP using the Pohlig-Hellman algorithm. Secondly it enables one to provably find a generator. Finally, it determines the small factors for which we apply Pollard's rho method, and the large factors for the linear algebra computation. Since the complexity of the Special Number Field Sieve [20] is much higher than the present DLP algorithms, it is unlikely that one can completely factorise $2^{\ell k n} - 1$ in cases of interest in a reasonable time. In these cases it is vital to at least know all the small prime factors of the group order, which can be accomplished using the Elliptic Curve Method [21] and the identity

$$2^{\ell k n} - 1 = \prod_{d \mid \ell k n} \Phi_d(2),$$

where $\Phi_d \in \mathbb{Z}[x]$ denotes the d-th cyclotomic polynomial.

3.2 Pohlig-Hellman and Pollard's Rho Method

In order to compute a discrete logarithm in a group G of order m we can use any factorisation of $m = m_1 \cdot \ldots \cdot m_r$ into pairwise coprime factors m_i and compute the discrete log modulo each factor. Indeed, if we are to compute $z = \log_\alpha \beta$ it suffices to compute $\log_{\alpha^{c_i}} \beta^{c_i}$ with $c_i = m/m_i$, which determines $z \bmod m_i$. With the information of $z \bmod m_i$ for all i one easily determines $z \pmod{m}$ by the Chinese Remainder theorem.

For the small prime (power) factors of m we use Pollard's rho method to compute the discrete logarithm modulo each factor. Regarding the large factors of m we find it most efficient to combine them into a single product m_*, so that in the linear algebra step of the index calculus method we work over the ring $\mathbb{Z}_{m_*}$. Note that each iteration of the Lanczos method that we use for the linear algebra problem requires the inversion of a random element in $\mathbb{Z}_{m_*}$; this is the reason why we separate the small factors of the group order from the large ones.

3.3   Linear Algebra

The relation generation phase of the index calculus method produces linear relations among the logarithms of the factor base elements. As the factor base logs
are also related by the automorphism group as explained in Sect. 2.2 the number
N of variables is reduced and the linear relations will have coefficients being
powers of 2. Once $M > N$ relations have been generated we have to find a
nonzero solution vector for the linear system. To ensure that the matrix is of
maximal rank $N - 1$ we generate $M \approx N + 100$ relations. As noted earlier the
number of variables N is expected to be about $\frac{q^k}{kn} \approx \frac{1}{k}q^{k-1}$.

We let B be the $M \times N$ matrix of the relations' coefficients, which is a matrix
of constant row-weight $q + 3$. We have to find a nonzero vector v of length N
such that $Bv = 0$ modulo m_*, the product of the large prime factors of the
group order m. A common approach in index calculus algorithms is to reduce
the matrix size at this stage by using a structured Gaussian elimination (SGE)
method. In our case, however, the matrix is not extremely sparse while its size
is quite moderate, hence the expected benefit from SGE would be minimal and
we refrained from this step.

We use the iterative Lanczos method [18,19] to solve the linear algebra problem, which we briefly describe here. Let $A = B^t B$, which is a symmetric $N \times N$
matrix. We let $v \in \mathbb{Z}_{m_*}^N$ be random, $w = Av$, and find a vector $x \in \mathbb{Z}_{m_*}^N$ such
that $Ax = w$ holds (since $A(x - v) = 0$ we have thus found a kernel element).
We compute the following iteration

$$w_0 = w, \quad v_0 = Aw_0, \quad w_1 = v_0 - \frac{(v_0, v_0)}{(v_0, w_0)}w_0$$

$$v_i = Aw_i, \quad w_{i+1} = v_i - \frac{(v_i, v_i)}{(v_i, w_i)}w_i - \frac{(v_i, v_{i-1})}{(v_{i-1}, w_{i-1})}w_{i-1}$$

and stop once $(v_j, w_j) = 0$; if $w_j \neq 0$ the algorithm fails, otherwise we find the
solution vector

$$x = \sum_{i=0}^{j-1} \frac{(w, w_i)}{(v_i, w_i)}w_i \,.$$

Performing the above iteration consists essentially of several matrix-vector
products, scalar-vector multiplications, and vector-vector inner products. As the
matrix is sparse and consists of entries being powers of 2 the matrix-vector
products can be carried out quite efficiently. Therefore, the scalar multiplications
and inner products consume a significant part of the computation time. We have
used a way to reduce the number of inner products per iteration, as was suggested
recently [23].

Indeed, using the A-orthogonality $(v_i, w_j) = w_i^t A w_j = 0$ for $i \neq j$ we find
that

$$(v_i, v_{i-1}) = (v_i, w_i) \quad \text{and} \quad (w, w_{i+1}) = -\frac{(v_i, v_i)}{(v_i, w_i)}(w, w_i) - \frac{(v_i, v_{i-1})}{(v_{i-1}, w_{i-1})}(w, w_{i-1}).$$

Now at each iteration, given w_i we compute the matrix-vector product Bw_i and
the inner product $a_i := (v_i, w_i) = (Bw_i, Bw_i)$, as well as $v_i = Aw_i = B^t(Bw_i)$

and $b_i := (v_i, v_i) = (Aw_i, Aw_i)$. We then have the simplified iteration

$$w_0 = w, \quad w_1 = v_0 - \frac{b_0}{a_0}w_0, \quad w_{i+1} = v_i - \frac{b_i}{a_i}w_i - \frac{a_i}{a_{i-1}}w_{i-1}$$

and the solution vector $x = \sum_{i=0}^{j-1} \frac{c_i}{a_i}w_i$, where $c_i := (w, w_i)$ can be computed by the iteration

$$c_0 = (w, w), \quad c_1 = a_0 - \frac{b_0}{a_0}c_0, \quad c_{i+1} = -\frac{b_i}{a_i}c_i - \frac{a_i}{a_{i-1}}c_{i-1}.$$

We see that each iteration requires merely two matrix-vector products, three scalar multiplications, and two inner products.

3.4 Target Element

In order to set ourselves a DLP challenge we construct the 'random' target element $\beta \in \mathbb{F}_{(q^k)^n}$ using the binary digits expansion of the mathematical constant π. More precisely, considering the q^k-ary expansion

$$\pi = 3 + \sum_{i=1}^{\infty} c_i\, q^{-ki} \quad \text{with} \quad c_i \in S_{q^k} := \{0, 1, \ldots, q^k - 1\}$$

we use a bijection between the sets S_{q^k} and $\mathbb{F}_{q^k}$, which is defined by the mappings $\varphi_q : \mathbb{F}_q \to \{0, \ldots, q-1\}$: $\sum_{i=0}^{\ell-1} a_i t^i \mapsto \sum_{i=0}^{\ell-1} a_i 2^i$ and $\varphi : \mathbb{F}_{q^k} \to S_{q^k}$: $\sum_{j=0}^{k-1} b_j w^j \mapsto \sum_{j=0}^{k-1} \varphi_q(b_j)q^j$, and construct in this way the target element

$$\beta_\pi := \sum_{i=0}^{n-1} \varphi^{-1}(c_{i+1})\, x^i \in \mathbb{F}_{(q^k)^n}.$$

4 Discrete Logarithms in $\mathbb{F}_{2^{6120}}$

In this section we document the breaking of a DLP in the case $\ell = 8$ and $k = 3$, i.e., in $\mathbb{F}_{2^{6120}}$. The salient features of the computation are:

- The relation generation for degree one elements took $15\,\mathrm{s}$[4].
- The corresponding linear algebra took 60.5 core-hours.
- In contrast to [12,15], we computed the logarithm of degree 2 irreducibles on the fly; each took on average 0.03 s.
- The descent was designed so as to significantly reduce the number of bottleneck (degree 6) eliminations. As a result, the individual logarithm phase took just under 689 core-hours.

---

[4] In our inital announcement [8] we stated a running time of 60 s for the relation generation. The reason for this higher running time was an unnecessary step of ordering the matrix entries, which we have discounted here.

4.1   Setup

We first defined $\mathbb{F}_{2^8}$ using the irreducible polynomial $T^8 + T^4 + T^3 + T + 1$. Letting t be a root of this polynomial, we defined $\mathbb{F}_{2^{24}}/\mathbb{F}_{2^8}$ using the irreducible polynomial $W^3 + t$. Letting w be a root of this polynomial, we finally defined $\mathbb{F}_{2^{6120}}/\mathbb{F}_{2^{24}}$ using the irreducible polynomial $X^{255} + w + 1$, where we denote a root of this polynomial by x.

We chose as a generator $g = x + w$, which has order $2^{6120} - 1$; this was proven via the prime factorisation of $2^{6120} - 1$, which is provided in [8]. As usual, the target element was set to be β_π as explained in Sect. 3.4.

4.2   Relation Generation

Our factor base is simply the set of degree one elements of $\mathbb{F}_{2^{6120}}/\mathbb{F}_{2^{24}}$. As detailed in Sect. 2.2, quotienting out by the action of the 8-th power of Frobenius produces 21,932 distinct orbits. To obtain relations, as explained in Sect. 2.3, we make essential use of the single polynomial $X^{257} + X + 1$, which splits completely over $\mathbb{F}_{2^{24}}$. In particular, letting $y := x^{256}$ so that $x = \frac{y}{w+1}$, the $\mathbb{F}_{2^{6120}}$ element $xy + ay + bx + c$ corresponds to $X^{257} + aX^{256} + bX + c$ on the one hand, and $\frac{X^2}{w+1} + aX + \frac{bX}{w+1} + c$ on the other. The first of these transforms to $X^{257} + X + 1$ if and only if $(a^{256} + b)^{257} = (ab + c)^{256}$. So for randomly chosen (a, b) we compute c and check whether the corresponding quadratic splits. If it does – which occurs with probability $1/2$ – we obtain a relation. Thanks to the simplicity of this approach, we collected 22,932 relations and wrote these to a matrix in 15 s using C++/NTL [24].

4.3   Linear Algebra

We took as our modulus the product of the largest 35 factors of $2^{6120} - 1$ listed in [8], which has bitlength 5121. We ran a parallelised C/GMP [9] implementation of Lanczos' algorithm on four of the Intel (Westmere) Xeon E5650 hex-core processors of ICHEC's SGI Altix ICE 8200EX Stokes cluster. This took 60.5 core-hours (just over 2.5 h wall time).

4.4   Individual Logarithm

Degree 2 Elimination. For computing the discrete logarithm of a degree two element $Q(x) = x^2 + q_1 x + q_0$ we try to equate $Q(x)$ with $x^{257} + ax^{256} + bx + c$, where $(a^{256} + b)^{257} = (ab + c)^{256}$. If this fails we apply the following strategy, making use of the fact that $\mathbb{F}_{2^{24}}$ can also be viewed as a field extension of $\mathbb{F}_{2^6}$. We consider $y = x^{256}$ and $\bar{x} = x^4$, so that $y = \bar{x}^{64}$ and $\bar{x} = (\frac{y}{\gamma})^4$ holds, and apply the large degree descent method to $\bar{Q}(X) := Q(\frac{X}{\gamma})$ (note that $\bar{Q}(y) = Q(x)$). Considering the lattice L (see Sect. 2.4) we construct a basis of the form $(X + u_0, u_1), (v_0, X + v_1)$, where $u_0, u_1, v_0, v_1 \in \mathbb{F}_{2^{24}}$. Then for $s \in \mathbb{F}_{2^{24}}$ we have lattice elements $(X + u_0 + sv_0, sX + u_1 + sv_1) \in L$. Now for each $B \in \mathbb{F}_{2^{24}}$ such that $X^{65} + BX + B$ splits, we solve for $s \in \mathbb{F}_{2^{24}}$ satisfying

$$(v_0 s^2 + (u_0 + v_1)s + u_1)^{64} = B(s^{64} + v_0 s + u_0)^{65},$$

which can be expressed as a quadratic system in the $\mathbb{F}_{2^6}$-components of s, and thus solved by a Gröbner basis computation over $\mathbb{F}_{2^6}$. We then have an equation

$$\bar{x}^{65} + a\bar{x}^{64} + b\bar{x} + c = \tfrac{1}{\gamma^4}(y^5 + by^4 + a\gamma^4 y + c\gamma^4)$$

with $a = s$, $b = \gamma s + q_1$, and $c = \frac{q_0}{\gamma}$, where the left-hand side polynomial splits, while the right-hand side polynomial contains $\bar{Q}(X)$.

The polynomial $X^5 + bX^4 + a\gamma^4 X + c\gamma^4 = \bar{Q}(X)R(X)$ has the property that $R(X)$ always factors into a linear and an irreducible quadratic polynomial over $\mathbb{F}_{q^k}$. Indeed, by a result of Bluher [2, Theorem 4.3], for any $B \in \mathbb{F}_{2^{24}}$ and any $d \geq 1$, the number of roots in $\mathbb{F}_{2^{24d}}$ of the polynomial $F_B(X) = X^5 + BX + B$ equals either 0, 1, 2, or 5. Since $X^5 + bX^4 + a\gamma^4 X + c\gamma^4$ can be rewritten as $X^5 + BX + B$ via a linear transformation (except when $a\gamma^4 = b^4$), the same holds also regarding the $\mathbb{F}_{2^{24d}}$-roots of this polynomial. Now applying Bluher's result for $d = 1$ we see that $R(X)$ can not split into linear factors, and by Bluher's result for $d = 3$ we conclude that $R(X)$ can not be irreducible. Hence, $R(X)$ is the product of linear and a quadratic polynomial, which we call $Q'(X)$.

Now if $Q'(X)$ is resolvable by the direct method, we have successfully eliminated the original polynomial $Q(X)$. The number of B such that $X^{65} + BX + B$ splits over $\mathbb{F}_q$ equals 64, according to Theorem 1, and by experiment, for each one the success probability to find a resolvable polynomial $Q'(X)$ is about 0.4.

Performing the Descent. Using C++/NTL we first used continued fractions to express the target element β_π as a ratio of two 27-smooth polynomials, which took 10 core-hours, and then we applied the three different descent strategies as explained in Sect. 2.4.

We used the large degree descent strategy to express all of the featured polynomials using polynomials of degree 6 or less. This took a further 495 core-hours. While we could have performed this part of the descent more efficiently, as noted above we opted to find expressions which resulted in a relatively small number of degree 6 polynomials – which are the bottleneck eliminations for the subsequent descent – namely 326.

For degrees 6 down to 3 we used the analogue of Joux's small degree elimination method, based on the same polynomial that we used for relation generation, i.e., $X^{257} + X + 1$, rather than the polynomial $X^{256} + X$ that was used in [15], since the resulting performance was slightly better. Finally, we performed the degree 2 elimination as outlined above.

For convenience we coded the eliminations of polynomials of degrees 6 down to 2 in Magma [3] V2.16-12, using Faugere's F4 algorithm [4]. The total time for this part was just over 183.5 core-hours on a 2 GHz AMD Opteron computer.

For the logarithm modulo the cofactor of our modulus we used either linear search or Pollard's rho method, which took 20 min in total in C++/NTL. Thus the total time for the descent was just under 689 h.

Finally, we found[5] that $\beta_\pi = g^{\log}$, with log =

13858759836397869262547571128312317100923636150389699236649593170451770028
01271780222348940986175813601314418350742563637306244268142932334742725215
98166126957928116825443110965404253837938808595404111035238027107772178822
93928187340345199973181514007348176651371535844927931455679735244624686031
79467501244756894744062749423560359365016740509334489092010298345222267322
47771897083223217282051573645013603613042367782716361877817938374393824313
01907362478638761841403754168112028404465938319290743685252639208772430477
54516312718252509681114514005027334043817696752552891273466393500982215708
44400380788516332496583882522436381918008200167032186350245107751346979596
31469615366671616895148194809106006673018476675813777394430387542983086720
54639181442568439117307472651461541934380416278336617397750571612363460962
36566875251277843062329973044475486561062204356908568471471279383781038538
81888446379698990607607984324812725202083970588643607121365057518670745694
85840723789169429253691408684171964795734810327114810217291628659735881740
96389913305607677858033996361734905537150362024720515772660781208855505434
33105576657001421187560294063357576385045750307908707437658530447052041132
02462922553757114575735552860602366993170394544793267182811289614232751427
87569425690532833283344049635521302596000897192512036695298807294032964530
95969137708720454634896013276009554410598019825524549320241283159389198478
81524179576919398171123661820636875299153651503611802144512343876568832561
49355994405051149585969163075307026647956035683671589546448539955132726112
03493865596129185620342224768038702907847352095116033447252547507168067262
36615872927203296061825120443121943571561392013409520378729752432544760815
54937002122953415949407262137232099852298394838422907643191397673290238344
18304604097585991592853653044569714531766804497370964833241561850441.

4.5 Total Running Time

The total running time is $689 + 60.5 = 749.5$ core-hours. Note that most of the computation (all except the linear algebra part) was performed on a personal computer. On a modern quad-core PC, the total running time would be around a week.

---

[5] Magma verification code for this solution is available from [8].

5   Complexity Considerations

In this section we prove a tighter complexity result than that given in [12] for the new small-degree stage of the descent. As stated in Sect. 1, the systems arising from the small-degree elimination in Sect. 2.4 are quadratic, but not bilinear. As such, they do not necessarily enjoy the same resolution complexity as bilinear quadratic systems, as given by a theorem due to Spaenlehauer [25, Corollary 6.30]. However, if one instead reverts to using the polynomial $X^q - X$, then one can argue as follows.

Let the fields under consideration be $\mathbb{F}_{(q^k)^n}$, with $k \geq 3$ fixed, $n \approx q\delta_1$ and $\delta_1 \geq 1$ a small integer, as per the field representation described in [6, Sect. 3.3], and $q \to \infty$. This is achieved by finding a polynomial p_1 of degree δ_1 such that $p_1(X^q) - X \equiv 0 \pmod{I(X)}$, with $I(X)$ irreducible of degree n. By letting $x \in \mathbb{F}_{(q^k)^n}$ be a root of $I(X)$ and $y := x^q$, one also has $x = p_1(y)$, and therefore two related representations of $\mathbb{F}_{(q^k)^n}$.

For simplicity we assume $\delta_1 = 1$; the case $\delta_1 > 1$ can be treated similarly. The cardinality of $\mathbb{F}_{(q^k)^n}$ is $\approx q^{kq}$ and we have

$$L_{q^{kq}}(1/4, c) = \exp\left((c + o(1))(kq \log q)^{1/4}(\log(kq \log q))^{3/4}\right)$$
$$= \exp\left((ck^{1/4} + o(1))\, q^{1/4} \log q\right). \tag{1}$$

We now recall Joux's elimination method. The final part of the descent starts with an element $Q(x)$ of degree $D \approx \alpha_1 q^{1/2}$ which is to be eliminated; here, α_1 is a constant that depends on the efficiency of the classical large-degree descent. For a parameter $1 < d < D/2$ yet to be optimised, we substitute $X = f(X)/g(X)$ into $X^q - X$ with $\deg(f) = d$ and $\deg(g) = D - d$, both with yet-to-be determined $\mathbb{F}_{q^k}$ coefficients. In this case one has the $\mathbb{F}_{(q^k)^n}$-relation

$$f(x)^q g(x) - f(x)g(x)^q = \left(f(x)^q g(x) - f(x)g(x)^q\right) \bmod I(x). \tag{2}$$

By the factorisation of $X^q - X$ over $\mathbb{F}_q$, the LHS of Eq. (2) has irreducible factors of degree at most $D - d$. On the RHS one stipulates that it be zero mod $Q(x)$. This condition can be expressed as a bilinear quadratic system in the dk $\mathbb{F}_q$-components of the coefficients of f and the $(D - d)k$ $\mathbb{F}_q$-components of the coefficients of g. Since $Q(x)$ has D coefficients in $\mathbb{F}_{q^k}$ one expects there to be $O(1)$ solutions to this system when both f and g are monic. Hence by varying the leading coefficient of one of them, one expects many solutions.

The degree of the RHS of Eq. (2) depends on the representation of the field $\mathbb{F}_{(q^k)^n}$. Recall that in Joux's field representation, one has $h_0(X)$, $h_1(X)$ of very low degree δ_{h_0}, δ_{h_1} such that $h_1(X)X^q - h_0(X) \equiv 0 \pmod{I(X)}$, with $I(X)$ irreducible of degree n and $n \approx q$. Now on the RHS of Eq. (2) one replaces each occurrence of x^q by $h_0(x)/h_1(x)$, and thus the cofactor of $Q(x)$ on the RHS has degree $(D - d)(\max\{\delta_{h_0}, \delta_{h_1}\} - 1)$. For each solution to the bilinear quadratic system, it is tested for $(D - d)$-smoothness, and when it is, one has successfully represented $Q(x)$ as a product of at most q field elements of degree at most $D - d$ (ignoring the negligible number of factors from the cofactor).

Using our field representation, recall that $y = x^q$ and hence

$$f(x)^q = \sum_{i=0}^{d} f_i^q y^i \quad \text{and} \quad g(x)^q = \sum_{j=0}^{D-d} g_j^q y^j .$$

Then also using $x = p_1(y)$, the RHS of Eq. (2) becomes:

$$\left(\sum_{i=0}^{d} f_i^q y^i \right) \left(\sum_{j=0}^{D-d} g_j p_1(y)^j \right) - \left(\sum_{i=0}^{d} f_i p_1(y)^i \right) \left(\sum_{j=0}^{D-d} g_j^q y^j \right),$$

so that the cofactor of $Q(y)$ has degree $(D - d)(\delta_1 - 1)$ in y.

By repeating the above elimination technique recursively for each element occurring in the product until only degree one or degree two elements remain, the logarithm of $Q(x)$ is computed. So what is the optimal d? Joux's analysis [12] indicates that $d = O(q^{1/4}(\log q)^{1/2})$ should be used, giving an overall complexity of $\exp\left((c' + o(1)) q^{1/4}(\log q)^{3/2}\right)$ for some c', which is $L_{q^{kq}}(1/4 + o(1), c')$, due to the presence of the extra $(\log q)^{1/2}$ factor, relative to Eq. (1).

However, one can instead set $d \approx \alpha_2 q^{1/4}$, as we now show (the constant α_2 is to be optimised later). Let $C(D, d)$ be the cost of expressing a degree D element as a product of elements of degree at most d, when the numerator f has degree d at each step. If $C_0(D, d)$ is the cost of resolving the corresponding bilinear quadratic system, we have

$$\begin{aligned}
C(D, d) &= C_0(D, d) + q \, C(D - d, d) \\
&= C_0(D, d) + q \left(C_0(D - d, d) + q \, C(D - 2d, d) \right) \\
&= \cdots = \sum_{i=0}^{\lfloor D/d \rfloor - 1} q^i C_0(D - id, d) .
\end{aligned}$$

Since $C_0(D - id, d) \leq C_0(D, d)$ for all i and since $\sum_{i=0}^{\lfloor D/d \rfloor - 1} q^i \leq q^{D/d}$ we get the upper bound

$$C(D, d) \leq q^{D/d} C_0(D, d) .$$

As in [12], we need the following essential lemma.

Lemma 1. ([25, Corollary 6.30]) *The arithmetic complexity (measured in $\mathbb{F}_q$-operations) of computing a Gröbner basis of a generic bilinear system $f_1, \ldots, f_{n_x + n_y} \in \mathbb{F}_q[x_0, \ldots, x_{n_x - 1}, y_0, \ldots, y_{n_y - 1}]$ with Faugere's F4 algorithm [4] is bounded by*

$$O\left(\min(n_x, n_y)(n_x + n_y) \binom{n_x + n_y + \min(n_x, n_y) + 2}{\min(n_x, n_y) + 2}^{\omega} \right),$$

where ω is the exponent of matrix multiplication.

Hence, using the estimate $\binom{a+2}{b+2} \leq (\frac{a}{b})^2 \binom{a}{b} \leq (\frac{a}{b})^2 (e\frac{a}{b})^b = e^b (\frac{a}{b})^{b+2}$, we have

$$C_0(D,d) = O\left(k^2 Dd\left(\frac{k(D+d)+2}{kd+2}\right)^\omega\right) = O\left(k^2 Dde^{k\omega d}\left(\frac{D+d}{d}\right)^{k\omega d + 2\omega}\right),$$

and, neglecting the lower order terms, we get

$$\log C_0(D,d) = \left(k\omega d \log(D/d)\right)(1 + o(1)).$$

Therefore, we have

$$\log C(D,d) = \left((D/d)\log q + k\omega d \log(D/d)\right)(1 + o(1))$$
$$= \left(\left(\frac{\alpha_1}{\alpha_2} + \frac{k\omega\alpha_2}{4}\right)q^{1/4}\log q\right)(1 + o(1)),$$

and in particular, for the optimal choice $\alpha_2 = (4\alpha_1/k\omega)^{1/2}$, we get

$$\log C(D,d) = \left((k\omega\alpha_1)^{1/2}q^{1/4}\log q\right)(1 + o(1)).$$

Thus, taking into account Eq. (1), we arrive at the complexity

$$C(D,d) = L_{q^{kq}}(1/4, \, k^{1/4}(\omega\alpha_1)^{1/2}). \tag{3}$$

Observe that the number of degree $d \approx \alpha_2 q^{1/4}$ elements in such an expression for the initial degree $D \approx \alpha_1 q^{1/2}$ element is $O(q^{(\alpha_1/\alpha_2)q^{1/4}})$. Note that this choice of d represents the optimal balance between the number of nodes in the descent tree at level d and the cost of resolving the bilinear systems.

Moreover, exactly the same argument shows that $C(\alpha_j q^{1/2^j}, \alpha_{j+1}q^{1/2^{j+1}}) = L_{q^{kq}}(1/2^{j+1})$, and so the cost of expressing each of the $L_{q^{kq}}(1/4)$ degree $\alpha_2 q^{1/4}$ elements in terms of elements of degree $\alpha_3 q^{1/8}$ is $L_{q^{kq}}(1/8)$, and therefore for any $j > 1$ the total cost down to degree $\alpha_j q^{1/2^j}$ never exceeds $L_{q^{kq}}(1/4)$. After $j = \lceil \log_2 \log_2 q \rceil$ of the above sequence of steps we have $\lfloor q^{1/2^j} \rfloor = 1$, and the total cost is precisely that given in Eq. (3).

As the complexity of the initial splitting of a target element into a product of elements of degree at most $\alpha_0 q^{3/4}$ is $L_{q^{kq}}(1/4)$, as is the complexity of classical descent from degree $\alpha_0 q^{3/4}$ to degree $\alpha_1 q^{1/2}$, the above tighter analysis demonstrates that for the fields considered, Joux's algorithm has complexity $L_{q^{kq}}(1/4)$ as well, for both his and our field representations. We have omitted the determination of the optimal parameters α_0 and α_1, since this is beyond our focus on proving that the full algorithm is $L(1/4)$.

References

1. Barreto, P.S.L.M., Galbraith, S.D., Ó' hÉigeartaigh, C., Scott, M.: Efficient pairing computation on supersingular abelian varieties. Des. Codes Cryptogr. 42(3), 239–271 (2007)

2. Bluher, A.W.: On $x^{q+1} + ax + b$. Finite Fields Appl. **10**(3), 285–305 (2004)
3. Bosma, W., Cannon, J., Playoust, C.: The magma algebra system. I. The user language. J. Symbolic Comput. **24**(3–4), 235–265 (1997)
4. Faugére, J.C.: A new efficient algorithm for computing Gröbner bases (F_4). J. Pure Appl. Algebra **139**(1–3), 61–88 (1999)
5. Gaudry, P., Hess, F., Smart, N.P.: Constructive and destructive facets of weil descent on elliptic curves. J. Cryptol. **15**(1), 19–46 (2002)
6. Göloğlu, F., Granger, R., McGuire, G., Zumbrägel, J.: On the function field sieve and the impact of higher splitting probabilities: application to discrete logarithms in $\mathbb{F}_{2^{1971}}$ and $\mathbb{F}_{2^{3164}}$. In: Canetti, R., Garay, J.A. (eds.) CRYPTO 2013, Part II. LNCS, vol. 8043, pp. 109–128. Springer, Heidelberg (2013)
7. Göloğlu, F., Granger, R., McGuire, G., Zumbrägel, J.: Discrete Logarithms in $GF(2^{1971})$. NMBRTHRY list, 19 Feb 2013
8. Göloğlu, F., Granger, R., McGuire, G., Zumbrägel, J.: Discrete Logarithms in $GF(2^{6120})$. NMBRTHRY list, 11 Apr 2013
9. Granlund, T.: The GMP development team: GNU MP: The GNU Multiple Precision Arithmetic Library, 5.0.5 edn. http://gmplib.org/ (2012)
10. Helleseth, T., Kholosha, A.: $x^{2^l+1} + x + a$ and related affine polynomials over (2^k). Cryptogr. Commun. **2**(1), 85–109 (2010)
11. Joux, A.: Faster index calculus for the medium prime case application to 1175-bit and 1425-bit finite fields. In: Johansson, T., Nguyen, P.Q. (eds.) EUROCRYPT 2013. LNCS, vol. 7881, pp. 177–193. Springer, Heidelberg (2013)
12. Joux, A.: A new index calculus algorithm with complexity $L(1/4 + o(1))$ in very small characteristic. Cryptology ePrint Archive, report 2013/095. http://eprint.iacr.org/ (2013)
13. Joux, A.: Personal communication (2013)
14. Joux, A.: Discrete Logarithms in $GF(2^{1778})$. NMBRTHRY list, 11 Feb 2013
15. Joux, A.: Discrete Logarithms in $GF(2^{4080})$. NMBRTHRY list, 22 Mar 2013
16. Joux, A.: Discrete Logarithms in $GF(2^{6168})$. NMBRTHRY list, 21 May 2013
17. Joux, A., Lercier, R.: The function field sieve in the medium prime case. In: Vaudenay, S. (ed.) EUROCRYPT 2006. LNCS, vol. 4004, pp. 254–270. Springer, Heidelberg (2006)
18. LaMacchia, B.A., Odlyzko, A.M.: Solving large sparse linear systems over finite fields. In: Menezes, A., Vanstone, S.A. (eds.) CRYPTO 1990. LNCS, vol. 537, pp. 109–133. Springer, Heidelberg (1991)
19. Lanczos, C.: An iteration method for the solution of the eigenvalue problem of linear differential and integral operators. J. Res. Nat. Bur. Stan. **45**, 255–282 (1950)
20. Lenstra, A.K., Lenstra Jr, H.W. (eds.): The Development of the Number Field Sieve. LNM, vol. 1554. Springer, Heidelberg (1993)
21. Lenstra Jr, H.W.: Factoring integers with elliptic curves. Ann. Math. (2) **126**(3), 649–673 (1987)
22. Lenstra Jr, H.W.: Finding isomorphisms between finite fields. Math. Comp. **56**(193), 329–347 (1991)
23. Popovyan, I.: Efficient parallelization of lanczos type algorithms. Cryptology ePrint Archive, Report 2011/416. http://eprint.iacr.org/ (2011)
24. Shoup, V.: NTL: A library for doing number theory, 5.5.2 edn. http://www.shoup.net/ntl/ (2009)
25. Spaenlehauer, P.J.: Solving multihomogeneous and determinantal systems algorithms - complexity - applications. Ph.D. thesis, Université Pierre et Marie Curie (UPMC) (2012)

Stream Ciphers
and Authenticated Encryption

How to Recover Any Byte of Plaintext on RC4

Toshihiro Ohigashi[1]([✉]), Takanori Isobe[2], Yuhei Watanabe[2],
and Masakatu Morii[2]

[1] Hiroshima University, 1-4-2 Kagamiyama,
Higashi-Hiroshima, Hiroshima 739-8511, Japan
ohigashi@hiroshima-u.ac.jp
[2] Kobe University, 1-1 Rokkoudai, Nada-ku, Kobe 657-8501, Japan
Takanori.Isobe@jp.sony.com
yuheiwatanabe@stu.kobe-u.ac.jp
mmorii@kobe-u.ac.jp

Abstract. In FSE 2013, Isobe et al. proposed efficient plaintext recovery
attacks on RC4 in the broadcast setting where the same plaintext is
encrypted with different user keys. Their attack is able to recover first
1000 terabytes of a plaintext with probability of almost one, given 2^{34}
ciphertexts encrypted by different keys. Since their attack essentially
exploits biases in the initial (1st to 257th) bytes of the keystream, it
does not work any more if such initial bytes are disregarded. This paper
proposes two advanced plaintext recovery attacks that can recover *any*
byte of a plaintext without relying on initial biases, i.e., our attacks are
feasible even if initial bytes of the keystream are disregarded. The first
attack is the modified Isobe et al.'s attack. Using the partial knowledge
of the target plaintext, e.g., only 6 bytes of the plaintext, the other bytes
can be recovered with the high probability from 2^{34} ciphertexts. The
second attack does not require any previous knowledge of a plaintext. In
order to achieve it, we develop a *guess-and-determine* plaintext recovery
method based on two strong long-term biases. Given 2^{35} ciphertexts, any
byte of a plaintext can be recovered with probability close to one.

Keywords: RC4 · Broadcast setting · Plaintext recovery attack · Bias ·
Guess-and-determine attack · Multi-session setting · RC4-drop

1 Introduction

RC4, designed by Rivest in 1987, is one of most widely used stream ciphers in
the world. It is adopted in many software applications and standard protocols
such as SSL/TLS, WEP, Microsoft Lotus and Oracle secure SQL. RC4 consists
of a key scheduling algorithm (KSA) and a pseudo-random generation algorithm
(PRGA). The KSA converts a user-provided variable-length key (typically, 5–32
bytes) into an initial state S consisting of a permutation of $\{0, 1, 2, \ldots, N-1\}$,
where N is typically 256. The PRGA generates a keystream Z_1, Z_2, $\ldots$, Z_r,
$\ldots$ from S, where r is a round number of the PRGA. Z_r is XOR-ed with the

T. Lange, K. Lauter, and P. Lisoněk (Eds.): SAC 2013, LNCS 8282, pp. 155–173, 2014.
DOI: 10.1007/978-3-662-43414-7_8, © Springer-Verlag Berlin Heidelberg 2014

r-th plaintext byte P_r to obtain the ciphertext byte C_r. The algorithm of RC4 is shown in Algorithm 1, where $+$ denotes arithmetic addition modulo N, ℓ is the key length, and i and j are used to point to the locations of S, respectively. Then, $S[x]$ denotes the value of S indexed x.

In FSE 2001, Mantin and Shamir proposed a plaintext recovery attack on RC4 in the broadcast setting where the same plaintext is encrypted with different user keys [12]. Using a bias of Z_2, a second byte of the plaintext is recovered from $\Omega(N)$ ciphertexts encrypted with randomly-chosen different keys. In FSE 2011, Maitra, Paul and Sen Gupta showed that $Z_3, Z_4, \ldots, Z_{255}$ are also biased to 0 [9]. The bytes 3 to 255 are also obtained in the broadcast setting, from $\Omega(N^3)$ ciphertexts. In FSE 2013, Isobe et al. introduced several new biases in the initial bytes of the RC4 keystream, and constructed a cumulative list of strong biases in the first 257 bytes with theoretical reasons [7]. They demonstrated plaintext recovery attacks using their strong biases set with typical parameters of $N = 256$ and $\ell = 16$ (128-bit key). 2^{32} ciphertexts encrypting the same plaintext enable to extract first 257 bytes of a plaintext with probability more than 0.8. Using these initial biases in conjunction with the digraph repetition bias proposed by Mantin in EUROCRYPT 2005 [11], the consecutive first 1000 terabytes of a plaintext is theoretically recovered with probability of almost one from 2^{34} ciphertexts encrypted by different keys. After that, AlFardan et al. also proposed similar plaintext recovery attack of the first 256 bytes [1] independently of [7], and this attack can recover first 256 bytes of a plaintext with probability more than 0.96 from 2^{32} ciphertexts encrypted by different keys. Note that broadcast attacks [1,7] can be converted into the attacks for the multi-session setting of SSL/TLS where the target plaintext blocks are repeatedly sent in the same position in the plaintexts in multiple sessions [3].

Previous plaintext recovery attacks essentially exploit biases in the 1st to 257th bytes of the keystream. If the initial 256/512/768 bytes of the keystream are disregarded, as recommended in case of RC4 usages, it does not work any more as mentioned in [7]. Thus, RC4 that disregards the first n bytes of a keystream seem to be secure against above attacks for $n > 257$.

This paper proposes two advanced plaintext recovery attacks that can recover *any* byte of a plaintext without relying on initial biases of the keystream, i.e., our attacks are feasible even if initial bytes of the keystream are disregarded, unlike Isobe et al. and AlFardan et al.'s attacks. To begin with, we improve Isobe et al.'s attack so that it works without initial biases of a keystream. In particular, we assume that an attacker knows some bytes of the target plaintext, e.g., fixed header information. Using the digraph repetition biases in forward and backward manners, the other bytes of the plaintext are recovered from the partial knowledge of the plaintext. In our attack, if only consecutive 6 bytes of the target plaintexts are known, 1000 terabytes of the target plaintext can be recovered with probability of about 0.636 from 2^{34} ciphertexts. The number of required ciphertexts of this attack is same as that of Isobe et al.'s attack, while Isobe et al.'s attack needs the initial 257 bytes of the keystream. The second attack does not require any previous knowledge of a plaintext. In order to achieve

---

Algorithm 1. RC4 Algorithm

KSA($K[0 \ldots \ell - 1]$):	PRGA(K):
for $i = 0$ to $N - 1$ do	$i \leftarrow 0$
$\quad S[i] \leftarrow i$	$j \leftarrow 0$
end for	$S \leftarrow KSA(K)$
$j \leftarrow 0$	loop
for $i = 0$ to $N - 1$ do	$\quad i \leftarrow i + 1$
$\quad j \leftarrow j + S[i] + K[i \bmod \ell]$	$\quad j \leftarrow j + S[i]$
$\quad$ Swap $S[i]$ and $S[j]$	$\quad$ Swap $S[i]$ and $S[j]$
end for	$\quad$ Output $Z \leftarrow S[S[i] + S[j]]$
	end loop

---

it, we develop a novel *guess-and-determine* plaintext recovery method based on two strong long-term biases, i.e., digraph repetition biases [11] and Fluhrer-McGrew biases [4]. The basic idea behind our guess-and-determine attack is that two biases are used for the detection the wrong candidates of plaintext bytes. Given 2^{35} ciphertext encrypted by different keys, any byte of a plaintext can be recovered with probability close to one[1].

We emphasize that our attacks are applicable even if any number of initial bytes of the keystream are disregarded, with almost same amount of ciphertexts as Isobe et al.'s attack. Therefore, our work reveals that the RC4 implementation that disregards the first n bytes of a keystream is also not secure even if n is enough large (e.g. $n = 3072$).

2 Preliminary

In this section, we introduce two known long-term biases, which occur in any keystream bytes, because our attacks are based on them. Then we describe previous plaintext recovery attacks on RC4 in the broadcast setting.

2.1 Long-term Bias

As a long-term bias, following two types of biases were proposed.

Bias of Digraph Probabilities (FM00 Bias). Fluhrer and McGrew showed a long-term bias of digraph probabilities in the RC4 keystream, called the *FM00 bias*. It is a bias of 2-byte word of the keystream with the condition of index i ($= r \bmod N$) [4], and consists of 12 positive or negative events. The detail of the FM00 bias is shown in Table 1.

---

[1] Independently of our work, other plaintext recovery attacks on RC4 implementation which disregards the first n bytes of a keystream, was recently reported in [1,2]. The attack uses only the Fluhrer-McGrew biases with the sophisticated count-up method, and obtains experimental results similar to that of our attack.

Table 1. Events of the FM00 bias with the condition of index i $(= r \bmod N)$

Condition of event	Digraph (Z_r, Z_{r+1})	$\Pr(Z_r \wedge Z_{r+1})$
$i = 1$	$(0,0)$	$N^{-2} \cdot (1 + 2 \cdot N^{-1})$
$i \neq 1, N-1$	$(0,0)$	$N^{-2} \cdot (1 + N^{-1})$
$i \neq 0, 1$	$(0,1)$	$N^{-2} \cdot (1 + N^{-1})$
$i \neq N-2$	$(i+1, N-1)$	$N^{-2} \cdot (1 + N^{-1})$
$i \neq 1, N-2$	$(N-1, i+1)$	$N^{-2} \cdot (1 + N^{-1})$
$i \neq 0, N-3, N-2, N-1$	$(N-1, i+2)$	$N^{-2} \cdot (1 + N^{-1})$
$i = N-2$	$(N-1, 0)$	$N^{-2} \cdot (1 + N^{-1})$
$i = N-1$	$(N-1, 1)$	$N^{-2} \cdot (1 + N^{-1})$
$i = 0, 1$	$(N-1, 2)$	$N^{-2} \cdot (1 + N^{-1})$
$i = 2$	$(N/2+1, N/2+1)$	$N^{-2} \cdot (1 + N^{-1})$
$i \neq N-2$	$(N-1, N-1)$	$N^{-2} \cdot (1 - N^{-1})$
$i \neq 0, N-1$	$(0, i+1)$	$N^{-2} \cdot (1 - N^{-1})$

The Digraph Repetition Bias ($ABSAB$ Bias). Mantin found another long-term bias of digraph distribution in the RC4 keystream [11], called the $ABSAB$ bias. Assuming A and B are two words of the keystream, the digraph AB tends to repeat with short gaps S between them, e.g., $ABAB$, $ABCAB$ and $ABCDAB$, where gap S is defined as zero, C, and CD, respectively. The detail of the $ABSAB$ bias is as follows,

$$Z_r \parallel Z_{r+1} = Z_{r+2+G} \parallel Z_{r+3+G} \quad \text{for } G \geq 0, \tag{1}$$

where $\parallel$ is a concatenation. The probability that Eq. (1) holds is given as Theorem 1.

Theorem 1 [11]. *For small values of G the probability of the pattern $ABSAB$ in RC4 keystream, where S is a G-byte string, is $(1 + e^{(-4-8G)/N}/N) \cdot 1/N^2$.*

2.2   Previous Works

This section briefly reviews known attacks on RC4 in the broadcast setting where the same plaintext is encrypted with different randomly-chosen keys.

Mantin-Shamir (MS) Attack. Mantin and Shamir first presented broadcast RC4 attacks. Their attacks exploit a bias of second byte of keystream, Z_2 [12] as follows.

Theorem 2 [12]. *Assume that the initial permutation S is randomly chosen from the set of all the possible permutations of $\{0, 1, 2, \ldots, N-1\}$. Then the probability that the second output byte of RC4 is 0 is approximately $\frac{2}{N}$.*

This probability is estimated as $\frac{2}{256}$ when $N = 256$. Based on this bias, a distinguishing attack and a plaintext recovery attack on RC4 in the broadcast setting are demonstrated by Theorems 3 and 4, respectively.

Theorem 3 [12]. *Let X and Y be two distributions, and suppose that the event e happens in X with probability p and in Y with probability $p \cdot (1 + q)$. Then for small p and q, $O(\frac{1}{p \cdot q^2})$ samples suffice to distinguish X from Y with a constant probability of success.*

In this case, p and q are given as $p = 1/N$ and $q = 1$. The number of samples is about $\frac{1}{p \cdot q^2} = N$.

Theorem 4 [12]. *Let P be a plaintext, and let $C^{(1)}, C^{(2)}, \ldots, C^{(k)}$ be the RC4 encryptions of P under k uniformly distributed keys. Then, if $k = \Omega(N)$, the second byte of P can be reliably extracted from $C^{(1)}, C^{(2)}, \ldots, C^{(k)}$.*

According to the relation $C_2^{(i)} = P_2^{(i)} \oplus Z_2^{(i)}$, if $Z_2^{(i)} = 0$ holds, then $C_2^{(i)}$ is same as $P_2^{(i)}$. From Theorem 2, $Z_2 = 0$ occurs with twice the expected probability of a random one. Thus, most frequent byte in amongst $C_2^{(1)}, C_2^{(2)}, \ldots, C_2^{(k)}$ is likely to be P_2 itself. When $N = 256$, it requires more than 2^8 ciphertexts encrypted with randomly-chosen keys.

Maitra-Paul-Sen Gupta (MPS) Attack. Maitra, Paul and Sen Gupta showed that $Z_3, Z_4, \ldots, Z_{255}$ are also biased to 0 [6,9]. Although Mantin and Shamir assume that an initial permutation S is random, Maitra et al. exploit biases of S after the KSA [10]. Then the 3rd to 255th bytes of a plaintext are obtained from $\Omega(N^3)$ ciphertexts encrypted with different keys.

Isobe-Ohigashi-Watanabe-Morii (IOWM) Attack. Isobe et al. proposed a full plaintext recovery attack, which is able to extract the full bytes of a plaintext on RC4 from ciphertexts in the broadcast setting [7]. Their attack consists of two phases: an initial byte recovery phase and a sequential recovery phase for finding later bytes of a plaintext.

In the initial byte recovery phase, the first 257 bytes of a plaintext are recovered by using the cumulative bias set of $Z_1, Z_2, \ldots, Z_{257}$. Their cumulative bias set includes a conditional bias $Z_1 = 0 | Z_2 = 0$ [7] and single byte biases $Z_2 = 0$ [12], $Z_3 = 131$ [7], $Z_r = 0$ for $3 \leq r \leq 255$ [6,9], $Z_r = r$ for $3 \leq r \leq 255$ [7], $Z_{16} = 240$ [5], $Z_r = (256 - r)$ for $r = 32, 48, 64, 80, 96, 112$ [7], and $Z_{256} \neq 0$ [7], $Z_{257} = 0$ [7] (when $N = 256$ and $\ell = 16$). Given 2^{32} ciphertexts encrypted by randomly-chosen keys, the first 257 bytes of a plaintext are extracted with probability more than 0.8.

In the sequential recovery phase, the later bytes (after P_{258}) are sequentially recovered with the first 257 bytes of the plaintext, which were already obtained in the initial byte recovery phase. The sequential algorithm effectively uses a long-term bias, the *ABSAB* bias [11]. In particular, *ABSAB* biases with different G are simultaneously used for enhancing the attack, using the following lemmas for the discrimination.

Lemma 1 [11]. *Let X and Y be two distributions and suppose that the independent events $\{e_i : 1 \leq i \leq k\}$ occur with probabilities $\Pr_X(e_i) = p_i$ in X and*

$\Pr_Y(e_i) = (1 + q_i) \cdot p_i$ in Y. Then the discrimination D of the distributions is $\sum_i p_i \cdot q_i^2$.

The number of required samples for distinguishing the biased distribution from the random distribution with probability of $1 - \alpha$ is given as the following lemma.

Lemma 2 [11]. *The number of samples that is required for distinguishing two distributions that have discrimination D with success rate $1 - \alpha$ (for both directions) is $(1/D) \cdot (1 - 2\alpha) \cdot log_2 \frac{1-\alpha}{\alpha}$.*

This lemma shows that in the broadcast RC4 attack, once the discrimination D and the number of samples k are given, the success probability $\Pr_{distinguish}$ for distinguishing the distribution of correct candidate plaintext byte (the biased distribution) from the distribution of one wrong candidate of plaintext byte (a random distribution) always becomes constant. The success probability for recovering plaintext bytes depends on $\Pr_{distinguish}$. Thus if k is fixed, the success probability only depends on D.

In their attack, the following equation regarding the $ABSAB$ bias is used.

$$(C_r \parallel C_{r+1}) \oplus (C_{r+2+G} \parallel C_{r+3+G})$$
$$= (P_r \oplus Z_r \parallel P_{r+1} \oplus Z_{r+1}) \oplus (P_{r+2+G} \oplus Z_{r+2+G} \parallel P_{r+3+G} \oplus Z_{r+3+G})$$
$$= (P_r \oplus P_{r+2+G} \oplus Z_r \oplus Z_{r+2+G} \parallel P_{r+1} \oplus P_{r+3+G} \oplus Z_{r+1} \oplus Z_{r+3+G}). \quad (2)$$

Assuming that Eq. (1) (event of the $ABSAB$ bias) holds, the relation of plaintexts and ciphertexts without keystreams is obtained, i.e., $(C_r \parallel C_{r+1}) \oplus (C_{r+2+G} \parallel C_{r+3+G}) = (P_r \oplus P_{r+2+G} \parallel P_{r+1} \oplus P_{r+3+G}) = (P_r \parallel P_{r+1}) \oplus (P_{r+2+G} \parallel P_{r+3+G})$. For combining these relations with different G to enhance the biases, the algorithm uses the knowledge of pre-guessed plaintext bytes. For example, in the cases of $(r = r'$ and $G = 1)$ and $(r = r' + 1$ and $G = 0)$, right parts of equations are given as $(P_{r'} \parallel P_{r'+1}) \oplus (P_{r'+3} \parallel P_{r'+4})$ and $(P_{r'+1} \parallel P_{r'+2}) \oplus (P_{r'+3} \parallel P_{r'+4})$, respectively. Then, if $P_{r'}, P_{r'+1}$, and $P_{r'+2}$ are already known, the two equations with respected to $(P_{r'+3} \parallel P_{r'+4})$ is obtained by transposing $P_{r'}, P_{r'+1}$, and $P_{r'+2}$ to the left part of the equation. Then, these equations with different G can be merged.

Suppose that $P_1, P_2, \ldots, P_{257}$ are guessed by the cumulative bias set. Then, the sequential algorithm for recovering P_r for $r = 258, 259, \ldots, P_{MAX}$, from k ciphertexts $C^{(1)}, C^{(2)}, \ldots, C^{(k)}$ encrypted by different keys, by using $ABSAB$ biases of $G = 0, 1, \ldots, G_{MAX}$ is given as follows.

Step 1 Obtain $C_{258-3-G_{MAX}}, C_{258-2-G_{MAX}}, \ldots, C_{P_{MAX}}$ in each ciphertext, and make frequency tables $T_{count}[r][G]$ of $(C_{r-3-G} \parallel C_{r-2-G}) \oplus (C_{r-1} \parallel C_r)$ for all $r = 258, 259, \ldots, P_{MAX}$ and $G = 0, 1, \ldots, G_{MAX}$, where $(C_{r-3-G} \parallel C_{r-2-G}) \oplus (C_{r-1} \parallel C_r) = (P_{r-3-G} \parallel P_{r-2-G}) \oplus (P_{r-1} \parallel P_r)$ only if Eq. (1) holds.

Step 2 Set $r = 258$.

Step 3 Guess the value of P_r.

Step 3.1 For $G = 0, 1, \ldots, G_{MAX}$, convert $T_{count}[r][G]$ into a frequency table $T_{marge}[r]$ of $(P_{r-1} \| P_r)$ by using pre-guessed values of $P_{r-3-G_{MAX}}$, $\ldots, P_{r-2}$, and merge counter values of all tables.

Step 3.2 Make a frequency table $T_{guess}[r]$ indexed by only P_r from $T_{marge}[r]$ with knowledge of the P_{r-1}. To put it more precisely, using a pre-guessed value of P_{r-1}, only tables $T_{marge}[r]$ corresponding to the value of P_{r-1} is taken into consideration. Finally, regard most frequency one in table $T_{guess}[r]$ as the correct P_r.

Step 4 Increment r. If $r = P_{MAX} + 1$, terminate this algorithm. Otherwise, go to Step 3.

Isobe et al. theoretically showed that this algorithm can recover consecutive 1000 terabytes of a plaintext from 2^{34} ciphertexts when $G_{MAX} = 63$ ($D = 2^{-28.03}$) is adopted.

Countermeasure. These attacks essentially exploit biases in the initial (1st to 257th) bytes of the RC4 keystream. If initial bytes of the keystream are disregarded, it does not work any more as mentioned in [7]. Thus, the RC4-drop(257) is considered as a countermeasure against previous plaintext recovery attacks, where RC4-drop(n) is an RC4 implementation that disregards the first n bytes of a keystream[2].

In addition, Mironov also recommended $n = 512$ or 768, and gave a conservative recommended parameter $n = 3072$ based on the experimental data for avoiding initial bytes biases [13].

3 Plaintext Recovery Attack Using Known Partial Plaintext Bytes

In this section, we propose a plaintext recovery attack that is feasible even if initial bytes of a keystream are disregarded, unlike previous attacks. We improve Isobe et al.'s attack so that it works without initial biases of the keystream. In particular, we suppose that an attacker has the partial knowledge of a target plaintext, e.g., fixed header information. This assumption is reasonable in the practical usage on RC4. Then, with partial knowledge of the target plaintext, the other bytes of the plaintext can be recovered by using $ABSAB$ biases.

For the simplification, the encryption on RC4-drop(n) denotes $C_r = P_r \oplus Z_{r+n} = P_r \oplus Z_{r^*}$ where $r^* = r + n$.

3.1 Attack Functions

We give two functions based on $ABSAB$ biases for recovering an unknown byte of the plaintext.

---

[2] RC4-drop(n) is a generalized implementation of the countermeasure written by [13], and this is defined at http://www.users.zetnet.co.uk/hopwood/crypto/scan/cs.html.

Algorithm 2. $f_{ABSAB\_F}()$

Require: r, /* round number of a plaintext to be guessed */
G_{MAX}, /* parameter of the ABSAB bias*/
$P_{r-G_{MAX}-3}, \ldots, P_{r-1}$, /* known plaintext bytes */
$(C_{r-G_{MAX}-3}, \ldots, C_r)$s of $C^{(1)}, C^{(2)}, \ldots, C^{(k)}$ /* bytes of k ciphertexts encrypted by different keys */

Ensure: P_r
1: **for** $G = 0$ **to** G_{MAX} **do**
2:    Make frequency tables $T_{count}[r][G]$ of $(C_{r-3-G} \| C_{r-2-G}) \oplus (C_{r-1} \| C_r)$ from all ciphertexts $C^{(1)}, C^{(2)}, \ldots, C^{(k)}$.
3:    Convert $T_{count}[r][G]$ into a frequency table $T_{marge}[r]$ of $(P_{r-1} \| P_r)$ by $P_{r-3-G_{MAX}}, \ldots, P_{r-2}$, and merge counter values of all tables.
4: **end for**
5: Make a frequency table $T_{guess}[r]$ indexed by only P_r from $T_{marge}[r]$ with knowledge of P_{r-1}. To put it more precisely, using a pre-guessed value of P_{r-1}, only tables $T_{marge}[r]$ corresponding to the value of P_{r-1} is taken into consideration.
6: Regard most frequency one in table $T_{guess}[r]$ as the correct P_r.
7: Output P_r

$f_{ABSAB\_F}()$: Find an unknown byte P_r from pre-known consecutive $(G_{MAX} + 3)$ bytes of a plaintext $P_{r-G_{MAX}-3}, \ldots, P_{r-1}$ (See Algorithm 2).
$f_{ABSAB\_B}()$: Find an unknown byte P_r from pre-known consecutive $(G_{MAX} + 3)$ bytes of a plaintext $P_{r+1}, \ldots, P_{r+G_{MAX}+3}$.

The algorithm of $f_{ABSAB\_B}()$ is given by replacing "−" of subscripts of variables in Algorithm 2 to "+". These functions can be obtained from Step 1 and Step 3 of the IOWM attack. Figure 1 (Fig. 3) illustrates the procedures of $f_{ABSAB\_F}()$ and $f_{ABSAB\_B}()$. By using above two functions, all plaintext bytes can be recovered from the partial knowledge of the plaintext and the corresponding ciphertexts.

3.2   Attack Procedure

Suppose that x bytes of a target plaintext, $P_r, \ldots P_{r+x-1}$, are given. An attacker aims to recover the next byte (P_{r+x}) or the previous byte (P_{r-1}) of the known plaintext bytes by using $f_{ABSAB\_F}()$ or $f_{ABSAB\_B}()$, respectively. If (P_{r+x}) or (P_{r-1}) is successfully recovered, the attacker recovers (P_{r+x+1}) or (P_{r-2}) with knowledge of (P_{r+x}) or (P_{r-1}). Since G_{MAX} increases, the probability for recovering a plaintext byte also increases in the next step.

Our attack repeats above procedure until the all plaintext bytes are found. After G_{MAX} reaches 63, G_{MAX} is fixed since the increase of D is converged around $G_{MAX} = 63$ as mentioned in [7]. Figure 2 shows that our plaintext recovery attack using known partial plaintext bytes when consecutive 6 bytes of a target plaintext are given.

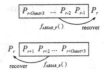

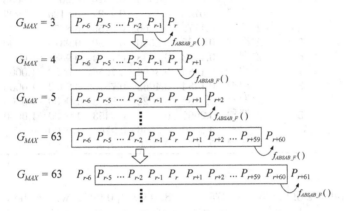

Fig. 1. Forward and backward functions for recovering one byte of a target plaintext using the partial knowledge of the plaintext and $ABSAB$ biases

Fig. 2. A plaintext recovery attack using the known partial plaintext bytes when consecutive 6 bytes of a target plaintext are known

3.3   Experimental Results

We evaluate our plaintext recovery attack on RC4-drop(n) in the broadcast setting by the computer experiment when $N = 256$ and $n = 3072$, which is a conservative recommended parameter given in [13]. Then, ciphertext C is expressed as $(C_1, C_2, \ldots, C_r, \ldots) = (P_1 \oplus Z_{1+3072}, P_2 \oplus Z_{2+3072}, \ldots, P_r \oplus Z_{r+3072}, \ldots)$.

In order to estimate the success probability of our attack, we evaluate the probabilities for recovering the one byte of the target plaintext by $f_{ABSAB\_F}()$ and $f_{ABSAB\_B}()$. The probabilities dependent on G_{MAX} and the number of obtained ciphertexts, but does not depend on the round number r. Thus, our experiment uses parameters such that $G_{MAX} = 0, 1, 2, 3, 4, 5, 6, 7, 8, 9, 15, 31, 63$ and $2^{31}, 2^{32}, \ldots, 2^{36}$ ciphertexts.

Table 2 shows the experimental result for 128 different plaintexts when $r = 128$, $n = 3072$, and the number of known plaintext bytes and the discrimination D and corresponding G_{MAX}. The success probability for recovering P_r increases with the increasing the value of G_{MAX} and D.

For the estimation of the impact in the realistic environment, let us consider the situation of Fig. 2 where an attacker knows consecutive *only 6 bytes* of a target plaintext. Suppose that 2^{34} ciphertexts encrypted by randomly-chosen keys are obtained, the probability for recovering P_r by $f_{ABSAB\_F}()$ with $G_{MAX} = 3$ is estimated as 0.8125. Similarly, $P_{r+1}, P_{r+2}, \ldots P_{r+5}$ are recovered by $f_{ABSAB\_F}()$

Table 2. The probabilities for recovering P_{128} by using $f_{ABSAB\_F}()$ and $P_{128-G_{MAX}-3}$, $\ldots, P_{127}$ when $n = 3072$

# of known plaintext bytes	G_{MAX}	D	# of ciphertexts					
			2^{31}	2^{32}	2^{33}	2^{34}	2^{35}	2^{36}
3	0	$2^{-32.05}$	0.0078	0.0547	0.0625	0.1250	0.4609	0.8750
4	1	$2^{-31.09}$	0.0156	0.0469	0.1797	0.4141	0.8516	0.9766
5	2	$2^{-31.55}$	0.0625	0.1484	0.3516	0.6641	0.9688	1.0000
6	3	$2^{-30.18}$	0.0703	0.1875	0.4297	0.8125	0.9922	1.0000
7	4	$2^{-29.90}$	0.1172	0.2266	0.5156	0.8750	0.9922	1.0000
8	5	$2^{-29.68}$	0.0938	0.2656	0.6250	0.9375	1.0000	1.0000
9	6	$2^{-29.50}$	0.1563	0.3438	0.7344	0.9688	1.0000	n/a
10	7	$2^{-29.35}$	0.1484	0.3594	0.7656	0.9922	1.0000	n/a
11	8	$2^{-29.22}$	0.1484	0.4063	0.7578	0.9922	1.0000	n/a
12	9	$2^{-29.11}$	0.1484	0.4922	0.8203	1.0000	1.0000	n/a
18	15	$2^{-28.66}$	0.2969	0.6172	0.9453	1.0000	1.0000	n/a
34	31	$2^{-28.21}$	0.3359	0.7656	0.9766	1.0000	n/a	n/a
66	63	$2^{-28.03}$	0.3672	0.7656	0.9766	1.0000	n/a	n/a

with probabilities of 0.8750, 0.9375, 0.9688, 0.9922, 0.9922, where these parameters are $G_{MAX} = 4, 5, 6, 7, 8$, respectively. Then, the attacker obtains the consecutive $12(= 6 + 6)$ bytes with probability of $(0.8125) \cdot (0.8750) \cdot (0.9375) \cdot (0.9688) \cdot (0.9922) \cdot (0.9922) \sim 0.636$. $P_{r+6}, P_{r+7}, \ldots, P_{r+59}$ are expected to be recovered by $f_{ABSAB\_F}()$ with probability of one from Table 2. After that, other bytes of the target plaintexts can be recovered with probability of one similar to the IOWM attack because the parameter becomes $G_{MAX} = 63$. Therefore, in our attack, the only knowledge of consecutive 6 bytes of the target plaintexts enables to recover 1000 terabytes of the target plaintext with probability of about 0.636 from 2^{34} ciphertexts. The number of required ciphertexts of this attack is same as that of IOWM attack, while IOWM attack uses the initial 257 bytes of the keystream.

4 Guess-and-Determine Plaintext Recovery Attack (GD Attack)

This section gives a plaintext recovery attack which does not require any previous knowledge of the plaintext unlike the attack in Sect. 3. In order to achieve it, we develop a *guess-and-determine* (GD) plaintext recovery method based on two strong long-term biases, the FM00 bias and the *ABSAB* bias. Generally, in stream ciphers, the guess-and-determine method is considered as a technique for internal state recovery attacks such that a part of an internal state is determined from the other parts by exploiting the relations between the state and keystream. Our method seems to be a new class of the guess-and-determine methods for the plaintext recovery attack.

Assuming P_r is the target byte, the overview of our GD attack is given as follows.

1. Guess the value of P_r.
2. Recover x bytes of the plaintext, $P_{r-x}, \ldots, P_{r-1}$, from P_r (guessed in Step 1) by using the FM00 bias.
3. Recover P'_r from $P_{r-x}, \ldots, P_{r-1}$ (guessed in Step 2) by using the $ABSAB$ bias.
4. If P'_r is not equal to P_r guessed in Step 1, the value is wrong. Otherwise the value is regarded as a candidate of correct P_r.

For each candidate of P_r, Step 1–4 are performed. The basic idea behind our GD attack is that if the value of P_r guessed in Step 1 is correct, P'_r is surely same as P_r guessed in Step 1. Two biases are used for the detection the wrong candidates of plaintext bytes.

In this section, we firstly give attack functions based on the FM00 bias for guess-and-determine methods. Then, we explain the detailed algorithm of guess-and-determine methods. Finally we evaluate this attack.

4.1 FM00 Bias for GD Attack

The FM00 bias is a two-word bias (See Table 1), and is relatively weaker than the $ABSAB$ bias. If the simple count-up method for guessing correct plaintext byte is used, the FM00 bias is not directly used for efficient plaintext recovery attacks, because some events indexed by same r^* are dependent each other.

For example, let us consider two events of $(Z_{r^*}, Z_{r^*+1}) = (0,0)$ and $(Z_{r^*}, Z_{r^*+1}) = (0,1)$, whose probabilities are same. Here, the relation of plaintext and ciphertext is given as $(P_r, P_{r+1}) = (C_r \oplus Z_{r^*}, C_{r+1} \oplus Z_{r^*+1})$. If the event of $(Z_{r^*}, Z_{r^*+1}) = (0,0)$ occurs, the relation of $(P_r, P_{r+1}) = (C_r, C_{r+1})$ hold. On the other hand, if the event of $(Z_{r^*}, Z_{r^*+1}) = (0,1)$ occurs, $(P_r, P_{r+1} \oplus 1) = (C_r, C_{r+1})$ holds. Since these probabilities are same, we can not determine whether most frequency (C_r, C_{r+1}) is equal to (P_r, P_{r+1}) or $(P_r, P_{r+1} \oplus 1)$ in the plaintext recovery attack[3].

Conditional Bias Regarding the FM00 Bias. So that FM00 biases can be independently used for the plaintext recovery attack, we convert the FM00 bias into conditional bias such that $\Pr(Z_{r^*+1}|Z_{r^*})$ (the forward) or $\Pr(Z_{r^*}|Z_{r^*+1})$ (the backward), assuming that one byte of the plaintext can be known. Here, we consider the forward and backward conditional biases for previous two events $(Z_{r^*}, Z_{r^*+1}) = (0,0)$ and $(Z_{r^*}, Z_{r^*+1}) = (0,1)$.

The backward conditional biases, $(Z_{r^*} = 0 | Z_{r^*+1} = 0)$ and $(Z_{r^*} = 0 | Z_{r^*+1} = 1)$, are independently used for the plaintext recovery attack. Suppose that P_{r+1}

---

[3] Yarrkov showed a plaintext recovery attack using the FM00 bias on his web page [15] before our results. However, the detailed description of attacks and estimations are not given, and only the source code is given.

Algorithm 3. $f_{FM00\_B}()$

Require: r, /* round number of plaintext to be guessed */
    P_{r+1}, /* known plaintext bytes */
    (C_r, C_{r+1})s of $C^{(1)}, C^{(2)}, \ldots, C^{(k)}$ /* bytes of k ciphertexts encrypted by different keys */
Ensure: P_r
1: Make frequency tables of $T_{count}[bias]$ of P_r and P_{r+1} for all FM00 biases regarding P_{r+1} from all ciphertexts $C^{(1)}, C^{(2)}, \ldots, C^{(k)}$.
2: Convert $T_{count}[bias]$ into a frequency table $T_{guess}[r]$ indexed by only P_r with knowledge of P_{r+1}. Here, we only deal with the bias independent of other biases.
3: Regard most frequency one in table $T_{guess}[r]$ as the correct P_r.
4: Output P_r

---

is obtained, the values of $Z_{r^*+1} = 0$ is computed by $Z_{r^*+1} = C_{r+1} \oplus P_{r+1}$. Then, two tables of $Z_{r^*} = 0$ are obtained from two backward conditional biases ($Z_{r^*} = 0 | Z_{r^*+1} = 0$) and ($Z_{r^*} = 0 | Z_{r^*+1} = 1$). In these tables, it is expected that most frequency values of these tables indicate same value of the plaintext, because source event Z_{r^*+1} are different. Thus, these frequency tables are efficiently merged to recover the plaintext byte P_r.

On the other hand, the forward conditional biases ($Z_{r^*+1} = 0 | Z_{r^*} = 0$) and ($Z_{r^*+1} = 1 | Z_{r^*} = 0$) are not independently used. Even if two tables of $Z_{r^*} = 0$ obtained from ($Z_{r^*+1} = 0 | Z_{r^*} = 0$) and ($Z_{r^*+1} = 1 | Z_{r^*} = 0$) are merged, it is expected that two peaks of $Z_{r^*+1} = 0$ and $Z_{r^*+1} = 1$ are observed due to same source event $Z_{r^*} = 0$.

Therefore, if the source events of conditional bias (the forward is Z_{r^*} and the backward is Z_{r^*+1}) are different, these events can be independently used. Note that events for positive bias and negative bias are not dependent even if the source events of conditional bias are same.

Attack Functions Based on the FM00 Bias. By using all the independent conditional biases, we construct the forward and backward functions for the guess-and-determine attack based on the FM00 bias as follows:

$f_{FM00\_F}()$: Find an unknown byte P_r from pre-known a byte of a plaintext P_{r-1}.
$f_{FM00\_B}()$: Find an unknown byte P_r from pre-known a byte of a plaintext P_{r+1} (See Algorithm 3).

The algorithm of $f_{FM00\_F}()$ is given by replacing "+" of subscripts of variables in Algorithm 3 to "−". Figure 3 illustrates the procedures of $f_{FM00\_F}()$ and $f_{FM00\_B}()$.

The number of independent events of the forward conditional bias N_f and that of the backward conditional bias N_b in each index i are shown in Table 3. When index $i = 0$, the all events of backward conditional bias are independent, and $N_b = 5$. On the other hand, two events of forward conditional bias $Z_{r^*+1} = 1 | Z_{r^*} = N - 1$ and $Z_{r^*+1} = 2 | Z_{r^*} = N - 1$ are not independent, and $N_f = $

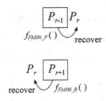

Fig. 3. The guess-and-determine methods based on the conditional bias of the FM00 bias

$5 - 2 = 3$. For all index i, N_b is larger than N_f. Hence, the success probability of $f_{FM00\_B}()$ is larger than that of $f_{FM00\_F}()$.

4.2 Plaintext Recovery Method for Recovering Any Plaintext Byte

Our GD attack utilizes the backward conditional bias of the FM00 bias and the forward $ABSAB$ bias.

To begin with, a plaintext byte P_r is guessed from N candidates. Then, our attack sequentially recovers $P_{r-1} \to P_{r-2} \to \ldots$ from P_r and the ciphertexts by using $f_{FM00\_B}()$ in the backward manner. Since the number of the candidates of P_x is N, the number of candidates of $(P_r, P_{r-1}, P_{r-2}, \ldots)$ is also N. In order to detect the wrong candidates of P_r, we use $f_{ABSAB\_F}()$, which is based on the other bias. In particular, P'_r is obtained from ciphertexts and the candidate of plaintext bytes $(P_{r-1}, P_{r-2}, \ldots)$ by using $f_{ABSAB\_F}()$ with G_{MAX}. If the number of ciphertexts is enough larger and P_r is correctly guessed, the relation of $P_r = P'_r$ surely holds. Otherwise the probability that $P_r = P'_r$ holds is $1/N$. After this method, about two candidates of P_r are expected to be left. If the number of the candidates of P_r is not one, the same method is repeated for $P'_{r-1}, P'_{r-2}, \ldots$, which are obtained by P_r. If P_r is correct, these method correctly works. In most cases, the number of repeating this method N_{repeat} is less than three. Figure 4 shows the procedure of our plaintext recovery attack for recovering any plaintext byte. The detail of our attack for recovering any plaintext byte P_r is given in Algorithm 4.

We consider the parameter G_{MAX} for the $ABSAB$ bias. It should be chosen so that $ABSAB$ bias is stronger than the FM00 bias to efficiently detect wrong candidates. From Lemma 2, given $1/D$ samples, $\Pr_{distinguish}$ become constant. Since the probability of the plaintext recovery attack depends on $\Pr_{distinguish}$, we evaluate our attack by the number of required ciphertexts for obtaining $1/D$ samples. For example, D of the backward conditional bias of the FM00 bias is estimated as $D = N^{-3} = 2^{-24}$ for $N = 256$ and $i = 3, 4, \ldots, N - 4$. From Table 3, there are seven independent events of the FM00 conditional biases in this case. As mentioned before, these biases are independently used. Thus, the probability that a ciphertext matches one of these source events is $7/N$. The number of the required ciphertexts is $(N/7) \cdot (1/D) = 2^{29.19}$ for $1/D$ samples. On the other hand, discriminations D of the $ABSAB$ bias and these number of

Table 3. Events of the conditional bias of the FM00 bias in each index i $(= r^* \bmod N)$

Index i	Z_{r^*}	Z_{r^*+1}	Conditional probability	N_f	N_b
	0	0	$N^{-1} \cdot (1 + N^{-1})$		
	1	$N-1$	$N^{-1} \cdot (1 + N^{-1})$		
0	$N-1$	1	$N^{-1} \cdot (1 + N^{-1})$	3	5
	$N-1$	2	$N^{-1} \cdot (1 + N^{-1})$		
	$N-1$	$N-1$	$N^{-1} \cdot (1 - N^{-1})$		
	0	0	$N^{-1} \cdot (1 + 2 \cdot N^{-1})$		
	2	$N-1$	$N^{-1} \cdot (1 + N^{-1})$		
1	$N-1$	3	$N^{-1} \cdot (1 + N^{-1})$	4	6
	$N-1$	2	$N^{-1} \cdot (1 + N^{-1})$		
	$N-1$	$N-1$	$N^{-1} \cdot (1 - N^{-1})$		
	0	2	$N^{-1} \cdot (1 - N^{-1})$		
	0	0	$N^{-1} \cdot (1 + N^{-1})$		
	0	1	$N^{-1} \cdot (1 + N^{-1})$		
	3	$N-1$	$N^{-1} \cdot (1 + N^{-1})$		
2	$N-1$	3	$N^{-1} \cdot (1 + N^{-1})$	4	8
	$N-1$	4	$N^{-1} \cdot (1 + N^{-1})$		
	$N/2+1$	$N/2+1$	$N^{-1} \cdot (1 + N^{-1})$		
	$N-1$	$N-1$	$N^{-1} \cdot (1 - N^{-1})$		
	0	3	$N^{-1} \cdot (1 - N^{-1})$		
	0	0	$N^{-1} \cdot (1 + N^{-1})$		
	0	1	$N^{-1} \cdot (1 + N^{-1})$		
	$i+1$	$N-1$	$N^{-1} \cdot (1 + N^{-1})$		
$3, 4, \ldots, N-4$	$N-1$	$i+1$	$N^{-1} \cdot (1 + N^{-1})$	3	7
	$N-1$	$i+2$	$N^{-1} \cdot (1 + N^{-1})$		
	$N-1$	$N-1$	$N^{-1} \cdot (1 - N^{-1})$		
	0	$i+1$	$N^{-1} \cdot (1 - N^{-1})$		
	0	0	$N^{-1} \cdot (1 + N^{-1})$		
	0	1	$N^{-1} \cdot (1 + N^{-1})$		
$N-3$	$N-2$	$N-1$	$N^{-1} \cdot (1 + N^{-1})$	4	6
	$N-1$	$N-2$	$N^{-1} \cdot (1 + N^{-1})$		
	$N-1$	$N-1$	$N^{-1} \cdot (1 - N^{-1})$		
	0	$N-2$	$N^{-1} \cdot (1 - N^{-1})$		
	0	0	$N^{-1} \cdot (1 + N^{-1})$		
$N-2$	0	1	$N^{-1} \cdot (1 + N^{-1})$	2	2
	$N-1$	0	$N^{-1} \cdot (1 + N^{-1})$		
	0	$N-1$	$N^{-1} \cdot (1 - N^{-1})$		
	0	1	$N^{-1} \cdot (1 + N^{-1})$		
	0	$N-1$	$N^{-1} \cdot (1 + N^{-1})$		
$N-1$	$N-1$	0	$N^{-1} \cdot (1 + N^{-1})$	1	3
	$N-1$	1	$N^{-1} \cdot (1 + N^{-1})$		
	$N-1$	$N-1$	$N^{-1} \cdot (1 - N^{-1})$		

Algorithm 4. Plaintext Recovery Attack for Recovering Any Plaintext Byte

Require: r, /* round number of plaintext to be guessed */
G_{MAX}, /* parameter of the ABSAB bias*/
$C^{(1)}, C^{(2)}, \ldots, C^{(k)}$ /* k ciphertexts encrypted by different keys */

Ensure: P_r

1: Set all N candidates of a plaintext byte P_r into table T_{cand}.
2: Set $N_{repeat} = 0$.
3: **for all** $P_r \in T_{cand}$ **do**
4:     Recover $G_{MAX} + 3 + N_{repeat}$ bytes of the plaintext, $P_{r-G_{MAX}-3-N_{repeat}}, \ldots, P_{r-1}$, from a candidate P_r by using $f_{FM00\_B}()$ and k ciphertexts $C^{(1)}, C^{(2)}, \ldots, C^{(k)}$.
5:     Recover $P'_{r-N_{repeat}}$ from $P_{r-G_{MAX}-3-N_{repeat}}, \ldots, P_{r-1-N_{repeat}}$ (guessed in Step 4) by using $f_{ABSAB\_F}()$ and k ciphertexts $C^{(1)}, C^{(2)}, \ldots, C^{(k)}$.
6:     **if** $P_{r-N_{repeat}} \neq P'_{r-N_{repeat}}$ **then**
7:         The candidate of P_r is removed from T_{cand}.
8:     **end if**
9: **end for**
10: **if** the number of candidates in T_{cand} is one **then**
11:     Output P_r, and the algorithm stops.
12: **else if** the number of candidates in T_{cand} is zero **then**
13:     Our attack fails, and the algorithm stops.
14: **else**
15:     Increment N_{repeat}, and go back to Step 3.
16: **end if**

required ciphertexts for recovering a plaintext byte are shown as ($D = 2^{-29.22}$, $1/D = 2^{29.22}$ ciphertexts) for $G_{MAX} = 8$ and ($D = 2^{-29.11}$, $1/D = 2^{29.11}$ ciphertexts) for $G_{MAX} = 9$. Therefore $G_{MAX} = 9$ is chosen for $N = 256$ and $i = 3, 4, \ldots, N - 4$.

4.3 Experimental Results

We perform the computer experiment for demonstrating the effectiveness of our attack with G_{MAX} on RC4-drop(n) in the broadcast setting when $N = 256$ and $n = 3072$. In this experiment, P_{128} is recovered from ciphertexts without the knowledge of the target plaintext. The parameters of the backward conditional bias of the FM00 bias, index i, satisfy $r^* \mod 256 = i \in \{3, 4, \ldots, N-4\}$. Hence, $G_{MAX} = 9$ is used as the parameter of the $ABSAB$ bias.

First, in order to evaluate $f_{FM00\_B}()$, we obtain the success probability for recovering $P_{114}, \ldots, P_{127}$ under the condition that the correct P_{128} is given. The success probabilities when 2^{29} to 2^{35} ciphertexts are given is shown in Table 4, where the number of tests is 256. The experimental result shows that all bytes of $P_{114}, \ldots, P_{127}$ are recovered from 2^{35} ciphertexts encrypted by randomly-chosen different keys with probability of one by using $f_{FM00\_B}()$. This results also shows that if one byte of the plaintext is known, 2^{33} ciphertexts enable to

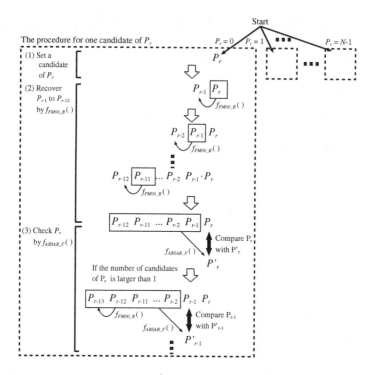

Fig. 4. The procedure of our plaintext recovery attack for recovering any plaintext byte ($G_{MAX} = 9$)

recover the other one byte with probability of about 0.8. Interestingly, it is more efficient than the attack in Sect. 3 when G_{MAX} is small. The attack in Sect. 3 are improved by using $f_{FM00\_B}()$. If consecutive 6 bytes of the plaintext are known, the other bytes can be recovered from 2^{34} with probability of about 0.984, while that of the attack in Sect. 3 is about 0.636.

Then, we estimate the success probability for recovering P_{128} from only ciphertexts by our plaintext recovery attack. The success probability when 2^{32} to 2^{35} ciphertexts are given is shown in Table 5, where the number of tests is 256. This experiment requires about one week with one CPU core (Intel(R) Core(TM) i7 CPU 920@ 2.67 GHz) to obtain the result of one plaintext. The experimental result shows that our attack can recover the target plaintext byte P_{128} with probability of one from 2^{35} ciphertexts encrypted by randomly-chosen different keys. Remaining plaintext bytes, namely $P_r(r \neq 128)$ can be recovered by repeating our attack or using our attack functions $f_{ABSAB\_F}()$, $f_{ABSAB\_B}()$, $f_{FM00\_F}()$, and $f_{FM00\_B}()$. Especially, in the cases of $i = N - 2, N - 1$, the success probabilities of conditional bias of the FM00 bias are relatively small than that of others cases. These bytes should be recovered by using $f_{ABSAB\_F}()$, $f_{ABSAB\_B}()$ for an efficient recovery attack after other bytes are recovered by using our GD attack.

Table 4. Success probabilities of $f_{FM00\_B}()$ for recovering $(P_{114}, \ldots, P_{127})$ under the condition that the correct P_{128} is given when $n = 3072$

	# of ciphertexts						
	2^{29}	2^{30}	2^{31}	2^{32}	2^{33}	2^{34}	2^{35}
P_{114}	0.0039	0.0039	0.0039	0.0078	0.0781	0.8750	1.0000
P_{115}	0.0039	0.0039	0.0078	0.0117	0.1055	0.8828	1.0000
P_{116}	0.0078	0.0000	0.0078	0.0117	0.1133	0.8828	1.0000
P_{117}	0.0039	0.0039	0.0078	0.0078	0.1328	0.8945	1.0000
P_{118}	0.0078	0.0195	0.0078	0.0078	0.1758	0.9023	1.0000
P_{119}	0.0078	0.0000	0.0078	0.0117	0.1992	0.9180	1.0000
P_{120}	0.0039	0.0039	0.0078	0.0156	0.2422	0.9258	1.0000
P_{121}	0.0039	0.0039	0.0117	0.0078	0.2773	0.9492	1.0000
P_{122}	0.0039	0.0078	0.0039	0.0117	0.3203	0.9570	1.0000
P_{123}	0.0000	0.0117	0.0117	0.0195	0.3672	0.9688	1.0000
P_{124}	0.0078	0.0039	0.0195	0.0391	0.4727	0.9844	1.0000
P_{125}	0.0078	0.0039	0.0078	0.0742	0.5820	0.9883	1.0000
P_{126}	0.0039	0.0078	0.0391	0.1602	0.6680	0.9922	1.0000
P_{127}	0.0430	0.0898	0.1719	0.3984	0.8008	0.9922	1.0000

Table 5. Success probabilities of our attack for recovering P_{128} when $n = 3072$

	# of ciphertexts			
	2^{32}	2^{33}	2^{34}	2^{35}
P_{128}	0.0039	0.1133	0.9102	1.0000

Given 2^{34} ciphertexts encrypted by randomly-chosen different keys, our attack can recover any plaintext byte with probability of about 0.91. The number of required ciphertexts are same as that of IOWM attack on original RC4, which does not discard initial keystream bytes. In addition, even if 2^{33} ciphertexts are given, our attack is more efficient than a random guess.

Also, this attack is applicable to original RC4 with constant success probability regardless of the position of plaintext bytes, while that of the IOWM attack decrease for the later plaintext byte. It is an advantage of our attack from the IOWM attack on the original RC4.

5   Conclusion

In this paper, we have evaluated the security of relatively secure RC4 implementation called RC4-drop(n), which discards the first n bytes of the keystream. We proposed two advanced plaintext recovery attacks that can recover *any* byte of a plaintext on RC4-drop(n) in the broadcast setting or the multi-session setting. The first attack is the modified IOWM attack. Using partial knowledge of the target plaintext, the other bytes can be recovered from ciphertexts encrypted by different keys. The attack can recover 1000 terabytes of a target plaintext with the high probability from 2^{34} ciphertexts encrypted by different keys if the knowledge of only consecutive 6 bytes of the target plaintext is given. The second attack does not rely on any previous knowledge of a plaintext. In order to achieve it, we developed a *guess-and-determine* plaintext recovery method based two strong long-term biases. Given 2^{35} ciphertext encrypted by different keys, any byte of a plaintext can be recovered with probability close to one from only ciphertexts. The amount of ciphertext is almost same as the IOWM attack on original RC4. Therefore, RC4 is not secure even if the enough initial keystream bytes are disregarded.

We recommend to replace RC4 with other stream ciphers [8] or the algorithms of authenticated encryption in the practical protocols and software applications.

A future work is to compare our attack with the method of [1,2] in the same conditions. In addition, we will combine our attack with the method of [1,2] for obtaining more efficient attacks.

Acknowledgments. This work was supported in part by Grant-in-Aid for Scientific Research (C) (KAKENHI 23560455) and Grant-in-Aid for Young Scientists (B) (KAKENHI 25730085) for Japan Society for the Promotion of Science.

References

1. AlFardan, N.J., Bernstein, D.J., Paterson, K.G., Poettering, B., Schuldt, J.C.N.: On the security of RC4 in TLS. In: USENIX Security 2013 (2013) (to appear)
2. AlFardan, N.J., Bernstein, D.J., Paterson, K.G., Poettering, B., Schuldt, J.C.N.: On the security of RC4 in TLS and WPA. http://www.isg.rhul.ac.uk/tls/RC4biases.pdf (2013)
3. Canvel, B., Hiltgen, A.P., Vaudenay, S., Vuagnoux, M.: Password interception in a SSL/TLS channel. In: Boneh, D. (ed.) CRYPTO 2003. LNCS, vol. 2729, pp. 583–599. Springer, Heidelberg (2003)
4. Fluhrer, S.R., McGrew, D.A.: Statistical analysis of the alleged RC4 keystream generator. In: Schneier [14], pp. 19–30
5. Sen Gupta, S., Maitra, S., Paul, G., Sarkar, S.: Proof of empirical RC4 biases and new key correlations. In: Miri, A., Vaudenay, S. (eds.) SAC 2011. LNCS, vol. 7118, pp. 151–168. Springer, Heidelberg (2012)
6. Sen Gupta, S., Maitra, S., Paul, G., Sarkar, S.: (Non-)random sequences from (Non-) random permutations - analysis of RC4 stream cipher. J. Cryptol. 1–42 (2012). http://dblp.uni-trier.de/rec/bibtex/journals/joc/GuptaMPS14
7. Isobe, T., Ohigashi, T., Watanabe, Y., Morii, M.: Full plaintext recovery attack on broadcast RC4. Preproceeding of Fast Software Encryption (FSE) (2013)
8. Josefsson, S., Strombergson, J., Mavrogiannopoulos, N.: The salsa20 stream cipher for transport layer security (TLS) and datagram transport layer security (DTLS). Network Working Group Internet-Draft, March 2013. http://tools.ietf.org/html/draft-josefsson-salsa20-tls-01 (2013)
9. Maitra, S., Paul, G., Sen Gupta, S.: Attack on broadcast RC4 revisited. In: Joux, A. (ed.) FSE 2011. LNCS, vol. 6733, pp. 199–217. Springer, Heidelberg (2011)
10. Mantin, I.: Analysis of the stream cipher RC4. Master's Thesis, The Weizmann Institute of Science, Israel. http://www.wisdom.weizmann.ac.il/itsik/RC4/rc4.html (2001)

11. Mantin, I.: Predicting and distinguishing attacks on RC4 keystream generator. In: Cramer, R. (ed.) EUROCRYPT 2005. LNCS, vol. 3494, pp. 491–506. Springer, Heidelberg (2005)
12. Mantin, I., Shamir, A.: A practical attack on broadcast RC4. In: Matsui, M. (ed.) FSE 2001. LNCS, vol. 2355, pp. 152–164. Springer, Heidelberg (2002)
13. Mironov, I.: (not so) random shuffles of RC4. In: Yung, M. (ed.) CRYPTO 2002. LNCS, vol. 2442, pp. 304–319. Springer, Heidelberg (2002)
14. Schneier, B. (ed.): FSE 2000. LNCS, vol. 1978. Springer, Heidelberg (2001)
15. Yarrkov, E.: Why the recent RC4 attack doesn't surprise me. https://cipherdev.org/rc4_2013-03-13.html (2013)

The LOCAL Attack: Cryptanalysis
of the Authenticated Encryption Scheme ALE

Dmitry Khovratovich[1] and Christian Rechberger[2]([⊠])

[1] University of Luxembourg, Walferdange, Luxembourg
dmitry.khovratovich@uni.lu
[2] DTU, Kongens Lyngby, Denmark
crec@dtu.dk

Abstract. We show how to produce a forged (ciphertext, tag) pair for the scheme ALE with data and time complexity of 2^{102} ALE encryptions of short messages and the same number of authentication attempts. We use a differential attack based on a local collision, which exploits the availability of extracted state bytes to the adversary. Our approach allows for a time-data complexity tradeoff, with an extreme case of a forgery produced after 2^{119} attempts and based on a single authenticated message. Our attack is further turned into a state recovery and a universal forgery attack with a time complexity of 2^{120} verification attempts using only a single authenticated 48-byte message.

1 Introduction

Cryptanalysis and design of authenticated encryption primitives are getting renewed interest, not least because of the CAESAR initiative [1]. Recently, at DIAC 2012 and FSE 2013, a proposal named ALE was presented by Bogdanov et al. [6]. ALE provides online single-pass encryption and authentication functionality with optional processing of associated data in a single primitive. The design borrows well tested ideas from Pelican-MAC [9] and the AES-based stream-cipher LEX [3]. From an implementation point of view it is an attractive proposal as it both lends itself to lightweight hardware implementation, and at the same time offers very high speed software implementations on platforms with AES instructions available.

The designers claim 128-bit security against state recovery, key recovery, or forgery attacks, under the assumptions that nonces are not re-used. Our cryptanalysis suggests that the security against forgery and state recovery attacks is less than expected and claimed. Even though the designers limited the amount of data that can be authenticated or both authenticated and encrypted to 2^{45} bytes, our forgery attack will likely succeed. In fact, for a variant of our approach, as little as 32 bytes of available data are enough. Furthermore our approach can be extended to recover the full 256-bit internal state of ALE.

Our methods. We use differential cryptanalysis despite the designers' intention of making these attacks unlikely. Their motivation comes from the good properties of the AES round function when iterated a few times, leading to very low

T. Lange, K. Lauter, and P. Lisoněk (Eds.): SAC 2013, LNCS 8282, pp. 174–184, 2014.
DOI: 10.1007/978-3-662-43414-7_9, © Springer-Verlag Berlin Heidelberg 2014

bounds for the probability of differential characteristics and differentials. Study of so-called extinguishing differentials in the context of Pelican-MAC backs up this analysis.

Our attack uses differentials of a particular type, called "local collisions", as they lead to the same tags for different plaintexts. These seem to have been first used in the collision search of SHA-0 [7], and more recently in related-key key-recovery attacks on AES-192 and AES-256 [4], and are also related to the aforementioned extinguishing differentials from the security analysis of Pelican-MAC [9]. However, as we discovered, using information that is leaked via the ciphertext these local collisions can be constructed much faster than expected, in turn leading to forgery attacks. Because of these properties, we call our method the **LOCAL** method: "LOcal-Collision Amplification via Leakage".

Outline of the paper and our results. We give a short introduction into the state of the art in the authenticated encryption in Sect. 2. We also provide a detailed description of ALE and discuss its similarities and differences to LEX. Then we proceed with the description of our attack in Sect. 3. We show that each encrypted message has many counterparts which yield the same tag with probability from 2^{-119} to 2^{-102}. Hence we can use a time-data tradeoff and demonstrate the fastest attack when 2^{102} messages are available, and the slowest with complexity 2^{119} when only a single message is available. In Sect. 4 we turn this attack into a stronger attack, allowing for state recovery and hence universal forgery. We discuss various repair strategies in Sect. 5 and conclude that a version of ALE resistant to our attack would have to suffer about 30 % in performance.

2   Authenticated Encryption Schemes and ALE

It has been known for a while that the encryption modes CBC, CFB, and CTR do not provide any sort of data integrity. Whenever a recipient of a ciphertext needs to check whether it was not modified by an adversary, a separate mechanism is needed. A traditional way to authenticate the ciphertext is to compute a message authentication code (MAC) of it, also called a tag. A secure way to do it, known as Encrypt-then-MAC, is to produce a MAC on another key and couple it with the ciphertext. A combination of a secure mode of operation and a secure MAC yields a secure authenticated encryption scheme [2], which provides

– Confidentiality (inability to distinguish the ciphertext from a random string);
– Ciphertext integrity (inability to find a valid pair (ciphertext, tag)).

Apart from using two different constructions, this approach has one clear disadvantage: it uses two different keys, which puts additional burden on the end user.

Since at least the year of 2000, cryptographers have tried to design an authenticated encryption scheme, which would use a single key and would be at least as efficient as Encrypt-then-MAC. The research went in two directions. The first one deals with new modes of operation which use an arbitrary block cipher.

The ISO standards GCM, CCM, and OCB are typical examples [16]. The patented OCB mode runs almost as fast as the counter encryption mode, which yields the speed below one cycle per byte on modern CPUs if used with AES [12]. The second approach deals with dedicated AE schemes, such as Nessie submissions like Helix or Sober-128, the eStream candidate Phelix, or Grain128a. Both approaches typically use probabilistic encryption to achieve confidentiality, and nonces are the usual source of randomness.

Modern authenticated encryption schemes are also able to authenticate so called *associated data* (AD) without encrypting it [15]. A typical application is Internet packets, whose contents are encrypted, whereas headers are not for routing purposes, while they still should be bound to the encrypted data.

Syntax of authenticated encryption. It is customary to use the following syntax for a nonce-based authenticated encryption scheme with associated data. The encryption function $\mathcal{E}$ operates as follows:

$$\mathcal{E} : \mathcal{K} \times \mathcal{M} \times \mathcal{N} \times \mathcal{A} \longrightarrow \mathcal{C},$$

where $\mathcal{K}$ is the key space, $\mathcal{M}$ is the message (plaintext) space, $\mathcal{N}$ is the nonce space, $\mathcal{A}$ is the associated data space, and $\mathcal{C}$ is the ciphertext space. The authentication part of the ciphertext may be syntactically separated and called a tag $T \in \mathcal{T}$.

The decryption function decrypts valid ciphertexts into plaintexts, and invalid ciphertexts into an error ($\perp$):

$$\mathcal{D} : \mathcal{K} \times \mathcal{C} \times \mathcal{N} \times \mathcal{A} \longrightarrow \mathcal{M} \cup \{\perp\}.$$

Security against forgery attacks comes from the inability of the computationally bounded adversary to produce a ciphertext that does not decrypt to $\perp$.

Attack model. Though particular applications may have their own restrictions, the security of the authenticated encryption scheme is defined with respect to a quite powerful adversary [15]. She may ask almost arbitrary requests to encryption and decryption oracles, with the main restriction that nonces do not repeat in encryption requests (so called nonce-respective adversary). Usually, no security is offered if the sender reuses the nonce. However, the receiver usually does not have technical means to check whether the nonce has not been used in another communication. Hence an adversary may ask to decrypt several tuples (C, N, A) with the same nonce (authenticating herself to distinct receivers if needed). A secure authenticated encryption scheme returns $\perp$ even in this case.

It is said that the adversary can create a *forgery*, if she is able to submit a tuple (C, N, A) to the decryption oracle such that

- It does not return $\perp$.
- There have been no encryption request which contained N and A and returned C.

This definition does not specify whether the adversary can choose the message she wants to be authenticated. From the practical point of view, we say that the adversary constructs a *universal forgery* if she indeed can choose the message at her own, and an *existential forgery* if she cannot.

Description of ALE

The authenticated encryption scheme ALE [6] is a dedicated scheme, which uses components of the AES-128 block cipher [8].

AES. AES-128 operates on a 16-byte block, which is traditionally represented as a matrix:

0	4	8	12
1	5	9	13
2	6	10	14
3	7	11	15

Plaintext of AES-128 undergoes a sequence of 10 rounds, each preceded with a subkey addition. One round consists of the following invertible transformations:

- SubBytes (SB) — nonlinear bytewise transformation. Each byte enters a so called S-box (the same for the whole cipher). S-box has a maximal differential probability of 2^{-6} (four conforming inputs), but the majority of differentials have probability of either 2^{-7} or zero;
- ShiftRows (SR) — rotates row i in the array (counting from 0) by i positions to the left;
- MixColumns (MC) — linear columnwise transformation. Is invertible, has branch number 5, i.e. two inputs differing in k bytes have outputs differing in at least $5 - k$ bytes, and vice versa.

The last, tenth round lacks MixColumns but is followed by another subkey addition. The key schedule of AES-128 is a lightweight transformation that produce subkeys in an invertible way.

ALE. ALE encrypts plaintexts up to 2^{45} bytes long. The nonces and keys are 128-bit strings. The encryption proceeds as follows (Fig. 1). During *the initialization phase* the 128-bit nonce N is encrypted on the 128-bit master key K to produce the temporary key K_1. The zero 128-bit string is encrypted on K to produce the temporary state S_1. The state S_1 is then encrypted on K_1 with 10 AES rounds. The last subkey of the latter encryption is denoted by K_2.

The associated data is appropriately padded and split into 16-byte blocks. The *associated data phase* alternates injecting the AD blocks into the state with encrypting the state with 4 AES rounds. The AD blocks are 16 bytes long and are simply xored into the internal state. The encryption subkeys are taken from the AES key schedule algorithm applied to K_2 and extended for as many rounds as needed (the original paper is a bit vague on the details, and we'll return to this issue in Sect. 4). This process continues in the message processing phase.

The message is partitioned into 16-byte blocks. For the sake of simplicity, we consider only the case where the message byte length is a multiple of 16. Then the *message processing phase* alternates groups of four leaking rounds with message block injections. Every odd round the scheme extracts bytes 0, 2, 8, 10, and every even round it extracts bytes 4, 6, 12, 14. The bytes are extracted after the SubBytes operation.

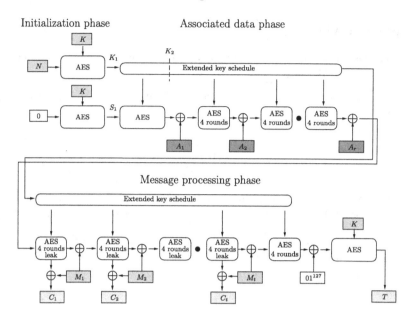

Fig. 1. Outline of authenticated encryption scheme ALE for messages multiple of block length.

A message block is xored to the internal state and is simultaneously xored to the last 16 bytes extracted, which forms a new block of ciphertext C. After the full message is processed, the scheme encrypts the state with four rounds using the previous subkeys, xors 0x70 to byte 0, and encrypts the state again with the key K for the full 10 rounds of AES-128. The result is declared the authentication tag T.

Security claims. ALE designers claim the following: *"Any forgery attack not involving key recovery/internal state recovery has a success probability at most 2^{-128}"*.

Differences between LEX and ALE and design weaknesses. ALE inherited a lot from the stream cipher LEX [3], which generates the keystream also by outputting specific bytes of the AES internal state. There are two crucial differences between them apart of the authentication option: first, LEX uses the same key in all its 10-group rounds, and second, LEX does not feed any data to the internal state. The former property led to distinguishing attacks on LEX based on colliding states [10]. Distinct keys in ALE make these attacks irrelevant.

However, the latter difference actually weakens the design, as the attacker is now able to manipulate the internal state, whose contents he has just observed via leakage. Even though the extracted bytes and the message injections are separated by subkey additions, a classical differential analysis bypasses this countermeasure, as we see below.

3   Forgery Attack

Outline. In this section we demonstrate a forgery attack on ALE. Our goal is to produce a fresh tuple (C, N, A) that does not decrypt to $\bot$ (here C includes the tag T). An adversary first asks for the encryption of some messages, and then attempts to forge the tag by modifying ciphertexts. Even though nonces repeat in forgery attempts, they do not repeat in encryption requests. Therefore, our attack operates in a standard model.

Attack overview. The attack proceeds as follows. We ask for the encryption of a message $M = (M_1, M_2)$:

$$\mathcal{E}_K(M, N, A) = C.$$

We do not care about the message contents, the nonce, and the associated data, so the attack can be entirely *known-plaintext* as long as the plaintexts are at least two blocks long. Then we attempt to construct a pair of differences $\Delta = (\Delta_1, \Delta_2)$, which yields a *local collision* in ALE if being applied to (M_1, M_2), meaning that the two differences compensate each other. If the local collision property holds, the authentication tag remains the same, and the ciphertext is simply xored with $\Delta_C = (\Delta_1, \Delta_2, 0^{128})$:

$$\mathcal{D}_K(C \oplus \Delta_C, N, A) = M.$$

If it does not hold, we repeat the procedure for another difference or another message, as explained below.

The designers of ALE supposedly ruled out such an attack, since the group of four rounds of AES between the message injection benefits from the wide trail strategy. The latter concept enables to prove that any 4-round differential trail activates at least 25 S-boxes, which yields the maximum probability of $2^{-25 \cdot 6} = 2^{-150}$. It should make any differential event, including the local collision, highly unlikely. However, this idea does not take into account the fact that as many as 16 bytes from the internal states have been extracted during these four rounds. Since they are known to the adversary, he can select the differential trail so that it has higher probability than the wide trail strategy offers. A differential trail is easily converted to a verification attempt.

Attack details. First we note that the extracted bytes are the S-box outputs (the inputs would work too). Hence whenever a trail activates an S-box whose value is extracted, the difference propagation is deterministic in this S-box, and it does not add a factor to the total probability. Thus we attempt to find a trail that has low weight and this weight consists of as many "extraction" S-boxes as possible.

We did not do an exhaustive search for all low-weight trails, but the following round weights are good enough for our purposes:

$$16 \xrightarrow{SR,MC} 4 \xrightarrow{SR,MC} 1 \xrightarrow{SR,MC} 4 \xrightarrow{SR,MC} 16.$$

The optimal layout for active S-boxes is to be determined, but the one at Fig. 2 is good enough, as only 17 active S-boxes out of 25 add a factor to the probability.

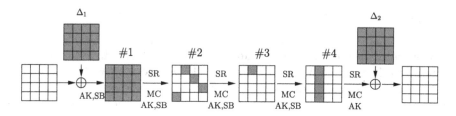

Fig. 2. Differential trail for a local collision: overview. Orange cells are active extraction S-boxes, violet cells are the other active S-boxes.

These trails can be constructed online very quickly in the start-from-the-middle framework [13]. We select a random difference in state #3 and expand it in both directions. Whenever we encounter extraction S-boxes or MixColumns, the difference evolves deterministically. For each active non-extraction S-box we select an output difference so that the differential probability equals the maximum 2^{-6}. Eventually, we obtain values of Δ_1 and Δ_2. Hence for every extraction tuple it is easy to obtain a differential trail that holds with probability $2^{-17 \cdot 6} = 2^{-102}$.

Therefore, for each encrypted 2-block message we can construct a counterpart that yields the same authentication tag with probability 2^{-102}. Hence we can construct a forgery for ALE with complexity of 2^{102} ALE encryptions of two-block messages and 2^{102} verification attempts. While it is enough to constitute a weakness in ALE, the data complexity should be reduced further to match the design restrictions.

Reducing the data complexity. The specification [6] requires that no more than 2^{40} 2-block messages be authenticated with a single key. In order to match this condition, we use a simple tradeoff by allowing some $r \leq 17$ S-boxes in a trail to have non-maximal differential probability. Instead of one choice per S-box, we now have 2^7 choices per non-optimal S-box, and hence many more trails for the same message. The value $r = 8$ yields $\binom{17}{8}2^{56} \approx 2^{70.5}$ trails with probability 2^{-110}. Hence we can use 2^{40} plaintexts to generate $2^{110.5}$ verification attempts with the total attack probability close to 1. By further increasing r we can work with very low data complexity up to the extreme case of one message block, where we have to use all the degrees of freedom in each S-box so that the attack complexity increases to $2^{7 \cdot 17} = 2^{119}$.

The memory complexity of our attack is negligible, as we store only several AES internal states and the S-box difference distribution table.

4   Turning the Forgery into a State Recovery Attack

The fact that the forgery from above is the result of a differential attack reveals much information about the internal state. Indeed, as long as the differential trail holds, each active S-boxes takes at most 4 possible values (2 if the probability is 2^{-7}). Hence we obtain at least $12 \cdot 7 + 4 \cdot 8 = 116$ bits of information about

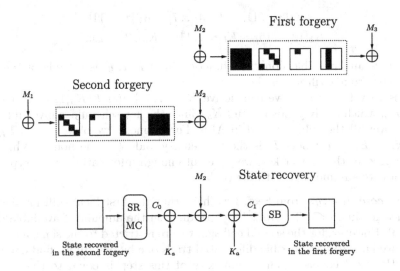

Fig. 3. Outline of the state recovery attack on ALE.

the state #1. This may seem insufficient to fully recover the state and the key, as they take 256 bits altogether.

However, we note that the local collision attack can be repeated for the same message but another pair of blocks (Fig. 3). Assume that we have mounted the forgery attack with a local collision based on blocks (M_2, M_3), whereas the first block is M_1. Then we attempt to construct another local collision based on blocks (M_1, M_2) with a trail of the following form (again, SB and AK are omitted):

$$4 \xrightarrow{SR,MC} 1 \xrightarrow{SR,MC} 4 \xrightarrow{SR,MC} 16 \xrightarrow{SR,MC} 16$$

As soon as we construct the second forged ciphertext, we obtain information about the internal state in the last round where all S-boxes are active. Having 4 S-boxes extracted, we obtain $12 \cdot 7 + 4 \cdot 8 = 116$ bits of information — the same as for the first local collision. Let us guess the unknown 12 bits in both fully active states and recompute the states towards the injection of M_2. Let us denote the subkeys encompassing the injection of M_2 by K_a and K_b. Then we obtain the following equation:

$$C_0 \oplus K_a \oplus M_2 \oplus K_b = C_1,$$

where C_0 and C_1 are known constants. Hence we obtain the value $K_a \oplus K_b$.

The original specification says that K_b is derived from K_a by applying an AES key schedule round with a specific constant:

$$K_b[0\ldots 3] = F(K_a[12\ldots 15]) \oplus K_a[0\ldots 3];$$
$$K_b[4\ldots 7] = K_b[0\ldots 3] \oplus K_a[4\ldots 7];$$

$$K_b[8\ldots 11] = K_b[4\ldots 7] \oplus K_a[8\ldots 11];$$
$$K_b[12\ldots 15] = K_b[8\ldots 11] \oplus K_a[12\ldots 15].$$

where F is an invertible nonlinear function, and $K[x..y]$ is a tuple of the key state bytes from x till y included.

It is easy to see that we can derive $K_b[0\ldots 11]$ and $F(K_a[12\ldots 15])$ from $K_a \oplus K_b$, which easily yields the full K_b. Since the key schedule is invertible, we can recover all the subkeys used in ALE. Furthermore, we obtain $S_1 = E_K(0)$ and $K_1 = E_K(N)$, where K is the master key and N is the nonce. While we cannot recover the master key, we have got enough information to encrypt and authenticate any message with nonce N.

Attack complexity. From Sect. 3 we have that the first local collision can be obtained in time from 2^{102} to 2^{119}, depending on the amount of available data (Sect. 3). However, for the second collision we are restricted to the same message. Hence we have to test possible differential trails one by one till we find one that yields the local collision. The complexity of this step is equal to that of the forgery attack with a single message — 2^{119}. As soon as both local collisions are constructed, the state recovery takes negligible time, as we only have to test 2^{24} state values conforming to the active S-boxes. The memory complexity is also negligible. The total time complexity equals 2^{120} forgery attempts of 48-byte messages.

5   Strengthening ALE

It is a natural question if ALE can be strengthened to prevent our attack. One may think that using five AES rounds would be enough, with the last round not extracting any values. Indeed, our trail would expand to a fully active state in the final round. However, there is a 5-round trail with only 26 active S-boxes, of which 8 ones are extracted:

$$1 \xrightarrow{SR,MC} 4 \xrightarrow{SR,MC} 16 \xrightarrow{SR,MC} 4 \xrightarrow{SR,MC} 1 \xrightarrow{SR,MC} 4.$$

The total probability of the trail hence decreases to 2^{-110} (see Fig. 4 for illustration). However, much fewer trails can be built for a single message. For each particular truncated differential trail we estimate with the rebound technique [14] that for each set of extracted values there are 2^{14} valid trails. Hence the data complexity would be about 2^{96}. By playing with the trail layout and by adding one more active S-box we can further reduce it to about 2^{80}. Even though it violates the data restriction, the security margin seems to be quite thin. Adding one more round seem to solve the problem completely, as the best trail seems to have 22 active non-extracted S-boxes. Hence we believe that at least 6 rounds are required to counteract our attack.

Another countermeasure could be to decrease the number of extracted bytes. If only 3 bytes are extracted at each round, so that 12 bytes are injected, it might be difficult to construct a trail that yields a local collision. A much more

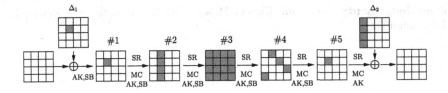

Fig. 4. Local collision trail for a 5-round variant of ALE.

elaborate analysis is needed to investigate this option. Still, it would give quite a penalty on the performance, but not that big as using 6 rounds instead of 4.

A third countermeasure could be to introduce key information into the round transformations with the aim to separate the leaked bytes from the S-boxes before and after the leak, as this has been done in ASC-1 [11]. This would affect the performance only very moderately, however depending on how exactly this key information would be derived, guess-and-determine extensions of the LOCAL approach would need to be considered as well.

6   Conclusion

We have demonstrated how to construct forgeries for ALE within the security claim limits. We show that the mere weight of a differential trail is a poor measure of the scheme resistance to differential attack as long as the values of active S-boxes are partially extracted or leaked. By choosing the trail values according to the extracted bytes, we can amplify its probability and eventually construct a forgery using 2^{45} encrypted messages and 2^{110} time. The inability of the receiver in a general case to avoid the nonce reuse enables us to reconstruct the internal state of the encryption out of two forgeries on the same message, which in turn leads to the universal forgery attack. One can hence say that ALE, similarly to GCM, has high reforgeability [5].

We have also proposed several ways to strengthen ALE against our attack, which include a larger number of rounds and a different leakage scheme (Table 1)

Table 1. Summary of attacks on ALE

Data	Verification attempts	Memory	Security claim
Forgery			
2^{102}	2^{102}	negl.	not violated
2^{40}	2^{110}	negl.	violated
1	2^{119}	negl.	violated
1	1	negl.	violated, success rate 2^{-102}
State recovery			
1	2^{120}	negl.	violated

Acknowledgements. We thank Florian Mendel and the anonymous reviewers for helpful comments.

References

1. http://competitions.cr.yp.to/caesar.html
2. Bellare, M., Namprempre, C.: Authenticated encryption: relations among notions and analysis of the generic composition paradigm. In: Okamoto, T. (ed.) ASIACRYPT 2000. LNCS, vol. 1976, pp. 531–545. Springer, Heidelberg (2000)
3. Biryukov, A.: The design of a stream cipher LEX. In: Biham, E., Youssef, A.M. (eds.) SAC 2006. LNCS, vol. 4356, pp. 67–75. Springer, Heidelberg (2007)
4. Biryukov, A., Khovratovich, D.: Related-key cryptanalysis of the full AES-192 and AES-256. In: Matsui, M. (ed.) ASIACRYPT 2009. LNCS, vol. 5912, pp. 1–18. Springer, Heidelberg (2009)
5. Black, J., Cochran, M.: MAC reforgeability. In: Dunkelman, O. (ed.) FSE 2009. LNCS, vol. 5665, pp. 345–362. Springer, Heidelberg (2009)
6. Bogdanov, A., Mendel, F., Regazzoni, F., Rijmen, V., Tischhauser, E.: ALE: AES-based lightweight authenticated encryption. In: FSE'13, to appear (2013)
7. Chabaud, F., Joux, A.: Differential collisions in SHA-0. In: Krawczyk, H. (ed.) CRYPTO 1998. LNCS, vol. 1462, pp. 56–71. Springer, Heidelberg (1998)
8. Daemen, J., Rijmen, V.: The Design of Rijndael: AES - The Advanced Encryption Standard. Springer, Heidelberg (2002)
9. Daemen, J., Rijmen, V.: The pelican MAC function. IACR Cryptology ePrint Archive 2005: 88 (2005)
10. Dunkelman, O., Keller, N.: A new attack on the LEX stream cipher. In: Pieprzyk, J. (ed.) ASIACRYPT 2008. LNCS, vol. 5350, pp. 539–556. Springer, Heidelberg (2008)
11. Jakimoski, G., Khajuria, S.: ASC-1: an authenticated encryption stream cipher. In: Miri, A., Vaudenay, S. (eds.) SAC 2011. LNCS, vol. 7118, pp. 356–372. Springer, Heidelberg (2012)
12. Krovetz, T., Rogaway, P.: The software performance of authenticated-encryption modes. In: Joux, A. (ed.) FSE 2011. LNCS, vol. 6733, pp. 306–327. Springer, Heidelberg (2011)
13. Mendel, F., Peyrin, T., Rechberger, C., Schläffer, M.: Improved cryptanalysis of the reduced grøstl compression function, ECHO permutation and AES block cipher. In: Jacobson Jr, M.J., Rijmen, V., Safavi-Naini, R. (eds.) SAC 2009. LNCS, vol. 5867, pp. 16–35. Springer, Heidelberg (2009)
14. Mendel, F., Rechberger, C., Schläffer, M., Thomsen, S.: The rebound attack: cryptanalysis of reduced whirlpool and grøstl. In: Dunkelman, O. (ed.) FSE 2009. LNCS, vol. 5665, pp. 260–276. Springer, Heidelberg (2009)
15. Rogaway, P.: Authenticated-encryption with associated-data. In: ACM Conference on Computer and Communications Security'02, pp. 98–107 (2002)
16. ISO/IEC 19772 JTC 1 SC 27. Information technology – Security techniques – Authenticated encryption (2009)

AEGIS: A Fast Authenticated Encryption Algorithm

Hongjun Wu[1](✉) and Bart Preneel[2]

[1] School of Physical and Mathematical Sciences,
Nanyang Technological University, Nanyang Link, Singapore
wuhj@ntu.edu.sg
[2] Dept. Elektrotechniek-ESAT/COSIC,
KU Leuven and iMinds, Leuven, Belgium
bart.preneel@esat.kuleuven.be

Abstract. This paper introduces a dedicated authenticated encryption algorithm AEGIS; AEGIS allows for the protection of associated data which makes it very suitable for protecting network packets. AEGIS-128 uses five AES round functions to process a 16-byte message block (one step); AES-256 uses six AES round functions. The security analysis shows that both algorithms offer a high level of security. On the Intel Sandy Bridge Core i5 processor, the speed of AEGIS is around 0.7 clock cycles/byte (cpb) for 4096-byte messages. This is comparable in speed to the CTR mode (that offers only encryption) and substantially faster than the CCM, GCM and OCB modes.

Keywords: Authenticated encryption · AEGIS · AES-NI

1 Introduction

The protection of a message typically requires the protection of both confidentiality and authenticity. There are two main approaches to authenticate and encrypt a message. One approach is to treat the encryption and authentication separately. The plaintext is encrypted with a block cipher or stream cipher, and a MAC algorithm is used to authenticate the ciphertext. For example, we may apply AES [17] in CBC mode [18] to the plaintext, then apply AES-CMAC [22] (or Pelican MAC [6] or HMAC [19]) to the ciphertext to generate an authentication tag. This approach is relatively easy to analyze since the security of authentication and encryption can be analyzed almost separately. Bellare and Namprempre have performed a detailed analysis of this type of authenticated encryption for randomized encryption [2]. Another approach is to apply an integrated authenticated encryption algorithm to the message; one can expect that this is more efficient since authentication and encryption can share part of the computation.

There are three approaches to design an integrated authenticated encryption algorithm. The first approach is to use a block cipher in a special mode (the block

T. Lange, K. Lauter, and P. Lisoněk (Eds.): SAC 2013, LNCS 8282, pp. 185–201, 2014.
DOI: 10.1007/978-3-662-43414-7_10, © Springer-Verlag Berlin Heidelberg 2014

cipher is treated as a black box). The research on this approach started about ten years ago [9,12,14]. There are now two NIST recommended modes of operation for authenticated encryption, namely, CCM [20] and GCM [21]. OCB [15,24,25] is a widely known authenticated encryption mode, and OCB2 is an ISO standard. The second approach is to use a stream cipher (the stream cipher is treated as a black box). The keystream is divided into two parts: one part for encryption and another part for authentication. A typical example of this approach is Grain-128a [1]. The third approach is to design dedicated authenticated encryption algorithms. In this approach, a message is used to update the state of the cipher, and message authentication can be achieved almost for free. Two examples of this approach are Helix [8] and Phelix [26]. The attack against Phelix [27] shows that it is unlikely that this type of authenticated encryption algorithm can withstand nonce-reuse attacks if it requires much less computation than a block cipher.

In this paper, we propose a dedicated authenticated encryption algorithm AEGIS following the third approach above. AEGIS is constructed from the AES encryption round function (not the last round). AEGIS-128 processes a 16-byte message block with 5 AES round functions, and AEGIS-256 uses 6 AES round functions. The computational cost of AEGIS is about half that of AES. AEGIS is very fast. On the Intel Sandy Bridge processor Core-i5, the encryption speeds of AEGIS-128 and AEGIS-256 are about 0.66 cpb and 0.70 cpb, respectively. The speeds are close to that of AES in counter (CTR) mode, and are about 8 times that of AES encryption in CBC mode. AEGIS offers a very high security. As long as the nonce is not reused, it is impossible to recover the AEGIS state and key faster than exhaustive key search (under the assumption that a 128-bit authentication tag is used, and the forgery attack cannot be repeated for the same key for more than 2^{128} times). AEGIS is suitable for network communication since it is straightforward to use AEGIS to protect a packet while leaving the packet header (associated data) unencrypted.

This paper is organized as follows. The operations, variables and functions are introduced in Sect. 2. The specifications of AEGIS-128 and AEGIS-256 are given in Sect. 3 and Sect. 4, respectively. Section 5 gives the security analysis of AEGIS-128 and AEGIS-256. The software performance of AEGIS is given in Sect. 6. The design rationale is given in Sect. 7. Section 8 concludes this paper.

2   Operations, Variables and Functions

2.1   Operations

The following operations are used in AEGIS:

$\oplus$: bit-wise exclusive OR
& : bit-wise AND
‖ : concatenation
$\lceil x \rceil$: ceiling operation, $\lceil x \rceil$ is the smallest integer not less than x

2.2 Variables and Constants

The following variables and constants are used in AEGIS:

AD : associated data (this data will not be encrypted or decrypted).
AD_i : a 16-byte associated data block (the last block may be a partial block).
$adlen$: bit length of the associated data with $0 \leq adlen < 2^{64}$.
C : ciphertext.
C_i : a 16-byte ciphertext block (the last block may be a partial block).
$const$: a 32-byte constant in the hexadecimal format; $const = 00 \parallel 01 \parallel 01 \parallel 02 \parallel$
              $03 \parallel 05 \parallel 08 \parallel 0d \parallel 15 \parallel 22 \parallel 37 \parallel 59 \parallel 90 \parallel e9 \parallel 79 \parallel 62 \parallel db \parallel 3d \parallel 18 \parallel$
              $55 \parallel 6d \parallel c2 \parallel 2f \parallel f1 \parallel 20 \parallel 11 \parallel 31 \parallel 42 \parallel 73 \parallel b5 \parallel 28 \parallel dd$. This is the
              Fibonacci sequence modulo 256.
$const_0$: first 16 bytes of $const$.
$const_1$: last 16 bytes of $const$.
IV_{128} : 128-bit initialization vector of AEGIS-128.
IV_{256} : 256-bit initialization vector of AEGIS-256.
$IV_{256,0}$: first half of IV_{256}.
$IV_{256,1}$: second half of IV_{256}.
K_{128} : 128-bit key of AEGIS-128.
K_{256} : 256-bit key of AEGIS-256.
$K_{256,0}$: first half of K_{256}.
$K_{256,1}$: second half of K_{256}.
$msglen$: bit length of the plaintext/ciphertext with $0 \leq msglen < 2^{64}$.
m_i : a 16-byte data block.
P : plaintext.
P_i : a 16-byte plaintext block (the last block may be a partial block).
S_i : state at the beginning of the ith step.
$S_{i,j}$: j-th 16-byte element of the state S_i. For AEGIS-128, $0 \leq j \leq 4$; for
              AEGIS-256, $0 \leq j \leq 5$.
T : authentication tag.
t : bit length of the authentication tag with $64 \leq t \leq 128$.
u : $u = \lceil \frac{adlen}{128} \rceil$.
v : $v = \lceil \frac{msglen}{128} \rceil$.

2.3 Functions

The AES encryption round function (not the last round) is used in AEGIS:

$AESRound(A, B)$: A is the 16-byte state, B is the 16-byte round key. This function mapping 2 16-byte inputs to a 16-byte output can be implemented efficiently on recent x86 processors using the AES instruction `_m128_aesenc_si128(A, B)`, where A and B are two 128-bit integers `_m128i`.

3 AEGIS-128

In this section, we describe AEGIS-128. With a 128-bit key and a 128-bit initialization vector, AEGIS-128 encrypts and authenticates a message. The associated data length and the plaintext length are less than 2^{64} bits. The authentication tag length is less than or equal to 128 bits. We strongly recommend the use of a 128-bit tag.

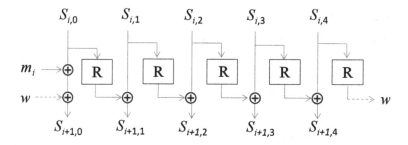

Fig. 1. The state update function of AEGIS-128. R indicates the AES encryption round function without XORing with the round key and w is a temporary 16-byte word.

3.1   The State Update Function of AEGIS-128

The state update function updates the 80-byte state S_i with a 16-byte message block m_i. $S_{i+1} = \texttt{StateUpdate128}(S_i, m_i)$ is given as follows:

$$S_{i+1,0} = AESRound(S_{i,4}, S_{i,0} \oplus m_i);$$
$$S_{i+1,1} = AESRound(S_{i,0}, S_{i,1});$$
$$S_{i+1,2} = AESRound(S_{i,1}, S_{i,2});$$
$$S_{i+1,3} = AESRound(S_{i,2}, S_{i,3});$$
$$S_{i+1,4} = AESRound(S_{i,3}, S_{i,4}).$$

The state update function is shown in Fig. 1.

3.2   The Initialization of AEGIS-128

The initialization of AEGIS-128 consists of loading the key and IV into the state, and running the cipher for 10 steps with the key and IV being used as message.

1. Load the key and IV into the state as follows:

$$S_{-10,0} = K_{128} \oplus IV_{128};$$
$$S_{-10,1} = const_1;$$
$$S_{-10,2} = const_0;$$
$$S_{-10,3} = K_{128} \oplus const_0;$$
$$S_{-10,4} = K_{128} \oplus const_1.$$

2. For $i = -5$ to -1, $m_{2i} = K_{128}$; $m_{2i+1} = K_{128} \oplus IV_{128}$.
3. For $i = -10$ to -1, $S_{i+1} = \texttt{StateUpdate128}(S_i, m_i)$.

3.3   Processing the Authenticated Data

After the initialization, the associated data AD is used to update the state.

1. If the last associated data block is not a full block, use 0 bits to pad it to 128 bits, and the padded full block is used to update the state. Note that if $adlen = 0$, the state will not be updated.
2. For $i = 0$ to $\lceil \frac{adlen}{128} \rceil - 1$, we update the state:

$$S_{i+1} = \texttt{StateUpdate128}(S_i, AD_i).$$

3.4   The Encryption of AEGIS-128

After processing the associated data, at each step of the encryption, a 16-byte plaintext block P_i is used to update the state, and P_i is encrypted to C_i.

1. If the last plaintext block is not a full block, use 0 bits to pad it to 128 bits, and the padded full block is used to update the state. But only the partial block is encrypted. Note that if $msglen = 0$, the state will not get updated, and there is no encryption.
2. Let $u = \lceil \frac{adlen}{128} \rceil$ and $v = \lceil \frac{msglen}{128} \rceil$. For $i = 0$ to $v - 1$, we perform encryption and update the state:

$$C_i = P_i \oplus S_{u+i,1} \oplus S_{u+i,4} \oplus (S_{u+i,2} \& S_{u+i,3});$$
$$S_{u+i+1} = \texttt{StateUpdate128}(S_{u+i}, P_i).$$

3.5   The Finalization of AEGIS-128

After encrypting all the plaintext blocks, we generate the authentication tag using seven more steps. The length of the associated data and the length of the message are used to update the state.

1. Let $tmp = S_{u+v,3} \oplus (adlen \parallel msglen)$, where $adlen$ and $msglen$ are represented as 64-bit integers.
2. For $i = u + v$ to $u + v + 6$, we update the state:

$$S_{i+1} = \texttt{StateUpdate128}(S_i, tmp).$$

3. We generate the authentication tag from the state S_{u+v+7} as follows:

$$T' = \bigoplus_{i=0}^{4} S_{u+v+7,i}.$$

The authentication tag T consists of the first t bits of T'.

3.6   The Decryption and Verification of AEGIS-128

The exact values of key size, IV size, and tag size should be known to the decryption and verification processes. The decryption starts with the initialization and the processing of authenticated data. Then the ciphertext is decrypted as follows:

1. If the last ciphertext block is not a full block, decrypt only the partial ciphertext block. The partial plaintext block is padded with 0 bits, and the padded full plaintext block is used to update the state.
2. For $i = 0$ to $v - 1$, we perform decryption and update the state.

$$P_i = C_i \oplus S_{u+i,1} \oplus S_{u+i,4} \oplus (S_{u+i,2} \& S_{u+i,3});$$
$$S_{u+i+1} = \texttt{StateUpdate128}(S_{u+i}, P_i).$$

The finalization in the decryption process is the same as that in the encryption process. We emphasize that if the verification fails, the ciphertext and the newly generated authentication tag should not be given as output; otherwise, the state of AEGIS-128 is vulnerable to known-plaintext or chosen-ciphertext attacks (using a fixed IV). This requirement also applies to AEGIS-256.

4   AEGIS-256

In this section, we describe AEGIS-256. With a 256-bit key and a 256-bit initialization vector, AEGIS-256 encrypts and authenticates a message. The associated data length and the plaintext length are less than 2^{64} bits. The authentication tag length is less than or equal to 128 bits. We strongly recommend the use of a 128-bit tag.

4.1   The State Update Function of AEGIS-256

The state update function updates the 96-byte state S_i with a 16-byte message block m_i. $S_{i+1} = \texttt{StateUpdate256}(S_i, m_i)$ is illustrated as follows:

$$S_{i+1,0} = AESRound(S_{i,5}, S_{i,0} \oplus m_i);$$
$$S_{i+1,1} = AESRound(S_{i,0}, S_{i,1});$$
$$S_{i+1,2} = AESRound(S_{i,1}, S_{i,2});$$
$$S_{i+1,3} = AESRound(S_{i,2}, S_{i,3});$$
$$S_{i+1,4} = AESRound(S_{i,3}, S_{i,4});$$
$$S_{i+1,5} = AESRound(S_{i,4}, S_{i,5}).$$

4.2   The Initialization of AEGIS-256

The initialization of AEGIS-256 consists of loading the key and IV into the state, and running the cipher for 16 steps with the key and IV being used as message.

1. Load the key and IV into the state as follows:

$$S_{-16,0} = K_{256,0} \oplus IV_{256,0};$$
$$S_{-16,1} = K_{256,1} \oplus IV_{256,1};$$
$$S_{-16,2} = const_1;$$
$$S_{-16,3} = const_0;$$
$$S_{-16,4} = K_{256,0} \oplus const_0;$$
$$S_{-16,5} = K_{256,1} \oplus const_1.$$

2. For $i = -4$ to -1,

$$m_{4i} = K_{256,0};$$
$$m_{4i+1} = K_{256,1};$$
$$m_{4i+2} = K_{256,0} \oplus IV_{256,0};$$
$$m_{4i+3} = K_{256,1} \oplus IV_{256,1}.$$

3. For $i = -16$ to -1, $S_{i+1} = \texttt{StateUpdate256}(S_i, m_i)$.

4.3 Processing the Authenticated Data

After the initialization, the associated data AD is used to update the state.

1. If the last associated data block is not a full block, use 0 bits to pad it to 128 bits, and the padded full block is used to update the state. Note that if $adlen = 0$, the state will not get updated.
2. For $i = 0$ to $\lceil \frac{adlen}{128} \rceil - 1$, we update the state.

$$S_{i+1} = \texttt{StateUpdate256}(S_i, AD_i).$$

4.4 The Encryption of AEGIS-256

After processing the associated data, at each step of the encryption, a 16-byte plaintext block P_i is used to update the state, and P_i is encrypted to C_i.

1. If the last plaintext block is not a full block, use 0 bits to pad it to 128 bits, and the padded full block is used to update the state. But only the partial block is encrypted. Note that if $msglen = 0$, the state will not get updated, and there is no encryption.
2. Let $u = \lceil \frac{adlen}{128} \rceil$ and $v = \lceil \frac{msglen}{128} \rceil$. For $i = 0$ to $v - 1$, we perform encryption and update the state:

$$C_i = P_i \oplus S_{u+i,1} \oplus S_{u+i,4} \oplus S_{u+i,5} \oplus (S_{u+i,2} \& S_{u+i,3});$$
$$S_{u+i+1} = \texttt{StateUpdate256}(S_{u+i}, P_i).$$

4.5 The Finalization of AEGIS-256

After encrypting all the plaintext blocks, we generate the authentication tag using seven more steps. The length of the associated data and the length of the message are used to update the state.

1. Let $tmp = S_{u+v,3} \oplus (adlen \parallel msglen)$, where $adlen$ and $msglen$ are represented as 64-bit integers.
2. For $i = u + v$ to $u + v + 6$, we update the state:

$$S_{i+1} = \texttt{StateUpdate256}(S_i, tmp).$$

3. We generate the authentication tag from the state S_{u+v+7} as follows:

$$T' = \bigoplus_{i=0}^{5} S_{u+v+7,i}.$$

The authentication tag T consists of the first t bits of T'.

5   The Security of AEGIS

The following requirements should be satisfied in order to use AEGIS securely.

1. Each key should be generated uniformly at random.
2. Each key and *IV* pair should not be used to protect more than one message; and each key and *IV* pair should not be used with two different tag sizes.
3. If verification fails, the decrypted plaintext and the wrong authentication tag should not be given as output.

If the above requirements are satisfied, we have the following security claims:

Claim 1. The success rate of a forgery attack is 2^{-t}, where t is the tag size. If the forgery attack is repeated n times, the success rate of a forgery attack is about $n \times 2^{-t}$.

Claim 2. The state and key cannot be recovered faster than exhaustive key search if the forgery attack is not successful. We recommend the use of a 128-bit tag size for AEGIS in order to resist repeated forgery attacks. (Note that with 128-bit tag, the state of AEGIS-256 can be recovered faster than exhaustive key search if a forgery attack is repeated for about 2^{128} times for the same key and *IV* pair.)

5.1   The Security of the Initialization

A difference in *IV* is the main threat to the security of the initialization of AEGIS. A difference in *IV* would eventually propagate into the ciphertexts, and thus it is possible to apply a differential attack against AEGIS. In AEGIS-128, there are 50 AES round functions (10 steps) in the initialization. If there is a difference in *IV*, the difference would pass through more than 10 AES round functions. In AEGIS-256, there are 96 AES round functions (16 steps) in the initialization. If there is a difference in *IV*, the difference would pass through more than 16 AES round functions. Furthermore, in order to prevent the difference in the state being eliminated completely in the middle of the initialization, we inject the *IV* difference repeatedly into the state (5 and 8 times into the state of AEGIS-128 and AEGIS-256, respectively). We expect that a differential attack against the initialization would be more expensive than exhaustive key search.

5.2   The Security of the Encryption Process

We emphasize here that AEGIS encryption is a stream cipher with a large state that is updated continuously. The attacks against a block cipher cannot be applied directly to AEGIS. The state update function involves five AES round functions in AEGIS-128, and six AES round functions in AEGIS-256. We should ensure that *IV* is not reused for the same key; otherwise, the states of AEGIS can be recovered easily with either known-plaintext attacks or chosen plaintext attacks. For example, if we re-use an *IV* and inject a difference into P_i, the difference would propagate into C_{i+2}, and part of the state can be attacked by analyzing the difference pair $(\Delta P_i, \Delta C_{i+2})$. If an authenticated encryption algorithm is secure for re-used IVs, we expect that such an algorithm can only be as fast as a block cipher, as pointed out in [27]. This can be argued as follows: once an IV is re-used, the attacks that are relevant for a block cipher can be applied to attack the state.

Statistical Attacks. If the IV is used only once for each key, it is impossible to apply a differential attack to the encryption process. It is extremely difficult to apply a linear attack (or correlation attack) to recover the secret state since the state of AEGIS is updated in a nonlinear way. In general, it would be difficult to apply any statistical attack to recover the secret state due to the nonlinear state update function (the statistical correlation between any two states vanishes quickly as the distance between them increases).

LEX [3,4] is an AES-based stream cipher that generates keystream from part of the state. We would like to mention here that AEGIS is not vulnerable to the attack against LEX [7]. There is a fundamental reason why LEX is vulnerable to a statistical attack while AEGIS is not: the round keys used in LEX are fixed, while the whole state of AEGIS is updated continuously in a nonlinear way.

5.3 The Security of Message Authentication

There are two main approaches to attack a MAC algorithm. One approach is to recover the secret key or secret state, another approach is to introduce/detect an internal state collision. Besides these two approaches, when we analyze the security of message authentication, we need to consider that the AEGIS encryption may affect the security of message authentication.

Recovering Key or State. From Sect. 5.1, we expect that the secret key cannot be recovered faster than exhaustive search by attacking the initialization. From Sect. 5.2, we expect that the state cannot be recovered faster than exhaustive search by attacking the encryption process if the IV is used only once. Similarly, we expect that the state cannot be recovered faster than exhaustive search by attacking the tag generation process if IV is not reused.

An attacker can still inject a difference into the state in the tag verification process and obtain the decrypted plaintext if the forgery attack is allowed to be repeated for multiple times for the same key and IV pair. In a forgery attack, the decrypted plaintext is known to the attacker with probability 2^{-t} (if the verification is successful). It becomes possible to recover the state if the forgery attack is repeated many times. We recommend the use of 128-bit tag so that recovering the state requires at least 2^{128} forgery attempts.

The security level of the AEGIS-256 state is only 128 bits with a 128-bit tag (if we consider that a forgery attack becomes successful). However, we believe that repeating the forgery attack for around 2^{128} times to recover a state is impractical.

Internal Collisions. A powerful attack against MAC is to introduce and detect internal collisions. A general approach based on the birthday attack was given by Preneel and van Oorschot [23]: an internal collision can be detected after a key is used to generate the authentication tags of about $2^{n/2}$ chosen messages, where n is the state size and tag size in bits. The internal collision can be exploited to forge the tags of new messages. The birthday attack was later applied to other MAC algorithms [28]. AEGIS resists this type of attacks due to its large state size. Another approach to introduce internal collision is through differential cryptanalysis. Suppose that the difference cancellation in the state occurs with probability 2^{-a}; then we can detect an internal collision after a secret key is used to generate the tags of those 2^a message pairs. The resulting internal collision can be used to forge the tags of new messages.

An attacker can inject a difference into the state in the decryption and tag verification process by modifying the ciphertext. However, AEGIS provides an extremely large security margin against this type of attack since differences are introduced into a large state. Obviously the security of AEGIS against forgery attack is stronger than that of Pelican MAC when the message or the tag gets modified. In Pelican MAC, four AES round functions are used to process each 16-byte message block; while in AEGIS, at least five AES round functions are used. Furthermore, the state size of AEGIS-128 is at least 5 times that of Pelican MAC, and it becomes much more difficult to eliminate the difference in the large state. A simple description of our analysis is given below. We notice that the first difference being injected into ciphertext would pass through five round functions without being affected by another ciphertext difference in AEGIS-128, and there are at least 26 active Sboxes being involved. Furthermore, when a difference passes through five AES round functions, the difference would be injected into each 16-byte element in the state. The difference cancellation in the state would involve at least 52 active Sboxes (at least 26 active Sboxes for generating the difference patterns, and 26 active Sboxes for generating the proper differences for difference cancellation). If we consider only a single differential path, the probability of the difference cancellation in the state is less than $2^{-6 \times 52} = 2^{-312}$. This means that generating a state collision in the verification process requires at least 2^{312} modifications to the ciphertext. Note that the differential attack here is slightly different from that against block cipher since the AEGIS verification process would guarantee that each forgery attack generates only one useful difference pair (the failed forgery attacks would not give outputs). The complexity 2^{312} is significantly larger than that of the forgery based key recovery attack (2^{128}, as illustrated at the beginning of Sect. 5.3). It shows that AEGIS-128 is strong against forgery attack when the ciphertext or tag gets modified. Multiple differential paths would not have a significant effect on the forgery attack here, since each differential path has to cancel its own differences being left in the state. Attacking AEGIS-256 is more difficult since it involves a larger state and more AES round functions.

We now analyze whether the noninvertible AEGIS state update function affects the security of the authentication of AEGIS. In AEGIS, a difference in

the state could be eliminated even if there is no difference being introduced
to cancel it. However, it would only happen if the difference in every 16-byte
element is able to eliminate the difference in the next element after passing
through an AES round function. It means that at least 26 active Sboxes are
involved in this difference elimination process in AEGIS-128, and generating
these particular differences in the state involves more than 26 additional active
Sboxes. We consider that this type of weak state difference has a negligible effect
on the security of the authentication of AEGIS.

The analysis given above shows that the authentication of AEGIS is very
strong.

5.4   Other Attacks

There are weak states in AEGIS. In one type of weak states, all the 16-byte
elements in a state are equal: consequently all the 16-byte elements in the next
state would be equal (if the message block is 0). However, there are only 2^{128} such
states, so this type of weak state appears with probabilities 2^{-512} and 2^{-640} for
AEGIS-128 and AEGIS-256, respectively. In another type of weak states, the four
columns in each 16-byte element are equal and every 16-byte element has such a
property: in this case, the same property would appear in the next state (if the
message block also has such a property). However, there are only $2^{32\times5} = 2^{160}$
such states in AEGIS-128 and $2^{32\times6} = 2^{192}$ such states in AEGIS-256, so we
expect that this type of weak state appears with probabilities 2^{-480} and 2^{-608}
for AEGIS-128 and AEGIS-256, respectively.

6   The Performance of AEGIS

To process a 16-byte message block, AEGIS-128 and AEGIS-256 use five and six
AES round functions, respectively. In AEGIS, the critical path for processing
a 16-byte message block is about one AES round. The computational cost of
AEGIS is about half that of AES for each message block, thus the speed of
AEGIS is about twice that of AES when they are implemented using table
lookups. For implementations based on bit-slicing techniques (e.g. Käsper and
Schwabe [13]), the difference is smaller as AEGIS allows for 5 or 6 parallel AES
operations rather than 8. AEGIS is very efficient when it is implemented using
the AES new instructions (AES-NI) available on some x86 processors since 2010.
With parallel AES round functions at each step, AEGIS can fully utilize the 3-
stage pipeline in AES-NI in Intel Westmere processor, and can utilize most of
the 8-stage pipeline in the AES-NI on the Intel Sandy Bridge processor. When
implemented using AES-NI on the Sandy Bridge processor, the speed of AEGIS
is about 8 times that of AES in CBC mode (encryption), and it is slightly faster
than AES-CTR.

We implemented AEGIS in C code using AES-NI. We tested the speed on
Intel Core i5-2540M 2.6 GHz processor (Sandy Bridge) running 64-bit Ubuntu
11.04 and turning off the Turbo Boost. The compiler being used is gcc 4.5.2, and

Table 1. The speed comparison (in cycles per byte) for different message length. A plus sign (+) indicates that the data are from the ALE designers and the performance is measured on the Intel i5-2400 microprocessor.

	64 B	128 B	256 B	512 B	1024 B	4096 B
AES-128-CTR$^+$	–	1.61	1.22	0.99	0.87	0.77
AES-128-CCM	7.26	6.31	5.65	5.19	5.17	5.05
AES-128-GCM$^+$	–	4.95	3.88	3.33	3.05	2.90
AES-128-OCB3$^+$	–	2.69	1.79	1.34	1.12	0.88
ALE$^+$	–	6.63	5.11	4.34	3.96	3.68
ASC-1$^+$	–	7.74	4.80	3.69	2.88	2.64
AEGIS-128(EA^a)	3.37	1.99	1.30	0.96	0.80	0.66
AEGIS-128(DV^b)	3.78	2.17	1.36	1.02	0.84	0.67
AEGIS-256(EA)	3.51	2.10	1.34	1.03	0.86	0.70
AEGIS-256(DV)	4.00	2.35	1.51	1.09	0.90	0.74

^{a}EA: Encryption-Authentication
^{b}DV: Decryption-Verification

the options "-O3 -msse2 -maes -mavx" are used. In our test, associated data is not considered, and 128-bit tag is used. The test is performed by processing a message repeatedly and printing out the final message. To ensure that the tag generation is not removed in the compiler optimization process, we use the tag as *IV* for the next message. To ensure that the tag verification is not removed in the compiler optimization process, we count the number of failed verifications and print out the final result.

The performance is given in Table 1. For 4096-byte messages, the speed of AEGIS is around 0.7 cpb. According to Table 1, the performance of AEGIS is better than that of CCM, GCM and OCB3, ALE [5] and ASC-1 [11]. ALE and ASC-1 are two new authenticated encryption algorithms using AES instructions. In Table 1, the speed for multiple messages is not included since it is a common practice to compare the speeds for a single message. (For multiple long messages, the speeds of ALE and CCM are 1.2 and 3.1 cpb, respectively [5].) Note that the speeds given in Table 1 are for reference only since the ciphers are not evaluated under the same conditions.

In Table 1, AEGIS decryption-verification is slightly slower than encryption-authentication for two reasons: a ciphertext block needs to be decrypted first before it can be applied to update the state; and the verification process is slightly more expensive than tag generation. AEGIS-128 is only slightly slower than AEGIS-256 for long messages, although the computational cost of AEGIS-256 is about 20 % more than that of AEGIS-128. The reason is that on the Sandy Bridge microprocessor, AES-NI is implemented with an eight-stage pipeline, and both AEGIS-128 and AEGIS-256 do not fully utilize the pipeline, so the performance of AEGIS-128 is close to that of AEGIS-256. On the Intel Westmere microprocessors with a 3-stage AES-NI, AEGIS-256 is about 20 % slower than AEGIS-128.

7   Design Rationale

The goal of AEGIS is to achieve high performance and strong security. To achieve high performance, we use the AES round function which is now implemented on the latest Intel and AMD microprocessors as Intel AES New Instructions (AES-NI). AES-NI is very efficient for achieving diffusion and confusion on a modern microprocessor. In the design of AEGIS, we use several parallel AES round functions in each step so as to use most of the pipeline stages in AES instruction. AES instructions are implemented on Intel Westmere (06_25H, 06_2CH, 06_2FH) microprocessors with a three-stage pipeline (6 clock cycles), and are implemented on Intel Sandy Bridge (06_2AH) microprocessors with an eight-stage pipeline (8 clock cycles) [10]. Using several parallel AES round functions in AEGIS significantly improves its performance by utilizing the pipeline of AES-NI.

To achieve strong encryption security, we ensure that the IV difference is randomized at the initialization stage, and the state cannot be recovered from the ciphertext. There are 10 steps and 16 steps in the initialization of AEGIS-128 and AEGIS-256, so we expect that the initialization of AEGIS is strong. To ensure that the state cannot be recovered from the ciphertext faster than brute force key search, we use a state in the design (80 bytes for AEGIS-128 and 96 bytes for AEGIS-256) in order to ensure that at least 20 and 30 AES round functions are involved in the state recovery attack against AEGIS-128 and AEGIS-256, respectively (the detailed analysis was omitted due to space restrictions). We avoid using a 64-byte state in AEGIS-128 since only 12 AES round functions would be involved in the state recovery attack, and we are not comfortable with its security.

To achieve strong authentication security, we try to ensure that any difference being introduced into the state would result in a particular difference with sufficiently small probability, so that it is difficult to launch a forgery attack. Our design is partly motivated by the design of Pelican MAC [6]. In Pelican MAC, a difference would pass through 4 AES round functions before meeting with another difference, so at least 25 active Sboxes are involved. The security proof against differential forgery attack is very simple for Pelican MAC (however, there is a birthday type attack against Pelican MAC due to its 128-bit size [28]). In AEGIS, the first difference in the state would pass through at least 5 AES round functions before being affected by another difference. In addition, when a difference passes through AES round functions, the differences are injected into every element in the state, so it becomes more difficult to eliminate the difference in the state.

8   Conclusion

In this paper, we introduced a dedicated authenticated encryption algorithm AEGIS. AEGIS is fast for both short and long messages, and it is the fastest authenticated encryption algorithm on the microprocessors with the AES instruction set. We performed a security analysis of the encryption and authentication of AEGIS. Our analysis shows that the encryption and authentication of AEGIS are strong. We welcome the security analysis of this new authenticated encryption algorithm.

Finally we state that AEGIS is not patented and it is freely available for all applications.

Acknowledgements. We would like to thank the anonymous reviewers for their helpful comments, especially the idea of fully utilizing the 8-stage pipeline of AES-NI on the Sandy Bridge processor to achieve higher performance by increasing the state size (this idea is not used in this paper since we have not fully analyzed its security). The second author has been funded in part by the Research Council KU Leuven (GOA TENSE) and the FWO Flanders.

A   Test Vectors

The test vectors (in hexadecimal format) of AEGIS-128 and AEGIS-256 are given below.

A.1   Test Vectors of AEGIS-128

```
associated data: 0 bits     plaintext: 128 bits
K128        = 00000000000000000000000000000000
IV128       = 00000000000000000000000000000000
plaintext   = 00000000000000000000000000000000
ciphertext  = 951b050fa72b1a2fc16d2e1f01b07d7e
tag         = a7d2a99773249542f422217ee888d5f1

associated data: 128 bits  plaintext: 128 bits
K128        = 00000000000000000000000000000000
IV128       = 00000000000000000000000000000000
assoc. data = 00000000000000000000000000000000
plaintext   = 00000000000000000000000000000000
ciphertext  = 10b0dee65a97d751205c128a992473a1
tag         = 46dcb9ee93c46cf13731d41b9646c131

associated data: 32 bits    plaintext: 128 bits
K128        = 00010000000000000000000000000000
IV128       = 00000200000000000000000000000000
assoc. data = 00010203
plaintext   = 00000000000000000000000000000000
ciphertext  = 2b78f5c1618da39afbb2920f5dae02b0
tag         = 74759cd0e19314650d6c635b563d80fd

associated data: 64 bits    plaintext: 256 bits
K128        = 10010000000000000000000000000000
```

```
IV128        = 1000020000000000000000000000000000
assoc. data  = 0001020304050607
plaintext    = 000102030405060708090a0b0c0d0e0f
               101112131415161718191a1b1c1d1e1f
ciphertext   = e08ec10685d63c7364eca78ff6e1a1dd
               fdfc15d5311a7f2988a0471a13973fd7
tag          = 27e84b6c4cc46cb6ece8f1f3e4aa0e78
```

A.2   Test Vectors of AEGIS-256

```
associated data: 0 bits     plaintext: 128 bits
K128         = 00000000000000000000000000000000
               00000000000000000000000000000000
IV128        = 00000000000000000000000000000000
               00000000000000000000000000000000
plaintext    = 00000000000000000000000000000000
ciphertext   = b98f03a947807713d75a4fff9fc277a6
tag          = a008acb1d372d73932ec5e6df9aca70a
```

```
associated data: 128 bits  plaintext: 128 bits
K128         = 00000000000000000000000000000000
               00000000000000000000000000000000
IV128        = 00000000000000000000000000000000
               00000000000000000000000000000000
assoc. data  = 00000000000000000000000000000000
plaintext    = 00000000000000000000000000000000
ciphertext   = b286705e6ccf368974ade9ff5550a4c5
tag          = 367f3f14897b31c6a66eb7b540eccc8b
```

```
associated data: 32 bits     plaintext: 128 bits
K128         = 00010000000000000000000000000000
               00000000000000000000000000000000
IV128        = 00000200000000000000000000000000
               00000000000000000000000000000000
assoc. data  = 00010203
plaintext    = 00000000000000000000000000000000
ciphertext   = 1f452a22fc07f2471ab4345d7ab121b1
tag          = 0d80d9c73cd4b8b3422b66cdaa45ae8a
```

```
associated data: 64 bits     plaintext: 256 bits
K128         = 10010000000000000000000000000000
               00000000000000000000000000000000
IV128        = 10000200000000000000000000000000
               00000000000000000000000000000000
assoc. data  = 0001020304050607
plaintext    = 000102030405060708090a0b0c0d0e0f
               101112131415161718191a1b1c1d1e1f
```

```
ciphertext  = f373079ed84b2709faee373584585d60
              accd191db310ef5d8b11833df9dec711
tag         = 787347bc96d3d0fdb33ddc8ee5ef4924
```

References

1. Ågren, M., Hell, M., Johansson, T., Meier, W.: Grain-128a: a new version of Grain-128 with optional authentication. Int. J. Wireless Mobile Comput. **5**(1), 48–59 (2011)
2. Bellare, M., Namprempre, C.: Authenticated encryption: relations among notions and analysis of the generic composition paradigm. In: Okamoto, T. (ed.) ASIACRYPT 2000. LNCS, vol. 1976, pp. 531–545. Springer, Heidelberg (2000)
3. Biryukov, A.: The design of a stream cipher LEX. In: Biham, E., Youssef, A.M. (eds.) SAC 2006. LNCS, vol. 4356, pp. 67–75. Springer, Heidelberg (2007)
4. Biryukov, A.: The Tweak for LEX-128, LEX-192, LEX-256. ECRYPT stream cipher project report 2006/037. http://www.ecrypt.eu.org/stream
5. Bogdanov, A., Mendel, F., Regazzoni, F., Rijmen, V., Tischhauser, E.: ALE: AES-based lightweight authenticated encryption. Fast Software Encryption - FSE 2013
6. Daemen, J., Rijmen, V.: The Pelican MAC function. IACR Cryptol. ePrint Arch. **2005**, 88 (2005)
7. Dunkelman, O., Keller, N.: A new attack on the LEX stream cipher. In: Pieprzyk, J. (ed.) ASIACRYPT 2008. LNCS, vol. 5350, pp. 539–556. Springer, Heidelberg (2008)
8. Ferguson, N., Whiting, D., Schneier, B., Kelsey, J., Lucks, S., Kohno, T.: Helix: fast encryption and authentication in a single cryptographic primitive. In: Johansson, T. (ed.) FSE 2003. LNCS, vol. 2887, pp. 330–346. Springer, Heidelberg (2003)
9. Gligor, V.D., Donescu, P.: Fast encryption and authentication: XCBC encryption and XECB authentication modes. In: Matsui, M. (ed.) FSE 2001. LNCS, vol. 2355, pp. 92–108. Springer, Heidelberg (2002)
10. Intel. Intel 64 and IA-32 Architectures Optimization Reference Manual. http://www.intel.com/content/dam/doc/manual/64-ia-32-architectures-optimization-manual.pdf
11. Jakimoski, G., Khajuria, S.: ASC-1: an authenticated encryption stream cipher. In: Miri, A., Vaudenay, S. (eds.) SAC 2011. LNCS, vol. 7118, pp. 356–372. Springer, Heidelberg (2012)
12. Jutla, C.S.: Encryption modes with almost free message integrity. In: Pfitzmann, B. (ed.) EUROCRYPT 2001. LNCS, vol. 2045, pp. 529–544. Springer, Heidelberg (2001)
13. Käsper, E., Schwabe, P.: Faster and timing-attack resistant AES-GCM. In: Clavier, C., Gaj, K. (eds.) CHES 2009. LNCS, vol. 5747, pp. 1–17. Springer, Heidelberg (2009)
14. Katz, J., Yung, M.: Unforgeable encryption and chosen ciphertext secure modes of operation. In: Schneier, B. (ed.) FSE 2000. LNCS, vol. 1978, pp. 284–299. Springer, Heidelberg (2001)
15. Krovetz, T., Rogaway, P.: The software performance of authenticated-encryption modes. In: Joux, A. (ed.) FSE 2011. LNCS, vol. 6733, pp. 306–327. Springer, Heidelberg (2011)
16. McGrew, D.A., Viega, J.: The security and performance of the Galois/Counter mode (GCM) of operation. In: Canteaut, A., Viswanathan, K. (eds.) INDOCRYPT 2004. LNCS, vol. 3348, pp. 343–355. Springer, Heidelberg (2004)

17. National Institute of Standards and Technology. Advanced Encryption Standard. FIPS 197
18. National Institute of Standards and Technology. Recommendation for Block Cipher Modes of Operation. NIST special publication 800-38A, 2001 Edition
19. National Institute of Standards and Technology. The Keyed-Hash Message Authentication Code (HMAC). FIPS PUB 198
20. National Institute of Standards and Technology. Recommendations for Block Cipher Modes of Operation: The CCM Mode for Authentication and Confidentiality. NIST special publication 800-38C, May 2004
21. National Institute of Standards and Technology. Recommendations for Block Cipher Modes of Operation: Galois/Counter Mode (GCM) and GMAC. NIST special publication 800-38D, Nov 2007
22. National Institute of Standards and Technology. Recommendation for Block Cipher Modes of Operation: The CMAC Mode for Authentication. NIST special publication 800-38B
23. Preneel, B., van Oorschot, P.C.: On the security of iterated message authentication codes. IEEE Trans. Inf. Theory 45(1), 188–199 (1999)
24. Rogaway, P., Bellare, M., Black, J.: OCB: a block-cipher mode of operation for efficient authenticated encryption. ACM Trans. Inf. Syst. Secur. 6(3), 365–403 (2003). Earlier version, with T. Krovetz, in CCS 2001
25. Rogaway, P.: Efficient instantiations of tweakable blockciphers and refinements to modes OCB and PMAC. In: Lee, P.J. (ed.) ASIACRYPT 2004. LNCS, vol. 3329, pp. 16–31. Springer, Heidelberg (2004)
26. Whiting, D., Schneier, B., Lucks, S., Muller, F.: Phelix: Fast Encryption and Authentication in a Single Cryptographic Primitive. eSTREAM, ECRYPT Stream Cipher Project, Report 2005/027
27. Wu, H., Preneel, B.: Differential-linear attacks against the stream cipher Phelix. In: Biryukov, A. (ed.) FSE 2007. LNCS, vol. 4593, pp. 87–100. Springer, Heidelberg (2007)
28. Yuan, Z., Wang, W., Jia, K., Xu, G., Wang, X.: New birthday attacks on some MACs based on block ciphers. In: Halevi, S. (ed.) CRYPTO 2009. LNCS, vol. 5677, pp. 209–230. Springer, Heidelberg (2009)

Post–quantum (Hash-Based and System Solving)

Fast Exhaustive Search for Quadratic Systems in $\mathbb{F}_2$ on FPGAs

Charles Bouillaguet[1], Chen-Mou Cheng[2], Tung Chou[3],
Ruben Niederhagen[4(✉)], and Bo-Yin Yang[4]

[1] Université de Lille, Lille, France
charles.bouillaguet@lifl.fr
[2] National Taiwan University, Taipei, Taiwan
doug@crypto.tw
[3] Technische Universiteit Eindhoven, Eindhoven, The Netherlands
blueprint@crypto.tw
[4] Academia Sinica, Taipei, Taiwan
ruben@polycephaly.org, by@crypto.tw

Abstract. In 2010, Bouillaguet *et al.* proposed an efficient solver for
polynomial systems over $\mathbb{F}_2$ that trades memory for speed [BCC+10].
As a result, 48 quadratic equations in 48 variables can be solved on
a graphics processing unit (GPU) in 21 min. The research question that
we would like to answer in this paper is how specifically designed
hardware performs on this task. We approach the answer by solving
multivariate quadratic systems on reconfigurable hardware, namely
Field-Programmable Gate Arrays (FPGAs). We show that, although the
algorithm proposed in [BCC+10] has a better asymptotic *time* complexity than traditional enumeration algorithms, it does not have a better
asymptotic complexity in terms of silicon *area*. Nevertheless, our FPGA
implementation consumes 20–25 times less energy than its GPU counterpart. This is a significant improvement, not to mention that the mon-
etary cost per unit of computational power for FPGAs is generally much
cheaper than that of GPUs.

Keywords: Multivariate quadratic polynomials · Solving systems of
equations · Exhaustive search · Parallelization · Field-Programmable
Gate Arrays (FPGAs)

1 Introduction

Solving a system of m nonlinear multivariate polynomial equations in n variables
over $\mathbb{F}_q$ is called the MP problem. It is known to be NP-hard even if $q = 2$ and if
we restrict ourselves to multivariate quadratic equations (in which case we call
the problem MQ). These problems are mathematical problems of natural interest
to cryptographers since an NP-hard problem whose random instances seem hard

See IACR ePrint Archive, Report 2013/436 [BCC+13], for an extended version.

T. Lange, K. Lauter, and P. Lisoněk (Eds.): SAC 2013, LNCS 8282, pp. 205–222, 2014.
DOI: 10.1007/978-3-662-43414-7_11, © Springer-Verlag Berlin Heidelberg 2014

could be used to design cryptographic primitives. Indeed, a seldom challenged standard conjecture is "any probabilistic Turing machine has negligible chance of successfully solving a random MQ instance with a given sub-exponential (in n) complexity when m/n is a constant" [BGP06].

This led to the development of *multivariate public-key cryptography* over the last decades, using one-way trapdoor functions to build cryptosystems such as HFE [Pat96], SFLASH [CGP02], and QUARTZ [PCG01]. It also led to the study of "provably-secure" stream ciphers like QUAD [BGP06].

In *algebraic cryptanalysis*, on the other hand, one distills from a cryptographic primitive a system of multivariate polynomial equations with the secret among the variables. This does not break AES as first advertised, but does break KeeLoq [CBW08], for a recent example. Fast solving would also be a very useful subroutine in attacks such as [BFJ+09].

Fast Exhaustive Search. When evaluating a quadratic system with n variables over $\mathbb{F}_2$, each variable can be chosen as either 0 or 1. Thus, a straight forward approach is to evaluate each equation for all of the 2^n choices of inputs and to return any input that is evaluated to 0 by every single equation. The 2^n inputs can be enumerated by, e.g., using the binary representation of a counter of n bits where bit i is used as value for x_i. Since there are $\frac{n \cdot (n-1)}{2}$ pairs of variables and since in a generic (random) system each coefficient is 1 with probability $\frac{1}{2}$, each generic equation has about $\frac{n \cdot (n-1)}{2} \cdot \frac{1}{2}$ quadratic terms. Therefore, this approach has an asymptotic time complexity of $O(2^n \cdot m \cdot \frac{n \cdot (n-1)}{2} \cdot \frac{1}{2})$. Obviously, the second equation only needs to be evaluated in case the first one evaluates to 0 which happens for about 50 % of the inputs. The third one only needs to be evaluated if the second one evaluated to 0 and so forth. The expected number of equations that need to be evaluated per iteration is $\sum_{i=1}^{m} 2^{1-i} < 2$. Thus, the overall complexity can be reduced to $O(2^n \cdot 2 \cdot \frac{n \cdot (n-1)}{2} \cdot \frac{1}{2}) = O(2^{n-1}(n-1)n)$ or more roughly $O(2^n n^2)$. Observe that the asymptotic time complexity is independent of m, the number of equations in the system, and only depends on n, the number of variables. This straight forward approach will be called *full-evaluation* approach in the remainder of this paper.

The full-evaluation approach requires a small amount of memory. The equation system is known beforehand and can be hard-coded into program code. It requires only n bits to store the current input value plus a small number of registers for the program state and temporary results. Thus, it has an asymptotic memory complexity of $O(n)$.

However, [BCC+10] suggests that we can trade memory for speed. The full-evaluation approach has the disadvantage that computations are repeated since the input of two consecutive computations may be only slightly different. For example, for a counter step from 16 (10000_b) to 17 (10001_b) only the least significant bit and thus the value of x_0 has changed; all the other inputs do not change, the computations not involving x_0 are exactly the same as in the previous step. In other examples, e.g., stepping from 15 (01111_b) to 16 (10000_b) more bits and therefore more variables are affected. Nevertheless, it is not important in which order the inputs are enumerated. The authors of [BCC+10] point out that, by enumerating the inputs in Gray-code order, we ensure that between two consecutive enumeration steps only exactly one bit and therefore only one variable is changed. Therefore only those parts of an equation need to be recomputed that are affected by the change of that single variable x_i. Being in $\mathbb{F}_2$, we only need to add $\frac{\partial f}{\partial x_i}(x)$ to the previous result. This reduces the computational cost from evaluating a *quadratic* multivariate equation in each enumeration step to evaluating a *linear* multivariate equation.

Furthermore, the authors of [BCC+10] prove that between two consecutive evaluations of $\frac{\partial f}{\partial x_i}(x)$ for a particular variable x_i only one other variable x_j of the input has changed. That is, the partial derivative of each variable is also evaluated in Gray-code order, and hence the trick can be applied *recursively*. Thus, by storing the result of the previous evaluation of $\frac{\partial f}{\partial x_i}(x)$, we only need to compute the change in regard to that particular variable x_j, i.e., the second derivative $\frac{\partial^2 f}{\partial x_i \partial x_j}(x)$, which is a *constant* value for quadratic equations.

Therefore, we can trade larger memory for less computation by storing the second derivatives in respect to all pairs of variables in a constant lookup table and by storing the first derivative in respect to each variable in registers. This requires $\frac{n\cdot(n-1)}{2}$ bits for the constant lookup table of the second derivatives and n bits of registers for the first derivatives. The computational cost of each iteration step is reduced to two additions in $\mathbb{F}_2$, one for updating the value of a particular first derivative and one for computing the result of the evaluation.

The computational cost for each equation is independent from the values of n and m and thus will be considered constant for asymptotic estimations. However, since a state is updated in every iteration, all equations need to be computed (in parallel, e.g., using the bitslicing technique as suggested in [BCC+10]) in every single iteration. Therefore, the asymptotic time complexity for this approach is $O(2^n \cdot m)$. The asymptotic memory complexity is $O(m \cdot (\frac{n(n-1)}{2} + n)) = O(\frac{mn(n+1)}{2})$ or more roughly $O(n^2 m)$.

Note that both the Gray-code approach and the full-evaluation approach can be combined by using only m_g equations for the Gray-code approach, thus producing about 2^{n-m_g} solution *candidates* to be tested by the remaining $m-m_g$ equations using full evaluation.

Lastly, we note that Gröbner-basis methods like XL [CKP+00] and F_5 [Fau02] using sparse linear solvers such as Wiedemann might have better performance than exhaustive search even over $\mathbb{F}_2$. For example, they are claimed to asymptotically outperform exhaustive search when $m = n$ with guessing of $\approx 0.45n$ variables [YCC04,BFS+13]. However, as with all asymptotic results, one must carefully check all explicit and implicit assumptions to see how they hold in practice. When taking into account the true cost of Gröbner-basis methods, e.g., communication involved in running large-memory machines, the cross-over point is expected to be much higher than $n = 200$ as predicted in [BFS+13]. However, even systems in 200 variables are out of reach for today's computing capabilities.

The Research Question. The implementation of the Gray-code approach described in [BCC+10] for x86 CPUs and GPUs solves 48 quadratic equations in 48 binary variables using one NVIDIA GTX 295 graphics card in 21 min. The research question that we would like to answer in this paper is *how specifically designed hardware would perform on this task.* We approach the answer by solving multivariate quadratic systems on reconfigurable hardware, namely Field-Programmable Gate Arrays (FPGAs).

While the Gray-code approach has a lower asymptotic time complexity than full evaluation and is — given a sufficient amount of memory — the best choice for a software implementation, we show in Sect. 2.2 that both approaches have the same asymptotic *area* complexity. Therefore, for an FPGA implementation the choice of using either Gray code or full evaluation depends on the specific parameters and the target architecture of the implementation. We motivate our choice and describe our implementation for the Xilinx Spartan-6 FPGA in Sect. 2.

For a massively parallel implementation on FPGAs, it is most efficient to work on a set of input values in a batch. This increases the probability of having collisions of solutions during the computation, i.e. cases in which more than one input value in a batch is a solution candidate for the equation system. The implementation must guarantee that no solution is silently dropped. We discuss this effect in detail in Sect. 3, followed by the discussion of the implementation results and the conclusion of this paper in Sect. 4.

Source Code. The source code of our implementation is available under MIT License at http://www.polycephaly.org/forcemq/.

2 Implementation

The target hardware platform of our implementation is a Xilinx FPGA of the Spartan-6 architecture, device xc6slx150, package fgg676, and speed grade -3. The Spartan-6 architecture offers three different types of logic slices: SLICEX, SLICEL, and SLICEM.

The largest amount with about 50 % of the slices is of type SLICEX. These slices offer four 6-input lookup tables (LUTs) and eight flip-flops. The LUTs can either be treated as logic or as memory: Seen as logic, each LUT-6 is computing the output value of any logical expression in 6 binary variables; seen as memory, each LUT-6 uses the 6 input wires to address a bit in a 64-bit read-only memory. Alternatively, each LUT-6 can be used as two LUT-5 with five identical input wires and two independent output wires.

About 25 % of the slices are of type SLICEL, additionally offering wide multiplexers and carry logic for large adders. Another roughly 25 % of the slices are of type SLICEM, which offer all of the above; in addition, the LUTs of these slices can be used as shift registers or as distributed *read-and-write* memory.

Please refer to [UG384] for more details on the Spartan-6 architecture.

2.1   Parallelization Using Accelerators

Exhaustive search for solutions of multivariate systems is embarrassingly parallel
— all inputs are independent from each other and can be tested in parallel on
as many computing devices as physically available. Furthermore, resources can
be shared during the computation of inputs that have the same value for some
of the variables.

Assume that we want to compute 2^i instances in parallel. We simply *clamp*
the values of i variables such that $x_{n-i}, \ldots, x_{n-1}$ are constant for each instance,
e.g., in case $i = 4$ for instance $5 = 0101_b$ variable $x_{n-1} = 0$, $x_{n-2} = 1$, $x_{n-3} = 0$,
and $x_{n-4} = 1$. Therefore, the 2^n inputs for computations of a system in n
variables can be split into 2^i new systems of 2^{n-i} inputs for $n - i$ variables
using precomputation. These 2^i independent systems can either be computed
in parallel on 2^i computing devices or sequentially on any smaller number of
devices. (Obviously there is a limit on the efficiency of this approach; choosing
$i = n$ would result in solving the whole original system during precomputation.)
The same procedure of fixing variables can be repeated to cut the workload into
parallel instances to exploit parallelism on each computing device.

After fixing variables $x_{n-i}, \ldots, x_{n-1}$, all 2^i instances of one polynomial share
the same quadratic terms; all terms involving $x_{n-i}, \ldots, x_{n-1}$ become either
linear terms or constant terms. Therefore, the computations of the quadratic
terms can be shared: For the Gray-code approach, the second derivatives can
be shared between all instances while one set of first derivatives needs to be
stored per instance; for full evaluation, the logic for the quadratic terms can be
shared while the logic for the linear terms differs between the instances. Sharing
resources requires communication between the instances and therefore is particularly suitable for computations on one single device. Given a sufficient amount
of instances, the total area consumption is dominated by the instances doing the
linear computations rather than by the shared computations on the quadratic
part; therefore, the computations on the linear part require the most attention
for an efficient implementation.

In the following, we investigate the optimal choices of n and m and the number of instances to exhaust the resources of *one single* FPGA most efficiently.
Larger values of n can easily be achieved by running such a design several times
or in parallel on several FPGAs. Larger values of m can be achieved by computing solutions for a subset of equations on the FPGA and forwarding those
solution candidates from the FPGA to a host computer to be checked for the
remaining equations. The flexibility in choosing n and m allows to cut the total
workload into pieces that take a moderate amount of computation time on a
single FPGA. This has the benefit of recovering from hardware failures or power
outages without loss of too many computations.

2.2   Full Evaluation or Gray Code?

The asymptotic time and memory complexities of the full-evaluation approach
and the Gray-code approach are summarized in Table 1. Considering a software

Table 1. Asymptotic complexities of the two approaches for exhaustive search.

	Time	Memory	Comp. logic	Area
Full evaluation	$O(2^n n^2)$	$O(n)$	$O(n^2 m)$	$O(n^2 m)$
Gray code	$O(2^n m)$	$O(n^2 m)$	$O(m)$	$O(n^2 m)$

implementation, for larger systems the Gray-code approach obviously is the more efficient choice, since it has a significantly lower time complexity and it is rather computational than memory bound. Because the memory complexity is much smaller than the time complexity, the memory demand can be handled easily by most modern architectures for such choices of parameters n and m that can be computed in realistic time.

However, a key measure for the complexity of a hardware design is the *area consumption* of the implementation: A smaller area consumption of a single instance of the implementation allows either to reduce cost or to increase the number of parallel instances and thus to reduce the total runtime. The area can be estimated as the sum of the area for computational logic and the area required for memory: The asymptotic complexity for the computational logic of the full-evaluation approach is about $O(n^2)$ for each equation, thus in total $O(n^2 m)$. The memory complexity is $O(n)$, so the area complexity is $O(n + n^2 m) = O(n^2 m)$. We point out that in contrast to the *time* complexity, the *area* complexity *depends* on m. The asymptotic complexity for the computational logic of the Gray-code approach is $O(m)$, the memory complexity is $O(n^2 m)$; the area complexity in total is $O(n^2 m + m) = O(n^2 m)$. Therefore, the asymptotic area complexity of the full-evaluation approach is equal to the area complexity of the Gray-code approach.

In contrast to a software implementation, it is not obvious from the asymptotic complexities, which approach eventually gives the best performance for specific hardware and specific values of n and m. The question is: which approach is using the resources of an FPGA more efficiently.

Choosing the Most Efficient Approach. For fixed parameters n and m we want to run as many parallel instances as possible on the given hardware. Since the quadratic terms are shared by the instances, the optimization goal is to minimize the resource requirements for the computations on the linear terms.

The main disadvantage of the Gray-code approach is that it requires access to *read-and-write memory* to keep track of the first derivatives. The on-chip memory resources, i.e., block memory and distributed memory using slices of type SLICEM, are quite limited. In contrast, the full-evaluation approach "only" requires *logic* that can be implemented using the LUTs of all types of slices.

However, each LUT in a SLICEM stores 64 bits; this is sufficient space for the first derivatives of 64 variables using the Gray-code approach. On the other hand, there are four times more logic-LUTs than RAM-LUTs. Four LUT-6 cover the evaluation of at most 24 variables. Therefore, the Gray-code approach is using the available input ports more efficiently. This is due to the fact that the inputs for the Gray-code approach are addresses of width $O(\log n)$, whereas full evaluation requires $O(n)$ inputs for the variables. Thus, the Gray-code approach requires smaller bus widths and buffer sizes for pipelining.

Finally, the Gray-code approach allows to easily reuse a placed and routed design for different equation systems by exchanging the data in the lookup tables. An area-optimized implementation of the full-evaluation approach only requires logic for those terms of an equation that have a non-zero coefficient. To be able to use the same design for different equation systems, one would have to provide logic for *all* terms regardless of their coefficients, thus roughly doubling the required logic compared to the optimal solution. The Xilinx tool chain does not include a tool to exchange the LUT data from a fully placed and routed design, so we implemented our own tool for this purpose.

All in all, the Gray-code approach has several benefits compared to the full-evaluation approach which make it more suitable and more efficient for an FPGA implementation on a Spartan-6. The figures might be different, e.g., for an ASIC implementation or for FPGAs with different LUT sizes. We decided to use the Gray-code approach for the main part of our implementation to produce a number of solution candidates from a subset of the equations. These candidates are then checked for the remaining equations using full evaluation, partly on the FPGA, partly on the host computer.

2.3 Implementation of the Gray-Code Approach

As described in Sect. 1, the Gray-code approach trades larger memory for less computation. Algorithm 1 shows the pseudo code of the Gray-code approach (see the extended version of [BCC+10]). In case of the FPGA implementation, the initialization (Algorithm 1, lines 20 to 35) is performed offline and is hard-coded into the program file. Figure 1 shows the structure of the module *solver* for solving a system of m equations in n variables with 2^i instances of m_g equations using the Gray-code approach and $m - m_g$ full evaluations for the remaining equations.

The implementation of the Gray-code approach works as follows: First and second derivatives in respect to each variable are stored in lookup tables d' and d'' (Algorithm 1, lines 27 and 32). The second derivatives are constant and thus only require read-only memory. They require a quadratic amount of bits depending on the number of variables n. The first derivatives are computed in each iteration step based on their previous value (Algorithm 1, line 16). Therefore, the first derivatives are stored in a relatively small random access memory with a size linear to n.

Due to the structure of the Gray code, when looking at two consecutive values v_{i-1}, v_i in Gray-code enumeration, the position k_1 of the least-significant non-zero bit in the binary representation of i is the particular bit that is toggled when stepping from v_{i-1} to v_i. Therefore, the first derivative $\frac{\partial f}{\partial x_{k_1}}$ in respect to variable x_{k_1} needs to be considered for the evaluation. Furthermore, since the last time the bit k_1 had toggled, only the bit at the position k_2 of the second

```
 1: function RUN(f, n)                    20: function INIT(f = a_{n-1,n-2}x_{n-1}x_{n-2} +
 2:    s ← INIT(f, n);                          a_{n-1,n-3}x_{n-1}x_{n-3} + · · · + a_{1,0}x_1x_0 +
 3:    while s.i < 2^n do                        a_{n-1}x_{n-1} + a_{n-2}x_{n-2} + · · · + a_0x_0 + a, n)
 4:       NEXT(s);                        21:    state s;
 5:       if s.y = 0 then                 22:    s.i ← 0;
 6:          return s.i ⊕ SHR_1(s.i);     23:    s.x ← 0;
 7:       end if                          24:    s.y ← a;
 8:    end while                          25:    for all k, 0 < k < n, do
 9: end function                          26:       for all j, 0 ⩽ j < k, do
10:                                       27:          s.d''[k, j] ← a_{k,j};
11: function NEXT(s)                      28:       end for
12:    s.i ← s.i + 1;                     29:    end for
13:    k_1 ← BIT_1(s.i);                  30:    s.d'[0] ← a_0;
14:    k_2 ← BIT_2(s.i);                  31:    for all k, 1 ⩽ k < n, do
15:    if k_2 valid then                  32:       s.d'[k] ← s.d''[k, k − 1] ⊕ a_k;
16:       s.d'[k_1] ← s.d'[k_1] ⊕ s.d''[k_1, k_2];  33:    end for
17:    end if                             34:    return s;
18:    s.y ← s.y ⊕ s.d'[k_1];            35: end function
19: end function
```

Algorithm 1. Pseudo code for the Gray-code approach (see [BCC+10]). The functions BIT_1 and BIT_2 return the positions of the first and second least-significant non-zero bits respectively and SHR_1 is a logical shift right by one position.

least-significant non-zero bit in i has changed. So we need to access $\frac{\partial^2 f}{\partial x_{k_1} \partial x_{k_2}}$ in the static lookup table.

To compute k_1 and k_2 (Algorithm 1, lines 13 and 14), we use a module *counter* (Fig. 1, bottom) that is incrementing a counter by 1 in each cycle (cf. Algorithm 1, line 12). The counter counts from 0 to 2^{n-i}. To determine its first and second least-significant non-zero bits, we feed the counter value to a module called *gray_tree* that derives the index positions of the first and the second non-zero bit based on a divide-and-conquer approach. The output of the *gray_tree* module are buses k_1 and k_2 of width $\lceil \log_2(n) \rceil$ and two wires $enable_1$ and $enable_2$ (not shown in the figure) indicating whether k_1 and k_2 contain valid information (e.g., for all counter values $2^j, j \geq 0$, the output k_2 is invalid since the binary representation of 2^j has only one non-zero bit).

Next, we compute the address *addr* of the second derivative in the lookup table from the values k_1 and k_2 as $addr = k_2(k_2 - 1)/2 + k_1$ (cf. Algorithm 1, line 16). The computation is implemented fully-pipelined to guarantee short data paths and a high frequency at runtime. The modules *counter* and *gray_tree* and the computation of the address for the lookup in the table are the same for all instances of all equations and therefore are required only once.

Now, the address is forwarded to the logic for the first equation eq_0. Here, the buses *addr* and k_1 are buffered and in the next cycle forwarded to the lookup table of equation eq_1 and so on. The address is fed to the constant memory that returns the value of the second derivative d_0''. We implement the constant

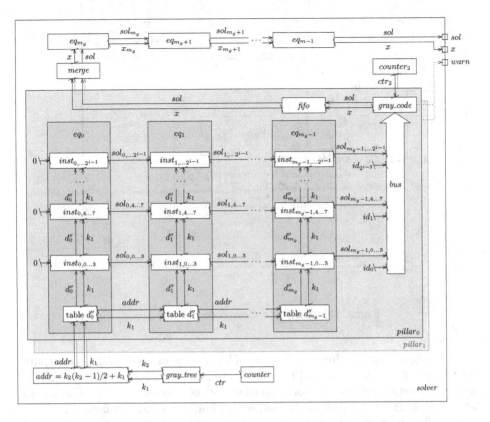

Fig. 1. Structure of the overall architecture.

memory using LUTs. The address of an element in the lookup table is split into segment and offset: The segment specifies the LUT that is storing the bit, the 6 least significant bits of the addresses are the offset of the bit in that LUT.

After value d_0'' of the second derivative of eq_0 has been read from the lookup table, it is forwarded together with k_1 to the first instance $inst_{0,0}$ of eq_0, where $inst_{j,k}$ denotes the k-th instance of equation eq_j. Here, d_0'' and k_1 are buffered and forwarded in the next clock cycle to the instance $inst_{0,1}$ of eq_0 and so on.

In instance $inst_{0,0}$, the value of the first derivative in respect to x_{k_1} is updated and its **xor** with the previous result y is computed. For the random access memory storing the first derivatives we are using distributed memory implemented by slices of type SLICEM. Figure 2 shows a schematic of a Gray-code instance $inst_{j,k}$. Storing the first derivative requires one single LUT-6 for up to 64 variables. Storing the result y of each iteration step requires a one-bit storage; we use a flip-flop for this purpose. The logic for updating the first derivative requires three inputs: d'', the first derivative d', and $enable_2$ to distinguish whether d'' is valid (see Algorithm 1, line 15 and 16). The logic for updating y requires two inputs, the new first derivative d' and the previous value of y (Algorithm 1, line 18). We combine both computations in one single LUT-6 by using one LUT-6 as

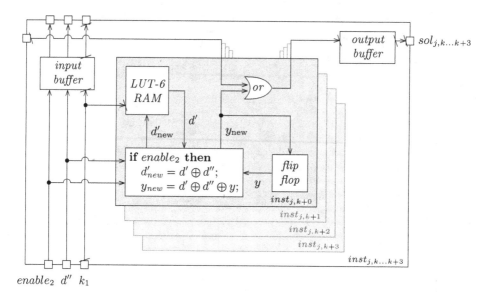

Fig. 2. Schematic of a Gray-code instance group.

two LUT-5, giving four inputs d'', d', $enable_2$, and y and receiving two outputs for the new first derivative and for the new y. Furthermore, we compute the **or** with the solutions of the previous equations as $sol_{j,k} = sol_{j-1,k} \vee y$. The inputs d'', $enable_2$, and k_1 as well as the output are buffered using flip-flops.

Finally, the buffered result $sol_{j,k}$ is forwarded to $inst_{j+1,k}$ of eq_{j+1} in the next cycle. After the result of $inst_{j+1,k}$ has been computed as described before, the cumulated result $sol_{j+1,k} = sol_{j,k} \vee y$ is computed and forwarded to instance $inst_{j+2,k}$ and so on.

Each SLICEM has four LUTs that can be addressed as memory. However, they can only be written to if they all share the same address wires as input. Therefore, we combine four instances $inst_{j,k...k+3}$ of an equation j in one SLICEM using the same data as input. As a side effect, this reduces the number of buffers that are required for the now four-fold shared inputs. All in all, for up to 64 variables, a group of four instances for one equation requires 4 slices, one of them being a SLICEM.

Eventually, the four results $sol_{m_g-1,k...k+3}$ of an instance group are put on a bus together with a group ID that defines the value of the clamped variables. If more than one instance group finds a solution candidate in the same enumeration step, there might be a collision on the bus. We describe these collisions and our counter measures in detail in Sect. 3.

In each cycle, the solution candidates together with their ID are forwarded from one bus segment to the next, each connected to an instance group, until they eventually are leaving the bus after the last segment has been reached.

We are using the remaining resources of the FPGA to compute the actual solutions of the equation system. The computations on a subset of m_g equations using the Gray-code approach drastically reduce the search space from 2^n to 2^{n-m_g}. Therefore, we only need single instances of the remaining equations to check the solution candidates we receive from the Gray-code part. Since the inputs are quasi-random, we use full evaluation to check the candidates. If the system has more equations than we can fit on the FPGA, the remaining solution candidates are eventually forwarded to the host for final processing.

In order to check a solution candidate on the FPGA, we need to compute the actual Gray code for the input first. Since the design is fully pipelined, the value of each solution candidate from the Gray-code part is uniquely defined by the cycle when it appears. Therefore, we use a second counter ($counter_2$) that runs in sync, delayed by the pipeline length, to the original counter ($counter$). We compute the corresponding Gray code from the value ctr_2 of this counter as $x = ctr_2 \oplus \mathrm{SHR}_1(ctr_2)$ (see Algorithm 1, line 6). This value is appended to the ID and $x_{m_g-1} = (id, x)$ is forwarded into a FIFO queue.

To give some flexibility when fitting the design to the physical resources on the FPGA, our design allows the instances to be split into several *pillars*, each with their own bus, *gray_code* module and FIFO queue. The data paths are merged by selecting one solution candidate per cycle from the FIFO queues in a round-robin fashion.

Each solution candidate is forwarded to a module eq_{m_g} which simply evaluates equation m_g for the given input. To implement the full evaluation, we use a Greedy algorithm to map the terms of each equation to as few LUTs as possible (for more details please refer to the extended version [BCC+13] of this paper). The result of eq_{m_g} is or-ed to sol_{m_g-1} and forwarded to eq_{m_g+1} together with a buffered copy of x_{m_g-1} and so on.

Eventually, a vector x, its solution *sol*, and a warning signal *warn* are returned by the module *solver*. In case *sol* is equal to zero, i.e., all equations evaluated to zero for input x, the vector x is sent to the host.

3   Collisions, or Overabundance of Solution Candidates

Our implementation is akin to a map-reduce process, wherein $V = 2^n$ input vectors (n being the number of variables) are passed to many instances that each screen a portion of the inputs against a subset of m_g equations. Solution candidates which pass this stage move to a stage where they are checked against the remaining equations.

As mentioned in the previous section, the solution candidates that are computed in the first stage are collected by a sequential bus that connects all instances. This bus must provide a sufficient amount of resources to transfer all solution candidates to the second stage. Problems occur, if two or more instances find a solution candidate in the same iteration step. Every input processed by each screening instance may become a solution candidate with probability 2^{-m_g}. This is a highly unlikely event for a specific instance, but with a large number of instances, the probability of finding a solution candidate grows.

3.1   Expected Collisions

Let us assume that each of $V = 2^n$ input vectors is checked against m_g equations by $I = 2^i$ instances. A reasonable setup on a Spartan-6 FPGA might have $(n, m_g, i) = (48, 28, 9)$ or $(n, m_g, i) = (48, 14, 10)$.

A back-of-the-envelope calculation would go as follows: There are approximately $V/2^{m_g} = 2^{n-m_g}$ solution candidates, randomly spread over $V/I = 2^{n-i}$ iteration steps. The birthday paradox says that we may reasonably expect one or more collisions from x balls (solution candidates) in y bins (iteration steps) as soon as $x \gtrsim \sqrt{2y}$. Therefore, we should expect a small but non-zero number of "collisions", iteration steps that have more than one solution candidate.

To articulate the above differently, each input vector has a probability of 2^{-m_g} to pass screening, and the event for each vector may be considered independent. Thus, the probability to have two or more solutions among I instances in the same iteration step is given by the sum of all coefficients of the quadratic and higher terms in the expansion of $(1 + (x - 1)/2^{m_g})^I$. The quadratic term represents the probability of having a collision of two values, the cubic term the probability of three values, and so on. The quadratic coefficient can be expected to be the largest and contribute to most of the sum. The expected number of collisions among all inputs is V/I times this sum, which is roughly

$$(V/I)\left[x^2\right]\left((1 - 2^{-m_g}) + 2^{-m_g}x\right)^I = (1 - 2^{-m_g})^{I-2}\frac{(I-1)}{2^{2m_g-n+1}} \approx 2^{i+n-2m_g-1},$$

where $\left[x^k\right] f(x)$ denotes the coefficient of x^k in the expansion of f.

The last approximation holds when $(1 - 2^{-m_g})^{I-2} \approx \exp\left(2^{-(m_g-i)}\right) \approx 1$ and $I \gg 1$. We can judge the quality of this approximation by the ratio between the quadratic and cubic term coefficients, which is $(I-2)2^{-m_g}/3 \lesssim 2^{-(m_g+1-i)}$. In other words, if $m_g - i > 3$, the number of expected collisions is roughly $2^{n+i-(2m_g+1)}$ with an error bar of 5 % or less. Similarly the expected number of c-collisions (with at least c solutions within the same iteration step) is

$$(V/I)\left[x^c\right]\left((1 - 2^{-m_g}) + 2^{-m_g}x\right)^I \approx 2^{n-ck+(c-1)i}/c!.$$

3.2   Choosing Parameters

In case of the Spartan-6 xc6slx150-fgg676-3 FPGA, the slices are physically located in a quite regular, rectangular grid of 128 columns and 192 rows. The grid has some large gaps on top and in the bottom as well as several vertical and horizontal gaps. By picking a subset of slices in the center of the FPGA we obtain a regular grid structure of 116 columns and 144 rows. Each row has 29 groups of 4 slices: one SLICEM, one SLICEL and two SLICEX. Such a group has enough resources for four Gray-code instances each. Therefore, the whole region can be used for up to $29 \cdot 4 \cdot 144 = 16,704$ Gray-code instances. The area below the slices for the Gray-code instances is used for the modules *counter* and *gray_tree*, for the computation of the address, and for the second-derivative tables. The area above the instances contains enough logic for evaluating the remaining equations using full evaluation and for the logic required for FPGA-to-host communication.

Using 128 rows, we could fit $I = 128 \cdot 4 = 512 = 2^9$ instances of $m_g = 28$ equations of the Gray-code approach onto the FPGA — one equation per column, four instances per row — while guaranteeing short signal paths, leaving space of four slice columns for the bus, and giving more space for full evaluation on the top. With 28 equations in 2^9 instances, collisions of two solutions during one cycle are very rare and easy to handle by the host CPU. The obvious optimization to double the performance is to double I, the number of system instances, and to halve m_g, the number of equations evaluated with the Gray-code approach. However, this optimization introduces additional complications: Even if we can fit $I = 2^{10}$ instances of $m_g = 14$ equations using the Gray-code approach into the FPGA, Sect. 3.1 shows that one collision appears every 2^{10} cycles on average. We can no longer use the simple approach of re-checking all blocks with collisions on the CPU, we have to handle collisions on the FPGA. We describe in the following how to achieve 2^{10} instances for up to 14 (actually only 12) equations.

3.3 Handling of Collisions

Due to the physical layout of the FPGA and in order to save space for input-buffers, our implementation groups four instances with the same inputs together into an instance group. Instead of resolving a collision within an instance group right away, we forward a word of four bits, one for each instance, to the bus and cope with those collision later.

Whenever there is a collision at a instance group j, i.e., there is already a solution candidate on the bus in bus segment j, the candidate of group j is postponed giving precedence to the candidate on the bus. However, the actual input giving this solution candidate is not stored in the Gray-code instances but is later derived from the cycle in which the solution was found. Therefore, delaying the solution distorts the computation of the input value. Computing the input value immediately at each bus segment would require a lot of logic and would increase the bus width to n. Instead, we count how many cycles each solution candidate is delayed before being placed on the bus. Since the resources are limited, we can use at most 4 bits for this counter. For a push-back of up to 14 cycles, we can compute the exact corresponding solution candidate from each counter value. In case of 15 or more cycles of push-back, 1111_b is put on the bus to signal an error condition to the follow-up logic.

Since the delay has a very limited maximum number of cycles, we can not use classical bus congestion techniques like exponential backoff; we must ensure that candidates are pushed onto the bus as soon as possible. This leads to high congestion in particular at the end of the bus.

Due to the push-back, our collision pool has become temporal as well as spatial. That is, it might happen that another solution candidate is produced by the same instance group before the previous one is handed to the bus. Therefore, we provide four buffer slots for each instance group to handle the rare cases where candidates are pushed back for several cycles while further candidates come up. If there are more candidates than there are buffer slots available, a warning signal is fired up and the involved input values are recomputed by the host.

All in all, the bus is transporting $i+7$ signals for 2^i instances; $i-2$ signals for the instance-group ID of the solution candidate, 4 signals for the push-back counter, 4 signals for the four outputs of a group of instances, and 1 warning signal.

Figure 3 shows a schematic of a bus segment. The solutions from an instance group of equation eq_{m_g-1} are sent in from the left using signal sol; the inputs from the previous bus segment are shown in the bottom. Whenever there is no signal on the bus, i.e., sol_in is all high, the control logic sets the signal $step$ to high and a buffered result is pushed onto the bus; further delayed results are forwarded to the next buffer. If an available result can not be sent to the bus because there is already data on the bus, the step signal is set to low and each cycle counter in the counter buffers is incremented by one.

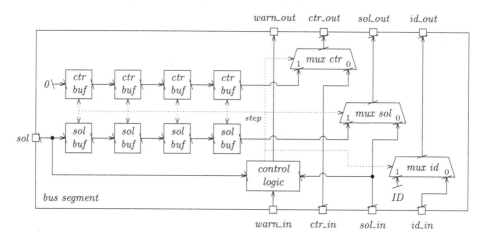

Fig. 3. Schematic of a bus segment.

The logic for each bus segment covering a group of 4 instances requires 10 slices (the area of 2.5 Gray-Code instance groups, i.e. four instances of a single equation) including buffers, counters, and multiplexers. Therefore, even though 29 Gray-Code instance groups would fit into one row on the FPGA, with two buses and two pillars of instances per row, we can only fit instances of 12 equations: $2 \cdot (12 + 2.5) = 29$. However, we achieve the goal of the desired $2^{10} = 1024$ parallel instances.

At the end of the buses, two FIFOs buffer the solution candidates so that the two data streams can be joined safely to forward a single data stream to the following logic for further handling of solution candidates (see Fig. 1). Here also the occasional collisions of solutions are resolved that might occur in an instance group of four instances as described above. Since the Gray-code part is using 2^{10} instances and 12 equations, there is one solution candidate on average every $2^{12-10} = 4$ cycles going into full evaluation.

With each bus averaging $1/8$ new entries and being capable of dispatching 1 entry every cycle, the buses should not suffer from too much congestion (confirmed by simulations and tests). With a push-back of at most 14 cycles, an unhandleable super-collision should only happen if 15 candidates appear within 15 consecutive 4-instance groups each with probability 2^{-10}, *all within 15 cycles*. We can do a back-of-the-envelope calculation for the probability like in Sect. 3.1 to find an upper bound of $\binom{225}{15} \left(2^{-10}\right)^{15} \approx 6.4 \times 10^{-21}$. Just to be very sure, such super-collisions are still detected and passed to the host CPU, which rechecks the affected inputs. In all our tests and simulations, we did not detect any super-collisions, which confirms that our push-back buffer and counter sizes are sufficient.

We are able to fit logic for full evaluation of at least 42 more equations on the chip, giving 54 equations in the FPGA in total. This reduces the amount of outgoing solution candidates from the FPGA to the host computer to a marginal amount. Therefore, the host computer is able to serve a large amount of FPGAs even for a large total amount of equations in the system.

4   Performance Results and Concluding Remarks

We tested our implementation on a "RIVYERA S6-LX150 FPGA Cluster" from SciEngines. The RIVYERA has a 19-inch chassis of 4U height with an off-the-shelf host PC that controls 16 to 128 Spartan-6 LX150 FPGAs (xc6slx150-fgg676-3) and up to 256 FPGAs in the high density version "RIVYERA S6-LX150 HD"; our RIVYERA S6-LX150 has 16 FPGAs. The FPGAs are mounted on extension cards of 8 FPGAs (16 in the HD version) each with an extra FPGA exclusively for the communication with the host via PCIe.

We are using LOC constraints to explicitly place the Gray-code instances. Therefore, we achieve a tight packing and short data paths which allows us to run our design at up to 200 MHz. Due to the overall architecture we can compute systems of up to 64 variables using 2^{10} instances on a single FPGA. At a clock frequency of 200 MHz, solving a system in 64 variables in a single run requires $2^{64-10}/200\,\text{MHz} \approx 1042\,\text{days}$; to reduce data loss in case of system failures or power outages, we recommend to divide the workload into smaller pieces with a shorter runtime. Our reference design is using $n = 54$ variables and $m = 54$ equations. In this case, a single run is finished after $2^{54-10}/200\,\text{MHz} \approx 24.5\,\text{h}$. Preparing and exchanging the LUT data in the program file using our tools takes about 10 s. Therefore a system of 64 variables can be solved in $2^{64-54} = 1024$ separate runs with a negligible overhead.

Area Consumption. The Spartan-6 LX150 FPGA has 23,038 slices. In total, our logic occupies 18,613 slices (80.79 %) of the FPGA. We are using 63.44 % of the LUTs and 44.47 % of the registers.

The logic for the Gray-code evaluation occupies the largest area with 15,281 slices (67.43 %). Only 253 of those slices are used for the second-derivative tables,

Table 2. Comparison of the runtime and cost for systems in 48, 64, and 80 variables.

		Time	Energy	Energy cost	
				Germany	USA
48 variables	Spartan-6	23 min	3.4 Wh	–	–
	GTX 295	21 min	82.3 Wh	–	–
64 variables	Spartan-6	1,042 days	216 kWh	€56	US$28
	GTX 295	956 days	5,390 kWh	€1,401	US$701
80 variables	Spartan-6	187,182 years	14.4 GWh	€3.7 mil.	US$1.9 mil.
	GTX 295	171,603 years	353.3 GWh	€91.8 mil.	US$45.9 mil.

the counter, and address calculation. The bus occupies 2,740 slices, the remaining 12,288 slices are used for the 1,024 instances of 12 equations.

The logic for full evaluation of the remaining 42 equations, the FIFO queues, and the remaining solver logic requires 1,702 slices (7.39 %). Each equation in 54 variables requires 88 LUTs for computational logic, thus about 22 slices. All these slices are located in an area above the Gray-code logic. More than 50 % of the slices in this area are still available, leaving space to evaluate more equations using full evaluation if required.

The logic for communication with the host using SciEngine's API requires 1,377 slices (5.98 %).

Performance Evaluation. Our Spartan-6 FPGA design runs at 200 MHz. The design is fully pipelined and evaluates 2^{10} input values in each clock cycle. Thus, we compute all solutions of a system of 48 variables and 48 equations by evaluating all possible 2^{48} input values in $2^{48-10}/200$ MHz = 23 min with a single FPGA. The GPU implementation of [BCC+10] computes all solutions on a GTX 295 graphics card in 21 min. Therefore, the Spartan-6 performs about the same as the GTX 295.

However, total runtime is not the only factor that affects the overall cost of the computation; power consumption is another important factor. We measured both the power consumptions of the Spartan-6 FPGA and the GTX 295 during computation: Our RIVYERA requires 305 W on average during the computation using all 16 FPGAs. The host computer with all FPGA cards removed requires 165 W. Therefore, a single FPGA requires (305 W − 165 W)/16 = 8.8 W on average, including communication overhead. We measured the power consumption of the GTX 295 in the same way: During computation on the GTX 295, the whole machine required 357W on average. Without the graphics card, the GPU-host computer requires 122 W. Therefore, the GTX 295 requires 235 W on average during computation. For a system of 48 variables, a single Spartan-6 FPGA requires 8.8 W · 23 min = 3.4 Wh for the whole computation. The GPU requires 235 W · 21 min = 82.3 Wh. Therefore, the Spartan-6 FPGA requires about 25 times less energy than the GTX 295 graphics card.

For a system of 64 variables, the very same FPGA design needs about $2^{64-10}/200$ MHz = 1042 days and therefore about 216 kWh. For this system, the

GPU requires about 965 days and roughly 5,390 kWh. A single kWh costs, e.g., about €0.26 in Germany[1] and about US$0.13 in the USA[2]. Therefore, solving a system of 64 variables with an FPGA costs about $216\,\text{kWh} \cdot e0.26/\text{kWh} = e56$ in Germany and $216\,\text{kWh} \cdot \text{US\$0.13}/\text{kWh} = \text{US\$28}$ in the US. Solving the same system using a GTX 295 graphics card costs €1,401 or US$701. Table 2 shows an overview for systems in 48, 64, and 80 variables.

Development of GPU Hardware. The GPU implementation of [BCC+10] from 2010 uses a GTX 295 graphics card. We also measured the performance of their CUDA program on a GTX 780 graphics card which is state-of-the-art in 2013. However, the computations took slightly more time, although the GTX 780 should be more than three times faster than the GTX 295: the GTX 780 has 2304 ALUs running at 863 MHz while the GTX 295 has 480 ALUs running at 1242 MHz.

We suspect that the relative decrease of SRAM compared to the number of ALUs and the new instruction scheduling of the new generation of NVIDIA GPUs is responsible for the tremendous performance gap. To get full performance on the GTX 780 a thorough adaption and hardware-specific optimization of the algorithm would be required; the claim of NVIDIA that CUDA kernels can just be recompiled to profit from new hardware generations does not apply.

Nevertheless, running the code from [BCC+10] on a GTX 780 graphics card requires about 20 % less energy than on the GTX 295, about 20 times more than our FPGA implementation.

80-bit Security. We want to point out that it is actually feasible to solve a system in 80 variables in a reasonable time: using $2^{80-64} = 2^{16} = 65{,}536$ FPGAs in parallel, such a system could be solved in 1042 days. Building such a large system is possible; e.g., the Tianhe-2 supercomputer has 80,000 CPUs.

Each RIVYERA S6-LX150 HD has up to 256 FPGAs; therefore, this computation would require $2^{16}/256 = 256$ RIVYERA-HD computers. The list price for one RIVYERA-HD is €110,000, about US$145,000; the price for 256 machines is at most $256 \cdot \text{US\$145,000} \approx \text{US\$37}$ million. Therefore, solving a system in 80 variables in 1042 days costs US$39 million, including the electricity bill of US$2 million for a continuous supply of $((256 \cdot 8.8\text{W}) + 165\text{W}) \cdot 256 = 620\text{kW}$. For comparison, the budget for the Tianhe-2 supercomputer was 2.4 billion Yuan (US$390 million), *not* including the electricity bill for its peak power consumption of 17.8 MW. Therefore, 80-bit security coming from solving 80-variable systems over $\mathbb{F}_2$ is, as more cryptographers gradually acknowledge, no longer secure against institutional attackers and today's computing technology.

Acknowledgments. We would like to thank SciEngines for their support to get our design running on the RIVYERA, Ralf Zimmermann for his answers to our FPGA-related questions, and the anonymous reviewers for their valuable feedback. This research was partially sponsored by Academia Sinica under Bo-Yin Yang's Career Award and by the National Science Council project 100-2628-E-001-004-MY3.

---

[1] Average in 2012 according to the Agentur für Erneuerbare Energien.
[2] Average in 2012 according to the Bureau of Labor Statistics.

References

[BCC+10] Bouillaguet, C., Chen, H.-C., Cheng, C.-M., Chou, T., Niederhagen, R., Shamir, A., Yang, B.-Y.: Fast exhaustive search for polynomial systems in $\mathbb{F}_2$. In: Mangard, S., Standaert, F.-X. (eds.) CHES 2010. LNCS, vol. 6225, pp. 203–218. Springer, Heidelberg (2010). Extended Version: http://www.lifl.fr/~bouillag/pub.html

[BCC+13] Bouillaguet, C., Cheng, C.-M., Chou, T., Niederhagen, R., Yang, B.-Y.: Fast exhaustive search for quadratic systems in $\mathbb{F}_2$ on FPGAs. Extended Version. IACR Cryptology ePrint Archive, Report 2013/436. http://eprint.iacr.org/2013/436 (2013)

[BFJ+09] Bouillaguet, C., Fouque, P.-A., Joux, A., Treger, J.: A family of weak keys in HFE (and the corresponding practical key-recovery). IACR Cryptology ePrint Archive, Report 2009/619. http://eprint.iacr.org/2009/619 (2009)

[BFS+13] Bardet, M., Faugère, J.-C., Salvy, B., Spaenlehauer, P.-J.: On the complexity of solving quadratic boolean systems. J. Complex. **29**(1), 53–75 (2013)

[BGP06] Berbain, C., Gilbert, H., Patarin, J.: QUAD: a practical stream cipher with provable security. In: Vaudenay, S. (ed.) EUROCRYPT 2006. LNCS, vol. 4004, pp. 109–128. Springer, Heidelberg (2006)

[CBW08] Courtois, N.T., Bard, G.V., Wagner, D.: Algebraic and slide attacks on KeeLoq. In: Nyberg, K. (ed.) FSE 2008. LNCS, vol. 5086, pp. 97–115. Springer, Heidelberg (2008)

[CGP02] Courtois, N., Goubin, L., Patarin, J.: SFLASH, A Fast Asymmetric Signature Scheme for Low-Cost Smartcards: Primitive Specification, Second Revised Version. https://www.cosic.esat.kuleuven.be/nessie/tweaks.html (2002)

[CKP+00] Courtois, N.T., Klimov, A.B., Patarin, J., Shamir, A.: Efficient algorithms for solving overdefined systems of multivariate polynomial equations. In: Preneel, B. (ed.) EUROCRYPT 2000. LNCS, vol. 1807, pp. 392–407. Springer, Heidelberg (2000)

[Fau02] Faugère, J.-C.: A new efficient algorithm for computing Gröbner bases without reduction to zero (F_5). In: International Symposium on Symbolic and Algebraic Computation – ISSAC 2002, July 2002, pp. 75–83. ACM Press (2002)

[Pat96] Patarin, J.: Hidden fields equations (HFE) and isomorphisms of polynomials (IP): two new families of asymmetric algorithms. In: Maurer, U.M. (ed.) EUROCRYPT 1996. LNCS, vol. 1070, pp. 33–48. Springer, Heidelberg (1996)

[PCG01] Patarin, J., Courtois, N.T., Goubin, L.: QUARTZ, 128-bit long digital signatures. In: Naccache, D. (ed.) CT-RSA 2001. LNCS, vol. 2020, pp. 282–297. Springer, Heidelberg (2001)

[UG384] Spartan-6 FPGA Configurable Logic Block — User Guide. v1.1 UG384. Xilinx Inc., Feb. 2010

[YCC04] Yang, B.-Y., Chen, J.-M., Courtois, N.T.: On asymptotic security estimates in XL and Gröbner bases-related algebraic cryptanalysis. In: López, J., Qing, S., Okamoto, E. (eds.) ICICS 2004. LNCS, vol. 3269, pp. 401–413. Springer, Heidelberg (2004)

Faster Hash-Based Signatures
with Bounded Leakage

Thomas Eisenbarth[1], Ingo von Maurich[2(✉)], and Xin Ye[1]

[1] Worcester Polytechnic Institute, Worcester, MA, USA
[2] Horst Görtz Institute for IT-Security, Ruhr-University Bochum, Bochum, Germany
{teisenbarth,xye}@wpi.edu, ingo.vonmaurich@rub.de

Abstract. Digital signatures have become a key component of many embedded system solutions and are facing strong security and efficiency requirements. At the same time side-channel resistance is essential for a signature scheme to be accepted in real-world applications. Based on the Merkle signature scheme and Winternitz one-time signatures we propose a signature scheme with bounded side-channel leakage that is secure in a post-quantum setting. Novel algorithmic improvements for the authentication path computation bound side-channel leakage and improve the average signature computation time by close to 50 % when compared to state-of-the-art algorithms. The proposed scheme is implemented on an Intel Core i7 CPU and an AVR ATxmega microcontroller with carefully optimized versions for the respective target platform. The theoretical algorithmic improvements are verified in the implementations and cryptographic hardware accelerators are used to achieve competitive performance.

Keywords: Hash-based cryptography · Signatures · Side-channel leakage · Software · Microcontroller · Post-quantum cryptography

1 Motivation

With the increasing popularity of contactless smart cards and near field communication, digital signature engines have become a key component of many embedded system solutions. The applications of digital signatures are numerous, ranging from identification over electronic payments to firmware updates and protection against product counterfeiting. Due to the high computational requirements for public-key cryptography, providing efficient signatures on embedded microprocessors without dedicated co-processors is a challenge. At the same time, side channel attacks are considered a serious threat for such embedded implementations. On the downside, adding effective protection against attacks like power or EM analysis is costly in terms of space and computation time. Hence, side-channel resistant public key engines are often just too bulky for widespread adoption. Exploring public key schemes that are both efficient on embedded platforms and offer inherent side-channel resistance can be a superior alternative to the prevailing choices of (EC-)DSA and RSA.

T. Lange, K. Lauter, and P. Lisoněk (Eds.): SAC 2013, LNCS 8282, pp. 223–243, 2014.
DOI: 10.1007/978-3-662-43414-7_12, © Springer-Verlag Berlin Heidelberg 2014

New research directions in theoretical cryptography, namely *leakage resilient* cryptographic schemes, suggest that performing cryptographic algorithms in a different way might make them inherently resistant against side-channel attacks without the need of further implementational countermeasures. Instead of protecting a key that is used over and over again, these schemes limit the leakage that an attacker can observe for a given key (or state) by limiting the number of accesses to it. The groundbreaking work of Faust et al. [9] shows a scheme that provides choosable many leakage resilient signatures. The approach builds on a signature scheme that only leaks an admissible amount of information when executed up to three times. The scheme does not explicitly propose or recommend an underlying signature scheme. But when instantiated with one of the prevailing signature schemes, the leakage resilient signature engine becomes practically infeasible: each generated leakage-resilient signature requires three signature generations and two key generations of the underlying signature.

Prior work by Rohde et al. [22] as well as by Hülsing et al. [11] suggest that the Merkle Signature Scheme (MSS) in combination with Winternitz One-Time Signatures (W-OTS) is a possible choice for a time-limited signature scheme and can be efficiently implemented in embedded systems. We analyze and extend the proposal by Rohde et al. and propose several modifications that lead to significant performance improvements and bounded side-channel leakage. One of the key components of the analyzed MSS engine is the Pseudo Random Number Generator (PRNG) used to generate the private signing key. The PRNG is a self-contained component and is desired to be leakage resilient. Another building block for the one-time signatures is a one-way function that needs to have bounded leakage. Other parts of the engine, such as a collision resistant hash function needed for the Merkle tree only process public knowledge and are thus leakage-agnostic.

Contribution. Compared to the state-of-the-art, the proposed scheme provides bounded leakage at comparable cost to an *unprotected* ECC engine, which enables and encourages a wide deployment. We implement the proposed signature scheme on two wide-spread platforms (Intel Core i7 CPU and low-cost AVR 8-bit microcontroller) targeting a security level of 80-bit and making use of available cryptographic hardware accelerators to gain maximum efficiency. Furthermore, we propose an improved algorithm for the authentication path computation of a Merkle tree which limits side-channel leakage when signature keys are generated using a secure PRNG. At the same time we decrease the average computation time by close to 50 % compared to the most efficient authentication path computation algorithm at the price of a slightly increased memory consumption. Explicit formulas are developed to quantify the amount each leaf of the Merkle tree is computed during the authentication path computation. The drawback of current authentication path computation algorithms is the unbalanced number of computations per leaf. Our improved algorithm mitigates this issue by reducing the number of computations for often used leaves and allows for more efficient computation of the authentication path.

2 Hash-Based Signatures

In the following we describe the foundations of the Merkle signature scheme. It was introduced in [19] and a detailed description of MSS can be found in [6]. Details about the implementation inspiring our work are given in [22]. We use Winternitz one-time signatures [8] for message signing. The one-time keys are generated using a PRNG to minimize storage requirements as proposed in [22].

The following components use an at least second preimage resistant, undetectable n-bit one-way function f and a cryptographic m-bit hash function g:

$$f : \{0,1\}^n \to \{0,1\}^n \ , \quad g : \{0,1\}^* \to \{0,1\}^m$$

2.1 The Merkle Signature Scheme

Given a One-Time Signature Scheme (OTSS) a tree height H is chosen to allow for the creation of 2^H signatures that are verifiable with the same verification key. Let the nodes of the Merkle tree be denoted as $\nu_h[s]$ with $h \in \{0, \ldots, H\}$ being the height of the node and $s \in \{0, \ldots, 2^{H-h} - 1\}$ being the node index on height h.

Key Generation. The 2^H leaves of the Merkle tree are defined to be digests $g(Y_i)$ of one-time verification keys Y_i. Starting from the leaves, the MSS verification key which is the root node of the Merkle tree $\nu_H[0]$ is generated following

$$\nu_{h+1}[i] = g(\nu_h[2i] \,\|\, \nu_h[2i+1]), \quad 0 \le h < H, \quad 0 \le i < 2^{H-h-1},$$

meaning that a parent node is generated by hashing the concatenation of its two child nodes.

Signature Generation. A Merkle signature $\sigma_s(d)$ of a digest $d = g(M)$ of a message M consists of a signature index s, a one-time signature σ_{OTS}, a one-time verification key Y_s, and an authentication path $(\text{AUTH}_0, \ldots, \text{AUTH}_{H-1})$ that allows the verification of the one-time signature with respect to the public MSS verification key, hence

$$\sigma_s(d) = (s, \sigma_{\text{OTS}}, Y_s, (\text{AUTH}_0, \ldots, \text{AUTH}_{H-1})).$$

The signature index $s \in \{0, \ldots, 2^H - 1\}$ is incremented with every issued signature. The OTSS is applied using signature key X_s to generate the signature $\sigma_{\text{OTS}} = \text{Sign}_{\text{OTS}}(d, X_s)$ of the message digest d. The authentication path for the sth leaf are all sibling nodes AUTH_h, $h \in \{0, \ldots, H-1\}$ on the path from leaf $\nu_0[s]$ to the root node $\nu_H[0]$. It enables the verifier to recompute the root node of the Merkle tree and authenticates the current one-time signature.

We would like to stress that the signature generation reflects the structure of an online/offline signature scheme. The authentication path only depends on the OTSS verification key Y_s which is known prior to the message and hence can be precomputed.

Signature Verification. Given a message digest $d = g(M)$ and a signature $\sigma_s(d)$ the verifier checks the one-time signature σ_{OTS} with the underlying one-time signature verification algorithm $\text{Verify}_{\text{OTS}}(d, \sigma_s(d))$. In addition, the root node is reconstructed using the provided authentication path

$$\phi_{h+1} = \begin{cases} g\left(\phi_h \,\|\, \text{AUTH}_h\right), & \text{if } \lfloor s/2^h \rfloor \equiv 0 \bmod 2 \\ g\left(\text{AUTH}_h \,\|\, \phi_h\right), & \text{if } \lfloor s/2^h \rfloor \equiv 1 \bmod 2 \end{cases}, \quad \phi_0 = \nu_0[s], \quad h = 0, \ldots, H-1.$$

If the one-time signature σ_{OTS} is successfully verified and ϕ_H is equal to $\nu_H[0]$ the MSS signature is accepted.

2.2 Winternitz One-Time Signatures

Winternitz OTS [8] are a convenient choice for the one-time signature scheme, as they reduce the overall signature length. The Winternitz parameter $w \geq 2$ determines how many bits are signed simultaneously and t determines of how many random n-bit strings x_i the Winternitz signature keys consist.

$$t = t_1 + t_2, \quad t_1 = \left\lceil \frac{n}{w} \right\rceil, \quad t_2 = \left\lceil \frac{\lfloor \log_2 t_1 \rfloor + 1 + w}{w} \right\rceil$$

Key Generation. A W-OTS signature key $X = (x_0, \ldots, x_{t-1})$ is generated by selecting t random bit strings $x_i \in \{0,1\}^n$, $0 \leq i < t$. The W-OTS verification key $Y = g(y_0 \,\|\, \cdots \,\|\, y_{t-1})$ is computed from the signature key by applying f $2^w - 1$ times to each x_i giving $y_i = f^{2^w - 1}(x_i)$, $0 \leq i < t$ and computing the hash of the concatenated y_i's. Note, the superscript denotes multiple executions of f, e.g., $f^2(x_i) = f(f(x_i))$ and $f^0(x_i) = x_i$.

Signature Generation. A signature for a message M is created by signing its digest $d = g(M)$ under key X. Digest d is divided into t_1 blocks $b_0, \ldots, b_{t_1-1}$ of length w and a checksum $c = \sum_{i=0}^{t_1-1} (2^w - b_i)$ is computed. Checksum c is divided into t_2 blocks $b_{t_1}, \ldots, b_{t-1}$ of length w (zero-padding to the left is applied if c or d are no multiples of w). The W-OTS signature $\sigma_{\text{W-OTS}} = (\sigma_0, \ldots, \sigma_{t-1})$ is computed with $\sigma_i = f^{b_i}(x_i)$, $0 \leq i < t$.

Signature Verification. Given a message digest $d = g(M)$, a signature $\sigma_{\text{W-OTS}}$ and a verification key Y_s the verifier generates blocks $b_0, \ldots, b_{t-1}$ from d as in signature generation and reconstructs

$$Y_s' = g\left(f^{2^w - 1 - b_0}(\sigma_0) \,\|\, \cdots \,\|\, f^{2^w - 1 - b_{t-1}}(\sigma_{t-1}) \right).$$

If Y_s' equals Y_s the signature is valid, otherwise it has to be rejected. When using W-OTS signatures in MSS, transmitting Y_s and comparing Y_s to Y_s' can be omitted. Y_s' can simply be used together with the nodes of the authentication path to recompute the root of the Merkle tree. If the recomputed root equals the MSS public key, then Y_s' is a valid OTS verification key.

2.3 Private Key Generation

Storing 2^H one-time signature or verification keys can be an infeasible task, especially on constrained implementation platforms. Generating keys on-the-fly by using a PRNG significantly reduces the required storage space (cf. [22]).

Each W-OTS signature key $X_i = (x_0, \ldots, x_{t-1})$, $0 \leq i < 2^H$ is generated by the PRNG from a seed $\text{SEED}_{\text{W-OTS}_i}$. These seeds in turn are also generated by the PRNG from a initial randomly selected seed $\text{SEED}_0 \in_R \{0,1\}^n$ which serves as the MSS signature key. On input of k_i the PRNG outputs a random string r_{i+1} and an updated seed k_{i+1}.

$$\text{PRNG} : \{0,1\}^n \rightarrow \{0,1\}^n \times \{0,1\}^n, k_i \rightarrow (k_{i+1}, r_{i+1}) \tag{1}$$

Starting from the initial SEED_0 the seeds for the signature keys $\text{SEED}_{\text{W-OTS}_i}$ are created by

$$(\text{SEED}_{i+1}, \text{SEED}_{\text{W-OTS}_i}) \leftarrow \text{PRNG}(\text{SEED}_i), \ 0 \leq i < 2^H.$$

The t n-bit strings of the i-th W-OTS signature key $X_i = (x_0, \ldots, x_{t-1})$, $0 \leq i < 2^H$ are then generated by

$$(\text{SEED}_{\text{W-OTS}_i}, x_j) \leftarrow \text{PRNG}(\text{SEED}_{\text{W-OTS}_i}), \ 0 \leq j < t.$$

2.4 Authentication Path Computation

Creating an authentication path for a specific leaf s can be accomplished by storing all tree nodes in memory and looking up the required nodes when needed. However, because of the exponential growth of nodes in tree height H this approach becomes infeasible for reasonable practical applications. Hence, algorithms for efficient on-the-fly authentication path computation during signature generation are required.

The currently best known algorithm for on-the-fly computation of authentication nodes is the BDS algorithm [6] (Algorithm 3, cf. Appendix). It makes use of several treehash algorithm instances TREEHASH_h for heights $0 \leq h \leq H - K - 1$. The treehash algorithm was introduced in [19] and modified in [25]. It allows to efficiently create (parts of) Merkle trees. In the BDS algorithm each instance is initialized with a leaf index s to which it computes the corresponding node value. Each instance is updated until the required authentication node is computed. During a treehash update the next leaf is created and parent nodes are computed if possible.

The generation of the authentication path is split up into two parts that go alongside with the key and signature generation of MSS. During key generation all treehash instances TREEHASH_h are initialized with ν_h [3] and the first authentication path stored is $\text{AUTH}_h = \nu_h$ [1], $0 \leq h \leq H - 1$.

The BDS algorithm generates left authentication nodes either by computing the leaf value or by one hash-function evaluation of the concatenation of two previously computed nodes that are held in memory. Right authentication nodes in contrast are computed from the leaf up, which is computationally more expensive. Since right nodes close to the top are expensive to compute a positive integer $K \geq 2, (H - K \text{ even})$ decides how many of these nodes are stored in RETAIN$_h$, $H - K \leq h \leq H - 2$ during key generation.

Authentication nodes change every 2^h steps for height h. During signature generation the treehash instances are updated and if a authentication node from a treehash instance is used, the instance is re-initialized to compute the next authentication node for that height.

2.5   Security of MSS

The security properties of the signature scheme described above is discussed in [6]. Specifically, the work shows that the Lamport-Diffie one-time signatures [15] are existentially unforgeable under an adaptive chosen message attack (i.e., CMA-secure), if the chosen one-way function is preimage resistant. The employed Merkle signature scheme is also CMA-secure if the underlying OTS is CMA-secure and if the underlying hash function is collision resistant. For increased efficiency (and shorter signatures) we chose Winternitz OTS rather than the classic Lamport-Diffie OTS. The security of the Winternitz one-time signatures is discussed in [4,8,10]. The findings in [4]and [10] show that Winternitz OTS are CMA-secure if used with pseudo-random functions or collision-resistant, undetectable one-way functions, respectively. The level of bit security lost by using a small Winternitz-parameter is in both cases rather small. In our case, the biggest Winternitz parameter is $w = 4$, hence we still provide a security level of approx. 95 bits for a 128-bit PRF or 116 bits for W-OTS+ [10]). Related discussions for a similar MSS scheme can also be found in [5].

2.6   Bounded Leakage for MSS

The presented design has several features that bound leakage of secret information. First, the design consists of many one-time signatures with *independent* keys. This means there is no key reuse, and hence leakage of one OTS key does not reveal information about the other keys. Major parts of the performed computations are in the Merkle tree. Since the Merkle tree is public, computations within the tree do not leak any secret information. Hence, leakage of g is not an issue.

Secret information is only processed during *signing* and *key generation*. Key generation usually takes place in a secure environment, as key generation is usually too costly to be performed on the embedded system. However, even if key generation leaks, it is a single sequence of leakage for all parts of the key, i.e., all one-time keys leak exactly once. Critical information leakage can only happen during signing. If all OTS keys would be stored, they could be chosen independently and would leak exactly once, when used for signing (assuming that *only computation leaks information* [20]). In this case, an adversary would get, at most, two observations per key (one during key generation and one at signing), outperforming the scheme described in [9]. However, as described in Sect. 2.3, the OTS keys are generated on-the-fly using a PRNG to achieve a scheme suited for embedded devices. In this case each signing operation consists of three steps: (i) performing one OTS, (ii) updating the state (requires recomputation of verification keys), and (iii) computing the authentication path. Since the Merkle tree is public, no secret information is revealed during authentication path computation. The OTS itself only leaks information about the current OTS key, i.e. one additional leakage for each key. The main leakage occurs during the state updates, which result in repeated execution of the PRNG and recomputation of verification keys that leak information about the corresponding OTS key.

Each PRNG update reveals information about one OTS key and the internal state of the PRNG. As the described scheme generates several one-time keys more than once, the PRNG can be executed l times on the *same* input, where l is determined by the parameters of the BDS algorithm. That is, each SEED_i has up to l leakages as PRNG input. The OTS keys x_i are derived from an initial seed $\text{SEED}_{\text{W-OTS}_i}$ by the same PRNG. The x_i serve as input for the one-way function f. That is, each $\text{SEED}_{\text{W-OTS}_i}$ has up to l leakages as input to PRNG; each x_i is either known by the adversary (as part of the signature) or has up to l leakages as input of f during verification key recomputation and signing.

3   Optimized Authentication Path Computation

Since the Merkle-tree is not stored, the parts of the Merkle tree needed for the authentication path must be generated. One optimized algorithm for this purpose is the BDS algorithm [6]. Its design goal was to minimize costly leaf computations. However, to minimize the leakage, it is also important to balance leaf computations. In the following we describe further optimizations that reduce the number of computations for each individual leaf, thereby minimizing the maximum leakage per private key computation. We furthermore reduce the overall computation time by close to 50 %, at the cost of a slightly increased memory usage.

3.1   Authentication Path Computation

The authentication path consists of nodes of the Merkle tree. For the computation of upcoming authentication nodes we use several stacks of nodes for different heights of the tree. Treehash instances TREEHASH_h are used for heights $0 \leq h \leq H - K - 1$. Each instance is initialized with a leaf index s and is updated in Algorithm 3 until the required authentication node is computed. During a treehash update the next leaf is created and parent nodes are computed by hashing previously created nodes if possible. Authentication nodes change every 2^h steps for height h and if an authentication node is used from a treehash instance, this instance is re-initialized to compute the following authentication node for that height.

Preliminaries. The total number of leaf computations that occur during execution of Algorithm 3 can be calculated by counting all invocations of LEAFCALC, a function that on input s outputs leaf $\nu_0[s]$. As mentioned in [6] it is possible to omit LEAFCALC in Step 3 of Algorithm 3 since the sth W-OTS key pair is used to sign the current message, hence the verification key can be computed from the signature and one additional hash computation yields leaf $\nu_0[s]$. If a different OTSS is used the verification key is part of the OTS and can be hashed to create $\nu_0[s]$. This saves 2^{H-1} LEAFCALC invocations. Careful analysis of Algorithm 3 leads to the total number of leaf computations in the BDS algorithm

$$N_{H,K_{\text{total}}} = \sum_{h=0}^{H-K-1} \left(2^{H-1} - 2^{h+1}\right) = (H-K)\,2^{H-1} - 2^{H-K+1} + 2.$$

In order to count the necessary computations for a specific leaf s during execution of Algorithm 3 we have to consider all occurrences of s as parameter of LEAFCALC, except for when s is a left leaf (Step 3 of Algorithm 3), as explained above. To determine if leaf s is computed in treehash instance TREEHASH$_h$ we make the following observation: TREEHASH$_0$ computes leaves $(5),(7),(9),\dots$, TREEHASH$_1$ computes leaves $(10,11),(14,15),\dots$, TREEHASH$_2$ computes leaves $(20,21,22,23),(28,29,30,31),\dots$ and so forth. Hence, the total number of computations for leaf s is given by

$$N_{H,K}(s) = \sum_{h=0}^{H-K-1} \left\lfloor \frac{s \bmod 2^{h+1}}{2^h} \right\rfloor \cdot \left\lceil \frac{\left\lfloor \frac{s}{5 \cdot 2^h} \right\rfloor}{2^H} \right\rceil$$

Drawbacks. A drawback of the BDS algorithm (Algorithm 3) is that it does not balance the computation of leaf nodes. There are leaves that are calculated various times, while others are barely touched. In terms of side-channel leakage this is undesirable. On average each leaf of the Merkle tree is computed $\overline{N_{H,K}} = N_{H,K_{\text{total}}}/2^H \approx \frac{1}{2}(H-K)$ times. However, the computations per leaf deviate from the average as shown in Fig. 1 for a Merkle tree ($H = 10, K = 2$) with 1024 leaves.

3.2 Balanced Authentication Path Computation

Since the rightmost nodes of each treehash instance are calculated most frequently, we propose to cache and reuse them for balancing the leaf computations. We use an array RIGHTNODES to store those nodes. Note, the root of each treehash instance and the complete treehash instance TREEHASH$_0$ are not stored since lower treehash instances do not require those nodes. Besides reducing the side-channel leakage for heavy duty leaves, this also leads to a significantly reduced computation time, at the cost of an increased memory consumption.

From TREEHASH$_1$ we store node $\nu_0[7]$, from TREEHASH$_2$ we store nodes $\nu_1[7]$ and $\nu_0[15]$ and so on. More generally, we store h nodes $\nu_j\left[2^{2+h-j}-1\right]$,

$j = 0, \ldots, h - 1$ for each instance TREEHASH$_h$, $1 \le h \le H - K - 1$. The required storage space is

$$S_{\text{RightNodes}}(H, K) = \sum_{h=1}^{H-K-1} h = \binom{H-K}{2} = \triangle_{H-K-1}.$$

Table 1 lists the storage requirements for common $H - K$ values. The initialization of the RIGHTNODES array is done during the computation of the public key of the Merkle tree. The updated initial setup is formalized in Algorithm 2.

Table 1. Storage space required by the RIGHTNODES array where the rightmost nodes of each treehash instance TREEHASH$_h$, $h = 1, \ldots, H - K - 1$ are stored for reusage by lower treehash instances.

$H - K$	$\triangle_{H-K-1}$	128-bit digest (byte)	160-bit digest (byte)	256-bit digest (byte)
6	15	240	300	480
8	28	448	560	896
10	45	720	900	1440
12	66	1056	1320	2112
14	91	1456	1820	2912
16	120	1920	2400	3840
18	153	2448	3060	4896

In Step 5 of Algorithm 3 the treehash instances receive updates if they are initialized and not finished. In every update one leaf is computed and higher nodes are generated if possible by hashing concatenated nodes from the stack. During the last update before the treehash instance is finished, the rightmost leaf of this treehash instance is computed and all other rightmost nodes of this treehash instance are consecutively generated. If the leaf index $s \equiv 2^h - 1 \mod 2^h$ in instance TREEHASH$_h$, we store the following nodes in the RIGHTNODES array starting from offset $h(h-1)/2$. An adapted version of the treehash update algorithm is given in Algorithm 1.

In every second re-initialization of treehash instances TREEHASH$_h$, $h = 0, \ldots$, $H - K - 2$ the authentication node can be copied from the RIGHTNODES array because it has been computed before by treehash instance TREEHASH$_{h+1}$. If $s + 1 \equiv 0 \mod 2^{h+2}$ the authentication node can be copied from the RIGHTNODES array and if $s + 1 \equiv 2^{h+1} \mod 2^{h+2}$ the authentication node has to be computed. If we can reuse nodes, we not only copy the authentication node (root of TREEHASH$_h$) but also its rightmost child nodes from RIGHTNODES, so they can be reused for instances TREEHASH$_j$, $j < h$. This improvement can be easily integrated into the BDS algorithm by modifying Step 4c) accordingly.

Comparison. In order to quantify our improvements, we give the total amount of leaf computations and show how to determine the leaf computations for a specific leaf s. As before, each instance $\textsc{Treehash}_h$ computes 2^h leaves until they are finished. The re-initializations however are halved for treehash instances $\textsc{Treehash}_h$, $h = 0, \ldots, H - K - 2$, to $2^{H-h-2} - 1$ re-initializations because in half of all cases previously computed nodes can be copied from the $\textsc{Rightnodes}$ array and the $\textsc{Leafcalc}$ computations are skipped. Hence, the number of calls to $\textsc{Leafcalc}$ from each $\textsc{Treehash}_h$ instance is $2^{H-2} - 2^h$ The treehash instance $\textsc{Treehash}_{H-K-1}$ cannot copy nodes from higher instances since it is the topmost treehash instance. It calls $\textsc{Leafcalc}$ as before, resulting in $2^{H-1} - 2^{H-K}$ computations. The total number of leaf computations is

$$N'_{H,K_{\text{total}}} = \sum_{h=0}^{H-K-2} \left(2^{H-2} - 2^h\right) + 2^{H-1} - 2^{H-K}$$

$$= (H - K + 1)\, 2^{H-2} - 3 \cdot 2^{H-K-1} + 1.$$

When compared to $N_{H,K_{\text{total}}}$ of the BDS algorithm this is nearly a 50 % reduction.

To retrieve the number of leaf computations in the improved version for a specific leaf s we have to check whether s is a left or a right leaf. If s is even, it is a left leaf and can be computed from the current one-time signature or verification key as mentioned in Sect. 3.1 for Step 3 of Algorithm 3. If s is odd, it is a right leaf thus $\textsc{Leafcalc}$ is not executed directly. To determine if s is computed in treehash instance $\textsc{Treehash}_h$, $h = 0, \ldots, H - K - 2$, we have to consider that in half of all cases it is copied and not computed. For this purpose we construct function $\delta'_{H,K}(s)$ that returns the number of times leaf s is computed in treehash instances $\textsc{Treehash}_h, h = 0, \ldots, H - K - 2$.

$$\delta'_{H,K}(s) = \sum_{h=0}^{H-K-2} \left\lfloor \frac{s \bmod 2^{h+1}}{2^h} \right\rfloor \cdot \left\lceil \frac{\left\lfloor \frac{s}{5 \cdot 2^h} \right\rfloor}{2^H} \right\rceil \cdot \left(1 - \left\lfloor \frac{s \bmod 2^{h+2}}{2^{h+1}} \right\rfloor\right)$$

The topmost treehash instance $\textsc{Treehash}_{H-K-1}$ cannot copy nodes from the $\textsc{Rightnodes}$ array because the required nodes have not been computed so far. Thus, we have to count the number of computations for this instance as in the unoptimized version. The total number of times leaf s is generated during the computation of all authentication nodes can now be summed up to

$$N'_{H,K}(s) = \left\lfloor \frac{s \bmod 2^{H-K}}{2^{H-K-1}} \right\rfloor \cdot \left\lceil \frac{\left\lfloor \frac{s}{5 \cdot 2^{H-K-1}} \right\rfloor}{2^H} \right\rceil + \delta'_{H,K}(s).$$

On average each leaf is now computed $\overline{N'_{H,K}} = N'_{H,K_{\text{total}}} / 2^H \approx \frac{1}{4}(H - K + 1)$ times. The reduced number of computations for each leaf is shown in Fig. 2. Visual comparison between Figs. 1 and 2 already gives an intuition of the reduction and balancing of leaf computations. For further comparisons see Fig. 3 in the appendix. Table 2 compares the total number of leaf computations, how often a leaf has to be computed in the worst-case, and the average number of leaf computations for common heights $H = \{10, 16, 20\}$ and $K = \{2, 4\}$. The total number of leaf

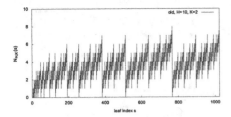

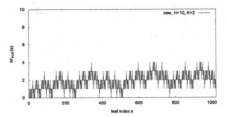

Fig. 1. Number of times each leaf is computed by the original BDS algorithm for a Merkle tree of height $H = 10$ and $K = 2$.

Fig. 2. Number of times each leaf is computed by our variation for a Merkle tree of height $H = 10$ and $K = 2$.

computations as well as the average computations per leaf are decreased by about 38–48 % for the chosen parameters of H and K. Both the worst-case computation time as well as the average signature computation time are decreased. E.g., battery-powered devices greatly profit from the reduced overall computation time which directly relates to the overall power consumption.

Table 2. Overview of the necessary computations for a Merkle tree with parameters H and K when executing Algorithm 3. Furthermore, the worst-case computations for a leaf is listed together with the average computations $\overline{N_{H,K}}$ and $\overline{N'_{H,K}}$. The variance of $N_{H,K}(s)$ and $N'_{H,K}(s)$ is denoted by $\sigma^2_{H,K}$ and $\sigma'^2_{H,K}$.

H	K	$N_{H,K_{tot}}$	$N'_{H,K_{tot}}$	$\overline{N_{H,K}}$	$\overline{N'_{H,K}}$	%	$\sigma^2_{H,K}$	$\sigma'^2_{H,K}$	%	max. $N_{H,K}(s)$	max. $N'_{H,K}(s)$	%
10	2	3586	1921	3.50	1.88	46.4	2.24	0.73	67.3	8	4	50.0
10	4	2946	1697	2.88	1.66	42.4	1.60	0.50	68.5	6	3	50.0
10	6	2018	1257	1.97	1.23	37.7	1.02	0.33	67.9	4	2	50.0
16	2	425986	221185	6.50	3.38	48.1	3.75	1.11	70.4	14	7	50.0
16	4	385026	206849	5.88	3.16	46.3	3.11	0.88	71.6	12	6	50.0
16	6	325634	178689	4.97	2.73	45.1	2.53	0.71	72.1	10	5	50.0
20	2	8912898	4587521	8.50	4.38	48.5	4.75	1.36	71.4	18	9	50.0
20	4	8257538	4358145	7.88	4.16	47.2	4.11	1.13	72.5	16	8	50.0
20	6	7307266	3907585	6.97	3.73	46.5	3.53	0.96	72.9	14	7	50.0

Since all but the topmost treehash instance only need to be computed every second time, the number of updates per signature (Algorithm 3, Step 5) can be reduced from $\lceil (H - K)/2 \rceil$ to $\lceil (H - K + 1)/4 \rceil$. As a result, the average update time is much better balanced than in Algorithm 3 and the worst case computation time is also improved. The BDS algorithm needs to store $3H + \lfloor H/2 \rfloor - 3K + 2^K - 2$ tree nodes and $2(H - K) + 1$ PRNG seeds as signature key. Due to storing the rightmost nodes our improved algorithm increases the

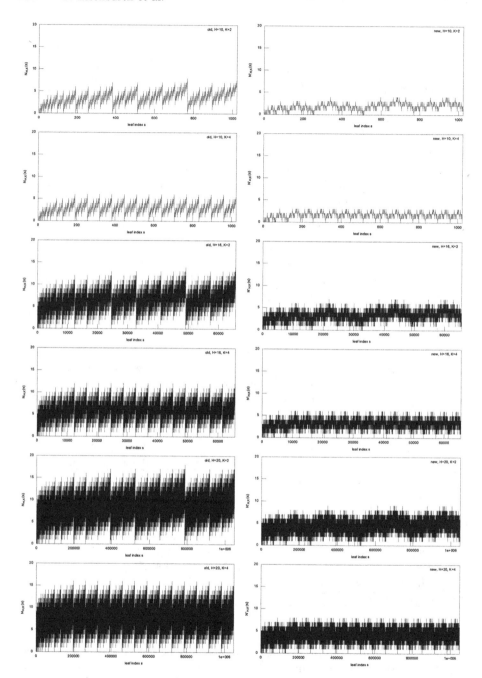

Fig. 3. Comparison of $N_{H,K}(s)$ and $N'_{H,K}(s)$ for $H = \{10, 16, 20\}$ and $K = \{2, 4\}$ for all leaves s of the respective tree.

number of tree nodes that have to be stored by $\binom{H-K}{2}$. Even if the additional memory is used to increase K for the original BDS algorithm, the speedup is still significant. E.g., comparing our $(H, K) = (16, 4)$ to BDS$(16, 6)$ gives comparable storage requirements, but still a speedup of 36 %. The verification key and signature sizes remain unaffected: the verification key size is m and the signature size remains at $t \cdot n + H \cdot m$.

4 Implementation and Results

In the following we describe our choices for the cryptographic primitives which we use to implement the proposed signature scheme described in Sects. 2 and 3. We then detail on the target platforms and give performance figures for key and signature generation as well as signature verification.

4.1 A Bounded Leakage Merkle Signature Engine

We implemented two versions with different *hash functions* g for the Merkle tree. Both versions use AES-128 in an MJH construction [16]. Using AES-128 as block cipher is favorable from a performance perspective as existing AES co-processors can be used. MJH is collision resistant for up to $\mathcal{O}\left(2^{\frac{2n}{3}-\log n}\right)$ queries when instantiated with a n-bit block cipher. With AES-128 as an ideal cipher, this results in 80 bits security [16]. On the downside, MJH produces 256-bit hash outputs which in the MSS setting leads to an increased key and signature size. Hence, we also implement a version that shortens the 256-bit output of MJH to 160-bit, resulting in smaller key and signature sizes. This also reduces the number of times the AES-engine needs to be called when creating nodes in the Merkle tree. Leakage of g is not an issue, since g only processes public information.

One-way function f is implemented based on AES-128 in an MMO [17,18] construction: $f(x_i) := \text{AES}_{\text{IV}}(x_i) \oplus x_i$. Unlike the PRNG, f is keyless. Hence, for independent inputs its leakage is inherently 1-limiting and f can thus be viewed as uniformly seed-preserving. The *PRNG* defined in (1) is implemented based on the leakage-2-limiting PRNG proposed in [24]. In particular, $\text{PRNG}(k_i) := (\text{AES}_{k_i}(0^{128}), \text{AES}_{k_i}(0^{127}||1))$, where AES_{k_i} denotes the AES-128 with a 128-bit key k_i, used as seed-preserving function.

Both PRNG and f handle secret inputs. The PRNG processes each SEED_s and $\text{SEED}_{\text{W-OTS}_s}$ as well as the x_i for s exactly $N'_{H,K}(s)$ times during state updates and one time during signing OTS_s. We exclude the key generation in this analysis, as it is performed off-chip, assumably in a secure environment. Both PRNG and f rely on AES-128 as cryptographic building block. The PRNG executes AES twice under the same secret key (i.e. the PRNG is 2-limiting), while f touches the secret input only once, making the signature engine overall leakage-2-limited. The strongest leakage will be observed for the SEED_i, resulting in a total of $l = 2 \cdot \left(\max(N'_{H,K}(s)) + 1\right)$ leakages. These l observations are on 2 different inputs, i.e., there are $l/2 = \max(N'_{H,K}(s)) + 1$ observations under the same input (i.e., leakage will only differ by noise). Classical side-channel attacks are further mitigated by the fact that intermediate values SEED_i of the key generation PRNG are not output. The adversary will only get access to a limited number of x_i.

4.2 Implementation Platforms

We implement the signature scheme on two different platforms. On the one side we choose a lightweight and low-cost 8-bit Atmel ATxmega microcontroller and on the other side a powerful Intel Core i7 notebook CPU.

Intel Core i7-2620M 64-bit CPU. Intel's off-the-shelf Core i7-2620M 64-bit Sandy Bridge notebook CPU [12] features two cores running at 2.70 GHz (with Turbo Boost technology up to 3.40 GHz). For accurate measurement, we disabled Turbo Boost and hyper-threading during our benchmarks. The CPU incorporates the recent extensions to the x86 instruction set that improve the performance when en-/decrypting data using AES. The extension is called AES-NI and consists of six additional instructions [13]. All standardized key lengths (128 bit, 192 bit, 256 bit) are supported for a block size of 128 bit.

Atmel AVR ATxmega128A1 8-bit Microcontroller. We are using the Atmel evaluation board AVR XPLAIN [3] that features an ATxmega128A1 microcontroller [1,2]. The ATxmega offers hardware accelerators for DES and AES and is clocked at 32 MHz. The hardware acceleration is limited to AES with 128-bit key and block size. A leakage analysis has been performed on this processor in Sect. 4.4, as it is a typical example for a low-power embedded platform.

4.3 Performance Results

In the following we give performance figures of the signature scheme for selected Merkle tree heights H and parameters K and w on both platforms.

CPU Performance. On the Intel CPU we measure the time it takes to create the root node of the Merkle tree, i.e., the verification key generation. We iterate over all leaves and sign random messages to measure the average computation time that is needed to create a valid MSS signature. Additionally, we measure the time it takes to verify an MSS signature. Signature computation includes creating the signing key, performing a one-time signature with the created signing key, and generating the next authentication path (the last step can be removed, as it can be precomputed at any time between two signing operations). The measurement is done for tree height $H = 16$ with $K = 2$ and $w = 2$. Note, due to the binary tree structure the root node computation can be parallelized if more than one CPU core is available, which would bring down the required

Table 3. Performance figures of a Merkle tree with parameters $H = 16, K = 2, w = 2$ on an Intel i7 CPU and $H = 10, K = 2, w = 2$ on an ATxmega microcontroller. f is implemented using a hardware-accelerated AES-128 (AES-NI instructions, ATxmega crypto accelerator) in MMO construction. g is implemented using AES-128 in an MJH-256 construction and with the output truncated to 160 bit. The Intel CPU was clocked at 2.7 GHz and the ATxmega at 32 MHz.

Hash g		MJH-256 w/ AES-128			MJH-160 w/ AES-128		
Target		[22]	our	Impr. (%)	[22]	our	Impr. (%)
Core i7	KeyGen	6546.9 ms	6037.5 ms	8	4218.7 ms	3886.3 ms	8
Core i7	Sign	743.9 us	401.3 us	46	487.1 us	256.2 us	47
Core i7	Verify	76.1 us	78.1 us	-3	50.8 us	49.3 us	3
AVR	Sign	110.0 ms	64.9 ms	41	70.7 ms	41.7 ms	41
AVR	Verify	18.4 ms	18.4 ms	0	11.0 ms	11.0 ms	0

computation time by roughly the factor of cores used. We compare our results against the originally proposed signature scheme [22] in Table 3.

Compared to the previous results of [22] our improved algorithm in combination with the exchanged PRNG yields on average a performance gain of 46–47 % for signature generation. The new PRNG improves the computation time on average by 8 %, the algorithmic changes to the authentication path computation algorithm yield 38–39 % points.

When generating verification keys an 8 % improvement can be observed. This is due to the exchanged PRNG which uses a hardware-accelerated AES-engine since our algorithmic improvements do not affect key generation. Signature verification is more or less stable, regardless of cipher/algorithm combinations and is about a factor of 5 faster than signature generation.

Microcontroller Performance. On the microcontroller we measure the average computation time that is needed to create a valid MSS signature (including next authentication path computation) and the time it takes to verify an MSS signature. We omit the verification key generation since for reasonable tree heights it is an infeasible task for the microcontroller. Verification keys have to be computed once on a computer platform when initializing the microcontroller. The code was compiled using avr-gcc version 3.3.0. We found optimization stage -O2 to provide the best tradeoff between runtime and code size.

The results on the microcontroller are in accordance with the results observed on the Intel CPU. The average signature generation time improves by 41 % when using our proposed changes. Signature verification remains stable and is four times faster than signature generation. The memory consumption is listed in Table 4. Compared to the setting of [22] we need more flash and SRAM memory due to the additional storage for the RightNodes array.

Table 5 compares key and signature sizes for different MSS implementations. Note that the increased signature sizes for [11] enable on-card key generation.

Table 4. Required memory on the ATxmega128A1 microcontroller. In total 128 kByte flash memory and 8 kByte SRAM are available on this device. Memory consumption is reported in bytes and includes the verification and signature keys.

		MJH-256 w/ AES-128				MJH-160 w/ AES-128			
		[22]		our		[22]		our	
H	K	Flash	SRAM	Flash	SRAM	Flash	SRAM	Flash	SRAM
10	2	10,608	1,486	12,070	2,382	10,204	1,066	11,352	1,626
10	4	10,726	1,604	11,768	2,084	10,250	1,112	11,138	1,412
10	6	11,994	2,874	12,752	3,066	11,018	1,878	11,726	1,998

Table 5. Comparison of signing key (sk), verification key (vk), and signature size (sig) between [22], our improvement, and XMSS$^+$ [11] for common (H, K, w) parameter sets. All sizes are reported in bytes.

			MJH-256			MJH-160			[22] (MJH-256)			[22] (MJH-160)			XMSS$^+$ [11]		
H	K	w	sk	vk	sig	sk	vk	sig	sk	vk	sig	sk	vk	sig	sk	vk	sig
16	2	2	5,335	32	2,640	3,547	20	1,680	2,423	32	2,640	1,727	20	1,680	3,760	544	3,476
16	2	4	5,335	32	1,584	3,547	20	1,008	2,423	32	1,584	1,727	20	1,008	3,200	512	1,892
20	4	2	7,049	32	2,768	4,649	20	1,760	3,209	32	2,768	2,249	20	1,760	4,303	608	3,540
20	4	4	7,049	32	1,712	4,649	20	1,088	3,209	32	1,712	2,249	20	1,088	3,744	576	1,956

4.4 Leakage Results

The *leakage* of the AVR ATxmega processors with respect to power analysis has been analyzed in [14]. The found leakage is weak: the best attack needs more than 3000 measurements on random known inputs to recover the secret key. However, the applied method is not the most powerful[1].

In order to get a more thorough leakage analysis of the target platform, we performed own side-channel experiments. Since all AES computations with critical leakage are performed by the AES co-processor of the ATxmega processor [2], we analyzed the leakage of that co-processor. Instead of a correlation based DPA, we applied a (univariate) template attack [7], the de-facto standard for power leakage evaluation [23]. The profiled intermediate state is $\Delta = p_0 \oplus k_0 \oplus p_1 \oplus k_1$, where one template was created for each possible Δ. This is the same intermediate state that was targeted in [14]. It appears to be the intermediate state with the strongest leakage. Each recovered Δ reveals one byte of key information. The maximum observable leakage is that of the 2-limiting PRNG, which is, at most, executed 10 times each on two different inputs (for $(H, K) = (20, 2)$). To capture this maximal leakage, the experiment builds univariate templates from 10,000 traces and tests over two groups of 10 traces (each group shares the same input). A total of 5000 experiments are conducted, resulting in a Guessing Entropy [23] of 85.06 or 6.41 bits for the correct Δ. This means that the adversary still has

---

[1] Both targeting the key xor and using correlation attack are not considered optimal methods of leakage extraction.

to test more than 85 hypotheses for that byte on average. The reduction in entropy is hence less than $0.6\,\mathrm{bit}^2$, resulting in well above $100\,\mathrm{bit}$ of remaining key entropy when considering univariate side-channel attacks.

An alternative to plain template attacks are algebraic side-channel attacks [21], which do not require known input and output and would be more applicable to attack the PRNG in this work. While being able to exploit several (close to 1000 in [21]) leakages during a single execution of AES, these methods are very sensitive to noise and need a much stronger leakage than the one observed here. Often, an almost noise-free Hamming weight leakage is assumed, which is more than 2.5 bits of information on a byte. This kind of information is not provided by the observed leakage of the hardware AES of the ATxmega processor.

The remaining point of attack is in the Winternitz signature, where the adversary actually gets access to hash outputs and some outputs of the PRNG used to generate the one-time keys. The observed leakage (10 observations for the same single input, same setup as for the PRNG) has a guessing entropy of 99.53, i.e. less than $0.4\,\mathrm{bit}$ of information per byte are revealed. Not much prior work on side-channel attacks on one-way functions has been performed which is most likely due to the fact that the adversary gets only single observations of the leakage.

5   Conclusion

We presented a novel algorithmic improvement for authentication path computation in MSS that balances leaf computations and reduces side-channel leakage. The proposed improvements have been implemented on two platforms and were compared to previous proposed algorithms showing significant improvements. Furthermore, we gave explicit formulas to quantify the number of leaf computations when using MSS and showed that the leakage of the secret state is bounded throughout the entire scheme. The leakage analysis of the ATxmega AES engine showed that no significant information can be extracted about the secret state, due to the bounded number of executions under the same key.

We stated theoretically achievable performance gains and verified them practically. The algorithmic improvement decreases the required computation time for signature creation in theory as well as in practice. The performance figures show that Merkle signatures are not only practical, but also resource-friendly and fast and have inherently bounded side-channel leakage. As such they are a advantageous choice for, e.g., digital signature smartcards.

Acknowledgments. This material is based in part upon work supported by the National Science Foundation under Grant No. 1261399 and by grant 01ME12025 Sec-Mobil of the German Federal Ministry of Economics and Technology. We would like to thank the anonymous reviewers for their helpful comments.

---

^{2} Note that the guessing entropy for a byte with 2^8 equiprobable states is 128, i.e. 7 bits as guessing entropy looks for the expected number of guesses.

A   Appendix

Algorithm 1. Improved treehash update

Input: Height h, current index s, RIGHTNODES array
Output: updated RIGHTNODES array, updated Treehash instance TREEHASH$_h$
Compute the sth leaf: NODE$_1$ ←LEAFCALC(s)

if $s \equiv 2^h - 1 \left(\bmod\, 2^h\right)$ **and** NODE$_1$.height$() < h$ **then**
   offset $= h\,(h-1)\,/2$
   RIGHTNODES[offset] ←NODE$_1$
end if
while NODE$_1$ has the same height as the top node on TREEHASH$_h$ **do**
   Pop the top node from the stack: NODE$_2$ ←TREEHASH$_h$.$pop()$
   Computer their parent node: NODE$_1$ ← $g($NODE$_2\|$NODE$_1)$
   if $s \equiv 2^h - 1 \left(\bmod\, 2^h\right)$ **then**
      offset $=$ offset $+1$
      RIGHTNODES[offset] ←NODE$_1$
   end if
end while
Push the parent node on the stack: TREEHASH$_h$.$push($NODE$_1)$

Algorithm 2. Key generation and initial setup for the improved traversal algorithm.

Input: H, K
Output: Public key $\nu_H\,[0]$, Authentication path, RIGHTNODES array, TREEHASH stacks, RETAIN stacks
1: **Public Key** Calculate and publish tree root, $\nu_H\,[0]$.
2: **Initial Right Nodes**
   $i = 0$
   for $h = 1$ to $H - K - 1$ **do**
      for $j = 0$ to $h - 1$ **do**
         Set RIGHTNODES$[i] = \nu_j\left[2^{2+h-j} - 1\right]$.
      $i = i + 1$
3: **Initial Authentication Nodes**
   for each $h \in \{0, 1, \ldots, H - 1\}$ **do**
      Set AUTH$_h = \nu_h\,[1]$.
4: **Initial Treehash Stacks**
   for each $h \in \{0, 1, \ldots, H - K - 1\}$ **do**
      Setup TREEHASH$_h$ stack with $\nu_h\,[3]$.
5: **Initial Retain Stacks**
   for each $h \in \{H - K, \ldots, H - 2\}$ **do**
      for each $j \in \left\{2^{H-h-1}, \ldots, 0\right\}$ **do**
         RETAIN$_h$.push($\nu_h\,[2j + 3]$).

Algorithm 3. Algorithm for authentication path computation as presented in [6]

Input: $s \in \left\{ 0, \ldots, 2^H - 2 \right\}$, H, K, and the algorithm state.

Output: Authentication path A_{s+1} for leaf $s + 1$.

1: Let $\tau = 0$ if leaf s is a left node or let τ be the height of the first parent of leaf s which is a left node: $\tau \leftarrow \max\{h : 2^h | (s + 1)\}$

2: If the parent of leaf s on height $\tau + 1$ is a left node, store the current authentication node on height τ in KEEP$_\tau$:
   if $\lfloor s/2^{\tau+1} \rfloor$ is even **and** $\tau < H - 1$ **then** KEEP$_\tau \leftarrow$ AUTH$_\tau$

3: If leaf s is a left node, it is required for the authentication path of leaf $s + 1$:
   if $\tau = 0$ **then** AUTH$_0 \leftarrow$ LEAFCALC(s)

4: Otherwise, if leaf s is a right node, the auth. path for leaf $s + 1$ changes on heights $0, \ldots, \tau$:
   if $\tau > 0$ **then**
   a) The authentication path for leaf $s + 1$ requires a new left node on height τ. It is computed using the current authentication node on height $\tau - 1$ and the node on height $\tau - 1$ previously stored in KEEP$_{\tau-1}$. The node stored in KEEP$_{\tau-1}$ can then be removed:
      AUTH$_\tau \leftarrow g$ (AUTH$_{\tau-1} \|$ KEEP$_{\tau-1}$), remove KEEP$_{\tau-1}$
   b) The authentication path for leaf $s + 1$ requires new right nodes on heights $h = 0, \ldots, \tau - 1$. For $h < H - K$ these nodes are stored in TREEHASH$_h$ and for $h \geq H - K$ in RETAIN$_h$:
      for $h = 0$ **to** $\tau - 1$ **do**
          if $h < H - K$ **then** AUTH$_h \leftarrow$ TREEHASH$_h$.pop()
          if $h \geq H - K$ **then** AUTH$_h \leftarrow$ RETAIN$_h$.pop()
   c) For heights $0, \ldots, \min\{\tau - 1, H - K - 1\}$ the Treehash instances must be initialized anew. The Treehash instance on height h is initialized with the start index $s + 1 + 3 \cdot 2^h < 2^H$:
      for $h = 0$ **to** $\min\{\tau - 1, H - K - 1\}$ **do**
          TREEHASH$_h$.initialize($s + 1 + 3 \cdot 2^h$)

5: Next we spend the budget of $(H - K)/2$ updates on the Treehash instances to prepare upcoming authentication nodes:
   repeat $(H - K)/2$ **times**
   a) We consider only stacks which are initialized and not finished. Let k be the index of the Treehash instance whose lowest tail node has the lowest height. In case there is more than one such instance we choose the instance with the lowest index:
      $k \leftarrow \min \left\{ h : \text{TREEHASH}_h.\text{height}() = \min_{j=0,\ldots,H-K-1} \{\text{TREEHASH}_j.\text{height}()\} \right\}$
   b) The Treehash instance with index k receives one update: TREEHASH$_k$.update()

6: The last step is to output the authentication path for leaf $s + 1$: **return** AUTH$_0, \ldots,$ AUTH$_{H-1}$.

References

1. Atmel. ATxmega128A1 Data Sheet. http://www.atmel.com/dyn/resources/prod_documents/doc8067.pdf
2. Atmel. AVR XMEGA A Manual. http://www.atmel.com/dyn/resources/prod_documents/doc8077.pdf
3. Atmel. AVR XPLAIN board. http://www.atmel.com/dyn/resources/prod_documents/doc8203.pdf
4. Buchmann, J., Dahmen, E., Ereth, S., Hülsing, A., Rückert, M.: On the security of the winternitz one-time signature scheme. In: Nitaj, A., Pointcheval, D. (eds.) Progress in Cryptology AFRICACRYPT 2011. LNCS, vol. 6737, pp. 363–378. Springer, Berlin / Heidelberg (2011)
5. Buchmann, J., Dahmen, E., Hülsing, A.: XMSS - a practical forward secure signature scheme based on minimal security assumptions. In: Yang, B.-Y. (ed.) PQCrypto 2011. LNCS, vol. 7071, pp. 117–129. Springer, Heidelberg (2011)

6. Buchmann, J., Dahmen, E., Szydlo, M.: Hash-based digital signature schemes. In: Bernstein, D.J., Buchmann, J., Dahmen, E. (eds.) Post-Quantum Cryptography, pp. 35–93. Springer, Heidelberg (2009)

7. Chari, S., Rao, J.R., Rohatgi, P.: Template Attacks. In: Kaliski, B.S., Koç, çK, Paar, C. (eds.) CHES 2002. LNCS, vol. 2523, pp. 13–28. Springer, Heidelberg (2003)

8. Dods, C., Smart, N.P., Stam, M.: Hash based digital signature schemes. In: Smart, N.P. (ed.) Cryptography and Coding 2005. LNCS, vol. 3796, pp. 96–115. Springer, Heidelberg (2005)

9. Faust, S., Kiltz, E., Pietrzak, K., Rothblum, G.N.: Leakage-resilient signatures. In: Micciancio, D. (ed.) TCC 2010. LNCS, vol. 5978, pp. 343–360. Springer, Heidelberg (2010)

10. Hülsing, A.: W-OTS+ - shorter signatures for hash-based signature schemes. In: Youssef, A., Nitaj, A., Hassanien, A.E. (eds.) AFRICACRYPT 2013. LNCS, vol. 7918, pp. 173–188. Springer, Heidelberg (2013)

11. Hülsing, A., Busold, C., Buchmann, J.: Forward secure signatures on smart cards. In: Knudsen, L.R., Wu, H. (eds.) SAC 2012. LNCS, vol. 7707, pp. 66–80. Springer, Heidelberg (2013)

12. Intel. Intel Core i7 2620M Specifications. http://ark.intel.com/products/52231/Intel-Core-i7-2620M-Processor-(4M-Cache-2_70-GHz)

13. Intel. Whitepaper on the Intel AES Instructions Set. http://software.intel.com/file/24917

14. Kizhvatov, I.: Side channel analysis of AVR XMEGA crypto engine. In: Proceedings of the 4th Workshop on Embedded Systems Security, WESS '09, pp. 8:1–8:7. ACM (2009)

15. Lamport, L.: Constructing digital signatures from a one-way function. Technical report, CSL-98, SRI, International (1979)

16. Lee, J., Stam, M.: MJH: a faster alternative to MDC-2. In: Kiayias, A. (ed.) Topics in Cryptology CT-RSA 2011. LNCS, vol. 6558, pp. 213–236. Springer, Berlin / Heidelberg (2011)

17. Matyas, S.M., Meyer, C.H., Oseas, J.: Generating strong one-way functions with cryptographic algorithm. IBM Tech. Discl. Bull. 27(10A), 5658–5659 (1985)

18. Menezes, A., Van Oorschot, P., Vanstone, S.: Handbook of Applied Cryptography. CRC Press, Boca Raton (1997). Algorithm 9.41

19. Merkle, R.C.: A certified digital signature. In: Brassard, G. (ed.) CRYPTO 1989. LNCS, vol. 435, pp. 218–238. Springer, Heidelberg (1990)

20. Micali, S., Reyzin, L.: Physically observable cryptography. In: Naor, M. (ed.) TCC 2004. LNCS, vol. 2951, pp. 278–296. Springer, Heidelberg (2004)

21. Renauld, M., Standaert, F.-X., Veyrat-Charvillon, N.: Algebraic side-channel attacks on the AES: why time also matters in DPA. In: Clavier, C., Gaj, K. (eds.) CHES 2009. LNCS, vol. 5747, pp. 97–111. Springer, Heidelberg (2009)

22. Rohde, S., Eisenbarth, T., Dahmen, E., Buchmann, J., Paar, C.: Fast hash-based signatures on constrained devices. In: Grimaud, G., Standaert, F.-X. (eds.) CARDIS 2008. LNCS, vol. 5189, pp. 104–117. Springer, Heidelberg (2008)

23. Standaert, F.-X., Malkin, T.G., Yung, M.: A unified framework for the analysis of side-channel key recovery attacks. In: Joux, A. (ed.) EUROCRYPT 2009. LNCS, vol. 5479, pp. 443–461. Springer, Heidelberg (2009)

24. Standaert, F.-X., Pereira, O., Yu, Y., Quisquater, J.-J., Yung, M., Oswald, E.: Leakage resilient cryptography in practice. In: Sadeghi, A.-R., Naccache, D., Basin, D., Maurer, U. (eds.) Towards Hardware-Intrinsic Security. Information Security and Cryptography, pp. 99–134. Springer, Heidelberg (2010)
25. Szydlo, M.: Merkle tree traversal in log space and time. In: Cachin, C., Camenisch, J.L. (eds.) EUROCRYPT 2004. LNCS, vol. 3027, pp. 541–554. Springer, Heidelberg (2004)

White Box Crypto

White-Box Security Notions
for Symmetric Encryption Schemes

Cécile Delerablée[1], Tancrède Lepoint[1,2],
Pascal Paillier[1], and Matthieu Rivain[1(✉)]

[1] CryptoExperts, 41 Boulevard des Capucines, 75002 Paris, France
{cecile.delerablee,tancrede.lepoint,
pascal.paillier,matthieu.rivain}@cryptoexperts.com
[2] École Normale Supérieure, 45 Rue D'Ulm, 75005 Paris, France

Abstract. White-box cryptography has attracted a growing interest from researchers in the last decade. Several white-box implementations of standard block-ciphers (DES, AES) have been proposed but they have all been broken. On the other hand, neither evidence of existence nor proofs of impossibility have been provided for this particular setting. This might be in part because it is still quite unclear what white-box cryptography really aims to achieve and which security properties are expected from white-box programs in applications. This paper builds a first step towards a practical answer to this question by translating folklore intuitions behind white-box cryptography into concrete security notions. Specifically, we introduce the notion of white-box compiler that turns a symmetric encryption scheme into randomized white-box programs, and we capture several desired security properties such as one-wayness, incompressibility and traceability for white-box programs. We also give concrete examples of white-box compilers that already achieve some of these notions. Overall, our results open new perspectives on the design of white-box programs that securely implement symmetric encryption.

Keywords: White-box cryptography · Security notions · Attack models · Security games · Traitor tracing

1 Introduction

Traditionally, to prove the security of a cryptosystem, cryptographers consider attack scenarios where an adversary is only given a *black-box* access to the cryptographic system, namely to the inputs and outputs of its underlying algorithms. Security notions are built on the standard paradigm that the algorithms are known and that computing platforms can be trusted to effectively protect the secrecy of the private key.

However attacks on *implementations* of cryptographic primitives have become a major threat due to side-channel information leakage (see for example [18, 28]) such as execution time, power consumption or electromagnetic emanations.

T. Lange, K. Lauter, and P. Lisoněk (Eds.): SAC 2013, LNCS 8282, pp. 247–264, 2014.
DOI: 10.1007/978-3-662-43414-7_13, © Springer-Verlag Berlin Heidelberg 2014

More generally, the increasing penetration of cryptographic applications onto untrusted platform (the end points being possibly controlled by a malicious party) makes the black-box model too restrictive to guaranty the security of *programs* implementing cryptographic primitives.

White-box cryptography was introduced in 2002 by Chow, Eisen, Johnson and van Oorschot [10,11] as the ultimate, *worst-case* attack model. This model considers an attacker far more powerful than in the classical black-box model (and thus more representative of real-world attackers); namely the attacker is given full knowledge and full control on both the algorithm and its execution environment. However, even such powerful capabilities should not allow her to e.g. extract the embedded key[1]. White-box cryptography can hence be seen as a restriction of general obfuscation where the function to protect belongs to some narrower class of cryptographic functions indexed by a secret key. From that angle, the ultimate goal of a white-box implementation is to leak nothing more than what a black-box access to the function would reveal. An implementation achieving this strong property would be as secure as in the black-box model, in particular it would resist *all existing and future* side-channel and fault-based attacks. Although we know that general obfuscation of any function is impossible to achieve [1], there is no known impossibility result for white-box cryptography and positive examples have even been discovered [7,15]. On the other hand, the work of Chow *et al.* gave rise to several proposals for white-box implementations of symmetric ciphers, specifically DES [10,21,32] and AES [6,11,19,33], even though all these proposals have been broken [3,13,16,20,22–24,31].

Our belief is that the dearth of promising white-box implementations is also a consequence of the absence of well-understood security goals to achieve. A first step towards a theoretical model was proposed by Saxena, Wyseur and Preneel [29], and subsequently extended by Wyseur in his PhD thesis [30]. These results show how to translate any security notion in the black-box model into a security notion in the white-box model. They introduce the *white-box property* for an obfuscator as the ability to turn a program (modeled as a polynomial Turing machine) which is secure with respect to some black-box notion into a program secure with respect to the corresponding white-box notion. The authors then give an example of obfuscator for a symmetric encryption scheme achieving the white-box equivalent of semantic security. In other words, the symmetric encryption scheme is turned into a secure asymmetric encryption scheme. While these advances describe a generic model to translate a given notion from the black-box to the white-box setting, our aim in this paper is to define explicit security notions that white-box cryptography should realize in practice. As a matter of fact, some of our security notions are not black-box notions that one would wish to preserve in the white-box setting, but arise from new features potentially introduced by the white-box compilation. Note that although we use a different formalism and pursue different goals, our work and those in [29,30] are not in contradiction but rather co-exist in a wider framework.

---

[1] Quoting [10], the "choice of the implementation is the sole remaining line of defense and is precisely what is pursued in white-box cryptography".

Our Contributions. We formalize the notion of *white-box compilers* for a symmetric encryption scheme and introduce several security notions for such compilers. As traditionally done in provable security (e.g. [2]), we consider separately various adversarial goals (e.g. decrypt some ciphertext) and attack models (e.g. chosen ciphertext attack), and then obtain distinct security definitions by pairing a particular goal with a particular attack model. We consider four different attack models in the white-box context: the chosen plaintext attack, the chosen ciphertext attack, the recompilation attack and the chosen ciphertext and recompilation attack. We formalize the main security objective of white-box cryptography which is to protect the secret key as a notion of *unbreakability*. We show that additional security notions should be considered in applications and translate folklore intuitions behind white-box cryptography into concrete security notions; namely the *one-wayness*, *incompressibility* and *traceability* of white-box programs. For the first two notions, we show an example of a simple symmetric encryption scheme over an RSA group for which an efficient white-box compiler exists that provably achieves both notions. We finally show that white-box programs are efficiently traceable by simple means assuming that functional perturbations can be hidden in them. Overall, our positive results shed more light on the different aspects of white-box security and provide concrete constructions that achieve them in a provable fashion.

2 Preliminaries

Symmetric Encryption. A symmetric encryption scheme is a tuple $\mathcal{E} = (\mathsf{K}, \mathsf{M}, \mathsf{C}, K, E, D)$ where K is the key space, M is the plaintext (or message) space, C is the ciphertext space, K is a probabilistic algorithm that returns a key $k \in \mathsf{K} = \mathsf{range}\,(K())$, E is a deterministic encryption function mapping elements of $\mathsf{K} \times \mathsf{M}$ to elements of C, D is a deterministic decryption function mapping elements of $\mathsf{K} \times \mathsf{C}$ to elements of M.

We require that for any $k \in \mathsf{K}$ and any $m \in \mathsf{M}$, $D(k, E(k, m)) = m$. Most typically, $\mathcal{E}$ refers to a block-cipher in which case all sets are made of binary strings of determined length and $\mathsf{C} = \mathsf{M}$.

Programs. A program is a word in the language-theoretic sense and is interpreted in the explicit context of a programming model and an execution model, the details of which we want to keep as abstracted away as possible. Programs differ from remote oracles in the sense that their code can be executed locally, read, copied and modified at will. Successive executions are inherently stateless and all the "system calls" that a program makes to external resources such as a random source or a system clock can be captured and responded arbitrarily. Execution can be interrupted at any moment and all the internal variables identified by the program's instructions can be read and modified arbitrarily by the party that executes the program.

For some function f mapping some set A to some set B, we denote by $\mathsf{prog}\,(f)$ the set of all programs implementing f. A program $P \in \mathsf{prog}\,(f)$ is said to be fully functional with respect to f when for any $a \in \mathsf{A}$, $P(a)$ returns $f(a)$ with probability 1. P is said to be δ-functional (with respect to f) when P is at distance at most $\delta \in [0,1]$ from f, i.e.

$$\Delta(P,f) \overset{\text{def}}{=} \Pr[a \overset{\$}{\leftarrow} \mathsf{A}; \quad b \leftarrow P(a) : b \neq f(a)] \leq \delta .$$

The set of δ-functional programs implementing f is noted $\delta\text{-prog}\,(f)$. Obviously $0\text{-prog}\,(f) = \mathsf{prog}\,(f)$.

Other Notations. If A is some set, $|\mathsf{A}|$ denotes its cardinality. If $\mathbb{A}$ is some generator i.e. a random source with some prescribed output range A, $H(\mathbb{A})$ denotes the output entropy of $\mathbb{A}$ as a source. Abusing notations, we may also denote it by $H(a)$ for $a \leftarrow \mathbb{A}(\cdots)$. Finally, when we write $\mathcal{O}(\cdot) = \epsilon$, we mean that $\mathcal{O}$ is the oracle which, on any input, returns the empty string ϵ.

3   White-Box Compilers

In this paper, we consider that a *white-box implementation* of the scheme $\mathcal{E}$ is a program produced by a publicly known compiling function $\mathbf{C}_{\mathcal{E}}$ which takes as arguments a key $k \in \mathsf{K}$ and possibly a diversifying nonce $r \in \mathsf{R}$ drawn from some randomness space R. We will denote the compiled program by $[E_k^r]$ (or $[E_k]$ when the random nonce r is implicit or does not exist), namely $[E_k^r] = \mathbf{C}_{\mathcal{E}}(k,r)$.

A compiler $\mathbf{C}_{\mathcal{E}}$ for $\mathcal{E}$ is *sound* when for any $(k,r) \in \mathsf{K} \times \mathsf{R}$, $[E_k^r]$ exactly implements the function $E(k,\cdot)$ (i.e. it is fully functional). Therefore $[E_k^r]$ accepts as input any $m \in \mathsf{M}$ and always returns the correct encryption $c = E(k,m)$. At this stage, we only care about sound compilers.

Remark 1. In the above definition, we consider white-box compilers for the encryption function. However, since we focus on deterministic encryption – $E(k,\cdot)$ and $D(k,\cdot)$ being inverse of one another, we can swap roles without loss of generality and get compilers for the decryption procedure. We will precisely do this in Sect. 7.

Note again that $[E_k]$ differs in nature from $E(k,\cdot)$. $E(k,\cdot)$ is a mapping from M to C, whereas $[E_k]$ is a word in some programming language (the details of which we want to keep away from) and has to fulfill some semantic consistency rules. Viewed as a binary string, it has a certain bitsize $\mathsf{size}\,([E_k]) \in \mathbb{N}$. Even though $E(k,\cdot)$ is deterministic, nothing forbids $[E_k]$ to collect extra bits from a random tape and behave probabilistically. For an input $m \in \mathsf{M}$ and random tape $\rho \in \{0,1\}^*$, $[E_k](m,\rho)$ takes a certain time $\mathsf{time}\,([E_k](m,\rho)) \in \mathbb{N}$ to complete execution.

3.1   Attack Models

The first step in specifying new security notions for white-box cryptography is to classify the threats. This section introduces four distinct attack models for an adversary $\mathcal{A}$ in the white-box model: the *chosen plaintext attack* (CPA), the *chosen ciphertext attack* (CCA), the *recompilation attack* (RCA) and the *chosen ciphertext and recompilation attack* (CCA+RCA). In all of these, we assume that the compiler $\mathbf{C}_{\mathcal{E}}$ is public, i.e. at any point in time, the adversary $\mathcal{A}$ can select any key $k \in \mathsf{K}$ and nonce $r \in \mathsf{R}$ of her choosing and generate a white-box implementation $[E_k^r] = \mathbf{C}_{\mathcal{E}}(k, r)$ by herself.

In a *chosen plaintext attack* (CPA) the adversary can encrypt plaintexts of her choice under $E(k, \cdot)$. Indeed, even though the encryption scheme $\mathcal{E}$ is a symmetric primitive, the attacks are defined with respect to the compiler that generates white-box programs implementing $E(k, \cdot)$: given any one of these programs, the adversary can always evaluate it on arbitrary plaintexts at will. So clearly, chosen plaintexts attacks cannot be avoided, very much like in the public-key encryption setting.

In a *chosen ciphertext attack* (CCA), in addition to the challenge white-box implementation $[E_k^r]$, we give $\mathcal{A}$ access to a decryption oracle $D(k, \cdot)$, i.e. she can send decryption queries $c_1, \ldots, c_q \in \mathsf{C}$ adaptively to the oracle and be returned the corresponding plaintexts $m_1, \ldots, m_q \in \mathsf{M}$ where $m_i = D(k, c_i)$. Notice that this attack includes the CPA attack when $q = 0$.

In a *recompilation attack* (RCA), in addition to the challenge white-box implementation $[E_k^r]$, we give $\mathcal{A}$ access to a recompiling oracle $\mathbf{C}_{\mathcal{E}}(k, \mathsf{R})$ that generates other programs $[E_k^{r'}]$ with key k for adversarially unknown random nonces $r' \xleftarrow{\$} \mathsf{R}$. In other words, we give $\mathcal{A}$ the ability to observe other programs compiled with the same key and different nonces.

In a *chosen ciphertext and recompilation attack* (CCA+RCA) we give $\mathcal{A}$ (the challenge white-box implementation $[E_k^r]$ and) simultaneous access to a decryption oracle $D(k, \cdot)$ and a recompiling oracle $\mathbf{C}_{\mathcal{E}}(k, \mathsf{R})$, both parametrized with the same key k.

Remark 2. We emphasize that the recompilation attack model is *not* artificial when dealing with white-box cryptography. Indeed, it seems reasonable to assume that user-related values can be embedded in the random nonce $r \in \mathsf{R}$ used to compile a (user-specific) white-box implementation. Thus a coalition of malicious users can be modeled as a single adversary with (possibly limited) access to a recompiling oracle producing white-box implementations under fresh random nonces $r' \in \mathsf{R}$.

3.2 The Prime Goal: Unbreakability

Chow *et al.* stated in [10,11] that the first security objective of white-box cryptography is, given a program $[E_k]$, to preserve the privacy of the key k embedded in the program (see also [17, Q1] and [30, Definition 2]). We define the following game to capture that intuition:

1. randomly generate a key $k \leftarrow K()$ and a nonce $r \xleftarrow{\$} \mathsf{R}$,
2. the adversary $\mathcal{A}$ is run on input $[E_k^r] = \mathbf{C}_{\mathcal{E}}(k, r)$,
3. $\mathcal{A}$ returns a guess $\hat{k} \in \mathsf{K}$,
4. $\mathcal{A}$ succeeds if $\hat{k} = k$.

Notice that at Step 2, the adversary may have access to the decryption oracle $D(k, \cdot)$ or to the recompiling oracle $\mathbf{C}_\mathcal{E}(k, \mathsf{R})$, or both, depending on the attack model.

Let us define more concisely and precisely the notion of unbreakability with respect to the attack model ATK (CPA, CCA, RCA or CCA+RCA).

Definition 1 (Unbreakability). *Let $\mathcal{E}$ be a symmetric encryption scheme as above, $\mathbf{C}_\mathcal{E}$ a white-box compiler for $\mathcal{E}$ and let $\mathcal{A}$ be an adversary. For ATK $\in$ $\{\mathsf{CPA}, \mathsf{CCA}, \mathsf{RCA}, \mathsf{CCA} + \mathsf{RCA}\}$, we define*

$$\mathsf{Succ}_{\mathcal{A},\mathbf{C}_\mathcal{E}}^{\mathsf{UBK}-\mathsf{ATK}} \stackrel{\text{def}}{=} \Pr\left[k \leftarrow K(); \quad r \stackrel{\$}{\leftarrow} \mathsf{R}; \quad [E_k^r] = \mathbf{C}_\mathcal{E}(k, r); \quad \hat{k} \leftarrow \mathcal{A}^\mathcal{O}([E_k^r]) : \hat{k} = k\right]$$

where

$$\begin{aligned}
\mathcal{O}(\cdot) &= \epsilon & \textit{if } \mathsf{ATK} &= \mathsf{CPA} \\
\mathcal{O}(\cdot) &= D(k, \cdot) & \textit{if } \mathsf{ATK} &= \mathsf{CCA} \\
\mathcal{O}(\cdot) &= \mathbf{C}_\mathcal{E}(k, \mathsf{R}) & \textit{if } \mathsf{ATK} &= \mathsf{RCA} \\
\mathcal{O}(\cdot) &= \{D(k, \cdot), \mathbf{C}_\mathcal{E}(k, \mathsf{R})\} & \textit{if } \mathsf{ATK} &= \mathsf{CCA} + \mathsf{RCA}.
\end{aligned}$$

We say that $\mathbf{C}_\mathcal{E}$ is (τ, ε)-secure in the sense of UBK-ATK if for any adversary $\mathcal{A}$ running in time at most τ, $\mathsf{Succ}_{\mathcal{A},\mathbf{C}_\mathcal{E}}^{\mathsf{UBK}-\mathsf{ATK}} \leq \varepsilon$.

Note that in our setting, a total break requires the adversary to output the whole key k embedded into $[E_k^r]$. Basing UBK on the semantic security of k makes no sense here since it is straightforward to ascertain, for some guess $\hat{k}$, that $\hat{k} = k$ by just checking whether the value returned by $[E_k^r](m)$ is equal to $E(\hat{k}, m)$ for sufficiently many plaintext(s) $m \in \mathsf{M}$. In other words, the distributions $\{k, [E_k^r]\}_{k \in \mathsf{K}, r \in \mathsf{R}}$ and $\{k', [E_k^r]\}_{(k,k') \in \mathsf{K}^2, r \in \mathsf{R}}$ are computationally distinguishable. As a result, one cannot prevent some information leakage about k from $[E_k^r]$, whatever the specification of the compiler $\mathbf{C}_\mathcal{E}$.

Remark 3. Although not required in the above definition, for a white-box compiler to be cryptographically sound, one would require that there exist some security parameter λ such that ε / τ be exponentially small in λ and $\mathsf{size}([E_k])$ and $\mathsf{time}([E_k](\cdot))$ be polynomial in λ. Otherwise said, one aims to get a negligible ε / τ while keeping fair $\mathsf{size}([E_k])$ and $\mathsf{time}([E_k](\cdot))$.

3.3   Security Notions Really Needed in Applications

When satisfied, unbreakability ensures that an adversary cannot extract the secret key of a randomly generated white-box implementation. Therefore any party should have to execute the program rather than simulating it with the secret key. While this property is the very least that can be expected from white-box cryptography, it is rather useless on its own. Indeed, knowing the white-box program amounts to knowing the key in some sense since it allows one to process the encryption without restriction. As discussed in [30, Sect. 3.1.3], an attacker only needs to isolate the cryptographic code in the implementation. This is a common threat in DRM applications, which is known as *code lifting*. Although some countermeasures can make code lifting a tedious task it is reasonable to assume that sooner or later a motivated attacker would eventually recover the cryptographic code. That is why, in order to make the white-box compilation useful, the availability of the white-box program should restrict the adversary capabilities compared to the availability of the secret key.

One-Wayness. A natural restriction is that although the white-box implementation allows one to encrypt at will, it should not enable decryption. In other words, it should be difficult to invert the program computations. In that case, the program is said to be *one-way*, to keep consistency with the notion of one-wayness (for a function or a cryptosystem) traditionally used in cryptography. As already noted in [17], a white-box compiler achieving one-wayness is of great interest as it turns a symmetric encryption scheme into a public-key encryption scheme. This is also one of the many motivations to design methods for general obfuscation [1,14].

Incompressibility of Programs. Another argument often heard in favor of white-box cryptography is that a white-box program is less convenient to store and exchange than a mere secret key due to its bigger size. As formulated in [30, Sect. 3.1.3], white-box cryptography allows to "hide a key in an even bigger key". For instance, Chow *et al.* implementation of AES [11] makes use of 800 KB of look-up tables, which represents a significant overhead compared to a 128-bit key. Suppose this implementation was unbreakable in the sense of Definition 1 (which we know to be false [3]), the question that would arise would be: what is the computationally achievable minimum size of a program functionally equivalent to this implementation? When a program is hard to compress beyond a certain prescribed size, we shall say that this program is *incompressible*. Section 6 shows an example of computationally incompressible programs for symmetric encryption.

Traceability of Programs. It is often heard that white-box compilation can provide traceability (see for instance [30, Sect. 5.5.1]). Specifically, white-box compilation should enable one to derive several functionally equivalent versions of the same encryption (or decryption) program. A typical use case for such a system is the distribution of protected digital content where every legitimate user gets a different version of some decryption software. If a malicious user shares its own program (e.g. over the Internet), then one can trace the so-called *traitor* by identifying its unique copy of the program. However, in a white-box context, a user can easily transform its version of the program while keeping the same functionality. Therefore to be effective, the tracing should be robust to such transformations, even in the case where several malicious users collude to produce an untraceable software. We show in Sect. 7 how to achieve such a robust tracing from a compiler that can *hide* functional perturbations in a white-box program. Accordingly, we define new security notions for such a white-box compiler. Combined with our tracing scheme, a compiler achieving these security notions is shown to provide traceable white-box programs.

4 One-Wayness

An adversarial goal of interest in white-box cryptography consists, given a white-box implementation $[E_k^r]$, in recovering the plaintext of a given ciphertext with respect to the embedded key k. This security notion is even essential when white-box implementations are deployed as an asymmetric primitive [17, Q4]. We define the following security game to capture that intuition:

1. randomly select a key $k \leftarrow K()$ and a nonce $r \xleftarrow{\$} \mathsf{R}$,
2. generate the white box program $[E_k^r] = \mathbf{C}_{\mathcal{E}}(k, r)$,
3. randomly select a plaintext $m \xleftarrow{\$} \mathsf{M}$
4. compute its encryption $c = E(k, m)$,
5. the adversary $\mathcal{A}$ is run on inputs $[E_k^r]$ and c,
6. $\mathcal{A}$ returns a guess $\hat{m}$,
7. $\mathcal{A}$ succeeds if $\hat{m} = m$.

Notice that at Step 5, the adversary may have access to the decryption oracle $D(k, \cdot)$ or to the recompiling oracle $\mathbf{C}_{\mathcal{E}}(k, \mathsf{R})$ (or both) depending on the attack model. When $\mathcal{A}$ is given access to the decryption oracle, the challenge ciphertext c itself shall be rejected by the oracle.

Let us define more precisely the notion of one-wayness with respect to the attack model ATK.

Definition 2 (One-Wayness). *Let $\mathcal{E}$ be a symmetric encryption scheme as above, $\mathbf{C}_{\mathcal{E}}$ a white-box compiler for $\mathcal{E}$ and $\mathcal{A}$ an adversary. For* ATK $\in \{$CPA, CCA, RCA, CCA + RCA$\}$, *let*

$$\mathsf{Succ}_{\mathcal{A}, \mathbf{C}_{\mathcal{E}}}^{\mathsf{OW-ATK}} \overset{\text{def}}{=} \Pr \begin{bmatrix} k \leftarrow K(); & r \xleftarrow{\$} \mathsf{R}; & [E_k^r] = \mathbf{C}_{\mathcal{E}}(k, r); \\ m \xleftarrow{\$} \mathsf{M}; & c = E(k, m); & \hat{m} \leftarrow \mathcal{A}^{\mathcal{O}}([E_k^r], c) \end{bmatrix} : \hat{m} = m$$

where

$$\begin{aligned} \mathcal{O}(\cdot) &= \epsilon & if\ \mathsf{ATK} = \mathsf{CPA} \\ \mathcal{O}(\cdot) &= D(k, \cdot) & if\ \mathsf{ATK} = \mathsf{CCA} \\ \mathcal{O}(\cdot) &= \mathbf{C}_{\mathcal{E}}(k, \mathsf{R}) & if\ \mathsf{ATK} = \mathsf{RCA} \\ \mathcal{O}(\cdot) &= \{D(k, \cdot), \mathbf{C}_{\mathcal{E}}(k, \mathsf{R})\} & if\ \mathsf{ATK} = \mathsf{CCA} + \mathsf{RCA}. \end{aligned}$$

We say that $\mathbf{C}_{\mathcal{E}}$ is (τ, ε)-secure in the sense of OW-ATK *if $\mathcal{A}$ running in time at most τ implies* $\mathsf{Succ}_{\mathcal{A}, \mathbf{C}_{\mathcal{E}}}^{\mathsf{OW-ATK}} \le \varepsilon$.

Similarly to the unbreakability notion, it is obvious that any incorrect guess $\hat{m}$ on m can be rejected by comparing the value returned by $[E_k^r](\hat{m})$ with c. In other words, the two distributions

$$\{[E_k^r], E(k, m), m\}_{k \in \mathsf{K}, r \in \mathsf{R}, m \in \mathsf{M}} \quad \text{and} \quad \{[E_k^r], E(k, m), m'\}_{k \in \mathsf{K}, r \in \mathsf{R}, m, m' \in \mathsf{M}}$$

are easily distinguishable. Moreover, there is an easy reduction from OW-ATK to UBK-ATK. Clearly, extracting k from $[E_k]$ enables one to use it and the challenge as inputs to the (publicly available) decryption function $D(\cdot, \cdot)$ and thus to recover m.

5 Incompressibility of White-Box Programs

In this section, we formalize the notion of incompressibility for a white-box compiler. What we mean by incompressibility here is the hardness, given a (large) compiled program $[E_k]$, of coming up with a significantly smaller program functionally close to $E(k, \cdot)$. A typical example is when a content provider distributes a large encryption program (e.g. 100 GB or more) and wants to make sure that no smaller yet equivalent program can be redistributed by subscribers to illegitimate third parties. The content provider cannot prevent the original program from being shared e.g. over the Internet; however, if compiled programs are provably incompressible then redistribution may be somewhat discouraged by the size of transmissions.

We define (λ, δ)-INC as the adversarial goal that consists, given a compiled program $[E_k]$ with $\text{size}([E_k]) \gg \lambda$, in building a smaller program P that remains satisfactorily functional, i.e. such that

$$\text{size}(P) < \lambda \qquad \text{and} \qquad P \in \delta\text{-prog}(E(k, \cdot)) \ .$$

This is formalized by the following game:

1. randomly select $k \leftarrow K()$ and $r \overset{\$}{\leftarrow} R$,
2. compile $[E_k^r] = \mathbf{C}_{\mathcal{E}}(k, r)$,
3. run $\mathcal{A}$ on input $[E_k^r]$,
4. $\mathcal{A}$ returns some program P,
5. $\mathcal{A}$ succeeds if $\Delta(P, E(k, \cdot)) \leq \delta$ and $\text{size}(P) < \lambda$.

Definition 3 ((λ, δ)-Incompressibility). *Let $\mathcal{E}$ be a symmetric encryption scheme, $\mathbf{C}_{\mathcal{E}}$ a white-box compiler for $\mathcal{E}$ and $\mathcal{A}$ an adversary. For* ATK $\in \{$CPA, CCA, RCA, CCA + RCA$\}$, *let*

$$\mathsf{Adv}_{\mathcal{A}, \mathbf{C}_{\mathcal{E}}}^{(\lambda, \delta) - \text{INC} - \text{ATK}} \overset{\text{def}}{=} \Pr \left[\begin{array}{l} k \leftarrow K(); \quad r \overset{\$}{\leftarrow} R; \\ [E_k^r] = \mathbf{C}_{\mathcal{E}}(k, r); \\ P \leftarrow \mathcal{A}^{\mathcal{O}}([E_k^r]) \end{array} : (\Delta(P, E(k, \cdot) \leq \delta) \wedge (\text{size}(P) < \lambda) \right]$$

where

$$\begin{aligned} \mathcal{O}(\cdot) &= \epsilon & \text{if } \mathsf{ATK} = \mathsf{CPA} \\ \mathcal{O}(\cdot) &= D(k, \cdot) & \text{if } \mathsf{ATK} = \mathsf{CCA} \\ \mathcal{O}(\cdot) &= \mathbf{C}_{\mathcal{E}}(k, \mathsf{R}) & \text{if } \mathsf{ATK} = \mathsf{RCA} \\ \mathcal{O}(\cdot) &= \{D(k, \cdot), \mathbf{C}_{\mathcal{E}}(k, \mathsf{R})\} & \text{if } \mathsf{ATK} = \mathsf{CCA} + \mathsf{RCA} \ . \end{aligned}$$

We say that $\mathbf{C}_{\mathcal{E}}$ is (τ, ε)-secure in the sense of (λ, δ)-INC-ATK if having $\mathcal{A}$ running in time at most τ implies that $\mathsf{Adv}_{\mathcal{A}, \mathbf{C}_{\mathcal{E}}}^{(\lambda, \delta) - \text{INC} - \text{ATK}} \leq \varepsilon$.

Notice that for some values of λ and δ, the (λ, δ)-incompressibility may be trivially broken. For example, the problem is trivial for $\delta = 1$ as the user can always construct any program smaller than λ bits with outputs unrelated to $E(k, \cdot)$. Even though the definition allows any $\delta \in [0, 1]$, the notion makes more sense (and surely is harder to break) when δ is taken small enough. In that case, the adversary has to output a program which correctly encrypts nearly all plaintexts (or at least a significant fraction).

It seems natural to hope that a reduction exists from INC-ATK to UBK-ATK: intuitively, extracting k from $[E_k]$ enables one to build a small program that implements $E(k, \cdot)$. Let $\lambda(k)$ be the size of that program; it is easily seen that $\lambda(k)$ is lower-bounded by

$$\lambda_0 = H(k) + \mathsf{size}\,(P_E)$$

where $H(k)$ is the average number of bits needed to represent the key k and P_E the smallest known program that implements the generic encryption function $E(\cdot, \cdot)$ that takes k, m as inputs and returns $E(k, m)$. When $\lambda_0 \leq \lambda$, a total break (i.e. recovering the key k) will allow to break $(\lambda, 0)$-incompressibility by outputting a program P composed of P_E and a string representing k, which will be of size at most $\lambda_0\ (\leq \lambda)$.

On the other hand, denoting

$$\lambda^+ = \sup_{k \in \mathsf{K}, r \in \mathsf{R}} \mathsf{size}\,([E_k^r]) \quad \text{and} \quad \lambda^- = \inf_{k \in \mathsf{K}, r \in \mathsf{R}} \mathsf{size}\,([E_k^r]) \ ,$$

we also see that when $\lambda \geq \lambda^+$, the challenge program $[E_k^r]$ given to $\mathcal{A}$ already satisfies the conditions of a satisfactorily compressed program and $\mathcal{A}$ may then return $P = [E_k^r]$ as a solution. (λ, δ)-INC is therefore trivial to break in that case. However, (λ, δ)-incompressibility for $\lambda \leq \lambda^-$ may not be trivial to break. To conclude, the (λ, δ)-incompressibility notion makes sense in practice for parameters $\lambda \in (\lambda_0, \lambda^-)$ and δ close to 0.

6   A Provably One-Way and Incompressible White-Box Compiler

In this section, we give an example of a symmetric encryption scheme for which there exists a efficient one-way and incompressible white-box compiler. This example is a symmetric-key variant of the RSA cryptosystem [27]. The one-wayness and incompressibility properties of the compiler are provably achieved based on standard hardness assumptions related to the integer factoring problem.

One-Way Compilers from Public-Key Encryption. It is worthwhile noticing that any *one-way public-key* encryption scheme straightforwardly gives rise to a symmetric encryption scheme for which a one-way compiler exists. The symmetric key is defined as the secret key of the asymmetric encryption scheme and encryption is defined as the function deriving the public key from the secret key composed with the encryption procedure. The white-box compiler then simply produces a program evaluating the encryption algorithm with the public key embedded in it. The one-wayness of the compiler comes directly from the one-wayness of the asymmetric scheme. Such an example of a one-way compiler is given in [29, Theorem 3],[30, Sect. 4.8.2].

We present hereafter another compiler obtained from the RSA cryptosystem and whose one-wayness straightforwardly holds by construction. The main interest of our example is to further satisfy $(\lambda, 0)$-incompressibility for any arbitrary λ. We first recall some background on RSA groups.

6.1 RSA Groups

We consider a (multiplicative) group $\mathcal{G}$ of unknown order ω, also called an *RSA group*. A typical construction for $\mathcal{G}$ is to take the group of invertible integers modulo a composite number or a carefully chosen elliptic curve over a ring. Practical RSA groups are known to be efficiently samplable in the sense that there exists a group generation algorithm $\mathbb{G}$ which, given a security parameter $n \in \mathbb{N}$, outputs the public description $\mathsf{desc}\,(\mathcal{G})$ of a random group $\mathcal{G}$ together with its order ω. Efficient means that the random selection

$$(\mathsf{desc}\,(\mathcal{G}), \omega) \leftarrow \mathbb{G}(1^n)$$

takes time polynomial in n. The parameter n determine the size of the returned order (i.e. $|\omega| = n$) and hence tunes the hardness of breaking the group. For security reasons, we require the returned order ω to have a low smoothness. More specifically, we require that it satisfy $\varphi(\omega) \geq \frac{1}{3}\omega$, where φ denotes the Euler's totient function.[2] The group descriptor $\mathsf{desc}\,(\mathcal{G})$ intends to contain all the necessary parameters for performing group operations. Obviously ω is excluded from the group description.

In the following, we shall make the usual hardness assumptions for RSA group generators. Namely, we assume that the groups sampled by $\mathbb{G}$ have the following properties (formal definitions for these security notions are provided in the full version of this paper [12]):

Unbreakability – UBK[$\mathbb{G}$]:
   It is hard to compute the secret order ω of $\mathcal{G}$ from $\mathsf{desc}\,(\mathcal{G})$.

Hardness of Extracting Orders – ORD[$\mathbb{G}$]:
   It is hard to compute the order of a random group element $x \xleftarrow{\$} \mathcal{G}$ (or a multiple thereof) from $\mathsf{desc}\,(\mathcal{G})$.

Hardness of Extracting Roots – RSA[$\mathbb{G}$]:
   For a random integer $e \in [0, \omega)$ such that $\gcd(e, \omega) = 1$, it is hard to compute the e-th root of a random group element $x \in \mathcal{G}$ from e and $\mathsf{desc}\,(\mathcal{G})$.

---

[2] In practice, it is well known how to generate such groups. For instance, the multiplicative group $\mathbb{Z}_{pq}^*$ with p and q being *safe primes* has order $\omega = (p-1)(q-1)$ with $\varphi(\omega) \approx \frac{1}{2}\omega$.

6.2   The White-Box Compiler

We consider the symmetric encryption scheme $\mathcal{E} = (\mathsf{K}, \mathsf{M}, \mathsf{C}, K, E, D)$ where:

1. $\mathcal{E}$ makes use of a security parameter $n \in \mathbb{N}$,
2. $K()$ randomly selects a group $(\mathsf{desc}\,(\mathcal{G}), \omega) \leftarrow \mathbb{G}(1^n)$ and a public exponent $e \in [0, \omega)$ such that $\gcd(e, \omega) = 1$, and returns $k = (\mathsf{desc}\,(\mathcal{G}), \omega, e)$,
3. plaintexts and ciphertexts are group elements i.e. $\mathsf{M} = \mathsf{C} = \mathcal{G}$,
4. given a key $k = (\mathsf{desc}\,(\mathcal{G}), \omega, e)$ and a plaintext $m \in \mathcal{G}$, $E(k, m)$ computes $m^e \mod \omega$ in the group and returns that value,
5. given a key $k = (\mathsf{desc}\,(\mathcal{G}), \omega, e)$ and a ciphertext $c \in \mathcal{G}$, $D(k, c)$ computes $c^{\frac{1}{e}} \mod \omega$ in the group and returns that value.

It is clear that $D(k, E(k, m)) = m$ for any $k \in \mathsf{K}$ and $m \in \mathsf{M}$. Our white-box compiler $\mathbf{C}_{\mathcal{E}}$ is then defined as follows:

1. $\mathbf{C}_{\mathcal{E}}$ makes use of an additional security parameter $h \in \mathbb{N}$,
2. the randomness space R is the integer set $[0, 2^h/\omega)$,
3. we define the *blinded exponent* f with respect to the public exponent e and a random nonce $r \in \mathsf{R}$ as the integer $f = e + r \cdot \omega$,
4. given a key $k = (\mathsf{desc}\,(\mathcal{G}), \omega, e) \in \mathsf{K}$, and a random nonce $r \in \mathsf{R}$, our white-box compiler $\mathbf{C}_{\mathcal{E}}$ generates a program $[E_k]$ which simply embeds $\mathsf{desc}\,(\mathcal{G})$ and f and computes m^f for any input $m \in \mathcal{G}$.

According to the above definition, we clearly have that the white-box program $[E_k]$ is a functional program with respect to the encryption function $E(k, \cdot)$. Moreover, we state (see proof in the full version [12]):

Theorem 1. *The white-box compiler $\mathbf{C}_{\mathcal{E}}$ is* UBK-CPA *secure under the assumption that* UBK[$\mathbb{G}$] *is hard, and* OW-CPA *secure under the assumption that* RSA[$\mathbb{G}$] *is hard.*

6.3   Proving Incompressibility Under Chosen Plaintext Attacks

We now show that $\mathbf{C}_{\mathcal{E}}$ is $(\lambda, 0)$-INC-CPA secure under UBK[$\mathbb{G}$] as long as the security parameter h is slightly greater than λ. We actually show a slightly weaker result: our reduction assumes that the program P output by the adversary is *algebraic*. An algebraic program P (see [5,26]) with respect to group $\mathcal{G}$ has the property that each and every group element $y \in \mathcal{G}$ output by P is computed as a linear combination of all the group elements $x_1, \ldots, x_t$ that were given to P as input in the same execution. Relying on the definition of [26], P must then admit an efficient extractor Extract (running in time τ_{Ex}) which, given the code of P as well as all its inputs and random tape for some execution, returns the coefficients α_i such that $y = x_1^{\alpha_1} \cdots x_t^{\alpha_t}$.

Theorem 2. *For every $h > \lambda + \log_2(3)$, the compiler $\mathbf{C}_{\mathcal{E}}$ is $(\tau_{\mathcal{A}}, \varepsilon_{\mathcal{A}})$-secure in the sense of $(\lambda, 0)$-INC-CPA under the assumption that* ORD[$\mathbb{G}$] *is (τ, ε)-hard, with*

$$\tau_{\mathcal{A}} = \tau - \tau_{\mathsf{Ex}} \quad \text{and} \quad \varepsilon_{\mathcal{A}} < \frac{3}{1 - 3 \cdot 2^{\lambda - h}}\, \varepsilon\,.$$

The proof of Theorem 2 is provided in the full version of the paper [12].

Remark 4. The white-box compiler can also be shown to be $(\lambda, 0)$-INC-CCA secure under the (gap) assumption that ORD[$\mathbb{G}$] remains hard when RSA[$\mathbb{G}$] is easy. The reduction would work similarly but with an oracle solving RSA[$\mathbb{G}$] that it would use to simulate decryption queries.

7   Traceability of White-Box Programs

One of the main applications of white-box cryptography is the secure distribution of valuable content through applications enforcing digital rights management (DRM). Namely, some digital content is distributed in encrypted form to legitimate users. A service user may then recover the content in clear using her own private white-box-secure decryption software.

However, by sharing their decryption software, users may collude and try to produce a pirate decryption software i.e. a non-registered utility capable of decrypting premium content. Traitor tracing schemes [4,8,9,25] were specifically designed to fight copyright infringement, by enabling a designated authority to recover the identity of at least one of the traitors in the malicious coalition who constructed the rogue decryption software. In this section, we show how to apply some of these techniques to ensure the full traceability of programs assuming that slight perturbations of the programs functionality by the white-box compiler can remain *hidden* to an adversary.

As opposed to previous sections, we interchange the roles of encryption and decryption, considering that for our purpose, user programs would implement decryption rather than encryption.

7.1   Programs with Hidden Perturbations

A program can be made traceable by unnoticeably modifying its functionality. The basic idea is to *perturbate* the program such that it returns an incorrect output for a small set of unknown inputs (which remains a negligible fraction of the input domain). The set of so-called *tracing inputs* varies according to the identity of end users so that running the decryption program over inputs from different sets and checking the returned outputs efficiently reveals the identity of a traitor. We consider tracing schemes that follow this approach to make programs traceable in the presence of pirate coalitions. Of course, one must consider collusions of several users aiming to produce an untraceable program from their own legitimate programs. A tracing scheme that resists such collusions is said to be *collusion-resistant*.

In the context of deterministic symmetric encryption schemes, one can generically describe functional perturbations with the following formalism. Consider a symmetric encryption scheme $\mathcal{E} = (\mathsf{K}, \mathsf{M}, \mathsf{C}, K, E, D)$ under the definition of Sect. 2. A white-box compiler $\mathbf{C}_\mathcal{E}$ with respect to $\mathcal{E}$ that *supports perturbation* takes as additional input an ordered list of dysfunctional ciphertexts $\boldsymbol{c} = \langle c_1, \ldots, c_u \rangle \in \mathsf{C}^u$ and returns a program

$$[D^r_{k,c}] = \mathbf{C}_{\mathcal{E}}(k, r; c)$$

such that $[D^r_{k,c}](c) = D(k, c)$ for any $c \in \mathsf{C} \setminus c$ and for $i \in [1, u]$, $[D^r_{k,c}](c_i)$ returns some incorrect plaintext randomly chosen at compilation. We will say that $\mathbf{C}_{\mathcal{E}}$ *hides* functional perturbations when, given a program instance $P = [D^r_{k,c}]$, an adversary cannot extract enough information about the dysfunctional input-output pairs to be able to correct P back to its original functionality. It is shown later that perturbated programs can be made traceable assuming that it is hard to recover the correct output of dysfunctional inputs. This is formalized by the following game:

1. randomly select $k \leftarrow K()$, $m \xleftarrow{\$} \mathsf{M}$ and $r \xleftarrow{\$} \mathsf{R}$,
2. compile $[D^r_{k,\langle c \rangle}] = \mathbf{C}_{\mathcal{E}}(k, r; \langle c \rangle)$ with $c = E(k, m)$,
3. run $\mathcal{A}$ on input $(c, [D^r_{k,\langle c \rangle}])$,
4. $\mathcal{A}$ return some message $\hat{m}$,
5. $\mathcal{A}$ succeeds if $\hat{m} = m$.

Definition 4 (Perturbation-Value Hiding). *Let $\mathcal{E}$ be a symmetric encryption scheme, $\mathbf{C}_{\mathcal{E}}$ a white-box compiler for $\mathcal{E}$ that supports perturbations, and let $\mathcal{A}$ be an adversary. Let*

$$\mathsf{Succ}^{\mathsf{PVH}}_{\mathcal{A},\mathbf{C}_{\mathcal{E}}} \overset{\text{def}}{=} \Pr \left[\begin{array}{c} k \leftarrow K(); \quad m \xleftarrow{\$} \mathsf{M}; \quad c = E(k, m); \\ r \xleftarrow{\$} \mathsf{R}; \quad [D^r_{k,\langle c \rangle}] = \mathbf{C}_{\mathcal{E}}(k, r; \langle c \rangle); \quad : \hat{m} = m \\ \hat{m} \leftarrow \mathcal{A}^{\mathcal{O}}(c, [D^r_{k,\langle c \rangle}]) \end{array} \right].$$

where $\mathcal{O}$ is a recompiling oracle $\mathcal{O}(\cdot) \overset{\text{def}}{=} \mathbf{C}_{\mathcal{E}}(k, \mathsf{R}; \langle c, \cdot \rangle)$ that takes as input a list of dysfunctional inputs containing c and returns a perturbated program accordingly, under adversarially unknown randomness. The white-box compiler $\mathbf{C}_{\mathcal{E}}$ is said (τ, ε)-secure in the sense of PVH if $\mathcal{A}$ running in time at most τ implies $\mathsf{Succ}^{\mathsf{PVH}}_{\mathcal{A},\mathbf{C}_{\mathcal{E}}} \leq \varepsilon$.

A second security notion that we will make use of for our tracing construction relates to the intuition that all perturbations should be equally hidden by the white-box compiler. Namely, it should not matter in which order the dysfunctional inputs are given to the compiler: they should all appear equally hard to recover to an adversary. When this property is realized, we say that the compiler achieves *perturbation-index hiding*. We formalize this notion with the following game, where $n > 1$ and $v \in [1, n-1]$ are fixed parameters:

1. randomly select $k \leftarrow K()$,
2. for $i \in [1, n]$, randomly select $m_i \xleftarrow{\$} \mathsf{M}$ and set $c_i = E(k, m_i)$,
3. for $i \in [1, n]$ with $i \neq v$, randomly select $r_i \xleftarrow{\$} \mathsf{R}$ and generate $P_i = \mathbf{C}_{\mathcal{E}}(k, r_i; \langle c_1, \ldots, c_i \rangle)$,
4. randomly pick $b \xleftarrow{\$} \{0, 1\}$,
5. run $\mathcal{A}$ on inputs $P_1, \ldots, P_{v-1}, P_{v+1}, \ldots, P_n$ and (m_{v+b}, c_{v+b}),
6. $\mathcal{A}$ returns a guess $\hat{b}$ and succeeds if $\hat{b} = b$.

Definition 5 (Perturbation-Index Hiding). *Let $\mathcal{E}$ be a symmetric encryption scheme, $\mathbf{C}_{\mathcal{E}}$ a white-box compiler for $\mathcal{E}$ that supports perturbations, and let $\mathcal{A}$ be an adversary. Let*

$$
\mathsf{Adv}^{\mathsf{PIH}}_{\mathcal{A},\mathbf{C}_{\mathcal{E}}} \stackrel{\text{def}}{=} \left| \Pr \left[\begin{array}{l} k \leftarrow K(); \quad m_i \stackrel{\$}{\leftarrow} \mathsf{M}; \quad c_i = E(k, m_i) \text{ for } i \in [1, n] \\ r_i \stackrel{\$}{\leftarrow} \mathsf{R}; \quad P_i = \mathbf{C}_{\mathcal{E}}(k, r_i; \langle c_1, \ldots, c_i \rangle) \text{ for } i \in [1, n], i \neq v : \hat{b} = b \\ b \stackrel{\$}{\leftarrow} \{0, 1\}; \quad \hat{b} \leftarrow \mathcal{A}(\{P_i\}_{i \neq v}, m_{v+b}, c_{v+b}) \end{array} \right] - \frac{1}{2} \right| .
$$

The white-box compiler $\mathbf{C}_{\mathcal{E}}$ is said to be (τ, ε)-secure in the sense of PIH if $\mathcal{A}$ running in time at most τ implies $\mathsf{Adv}^{\mathsf{PIH}}_{\mathcal{A},\mathbf{C}_{\mathcal{E}}} \leq \varepsilon$.

Note that in a PIH-secure white-box compiler, all entries in the list of its dysfunctional inputs can be permuted with no (non-negligible) impact on the security of the compiler.

7.2 A Generic Tracing Scheme

We now give an example of a tracing scheme $\mathcal{T}$ for programs generated by a white-box compiler $\mathbf{C}_{\mathcal{E}}$ that supports hidden perturbations. We formally prove that the identification of at least one traitor is computationally enforced assuming that $\mathbf{C}_{\mathcal{E}}$ is secure in the sense of PVH and PIH, independently of the total number n of issued programs. Under these assumptions, $\mathcal{T}$ therefore resists collusions of up to n users i.e. is maximally secure. As usual in traitor-tracing schemes, $\mathcal{T}$ is composed of a setup algorithm $\mathcal{T}$.setup and a tracing algorithm $\mathcal{T}$.trace. These algorithms are defined as follows.

Setup Algorithm. A random key $k \stackrel{\$}{\leftarrow} K()$ is generated as well as n random input-output pairs (m_i, c_i) where $m_i \stackrel{\$}{\leftarrow} \mathsf{M}$ and $c_i = E(k, m_i)$ for $i \in [1, n]$. $\mathcal{T}$ keeps perturbations $= ((m_1, c_1), \ldots, (m_n, c_n))$ as private information for later tracing. For $i \in [1, n]$, user i is (securely) given the i-perturbated program $P_i = \mathbf{C}_{\mathcal{E}}(k, r_i; \langle c_1, \ldots, c_i \rangle)$ where $r_i \stackrel{\$}{\leftarrow} \mathsf{R}$. It is easily seen that all P_i's correctly decrypt any $c \notin \{c_i, i \in [1, n]\}$. However when $c = c_i$, user programs $P_i, \ldots, P_n$ return junk while $P_1, \ldots, P_{i-1}$ remain functional. Therefore $\mathcal{T}$ implements a private linear broadcast encryption (PLBE) scheme in the sense of [4].

Tracing Algorithm. Given a rogue decryption program Q constructed from a set of user programs $\{P_j \mid j \in T \subseteq [1, n]\}$, $\mathcal{T}$.trace uses its knowledge of k and perturbations to identify a traitor $j \in T$ in $O(\log n)$ evaluations of Q as follows. Since Q is just a program and is therefore stateless, the general tracing techniques of [4,25] are applicable. $\mathcal{T}$.trace makes use of two probability estimators as subroutines:

1. a probability estimator $\widehat{p_0}$ which intends to measure the actual probability

$$
p_0 = \Pr \left[m \stackrel{\$}{\leftarrow} \mathsf{M}; \quad c = E(k, m) : Q(c) = m \right]
$$

---

1. evaluate $\widehat{p_0}$ and $\widehat{p_n}$
2. set $a = 0$ and $b = n$
3. while $a \neq b - 1$
   3.1. set $v = \lceil (a+b)/2 \rceil$
   3.2. evaluate $\widehat{p_v}$
   3.3. if $|\widehat{p_v} - \widehat{p_a}| > |\widehat{p_v} - \widehat{p_b}|$ then set $b = v$ else set $a = v$
4. return b as the identified traitor.

Fig. 1. Dichotomic search implemented by $\mathcal{T}$.trace

when all calls Q makes to an external random source are fed with a perfect source. Since the pirate decryption program is assumed to be fully or almost fully functional, p_0 must be significantly close to 1. It is classical to require from Q that $p_0 \geq 1/2$.

2. a probability estimator $\widehat{p_v}$ which, given $v \in [1, n]$, estimates the actual probability

$$p_v = \Pr\left[Q(c_v) = m_v\right]$$

where Q is run over a perfect random source again.

To estimate p_v for $v \in [0, n]$, Q is executed θ times (on fresh random tapes), where θ is an accuracy parameter. Then, one counts how many times, say ν, the returned output is as expected and $\widehat{p_v}$ is set to ν/θ. Finally, $\mathcal{T}$.trace implements a dichotomic search as shown on Fig. 1.

We state (see proof in the full version [12]):

Theorem 3. *Assume* $\mathbf{C}_{\mathcal{E}}$ *is secure in the sense of both* PVH *and* PIH. *Then for any subset of traitors* $T \subseteq [1, n]$, $\mathcal{T}$.trace *correctly returns a traitor* $j \in T$ *with overwhelming probability after* $O(\log n)$ *executions of the pirate decryption program* Q.

This result validates the folklore intuition according to which cryptographic programs can be made efficiently traceable when properly obfuscated and assuming that slight alterations can be securely inserted in them. It also identifies clearly which sufficient security properties must be fulfilled by the white-box compiler to achieve traceability even when all users collude i.e., in the context of total piracy.

Acknowledgements. This work has been financially supported by the French national FUI12 project MARSHAL+. The authors would like to thank Jean-Sébastien Coron and Louis Goubin for interesting discussions and suggestions.

References

1. Barak, B., Goldreich, O., Impagliazzo, R., Rudich, S., Sahai, A., Vadhan, S., Yang, K.: On the (im)possibility of obfuscating programs. In: Kilian, J. (ed.) CRYPTO 2001. LNCS, vol. 2139, pp. 1–18. Springer, Heidelberg (2001)

2. Bellare, M., Desai, A., Pointcheval, D., Rogaway, P.: Relations among notions of security for public-key encryption schemes. In: Krawczyk, H. (ed.) CRYPTO 1998. LNCS, vol. 1462, pp. 26–45. Springer, Heidelberg (1998)

3. Billet, O., Gilbert, H., Ech-Chatbi, C.: Cryptanalysis of a white Box AES implementation. In: Handschuh, H., Hasan, M.A. (eds.) SAC 2004. LNCS, vol. 3357, pp. 227–240. Springer, Heidelberg (2005)

4. Boneh, D., Sahai, A., Waters, B.: Fully collusion resistant traitor tracing with short ciphertexts and private keys. In: Vaudenay, S. (ed.) EUROCRYPT 2006. LNCS, vol. 4004, pp. 573–592. Springer, Heidelberg (2006)

5. Boneh, D., Venkatesan, R.: Breaking RSA may not be equivalent to factoring. In: Nyberg, K. (ed.) EUROCRYPT 1998. LNCS, vol. 1403, pp. 59–71. Springer, Heidelberg (1998)

6. Bringer, J., Chabanne, H., Dottax, E.: White box cryptography: another attempt. Cryptology ePrint Archive, Report 2006/468 (2006). http://eprint.iacr.org/

7. Chandran, N., Chase, M., Vaikuntanathan, V.: Functional re-encryption and collusion-resistant obfuscation. In: Cramer, R. (ed.) TCC 2012. LNCS, vol. 7194, pp. 404–421. Springer, Heidelberg (2012)

8. Chor, B., Fiat, A., Naor, M.: Tracing traitors. In: Desmedt, Y.G. (ed.) CRYPTO 1994. LNCS, vol. 839, pp. 257–270. Springer, Heidelberg (1994)

9. Chor, B., Fiat, A., Naor, M., Pinkas, B.: Tracing traitors. IEEE Trans. Inf. Theory 46(3), 893–910 (2000)

10. Chow, S., Eisen, P., Johnson, H., van Oorschot, P.C.: A White-box DES implementation for DRM applications. In: Feigenbaum, J. (ed.) DRM 2002. LNCS, vol. 2696, pp. 1–15. Springer, Heidelberg (2003)

11. Chow, S., Eisen, P., Johnson, H., van Oorschot, P.C.: White-box cryptography and an AES implementation. In: Nyberg, K., Heys, H. (eds.) SAC 2002. LNCS, vol. 2595, pp. 250–270. Springer, Heidelberg (2003)

12. Delerablée, C., Lepoint, T., Paillier, P., Rivain, M.: White-box security notions for symmetric encryption schemes. Cryptology ePrint Archive (2013). http://eprint.iacr.org/

13. Goubin, L., Masereel, J.-M., Quisquater, M.: Cryptanalysis of white box des implementations. In: Adams, C., Miri, A., Wiener, M. (eds.) SAC 2007. LNCS, vol. 4876, pp. 278–295. Springer, Berlin Heidelberg (2007)

14. Hofheinz, D., Malone-Lee, J., Stam, M.: Obfuscation for cryptographic purposes. J. Cryptol. 23(1), 121–168 (2010)

15. Hohenberger, S., Rothblum, G.N., Shelat, A., Vaikuntanathan, V.: Securely obfuscating re-encryption. In: Vadhan, S.P. (ed.) TCC 2007. LNCS, vol. 4392, pp. 233–252. Springer, Heidelberg (2007)

16. Jacob, M., Boneh, D., Felten, E.: Attacking an obfuscated cipher by injecting faults. In: Feigenbaum, J. (ed.) DRM 2002. LNCS, vol. 2696, pp. 16–31. Springer, Heidelberg (2003)

17. Joye, M.: On white-box cryptography. In: Preneel, B., Elçi, A., Ors, S.B. (eds.) Security of Information and Networks, pp. 7–12. Trafford Publishing (2008)

18. Joye, M.: Basics of side-channel analysis. In: Koç, C.K. (ed.) Cryptographic Engineering, pp. 365–380. Springer, New York (2009)

19. Karroumi, M.: Protecting white-box AES with dual ciphers. In: Rhee, K.-H., Nyang, D. (eds.) ICISC 2010. LNCS, vol. 6829, pp. 278–291. Springer, Heidelberg (2011)

20. Lepoint, T., Rivain, M., De Mulder, Y., Roelse, P., Preneel, B.: Two Attacks on a White-Box AES Implementation. In: Lange, T., Lauter, K., Lisonek, P. (eds.) SAC 2013. LNCS. Springer (2013)

21. Link, H.E., Neumann, W.D.: Clarifying obfuscation: improving the security of white-box DES. In: ITCC 2005, vol. 1, pp. 679–684 (2005)
22. Michiels, W., Gorissen, P., Hollmann, H.D.L.: Cryptanalysis of a generic class of white-box implementations. In: Avanzi, R.M., Keliher, L., Sica, F. (eds.) SAC 2008. LNCS, vol. 5381, pp. 414–428. Springer, Heidelberg (2009)
23. De Mulder, Y., Roelse, P., Preneel, B.: Cryptanalysis of the xiao - lai white-box aes implementation. In: Knudsen, L.R., Huapeng, W. (eds.) SAC 2012. LNCS, vol. 7707, pp. 34–49. Springer, Heidelberg (2013)
24. De Mulder, Y., Wyseur, B., Preneel, B.: Cryptanalysis of perturbated white-box AES implementation. In: Gong, G., Gupta, K.C. (eds.) INDOCRYPT 2010. LNCS, vol. 6498, pp. 292–310. Springer, Heidelberg (2010)
25. Naor, D., Naor, M., Lotspiech, J.: Revocation and tracing schemes for stateless receivers. In: Kilian, J. (ed.) CRYPTO 2001. LNCS, vol. 2139, pp. 41–62. Springer, Heidelberg (2001)
26. Paillier, P., Vergnaud, D.: Discrete-log-based signatures may not be equivalent to discrete log. In: Roy, B. (ed.) ASIACRYPT 2005. LNCS, vol. 3788, pp. 1–20. Springer, Heidelberg (2005)
27. Rivest, R.L., Shamir, A., Adleman, L.M.: A method for obtaining digital signatures and public-key cryptosystems. Commun. ACM **21**(2), 120–126 (1978)
28. Rohatgi, P.: Improved techniques for side-channel analysis. In: Kçc, C.K. (ed.) Cryptographic Engineering, pp. 381–406. Springer, New York (2009)
29. Saxena, A., Wyseur, B., Preneel, B.: Towards security notions for white-box cryptography. In: Samarati, P., Yung, M., Martinelli, F., Ardagna, C.A. (eds.) ISC 2009. LNCS, vol. 5735, pp. 49–58. Springer, Heidelberg (2009)
30. Wyseur, B.: White-box cryptography. Ph.D. thesis, Katholieke Universiteit Leuven (2009)
31. Wyseur, B., Michiels, W., Gorissen, P., Preneel, B.: Cryptanalysis of white-box des implementations with arbitrary external encodings. In: Adams, C., Miri, A., Wiener, M. (eds.) SAC 2007. LNCS, vol. 4896, pp. 264–277. Springer, Heidelberg (2007)
32. Wyseur, B., Preneel, B.: Condensed white-box implementations. In: Proceedings of the 26th Symposium on Information Theory in the Benelux, pp. 296–301 (2005)
33. Yaying, X., Xuejia, X.: A secure implementation of white-box AES. In: CSA 2009, pp.1–6 (2009)

Two Attacks on a White-Box AES Implementation

Tancrède Lepoint[1,2], Matthieu Rivain[1], Yoni De Mulder[3(✉)],
Peter Roelse[4], and Bart Preneel[3]

[1] CryptoExperts, Paris, France
`{tancrede.lepoint,matthieu.rivain}@cryptoexperts.com`
[2] École Normale Supérieure, Paris, France
[3] KU Leuven and iMinds, Heverlee, Belgium
`{yoni.demulder,bart.preneel}@esat.kuleuven.be`
[4] Irdeto B.V., Hoofddorp, The Netherlands
`peter.roelse@irdeto.com`

Abstract. White-box cryptography aims to protect the secret key of a
cipher in an environment in which an adversary has full access to the
implementation of the cipher and its execution environment. In 2002,
Chow, Eisen, Johnson and van Oorschot proposed a white-box implementation of AES. In 2004, Billet, Gilbert and Ech-Chatbi presented an
efficient attack (referred to as the BGE attack) on this implementation,
extracts extracting its embedded AES key with a work factor of 2^{30}. In
2012, Tolhuizen presented an improvement of the most time-consuming
phase of the BGE attack. The present paper includes three contributions. First we describe several improvements of the BGE attack. We
show that the overall work factor of the BGE attack is reduced to 2^{22}
when all improvements are implemented. This paper also presents a new
attack on the initial white-box implementation of Chow *et al.* This attack
exploits collisions occurring on internal variables of the implementation
and it achieves a work factor of 2^{22}. Eventually, we address the white-
box AES implementation presented by Karroumi in 2010 which aims to
withstand the BGE attack. We show that the implementations of Karroumi and Chow *et al.* are the same, making them both vulnerable to
the same attacks.

Keywords: White-box cryptography · AES implementation · Dual
cipher · Cryptanalysis

1 Introduction

In 2002, Chow *et al.* introduced the concept of white-box cryptography by presenting a white-box implementation of AES [5]. White-box cryptography aims to

---

The present paper is a merged abstract of two independent but overlapping works: a
paper by De Mulder, Roelse and Preneel [11] and a paper by Lepoint and Rivain [7].

T. Lange, K. Lauter, and P. Lisoněk (Eds.): SAC 2013, LNCS 8282, pp. 265–285, 2014.
DOI: 10.1007/978-3-662-43414-7_14, © Springer-Verlag Berlin Heidelberg 2014

protect the confidentiality of the secret key of a cipher in a white-box model, i.e., where an adversary is assumed to have full access to the implementation of the cipher and its execution environment. For example, in a white-box context the adversary can use tools such as decompilers and debuggers to reverse engineer the implementation of the cipher, and to read and alter values of intermediate results of the cipher during its execution. A typical example of an application in which a cipher is implemented in a white-box environment is a content protection system in which a client is executed on the main processor of a PC, a tablet, a mobile device, or a set-top box.

In 2004, Billet *et al.* [3] presented an attack on the white-box AES implementation of Chow *et al.*. The BGE attack assumes that the order of the bytes of the intermediate AES results is randomized in the white-box implementation, and extracts its embedded AES key with a work factor of 2^{30}. In 2012, Tolhuizen [12] proposed an improvement to the most time-consuming phase of the BGE attack, reducing the work factor of this phase to 2^{19}. If the improvement of Tolhuizen is implemented, then the work factor of the BGE attack is dominated by the other phases of the BGE attack, and equals 2^{29}. This paper presents several improvements to the other phases of the BGE attack, and shows that the work factor of the BGE attack is reduced to 2^{22} when Tolhuizen's improvement and the improvements presented in this paper are implemented.

This paper also presents a new attack on the white-box implementation of Chow *et al.* The key idea is to exploit collisions in output of the first round in order to construct sparse linear systems. Solving these systems then reveals the byte encodings and secret key byte(s) involved in some target look-up tables. Applied to the original scheme, we get an attack of complexity 2^{22}.

The BGE attack triggered the design of new white-box AES implementations, such as the ones proposed by Xiao and Lai in 2009 [13] and by Karroumi in 2010 [6]. In [10], De Mulder, Roelse and Preneel presented a cryptanalysis of Xiao and Lai's white-box AES implementation, showing that this implementation is insecure.

In [6], Karroumi uses the concept of dual ciphers [1,2,4] and the white-box techniques of Chow *et al.* to design a new white-box AES implementation. In [6], Karroumi argues that the additional secrecy introduced by the dual cipher increases the work factor of the BGE attack to 2^{93}. This paper shows that the white-box AES implementations of Chow *et al.* and Karroumi are the same. As a direct consequence, Karroumi's white-box AES implementation is vulnerable to the same attacks, including the original BGE attack and the attacks presented in this paper.

Paper organization. Section 2 describes aspects of AES, the white-box AES implementation of Chow *et al.*, and the BGE attack that are relevant to this paper. The improvements of the BGE attack and their work factor are presented in Sect. 3. The new attack based on collisions is presented in Sect. 4. The insecurity of Karroumi's scheme is shown in Sect. 5. Finally, concluding remarks are provided in Sect. 6

2   Preliminaries

2.1   AES

AES [8] is a key-iterated block cipher operating on 16-byte blocks. This paper assumes throughout and without loss of generality that the AES variant in [8] with a 128-bit key is used. AES consists of 10 rounds and has 11 round keys which are derived from the secret key using a key scheduling process. Each AES round and the operations within a round update a 16-byte state; the initial and final state are the AES plaintext and ciphertext, respectively. AES can be described elegantly by interpreting the bytes of the state as elements of the finite field $\mathbf{F}_{256}$, and by defining AES operations as mappings over this field (see also [8]). As the final round is not relevant for the discussion in this paper, only the first 9 rounds are considered in the following text. Each round r with $1 \leq r \leq 9$ comprises four operations:

ShiftRows: a permutation on the indices of the 16 bytes of the state;

AddRoundKey: a byte-wise addition of 16 round key bytes $k_i^{(r,j)}$ $(0 \leq i, j \leq 3)$ and the 16-byte state;

SubBytes: applies the AES S-box, denoted by S, to every byte of the 16-byte state;

MixColumns: a linear operation on $\mathbf{F}_{256}^{16}$. The MixColumns operation is represented by a 4×4 matrix MC over $\mathbf{F}_{256}$; the linear operation applies 4 instances of this matrix in parallel to the 16-byte state. The 16 coefficients of MC are denoted by mc_{ij} for $0 \leq i, j \leq 3$.

In literature, the boundaries between rounds are defined in different ways. In this paper, ShiftRows and MixColumns are the first and final operations within a round, respectively. That is, the order of the operations within a round is identical to the order used to describe the operations above. For details about AES, refer to [8].

AES Subrounds. The mappings in the following definition will be used to describe the white-box AES implementations and the attacks on the implementations. In the following text, the finite field representation as defined in [8] is referred to as the AES polynomial representation, and $\oplus$ and $\otimes$ denote the addition and multiplication operations in this representation, respectively.

Definition 1. *Let $x_i, y_i \in \mathbf{F}_{256}$ for $0 \leq i \leq 3$ be represented using the AES polynomial representation. The mapping $AES^{(r,j)} : \mathbf{F}_{256}^4 \rightarrow \mathbf{F}_{256}^4$ for $1 \leq r \leq 9$ and $0 \leq j \leq 3$, called an AES subround, is defined by $(y_0, y_1, y_2, y_3) = AES^{(r,j)}(x_0, x_1, x_2, x_3)$ with*

$$y_i = mc_{i0} \otimes S\big(x_0 \oplus k_0^{(r,j)}\big) \oplus mc_{i1} \otimes S\big(x_1 \oplus k_1^{(r,j)}\big) \oplus$$
$$mc_{i2} \otimes S\big(x_2 \oplus k_2^{(r,j)}\big) \oplus mc_{i3} \otimes S\big(x_3 \oplus k_3^{(r,j)}\big) \ ,$$

for $0 \leq i \leq 3$.

Observe that an AES subround consists of the key additions, the S-box operations and the MixColumns operations in an AES round that are associated with a single MixColumns matrix operation, and that one AES round comprises four AES subrounds. The subrounds are indexed by j in Definition 1, and this paper assumes throughout that the four subrounds in a round are numbered left to right. The bytes $k_i^{(r,j)}$ for $0 \leq i, j \leq 3$ are the 16 bytes of the AES round key of round r.

2.2 Chow *et al.*'s White-Box AES Implementation and the BGE Attack

This section describes aspects of Chow *et al.*'s white-box AES implementation [5] and the BGE attack [3] that are relevant to this paper. For an in-depth tutorial on how Chow *et al.*'s white-box AES implementation is constructed, refer to [9].

Encoded AES Subrounds. In the following text, $P_i^{(r,j)}$ and $Q_i^{(r,j)}$ for $0 \leq i \leq 3$ denote bijective mappings on the vector space $\mathbf{F}_2^8$, referred to as *encodings* in white-box cryptography. The encodings are generated randomly and are kept secret in a white-box implementation (for details about encodings, refer to [5,9]). A vector of four mappings, such as $(P_0^{(r,j)}, P_1^{(r,j)}, P_2^{(r,j)}, P_3^{(r,j)})$ or $(Q_0^{(r,j)}, Q_1^{(r,j)}, Q_2^{(r,j)}, Q_3^{(r,j)})$, denotes the mapping defined by applying the i-th element of the vector to its i-th input byte for $0 \leq i \leq 3$. For $a \in \mathbf{F}_2^n$ the mapping $\oplus_a \colon \mathbf{F}_2^n \to \mathbf{F}_2^n$ denotes the addition with a. With slight abuse of notation, an input to $AES^{(r,j)}$ is considered to be an element of $\mathbf{F}_{256}^4$ using the AES polynomial representation in the following definition, and an output of $AES^{(r,j)}$ is considered to be an element of $(\mathbf{F}_2^8)^4$.

Definition 2. *The mapping* $AES_{enc}^{(r,j)} \colon (\mathbf{F}_2^8)^4 \to (\mathbf{F}_2^8)^4$ *for* $1 \leq r \leq 9$ *and* $0 \leq j \leq 3$, *called an encoded AES subround, is defined by*

$$AES_{enc}^{(r,j)} = (Q_0^{(r,j)}, Q_1^{(r,j)}, Q_2^{(r,j)}, Q_3^{(r,j)}) \circ$$
$$AES^{(r,j)} \circ (P_0^{(r,j)}, P_1^{(r,j)}, P_2^{(r,j)}, P_3^{(r,j)}) .$$

In Chow *et al.*'s white-box AES implementation, the output encodings $Q_i^{(r-1,j)}$ and input encodings $P_i^{(r,j)}$ for $0 \leq i, j \leq 3$ of successive AES rounds are pairwise annihilating to maintain the functionality of AES. The data-flow of the white-box implementation between successive AES rounds $r-1$ and r determines the 16 pairs of output/input encodings which are pairwise annihilating.

Remark 1. Although not explicitly mentioned by Chow *et al.* [5], one can use a randomization of the order of the subrounds in an AES round and in the order of the bytes within each subround to add confusion to the implementation. This can be implemented without increasing the size and without decreasing the performance of the white-box implementation. We capture such a randomization in the next definition of encoded subround where permutations $\Pi_i^{(r,j)} : (\mathbf{F}_2^8)^4 \to (\mathbf{F}_2^8)^4$ ($i = 1, 2$) for $1 \leq r \leq 9$ and $0 \leq j \leq 3$ are added to randomize the order of the input bytes and output bytes of an AES subround. Moreover, permutations $\pi^{(r)} : \{0, 1, 2, 3\} \to \{0, 1, 2, 3\}$ for $1 \leq r \leq 9$ randomize the order of the four AES subrounds within an AES round. These permutations are randomly chosen and kept secret in a white-box implementation.

Definition 3. *The mapping* $\overline{AES}_{enc}^{(r,j)} : (\mathbf{F}_2^8)^4 \to (\mathbf{F}_2^8)^4$ *for* $1 \leq r \leq 9$ *and* $0 \leq j \leq 3$, *called an encoded AES subround with byte permutations, is defined by*

$$\overline{AES}_{enc}^{(r,j)} = (Q_0^{(r,j)}, Q_1^{(r,j)}, Q_2^{(r,j)}, Q_3^{(r,j)}) \circ$$
$$\overline{AES}^{(r,j)} \circ (P_0^{(r,j)}, P_1^{(r,j)}, P_2^{(r,j)}, P_3^{(r,j)}) ,$$

where the mapping $\overline{AES}^{(r,j)}$ *is defined by*

$$\Pi_2^{(r,j)} \circ AES^{(r,\pi^{(r)}(j))} \circ \Pi_1^{(r,j)} = MC^{(r,j)} \circ (S, S, S, S) \circ \oplus_{[\bar{k}_i^{(r,j)}]_{0 \leq i \leq 3}} ,$$

$$\text{with} \quad [\bar{k}_i^{(r,j)}]_{0 \leq i \leq 3} = (\Pi_1^{(r,j)})^{-1}([k_i^{(r,\pi^{(r)}(j))}]_{0 \leq i \leq 3})$$
$$\text{and} \quad MC^{(r,j)} = \Pi_2^{(r,j)} \circ MC \circ \Pi_1^{(r,j)} .$$

In [3], Billet *et al.* described a cryptanalysis of Chow *et al.*'s white-box AES implementation [5] with byte permutations and subround permutations. The starting point of their attack is that for rounds $1 \leq r \leq 9$, it is possible to compose certain white-box look-up tables in such a way that an adversary has access to the encoded AES subrounds of each round.

BGE Attack. As indicated above, the adversary has access to the encoded AES subrounds $\overline{AES}_{enc}^{(r,j)}$ for $1 \leq r \leq 9$ and $0 \leq j \leq 3$. Next, the BGE attack [3] comprises the following three phases: Phases 1 and 2 retrieve the bytes of the AES round key associated with round r for some r with $2 \leq r \leq 9$, and Phase 3 determines the correct order of the round key bytes and extracts the AES key.

Phase 1 retrieves the encodings $Q_i^{(r,j)}$ ($0 \leq i \leq 3$) up to an affine part for each encoded AES subround j ($0 \leq j \leq 3$). Because of the pairwise annihilating property of the encodings between successive rounds, the encodings $P_i^{(r,j)}$ ($0 \leq i, j \leq 3$) can be retrieved up to an affine part by applying the same technique to the encoded AES subrounds of the previous round.

Phase 2 assumes that all encodings of an encoded AES round are affine mappings (as the other parts have been retrieved in Phase 1). Phase 2 first retrieves the affine encodings $Q_i^{(r,j)}$ ($0 \leq i \leq 3$) for each encoded AES subround j ($0 \leq j \leq 3$). During this process, the key-dependent affine mappings $\widetilde{P}_i^{(r,j)}(x) = P_i^{(r,j)}(x) \oplus \bar{k}_i^{(r,j)}$ ($0 \leq i, j \leq 3$) are obtained as well. As in Phase 1, the affine encodings $P_i^{(r,j)}$ ($0 \leq i, j \leq 3$) are retrieved by applying the same technique to the encoded

AES subrounds of the previous round. This enables the adversary to compute the round key bytes $\bar{k}_i^{(r,j)} = \widetilde{P}_i^{(r,j)}(0) \oplus P_i^{(r,j)}(0)$ for $0 \le i,j \le 3$.

Phase 3 retrieves the round key bytes of round $r+1$ as discussed above in Phases 1 and 2, and uses the fact that the round key bytes of rounds r and $r+1$ are related to each other via both the data-flow of the white-box implementation and the AES key scheduling algorithm to retrieve the AES round key. Finally, assuming that the AES variant with a 128-bit key is used, the adversary can use the property of the AES key scheduling algorithm that the AES key can be computed if one of the round keys is known.

Work factor of the BGE attack. In [3], the authors claim that the work factor associated with the three phases of the BGE attack is around 2^{30}. As a result, the white-box AES implementation of Chow *et al.* is insecure. For detailed information about the BGE attack, refer to [3].

3   Reducing the Work Factor of the BGE Attack

In this section, an encoded AES subround is defined as in Definition 3. In 2012, Tolhuizen [12] presented an improvement of the first phase of the BGE attack. If the improvement of Tolhuizen is implemented, then the work factor of the BGE attack is dominated by the second phase. In this section we present several improvements to the other phases of the BGE attack:

1. A method to reduce the expected work factor of Phase 2 of the BGE attack;
2. An efficient method to retrieve the round key bytes of round $r+1$ after the round key bytes of round r are extracted;
3. An efficient method to determine the correct order of the round key bytes, given the round key bytes of two consecutive rounds.

As the work factors of Phases 1 and 2 of the BGE attack are reduced by Tolhuizen's improvement and the first improvement above, respectively, it is now important to have an efficient method for Phase 3 of the BGE attack as well, as otherwise the work factor of this phase could dominate the overall work factor. The second and third improvements above comprise such a method for Phase 3. It will be shown that Tolhuizen's improvement to Phase 1 of the BGE attack and the above improvements to the other phases reduce the work factor of the BGE attack to 2^{22}. The improved BGE attack comprises the following four (instead of three) phases:

Phases 1 and 2: Retrieve the Round Key Bytes $\bar{k}_i^{(r,j)}$ ($0 \le i,j \le 3$) Associated with Round r ($2 \le r \le 8$)

The first two phases are the ones of the BGE attack [3] using Tolhuizen's improvement, and retrieve the round key bytes $\bar{k}_i^{(r,j)}$ for $0 \le i,j \le 3$ associated with round r for some r with $2 \le r \le 8$.

Work factor of Phase 1. Tolhuizen's improvement [12] reduces the work factor of Phase 1 to around $2 \cdot 4 \cdot 4 \cdot (35 \cdot 2^8) < 2^{19}$. The first three factors (i.e., $2 \cdot 4 \cdot 4$) denote the number of encodings involved in Phase 1, i.e., four encodings for each of the four subrounds for each of the two consecutive rounds. The fourth factor (i.e., $35 \cdot 2^8$) denotes the work factor required to retrieve one encoding up to an affine part using Tolhuizen's method.

Work factor of Phase 2. The expected work factor F of the second phase as described in [3] equals approximately $2 \cdot 4 \cdot 4 \cdot 2^{15} \cdot 2^8 = 2^{28}$, and is measured in the number of evaluations of mappings on $\mathbf{F}_2^8$. The evaluations are required to determine if a mapping on $\mathbf{F}_2^8$ is affine. The mappings f that need to be tested for being affine are listed in [3, Proposition 3]. Each f is associated with a secret encoding $P_i^{(r,j)}$ ($0 \leq i, j \leq 3$) of a round r. As Phase 2 needs to be applied to two consecutive rounds, this involves a total of $2 \cdot 4 \cdot 4$ mappings (which corresponds to the first three factors in F). The mappings f are permutations on $\mathbf{F}_2^8$ and have the structure

$$f = S^{-1} \circ Q_{(c,d)}^{-1} \circ Q \circ S \circ \oplus_k \circ P , \tag{1}$$

where S denotes the AES S-box mapping (viewed as a permutation on $\mathbf{F}_2^8$), k denotes a key byte, P and Q denote bijective affine mappings on $\mathbf{F}_2^8$, and $Q_{(c,d)}^{-1}$ denotes a bijective affine mapping on $\mathbf{F}_2^8$ for each pair $(c,d) \in \mathbf{F}_{256}^2$. Furthermore, $Q_{(c,d)}^{-1} = Q^{-1}$ for one specific pair $(c,d) \in \mathbf{F}_{256}^2$. An affine-test is performed for each possible pair $(c,d) \in \mathbf{F}_{256}^2$ until the corresponding mapping f is affine. The expected number of pairs for which the test is performed equals approximately 2^{15}, which is the fourth factor in F. The fifth factor in F, i.e., 2^8, is associated with the test used in [3].

Instead of the test used in [3], which requires 2^n evaluations to determine if $f : \mathbf{F}_2^n \to \mathbf{F}_2^n$ is affine, we use the following algorithm to reduce the expected number of evaluations. If e_i ($1 \leq i \leq n$) denotes the i-th unit vector in $\mathbf{F}_2^n$, then the algorithm first verifies if the equation

$$f(e_1 \oplus e_2) = f(0) \oplus f(e_1) \oplus f(e_2) \tag{2}$$

holds true. If this equation does not hold true, then the algorithm terminates with "f is not affine". Observe that the algorithm requires 4 evaluations of f in this case. If Eq. 2 holds true, then the algorithm applies the method used in [3] to determine if f is affine (with the only difference that f is not re-evaluated for the four input values $0, e_1, e_2$ and $e_1 \oplus e_2$). In this case 2^n evaluations of f are required.

To show the correctness of this algorithm, it is sufficient to show that an affine mapping always satisfies Eq. 2. If f is affine, then $f(x) = A(x) \oplus b$ for some $A \in \mathbf{F}_2^{n \times n}$ and some $b \in \mathbf{F}_2^n$. It follows that $f(0) \oplus f(e_1) \oplus f(e_2) = b \oplus A(e_1) \oplus b \oplus A(e_2) \oplus b = A(e_1 \oplus e_2) \oplus b = f(e_1 \oplus e_2)$.

Lemma 1. *If f is a random permutation on $\mathbf{F}_2^n$ and if $E(n)$ denotes the expected number of evaluations of f required by the algorithm described above, then $E(n) < 5$.*

Proof. Let $p(n)$ denote the probability that Eq. 2 holds true for a random permutation. To determine $p(n)$, note that $f(0), f(e_1), f(e_2)$ and $f(e_1 \oplus e_2)$ are four distinct elements of $\mathbf{F}_2^n$ if f is a permutation. From this it follows that $f(0) \oplus f(e_1) \oplus f(e_2)$ and $f(e_1 \oplus e_2)$ are both elements of $\mathbf{F}_2^n \setminus \{f(0), f(e_1), f(e_2)\}$. Further, as f is a random permutation, $f(e_1 \oplus e_2)$ is a random element of this set. Hence, $p(n) = 1/(2^n - 3)$ and $E(n) = 4(1 - p) + 2^n p = 4 + (2^n - 4)/(2^n - 3) < 5$. ∎

Under the assumption that f in Eq. 1 behaves as a random permutation on $\mathbf{F}_2^8$ for every incorrect guess for (c, d), the expected work factor of the affine-test is reduced from 2^8 to approximately 5 evaluations if f is not affine and the work factor is 2^8 if f is affine. This implies that the fifth factor in F is reduced to approximately 5. That is, the expected work factor of Phase 2 of the BGE attack is now approximately $2 \cdot 4 \cdot 4 \cdot 2^{15} \cdot 5 \approx 2^{22}$.

Phase 3: Retrieve the Round Key Bytes $\bar{k}_i^{(r+1,j)}$ ($0 \le i, j \le 3$) Associated with Round $r + 1$

As mentioned in the description of the BGE attack in Sect. 2.2, [3] obtains the round key bytes of round $r + 1$ by applying Phases 1 and 2 to round $r + 1$ as well. Here, we present a more efficient method based on the affine-test described above. The method comprises the following three steps for each encoded AES subround j ($0 \le j \le 3$) associated with round $r + 1$ to retrieve the round key bytes $\bar{k}_i^{(r+1,j)}$ ($0 \le i, j \le 3$):

Step 1 applies Phase 1 (using Tolhuizen's improvement) to round $r + 1$ in order to retrieve the encodings $Q_i^{(r+1,j)}$ ($0 \le i \le 3$) up to an affine part.

Step 2 first removes the non-affine part of the output encodings as recovered in Step 1 from the encoded AES subround. Next, Step 2 removes the input encodings $P_i^{(r+1,j)}$ ($0 \le i \le 3$) from the encoded AES subround (observe that the inverses of these input encodings were obtained in Phases 1 and 2). The resulting mapping $f^{(r+1,j)} : (\mathbf{F}_2^8)^4 \to (\mathbf{F}_2^8)^4$ is given by

$$f^{(r+1,j)} = \left(\hat{Q}_0^{(r+1,j)}, \hat{Q}_1^{(r+1,j)}, \hat{Q}_2^{(r+1,j)}, \hat{Q}_3^{(r+1,j)} \right) \circ \overline{AES}^{(r+1,j)} ,$$

where $\hat{Q}_i^{(r+1,j)}$ ($0 \le i \le 3$) are affine output encodings.

Step 3 retrieves the round key bytes $\bar{k}_i^{(r+1,j)}$ ($0 \le i \le 3$). To find a key byte, say $\bar{k}_0^{(r+1,j)}$, fix the other three input bytes to $f^{(r+1,j)}$ (e.g., to zero), search over all possible 2^8 values of the key byte k and verify if

$$g_k(x) = f^{(r+1,j)}\left(k \oplus S^{-1}(x), 0, 0, 0 \right)$$

is affine using the test described above. In case $g_k(x)$ is affine, then $\bar{k}_0^{(r+1,j)} = k$. Repeat this for $\bar{k}_i^{(r+1,j)}$ ($i = 1, 2, 3$).

The correctness of Step 3 uses the fact that the mapping $S(c \oplus S^{-1}(x))$ is non-affine for all non-zero values of c. This has already been proven in [3, proof of Proposition 3].

Work factor of Phase 3. The work factor of Step 3 equals $4 \cdot 4 \cdot 2^7 \cdot 5 \approx 2^{13}$, where $4 \cdot 4$ denotes the number of round key bytes, 2^7 denotes the expected number of key values for which the affine-test is performed and 5 denotes the expected number of evaluations of the affine-test if g_k is not affine. The work factor of Step 1 is $4 \cdot 4 \cdot (35 \cdot 2^8) < 2^{18}$, where the first two factors denote the number of output encodings involved in Step 1. As a result, the work factor of Phase 3 is dominated by Step 1 and is less than 2^{18}.

Phase 4: Determine the Correct Order of the Round Key Bytes and Extract the Secret AES Key

After Phases 1–3, the values of the round key bytes of two consecutive rounds r and $r + 1$ are known. However, for each round, the order of the round key bytes of each subround and the order of the four subrounds are still unknown. Notice that there are still $(4!)^5 \approx 2^{23}$ possibilities for the round key if only the bytes of that round key are considered. In [3], it is indicated how the correct order can be determined given the "shuffled" round key bytes of rounds r and $r + 1$. However, [3] does not contain an explicit description of such a method. As the work factor of the first three phases equals 2^{22}, it is desirable to have a method to determine the correct order of the round key bytes with a work factor that is less than 2^{22}. Below we present such a method, comprising the following three steps:

Step 1 retrieves $\mathrm{MC}^{(r,j)}$ associated with each subround j $(0 \leq j \leq 3)$ of round r. Recall that the encodings $P_i^{(r,j)}$ and $Q_i^{(r,j)}$ $(0 \leq i, j \leq 3)$ were obtained in Phases 1 and 2. Together with the knowledge of the round key bytes $\bar{k}_i^{(r,j)}$ $(0 \leq i, j \leq 3)$, compute

$$\mathrm{MC}^{(r,j)} = \left(Q_0^{(r,j)}, Q_1^{(r,j)}, Q_2^{(r,j)}, Q_3^{(r,j)}\right)^{-1} \circ \overline{AES}_{enc}^{(r,j)} \circ$$
$$\left(P_0^{(r,j)}, P_1^{(r,j)}, P_2^{(r,j)}, P_3^{(r,j)}\right)^{-1} \circ \oplus_{[\bar{k}_i^{(r,j)}]_{0 \leq i \leq 3}} \circ (S, S, S, S)^{-1} ,$$

for $j = 0, 1, 2, 3$.

Step 2 computes for each $\mathrm{MC}^{(r,j)}$ $(0 \leq j \leq 3)$ the permutations $\Pi_1, \Pi_2 : (\mathbf{F}_2^8)^4 \to (\mathbf{F}_2^8)^4$ such that

$$\mathrm{MC}^{(r,j)} = \Pi_2 \circ \mathrm{MC} \circ \Pi_1 . \tag{3}$$

Let $(\Pi^{(1)}, \Pi^{(2)})$ denote the pairs of permutations for which MC remains invariant, i.e., $\mathrm{MC} = \Pi^{(2)} \circ \mathrm{MC} \circ \Pi^{(1)}$. It is easily verified that there are exactly four such pairs. The four permutations $\Pi^{(1)}$ are the four different circular shifts on the indices of a 4-byte vector, and $\Pi^{(2)} = (\Pi^{(1)})^{-1}$ for each of these pairs. This implies that there are also exactly four different pairs of permutations satisfying Eq. 3, given by

$$\left(\varPi^{(1)} \circ \varPi_1 \, , \, \varPi_2 \circ \varPi^{(2)} \right) . \tag{4}$$

As a consequence, finding one pair of permutation matrices satisfying Eq. 3 suffices to find the remaining three as well. Notice that exactly one of these four pairs of permutations equals the pair $(\varPi_1^{(r,j)}, \varPi_2^{(r,j)})$ of the encoded subround (see also Definition 3); in other words, one of these pairs is the correct pair.

After this, the order of the round key bytes associated with each subround is known up to an uncertainty of four possibilities (circular shifts). Observe that the order of the four subrounds is still unknown.

Step 3 determines the correct order of the round key bytes. For each of the possible orderings of the four AES subrounds of round r and the round key bytes within these subrounds (as determined in Step 2), obtain a candidate for the $(r+1)^{th}$ round key using the following two methods: (i) the AES key scheduling algorithm and (ii) the data-flow of the white-box AES implementation between the encoded subrounds of rounds r and $r+1$. Notice that once an order of the round key bytes of round r is selected, the order of the round key bytes of round $r+1$ can be determined using the corresponding pair of permutations of each of the subrounds of round r (see also Eq. 4) and the data-flow of the white-box implementation. With overwhelming probability, only one ordering of round key bytes of round r results in the same $(r+1)^{th}$ round key; this ordering corresponds to the correct round key of round r. Finally, use the property of the AES key scheduling algorithm that the AES key can be computed if one of the round keys is known.

Work factor of Phase 4. A naive approach yields an expected work factor of $(4!)^2 \approx 2^9$ for Step 2 by searching over all possible pairs of permutations. Step 2 reduces the number of possible orderings of the round key bytes from 2^{23} to $4^4 \cdot 4! < 2^{13}$ (where the first and second factor denote the possible orderings of round key bytes within each subround and of the four subrounds, respectively), which equals the work factor of Step 3. As a result, the overall work factor of Phase 4 is dominated by the work factor of Step 3 and hence is less than 2^{13}.

3.1   Conclusion

The work factor of the improved BGE attack is dominated by the work factor of the second phase and equals 2^{22}.

Note that the uncertainty in the order of the round key bytes results in the need to retrieve key bytes of two consecutive rounds. This affects the work factor of the original BGE attack. In the improved BGE attack this is no longer the case, as the work factors of the phases that determine the correct order (i.e. Phases 3 and 4) are negligible compared to the work factor of Phase 2. A consequence of Tolhuizen's improvement is that the use of non-affine white-box encodings has a negligible impact on the overall work factor of the improved BGE attack.

4   A New Attack Exploiting Internal Collisions

In this section we propose a new attack on the initial Chow *et al.* implementation exploiting collisions in output of the first AES round. Note that unlike the BGE attack, the description below only considers the basic implementation, i.e., without byte permutations. In this section, an encoded AES subround is defined as in Definition 2.

According to Sect. 2, applying a set of successive look-up tables, one can compute the first encoded AES subround $AES_{enc}^{(1,0)}$, which is denoted by f' in the following for the sake of clarity (and in accordance to notations in [7]):

$$f' = (Q_0^{(1,0)}, Q_1^{(1,0)}, Q_2^{(1,0)}, Q_3^{(1,0)}) \circ AES^{(1,0)} \circ (P_0^{(1,0)}, P_1^{(1,0)}, P_2^{(1,0)}, P_3^{(1,0)}) . \quad (5)$$

Let us denote by f'_ℓ the coordinate functions of f' such that $f' = (f'_0, f'_1, f'_2, f'_3)$. Let us further denote by S_i the function defined as

$$S_i(\cdot) = S(k_i^{(1,0)} \oplus (P_i^{(1,0)})(\cdot)) , \quad (6)$$

for $0 \le i \le 3$.

4.1   Recovering the S_i Functions

Our attack consists in finding collisions in output of the coordinate functions f'_ℓ in order to recover functions S_0, S_1, S_2 and S_3 and associated key bytes. For the sake of clarity, we drop all the surperscripts $(1,0)$ in the following. We start with the recovery of S_0 and S_1 by looking for collision of the form

$$f'_0(\alpha, 0, 0, 0) = f'_0(0, \beta, 0, 0) . \quad (7)$$

By definition of the MixColumns transformation, the above equation can be rewritten as

$$Q_0 (02 \otimes S_0(\alpha) \oplus 03 \otimes S_1(0) \oplus c) = Q_0 (02 \otimes S_0(0) \oplus 03 \otimes S_1(\beta) \oplus c)$$

where $c = S_2(0) \oplus S_3(0)$, implying

$$02 \otimes S_0(\alpha) \oplus 03 \otimes S_1(0) = 02 \otimes S_0(0) \oplus 03 \otimes S_1(\beta) . \quad (8)$$

Collecting several such equations, we can construct a linear system to recover S_0 and S_1. Let $u_0, u_1, \ldots, u_{255}$ and $v_0, v_1, \ldots, v_{255}$ denote the unknowns associated to the outputs of S_0 and S_1 (*i.e.* $u_i = S_0(i)$ and $v_i = S_1(i)$). Then (8) can be rewritten as

$$02 \otimes (u_0 \oplus u_\alpha) \oplus 03 \otimes (v_0 \oplus v_\beta) = 0 . \quad (9)$$

Then we can easily obtain a system involving all the u_i and all the v_i. Indeed, the functions $\alpha \mapsto f'_0(\alpha, 0, 0, 0)$ and $\beta \mapsto f'_0(0, \beta, 0, 0)$ are bijections, so we get exactly 256 collisions between $f'_0(\alpha, 0, 0, 0)$ and $f'_0(0, \beta, 0, 0)$ while α and β vary over $\mathbf{F}_{256}$. Discarding the irrelevant collision for $(\alpha, \beta) = (0,0)$, we get 255 pairs (α, β) satisfying $f_0'(\alpha, 0, 0, 0) = f_0'(0, \beta, 0, 0)$ and providing an equation of the form of (9). Moreover, every unknown u_α and v_β appears once for $\alpha, \beta > 0$ and the unknowns u_0 and v_0 appear in each equation. We proceed similarly for coordinates f_ℓ' with $\ell \in \{1, 2, 3\}$, for which the collisions give rise to similar equations but with different pairs of coefficients in $\{01, 02, 03\}$. For instance a collision $f_1'(\alpha, 0, 0, 0) = f_1'(0, 0, \beta, 0)$ yields an equation

$$01 \otimes (u_0 \oplus u_\alpha) \oplus 02 \otimes (v_0 \oplus v_\beta) = 0 .$$

We hence get 4×255 linear equations involving all the 512 unknowns. However, this system is not of full rank. Consider the 2×255 unknowns $u_i' = u_0 \oplus u_i$ and $v_i' = v_0 \oplus v_i$ for $i \in \{1, 2, \ldots, 255\}$. Every equation of the form of (9) can be rewritten as

$$02 \otimes u_\alpha' \oplus 03 \otimes v_\beta' = 0 .$$

This shows that the system can be rewritten in terms of 510 unknowns and is hence of rank at most 510. But the system has still at least one degree of freedom left, since more than one solution is still possible. For instance, the system is solved by $u_i' = 0$ and $v_i' = 0$ for every i, and it is also solved by the solution we are looking for (i.e. $u_i' = S_0(0) \oplus S_0(i)$ and $v_i' = S_1(0) \oplus S_1(i)$), which is such that $u_i' \neq 0$ and $v_i' \neq 0$ by bijectivity of S_0 and S_1. The obtained system is hence of rank at most 509.

In all our experiments, the 4×255 available linear equations always yielded a system of rank 509. From such a system, all the unknowns can be expressed in function of one unknown, say u_1'. And since all the unknowns are linearly linked, there exist coefficients a_i and b_i such that $u_i' = a_i \otimes u_1'$ and $v_i' = b_i \otimes u_1'$. These coefficients can be easily recovered by solving the system for $u_1' = 1$. We then get

$$u_i = a_i \otimes (u_0 \oplus u_1) \oplus u_0 , \tag{10}$$

and

$$v_i = b_i \otimes (u_0 \oplus u_1) \oplus v_0 . \tag{11}$$

From the a_i coefficients and from Equation (10), we can recover the overall function S_0 by exhaustive search on the pair (u_0, u_1). In order to determine the good solution, we use the particular structure of the function S_0. Specifically, we use the relation

$$S^{-1} \circ S_0(\cdot) = P_0(\cdot) \oplus k_0 .$$

By definition of P_0, the above function has algebraic degree at most 4. We then use the following lemma.

Lemma 2. *Let g be a function from $\{0, 1\}^8$ to itself with algebraic degree at most 4. The map*

$$\varphi : x \mapsto \bigoplus_{\alpha=0}^{15} g(x \oplus \alpha) ,$$

is the null function $x \mapsto 0$.

Proof. The map φ is a 4th-order derivative of the function g (specifically $\varphi = D_1 D_2 D_4 D_8(g)$) and since g has algebraic degree at most 4, all its 4th-order derivatives are null. $\qquad\square$

Remark 2. For a wrong pair (u_0, u_1), the candidate function $\hat{S}_0$ obtained from (10) is affine equivalent to S_0. Namely there exist a and b such that $\hat{S}_0(\cdot) = a \otimes S_0(\cdot) \oplus b$, with $a \neq 0$ and $(a, b) \neq (0, 1)$. The function $S^{-1} \circ \hat{S}_0$ then satisfies

$$S^{-1} \circ \hat{S}_0(\cdot) = S^{-1}\big(a \otimes S(k_0 \oplus P_0(\cdot)) \oplus b\big) \ ,$$

and it has an algebraic degree greater than 4 with overwhelming probability.[1]

According to Lemma 2 and the above remark, we can easily determine the good pair (u_0, u_1) by computing the 4th-order derivative $\hat{\varphi}$ of the associated function $\hat{g} = S^{-1} \circ \hat{S}_0$, which satisfies

$$\hat{\varphi}(x) = \bigoplus_{\alpha=0}^{15} S^{-1}\big(a_{x \oplus \alpha} \otimes (u_0 \oplus u_1) \oplus u_0\big) \ .$$

For the sake of efficiency, we first compute $\hat{\varphi}(0)$ and check whether it equals 0 or not. If we get $\hat{\varphi}(0) = 0$, we step forwards and compute $\hat{\varphi}(x)$ for another x. Note that we only need to compute $\hat{\varphi}$ for 16 inputs at most since for every x we have $\hat{\varphi}(x) = \hat{\varphi}(x \oplus 01) = \cdots = \hat{\varphi}(x \oplus 15)$. Getting $\hat{\varphi}(x) = 0$ for a wrong pair (u_0, u_1) should roughly occur with probability $1/256$, so wrong guesses are quickly discarded.

Once S_0 has been recovered, we can recover S_1 from (11) by exhaustive search on v_0. Here again, the good solution is determined using Lemma 2 and the above approach. The remaining functions S_2 and S_3 are recovered similarly by solving the linear systems arising from collisions of the form $f'_\ell(\alpha, 0, 0, 0) = f'_\ell(0, 0, \beta, 0)$ and $f'_\ell(\alpha, 0, 0, 0) = f'_\ell(0, 0, 0, \beta)$. Since S_0 is already known, we get the same situation as for the recovery of S_1. Namely, all the elements of S_2 (resp. S_3) can be expressed as affine functions of $S_2(0)$ (resp. $S_3(0)$), and we can recover the overall function by exhaustive search on this value and with the selection criterion of Lemma 2.

4.2   Recovering the Secret Key

Once the S_i functions have been recovered, one can easily recover the byte-encodings Q_i in output of the first round. For instance evaluating $f'_0(\alpha, 0, 0, 0)$ one gets the value $Q_0(\psi(\alpha))$ where

$$\psi \colon \alpha \mapsto 02 \otimes S_0(\alpha) \oplus 03 \otimes S_1(0) \oplus S_2(0) \oplus S_3(0)$$

is a bijective function. We hence get $Q_0(\cdot) = f'_0(\psi^{-1}(\cdot), 0, 0, 0)$ which enables to fully retrieve Q_0 by looping on the 256 input values. Each byte-encoding $Q_i^{(1,j)}$ in output of the first round can be recovered in a similar way.

---

[1] We ran a few million tests and never obtained a function with algebraic degree 4 or less.

Since the output byte-encodings of the first round are the inverse of the input byte-decodings of the second round, we now show how to retrieve the key bytes in the second round from that knowledge. In what follows, we shall slightly change the definition of f' and the S_i's given in (5) and (6). Namely, f' shall denote the first encoded subround of the second round (rather that of the first round), and S_i the associated functions, that is $f' = AES_{enc}^{(2,0)}$ and $S_i(\cdot) = S(k_i^{(2,0)} \oplus (P_i^{(2,0)})(\cdot))$ for $0 \le i \le 3$. As in the previous section, we shall further drop all the surperscripts $(2,0)$ for the sake of clarity.

For the recovery of k_0, we use the following distinguisher. Consider the function g associated to k_0 and defined as:

$$g = f_0'(P_0^{-1}(S^{-1}(\cdot) \oplus k_0), 0, 0, 0) .$$

This function satisfies

$$g(x) = Q_0(02 \otimes x \oplus c) \qquad \text{where } c = 03 \otimes S_1(0) \oplus S_2(0) \oplus S_3(0) ,$$

and it has algebraic degree at most 4 by definition of Q_0 (since multiplying and adding constant coefficients are linear). Therefore, according to Lemma 2, the 4th-order derivative $\varphi \colon x \mapsto \bigoplus_{\alpha=0}^{15} g(x \oplus \alpha)$ equals the null function. On the other hand, consider the function $\hat{g}$ associated to a wrong guess $\hat{k}_0 \neq k_0$, that is

$$\hat{g}(x) = f_0'(P_0^{-1}(S^{-1}(x) \oplus \hat{k}_0), 0, 0, 0) = Q_0(02 \otimes S(S^{-1}(x) \oplus \hat{k}_0 \oplus k_0) \oplus c) .$$

This function has algebraic degree greater than 4 with overwhelming probability.[2] This way, we can easily recover k_0 by exhaustive search while testing for every candidate whether the function $\hat{g}$ is of algebraic degree 4 or not. Namely, for every guess $\hat{k}_0$, we test whether the function

$$\hat{\varphi}(x) = \bigoplus_{\alpha=0}^{15} f_0'(P_0^{-1}(S^{-1}(x) \oplus \hat{k}_0), 0, 0, 0)$$

equals the null function $x \mapsto 0$, or not. As for the previous recovery of the S_i functions, this is done at most for 16 different values of x since we have $\hat{\varphi}(x) = \hat{\varphi}(x \oplus 01) = \cdots = \hat{\varphi}(x \oplus 15)$. Moreover, as for the recovery of the S_i, we only need to compute $\hat{\varphi}$ for 16 inputs at most since for every x we have $\hat{\varphi}(x) = \hat{\varphi}(x \oplus 01) = \cdots = \hat{\varphi}(x \oplus 15)$. Moreover getting $\hat{\varphi}(x) = 0$ for a wrong guess $\hat{k}_0$ roughly occur with probability $1/256$, so wrong guesses are quickly discarded.

The key bytes k_1, k_2 and k_3 can be retrieved similarly; only the definition of the function g shall change. For instance, g is defined as $f_0'(0, P_1^{-1}(S^{-1}(\cdot) \oplus k_1), 0, 0)$ for k_1, and so on for k_2 and k_3. And the other key bytes $k_i^{(2,j)}$ for $j \ge 1$ can be recovered in the exact same way. Eventually, from the second round key, one can easily recover the full AES secret key by inverting the key schedule process.

---

[2] Here again, we ran a few million tests and never obtained a function with algebraic degree 4 or less.

4.3   Attack Complexity

The bottleneck of our attack is the exhaustive search to recover the functions S_i in the first round. Indeed, the previous system to solve for the recovery of the a_i and b_i coefficients is very sparse and it can hence be solved with Gaussian elimination in linear complexity (*i.e.* in 512 times a few operations). To recover S_0, one loops on the 2^{16} candidate values for (u_0, u_1), and for each value test whether $\hat{\varphi}(x) = 0$ (which is a XOR over 16 elements) for at most 16 values x. We use laziness, namely we test whether $\hat{\varphi}(0) = 0$ first, if false we stop and if true we step forwards to the next x, and so on and so forth. Now getting $\hat{\varphi}(x) = 0$ for a wrong pair (u_0, u_1) roughly occurs with probability $1/256$, therefore the expected number of tests is $1 + 1/256 + \cdots + 1/(256^{15}) \leq 1.004$. The complexity of the recovery of S_0 is hence of

$$2^{16} \cdot 1.004 \cdot 2^4 \approx 2^{20} .$$

Then the recovery of S_1 (resp. S_2, S_3) from S_0 only requires an exhaustive search on v_0, which makes a complexity of $2^8 \cdot 1.004 \cdot 2^4 \approx 2^{12}$. We hence get a complexity of $2^{20} + 3 \cdot 2^{12} \approx 2^{20}$ for the recovery of S_0, S_1, S_2 and S_3. This computation must be performed for each subround of the first AES round, which makes a total complexity of $4 \times 2^{20} = 2^{22}$.

The recovery of the key bytes has a negligible complexity compared to the recovery of the S_i functions in the first round. Indeed, according to the above analysis, the recovery of one key byte is roughly of $2^8 \cdot 1.004 \cdot 2^4 \approx 2^{12}$. This must be done 16 times, yielding a complexity of $16 \cdot 2^{12} \ll 2^{22}$.

5   Karroumi's White-Box AES Implementation

Karroumi's method to generate a white-box AES implementation [6] can be divided into two phases; *Phase 1* generates a dual AES cipher from a key-instantiated AES cipher, and *Phase 2* applies the white-box techniques presented by Chow *et al.* to the dual AES cipher. Below, aspects of these phases that are relevant to this paper are described.

Phase 1: Dual AES Cipher

In this section we give a description of the set of dual AES ciphers used by Karroumi in [6]. First, we define a dual AES subround. The following notation is used: $m_\alpha : \mathbf{F}_{256} \to \mathbf{F}_{256}$ with $\alpha \in \mathbf{F}_{256}^*$ is defined by $m_\alpha(x) = \alpha \otimes x$, and $f_t : \mathbf{F}_{256} \to \mathbf{F}_{256}$ defined by $f_t(x) = x^{2^t}$ for $0 \leq t \leq 7$ are the automorphisms of $\mathbf{F}_{256}$ over $\mathbf{F}_2$. Further, $R_l : \mathbf{F}_{256} \to \mathbf{F}_{256}$ are the isomorphisms mapping elements in the AES polynomial representation to field elements in one of the polynomial representations of $\mathbf{F}_{256}$. There are 30 irreducible polynomials of degree 8 over $\mathbf{F}_2$, each one resulting in a unique polynomial representation of $\mathbf{F}_{256}$ (one of these representations being the AES polynomial representation), hence in total there are 30 distinct isomorphisms R_l $(1 \leq l \leq 30)$. The addition and multiplication operations in the polynomial representation associated with R_l are denoted by $\oplus_l$ and $\otimes_l$, respectively ($\oplus_l$ and $\otimes_l$ being equal to $\oplus$ and $\otimes$ for exactly one value of l with $1 \leq l \leq 30$). Finally, the definition of a dual AES subround uses a set of mappings, denoted by $\mathcal{T}$, and defined by

$$\mathcal{T} = \{R_l \circ m_\alpha \circ f_t \mid 1 \leq l \leq 30, \alpha \in \mathbf{F}_{256}^* \text{ and } 0 \leq t \leq 7\} \ .$$

Observe that an element of $\mathcal{T}$ maps elements in the AES polynomial representation to elements in one of the 30 polynomial representations of $\mathbf{F}_{256}$.

Definition 4. *Let $\Delta_{r,j} \in \mathcal{T}$ with $\Delta_{r,j} = R_l \circ m_\alpha \circ f_t$ for some triple (l, α, t) with $1 \leq l \leq 30, \alpha \in \mathbf{F}_{256}^*$ and $0 \leq t \leq 7$, and let $\delta_{r,j} = R_l \circ f_t$. Further, let $v_i, w_i \in \mathbf{F}_{256}$ for $0 \leq i \leq 3$ be represented using the polynomial representation associated with R_l. The mapping $AES^{(r,j,\Delta_{r,j})} : \mathbf{F}_{256}^4 \to \mathbf{F}_{256}^4$ for $1 \leq r \leq 9$ and $0 \leq j \leq 3$, called a dual AES subround, is defined by $(w_0, w_1, w_2, w_3) = AES^{(r,j,\Delta_{r,j})}(v_0, v_1, v_2, v_3)$ with*

$$w_i = \delta_{r,j}(mc_{i0}) \otimes_l \Delta_{r,j} \circ S \circ \Delta_{r,j}^{-1}\big(v_0 \oplus_l \Delta_{r,j}(k_0^{(r,j)})\big)$$
$$\oplus_l \delta_{r,j}(mc_{i1}) \otimes_l \Delta_{r,j} \circ S \circ \Delta_{r,j}^{-1}\big(v_1 \oplus_l \Delta_{r,j}(k_1^{(r,j)})\big)$$
$$\oplus_l \delta_{r,j}(mc_{i2}) \otimes_l \Delta_{r,j} \circ S \circ \Delta_{r,j}^{-1}\big(v_2 \oplus_l \Delta_{r,j}(k_2^{(r,j)})\big)$$
$$\oplus_l \delta_{r,j}(mc_{i3}) \otimes_l \Delta_{r,j} \circ S \circ \Delta_{r,j}^{-1}\big(v_3 \oplus_l \Delta_{r,j}(k_3^{(r,j)})\big) \ ,$$

for $0 \leq i \leq 3$.

The following lemma presents a property that is required to show that a dual AES cipher maintains the functionality of AES. As the lemma is also used in the cryptanalysis in this paper, and as a formal proof of this property is omitted in [4] and [6], we include a proof as well.

Lemma 3. *If $\Delta_{r,j} \in \mathcal{T}$, then*

$$AES^{(r,j,\Delta_{r,j})} \circ (\Delta_{r,j}, \Delta_{r,j}, \Delta_{r,j}, \Delta_{r,j}) = (\Delta_{r,j}, \Delta_{r,j}, \Delta_{r,j}, \Delta_{r,j}) \circ AES^{(r,j)} \ ,$$

for $1 \leq r \leq 9$ and $0 \leq j \leq 3$.

Proof. Let x_i for $0 \leq i \leq 3$ be elements of $\mathbf{F}_{256}$ using the AES polynomial representation, let w_i for $0 \leq i \leq 3$ be elements of $\mathbf{F}_{256}$ using the polynomial representation associated with R_l (assuming that $\Delta_{r,j} = R_l \circ m_\alpha \circ f_t$), and let

$$(w_0, w_1, w_2, w_3) = AES^{(r,j,\Delta_{r,j})} \circ (\Delta_{r,j}, \Delta_{r,j}, \Delta_{r,j}, \Delta_{r,j})(x_0, x_1, x_2, x_3) \ .$$

Substituting $v_i = \Delta_{r,j}(x_i)$ for $0 \leq i \leq 3$ in the equation in Definition 4 yields

$$w_i = \bigoplus_{z=0}^{3} \delta_{r,j}(mc_{iz}) \otimes_l \Delta_{r,j} \circ S \circ \Delta_{r,j}^{-1}\big(\Delta_{r,j}(x_z) \oplus_l \Delta_{r,j}(k_z^{(r,j)})\big) \ ,$$

for $0 \leq i \leq 3$. Next, observe that $\Delta_{r,j}(a) \oplus_l \Delta_{r,j}(b) = R_l \circ m_\alpha \circ f_t(a) \oplus_l R_l \circ m_\alpha \circ f_t(b) = R_l(m_\alpha \circ f_t(a) \oplus m_\alpha \circ f_t(b)) = R_l(m_\alpha(f_t(a) \oplus f_t(b))) = R_l(m_\alpha(f_t(a \oplus b)))$

$= \Delta_{r,j}(a \oplus b)$ for all $a, b \in \mathbf{F}_{256}$ and all $\alpha \in \mathbf{F}_{256}^*$; the second equality holds true since R_l is an isomorphism, the third equality holds true as $\alpha(a \oplus b) = \alpha(a) \oplus \alpha(b)$ for all $a, b \in \mathbf{F}_{256}$ and the fourth equality holds true since f_t is an automorphism. It follows that

$$w_i = \bigoplus_{z=0}^{3} \delta_{r,j}(mc_{iz}) \otimes_l \Delta_{r,j} \circ S(x_z \oplus k_z^{(r,j)}) \;,$$

for $0 \leq i \leq 3$. Next, note that $\delta_{r,j}(a) \otimes_l \Delta_{r,j}(b) = R_l \circ f_t(a) \otimes_l R_l \circ m_\alpha \circ f_t(b) = R_l(f_t(a) \otimes m_\alpha \circ f_t(b)) = R_l(m_\alpha(f_t(a \otimes b))) = \Delta_{r,j}(a \otimes b)$ for all $a, b \in \mathbf{F}_{256}$; the second equality holds true since R_l is an isomorphism and the third equality uses the fact that $a^{2^t} \otimes \alpha b^{2^t} = \alpha(ab)^{2^t}$ for all $a, b \in \mathbf{F}_{256}$ and all $\alpha \in \mathbf{F}_{256}^*$. It follows that

$$w_i = \bigoplus_{z=0}^{3} \Delta_{r,j} \left(mc_{iz} \otimes S(x_z \oplus k_z^{(r,j)}) \right) \;,$$

for $0 \leq i \leq 3$. From this, $\Delta_{r,j}(a) \oplus_l \Delta_{r,j}(b) = \Delta_{r,j}(a \oplus b)$ for all $a, b \in \mathbf{F}_{256}$, and the definition of y_i in Definition 1, it follows that $w_i = \Delta_{r,j}(y_i)$ for $0 \leq i \leq 3$. □

Now, Karroumi [6] obtains a dual AES cipher as follows:

Step 1 assigns a randomly chosen $\Delta_{r,j} \in \mathcal{T}$ to each AES subround $AES^{(r,j)}$ ($1 \leq r \leq 9$ and $0 \leq j \leq 3$). Based on $\Delta_{r,j}$, the corresponding dual AES subround $AES^{(r,j,\Delta_{r,j})}$ is implemented as specified by Definition 4. The mappings $\Delta_{r,j}$ and $\delta_{r,j}$ (and the implementation of the dual cipher) are kept secret.

Step 2 ensures that the functionality of AES is maintained by including an additional operation (referred to as ChangeDualState) between ShiftRows and AddRoundKey operations of round r for $1 \leq r \leq 9$. If the inverse ShiftRows operation is defined by the mapping $sr(i,j) = (j+i) \bmod 4$ for $0 \leq i, j \leq 3$, then the ChangeDualState operation of round r applies the mapping $C_i^{(r,j)} : \mathbf{F}_{256} \rightarrow \mathbf{F}_{256}$ to the byte of the state associated with the i-th input byte of $AES^{(r,j,\Delta_{r,j})}$ for $0 \leq i, j \leq 3$, defined by $C_i^{(1,j)} = \Delta_{1,j}$ and $C_i^{(r,j)} = \Delta_{r,j} \circ \Delta_{r-1,sr(i,j)}^{-1}$ if $2 \leq r \leq 9$. Observe that for $2 \leq r \leq 9$, $C_i^{(r,j)}$ maps elements from $\mathbf{F}_{256}$ using the polynomial representation associated with $\Delta_{r-1,sr(i,j)}$ to elements of $\mathbf{F}_{256}$ using the polynomial representation associated with $\Delta_{r,j}$.

Karroumi presents two different but equivalent methods (from a security point of view) in [6] to perform the ChangeDualState operation, and specifies the white-box AES implementation using one of these methods. In this paper we use the specification as in [6]; the cryptanalysis can easily be adapted if the other method is used.

Phase 2: Apply the Techniques of Chow *et al.*

The following description of Karroumi's white-box AES implementation is equivalent to the description in [6]:

Step 1 applies the techniques of Chow *et al.* to write the dual AES cipher (with a fixed key) obtained in Phase 1 as a series of lookup tables. In particular, the dual AES key addition operations and the dual S-box operations are merged into key-dependent bijective mappings $T_i^{(r,j,\Delta_{r,j})}$ for $0 \leq i, j \leq 3$ and $1 \leq r \leq 9$. These mappings are referred to as dual T-boxes and are defined by

$$T_i^{(r,j,\Delta_{r,j})} = \Delta_{r,j} \circ S \circ \Delta_{r,j}^{-1} \circ \oplus_{\Delta_{r,j}(k_i^{(r,j)})} \circ C_i^{(r,j)} \ ,$$

where each dual T-box mapping is implemented as a table mapping 8 input bits to 8 output bits. Recall that the mappings $C_i^{(r,j)}$ define the `ChangeDualState` operation. Next, write the other part of the dual AES cipher as a series of lookup tables as indicated by Chow *et al.* in [5]. The number and types of tables (including the tables representing the dual T-boxes) and the data-flow between tables are the same as in the lookup table implementation of AES in [5]. The only difference is that the values of the table entries of the dual AES implementation are likely to be different from the values of the corresponding entries in the AES implementation in [5] due to the dual version of the AES operations.

Step 2 applies the white-box encoding techniques of Chow *et al.* in [5] to this lookup table implementation of dual AES. As these white-box encoding techniques do not depend on the values of the table entries, the number and types of white-box tables, and the data-flow of Karroumi's white-box AES implementation are the same as in the white-box AES implementation of Chow *et al.* in [5].

In [6], Karroumi argues that the secrecy of the mappings $\Delta_{r,j}$, randomly selected from the set $\mathcal{T}$ and used to generate the dual cipher, increases the work factor of the BGE attack to 2^{93}.

5.1   Insecurity

This section shows that Karroumi's white-box AES implementation [6] is insecure. Recall that Karroumi's white-box AES implementation uses the same number and types of white-box tables, and that the data-flow of the implementation is the same as in Chow *et al.*'s white-box AES implementation in [5]. As a result, the techniques of Billet *et al.* can be applied directly to compose lookup tables in Karroumi's implementation to obtain access to the encoded dual AES subrounds (instead of the encoded AES subrounds in case of Chow *et al.*'s implementation) for rounds $1 \leq r \leq 9$. In the following definition, $A_i^{(r,j)}$ and $B_i^{(r,j)}$ for $0 \leq i \leq 3$ denote bijective mappings (or encodings) on the vector space $\mathbf{F}_2^8$. Further, with slight abuse of notation, an output of $A_i^{(r,j)}$ is considered to be an element of $\mathbf{F}_{256}$ using the polynomial representation associated with the mapping R_l as defined by $\Delta_{r-1,\mathrm{sr}(i',j')}$, and an output of $AES^{(r,j,\Delta_{r,j})}$ is considered to be an element of $(\mathbf{F}_2^8)^4$. In the following definition, $\Pi_1^{(r,j)}, \Pi_2^{(r,j)}$ and $\pi^{(r)}$ are the permutations as used in Definition 3.

Definition 5. *The mapping* $\overline{AES}_{enc}^{(r,j,\Delta_{r,j})} : (\mathbf{F}_2^8)^4 \to (\mathbf{F}_2^8)^4$ *for* $1 \leq r \leq 9$ *and* $0 \leq j \leq 3$, *called an encoded dual AES subround, is defined by*

$$\overline{AES}_{enc}^{(r,j,\Delta_{r,j})} = (B_0^{(r,j)}, B_1^{(r,j)}, B_2^{(r,j)}, B_3^{(r,j)}) \circ \overline{AES}^{(r,j,\Delta_{r,j})} \circ \tag{12}$$
$$(A_0^{(r,j)}, A_1^{(r,j)}, A_2^{(r,j)}, A_3^{(r,j)}) \,,$$

where the mapping $\overline{AES}^{(r,j,\Delta_{r,j})}$ *is defined by*

$$\Pi_2^{(r,j)} \circ AES^{(r,j',\Delta_{r,j'})} \circ (C_0^{(r,j')}, C_1^{(r,j')}, C_2^{(r,j')}, C_3^{(r,j')}) \circ \Pi_1^{(r,j)} \,, \tag{13}$$

with $j' = \pi^{(r)}(j)$.

The next lemma shows that an encoded dual AES subround can be represented by an encoded AES subround using the same key bytes:

Lemma 4. *An encoded dual AES subround* $\overline{AES}_{enc}^{(r,j,\Delta_{r,j})}$ *is an encoded AES subround* $\overline{AES}_{enc}^{(r,j)}$ *as in Definition 3 with*

$$P_i^{(1,j)} = A_i^{(1,j)} \quad and \quad P_i^{(r,j)} = \Delta_{r-1,\text{sr}(i',j')}^{-1} \circ A_i^{(r,j)} \quad if \;\; 2 \leq r \leq 9 \,,$$

and

$$Q_i^{(r,j)} = B_i^{(r,j)} \circ \Delta_{r,j'} \,,$$

for $0 \leq i, j \leq 3$ *and* $1 \leq r \leq 9$, *with* $i' = (\pi_1^{(r,j)})^{-1}(i)$ *and* $j' = \pi^{(r)}(j)$ *where* $(\pi_1^{(r,j)})^{-1}$ *denotes the permutation on the indices of a 4-byte vector as a result of the application of* $(\Pi_1^{(r,j)})^{-1}$.

Proof. The proof is given for the case $2 \leq r \leq 9$; similar reasoning applies to the case $r = 1$. From the definition of the ChangeDualState operation (see Step 2 of Phase 1 of Karroumi's implementation) it follows that

$$(C_0^{(r,j')}, C_1^{(r,j')}, C_2^{(r,j')}, C_3^{(r,j')}) = (\Delta_{r,j'}, \Delta_{r,j'}, \Delta_{r,j'}, \Delta_{r,j'}) \circ$$
$$(\Delta_{r-1,\text{sr}(0,j')}^{-1}, \Delta_{r-1,\text{sr}(1,j')}^{-1}, \Delta_{r-1,\text{sr}(2,j')}^{-1}, \Delta_{r-1,\text{sr}(3,j')}^{-1}) \quad if \; 2 \leq r \leq 9,$$

for $0 \leq j \leq 3$. Substituting the above expression for the ChangeDualState operation in Eq. 13 and applying Lemma 3 gives

$$\overline{AES}^{(r,j,\Delta_{r,j})} = \Pi_2^{(r,j)} \circ (\Delta_{r,j'}, \Delta_{r,j'}, \Delta_{r,j'}, \Delta_{r,j'}) \circ AES^{(r,j')} \circ$$
$$(\Delta_{r-1,\text{sr}(0,j')}^{-1}, \Delta_{r-1,\text{sr}(1,j')}^{-1}, \Delta_{r-1,\text{sr}(2,j')}^{-1}, \Delta_{r-1,\text{sr}(3,j')}^{-1}) \circ \Pi_1^{(r,j)} \,.$$

Observe that $\Pi_2^{(r,j)}$ and $(\Delta_{r,j'}, \Delta_{r,j'}, \Delta_{r,j'}, \Delta_{r,j'})$ commute and thus can be swapped. By applying the equation

$$(\Delta_{r-1,\text{sr}(0,j')}^{-1}, \Delta_{r-1,\text{sr}(1,j')}^{-1}, \Delta_{r-1,\text{sr}(2,j')}^{-1}, \Delta_{r-1,\text{sr}(3,j')}^{-1}) \circ \Pi_1^{(r,j)} =$$
$$\Pi_1^{(r,j)} \circ (\Delta_{r-1,\text{sr}(0',j')}^{-1}, \Delta_{r-1,\text{sr}(1',j')}^{-1}, \Delta_{r-1,\text{sr}(2',j')}^{-1}, \Delta_{r-1,\text{sr}(3',j')}^{-1}) \,,$$

where $i' = (\pi_1^{(r,j)})^{-1}(i)$ for $i = 0, 1, 2, 3$ where $(\pi_1^{(r,j)})^{-1}$ denotes the permutation on the indices of a 4-byte vector as a result of the application of $\left(\Pi_1^{(r,j)}\right)^{-1}$, one gets the result of Lemma 4. □

From the discussion above it follows that Karroumi's white-box AES implementation and the white-box AES implementation of Chow *et al.* are the same. As a consequence, Karroumi's white-box AES implementation is vulnerable to the original BGE attack and the attacks presented in this paper.

6   Conclusion

The BGE attack on the white-box AES implementation of Chow *et al.* extracts the AES key from such an implementation with a work factor of 2^{30}. Taking Tolhuizen's improvement to the most time-consuming phase of the BGE attack as the starting point, Sect. 3 presented several improvements to the other phases of the BGE attack. It was shown that the overall work factor of the BGE attack is reduced to 2^{22} when all improvements are implemented. Unlike the original BGE attack, the use of non-affine white-box encodings and the randomization in the order of the bytes of the intermediate results in AES have a negligible contribution to the overall work factor of the improved BGE attack.

Section 4 presented a new attack on the white-box implementation of Chow *et al.* based on collisions occurring in the output bytes of an encoded AES round. It was shown that the new attack also has a work factor of 2^{22}.

Karroumi's white-box AES implementation was designed to withstand the BGE attack. Section 5 showed that the white-box AES implementations of Chow *et al.* and Karroumi are the same. As a result, the original BGE attack and the attacks presented in this paper can be applied directly to extract the key from Karroumi's white-box AES implementation, implying that this implementation is insecure.

Acknowledgments. This work was supported in part by the Research Council KU Leuven: GOA TENSE (GOA/11/007). In addition, this work was supported by the Flemish Government, FWO WET G.0213.11N and IWT GBO SEC SODA. Yoni De Mulder was supported in part by a research grant of iMinds of the Flemish Government.

References

1. Barkan, E., Biham, E.: In how many ways can you write Rijndael? In: Zheng, Y. (ed.) ASIACRYPT 2002. LNCS, vol. 2501, pp. 160–175. Springer, Heidelberg (2002)
2. Barkan, E., Biham, E.: The book of Rijndaels. IACR Cryptology ePrint Archive, 2002:158. http://eprint.iacr.org/2002/158 (2002)
3. Billet, O., Gilbert, H., Ech-Chatbi, C.: Cryptanalysis of a white box AES implementation. In: Handschuh, H., Hasan, M.A. (eds.) SAC 2004. LNCS, vol. 3357, pp. 227–240. Springer, Heidelberg (2004)

4. Biryukov, A., De Cannière, C., Braeken, A., Preneel, B.: A toolbox for cryptanalysis: linear and affine equivalence algorithms. In: Biham, E. (ed.) EUROCRYPT 2003. LNCS, vol. 2656, pp. 33–50. Springer, Heidelberg (2003)

5. Chow, S., Eisen, P., Johnson, H., Van Oorschot, P.C.: White-box cryptography and an AES implementation. In: Nyberg, K., Heys, H. (eds.) SAC 2002. LNCS, vol. 2595, pp. 250–270. Springer, Heidelberg (2003)

6. Karroumi, M.: Protecting white-box AES with dual ciphers. In: Rhee, K.-H., Nyang, D. (eds.) ICISC 2010. LNCS, vol. 6829, pp. 278–291. Springer, Heidelberg (2011)

7. Lepoint, T., Rivain, M.: Another nail in the coffin of white-box AES implementations. Cryptology ePrint Archive, Report 2013/455. http://eprint.iacr.org/2013/455.pdf (2013)

8. National Institute of Standards and Technology: Advanced encryption standard. In: Federal Information Processing Standard (FIPS), Publication 197, U.S. Department of Commerce, Washington, DC (November 2001). http://csrc.nist.gov/publications/fips/fips197/fips-197.pdf

9. Muir, J.A.: A tutorial on white-box AES. In: Kranakis, E. (ed.) Advances in Network Analysis and its Applications. Mathematics in Industry, pp. 209–229. Springer, Heidelberg (2013). http://www.ccsl.carleton.ca/ jamuir/papers/wb-aes-tutorial.pdf

10. De Mulder, Y., Roelse, P., Preneel, B.: Cryptanalysis of the Xiao - Lai white-box AES implementation. In: Knudsen, L.R., Wu, H. (eds.) SAC 2012. LNCS, vol. 7707, pp. 34–49. Springer, Heidelberg (2013)

11. De Mulder, Y., Roelse, P., Preneel, B.: Revisiting the BGE attack on a white-box AES implementation. Cryptology ePrint Archive, Report 2013/450. http://eprint.iacr.org/2013/450.pdf (2013)

12. Tolhuizen, L.: Improved cryptanalysis of an AES implementation. In: 33rd WIC Symposium on Information Theory in the Benelux (2012)

13. Xiao, Y., Lai, X.: A secure implementation of white-box AES. In: 2nd International Conference on Computer Science and its Applications (CSA 2009), pp. 1–6. IEEE (2009)

Block Ciphers

Extended Generalized Feistel Networks
Using Matrix Representation

Thierry P. Berger[1], Marine Minier[2], and Gaël Thomas[1(✉)]

[1] XLIM (UMR CNRS 7252), Université de Limoges, 123 avenue Albert Thomas,
87060 Limoges Cedex, France
{thierry.berger,gael.thomas}@unilim.fr
[2] CITI, INSA-Lyon, INRIA, Université de Lyon, F-69621 Villeurbanne, France
marine.minier@insa-lyon.fr

Abstract. While Generalized Feistel Networks have been widely studied in the literature as a building block of a block cipher, we propose in this paper a unified vision to easily represent them through a matrix representation. We then propose a new class of such schemes called Extended Generalized Feistel Networks well suited for cryptographic applications. We instantiate those proposals into two particular constructions and we finally analyze their security.

Keywords: Generalized feistel networks · Matrix representation · Scheme proposal · Security analysis

Introduction

While a classical Feistel network, such as DES [23] or Camellia [2], divides a plaintext into 2 n-bit-long halves, a Generalized Feistel Network (GFN) divides it into $k \geq 2$ n-bit-long subblocks. Various GFNs exist in the literature. This includes Source-Heavy (SH) as in RC2 [25] and SHA-1 [29]; Target-Heavy (TH) as in MARS [7]; Type-1 as in CAST-256 [1] and Lesamnta [11]; Type-2 as in RC6 [26], HIGHT [13] and CLEFIA [28]; Type-3 and Nyberg's GFNs [24]. Pseudo-randomness of these constructions is studied in [12,21,33] for Type-1, Type-2 and Type-3, in [12,22] for SH GFN and [12,21] for TH GFN. Figure 1 gives an example of Type-3 GFN. Usually GFNs perform a block-wise cyclic shift in their permutation layer.

In [30], Suzaki and Minematsu proposed to use a non-cyclic permutation instead and applied it to Type-2 GFNs. More precisely, they studied the maximum diffusion round. Roughly speaking, it is the minimum number of rounds such as every output block depends on every input block. They exhaustively searched all the optimum permutations for $k \leq 16$ and found that the diffusion in Type-2 GFNs can be improved. They also showed a lower bound on the

This work was partially supported by the French National Agency of Research: ANR-11-INS-011.

T. Lange, K. Lauter, and P. Lisoněk (Eds.): SAC 2013, LNCS 8282, pp. 289–305, 2014.
DOI: 10.1007/978-3-662-43414-7_15, © Springer-Verlag Berlin Heidelberg 2014

maximum diffusion round of Type-2 GFNs and when k is a power of 2, they gave a generic construction based on de Bruijn graphs whose maximum diffusion round is close to the lower bound they found. Besides, they studied the pseudorandomness of these GFNs and their resistance against classical attacks and showed that it is actually improved as well. One of these Type-2 GFNs is used in TWINE [31].

Following the work of [30], Yanagihara and Iwata [32] studied the case of Type-1, Type-3, SH and TH GFNs with non-cyclic permutation. For Type-1 and Type-3 GFNs, they showed that the maximum diffusion round can be improved by changing the permutation while for SH and TH GFNs it cannot. Besides, for Type-1 GFNs, they gave an optimum generic construction for any k and identified a necessary and sufficient condition for improved Type-3 to have a finite maximum diffusion round. They also evaluated the resistance of all those GFNs against classical attacks and showed that it can be improved in the Type-1 and Type-3 cases.

In this paper, we first investigate a unified vision of GFNs using a matrix representation and use it to further study the diffusion properties of GFNs. We then extend this matrix representation and propose a broader class of Feistel networks that we call Extended Generalized Feistel Networks (EGFNs). We finally propose one particular EGFN with good diffusion properties and study the security of this proposal.

This paper is organized as follows: Sect. 1 gives the matrix representation of a GFN, its link with diffusion and shows how each possible GFN could be represented using a particular matrix. Section 2 extends GFNs into EGFNs and contains a particular EGFN proposal with good diffusion properties. In Sect. 3 we present a complete security analysis concerning this proposal.

1   Matrix Representation of Feistel Networks

Before defining the matrix representation of a GFN, let us introduce a few notations.

1.1   Definitions and Notations

A GFN divides its input into $k \geq 2$ blocks of n bits each. Let $x_0, \cdots, x_{k-1}$ denote the input blocks of a GFN round and $y_0, \cdots, y_{k-1}$ the corresponding output blocks. A GFN can be separated into two successive layers, as done in [30,32]: a round-function layer and a permutation layer, as on Fig. 1. The round-function layer is made of key-dependent functions whose inputs are some of the blocks and whose outputs are added (x-ored) to some other blocks. The permutation layer is a block-wise permutation of the k blocks. How the different round-functions are arranged depends on the type of GFN considered, while the permutation is usually the cyclic shift. We further denote by y_i^r the content of the i-th block after r rounds.

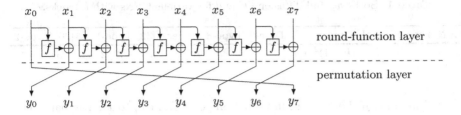

Fig. 1. One round of a Type-3 GFN with $k = 8$ blocks.

1.2 Diffusion Delay

We say input block x_i affects output block y_j^r if x_i effectively appears in the expression of y_j^r seen as a function of $x_0, \cdots, x_{k-1}$. We say x_i has diffused at round r if x_i affects every y_j^r for $0 \le j \le k - 1$. If every input block x_i has diffused at round r, we say the GFN has reached full diffusion, that is every output block y_j^r depends on every input block x_i. We call full diffusion delay the minimum number of rounds required to reach full diffusion and denote it d^+. In fact, the notion of full diffusion delay is a general notion that can be applied to any automaton as done in [3]. In the particular case of GFNs, this is exactly the same notion as the maximum diffusion round introduced in [30].

Another way to see the full diffusion delay is from a graph point of view. For a k-block GFN, let us define the associated directed graph as the graph with vertex set $\{0, \cdots, k - 1\}$ and such that (i, j) is an edge if the output y_j depends on the input x_i (directly or via a round-function). In other words, this is simply the usual Feistel schemes with outputs folded onto the input with same index. Knowing that, it is easy to see that the notion of *block x_i affecting block y_j^r* becomes *there exists a path of length exactly r going from i to j*. Thus the full diffusion delay d^+ can be alternately defined as the smallest integer r such that for all ordered pair of vertices (i, j) there exists a path of length exactly r going from i to j. Two things should now be noticed. First, if a GFN is in a full diffusion state at round r then it will remain so at round $r + 1$. Second, the full diffusion delay of a GFN depends solely on the structure of this graph and not on the round-functions used in the GFN.

Similarly, we can define full diffusion delay when considering decryption instead of encryption and denote it d^-. Following the work of [30], we consider the both-way full diffusion delay $d = \max(d^+, d^-)$. The both-way full diffusion delay d for the different classical GFNs is summed up in Table 1. For security reasons, it is necessary that d be finite.

1.3 Matrix Representation of Feistel Networks

Recall that a GFN is divided into two distinct transformations: first, the round-function layer and second, the permutation layer, represented by a permutation matrix $\mathcal{P}$. We call matrix representation of the round-function layer, the matrix denoted $\mathcal{F}$ with an all-one diagonal and with a parameter we call F at position

Table 1. Both-way full diffusion delay d for various GFNs with k blocks.

GFN Type	SH	TH	Type-1	Type-2	Type-3	Nyberg [32]	Type-1	[30] Type-2
d	k	k	$(k-1)^2+1$	k	k	k	$k(k+2)/2-2$	$2\log_2 k$

(i,j) if and only if there is a round-function going from x_j to x_i. The parameter F is a formal parameter, meaning it merely indicates the presence of a round-function in the GFN, the same F is used for all the different round-functions used throughout the cipher. If one follows the matrix representation idea, one would define the matrix of the whole GFN as $\mathcal{M} = \mathcal{P} \times \mathcal{F}$.

In other words, for a GFN with k blocks, let $\mathcal{M}$ be the $k \times k$ matrix over $\mathbb{Z}[F]$ defined as follows: for indices $0 \le i, j \le k-1$, coefficient at row i and column j of $\mathcal{M}$ is either a 1 if output y_i directly depends on x_j, that is without going through a round-function, or a formal parameter F, if y_i depends on x_j via a round-function, or 0 otherwise. This corresponds to the definition of Encryption Characteristic Matrix given in [14]. E.g. Fig. 2 gives the matrices $\mathcal{M}$, $\mathcal{P}$ and $\mathcal{F}$ of the GFN on Fig. 1.

$$\mathcal{M} = \begin{pmatrix} F & 1 & & & & & & \\ & F & 1 & & & & & \\ & & F & 1 & & & & \\ & & & F & 1 & & & \\ & & & & F & 1 & & \\ & & & & & F & 1 & \\ & & & & & & F & 1 \\ 1 & & & & & & & \end{pmatrix} \quad \mathcal{P} = \begin{pmatrix} & 1 & & & & & & \\ & & 1 & & & & & \\ & & & 1 & & & & \\ & & & & 1 & & & \\ & & & & & 1 & & \\ & & & & & & 1 & \\ & & & & & & & 1 \\ 1 & & & & & & & \end{pmatrix} \quad \mathcal{F} = \begin{pmatrix} 1 & & & & & & & \\ F & 1 & & & & & & \\ & F & 1 & & & & & \\ & & F & 1 & & & & \\ & & & F & 1 & & & \\ & & & & F & 1 & & \\ & & & & & F & 1 & \\ & & & & & & F & 1 \end{pmatrix}$$

Fig. 2. Decomposition of the transition matrix of the Type-2 GFN given on Fig. 1

As round-functions in a GFN are unlikely to be linear, such a matrix is not an exact representation. However it still retains enough information to evaluate diffusion; namely which output block y_i is influenced by which input block x_j and whether this done directly or via a round-function.

An important feature of GFNs is to transform a set of non-invertible round-functions into an invertible permutation. Hence the matrix of the GFN in decryption mode $\mathcal{M}^{-1}$ should not contain inverses of expressions containing a F. This translates into $\det(\mathcal{M})$ is independent of F, or equivalently $\det(\mathcal{F}) = \pm 1$, as $\mathcal{P}$ is a permutation matrix. This is the case for all of the classical GFNs (SH, TH,...) including those of [30,32] because the matrix $\mathcal{F}$ is lower triangular with an all-one diagonal.

An other feature of many GFNs is quasi-involutiveness, that is encryption/decryption is roughly the same process, up to using the direct/inverse permutation layer $\mathcal{P}$. To ensure that, one asks that the round-function layer be quasi-involutive. Except the Type-3 GFNs where the round-functions must be evaluated sequentially, all GFNs round-function layers are quasi-involutive. We choose to focus on GFNs that satisfy this property:

Definition 1. *A matrix $\mathcal{M}$ with coefficients in $\{0, 1, F\} \subset \mathbb{Z}[F]$ is a GFN matrix if it can be written as $\mathcal{M} = \mathcal{P}\mathcal{F}$ such that $\mathcal{P}$ is a permutation matrix and the matrix $\mathcal{F}$ satisfies the following conditions:*

1. *the main diagonal is filled with 1,*
2. *the off-diagonal coefficients are either 0 or F,*
3. *for each index i, row i and column i cannot both have an F coefficient.*

In other words, the blocks of the GFN can be partitioned into three categories: blocks that emit (through a round-function), blocks that receive and blocks that do not emit nor receive. This definition encompasses most of the known GFNs, with the exception of the Type-3. The property of quasi-involutiveness comes from the following theorem.

Theorem 1. *Let $\mathcal{M} = \mathcal{P}\mathcal{F}$ be a GFN according to Definition 1. Then $\mathcal{F}$ is invertible and $\mathcal{F}^{-1} = 2\mathcal{I} - \mathcal{F}$, where $\mathcal{I}$ stands for the identity matrix.*

Proof. To prove $\mathcal{F}$ is invertible, we compute $\det(\mathcal{F})$. Because of Condition 3 of Definition 1, for each index i either row i or column i is all-zero except for the diagonal coefficient. Thus by successively expanding the determinant along either row i or column i, $\det(\mathcal{F}) = 1$.

To prove $\mathcal{F}^{-1} = 2\mathcal{I} - \mathcal{F}$, we equivalently prove $(\mathcal{F} - \mathcal{I})^2 = 0$. Let $f_{i,j}$ (resp. $f'_{i,j}$) denote the coefficient of $\mathcal{F} - \mathcal{I}$ (resp. $(\mathcal{F} - \mathcal{I})^2$) at row i and column j. By definition of the matrix product, for all i and j, we have $f'_{i,j} = f_{i,i}f_{i,j} + f_{i,j}f_{j,j} + \sum_{\substack{\ell \neq i \\ \ell \neq j}} f_{i,\ell}f_{\ell,j} = \sum_{\substack{\ell \neq i \\ \ell \neq j}} f_{i,\ell}f_{\ell,j}$. In the sum, consider one term $f_{i,\ell}f_{\ell,j}$. As $\ell \neq i$, $f_{i,\ell}$ can either be zero or F. But, if $f_{i,\ell}$ is non-zero then the ℓ-th column of $\mathcal{F}$ contains an F thus, by Condition 3 the ℓ-th row must not contain any F, implying $f_{\ell,j} = 0$ for all $j \neq \ell$. Thus, each term $f_{i,\ell}f_{\ell,j}$ is zero, so $f'_{i,j} = 0$.   □

Notice that in the case where the outputs of round-functions are xored with other blocks, then matrix $\mathcal{F}^{-1} = 2\mathcal{I} - \mathcal{F}$ is simply $\mathcal{F}$ itself. Besides, we can characterize the matrices $\mathcal{F}$ for which $\mathcal{F}^{-1} = 2\mathcal{I} - \mathcal{F}$ holds.

Theorem 2. *Let $\mathcal{F}$ be a matrix that verifies Conditions 1 and 2 of Definition 1. If $(\mathcal{F} - \mathcal{I})^2 = 0$ then $\mathcal{F}$ also verifies Condition 3.*

Proof. Let $f_{i,j}$ be the coefficient of $\mathcal{F} - \mathcal{I}$ at row i and column j. For all i and j, we have $0 = \sum_{\ell=0}^{k-1} f_{i,\ell}f_{\ell,j} = \sum_{\ell \neq i,j} f_{i,\ell}f_{\ell,j}$. All the coefficients $f_{i,\ell}$ and $f_{\ell,j}$ in the previous equation are off-diagonal, thus are either F or 0. Hence the sum can be zero only if all its terms are zero. For each index ℓ, we need to prove that row ℓ and column ℓ cannot both have an F coefficient. Suppose column ℓ has an F coefficient, say $f_{i,\ell}$ with $i \neq \ell$. This implies that for all $j \neq \ell$, $f_{\ell,j} = 0$. Thus row ℓ has no F coefficient. By transposing, the same goes when considering rows instead of columns.   □

In other words, the GFNs round-function layer matrices $\mathcal{F}$ which are quasi-involutive are exactly those where Condition 3 of Definition 1 holds.

Recall that the full diffusion delay can be expressed in term of distance in a directed graph. In fact, if one evaluates the matrix $\mathcal{M}$ of the GFN in $F = 1$, we obtain the adjacency matrix of this graph. The full diffusion delay d^+ is then the smallest integer such that $\mathcal{M}^{d^+}$ has no zero coefficient. The same goes for the decryption full diffusion delay d^-, using $\mathcal{M}^{-d^-}$.

1.4 Matrix Equivalences

Now that we have matrices representing GFNs, we define an equivalence relations on them that will help us to find GFNs.

Definition 2. *Two GFNs matrices $\mathcal{M}$ and $\mathcal{M}'$ are equivalent if there exists a permutation (matrix) π of the k blocks such that $\pi \mathcal{M} \pi^{-1} = \mathcal{M}'$.*

In other words, two GFNs are equivalent if they are the same up to block reindexation and thus share the same properties, such as a common full diffusion delay. We then have the property of "equivalent decompositions":

Theorem 3. *Let $\mathcal{M} = \mathcal{P}\mathcal{F}$ and $\mathcal{M}' = \mathcal{P}'\mathcal{F}'$ be two GFNs according to Definition 1 and equivalent under Definition 2. Let also be π such that $\pi \mathcal{M} \pi^{-1} = \mathcal{M}'$. Then $\pi \mathcal{P} \pi^{-1} = \mathcal{P}'$ and $\pi \mathcal{F} \pi^{-1} = \mathcal{F}'$.*

Proof. By hypothesis, we have $\pi \mathcal{P}\mathcal{F} \pi^{-1} = \mathcal{P}'\mathcal{F}'$. Also by definition, $\mathcal{F}$ and $\mathcal{F}'$ have an all-one diagonal and either F or zero elsewhere. Hence $\mathcal{F}$ and $\mathcal{F}'$ both evaluate to the identity matrix $\mathcal{I}$ in $F = 0$. Thus, specifying the above equation in zero, we obtain $\pi \mathcal{P} \pi^{-1} = \mathcal{P}'$, which implies $\pi \mathcal{F} \pi^{-1} = \mathcal{F}'$.   □

In other words, two GFNs are equivalent if and only if both layers are equivalent with same conjugating element. For example, if one studies a class of GFNs with a fixed $\mathcal{F}$ matrix, as done in [30,32], Theorem 3 allows to define an equivalence relation on the permutation layer.

1.5 Exhaustive Search of Feistel Networks

We investigated all the GFNs according to Definition 1 with $k = 8$ blocks up to equivalence. We consider three parameters:

- the full diffusion delay d,
- the number of round-functions per round s,
- the cost for full diffusion, i.e the total number of round-functions required for full diffusion, $c = d \times s$.

We found there is no GFN with cost $c < 24$. However, there are cases where the number of rounds d is a more important criterion than the total cost c. For each possible value of $d \leq 12$, Table 2 gives the minimum number of round-functions s required for an 8-block GFN to fully diffuse in d rounds. It also gives

Table 2. Minimum number s of functions per round required to have a full diffusion in d rounds and corresponding total cost $c = s \times d$. For each case, the number of different $\mathcal{F}$ matrices ($\#\mathcal{F}$) and the total number of GFNs ($\#\mathcal{M}$) are also given up to equivalence.

d	1,2	3	4	5	6	7	8	9	10	11	12
s	∞	16	7	6	4	4	4	3	3	3	2
c	∞	48	28	30	24	28	32	27	30	33	24
$\#\mathcal{F}$	0	1	1	8	3	13	13	1	6	6	1
$\#\mathcal{M}$	0	5	3	26	9	101	652	18	100	56	5

the number of GFNs that achieve such diffusion, splitted into the number of different $\mathcal{F}$ matrices (row $\#\mathcal{F}$) and the total number of GFNs (row $\#\mathcal{M}$), up to equivalence.

Note that among the GFNs that fully diffuse in $d = 6$, with $s = 4$ round-functions, are the Type-2 GFNs with non-cyclic permutation given in [30], which are then diffusion-optimum among the GFNs of Definition 1.

2   New Feistel Network Proposals

2.1   Extended Generalized Feistel Networks

For a GFN $\mathcal{M} = \mathcal{PF}$, to achieve quicker diffusion, one can increase the number of round-functions in $\mathcal{F}$. However, this also makes costlier GFNs. The other possibility is to look at the permutation layer $\mathcal{P}$. Definition 1 already allows for block-wise permutations. A possible generalization is to use a linear mapping instead, thus looking for GFNs $\mathcal{M} = \mathcal{GF}$ with $\mathcal{G}$ an invertible $k \times k$ matrix. This is however much costlier than a simple block-wise permutation and besides it loses the quasi-involutive property. What we propose is to have a $\mathcal{G}$ which is itself a GFN but with the identity mapping as round-functions. In other words, we write $\mathcal{G} = \mathcal{PL}$ where $\mathcal{P}$ is a permutation matrix and $\mathcal{L}$ is matrix similar to $\mathcal{F}$ but with I off-diagonal non-zero coefficients instead of F. We call this matrix $\mathcal{L}$ the linear layer. In that case, the whole Feistel network matrix becomes $\mathcal{M} = \mathcal{PLF}$, e.g. Fig. 3. Because matrices $\mathcal{L}$ and $\mathcal{F}$ have common structure, we regroup them into a single matrix $\mathcal{N} = \mathcal{LF}$, and write $\mathcal{M} = \mathcal{PN}$. The matrix $\mathcal{N}$ is the new round-function part of the Feistel network but now has two formal parameters: F for non-linear round-functions to provide cryptographic security and I for identity round-functions to provide quick diffusion. We call these new schemes Extended Generalized Feistel Networks (EGFNs).

As done in Sect. 1.3 for GFNs, to be considered an EGFN we require that matrix $\mathcal{M} = \mathcal{PN}$ is invertible and that $\det(\mathcal{M})$ does not depend on F nor I, which translates into $\det(\mathcal{N}) = \pm 1$. Again, we choose to focus on EGFNs that are quasi-involutive. Hence the following definition.

Definition 3. *A matrix $\mathcal{M}$ with coefficients in $\{0, 1, F, I\} \subset \mathbb{Z}[F, I]$ is an Extended Generalized Feistel Network (EGFN) matrix if it can be written as*

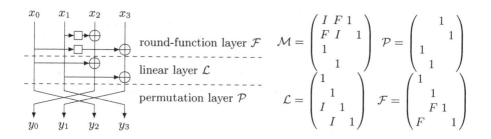

Fig. 3. Overview of an EGFN three layers and corresponding matrices (right).

$\mathcal{M} = \mathcal{PN}$ such that $\mathcal{P}$ is a permutation matrix and the matrix $\mathcal{N}$ satisfies the following conditions:

1. the main diagonal is filled with 1,
2. the off-diagonal coefficients are either 0, F or I,
3. for each index i, row i and column i cannot both contain a non-zero coefficient other than on the diagonal,
4. for each index i, if row i contains an I then it also contains an F.

As in Sect. 1.3, Condition 3 allows to partition the blocks into emitters and receivers. Condition 4 ensures that the pseudorandomness evaluation of EGFNs can be computed (see Sect. 3.1). Because Definition 3 is essentially the same as Definition 1, the following theorem on quasi-involutiveness is straightforward.

Theorem 4. Let $\mathcal{M} = \mathcal{PN}$ be an EGFN according to Definition 3. Then $\det(\mathcal{N}) = 1$ and $\mathcal{N}^{-1} = 2\mathcal{I} - \mathcal{N}$.

Proof. Same as Theorem 1, since Conditions 1, 2 and 3 of Definition 3 are essentially the same as in Definition 1.   □

Besides, define matrices $\mathcal{L}$ and $\mathcal{F}$ for the EGFNs of Definition 3.

Definition 4. Let $\mathcal{M} = \mathcal{PN}$ be a EGFN according to Definition 3. Then define matrix $\mathcal{F} \in \mathbb{Z}[F]$ as the evaluation of $\mathcal{N}$ in $I = 0$ and similarly matrix $\mathcal{L} \in \mathbb{Z}[I]$ as the evaluation of $\mathcal{N}$ in $F = 0$.

Theorem 5 verifies this definition works as intended, that is $\mathcal{M} = \mathcal{PLF}$.

Theorem 5. Let $\mathcal{N}$, $\mathcal{F}$ and $\mathcal{L}$ be defined as in Definition 4, then $\mathcal{N} = \mathcal{L} + \mathcal{F} - \mathcal{I}$ and $\mathcal{N} = \mathcal{L} \times \mathcal{F} = \mathcal{F} \times \mathcal{L}$.

Proof. The first equation is a straightforward consequence of the definition of $\mathcal{N}$, $\mathcal{L}$ and $\mathcal{F}$. As for the second, let $a_{i,j}$ be the coefficient at row i and column j of matrix $\mathcal{LF}$ and show that $a_{i,i} = 1$ and $a_{i,j} = \mathcal{L}_{i,j} + \mathcal{F}_{i,j}$ otherwise (with obvious notations). Write $a_{i,i} = \mathcal{L}_{i,i}\mathcal{F}_{i,i} + \sum_{\ell \neq i} \mathcal{L}_{i,\ell}\mathcal{F}_{\ell,i}$. Then $a_{i,i} = \mathcal{L}_{i,i}\mathcal{F}_{i,i} = 1$ because all terms in the rightmost sum are 0 as a consequence of Condition 3 of Definition 3. For the same reason, if $i \neq j$, $a_{i,j} = \mathcal{L}_{i,i}\mathcal{F}_{i,j} + \mathcal{L}_{i,j}\mathcal{F}_{j,j} + \sum_{\substack{\ell \neq i \\ \ell \neq j}} \mathcal{L}_{i,\ell}\mathcal{F}_{\ell,j}$ and then $a_{i,j} = \mathcal{L}_{i,j} + \mathcal{F}_{i,j}$.   □

Finally, the last thing to update to EGFNs is the equivalence relation. The definition of two equivalent EGFNs $\mathcal{M}$ and $\mathcal{M}'$ is the same as for GFNs, the only difference being that $\mathcal{M}$ and $\mathcal{M}'$ now also have I coefficients. In other words, a conjugating element π of $\mathcal{M}$ and $\mathcal{M}'$ exchanges the positions of F's, as well as the positions of I's but it cannot exchange an F and an I. The analogous of Theorem 3 is straightforward.

Theorem 6. *Let $\mathcal{M} = \mathcal{PLF}$ and $\mathcal{M}' = \mathcal{P}'\mathcal{L}'\mathcal{F}'$ be two equivalent EGFNs defined by Definition 3. Let also π be such that $\pi\mathcal{M}\pi^{-1} = \mathcal{M}'$. Then $\pi\mathcal{P}\pi^{-1} = \mathcal{P}'$, $\pi\mathcal{L}\pi^{-1} = \mathcal{L}'$ and $\pi\mathcal{F}\pi^{-1} = \mathcal{F}'$.*

Proof. Same as Theorem 3 by evaluating I, F or both in 0. □

2.2 An Efficient Example

We give here a particular case of EGFN with good full diffusion delay and cheap cost. This EGFN with k blocks is depicted on Figs. 4 and 5. Its diffusion is issued in Theorem 7. Besides Sect. 3 studies the security of this EGFN.

$$\mathcal{M} = \begin{pmatrix}
 & & & & F & 1 & & & & \\
 & (0) & & F & I & & 1 & & & \\
 & & \iddots & & I & & & \ddots & & \\
 & F & & (0) & \vdots & & & & 1 & \\
F & I & I & \cdots & I & & & & & 1 \\
1 & & & & & & & & & \\
 & 1 & & & & & & & & \\
 & & \ddots & & & & & (0) & & \\
 & & & 1 & & & & & & \\
 & & & & 1 & & & & &
\end{pmatrix}$$

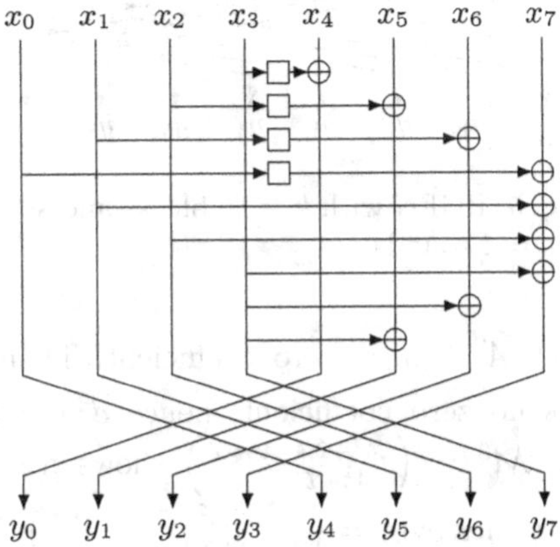

Fig. 4. EGFN matrix $\mathcal{M}$ (left) with $s = \frac{k}{2}$ round-functions with the corresponding diagram (right) that reaches full diffusion in $d = 4$ rounds.

Theorem 7. *For an even integer k, let $\mathcal{M}$ be the k-block EGFN defined on Fig. 4 and let d be its full diffusion delay. Then if $k = 2$ then $d = 2$ and if $k \geq 4$ then $d = 4$.*

Proof. Write $\mathcal{M} = \left(\begin{smallmatrix} \mathcal{A} & \mathcal{I} \\ \mathcal{I} & 0 \end{smallmatrix}\right) \in \mathbb{Z}[F, I]$ where $\mathcal{I}$ stands for the $\frac{k}{2} \times \frac{k}{2}$ identity matrix and the upper left quarter of $\mathcal{M}$ is $\mathcal{M}$ is $\mathcal{A} = \begin{pmatrix}
 & & & & F \\
 & (0) & & F & I \\
 & & \iddots & & I \\
 & F & & (0) & \vdots \\
F & I & I & \cdots & I
\end{pmatrix}$. Note

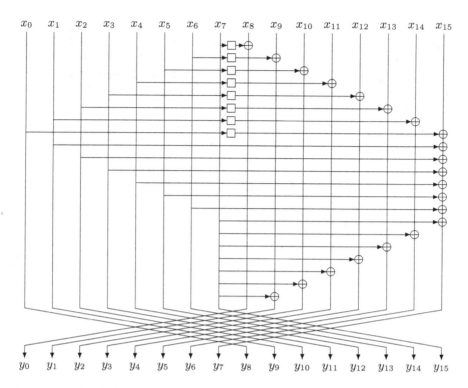

Fig. 5. EGFN with $k = 16$ blocks and $s = 8$ round-functions that reaches full diffusion in $d = 4$ rounds.

that $\mathcal{A}^2$ has no zero coefficient. Then $\mathcal{M}^2 = \begin{pmatrix} \mathcal{A}^2+\mathcal{I} & \mathcal{A} \\ \mathcal{A} & \mathcal{I} \end{pmatrix}$. If $k = 2$ then $\mathcal{M}^2$ has no zero coefficient, hence $d^+ = 2$. But if $k > 2$, it still has. Computing $\mathcal{M}^3 = \begin{pmatrix} \mathcal{A}^3+2\mathcal{A} & \mathcal{A}^2+\mathcal{I} \\ \mathcal{A}^2+\mathcal{I} & \mathcal{A} \end{pmatrix}$ shows it still has zero coefficients, as $\mathcal{A}$ does. Compute then $\mathcal{M}^4 = \begin{pmatrix} \mathcal{A}^4+3\mathcal{A}^2+\mathcal{I} & \mathcal{A}^3+2\mathcal{A} \\ \mathcal{A}^3+2\mathcal{A} & \mathcal{A}^2+\mathcal{I} \end{pmatrix}$. Thus $\mathcal{M}^4$ has no zero coefficient, hence if $k \geq 4$, $d^+ = 4$. To conclude, just note that $\mathcal{M}^{-1} = \begin{pmatrix} 0 & \mathcal{I} \\ \mathcal{I} & -\mathcal{A} \end{pmatrix}$, which implies $d^- = d^+ = d$. □

Thanks to Theorem 7, we then have a family of EGFNs with $s = \frac{k}{2}$ round-functions and a diffusion delay of $d = 4$, thus with total cost $c = 2k$. In comparison, [30] gives a family of Type-2 GFNs that diffuse in $d = 2\log_2 k$ rounds. Their total cost is then $c = k\log_2 k$. For $k > 4$, we achieve full diffusion at a cheaper cost than they do.

3   Security Analysis of Our Proposed Feistel Scheme

As done in [30], we analyze the proposed scheme with essentially $k = 8$ and $k = 16$ as parameters regarding first the pseudorandomness of the scheme and second its resistance to classical attacks.

3.1 Pseudorandomness

As we have defined a new block cipher structure, it is legitimate to introduce the pseudo-random-permutation advantage (prp-advantage) and the strong-pseudo-random-permutation advantage (sprp-advantage) of an adversary as done in several works such as [10,16,21]. For this purpose, we introduce the two advantage notations as:

$$\text{Adv}_C^{\text{prp}}(q) =_{\text{def}} \max_{A:q\text{-CPA}} \left| \Pr[A^C = 1] - \Pr[A^{P_n} = 1] \right| \tag{1}$$

$$\text{Adv}_C^{\text{sprp}}(q) =_{\text{def}} \max_{A:q\text{-CCA}} \left| \Pr[A^{C,C^{-1}} = 1] - \Pr[A^{P_n,P_n^{-1}} = 1] \right| \tag{2}$$

where C is the encryption function of an n-bit block cipher composed of uniform random functions (URFs) as internal modules [16] whereas C^{-1} is its inverse; P_n is an n-bit uniform random permutation (URP) uniformly distributed among all the n-bit permutations; P_n^{-1} is its inverse. The adversary, A, tries to distinguish C from P_n using q queries in a CPA (Chosen Plaintext Attack) attack and tries to distinguish, always using q queries, (C, C^{-1}) from (P_n, P_n^{-1}) in a CCA (Chosen Ciphertext Attack) attack. The notation means that the final guess of the adversary A is either 0 if A thinks that the computations are done using P_n, or 1 if A thinks that the computations are done using C. The maximums of Eqs. (1,2) are taken over all possible adversaries A with q queries and an unbounded computational power. Many results [10,16,21] have appear evaluating the security of Feistel variants in this model. For example, Luby and Rackoff in their seminal work [16] proved the security of a $2n$-bit classical Feistel cipher with 3 rounds in the prp model and with 4 rounds in the sprp model considering that the classical Feistel cipher is composed of n-bit-to-n-bit URFs (the bounds they found are in $\mathcal{O}(q^2/2^n)$ for both cases). Those initial results have been generalized in many ways [19,33].

To prove the bounds of our scheme in those models, we follow the methodology of [30] based on the results of [20]. To do so, we introduce the following notations: Let $\Phi_{kn,r}$ denote our k-block scheme acting on n-bit blocks, using r rounds and with diffusion delay d. We first introduce the following definition that will be useful for the next lemma:

Definition 5. *Let H be a keyed permutation over $(\{0,1\}^n)^k$ and let $\boldsymbol{x} = (x_0, \cdots, x_{k-1}) \in (\{0,1\}^n)^k$ with $\boldsymbol{x}_{[i]} = x_i$. H is said to be an ϵ-AU (ϵ Almost Universal) function if:*

$$\max_{\boldsymbol{x} \neq \boldsymbol{x}'} \Pr[H(\boldsymbol{x})_{[i]} = H(\boldsymbol{x}')_{[i]}, \text{for } i \in \{0, \cdots, k-1\}] \leq \epsilon$$

Lemma 1. *Let H and H' be two keyed permutations over $(\{0,1\}^n)^k$ that are respectively ϵ-AU and ϵ'-AU; Let denote by $\Phi_{kn,r}$ our r-round EGFN with k branches acting on n-bit blocks with a diffusion delay d where all n-bit round-functions are independent URFs. Then we have:*

$$\text{Adv}^{\text{prp}}_{\Phi_{kn,2} \circ H}(q) \leq \left(\epsilon + \frac{k}{2^n}\right) \cdot \binom{q}{2} \tag{3}$$

$$\text{Adv}^{\text{sprp}}_{H'^{-1} \circ \Phi_{kn,2} \circ H}(q) \leq \left(\epsilon + \epsilon' + \frac{k}{2^{n-1}}\right) \cdot \binom{q}{2} \tag{4}$$

Proof. Intuitively, for Eq. (3), this lemma uses the fact that after the application of H the inputs of function $\Phi_{kn,2}$ are sufficiently distinct and are random strings. We then have rare collisions at the outputs of $\Phi_{kn,2}$. For Eq. (4), same arguments hold in both directions. The proof of this lemma is omitted as it is similar to those of Theorem 3.1 and Theorem 3.2 of [22] or is a direct extension of Lemma 9 and Theorem 7 of [19].   □

Theorem 8. *Given the r-round EGFN $\Phi_{kn,r}$ with k branches acting on n-bit blocks with a diffusion delay d where all n-bit round functions are independent URFs. Then we have:*

$$\text{Adv}^{\text{prp}}_{\Phi_{kn,d+2}}(q) \leq \frac{kd}{2^n} q^2 \tag{5}$$

$$\text{Adv}^{\text{sprp}}_{\Phi_{kn,2d+2}}(q) \leq \frac{kd}{2^{n-1}} q^2 \tag{6}$$

Proof. To demonstrate Theorem 8, we have first to show that $\Phi_{kn,d}$ is an ϵ-AU function and second that $\overline{\Phi_{kn,d}}$ which is $\Phi^{-1}_{kn,d}$ without the final shuffle is also an ϵ-AU function.

Let us first demonstrate (as done in [30]) that

$$\Pr[\Phi_{kn,d}(\mathbf{x})_{[i]} = \Phi_{kn,d}(\mathbf{x'})_{[i]}] \leq \frac{d}{2^n}, \text{ for all } i \in \{0, \cdots, k-1\}] \tag{7}$$

We assume that $(x_{k/2-1}, x_{k/2-2}, x_{k/2+1}) \neq (x'_{k/2-1}, x'_{k/2-2}, x'_{k/2+1})$, without loss of generality. We then estimate the probability that $\Phi_{kn,d}(\mathbf{x})_{[0]} = \Phi_{kn,d}(\mathbf{x'})_{[0]}$. By definition of d, there is an appropriate path of length d on the graph of $\Phi_{kn,d}$ starting and finishing at vertex 0. For $h = 1, \cdots, d$, we can define a sequence of internal inputs $Y_h = \Phi_{kn,h}(\mathbf{x})_{[s(h)]}$ following the appropriate path. It is straightforward to see that $\Pr[Y_1 = Y'_1] = \Pr[F(x_{k/2-2}) \oplus x_{k/2-1} \oplus x_{k/2+1} = F(x'_{k/2-2}) \oplus x'_{k/2-1} \oplus x_{k/2+1}] \leq 1/2^n$ because the round function F is a URF (using the same reasoning, this result also holds for probabilities of the other branches, even the branch x_{k-1} due to the presence of an F function). Then, $\Pr[Y_d = Y'_d]$ is over bounded by $\sum_{j=2}^{d} \Pr[Y_j = Y'_j | Y_{j-1} \neq Y'_{j-1}] + \Pr[Y_1 = Y'_1] \leq d/2^n$ because all round functions are independent, i.e. $\Pr[Y_j = Y'_j | Y_{j-1} \neq Y'_{j-1}] \leq 1/2^n$. This proves Eq. (7). Thus, $\Phi_{kn,h}$ is a $\frac{kd}{2^n}$-AU function. Equation (5) of Theorem 8 is straightforwardly proved using Eq. (3) of Lemma 1.

To prove the second equation of Theorem 8, we use exactly the same reasoning on $\overline{\Phi_{kn,d}}$ to show that $\Pr[Y_d = Y'_d] \leq d/2^n$ with $Y_h = \overline{\Phi_{kn,h}}(\mathbf{x})_{[s(h)]}$ for $h = 1, \cdots, d$. We then deduce that $\overline{\Phi_{kn,d}}$ is a $\frac{kd}{2^n}$-AU function. Combining the fact that $\Phi_{kn,d}$ is a $\frac{kd}{2^n}$-AU function and that $\overline{\Phi_{kn,d}}$ is a $\frac{kd}{2^n}$-AU function through Eq. (4) of Lemma 1, we obtain Eq. (6).   □

3.2 Evaluation of Security Against Classical Attacks

Differential/Linear Cryptanalysis. Differential and linear cryptanalysis are the most famous attacks on block ciphers. They have been introduced respectively in [5] and in [18]. Since their discovery, many works have been done to first show the links between both forms of cryptanalysis [8] and to find better ways to prevent those attacks from happening for a given cipher [9]. The usual consensus about this last point is to count the minimal number of active S-boxes crossed all along the cipher by differential and linear characteristics and thus to estimate the induced maximal differential/linear probability, under the independence assumption.

If the maximal differential/linear probability of an S-box is denoted by DP/LP and if the minimal number of active S-boxes is N, then the best differential/linear attack against the cipher has a complexity of about $1/(DP^N)$ (resp. $1/(LP^N)$) operations. Thus, a cipher is supposed to be secure against differential/linear cryptanalysis as soon as $1/(DP^N)$ (resp. $1/(LP^N)$) is greater than the entire codebook, equal here to 2^{kn}.

In Table 3, we evaluate the minimal number of active S-boxes up to 20 rounds for our scheme and compare it the results of [30] for their optimal construction. We obtain a greater number of active S-boxes in our case.

Table 3. Number of active S-boxes for every round compared with results of [30].

Round	1	2	3	4	5	6	7	8	9	10	11	12	13	14	15	16	17	18	19	20
$k = 8$ [30]	0	1	2	3	4	6	8	10	12	12	14	16	16	18	20	20	22	24	24	26
$k = 8$ Ours	0	1	2	6	9	9	12	14	15	19	19	22	24	25	29	29	32	34	35	39
$k = 16$ [30]	0	1	2	3	4	6	8	11	14	19	21	24	25	27	30	31	33	36	37	39
$k = 16$ Ours	0	1	2	10	17	17	18	26	33	33	34	42	49	49	50	58	65	65	66	74

Finally, if we want to estimate the number of rounds that could be attacked using differential/linear cryptanalysis, we could estimate DP and LP for classical n-bit S-box construction, i.e. we write F the internal n-bit function as $F(x) = S(K \oplus x)$ where K is a subkey different at each round. We have the following bounds on DP and LP for such an F function: if we assume n is even, then DP and LP are over bounded by 2^{-n+2}; if n is odd then DP and LP are over bounded by 2^{-n+1}. For example, if we assume that F works on 8-bit words with $k = 8$, our scheme ciphers 64-bit plaintexts. We have $DP = LP = 2^{-6}$ and the maximal number of active S-boxes that could be crossed is equal to 10 to have $2^{64} > 1/(DP^N) = 2^{6 \cdot 10}$. From Table 3, we could deduce that, under those hypotheses, our scheme is resistant to differential/linear cryptanalysis as soon as 7 rounds have been performed. In the same way, with $k = 16$ and $n = 4$, $DP = LP = 2^{-2}$, the maximal number of S-boxes that could be crossed is equal to 31 and at least 9 rounds of our 16 branches scheme must at least be performed.

The total number of rounds to perform for preventing differential/linear attacks is smaller than the one required for the schemes proposed in [30] because the number of S-boxes crossed at each round is more important.

Integral Attack. In [15] L. Knudsen and D. Wagner analyze integral cryptanalysis as a dual to differential attacks particularly applicable to block ciphers with bijective components. A first-order integral cryptanalysis considers a particular collection of m words in the plaintexts and ciphertexts that differ on a particular component. The aim of this attack is thus to predict the values in the sums (i.e. the integral) of the chosen words after a certain number of rounds of encryption. The same authors also generalize this approach to higher-order integrals: the original set to consider becomes a set of ml vectors which differ in l components and where the sum of this set is predictable after a certain number of rounds. The sum of this set is called an lth-order integral. In [27], the authors improve the already known results in the case of Feistel structure noticing that computations of the XOR sum of the partial decryptions can be divided into two independent parts through a meet-in-the-middle approach. We define the following properties for a set of 2^n n-bit words:

- 'C' (for Constant) in the ith entry, means that the values of all the ith words in the collection of texts are equal.
- 'A' (for All) means that all words in the collection of texts are different.
- '?' means that the sum of words can not be predicted.
- 'B' (for Balanced) means that the sum of all words taken on a particular word is equal to 0.

Integral characteristics are of the form $(\alpha \to \beta)$ with $\alpha \in \{C, A\}^k$ containing at least one A and $\beta \in \{C, A, ?, B\}^k$ containing at least one A or one C or one B. To find integral characteristics, we apply the method and the properties described in [6]. We first look at characteristics α containing exactly one A subblock, the other ones being C. By definition of d, the state after d rounds does not contain C. If we assume that the state after d rounds contains two As for the most favorable n-bit blocks, say i and j (for example blocks with indices $k/2 - 1$ and $k - 1$), then by adding one more round, the state at the subblock $s = \mathcal{P}(j)$ becomes a $B = (F(A) \oplus A)$ or a $B = (F(A) \oplus A \oplus A)$ subblock for the simplest transformations, the other transformations straightforwardly give same kind of results. After one more round, the state at indice $t = \mathcal{P}(s)$ is of the same form because no F function has been crossed. Adding another round transforms this state into a state of the form $? = F(B) \oplus ?$ or $? = F(B) \oplus B \oplus ?$ or more complicated expressions for y_1. Therefore, an integral characteristic (containing one A and $k - 1$ Cs) exists for at most $d + 2$ rounds. If we try to extend at the beginning this first order characteristic into an lth-order characteristic, we could add at most d rounds at the beginning due to the definition of d. Thus, the maximum number of rounds that could be reach by an lth order integral characteristic is $d + d + 2 = 2d + 2$. We confirm this bound by experimental analysis being able to find a first order integral characteristic for at most $d + 2$ rounds.

Impossible Differential Attack. Impossible differential cryptanalysis [4] is a form of differential cryptanalysis for block ciphers. While ordinary differential cryptanalysis tracks differences that propagate through the cipher with a probability as large as possible, impossible differential cryptanalysis exploits differences with 0 probability in intermediate rounds of the cipher to sieve wrong key candidates.

More formally, impossible differential attacks are represented by a differential transition $\alpha \nrightarrow \beta$ with $\alpha, \beta \in (\{0,1\}^n)^k$ for a cipher E with k n-bit blocks with $Pr[E(x) + E(x + \alpha) = \beta] = 0$ for any x. Intuitively, if we want to form an impossible differential transition for our EGFN, we need to first form the first part of the impossible differential on r_1 rounds between the input differential $\alpha^0 = (\alpha_0^0, \cdots, \alpha_{k-1}^0)$ and the output differential after r_1 rounds $\alpha^{r_1} = (\alpha_0^{r_1}, \cdots, \alpha_{k-1}^{r_1})$. Then, we form the second part of the impossible differential in the decryption direction on r_2 rounds between $\beta^0 = (\beta_0^0, \cdots, \beta_{k-1}^0)$ and $\beta^{r_2} = (\beta_0^{r_2}, \cdots, \beta_{k-1}^{r_2})$. Then, the impossible differential on $r_1 + r_2$ rounds is $\alpha^0 \nrightarrow \beta^0$ if the differences α^{r_1} and β^{r_2} are not compatible in the middle of the cipher.

From the $\mathcal{U}$-method of [14] or the UID-method of [17], the differences α^{r_1} and β^{r_2} could be of the types: zero difference (denoted 0), nonzero unfixed difference (denoted δ), non zero fixed difference (denoted γ), exclusive-or of nonzero fixed and nonzero unfixed difference (denoted by $\delta + \gamma$), and unfixed difference (denoted t). As done in [30], we could determine the maximal number of rounds for an impossible differential attack using the $\mathcal{U}$-method described in [14]. This number of rounds mainly depends on d as shown below:

- If α_i^d for i in $\{k/2, \cdots, k-1\}$ has type γ, there exists a data path, P that does not pass through any F (i.e. the equation corresponding to this path does not contain α_i^0 as a part of arguments of F). If α_j^0 for j in $\{0, \cdots, k/2 - 1\}$ has type δ then α_l^{d+1} with $l = \mathcal{P}(i)$ has type $\delta + \gamma$. If β_k^d has type γ, we are able to construct an impossible differential attack on $2d + 1$ rounds.
- If all the data paths pass through at least one F function, then both α^d and β^d do not contain differences of type neither γ nor 0. Thus, we could only mount differences on $d - 1$ rounds for the direct sens (i.e. α difference) and on d rounds for the decryption sens (i.e. β difference). The maximal number of rounds for this type of impossible differential attack is $2d - 1$ rounds.
- By definition of d, there exists α^0 such that α_i^{d-1} has type γ for some i. Similarly, there exists β^0 with β_j^{d-1} has type γ' for some j. If $i = j$ and $\gamma \neq \gamma'$, we can construct an impossible differential attack on $2d - 2$ rounds.

Finally, the implementation of the $\mathcal{U}$-method gives us the same results: the maximal number of rounds for our scheme looking at impossible differential attack is equal to $2d - 2$, $2d - 1$ or $2d + 1$.

4   Conclusion

In this article, we have introduced a generic matrix representation that captures most existing Generalized Feistel Networks. We explained diffusion properties of those schemes through this representation. We then introduce a new kind of schemes called Extended Generalized Feistel Networks that adds a diffusion layer to the classical GFNs. We finally instantiated this class of schemes into two proposals and proved the security of them under classical security and attack models.

Our further work will be to propose a complete block cipher using small S-boxes for round-functions and based on our EGFNs proposals that have proved security bounds and provide a more efficient diffusion with a reasonable additional cost, and confront our theoretical study to the ruthless world of cryptanalysis and of cryptanalysts.

References

1. Adams, C., Gilchrist, J.: The CAST-256 encryption algorithm. Network Working Group, RFC 2612, June 1999. http://tools.ietf.org/html/rfc2612 (1999)
2. Aoki, K., Ichikawa, T., Kanda, M., Matsui, M., Moriai, S., Nakajima, J., Tokita, T.: Camellia: a 128-bit block cipher suitable for multiple platforms - design and analysis. In: Stinson, D.R., Tavares, S. (eds.) SAC 2000. LNCS, vol. 2012, pp. 39–56. Springer, Heidelberg (2001)
3. Arnault, F., Berger, T.P., Minier, M., Pousse, B.: Revisiting LFSRs for cryptographic applications. IEEE Trans. Info. Theory 57(12), 8095–8113 (2011)
4. Biham, E., Biryukov, A., Shamir, A.: Cryptanalysis of skipjack reduced to 31 rounds using impossible differentials. In: Stern, J. (ed.) EUROCRYPT 1999. LNCS, vol. 1592, pp. 12–23. Springer, Heidelberg (1999)
5. Biham, E., Shamir, A.: Differential cryptanalysis of DES-like cryptosystems. In: Menezes, A., Vanstone, S.A. (eds.) CRYPTO 1990. LNCS, vol. 537, pp. 2–21. Springer, Heidelberg (1991)
6. Biryukov, A., Shamir, A.: Structural cryptanalysis of SASAS. In: Pfitzmann, B. (ed.) EUROCRYPT 2001. LNCS, vol. 2045, pp. 394–405. Springer, Heidelberg (2001)
7. Burwick, C., Coppersmith, D., D'Avignon, E., Gennaro, R., Halevi, S., Jutla, C., Matyas Jr, S.M., O'Connor, L., Peyravian, M., Stafford, D., Zunic, N.: MARS - a candidate cipher for AES. NIST AES Proposal (1999)
8. Chabaud, F., Vaudenay, S.: Links between differential and linear cryptanalysis. In: De Santis, A. (ed.) EUROCRYPT 1994. LNCS, vol. 950, pp. 356–365. Springer, Heidelberg (1995)
9. FIPS 197. Advanced encryption standard. Federal Information Processing Standards Publication 197, Department of Commerce/N.I.S.T., U.S. (2001)
10. Gilbert, H., Minier, M.: New results on the pseudorandomness of some blockcipher constructions. In: Matsui, M. (ed.) FSE 2001. LNCS, vol. 2355, pp. 248–266. Springer, Heidelberg (2002)
11. Hirose, S., Kuwakado, H., Yoshida, H.: SHA-3 Proposal: Lesamnta. http://www.hitachi.com/rd/yrl/crypto/lesamnta/index.html (2008)
12. Hoang, V.T., Rogaway, P.: On generalized feistel networks. In: Rabin, T. (ed.) CRYPTO 2010. LNCS, vol. 6223, pp. 613–630. Springer, Heidelberg (2010)
13. Hong, D., Sung, J., Hong, S.H., Lim, J.-I., Lee, S.-J., Koo, B.-S., Lee, C.-H., Chang, D., Lee, J., Jeong, K., Kim, H., Kim, J.-S., Chee, S.: HIGHT: a new block cipher suitable for low-resource device. In: Goubin, L., Matsui, M. (eds.) CHES 2006. LNCS, vol. 4249, pp. 46–59. Springer, Heidelberg (2006)

14. Kim, J., Hong, S., Lim, J.: Impossible differential cryptanalysis using matrix method. Discrete Math. **310**(5), 988–1002 (2010)
15. Knudsen, L.R., Wagner, D.: Integral cryptanalysis. In: Daemen, J., Rijmen, V. (eds.) FSE 2002. LNCS, vol. 2365, pp. 112–127. Springer, Heidelberg (2002)
16. Luby, M., Rackoff, C.: How to construct pseudorandom permutations from pseudorandom functions. SIAM J. Comput. **17**(2), 373–386 (1988)
17. Luo, Y., Wu, Z., Lai, X., Gong, G.: A unified method for finding impossible differentials of block cipher structures. IACR Cryptology ePrint Archive 2009:627 (2009)
18. Matsui, M.: Linear cryptanalysis method for DES cipher. In: Helleseth, T. (ed.) EUROCRYPT 1993. LNCS, vol. 765, pp. 386–397. Springer, Heidelberg (1994)
19. Maurer, U.M.: Indistinguishability of random systems. In: Knudsen, L.R. (ed.) EUROCRYPT 2002. LNCS, vol. 2332, pp. 110–132. Springer, Heidelberg (2002)
20. Mitsuda, A., Iwata, T.: Tweakable pseudorandom permutation from generalized feistel structure. In: Baek, J., Bao, F., Chen, K., Lai, X. (eds.) ProvSec 2008. LNCS, vol. 5324, pp. 22–37. Springer, Heidelberg (2008)
21. Moriai, S., Vaudenay, S.: On the pseudorandomness of top-level schemes of block ciphers. In: Okamoto, T. (ed.) ASIACRYPT 2000. LNCS, vol. 1976, pp. 289–302. Springer, Heidelberg (2000)
22. Naor, M., Reingold, O.: On the construction of pseudorandom permutations: Luby-Rackoff revisited. J. Cryptol. **12**(1), 29–66 (1999)
23. National Bureau of Standards: U.S. Department of Commerce. Data Encryption Standard (1977)
24. Nyberg, K.: Generalized feistel networks. In: Kim, K., Matsumoto, T. (eds.) ASIACRYPT 1996. LNCS, vol. 1163, pp. 91–104. Springer, Heidelberg (1996)
25. Rivest, R.L.:. A description of the RC2(r) encryption algorithm. Network Working Group, RFC 2268, March 1998. http://tools.ietf.org/html/rfc2268 (1998)
26. Rivest, R.L., Robshaw, M.J.B., Sidney, R., Yin, Y.L.: The RC6 block cipher, august 1998. http://people.csail.mit.edu/rivest/pubs/RRSY98.pdf (1998)
27. Sasaki, Y., Wang, L.: Meet-in-the-middle technique for integral attacks against feistel ciphers. In: Knudsen, L.R., Wu, H. (eds.) SAC 2012. LNCS, vol. 7707, pp. 234–251. Springer, Heidelberg (2013)
28. Shirai, T., Shibutani, K., Akishita, T., Moriai, S., Iwata, T.: The 128-bit blockcipher CLEFIA (Extended Abstract). In: Biryukov, A. (ed.) FSE 2007. LNCS, vol. 4593, pp. 181–195. Springer, Heidelberg (2007)
29. SHS. Secure hash standard. In: FIPS PUB 180-4, Federal Information Processing Standards Publication (2012)
30. Suzaki, T., Minematsu, K.: Improving the generalized feistel. In: Hong, S., Iwata, T. (eds.) FSE 2010. LNCS, vol. 6147, pp. 19–39. Springer, Heidelberg (2010)
31. Suzaki, T., Minematsu, K., Morioka, S., Kobayashi, E.: TWINE: a lightweight block cipher for multiple platforms. In: Knudsen, L.R., Wu, H. (eds.) SAC 2012. LNCS, vol. 7707, pp. 339–354. Springer, Heidelberg (2013)
32. Yanagihara, S., Iwata, T.: Improving the permutation layer of Type 1, Type 3, Source-Heavy, and Target-Heavy generalized feistel structures. IEICE Trans. **96–A**(1), 2–14 (2013)
33. Zheng, Y., Matsumoto, T., Imai, H.: On the construction of block ciphers provably secure and not relying on any unproved hypotheses. In: Brassard, G. (ed.) CRYPTO 1989. LNCS, vol. 435, pp. 461–480. Springer, Heidelberg (1990)

Zero-Correlation Linear Cryptanalysis with FFT and Improved Attacks on ISO Standards Camellia and CLEFIA

Andrey Bogdanov[1](✉), Huizheng Geng[2](✉), Meiqin Wang[2](✉), Long Wen[2](✉), and Baudoin Collard[3]

[1] Technical University of Denmark, Kongens Lyngby, Denmark
anbog@dtu.dk
[2] Key Laboratory of Cryptologic Technology and Information Security,
Ministry of Education, Shandong University, Jinan 250100, China
{huizhenggeng,longwen}@mail.sdu.edu.cn, mqwang@sdu.edu.cn
[3] Université Catholique de Louvain, Louvain-la-Neuve, Belgium

Abstract. Zero-correlation linear cryptanalysis is based on the linear approximations with correlation exactly zero, which essentially generalizes the integral property, and has already been applied to several block ciphers — among others, yielding best known attacks to date on round-reduced TEA and CAST-256 as published in FSE'12 and ASIACRYPT'12, respectively.

In this paper, we use the FFT (Fast Fourier Transform) technique to speed up the zero-correlation cryptanalysis. First, this allows us to improve upon the state-of-the-art cryptanalysis for the ISO/IEC standard and CRYPTREC-portfolio cipher Camellia. Namely, we present zero-correlation attacks on 11-round Camellia-128 and 12-round Camellia-192 with FL/FL^{-1} and whitening key starting from the first round, which is an improvement in the number of attacked rounds in both cases. Moreover, we provide multidimensional zero-correlation cryptanalysis of 14-round CLEFIA-192 and 15-round CLEFIA-256 that are attacks on the highest numbers of rounds in the classical single-key setting, respectively, with improvements in memory complexity.

Keywords: Block cipher · Zero-correlation cryptanalysis · FFT · Multidimesional linear cryptanalysis · Camellia · CLEFIA

1 Introduction

Zero-correlation linear cryptanalysis proposed by Bogdanov and Rijmen in [2] has its theoretical foundation in the availability of numerous key-independent unbiased linear approximations with correlation zero for many ciphers. (If p is the probability for a linear approximation to hold, its correlation is defined as $c = 2p - 1$). Though the initial distinguisher of [2] had some limitations in terms of data complexity, they were overcome in the FSE'12 paper [3], where the existence of multiple linear approximations with correlation zero in target ciphers

T. Lange, K. Lauter, and P. Lisoněk (Eds.): SAC 2013, LNCS 8282, pp. 306–323, 2014.
DOI: 10.1007/978-3-662-43414-7_16, © Springer-Verlag Berlin Heidelberg 2014

was used to propose a more data-efficient distinguisher. This resulted in improved attacks on reduced-round TEA and XTEA. The zero-correlation attack on 21 (resp. 23) rounds of TEA remains the attack breaking most rounds of TEA in the single secret-key setting. In a follow-up work at ASIACRYPT'12 [4], zero-correlation cryptanalysis was shown to apply to CAST-256 and to break the highest number of rounds here as well. Moreover, fundamental links of integral cryptanalysis to zero-correlation cryptanalysis have been revealed. Namely, integrals (similar to saturation or multiset distinguishers) have been demonstrated to be essentially a special case of the zero-correlation property. On top of that, a multidimensional distinguisher has been constructed for the zero-correlation property, which removed the unnecessary independency assumptions on the distinguishing side.

While the question of coping with the data requirements of zero-correlation distinguishers has been studied in detail, the *key recovery techniques* used so far on top of those statistical distinguishers remain quite rudimentary. To attack as many rounds as possible, the attackers choose to span the zero-correlation property over a high number of rounds, which usually yields a decrease in the number of zero-correlation linear approximations available. Moreover, for the same reason, the cryptanalysts tend to partially encrypt/decrypt over as many rounds as possible, which gives a high number of (sub)key bits that need to be guessed. Now, in a cryptanalytic effort based on correlation zero, one has to evaluate the sample correlation of all linear approximations (usually, a rather low number) for all plaintext-ciphertext pairs (usually, a significantly higher number) and all key guesses (which can be very high). In terms of computational complexity, this is the bottle neck of zero-correlation attacks so far. And this is exactly the point where the Discrete Fast Fourier Transform comes in handy.

Contributions. The contributions of this paper are three-fold:

Zero-correlation cryptanalysis with FFT: We use Discrete Fast Fourier Transform — that has been previosly used in linear cryptanalysis in [7] — to improve the time complexity of zero-correlation attacks. It relies on eliminating the redundant computations from the partial encryption/decryption in the course of zero-correlation key recovery. For that, an auxiliary $\{-1, 1\}$-matrix with a level-circulant structure is defined such that the evaluation of the sample correlation can be done by matrix-vector multiplication for different keys. By making use of this special structure, the matrix-vector multiplication can be computed efficiently with FFT. This technique is described in Sect. 3.

Improved cryptanalysis of Camellia: We apply this FFT technique to the block cipher Camellia and obtain an improvement in the number of attacked rounds for Camellia-128 and Camellia-192.

Camellia is a block cipher jointly proposed by Mitsubishi and NTT in 2000 [1]. It was adopted as international standard by ISO/IEC [8]. Camellia is a CRYPTREC-recommended cipher for Japanese e-Government applications and is a part of the NESSIE project portfolio. It has a 128-bit block and supports a variable key size. The number of rounds depends on the key size: 18 rounds for 128-bit keys, 24 rounds for 192-bit keys, and 24 rounds for 256-bit keys. The basic Feistel structure is used and a logical keyed transformation layer FL/FL^{-1} is applied every six rounds.

Camellia has received a great deal of attention from cryptanalysts with dozens of attacks on reduced-round variants published alone in the recent years. However, to be able to claim more attacked rounds, most of the existing attacks do not consider FL/FL^{-1} and whitening key. Moreover, some of them only include FL/FL^{-1} but no whitening keys. As opposed to that, in this paper, we only discuss attacks on *Camellia with FL/FL^{-1} and whitening key starting from the first round*. Rather recently, some attacks on reduced-round Camellia with FL/FL^{-1} and whitening key have been introduced [6,11,12]. In this setting, the best attack on Camellia-128 is the impossible differential attack on 10 rounds [11]. A similar attack can break 11 rounds of Camellia-192 [11].

Table 1. Summary of attacks on Camellia with FL/FL^{-1} and whitening key

Key	Attack Type	Rounds	Data	Time (*Ens.*)	Memory (*Bytes*)	Source
128	Imp. Diff	10	$2^{113.8}$CPs	$2^{120.0}$	$2^{84.8}$	[11]
	ZC. FFT	**11**	$2^{125.3}$**KPs**	$2^{125.8}$	$2^{112.0}$	Sect. 4.2
192	Imp. Diff	10	$2^{121.0}$CPs	$2^{175.3}$	$2^{155.2}$	[6]
	Imp. Diff	10	$2^{118.7}$CPs	$2^{130.4}$	$2^{135.0}$	[9]
	Imp. Diff	11	$2^{114.6}$CPs	$2^{184.0}$	$2^{141.6}$	[11]
	ZC. FFT	**12**	$2^{125.7}$**KPs**	$2^{188.8}$	$2^{112.0}$	Sect. 4.3

CPs: Chosen Plaintexts, KPs: Known Plaintexts

In this paper, with the FFT zero-correlation technique, we propose an attack on 11 rounds of Camellia-128. Moreover, we propose an FFT zero-correlation attack on 12-round Camellia-192, while previously only 11 rounds could be attacked. The attacks are given in Sect. 4. Our improvements upon the state-of-the-art cryptanalysis for Camellia are summarized in Table 1.

Improved cryptanalysis of CLEFIA: Multidimensional zero-correlation attacks on 14-round CLEFIA-192 and 15-round CLEFIA-256 with better memory complexities than the currently best published cryptanalysis are reported, while the time and data complexities are almost identical, featuring a rather high data complexity though.

CLEFIA is a block cipher proposed in 2007 by Sony Corporation [15] and has been adopted as ISO/IEC international standard in lightweight cryptography. The block size is 128 bits and the key size is 128, 192, or 256 bits. The numbers of rounds for CLEFIA-128, CLEFIA-192 and CLEFIA-256 are 18, 22 and 26, respectively. Despite CLEFIA's relatively recent publication, the cryptanalysts have been active attacking it [10,17–20] with the best attack to date being the improbable differential cryptanalysis that can break 14-round CLEFIA-192 and 15-round CLEFIA-256 [16].

With the multidimensional zero-correlation cryptanalysis, we can attack 14-round CLEFIA-192 and 15-round CLEFIA-256 with significantly reduced

Table 2. Summary of attacks on CLEFIA

Key size	Attack type	Rounds	Data	Time ($Ens.$)	Memory ($Bytes$)	Source
192	Imp. Diff	13	$2^{111.8}$CPs	2^{155}	2^{116}	[18]
	Imp. Diff	13	$2^{116.6}$CPs	2^{171}	2^{101}	[18]
	Imp. Diff	13	$2^{108.6}$CPs	2^{179}	2^{113}	[18]
	Imp. Diff	13	$2^{108.6}$CPs	2^{171}	2^{109}	[18]
	Integral	13	2^{113}CPs	$2^{180.5}$	N/A	[10]
	Imp. Diff	13	$2^{119.8}$CPs	2^{146}	2^{120}	[17]
	Improbable	14	$2^{127.0}$CPs	$2^{183.2}$	$2^{127.0}$	[16]
	Multidim. ZC	**14**	$2^{127.5}$**KPs**	$2^{180.2}$	2^{115}	Sect. 5.3
256	Imp. Diff	14	$2^{112.3}$CPs	2^{220}	2^{117}	[18]
	Imp. Diff	14	$2^{117.0}$CPs	2^{236}	2^{121}	[18]
	Imp. Diff	14	$2^{109.0}$CPs	2^{244}	2^{113}	[18]
	Imp. Diff	14	$2^{109.0}$CPs	2^{236}	2^{113}	[18]
	Integral	14	2^{113}CPs	$2^{244.5}$	N/A	[10]
	Imp. Diff	14	$2^{120.3}$CPs	2^{212}	2^{121}	[17]
	Improbable	15	$2^{127.4}$CPs	$2^{247.5}$	$2^{127.4}$	[16]
	Multidim. ZC	**15**	$2^{127.5}$**KPs**	$2^{244.2}$	2^{115}	Sect. 5.4

CPs: Chosen Plaintexts, KPs: Known Plaintexts

memory complexities, while keeping the time and data complexities virtually unchanged. The results are given in Sect. 5 and are outlined in Table 2.

Organization of the Paper. The remainder of this paper is organized as follows. Section 2 recalls the techniques of zero-correlation linear cryptanalysis. Section 3 describes how to use Fast Fourier Transform in zero-correlation linear cryptanalysis. Section 4 derives the zero-correlation linear cryptanalysis with FFT of 11-round Camellia-128 and 12-round Camellia-192. Section 5 reports the multidimensional zero-correlation linear cryptanalysis of 14-round CLEFIA-192 and 15-round CLEFIA-256. We conclude in Section 6.

2 Preliminaries

In this section, we briefly recall what zero-correlation linear approximations are (Subsect. 2.1) and how they can be used to build distinguishers for block ciphers with multiple zero-correlation approximations (Subsect. 2.2) and a multidimensional approach (Subsect. 2.3). This summarizes the state-of-the-art of zero-correlation cryptanalysis.

2.1 Basics of Zero-Correlation Linear Cryptanalysis

Consider an n-bit block cipher f_K with key K. Let P denote a plaintext which is mapped to a ciphertext C under key K, $C = f_K(P)$ [2]. If Γ_P and Γ_C are nonzero plaintext and ciphertext linear masks of n bits each, we denote by $\Gamma_P \rightarrow \Gamma_C$ the linear approximation $\Gamma_P^T \cdot P \oplus \Gamma_C^T \cdot C = 0$. Here, $\Gamma_A^T \cdot A$ denotes the multiplication of the transposed bit vector Γ_A by a column bit vector A over $\mathbb{F}_2$. The linear approximation $\Gamma_P \rightarrow \Gamma_C$ has probability

$$p_{\Gamma_P, \Gamma_C} = \Pr_{P \in \mathbb{F}_2^n} \{\Gamma_P^T \cdot P \oplus \Gamma_C^T \cdot C = 0\}.$$

The value $c_{\Gamma_P, \Gamma_C} = 2p_{\Gamma_P, \Gamma_C} - 1$ is called the *correlation* of linear approximation $\Gamma_P \rightarrow \Gamma_C$. Note that $p_{\Gamma_P, \Gamma_C} = 1/2$ is equivalent to *zero correlation* $c_{\Gamma_P, \Gamma_C} = 0$.

Given a distinguisher of zero-correlation linear approximation(s) over a part of the cipher (detailed upon in the next two subsections), the basic key recovery can be done with a technique similar to that of Matsui's Algorithm 2 [14], partially encrypting/decrypting from the plantext/ciphertext up to the boundaries of the property. This is the key recovery approach used in all zero-correlation attacks so far. In this paper, we aim to improve upon this by using an FFT technique to reduce the computational complexity of attacks.

2.2   Zero-Correlation Linear Cryptanalysis with Multiple Linear Approximations

Let the number of available zero-correlation linear approximations for an n-bit block cipher be denoted by ℓ [3]. Let the number of required known plaintexts be N. For each of the ℓ given linear approximations, the adversary computes the number T_i of times that linear approximation i is fulfilled on N plaintexts and ciphertexts, $i \in \{1, \ldots, \ell\}$. Each T_i suggests an empirical correlation value $\hat{c}_i = 2\frac{T_i}{N} - 1$. Then, the adversary evaluates the statistic:

$$\sum_{i=1}^{\ell} \hat{c}_i^2 = \sum_{i=1}^{\ell} \left(2\frac{T_i}{N} - 1\right)^2.$$

Under a statistical independency assumption, the value $\sum_{i=1}^{\ell} \hat{c}_i^2$ for the right key approximately follows a normal distribution with mean $\mu_0 = \frac{\ell}{N}$ and standard deviation $\sigma_0 = \frac{\sqrt{2\ell}}{N}$ while for the wrong key the distribution is approximately a normal distribution with mean $\mu_1 = \frac{\ell}{N} + \frac{\ell}{2^n}$ and standard deviation $\sigma_1 = \frac{\sqrt{2\ell}}{N} + \frac{\sqrt{2\ell}}{2^n}$.

If we denote the probability of false positives and the probability of false negatives to distinguish between a wrong key and a right key as β_1 and β_0, respectively, and we consider the decision threshold $\tau = \mu_0 + \sigma_0 z_{1-\beta_0} = \mu_1 - \sigma_1 z_{1-\beta_1}$ ($z_{1-\beta_0}$ and $z_{1-\beta_1}$ are the quantiles of the standard normal distribution), then the number of known plaintexts N should be approximately:

$$N \approx \frac{2^n (z_{1-\beta_0} + z_{1-\beta_1})}{\sqrt{\ell/2} - z_{1-\beta_1}}. \tag{1}$$

2.3 Multidimensional Zero-Correlation Linear Cryptanalysis

Now we treat the zero-correlation linear approximations available as a linear space spanned by m base zero-correlation linear approximations such that all $\ell = 2^m - 1$ non-zero linear combinations of them have zero correlation [4]. For each of the 2^m data values $z \in \mathbb{F}_2^m$, the attacker initializes a counter $V[z]$, $z = 0, 1, 2, \ldots, 2^m - 1$, to value zero. Then, for each distinct plaintext, the attacker computes the corresponding data value in $\mathbb{F}_2^m$ by evaluating the m basis linear approximations and increments the counter $V[z]$ of this data value by one. Then the attacker computes the statistic T:

$$T = \sum_{i=0}^{2^m - 1} \frac{(V[z] - N2^{-m})^2}{N2^{-m}(1 - 2^{-m})}.$$

The statistic T for the right key guess follows a χ^2-distribution with mean $\mu_0 = (\ell - 1)\frac{2^n - N}{2^n - 1}$ and variance $\sigma_0^2 = 2(\ell - 1)\left(\frac{2^n - N}{2^n - 1}\right)^2$, while for the wrong key guess it follows a χ^2-distribution with mean $\mu_1 = \ell - 1$ and variance $\sigma_1^2 = 2(\ell - 1)$.

If we denote the probability of false positives and the probability of false negatives to distinguish between a wrong key and a right key as β_1 and β_0, respectively, and we consider the decision threshold $\tau = \mu_0 + \sigma_0 z_{1-\beta_0} = \mu_1 - \sigma_1 z_{1-\beta_1}$, then the number of known plaintexts N should be about

$$N \approx \frac{(2^n - 1)(z_{1-\beta_0} + z_{1-\beta_1})}{\sqrt{(\ell - 1)/2} + z_{1-\beta_0}} + 1. \tag{2}$$

Note that in both (1) and (2), the number of approximations used is the same and equals ℓ. While in the first case we take those individually, the multidimensional treatment considers them as a linear space spanned by m base approximations.

3 Fast Fourier Transform for Zero Correlation

In this section, we describe an FFT-based technique of computational complexity reduction for zero-correlation cryptanalysis. It relies on eliminating the redundant computations from the partial encryption/decryption in the course of zero-correlation linear cryptanalysis. Let $\chi_P \rightarrow \chi_D$ be the linear approximation for the first $R - 1$ rounds of an R-round block cipher f_K.

After partial decryption of the last round, the linear approximation to be evaluated becomes: $\chi_P^T \cdot P \oplus \chi_D^T \cdot S^{-1}(C \oplus K)$, where $S^{-1}(\cdot)$ represents a partial decryption of the last round for the k bits of C and K that influence the value of $\chi_D^T \cdot D$.

We define the $2^k \times 2^k$ matrix M as follows:

$$M(C, K) = (-1)^{\chi_D^T \cdot S^{-1}(C \oplus K)}, \text{ for all } C, K \in \{0, \ldots, 2^k - 1\}.$$

Then, the bias of the linear approximation can be evaluated as the matrix vector product $M \cdot x$. As shown in [7], the matrix M has a level-circulant structure and, consequently, this matrix-vector product can be computed efficiently using the Fast Walsh-Hadamard Transform (equivalent to a k-dimensional Fast Fourier Transform) with $\mathcal{O}(3k \cdot 2^k)$ time complexity. The level-circulant structure results from the XOR between the ciphertext and the key guess. Therefore, the matrix can be expressed as a function of $C \oplus K$. The detail of computing matrix-vector product with FFT is shown in Appendix A of the full version of this paper [5].

The objective of using FFT is to compute the correlation for different subkey guesses with matrix-vector multiplications. The key recovery part in zero-correlation linear cryptanalysis can be done with the similar method utilized by Matsui's Algorithm 2 [14], as shown in [3]. Since the zero correlation attack with multiple linear approximations computes the statistic which reveals correlation directly, we can use the FFT speed-up to improve the computational complexity as described above.

4 Zero-Correlation Cryptanalysis of Camellia with FFT

Camellia is a block cipher jointly proposed by Mitsubishi and NTT in 2000 [1] which has been approved for use by ISO/IEC. It features the basic Feistel structure. The block size is 128 bits and the key size is variable. The number of rounds depends on the key size, i.e., 18 rounds for 128-bit key and 24 rounds for 192/256-bit key. Every six rounds, a logical keyed transformation layer FL/FL^{-1} is applied and the round function uses a SPN structure, including the XOR operation with the round subkey, the nonlinear transformation consisting of eight parallel S-boxes (8×8) and the linear permutation P. The cipher also uses input and output key whitening. Encryption process and key schedule are illustrated in Appendix B of the full version of this paper [5].

4.1 Zero-Correlation Linear Approximations for 7-Round Camellia

In this subsection, some zero-correlation linear approximations for 7-round Camellia with FL/FL^{-1} are derived. First, we will introduce some properties for FL/FL^{-1} of Camellia.

Property 1. If the input mask of FL is $IM = (0|0|0|0|0|0|0|i)$, then the output mask of FL is $OM = (?|0|0|?|?|0|0|?)$, where '?' is an unknown value, see Fig. 1(a).

Property 2. For the output mask of FL^{-1} is $OM = (0|0|0|0|0|0|0|i)$, then the input mask of FL^{-1} is $IM = (?|0|0|?|?|0|0|?)$, where '?' is an unknown value, see Fig. 1(b).

With these properties, we can derive zero-correlation linear approximations for 7-round Camellia.

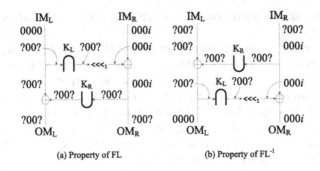

(a) Property of FL   (b) Property of FL^{-1}

Fig. 1. Property of FL/FL^{-1}

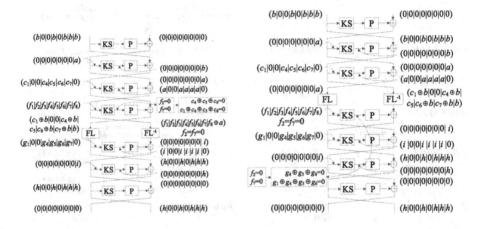

Fig. 2. $4 + 3$ rounds   **Fig. 3.** $3 + 4$ rounds

Property 3. For 7-round Camellia consisting of $(F|F|F|F|FL/FL^{-1}|F|F|F)$ as in Fig. 2 or $(F|F|F|FL/FL^{-1}|F|F|F|F)$ as in Fig. 3, if the input mask of the first round is $(b|0|0|b|0|b|b|b, 0|0|0|0|0|0|0|0)$ and the output mask of the last round is $(0|0|0|0|0|0|0|0, h|0|0|h|0|h|h|h)$, then the correlation of the linear approximations is zero, where $b, h \in \mathbb{F}_2^8, b \neq 0, h \neq 0$.

The proofs of Property 1, Property 2 and Property 3 are given in Appendix C of the full version of this paper [5].

4.2   Key Recovery for 11-Round Camellia-128

Using the FFT technique, we can attack 11-round Camellia-128 with FL/FL^{-1} and whitening key starting from the first round by placing the zero-correlation linear approximations of 7-round $(4 + 3)$ Camellia in rounds 3–9 as demonstrated in Fig. 3. This is clarified in Fig. 4(a). Note that in Fig. 4(a), the byte values to be computed are denoted as '$*$' while the bytes denoted as '0' do not require computation.

In the following, we will use some notations. $P^{i_1,i_2,\cdots}$, $C^{i_1,i_2,\cdots}$ and $K^{i_1,i_2,\cdots}$ denote the concatenation of i_1-th, i_2-th,... bytes of the plaintext word, ciphertext word or subkey word respectively. S^j denotes the output of the j-th S-box, F_r denotes the round function for the r-th round and F_r^l is a function and it computes the l-th output byte of the round function for the r-th round. We denote $K_0 = k^{w1} \oplus k_1$, $K_1 = k^{w2} \oplus k_2$, $K_2 = k^{w3} \oplus k_{10}$, and $K_3 = k^{w4} \oplus k_{11}$, where k_1, k_2, k_{10} and k_{11} are 64-bit subkeys for round 1, 2, 10 and 11, respectively, and $k^{wi}, 1 \le i \le 4$ is the 64-bit whitening subkey.

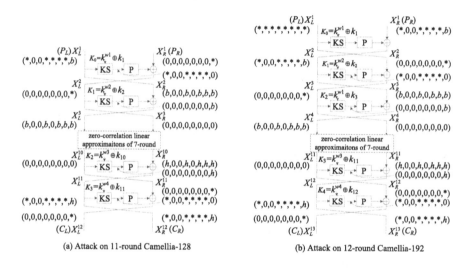

(a) Attack on 11-round Camellia-128   (b) Attack on 12-round Camellia-192

Fig. 4. Attacks on 11-round Camellia-128 and 12-round Camellia-192

In our attack, we guess the subkey and evaluate the linear approximation $(\mathbf{b}|0|0|\mathbf{b}|0|\mathbf{b}|\mathbf{b}|\mathbf{b}) \cdot X_L^3 \oplus (\mathbf{h}|0|0|\mathbf{h}|0|\mathbf{h}|\mathbf{h}|\mathbf{h}) \cdot X_R^{10} = 0$ with

$$u = \mathbf{b}^T \cdot P_L^8 \oplus \mathbf{h}^T \cdot C_R^8 \oplus \alpha^T \cdot P_L^{1,4,6,7} \oplus \beta^T \cdot C_R^{1,4,6,7}$$
$$\oplus \mathbf{b}^T \cdot S^8[P_R^8 \oplus K_1^8 \oplus F_1^8(P_L^{1,4,5,6,7} \oplus K_0^{1,4,5,6,7})]$$
$$\oplus \mathbf{h}^T \cdot S^8[C_L^8 \oplus K_2^8 \oplus F_{11}^8(C_R^{1,4,5,6,7} \oplus K_3^{1,4,5,6,7})] = 0,$$

where $\alpha = (\mathbf{b}, \mathbf{b}, \mathbf{b}, \mathbf{b})$, $\beta = (\mathbf{h}, \mathbf{h}, \mathbf{h}, \mathbf{h})$, $\mathbf{b}$ and $\mathbf{h}$ are non-zero bytes. In order to take the full advantage of the FFT technique to reduce the time complexity, we transform u to v by XORing $\alpha^T \cdot K_0^{1,4,6,7} \oplus \beta^T \cdot K_3^{1,4,6,7}$:

$$v = \mathbf{b}^T \cdot P_L^8 \oplus \mathbf{h}^T \cdot C_R^8 \oplus \alpha^T \cdot (P_L^{1,4,6,7} \oplus K_0^{1,4,6,7}) \oplus \beta^T \cdot (C_R^{1,4,6,7} \oplus K_3^{1,4,6,7})$$
$$\oplus \mathbf{b}^T \cdot S^8[P_R^8 \oplus K_1^8 \oplus F_1^8(P_L^{1,4,5,6,7} \oplus K_0^{1,4,5,6,7})] \qquad (3)$$
$$\oplus \mathbf{h}^T \cdot S^8[C_L^8 \oplus K_2^8 \oplus F_{11}^8(C_R^{1,4,5,6,7} \oplus K_3^{1,4,5,6,7})].$$

Obviously, the absolute of correlation of the linear approximation $u = 0$ equals to that of the linear approximation $v = 0$, so our attack is equivalent to evaluating the correlation of the linear approximation $v = 0$. As described in Sect. 3, the correlation of the linear approximation $v = 0$ can be evaluated as the matrix vector product where the matrix is:

$$M(P_L^{1,4,5,6,7}|P_R^8|C_L^8|C_R^{1,4,5,6,7}, K_0^{1,4,5,6,7}|K_1^8|K_2^8|K_3^{1,4,5,6,7}) = (-1)^v. \qquad (4)$$

To reduce the time complexity, we choose 2^{14} linear approximations where **h** takes all possible non-zero values while **b** only takes all non-zero values for the six least significant bits and zero value for the two most significant bits. Then the attack is performed as follows:

1. Allocate the vector of counters C_κ of the experimental correlation for every subkey candidate $\kappa = (K_0^{1,4,5,6,7}|K_1^8|K_2^8|K_3^{1,4,5,6,7})$.
2. For each of the 2^{110} values of $i = (P_L^{1,4,5,6,7}|P_L^8[1,2,3,4,5,6]|P_R^8|C_L^8|C_R^{1,4,5,6,7,8})$, define a vector of 2^{110} counters **x**, where $P_L^8[1,2,3,4,5,6]$ is the six least significant bits of P_L^8.
3. For each of N plaintext-ciphertext pairs, extract the 110-bit value

$$i = (P_L^{1,4,5,6,7}|P_L^8[1,2,3,4,5,6]|P_R^8|C_L^8|C_R^{1,4,5,6,7,8})$$

   and increment the counter x_i according to the value of i.
4. For each of the 2^{14} linear approximations
   (a) Perform the data counting phase
     i. For each of the 2^{96} values of $j = (P_L^{1,4,5,6,7}|P_R^8|C_L^8|C_R^{1,4,5,6,7})$, define a vector of 2^{96} counters **y**.
     ii. For each of the 2^{110} values of $i = (P_L^{1,4,5,6,7}|P_L^8[1,2,3,4,5,6]|P_R^8|C_L^8|C_R^{1,4,5,6,7,8})$, extract 96-bit value $j = (P_L^{1,4,5,6,7}|P_R^8|C_L^8|C_R^{1,4,5,6,7})$ and add x_i to or subtract x_i from the counter y_j according to the parity of $\mathbf{b}^T \cdot P_L^8 \oplus \mathbf{h}^T \cdot C_R^8$.
   (b) Perform the key counting phase
     i. Compute the first column of M using (3) and (4). As M is a 96-level circulant matrix, this information is sufficient to define M completely (requires 2^{96} operations).
     ii. Evaluate the vector $\epsilon = M \cdot \mathbf{y}$ (requires $3 \cdot 96 \cdot 2^{96}$ operations).
     iii. Let $C = C + (\epsilon/N)^2$.
5. If $C_\kappa < \tau$, then the corresponding κ is a possible subkey candidate and all master keys are tested exhaustively.

After Step 4, we obtain 2^{96} counters C_κ which are the sum of squares of correlations for 2^{14} linear approximations under each κ. The correct subkey is then selected from the candidates with C_κ less than the threshold $\tau = \sigma_0 \cdot z_{1-\beta_0} + \mu_0 = \frac{\sqrt{2\ell}}{N} \cdot z_{1-\beta_0} + \frac{\ell}{N}$.

If we set $\beta_0 = 2^{-2.7}$ and $\beta_1 = 2^{-96}$, we get $z_{1-\beta_0} \approx 1$ and $z_{1-\beta_1} \approx 11.3$. Since the block size $n = 128$ and we have $\ell = 2^{14}$ linear approximations, according to Eq. (1) the number of known plaintext-ciphertext pairs N should be about $2^{125.3}$.

In Step 5, only about $2^{96} \cdot 2^{-96} = 1$ guess is expected to survive for the 96-bit target subkey. According to the key schedule of Camellia (e.g. outlined in Appendix B of the full version of this paper [5]), the recovered 96-bit subkey $K_0^{1,4,5,6,7}$, K_1^8, K_2^8 and $K_3^{1,4,5,6,7}$ can be expressed in k_A and k_L as follows,

$$
\begin{aligned}
K_0^{1,4,5,6,7} &= [k^{w1} \oplus k_1]^{1,4,5,6,7} &&= [(k_L)_L \oplus (k_A)_L]^{1,4,5,6,7}, \\
K_1^8 &= [k^{w2} \oplus k_2]^8 &&= [(k_L)_R \oplus (k_A)_R]^8, \\
K_2^8 &= [k^{w3} \oplus k_{10}]^8 &&= [(k_A \lll 111)_L \oplus (k_L \lll 60)_R]^8, \\
K_3^{1,4,5,6,7} &= [k^{w4} \oplus k_{11}]^{1,4,5,6,7} &&= [(k_A \lll 111)_R \oplus (k_A \lll 60)_L]^{1,4,5,6,7}.
\end{aligned}
\tag{5}
$$

One can see that $K_3^{1,4,5,6,7}$ is only related to 61 bits of k_A. So we first guess these 61 bits of k_A and compute $K_3^{1,4,5,6,7}$. Then only about $2^{61} \cdot 2^{-40} = 2^{21}$ values for 61-bit k_A will survive. Second, we guess the other 67 bits of k_A. Then the master key k_L could be computed with four 1-round Camellia encryptions using (6) as proposed in [13]:

$$
\begin{aligned}
k_L^R &= F_{C_2}^{-1}(k_A^L \oplus F_{C_4}(k_A^R)) \oplus k_A^R \oplus F_{C_3}(k_A^L \oplus F_{C_4}(k_A^R)), \\
k_L^L &= F_{C_1}^{-1}(k_A^R \oplus F_{C_3}(k_A^L \oplus F_{C_4}(k_A^R))),
\end{aligned}
\tag{6}
$$

where $C_i, 1 \leq i \leq 4$ is the constant value used in the key schedule. The complexity of this procedure is about $2^{21} \cdot 2^{67} \cdot \frac{4}{11} \approx 2^{86.5}$ 11-round Camellia encryptions.

The complexities for Step 3, Step 4(a), Step 4(b) and Step 5 are $2^{125.3}$ memory accesses, 2^{124} memory accesses, $2^{14} \cdot 4 \cdot 96 \cdot 2^{96} = 2^{118.6}$ 11-round encryptions, $2^{86.5}$ 11-round encryptions, respectively. If we assume that one time of memory access is equivalent to one 11-round Camellia encryption, then the total time complexity is about $2^{125.8}$ encryptions. The memory requirements are about 2^{112} bytes.

All in all, the data complexity is about $2^{125.3}$ known plaintexts, the time complexity is about $2^{125.8}$ encryptions and the memory requirements are 2^{112} bytes.

4.3   Key Recovery for 12-Round Camellia-192

Now we will use the 7-round zero-correlation linear approximations of type (3+4) as given in Fig. 3 to attack 12-round Camellia-192 starting from the first round. By placing these 7-round zero-correlation linear approximations in rounds 4 to 10, we can attack Camellia-192 from round 1 to round 12. This is illustrated in Fig. 4(b).

First, we guess the 64-bit subkey of the first round K_0 and then we proceed with the steps similar as those in the attack on 11-round Camellia-128. Hence, we have to guess 160-bit subkey:

$$
K_0^{1,2,3,4,5,6,7,8} = [k^{w1} \oplus k_1]^{1,2,3,4,5,6,7,8} = [(k_L)_L \oplus (k_B)_L]^{1,2,3,4,5,6,7,8}, \tag{7}
$$

$$
K_1^{1,4,5,6,7} = [k^{w2} \oplus k_2]^{1,4,5,6,7} = [(k_L)_R \oplus (k_B)_R]^{1,4,5,6,7}, \tag{8}
$$

$$
K_2^8 = [k^{w1} \oplus k_3]^8 = [(k_L)_L \oplus (k_R \lll 15)_L]^8, \tag{9}
$$

$$
K_3^8 = [k^{w3} \oplus k_{11}]^8 = [(k_B \lll 111)_L \oplus (k_A \lll 45)_L]^8, \tag{10}
$$

$$
K_4^{1,4,5,6,7} = [k^{w4} \oplus k_{12}]^{1,4,5,6,7} = [(k_B \lll 111)_R \oplus (k_A \lll 45)_R]^{1,4,5,6,7}. \tag{11}
$$

Note that in this attack we set $\beta_0 = 2^{-2.7}$ and $\beta_1 = 2^{-160}$, we get $z_{1-\beta_0} \approx 1$ and $z_{1-\beta_1} \approx 14.7$. Since the block size $n = 128$ and we have $\ell = 2^{14}$ linear approximations, then N should be about $\approx 2^{125.7}$ from (1). Similar to the attack on 11-round Camellia-128, only about $2^{160} \cdot 2^{-160} = 1$ guess for the 160-bit target subkey is expected to survive. The complexity of these steps is about $2^{64} \cdot 2^{124.8} = 2^{188.8}$ 12-round Camellia encryptions since the attack on 12-round Camellia-192 is basically the same as the attack on 11-round Camellia-128 except that we have to guess the extra 64-bit $K_0^{1,2,3,4,5,6,7,8}$.

To recover the master key consisting of 128-bit k_L and 64-bit $(k_R)_L$, we first guess 128-bit k_B, compute k'_B according to key schedule. We compute the value of $(k_L)_L$ according to (7). Then we get $(k_R \lll 15)_L^8$ with (9), guess 56-bit $(k_R \lll 15)_L^{1,2,3,4,5,6,7}$ and compute $k_A = k'_B \oplus k_R$. Now we get the value of k_A and k_B according to the key schedule. Using (10, 11), we filter out 2^{-48} values of k_A and k_B. After this step, there are about $2^{128} \cdot 2^{56} \cdot 2^{-48} = 2^{136}$ possible values for k_A, k_B and k_R. k_L can be computed with a cost of four 1-round Camellia encryptions for each of 2^{136} values of k_A, k_B and k_R. With (8), we filter out 2^{-40} wrong candidates. Then we have 2^{96} right key candidates at this time. By verifying with one plaintext-ciphertext pair, only the right key will remain. The dominant time complexity of the above procedure lies in the computation of k_A after guessing 128-bit k_B and 56-bit $(k_R \lll 15)_L^{1,2,3,4,5,6,7}$, which is about 2^{184} XORs of two 128-bit values. Compared to $2^{188.8}$ 12-round Camellia-192 encryptions, this time complexity is negligible.

Thus, the data complexity is $2^{125.7}$ known plaintexts, the memory requirements are about 2^{112} bytes, and the time complexity is $2^{188.8}$ encryptions.

5   Multidimensional Zero-Correlation Cryptanalysis of CLEFIA

CLEFIA is a block cipher proposed in 2007 by Sony Corporation [15] and has been adopted as one of the ISO/IEC international standards in lightweight cryptography. The block size is 128-bit and the key size could be 128, 192 or 256 bits. Accordingly, they are denoted as CLEFIA-128, CLEFIA-192 and CLEFIA-256 and the number of rounds for them are 18, 22 and 26, respectively. CLEFIA employs a four-branch generalized Feistel structure with two parallel F functions (F_0, F_1). The 128-bit ciphertext $(C_0|C_1|C_2|C_3)$ is generated from 128-bit plaintext $(P_0|P_1|P_2|P_3)$ along with $2r$ 32-bit subkey keys $(RK_0, \ldots, RK_{2r-1})$ and four 32-bit whitening keys (WK_0, WK_1, WK_2, WK_3), where r is the total round number. Here we denote a 128-bit value as concatenation of four 32-bit words. The encryption process and key schedule of CLEFIA are shown in Appendix D of the full version of this paper [5].

There are two types of round functions consisting of subkey XOR, S-boxes and the linear transformation, where the linear transformations for them are defined as M_0 and M_1, respectively:

$$M_0 = \begin{pmatrix} 0x1 & 0x2 & 0x4 & 0x6 \\ 0x2 & 0x1 & 0x6 & 0x4 \\ 0x4 & 0x6 & 0x1 & 0x2 \\ 0x6 & 0x4 & 0x2 & 0x1 \end{pmatrix} \text{ and } M_1 = \begin{pmatrix} 0x1 & 0x8 & 0x2 & 0xa \\ 0x8 & 0x1 & 0xa & 0x2 \\ 0x2 & 0xa & 0x1 & 0x8 \\ 0xa & 0x2 & 0x8 & 0x1 \end{pmatrix}.$$

5.1   Zero-Correlation Linear Approximations of 9-Round CLEFIA

In [2], zero-correlation linear approximations of 9-round CLEFIA have been given. If the input mask is $(\mathbf{a}, \mathbf{0}, \mathbf{0}, \mathbf{0})$ and the output mask is $(\mathbf{0}, \mathbf{0}, \mathbf{0}, \mathbf{a})$, then the correlation of the linear approximations is zero. The details of the zero-correlation linear approximations of 9-round CLEFIA are shown in Fig. 5.

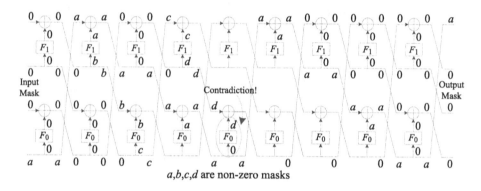

Fig. 5. Zero-correlation linear approximations of 9-Round CLEFIA

5.2   Multidimensional Zero-Correlation Cryptanalysis of 14-Round CLEFIA-192 and 15-Round CLEFIA-256

For the zero-correlation linear approximations of 9-round CLEFIA $(\mathbf{a}, \mathbf{0}, \mathbf{0}, \mathbf{0})$ $\longrightarrow 9r(\mathbf{0}, \mathbf{0}, \mathbf{0}, \mathbf{a})$, if we take all non-zero values for $\mathbf{a}$, then there are so many guessed subkey bits involved in the key recovery process that the time complexity will be greater than exhaustive search. Therefore, in order to reduce the number of guessed subkey bits, we only use the linear approximations where $\mathbf{a}$ satisfies the following condition:

$$(x, 0, 0, 0), (0, x, 0, 0), (0, 0, x, 0) \text{ or } (0, 0, 0, x) \longrightarrow M_1 \mathbf{a}, x \in \mathbb{F}_2^8, x \neq 0, \mathbf{a} \in \mathbb{F}_2^{32}, \mathbf{a} \neq 0,$$
$$(y_0, y_1, y_2, y_3) \longrightarrow M_0 \mathbf{a}, y_i \in \mathbb{F}_2^8, 0 \leq i \leq 3, y_i \neq 0.$$

We will use the above four groups of $\mathbf{a}$ in our attack and there are 255 such linear approximations for each group discovered in our test. In the following, we use $\mathbf{a}_g, 0 \leq g \leq 3$ to denote the four groups where only the g-th byte's input mask of M_1 is nonzero in $\mathbf{a}_g$, e.g. $(x, 0, 0, 0) \in \mathbf{a}_0$ and $(0, 0, x, 0) \in \mathbf{a}_2$. In this way, if the output mask of the round function F_1 is $\mathbf{a}$, then the input mask of the linear

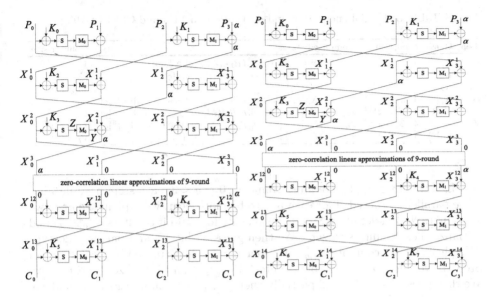

Fig. 6. Attack on 14-round CLEFIA-192   **Fig. 7.** Attack on 15-round CLEFIA-256

transformation M_1 of this round function is $(x, 0, 0, 0)$, $(0, x, 0, 0)$, $(0, 0, x, 0)$ or $(0, 0, 0, x)$. In this way, there is only one active S-box in F_1 round function in the 1st and 13th rounds, only one subkey byte is required to be guessed instead of four subkey bytes. Four groups of $\mathbf{a}_g$ will be used one by one to sieve wrong subkeys. The right subkey candidates are those survived after the filteration by four groups of $\mathbf{a}$.

5.3 Key Recovery for 14-Round CLEFIA-192

We put the zero-correlation linear approximations of 9-round CLEFIA in rounds 4–12 and attack 14-round CLEFIA-192 starting from the first round, see Fig. 6.

Assume that N known plaintexts are used, the partial encryption and decryption using the partial sum technique are proceeded as in Table 3. Note that X_j^r denotes the j-th branch of the r-th round, the number in square bracket denotes the byte of a 32-bit word, e.g. $P_2[g], 0 \leq g \leq 3$ is the g-th byte of 32-bit P_2. Y and Z are the intermediate states in the third round shown in Fig. 6. In Table 3, the second column stands for the subkey bytes that have to be guessed in each step, the third column denotes the time complexity of corresponding step measured in 1/4 round encryption. In each step, we save the values of the intermediate state $x_{i,g}, 1 \leq i \leq 7, 0 \leq g \leq 3$, during the encryption and decryption process and these are shown in column "Computed States". For each possible value of $x_{i,g}$, the counter (partial sum) $V_{i,g}[x_{i,g}]$ will record how many plaintext-ciphertext pairs can produce the corresponding intermediate state $x_{i,g}$. The counter size for each $x_{i,g}$ is shown in the last column.

Table 3. Partial encryption and decryption on 14-round CLEFIA-192

Step	Guess	Complexity	Computed states	Counter-size
I	K_5	$4 \cdot N \cdot 2^{32}$	$x_{1,g} = (P_0|P_1|P_2|(M_1^{-1}(P_3 \oplus C_2))[g]|X_1^{13}[g])$	$V_{1,g} - 2^{112}$
II	K_0	$4 \cdot 2^{112} \cdot 2^{64}$	$x_{2,g} = (X_0^1|P_2|(M_1^{-1}(P_3 \oplus C_2))[g]|X_1^{13}[g])$	$V_{2,g} - 2^{80}$
III	K_2	$4 \cdot 2^{80} \cdot 2^{96}$	$x_{3,g} = (X_0^2|P_2[g]|(M_1^{-1}(P_3 \oplus C_2))[g]|X_1^{13}[g])$	$V_{3,g} - 2^{56}$
IV	$K_3[0]$	$4 \cdot 2^{56} \cdot 2^{104}$	$x_{4,g} = (X_0^2[1,2,3]|Z[0]|P_2[g]|(M_1^{-1}(P_3 \oplus C_2))[g]|X_1^{13}[g])$	$V_{4,g} - 2^{56}$
V	$K_3[1]$	$4 \cdot 2^{56} \cdot 2^{112}$	$x_{5,g} = (X_0^2[2,3]|Z[1,0]|P_2[g]|(M_1^{-1}(P_3 \oplus C_2))[g]|X_1^{13}[g])$	$V_{5,g} - 2^{56}$
VI	$K_3[2]$	$4 \cdot 2^{56} \cdot 2^{120}$	$x_{6,g} = (X_0^2[3]|Z[0,1,2]|P_2[g]|(M_1^{-1}(P_3 \oplus C_2))[g]|X_1^{13}[g])$	$V_{6,g} - 2^{56}$
VII	$K_3[3]$	$4 \cdot 2^{56} \cdot 2^{128}$	$x_{7,g} = (P_2[g]|(M_1^{-1}(Y \oplus P_3 \oplus C_2))[g]|X_1^{13}[g])$	$V_{7,g} - 2^{24}$

Since we are going to use four groups $\mathbf{a}_g, 0 \leq g \leq 3$, each step in Table 3 has to be parallelly proceeded for each $\mathbf{a}_g$. To be more clear, we explain the first two steps in Table 3 in detail. In Step I, we allocate four 16-bit counters $V_{1,g}[x_{1,g}]$ and initialize these counters to zero. We then guess 32-bit K_5 and partially decrypt N ciphertexts to compute $x_{1,g}$, and increment the corresponding counters. In Step II, we allocate four 48-bit counters $V_{2,g}[x_{2,g}]$ and initialize them to zero. We then guess 32-bit K_0 and partially encrypt $x_{1,g}$ to compute $x_{2,g}$ and add the corresponding $V_{1,g}$ to $V_{2,g}$.

Key Recovery. We set $\beta_0 = 2^{-4.6}$ and $\beta_1 = 2^{-48}$, then $z_{1-\beta_0} \approx 1.7, z_{1-\beta_1} = 7.8$. Since $n = 128$ and $\ell = 255$, then according to (2), the data complexity N is about $2^{127.5}$. To recover the master key, we perform the following steps.

(A) Partial encryption and decryption for $2^{127.5}$ plaintext-ciphertext pairs as specified by Step I~VII in Table 3. After Step VII, we get counters $V_{7,0}[x_{7,0}]$, $V_{7,1}[x_{7,1}]$, $V_{7,2}[x_{7,2}]$ and $V_{7,3}[x_{7,3}]$.

(B) Wrong subkeys filteration with $\mathbf{a}_0$ as specified in Algorithm 1. There are 16 new guessed subkey bits involved in this step, and thus about $2^{128+16} \cdot 2^{-48} = 2^{96}$ values for guessed 144-bit subkey will survive after this step.

(C) Wrong subkeys filteration with $\mathbf{a}_1$ as specified in Algorithm 1. After this step, $2^{96+16} \cdot 2^{-48} = 2^{64}$ values for guessed 160-bit subkey will survive.

(D) Wrong subkeys filteration with $\mathbf{a}_2$ as specified in Algorithm 1. $2^{64+16} \cdot 2^{-48} = 2^{32}$ values for guessed 176-bit subkey are expected to survive after this step.

(E) Wrong subkeys filteration with $\mathbf{a}_3$ as specified in Algorithm 1. Only $2^{32+16} \cdot 2^{-48} = 1$ value for guessed 192-bit subkey is supposed to remain.

(F) According to the key schedule of CLEFIA-192, we can recover the master key from this unique 192-bit subkey.

The dominant time complexity in Step (A) lies in Step VII, which is about $4 \cdot 2^{56} \cdot 2^{128} \cdot \frac{1}{4} \cdot \frac{1}{14} \approx 2^{180.2}$ 14-round CLEFIA-192 encryptions. The time complexity of Step (B) is about $(2^{128+8} \cdot 2^{24} + 2^{128+16} \cdot 2^{16}) \cdot \frac{1}{4} \cdot \frac{1}{14} \approx 2^{155.2}$ 14-round CLEFIA-192 encryptions. The time complexity of Step (C) is about $(2^{96+8} \cdot 2^{24} + 2^{96+16} \cdot 2^{16}) \cdot \frac{1}{4} \cdot \frac{1}{14} \approx 2^{123.2}$ 14-round CLEFIA-192 encryptions. The time complexity of Step (D) and (E) is negligible.

For the time complexity of Step (F), we need to consider the key schedule of CLEFIA-192. The six subkeys guessed, $K_i, 0 \leq i \leq 5$ are RK_0, RK_1, $RK_2 \oplus$

Algorithm 1. Filter out wrong subkeys with a_g

1: Allocate 128-bit counter $V_{8,g}$ for 16-bit $x_{8,g} = ((M_1^{-1}(Y \oplus X_2^1 \oplus C_2))[g]|X_1^{13}[g])$
   and initialize to zero
2: Guess 8-bit $K_1[g]$, compute $x_{8,g}$ with $x_{7,g}$, then $V_{8,g}[x_{8,g}]+ = V_{7,g}[x_{7,g}]$
3: Allocate 128-bit counter $V_{9,g}$ for 8-bit $x_{9,g} = ((M_1^{-1}(Y \oplus X_2^1 \oplus X_3^{12}))[g])$ and
   initialize to zero
4: Guess 8-bit $K_4[g]$, compute $x_{9,g}$ with $x_{8,g}$, then $V_{9,g}[x_{9,g}]+ = V_{8,g}[x_{8,g}]$
5: Allocate 128-bit counter $V_g[z]$ for 8-bit z and initialize to zero
   {z is the concatenation of evaluations of 8 basis zero-correlation masks}
6: Compute z from $x_{9,g}$ with 8 basis zero-correlation masks, then $V_g[z]+ = V_{9,g}[x_{9,g}]$
7: Compute $T = N \cdot 2^8 \cdot \sum_{z=0}^{2^8-1} \left(\frac{V_g[z]}{N} - \frac{1}{2^8} \right)^2$
8: **if** $T < \tau$ **then**
9:     Guessed subkey values are possible right subkey candidates
10: **end if**

WK_0, RK_4, $RK_{25} \oplus WK_2$ and RK_{26}, respectively. According to the key schedule in Appendix D of the full version of this paper [5], RK_0, RK_1 and RK_{26} is only related with the intermediate key value L. Then after Step (E), we obtained 96-bit L since there is only one value for the 192-bit subkey left. To recover the 192-bit key K from the key schedule, we guess other 160-bit L and compute K with cost equivalent to 20 one-round CLEFIA encryptions. K could then be verified with at most two plaintext-ciphertext pairs. The complexity to recover the master key from the 192-bit subkey we obtained after Step (E) is $2^{160} \cdot \frac{20}{14} + 2^{160} + 2^{160-128} \approx 2^{161.3}$ 14-round CLEFIA-192 encryptions.

All in all, the time complexity of our attack on 14-round CLEFIA-192 is about $2^{180.2}$ 14-round CLEFIA-192 encryptions, the data complexity is $2^{127.5}$ known plaintexts and the memory requirements are about 2^{115} bytes to store the counters in Step I.

5.4 Key Recovery for 15-Round CLEFIA-256

We also place the zero-correlation linear approximations of 9-round CLEFIA in rounds 4 to 12 and attack 15-round CLEFIA-256 starting from the first round, see Fig. 7.

For the attack on 15-round CLEFIA-256, we need to guess 32-bit K_6 and 32-bit K_7 and decrypt N pairs of texts to get $(X_0^{14}, X_1^{14}, X_2^{14}, X_3^{14})$. The remaining procedure is similar as the attack on 14-round CLEFIA-192, where we still set $\beta_0 = 2^{-4.6}$ and $\beta_1 = 2^{-48}$.

The time complexity from Step (A) to Step (E) for the attack on 15-round CLEFIA-256 is about 2^{64} times of the time complexity in the corresponding step for the attack on 14-round CLEFIA-192. So the total complexity for Step (A)~(E) is about $2^{180.2} \cdot 2^{64} \approx 2^{244.2}$ 15-round CLEFIA-256 encryptions.

For the time complexity of Step (F), the key schedule of CLEFIA-256 should be considered. The guessed eight subkeys, $K_i, 0 \leq i \leq 7$ are RK_0, RK_1, $RK_2 \oplus WK_0$, RK_4, RK_{25}, $RK_{26} \oplus WK_3$, RK_{28} and RK_{29}, respectively. From the key schedule of Appendix D of the full version of this paper [5], the guessed subkey RK_0, RK_1 and RK_{25} are only related with the intermediate key value L. Then after Step (E), we obtained 2^{64} values for 96-bit L since there are 2^{64} guesses for the 256-bit subkey left. To recover the 256-bit key K, we guess other 160-bit L and compute K with cost equivalent to 20 one-round CLEFIA encryptions. K could then be verified with at most two plaintext-ciphertext pairs. The complexity to recover the master key from the 256-bit subkey we obtained after Step (E) is about $2^{64} \cdot 2^{160} \cdot \frac{20}{15} + 2^{64} \cdot 2^{160} + 2^{64} \cdot 2^{160} \cdot 2^{-128} \approx 2^{185.2}$ 15-round CLEFIA-256 encryptions.

All in all, the time complexity of our attack on 15-round CLEFIA-256 is about $2^{244.2}$ 15-round CLEFIA-256 encryptions, the data complexity is $2^{127.5}$ known plaintexts and the memory requirements are about 2^{115} bytes to store the counters in Step I.

6 Conclusion

In this paper, we use the Discrete Fast Fourier Transform to enhance zero-correlation linear cryptanalysis by a faster key recovery. We improve upon the state-of-the-art cryptanalysis for Camellia and CLEFIA by breaking more rounds for Camellia-128 and Camellia-192 than was possible previously as well as by reducing time and memory complexities for CLEFIA-192 and CLEFIA-256.

It is our hope that the FFT zero correlation cryptanalysis will lead to a reevaluation of security level for further ciphers as well.

Acknowledgments. This work has been supported by the National Basic Research 973 Program of China under Grant No. 2013CB834205, the National Natural Science Foundation of China under Grant Nos. 61133013, 61070244, the Program for New Century Excellent Talents in University of China under Grant No. NCET-13-0350, as well as the Interdisciplinary Research Foundation of Shandong University of China under Grant No. 2012JC018.

References

1. Aoki, K., Ichikawa, T., Kanda, M., Matsui, M., Moriai, S., Nakajima, J., Tokita, T.: *Camellia*: a 128-bit block cipher suitable for multiple platforms - design and analysis. In: Stinson, D.R., Tavares, S. (eds.) SAC 2000. LNCS, vol. 2012, pp. 39–56. Springer, Heidelberg (2001)
2. Bogdanov, A., Rijmen, V.: Linear hulls with correlation zero and linear cryptanalysis of block ciphers. Des. Codes Crypt. **70**(3), 369–383 (2014)
3. Bogdanov, A., Wang, M.: Zero correlation linear cryptanalysis with reduced data complexity. In: Canteaut, A. (ed.) FSE 2012. LNCS, vol. 7549, pp. 29–48. Springer, Heidelberg (2012)
4. Bogdanov, A., Leander, G., Nyberg, K., Wang, M.: Integral and multidimensional linear distinguishers with correlation zero. In: Wang, X., Sako, K. (eds.) ASIACRYPT 2012. LNCS, vol. 7658, pp. 244–261. Springer, Heidelberg (2012)

5. Bogdanov, A., Geng, H., Wang, M., Wen, L., Collard, B.: Zero-correlation linear cryptanalysis with FFT and improved attacks on ISO standards Camellia and CLEFIA. IACR ePrint Archive report (2013)
6. Chen, J., Jia, K., Yu, H., Wang, X.: New impossible differential attacks of reduced-round Camellia-192 and Camellia-256. In: Parampalli, U., Hawkes, P. (eds.) ACISP 2011. LNCS, vol. 6812, pp. 16–33. Springer, Heidelberg (2011)
7. Collard, B., Standaert, F.-X., Quisquater, J.-J.: Improving the time complexity of Matsui's linear cryptanalysis. In: Nam, K.-H., Rhee, G. (eds.) ICISC 2007. LNCS, vol. 4817, pp. 77–88. Springer, Heidelberg (2007)
8. ISO/IEC 18033-3:2005 Information technology – Security techniques – Encryption algrithm – Part 3: Block Ciphers (July 2005)
9. Li, L., Chen, J., Jia, K.: New impossible differential cryptanalysis of reduced-round Camellia. In: Lin, D., Tsudik, G., Wang, X. (eds.) CANS 2011. LNCS, vol. 7092, pp. 26–39. Springer, Heidelberg (2011)
10. Li, Y., Wu, W., Zhang, L.: Improved integral attacks on reduced-round clefia block cipher. In: Jung, S., Yung, M. (eds.) WISA 2011. LNCS, vol. 7115, pp. 28–39. Springer, Heidelberg (2012)
11. Liu, Y., Li, L., Gu, D., Wang, X., Liu, Z., Chen, J., Li, W.: New observations on impossible differential cryptanalysis of reduced-round Camellia. In: Canteaut, A. (ed.) FSE 2012. LNCS, vol. 7549, pp. 90–109. Springer, Heidelberg (2012)
12. Liu, Y., Gu, D., Liu, Z., Li, W.: Improved results on impossible differential cryptanalysis of reduced-round Camellia-192/256. J. Syst. Softw. **85**(11), 2451–2458 (2012)
13. Mala, H., Shakiba, M., Dakhilalian, M., Bagherikaram, G.: New results on impossible differential cryptanalysis of reduced–round Camellia–128. In: Jacobson Jr, M.J., Rijmen, V., Safavi-Naini, R. (eds.) SAC 2009. LNCS, vol. 5867, pp. 281–294. Springer, Heidelberg (2009)
14. Matsui, M.: Linear cryptanalysis method for DES cipher. In: Helleseth, T. (ed.) EUROCRYPT 1993. LNCS, vol. 765, pp. 386–397. Springer, Heidelberg (1994)
15. Shirai, T., Shibutani, K., Akishita, T., Moriai, S., Iwata, T.: The 128-bit blockcipher CLEFIA (extended abstract). In: Biryukov, A. (ed.) FSE 2007. LNCS, vol. 4593, pp. 181–195. Springer, Heidelberg (2007)
16. Tezcan, C.: The improbable differential attack: cryptanalysis of reduced round CLEFIA. In: Gong, G., Gupta, C.K. (eds.) INDOCRYPT 2010. LNCS, vol. 6498, pp. 197–209. Springer, Heidelberg (2010)
17. Tsunoo, Y., Tsujihara, E., Shigeri, M., Saito, T., Suzaki, T., Kubo, H.: Impossible differential cryptanalysis of CLEFIA. In: Nyberg, K. (ed.) FSE 2008. LNCS, vol. 5086, pp. 398–411. Springer, Heidelberg (2008)
18. Tsunoo, Y., Tsujihara, E., Shigeri, M., Suzaki, T., Kawabata, T.: Cryptanalysis of CLEFIA using multiple impossible differentials. ISITA **2008**, 1–6 (2008)
19. Wang, W., Wang, X.: Saturation cryptanalysis of CLEFIA. J. Commun. **29**(10), 88–92 (2008)
20. Zhang, W., Han, J.: Impossible differential analysis of reduced round CLEFIA. In: Yung, M., Liu, P., Lin, D. (eds.) INSCRYPT 2008. LNCS, vol. 5487, pp. 181–191. Springer, Heidelberg (2009)

Implementing Lightweight Block Ciphers
on x86 Architectures

Ryad Benadjila[1], Jian Guo[2], Victor Lomné[1($\boxtimes$)], and Thomas Peyrin[2]

[1] ANSSI, Paris, France
{ryad.benadjila,victor.lomne}@ssi.gouv.fr
[2] Division of Mathematical Sciences, School of Physical and Mathematical Sciences,
Nanyang Technological University, Singapore, Singapore
{ntu.guo,thomas.peyrin}@gmail.com

Abstract. Lightweight block ciphers are designed so as to fit into very constrained environments, but usually not really with software performance in mind. For classical lightweight applications where many constrained devices communicate with a server, it is also crucial that the cipher has good software performance on the server side. Recent work has shown that bitslice implementations applied to `Piccolo` and `PRESENT` led to very good software speeds, thus making lightweight ciphers interesting for cloud applications. However, we remark that bitslice implementations might not be interesting for some situations, where the amount of data to be enciphered at a time is usually small, and very little work has been done on non-bitslice implementations.

In this article, we explore general software implementations of lightweight ciphers on `x86` architectures, with a special focus on `LED`, `Piccolo` and `PRESENT`. First, we analyze table-based implementations, and we provide a theoretical model to predict the behavior of various possible trade-offs depending on the processor cache latency profile. We obtain the fastest table-based implementations for our lightweight ciphers, which is of interest for legacy processors. Secondly, we apply to our portfolio of primitives the `vperm` implementation trick for 4-bit Sboxes, which gives good performance, extra side-channels protection, and is quite fit for many lightweight primitives. Finally, we investigate bitslice implementations, analyzing various costs which are usually neglected (bitsliced form (un)packing, key schedule, etc.), but that must be taken in account for many lightweight applications. We finally discuss which type of implementation seems to be the best suited depending on the applications profile.

Keywords: Lightweight cryptography · Software · `vperm` · Bitslice · `LED` · `Piccolo` · `PRESENT`

1 Introduction

RFID tags and very constrained computing devices are expected to become increasingly important for many applications and industries. In parallel to this

J. Guo and T. Peyrin - Supported by the Singapore National Research Foundation Fellowship 2012 (NRF-NRFF2012-06).

T. Lange, K. Lauter, and P. Lisoněk (Eds.): SAC 2013, LNCS 8282, pp. 324–351, 2014.
DOI: 10.1007/978-3-662-43414-7_17, © Springer-Verlag Berlin Heidelberg 2014

general trend, the growth of ubiquitous computing and communication inter-connections naturally leads to more entry points and increased potential damage for attackers. Security is crucial for many situations, but often left apart due to cost and feasibility constraints. In order to fulfill the need in cryptographic primitives that can be implemented and executed in very constrained environments (area, energy consumption, etc.), aka lightweight cryptography, the research community has recently made significant advances in particular in the domain of symmetric-key cryptography.

Current NIST standards for block cipher (AES [10]) or hash function (SHA-2 [25] or SHA-3 [3]) are not really fit for very constrained environments and several alternatives have been proposed, such as PRESENT [5], KATAN [7], LED [13], Piccolo [23], TWINE [24] for block ciphers and QUARK [1], PHOTON [12], SPONGENT [4] for hash functions. Notably, PRESENT block cipher is now part of an ISO standard [17]. All these different proposals greatly improved our knowledge in lightweight designs and many already achieve close to optimal performance for certain metrics such as area consumption.

In practice, the constrained devices will be either communicating with other constrained devices or more probably with a server. In the latter case, the server is likely to have to handle an important number of devices, and while cryptography might be used in a protocol to secure the communications, other applications operations have to be performed by the server. Therefore, it is crucial that the server does not spend too much time performing cryptographic operations, even when communicating with many clients, and thus software performance does matter for lightweight cryptography.

At CHES 2012, Matsuda and Moriai [19] have studied the application of bitslice implementations to PRESENT and Piccolo block ciphers, concluding that current lightweight ciphers can be surprisingly competitive for cloud applications. Bitslice implementations allow impressive speed results and are also valuable for their inherent protection against various side-channel cryptanalysis. However, we argue that they might not really fit all the lightweight cryptography use cases, where a server has to communicate with many devices. Indeed, constrained devices usually encipher a very small amount of data at a time. For example, in its smallest form, an Electronic Product Code (EPC), which is thought to be a replacement for bar codes using low-cost passive RFID-tags, uses 64, 96 or 125 bits as a unique identifier for any physical item. Small data enciphering makes the cost of data transformation into bitsliced form and key schedule process very expensive (these costs are usually omitted by assuming that a rather large number of blocks will be enciphered).

Therefore, it is interesting to explore the software efficiency profile of lightweight ciphers not only for cloud applications but also for classical lightweight applications and, surprisingly, apart from embedded 8-bit architectures, they are not really meant to perform well in software on mid-range or high-end processors. For example, the currently best non-bitslice AES implementations reaches about 14 cycles per byte (c/B) on a 32-bit Pentium III CPU [20], while the currently best non-bitslice PRESENT implementations only runs in 130 c/B on the same processor (the implementation in [21] reports a performance of 16.2 cycles per bit). Therefore, we believe a gap exists in this area, even if very recent proposals such as TWINE do report good non-bitsliced software performances.

Our Contributions. In this article, we provide three main contributions for lightweight ciphers software implementations on x86 architectures, with a special focus on LED, PRESENT and Piccolo. First, in Sect. 2, we argue that table-based implementations are still valuable in particular situations (some servers with "legacy" CPUs, pre Core2, might lack the necessary SSE instructions set that is used in optimized bitslice or vperm implementations) and we propose new interesting trade-offs, with a theoretical cache modeling to better predict which trade-off will be suitable depending on the target processor. Our model is backed up by our experiments and we obtain the best known table-based implementations for the studied lightweight ciphers.

Then, in Sect. 3, we further push software implementations of lightweight ciphers by exploring the vperm implementation trick for 4-bit Sboxes that has already proven to be interesting for AES [14] or TWINE [24], and which provides cache-timing attack resistance. We propose a strategy for our portfolio of lightweight ciphers, and we conclude that the linear layer, usually not the part contributing a lot in the amount of computations, can have a significant impact on the performances for this type of implementation. We note that these implementations are interesting because they apply to almost all lightweight ciphers and they produce very efficient code.

Thirdly, in Sect. 4, we explore bitslice implementations for lightweight ciphers and we show that for some common use cases they are less interesting than for cloud applications [19]. In fact, bitslice implementations can be slower than table-based of vperm in some situations, for example when only a low number of blocks is enciphered per device. Moreover, previous bitslice analysis usually neglects the key schedule part, so we provide bitsliced versions of the key schedules. However, even in a bitsliced version, the key schedule can have a significant impact on the overall performance. We therefore revisit this type of implementation by taking into account various factors that are important in practice, such as the amount of distinct keys, the amount of blocks to be enciphered, etc. We note that we provide the first bitslice implementation of LED, greatly improving over the best known software performance of this cipher.

For all three primitives LED, PRESENT and Piccolo, we have coded all three versions of implementation with various tradeoffs. Then, for various crucial use cases presented in Sect. 5, we compare the different implementation strategies and we discuss our results in Sect. 6. For the readers not familiar with them, we quickly explain in Appendix A the three lightweight ciphers that we take as example for our implementations and refer to the specification documents [5,13, 23] for a complete description. As many other lightweight ciphers, LED, PRESENT and Piccolo are 64-bit ciphers based on the repetition of a round function built upon a 4-bit Sbox and a linear diffusion layer, while the key schedule is very simple if not inexistent. All these design choices are justified by the reduction of the area consumption and while smaller Sboxes are possible, 4 bits is a sensitive choice which can provide very small area in hardware as well as ease of implementation in software.

The reader will find more details and code illustrations in the extended version of this paper [2]. Furthermore, the full source codes of the implementations presented in this paper are available online at https://github.com/rb-anssi/lightweight-crypto-lib.

2 Table-Based Implementations

2.1 Core Ideas

State of the Art. Tabulating operations for efficiency purposes is an old method well known by programmers. When applied to block ciphers, the goal is to tabulate as much as possible the different operations composing one round, such that its computation consists in:

- selecting slices of the internal state by shift and mask operations;
- performing several table lookups to achieve the round transformation;
- aggregating lookup table outputs to get the updated internal state;
- performing the key addition layer.

Such an approach has for instance been proposed by Daemen and Rijmen in [10] to perform efficiently AES operations on 32-bit processors. Thus, an AES round can be computed with 16 table lookups, using 4 tables of 8-bit inputs and 32-bit outputs (each table having a size of about 1 KB).

Table Size Tradeoffs. Many lightweight ciphers have in common 64-bit block and 4-bit Sbox, which allows a lot of tradeoffs when implemented on 32 or 64-bit processors with a table-based approach. It can be tedious to implement all these tradeoffs and check which one provides the best results. Thus, in the following, we propose a model to directly find the most efficient implementation strategy. We emphasize that such a modeling method can be applied on all 32 or 64-bit architectures, but here we focus specifically on Intel x86 ones. If one considers a generic Substitution and Permutation Network (SPN) based lightweight cipher (like LED or PRESENT), the round function can be performed, following the table-based approach, as follows (the internal state being divided into $64/m$ slices of m bits each, T0, T1, ... being tables with m-bit input and 64-bit output, and MASKm being a mask with m consecutive least significant bits at 1):

```
// Computation of a generic SPN lightweight cipher round
// Input: 64-bit state  ---  Output: updated 64-bit state
t0 = T0[ state       & MASKm];
t1 = T1[(state >>  m) & MASKm];
t2 = T2[(state >> 2m) & MASKm];
...
state = t0 ^ t1 ^ t2 ^ ...;
```

Note that the choice of 64-bit output tables exactly fits with the size of the cipher internal state, and thus one can directly include the linear layer when doing the table lookup. One round will then roughly be computed with shift, mask, table lookup and XOR operations, whose amount will depend on the size of the tables (each table T will have a size $S_T = 2^m \times 8$ bytes). The main issue will be to choose the best tradeoff for m. Indeed, the bigger are the tables, the smaller is the amount of operations to compute during the round function, but the bigger are the latencies of the table lookups. Furthermore, depending on m, the Intel x86 instruction set allows some tricks (like mask-and-move instructions) reducing the number of operations. We then focus on the assembly pseudo-code corresponding to one line (for $m = 4, 12, 16$) or two lines (for $m = 8$) of the previous generic SPN round functions on m (the assembly is Intel syntax):

```
// m=8 (2 rounds)
shr state, 16
// m=4 or 12 (1 round)          movzbl tmp1, state          // m=16 (1 round)
shr state, m                    movzbh tmp2, state          // The state is in rax
mov tmp, state                  mov/xor accumulator, [T+8*tmp1]   shr rax, 16
and tmp, MASKm                  mov/xor accumulator, [T+8*tmp2]   mov tmp, ax
mov/xor accumulator, [T+8*tmp]  ...                         mov/xor accumulator, [T+8*tmp]
...                                                         ...
```

It is to be noted that these pseudo-codes are for x86 64-bit architectures (on 32-bit ones, more mov and xor are required due to the fact that table lookups only get 32-bit words – refer to table under section "Results" (footnote a) for more details about this –).

Cache Latency Model. To perform efficiently memory accesses, modern processors have different cache memory levels ($L1$, $L2$ and sometimes $L3$). According to cache policy rules, the most used data will be stored in $L1$, then in $L2$, etc... When considering a table T of size $|T|$, the probability P_{L1} that an element of T is in $L1$ (cache of size $|L1|$) is $P_{L1} = \frac{|L1|}{|T|}$ if $|T| > |L1|$ and $P_{L1} = 1$ otherwise. Furthermore, the probability P_{L2} that an element of T is in $L2$ and not in $L1$ (considering that the element is either in $L1$ or in $L2$[1], i.e. $|T| \leq |L1| + |L2|$) is $P_{L2} = 1 - P_{L1}$. Thus, one can simply deduce the average latency l_T to load an element of T during a random access (which is the case for block ciphers):

$$l_T = l_{L1} \times P_{L1} + l_{L2} \times P_{L2} = l_{L1} \times P_{L1} + l_{L2} \times (1 - P_{L1}) \qquad (1)$$

with l_{L1} and l_{L2} denoting the latencies of $L1$ and $L2$ caches respectively. Since in this work we focus on x86 architectures, and more precisely on Intel ones, we now have to consider the size and the latency of their different cache memories. These numbers for several microarchitectures are given in the table below.

---

[1] For the sake of simplicity, we consider an exclusive cache model. Considering inclusive or hybrid models would not change the equation much.

Microarchitecture	L1 size (KB)	L1 latency (cycles)	L2 size (KB)	L2 latency (cycles)
Intel P6	16 or 32	3	512	8
Intel Core	32	3	1500	15
Intel Nehalem/Westmere[a]	32	4	256	10
Intel Sandy/Ivy Bridge[a]	32	5[b]	256	12

[a] Westmere is the 32 nm die shrink of the Nehalem microarchitecture, and Ivy Bridge is the 22 nm die shrink of Sandy Bridge.
[b] Sandy and Ivy Bridge data L1 cache latency can drop to 4 cycles when the offset from the base address is less than 2048 bytes (see [16] for more details). However, rounding this to a fixed 5 cycles gives a reasonable first-order approximation for our model.

Results. From the generic SPN round pseudo-code given above (and its assembly decomposition), one can compute the number of instructions required for such a round according to the value m of a block slice and the microarchitecture cache memory characteristics. We can weight each instruction by its latency. We assume that a register to register shift, move and XOR have a latency of one cycle, whereas a table lookup has an average latency l_T defined in Eq. (1). An average theoretical latency of one round, for different microarchitectures, is given in the table below (for each architecture, the average latency is obtained by summing all the operations latencies).

Instruction type	Theoretical number of instructions for one round (for different table input sizes m)			
	$m = 4$ bits	$m = 8$ bits	$m = 12$ bits	$m = 16$ bits
Shift	15	3	5	3
Move/xor	15	8	5	3
Mask	16	0	5	0
Table lookup[a]	16 (32)	8 (16)	6 (12)	4 (8)

Microarchitecture	Theoretical average round latency (for different table input sizes m)			
	$m = 4$ bits	$m = 8$ bits	$m = 12$ bits	$m = 16$ bits
Intel P6	142	59	99	93
Intel Core	94	35	91	264
Intel Nehalem/Westmere	110	43	68	186
Intel Sandy/Ivy Bridge	126	51	79	114

[a] The number in brackets denotes the cost for 32-bit architectures, where two table lookups need to be performed in order to obtain an entire 64-bit output. This however holds if we only consider **general purpose registers** loads: only one table lookup is needed when using SIMD registers, at the expense of additional loads to save back the state from SSE to general purpose registers. For the sake of simplicity, we only focus on general purpose registers code latency in this section.

Note that for $m = 16$ bits, we might have to also consider the $L3$ or RAM latency depending on the $L2$ size, and naturally extend the Eq. (1). We verified experimentally these values by implementing and running such a generic SPN round for the different m values considered. We could confirm the results on each of the considered microarchitectures. Note however that the experimental results do not exactly match the theoretical ones due to the superscalar property of the Intel architectures[2]. Nevertheless, we emphasize the fact that this model is sufficient for our purpose: one can deduce that 8-bit slices seem to be the best tradeoff from an efficiency point-of-view, whatever the microarchitecture, and we will apply this tradeoff on each of the three lightweight ciphers from our portfolio. One can also notice that some theoretical counter-intuitive results are experimentally verified: for instance, 16-bits input tables outperform 4-bit input tables on some microarchitectures though a lot of data are outside $L1$ and $L2$ (this is due to the reduced number of shift/move/mask operations compensating the bad average table access latency). Even though this is not the core subject of our paper, this theoretical model can be used for performance comparisons of table based implementations on other architectures such as ARM, SPARC or PowerPC.

Finally, table-based implementations specificities for each cipher are described in the following sections.

2.2   LED

We build eight tables, each one taking as input two row-wise adjacent 4-bit Sbox words (thus 8-bit input), and providing 64-bit output words. We give as example the description of the first table T_0, that takes as input the two least significant 4-bit words of the internal state (we denote a_0 and a_1 these two words, while SB represents the Sbox and $\otimes$ the multiplication in $GF(2^4)$):

$$
T_0(a_0, a_1) = \begin{bmatrix} 4 \otimes SB[a_0] & 4 \otimes SB[a_1] & 0 & 0 \\ 8 \otimes SB[a_0] & 8 \otimes SB[a_1] & 0 & 0 \\ B \otimes SB[a_0] & B \otimes SB[a_1] & 0 & 0 \\ 2 \otimes SB[a_0] & 2 \otimes SB[a_1] & 0 & 0 \end{bmatrix}
$$

Note that the 4-bit input words row-wise packing and the 64-bit output words allow to include the ShiftRows operation directly inside the table, by carefully placing the meaningful output bits at their correct position. Thus, the three round operations SubCells, ShiftRows and MixColumnsSerial are performed with 7 shifts and 8 masks (to select the eight 8-bit slices of the internal state), 8 table lookups (to perform the three round operations) and 7 XORs to agglomerate the eight table outputs.

Furthermore one extra table of 31 or 48 64-bit words (respectively in the case of LED-64 and LED-128) allows to perform the AddConstants operation with only

---

[2] One should consider the throughput of the instructions instead of their latencies for accurate performance estimates.

one table lookup and one XOR (again, we manipulate 64-bit words in order to directly place the 4-bit constants at their correct position).

To summarize, one round of LED with 64-bit keys (resp. 128-bit keys) can be implemented with 7 shifts, 8 masks, 8 XORs[3] and 9 table lookups, and with memory requirements of 16640 bytes (resp. 16768 bytes). The tables are therefore small enough to fit mostly or even entirely in the L1 cache of the processor. We provide the pseudo-code for the ith round computation (T_cst being the table computing the AddConstants operation, and T0, T1, T2, T3, T4, T5, T6 and T7 being the eight tables performing the SubCells, ShiftRows and MixColumnsSerial operations):

```
// Computation of the LED round i
// Input: 64-bit state St, round number i  --- Output: updated 64-bit state St
St ^= T_cst[i];
t0 = T0[St        & 0xff];   t1 = T1[(St >>  8) & 0xff];
t2 = T2[(St >> 16) & 0xff];   t3 = T3[(St >> 24) & 0xff];
t4 = T4[(St >> 32) & 0xff];   t5 = T5[(St >> 40) & 0xff];
t6 = T6[(St >> 48) & 0xff];   t7 = T7[(St >> 56) & 0xff];
St = t0 ^ t1 ^ t2 ^ t3 ^ t4 ^ t5 ^ t6 ^ t7;
```

2.3 PRESENT

Encryption. Having a very similar structure to LED, we use the same implementation strategy for PRESENT. Eight tables are built, each one taking as input two adjacent Sbox 4-bit words (8-bit inputs), and providing 64-bit output words, such that the tables also take into account the permutation layer. The round computation pseudo-code is exactly the same as for LED, except that there is no constant addition in the round function. Therefore, one PRESENT round is performed with 7 shifts, 8 masks, 8 table lookups and 7 XORs[3] and requires eight tables of 2048 bytes each, thus 16384 bytes in total. The tables are therefore small enough to fit mostly or even entirely in L1 cache. An example of how to build the tables is provided in Appendix C.1 of [2].

Key Schedule. The PRESENT key schedule is quite costly in software, due to the 61-bit rotation over the full size of the master key (especially for the 80-bit key version, which does not fit exactly within a multiple of a x86 general purpose register size). Using two small tables of 31 and 16 64-bit words, one can compute the round counter addition and the key schedule Sbox lookup with only a single table lookup and a XOR (the 128-bit key version performs two adjacent Sbox calls in the key schedule, thus the second table will contain 256 elements in the case of PRESENT-128). We provide the pseudo-code of the 80-bit version in Appendix C.1 of [2].

2.4 Piccolo

Encryption. The table-based implementation of Piccolo is slightly different from that of LED or PRESENT since Piccolo has a Feistel network structure. In

---

[3] These figures correspond to high level pseudo-code, but are slightly changed in assembly as reflected in the cache model results thanks to mask-and-move instructions.

order to tabulate as much as possible the internal function F, we divide it in two parts. The first one packs the first Sbox layer of F and also the subsequent diffusion layer. It yields two tables of 8-bit input and 32-bit output (two Sbox inputs are handled at a time), which can be used to perform the first part of F in both branches of the Feistel. The second part computes the second Sbox layer only. It is therefore implemented using four tables of 8-bit input and 64-bit output (two tables per branch), allowing again to place the 16-bit branches at their correct positions before the byte permutation at the end of the round. We explain in Appendix C.2 of [2] how to build these tables, and the total amount of memory required is 10240 bytes, which is small enough to fit entirely in the L1 cache of the processor. The final byte permutation of a `Piccolo` round can then be computed efficiently with two masks, two 16-bit rotations and one XOR. We provide the pseudo-code for the ith round computation of `Piccolo` in Appendix C.2 of [2].

Key Schedule. The 80-bit and 128-bit versions of the `Piccolo` key schedule are slightly different, nevertheless they have a similar core which consists in selecting 16-bit slices of the master key and XORing them with constant values. Hence, we build one extra small table made of 25 64-bit words (or 31 words for `Piccolo`-128) corresponding to the constant values. Then, we prepare several 16-bit slices of the master key in 64-bit words, and one can perform the key schedule with only a single table lookup and one XOR operation. Note that the permutation used in the 128-bit version of the key schedule can be efficiently implemented with two masks, two 16-bit rotations and one XOR.

3   Implementations Using `vperm` Technique

3.1   Introducing the `vperm` Technique

Vector Permute, abbreviated `vperm`, is a technique that uses vector permutation instructions in order to implement table lookups by taking advantage of the SIMD engine present inside modern CPUs. The main advantages of the `vperm` technique are parallel table lookups and timing attacks side-channel resistance. This technique, applied to block cipher implementations, comes originally from [14]. It has also proven to be efficient for multivariate cryptography [8].

The main idea behind the `vperm` technique is to use shuffling instructions for looking into small size tables. Though this technique can be used in different architectures where SIMD shuffling instructions are present (for instance AltiVec on PowerPC, or NEON on ARM), we will exclusively focus on their x86 flavor, namely the `pshufb` instruction. This instruction has been introduced with the SSSE3 extension that came with the Intel Core microarchitecture.

Regarding the lightweight block ciphers, the `vperm` technique has already been applied to TWINE [24], yielding in very competitive results on the x86 platform (6.87 c/B for a 2-message encryption). However, there are no results available for other lightweight block ciphers. In the following subsections, we study how the vperm technique fits for LED, Piccolo and PRESENT. We will show that, though the confusion layer is quite straightforward to implement using vperm, the linear diffusion layer can be challenging.

3.2   Core Ideas for vperm Applied to Lightweight Block Ciphers

In this section, we briefly describe the main implementation ideas that are common to LED, PRESENT and Piccolo (as well as to many lightweight block ciphers).

The pshufb Instruction. pshufb is a byte shuffling instruction that takes two 128-bit operands as input, e.g. xmm0 and xmm1 registers (see Fig. 1). The destination operand xmm0 bytes are shuffled according to the source operand: xmm1 is used as a permutation mask selecting bytes inside xmm0. Only the low nibbles of bytes in xmm1 are used, and if the MSB is set the resulting byte is nullified. The result of the shuffling is stored inside xmm0. The second operand can be a memory reference. There is an AVX variant vpshufb of pshufb that takes three operands as input, the first operand being the destination. This saves a movdqa operation that is normally required to avoid overwriting the destination, thus saving some CPU cycles.

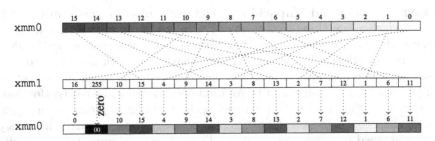

Fig. 1. Result of "pshufb xmm0, xmm1": bytes in xmm0 are shuffled according to the content of xmm1. Only the low nibble of bytes in xmm1 are used as index: index 0x10=16 in the example translates to 0. When the byte index inside xmm1 $\geq$ 128 (i.e. the high bit of the byte is set, 255 on the example), the destination byte is zeroed.

Sbox Implementation. Most lightweight block ciphers use Sboxes on $GF(2^4)$, meaning that the Sbox is a table of 16 possible output values selected by the input. It is straightforward to implement such an operation on 16 nibbles, in parallel, using the pshufb instruction (see Fig. 1). The piece of code in Fig. 2 performs 16 parallel Sbox lookups on the 16 low nibbles of the r register (the high nibbles of each byte r_i are supposed to be zero). The same technique can be used for any function from $GF(2^4)$ to itself (including multiplications over the field), or even any function from $GF(2^4)$ to $GF(2^8)$ without any loss of parallelism since one xmm register is 16-byte long. Hence, the MixColumns-like multiplications can be stored inside 16-byte tables. More specifically, we can store the composition of the Sbox and the multiplication inside a single 16-element table, as explained in Sect. 2.

```
// Input: r as input, s as the sbox,
// e.g sbox={0x0c, 0x05, ..., 0x02}
// for PRESENT and LED
// Output: t
movdqa t, s
pshufb t, r
```

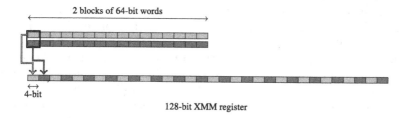

| s_{15} | s_{14} | s_{13} | s_{12} | s_{11} | s_{10} | s_9 | s_8 | s_7 | s_6 | s_5 | s_4 | s_3 | s_2 | s_1 | s_0 | s |

| r_{15} | r_{14} | r_{13} | r_{12} | r_{11} | r_{10} | r_9 | r_8 | r_7 | r_6 | r_5 | r_4 | r_3 | r_2 | r_1 | r_0 | r |

| s_{r15} | s_{r14} | s_{r13} | s_{r12} | s_{r11} | s_{r10} | s_{r9} | s_{r8} | s_{r7} | s_{r6} | s_{r5} | s_{r4} | s_{r3} | s_{r2} | s_{r1} | s_{r0} | t |

Fig. 2. Using `pshufb` for 16 parallel Sbox lookups (high nibbles of bytes r_i are supposed to be zero).

Extending to Bigger Tables. `pshufb` can be utilized in order to compute a 4-bit to 8-bit function and it is possible to use the same technique for lookups inside tables with even bigger output size (but multiple of 8 bits). As presented on Fig. 8 in Appendix D.1 of [2], if we consider, for instance, a 16-bit output table, we can pack this table inside two 128-bit `xmm` registers s^0 and s^1. Then, the ith entry of the table ($0 \leq i \leq 15$) is represented by the 16-bit value formed by s_i^0 and s_i^1. Therefore, one can perform 16 parallel table lookups (with 16 output bits) by using two `pshufb` in a row, the first one getting the first half of the word in t^0, and the second one getting the second half in t^1.

Message Packing and Unpacking. Lightweight block ciphers states are 64-bit long, which means that two of them can be stored inside a 128-bit `xmm` register. However, the natural packing concatenating the two states side by side inside a register is not optimal. This is due to the fact that the algorithms we focus on use nibble-based permutations as part of their linear diffusion layer. Implementing such permutations by using shift or rotation operations can be costly. However, if the two states are packed by interleaving their nibbles as presented in Fig. 3, it is possible to realize any nibble permutation by using `pshufb`, since they are now mapped to a byte permutation. The packing and unpacking are easily implemented using some shift and `pshufb` operations. Their cost, around ten cycles, is marginal compared to the encryption process. Using this packing, one can apply 32 Sbox lookups on the two states by using two `pshufb`, two `pand` masks and one 4-bit left shift `psrlw` to isolate low and high nibbles, and one `pxor` to merge the two results. As we will explain, this packing will be applied to `Piccolo` and `PRESENT`, but not to `LED`.

2 blocks of 64-bit words

4-bit

128-bit XMM register

Fig. 3. Packing for the 2-parallel `vperm` implementation of `PRESENT` and `Piccolo`. Each rectangle represents a 4-bit nibble.

Using AVX Extensions. On the two last Intel CPU generations (Sandy and Ivy Bridge), a new instruction set has been added to extend Westmere's SSE 4.2. The 128-bit xmm registers have also been extended to 256-bit ymm registers, most of the instructions do however not operate on the full ymm registers, but only on their low 128-bit part. The full AVX extensions operating on ymm will be introduced on the forthcoming Haswell architecture with AVX2. All the presented encryption algorithms and their key schedules can still benefit from AVX on Sandy and Ivy Bridge by using the three operands form of the instructions, which saves registers backup. For instance, table lookups can be performed with one instruction "vpshufb t, s, r" instead of the two instructions "movdqa t, s; pshufb t, r"[4].

3.3 LED

The LED block cipher does not have a key schedule *per se* and since the decryption process is not more complex than the encryption one (the coefficients for the inverse diffusion matrix are the same as for the original matrix), we will only focus on the latter case. As explained previously, the 4-bit Sbox layer can be implemented in a few cycles by using pshufb, masks and shifts. The ShiftRows is also immediate with a pshufb by using the interleaved nibbles packing described above. However, the MixColumnsSerial step uses field multiplications with 11 different constants (4, 2, B ...). Using as many as 11 lookup tables as multiplicative constants would be too costly as they would not leave room for the state and other operations inside the xmm registers. We could also use the fact that LED's MDS matrix is a power of a simpler sparse matrix, using less constants: the drawback is that raising to the power 4 would mean that the all operations would have to be applied four times.

We found out that there is a better implementation strategy for LED: we can use the table-based tricks to store the Sbox and MixColumnsSerial layers inside xmm register-based tables. Each column can be stored inside a $2^4 \times 2 = 32$ bytes table (thus 2 xmm registers). Hence, 4 pairs of xmm registers will store the 4 tables needed to perform a round of LED, and lookups inside each table will be performed in a vectorized way for each nibble of the state using two pshufb as described in Sect. 3.2. The drawback is that the output words will be on different xmm registers, but the repacking of this step can be combined with the ShiftRows layer that shuffles the columns. We also use por masking to force the MSB of bytes that are not concerned with a lookup in a specific table. For each LED round, 8 pshufb instructions are used for the lookups, and 6 pshufb for the shifting layer (ShiftRows and repacking). This implementation strategy does not use the specific state packing from Fig. 3 since shuffling for the ShiftRows and table repacking can be expressed using pshufb. However, one should notice that there is a small message packing cost for LED due to its row oriented message

---

[4] The expected throughput improvement would however vary across the considered microarchitectures (mainly depending on the pipeline stage where register-to-register moves are performed, as well as the front end instruction decoder throughput).

loading in the state: the input message is packed in a column wise fashion, and the ciphertext is packed back to row wise.

3.4 PRESENT

PRESENT can benefit from the vperm technique in both encryption and key schedule, since the latter uses Sbox lookups for subkeys computations.

Encryption. As explained in [21] and on Fig. 4, PRESENT's pLayer permutation can be seen as the composition of two permutations: one acting on bits inside groups of 16 bits, and one shuffling the nibbles inside the 64-bit state. As for the table-based implementations of LED, it would be possible to compute a PRESENT round by using 4-bit to 16-bit tables that merge the Sbox and the first permutation of the pLayer acting on 16-bit groups. Nevertheless, we have found that this permutation can be implemented in a more efficient way by moving groups of bits (see the code on Fig. 4 for more details). The second permutation, mapped to a byte permutation thanks to the message packing from Fig. 3, can be expressed as one pshufb.

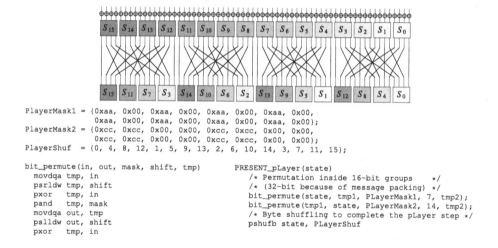

```
PlayerMask1 = {0xaa, 0x00, 0xaa, 0x00, 0xaa, 0x00, 0xaa, 0x00,
               0xaa, 0x00, 0xaa, 0x00, 0xaa, 0x00, 0xaa, 0x00};
PlayerMask2 = {0xcc, 0xcc, 0x00, 0x00, 0xcc, 0xcc, 0x00, 0x00,
               0xcc, 0xcc, 0x00, 0x00, 0xcc, 0xcc, 0x00, 0x00};
PlayerShuf  = {0, 4, 8, 12, 1, 5, 9, 13, 2, 6, 10, 14, 3, 7, 11, 15};
```

```
bit_permute(in, out, mask, shift, tmp)        PRESENT_pLayer(state)
    movdqa  tmp, in                               /* Permutation inside 16-bit groups   */
    psrldw  tmp, shift                            /* (32-bit because of message packing) */
    pxor    tmp, in                               bit_permute(state, tmp1, PLayerMask1, 7, tmp2);
    pand    tmp, mask                             bit_permute(tmp1, state, PLayerMask2, 14, tmp2);
    movdqa  out, tmp                              /* Byte shuffling to complete the pLayer step */
    pslldw  out, shift                            pshufb state, PLayerShuf
    pxor    tmp, in
```

Fig. 4. PRESENT's pLayer representation as two permutations.

Key Schedule. A straightforward method for implementing PRESENT's keys schedules for 80-bit and 128-bit keys would be to store the master key inside one xmm register and compute all the subkeys by using rotations on the register (80-bit or 128-bit rotations depending on the key size), and extract the high part to get each subkey. However, the SSE instruction set lacks a rotation instruction. One could implement the rotation with two shifts and one XOR (and one AND for the 80-bit key case), but the shift instructions ps(r/l)ldq that operate on the entire 128-bit xmm register can only handle shift values that are multiples of 8 bits. Since PRESENT's key schedules use a 61-bit rotation, using such instructions is therefore too costly. Instead, we split the high and low key parts in two xmm register halves, which allows us to perform the 61-bit rotation with the quadword shift instructions ps(r/l)lq. It is possible to vectorize the key schedule on two keys by using this trick, since the high parts of the two xmm registers can be used to store high and low keys of the second master key:

| keylow2 | keylow1 | xmm0 |
| keyhigh2 | keyhigh1 | xmm1 |

One should notice that since the PRESENT vperm encryption part uses packed messages, the scheduled keys that will be XORed to the cipher state must be packed in the same way. However, the 61-bit rotation is not compatible with the nibble interleaving packing from Fig. 3, which means that the key schedule cannot be easily performed with this data packing. This implies that all the subkeys are to be packed after they have been generated and this explains the high key schedule packing cost reported in Appendix B.

3.5 Piccolo

Encryption. Piccolo's F function uses a circulant MixColumns matrix over $GF(2^4)$, which allows using three 16 bytes tables, namely the Sbox, the Sbox composed with the multiplication by 2 in the field, and the Sbox composed with the multiplication by 3. Two states of Piccolo are stored in one xmm register with the nibbles interleaved as in Fig. 3. It is then possible to implement one Piccolo round with two F functions in parallel inside the xmm register, by using three pshufb for the three multiplications lookups (by 1, 2, and 3). Three more pshufb on the results and three pxor are necessary in order to perform the columns mixing according to the circulant nature of the MixColumns matrix. The second layer of Sbox lookups in F can be performed with only one pshufb. Finally, Piccolo's Round Permutation is realized with a unique pshufb, since it is a byte permutation. The piece of code given in Appendix D. 2 of [2] illustrates these steps (it is suited for the low nibbles of the state, almost the same code is used for the high nibbles).

Key Schedule. Piccolo's key schedules for 80 and 128-bit keys do not really benefit from the vperm technique, since no Sbox lookup nor field multiplication over $GF(2^4)$ is performed. The same implementation tricks as presented in Sect. 2.4 are used in order to minimize the number of operations extracting the master key subparts. The main difference with the table-based implementations key schedule is that in the case of vperm, the process is performed inside xmm registers with SSE instructions: the main benefit being that one can vectorize the key schedule for two master keys, performing all the operations with the nibbles interleaved packing format from Fig. 3. This results in an optimized key schedule for two keys that requires almost the same number of cycles than the table-based implementation on one key (see results in Appendix B).

4   Bitslice Implementations

Bitslice implementations often lead to impressive performance results, as shown for example in [19] for PRESENT and Piccolo. However, we would like to also take into account the key schedule cost that might not be negligible in several typical lightweight cryptography use cases, such as short data or independent keys for different data blocks (see 5.2 for specific examples). As a consequence, exploring the bitslice possibilities for the various key schedules is of interest. In particular, many distinct keys might be used for the encryption and non-bitsliced key schedules might kill the parallelism gain if one does the packing for each round key (packing/unpacking takes comparable cycles as for encryption in most of the cases). This bitsliced key scheduling has never been studied for lightweight block ciphers to our knowledge, and we provide some results for the three ciphers in this section. One of our conclusions is that some key schedules can significantly slow down performances depending on the use case, which somehow moderates the results exposed in [19].

4.1   The Packing/unpacking

The choice of an appropriate packing inside the xmm registers is important for a bitslice implementation. For the LED bitsliced version with 16 parallel blocks, we use the packing described in Fig. 9 in Appendix E.4 of [2]. The packing for 32 parallel blocks is identical (see Fig. 11 of [2]). It is to be noted that the packing used for PRESENT is the same as for LED (such a packing can be obtained with a little more than one hundred of instructions).

The (un)packing for Piccolo with 16-parallel blocks depicted in Fig. 10 of [2] is very similar and requires a few more instructions. The reader can refer to [19] for details and code about this.

4.2   The Encryption

An important part of the encryption cost are the Sboxes, but the bitslice representation allows to compute many of them in parallel within a few clock cycles. We recall the logical instructions sequences proposed by [19] in Appendix E.1 of [2] for the LED and PRESENT Sbox, and in Appendix E.2 of [2] for the Piccolo Sbox.

The second part of an encryption round is the linear diffusion layer. For LED, the ShiftRows is simply performed with a few pshufb operations and the Mix-ColumnsSerial are handled with the same method as in [18] for AES or in [19] for Piccolo diffusion matrices. In the case of LED, one also has to consider the XOR-ing of round dependent constants during the AddConstants function, but this can be done easily by preparing in advance the constants in bitsliced form. For PRESENT, the bit permutation function pLayer can be performed by just reorganizing the positions of the 16-bit (or 32-bit) words in the xmm registers in bitsliced form. This can be executed efficiently [19] using a few pshufd, punpck(h/l)dq and punpck(h/l)qdq instructions (see the pseudo-code in Appendix E.3 of [2] for 8-parallel data blocks). For `Piccolo`, the nibble position permutation (performed with a few `pshufd` instructions) and the matrix multiplication are similar to the ones in [19].

4.3   The Key Schedule

As previously explained, the key schedule cost can be prohibitive in certain use cases when it comes to bitslicing. Thus, it seems reasonable to design **bitsliced versions** of the key schedule: this would leverage possible parallelism when many keys are processed, and this will prepare these keys in their packed format so that XORing them with the bitsliced state is straightforward. As a matter of consequence, the bitslice format for the key must be the same as for the data, or at least very similar so that the repacking cost is small. To minimize the key schedule cost, the packing is only performed once for the original keys, from which the subkeys are produced by shift and masking operations.

LED. No key schedule is defined for LED. Only the original secret key has to be packed in the data bitsliced format (one 64-bit key for LED-64 and two 64-bit keys for LED-128, other sizes use a sliding window requiring some additional shifts and masks).

`Piccolo`. The key schedule is very light: it basically consists in selecting 16-bit chunks from the original secret key and XORing them with round constants. Similarly to LED, our implementation first prepares the 16-bit chunks in bitsliced format once and for all. Thanks to the adapted packing, the two 16-bit key words appear in the same registers. For instance, when parallelism is of 16 blocks, 8 `xmm` registers are required to store the data and each round key, however, 4 are required only for storing one round-key in our case, because the other 4 contain only 0s, which can be discarded. This saves storage, and also key-addition operations by half. Another important observation is that even-number indexed chunks appear only in the left part of the round keys, and odd-number indexed chunks appear only in their right parts. Hence, we can pre-position these chunks only once, and the key schedule would involve only XORing the appropriate two chunks and the constants. To reduce the number of packing operations, we first pack all the original secret keys without re-positioning, and then do the pre-positioning for subkeys. These arrangements minimize the overall operations required by the key schedule.

PRESENT. The key schedule of PRESENT is not well suited for software, and even less suited when the key data has to be in bitsliced format. We divide the keys in two chunks (64 and 16 bits for PRESENT-80 and two 64-bit chunks for PRESENT-128) and prepare them in bitsliced format using the same packing as the data (each first chunks of the keys are packed together and each second chunks of the keys are packed together). The subkey to be XORed every round to the cipher internal state is located in the first chunk. The constants addition of the key schedule update function is simply handled by pre-formatting the constants in the bitsliced format and XORing them to the chunks (in fact only one chunk will be impacted if one does this step before the rotation). Then, the Sbox layer is performed by using the same Sbox function as for the internal cipher, just making sure with a mask that only a single Sbox is applied. Finally, the 61-bit rotation is separated in two parts, since only rotations of a multiple of 4 bits are easy to handle in bitslice packing. First, a 60-bit rotation is applied using several `pshufb` instructions (together with masking and XORs). Then, a single bit rotation is computed by changing the ordering of the xmm registers (the xmm registers containing the third Sbox bits will now contain the second Sbox bits, etc.). An adjustment is eventually required as some bits will go beyond the register limit and should switch to another one (this can be done with more shifts, masks and XORs). We provide the pseudo-code for the bitsliced key schedule implementation of PRESENT-80 in Appendix E.5 of [2].

4.4 Discussions

To have a fair view on the workload of the key schedules, we minimized the number of packing operations in each implementation. The Table below, deduced from Table 2, shows the ratio of the key schedule (including the packing of the keys and subkeys generations) over one data block encryption (including plaintext packing, encryption, ciphertext unpacking) for 16 blocks parallelism. In other words, it represents the workload increase when taking key schedule into account. LED is affected only slightly, Piccolo by a quarter and PRESENT by more than half.

	LED-64	LED-128	Piccolo-80	Piccolo-128	PRESENT-80	PRESENT-128
Key schedule ratio	3.3 %	4.1 %	20.2 %	26.7 %	55.2 %	59.9 %

5 Analyzing the Performance

5.1 Framework for Performance Evaluation

In order to compare various implementation techniques, we will consider that a server is communicating with D devices, each using a distinct key. For each device, the server has to encipher/decipher B 64-bit blocks of data. Moreover, we distinguish between the cases where the enciphered data comes from a parallel operating mode (like CTR) or a serial one (like CBC).

Now, we would like to take in account the fact that some implementations can be faster when some parallelism is possible (like bitslice technique). Let t_E be the time required by the implementation to perform the encryption process (without the key schedule and without the packing/unpacking of the input/output data). Let P_E denote the number of blocks that the implementation enciphers at a time in an encryption process (i.e. the number of blocks the implementation was intended to be used with). Similarly, let t_{KS} be the time required by the implementation to perform the key schedule process (without the packing of the key data) and we naturally extend the notation to P_{KS}.

We remark that ciphering a lower number of blocks than P_E (resp. P_{KS}) will still require time t_E (resp. t_{KS}). However, contrary to the encryption or key schedule process, the packing/unpacking time of the input/output data will strongly depend on the number of blocks involved. Therefore, if we denote by t_{pack} the time required to pack one block of data, we get that packing x blocks simply requires $x \cdot t_{pack}$. Similarly, we denote t_{unpack} the time required to unpack one block of data and unpacking x blocks simply requires $x \cdot t_{unpack}$. For the key schedule, t_{packKS} denotes the time to pack the key data, and packing x keys requires $x \cdot t_{packKS}$ (there is no need to unpack the key).

Finally, depending on D and B, the average time per block required to encrypt all $D \cdot B$ data blocks with a parallel operating mode is given by:

$$s_{parallel}(D, B) = \frac{\text{total encryption time}}{\text{number of data blocks enciphered}}$$

$$= \frac{\left\lceil \frac{D \cdot B}{P_E} \right\rceil \cdot t_E + \left\lceil \frac{D}{P_{KS}} \right\rceil \cdot t_{KS} + D \cdot B \cdot (t_{pack} + t_{unpack}) + D \cdot t_{packKS}}{D \cdot B}$$

$$= \frac{\left\lceil \frac{D \cdot B}{P_E} \right\rceil \cdot t_E + \left\lceil \frac{D}{P_{KS}} \right\rceil \cdot t_{KS}}{D \cdot B} + t_{pack} + t_{unpack} + \frac{t_{packKS}}{B}.$$

However, when using a serial operating mode, the average time per block required to encrypt all $D \cdot B$ data blocks is given by:

$$s_{serial}(D, B) = \frac{\text{total encryption time}}{\text{number of data blocks enciphered}}$$

$$= \frac{\left\lceil \frac{D}{P_E} \right\rceil \cdot B \cdot t_E + \left\lceil \frac{D}{P_{KS}} \right\rceil \cdot t_{KS} + D \cdot B \cdot (t_{pack} + t_{unpack}) + D \cdot t_{packKS}}{D \cdot B}$$

$$= \frac{\left\lceil \frac{D}{P_E} \right\rceil \cdot t_E}{D} + \frac{\left\lceil \frac{D}{P_{KS}} \right\rceil \cdot t_{KS}}{D \cdot B} + t_{pack} + t_{unpack} + \frac{t_{packKS}}{B}.$$

Since table-based implementations are usually not faster when offered the possibility to encipher several blocks at a time, we have that $P_E = P_{KS} = 1$ and $t_{pack} = t_{unpack} = t_{packKS} = 0$. Therefore, we conclude that for table-based implementations we have $s(D, B) = t_E + t_{KS}/B$. On the opposite, for bitslice implementations, many data blocks will be enciphered in parallel. Note that vperm implementations will stand in between table-based and bitsliced versions, since a slight parallelism might increase the speed.

For previous bitslice implementations, since many blocks are assumed to be enciphered, the key schedule cost is usually omitted. However, in this article, we are interested in use cases where for example B can be a small value, like a single block. When B is small, one can see that the relative cost of the key schedule has to be taken in account.

5.2 The Use Cases

In order to have a clearer picture of the various scenarios that might be encountered in practice, we chose to study six distinct and meaningful use cases, depending on the value of D, B and the type of encryption operating mode. The six situations are given in Table 1 together with some examples. One might argue that the first use case is not really interesting since with only few blocks and few devices the server would not be overloaded by the encryption/decryption work. However, latency can be an important criterion for many applications, and thus this use case checks the ability of the server to perform the cryptographic operation rapidly in software.

Table 1. Six device/server use cases for lightweight encryption. For the practical measurements given in Table 2 in Appendix B, the notation "big/small" refers to more/less than 10 on average. For the experimentations in Table 2 we used 1000 and 1

	D	B	Op. mode	Example	LED	PRESENT	Piccolo
①	Small	Small	-	Authentication/access control/secure traceability (industrial assembly line)	Table/ **vperm**	Table/ **vperm**	Table/ **vperm**
②	Small	Big	Parallel	Secure streaming communication (medical device sending continuously sensitive data to a server, tracking data, etc.)	Bitslice	Bitslice	Bitslice
③	Small	Big	Serial	Secure serial communication	Table/ **vperm**	Table/ **vperm**	Table/ **vperm**
④	Big	Small	-	Multi-user authentication/secure traceability (parallel industrial assembly lines)	Bitslice	Bitslice	Bitslice
⑤	Big	Big	Parallel	Multi-user secure streaming communication/cloud computing/smart meters server/sensors network/internet of things	Bitslice	Bitslice	Bitslice
⑥	Big	Big	Serial	Multi-user secure serial communication	Bitslice	Bitslice	Bitslice

6 Results and Discussions

6.1 Implementation Results

We have performed measurements of our three types of implementations for our three lightweight candidates. For more precision, the encryption times have been measured with a differential method, checking the consistency by verifying that the sum of the subparts is indeed equal to the entire encryption. Moreover, the measurements have been performed with the Turbo-Boost option *disabled*, in order to avoid any dynamic upscale of the processor's clock rate (this technology was implemented in certain processor versions since Intel Nehalem CPU generation). We observe that our bitslice implementations timings for Piccolo and PRESENT are consistent with the ones provided in [19]. Moreover, we greatly improve over the previously best known LED software implementations (about 57 c/B on Core i7-720QM [13]), since our bitsliced version can reach speeds up to 12 c/B.

We give in Table 2 in Appendix B all the implementation results on Core i3-2367M (Sandy Bridge microarchitecture), XEON X5650 (Westmere microarchitecture) and Core 2 Duo P8600 (Core microarchitecture) processors. Using the measurements for t_E, t_{KS}, t_{pack}, t_{unpack}, t_{packKS} in our framework from Sect. 5, we can infer the performances for the 6 use cases.

6.2 Comparing the implementations types and the ciphers

We can extract general tendencies from our measurements (see Table 1) and one can remark that bitslice implementations will perform better than table-based or vperm ones except for use cases ① and ③, where only few devices are involved and data blocks can only be handled one at a time (bitslice implementations are naturally not fit for low latency and single block). More surprisingly, even for the use cases ④ and ⑥, the gain of bitslice over table-based or vperm implementations is only clear for more than 10 devices.

For bitslice implementations, the cost of bitsliced form transposition on the server can be removed if the device also enciphers in bitsliced format. However, depending on the type of constrained device, the bitsliced algorithm might perform very poorly and the communication cost would increase if a serial mode is used or if a small amount of data is enciphered. Moreover, this solution would reduce the compatibility if other participants have to decipher in non-bitsliced form. The same compatibility issue is true for the keys in the server database, if one directly stores the keys or subkeys in bitsliced form. Finally, it is to be noted that bitsliced versions of the key schedule are especially interesting when all the keys are changed at the same time (i.e. fixed message length, messages synchronized in time).

We can see that from a software implementation perspective, all three ciphers perform reasonably well and are in the same speed range. Their internal round function is quite fit for x86 architectures. Table-based implementations are helped by the small 64-bit internal state size. The vperm implementations are fast thanks to the use of small 4-bit Sboxes, even though the linear diffusion layer can significantly impact the performance (which is the reason why TWINE has very good vperm implementation performances). For PRESENT the bit permutation layer is not really suited for software, the LED diffusion matrix has complex coefficients when not in its serial form, and the Piccolo F function with two layers of Sboxes reduces the possibilities of improvements. Concerning the key schedule, having a byte oriented or no key schedule is an advantage and bitwise rotation as in PRESENT is clearly difficult to handle in software.

Lots of research has been conducted on block cipher constructions and building a good cryptographic permutation is now well understood by the community. However, this is not the case of the key schedule and, usually, block ciphers designers try to build a key schedule very different from the round function, in a hope to avoid any unpredicted relation that might arise between the two components. However, we remark that this is in contradiction with efficient parallel implementations (like bitslice), since the packing of the key and the block cipher internal state must be (almost) the same (otherwise the repacking cost for every generated subkey would be prohibitive).

It is also to be noted that when analyzing ciphers software performances on the server side, it is more likely that decryption will have to be performed instead of encryption. We emphasize that the decryption process would have the same performances as our encryption implementations in the case of PRESENT. For LED and Piccolo, the inverse matrix for the diffusion layer will have more complex coefficients than the encryption one (only the non-serialized matrix for LED), but this shall not impact table-based implementations. However, we remark that this might have an impact on our best performing implementations for Piccolo and their decryption counterpart are likely to be somewhat slower than encryption mode.

6.3   Future Implementations

The forthcoming Haswell architecture will introduce the new AVX2 instruction set. As discussed in Sect. 3.2, this extension will permit most of the existing SSE instructions to operate on the full 256-bit ymm registers. Apart from the three operands improvement already utilized in our vperm versions (Sect. 3.2), the three types of implementations studied in this paper will probably gain from AVX2.

- **Table-based implementations:** with the new vgatherqq instruction, it is possible to perform 4 parallel table lookups by using 4 indexes inside the ymm quadwords. The resulting quadwords, after the lookups, are stored inside the ymm source register. Such a technique has been applied to the Grøstl hash function in [15]. When applied to lightweight block ciphers, 4 internal states can be stored inside a single ymm register. One can isolate the 8-bit indexes (if we use 8-bit tables) by using the vpshufb instruction, perform the 4 lookups in parallel, and merge the results by XORing it within an accumulator. As we can see, this will result in a 4-way vectorized block cipher. According to [16], vgatherqq will have a latency of 16 cycles and a throughput of 10 cycles when data is in L1. A very rough estimation of the results on Haswell CPU is thus a 1.5 to 2 times improvement over the table-based implementations results provided in Appendix B (since the mov instruction has a latency of 4 cycles in L1).

- **vperm based implementations:** extending the vperm technique to 256-bit ymm registers is straightforward, since one would store 4 states instead of 2 in one register. As for table-based, vperm implementations will be vectorized on 4 states providing a 2 times performance improvement for at least 4 parallel message blocks.
- **Bitslice implementations:** as for the vperm technique, bitslicing can naturally take advantage of the AVX2 extension to 256-bit registers by performing in the high 128-bit parts of ymm the exact same operations as on the low parts (if N message blocks are to be packed, $N/2$ are packed as previously presented in the low part of ymm, and $N/2$ are packed in the high part). This would roughly give a 2 times improvement for the performance (however requiring, as for vperm, twice more parallel message blocks).

Conclusion and Future Works

In this article, we have studied the software implementation of lightweight block ciphers on x86 architectures, with special focus on LED, Piccolo and PRESENT. We provided table-based, vperm and bitslice implementations and compared these three methods according to different common lightweight block ciphers use cases. We believe our work helps to get a more complete picture on lightweight block ciphers and we identified several possible future researches.

First, we remark that our cache latency model for table-based implementations predicts that new and future processors with an important amount of L2 cache might enable new fast primitives that utilize 16-bit Sboxes (which could then be implemented using big table lookups). Moreover, this remark might also improve current ciphers such as LED or PRESENT, by imagining a "Super-Sbox" type of implementation: two rounds can be seen as only composed of the applications of four parallel 16-bit Sboxes, and thus can be perfomed with only 4 table lookups.

Secondly, in the future, it would be interesting to use this kind of modeling to compare different implementation tradeoffs without tedious implementation for all of them (this would be also true for hardware implementations). Table-based is a simple case we leave as open problem if more complex implementations can be studied the same way.

Finally, another future work is to study other recently proposed block cipher designs such as PRINCE [6] or Zorro [11], and the lightweight SPN-based hash functions such as PHOTON [12] or SPONGENT [4]. The analysis of hash functions would be quite different since their internal state sizes (which vary with the intended output size) is bigger than 64 bits. Therefore, the amount of memory required to store the tables for table-based implementations is likely to be bigger, and vperm or bitslice implementations would be impacted as well since the packing would be more complex and would use more xmm registers.

Acknowledgements. The authors would like to thank the anonymous referees for their helpful comments.

Appendix

A   LED, PRESENT and Piccolo

A.1   LED

LED is a 64-bit block cipher that applies 32 rounds for the 64-bit key version and 48 rounds for bigger key sizes (up to 128 bits). The internal state is conceptually arranged in a (4×4) grid where each nibble represents an element from $GF(2^4)$ with the underlying polynomial for field multiplication given by $X^4 + X + 1$. A step is composed of 4 rounds and the key is XORed to the internal state before each step and also after the last step (there is no key schedule so if the key K is larger than 64 bits, the subkey material that is XORed every step is selected from K by a 64-bit sliding window).

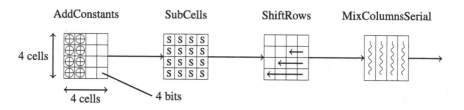

Fig. 5. An overview of a single round of LED.

One round is composed of four steps: AddConstants, SubCells, ShiftRows and MixColumnsSerial as illustrated in Fig. 5. The first function XORs a fixed constant to the first column and a round-dependent constant to the second column of the internal state. The SubCells function applies the 4-bit Sbox to every nibble of the state, the Sbox being the same as in PRESENT and given in Appendix E.1 of [2]. The ShiftRows function just shifts left by i position all the nibbles located in row i. Finally, the linear function MixColumnsSerial applies a MDS diffusion matrix M to every column of the state independently, where

$$M = \begin{bmatrix} 4 & 1 & 2 & 2 \\ 8 & 6 & 5 & 6 \\ B & E & A & 9 \\ 2 & 2 & F & B \end{bmatrix} = \begin{bmatrix} 0 & 1 & 0 & 0 \\ 0 & 0 & 1 & 0 \\ 0 & 0 & 0 & 1 \\ 4 & 1 & 2 & 2 \end{bmatrix}^4$$

A.2   PRESENT

PRESENT is a 64-bit block cipher that applies 31 rounds for both its 80 and 128-bit key versions. One round is composed of three steps: addRoundKey, sBoxLayer and pLayer as illustrated in Fig. 6. The first function just XORs the incoming subkey to the internal state and the sBoxLayer applies the 4-bit Sbox (given in

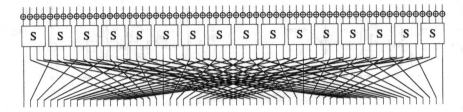

Fig. 6. An overview of a single round of PRESENT.

Appendix E.1 of [2]) to all nibbles. The pLayer function is a bit permutation where a bit located at position i is moved to position $j = i \cdot 16 \mod 63$ when $i \in \{0, \ldots, 62\}$ and $j = i$ if $i = 63$. After the last round, a last addRoundKey layer is performed.

The key schedule generating the subkeys is composed of four steps. Firstly, the subkey is obtained from the key state by extracting the 64 leftmost bits. Then, the key state is rotated to the left by 61 bit positions and the Sbox is applied to the leftmost nibble (the Sbox is also applied to the second-leftmost nibble for the 128-bit key version). Finally, a 5-bit round counter is XORed from bit positions 15 to 19 of the key state (from bit positions 62 to 66 for the 128-bit key version).

A.3 Piccolo

Piccolo is a 64-bit block cipher that applies respectively 25 and 31 rounds for the 80 and 128-bit key versions. The round function is a 4-line type-II generalized Feistel network variant, so one can view the internal state as four 16-bit branches. The three steps in one round are illustrated in Fig. 7. The first function applies a transformation F to the first branch (resp. third branch) and XORs the result to the second branch (resp. fourth branch). Then two incoming 16-bit subkeys are XORed to the second and fourth branches respectively. Finally, a permutation on the nibble position is performed, where a nibble at position i is moved to position $T[i]$ with $T = [4, 5, 14, 15, 8, 9, 2, 3, 12, 13, 6, 7, 0, 1, 10, 11]$. The 16-bit function F itself applies a 4-bit Sbox (given in Appendix E.2 of [2]) to every nibble, then multiplies the current vector by an MDS diffusion matrix M, and applies again the 4-bit Sbox to every nibble. The matrix M is

$$M = \begin{bmatrix} 2 & 3 & 1 & 1 \\ 1 & 2 & 3 & 1 \\ 1 & 1 & 2 & 3 \\ 3 & 1 & 1 & 2 \end{bmatrix}$$

where each nibble represents an element from $GF(2^4)$ with the underlying polynomial for field multiplication given by $X^4 + X + 1$. Finally, two 16-bit whitening keys are incorporated to the first and third branches respectively, at the beginning and at the end of the ciphering process.

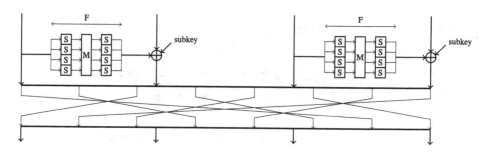

Fig. 7. An overview of a single round of `Piccolo`.

The key schedule generating the subkeys simply selects two 16-bit chunks from the original key and XORs them with some round-dependent constants.

B Results Tables

Table 2. Implementation results for `LED`, `PRESENT` and `Piccolo` on various `x86` architectures.

Cipher	Implementation type	t_E (cycles)	t_{KS} (cycles)	P_E	P_{KS}	t_{pack} (cycles)	t_{unpack} (cycles)	t_{packKS} (cycles)	use cases speed (cycles/byte) ①	②	③	④	⑤	⑥
\multicolumn{15}{c}{Implementation results for LED, PRESENT and Piccolo on Core i3–2367M @ 1.4 GHz}
LED-64	Table	608	0	1	1	0.0	0.0	0.0	76.0	76.0	76.0	76.0	76.0	76.0
	vperm	560	0	2	2	4.0	4.0	4.0	71.5	36.0	71.0	36.5	36.0	36.0
	Bitslice	2443	0	16	16	5.1	6.3	5.4	307.5	20.7	306.8	21.3	20.5	20.7
	Bitslice	2604	0	32	32	5.7	8.4	5.8	328.0	12.2	327.3	12.9	11.9	12.2
LED-128	Table	906	0	1	1	0.0	0.0	0.0	113.3	113.3	113.3	113.3	113.3	113.3
	vperm	858	0	2	2	4.0	4.0	9.0	109.4	54.6	108.3	55.8	54.6	54.6
	Bitslice	3671	0	16	16	5.1	6.6	9.9	461.6	30.4	460.3	31.6	30.1	30.4
	Bitslice	3967	0	32	32	5.8	8.4	11.9	499.1	17.6	497.7	19.1	17.3	17.6
Piccolo-80	Table	671	38	1	1	0.0	0.0	0.0	88.6	83.9	83.9	88.6	83.9	83.9
	vperm	512	55	2	2	6.0	4.5	7.5	73.1	33.3	65.3	37.7	33.3	33.3
	Bitslice	977	0	16	16	5.4	6.9	14.8	125.5	9.2	123.7	11.1	9.2	9.2
Piccolo-128	Table	829	57	1	1	0.0	0.0	0.0	110.8	103.6	103.6	110.8	103.6	103.6
	vperm	644	55	2	2	9.0	2.0	6.5	89.6	41.6	81.9	45.9	41.6	41.6
	Bitslice	1196	0	16	16	5.2	6.7	23.1	153.9	10.9	151.0	13.8	10.8	10.9
PRESENT-80	Table	580	408	1	1	0.0	0.0	0.0	123.5	72.6	72.6	123.5	72.6	72.6
	vperm	540	350	2	2	6.5	3.5	87.5	123.4	35.1	68.8	67.8	35.0	35.0
	Bitslice	1333	706	8	8	9.0	8.3	15.8	259.0	23.1	168.9	36.0	23.0	23.0
	Bitslice	2038	1100	16	16	5.1	5.6	7.4	394.5	17.5	256.2	27.0	17.3	17.4
PRESENT-128	Table	580	334	1	1	0.0	0.0	0.0	114.3	72.5	72.5	114.3	72.5	72.5
	vperm	540	296	2	2	6.5	3.5	103.0	118.6	35.0	68.8	66.4	35.0	35.0
	Bitslice	1313	738	8	8	9.4	8.5	15.8	260.6	22.8	166.5	36.3	22.8	22.8
	Bitslice	2221	1286	16	16	5.3	5.8	9.4	440.9	19.0	279.2	30.2	18.7	18.9

Table 2. (*Continued*)

Cipher	Implementation type	t_E (cycles)	t_{KS} (cycles)	P_E	P_{KS}	t_{pack} (cycles)	t_{unpack} (cycles)	t_{packKS} (cycles)	use cases speed (cycles/byte)					
									①	②	③	④	⑤	⑥
Implementation results for LED, PRESENT and Piccolo on XEON X5650 @ 2.67 GHz														
LED-64	Table	567	0	1	1	0.0	0.0	0.0	70.9	70.9	70.9	70.9	70.9	70.9
	vperm	749	0	2	2	5.0	5.0	10.0	96.1	48.1	94.9	49.3	48.1	48.1
	Bitslice	2445	0	16	16	5.0	6.3	5.1	307.7	20.7	307.0	21.3	20.5	20.7
	Bitslice	2846	0	32	32	5.8	8.2	6.0	358.2	13.1	357.5	13.9	12.9	13.1
LED-128	Table	847	0	1	1	0.0	0.0	0.0	105.9	105.9	105.9	105.9	105.9	105.9
	vperm	1058	0	2	2	5.0	5.0	18.5	135.8	67.4	133.5	69.7	67.4	67.4
	Bitslice	3674	0	16	16	5.0	6.3	9.7	461.9	30.3	460.7	31.6	30.1	30.3
	Bitslice	4306	0	32	32	5.9	8.2	12.2	541.5	19.0	540.0	20.5	18.6	19.0
Piccolo-80	Table	568	39	1	1	0.0	0.0	0.0	75.9	71.0	71.0	75.9	71.0	71.0
	vperm	580	47	2	2	2.5	7.0	13.5	81.3	37.4	73.7	42.1	37.4	37.4
	Bitslice	1038	0	16	16	5.4	6.7	14.4	133.1	9.7	131.3	11.5	9.6	9.7
Piccolo-128	Table	700	62	1	1	0.0	0.0	0.0	95.3	87.5	87.5	95.3	87.5	87.5
	vperm	724	77	2	2	10.5	7.0	8.0	103.3	47.4	92.7	53.3	47.4	47.4
	Bitslice	1400	0	16	16	5.3	6.6	22.8	179.3	12.5	176.5	15.4	12.4	12.5
PRESENT-80	Table	525	398	1	1	0.0	0.0	0.0	115.4	65.7	65.7	115.4	65.7	65.7
	vperm	650	441	2	2	6.0	5.5	99.5	150.3	42.1	82.8	82.1	42.1	42.1
	Bitslice	1360	600	8	8	9.5	6.0	15.9	249.3	23.6	172.4	34.9	23.6	23.6
	Bitslice	2453	1437	16	16	5.0	6.0	8.4	488.7	20.9	308.2	33.1	20.6	20.7
PRESENT-128	Table	525	304	1	1	0.0	0.0	0.0	103.6	65.7	65.7	103.6	65.7	65.7
	vperm	650	408	2	2	6.0	5.5	152.5	152.8	42.1	82.8	86.6	42.1	42.1
	Bitslice	1389	674	8	8	8.8	9.0	16.0	262.1	24.0	175.9	36.5	23.9	23.9
	Bitslice	2882	1888	16	16	5.3	5.9	9.6	598.8	24.3	361.9	40.2	23.9	24.1
Implementation results for LED, PRESENT and Piccolo on Core 2 Duo P8600 @ 2.4 GHz														
LED-64	Table	502	0	1	1	0.0	0.0	0.0	62.8	62.8	62.8	62.8	62.8	62.8
	vperm	751	0	2	2	2.0	2.0	4.0	94.9	47.4	94.4	47.9	47.4	47.4
	Bitslice	2880	0	16	16	6.6	9.4	6.6	362.6	24.7	362.0	25.5	24.5	24.7
	Bitslice	3029	0	32	32	6.3	10.3	6.7	381.5	14.2	380.7	15.0	13.9	14.2
LED-128	Table	748	0	1	1	0.0	0.0	0.0	93.5	93.5	93.5	93.5	93.5	93.5
	vperm	1091	0	2	2	2.0	2.0	25.0	140.0	68.7	136.9	71.8	68.7	68.7
	Bitslice	4219	0	16	16	6.5	9.5	12.8	531.0	35.2	529.4	36.8	35.0	35.2
	Bitslice	4521	0	32	32	6.5	10.5	13.4	568.9	20.2	567.3	21.9	19.8	20.2
Piccolo-80	Table	537	41	1	1	0.0	0.0	0.0	72.3	67.1	67.1	72.3	67.1	67.1
	vperm	594	44	2	2	4.0	5.0	15.0	82.8	38.3	75.4	42.9	38.3	38.3
	Bitslice	1100	0	16	16	7.1	9.4	16.9	141.7	10.7	139.6	12.8	10.7	10.7
Piccolo-128	Table	669	65	1	1	0.0	0.0	0.0	91.8	83.6	83.6	91.8	83.6	83.6
	vperm	739	73	2	2	4.0	4.0	8.0	103.5	47.2	93.4	52.8	47.2	47.2
	Bitslice	1400	0	16	16	6.3	9.4	25.6	180.2	13.0	177.0	16.2	12.9	13.0
PRESENT-80	Table	476	359	1	1	0.0	0.0	0.0	104.4	59.5	59.5	104.4	59.5	59.5
	vperm	651	384	2	2	8.5	4.0	105.5	144.1	42.3	83.0	79.4	42.3	42.3
	Bitslice	1446	731	8	8	11.0	11.1	17.6	277.1	25.5	183.6	39.0	25.4	25.4
	Bitslice	2438	1250	16	16	6.3	8.3	10.0	464.1	21.2	306.7	32.1	20.9	21.0
PRESENT-128	Table	476	285	1	1	0.0	0.0	0.0	95.1	59.5	59.5	95.1	59.5	59.5
	vperm	652	386	2	2	7.0	5.5	124.0	146.8	42.4	83.1	81.9	42.4	42.4
	Bitslice	1472	812	8	8	10.4	11.5	17.8	290.5	25.8	186.8	40.6	25.7	25.7
	Bitslice	2830	1631	16	16	6.0	8.1	11.1	560.8	24.3	355.7	38.3	23.9	24.1

References

1. Aumasson, J.-P., Henzen, L., Meier, W., Naya-Plasencia, M.: QUARK: a lightweight hash. In: Mangard, S., Standaert, F.-X. (eds.) CHES 2010. LNCS, vol. 6225, pp. 1–15. Springer, Heidelberg (2010)
2. Benadjila, R., Guo, J., Lomné, V., Peyrin, T.: Implementing lightweight block ciphers on x86 architectures. Cryptology ePrint Archive, Report 2013/445, full version. http://eprint.iacr.org/2013/445.pdf (2013)
3. Bertoni, G., Daemen, J., Peeters, M., Van Assche, G.: Keccak specifications. Submission to NIST. http://keccak.noekeon.org/Keccak-specifications.pdf (2008)
4. Bogdanov, A., Knezevic, M., Leander, G., Toz, D., Varici, K., Verbauwhede, I.: SPONGENT: a lightweight hash function. In: Preneel, B., Takagi, T. (eds.) [22], pp. 312–325
5. Bogdanov, A.A., Knudsen, L.R., Leander, G., Paar, Ch., Poschmann, A., Robshaw, M., Seurin, Y., Vikkelsoe, C.: Present: an ultra-lightweight block cipher. In: Paillier, P., Verbauwhede, I. (eds.) CHES 2007. LNCS, vol. 4727, pp. 450–466. Springer, Heidelberg (2007)
6. Borghoff, J., Canteaut, A., Güneysu, T., Kavun, E.B., Knezevic, M., Knudsen, L.R., Leander, G., Nikov, V., Paar, Ch., Rechberger, Ch., Rombouts, P., Thomsen, S.S., Yalçın, T.: PRINCE – a low-latency block cipher for pervasive computing applications. In: Wang, X., Sako, K. (eds.) ASIACRYPT 2012. LNCS, vol. 7658, pp. 208–225. Springer, Heidelberg (2012)
7. De Cannière, C., Dunkelman, O., Knezevic, M.: KATAN and KTANTAN - a family of small and efficient hardware-oriented block ciphers. In: Clavier, C., Gaj, K. (eds.) [9], pp. 272–288
8. Chen, A.I.-T., Chen, M.-S., Chen, T.-R., Cheng, C.-M., Ding, J., Kuo, E.L.-H., Lee, F.Y.-S., Yang, B.-Y.: SSE implementation of multivariate PKCs on modern x86 CPUs. In: Clavier, C., Gaj, K. (eds.) [9], pp. 33–48
9. Clavier, C., Gaj, K. (eds.): CHES 2009. LNCS, vol. 5747. Springer, Heidelberg (2009)
10. Daemen, J., Rijmen, V.: The Design of Rijndael: AES - The Advanced Encryption Standard. Springer, Heidelberg (2002)
11. Gérard, B., Grosso, V., Naya-Plasencia, M., Standaert, F.-X. : Block ciphers that are easier to mask: how far can we go? Cryptology ePrint Archive, Report 2013/369. http://eprint.iacr.org/ (2013)
12. Guo, J., Peyrin, T., Poschmann, A.: The photon family of lightweight hash functions. In: Rogaway, P. (ed.) CRYPTO 2011. LNCS, vol. 6841, pp. 222–239. Springer, Heidelberg (2011)
13. Guo, J., Peyrin, T., Poschmann, A., Robshaw, M.J.B.: The LED block cipher. In: Preneel, B., Takagi,T. [22], pp. 326–341
14. Hamburg, M.: Accelerating AES with vector permute instructions. In: Clavier, C., Gaj, K. (eds.) [9], pp. 18–32
15. Holzer-Graf, S., Krinninger, T., Pernull, M., Schläffer, M., Schwabe, P., Seywald, D., Wieser, W.: Efficient vector implementations of aes-based designs: a case study and new implemenations for Grøstl. In: Dawson, E. (ed.) CT-RSA 2013. LNCS, vol. 7779, pp. 145–161. Springer, Heidelberg (2013)
16. Intel. Intel 64 and IA-32 Architectures Optimization Reference Manual, 2013.
17. International Organization for Standardization. ISO/IEC 29192–2:2012, Information technology - Security techniques - Lightweight cryptography - Part 2: Block ciphers, 2012

18. Käsper, E., Schwabe, P.: Faster and timing-attack resistant AES-GCM. In: Clavier, C., Gaj, K. (eds.) [9], pp. 1–17
19. Matsuda, S., Moriai, S.: Lightweight cryptography for the cloud: exploit the power of bitslice implementation. In: Prouff, E., Schaumont, P. (eds.) CHES 2012. LNCS, vol. 7428, pp. 408–425. Springer, Heidelberg (2012)
20. Osvik, D.A.: Fast assembler implementations of the AES (2003)
21. Poschmann, A.: Lightweight cryptography - cryptographic engineering for a pervasive world. Cryptology ePrint Archive, Report 2009/516. http://eprint.iacr.org/ (2009)
22. Preneel, B., Takagi, T. (eds.): CHES 2011. LNCS, vol. 6917. Springer, Heidelberg (2011)
23. Shibutani, K., Isobe, T., Hiwatari, H., Mitsuda, A., Akishita, T., Shirai, T.: Piccolo: an ultra-lightweight blockcipher. In: Preneel, B., Takagi, T. (eds.) CHES 2011. LNCS, vol. 6917, pp. 342–357. Springer, Heidelberg (2011)
24. Suzaki, T., Minematsu, K., Morioka, S., Kobayashi, E.: *twine*: a lightweight block cipher for multiple platforms. In: Knudsen, L.R., Wu, H. (eds.) SAC 2012. LNCS, vol. 7707, pp. 339–354. Springer, Heidelberg (2013)
25. U.S. Department of Commerce, National Institute of Standards and Technology. Secure Hash Standard (SHS) (Federal Information Processing Standards Publication 180–4). http://csrc.nist.gov/publications/fips/fips180-4/fips-180-4.pdf (2012)

Invited Talk

A New Index Calculus Algorithm
with Complexity $L(1/4 + o(1))$
in Small Characteristic

Antoine Joux[✉]

Laboratoire PRISM, CryptoExperts and Université de Versailles
Saint-Quentin-en-Yvelines, 45 Avenue des États-Unis, 78035 Versailles Cedex, France
antoine.joux@m4x.org

Abstract. In this paper, we describe a new algorithm for discrete logarithms in small characteristic. This algorithm is based on index calculus and includes two new contributions. The first is a new method for generating multiplicative relations among elements of a small smoothness basis. The second is a new descent strategy that allows us to express the logarithm of an arbitrary finite field element in terms of the logarithm of elements from the smoothness basis. For a small characteristic finite field of size $Q = p^n$, this algorithm achieves heuristic complexity $L_Q(1/4 + o(1))$. For technical reasons, unless n is already a composite with factors of the right size, this is done by embedding $\mathbb{F}_Q$ in a small extension $\mathbb{F}_{Q^e}$ with $e \leq 2\lceil \log_p n \rceil$.

1 Introduction

The discrete logarithm problem is one of the major hard problems used in cryptography. In this paper, we show that for finite fields of small characteristic, this problem can be solved with heuristic complexity $L(1/4 + o(1))$. Moreover, the algorithm yields very practical improvements compared to the previous state-of-the-art.

One of the two main ideas used for our algorithm is a generalization of the pinpointing technique proposed in [10]. Another independent algorithm for characteristic 2 was proposed in [5], yielding an algorithm with complexity $L_Q(1/3)$, with a better constant than the Function Field Sieve.

2 A Reminder of Discrete Logarithm Algorithms in Small Characteristic

As usual when studying index calculus algorithms, we write:

$$L_Q(\beta, c) = \exp((c + o(1))(\log Q)^\beta (\log \log Q)^{1-\beta}),$$

where $Q = p^n$ denotes the size of the finite field.

T. Lange, K. Lauter, and P. Lisoněk (Eds.): SAC 2013, LNCS 8282, pp. 355–379, 2014.
DOI: 10.1007/978-3-662-43414-7_18, © Springer-Verlag Berlin Heidelberg 2014

When considering the computation of discrete logarithms, in fields of the form $\mathbb{F}_Q$, where p is relatively small compared to Q, the state of the art choice is to use one of the numerous variation of the function field sieve. For larger values of p, it becomes preferable to use a variation of the number field sieve. The choice between the two family of algorithms is made by comparing p and $L_Q(\frac{1}{3})$ (see [12]).

All these variants of the function field sieve find multiplicative relations by factoring various polynomials into polynomials of low degree. A classical useful result is the logarithm of the probability that a **random** polynomial of degree n decomposes into factors of degree m over a finite field is close to:

$$-\frac{n}{m} \log\left(\frac{n}{m}\right),$$

for a wide range of parameters [13].

When using function field sieve algorithms, a standard *heuristic assumption* is to assume that all polynomials that arise in the algorithm also follow this smoothness probability. In the new algorithm presented here, this is false by construction, because we consider polynomials than decompose more frequently than usual. However, we still use the heuristic assumption on some polynomials: those for which there is no known reason to expect that they would deviate from the normal behavior.

Despite the new ingredients we are using, there are deep similarities between our algorithm and its predecessors. In particular, some features are reminiscent of Coppersmith's algorithm [3], while others are inspired from [11]. In the present section, we recall these two algorithms.

2.1   Coppersmith's Algorithm

Coppersmith's Algorithm was published in 1984 in [3]. Historically, it was the first discrete logarithm algorithm to achieve complexity $L(1/3)$. In its original presentation, this algorithm is dedicated to characteristic 2, but it can easily be generalized to any fixed characteristic [14].

Consider as usual a finite field of size $Q = p^n$. Coppersmith assumes that $\mathbb{F}_Q$ is constructed using a polynomial $P(x) = x^n - P_0(x)$, where $P_0(x)$ is a polynomial of low degree. He then chooses k a power of p close to $\sqrt{n}$ and writes $n = hk - n_0$, with $0 \le n_0 < k$.

Let A and B be two polynomials of low degree. Coppersmith considers the polynomial $C(x) = x^h A(x) + B(x)$, let $D = C^k$ and remarks that since k is a power of p, the linearity of the Frobenius map implies:

$$
\begin{aligned}
D(x) &= C(x)^k \\
&= x^{hk} A(x)^k + B(x)^k \pmod{P(x)} \\
&= x^{n_0} P_0(x) A(x)^k + B(x)^k \pmod{P(x)}
\end{aligned}
$$

As a consequence, both C and D have moderate degrees $O(\sqrt{n})$. If both factors into low degree polynomials, we obtain a multiplicative relation between the factors; in this relation, the factors of C are raised to the power k.

The complexity of Coppersmith's index calculus algorithm is $L(1/3, c)$ with a value of c that depends on the extension degree n. This constant is minimized when n is close to a power of p^2.

2.2   Function Field Sieve

The general function field sieve algorithm was proposed in 1999 by Adleman and Huang in [1]. It improves on Coppermith's algorithm when the extension degree n is not close to a power of p^2. In its general form, it uses multiplicative relations between ideals in function fields and technicalities arise due to this. A simplified version was proposed in [11]. This simplified version only involves polynomial rings (instead of function fields), which has the merit of removing most of these technicalities.

The algorithm from [11] is particularly well suited to the computation of discrete logarithms in fields that contain a medium-sized subfield (not necessarily prime). To emphasize this, we write the finite field as $\mathbb{F}_{q^n}$, a degree n extension of the medium-sized field $\mathbb{F}_q$. In the optimal case where $q = L_{q^n}(1/3)$, the constant in the complexity can even be reduced compared to usual function field sieve.

By convention, in the rest of the section, X and Y are formal variables, while x and y are elements of $\mathbb{F}_{q^n}$. In order to define the extension field $\mathbb{F}_{q^n}$, the algorithm selects g_1 and g_2 two univariate polynomials of respective degree d_1 and d_2 with coefficients in $\mathbb{F}_q$. If the polynomial $-g_2(g_1(Y)) + Y$ has an irreducible factor $\mathcal{I}(Y)$ of degree n over $\mathbb{F}_q$, then $\mathcal{I}$ can be used to define $\mathbb{F}_{q^n}$ and we denote by y a root of $\mathcal{I}$ in this field. When this occurs, $-g_1(g_2(X)) + X$ also has an irreducible factor $\mathcal{I}'(X)$ of degree n over $\mathbb{F}_q$. Moreover, $x = g_1(y)$ is a root of $\mathcal{I}'$ in $\mathbb{F}_{q^n}$. Abstractly, we consider that the algorithm is, in fact, defining the finite field $\mathbb{F}_{q^n}$ implicitly by the two relations:

$$x = g_1(y), \quad y = g_2(x), \tag{1}$$

As explained in [11], it is easy to find polynomials g_1 and g_2 that satisfy this requirement. This definition of the finite field induces the commutative diagram in Fig. 1. On the right-hand side, we use the $\mathcal{I}(Y)$ to define $\mathbb{F}_{q^n}$ and on the left-hand side, we use $\mathcal{I}'(X)$.

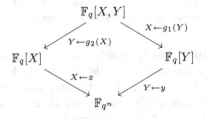

Fig. 1. Commutative diagram for the algorithm of [11]

The relative degrees of d_1 and d_2 in the construction are controlled by an extra parameter D, whose choice is determined by the size of q compared to q^n. More precisely, we have $d_1 \approx \sqrt{Dn}$ and $d_2 \approx \sqrt{n/D}$. The simplest and most efficient case occurs when we can choose $D = 1$, i.e. $d_1 \approx d_2 \approx \sqrt{n}$.

Starting from this definition of the finite field, the medium prime field algorithms consider objects of the form $\mathcal{A}(Y)\,X + \mathcal{B}(Y)$, where $\mathcal{A}$ and $\mathcal{B}$ are univariate polynomials of degree D and $\mathcal{A}$ is unitary. Substituting $g_1(Y)$ for X on one side and $g_2(X)$ for Y on the other, we obtain two univariate polynomials whose images in $\mathbb{F}_{q^n}$ are equal, i.e. an equation:

$$\mathcal{A}(y)\,g_1(y) + \mathcal{B}(y) = \mathcal{A}(g_2(x))\,x + \mathcal{B}(g_2(x)).$$

This relates the images of a polynomial of degree $d_1 + D$ in Y and a polynomial of degree $Dd_2 + 1$ in X.

Following [11] , we only keep the relations, where $\mathcal{A}(Y)\,g_1(Y) + \mathcal{B}(Y)$ and $\mathcal{A}(g_2(X))\,X + \mathcal{B}(g_2(X))$ both factor into unitary polynomials of degree at most D in X or Y. This yields multiplicative relations between the images in $\mathbb{F}_{q^n}$ of these low-degree polynomials, which form the smoothness basis. Classically the good pairs $(\mathcal{A}, \mathcal{B})$ are found using a sieving approach[1].

Complexity. To express the complexity, [11] let $Q = q^n$ and assumes that there exists a parameter α such that:

$$n = \frac{1}{\alpha} \cdot \left(\frac{\log Q}{\log \log Q} \right)^{2/3}, \qquad q = \exp\left(\alpha \cdot \sqrt[3]{\log Q \cdot \log^2 \log Q} \right).$$

In this setting, the heuristic asymptotic complexity of the sieving phase is $L_{q^n}(\frac{1}{3}, c_1)$ and the complexity of the linear algebra is $L_{q^n}(\frac{1}{3}, c_2)$, with:

$$c_1 = \frac{2}{3\sqrt{\alpha D}} + \alpha D \quad \text{and} \quad c_2 = 2\alpha D.$$

Note that the algorithm with parameter D only works under the condition that we can obtain enough linear equations to build the linear system of equations. This requires:

$$(D + 1)\alpha \geq \frac{2}{3\sqrt{\alpha D}}. \tag{2}$$

For a given finite field $\mathbb{F}_{q^n}$, [11] indicates that the best possible complexity is obtained by choosing the smallest acceptable value for the parameter D.

Individual Logarithms Phase. Another very important phase that appears in index calculus algorithms is the individual discrete logarithms phase which allows to compute the logarithm of an arbitrary finite field element by finding a multiplicative relation which relates this element to the elements of the smoothness basis whose logarithms have already been computed.

---

[1] Asymptotically, exhaustive search of good pairs is as efficient. However, using sieving improves things by a large constant factor.

We now detail this phase in the case of [11]. The ultimate goal of expressing a given element as a product of elements from the smoothness basis is not achieved in a single pass. Instead, it is done by first expressing the desired element in $\mathbb{F}_{q^n}$ as a product of univariate polynomials in either x or y and with degree smaller than that of the desired element. These polynomials can in turn be related to polynomials of a lower degree and so on, until hitting degree $\leq D$, i.e. elements of the smoothness basis. For this reason, the individual logarithm phase is also called the descent phase.

In order to create relations between a polynomial in either X or Y (i.e. coming either from the left or right side of a previous equation) and polynomials of lower degree, [11] proceeds as follows: Let $\mathcal{Q}(X)$ (resp. $\mathcal{Q}(Y)$) denote the polynomial that represent the desired element. One considers a set of monomials $S_{\mathcal{Q}} = \{X^i Y^j | i \in [0 \cdots D_x(\mathcal{Q})], j \in [0 \cdots D_y(\mathcal{Q})]\}$, where $D_x(\mathcal{Q})$ and $D_y(\mathcal{Q})$ are parameters that we determine later on. Each monomial in $S_{\mathcal{Q}}$ can be expressed as a univariate polynomial in X (resp. Y), after replacing Y by $g_2(X)$ (or X by $g_1(Y)$). For a monomial m we denote by $V_{\mathcal{Q}}(m)$ the value modulo $\mathcal{Q}$ of the univariate polynomial corresponding to m. Clearly, $V_{\mathcal{Q}}(m)$ can be represented by a vector of $\deg \mathcal{Q}$ finite field elements. We now build a matrix $M_{\mathcal{Q}}$ by assembling all the vectors $V_{\mathcal{Q}}(m)$ for $m \in S_{\mathcal{Q}}$. Any vector in the kernel of $M_{\mathcal{Q}}$ can then be interpreted as a polynomial whose univariate representation is divisible by $\mathcal{Q}$. If both the quotient after dividing by $\mathcal{Q}$ and the univariate representation in the other unknown decompose into products of polynomials of low enough degree, we obtain the desired relation.

Clearly, this approach requires us to take enough monomials to make sure that the kernel contains sufficiently many polynomials in order to find a satisfying relation. This can be achieved by choosing $D_x(\mathcal{Q})$ and $D_y(\mathcal{Q})$ such that $D_x(\mathcal{Q})D_y(\mathcal{Q}) \geq \deg \mathcal{Q}$. Moreover to balance the degrees after replacing X or Y, we make sure that $D_y(\mathcal{Q})/D_x(\mathcal{Q}) \approx D$. With these choices, the degree on each side after replacement is close to $\sqrt{n \deg \mathcal{Q}}$. The logarithm of the probability that each of the two sides decompose into polynomials of degree at most $\mu \deg \mathcal{Q}$ (after factoring out $\mathcal{Q}$) is estimated by:

$$-\frac{2}{\mu}\sqrt{\frac{n}{\deg \mathcal{Q}}} \log\left(\frac{2}{\mu}\sqrt{\frac{n}{\deg \mathcal{Q}}}\right).$$

The cost of this descent step increases when the degree of $\mathcal{Q}$ decreases. As a consequence, the total cost of the descent is dominated by the lowest degree polynomials that still need to be processed. In [11], the descent is used all the way down to constant degree D. As a consequence, with the relative sizes of n and q that [11] considers, the asymptotic complexity of the descent is $L_Q(1/3)$.

3   New Algorithm: Basic Ideas

The new index calculus algorithms proposed in this paper hinges on a few basic ideas, which can be arranged into a functional discrete logarithm algorithm.

Basic idea 1: Homographies. In [10], it was remarked that a single polynomial f that nicely factors can be transformed into several such polynomials, simply by a linear change of variable: $f(X) \longrightarrow f(aX)$, for any non-zero constant a.

Our first idea consists in remarking that this is also true for a larger class of change of variables. Basically, we consider changes induced by homographies:

$$X \longrightarrow \frac{aX + b}{cX + d}.$$

The reader might object that an homography is not going to transform f into polynomial. To cover this, we instead perform homogeneous evaluation of f at $(aX + b)/(cX + d)$.

In other words, we consider the polynomial:

$$F_{abcd}(X) = (cX + d)^{\deg f} f\left(\frac{aX + b}{cX + d}\right).$$

Theorem 1. *Let $f(Y)$ be a monic polynomial of degree D over $\mathbb{F}_q$ and $\mathbb{F}_{q^k}$ be an extension field of $\mathbb{F}_q$. Let $F_{abcd}(X) = (cX+d)^{\deg f} f\left(\frac{aX+b}{cX+d}\right)$ with $(a, b, c, d) \in \mathbb{F}_{q^k}^4$ and $ad \neq bc$. Write the factorization of f into monic irreducible polynomials as $f(Y) = \prod_{i=1}^{k} F_i(Y)^{e_i}$. It induces a factorization of F_{abcd}*

$$F_{abcd}(X) = \prod_{i=1}^{k} \left((cX + d)^{\deg F_i} F_i\left(\frac{aX + b}{cX + d}\right)\right)^{e_i}.$$

Note that the factors in this decomposition are not necessary monic, not necessary irreducible and may have a lower degree than the corresponding factor in F_i.

Proof. The induced factorization is clear. It suffices to perform the change of variable on both sides and remark that the grouped terms

$$(cX + d)^{\deg F_i} F_i\left(\frac{aX + b}{cX + d}\right)$$

are indeed polynomials.

It is also clear that the transformed factors have no reason to be irreducible in the extension field $\mathbb{F}_{q^k}$.

Remark that when $c \neq 0$ the coefficient of $X^{\deg F_i}$ in the factor coming from F_i is $c^{\deg F_i} F_i(a/c)$. Since this is not necessarily 1 and can even be 0, we see that the transformed polynomials are not necessarily monic and may have degree strictly smaller than the corresponding F_i. □

Thanks to this, it is now possible to amplify a single polynomial to a much larger extend than previously. More precisely, with a linear change of variables, the number of amplified copies of a single polynomial is close to the size of the finite field in which a is picked. With homographies, the number of copies becomes larger (see Sect. 4.2 for a detailed analysis).

Basic idea 2: Systematic polynomial splitting. The second idea directly stems from this fact. Since it is possible to make so many copies of one polynomial, it suffices to start from a single polynomial f. Thus, instead of considering many polynomials until we find some candidate, we are going to choose a polynomial with factors by design. Over a small finite field $\mathbb{F}_q$, an extremely natural candidate to consider is:

$$f(X) = X^q - X.$$

It is well-known that this polynomial splits into linear factors, since any element of $\mathbb{F}_q$ is a root of f.

Geometrically, using the homogeneous evaluation of f (with multiplication by $(cX + d)^{q+1}$) at an homography h is equivalent to considering the image of the projective line (including its point at infinity) $\mathbb{P}_1(\mathbb{F}_q)$ by h.

Basic idea 3: Field definition The image of $X^q - X$ by an homography is a polynomial which only contains the monomials X^{q+1}, X^q, X and 1. To obtain a multiplicative relation, it is thus desirable to find a finite field representation that transforms such a polynomial into a low degree polynomial. This can be achieved by choosing the finite field representation in a way that is reminiscent both of Coppersmith's algorithm and of [11].

More precisely, we ask for a relation in $\mathbb{F}_{q^n}$ of the form:

$$x^q = \frac{h_0(x)}{h_1(x)}.$$

This defines the finite field $\mathbb{F}_{q^n}$, if and only if, $h_1(X)X^q - h_0(X)$ admits an irreducible factor of degree n.

This construction is similar to Coppersmith's Algorithm, since we require a simple expression of the Frobenius map $x \to x^q$. It is similar to [11], because we do not ask for the relation to directly give an irreducible polynomial but only require a factor of the proper degree.

The rest of the paper gives the details of how to put together these basic ideas into a working discrete logarithm algorithm. Another application of the same ideas has been described in [7], where a new deterministic algorithm (based on similar heuristics to ours) is proposed to find a provable multiplicative generator of a finite field.

4   Description of the New Algorithm

In this section, we present the new discrete logarithm algorithm for small characteristic fields that arises when putting together the basic ideas from the previous section. We first describe the general setting of our algorithm, before considering its relation collection phase. We skip the description of the linear algebra phase that takes as input the relations and outputs logarithms of the elements of our factor basis, since it is left unchanged compared to previous algorithms. Finally, we study the computation of individual discrete logarithms, for arbitrary field elements. This phase relies on a descent method which contains two main strategies. For elements with representations of high degree, one proceeds as in [11], while for lower degrees we introduce a new strategy based on the resolution of multivariate systems of bilinear equations.

4.1   Choosing the Parameters

Given a small characteristic finite field $\mathbb{F}_{p^n}$, we start be embedding it into a field of the form $\mathbb{F}_{q^{2k}}$, with $k \leq q$. This can be achieved by taking a degree e extension of $\mathbb{F}_{p^n}$, with $e \leq 2\lceil \log_p n \rceil$.

After this initial embedding, the finite field $\mathbb{F}_{q^{2k}}$ is constructed has a degree k extension of $\mathbb{F}_{q^2}$. This degree k extension is obtained by using a irreducible factor of a low degree bivariate polynomial, evaluated at (X, X^p). More precisely, we follow the third idea of Sect. 3 and choose two low degree polynomials $h_0(X)$ and $h_1(X)$ with coefficients in $\mathbb{F}_{q^2}$ such that $h_1(X)X^q - h_0(X)$ has an irreducible factor $\mathcal{I}(X)$ of degree k. This field representation leads to the commutative diagram in Fig. 2. *Heuristically,* we expect arbitrary extension degrees to appear with this form of definition polynomials. Indeed, we expect that a fraction close to $1/k$ of random polynomials has a factor of degree k. Thus considering polynomials h_0 and h_1 of degree 2, we have a very large number of degrees of freedom and expect to get a good representation. However, this argument is not a proof. This is emphasized by the fact that with linear polynomials h_0 and h_1 we can only reach a fraction of the possible extension degrees (see the simple cases below).

In order to increase the confidence level in this heuristic hypothesis, we have performed some experiments in characteristic 2. This yields some numerical evidence supporting the heuristic which is described in Appendix B.

Moreover, since we have also the option of raising the degree of h_0 and h_1 to an arbitrary constant, it should be easy to achieve any extension degree k (up to $q + \deg(h_1)$.)

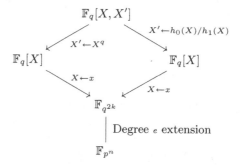

Fig. 2. Commutative diagram for our new algorithm

Illustration of Some Simple Cases. Some kind of extensions are especially well-suited to this form of representation. To illustrate our construction, we now describe these simple cases.

A first example concerns extensions of degree $k = q - 1$. They can be represented as Kummer extensions by an irreducible polynomial $\mathcal{I}(X) = X^{q-1} - g$, where g is a generator of the multiplicative group $\mathbb{F}_q^*$. This can be achieved easily in our setting by letting $h_0(X) = gX$ and $h_1(X) = 1$.

Similarly extensions of degree $k = q + 1$ can be represented by a Kummer extension by an irreducible polynomial $\mathcal{I}(X) = X^{q+1} + G^{q-1}$, where G is a generator of the multiplicative group $\mathbb{F}_{q^2}^*$. This can be achieved easily in our setting by letting $h_0(X) = -G^{q-1}$ and $h_1(X) = X$.

Alternatively, extensions of degree $q + 1$ can also be represented using a "twisted Kummer" form, i.e. using an irreducible polynomial of the form $X^{q+1} - AX - B$, with coefficients A and B in $\mathbb{F}_q$. This twisted Kummer form is used for the record computation presented in Sect. 8.

Another special case is $k = p$, which can be represented by an Artin-Schreier extension with $\mathcal{I}(X) = X^p - X - 1$. This can be achieved by choosing $h_0(X) = -(X + 1)$ and $h_1(X) = 1$. However, since our algorithm is dedicated to small characteristic, this only leads to low degree extensions.

Action of Frobenius. When using Kummer, twisted Kummer or Artin-Schreier extensions, the fact that the Frobenius maps X to an homography in X allows to reduce the size of the factor basis by a factor close to the extension degree. Indeed, we can remark that:

1. In the Kummer case:

$$(x + \theta)^q = x^q + \theta^q = g(x + \theta^q/g).$$

2. In the twisted Kummer case:

$$(x + \theta)^q = x^q + \theta^q = \frac{1}{x}((\theta + A)x + B).$$

3. In the Artin-Schreier case:

$$(x + \theta)^p = x^p + \theta^p + 1.$$

These relations yield simple linear relations between the elements of the smoothness basis and allow to reduce its size. It is easy to check that similar relations also relate polynomials of degree 2 in x.

4.2   Logarithms of Linear Polynomials

The first step in the algorithm is to generate the logarithms of all linear polynomials in the finite field. As usual in index calculus, we construct multiplicative relations between these elements. These equations can be viewed as linear equations on the values of their logarithms which are then obtained by linear algebra.

In order to generate the relations, we start from the polynomial identity:

$$\prod_{\alpha \in \mathbb{F}_q} (Y - \alpha) = Y^q - Y, \tag{3}$$

and perform a change of variable $Y = \frac{aX+b}{cX+d}$, with $(a, b, c, d) \in \mathbb{F}_{q^2}^4$ satisfying $ad - bc \neq 0$.

Evaluating Eq. (3) and multiplying by $(cX + d)^{q+1}$, we find that:

$$(cX + d) \prod_{\alpha \in \mathbb{F}_q} ((a - \alpha c)X + (b - \alpha d)) = (cX + d)(aX + b)^q - (aX + b)(cX + d)^q.$$

Moreover the right-hand side can be evaluated to:

$$(ca^q - ac^q)X^{q+1} + (da^q - bc^q)X^q + (cb^q - ad^q)X + (db^q - bd^q)$$
$$\equiv$$
$$\frac{(ca^q - ac^q)Xh_0(X) + (da^q - bc^q)h_0(X) + (cb^q - ad^q)Xh_1(X) + (db^q - bd^q)h_1(X)}{h_1(X)}$$
$$(\mathrm{mod}\ \mathcal{I}(X)). \tag{4}$$

As a consequence, we get an equality in $\mathbb{F}_{q^{2k}}$ between a product of linear polynomials and a fraction with low-degree numerator and constant denominator. Considering $h_1(X)$ as an extra element of the smoothness basis, we get a multiplicative relation whenever the right-hand side's numerator factors into linear factors.

Counting the Relation Candidates. The above description that generates a candidate relation from a quadruple (a, b, c, d) disregards some important structure in the set of candidates. In particular, the reader should be aware that the same relation may be encountered several times (with different quadruples (a, b, c, d)). Typically, when $(a, b, c, d) \in \mathbb{F}_q^4$, we obtain a trivial equation. Indeed, in this case, for each v in $\{a, b, c, d\}$, we have $v^q = v$. As a consequence, after evaluation, we obtain the polynomial $(ad - bc)(X^q - X)$. Since this a just a multiple of the basic polynomial $X^q - X$, this cannot form a new relation.

This is the reason why we need to take coefficients[2] (a, b, c, d) in $\mathbb{F}_{q^2}$ and to consider a smoothness basis with coefficients in $\mathbb{F}_{q^2}$.

To understand the way Eq. (3) is transformed, we need to recall a few facts about the geometric action of homographies on a projective line. Given a nonsingular matrix M with coefficients in a field $\mathbb{K}$ and a point P on the projective line $\mathbb{P}_1(\mathbb{K})$ with homogeneous coordinates (X_P, Y_P), we define the image of P by M to be the point MP, whose coordinates are obtained by multiplying the matrix M and the vector of coordinates of P. In other words, when

$$M = \begin{pmatrix} a & b \\ c & d \end{pmatrix},$$

---

[2] At this point, there is nothing really special with $\mathbb{F}_{q^2}$, it is just the smallest superfield of $\mathbb{F}_q$. A larger superfield would also work.

MP is defined as the point with homogeneous coordinates $(aX_P + bY_P, cX_P + dY_P)$. It is clear that multiplying M by an arbitrary non-zero scalar does not change the induced geometric action. Since the scalar matrices form a normal subgroup of the invertible matrices, it is better to consider M as an element from the corresponding quotient group which is traditionally called $PGL_2(\mathbb{K})$. It is well known that for a finite field $\mathbb{K}$, the cardinality of $PGL_2(\mathbb{K})$ is $(|\mathbb{K}|^2 - 1) \cdot |\mathbb{K}|$.

Geometrically, the change of variables we considered in the Eq. (3) is equivalent to writing a polynomial equation for the image of the projective line $\mathbb{P}_1(\mathbb{F}_q)$ by an element of $PGL_2(\mathbb{F}_{q^2})$. Since $PGL_2(\mathbb{F}_q)$ leaves $\mathbb{P}_1(\mathbb{F}_q)$ globally invariant, it is now clear that the same equation can arise multiple times. More precisely, for any M in $PGL_2(\mathbb{F}_{q^2})$ and any N in $PGL_2(\mathbb{F}_q)$, M and NM send $\mathbb{P}_1(\mathbb{F}_q)$ to the same image and induce the same equation. Since $PGL_2(\mathbb{F}_q)$ is not a distinguished subgroup of $PGL_2(\mathbb{F}_{q^2})$, we cannot form a quotient group. Instead, we need to regroup the matrices of $PGL_2(\mathbb{F}_{q^2})$ into orbits induced by the (left-)action of $PGL_2(\mathbb{F}_q)$. One can check that this action is free and thus that the cardinality of the set of orbits is simply the quotient of the cardinalities of $PGL_2(\mathbb{F}_{q^2})$ and $PGL_2(\mathbb{F}_q)$. As a consequence, the number of orbits and, thus, of candidate equations is:

$$\frac{q^6 - q^2}{q^3 - q} = q^3 + q.$$

Cost of relation finding. We now would like to estimate the probability of finding a relation for a random quadruple. Under the usual heuristic that the right-hand side's numerator factors into linear with a probability close to a random polynomial of the same degree, we need to perform $D!$ trials, where D denotes the degree of the right-hand numerator. We note that $D \leq 1 + \max(\deg h_0, \deg h_1)$.

As a consequence, since D can heuristically be chosen as a constant, we expect to find enough relations by considering $O(q^2)$ quadruples. To avoid duplicates, we can either use the structure of the orbits of $PGL_2(\mathbb{F}_{q^2})$ under the action of $PGL_2(\mathbb{F}_q)$ or simply keep hash values of the relations to remove collisions. Since we only need $O(q^2)$ distinct elements in a set of size close to q^3, the number of expected collisions between relations for randomly chosen quadruples (a, b, c, d) is $O(q)$. As a consequence, dealing with these collisions does not induce any noticeable slow-down.

4.3   Extending the Basis to Degree 2 Polynomials

The above process together with linear algebra can thus give us the logarithms of linear polynomials. Unfortunately, this is not enough. Indeed, we do not know, in general, how to compute arbitrary logarithms using a smoothness basis that only contains linear polynomials. Instead, we extend our basis of known logarithms to include polynomials of degree 2.

We first describe a natural approach that does not work, before proposing a successful approach that requires some additional linear algebra steps.

A Natural Strategy that Fails. The idea of this strategy is to reconsider the relations produced for finding the linear polynomials. But, instead of keeping the relations with a right-hand side that splits into linear factors, it also keeps relations with a single degree 2 factor and some linear factors. This clearly allows us to compute the logarithm of the degree 2 polynomial.

A simple counting argument shows that in general, this approach must fail. Indeed, on the one-hand, the number of quadratic polynomials with coefficients in $\mathbb{F}_{q^2}$ is $O(q^4)$, while on the other hand, the number of relations that can be obtained from homographies with coefficients in $\mathbb{F}_{q^2}$ is close to q^3 when removing the duplicates arising from homographies with coefficients in $\mathbb{F}_q$. As a consequence, it is not possible to derive the logarithms of all quadratic polynomials in this way.

It is interesting to note that if we replace the field $\mathbb{F}_{q^2}$ by a larger field for the coefficients of the homographies, the natural approach becomes workable. However, we can see that the same counting argument shows that, in general, using $\mathbb{F}_{q^3}$ is not good enough since a fraction of the equation are lost due to the right-hand side splitting probability. Thus, to be able to recover the degree 2 polynomials with the simple strategy we need to, at least, use $\mathbb{F}_{q^4}$ as our basefield. Since the number of linear polynomials in this case is q^4, it is clearly preferable to stay with $\mathbb{F}_{q^2}$ and pay the price of constructing quadratic polynomials with the strategy below.

A Working Strategy. For this second strategy, we produce some extra equations, using the same approach as for linear polynomials together with a slightly more general change of variable. More precisely, we consider changes of the form:

$$Y = \frac{aX^2 + bX + c}{dX^2 + eX + f}.$$

With this choice, the left-hand side factors into polynomials of degree at most 2. If the left-hand side also factors into polynomials of degree at most 2, we obtain an equation that involves the extended basis. Once we get enough equations, it suffices to perform a linear algebra step to recover the extra logarithms.

However, this linear algebra step is much bigger than the first one. In fact, it is almost as expensive as initially building all linear polynomials over the larger basefield $\mathbb{F}_{q^4}$. Thankfully, it is often possible to improve this, by separating the degree 2 polynomials into several subsets which can be addressed independently. Basically, the idea is to choose

$$Y = \frac{a(X^2 + \alpha X) + b}{c(X^2 + \alpha X) + d}.$$

With this choice, thanks to the repetition of $X^2 + \alpha X$ in the numerator and denominator, all the degree 2 factors on the left are of the form $X^2 + \alpha X + K$. If we only keep relations with a right-hand side that factors into linear polynomials, a set of relations that all share the same value for α then produce a much smaller linear system. Indeed, the unknowns are the logarithms of irreducible polynomials of degree 2 from the subset $X^2 + \alpha X + K$, with a fixed α. As a consequence, instead of solving a large system of size $O(q^4)$, we need to solve q^2 smaller system (on for each α), of size $O(q^2)$. This system is obtained by selecting equations with a smooth left-hand side in a set of $O(q^3)$ candidates.

Depending on the exact parameters of the finite field and the number of logarithms that need to be computed, it might also be useful to further extend the smoothness basis and include polynomials of higher degree (3 or more).

5   New Algorithm: Descent Phase

Once the logarithms of smoothness basis elements are known, we want to be able to compute the logarithm of an arbitrary element of the finite field. We wish to proceed using a descent approach similar to [11]. The basic idea is to first obtain a good representation of the desired element into a product of polynomials whose degrees are not too high. Then, proceeding recursively, we express the logarithms of those polynomials as sums of logarithms of polynomials of decreasing degree. Once we reach the polynomials of the smoothness basis, we are done.

In our context, we cannot, in general, use the preexisting method for this descent step. Yet, we first recall this method, discuss when it can be used and explain why we cannot use it generally. Then, we propose an alternative method that is more suited to the field representations we are using. This new method involves the resolution of bilinear multivariate systems of equations over $\mathbb{F}_{q^2}$. The resolution of such systems has been analyzed carefully in Spaenlehauer's PhD thesis [15] and in [4].

5.1   Practical Preliminary Step

Before going into the descent itself, it is useful to start by finding a good representation of the element Z whose logarithm is desired. Initially, Z is expressed as a polynomial of degree up to $k - 1$ over $\mathbb{F}_{q^2}$. Assuming that g denotes a generator of $\mathbb{F}_{q^{2k}}$, we consider the decomposition of the polynomials that represent $g^i Z$, until we find one which decomposes into elements of reasonably low degree. These lower degree elements are then processed by the descent step.

A classical improvement on this is to use a continued fraction algorithm to first express $g^i Z$ as a quotient of two polynomials of degree at most $k/2$.

This preliminary step gives no improvement on the asymptotic complexity of the descent phase.

5.2   Classical Descent Method

The classical descent technique as described in [11] and recalled in Sect. 2.2 is based on Special-Q sieving. More precisely, it creates relations in a linear subspace where by construction one side of the equation is divisible by the desired polynomial.

In the description of this method, we have two related variables X and Y. The relations are constructed by considering bivariate polynomials $h(X, Y)$, which can lead to relations of the form $h(X, f_1(X)) = h(f_2(Y), Y)$. To create a relation that involves a fixed polynomial $Q(X)$, we want to enforce the condition $h(X, f_1(X)) \equiv 0 \pmod{Q(X)}$. This condition is equivalent to $\deg(Q)$ linear equations on the coefficients of h. When the basefield is not too small, to get enough equations, it suffices to build the polynomials h as linear combination of $\deg(Q) + 2$ monomials.

In general characteristic, we cannot use this method in our context, because we do not known how to create two related variables X and Y to use in this descent step. However, with small characteristic fields, this become possible. Let p denote the characteristic of the finite field. We can then write $q = p^\ell$ and let $Y = X^{p^r}$, where $r = \lfloor \ell/2 \rfloor$. Then following our construction, we see that:

$$Y^{q \cdot p^{-r}} = X^q = \frac{h_0(X)}{h_1(X)}.$$

For the Kummer (or Artin-Schreier) case, where h_0 and h_1 have degree at most one, this directly gives X as a polynomial g in Y and the usual descent can be applied without modification. When h_0 or h_1 have higher degree, the method still works, but we need to use a slight variation. Instead of considering the relation $h(X, X^{p^r}) = h(g(Y), Y)$, we consider a relation $(h(X, X^{p^r}))^{q \cdot p^{-r}} = h'(X^{q \cdot p^{-r}}, h_0(X)/h_1(X))$, where h' is obtained from h by raising the coefficient to the power $q \cdot p^{-r}$. This has the additional advantage of completely eliminating the auxiliary variable Y.

As seen in Sect. 2.2, this becomes less and less efficient as the degree of Q decreases and the complexity is dominated by the lowest degree of Q that we consider.

However, by itself, this method cannot descend to very low degrees which is a problem when we want to keep a small smoothness basis. As a consequence, we combine it with a newer method described below, which works better on low degree polynomials.

5.3   Bilinear System Based Descent

The basic idea of the new descent method we propose to complement the classical descent works as follows: given a polynomial Q, we search for a pair of polynomials of lower degree, k_1 and k_2 such that $Q(X)$ divides $(k_1(X)^q k_2(X) - k_1(X)k_2(X)^q) \bmod \mathcal{I}(X)$. As a consequence, the relation:

$$(k_1(X)^q k_2(X) - k_1(X)k_2(X)^q) \equiv (k_1(X)^q k_2(X) - k_1(X)k_2(X)^q) \bmod I(x),$$

has a factor equal to Q on the right-hand side and factors of degree at most $D_m = \max(\deg k_1, \deg k_2)$ on the left-hand side. Since the total degree of the right-hand side is bounded by a small multiple of D_m (related to the degrees of h_0 and h_1 the polynomials which defined out extension field), with good probability, we obtain a relation between Q and polynomials of degree at most D_m.

The question is thus to construct such polynomials k_1 and k_2. We remark that the condition that $(k_1(X)^q k_2(X) - k_1(X) k_2(X)^q) \bmod \mathcal{I}(X)$ vanishes modulo Q can be rewritten as a quadratic system of multivariate equations over $\mathbb{F}_q$. In fact, this system is even bilinear, since each monomial that appear in it contains at most one unknown for each of k_1 and k_2. As a consequence, this system can be quite efficiently solved using a Gröbner basis algorithm. More precisely, consider each coefficient of k_1 and k_2 as a formal unknown belonging to the field of coefficients $\mathbb{F}_{q^2}$. If x is one of these unknowns, we express x as $x_0 + z x_1$, where $(1, z)$ is a polynomial basis for $\mathbb{F}_{q^2}$ over $\mathbb{F}_q$, x_0 and x_1 are unknowns belonging to $\mathbb{F}_q$. With this convention, we have $x^q = x_0 + z^q x_1$ and we can check that our polynomial system of equations is indeed bilinear over $\mathbb{F}_q$. This system contains $\deg Q$ equations over $\mathbb{F}_{q^2}$ which are rewritten as $2 \deg Q$ equations over $\mathbb{F}_q$. Assuming k_1 to be unitary, the maximal number of unknowns that can fit in k_1 and k_2 is $2(\deg k_1 + \deg k_2 + 1)$. However, due to the action of $\mathrm{PGL}_2(\mathbb{F}_q)$, several distinct pairs k_1, k_2 yield the same polynomial for $(k_1(X)^q k_2(X) - k_1(X) k_2(X)^q)$. To avoid this issue, we need to fix at least one of the unknowns over $\mathbb{F}_{q^2}$ to an element of $\mathbb{F}_{q^2} - \mathbb{F}_q$. After this, the number of remaining unknowns over $\mathbb{F}_q$ is $2(\deg k_1 + \deg k_2)$.

At this point, we need a new heuristic argument concerning the resulting system of equations. Namely, we require two important properties of the system that arise after fixing any additional unknowns to values. The resulting system is bilinear and its number of unknowns N is equal to its number of equations. We ask that with good probability this system should be zero-dimensional with at least one solution with values in the finite field $\mathbb{F}_q$. In order to apply this heuristic, we need at least one extra unknown over $\mathbb{F}_{q^2}$ that can be set to a random value. As a consequence, we require $\deg k_1 + \deg k_2 \geq \deg Q + 1$.

Under this heuristic, we can analyze the cost of the bilinear descent by studying the complexity of solving one such system. The main result from [4,15] is that this complexity is exponential in $\min(\deg k_1, \deg k_2)$. For this reason, we do not use our descent strategy with balanced degrees $\deg k_1 \approx \deg k_2$), instead we let $d = \deg k_2$ parametrize the smallest of the two degrees and fix $\deg k_1 = \deg Q + 1 - d$.

We recall the complexity analysis given in [4,15]:

Theorem 2 [Corollary 3 from [4]].
The arithmetic complexity of computing a Gröbner basis of a generic bilinear system $f_1, \cdots, f_{n_x + n_y} \in \mathbb{K}[x_0, \cdots, x_{n_x - 1}, y_0, \cdots, y_{n_y - 1}]$ with the F_5 algorithm is upper bounded by:

$$O\left(\left(\frac{n_x + n_y + \min(n_x + 1, n_y + 1)}{\min(n_x + 1, n_y + 1)} \right)^{\omega} \right),$$

where $2 \leq \omega \leq 3$ is the linear algebra constant.

In our application, we have $n_x = 2(\deg \mathcal{Q} + 1 - d)$, $n_y = 2d$ and $\min(n_x, n_y) = 2d$. Thus, the cost of one descent step becomes:

$$\left(\frac{2 \deg \mathcal{Q} + 3}{2d + 1} \right)^{\omega}.$$

An asymptotic choice for d is given in Sect. 6. It is obtained by making d large enough to make sure that the top level nodes of the descent tree dominate the total cost. Note that, in practical computations, the best choice is usually to make d as large as feasible. Indeed, the feasibility of the Gröbner step mostly depends on the available amount of memory and it is important to descent as steeply as possible to minimize the total cost.

6   Complexity Analysis

According to the heuristic argument of Sect. 4.1, the creation of the finite field representation runs in randomized polynomial time, just by trying random polynomials h_0 and h_1 of degree 2 (or higher constant degree). Similarly, the creation of the logarithms of linear and quadratic elements can be done in polynomial time. The dominating part of this initial creation of logarithms is dominated by the linear algebra required for the quadratic elements. Since we are solving q^2 linear systems of dimension $O(q^2)$ with $O(q)$ entries per line, the total cost of this polynomial part is $O(q^7)$ arithmetic operations. Note that for Kummer extensions, the number of linear systems is reduced to $O(q)$, which lowers the cost to $O(q^6)$.

A similar polynomial time behavior for computing the logarithms of the smoothness basis is also given in [5].

The rest of this section analyzes the descent phases which dominates the asymptotic cost of our algorithm.

6.1   Individual Logarithms

To analyze this phase it is convenient to write $k = \alpha q$, for some constant $\alpha \leq 1 + \frac{\deg h_1}{q}$. Under this hypothesis, remark that:

$$L_{q^{2k}}(\beta, c) = \exp((c + o(1))(2k \log q)^{\beta}(\log(2k \log q))^{1-\beta})$$
$$\approx \exp((c' + o(1))q^{\beta} \log(q)), \quad \text{where } c' = (2\alpha)^{\beta} \cdot c$$

We now give the analysis of the complexity, which shows that we can reach complexity $L(1/4 + o(1))$ when the characteristic is small enough. Namely, we require $q = p^{\ell}$ for some $\ell \geq 2$.

We start with the classical descent approach, which it is compatible with our algorithm when $\ell \geq 2$. The analysis of this method is recalled in Sect. 2.2. Since the cost increases when $\deg \mathcal{Q}$ decreases, it suffices to write the cost for the lowest degree we wish to attain, namely $c_c\sqrt{q/\log q}$ for some constant c_c. The total cost in this case becomes:

$$\exp\left(\frac{1}{2\mu}\sqrt{\frac{\alpha}{c_c}}q^{1/4}\log q^{5/4}\right),$$

where $\mu < 1$.

Of course stopping at polynomials of degree $O(q^{1/2})$ is not enough to finish the computation. To continue the descent, we use the newer approach, starting from polynomials of degree $\deg\mathcal{Q} = c_c\sqrt{q/\log q}$. We need to determine the value of the parameter $d = \deg k_2$ introduced in Sect. 5.3. The left-hand side in the bilinear descent contains $q+1$ polynomials of degree at most $\deg k_1 = \deg\mathcal{Q} + 1 - d$. The degree of the right-hand side is bounded by $\deg k_1(\max(\deg h_0, \deg h_1) + 1)$, i.e., by a small multiple of $\deg\mathcal{Q}$, a solution of the system yields with heuristic constant probability a new equation relating the desired polynomial to polynomials of degree at most $\deg k_1$. The total number of polynomials of degree between $\deg k_1 - d$ and $\deg k_1$ after decomposing each side into irreducible polynomial is at most $q + O(1)$. Note that the contribution of lower degree polynomials to the complexity is negligible, since the computation of their logarithms is deferred to a lower level of the computation tree, where they represent a tiny fraction of the polynomials to be addressed.

Thus, the running time to compute the logarithm of a degree $D_\mathcal{Q} = \deg\mathcal{Q}$ polynomial is $T(D_\mathcal{Q}, d) \approx T_0(D_\mathcal{Q}, d) + qT(D_\mathcal{Q} - d, d)$. In Sect. 5.3, we find that:

$$T_0(D_\mathcal{Q}, d) = \binom{2D_\mathcal{Q} + 3}{2d + 1}^\omega.$$

We now choose d to ensure that $T_0(D_\mathcal{Q}, d)$ dominates the computation. This requires d to be large enough to be able to neglect the powers of q in the sum (when the expression of $T(D_\mathcal{Q}, d)$ is unrolled). To simplify the analysis, we replace T_0 by $T_1(D_\mathcal{Q}, d) = D_\mathcal{Q}^{6(d+1)}$, which is asymptotically larger. We find that we need to choose d such that:

$$q\left(D_q - d\right)^{6(d+1)} \leq D_\mathcal{Q}^{6(d+1)}.$$

Taking the logarithm, and using $-\log(1 - \epsilon) \approx \epsilon$, it asymptotically suffices to have

$$d^2 \geq \frac{D_\mathcal{Q}\log q}{6}.$$

With $D_\mathcal{Q} = c_c\sqrt{q/\log q}$, we can choose $d = \left\lceil\left(\frac{c_c}{6}\sqrt{q\log q}\right)^{1/2}\right\rceil$.

This yields:

$$T_1(D_\mathcal{Q}, d) = \exp\left(\left(\frac{\sqrt{6c_c}}{4} + o(1)\right)q^{1/4}\log^{5/4}q\right).$$

Of course, this cost should be multiplied by the number of polynomials after the classical descent. When $\mu < 1$, the number of levels in the classical descent tree is logarithmic in q and each level multiplies the number of polynomials by a constant. As a consequence, the total number of polynomials after the classical descent is polynomial in q and vanishes into the $o(1)$ in the exponent of the complexity. In order the balance the two phases of the descent, we can take:

$$c_c = \frac{1}{\mu}\sqrt{\frac{2\alpha}{3}},$$

which achieves complexity:

$$\exp\left(\left(\frac{1}{2\sqrt{\mu}}\cdot\left(\frac{3\alpha}{2}\right)^{1/4}+o(1)\right)q^{1/4}\log^{5/4}q\right).$$

The constant in the above complexity could be improved by taking into account a value of the linear algebra constant $\omega < 3$ and letting μ tend toward 1. Note that due to the presence of an extra $\log^{1/2}(q)$ term, this is strictly bigger than $L(1/4)$. However, it can be rewritten as $L(1/4 + o(1))$.

Impact of more efficient algorithms to solve the bilinear systems. It is important to remark that given an oracle (or efficient algorithm) to solve the bilinear systems, we could use a much faster descent from degree $\deg \mathcal{Q}$ to $\lceil(\deg \mathcal{Q}+1)/2\rceil$ at each step. In this case, the complexity would be dominated by the number of nodes in the descent tree, i.e. $q^{\log D}$. Starting directly from $\deg \mathcal{Q} = k - 1$ would then give a **quasi-polynomial** complexity $\exp(O(\log^2 q))$.

Moreover, this would get rid of the use of classical descent, together with the constraint of having $q = p^\ell$, with $\ell \geq 2$.

7   Remarks on the Special Case of $\mathbb{F}_{p^k}$, p and k Prime

As already mentioned, in order to use our algorithm, we need to embed $\mathbb{F}_{p^k}$ with p and k prime into a small extension $\mathbb{F}_{q^{2k}}$, with $q = p^e$ and $e = 2\lceil\log k\rceil$. From an asymptotic point of view, this is of little impact, indeed the complexity would become:

$$\exp\left(Ck^{1/4}\log^{5/4}k\right),$$

for some constant C. Since $\log p^k = k\log p \geq k/2$, expressed as a function of p^k, it becomes:

$$\exp\left(C'\log^{1/4}p^k\log\log^{5/4}p^k\right) = L_{p^k}(1/4 + o(1)).$$

In practice, it is also interesting to consider computations in $\mathbb{F}_{2^p}$ with $1024 < p < 2048$ prime. We know from Appendix B that this can be done by taking $q = 2^{11}$ and having polynomials h_0 and h_1 of degree 2. In this case, we expect the complexity to be dominated by the computation of logarithms of quadratic polynomials. This would require approximately 2^{77} arithmetic operations on numbers of p bits, since we only need the value of logarithms modulo $2^p - 1$. Comparing with the most recent data of the function field sieve [2], this $L(1/3)$ algorithm remains more efficient in this range.

8 A Couple of Experiments on Kummer Extensions in Characteristic 2

For practical experiments, it is very convenient to use finite fields containing a subfield of adequate size and to chose an extension that can be represented with polynomials h_0 and h_1 of degree 1. In practice, this means choosing a Kummer or twisted Kummer extension, which also a reduction of the size of the smoothness basis by a nice factor. We recently announce two computation records that illustrate the algorithm described here in this context. For numerical details about these records, we refer the reader to [8,9].

8.1 A Kummer Extension $\mathbb{F}_{256^{2 \cdot 255}}$

Our first example is representative of our algorithm in the special case of Kummer extension. More precisely, we let $q = 256$ and consider the finite field $\mathbb{F}_{q^{2k}}$, with $k = q - 1$.

In this computation, the most costly part is the linear algebra step for computing the discrete logarithms of approximately 2^{22} quadratic polynomials. This is decomposed into 129 independent linear systems, one containing 2^{14} elements and 128 with 2^{15} elements. On average, these system contain 128 non-zero coefficients per line.

An initial phase of continued fractions reduced the problem to computed logarithms of polynomials of degree at most 29. The classical descent step was used to reduce this down to degree 12. The bilinear system approach permitted to conclude the computation.

The total cost of the individual logarithm was approximately one half of the cost of linear algebra. However, by using improved parameter choices (as in the next computation), it would be possible to reduce this by a large factor.

8.2 A Twisted Kummer Extension $\mathbb{F}_{256^{3 \cdot 257}}$

This second example is interesting because it shows that pairing-based cryptography over $\mathbb{F}_{2^{257}}$ cannot be secure. However, it is too specific to be representative, indeed, it crucially relies on the fact that $\mathbb{F}_{256^3} = \mathbb{F}_{64^4}$.

The main specificity of this computation is a descent strategy, similar to the one presented in [6], that allows a descent from polynomials of degree 2 to polynomials of degree 1. This requires 3 conditions, the use of a Kummer or twisted Kummer extension, the replacement of the field of coefficients $\mathbb{F}_{q^2}$ by $\mathbb{F}_{q^3}$ and the use of two different polynomials to generate the systematic side of relations. Namely, we used both $X^{256} + X$ and $(X^{64} + X)^4$.

As a direct consequence, the costly phase of generating quadratic polynomials as a whole is removed. Thus, the computation becomes dominated by the descent phase. Compared to the previous computation, this was largely optimized. Indeed, the cost of the descent in this computation is about 1/10 of the descent in the previous example.

Acknowledgements. We acknowledge that the results in this paper have been achieved using the PRACE Research Infrastructure resource Curie based in France at TGCC, Bruyères-le-Chatel (project number 2011050868) and the PRACE Research Infrastructure resource Jugene/Juqueen based in Germany at the Jülich Supercomputing Centre (project number 2011050868).

Appendix

A   Alternative Polynomials

Throughout the paper, we used the polynomial $X^q - X$ as our starting point. However, it is also possible to use other polynomials for this purpose. In order to be usable in our algorithm, a polynomial needs to satisfy two basic properties. First, it should factor into linear factors over a small degree extension of $\mathbb{F}_q$. Second, it should be possible to write it as a low degree polynomial in X and X^q.

Two possible alternative polynomials are $X^{q+1} - 1$ and $X^{q+1} + 1$ which factor into linear terms over $\mathbb{F}_{q^2}$. Another possibility is to use $X^{q+1} - X + 1$ or $X^{q+1} + X + 1$ which factor into linear terms over $\mathbb{F}_{q^3}$. For example, let us this factorization in the case of $X^{q+1} - X + 1$. Let x denote a root of this polynomial in $\overline{\mathbb{F}}_q$. It is clear that x satisfies:

$$x^q = \frac{x-1}{x}.$$

As a consequence:

$$x^{q^2} = \frac{x^q - 1}{x^q} = \frac{-1}{x-1},$$

and

$$x^{q^3} = \frac{-1}{x^q - 1} = x.$$

Thus x belongs to $\mathbb{F}_{q^3}$. The polynomials $X^{q+1} \pm X + 1$ are very closely related to the discrete logarithm approach proposed in [5].

A.1   Equivalence of Using the Alternative Polynomials

Assume that we are working with a subfield $\mathbb{F}_q$ of characteristic q. Define v to be a root of $X^{q+1} - 1$ in $\mathbb{F}_{q^2}$. Consider now the homography given by the quadruple $(a, b, c, d) = (v, 1, 1, v)$. It is easy to check that the image of $X^q - X$ by this homography is:

$$
(ca^q - ac^q)X^{q+1} + (da^q - bc^q)X^q + (cb^q - ad^q)X + (db^q - bd^q) \equiv \\
(v^q - v)X^{q+1} + (v^{q+1} - 1)X^q + (1 - v^{q+1})X + (v - v^q) \equiv \\
(v^q - v)(X^{q+1} - 1).
$$

Up to a multiplicative constant, this yields the polynomial $X^{q+1} - 1$.

Similarly, if v denotes a root of $X^{q+1} + 1$ in $\mathbb{F}_{q^2}$, consider the homography induced by the quadruple $(a, b, c, d) = (v, -1, 1, v)$. The image of $X^q - X$ is:

$$(ca^q - ac^q)X^{q+1} + (da^q - bc^q)X^q + (cb^q - ad^q)X + (db^q - bd^q) \equiv$$
$$(v^q - v)X^{q+1} + (v^{q+1} + 1)X^q + (-1 - v^{q+1})X + (-v + v^q) \equiv$$
$$(v^q - v)(X^{q+1} + 1).$$

As a consequence, the polynomials $X^{q+1} \pm 1$ can be obtained by applying a well-chosen homography to $X^q - X$. Thus, they do not generate any extra multiplicative relations in the finite field.

Similarly, the use of $X^{q+1} \pm X + 1$ is equivalent to the use of $X^q - X$ when taking coefficients in $\mathbb{F}_{q^3}$. To see that, define v to be a root of $X^{q+1} - X + 1$ in $\mathbb{F}_{q^3}$. Consider the homography given by $(a, b, c, d) = (v, v - 1, 1, v)$. We see that after applying the homography, $X^q - X$ becomes:

$$(ca^q - ac^q)X^{q+1} + (da^q - bc^q)X^q + (cb^q - ad^q)X + (db^q - bd^q) \equiv$$
$$(v^q - v)X^{q+1} + (v^{q+1} - v + 1)X^q + (v^q - 1 - v^{q+1})X + (v^{q+1} - v - v^{q+1} + v^q) \equiv$$
$$(v^q - v)(X^{q+1} + X + 1).$$

Finally, with v a root of $X^{q+1} + X + 1$ in $\mathbb{F}_{q^3}$ and the homography given by $(a, b, c, d) = (v, -v - 1, 1, v)$, we find after applying the homography:

$$(ca^q - ac^q)X^{q+1} + (da^q - bc^q)X^q + (cb^q - ad^q)X + (db^q - bd^q) \equiv$$
$$(v^q - v)X^{q+1} + (v^{q+1} + v + 1)X^q + (-v^q - 1 - v^{q+1})X + (-v^{q+1} - v + v^{q+1} + v^q)$$
$$\equiv$$
$$(v^q - v)(X^{q+1} - X + 1).$$

As a consequence, we see that the four natural alternative polynomials that can be used with coefficients in $\mathbb{F}_{q^2}$ or $\mathbb{F}_{q^3}$ turn out to be equivalent to the use of $X^q - X$.

B   Evidence for the Existence of the h_0 and h_1 Polynomials

Since our algorithm replies on the existence of low degree polynomials h_0 and h_1 such that $h_1(X) \cdot X^q - h_0(X)$ has a factor of degree k, it is important to study this heuristic hypothesis in more details.

In this appendix, we give some practical evidence for the existence of such polynomials in some practically interesting case. Assume that we wish to compute discrete logarithm in $\mathbb{F}_{2^p}$ for a prime p in the interval $[2^{10}, 2^{11}]$. We expect this to be achievable by embedding the finite field in $\mathbb{F}_{2^{11p}}$, i.e. by taking $q = 2^{11}$. We define the finite field $\mathbb{F}_q$ as $\mathbb{F}_2[a]$, with $a^{11} + a^2 + 1 = 0$, and search for good polynomials h_0 and h_1 with coefficient in $\mathbb{F}_q$.

The result of this search is given in Table 1. It shows that all of the desired extension fields can be represented with polynomials h_0 and h_1 of degree 2.

Table 1. Representation of $\mathbb{F}_{q^p}$ by $X^q = h_0(X)/h_1(X)$ for $q = 2^{11}$

Extension degree	h_0	h_1	Extension degree	h_0	h_1
1031	$X^2 + a^{1555} X + a^{148}$	$X^2 + a^{1962} X + a^{1465}$	1033	$X^2 + a^{277} X + a^{702}$	$X^2 + a^{131} X + a^{1619}$
1039	$X^2 + a^{1161} X + a^{498}$	$X^2 + a^{1519} X + a^{1482}$	1049	$X^2 + a^{1768} X + a^{709}$	$X^2 + a^{131} X + a^{283}$
1051	$X^2 + a^{1967} X + a^{1919}$	$X^2 + a^{304} X + a^{272}$	1061	$X^2 + a^{638} X + a^{1905}$	$X^2 + a^{347} X + a^{651}$
1063	$X^2 + a^{1079} X + a^{525}$	$X^2 + a^{904} X + a^{2029}$	1069	$X^2 + a^{1050} X + a^{1725}$	$X^2 + a^{1842} X + a^{1551}$
1087	$X^2 + a^{421} X + a^{1405}$	$X^2 + a^{1404} X + a^{901}$	1091	$X^2 + a^{609} X + a^{1744}$	$X^2 + a^{1945} X + a^{781}$
1093	$X^2 + a^{608} X + a^{468}$	$X^2 + a^{342} X + a^{1200}$	1097	$X^2 + a^{1603} X + a^{452}$	$X^2 + a^{1910} X + a^{1892}$
1103	$X^2 + a^{155} X + a^{1694}$	$X^2 + a^{732} X + a^{779}$	1109	$X^2 + a^{414} X + a^{612}$	$X^2 + a^{656} X + a^{1029}$
1117	$X^2 + a^{409} X + a^{1303}$	$X^2 + a^{1591} X + a^{1159}$	1123	$X^2 + a^{46} X + a^{1131}$	$X^2 + a^{1615} X + a^{1379}$
1129	$X^2 + a^{194} X + a^{315}$	$X^2 + a^{1379} X + a^{1184}$	1151	$X^2 + a^{394} X + a^{391}$	$X^2 + a^{1305} X + a^{125}$
1153	$X^2 + a^{1673} X + a^{171}$	$X^2 + a^{870} X + a^{302}$	1163	$X^2 + a^{694} X + a^{1368}$	$X^2 + a^{220} X + a^{24}$
1171	$X^2 + a^{771} X + a^{1996}$	$X^2 + a^{306} X + a^{805}$	1181	$X^2 + a^{506} X + a^{2018}$	$X^2 + a^{326} X + a^{1698}$
1187	$X^2 + a^{1351} X + a^{1709}$	$X^2 + a^{1810} X + a^{1518}$	1193	$X^2 + a^{845} X + a^{42}$	$X^2 + a^{572} X + a^{900}$
1201	$X^2 + a^{1053} X + a^{175}$	$X^2 + a^{734} X + a^{1402}$	1213	$X^2 + a^{1562} X + a^{1541}$	$X^2 + a^{597} X + a^{704}$
1217	$X^2 + a^{715} X + a^{1251}$	$X^2 + a^{1085} X + a^{147}$	1223	$X^2 + a^{807} X + a^{1818}$	$X^2 + a^{599} X + a^{162}$
1229	$X^2 + a^{397} X + a^{1837}$	$X^2 + a^{823} X + a^{245}$	1231	$X^2 + a^{1750} X + a^{356}$	$X^2 + a^{59} X + a^{724}$
1237	$X^2 + a^{572} X + a^{922}$	$X^2 + a^{1784} * X + a^{2037}$	1249	$X^2 + a^{673} X + a^{902}$	$X^2 + a^{43} X + a^{877}$
1259	$X^2 + a^{1700} X + a^{1480}$	$X^2 + a^{1780} X + a^{1750}$	1277	$X^2 + a^{1380} X + a^{1484}$	$X^2 + a^{1861} X + a^{538}$
1279	$X^2 + a^{431} X + a^{1433}$	$X^2 + a^{1695} X + a^{438}$	1283	$X^2 + a^{493} X + a^{208}$	$X^2 + a^{85} X + a^{1672}$
1289	$X^2 + a^{1934} X + a^{1863}$	$X^2 + a^{1273} X + a^{1829}$	1291	$X^2 + a^{375} X + a^{524}$	$X^2 + a^{1236} X + a^{1945}$
1297	$X^2 + a^{1921} X + a^{1736}$	$X^2 + a^{598} X + a^{1530}$	1301	$X^2 + a^{1029} X + a^{478}$	$X^2 + a^{1434} X + a^{1418}$
1303	$X^2 + a^{1194} X + a^{1801}$	$X^2 + a^{208} X + a^{1592}$	1307	$X^2 + a^{1754} X + a^{626}$	$X^2 + a^{235} X + a^{979}$
1319	$X^2 + a^{1437} X + a^{282}$	$X^2 + a^{148} X + a^{744}$	1321	$X^2 + a^{982} X + a^{1089}$	$X^2 + a^{1632} X + a^{1598}$

Table 1. (*Continued*)

Extension degree	h_0	h_1	Extension degree	h_0	h_1
1327	$X^2 + a^{1455} X + a^{181}$	$X^2 + a^{508} X + a^{373}$	1361	$X^2 + a^{1451} X + a^{882}$	$X^2 + a^{1035} X + a^{634}$
1367	$X^2 + a^{331} X + a^{198}$	$X^2 + a^{1167} X + a^{1818}$	1373	$X^2 + a^{459} X + a^{1461}$	$X^2 + a^{946} X + a^{957}$
1381	$X^2 + a^{45} X + a^{1524}$	$X^2 + a^{1816} X + a^{766}$	1399	$X^2 + a^{684} X + a^{1574}$	$X^2 + a^{580} X + a^{1611}$
1409	$X^2 + a^{1439} X + a^{454}$	$X^2 + a^{1599} X + a^{1039}$	1423	$X^2 + a^{792} X + a^{1028}$	$X^2 + a^{940} X + a^{1662}$
1427	$X^2 + a^{345} X + a^{908}$	$X^2 + a^{1392} X + a^{864}$	1429	$X^2 + a^{667} X + a^{1656}$	$X^2 + a^{1867} X + a^{830}$
1433	$X^2 + a^{219} X + a^{362}$	$X^2 + a^{141} X + a^{1881}$	1439	$X^2 + a^{1417} X + a^{1761}$	$X^2 + a^{1224} X + a^{766}$
1447	$X^2 + a^{994} X + a^{1216}$	$X^2 + a^{15} X + a^{756}$	1451	$X^2 + a^{718} X + a^{766}$	$X^2 + a^{509} X + a^{702}$
1453	$X^2 + a^{1180} X + a^{129}$	$X^2 + a^{130} X + a^{1659}$	1459	$X^2 + a^{619} X + a^{782}$	$X^2 + a^{1423} X + a^{793}$
1471	$X^2 + a^{757} X + a^{210}$	$X^2 + a^{1192} X + a^{1976}$	1481	$X^2 + a^{1880} X + a^{882}$	$X^2 + a^{773} X + a^{339}$
1483	$X^2 + a^{670} X + a^{20}$	$X^2 + a^{24} X + a^{1514}$	1487	$X^2 + a^{1972} X + a^{1964}$	$X^2 + a^{1370} X + a^{528}$
1489	$X^2 + a^{1501} X + a^{116}$	$X^2 + a^{866} X + a^{694}$	1493	$X^2 + a^{1957} X + a^{987}$	$X^2 + a^{979} X + a^{781}$
1499	$X^2 + a^{1456} X + a^{1644}$	$X^2 + a^{1479} X + a^{600}$	1511	$X^2 + a^{279} X + a^{1360}$	$X^2 + a^{591} X + a^{1944}$
1523	$X^2 + a^{810} X + a^{25}$	$X^2 + a^{1924} X + a^{927}$	1531	$X^2 + a^{1415} X + a^{632}$	$X^2 + a^{1575} X + a^{911}$
1543	$X^2 + a^{1957} X + a^{1106}$	$X^2 + a^{1098} X + a^{1111}$	1549	$X^2 + a^{140} X + a^{498}$	$X^2 + a^{513} X + a^{1876}$
1553	$X^2 + a^{1109} X + a^{883}$	$X^2 + a^{1256} X + a^{524}$	1559	$X^2 + a^{485} X + a^{1312}$	$X^2 + a^{1102} X + a^{847}$
1567	$X^2 + a^{908} X + a^{128}$	$X^2 + a^{188} X + a^{194}$	1571	$X^2 + a^{29} X + a^{1916}$	$X^2 + a^{1825} X + a^{1266}$
1579	$X^2 + a^{953} X + a^{1192}$	$X^2 + a^{1113} X + a^{1334}$	1583	$X^2 + a^{792} X + a^{1459}$	$X^2 + a^{1115} X + a^{645}$
1597	$X^2 + a^{874} X + a^{1697}$	$X^2 + a^{387} X + a^{763}$	1601	$X^2 + a^{138} X + a^{1728}$	$X^2 + a^{1623} X + a^{961}$
1607	$X^2 + a^{737} X + a^{119}$	$X^2 + a^{1858} X + a^{1788}$	1609	$X^2 + a^{1641} X + a^{355}$	$X^2 + a^{1823} X + a^{963}$
1613	$X^2 + a^{801} X + a^{730}$	$X^2 + a^{193} X + a^{292}$	1619	$X^2 + a^{1715} X + a^{167}$	$X^2 + a^{510} X + a^{1166}$
1621	$X^2 + a^{1359} X + a^{745}$	$X^2 + a^{1157} X + a^{145}$	1627	$X^2 + a^{1560} X + a^{1074}$	$X^2 + a^{1631} X + a^{1624}$
1637	$X^2 + a^{575} X + a^{1741}$	$X^2 + a^{1620} X + a^{110}$	1657	$X^2 + a^{1727} X + a^{1064}$	$X^2 + a^{1968} X + a^{1714}$
1663	$X^2 + a^{960} X + a^{270}$	$X^2 + a^{744} X + a^{157}$	1667	$X^2 + a^{176} X + a^{536}$	$X^2 + a^{1208} X + a^{1919}$
1669	$X^2 + a^{229} X + a^{407}$	$X^2 + a^{1723} X + a^{1999}$	1693	$X^2 + a^{73} X + a^{642}$	$X^2 + a^{889} X + a^{489}$

Table 1. (*Continued*)

Extension degree	h_0	h_1	Extension degree	h_0	h_1
1697	$X^2 + a^{441}X + a^{722}$	$X^2 + a^{1454}X + a^{1566}$	1699	$X^2 + a^{387}X + a^{1300}$	$X^2 + a^{44}X + a^{684}$
1709	$X^2 + a^{1475}X + a^{1582}$	$X^2 + a^{63}X + a^{1779}$	1721	$X^2 + a^{1051}X + a^{846}$	$X^2 + a^{1536}X + a^{1506}$
1723	$X^2 + a^{1493}X + a^{1551}$	$X^2 + a^{1293}X + a^{1781}$	1733	$X^2 + a^{1536}X + a^{708}$	$X^2 + a^{836}X + a^{1518}$
1741	$X^2 + a^{1215}X + a^{455}$	$X^2 + a^{2013}X + a^{1400}$	1747	$X^2 + a^{978}X + a^{1676}$	$X^2 + a^{1444}X + a^{1102}$
1753	$X^2 + a^{450}X + a^{1685}$	$X^2 + a^{392}X + a^{136}$	1759	$X^2 + a^{1010}X + a^{1438}$	$X^2 + a^{1215}X + a^{63}$
1777	$X^2 + a^{1293}X + a^{249}$	$X^2 + a^{569}X + a^{554}$	1783	$X^2 + a^{150}X + a^{1608}$	$X^2 + a^{1185}X + a^{1061}$
1787	$X^2 + a^{1563}X + 1$	$X^2 + a^{1766}X + a^{1790}$	1789	$X^2 + a^{1435}X + a^{1084}$	$X^2 + a^{264}X + a^{770}$
1801	$X^2 + a^{1713}X + a^{678}$	$X^2 + a^{1656}X + a^{1626}$	1811	$X^2 + a^{1809}X + a^{2036}$	$X^2 + a^{1859}X + a^{525}$
1823	$X^2 + a^{659}X + a^{567}$	$X^2 + a^{147}X + a^{962}$	1831	$X^2 + a^{1384}X + a^{170}$	$X^2 + a^{550}X + a^{2035}$
1847	$X^2 + a^{885}X + a^{964}$	$X^2 + a^{701}X + a^{1221}$	1861	$X^2 + a^{1932}X + a^{1701}$	$X^2 + a^{158}X + a^{1250}$
1867	$X^2 + a^{1363}X + a^{1836}$	$X^2 + a^{307}X + a^{735}$	1871	$X^2 + a^{749}X + a^{1955}$	$X^2 + a^{499}X + a^{166}$
1873	$X^2 + a^{757}X + a^{200}$	$X^2 + a^{971}X + a^{601}$	1877	$X^2 + a^{758}X + a^{500}$	$X^2 + a^{943}X + a^{1832}$
1879	$X^2 + a^{289}X + a^{1359}$	$X^2 + a^{913}X + a^{840}$	1889	$X^2 + a^{1076}X + a^{1002}$	$X^2 + a^{1431}X + a^{476}$
1901	$X^2 + a^{752}X + a^{1060}$	$X^2 + a^{269}X + a^{1793}$	1907	$X^2 + a^{1954}X + a^{1856}$	$X^2 + a^{255}X + a^{316}$
1913	$X^2 + a^{1142}X + a^{578}$	$X^2 + a^{1118}X + a^{1052}$	1931	$X^2 + a^{1529}X + a^{777}$	$X^2 + a^{1631}X + a^{285}$
1933	$X^2 + a^{600}X + a^{509}$	$X^2 + a^{1477}X + a^{598}$	1949	$X^2 + a^{839}X + a^{1766}$	$X^2 + a^{1232}X + a^{226}$
1951	$X^2 + a^{1016}X + a^{1143}$	$X^2 + a^{1624}X + a^{1871}$	1973	$X^2 + a^{722}X + a^{769}$	$X^2 + a^{834}X + a^{1277}$
1979	$X^2 + a^{1007}X + a^{1464}$	$X^2 + a^{966}X + a^{912}$	1987	$X^2 + a^{1002}X + a^{682}$	$X^2 + a^{1255}X + a^{1006}$
1993	$X^2 + a^{709}X + a^{1676}$	$X^2 + a^{638}X + a^{957}$	1997	$X^2 + a^{1653}X + a^{1899}$	$X^2 + a^{29}X + a^{867}$
1999	$X^2 + a^{104}X + a^{1482}$	$X^2 + a^{1019}X + a^{649}$	2003	$X^2 + a^{328}X + a^{701}$	$X^2 + a^{554}X + a^{176}$
2011	$X^2 + a^{1510}X + a^{1241}$	$X^2 + a^{1524}X + a^{741}$	2017	$X^2 + a^{1572}X + a^{1645}$	$X^2 + a^{814}X + a^{298}$
2027	$X^2 + a^{1878}X + a^{1243}$	$X^2 + a^{1474}X + a^{1124}$	2029	$X^2 + a^{1502}X + a^{1998}$	$X^2 + a^{982}X + a^{721}$
2039	$X^2 + a^{1871}X + a^{1848}$	$X^2 + a^{1346}X + a^{1272}$			

References

1. Adleman, L.M., Huang, M.-D.A.: Function field sieve method for discrete logarithms over finite fields. Inf. Comput. **151**, 5–16 (1999). (Academic Press)
2. Barbulescu, R., Bouvier, C., Detrey, J., Gaudry, P., Jeljeli, H., Thomé, E., Videau, M., Zimmermann, P.: Discrete logarithm in $GF(2^{809})$ with FFS. IACR Cryptol. ePrint Arch. **2013**, 197 (2013)
3. Coppersmith, D.: Fast evaluation of logarithms in fields of characteristic two. IEEE Trans. Inf. Theor. **IT-30**(4), 587–594 (1984)
4. Faugère, J.-C., Din, M.S.E., Spaenlehauer, P.-J.: Gröbner bases of bihomogeneous ideals generated by polynomials of bidegree (1,1): algorithms and complexity. J. Symbolic Comput. **46**(4), 406–437 (2011)
5. Göloglu, F., Granger, R., McGuire, G., Zumbrägel, J.: On the function field sieve and the impact of higher splitting probabilities: application to discrete logarithms in 2^{1971}. IACR Cryptol. ePrint Arch. **2013**, 74 (2013)
6. Göloglu, F., Granger, R., McGuire, G., Zumbrägel, J.: Solving a 6120-bit DLP on a desktop computer. IACR Cryptol. ePrint Arch. **2013**, 306 (2013)
7. Huang, M.-D., Narayanan, A.K.: Finding primitive elements in finite fields of small characteristic. CoRR abs/1304.1206 (2013)
8. Joux, A.: Discrete logarithms in $GF(2^{4080})$. NMBRTHRY list, March 2013
9. Joux, A.: Discrete logarithms in $GF(2^{6168}) = GF((2^{257})^{24})$. NMBRTHRY list, May 2013
10. Joux, A.: Faster index calculus for the medium prime case application to 1175-bit and 1425-bit finite fields. In: Johansson, T., Nguyen, P.Q. (eds.) EUROCRYPT 2013. LNCS, vol. 7881, pp. 177–193. Springer, Heidelberg (2013)
11. Joux, A., Lercier, R.: The function field sieve in the medium prime case. In: Vaudenay, S. (ed.) EUROCRYPT 2006. LNCS, vol. 4004, pp. 254–270. Springer, Heidelberg (2006)
12. Joux, A., Lercier, R., Smart, N.P., Vercauteren, F.: The number field sieve in the medium prime case. In: Dwork, C. (ed.) CRYPTO 2006. LNCS, vol. 4117, pp. 326–344. Springer, Heidelberg (2006)
13. Panario, D., Gourdon, X., Flajolet, P.: An analytic approach to smooth polynomials over finite fields. In: Buhler, J.P. (ed.) ANTS 1998. LNCS, vol. 1423, pp. 226–236. Springer, Heidelberg (1998)
14. Semaev, I.: An algorithm for evaluation of discrete logarithms in some nonprime finite fields. Math. Comput. **67**, 1679–1689 (1998)
15. Spaenlehauer, P.-J.: Solving multi-homogeneous and determinantal systems Algorithms - Complexity - Applications. Ph.D. thesis, Université Pierre et Marie Curie (UPMC) (2012)

Lattices Part II

High Precision Discrete Gaussian Sampling on FPGAs

Sujoy Sinha Roy$^{(\boxtimes)}$, Frederik Vercauteren, and Ingrid Verbauwhede

ESAT/COSIC and iMinds, KU Leuven,
Kasteelpark Arenberg 10, B-3001 Leuven-Heverlee, Belgium
{sujoy.sinharoy,frederik.vercauteren,ingrid.verbauwhede}@esat.kuleuven.be

Abstract. Lattice-based public key cryptography often requires sampling from discrete Gaussian distributions. In this paper we present an efficient hardware implementation of a discrete Gaussian sampler with high precision and large tail-bound based on the Knuth-Yao algorithm. The Knuth-Yao algorithm is chosen since it requires a minimal number of random bits and is well suited for high precision sampling. We propose a novel implementation of this algorithm based on an efficient traversal of the discrete distribution generating (DDG) tree. Furthermore, we propose optimization techniques to store the probabilities of the sample points in near-optimal space. Our implementation targets the Gaussian distribution parameters typically used in LWE encryption schemes and has maximum statistical distance of 2^{-90} to a true discrete Gaussian distribution. For these parameters, our implementation on the Xilinx Virtex V platform results in a sampler architecture that only consumes 47 slices and has a delay of 3 ns.

Keywords: Lattice-based cryptography · Discrete gaussian sampler · Hardware implementation · Knuth-Yao algorithm · Discrete distribution generating (DDG) tree

1 Introduction

Lattice-based cryptography has become one of the main research tracks in cryptography due to its wide applicability (see [19] for some applications) and the fact that its security is based on worst-case computational assumptions that remain hard even for quantum computers. The significant advancements in theoretical lattice-based cryptography [14,15,17] have more recently been complemented with practical implementations [5,9,16] both in software and hardware.

Lattice-based cryptosystems often require sampling from discrete Gaussian distributions. The implementation of such a discrete Gaussian sampler for cryptographic applications faces several challenges [7]. Firstly, most existing sampling algorithms require a large number of random bits, which could become a limitation for lattice-based cryptosystems on a computationally weak platform. Secondly, the sampling should be of high precision, i.e. the statistical distance to the true distribution should be negligible for the provable security results

T. Lange, K. Lauter, and P. Lisoněk (Eds.): SAC 2013, LNCS 8282, pp. 383–401, 2014.
DOI: 10.1007/978-3-662-43414-7_19, © Springer-Verlag Berlin Heidelberg 2014

to hold [4]. Sampling with negligible statistical distance however either requires high precision floating arithmetic or large precomputed tables.

There are various methods for sampling from a non-uniform distribution [1]. Rejection sampling and inversion sampling are the best known algorithms. In practice, rejection sampling for a discrete Gaussian distribution is slow due to the high rejection rate for the sampled values which are far from the center of the distribution [9]. Moreover, for each trial, many random bits are required which is very time consuming on a constrained platform.

The inversion method first generates a random probability and then selects a sample value such that the cumulative distribution up to that sample point is just larger than the randomly generated probability. Since the random probability should be of high precision, this method also requires a large number of random bits. Additionally, the size of the comparator circuit increases with the precision of the probabilities used. A recent work [3] shows that the number of random bits can be reduced by performing table lookup in a lazy fashion.

In [11], Knuth and Yao proposed a random walk model for sampling from any non-uniform distribution. They showed that the number of random bits required by the sampling algorithm is close to the entropy of the distribution and thus near-optimal. However the method requires the probabilities of the sample points to be stored in a table. In case of a discrete Gaussian distribution, the binary representations of the probabilities are infinitely long. For security reasons, the probability expansions should be stored with high precision to keep the statistical distance between the true Gaussian distribution and its approximation small [4]. Hence the storage required for the probabilities becomes an issue on constrained platforms. In [7], Galbraith and Dwarkanath observed that the probability expansions for a discrete Gaussian distribution contain a large number of leading zeros which can be compressed to save space. The authors proposed a block variant of the Knuth-Yao algorithm which partitions the probabilities in different blocks having roughly the same number of leading zero digits. The paper however does not report on an actual implementation.

Although there are several hardware implementations of continuous Gaussian samplers [6,10], these implementations have low precisions and are not suitable for sampling from discrete Gaussian distributions. To the best of our knowledge, the only reported hardware implementation of a discrete Gaussian sampler can be found in [9]. The hardware architecture uses a Gaussian distributed array and an LFSR as a pseudo-random bit generator to generate a random index of the array. However the sampler has rather low precision and samples up to a tail bound which is small ($2s$). This results in a large statistical distance to the true discrete Gaussian distribution which invalidates worst case security proofs [4].

Our contributions. In this paper we propose a hardware implementation of a discrete Gaussian sampler based on the Knuth-Yao algorithm [11]. To the best of our knowledge, this is the first hardware implementation of Knuth-Yao sampling. The implementation targets sampling from discrete Gaussian distributions with small standard deviations that are typically used in LWE encryption

systems [12,18]. The proposed hardware architecture for the sampler has high
precision and large tail-bound to keep the statistical distance below 2^{-90} to the
true Gaussian distribution for the LWE cryptosystem parameter set [9]. Furthermore, this paper proposes the following optimizations which are novel:

1. An implementation of the discrete distribution generating (DDG) tree [11]
   data structure at run time in hardware is challenging and costly. We use specific properties of the DDG tree to devise a simpler approach to traverse the
   DDG tree at run time using only the relative distance between the intermediate nodes.
2. The Knuth-Yao sampling algorithm assembles the binary expansions of the
   probabilities of the sample points in a bit matrix. How this bit matrix is
   stored in ROM greatly influences the performance of the sampling operation.
   Unlike the conventional row-wise approach, we propose a column-wise method
   resulting in much faster sampling.
3. Unlike the block variant of the Knuth-Yao method in [7], we perform column-
   wise compression of the zeros present in the probability matrix due to the
   ROM specific storage style. A *one-step* compression method is proposed which
   results in a near-optimal space requirement for the probabilities.

   The remainder of the paper is organized as follows: Sect. 2 has a brief mathematical background. Implementation strategies for the Knuth-Yao sampler architecture are described in Sect. 3. The hardware architecture for the discrete
Gaussian sampler is presented in Sect. 4 and experimental results are given in
Sect. 5. Finally, Sect. 6 has the conclusion.

2   Background

Here we recall the mathematical background required to understand the paper.

2.1   Discrete Gaussian Distribution

The continuous Gaussian distribution with standard deviation $\sigma > 0$ and mean
$c \in \mathbb{R}$ is defined as follows: let E be a random variable on $\mathbb{R}$, then for $x \in \mathbb{R}$
we have $Pr(E = x) = \frac{1}{\sigma\sqrt{2\pi}} e^{-(x-c)^2/2\sigma^2}$. The discrete version of the Gaussian
distribution over $\mathbb{Z}$ with mean 0 and standard deviation $\sigma > 0$ is denoted by
$D_{\mathbb{Z},\sigma}$ and is defined as follows: let E be a random variable on $\mathbb{Z}$, then

$$Pr(E = z) = \frac{1}{S} e^{-z^2/2\sigma^2} \quad \text{where } S = 1 + 2\sum_{z=1}^{\infty} e^{-z^2/2\sigma^2}$$

Here S is a normalization factor and is approximately $\sigma\sqrt{2\pi}$. Some authors use a
slightly different normalization and define $Pr(E = z)$ proportional to $e^{-\pi z^2/s^2}$.
Here $s > 0$ is called the parameter of the distribution and is related to the
standard deviation σ by $s = \sigma\sqrt{2\pi}$.

The discrete Gaussian distribution $D_{L,\sigma}$ over a lattice L with standard deviation $\sigma > 0$ assigns a probability proportional to $e^{-|\mathbf{x}|^2/2\sigma^2}$ to each element $\mathbf{x} \in L$. Specifically when $L = \mathbb{Z}^m$, the discrete Gaussian distribution is the product distribution of m independent copies of $D_{\mathbb{Z},\sigma}$.

2.2   Tail Bound of the Discrete Gaussian Distribution

The tail of the Gaussian distribution is infinitely long and cannot be covered by any sampling algorithm. Indeed we need to sample up to a bound known as the *tail bound*. A finite tail-bound introduces a statistical difference with the true Gaussian distribution. The tail-bound depends on the maximum statistical distance allowed by the security parameters. As per Lemma 4.4 in [13], for any $c > 1$ the probability of sampling $\mathbf{v}$ from $D_{\mathbb{Z}^m,\sigma}$ satisfies the following inequality.

$$Pr(|\mathbf{v}| > c\sigma\sqrt{m}) < c^m e^{\frac{m}{2}(1-c^2)} \tag{1}$$

2.3   Precision Bound of the Discrete Gaussian Distribution

The probabilities in a discrete Gaussian distribution have infinitely long binary representations and hence no algorithm can sample according to a true discrete Gaussian distribution. Secure applications require sampling with high precision to maintain negligible statistical distance from actual distribution. Let ρ_z denote the true probability of sampling $z \in \mathbb{Z}$ according to the distribution $D_{\mathbb{Z},\sigma}$. Assume that the sampler selects z with probability p_z where $|p_z - \rho_z| < \epsilon$ for some error-constant $\epsilon > 0$. Let $\tilde{D}_{\mathbb{Z},\sigma}$ denote the approximate discrete Gaussian distribution corresponding to the finite-precision probabilities p_z. The approximate distribution $\tilde{D}_{\mathbb{Z}^m,\sigma}$ corresponding to m independent samples from $\tilde{D}_{\mathbb{Z},\sigma}$ has the following statistical distance Δ to the true distribution $D_{\mathbb{Z}^m,\sigma}$ [7]:

$$\Delta(\tilde{D}_{\mathbb{Z}^m,\sigma}, D_{\mathbb{Z}^m,\sigma}) < 2^{-k} + 2mz_t\epsilon. \tag{2}$$

Here $Pr(|\mathbf{v}| > z_t : \mathbf{v} \leftarrow D_{\mathbb{Z}^m,\sigma}) < 2^{-k}$ represents the tail bound.

2.4   Sampling Methods and the Knuth-Yao Algorithm

Rejection and inversion sampling are the best known techniques to sample from a discrete Gaussian distribution [1]. However both sampling methods require a large number of random bits. On the other hand, the Knuth-Yao algorithm performs sampling from non-uniform distributions using a near-optimal number of random bits. A detailed comparative analysis of different sampling methods can be found in [7]. Since our proposed hardware architecture uses the Knuth-Yao algorithm, we mainly focus on the Knuth-Yao method.

The Knuth-Yao algorithm uses a random walk model to perform sampling using the probabilities of the sample space elements. The method is applicable for any non-uniform distribution. Let the sample space for a random variable X

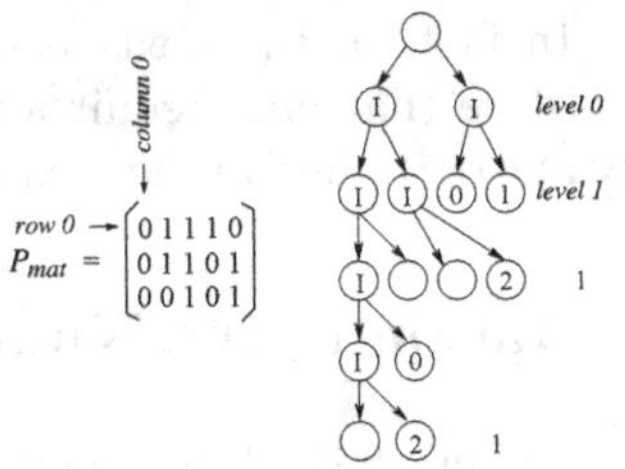

Fig. 1. Probability matrix and corresponding DDG-tree

consist of n elements $0 \leq r \leq n-1$ with probabilities p_r. The binary expansions of the probabilities are written as a matrix which we call the *probability matrix* P_{mat}. The rth row of the probability matrix corresponds to the binary expansion of p_r. An example of the probability matrix for a sample space containing three sample points $\{0,1,2\}$ with probabilities $p_0 = 0.01110$, $p_1 = 0.01101$ and $p_2 = 0.00101$ is shown in Fig. 1.

A rooted binary tree known as a discrete distribution generating (DDG) tree is constructed from the probability matrix. Each level of the DDG tree can have two types of nodes: intermediate nodes (I) and terminal nodes. The number of terminal nodes in the ith level of the DDG tree is equal to the Hamming weight of ith column in the probability matrix. Here we provide an example of the DDG tree construction for the given probability distribution in Fig. 1. The root of the DDG tree has two children which form the 0th level. Both the nodes in this level are marked with I since the 0th column in P_{mat} does not contain any non-zero. These two intermediate nodes have four children in the 1st level. To determine the type of the nodes, the 1st column of P_{mat} is scanned from the bottom. In this column only the row numbers '1' and '0' are non-zero; hence the right-most two nodes in the 1st level of the tree are marked with '1' and '0' respectively. The remaining two nodes in this level are thus marked as intermediate nodes. Similarly the next levels are also constructed. The DDG tree corresponding to P_{mat} is given in Fig. 1. In any level of the DDG tree, the terminal nodes (if present) are always on the right hand side.

The sampling operation is a random walk which starts from the root; visits a left-child or a right-child of an intermediate node depending on the random input bit. The sampling process completes when the random walk hits a terminal node and the output of the sampling operation is the value of the terminal node. By construction, the Knuth-Yao random walk samples accurately from the distribution defined by the probability matrix.

The DDG tree requires $O(nk)$ space where k is the number of columns in the probability matrix [7]. This can be reduced by constructing the DDG tree at run time during the sampling process. As shown in Fig. 1, the ith level of the DDG tree is completely determined by the $(i-1)^{th}$ level and the ith column of the probability matrix. Hence it is sufficient to store only one level of the DDG tree during the sampling operation and construct the next level (if required) using the probability matrix [11]. In fact, in the next section we introduce a novel method to traverse the DDG tree that only requires the current node and the ith column of the probability matrix to derive the next node in the tree traversal.

3   Efficient Implementation of the Knuth-Yao Algorithm

In this section we propose an efficient hardware-implementation of the Knuth-Yao based discrete Gaussian sampler which samples with high precision and large tail-bound. We describe how the DDG tree can be traversed efficiently in hardware and then propose an efficient way to store the probability matrix such that it can be scanned efficiently and also requires near-optimal space. Before we describe the implementation of the sampler, we first recall the parameter set for the discrete Gaussian sampler from the LWE implementation in [9].

3.1   Parameter Sets for the Discrete Gaussian Sampler

Table 1 shows the tail bound $|z_t|$ and precision ϵ required to obtain a statistical distance of less than 2^{-90} for the Gaussian distribution parameters in Table 1 of [9]. The standard deviation σ in Table 1 is derived from the parameter s using the equation $s = \sigma\sqrt{2\pi}$. The tail bound $|z_t|$ is calculated from Eq. 1 for the right-hand upper bound 2^{-100}. For a maximum statistical distance of 2^{-90} and a tail bound $|z_t|$, the required precision ϵ is calculated using Eq. 2.

Table 1. Parameter sets and precisions to achieve statistical distance less than 2^{-90}

m	s	σ	$|z_t|$	ϵ
256	8.35	3.33	84	106
320	8.00	3.192	86	106
512	8.01	3.195	101	107

However in practice the tail bounds are quite loose for the precision values in Table 1. The probabilities are zero (upto the mentioned precision) for the sample points greater than 39 for all three distributions. Given a probability distribution, the Knuth-Yao random walk always hits a sample point when the sum of the probabilities is one [11]. However if the sum is less than one, then the random walk may not hit a terminal node in the corresponding DDG tree. Due to finite range and precision in Table 1, the sum of the discrete Gaussian probability expansions (say P_{sum}) is less than one. We take an difference $(1 - P_{sum})$ as another sample point which indicates *out of range* event. If the Knuth-Yao random walk hits this sample point, the sample value is discarded. This *out of range* event has probability less than 2^{-100} for all three distribution sets.

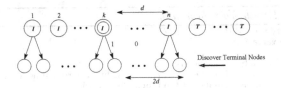

Fig. 2. DDG tree construction

3.2   Construction of the DDG Tree During Sampling

During the Knuth-Yao random walk, the DDG tree is constructed at run time. The implementation of DDG tree as a binary tree data structure is an easy problem [21] in software, but challenging on hardware platforms. As described in Sect. 2.4, the implementation of the DDG tree requires only one level of the DDG tree to be stored. However the ith level of a DDG tree may contain as many as 2^i nodes (where $2^i < nk$). On software platforms, dynamic memory allocation can be used at run time to allocate sufficient memory required to store a level of the DDG tree. But in hardware, we need to design the sampler architecture for the worst case storage requirement which makes the implementation costly.

We propose a hardware implementation friendly traversal based on specific properties of the DDG tree. We observe that in a DDG tree, all the intermediate nodes are on the left hand side; while all the terminal nodes are on the right hand side. This observation is used to derive a simple algorithm which identifies the nodes in the DDG tree traversal path instead of constructing each level during the random walk. Figure 2 describes the $(i-1)^{th}$ level of the DDG tree. The intermediate nodes are I, while the terminal nodes are T. The node visited at this level during the sampling process is highlighted by the double circle in the figure. Assume that the visited node is not a terminal node. This assumption is obvious because if the visited node is a terminal node, then we do not need to construct the ith level of the DDG tree. At this level, let there be n intermediate nodes and the visited node is the kth node from the left. Let $d = n - k$ denote the distance of the right most intermediate node from the visited node.

In the next step, the sampling algorithm reads a random bit and visits a child node on the ith level of the DDG tree. If the visited node is a left child, then it has $2d+1$ nodes to its right side. Otherwise, it will have $2d$ nodes to its right side (as shown in the figure). To determine whether the visited node is a terminal node or an intermediate node, the ith column of the probability matrix is scanned. The scanning process detects the terminal nodes from the right side of the ith level and the number of terminal nodes is equal to the Hamming weight h of the ith column of the probability matrix. The left child is a terminal node if $h > (2d+1)$ and the right child is a terminal node if $h > 2d$. If the visited node is a terminal node, we output the corresponding row number in the probability matrix as the result of sampling process. When the visited node in the ith level is internal, its visited-child in the $(i+1)^{th}$ level is checked in a similar way. From the analysis of DDG tree construction, we see the following points :

Algorithm 1. *Knuth-Yao Sampling*

Input: Probability matrix P
Output: Sample value S
1 **begin**
2    $d \leftarrow 0$; /* Distance between the visited and the rightmost internal node */
3    $Hit \leftarrow 0$; /* This is 1 when the sampling process hits a terminal node */
4    $col \leftarrow 0$;   /* Column number of the probability matrix */
5   **while** $Hit = 0$ **do**
6      $r \leftarrow RandomBit()$;
7      $d \leftarrow 2d + \bar{r}$;
8   **for** $row = MAXROW$ *down to* 0 **do**
9        $d \leftarrow d - P[row][col]$;
10   **if** $d = -1$ **then**
11         $S \leftarrow row$;
12         $Hit \leftarrow 1$;
13         $ExitForLoop()$;
14   **end**
15   **end**
16     $col \leftarrow col + 1$;
17   **end**
18 **end**

---

1. The sampling process is independent of the internal nodes that are to the left of the visited node.
2. The terminal nodes on the $(i-1)^{th}$ level have no influence on the construction of the ith level of the DDG tree.
3. The distance d between the right most internal node and the visited node on the $(i-1)^{th}$ level of the DDG tree is sufficient (along with the Hamming weight of the ith column of the probability matrix) to determine whether the visited node on the ith level is an internal node or a terminal node.

During the Knuth-Yao sampling we do not store an entire level of the DDG tree. Instead, the difference d between the visited node and the right-most intermediate node is used to construct the visited node on the next level. The steps of the Knuth-Yao sampling operation are described in Algorithm 1. In Line 6, a random bit r is used to jump to the next level of the DDG tree. On this new level, the distance between the visited node and the rightmost node is initialized to either $2d$ or $2d + 1$ depending on the random bit r. In Line 8, the *for*-loop scans a column of the probability matrix to detect the terminal nodes. Whenever the algorithm finds a 1 in the column, it detects a terminal node. Hence, the relative distance between the visited node and the right most internal node is decreased by one (Line 9). When d is reduced to -1, the sampling algorithm hits a terminal node. Hence, in this case the sampling algorithm stops and returns the corresponding row number as the output. In the other case, when d is positive after completing the scanning of an entire column of the probability matrix, the sampling algorithm jumps to the next level of the DDG tree.

3.3 Storing the Probability Matrix Efficiently

The Knuth-Yao algorithm reads the probability matrix of the discrete Gaussian distribution during formation of the DDG tree. A probability matrix having r

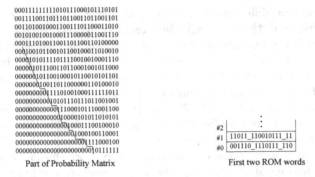

Fig. 3. Storing probability matrix

rows and c columns requires rc bits of storage. This storage could be significant when both r (depends on the tail-bound) and c (depends on the precision) are large. Figure 3 shows a portion of the probability matrix for the probabilities of $0 \leq |z| \leq 17$ with 30-bits precision according to the discrete Gaussian distribution with parameter $s = 8.01$. In [7] the authors observed that the leading zeros in the probability matrix can be compressed. The authors partitioned the probability matrix in different blocks having equal (or near-equal) number of leading zeros. Now for any row of the probability matrix, the conditional probability with respect to the block it belongs to is calculated and stored. In this case the conditional probability expansions do not contain a long sequence of leading zeros. The precision of the conditional probabilities is less than the precision of the absolute probabilities by roughly the number of leading zeros present in the absolute probability expansions. The sampling of [7] then applies two rounds of the Knuth-Yao algorithm: first to select a block and then to select a sample value according to the conditional probability expansions within the block.

However the authors of [7] do not give any actual implementation details. In hardware, ROM is ideal for storing a large amount of fixed data. To minimize computation time, data fetching from ROM should be minimized as much as possible. The pattern in which the probability expansions are stored in ROM determines the number of ROM accesses (thus performance) during the sampling process. During the sampling process the probability matrix is scanned column by column. Hence to ease the scanning operation, the probability expansions should be stored in a column-wise manner in ROM.

In Fig. 3, the probability matrix for a discrete Gaussian distribution contains large chunks of zeros near the bottom of the columns. Since we store the probability matrix in a column-wise manner in ROM, we perform compression of zeros present in the columns. The *column length* is the length of the top portion after which the chunk of bottom zeros start. We target to optimize the storage requirement by storing only the upper portions of the columns in ROM. Since the columns have different lengths, we also store the lengths of the columns. The number of bits required to represent the length of a column can be reduced by storing only the difference in column length with respect to the previous column. In this case, the number of bits required to represent the differential column length is the number of bits in the maximum deviation and a sign bit. For the discrete Gaussian distribution matrix shown in Fig. 3, the maximum deviation is three and hence three bits are required to represent the differential column lengths. Hence the total number of bits required to store the differential column lengths of the matrix (Fig. 3) is 86 (ignoring the first two columns).

For the discrete Gaussian distribution matrix, we observe that the difference between two consecutive column lengths is one for most of the columns. This observation is used to store the distribution matrix more efficiently in ROM. We consider only non-negative differences between consecutive column lengths; the length of a column either increases or remains the same with respect to its left column. When there is a decrement in the column length, the extra zeros are also considered to be part of the column to keep the column length the same as its left neighbor. In Fig. 3 the dotted line is used to indicate the lengths of the columns. It can be seen that the maximum increment in the column length happens to be one between any two consecutive columns (except the initial few columns). In this representation only one bit per column is needed to indicate the difference with respect to the left neighboring column: 0 for no-increment and 1 for an increment by one. With such a representation, 28 bits are required to represent the increment of the column lengths for the matrix in Fig. 3. Additionally, 8 redundant zeros are stored at the bottom of the columns due to the decrease in

---

Algorithm 2. *Knuth-Yao Sampling in Hardware Platform*

Input: Probability matrix P
Output: Sample value S

```
 1  begin
 2      d ← 0;      /* Distance between the visited and the rightmost internal node */
 3      Hit ← 0;    /* This is 1 when the sampling process hits a terminal node */
 4      ColLen ← INITIAL;    /* Column length is set to the length of first column */
 5      address ← 0;    /* This variable is the address of a ROM word */
 6      i ← 0;    /* This variable points the bits in a ROM word */
 7      while Hit = 0 do
 8          r ← RandomBit() ;
 9          d ← 2d + r̄ ;
10          ColLen ← ColLen + ROM[address][i] ;
11          for row = ColLen − 1 down to 0 do
12              i ← i + 1 ;
13              if i = w then
14                  address ← address + 1 ;
15                  i ← 0 ;
16              end
17              d ← d − ROM[row][i] ;
18              if d = −1 then
19                  S ← row ;
20                  Hit ← 1 ;
21                  ExitForLoop() ;
22              end
23          end
24      end
25      return (S)
26  end
```

column length in a few columns. Thus, a total of 36 bits are stored in addition to the pruned probability matrix. There is one more advantage of storing the probability matrix in this way in that we can use a simple binary counter to represent the length of the columns. The binary counter increments by one or remains the same depending on the column-length increment bit.

In ROM, we only store the portion of a column above the partition-line in Fig. 3 along with the column length difference bit. The column-length difference bit is kept at the beginning and then the column is kept in reverse order (bottom-to-top). As the Knuth-Yao algorithm scans a column from bottom to top, the column is stored in reverse order. Figure 3 shows how the columns are stored in the first two ROM words (word size 16 bits). During the sampling process, a variable is used to keep track of the column-lengths. This variable is initialized to the length of the first non-zero column. For the probability matrix in Fig. 3, the initialization value is 5 instead of 4 as the length of the next column is 6. Whilst scanning a new column, this variable is either incremented (starting bit 1) or kept the same (starting bit 0). Algorithm 2 summarizes the steps when a ROM of word size w is used as a storage for the probability matrix.

4   Hardware Architecture

Figure 4 shows the different components of the hardware architecture for the Knuth-Yao sampling. The ROM block has word size 32 bits and is used to store the probability matrix as described in Sect. 3.3. Addressing of the ROM words is done using a ROM-Address counter. Initially the counter is cleared and later incremented by one to fetch data from higher ROM locations.

The scanning operation is performed using the 32-bit register present in the *Scan ROM Word* block. First a word is fetched from the ROM and then stored in the scan register. The scan register is a left-shift register and the MSB of the register is used by the *Control Unit*. A 5-bit counter (Word-Bit) is used to count the number of bits scanned from a ROM word. When all 32 bits are read from a ROM word, the counter reaches the value 31. This event triggers data reloading from next ROM word into the scan register.

Random (or pseudo random) bits are required during the traversal of the DDG tree. We have used a true random bit generator based on the approach by Golic [8]. The quality of the random bit generator is not the main focus of this paper; the random bit generator can be replaced by any other true random bit generator [2,20] or pseudo-random bit generators based on LFSRs. The random bit generator can be slow since only five random bits are required on average during sampling from the distributions in Table 1.

An up-counter *Column Length* is used to store the lengths of the different columns of the probability matrix. This counter is first initialized to the length of the first non-zero column of the probability matrix. During the random walk, the counter increments or remains the same depending on the column-length bit. To count the number of rows during a column scanning operation, one down counter *Row Number* is used. At the start of the column-scanning, this counter is

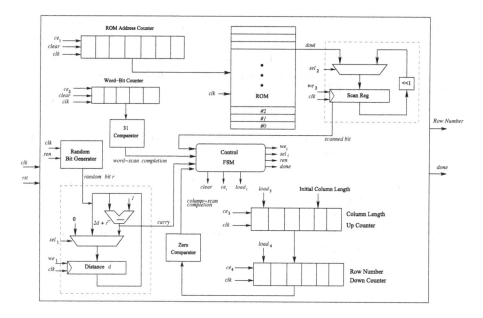

Fig. 4. Hardware architecture for Knuth-Yao sampler

initialized to the length of that column; later the counter decrements. A column scanning is completed when the *Row Number* counter reaches zero.

During construction of any level of the DDG tree, the relative position d of the right most intermediate node with respect to the visited node is kept in the register *Distance*. During the Knuth-Yao random walk, the *Distance* register is first updated to $2d$ or $2d + 1$ according to the input random bit. Later each detection of a terminal node by the scanning operation decrements the register by one. A subtracter is used for this purpose. The carry from the subtracter is an input to the control FSM. When the carry flag is set ($d < 0$), the control FSM stops the random walk and indicates completion of the sampling operation. After completion, the value present in *Row Number* is the magnitude of the sample output. One random bit is used as a sign of the value of the sample output.

The hardware architecture is driven by the control FSM. The FSM generates the selection signals for the multiplexers, the write enable signals for the registers and the enable/clear/load signals for the counters present in the architecture.

Speeding up the Sampling Operation. The sampling operation spends most time in scanning columns for which we propose two possible improvements.

1. Skipping Unnecessary Column Scanning. The sampling operation hits a terminal node when the initial value of the distance d in that level is smaller than the Hamming weight of the respective column in the probability matrix (Algorithm 1). The initial columns which have smaller Hamming weight than d

can thus be skipped; scanning is performed only for the first column that has larger Hamming weight than d. As such, unnecessary column scanning can be avoided by storing the Hamming weights of the columns.

There are two issues that make this strategy costly in terms of area. Firstly, extra memory is required to store the Hamming weights of the columns. Secondly, the shifting mechanism (to skip a column) for the *Scan Reg* (Fig. 4) becomes complicated due to the varying lengths of the columns. This also increases the size of the multiplexer for the *Scan Reg*. Since the scan register is 32 bits wide, the area overhead is significant with respect to the overall area.

2. Window-based Scanning of Columns. In hardware we can scan and process several bits of a column in a single clock cycle. Using a window-based scanning block, we can therefore reduce the computation time nearly by a factor equal to the size of the window. We can implement the window-based scanning operation by performing a minor modification in the sampler architecture shown in Fig. 4. The modifications required for window size four are shown in Fig. 5. The first four bits (bit[3] to bit[0]) near the MSB of the *Scan Reg* are scanned simultaneously and shift operations are always performed by four bits. During a column scanning operation, the register *Distance* is decremented by the sum of the bits. The register *Row Number* is decremented by four. However fast-scanning is affected when the following events occur: 1) *carry#d* is set, 2) *carry#row* is set, and 3) the wire *rowin* is zero. When only event 1 occurs, the sampling algorithm hits a terminal node and generates a sample value. Event 2 occurs when the four bits are from two columns: the end bits of the present column and the starting bits of the next column. For such events (1 or 2 or both), the control FSM suspends any register write operation and jumps to a *slow-scan* state. Now the FSM scans the bits $b[i]$ sequentially (similar to the architecture in Fig. 4) using the selection signal sel_4. Operations in this phase are similar to the basic bit-by-bit scanning method described previously. Event 3 indicates that the scanned four bits are actually the last four bits of the column. In this case, the FSM updates the registers and then performs slow-scanning for the next four bits (the first bit is the column length change bit for the new column).

The window-based scanning requires a few extra multiplexers as shown in Fig. 5 compared to the bit-by-bit method in Fig. 4. However the *Word-Bit* counter size reduces to three as one scanning operation for 32 bits requires eight shifting operations. The respective comparator circuit size also reduces. Since the multiplexers are small in size (1 and 3 bits wide), the strategy has very small area overhead and is thus more cost effective compared to the Skip-Column method.

5 Experimental Results

We have evaluated the proposed discrete Gaussian sampler architectures on Xilinx Virtex V FPGAs for the distribution parameter sets given in Table 1. The results are obtained from the ISEv11.1 tool after place and route analysis. Since

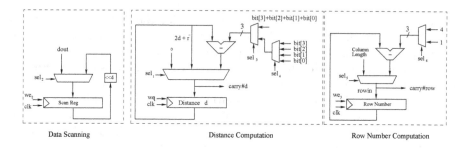

Fig. 5. Modifications required to perform 4-window scanning operation

Table 2. Width of the components in Fig. 4 for the distributions in Table 1

ROM address	Word-Bit	Scan-Reg	Column length	Row number	Distance
7	5 or 3	32	6	6	6

Table 3. Performance of the discrete Gaussian sampler on xc5vlx30

Architecture	FFs	Slices		LUTs		Delay (ns)	Clock
		Core	ROM	Core	ROM		Cycles
Figure 4	66	30	17	76	64	3	17
Figure 5	69	36	17	85	64	3.3	16

the parameter sets in Table 1 have similar standard deviations, the same architecture is used to implement all the samplers; only the ROM contents are different. In case of a given Gaussian distribution parameter, the width of the counters, registers and arithmetic circuits can be pre-determined. Table 2 shows the width of the registers present in the proposed sampler architectures.

The area, delay and average case clock cycle requirements for the two sampler architectures (Sect. 4) are shown in Table 3. The results do not include the random bit generator. The core of the bit-by-bit scanning sampler (excluding the ROM and the random bit generator in Fig. 4) consumes only 30 slices; while the core of the 4-window based fast architecture requires 6 extra slices.

On Xilinx FPGAs, ROM can be generated using LUTs or block-RAM slices. For the parameter set in Table 1, a block ROM requires only one RAMB slice. If LUT-based ROM is used, then a 32-by-96 ROM is sufficient for the distribution in Table 1. On Virtex V FPGAs, the distributed ROM consumes 17 slices.

Time spent in a sampling operation is mainly the time involved in scanning the column bits of the probability matrix. The number of bits scanned during a sampling operation depends on the number of levels jumped (equal to the number of random bits consumed) by the Knuth-Yao random walk along the DDG tree. Hence the number of bits scanned in a sampling operation increases with the number of levels jumped by random walk. However the probability of a jump from a level to its next level reduces exponentially with increase in the number of levels. Knuth and Yao showed that the expected number of random bits required (i.e the number of levels jumped) is at most two more than the entropy of the given distribution [11]. For the LWE parameter sets in Table 1, the entropy of the distributions is less than three (for $\sigma = 3.33$ the entropy is 2.9) and thus the average number of random bits required per sampling is at most five. When the Knuth-Yao random walk hits a terminal node during scanning of the fifth column of the probability matrix (Appendix A), then total number of bits scanned (column bits + column length bits) is in the range of 14 to 21.

In Appendix B, we performed a software simulation to know the average number of bits scanned. As per experimental results, on average 4.3 random bits are required and 13.5 memory-bits are scanned to generate a sample point. This experimental values support the Knuth-Yao *upper bound* for the average case. To scan the first 14 memory-bits, the bit-by-bit scanning architecture (Fig. 4) consumes 17 clock cycles, while the 4-window based fast scanning architecture (Fig. 5) spends 16 clock cycles. These average case clock cycle requirements for the two samplers are shown in Table 3.

The number of clock cycles saved by the fast architecture compared to the basic architecture is only 6 % in average case. This is due to frequent *slow-scanning* operations for the initial columns which have small lengths. The savings of the fast architecture increases with the number of levels jumped by the Knuth-Yao random walk increases. For example, when sample point is found during scanning of the 7th column of the probability matrix, the fast architecture takes only 24 cycles compared to 43 cycles (44 % saving) required by the basic architecture. Thus the fast architecture provides drastic speedup when the Knuth-Yao random walk goes beyond the average case.

Performance of the Sampler in Ring-LWE. Here we present an estimated performance analysis for the proposed sampling architectures in a ring-LWE encryption system [12]. In ring-LWE encryption, the major computations are: (1) two polynomial multiplications and (2) construction of three error polynomials using discrete Gaussian sampling. A feasible solution to implement a high-performance ring-LWE cryptosystem is to keep the multiplier and the sampler in a pipeline; the sampler stores sampled values in a buffer and the multiplier reads the buffer. Due to small delay, the sampler architecture can be integrated easily with a high-frequency polynomial multiplier.

The proposed 4-window based sampling architecture requires around 12,300 and 24,600 clock cycles on average to compute the three error polynomials [12] for the LWE parameters $m = 256$ and $m = 512$ (Table 1) respectively. The two polynomial multiplications using the NTT-based multipliers [16] require 4,800 and 10,000 clock cycles for $m = 256$ and $m = 512$ respectively. Thus the sampler architecture is slower compared to the polynomial multipliers in [16]. However, we note that our implementation is optimized for area and not speed. Since the the sampler has a very small area (compared to the multiplier) and requires random bits only occasionally, we can simply parallelize the sampling operations. In such a parallel implementation, the ROM and the random bit generator will be shared by the parallel sampling cores.

6   Conclusion

In this paper we showed that for small standard deviation, high precision discrete Gaussian samplers can be implemented in hardware using an adaptation of the Knuth-Yao algorithm. We introduced a hardware implementation friendly strategy to traverse the DDG tree in the Knuth-Yao sampling operation and proposed an optimization technique to reduce the space required to store the probabilities of the sample points in the discrete Gaussian distribution. Finally, we presented efficient hardware architectures for the discrete Gaussian distribution samplers used in LWE encryption systems. The proposed sampler architectures are small, fast and have very high precision to obtain a negligible statistical distance to a true discrete Gaussian distributions.

Acknowledgment. This work was supported in part by the Research Council KU Leuven: TENSE (GOA/11/007), by iMinds, by the Flemish Government, FWO G.0550.12N and by the Hercules Foundation AKUL/11/19. Sujoy Sinha Roy is funded by an Erasmus Mundus fellowship. We are thankful to Thomas Pöppelmann and Tim Güneysu for their suggestions to improve the quality of our paper.

Appendix A

Probability matrix for the discrete Gaussian distribution with parameter $s = 8.01$ used in the LWE crypto system of dimension $n = 512$ is shown in Fig. 6. The portion above the partition line is stored in ROM.

Appendix B

To know the average number of random bits required per sampling operation, we have performed a C-program simulation of the Knuth-Yao random walk for the distribution parameter $s = 8.01$. Column 1 and 2 in Table 4 shows the number of random bits required per sampling operation and the corresponding number of events in total 10^6 runs of the random walk. As per the experimental data in Table 4, on average 4.3 random bits are consumed and 13.5 bits are scanned from memory to sample a value from the discrete Gaussian distribution.

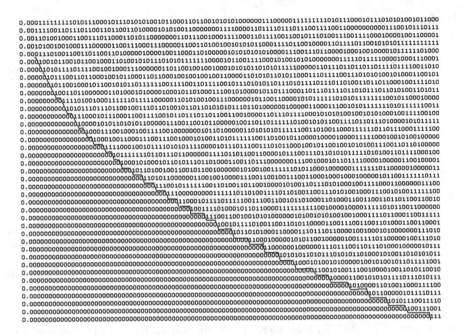

Fig. 6. Probability matrix for the discrete Gaussian distribution with $s = 8.01$

Table 4. Number of random bits required per sampling operation in 10^6 runs

Number of random bits	Occurrences
3	375097
4	312928
5	156405
6	77969
7	31093
8	19367
9	13510
10	6827
11	3380
12	1445
13	990
14	495
15	242
16	149
17	59
18	21
19	12
20	5
21	3
22	2
23	1

References

1. Devroye, L.: Non-Uniform Random Variate Generation. Springer, New York (1986)
2. Dichtl, M., Golić, J.D.: High-speed true random number generation with logic gates only. In: Paillier, P., Verbauwhede, I. (eds.) CHES 2007. LNCS, vol. 4727, pp. 45–62. Springer, Heidelberg (2007)
3. Ducas, L., Durmus, A., Lepoint, T., Lyubashevsky, V.: Lattice signatures and bimodal Gaussians. Cryptology ePrint Archive, Report 2013/383 (2013). http://eprint.iacr.org/
4. Ducas, L., Nguyen, P.Q.: Faster gaussian lattice sampling using lazy floating-point arithmetic. In: Wang, X., Sako, K. (eds.) ASIACRYPT 2012. LNCS, vol. 7658, pp. 415–432. Springer, Heidelberg (2012)
5. Frederiksen, T.: A practical implementation of Regev's LWE-based cryptosystem. In: http://daimi.au.dk/~jot2re/lwe/resources/ (2010)
6. Zhang, G., Leong, P., et al.: Ziggurat-based hardware Gaussian random number generator. In: Proceedings of the International Conference on Field Programmable Logic and Applications (FPL 2005), pp. 275–280 (2005)
7. Galbraith, S.D., Dwarakanath, N.C.: Efficient sampling from discrete Gaussians for lattice-based cryptography on a constrained device. Preprint
8. Golic, J.D.: New methods for digital generation and postprocessing of random data. IEEE Trans. Comput. 55(10), 1217–1229 (2006)
9. Göttert, N., Feller, T., Schneider, M., Buchmann, J., Huss, S.: On the design of hardware building blocks for modern lattice-based encryption schemes. In: Prouff, E., Schaumont, P. (eds.) CHES 2012. LNCS, vol. 7428, pp. 512–529. Springer, Heidelberg (2012)
10. Edrees, H.M., Cheung, B., Sandora, M., et al.: Hardware-optimized Ziggurat algorithm for high-speed Gaussian random number generators. In: Proceedings of the International Conference on Engineering of Reconfigurable Systems and Algorithms, pp. 254–260 (2009)
11. Knuth, D.E., Yao, A.C.: The complexity of non-uniform random number generation. In: Traub, J.F. (ed.) Algorithms and Complexity: New Directions and Recent Results, pp. 357–428. Academic Press, New York (1976)
12. Lindner, R., Peikert, C.: Better key sizes (and attacks) for LWE-based encryption. In: Kiayias, A. (ed.) CT-RSA 2011. LNCS, vol. 6558, pp. 319–339. Springer, Heidelberg (2011)
13. Lyubashevsky, V.: Lattice signatures without trapdoors. In: Pointcheval, D., Johansson, T. (eds.) EUROCRYPT 2012. LNCS, vol. 7237, pp. 738–755. Springer, Heidelberg (2012)
14. Micciancio, D.: Lattices in Cryptography and Cryptanalysis (2002)
15. Nguyên, P.Q., Stern, J.: The two faces of lattices in cryptology. In: Silverman, J.H. (ed.) CaLC 2001. LNCS, vol. 2146, p. 146. Springer, Heidelberg (2001)
16. Pöppelmann, T., Güneysu, T.: Towards efficient arithmetic for lattice-based cryptography on reconfigurable hardware. In: Hevia, A., Neven, G. (eds.) LATIN-CRYPT 2012. LNCS, vol. 7533, pp. 139–158. Springer, Heidelberg (2012)
17. Regev, O.: Quantum computation and lattice problems. SIAM J. Comput. 33(3), 738–760 (2004)
18. Regev, O.: On lattices, learning with errors, random linear codes, and cryptography. In: Proceedings of the Thirty-Seventh Annual ACM Symposium on Theory of Computing, STOC '05, pp. 84–93. ACM, New York (2005)

19. Regev, O.: Lattice-based cryptography. In: Dwork, C. (ed.) CRYPTO 2006. LNCS, vol. 4117, pp. 131–141. Springer, Heidelberg (2006)
20. Schellekens, D., Preneel, B., Verbauwhede, I.: FPGA vendor agnostic true random number generator. In: International Conference on Field Programmable Logic and Applications, FPL '06, pp. 1–6 (2006)
21. Rivest, R.L., Cormen, T.H., Leiserson, C.E., Stein, C.: Introduction to Algorithms, 2nd edn. MIT Press, Cambridge (2001)

Discrete Ziggurat: A Time-Memory Trade-Off for Sampling from a Gaussian Distribution over the Integers

Johannes Buchmann, Daniel Cabarcas,
Florian Göpfert[✉], Andreas Hülsing, and Patrick Weiden

Technische Universität Darmstadt, Darmstadt, Germany
{buchmann,fgoepfert,pweiden}@cdc.informatik.tu-darmstadt.de,
dcabarc@unal.edu.co, a.t.huelsing@tue.nl

Abstract. Several lattice-based cryptosystems require to sample from a discrete Gaussian distribution over the integers. Existing methods to sample from such a distribution either need large amounts of memory or they are very slow. In this paper we explore a different method that allows for a flexible time-memory trade-off, offering developers freedom in choosing how much space they can spare to store precomputed values. We prove that the generated distribution is close enough to a discrete Gaussian to be used in lattice-based cryptography. Moreover, we report on an implementation of the method and compare its performance to existing methods from the literature. We show that for large standard deviations, the Ziggurat algorithm outperforms all existing methods.

Keywords: Lattice-based cryptography · Gaussian sampling · Practicality · Implementation

1 Introduction

The object of study of this paper is the discrete Gaussian probability distribution over the integers. Sampling elements from such a distribution is widely used in lattice-based cryptography [GPV08, LP11, BGV12, GGH12]. It is a critical technical challenge to sample from a discrete Gaussian over the integers accurately and efficiently. Weiden et al. [WHCB13] report that sampling from it takes more than 50 % of the running time of the signing algorithm in their implementation of Lyubashevsky's signature scheme [Lyu12].

All existing methods to sample from a Gaussian distribution over the integers either need large amounts of memory or they are very slow. For example, Galbraith and Dwarakanath estimate that Peikert's sampler [Pei10] requires around 12 MB of storage [GD12] for some parameters. Such a large memory requirement might be acceptable on a PC but not on the diversity of devices that demand cryptographic solutions today.

In this paper we explore a different alternative for sampling from a Gaussian distribution over the integers that offers a flexible trade-off between speed and

T. Lange, K. Lauter, and P. Lisoněk (Eds.): SAC 2013, LNCS 8282, pp. 402–417, 2014.
DOI: 10.1007/978-3-662-43414-7_20, © Springer-Verlag Berlin Heidelberg 2014

memory. Moreover, for big standard deviations, this method beats commonly used methods. We call the method discrete Ziggurat because it adapts the Ziggurat algorithm [MT00] for the discrete case.

The discrete Ziggurat is specially appealing for cryptographic applications because of its flexibility. The method uses precomputed rectangles of equal 'size' to cover the area under the probability density function (PDF). Increasing the number of rectangles increases speed but also increases the memory used. Therefore, it offers an easy-to-tune trade-off between speed and memory. This is a desirable property because developers of cryptographic primitives can easily adjust it to fit the particular characteristics of different devices. On memory constraint devices like smartcards or microcontrollers they could use a low-memory low-speed setting, while on a high performing server they could use a high-memory high-speed configuration.

Originally, the Ziggurat sampler was developed for a continuous distribution. In order to adapt it to the discrete case some care must be taken. In particular the notion of 'size' of a rectangle must be redefined from the narrow concept of 'area' to the more general "probability to sample points inside the rectangle". We discuss the implications of this generalization.

It is also challenging to analyze the quality of the discrete Ziggurat because of the subtleties of an actual implementation. In this paper we provide a careful analysis that takes into consideration the loss of precision due to the tail-cut, the precision in sampling from the y-axis and the precision in calculating the PDF. The techniques used and the way they are combined in this analysis might show valuable for the analysis of other samplers. For developers we explain how to achieve a desired accuracy by setting the precision for representing numbers.

We implemented the discrete Ziggurat in C++ using the Number Theory Library (NTL) [Sho]. The implementation can be downloaded at the authors' homepage[1]. We compare the efficiency of the discrete Ziggurat with existing methods and analyze the speed-memory trade-off. For example, we used the parameters proposed by Galbraith and Dwarakanath [GD12] for the normal distribution in Lyubashevsky's signature scheme [Lyu12]. For this illustrative setting, the discrete Ziggurat produces about 1.13 million samples per second, using only 524 KB of memory. In comparison, Peikert's sampler outputs 281,000 samples per second for a memory usage of 33.55 MB. The Knuth-Yao algorithm is only slightly faster (it produces about 4 % more samples), but increases the memory-consumption by a factor of more than 400.

Related Work. We briefly survey existing alternatives to sample from a discrete Gaussian probability distribution over the integers, denoted D_σ. For parameter $\sigma > 0$, D_σ assigns $x \in \mathbb{Z}$ a probability proportional to $\rho_\sigma(x) = \exp(-\frac{1}{2}x^2/\sigma^2)$. It is important to note that sampling from D_σ is different to sampling from

---

[1] In particular at https://www.cdc.informatik.tu-darmstadt.de/~pschmidt/ implementations/ziggurat/ziggurat-src.zip.

a (continuous) normal distribution [TLLV07]. Another related problem is that of sampling from a Gaussian distribution over a generic lattice, a more complex problem, whose solutions often require sampling from D_σ as a subroutine [GPV08, Pei10, DN12, AGHS12].

For cryptographic applications it is sufficient to sample from the bounded subset $B := \mathbb{Z} \cap [-t\sigma, t\sigma]$, where the tailcut $t > 0$ is chosen large enough to guarantee a desired precision [GPV08]. One alternative to sample from D_σ is to do rejection sampling on B. Another alternative is to precompute the cumulative distribution function (CDF) for $x \in B$, sample a uniform element $y \in [0, 1)$ and perform a binary search on the CDF table to output the "inverse CDF" of y [Pei10]. To the best of our knowledge, no work analyzes the accuracy or efficiency of any of these methods in detail.

Yet another alternative, explored by Galbraith and Dwarakanath [GD12], is the Knuth-Yao algorithm. The algorithm first precomputes a binary tree with leaves labeled by the elements of B. For $x \in B$, if the probability of sampling x has a one in the i-th place of its binary representation, there is a leaf labeled x at height i of the tree. Then it samples by walking down the tree using one uniform bit at each step to decide which of the two children to move to. Galbraith and Dwarakanath present a very detailed analysis of the accuracy of the sampler and of the number of random bits it uses. They also propose ways to reduce the memory requirements. However, they do not assess the speed of the sampler.

Ducas and Nguyen propose an enhancement for rejection sampling. They observe that the sampler can compute at a low precision by default and only use high precision computation when a certain threshold is reached [DN12]. To the best of our knowledge, no work evaluates the effect of this enhancement in detail.

Organization. In Sect. 2 we explain the Ziggurat algorithm and we describe in detail its discrete variant. In Sect. 3 we analyze the quality of the distribution. Finally, in Sect. 4 we report on experimental results.

2   The Discrete Ziggurat Algorithm

The Ziggurat algorithm belongs to the class of rejection sampling algorithms and was introduced by Marsaglia and Tsang for sampling from a continuous Gaussian distribution [MT00]. Here we adapt it for the discrete case. After explaining the setting, we give a short overview over Ziggurat in the continuous case and shortly explain how to control the trade-off. Afterwards, we show how we adapted it to the discrete case and explain how to perform the necessary precomputing. Subsequently, we discuss the implementation-details and finish the section with further improvements.

2.1   Setting

We are concerned with sampling from a discrete Gaussian distribution centered at zero with bounded support $B := [-t\sigma, t\sigma] \cap \mathbb{Z}$ for some parameter $t > 0$. This bounded support is sufficient for the application in lattice-based cryptography as long as t is chosen large enough. Moreover, we show in Sect. 3.2 how to select parameters such that the sampled distribution is within a certain statistical distance to a (truly) discrete Gaussian distribution. The assumption that the distribution is centered at zero is also fine, as we can add a constant offset to transform samples into a distribution centered around any other integer.

2.2   Intuition

We briefly review the continuous Ziggurat for the above setting to give some intuition. As the target distribution is symmetric, we can proceed as follows. We use the method to sample a value $x \leq t\sigma$ within $\mathbb{R}_0^+$. Afterwards, if $x = 0$ we accept with probability $1/2$. Otherwise, we sample a sign $s \in \{-1, 1\}$ and return the signed value sx.

Now, how do we sample x within $\mathbb{R}_0^+$? During set-up, we enclose the area of the probability density function (PDF) in an area A consisting of m horizontal rectangles with equal area as shown in Fig. 1. How the rectangles are computed is described below. Next, we store the coordinates (x_i, y_i) of the lower right corner of each rectangle R_i, $1 < i < m - 1$. Please note that each rectangle R_i can be split into a left rectangle R_i^l that lies completely within the area of the PDF and a right rectangle R_i^r that is only partially covered by the PDF. For an example, see R_3 in Fig. 1.

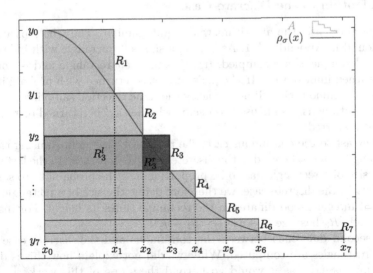

Fig. 1. Ziggurat for $m = 7$ with covering area A and the partition into rectangles.

Now, to actually sample a value $x \leq t\sigma$ within $\mathbb{R}_0^+$ we first sample an integer $1 \leq i \leq m$ uniformly at random, to select a random rectangle. Next, we sample an x-coordinate inside R_i, by sampling a uniformly random x' within $[0, x_i]$. If $x' \leq x_{i-1}$, i.e. if x' is inside R_i^l, we directly accept and return x'. Otherwise, x' lies within R_i^r. In this case, we do rejection sampling. Namely, we sample a value γ within $[y_{i+1}, y_i]$ uniformly at random. Then, if $\gamma + y_{i+1} \leq \rho_\sigma(x')$, i.e. we hit a point in the area below the PDF, we accept and return x'. Otherwise, we reject and restart the whole process by sampling a new i.

In order to understand why this sampling-algorithm works, think of it as an efficient implementation of rejection-sampling in the area A. More precisely, the implementation of the first step (sampling a point in the enclosing area) is improved. Since all the rectangles have equal size, the probabilities of sampling a point in a given rectangle are equal. Therefore, one can sample the rectangle first and a point in the rectangle afterwards.

The expensive part of the algorithm is computing $\rho_\sigma(x')$ if x' does not lie within R_i^l. It becomes even more expensive whenever a value is rejected. For this reason Ziggurat provides a time-memory trade-off, which is controlled by the number of rectangles used, as follows. If we use more rectangles, the ratio between the left and the right rectangle within one rectangle is changed in such a way that the left rectangle becomes comparatively bigger. Hence, we accept an x' without computing $\rho_\sigma(x')$ with higher probability. Moreover, using more rectangles, the area A tighter encloses the area C below the PDF. Thereby, the area $A \setminus C$ that leads to a rejection shrinks and with it the overall probability of a rejection. However, for each additional rectangle the coordinates of one additional point have to be stored, increasing the memory requirements.

2.3 Adaption to the Discrete Case

In the discrete case, the algorithm works quite similar. The whole pseudocode can be found in Appendix A.1. As before, a sign s, a rectangle with index i and a potential sample x' are sampled. If x' lies in a left rectangle and is non-zero, sx' is returned immediately. If x' equals zero, it is returned with probability $1/2$, like in the continuous case. If not, exactly the same rejection sampling procedure as in the continuous case is used to decide whether sx' is returned or the whole process is restarted.

In contrast to the continuous case, the notion of 'size' defined using the area of a rectangle can not be used in the discrete case. We have seen in the last section that the size of a rectangle has to be proportional to the probability to sample a point in it. In the discrete case, we therefore define the size of a rectangle as the number of integer x-coordinates in the rectangle times its height. For instance, the rectangle R_3 has size $(1 + \lfloor x_3 \rfloor) \cdot (y_2 - y_3)$.

The second difference between the continuous and the discrete case is the way the rectangles are computed. While we did not explain how this is done in the continuous case, as it would go beyond the scope of this work, we give a description for the discrete case. We explain how to obtain a partition for the Ziggurat algorithm for a given number of m rectangles where each rectangle has exactly the same 'size' S. Therefore, we set

$$y_m := 0, \qquad x_0 := 0 \qquad \text{and} \qquad x_m := t\sigma,$$

and we iteratively compute a possible partition "from right to left" via

$$y_{m-1} = \frac{S}{1 + \lfloor x_m \rfloor}, \qquad x_{m-1} = \rho_\sigma^{-1}(y_{m-1}),$$

$$\text{for } i = m-2, \ldots, 1: \qquad y_i = \frac{S}{1 + \lfloor x_{i+1} \rfloor} + y_{i+1}, \qquad x_i = \rho_\sigma^{-1}(y_i),$$

$$y_0 = \frac{S}{1 + \lfloor x_1 \rfloor} + y_1.$$

Recall that ρ_σ is a scaled density function with $\rho_\sigma(0) = 1$. Therefore, a valid partition for Ziggurat requires $y_0 \geq 1$, since only then the partition completely covers the area under the curve ρ_σ on the support $B_0^+ := [0, t\sigma] \cap \mathbb{Z}_0^+$. Since the value y_0 depends on the 'size' S of the rectangles, any value of S for which $y_0 \geq 1$ leads to a valid partition. We heuristically determine S as follows. We set $S = \sigma/(m \cdot \sqrt{\pi/2}) \cdot c$ with initial value $c = 1$, compute the corresponding partition, and increase c stepwise as long as $y_0 < 1$. (To improve the quality of the input partition, i.e. minimizing $y_0 - 1$, one can perform a binary search for S in $[\sigma/(m \cdot \sqrt{\pi/2}), t\sigma + 1]$.) In the case that no valid partition is found, we increase x_m by one and restart the whole process. Reaching $x_m = (t + 1)\sigma$, we abort. We note that this method ended with no partition being output in only about 1.3 % of our computations. In these cases, i.e. when no valid partition is found, one can re-run the procedure with one or more of the following changed: number of rectangles m, Gaussian parameter σ (if possible), or upper bound on x_m.

2.4   Implementation

For an implementation, we have to analyze the effect of computing with limited precision. We use a dash over numbers or functions to indicate the use of their corresponding n-bit fixed-point approximation, e.g. $\bar{y}$ and $\bar{\rho}_\sigma$ denote the n-bit approximation of $y \in \mathbb{R}$ and the function ρ_σ, respectively. Since we can exactly calculate $\bar{\rho}_\sigma$, we can find a partition such that the rectangles have exactly the same 'size' and represent it with the vertical bounds $\bar{y}_i$ (which we store with n bits fixed point precision) and the rounded horizontal borders $\lfloor x_i \rfloor$. The last problem is to sample uniformly at random in the infinite sets $[\bar{y}_i, \bar{y}_{i-1}]$. Our solution is to discretize the set: We define $\bar{h}_i := \bar{y}_{i-1} - \bar{y}_i$ to be the height of the i-th rectangle, sample $y' \xleftarrow{\$} \{0, 1, \ldots, 2^\omega - 1\}$ for a parameter $\omega \in \mathbb{Z}_0^+$ and transform the samples to $\bar{y} = \bar{h}_i y' \in [0, 2^\omega \bar{h}_i]$. Instead of transforming $\bar{y}$ into

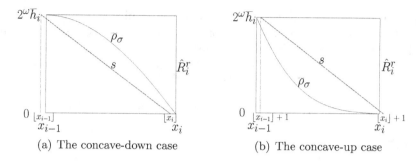

Fig. 2. Optimization to discrete Ziggurat ($\hat{R}_i^r$ is R_i^r vertically shifted and stretched)

the interval $[\overline{y}_i, \overline{y}_{i-1}]$ we replace the condition $\overline{y} \leq \overline{\rho}_\sigma(x)$ for $\overline{y} \in [\overline{y}_i, \overline{y}_{i-1}]$ with $\overline{y} \leq 2^\omega (\overline{\rho}_\sigma(x) - \overline{y}_i)$ for $\overline{y} \in [0, 2^\omega \overline{h}_i]$. We show in Sect. 3 how to choose the parameters t, ω and n in order to bound the statistical distance between the distribution defined by our algorithm and D_σ by a given value.

2.5   Further Improvement

Since the most time-consuming part of the discrete Ziggurat is the computation of $\overline{\rho}_\sigma$, we want to avoid it as often as possible. As mentioned above, it is only necessary if (x, y) is contained in a right rectangle R_i^r. But even in this case, depending on the shape of $\overline{\rho}_\sigma$ inside of R_i^r, we can avoid the evaluation of $\overline{\rho}_\sigma$ in nearly half of the cases and more easily reject or accept x as follows.

We divide R_i^r by connecting its upper left and lower right corner by a straight line s. Since $\overline{\rho}_\sigma$ has inflection point σ, it is concave-down for $x \leq \sigma$, and concave-up otherwise. In the concave-down case ($x_i \leq \sigma$) all points (x, y) in R_i^r below s implicitly fulfill the acceptance condition, thus x is instantly output. In the concave-up case ($\sigma \leq x_{i-1}$) all points above s lead to immediate rejection. In all other cases we have to evaluate $\overline{\rho}_\sigma(x)$ and check the acceptance condition. For the discrete Ziggurat we have to adjust this approach to our way of sampling $\overline{y}_i$ and our use of the values $\lfloor x_i \rfloor$ instead of x_i (for an idea how to accomplish this see Fig. 2).

3   Quality of Our Sampler

In this section, we show how to choose parameters for the algorithm such that it achieves a given quality in the sense of statistical distance to a discrete normal distribution. We begin with a theorem that bounds the statistical distance between the distribution produced by the sampler and a discrete normal distribution. Afterwards, we show as an example how to select parameters such that the statistical distance is smaller than 2^{-100}. The methodology can be used to select parameters for any given statistical distance.

3.1 Statistical Distance Between Sampled and Gaussian Distribution

No practical algorithm outputs samples exactly distributed according to a Gaussian distribution. Therefore, it is important to understand how much the produced output distribution differs from the normal distribution. This difference is measured by the statistical distance. Recall that t determines the tailcut and ω the precision of the sampled y-values. As explained before, we use numbers with n-bit fixed-point precision. Similar to the definition of the support $B_0^+ = [0, t\sigma] \cap \mathbb{Z}_0^+$, we define $B^+ := [0, t\sigma] \cap \mathbb{Z}^+$. The next theorem gives a lower bound on the quality of our sampler depending on the used parameters.

Theorem 1. *The statistical distance between the discrete Gaussian distribution D_σ and the distribution $\overline{D}_\sigma$ output by our algorithm is bounded by*

$$\Delta(D_\sigma, \overline{D}_\sigma) < te^{(1-t^2)/2} + \frac{|B_0^+|}{\overline{\rho}_\sigma(B^+) + \frac{1}{2}}(2^{-\omega+1} + 2^{-n}). \tag{1}$$

Because of the restricted space, we omit the proof of the result here. It can be found in the full version of this paper[2]. The main idea of the proof is to introduce intermediary distributions. The first intermediary distribution differs from a Gaussian distribution by the tailcut. The second intermediary distribution takes the limited precision of the stored numbers and the sampled y-values into consideration. After bounding the statistical distances between the consecutive distributions, we apply the triangle inequality to show the main result.

3.2 Parameter Selection

We now show how to choose t, n and ω such that the statistical distance of our distribution and the discrete Gaussian distribution is below 2^{-100} for $\sigma = 10$. We choose t to be the smallest positive integer such that $t\exp((1 - t^2)/2) < 2^{-101}$, which is $t = 13$. Furthermore, we choose $\omega = n + 1$ and obtain $2^{-\omega+1} + 2^{-n} = 2^{-n+1}$. We can now find an n such that the second addend of inequality (1) is bounded by 2^{-101}. Since this calculation is a little bit complex, we try to get a feeling for the expected result first. Since t was chosen such that the probability of sampling an element in the tail is extremely small, we obtain

$$\overline{\rho}_\sigma(B^+) + \frac{1}{2} \approx \rho_\sigma(B^+) + \frac{1}{2} \approx \rho_\sigma(\mathbb{Z}_0^+) \approx \int_0^\infty \rho_\sigma(x)dx = \sigma\sqrt{\frac{\pi}{2}}$$

and expect

$$2^{-n+1}\frac{|B_0^+|}{\overline{\rho}_\sigma(B^+)} \approx 2^{-n+1}\frac{t\sigma}{\sigma\sqrt{\pi/2}} \approx 2^{-n+1}t \approx 2^{-n+5}.$$

The smallest n satisfying $5 - n \leq -101$ is $n = 106$. An exact calculation shows indeed that $n = 106$ suffices.

---

[2] The full version is available at http://eprint.iacr.org/2013/510.pdf.

4   Experiments and Results

In this section we discuss the performance of our implementation of the discrete Ziggurat algorithm. We first describe the experiments we performed to test the efficiency, then present their results and analyze the gathered data. Furthermore, we compare our sampler to implementations of existing samplers for discrete Gaussians.

4.1   Environment and Setup

The experiments were carried out on a Sun XFire 4400 server with 16 Quad-Core AMD Opteron 8356 CPUs running at 2.3 GHz (we only used one CPU), having in total 64GB of RAM and running a 64 bit Debian 7.1. All implementations use the Number Theory Library (NTL, cf. [Sho]) with precision $n = 106$ bits in consistency to our choice of parameters in Sect. 3.2 to assure a statistical distance for Ziggurat of at most 2^{-100}. Furthermore, we used the tailcut $t = 13$ and the discrete Gaussian parameters $\sigma \in \{10, 32, 1000, 1.6 \cdot 10^5\}$. The value $\sigma = 32$ maintains the worst-to-average-case reduction [Reg05] in several schemes for a certain parameter set, and the rather large value $\sigma = 1.6 \cdot 10^5$ is chosen according to Galbraith and Dwarakanath [GD12]. The other two values $\sigma = 10, 1000$ were chosen arbitrarily inbetween and at the lower end to allow a better comparison.

We queried each algorithm iteratively 1 million times to output a single sample per call. These experiments were applied to the discrete Ziggurat with the

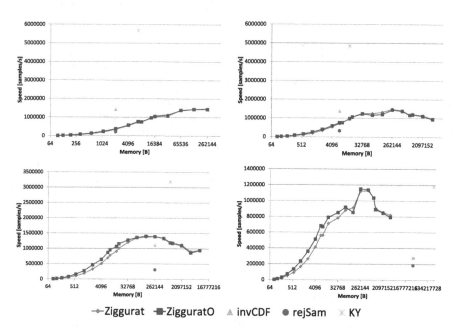

Fig. 3. Results for inverse CDF, rejection sampling, Knuth-Yao, and discrete Ziggurat with and without optimization for parameters $\sigma = 10, 32, 1000, 1.6 \cdot 10^5$, respectively.

optimization using the straight line s (ZigguratO), discrete Ziggurat without optimization (Ziggurat), inverse CDF (invCDF), rejection sampling with pre-computed lookup-table (rejSam), and Knuth-Yao (KY). Furthermore we tested both Ziggurat algorithms with a precomputed lookup-table for the support B_0^+ (ZigguratOP and ZigguratP, respectively).

For each algorithm we measured the running time using the (Linux-internal) function `clock_gettime` with clock `CLOCK_PROCESS_CPUTIME_ID`. In order to have non-distorted results we excluded all pre- and post-computations (e.g. setting up lookup-tables) from the measurements. Regarding the memory, we did not perform per-runtime analyses, but computed the amount of memory by adding up the number of fixed variables in regard to their types in NTL. For our choice of parameters, in Ziggurat(O) the values on the x-axis need 8 bytes and on the y-axis 24 bytes of memory. With m rectangles the total amount of memory is thus $32(m+2)$ bytes (including σ, t, ω, m). For both invCDF and rejSam we need to store a lookup-table of $t\sigma$ values à 16 bytes, resulting in 2080 bytes for $\sigma = 10$. The same amount of memory is used by Ziggurat(O) with $m = 63$ rectangles. The size of Knuth-Yao is approximated by (#intermediates + #leaves)$/2$ bits, where #intermediates $= n \cdot 2^{\lceil \log \log(n \cdot t\sigma) \rceil}$ and #leaves $= n \cdot 2^{\lceil \log \log(t\sigma) \rceil}$ for precision $n = 106$ bits as above.

4.2   Results

Figure 3 shows results for inverse CDF, rejection sampling, Knuth-Yao, and discrete Ziggurat with and without optimizations for different numbers of rectangles. It shows four different graphs for different values of σ. For small values of σ, the inverse CDF method outperforms both discrete Ziggurat and rejection sampling for the same fixed amount of memory. For example, our implementation invCDF samples about 1.37 million samples per second for $\sigma = 32$. On the other hand, rejection sampling is quite slow due to a large rejection area. Even with a precomputed lookup-table, rejSam only achieves about 327,000 samples per second, which is a factor 4.2 slower than invCDF. The naïve approach without lookup-table solely achieves 2,500 samples per second, being a factor 558 slower than invCDF. For the same amount of memory, ZigguratO achieves an overall number of about 753,000 samples per second, while Ziggurat outputs 718,000 samples per second. Compared to the other two methods, Ziggurat is 1.91 times slower than invCDF and a factor 2.19 faster than rejSam. Our implementation of Knuth-Yao outperforms all the other methods by at least a factor of 3.53, outputting 4.85 million samples per second. This comes at the cost of nearly doubled memory usage.

In the extreme case $\sigma = 1.6 \cdot 10^5$, the fastest instantiation of Ziggurat outputs 1.13 million samples per second with a memory usage of 524 KB. Inverse CDF creates 281,000 samples per second while using 33.55 MB, thus being about a factor 4 slower than Ziggurat. For rejSam the situation is even worse: Using the same amount of memory as invCDF, it only outputs 185,000 samples per second – a factor 6.1 slower than Ziggurat. The Knuth-Yao algorithm still performs better than Ziggurat, but only by 4.26 %. On the other hand, KY needs more than 424 times the memory storage of Ziggurat. Concluding we state that for larger values of σ the Ziggurat algorithm beats both inverse CDF and rejection sampling. Compared to Knuth-Yao, Ziggurat achieves almost the same speed but reduces the memory consumption by a factor of more than 400.

Figure 3 shows that we can beat invCDF in terms of speed and compete with Knuth-Yao. The reason for this is the simplicity of the algorithm. If many rectangles are stored, the rejection-probability gets very small. Likewise, the probability to sample an x in a right rectangle R_i^r gets very small. Therefore, the algorithm only samples a rectangle and afterwards samples a value within this rectangle, which can be done very fast.

As one can furthermore see in Fig. 3, the discrete Ziggurat algorithm shows a large flexibility in regard to the speed-memory trade-off. For a small amount of memory (i.e. number of rectangles) it is quite slow, e.g. for $\sigma = 32$ and 8 rectangles it obtains about 57,000 samples per second. For increasing memory allocation the speed of Ziggurat(O) increases. This statement holds for all values of σ we tested. As can be seen by the graphs, the speed of Ziggurat decreases for increasing number of rectangles. This was first surprising to us. Further analysis showed that this is due to the fact that with increasing number of rectangles (i.e. amount of allocated memory) the processor cannot keep the partition table in the fast caches, but has to obtain requested memory addresses from slower caches on demand. In addition, the large number of rectangles requires more bits to be sampled in a single step of the algorithm.

The trade-off provided by the Ziggurat-algorithms is indeed a property the other approaches do not share. InvCDF assigns every possible value to an interval on the y-axis. Consequently, one has to store at least the borders if the intervals. Decreasing the precision of the borders will decrease the memory consumption, but as well decrease the quality of the sampler. Increasing the precision

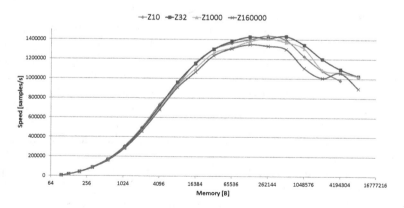

Fig. 4. Discrete Ziggurat for different parameters σ (ZX denotes Ziggurat for $\sigma = X$).

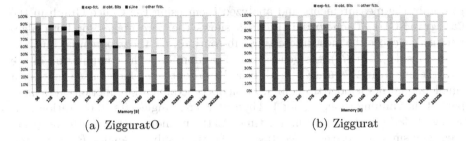

(a) ZigguratO   (b) Ziggurat

Fig. 5. Time-split of discrete Ziggurat with and without optimization

or storing intermediate values, on the other hand, will not decrease the running time. The same happens to rejection sampling if the precision of the precomputed values is changed. Knuth-Yao stores for every element in the support the probability to sample this element. Decreasing the precision of the stored probabilities would (like for invCDF) decrease the quality of the sampler. While there might be efficient ways to store those values, there is a minimal amount of space required to store this information. Knuth-Yao as well as invCDF and rejection sampling therefore only provide a trade-off between quality and speed/ memory consumption.

In Fig. 4 we draw the time-memory trade-off for the Ziggurat algorithm for different values of σ. One can see that the performance of the Ziggurat algorithm decreases for larger σ. What is interesting in the graph is that the Ziggurat algorithm for $\sigma = 10$ is slower for a large amount of rectangles than for $\sigma = 32$. This is puzzling as we cannot directly explain the described behaviour. We want to state that during our experiments we saw quite large fluctuations for several runs of the algorithm. Maybe this could explain the better performance for $\sigma = 32$ in comparison to $\sigma = 10$.

We also compared ZigguratO and Ziggurat in regard to speed.[3] The improvement rate increases up to 30 % for a total memory of 320 bytes, then decreases to around 6 % for 2080 bytes, until finally for 130KB and bigger there is no improvement. Overall, the described behaviour is not surprising since for increased memory the number of rectangles gets larger, so that the rejection area is very small. This leads to nearly no evaluations in the right sub-rectangles R_i^r and therefore to no computation of the straight line s (or even $\overline{\rho}_\sigma$).

Additionally, we compared ZigguratO to ZigguratOP, which operates with at least 2176 bytes of memory. ZigguratOP is slower until about 2.5 KB of memory, but then it beats ZigguratO with a speedup of up to 40 %, until for memory larger than 262 KB there seems to be no speedup at all. This behaviour is reasonable since the lookup-table requires more storage, but simultaneously affects the speed due to replacing $\overline{\rho}_\sigma$ by table-lookups.

At last, we give insights on the time-split for our implementations Ziggurat and ZigguratO. We used the tool suite `Valgrind` with the tool `Callgrind`

---

[3] For additional Figures see Appendix A.2.

to obtain the measurements and analyzed them using the Callee Graph in the Callgrind-GUI KCachegrind. Figure 5 shows the percentages for both algorithms. We chose the most interesting sub-routines, i.e. the exponential function (called inside $\bar{\rho}_\sigma$ in R_i^r), the generation of random bits, the computation of the straight line s (in ZigguratO), and 'other' sub-routines. One can see that for a small amount of memory the computation of the exponential function takes most part of the running time, e.g. for 104 bytes (two rectangles) its computation consumes 80–90 % of the total running time. As the memory increases, the rejection area gets smaller, i.e. the percentage of the right sub-rectangles R_i^r compared to their super-rectangles R_i. Thus, the number of integers sampled inside the R_i^r's decreases. Additionally, the exponential function has to be called less often. Nevertheless, the graphs show that the use of the straight line s decreases the use of the exponential function (or call to $\bar{\rho}_\sigma$) in ZigguratO in comparison to Ziggurat considerably, while at the same time the computational complexity of s is not high (at most 6.77 %).

A   Appendix

In this Appendix we present the pseudocode for the discrete Ziggurat algorithm and give additional Figures in regard to our experimental results.

A.1   Pseudocode for Discrete Ziggurat

In Fig. 6 we present the pseudocode for our implementation of the discrete Ziggurat algorithm of Sect. 2. In particular, we give the pseudocode for ZigguratO. From this, one obtains pseudocode for Ziggurat by removing lines 11–17, 19 and 20.

A.2   Additional Figures Regarding Results

In Fig. 7 we present the rate of improvement of Ziggurat with optimization (ZigguratO) over Ziggurat without the straight line approach. For a small amount of memory, the improvement using the straight line approach is quite good (around 20–30 % for memory usage between 128 and 576 bytes), while for larger memory, i.e. higher number of rectangles, the improvement vanishes due to nearly no rejection area.

Figure 8 shows the speed of ZigguratO and its corresponding variant ZigguratOP with precomputed lookup-table. ZigguratOP can perform only with memory larger or equal to 2176 bytes due to the size of the lookup-table. Thus, given a small amount of memory, it is not possible to apply ZigguratOP. But for available memory larger than 2.5 KB ZigguratOP outperforms ZigguratO up to 40 %.

Algorithm 1: ZigguratO

Input: m, σ, $\lfloor x_1 \rfloor, \ldots, \lfloor x_m \rfloor$, $\overline{y}_0, \overline{y}_1, \ldots, \overline{y}_m$, ω
Output: number distributed according to a discrete Gaussian distribution

1 **while** *true* **do**
2      $i \xleftarrow{\$} \{1, \ldots, m\}$, $s \xleftarrow{\$} \{-1, 1\}$, $x \xleftarrow{\$} \{0, \ldots, \lfloor x_i \rfloor\}$;
     // choose rectangle, sign and value
3   **if** $0 < x \le \lfloor x_{i-1} \rfloor$ **then return** sx;
4   **else**
5   **if** $x = 0$ **then**
6              $b \xleftarrow{\$} \{0, 1\}$;
7   **if** $b = 0$ **then return** sx;
8   **else continue**;
9   **else**
             // in rejection area R_i^r now
10              $y' \xleftarrow{\$} \{0, \ldots, 2^\omega - 1\}$, $\overline{y} = y' \cdot (\overline{y}_{i-1} - \overline{y}_i)$;
11   **if** $\lfloor x_i \rfloor + 1 \le \sigma$ **then**
                 // in concave-down case
12   **if**
                 $\overline{y} \le 2^\omega \cdot sLine(\lfloor x_{i-1} \rfloor, \lfloor x_i \rfloor, \overline{y}_{i-1}, \overline{y}_i; x) \vee \overline{y} \le 2^\omega \cdot (\overline{\rho}_\sigma(x) - \overline{y}_i)$
                 then return sx;
13   **else continue**;
14   **else if** $\sigma \le \lfloor x_{i-1} \rfloor$ **then**
                 // in concave-up case
15   **if**
                 $\overline{y} \ge 2^\omega \cdot sLine(\lfloor x_{i-1} \rfloor, \lfloor x_i \rfloor, \overline{y}_{i-1}, \overline{y}_i; x-1) \vee \overline{y} > 2^\omega \cdot (\overline{\rho}_\sigma(x) - \overline{y}_i)$
                 then continue;
16   **else return** sx;
17   **else**
18   **if** $\overline{y} \le 2^\omega \cdot (\overline{\rho}_\sigma(x) - \overline{y}_i)$ **then return** sx;
19   **else continue**;
20   **end**
21   **end**
22   **end**
23 **end**

Algorithm 2: sLine($\lfloor x_{i-1} \rfloor, \lfloor x_i \rfloor, \overline{y}_{i-1}, \overline{y}_i; x$)

1 **if** $\lfloor x_i \rfloor = \lfloor x_{i-1} \rfloor$ **then return** -1;
2 Set $\hat{y}_i = \overline{y}_i$ and $\hat{y}_{i-1} = \begin{cases} \overline{y}_{i-1} & i > 1 \\ 1 & i = 1 \end{cases}$
3 **return** $\dfrac{\hat{y}_i - \hat{y}_{i-1}}{\lfloor x_i \rfloor - \lfloor x_{i-1} \rfloor} \cdot (x - \lfloor x_i \rfloor)$

Fig. 6. The discrete Ziggurat algorithm with optimization (ZigguratO)

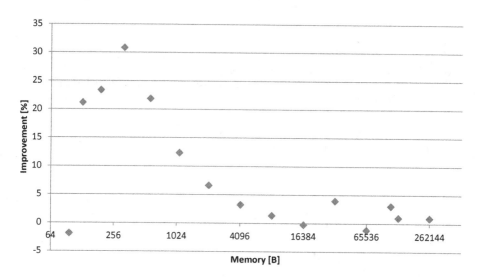

Fig. 7. Improvement rate of ZigguratO over Ziggurat

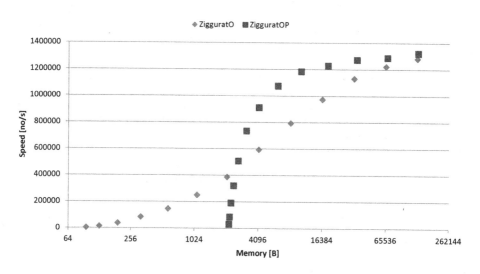

Fig. 8. Comparison of ZigguratO and ZigguratOP

References

[AGHS12] Agrawal, S., Gentry, C., Halevi, S., Sahai, A:. Discrete Gaussian left-over hash lemma over infinite domains. Cryptology ePrint Archive, Report 2012/714 (2012). http://eprint.iacr.org/

[BGV12] Brakerski, Z., Gentry, C., Vaikuntanathan, V.: (Leveled) fully homomorphic encryption without bootstrapping. In: Proceedings of the 3rd Innovations in Theoretical Computer Science Conference, ITCS '12, pp. 309–325. ACM, New York (2012)

[DN12]   Ducas, L., Nguyen, P.Q.: Faster Gaussian lattice sampling using lazy floating-point arithmetic. In: Wang, X., Sako, K. (eds.) ASIACRYPT 2012. LNCS, vol. 7658, pp. 415–432. Springer, Heidelberg (2012)

[GD12]   Galbraith, S.D., Dwarakanath, N.C.: Efficient sampling from discrete Gaussians for lattice-based cryptography on a constrained device. Preprint (2012)

[GGH12] Garg, S., Gentry, C., Halevi, S.: Candidate multilinear maps from ideal lattices. Cryptology ePrint Archive, Report 2012/610 (2012). http://eprint.iacr.org/

[GPV08] Gentry, C., Peikert, C., Vaikuntanathan, C.: Trapdoors for hard lattices and new cryptographic constructions. In: Ladner, R.E., Dwork, C. (ed.) 40th ACM STOC Annual ACM Symposium on Theory of Computing, Victoria, British Columbia, Canada, 17–20 May 2008, pp. 197–206. ACM Press (2008)

[LP11]   Lindner, R., Peikert, Ch.: Better key sizes (and attacks) for LWE-based encryption. In: Kiayias, A. (ed.) CT-RSA 2011. LNCS, vol. 6558, pp. 319–339. Springer, Heidelberg (2011)

[Lyu12] Lyubashevsky, V.: Lattice signatures without trapdoors. In: Pointcheval, D., Johansson, T. (eds.) EUROCRYPT 2012. LNCS, vol. 7237, pp. 738–755. Springer, Heidelberg (2012)

[MT00]   Marsaglia, G., Tsang, W.W.: The Ziggurat method for generating random variables. J. Stat. Softw. 5(8), 1–7, 10 (2000)

[Pei10] Peikert, Ch.: An efficient and parallel Gaussian sampler for lattices. In: Rabin, T. (ed.) CRYPTO 2010. LNCS, vol. 6223, pp. 80–97. Springer, Heidelberg (2010)

[Reg05] Regev, O.: On lattices, learning with errors, random linear codes, and cryptography. In: Proceedings of the Thirty-Seventh Annual ACM Symposium on Theory of Computing, STOC '05, pp. 84–93. ACM, New York (2005)

[Sho]   Shoup, V.: Number Theory Library (NTL) for C++. http://www.shoup.net/ntl/

[TLLV07] Thomas, D.B., Luk, W., Leong, P.H.W.: Gaussian random number generators. ACM Comput. Surv. 39(4), 11:1–11:38 (2007)

[WHCB13] Weiden, P., Hülsing, A., Cabarcas, D., Buchmann, J.: Instantiating treeless signature schemes. Cryptology ePrint Archive, Report 2013/065 (2013). http://eprint.iacr.org/

Elliptic Curves, Pairings and RSA

A High-Speed Elliptic Curve Cryptographic Processor for Generic Curves over GF(p)

Yuan Ma[1,2]($\boxtimes$), Zongbin Liu[1], Wuqiong Pan[1,2], and Jiwu Jing[1]

[1] State Key Laboratory of Information Security,
Institute of Information Engineering, CAS, Beijing, China
[2] University of Chinese Academy of Sciences, Beijing, China
{yma,zbliu,wqpan,jing}@lois.cn

Abstract. Elliptic curve cryptography (ECC) is preferred for high-speed applications due to the lower computational complexity compared with other public-key cryptographic schemes. As the basic arithmetic, the modular multiplication is the most time-consuming operation in public-key cryptosystems. The existing high-radix Montgomery multipliers performed a single Montgomery multiplication either in approximately $2n$ clock cycles, or approximately n cycles but with a very low frequency, where n is the number of words. In this paper, we first design a novel Montgomery multiplier by combining a quotient pipelining Montgomery multiplication algorithm with a parallel array design. The parallel design with one-way carry propagation can determine the quotients in one clock cycle, thus one Montgomery multiplication can be completed in approximately n clock cycles. Meanwhile, by the quotient pipelining technique applied in digital signal processing (DSP) blocks, our multiplier works in a high frequency. We also implement an ECC processor for generic curves over GF(p) using the novel multiplier on FPGAs. To the best of our knowledge, our processor is the fastest among the existing ECC implementations over GF(p).

Keywords: FPGA · Montgomery multiplier · DSP · High-speed · ECC

1 Introduction

Elliptic curve cryptography has captured more and more attention since the introduction by Koblitz [8] and Miller [12] in 1985. Compared with RSA or discrete logarithm schemes over finite fields, ECC uses a much shorter key to achieve an equivalent level of security. Therefore, ECC processors are preferred for high-speed applications owing to the lower computational complexity and other nice properties such as less storage and power consumption. Hardware accelerators

This work is supported by National Natural Science Foundation of China grant 70890084/G021102 and 61003274, Strategy Pilot Project of Chinese Academy of Sciences sub-project XDA06010702, and National High Technology Research and Development Program of China (863 Program, No. 2013AA01A214 and 2012AA013104).

T. Lange, K. Lauter, and P. Lisoněk (Eds.): SAC 2013, LNCS 8282, pp. 421–437, 2014.
DOI: 10.1007/978-3-662-43414-7_21, © Springer-Verlag Berlin Heidelberg 2014

are the most appropriate solution for the high-performance implementations with acceptable resource and power consumption. Among them, field-programmable gate arrays (FPGAs) are well-suited for this application due to their reconfigurability and versatility.

Point multiplication dominates the overall performance of the elliptic curve cryptographic processors. Efficient implementations of point multiplication can be separated into three distinct layers [6]: the finite field arithmetic, the elliptic curve point addition and doubling and the scalar multiplication. The fundamental finite field arithmetic is the basis of all the others. Finite field arithmetic over $GF(p)$ consists of modular multiplications, modular additions/subtractions and modular inversions. By choosing an alternative representation, called the projective representation, for the coordinates of the points, the time-consuming finite field inversions can be eliminated almost completely. This leaves the modular multiplication to be the most critical operation in ECC implementations over $GF(p)$. One of the widely used algorithms for efficient modular multiplications is the Montgomery algorithm which was proposed by Peter L. Montgomery [16] in 1985.

Hardware implementations of the Montgomery algorithm have been studied for several decades. From the perspective of the radix, the Montgomery multiplication implementations can be divided into two categories: radix-2 based [7,21] and high-radix based [1,2,9,11,17,19,20,22,23]. Compared with the former one, the latter, which can significantly reduce the required clock cycles, are preferred for high-speed applications.

For high-radix Montgomery multiplication, the determination of quotients is critical for speeding up the modular multiplication. For simplifying the quotient calculation, Walter et al. [3,23] presented a method that shifted up of modulus and multiplicand, and proposed a systolic array architecture. Following the similar ideas, Orup presented an alternative to systolic architecture [18], to perform high-radix modular multiplication. He introduced a rewritten high-radix Montgomery algorithm with quotient pipelining and gave an example of a non-systolic (or parallel) architecture, but the design is characterized by low frequency due to global broadcast signals. In order to improve the frequency, DSP blocks widely dedicated in modern FPGAs have been employed for high-speed modular multiplications since Suzuki's work [19] was presented. However, as a summary, the existing high-radix Montgomery multipliers perform a single Montgomery multiplication for n-word multiplicand either in approximately $2n$ clock cycles, or approximately n cycles but with a low frequency.

To design a high-speed ECC processor, our primary goal is to propose a new Montgomery multiplication architecture which is able to simultaneously process one Montgomery multiplication within approximately n clock cycles and improve the working frequency to a high level.

Key Insights and Techniques. One key insight is that the parallel array architecture with one-way carry propagation can efficiently weaken the data dependency for calculating quotients, yielding that the quotients can be determined in a *single* clock cycle. Another key insight is that a high working frequency can be achieved by employing quotient pipelining inside DSP blocks. Based on these insights, our Montgomery multiplication design is centered on the novel techniques: combining the parallel array design and the quotient pipelining inside DSP blocks.

We also implement an ECC processor for generic curves over $GF(p)$ using the novel multiplier on FPGAs. Due to the pipeline characteristic of the multiplier, we reschedule the operations in elliptic curve arithmetic by overlapping successive Montgomery multiplications to further reduce the number of operation cycles. Additionally, side-channel analysis (SCA) resistance is considered in our design. Experimental results indicate that our ECC processor can perform a 256-bit point multiplication in 0.38 ms at 291 MHz on Xilinx Virtex-5 FPGA.

Our Contributions. In summary, the main contributions of this work are as follows.

- We develop a novel architecture for Montgomery multiplication. As far as we know, it is the first Montgomery multiplier that combining the parallel array design and the quotient pipelining using DSP blocks.
- We design and implement our ECC processor on modern FPGAs using the novel Montgomery multiplier. To the best of our knowledge, our ECC processor is the fastest among the existing hardware implementations over $GF(p)$.

Structure. The rest of this paper is organized as follows. Section 2 presents the related work for high-speed ECC implementations and high-radix Montgomery multiplications. Section 3 describes a processing method for pipelined implementation, and a high-speed architecture is proposed in Sect. 4. Section 5 gives implementation results and detailed comparisons with other designs. Section 6 concludes the paper.

2   Related Work

2.1   High-Speed ECC Implementations over $GF(p)$

Among the high-speed ECC hardware implementations over $GF(p)$, the architectures in [5] and [4] are the fastest two. For a 256-bit point multiplication they reached latency of 0.49 ms and 0.68 ms in modern FPGAs Virtex-4 and Stratix II, respectively. The architectures in [5] are designed for NIST primes using fast reduction. By forcing the DSP blocks to run at their maximum frequency (487 MHz), the architectures reach a very low latency for one point multiplication. Nevertheless, due to the characteristics of dual clock and the complex control inside DSP blocks, the architecture can be only implemented in FPGA platforms. Furthermore, due to the restriction on primes, the application scenario of [5] is limited in NIST prime fields. For generic curves over $GF(p)$, [4] combines residue number systems (RNS) and Montgomery reduction for ECC implementation. The design achieves 6-stage parallelism and high frequency with a large number of DSP blocks, resulting in the fastest ECC implementation for generic curves. In addition, the design in [4] is resistant to SCA.

As far as we know, the fastest ECC implementation based on Montgomery multiplication was presented in [11], which was much slower than the above two designs. The main reason is that the frequency is driven down to a low level although the number of cycles for a single multiplication is approximately n. In an earlier FPGA device Virtex-2 Pro, the latency for a 256-bit point multiplication is 2.27 ms without the SCA resistance, and degrades to 2.35 ms to resist SCA.

2.2 High-Radix Montgomery Multiplication

Up to now, for speeding up high-radix Montgomery multiplications, a wealth of methods have been proposed either to reduce the number of processing cycles or to shorten the critical path in the implementations.

The systolic array architecture seems to be the best solution for modular multiplications with very long integers. Eldridge and Walter performed a shift up of the multiplicand to speed up modular multiplication [3], and Walter designed a systolic array architecture with a throughput of one modular multiplication every clock cycle and a latency of $2n + 2$ cycles for n-word multiplicands [23]. Suzuki introduced a Montgomery multiplication architecture based on DSP48, which is a dedicated DSP unit in modern FPGAs [19]. In order to achieve scalability and high performance, complex control signals and dual clocks were involved in the design. However, the average number of processing cycles per multiplication are approximately $2n$ at least. In fact, this is a common barrier in the high-radix Montgomery algorithm implementations: the quotient is hard to generate in a single clock cycle. This barrier also exists in other systolic high-radix designs [9,22].

On the contrary, some non-systolic array architectures were proposed for speeding up the process of quotient determination, but the clock frequency is a concern. Orup introduced a rewritten high-radix Montgomery algorithm with quotient pipelining and gave an example of a non-systolic architecture [18]. Another high-speed parallel design was proposed by Mentens [11], where the multiplication result was written in a special carry-save form to shorten the long computational path. The approach was able to process a single n-word Montgomery multiplication in approximately n clock cycles. But the maximum frequency was reduced to a very low level, because too many arithmetic operations have to be completed within one clock cycle. Similar drawbacks in frequency can also be found in [2,17].

3   Processing Method

In this section, we propose a processing method for pipelined implementation by employing DSP blocks.

3.1   Pipelined Montgomery Algorithm

Montgomery multiplication [16] is a method for performing modular multiplication without the need to perform division by the modulus. A high-radix version of Montgomery's algorithm with quotient pipelining [18] is given as Algorithm 1. The algorithm provides a way to apply pipelining techniques in Montgomery modular multiplication to shorten the critical path.

Algorithm 1. Modular Multiplication with Quotient Pipelining [18]

Input:

A modulus $M > 2$ with $\gcd(M, 2) = 1$ and positive integers k, n such that $4\tilde{M} < 2^{kn} = R$, where $\tilde{M}$ is given by $\tilde{M} = (\bar{M} \bmod 2^{k(d+1)})M$ and integer $d \geq 0$ is a delay parameter.

Integer R^{-1}, where $2^{kn}R^{-1} \bmod M = 1$

Integer $\bar{M}, M'$, where $(-M\bar{M}) \bmod 2^{k(d+1)} = 1$, $M' = (\tilde{M} + 1) \operatorname{div} 2^{k(d+1)}$

Integer multiplicand A, where $0 \leq A \leq 2\tilde{M}$

Integer multiplier $B = \sum_{i=0}^{n+d}(2^k)^i b_i$, where digit $b_i \in \{0, 1, \ldots, 2^k - 1\}$ for $0 \leq i < n$, $b_i = 0$ for $i \geq n$ and $0 \leq B \leq 2\tilde{M}$.

Output:

Integer S_{n+d+2} where $S_{n+d+2} \equiv ABR^{-1} \pmod{M}$ and $0 \leq S_{n+d+2} < 2\tilde{M}$

1: $S_0 = 0; q_{-d} = 0; q_{-d+1} = 0; \ldots; q_{-1} = 0;$

2: **for** $i = 0$ to $n + d - 1$ **do**

3:   $q_i = S_i \bmod 2^k;$

4:   $S_{i+1} = S_i \operatorname{div} 2^k + q_{i-d}M' + b_i A;$

5: **end for**

6: $S_{n+d+2} = 2^{kd}S_{n+d+1} + \sum_{j=0}^{d+1} q_{n+j+1}2^{kj}$

The calculation of the right q_i is crucial for Montgomery multiplication, and it is the most time-consuming operation for hardware implementations. In order to improve the maximum frequency, a straightforward method is to divide the computational path into α stages for pipelining. The processing clock cycles, however, increase by a factor of α, since q_i is generated every α clock cycles. That is to say, the pipeline does not work due to data dependency. The main idea of Algorithm 1 is using the preset values $q_{-d} = 0, q_{-d+1} = 0, \ldots, q_{-1} = 0$ to replace q_1 to start the pipeline in the first d clock cycles. Then, in the $(d+1)^{th}$ cycle, the right value q_1 is generated and fed into the calculation of the next round. After that, one q_i is generated per clock cycle in pipelining mode. Compared to the traditional Montgomery algorithm, the cost of Algorithm 1 is a few extra iteration cycles, additional pre-processing and a wider range of the final result.

3.2   DSP Blocks in FPGAs

Dedicated multiplier units in older FPGAs have been adopted in the high-radix Montgomery multiplication implementations for years. In modern FPGAs, such as Xilinx Virtex-4 and later FPGAs, instead of traditional multiplier units, arithmetic hardcore accelerators - DSP blocks have been embedded. DSP blocks can

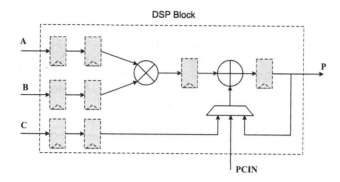

Fig. 1. Generic structure of DSP blocks in modern FPGAs

be programmed to perform multiplication, addition, and subtraction of integers in a more flexible and advanced fashion.

Figure 1 shows the generic DSP block structure in modern FPGAs. By using different data paths, DSP blocks can operate on external inputs A, B, C as well as on feedback values from P or results $PCIN$ from a neighboring DSP block. Notice that all the registers, labeled in gray in Figure 1, can be added or bypassed to control the pipeline stages, which is helpful to implement the pipelined Montgomery algorithm. Here, for the sake of the brevity and portability of the design, we do not engage dual clock and complex control signals like [5,19] which force DSP blocks to work in the maximum frequency.

3.3   Processing Method for Pipelined Implementation

According to the features of DSP resources, the processing method for pipelined implementation is presented in Algorithm 2. From Algorithm 1, we observe that M' is a pre-calculated integer, and the bit length m of $M' = \sum_{i=0}^{m-1}(2^k)^i m_i'$ equals that of modulus M, and the last statement in Algorithm 1 is just a left shift of S_{n+d+1} where the d last quotient digits are shifted in from the right. Here, the radix is set to 2^{16} and the delay parameter $d = 3$, yielding that $n \leq m + d + 2 = m + 5$. The remaining inputs appearing in Algorithm 1 are omitted.

Now we explain the consistency between Algorithms 1 and 2. There are three phases in Algorithm 2: *Phase 0* for initialization, *Phase 1* for iteration and *Phase 2* for the final addition. The initialization should be executed before each multiplication begins. In *Phase 1*, a four-stage pipeline is introduced in order to utilize the DSP blocks, so the total of the surrounding loops becomes $n + 6$ from $n + 3$. The inner loop from 0 to $n - 1$ represents the operations of n Processing Elements (PEs). In the pipeline, referring to Algorithm 1, we can see that *Stage 1* to *Stage 3* are used to calculate $w_i = q_{i_d}M' + b_iA$, and *Stage 4* is used to calculate $(S_i \bmod 2^k + w_i)$. Here, $(S_i \bmod 2^k)$ is divided into two parts: $c_{(i+3,j)}$ inside the PE itself and $s_{(i+3,j+1)}$ from the neighboring higher PE. The delay

---

Algorithm 2. Processing Method for Pipelined Implementation

Input:

    radix $2^k = 2^{16}$, delay parameter $d = 3$

    $M' = \sum_{i=0}^{m-1}(2^k)^i m'_i$, $A = \sum_{i=0}^{n-1}(2^k)^i a_i$, $B = \sum_{i=0}^{n+d}(2^k)^i b_i$

Output:

    Integer S_{n+5} where $S_{n+5} \equiv ABR^{-1} \pmod{M}$ and $0 \le S_{n+5} < 2\tilde{M}$

    /* *Phase 0*: Initialization */

1: **for** $j = 0$ to $n - 1$ **do**

2:    $u_{(0,j)} = 32'b0, v_{(0,j)} = 32'b0$;

3:    $w_{(0,j)} = 33'b0$;

4:    $s_{(0,j)} = 16'b0, c_{(0,j)} = 17'b0$;

5: **end for**

    /* *Phase 1* */

6: **for** $i = 0$ to $n + 6$ **do**

7:    $q_{i-3} = s_{(i,0)}$;

8:    **for** $j = 0$ to $n - 1$ **do**

9:        ***Stage 1:*** $u_{(i+1,j)} = q_{i-3}m'_j$;

10:      ***Stage 2:*** $v_{(i+1,j)} = a_j b_i$;

11:      ***Stage 3:*** $w_{(i+1,j)} = u_{(i,j)} + v_{(i,j)}$;

12:      ***Stage 4:*** $\{c_{(i+1,j)}, s_{(i+1,j)}\} = w_{(i,j)} + c_{(i,j)} + s_{(i,j+1)}$;

13:    **end for**

14: **end for**

    /* *Phase 2* */

15: $S_{n+4} = \sum_{j=0}^{n-4}(2^{16})^j \{c_{(n+7,j)}, s_{(n+7,j)}\}$;

16: $S_{n+5} = \{S_{n+4}, q_{n+3}, q_{n+2}, q_{n+1}\}$;

---

is caused by the pipeline. In *Stage 4*, S_i is represented by $s_{(i+3,j)}$ and $c_{(i+3,j)}$ in a redundant form, where $s_{(i+3,j)}$ represents the lower k bits and $c_{(i+3,j)}$ the $k + 1$ carry bits. Note that the carry bits from lower PEs are not transferred to higher PEs, because this interconnection would increase the data dependency for calculating q_i implying that q_i cannot be generated per clock cycle. Therefore, except for q_{i-3}, the transfer of $s_{(i,j+1)}$ in *Stage 4* is the only interconnection among the PEs, ensuring that q_{i-3} can be generated per cycle. The carry bits from lower PEs to higher PEs which are saved in $c_{(i,j)}$ are processed in *Phase 2*. In brief, the goal of *Phase 1* is to generate the right quotient per clock cycle for running the iteration regardless of the representation of S_i, while by simple additions *Phase 2* transforms the redundant representation to non-redundant representation of the final value S_{n+4}. The detailed hardware architecture is presented in the next section.

4 Proposed Architecture

4.1 Montgomery Multiplier

Processing Element. The Processing Elements, each of which processes k-bit block data, form the modular multiplication array. As the input $A \le 2\tilde{M}$, n PEs are needed to compose the array. Figure 2 provides the structure of the jth PE.

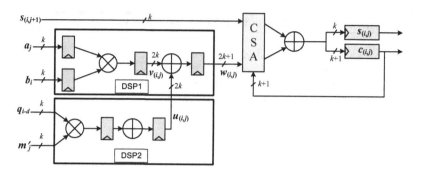

Fig. 2. The structure of the jth PE

In the first three pipeline stages, the arithmetic operations $q_{i-d}M' + b_i A$, are located in the two DSP blocks named DSP1 and DSP2. In order to achieve high frequency, two stage registers are inserted in DSP2 which calculates the multiplication of q_{i-d} and m'_j. Accordingly, another stage of registers are added in DSP1 in order to wait for the multiplication result $u_{(i,j)}$ from DSP2. The addition of $u_{(i,j)}$ and $v_{(i,j)}$ is performed by DSP1 as shown in Fig. 2. In the fourth stage, the three-number addition $w_{(i,j)} + c_{(i,j)} + s_{(i,j+1)}$ is performed by using the carry-save adder (CSA). In FPGAs, CSA can be implemented by one-stage look-up tables (LUTs) and one carry propagate adder (CPA). Because the computational path between the DSP registers is shorter than the CSA, the critical path only includes three-number addition, i.e. CSA. Therefore, in this way, the PE can work in a high frequency due to the very short critical path.

Parallel PE Array. n PEs named PE_0 to PE_{n-1} have been connected to form a parallel array which performs *Phase 1* in Algorithm 2, as shown in Fig. 3. The quotient is generated from PE_0 and fed to the following PEs. Especially, in PE_m to PE_{n-1}, DSP2 and q_{i-d} are no more required since m'_j equals to zero for these PEs. The PE outputs $c_{(i,j)}$ are omitted in Fig. 3, as they only need to be outputted when the iteration in *Phase 1* finishes. Unlike the high-radix systolic array [9] and the design in [19], the PE array works in parallel for the iteration, resulting in the consumed clock cycles for transferring the values from lower PEs to higer PEs are saved.

Now we analyze the performance of the PE array. According to Algorithm 2, the number of iteration rounds of *Phase 1* is $n + 7$. Together with the one clock cycle for initialization, the processing cycles of the PE array are $n + 8$. Regarding the consumed hardware resources, $n + m$ DSP blocks are required for forming the PE array.

Although the frequency may decrease due to the global signals and large bus width, fortunately we find that these factors do not have a serious impact on the hardware performance, owing to the small bit size (256 or smaller) of the operands of ECC. The impact has been verified in our experiment as shown in Sect. 5.1.

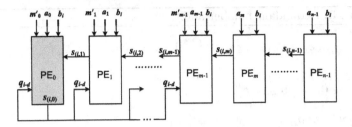

Fig. 3. The structure of the parallel PE array

The outputs of PEs are the redundant representation of the final result S_{n+4}. So some addition operations (cf. *Phase 2*) have to be performed to get the non-redundant representation before it can be used as input for a new multiplication. Here we use another circuit module - redundant number adder (RNA) to implement the operation of *Phase 2*. Actually, the PE array and RNA that work in an alternative form can be pipelined for processing independent multiplications which are inherent in the elliptic curve point calculation algorithms. Therefore, the average number of processing clock cycles for one multiplication are only $(n + 8)$ in our ECC processor.

Redundant Number Adder. The outputs of PEs should be added in an interleaved form to obtain the final result S_{n+4} by the RNA. The redundant number addition process is shown in Algorithm 3. For simplicity we rename $s_{n+7,j}$ and $c_{n+7,j}$ as s_j and c_j, respectively. Notice that there is a 1-bit overlap between c_j and c_{j+1} due to the propagation of the carry bit. Obviously, s_0 can be directly outputted. We rewrite the s_j and c_j to form three long integers SS, CL and CH in Algorithm 3, where $c_j[k-1:0]$ and $c_j[k]$ are the lowest k bits and the highest bit of c_j, respectively. Before being stored into the registers for addition, the three integers are converted to two integers by using CSA within one clock cycle. Then the addition of the two integers can be performed by a l-bit CPA in $\lceil \frac{(n-3)k}{l} \rceil$ clock cycles. For balancing the processing cycles and working frequency, the path delay of l-bit CPA is configured close to the addition of three numbers in PE. In our design, the width l is set to a value between $3k$ and $4k$.

4.2 ECC Processor Architecture

The architecture of the ECC processor based on our Montgomery modular multiplier is described in Fig. 4, where the Dual Port RAM is used to store arithmetic data. By reading a pre-configured program ROM, the Finite State Machine (FSM) controls the modular multiplier and the modular adder/subtracter (ModAdd/Sub), as well as the RAM state. Note that the widths of the data interfaces among the Dual Port RAM and the arithmetic units are all kn bits due to the parallelism of the multiplier.

Algorithm 3. Redundant number addition

Input:

$\quad s_j = s_{(n+7,j)}, c_j = c_{(n+7,j)}, j \in [0, n-4]$

Output:

$\quad S = \sum_{j=0}^{n-4}(2^k)^j \{c_j, s_j\}$

$\quad$ /*Forming three integers*/

1: $SS = \sum_{j=1}^{n-4}(2^k)^j s_j$

2: $CL = \sum_{j=0}^{n-4}(2^k)^j c_j[k-1:0]$

3: $CH = \sum_{j=0}^{n-4}(2^k)^{j+1} c_j[k]$

$\quad$ /*CSA*/

4: $X = SS \oplus CL \oplus CH$

5: $C = (SS\&CL)|(SS\&CH)|(CL\&CH)$

$\quad$ /*l-bit CPA*/

6: carry $= 1'b0$

7: **for** $i = 0$ to $\lceil \frac{(n-3)k}{l} \rceil - 1$ **do**

8: $\quad \{carry, S_i\} = X_i + C_i + carry,$

$\quad\quad$ where S_i, X_i, C_i represent the ith l-bit block of S, X, C, respectively.

9: **end for**

Modular Adder/Subtracter. In elliptic curve arithmetic, modular additions and subtractions are interspersed among the modular multiplication arithmetic. According to Algorithm 1, for the inputs in the range of $[0, 2\tilde{M}]$ the final result S_{n+d+2} will be reduced to the range of $[0, 2\tilde{M}]$.

In our design, ModAdd/Sub performs actually straightforward integer addition/subtraction without modular reduction. As an alternative, the modular reduction is performed by the Montgomery multiplication with an expanded R. After a careful observation and scheduling, the results of ModAdd/Sub are restricted to the range of $(0, 8\tilde{M})$, as shown in Appendix A, where the squaring is treated as the generic multiplication with two identical multiplicands. The range of $(0, 8M)$ is determined by the rescheduling of elliptic curve arithmetic. For example, for calculating $8(x \times y)$ where $x, y < 2\tilde{M}$, the process is rescheduled as $(4x) \times (2y)$ to narrow the range of the result. In this case, parameter R should be expanded to $R > 64\tilde{M}$ to guarantee that for inputs in the range of $(0, 8\tilde{M})$ the result of Montgomery multiplication S still satisfies: $S < 2\tilde{M}$. The proof is omitted here.

For $A + B \bmod \tilde{M}$, the range of the addition result is $(0, 8\tilde{M})$ due to the calculation of $4x$ where $x \in (0, 2\tilde{M})$ is an output of the multiplier. Therefore, the modular addition is simplified to the integer addition $A + B$, as shown in Eq. (1). For $A - B \bmod \tilde{M}$, the range of the subrahend B is $(0, 4\tilde{M})$ after specific scheduling, so $4\tilde{M}$ should be added to ensure that the result is positive, as shown in Eq. (2). Especially, for calculating $x - (y - z)$ where $x, y, z < 2\tilde{M}$, the process is rescheduled as $(x - y) + z \rightarrow (x - y + 4\tilde{M}) + z \in (0, 8\tilde{M})$.

$$A + B \bmod M \rightarrow A + B \in (0, 8\tilde{M}) \tag{1}$$

$$A - B \bmod M \rightarrow A - B + 4\tilde{M} \in (0, 8\tilde{M}) \tag{2}$$

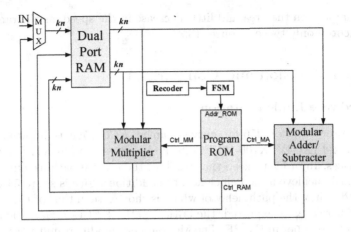

Fig. 4. The architecture of the ECC processor

Point Doubling and Addition. The point doubling and addition are implemented in Jacobian projective coordinates, under which the successive multiplications can be performed independently. The process of point doubling and addition with specific scheduling is presented in Appendix A. In the process, the dependencies of adjacent multiplications are avoided to fully exploit the multiplier, and the range of the modular addition/subtraction output satisfies the required conditions. After the above optimizations, completing one point doubling operation needs the processing cycles of 8 multiplications, and completing one point addition operation needs the processing cycles of 16 multiplications and 2 subtractions/additions.

SCA Resistance. Considering the SCA resistance and the efficiency, we combine randomized Jacobian coordinates method and a window method [13] against differential power analysis (DPA) and simple power analysis (SPA), respectively. The randomization technique transforms the base point $(x, y, 1)$ of projective coordinates to (r^2x, r^3y, r) with a random number $r \neq 0$. The window method in [13] based on a special recoding algorithm makes minimum information leak in the computation time, and it is efficient under Jacobian coordinates with a pre-computed table. A more efficient method was presented in [14], and a security enhanced method, which avoided a fixed table and achieved comparative efficiency, was proposed in [15]. For computing point multiplication, the window-based method [13] requires $2^{w-1} + tw$ point doublings and $2^{w-1} - 1 + t$ point additions, where w is the window size and t is the number of words after recoding. The pre-computing time has been taken into account, and the base point is not assumed to be fixed. The pre-computed table with $2^w - 1$ points can be easily implemented by block RAMs which are abundant in modern FPGAs, and the cost is acceptable for our design. Note that the randomization technique causes no impact on the area and little decrease in the speed, as the randomization is executed only twice or once [13].

5   Implementation and Comparison

5.1   Hardware Implementation

Our ECC processor for 256-bit curves named *ECC-256p* is implemented on Xilinx Virtex-4 (XC4VLX100-12FF1148) and Virtex-5 (XC5LX110T-3FF1136) FPGA devices. In order to keep the length of the critical path as expected and simultaneously achieve a high efficiency, the addition width is set to 54 for RNA and ModAdd/Sub, the path delay of which is shorter than that of three number addition. Therefore, as expected, the critical path of *ECC-256p* is the addition of three 32-bit number in the PE. The Montgomery modular multiplier can complete one operation in $n + 14$ clock cycles that consists of $n + 8$ cycles for the PE array and 6 cycles for the RNA, and the former is the average number of clock cycles for ECC point calculation. For the window-based algorithm of point multiplications, the window size w is set to 4, and the maximum t after recoding is 64 for 256-bit prime fields. In this case, one point multiplication requires 264 doublings and 71 additions at the cost of a pre-computed table with 15 points.

Table 1. Clock cycles for *ECC-256p* under Jacobian projective coordinates

Operation	*ECC-256p*
MUL	35 (average 29)
ADD/SUB	7
Point Doubling (Jacobian)	232
Point Addition (Jacobian)	484
Inversion (Fermat)	13685
Point Multiplication (Window)	109297

The number of clock cycles for the operations are shown in Table 1, and Post and Route (PAR) results on Virtex-4 and Virtex-5 are given in Table 2. In our results, the final inversion at the end of the scalar multiplication is taken into account. We use Fermats little theorem to compute the inversion. According to Table 2, *ECC-256p* can process one point multiplication in 109297 cycles under 250 MHz and 291 MHz frequency, meaning that the operation can be completed within 0.44 ms and 0.38 ms on Virtex-4 and Virtex-5, respectively. Note that the amounts of consumed hardware resource are different in the two devices, since the Virtex-5 resource units, such as slice, LUT and BRAM, have larger capacity. In particular, each slice in Virtex-5 contains four LUTs and flip-flops, while the number is two in Virtex-4 slice. Therefore, the total occupied slices are significantly reduced when the design is implemented on Virtex-5.

Table 2. PAR results of *ECC-256p* on Virtex-4 and Virtex-5

	Virtex-4	Virtex-5
Slices	4655	1725
LUTs	5740 (4-input)	4177 (6-input)
Flip-flops	4876	4792
DSP blocks	37	37
BRAMs	11 (18 Kb)	10 (36 Kb)
Frequency (Delay)	250 MHz (0.44 ms)	291 MHz (0.38 ms)

5.2 Performance Comparison and Discussion

The comparison results are shown in Table 3, where the first three works support generic elliptic curves, while the last two only support NIST curves. In addition, our work and [4, 11] are SCA resistant, while the others are not. We have labeled these differences in Table 3.

As far as we know, the fastest ECC processor for generic curves is [4], which uses RNS representations to speed up the computation. Substantial hardware resources (96 DSP blocks and 9177 ALM) in Stratix II FPGA are used for the implementation. In fact, Stratix II and Virtex-4 are at the same level, since the process nodes of the two devices are both $90\,nm$. Assuming that a Stratix II ALM and a Virtex-4 Slice are equivalent, our processor saves more than half resources compared with [4]. In the aspect of speed, our design is faster than [4] by more than 40 % from the perspective of implementation results. However, note that employing different SCA protections makes the performance quite different. In [4], Montgomery ladder which is a time-hungry technique against SPA and error-injection attacks was engaged. As the speed is the main concern, in our design it is not optimal (or even a waste) to adopt those countermeasures such as indistinguishable point addition formulae and Montgomery ladder, because the point doubling operation is nearly twice faster than the addition under Jacobian coordinates. In addition, our design has great advantages in area over [4]. Therefore, we use the window-based method which is a type of resource-consuming but efficient countermeasure against SPA. In brief, for generic curves over GF(p), our work provides an efficient alternative to achieve a higher speed and competitive security with a much more concise design.

The designs in [10, 11] are both based on the classic Montgomery algorithm, and implemented in earlier FPGAs Virtex-2 Pro, which did not supported DSP blocks yet. To our best knowledge, the architecture [11] is the fastest among the implementations based on the Montgomery multiplication for generic curves. In [11], the multiplication result was written in a special carry-save form to shorten the long computational path. But the maximum frequency was reduced to a very low level. As the targeted platform of our design is more advanced than that of [11], it is necessary to explain that our frequency is higher than [11] by a large margin from the aspect of the critical path. The critical path of [11] is composed of one adder, two 16-bit multipliers and some stage LUTs for 6-2 CSA, whereas

Table 3. Hardware performance comparison of this work and other ECC cores

	Curve	Device	Size (DSP)	Frequency (MHz)	Delay (ms)	SCA res.
Our	256 any	Virtex-5	1725 Slices (37 DSPs)	291	0.38	Yes
work	256 any	Virtex-4	4655 Slices (37 DSPs)	250	0.44	Yes
[4]	256 any	Stratix II	9177 ALM (96 DSPs)	157	0.68	Yes
[11]	256 any	Virtex-2 Pro	3529 Slices (36 MULTs)	67	2.35	Yes
[10]	256 any	Virtex-2 Pro	15755 Slices (256 MULTs)	39.5	3.84	No
[5]	256 NIST	Virtex-4	1715 Slices (32 DSPs)	487	0.49	No
[17]	192 NIST	Virtex-E	5708 Slices	40	3	No

the critical path in our design is only one stage LUTs for 3-2 CSA and one 32-bit adder. As a result, owing to the quotient pipelining technique applied in DSP blocks, the critical path is shortened significantly in our design.

The architecture described in [5] is the fastest FPGA implementation of elliptic curve point multiplication over $GF(p)$, but with restrictions on primes. It computes point multiplication over NIST curves which are widely used and standardized in practice. It is a dual clock design, and shifts all the field arithmetic operations into DSP blocks, thus the design occupies a small area and runs at a high speed (487 MHz) on Virtex-4. Our design extends the application to support generic curves at a higher speed, and our architecture is not limited in FPGA platforms. In fact, our architecture can be easily transferred to application specific integrated circuits (ASICs) by replacing the multiplier cores, i.e. DSP blocks with excellent pipelined multiplier IP cores. It will be more flexible on ASICs to configure the delay parameter and the radix to maximize the hardware performance. Furthermore, notice that the drawbacks of the pipelined Montgomery algorithm, i.e. the wider range and additional iteration cycles mentioned in Sect. 2.1, can be eliminated for commonly used pseudo Mersenne primes. Taking NIST prime P-256 $= 2^{256} - 2^{224} + 2^{192} + 2^{96} - 1$ as an example, the least 96 significant bits are all '1', so the parameter $\bar{M}$ equals 1 in Algorithm 1 for k, d satisfying $2^{k(d+1)} \leq 2^{96}$ and then $\tilde{M}$ is reduced to $\tilde{M} = M$. In this case, the range of pre-computed parameters are corresponding to the width in the traditional Montgomery algorithm. Therefore, if our architecture is designed for P-256, the performance will be further improved.

6   Conclusion and Future Work

This paper presents a high-speed elliptic curve cryptographic processor for generic curves over $GF(p)$ based on our novel Montgomery multiplier. We combine the quotient pipelining Montgomery multiplication algorithm with our new parallel array design, resulting in our multiplier completes one single Montgomery multiplication in approximately n clock cycles and also works in a high frequency. Also, employing the multiplier, we implement the ECC processor for scalar multiplications on modern FPGAs. Experimental results indicate that the design is faster than other existing ECC implementations over $GF(p)$ on FPGAs. From the comparison results, we can see that pipelined Montgomery based scheme is a better choice than the classic Montgomery based and RNS based ones in terms of speed or consumed resources for ECC implementations. In future work, we will implement the architecture in more advanced FPGAs such as Virtex-6 and Virtex-7, and transfer it to ASIC platforms.

Acknowledgements. The authors would like to acknowledge the contributions of Doctor Zhan Wang, Jingqiang Lin, and Chenyang Tu for useful discussions. The authors also would like to thank Professor Tanja Lange from Technische Universiteit Eindhoven in the Netherlands for helpful proofreading and comments. Finally, we are grateful to the anonymous reviewers for their invaluable suggestions and comments to improve the quality and fairness of this paper.

A   Rescheduling of Point Addition and Doubling in Jacobian Projective Coordinates

Given the Weierstrass equation of an elliptic curve $E : y^2 = x^3 + ax + b$ defined over $\mathrm{GF}(p)$, the projective point $(X : Y : Z)$, $Z \neq 0$ corresponds to the affine

Table 4. Scheduling process of point addition and doubling

	Point Addition		Point Doubling	
Step	MUL	ADD/SUB	MUL	ADD/SUB
1	$L_1 = Z_2 \times Z_2$		$L_1 = Z_1 \times Z_1$	$L_2 = Y_1 + Y_1$
2	$L_2 = Z_1 \times Z_1$		$L_3 = L_2 \times L_2$	$L_4 = X_1 + L_1$
				$L_5 = X_1 - L_1$
3	$\lambda_1 = X_1 \times L_1$		$L_{13} = L_4 \times L_5$	$L_6 = X_1 + X_1$
4	$\lambda_2 = X_2 \times L_2$		$\lambda_2 = L_3 \times L_6$	$\lambda_1 = 3L_{13}$
5	$L_3 = Y_1 \times Z_2$	$\lambda_3 = \lambda_1 - \lambda_2$	$L_9 = \lambda_1 \times \lambda_1$	$L_7 = \lambda_2/2$
		$\lambda_7 = \lambda_1 + \lambda_2$		$L_8 = \lambda_2 + L_7$
6	$L_4 = Z_1 \times Y_2$		$L_{10} = L_3 \times L_3$	$L_{11} = L_8 - L_9$
7	$\lambda_4 = L_1 \times L_3$		$L_{12} = L_{11} \times \lambda_1$	$\lambda_3 = L_{10}/2$
				$X_3 = L_9 - \lambda_2$
8	$\lambda_5 = L_2 \times L_4$		$Z_3 = L_2 \times Z_1$	$Y_3 = L_{12} - \lambda_3$
9	$L_5 = Z_1 \times Z_2$	$\lambda_6 = \lambda_4 - \lambda_5$		
		$\lambda_8 = \lambda_4 + \lambda_5$		
10	$L_6 = \lambda_3 \times \lambda_3$			
11	$L_7 = \lambda_6 \times \lambda_6$	$L_8 = \lambda_7 + \lambda_7$		
12	$L_9 = L_6 \times L_8$			
13	$L_{10} = \lambda_3 \times L_6$	$L_{11} = L_9/2$		
		$L_{12} = L_{11} + L_9$		
		$L_{13} = L_7 + L_7$		
14	$Z_3 = \lambda_3 \times L_5$	$X_3 = L_7 - L_{11}$		
		$L_{15} = L_{12} - L_{13}$		
15	$L_{14} = \lambda_8 \times L_{10}$			
16	$L_{16} = L_{15} \times \lambda_6$			
17		$Y_3 = L_{16} - L_{14}$		
18		$Y_3 = Y_3/2$		

point $(X/Z^2, Y/Z^3)$ in Jacobian projective coordinates. Here we assume that the elliptic curve $y^2 = x^3 + ax + b$ has $a = -3$ without much loss of generality. Given two points $P_1 = (X_1, Y_1, Z_1)$, $P_2 = (X_2, Y_2, Z_2)$ in Jacobian coordinates, sum $P_3 = P_1 + P_2$. The point addition calculation process for $P_1 \neq P_2$ and point doubling calculation process for $P_1 = P_2$ are scheduled as given in Table 4.

References

1. Blum, T., Paar, C.: High-radix montgomery modular exponentiation on reconfigurable hardware. IEEE Trans. Comput. **50**(7), 759–764 (2001)
2. Daly, A., Marnane, W.P., Kerins, T., Popovici, E.M.: An FPGA implementation of a GF(p) ALU for encryption processors. Microprocess. Microsyst. **28**(5–6), 253–260 (2004)
3. Eldridge, S.E., Walter, C.D.: Hardware implementation of montgomery's modular multiplication algorithm. IEEE Trans. Comput. **42**(6), 693–699 (1993)
4. Guillermin, N.: A high speed coprocessor for elliptic curve scalar multiplications over $\mathbb{F}_p$. In: Mangard, S., Standaert, F.-X. (eds.) CHES 2010. LNCS, vol. 6225, pp. 48–64. Springer, Heidelberg (2010)
5. Güneysu, T., Paar, Ch.: Ultra high performance ECC over NIST primes on commercial FPGAs. In: Oswald, E., Rohatgi, P. (eds.) CHES 2008. LNCS, vol. 5154, pp. 62–78. Springer, Heidelberg (2008)
6. Hankerson, D., Vanstone, S., Menezes, A.J.: Guide to elliptic curve cryptography. Springer, New York (2004)
7. Huang, M., Gaj, K., Kwon, S., El-Ghazawi, T.: An optimized hardware architecture for the montgomery multiplication algorithm. In: Cramer, R. (ed.) PKC 2008. LNCS, vol. 4939, pp. 214–228. Springer, Heidelberg (2008)
8. Koblitz, N.: Elliptic curve cryptosystems. Math. Comput. **48**(177), 203–209 (1987)
9. McIvor, C., McLoone, M., McCanny, J.V.: High-radix systolic modular multiplication on reconfigurable hardware. In: Brebner, G.J., Chakraborty, S., Wong, W.F. (eds) FPT 2005, pp. 13–18. IEEE (2005)
10. McIvor, C.J., McLoone, M., McCanny, J.V.: Hardware elliptic curve cryptographic processor over GF(p). IEEE Trans. Circ. Syst. I: Regul. Pap. **53**(9), 1946–1957 (2006)
11. Mentens, N.: Secure and efficient coprocessor design for cryptographic applications on FPGAs. Ph.D. thesis, Katholieke Universiteit Leuven (2007)
12. Miller, V.S.: Use of elliptic curves in cryptography. In: Williams, H.C. (ed.) CRYPTO 1985. LNCS, vol. 218, pp. 417–426. Springer, Heidelberg (1986)
13. Möller, B.: Securing elliptic curve point multiplication against side-channel attacks. In: Davida, G.I., Frankel, Y. (eds.) ISC 2001. LNCS, vol. 2200, pp. 324–334. Springer, Heidelberg (2001)
14. Möller, B.: Securing elliptic curve point multiplication against side-channel attacks, addendum: Efficiency improvement. http://pdf.aminer.org/000/452/864/securing_elliptic_curve_point_multiplication_against_side_channel_attacks.pdf (2001)
15. Möller, B.: Parallelizable elliptic curve point multiplication method with resistance against side-channel attacks. In: Chan, A.H., Gligor, V.D. (eds.) ISC 2002. LNCS, vol. 2433, pp. 402–413. Springer, Heidelberg (2002)
16. Montgomery, P.L.: Modular multiplication without trial division. Math. Comput. **44**(170), 519–521 (1985)

17. Orlando, G., Paar, C.: A scalable GF(p) elliptic curve processor architecture for programmable hardware. In: Koç, Ç.K., Naccache, D., Paar, C. (eds.) CHES 2001. LNCS, vol. 2162, pp. 348–363. Springer, Heidelberg (2001)
18. Orup, H.: Simplifying quotient determination in high-radix modular multiplication. In: IEEE Symposium on Computer Arithmetic, pp. 193–199 (1995)
19. Suzuki, D.: How to maximize the potential of FPGA resources for modular exponentiation. In: Paillier, P., Verbauwhede, I. (eds.) CHES 2007. LNCS, vol. 4727, pp. 272–288. Springer, Heidelberg (2007)
20. Tang, S.H., Tsui, K.S., Leong, P.H.W.: Modular exponentiation using parallel multipliers. In: FPT 2003, pp. 52–59. IEEE (2003)
21. Tenca, A.F., Koç, Ç.K.: A scalable architecture for montgomery multiplication. In: Koç, Ç.K., Paar, Ch. (eds.) CHES 1999. LNCS, vol. 1717, pp. 94–108. Springer, Heidelberg (1999)
22. Tenca, A.F., Todorov, G., Koç, Ç.K.: High-radix design of a scalable modular multiplier. In: Koç, Ç.K., Naccache, D., Paar, Ch. (eds.) CHES 2001. LNCS, vol. 2162, pp. 185–201. Springer, Heidelberg (2001)
23. Walter, C.D.: Systolic modular multiplication. IEEE Trans. Comput. **42**(3), 376–378 (1993)

Exponentiating in Pairing Groups

Joppe W. Bos, Craig Costello$^{(\boxtimes)}$, and Michael Naehrig

Microsoft Research, Redmond, USA
{jbos,craigco,mnaehrig}@microsoft.com

Abstract. We study exponentiations in pairing groups for the most common security levels and show that, although the Weierstrass model is preferable for pairing computation, it can be worthwhile to map to alternative curve representations for the non-pairing group operations in protocols.

1 Introduction

At the turn of the century it was shown that elliptic curves can be used to build powerful cryptographic primitives: bilinear pairings [14,36,49]. *Pairings* are used in a large variety of protocols, and even when considering the recent breakthrough paper which shows how to instantiate multilinear maps using ideal lattices [26], pairings remain the preferred choice for a bilinear map due to their superior performance. Algorithms to compute cryptographic pairings involve computations on elements in all three pairing groups, $\mathbb{G}_1$, $\mathbb{G}_2$ and $\mathbb{G}_T$, but protocols usually require many additional standalone exponentiations in any of these three groups. In fact, protocols often compute only a single pairing but require many operations in any or all of $\mathbb{G}_1$, $\mathbb{G}_2$ and $\mathbb{G}_T$ [13,28,47]. In this work, we use such scenarios as a motivation to enhance the performance of group operations that are not the pairing computation.

Using non-Weierstrass models for elliptic curve group operations can give rise to significant speedups (cf. [9,10,31,43]). Such alternative models have not found the same success within pairing computations, since Miller's algorithm [42] not only requires group operations, but also relies on the computation of functions with divisors corresponding to these group operations. These functions are somewhat inherent in the Weierstrass group law, which is why Weierstrass curves remain faster for the pairings themselves [17]. Nevertheless, this does not mean that alternative curve models cannot be used to give speedups in the standalone group operations in pairing-based protocols. The purpose of this paper is to determine which curve models are applicable in the most popular pairing scenarios, and to report the speedups achieved when employing them. In order to obtain meaningful results, we have implemented curve arithmetic in different models that target the 128-, 192- and 256-bit security levels. Specifically, we have implemented group exponentiations and pairings on BN curves [4] (embedding degree $k = 12$), KSS curves [38] ($k = 18$) and BLS curves [3] ($k = 12$ and $k = 24$). We use GLV [25] and GLS [23] decompositions of dimensions 2, 4, 6 and 8 to speed up the scalar multiplication.

T. Lange, K. Lauter, and P. Lisoněk (Eds.): SAC 2013, LNCS 8282, pp. 438–455, 2014.
DOI: 10.1007/978-3-662-43414-7_22, © Springer-Verlag Berlin Heidelberg 2014

The goal of this work is *not* to set new software speed records, but to illustrate the improved performance that is possible from employing different curve models in the pairing groups $\mathbb{G}_1$ and $\mathbb{G}_2$. In order to provide meaningful benchmark results, we have designed our library using recoding techniques [21,29] such that all code runs in constant-time, i.e. the run-time of the code is independent of any secret input material. Our implementations use state-of-the-art algorithms for computations in the various groups [24] and for evaluating the pairing [2]. For any particular curve or security level, we assume that the *ratios* between our various benchmark results remain (roughly) invariant when implemented for different platforms or when the bottleneck arithmetic functions are converted to assembly. We therefore believe that our table of timings provides implementers and protocol designers with good insight as to the relative computational expense of operating in pairing groups versus computing the pairing(s).

2   Preliminaries

A cryptographic pairing $e : \mathbb{G}_1 \times \mathbb{G}_2 \rightarrow \mathbb{G}_T$ is a bilinear map that relates the three groups $\mathbb{G}_1$, $\mathbb{G}_2$ and $\mathbb{G}_T$, each of prime order r. These groups are defined as follows. For distinct primes p and r, let k be the smallest positive integer such that $r \mid p^k - 1$. Assume that $k > 1$. For an elliptic curve $E/\mathbb{F}_p$ such that $r \mid \#E(\mathbb{F}_p)$, we can choose $\mathbb{G}_1 = E(\mathbb{F}_p)[r]$ to be the order-r subgroup of $E(\mathbb{F}_p)$. We have $E[r] \subset E(\mathbb{F}_{p^k})$, and $\mathbb{G}_2$ can be taken as the (order-r) subgroup of $E(\mathbb{F}_{p^k})$ of p-eigenvectors of the p-power Frobenius endomorphism on E. Let $\mathbb{G}_T$ be the group of r-th roots of unity in $\mathbb{F}_{p^k}^*$. The *embedding degree* k is very large (i.e. $k \approx r$) for general curves, but must be kept small (i.e. $k < 50$) if computations in $\mathbb{F}_{p^k}$ are to be feasible in practice – this means that so-called *pairing-friendly* curves must be constructed in a special way. In Sect. 2.1 we recall the best known techniques for constructing such curves with embedding degrees that target the 128-, 192- and 256-bit security levels – k is varied to optimally balance the size of r and the size of $\mathbb{F}_{p^k}$, which respectively determine the complexity of the best known elliptic curve and finite field discrete logarithm attacks.

2.1   Parameterized Families of Pairing-Friendly Curves with Sextic Twists

The most suitable pairing-friendly curves for our purposes come from parameterized families, such that the parameters to find a suitable curve $E(\mathbb{F}_p)$ can be written as univariate polynomials. For the four families we consider, we give below the polynomials $p(x)$, $r(x)$ and $t(x)$, where $t(x)$ is such that $n(x) = p(x)+1-t(x)$ is the cardinality of the desired curve, which has $r(x)$ as a factor. All of the curves found from these constructions have j-invariant zero, which means they can be written in Weierstrass form as $y^2 = x^3 + b$. Instances of these pairing-friendly families can be found by searching through integer values x of an appropriate size until we find $x = x_0$ such that $p = p(x_0)$ and $r = r(x_0)$ are simultaneously prime, at which point we can simply test different values for b until the curve $E : y^2 = x^3 + b$ has an n-torsion point.

To target the 128-bit security level, we use the BN family [4] ($k = 12$), for which

$$p(x) = 36x^4 + 36x^3 + 24x^2 + 6x + 1, t(x) = 6x^2 + 1, r(x) = p(x) + 1 - t(x). \quad (1)$$

At the 192-bit security level, we consider BLS curves [3] with $k = 12$, for which

$$p(x) = (x-1)^2(x^4 - x^2 + 1)/3 + x, \quad t(x) = x + 1, \quad r(x) = x^4 - x^2 + 1, \quad (2)$$

where $x \equiv 1 \bmod 3$, and KSS curves [38] with $k = 18$, which are given by

$$p(x) = (x^8 + 5x^7 + 7x^6 + 37x^5 + 188x^4 + 259x^3 + 343x^2 + 1763x + 2401)/21,$$
$$t(x) = (x^4 + 16x + 7)/7, \quad r(x) = (x^6 + 37x^3 + 343)/7^3, \quad (3)$$

with $x \equiv 14 \bmod 42$. At the 256-bit security level, we use curves from the BLS family [3] with embedding degree $k = 24$, which have the parametrization

$$p(x) = (x-1)^2(x^8 - x^4 + 1)/3 + x, \quad t(x) = x + 1, \quad r(x) = x^8 - x^4 + 1, \quad (4)$$

with $x \equiv 1 \bmod 3$.

For the above families, which all have $k = 2^i 3^j$, the best practice to construct the full extension field $\mathbb{F}_{p^k}$ is to use a tower of (intermediate) quadratic and cubic extensions [5,40]. Since $6 \mid k$, we can always use a *sextic twist* $E'(\mathbb{F}_{p^{k/6}})$ to represent elements of $\mathbb{G}_2 \subset E(\mathbb{F}_{p^k})[r]$ as elements of an isomorphic group $\mathbb{G}'_2 = E'(\mathbb{F}_{p^{k/6}})[r]$. This shows that group operations in $\mathbb{G}_2$ can be performed on points with coordinates in an extension field with degree one sixth the size, which is the best we can do for elliptic curves [50, Proposition X.5.4].

In all cases considered in this work, the most preferable sextic extension from $\mathbb{F}_{p^{k/6}} = \mathbb{F}_p(\xi)$ to $\mathbb{F}_{p^k} = \mathbb{F}_{p^{k/6}}(z)$ is constructed by taking $z \in \mathbb{F}_{p^k}$ as a root of the polynomial $z^6 - \xi$, which is irreducible in $\mathbb{F}_{p^{k/6}}[z]$. We describe the individual towers in the four cases as follows: the BN and BLS cases with $k = 12$ preferably take $p \equiv 3 \bmod 4$, so that $\mathbb{F}_{p^2}$ can be constructed as $\mathbb{F}_{p^2} = \mathbb{F}_p[u]/(u^2 + 1)$, and take $\xi = u + 1$ for the sextic extension to $\mathbb{F}_{p^{12}}$. For $k = 18$ KSS curves, we prefer that 2 is not a cube in $\mathbb{F}_p$, so that $\mathbb{F}_{p^3}$ can be constructed as $\mathbb{F}_{p^2} = \mathbb{F}_p[u]/(u^3 + 2)$, before taking $\xi = u$ to extend to $\mathbb{F}_{p^{18}}$. For $k = 24$ BLS curves, we again prefer to construct $\mathbb{F}_{p^2}$ as $\mathbb{F}_{p^2} = \mathbb{F}_p[u]/(u^2 + 1)$, on top of which we take $\mathbb{F}_{p^4} = \mathbb{F}_{p^2}[v]/(v^2 - (u+1))$ (it is easily shown that $v^2 - u$ cannot be irreducible [18, Proposition 1]), and use $\xi = v$ for the sextic extension. All of these constructions agree with the towers used in the "speed-record" literature [1,2,18,48].

2.2   The GLV and GLS Algorithms

The GLV [25] and GLS [23] methods both use an efficient endomorphism to speed up elliptic curve scalar multiplications. The GLV method relies on endomorphisms specific to the shape of the curve E that are unrelated to the Frobenius endomorphism. On the other hand, the GLS method works over extension fields where Frobenius becomes non-trivial, so it does not rely on E having a special shape. However, if E is both defined over an extension field and has a special shape, then the two can be combined [23, Sect. 3] to give higher-dimensional decompositions, which can further enhance performance.

Since in this paper we have $E/\mathbb{F}_p : y^2 = x^3 + b$ and $p \equiv 1 \bmod 3$, we can use the GLV endomorphism $\phi : (x, y) \mapsto (\zeta x, y)$ in $\mathbb{G}_1$ where $\zeta^3 = 1$ and $\zeta \in \mathbb{F}_p \setminus \{1\}$. In this case ϕ satisfies $\phi^2 + \phi + 1$ in the endomorphism ring $\mathrm{End}(E)$ of E, so on $\mathbb{G}_1$ it corresponds to scalar multiplication by λ_ϕ, where $\lambda_\phi^2 + \lambda_\phi + 1 \equiv 0 \bmod r$, meaning we get a 2-dimensional decomposition in $\mathbb{G}_1$. Since $\mathbb{G}_2'$ is always defined over an extension field herein, we can combine the GLV endomorphism above with the Frobenius map to get higher-dimensional GLS decompositions. The standard way to do this in the pairing context [24] is to use the untwisting isomorphism Ψ to move points from $\mathbb{G}_2'$ to $\mathbb{G}_2$, where the p-power Frobenius π_p can be applied (since E is defined over $\mathbb{F}_p$, while E' is not), before using the twisting isomorphism Ψ^{-1} to move this result back to $\mathbb{G}_2'$. We define ψ as $\psi = \Psi^{-1} \circ \pi_p \circ \Psi$, which (even though Ψ and Ψ^{-1} are defined over $\mathbb{F}_{p^k}$) can be explicitly described over $\mathbb{F}_{p^{k/6}}$. The GLS endomorphism ψ satisfies $\Phi_k(\psi) = 0$ in $\mathrm{End}(E')$ [24, Lemma 1], where $\Phi_k(\cdot)$ is the k-th cyclotomic polynomial, so it corresponds to scalar multiplication by λ_ψ, where $\Phi_k(\lambda_\psi) \equiv 0 \bmod r$, i.e. λ_ψ is a primitve k-th root of unity modulo r. For the curves with $k = 12$, we thus obtain a 4-dimensional decomposition in $\mathbb{G}_2' \subset E'(\mathbb{F}_{p^2})$; for $k = 18$ curves, we get a 6-dimensional decomposition in $\mathbb{G}_2' \subset E'(\mathbb{F}_{p^3})$; and for $k = 24$ curves, we get an 8-dimensional decomposition in $\mathbb{G}_2' \subset E'(\mathbb{F}_{p^4})$.

To compute the scalar multiple $[s]P_0$, a $d = 2$ dimensional GLV or $d = \varphi(k)$ dimensional GLS decomposition starts by computing the $d - 1$ additional points $P_i = \psi^i(P_0) = \psi(P_{i-1}) = [\lambda_\psi^i]P_0$, $1 \leq i \leq d - 1$. One then seeks a vector $(\hat{s}_0, \hat{s}_1) \in \mathbb{Z}^2$ in the "GLV lattice" L_ϕ that is close to $(s, 0) \in \mathbb{Z}^2$, or $(\hat{s}_0, \ldots, \hat{s}_{\varphi(k)-1}) \in \mathbb{Z}^{\varphi(k)}$ in the "GLS lattice" L_ψ that is close to $(s, 0, \ldots, 0) \in \mathbb{Z}^{\varphi(k)}$. The bases B_ϕ and B_ψ (for L_ϕ and L_ψ) are given as (see [22, p. 229–230])

$$
B_\phi = \begin{pmatrix} r & 0 \\ -\lambda_\phi & 1 \end{pmatrix}; \qquad
B_\psi = \begin{pmatrix} r & 0 \ldots 0 \\ -\lambda_\psi & 1 \ldots 0 \\ \vdots & \vdots \ddots \vdots \\ -\lambda_\psi^{d-1} & 0 \ldots 1 \end{pmatrix}. \tag{5}
$$

Finding close vectors in these lattices is particularly easy in the case of BLS $k = 12$ and $k = 24$ curves [24, Example 3,4]. For BN curves, we can use the special routine described by Galbraith and Scott [24, Example 5], which bears resemblance to the algorithm proposed in [46], which is what we use for the GLS decomposition on KSS curves.

To obtain the d mini-scalars $s_0, \ldots, s_{d-1}$ from the scalar s and the close vector $(\hat{s}_0, \ldots, \hat{s}_{d-1})$, we compute $(s_0, \ldots s_{d-1}) = (s, 0, \ldots, 0) - (\hat{s}_0, \ldots, \hat{s}_{d-1})$ in $\mathbb{Z}^d$. We can then compute $[s]P_0$ via the multi-exponentiation $\sum_{i=0}^{d-1}[s_i]P_i$. The typical way to do this is to start by making all of the s_i positive: we simultaneously negate any (s_i, P_i) pair for which $s_i < 0$ (this can be done in a side-channel resistant way using bitmasks). We then precompute all possible sums $\sum_{i=0}^{d-1} [b_i] P_i$, for the 2^d combinations of $b_i \in \{0, 1\}$, and store them in a lookup table. When simultaneously processing the j-th bits of the d mini-scalars, this allows us to update the running value with only one point addition, before performing a single point doubling. In each case however, this standard approach requires individual attention for further optimization – this is what we describe in Sect. 3.

We aim to create constant-time programs: implementations which have an execution time independent of any secret material (e.g. the scalar). This means that we always execute exactly the same amount of point additions and duplications independent of the input. In order to achieve this in the setting of scalar multiplication using the GLV/GLS method, we use the recoding techniques from [21,29]. This recoding technique not only guarantees that the program performs a constant number of point operations, but that the recoding itself is done in constant time as well. Furthermore, an advantage of this method is that the lookup table size is reduced by a factor of two, since we only store lookup elements for which the multiple of the first point P_0 is odd. Besides reducing the memory, this reduces the time to create the lookup table.

3   Strategies for GLV in $\mathbb{G}_1$ and GLS in $\mathbb{G}_2$

This section presents our high-level strategy for 2-GLV on $\mathbb{G}_1$, 4-GLS in $\mathbb{G}_2$ in the two $k = 12$ families, 6-GLS in $\mathbb{G}_2$ for the KSS curves with $k = 18$, and 8-GLS in $\mathbb{G}_2$ for the BLS curves with $k = 24$. We use the following abbreviations for elliptic curve operations that we require: DBL – for the doubling of a projective point, ADD – for the addition between two projective points, MIX – for the addition between a projective point and an affine point, and AFF – for the addition between two affine points to give a projective point.

3.1   2-GLV on $\mathbb{G}_1$

For the 2-GLV routines we compute the multi-exponentiation $[s_0]P_0 + [s_1]P_1$. Recoding our mini-scalars and proceeding in the naive way would give a lookup table consisting of two elements: P_0 and $P_0 + P_1$. However, the number of point additions can be further reduced by using a large window size [16] (see [23,24] for a description in the context of GLV/GLS). Specifically, we can reduce the number of point additions in the scalar processing phase by a factor of w if we generate a lookup table of size 2^{2w-1}. Since computing an element in the lookup table costs roughly one addition, one can compute the optimal window size given the maximum size of the mini-scalars (see Table 3). For 2-GLV in $\mathbb{G}_1$, we found a fixed window size of $w = 3$ to be optimal in all cases except BN curves (where we use $w = 2$ due to the smaller maximum size of the mini-scalars). In Algorithms 1 and 2 we give the algorithms for computing the 2-GLV

Algorithm 1. Generating the lookup table for 2-GLV with window size $w = 2$ (cost: 6 MIX + 1 AFF + 1 DBL).

Input: $P_0, P_1 \in \mathbb{G}_1$.
Output: The 2-GLV lookup table, T, for window size $w = 2$.

$$
\begin{aligned}
&t_0 \leftarrow \text{DBL}(P_0), & &T[0] \leftarrow P_0, & &T[1] \leftarrow \text{MIX}(t_0, P_0), \\
&T[2] \leftarrow \text{AFF}(P_0, P_1), & &T[3] \leftarrow \text{MIX}(T[1], P_1), & &T[4] \leftarrow \text{MIX}(T[2], P_1), \\
&T[5] \leftarrow \text{MIX}(T[3], P_1), & &T[6] \leftarrow \text{MIX}(T[4], P_1), & &T[7] \leftarrow \text{MIX}(T[5], P_1).
\end{aligned}
$$

---

lookup tables using $w = 2$ and $w = 3$, respectively. Algorithm 1 outlines how to compute $T[\lfloor \frac{a}{2} \rfloor + 2 \cdot b] = [a]P_0 + [b]P_1$ for $a \in \{1, 3\}$ and $b \in \{0, 1, 2, 3\}$, where T consists of eight elements. Algorithm 2 computes $T[\lfloor \frac{a}{2} \rfloor + 4 \cdot b] = [a]P_0 + [b]P_1$ for $a \in \{1, 3, 5, 7\}$ and $b \in \{0, 1, 2, 3, 4, 5, 6, 7\}$, where T consists of 32 elements.

For both BLS families and the KSS family, we get a simple GLV scalar decomposition and obtain the mini-scalars by writing s as a linear function in λ_ϕ. This has the additional advantage that both s_0 and s_1 are positive. For BN curves, we use the algorithm from [46] for the decomposition. In this setting, the mini-scalars can be negative, so we must ensure that they become positive (see Sect. 2.2) before using Algorithm 1 to generate the lookup table.

3.2 4-GLS on $\mathbb{G}_2$ for BN and BLS Curves with $k = 12$

In the BLS case, we have $\lambda_\psi(x) = x$, which means $|\lambda_\psi| \approx r^{1/4}$, so we get a 4-dimensional decomposition in $\mathbb{G}_2$ by writing the scalar $0 \leq s < r$ in base $|\lambda_\psi|$ as $s = \sum_{i=0}^{3} s_i |\lambda_\psi|^i$, with $0 \leq s_i < |\lambda_\psi|$ [24, Example 3]. On the other hand, the mini-scalars resulting from the decomposition on BN curves in [24, Example 5] can be negative.

Deciding on the best window size for 4-GLS is trivial since a window size of $w = 2$ requires a lookup table of 128 entries, where generating each entry costs an addition. This is far more than the number of additions saved from using this larger window. In Algorithm 3, we state how to generate the lookup table for $w = 1$ of size eight, which consists of the elements $T[\sum_{i=1}^{3} b_i 2^{i-1}] = P_0 + \sum_{i=1}^{3} [b_i]P_i$, for all combinations of $b_i \in \{0, 1\}$.

Algorithm 2. Generating the lookup table for 2-GLV with window size $w = 3$ (cost: 29 MIX + 2 ADD + 1 DBL).

Input: $P_0, P_1 \in \mathbb{G}_1$.
Output: The 2-GLV lookup table, T, for window size $w = 3$.

$$
\begin{aligned}
&t_0 \leftarrow \text{DBL}(P_0), & &T[0] \leftarrow P_0, & &T[1] \leftarrow \text{MIX}(t_0, P_0), \\
&T[2] \leftarrow \text{ADD}(t_0, T[1]), & &T[3] \leftarrow \text{ADD}(t_0, T[2]),
\end{aligned}
$$

for $i = 1$ to 7 **do**
    for $j = 0$ to 3 **do**
        $T[4i + j] \leftarrow \text{MIX}(T[4(i - 1) + j], P_1)$

Algorithm 3. Generating the lookup table for 4-GLS with window size $w = 1$ (cost: 4 MIX + 3 AFF).

Input: $P_0, P_1, P_2, P_3 \in \mathbb{G}_2$.
Output: The 4-GLS lookup table T.

$T[0] \leftarrow P_0,$ $\qquad\qquad$ $T[1] \leftarrow \text{AFF}(T[0], P_1),$ $\qquad$ $T[2] \leftarrow \text{AFF}(T[0], P_2),$
$T[3] \leftarrow \text{MIX}(T[1], P_2),$ $\qquad$ $T[4] \leftarrow \text{AFF}(T[0], P_3),$ $\qquad$ $T[5] \leftarrow \text{MIX}(T[1], P_3),$
$T[6] \leftarrow \text{MIX}(T[2], P_3),$ $\qquad$ $T[7] \leftarrow \text{MIX}(T[3], P_3).$

3.3   6-GLS on $\mathbb{G}_2$ for KSS Curves with $k = 18$

To decompose the scalar for 6-GLS on $\mathbb{G}_2$ for KSS curves, we use the technique[1] from [46], after which we must ensure all the s_i are non-negative according to Sect. 2.2. In this case, the decision of the window size (being $w = 1$) is again trivial, since a window of size $w = 2$ requires a lookup table of size 2^{11}. On input of P_i corresponding to $s_i > 0$, for $0 \le i \le 5$, we generate the 32 elements of the lookup table as follows. We use Algorithm 3 to produce $T[0], \ldots, T[7]$ (using $P_0, \ldots, P_3$). We compute $T[8] \leftarrow \text{AFF}(T[0], P_4)$ and $T[i] \leftarrow \text{MIX}(T[i-8], P_4)$ for $9 \le i \le 15$. Next, we compute $T[16] \leftarrow \text{AFF}(T[0], P_5)$ and $T[i] \leftarrow \text{MIX}(T[i - 16], P_5)$ for $17 \le i \le 31$.

3.4   8-GLS on $\mathbb{G}_2$ for BLS Curves $k = 24$

BLS curves with $k = 24$ have $\lambda_\psi(x) = x$, which means $|\lambda_\psi| \approx r^{1/8}$, so one can compute an 8-dimensional decomposition in $\mathbb{G}_2$ by writing the scalar $0 \le s < r$ in base $|\lambda_\psi|$ as $s = \sum_{i=0}^{7} s_i |\lambda_\psi|^i$, with $0 \le s_i < |\lambda_\psi|$ [24, Example 4]. We use the 8-dimensional decomposition strategy studied in [15]: the idea is to split the lookup table (a single large lookup table would consist of 128 entries) into two lookup tables consisting of eight elements each. In this case, we need to compute twice the amount of point additions when simultaneously processing the mini-scalars (see Table 3), but we save around 120 point additions in generating the lookup table(s). Let T_1 be the table consisting of the 8 entries $P_0 + \sum_{i=1}^{3} [b_i] P_i$, for $b_i \in \{0, 1\}$, which is generated using Algorithm 3 on $P_0, \ldots, P_3$. The second table, T_2, consists of the 8 entries $P_4 + \sum_{i=5}^{7} [b_i] P_i$ for $b_i \in \{0, 1\}$, and can be pre-computed as $T_2[j] \leftarrow \psi^4(T_1[j])$, for $j = 0, \ldots, 7$. With the specific tower construction for $k = 24$ BLS curves (see Sect. 2.1), the map $\psi^4 : \mathbb{G}_2 \to \mathbb{G}_2$ significantly simplifies to $\psi^4 : (x, y) \mapsto (c_x x, c_y y)$, where the constants c_x and c_y are in $\mathbb{F}_p$.

---

[1] We note that for particular KSS $k = 18$ curves, large savings may arise in this algorithm due to the fact that the $\alpha = \sum_{i=0}^{5} a_i \psi^i$ (from Sect. 5.2 of [46]) have some of the a_i being zero. In the case of the KSS curve we use, around $2/3$ of the computations vanish due to $a_2 = a_4 = a_5 = 0$ and $a_1 = 1$.

4 Alternate Curve Models for Exponentiations in Groups $\mathbb{G}_1$ and $\mathbb{G}_2$

An active research area in ECC involves optimizing elliptic curve arithmetic through the use of various curve models and coordinate systems (see [9,31] for an overview). For example, in ECC applications the fastest arithmetic to realize a group operation on Weierstrass curves of the form $y^2 = x^3 + b$ requires 16 field multiplications [9], while a group addition on an Edwards curve can incur as few as 8 field multiplications [33]. While alternative curve models are not favorable over Weierstrass curves in the pairing computation itself [17], they can still be used to speed up the elliptic curve operations in $\mathbb{G}_1$ and $\mathbb{G}_2$.

4.1 Three Non-Weierstrass Models

Unlike the general Weierstrass model which covers all isomorphism classes of elliptic curves over a particular field, the non-Weierstrass elliptic curves usually only cover a subset of all such classes. Whether or not an elliptic curve E falls into the classes covered by a particular model is commonly determined by the existence of a Weierstrass point with a certain order on E. In the most popular scenarios for ECC, these orders are either 2, 3 or 4. In this section we consider the fastest model that is applicable in the pairing context in each of these cases.

- $\mathcal{W}$ - **Weierstrass**: all curves in this paper have j-invariant zero and Weierstrass form $y^2 = x^3 + b$. The fastest formulas on such curves use Jacobian coordinates [8].
- $\mathcal{J}$ - **Extended Jacobi quartic**: if an elliptic curve has a point of order 2, then it can be written in (extended) Jacobi quartic form as $\mathcal{J}: y^2 = dx^4 + ax^2 + 1$ [11, Sect. 3] – these curves were first considered for cryptographic use in [11, Sect. 3]. The fastest formulas work on the corresponding projective curve given by $\mathcal{J}: Y^2 Z^2 = dX^4 + aX^2 Z^2 + Z^4$ and use the 4 extended coordinates $(X : Y : Z : T)$ to represent a point, where $x = X/Z$, $y = Y/Z$ and $T = X^2/Z$ [34].
- $\mathcal{H}$ - **Generalized Hessian**: if an elliptic curve (over a finite field) has a point of order 3, then it can be written in generalized Hessian form as $\mathcal{H}: x^3 + y^3 + c = dxy$ [20, Theorem 2]. The authors of [37,51] studied Hessian curves of the form $x^3 + y^3 + 1 = dxy$ for use in cryptography, and this was later generalized to include the parameter c [20]. The fastest formulas for ADD/MIX/AFF are from [7] while the fastest DBL formulas are from [32] – they work on the homogeneous projective curve given by $\mathcal{H}: X^3 + Y^3 + cZ^3 = dXYZ$, where $x = X/Z$, $y = Y/Z$. We note that the j-invariant zero version of $\mathcal{H}$ has $d = 0$ (see Sect. 4.3), so in Table 1 we give updated costs that include this speedup.
- $\mathcal{E}$ - **Twisted Edwards**: if an elliptic curve has a point of order 4, then it can be written in twisted Edwards form as $\mathcal{E}: ax^2 + y^2 = 1 + dx^2 y^2$ [6, Theorem 3.3]. However, if the field of definition, K, has $\#K \equiv 1 \bmod 4$, then $4 \mid E$ is enough to write E in twisted Edwards form [6, Sect. 3] (i.e. we do not necessarily need a point of order 4). Twisted Edwards curves [19] were introduced to cryptography in [6,10] and the best formulas are from [33].

Table 1. The costs of necessary operations for computing group exponentiations on four models of elliptic curves. Costs are reported as $T_{M,S,d,a}$, where M is the cost of a field multiplication, S is the cost of a field squaring, d is the cost of multiplication by a curve constant, a is the cost of a field addition (we have counted multiplications by 2 as additions), and T is the total number of multiplications, squarings, and multiplications by curve constants.

Model/coords	Requires	DBL cost	ADD cost	MIX cost	AFF cost
$\mathcal{W}$/Jac.	-	$7_{2,5,0,14}$	$16_{11,5,0,13}$	$11_{7,4,0,14}$	$6_{4,2,0,12}$
$\mathcal{J}$/ext.	pt. of order 2	$9_{1,7,1,12}$	$13_{7,3,3,19}$	$12_{6,3,3,18}$	$11_{5,3,3,18}$
$\mathcal{H}$/proj.	pt. of order 3	$7_{6,1,0,11}$	$12_{12,0,0,3}$	$10_{10,0,0,3}$	$8_{8,0,0,3}$
$\mathcal{E}$/ext.	pt. of order 4, or	$9_{4,4,1,7}$	$10_{9,0,1,7}$	$9_{8,1,0,7}$	$8_{7,0,1,7}$
	$4 \mid E$ and $\#K \equiv 1 \bmod 4$				

For each model, we summarize the cost of the required group operations in Table 1. The total number of field multiplications are reported in bold for each group operation – this includes multiplications, squarings and multiplications by constants. We note that in the context of plain ECC these models have been studied with small curve constants; in pairing-based cryptography, however, we must put up with whatever constants we get under the transformation to the non-Weierstrass model. The only exception we found in this work is for the $k = 12$ BLS curves, where $\mathbb{G}_1$ can be transformed to a Jacobi quartic curve with $a = -1/2$, which gives a worthwhile speedup [34].

4.2 Applicability of Alternative Curve Models for $k \in \{12, 18, 24\}$

In this section we prove the existence or non-existence of points of orders 2, 3 and 4 in the groups $E(\mathbb{F}_p)$ and $E'(\mathbb{F}_{p^{k/6}})$ for the pairing-friendly families considered in this work. These proofs culminate in Table 2, which summarizes the alternative curve models that are available for $\mathbb{G}_1$ and $\mathbb{G}_2$ in the scenarios we consider. We can study $\#E(\mathbb{F}_p)$ directly from the polynomial parameterizations in Sect. 2.1, while for $\#E'(\mathbb{F}_{p^e})$ (where $e = k/6$) we do the following. With the explicit recursion in [12, Corollary VI.2] we determine the parameters t_e and f_e which are related by the CM equation $4p^e = t_e^2 + 3f_e^2$ (since all our curves have CM discriminant $D = -3$). This allows us to compute the order of the correct sextic twist, which by [30, Proposition 2] is one of $n'_{e,1} = p^e + 1 - (3f_e + t_e)/2$ or $n'_{e,2} = p^e + 1 - (-3f_e + t_e)/2$. For $k = 12$ and $k = 24$ BLS curves, we assume that $p \equiv 3 \bmod 4$ so that $\mathbb{F}_{p^2}$ can be constructed (optimally) as $\mathbb{F}_{p^2} = \mathbb{F}_p[u]/(u^2 + 1)$. Finally, since $p \equiv 3 \bmod 4$, $E(\mathbb{F}_p)$ must contain a point of order 4 if we are to write E in twisted Edwards form; however, since E' is defined over $\mathbb{F}_{p^e}$, if e is even then $4 \mid E'$ is enough to write E' in twisted Edwards form (see Sect. 4.1).

Proposition 1. Let $E/\mathbb{F}_p$ be a BN curve with sextic twist $E'/\mathbb{F}_{p^2}$. The groups $E(\mathbb{F}_p)$ and $E'(\mathbb{F}_{p^2})$ do not contain points of order 2, 3 or 4.

Proof. From (1) we always have $\#E(\mathbb{F}_p) \equiv 1 \bmod 6$. Remark 2.13 of [44] shows that we have $\#E'(\mathbb{F}_{p^2}) = (p + 1 - t)(p - 1 + t)$, which from (1) gives that $\#E'(\mathbb{F}_{p^2}) \equiv 1 \bmod 6$. $\qquad\square$

Proposition 2. *For $p \equiv 3 \bmod 4$, let $E/\mathbb{F}_p$ be a $k = 12$ BLS curve with sextic twist $E'/\mathbb{F}_{p^2}$. The group $E(\mathbb{F}_p)$ contains a point of order 3 and can contain a point of order 2, but not 4, while the group $E'(\mathbb{F}_{p^2})$ does not contain a point of order 2, 3 or 4.*

Proof. From [12, Corollary VI.2] we have $t_2(x) = t(x)^2 - 2p(x)$, which with (2) and $4p(x)^2 = t_2(x)^2 + 3f_2(x)^2$ allows us to deduce that the correct twist order is $n'_{2,2}$, which gives $n'_{2,2}(x) \equiv 1 \bmod 12$ for $x \equiv 1 \bmod 3$, i.e. E' does not have points of order 2, 3 or 4. For E, (2) reveals that $3 \mid \#E$, and furthermore that $x \equiv 4 \bmod 6$ implies $\#E$ is odd, while for $x \equiv 1 \bmod 6$ we have $4 \mid \#E$. The assumption $p \equiv 3 \bmod 4$ holds if and only if $x \equiv 7 \bmod 12$, which actually implies $p \equiv 7 \bmod 12$. Now, to have a point of order 4 on $E/\mathbb{F}_p : y^2 = x^3 + b$, the fourth division polynomial $\psi_4(x) = 2x^6 + 40bx^3 - -8b^2$ must have a root $\alpha \in \mathbb{F}_p$, which happens if and only if $\alpha^3 = -10b \pm 6b\sqrt{3}$. However, [35, Sect. 5, Theorem 2-(b)] says that 3 is a quadratic residue in $\mathbb{F}_p$ if and only if $p \equiv \pm b^2 \bmod 12$, where b is co-prime to 3, which cannot happen for $p \equiv 7 \bmod 12$, so E does not have a point of order 4. $\qquad\square$

Proposition 3. *Let $E/\mathbb{F}_p$ be a $k = 18$ KSS curve with sextic twist $E'/\mathbb{F}_{p^3}$. The group $E(\mathbb{F}_p)$ does not contain a point of order 2, 3 or 4, while the group $E'(\mathbb{F}_{p^3})$ contains a point of order 3 but does not contain a point of order 2 or 4.*

Proof. From [12, Corollary VI.2] we have $t_3(x) = t(x)^3 - 3p(x)t(x)$. With (3) and $4p(x)^3 = t_3(x)^2 + 3f_3(x)^2$) it follows that $n'_{3,1}(x)$ is the correct twist order. We have $n'_{3,1}(x) \equiv 3 \bmod 12$ for $x \equiv 14 \bmod 42$, i.e. E' has a point of order 3 but no points of order 2 or 4. For E we have $\#E \equiv 1 \bmod 6$ from (3), which means there are no points of order 2, 3, or 4. $\qquad\square$

Proposition 4. *For $p \equiv 3 \bmod 4$, let $E/\mathbb{F}_p$ be a BLS curve with $k = 24$ and sextic twist $E'/\mathbb{F}_{p^4}$. The group $E(\mathbb{F}_p)$ can contain points of order 2 or 3 (although not simultaneously), but not 4, while the group $E'(\mathbb{F}_{p^4})$ can contain a point of order 2, but does not contain a point of order 3 or 4.*

Proof. Again, [12, Corollary VI.2] gives $t_4(x) = t(x)^4 - 4p(x)t(x)^2 + 2p(x)^2$, and from (4) and $4p(x)^4 = t_4(x)^2 + 3f_4(x)^2$ we get $n'_{4,1}(x)$ as the correct twist order. For $x \equiv 1 \bmod 6$ we have $n'_{4,1}(x) \equiv 1 \bmod 12$ (so no points of order 2, 3, or 4), while for $x \equiv 4 \bmod 6$ we have $n'_{4,1}(x) \equiv 4 \bmod 12$. Recall from the proof of Proposition 2 that $(\alpha, \beta) \in E'(\mathbb{F}_{p^4})$ is a point of order 4 if we have $\alpha \in \mathbb{F}_{p^4}$ such that $\alpha^3 = (-10 \pm 6\sqrt{3})b'$. The curve equation gives $\beta^2 = (-9 \pm 6\sqrt{3})b'$, i.e. b' must be a square in $\mathbb{F}_{p^4}$, which implies that $(0, \pm\sqrt{b'})$ are points of order 3 on $E'(\mathbb{F}_{p^4})$, which contradicts $n'_{4,1}(x) \equiv 1 \bmod 3$. Thus, $E'(\mathbb{F}_{p^4})$ cannot have points of order 3 or 4. For E, from (4) we have $\#E(\mathbb{F}_p) \equiv 3 \bmod 12$ if $x \equiv 4 \bmod 6$, but $\#E \equiv 0 \bmod 12$ if $x \equiv 1 \bmod 6$. Thus, there is a point of order 3 on E,

Table 2. Optional curve models for $\mathbb{G}_1$ and $\mathbb{G}_2$ in popular pairing implementations.

Family-k	$\mathbb{G}_1$ Algorithm	Models avail.	$\mathbb{G}_2$ Algorithm	Models avail.	Follows from
BN-12	2-GLV	$\mathcal{W}$	4-GLS	$\mathcal{W}$	Proposition 1
BLS-12	2-GLV	$\mathcal{H}, \mathcal{J}, \mathcal{W}$	4-GLS	$\mathcal{W}$	Proposition 2
KSS-18	2-GLV	$\mathcal{W}$	6-GLS	$\mathcal{H}, \mathcal{W}$	Proposition 3
BLS-24	2-GLV	$\mathcal{H}, \mathcal{J}, \mathcal{W}$	8-GLS	$\mathcal{E}, \mathcal{J}, \mathcal{W}$	Proposition 4

as well as a point of order 2 if $x \equiv 1 \bmod 6$. So it remains to check whether there is a point of order 4 when $x \equiv 1 \bmod 6$. Taking $x \equiv 1 \bmod 12$ gives rise to $p \equiv 1 \bmod 4$, so take $x \equiv 7 \bmod 12$. This implies that $p \equiv 7 \bmod 12$, and the same argument as in the proof of Proposition 2 shows that there is no point of order 4. □

In Table 2 we use the above propositions to summarize which (if any) of the non-Weierstrass models from Sect. 4.1 can be applied to our pairing scenarios.

4.3   Translating Endomorphisms to the Non-Weierstrass Models

In this section we investigate whether the GLV and GLS endomorphisms from Sect. 2.2 translate to the Jacobi quartic and Hessian models. Whether the endomorphisms translate desirably depends on how efficiently they can be computed on the non-Weierstrass model. It is not imperative that the endomorphisms do translate desirably, but it can aid efficiency: if the endomorphisms are not efficient on the alternative model, then our exponentiation routine also incurs the cost of passing points back and forth between the two models – this cost is small but could be non-negligible for high-dimensional decompositions. On the other hand, if the endomorphisms are efficient on the non-Weierstrass model, then the groups $\mathbb{G}_1$ and/or $\mathbb{G}_2$ can be defined so that all exponentiations take place directly on this model, and the computation of the pairing can be modified to include an initial conversion back to Weierstrass form.

We essentially show that the only scenario in which the endomorphisms are efficiently computable on the alternative model is the case of the GLV endomorphism ϕ on Hessian curves.

Endomorphisms on the Hessian Model. We modify the maps given in [20, Sect. 2.2] to the special case of j-invariant zero curves, where we have $d = 0$ on the Hessian model. Assume that $(0: \pm\alpha: 1)$ are points of order 3 on $\mathcal{W}: Y^2 Z = X^3 + \alpha^2 Z^3$, which is birationally equivalent to $\mathcal{H}: U^3 + V^3 + 2\alpha Z^3 = 0$. We define the constants $h_0 = \zeta - 1$, $h_1 = \zeta + 2$, $h_2 = -2(2\zeta + 1)\alpha$, where $\zeta^3 = 1$ and $\zeta \neq 1$. The map $\tau : \mathcal{W} \to \mathcal{H}$, $(X: Y: Z) \mapsto (U: V: W)$ is given as

$$U \leftarrow h_0 \cdot (Y + \alpha Z) + h_2 \cdot Z, \qquad V \leftarrow -U - 3(Y + \alpha Z), \qquad W \leftarrow 3X, \quad (6)$$

where $\tau(0\colon \pm \alpha\colon 1) = \mathcal{O} \in \mathcal{H}$. The inverse map $\tau^{-1}\colon \mathcal{H} \to \mathcal{W}$, $(U\colon V\colon W) \mapsto (X\colon Y\colon Z)$ is

$$X \leftarrow h_2 \cdot W, \qquad Z \leftarrow h_0 \cdot V + h_1 \cdot U, \qquad Y \leftarrow -h_2 \cdot (U + V) - \alpha \cdot Z. \quad (7)$$

It follows that the GLV endomorphism $\phi_{\mathcal{W}} \in \mathrm{End}(\mathcal{W})$ translates into $\phi_{\mathcal{H}} \in \mathrm{End}(\mathcal{H})$, where $\phi_{\mathcal{W}}\colon (X\colon Y\colon Z) \mapsto (\zeta X\colon Y\colon Z)$ becomes $\phi_{\mathcal{H}}\colon (U\colon V\colon W) \mapsto (U\colon V\colon \zeta W)$. However, we note that when computing $\phi_{\mathcal{H}}$ on an affine point, it can be advantageous to compute $\phi_{\mathcal{H}}$ as $\phi_{\mathcal{H}}\colon (u\colon v\colon 1) \mapsto (\zeta^2 u\colon \zeta^2 v\colon 1)$, where ζ^2 is the (precomputed) other cube root of unity, which produces an affine result.

For GLS on Hessian curves, there is no obvious or simple way to perform the analogous untwisting or twisting isomorphisms directly between $\mathcal{H}'(\mathbb{F}_{p^{k/6}})$ and $\mathcal{H}(\mathbb{F}_{p^k})$, which suggests that we must pass back and forth to the Weierstrass curve/s to determine the explicit formulas for the GLS endomorphism on $\mathcal{H}'$. The composition of these maps $\psi_{\mathcal{H}'} = \tau \circ \Psi_{\mathcal{W}}^{-1} \circ \pi_p \circ \Psi_{\mathcal{W}} \circ \tau^{-1}$ does not appear to simplify to be anywhere near as efficient as the GLS endomorphism is on the Weierstrass curve. Consequently, our GLS routine will start with a Weierstrass point in $\mathcal{W}'(\mathbb{F}_{p^{k/6}})$, where we compute $d - 1$ applications of $\psi \in \mathrm{End}(\mathcal{W}')$, before using (6) to convert the d points to $\mathcal{H}'(\mathbb{F}_{p^{k/6}})$, where the remainder of the routine takes place (save the final conversion back to $\mathcal{W}'$). Note that since we are converting affine Weierstrass points to $\mathcal{H}'$ via (6), this only incurs two multiplications each time. However, the results are now projective points on $\mathcal{H}'$ meaning that the more expensive full addition formulas must be used to generate the remainder of the lookup table.

Endomorphisms on the Jacobi Quartic Model. Unlike the Hessian model where the GLV endomorphism was efficient, for the Jacobi quartic model it appears that neither the GLV nor GLS endomorphisms translate to be of a similar efficiency as they are on the Weierstrass model. Thus, in all cases where Jacobi quartic curves are a possibility, we start and finish on $\mathcal{W}$, and only map to $\mathcal{J}$ after computing all applications of ϕ or ψ on the Weierstrass model. We adapt the maps given in [31, p. 17] to our special case as follows. Let $(-\theta\colon 0\colon 1)$ be a point of order 2 on $\mathcal{W}\colon Y^2 Z = X^3 + \theta^3 Z^3$ and let $a = 3\theta/4$ and $d = -3\theta^2/16$. The curve $\mathcal{W}$ is birationally equivalent to the (extended) Jacobi quartic curve $\mathcal{J}\colon V^2 W^2 = dU^4 + 2aU^2 W^2 + W^4$, with the map $\tau\colon \mathcal{W} \to \mathcal{J}$, $\tau\colon (X\colon Y\colon Z) \mapsto (U\colon V\colon W)$ given as

$$U \leftarrow 2YZ, \quad W \leftarrow X^2 - X\theta Z + \theta^2 Z^2, \quad V \leftarrow 6XZ\theta + W - 4aZ(\theta Z + X), \quad (8)$$

where $\tau((-\theta\colon 0\colon 1)) = (0\colon -1\colon 1) \in \mathcal{J}$. The inverse map $\tau^{-1}\colon \mathcal{J} \to \mathcal{W}$, $\tau^{-1}\colon (U\colon V\colon W) \mapsto (X\colon Y\colon Z)$, is given by

$$X \leftarrow (2V + 2)U + 2aU^3 - \theta U^3, \quad Y \leftarrow (4V + 4) + 4aU^2, \quad Z \leftarrow U^3, \quad (9)$$

where $\tau^{-1}((0\colon -1\colon 1)) = (-\theta\colon 0\colon 1) \in \mathcal{W}$ and the neutral point on $\mathcal{J}$ is $\mathcal{O}_{\mathcal{J}} = (0\colon 1\colon 1)$.

Endomorphisms on the Twisted Edwards Model. Similarly to the Jacobi-quartic model, endomorphisms on $\mathcal{E}$ are not nearly as efficiently computable as they are on $\mathcal{W}$, so we only pass across to $\mathcal{E}$ after the endomorphisms are applied on $\mathcal{W}$. Here we give the back-and-forth maps that are specific to our case(s) of interest. Namely, since we are unable to use twisted Edwards curves over the ground field (see Table 2), let $\mathcal{W}/\mathbb{F}_{p^e} : Y^2 Z = X^3 + b'Z^3$ for $p \equiv 3 \bmod 4$ and e being even. Since we have a point of order 2 on $\mathcal{W}$, i.e. $(\alpha : 0 : 1)$ with $\alpha = \sqrt[3]{-b'} \in \mathbb{F}_{p^e}$, then take $s = 1/(\alpha\sqrt{3}) \in \mathbb{F}_{p^e}$. The twisted Edwards curve $\mathcal{E} : aU^2W^2 + V^2W^2 = W^4 + dU^2V^2$ with $a = (3\alpha s + 2)/s$ and $d = (3\alpha s - 2)/s$ is isomorphic to $\mathcal{W}$, with the map $\tau : \mathcal{W} \to \mathcal{E}, (X:Y:Z) \mapsto (U:V:W)$ given as

$$U \leftarrow s(X - \alpha Z)(sX - s\alpha Z + Z), \quad V \leftarrow sY(sX - s\alpha Z - Z), \quad W \leftarrow sY(sX - s\alpha Z + Z),$$

with inverse map $\tau : \mathcal{E} \to \mathcal{W}, (U:V:W) \mapsto (X:Y:Z)$, given as

$$X \leftarrow -U(-W - V - \alpha s(W - V)), \quad Y \leftarrow (W + V)W, \quad Z \leftarrow sU(W - V).$$

4.4 Curve Choices for Pairings at the 128-, 192- and 256-bit Security Levels

The specific curves we choose in this section can use any of the alternative models that are available in the specific cases as shown in Table 2. The only exception occurs for $k = 24$, for which we are forced to choose between having a point of order 2 or 3 (see Proposition 4) in $\mathbb{G}_1$ – we opt for the point of order 3 and the Hessian model, as this gives enhanced performance. Note that these curves do not sacrifice any efficiency in the pairing computation compared to previously chosen curves in the literature (in terms of the field sizes, hamming-weights and towering options).

The $k = 12$ BN Curve. Since no alternative models are available for the BN family, we use the curve that was first seen in [45] and subsequently used to achieve speed records at the 128-bit security level [2], which results from substituting $x = -(2^{62} + 2^{55} + 1)$ into (1), and taking $E/\mathbb{F}_p : y^2 = x^3 + 2$ and $E'/\mathbb{F}_{p^2} : y^2 = x^3 + (1 - u)$, where $\mathbb{F}_{p^2} = \mathbb{F}_p[u]/(u^2 + 1)$.

The $k = 12$ BLS Curve. Setting $x = 2^{106} - 2^{72} + 2^{69} - 1$ in (2) gives a 635-bit prime p and a 424-bit prime r. Let $\mathbb{F}_{p^2} = \mathbb{F}_p[u]/(u^2 + 1)$ and let $\xi = u + 1$. The Weierstrass forms corresponding to $\mathbb{G}_1$ and $\mathbb{G}_2$ are $\mathcal{W}/\mathbb{F}_p : y^2 = x^3 + 1$ and $\mathcal{W}'/\mathbb{F}_{p^2} : y^2 = x^3 + \xi$. Only $\mathbb{G}_1$ has options for alternative models (see Table 2): the Hessian curve $\mathcal{H}/\mathbb{F}_p : x^3 + y^3 + 2 = 0$ and the Jacobi quartic curve $\mathcal{J}/\mathbb{F}_p : y^2 = \frac{-3}{16}x^4 + \frac{3}{4}x^2 + 1$ are both isomorphic to $\mathcal{W}$ over $\mathbb{F}_p$.

The $k = 18$ KSS Curve. Setting $x = 2^{64} - 2^{51} + 2^{47} + 2^{28}$ in (3) gives a 508-bit prime p and a 376-bit prime r. Let $\mathbb{F}_{p^3} = \mathbb{F}_p[u]/(u^3 + 2)$. The Weierstrass forms for $\mathbb{G}_1$ and $\mathbb{G}_2$ are $\mathcal{W}/\mathbb{F}_p : y^2 = x^3 + 2$ and $\mathcal{W}'/\mathbb{F}_{p^3} : y^2 = x^3 - u^2$. Only $\mathbb{G}_2$ allows for an alternative model (see Table 2): the Hessian curve $\mathcal{H}'/\mathbb{F}_{p^3} : x^3 + y^3 + 2u\sqrt{-1} = 0$ is isomorphic to $\mathcal{W}'$ over $\mathbb{F}_{p^3}$.

The $k = 24$ BLS Curve. Setting $x = 2^{63} - 2^{47} + 2^{38}$ in (3) gives a 629-bit prime p and a 504-bit prime r. Let $\mathbb{F}_{p^2} = \mathbb{F}_p[u]/(u^2+1)$ and $\mathbb{F}_{p^4} = \mathbb{F}_{p^2}[v]/(v^2 - (u+1))$. The Weierstrass forms corresponding to $\mathbb{G}_1$ and $\mathbb{G}_2$ are $\mathcal{W}/\mathbb{F}_p : y^2 = x^3 + 4$ and $\mathcal{W}'/\mathbb{F}_{p^4} : y^2 = x^3 + 4v$. This gives us the option of a Hessian model in $\mathbb{G}_1$: the curve $\mathcal{H}/\mathbb{F}_p : x^3 + y^3 + 4 = 0$ is isomorphic to $\mathcal{W}$ over $\mathbb{F}_p$. In $\mathbb{G}_2$ we have both the Jacobi quartic and twisted Edwards models as options. Let $\theta = (u+1)v$ and set $a = -3\theta/4$ and $d = (4A^2 - 3\theta^2)/4$. The curve $\mathcal{J}/\mathbb{F}_{p^4} : y^2 = dx^4 + ax^2 + 1$ is isomorphic to $\mathcal{W}'$ over $\mathbb{F}_{p^4}$. For the twisted Edwards model, we take $\alpha = \theta = (u+1)v$, $s = 1/(\alpha\sqrt{3}) \in \mathbb{F}_{p^4}$, $a' = (3\alpha s + 2)/s$ and $d' = (3\alpha s - 2)/s$; the curve $\mathcal{E}/\mathbb{F}_{p^4} : a'x^2 + y^2 = 1 + d'x^2y^2$ is then isomorphic to $\mathcal{W}'$.

5   Exponentiations in $\mathbb{G}_T$

For the scenarios in this paper, Galbraith and Scott [24] remark that the best known method for exponentiations in $\mathbb{G}_T \subset \mathbb{F}_{p^k}$ is to use the same $\varphi(k)$-dimensional decomposition that is used for GLS in $\mathbb{G}_2$. This means the same techniques for multi-exponentiation can be applied directly. The recoding technique (see Sect. 2.2) also carries across analogously, since inversions of $\mathbb{G}_T$-elements (which are conjugations over $\mathbb{F}_{p^{k/2}}$) are almost for free [24, Sect. 7], just as in the elliptic curve groups. For example, while the GLS map ψ on curves with $k = 12$ gives $\psi^4(Q') - \psi^2(Q') + Q' = \mathcal{O}$ for all $Q' \in \mathbb{G}_2'$, in $\mathbb{G}_T$ we use the p-power Frobenius map π_p, which gives $f \cdot \pi_p^4(f)/\pi_p^2(f) = 1$ for all $f \in \mathbb{G}_T$. Finally, $\mathbb{G}_T$ is contained in the cyclotomic subgroup of $\mathbb{F}_{p^k}^*$, in which much faster squarings are available [27,39]. The optimal choices of window sizes for the multi-exponentiation in $\mathbb{G}_T$ remain equal to those in $\mathbb{G}_2$ (see Sect. 3).

6   Results

In Table 3 we summarize the optimal curve choices in each scenario. We first note that Jacobi quartic curves were unable to outperform the Weierstrass, Hessian or twisted Edwards curves in any of the scenarios. This is because the small number of operations saved in a Jacobi quartic group addition were not enough to outweigh the slower Jacobi quartic doublings (see Table 1), and because of

Table 3. Optimal scenarios for group exponentiations. For both GLV on $\mathbb{G}_1$ and GLS on $\mathbb{G}_2$ in all four families, we give the decomposition dimension d, the maximum sizes of the mini-scalars $\|s_i\|_\infty$, the optimal window size w, and the optimal curve model.

Sec. level	Family-k	Exp. in $\mathbb{G}_1$				Exp. in $\mathbb{G}_2$			
		d	$\|s_i\|_\infty$	w	Curve	d	$\|s_i\|_\infty$	w	Curve
128-bit	BN-12	2	128	2	Weierstrass	4	64	1	Weierstrass
192-bit	BLS-12	2	212	3	Hessian	4	106	1	Weierstrass
	KSS-18	2	192	3	Weierstrass	6	63	1	Hessian
256-bit	BLS-24	2	252	3	Hessian	8	63	1	twisted Edwards

Table 4. Benchmark results for an optimal ate pairing and group exponentiations in $\mathbb{G}_1$, $\mathbb{G}_2$ and $\mathbb{G}_T$ in millions (M) of clock cycles for the best curve models. These results have been obtained on an Intel Core i7-3520M CPU averaged over thousands of random instances.

Sec. level	Family-k	Pairing e	Exp. in $\mathbb{G}_1$	Exp. in $\mathbb{G}_2$	Exp. in $\mathbb{G}_T$
128-bit	BN-12	7.0	0.9 ($\mathcal{W}$)	1.8 ($\mathcal{W}$)	3.1
192-bit	BLS-12	47.2	4.4 ($\mathcal{H}$)	10.9 ($\mathcal{W}$)	17.5
	KSS-18	63.3	3.5 ($\mathcal{W}$)	9.8 ($\mathcal{H}$)	15.7
256-bit	BLS-24	115.0	5.2 ($\mathcal{H}$)	27.6 ($\mathcal{E}$)	47.1

the extra computation incurred by the need to pass back and forth between $\mathcal{J}$ and $\mathcal{W}$ to compute the endomorphisms (see Sect. 4.3). On the other hand, while employing the Hessian and twisted Edwards forms also requires us to pass back and forth to compute the endomorphisms, the group law operations on these models are significantly faster than Weierstrass operations across the board, so Hessian and twisted Edwards curves reigned supreme whenever they were able to be employed – we give the concrete comparisons below. In Table 3 we also present the bounds we used on the maximum sizes of the mini-scalars resulting from a d-dimensional decomposition. In some cases, like those where decomposing s involves writing s in base λ_ϕ or λ_ψ, these bounds are trivially tight. However, in both the GLV and GLS on BN curves, and in the GLS on KSS curves, the bounds presented are those we obtained experimentally from hundreds of millions of scalar decompositions, meaning that the theoretical bounds could be a few bits larger – determining such bounds could be done using similar techniques to those in [41].

In Table 4 we present our timings for pairing computations and exponentiations in the three groups $\mathbb{G}_1$, $\mathbb{G}_2$ and $\mathbb{G}_T$, for the four families considered. We note that for 2-GLV on $k = 12$ BLS curves, Hessian curves gave a factor 1.23 speedup over Weierstrass curves (4.4M versus 5.4M cycles); for 6-GLS on $k = 18$ KSS curves, using Hessian curves gave a factor 1.11 speedup (9.8M versus 10.9M cycles); for 2-GLV on $k = 24$ BLS curves, Hessian curves gave a factor 1.19 speedup (5.2M versus 6.2M cycles); lastly, for 8-GLS on $k = 24$ BLS curves, twisted Edwards curves gave a factor 1.16 speedup (27.6M versus 31.9M cycles). The Hessian and twisted Edwards timings include the conversion from the Weierstrass model after the endomorphisms have been computed, and to the Weierstrass model at the end of the scalar multiplication routine.

In [1] it was first proposed to use $k = 12$ BLS curves for the 192-bit security level, by showing that pairings on these curves are significantly faster than pairings on $k = 18$ KSS curves. Our pairing timings add further weight to their claim. However, our timings also show that KSS curves are slightly faster for exponentiations in all three groups. There are many circumstances where Table 4 could guide implementers to make more efficient decisions when deploying a protocol. As one example, we refer to Boneh and Franklin's original identity-based encryption scheme [14, Sect. 4.1], where the sender computes a pairing between a public element P_{pub} and an identities' public key Q_{ID}, i.e. the sender computes

$g_{\text{ID}} = e(P_{\text{pub}}, Q_{\text{ID}})$. The sender then chooses a random exponent s and computes g_{ID}^s (which is hashed to become part of a ciphertext). In this case Table 4 shows that the sender would be much better off computing the scalar multiplication $[s]P_{\text{pub}}$ (assuming $P_{\text{pub}} \in \mathbb{G}_1$, or else we could compute $[s]Q_{\text{ID}}$) before computing the pairing $e([s]P_{\text{pub}}, Q_{\text{ID}}) = g_{\text{ID}}^s$.

Acknowledgment. We thank the reviewer who pointed out that having $4 \mid \#E(K)$ and $\#K \equiv 1 \bmod 4$ is sufficient to write E/K in twisted Edwards form.

References

1. Aranha, D.F., Fuentes-Castañeda, L., Knapp, E., Menezes, A., Rodríguez-Henríquez, F.: Implementing pairings at the 192-bit security level. In: Abdalla, M., Lange, T. (eds.) Pairing 2012. LNCS, vol. 7708, pp. 177–195. Springer, Heidelberg (2013)
2. Aranha, D.F., Karabina, K., Longa, P., Gebotys, C.H., López, J.: Faster explicit formulas for computing pairings over ordinary curves. In: Paterson, K.G. (ed.) EUROCRYPT 2011. LNCS, vol. 6632, pp. 48–68. Springer, Heidelberg (2011)
3. Barreto, P.S.L.M., Lynn, B., Scott, M.: Constructing elliptic curves with prescribed embedding degrees. In: Cimato, S., Galdi, C., Persiano, G. (eds.) SCN 2002. LNCS, vol. 2576, pp. 257–267. Springer, Heidelberg (2003)
4. Barreto, P.S.L.M., Naehrig, M.: Pairing-friendly elliptic curves of prime order. In: Preneel, B., Tavares, S. (eds.) SAC 2005. LNCS, vol. 3897, pp. 319–331. Springer, Heidelberg (2006)
5. Benger, N., Scott, M.: Constructing tower extensions of finite fields for implementation of pairing-based cryptography. In: Hasan, M.A., Helleseth, T. (eds.) WAIFI 2010. LNCS, vol. 6087, pp. 180–195. Springer, Heidelberg (2010)
6. Bernstein, D.J., Birkner, P., Joye, M., Lange, T., Peters, C.: Twisted Edwards curves. In: Vaudenay, S. (ed.) AFRICACRYPT 2008. LNCS, vol. 5023, pp. 389–405. Springer, Heidelberg (2008)
7. Bernstein, D.J., Kohel, D., Lange, T.: Twisted Hessian curves. http://www.hyperelliptic.org/EFD/g1p/auto-hessian-standard.html#addition-add-2001-jq
8. Bernstein, D.J., Lange, T.: Analysis and optimization of elliptic-curve single-scalar multiplication. In: Mullen, G., Panario, D., Shparlinski, I. (eds.) Finite Fields and Applications. Contemporary Mathematics Series, vol. 461, pp. 1–20. AMS, Providence (2007)
9. Bernstein, D.J., Lange, T.: Explicit-formulas database. http://www.hyperelliptic.org/EFD (2007)
10. Bernstein, D.J., Lange, T.: Faster addition and doubling on elliptic curves. In: Kurosawa, K. (ed.) ASIACRYPT 2007. LNCS, vol. 4833, pp. 29–50. Springer, Heidelberg (2007)
11. Billet, O., Joye, M.: The Jacobi model of an elliptic curve and side-channel analysis. In: Fossorier, M.P.C., Høholdt, T., Poli, A. (eds.) AAECC 2003. LNCS, vol. 2643, pp. 34–42. Springer, Heidelberg (2003)
12. Blake, I., Seroussi, G., Smart, N.: Elliptic Curves in Cryptography, vol. 265. Cambridge University Press, New York (1999)
13. Boneh, D., Boyen, X., Goh, E.-J.: Hierarchical identity based encryption with constant size ciphertext. In: Cramer, R. (ed.) EUROCRYPT 2005. LNCS, vol. 3494, pp. 440–456. Springer, Heidelberg (2005)

14. Boneh, D., Franklin, M.K.: Identity-based encryption from the Weil pairing. SIAM J. Comput. **32**(3), 586–615 (2003)
15. Bos, J.W., Costello, C., Hisil, H., Lauter, K.: High-performance scalar multiplication using 8-dimensional GLV/GLS decomposition. In: Bertoni, G., Coron, J.-S. (eds.) CHES 2013. LNCS, vol. 8086, pp. 331–348. Springer, Heidelberg (2013)
16. Brauer, A.: On addition chains. Bull. Am. Math. Soc. **45**, 736–739 (1939)
17. Costello, C., Lange, T., Naehrig, M.: Faster pairing computations on curves with high-degree twists. In: Nguyen, P.Q., Pointcheval, D. (eds.) PKC 2010. LNCS, vol. 6056, pp. 224–242. Springer, Heidelberg (2010)
18. Costello, C., Lauter, K., Naehrig, M.: Attractive subfamilies of BLS curves for implementing high-security pairings. In: Bernstein, D.J., Chatterjee, S. (eds.) INDOCRYPT 2011. LNCS, vol. 7107, pp. 320–342. Springer, Heidelberg (2011)
19. Edwards, H.M.: A normal form for elliptic curves. Bull. Am. Math. Soc. **44**(3), 393–422 (2007)
20. Farashahi, R.R., Joye, M.: Efficient arithmetic on Hessian curves. In: Nguyen, P.Q., Pointcheval, D. (eds.) PKC 2010. LNCS, vol. 6056, pp. 243–260. Springer, Heidelberg (2010)
21. Faz-Hernandez, A., Longa, P., Sanchez, A.H.: Efficient and secure algorithms for GLV-based scalar multiplication and their implementation on GLV-GLS curves. Cryptology ePrint Archive, Report 2013/158. http://eprint.iacr.org/ (2013). CT-RSA 2014, DOI:10.1007/978-3-319-04852-9_1
22. Galbraith, S.D.: Mathematics of Public Key Cryptography. Cambridge University Press, Cambridge (2012)
23. Galbraith, S.D., Lin, X., Scott, M.: Endomorphisms for faster elliptic curve cryptography on a large class of curves. J. Cryptol. **24**(3), 446–469 (2011)
24. Galbraith, S.D., Scott, M.: Exponentiation in pairing-friendly groups using homomorphisms. In: Galbraith, S.D., Paterson, K.G. (eds.) Pairing 2008. LNCS, vol. 5209, pp. 211–224. Springer, Heidelberg (2008)
25. Gallant, R.P., Lambert, R.J., Vanstone, S.A.: Faster point multiplication on elliptic curves with efficient endomorphisms. In: Kilian, J. (ed.) CRYPTO 2001. LNCS, vol. 2139, pp. 190–200. Springer, Heidelberg (2001)
26. Garg, S., Gentry, C., Halevi, S.: Candidate multilinear maps from ideal lattices. In: Johansson, T., Nguyen, P.Q. (eds.) EUROCRYPT 2013. LNCS, vol. 7881, pp. 1–17. Springer, Heidelberg (2013)
27. Granger, R., Scott, M.: Faster squaring in the cyclotomic subgroup of sixth degree extensions. In: Nguyen, P.Q., Pointcheval, D. (eds.) PKC 2010. LNCS, vol. 6056, pp. 209–223. Springer, Heidelberg (2010)
28. Groth, J.: Short pairing-based non-interactive zero-knowledge arguments. In: Abe, M. (ed.) ASIACRYPT 2010. LNCS, vol. 6477, pp. 321–340. Springer, Heidelberg (2010)
29. Hamburg, M.: Fast and compact elliptic-curve cryptography. Cryptology ePrint Archive, Report 2012/309. http://eprint.iacr.org/ (2012)
30. Hess, F., Smart, N.P., Vercauteren, F.: The Eta pairing revisited. IEEE Trans. Inf. Theor. **52**(10), 4595–4602 (2006)
31. Hisil, H.: Elliptic curves, group law, and efficient computation. Ph.D. thesis, Queensland University of Technology (2010)
32. Hisil, H., Carter, G., Dawson, E.: New formulae for efficient elliptic curve arithmetic. In: Srinathan, K., Rangan, C.P., Yung, M. (eds.) INDOCRYPT 2007. LNCS, vol. 4859, pp. 138–151. Springer, Heidelberg (2007)

33. Hisil, H., Wong, K.K.-H., Carter, G., Dawson, E.: Twisted Edwards curves revisited. In: Pieprzyk, J. (ed.) ASIACRYPT 2008. LNCS, vol. 5350, pp. 326–343. Springer, Heidelberg (2008)

34. Hisil, H., Wong, K.K.-H., Carter, G., Dawson, E.: Jacobi quartic curves revisited. In: Boyd, C., González Nieto, J. (eds.) ACISP 2009. LNCS, vol. 5594, pp. 452–468. Springer, Heidelberg (2009)

35. Ireland, K., Rosen, M.: A Classical Introduction to Modern Number Theory. Graduate Texts in Mathematics, vol. 84. Springer, New York (1990)

36. Joux, A.: A one round protocol for tripartite Diffie-Hellman. J. Cryptol. **17**(4), 263–276 (2004)

37. Joye, M., Quisquater, J.-J.: Hessian elliptic curves and side-channel attacks. In: Koç, Ç.K., Naccache, D., Paar, C. (eds.) CHES 2001. LNCS, vol. 2162, pp. 402–410. Springer, Heidelberg (2001)

38. Kachisa, E.J., Schaefer, E.F., Scott, M.: Constructing Brezing-Weng pairing-friendly elliptic curves using elements in the cyclotomic field. In: Galbraith, S.D., Paterson, K.G. (eds.) Pairing 2008. LNCS, vol. 5209, pp. 126–135. Springer, Heidelberg (2008)

39. Karabina, K.: Squaring in cyclotomic subgroups. Math. Comput. **82**(281), 555–579 (2013)

40. Koblitz, N., Menezes, A.: Pairing-based cryptography at high security levels. In: Smart, N.P. (ed.) Cryptography and Coding 2005. LNCS, vol. 3796, pp. 13–36. Springer, Heidelberg (2005)

41. Longa, P., Sica, F.: Four-dimensional Gallant-Lambert-Vanstone scalar multiplication. In: Wang, X., Sako, K. (eds.) ASIACRYPT 2012. LNCS, vol. 7658, pp. 718–739. Springer, Heidelberg (2012)

42. Miller, V.S.: The Weil pairing, and its efficient calculation. J. Cryptol. **17**(4), 235–261 (2004)

43. Montgomery, P.L.: Speeding the Pollard and elliptic curve methods of factorization. Math. Comput. **48**(177), 243–264 (1987)

44. Naehrig, M.: Constructive and computational aspects of cryptographic pairings. Ph.D. thesis, Eindhoven University of Technology (2009)

45. Nogami, Y., Akane, M., Sakemi, Y., Kato, H., Morikawa, Y.: Integer variable χ-based Ate pairing. In: Galbraith, S.D., Paterson, K.G. (eds.) Pairing 2008. LNCS, vol. 5209, pp. 178–191. Springer, Heidelberg (2008)

46. Park, Y.-H., Jeong, S., Lim, J.-I.: Speeding up point multiplication on hyperelliptic curves with efficiently-computable endomorphisms. In: Knudsen, L.R. (ed.) EUROCRYPT 2002. LNCS, vol. 2332, pp. 197–208. Springer, Heidelberg (2002)

47. Parno, B., Gentry, C., Howell, J., Raykova, M.: Pinocchio: nearly practical verifiable computation. In: Proceedings of the IEEE Symposium on Security and Privacy. IEEE (2013)

48. Pereira, G.C.C.F., Simplício Jr, M.A., Naehrig, M., Barreto, P.S.L.M.: A family of implementation-friendly BN elliptic curves. J. Syst. Softw. **84**(8), 1319–1326 (2011)

49. Sakai, R., Ohgishi, K., Kasahara, M.: Cryptosystems based on pairing. In: The 2000 Symposium on Cryptography and Information Security, Okinawa, Japan, pp. 135–148 (2000)

50. Silverman, J.H.: The Arithmetic of Elliptic Curves. Graduate Texts in Mathematics, vol. 106, 2nd edn. Springer, New York (2009)

51. Smart, N.P.: The Hessian form of an elliptic curve. In: Koç, Ç.K., Naccache, D., Paar, C. (eds.) CHES 2001. LNCS, vol. 2162, pp. 118–125. Springer, Heidelberg (2001)

Faster Repeated Doublings on Binary Elliptic Curves

Christophe Doche$^{(\boxtimes)}$ and Daniel Sutantyo

Department of Computing, Macquarie University, Sydney, Australia
{christophe.doche,daniel.sutantyo}@mq.edu.au

Abstract. The use of precomputed data to speed up a cryptographic protocol is commonplace. For instance, the owner of a public point P on an elliptic curve can precompute various points of the form $[2^k]P$ and transmit them together with P. One inconvenience of this approach though may be the amount of information that needs to be exchanged. In the situation where the bandwidth of the transmissions is limited, this idea can become impractical. Instead, we introduce a new scheme that needs only one extra bit of information in order to efficiently and fully determine a point of the form $[2^k]P$ on a binary elliptic curve. It relies on the *x-doubling* operation, which allows to compute the point $[2^k]P$ at a lower cost than with k regular doublings. As we trade off regular doublings for x-doublings, we use multi-scalar multiplication techniques, such as the Joint Sparse Form or interleaving with NAFs. This idea gives rise to several methods, which are faster than Montgomery's method in characteristic 2. A software implementation shows that our method called x-JSF$_2$ induces a speed-up between 4 and 18 % for finite fields $\mathbb{F}_{2^d}$ with d between 233 and 571. We also generalize to characteristic 2 the scheme of Dahmen et al. in order to precompute all odd points $[3]P$, $[5]P, \ldots, [2t-1]P$ in affine coordinates at the cost of a single inversion and some extra field multiplications. We use this scheme with x-doublings as well as with the window NAF method in López–Dahab coordinates.

Keywords: Public key cryptography · Elliptic curves · Scalar multiplication.

1 Introduction

We refer readers to [28] for Sutantyo, Daniel a general introduction to elliptic curves. An ordinary elliptic curve E defined over the finite field $\mathbb{F}_{2^d}$ can always be written with an equation of the form

$$E : y^2 + xy = x^3 + a_2 x^2 + a_6, \text{ with } a_2 \in \{0,1\}, a_6 \in \mathbb{F}_{2^d}^*. \tag{1}$$

This work was partially supported by ARC Discovery grant DP110100628.

This is an example of a curve in Weierstraß form. A point $P = (x_1, y_1)$ satisfying (1) is an *affine point* and the set of rational points of E, denoted by $E(\mathbb{F}_{2^d})$, corresponds to

$$E(\mathbb{F}_{2^d}) = \{(x_1, y_1) \in \mathbb{F}_{2^d} \times \mathbb{F}_{2^d} \mid y_1^2 + x_1 y_1 = x_1^3 + a_2 x_1^2 + a_6\} \cup P_\infty,$$

where P_∞ is a special point called the *point at infinity*. The set $E(\mathbb{F}_{2^d})$ can be endowed with an abelian group structure under a point addition operation, denoted by $+$, with P_∞ as the identity element. Naturally, this addition leads to the *scalar multiplication*

$$[n]P = \underbrace{P + P + \cdots + P}_{n \text{ times}},$$

for an integer $n \geqslant 1$ and a point $P \in E(\mathbb{F}_{2^d})$. Given n and P, there are very efficient techniques to compute $[n]P$, see Sect. 2.3. But the converse problem, known as the *Elliptic Curve Discrete Logarithm Problem* (ECDLP), appears to be intractable for a well chosen elliptic curve defined over $\mathbb{F}_{2^d}$ with d prime. Therefore the security of many protocols in elliptic curve cryptography relies on the hardness of the ECDLP. This makes scalar multiplication the most ubiquitous operation in any elliptic curve based protocols. See [3,5,6,14] for further discussions specific to the use of elliptic curves in cryptography.

2   State of the Art

2.1   Affine and López–Dahab Coordinates

Consider the elliptic curve E as in (1) and the point $P = (x_1, y_1) \in E(\mathbb{F}_{2^d})$. The double $P_2 = [2]P$ with coordinates (x_2, y_2) can be obtained with one inversion, two multiplications and one squaring. We abbreviate this as I+2M+S. There are similar formulas to compute the addition of two points at the cost of $I + 2M + S$ as well. In $\mathbb{F}_{2^d}$, represented by a polynomial basis, a squaring involves only a reduction. Thus it costs much less than a generic multiplication. Computing the inverse of an element $\alpha \in \mathbb{F}_{2^d}$ is more complex. We rely usually on the Extended Euclidean gcd algorithm or on the relation $\alpha^{-1} = \alpha^{2^d - 2}$. In software, an inversion can be cheaper than 10M, whereas the same operation can be extremely time consuming on platforms such as embedded devices. This explains why an alternate representation of E in projective coordinates is often considered. The equation

$$Y^2 + XYZ = X^3 Z + a_2 X^2 Z^2 + a_6 Z^4 \tag{2}$$

is an homogenized version of the equation E where the point P is represented in projective-like *López–Dahab* (LD) coordinates [17] by the triple $(X_1 : Y_1 : Z_1)$. When $Z_1 = 0$, the point P is the point at infinity whereas for $Z_1 \neq 0$, P corresponds to the affine point $(X_1/Z_1, Y_1/Z_1^2)$. The complexity of a doubling in LD coordinates is $3M + 1 \times a_6 + 5S$, including one multiplication by the fixed element a_6.

The addition of two points requires $13M + 4S$ in general, but only $8M + 5S$ in case at least one of the points is in affine coordinates, or in other words its Z-coordinate is equal to 1. This operation, that is very useful in practice, is referred to as a *mixed addition* [8]. See [4] for all the corresponding formulas.

2.2   Decompression Techniques in LD Coordinates

In the following, we show how the x-coordinate of a point together with one extra bit is enough to fully recover the point in affine coordinates. Indeed, let us consider a point P that is not the point at infinity nor a point of order 2 and which is represented by $(X_1 : Y_1 : Z_1)$ in LD coordinates. Assuming that we ignore Y_1 but know X_1 and Z_1 as well as the last bit of $Y_1/(X_1Z_1)$, let us see how to determine the affine coordinates x_1 and y_1 of P. Before we start, note that $Y_1/(X_1Z_1)$ is equal to y_1/x_1, so it is independent of the choice of the Z-coordinate of P in LD format.

Since P is on (2), it follows that Y_1 is a root of the quadratic equation

$$T^2 + TX_1Z_1 = X_1^3Z_1 + a_2X_1^2Z_1^2 + a_6Z_1^4.$$

The other root is $Y_1 + X_1Z_1$. The two solutions correspond to the points P and $-P$. Because of the assumption on P, we have $X_1Z_1 \neq 0$ so the change of variable $U = T\alpha$ where $\alpha = 1/(X_1Z_1)$ is valid and leads to the new equation

$$U^2 + U = \beta \qquad (3)$$

with $\beta = \alpha X_1^2 + a_2 + \alpha^2 a_6 Z_1^4$. To solve this equation let us introduce the half-trace function H defined by

$$H(\gamma) = \sum_{i=1}^{(d-1)/2} \gamma^{2^{2i}}.$$

When d is odd, it is well known that the solutions of Eq. (3) are $H(\beta)$ and $H(\beta) + 1$.

Clearly, we have $x_1 = \alpha X_1^2$. Now, let us explain how to find the correct value of y_1. It is easy to see that the solutions of (3) correspond to y_1/x_1 and $y_1/x_1 + 1$. So we can use the least significant bit of a root to identify the correct y_1. Let b be the last bit of y_1/x_1, then if the last bit of $H(\beta)$ is equal to b, set $y_1 = H(\beta)x_1$, otherwise $y_1 = (H(\beta) + 1)x_1$. The public point P can therefore be represented as (x_1, b) and we can fully determine P in affine coordinates with $I + H + 4M + 1 \times \sqrt{a_6} + 2S$, where H is the complexity to evaluate the half-trace function.

As the half-trace function is linear, its computation can be sped up significantly provided that there is enough memory to store some precomputed values. With those enhancements, we have in general $H \sim M$. See [2,14,15] for details.

Next, we review how to compute $[n]P$. Note that throughout the paper the coordinates of $[n]P$ are denoted by (x_n, y_n) or $(X_n : Y_n : Z_n)$.

2.3   Classical Scalar Multiplication Techniques

The simplest, yet efficient, way to perform a scalar multiplication $[n]P$ is the *double and add* method, which is a straightforward adaptation of the square and multiply algorithm used to compute an exponentiation. Given the binary representation of n, denoted by $(n_{\ell-1} \ldots n_0)_2$, a doubling is performed at each step followed by an addition if $n_i = 1$. The double and add method is therefore intrinsically linked to the binary representation of n. This is no surprise as the method used to perform the scalar multiplication $[n]P$ is often related to the representation of the integer n. Other choices are available to represent n, for instance in base 2^k for a fixed parameter k, or signed digits. A signed-digit expansion for an integer n is of the form

$$n = \sum_{i=0}^{\ell-1} c_i 2^i, \text{ with } c_i \in S,$$

where S is a finite set of acceptable coefficients. This is particularly interesting as a negative coefficient $-c$ in the representation of n induces the use of the point $-[c]P$ in the computation of $[n]P$. Note that $-[c]P$ can be obtained virtually for free from the point $[c]P$ in affine coordinates. The *Non-Adjacent Form* (NAF) [20,21] is especially relevant as the density of the expansion, i.e. the number of nonzero terms divided by the total length is equal to $\frac{1}{3}$ on average. Also for a given n, the NAF has the lowest density among all signed-digit expansions of n with coefficients in $\{-1, 0, 1\}$. A generalization of the NAF, called *window NAF of size w* [18,23,27] and denoted by NAF_w achieves an average density equal to $\frac{1}{w+1}$ for the set S of digits containing 0 and all the odd integers strictly less than 2^{w-1} in absolute value. For maximal efficiency, the points $[c]P$ are precomputed in affine coordinates for all the positive c in S. See [11] or [14] for more details on NAF and window NAF expansions.

It is often required, for instance during the verification phase of the ECDSA signature protocol, to perform a double-scalar multiplication of the form $[n_1]Q_1 + [n_0]Q_0$. Instead of computing each scalar multiplication separately, it is more efficient to combine the binary expansions of n_1 and n_0 in

$$\binom{n_1}{n_0} = \binom{u_{k-1} \ldots u_0}{v_{k-1} \ldots v_0}.$$

Mimicking the double and add method, we process a sequence of joint-bits, instead of a sequence of bits. At each step, a doubling is then followed by an addition of Q_1, Q_0, or $Q_1 + Q_0$ depending on the value of the joint-bit that is considered, i.e. $\binom{1}{0}$, $\binom{0}{1}$, or $\binom{1}{1}$. This idea, often attributed to Shamir is in fact a special case of an idea of Straus [26]. Mixing this idea with signed-digit representations gives birth to the *Joint Sparse Form* (JSF) [24] that can be seen as a generalization of the NAF for double-scalar multiplication. Indeed, the joint-density of the JSF is equal to $\frac{1}{2}$ on average and is optimal across all the joint signed-digit representations of n_1 and n_0. Note that the points Q_1, Q_0, $Q_1 + Q_0$, and $Q_1 - Q_0$ must be precomputed in affine coordinates for maximal efficiency. The JSF method is the standard way for computing a double-scalar multiplication when both points are not known in advance or when the amount of memory available on the device performing the computation is limited and does not allow the use of more precomputed values. Otherwise, *interleaving with NAFs* [14, Algorithm 3.51] gives excellent results. The principle of this approach is simply to form

$$\begin{pmatrix} n_1 \\ n_0 \end{pmatrix} = \begin{pmatrix} v_{k-1} \dots v_0 \\ u_{k-1} \dots u_0 \end{pmatrix}$$

where $(v_{k-1} \dots v_0)$ and $(u_{k-1} \dots u_0)$ are the window NAF expansions of n_1 and n_0, possibly padded with a few zeroes at the beginning. Note that we precompute only the points $[3]Q_i$, $[5]Q_i, \dots, [2^w - 1]Q_i$ for $i = 0$ and 1 and not all the combinations $[2s+1]Q_1 \pm [2t+1]Q_0$ as this option is too costly in most situations. It remains to compute all the doublings together and then perform at most two mixed additions at each step. Obviously, it is easy to generalize this idea to efficiently compute the $k + 1$ scalar multiplications $[n_k]Q_k + \cdots + [n_0]Q_0$ simultaneously provided that the points $[3]Q_i$, $[5]Q_i$, $\dots$, $[2^w - 1]Q_i$, for $i = 0, \dots, k$ are all precomputed.

2.4   Fixed Point Scalar Multiplication Using Precomputations

There are faster scalar multiplications techniques when the point P is known in advance and when some precomputations are available. For instance, we could considerably reduce the number of doublings, if not totally avoid them, by considering precomputed points of the form $[2^{ki}]P$ for a fixed k. Three methods, namely the Euclidean, Yao, and fixed-base comb, make use of this space-time trade-off to greatly reduce the complexity of a scalar multiplication. See [11, Sect. 9.3] for a presentation of those different methods.

If we consider a specific protocol such as ECDSA, Antipa et al. [1] show how to speed up the signature verification process by introducing the precomputed multiple $[2^k]P$ of the public point P, with $k = \lceil \ell/2 \rceil$. Tests show that the speed-up is significant, more than 35 % of the time saved, but this approach shares a drawback with the techniques discussed so far: it requires to transmit an important amount of additional data on top of the public point P.

When exchanging large volume of data is not practical, for instance because the bandwidth of the network is limited, the methods described in this part do not apply, even if the point P is known in advance. Instead, Montgomery's method is perfectly suited, as it allows to perform arithmetic on an elliptic curve using only the x-coordinate of P.

2.5   Montgomery's Method

Montgomery developed an efficient arithmetic for special elliptic curves defined over a prime field [19]. Ultimately, it relies on the possibility to derive the x-coordinate of $P + Q$ from the x-coordinates of P, Q, and $P - Q$. This approach has been generalized to binary curves by López and Dahab [16]. Indeed, starting from P in LD coordinates and assuming that we know at each step the X and Z coordinates of $[u]P$ and of $[u+1]P$, we can determine the X and Z coordinates of $[2u]P$ and $[2u+1]P$. See [16,25] for the actual formulas. The full scalar multiplication $[n]P$ can then be computed with Montgomery's ladder, which requires an addition and a doubling at each step. If the square root of a_6 is precomputed, the complexity of the scheme is $(5M + 1 \times \sqrt{a_6} + 4S)$ per bit of the scalar.

3   Applications of x-doublings to Scalar Multiplication

We have just seen that the x-coordinate of $[2]P$ only depends on the x-coordinate of the point P itself. Namely, if $P = (X_1 : Y_1 : Z_1)$, we have $[2]P$ given by $X_2 = X_1^4 + a_6 Z_1^4 = (X_1^2 + \sqrt{a_6} Z_1^2)^2$ and $Z_2 = X_1^2 Z_1^2$. In the following, we refer to this operation as an x-*doubling*. We can compute an x-doubling with $M + 1 \times \sqrt{a_6} + 3S$. This means that an x-doubling saves $2M + 2S$ compared to a regular doubling in LD coordinates. A doubling in LD coordinates costs $3M + 1 \times a_6 + 5S$ in the same conditions. From now on, we assume that $\sqrt{a_6}$ is precomputed and does not enjoy any special property so that $1 \times \sqrt{a_6} = 1M$.

We propose to speed up the scalar multiplication $[n]P$ by replacing some regular LD doublings with x-doublings. To take full advantage of this operation, our idea is to determine the x-coordinate of $[2^k]P$ using k successive x-doublings and then recover the y-coordinate using decompression techniques and one extra known bit of information.

3.1   Double Scalar Multiplication and x-Doublings

Let ℓ be the bit size of the order of a point P and $k = \lfloor \ell/2 \rfloor$. Let (x_1, b) be the public information corresponding to the point P, as explained in Sect. 2.2. We assume that the owner of the point P has also precomputed b_k, i.e. the last bit of y_{2^k}/x_{2^k}, and made it public.

Let n be an integer of size ℓ bits. It is clear that $[n]P = [n_1]Q_1 + [n_0]Q_0$ where $n = 2^k n_1 + n_0$, $Q_1 = [2^k]P$, and $Q_0 = P$. The X and Z coordinates of Q_1 can be obtained with k straight x-doublings at a cost of $(2M+3S)k$. Then we can recover the y-coordinates of Q_0 and Q_1 using b and b_k with decompression techniques. For that, we compute $\beta = \alpha x_1^2 + a_2 + a_6 \alpha^2$ and $\beta_k = \alpha_k X_{2^k}^2 + a_2 + a_6 \alpha_k^2 Z_k^4$ where $\alpha = 1/x_1$ and $\alpha_k = 1/(X_{2^k} Z_{2^k})$. Montgomery's trick [19] allows to obtain α and α_k with only one inversion and three extra multiplications. Then we compute the half-trace of β and β_k and identify the correct root with the bits b and b_k. Assuming that a_6 is a random element of $\mathbb{F}_{2^d}$ and that $\sqrt{a_6}$ has been precomputed, the complexity to determine Q_0 and Q_1 in affine coordinates is $I+2H+12M+4S$. This approach can easily be generalized to retrieve an arbitrary number of points. It then takes $I + tH + (7t - 2)M + 2tS$ to fully determine Q_0, $Q_1, \ldots, Q_{t-1}$ in affine coordinates once the X and Z coordinates of those points have been obtained using x-doublings.

Now that we have Q_0 and Q_1 in affine coordinates, we can compute $[n]P = [n_1]Q_1 + [n_0]Q_0$ with any standard double scalar multiplication technique, for instance the JSF, see Sect. 2.3. In this case, the complexity is approximately $\ell/2$ x-doublings, $\ell/2$ regular doublings, and $\ell/4$ mixed additions using the four points Q_0, Q_1, $Q_0 + Q_1$, and $Q_0 - Q_1$. Note that $Q_0 + Q_1$ and $Q_0 - Q_1$ should be computed simultaneously with $I + 4M + 2S$.

This new approach, called x-JSF, compares favorably against the window NAF_w method in LD coordinates and Montgomery's approach. Both are very popular methods in practice for a wide range of extension degrees when only the x-coordinate of the point P is transmitted. The x-JSF requires essentially $5M + 5.25S$ per bit compared to $6M + 4S$ for Montgomery's method. Adding the complexities of all the steps involved, including the cost of precomputations, and assuming that $H = M$, we obtain the following result.

Proposition 1. *Let n be an integer of binary length ℓ. The average complexity of the x-JSF method to compute the scalar multiplication $[n]P$ is*

$$\left(5M + \tfrac{21}{4}S\right)\ell + 3I + 20M + 7S.$$

Proof. Starting from the x-coordinate of P, we do $\tfrac{\ell}{2}$ consecutive x-doublings with $\left(M + \tfrac{3}{2}S\right)\ell$. We need $I + 12M + 4S$ to form the two quadratic equations and $2M$ to solve them in order to obtain P and $[2^{\lfloor \ell/2 \rfloor}]P$ in affine coordinates. We then need $I + 4M + 2S$ to compute the sum and difference of those two points in affine coordinates again. Then, we perform $\tfrac{\ell}{2}$ regular doublings, with $\left(2M + \tfrac{5}{2}S\right)\ell$, and $\tfrac{\ell}{4}$ mixed additions on average, with $\left(2M + \tfrac{5}{4}S\right)\ell$. Finally, we express the point in affine coordinates with $I + 2M + S$. $\square$

3.2   Trading Off More Doublings for x-Doublings

Previously, we explained how to replace approximately 50 % of normal doublings by x-doublings. Since an x-doubling is significantly cheaper than a doubling, it is natural to try to increase this ratio, i.e. replace more doublings with x-doublings. A simple idea is for instance to work with three shares instead of two, i.e. fix $k = \lfloor \ell/3 \rfloor$ and write $n = 2^{2k}n_2 + 2^k n_1 + n_0$. If we fix $Q_0 = P$, $Q_1 = [2^k]P$ and $Q_2 = [2^{2k}]P$, we see that $[n]P = [n_2]Q_2 + [n_1]Q_1 + [n_0]Q_0$. We denote by w-w-w the generalization of the interleaving with NAFs method, where the NAF_w expansions of n_2, n_1, and n_0 are stacked together as follows

$$\begin{pmatrix} n_2 \\ n_1 \\ n_0 \end{pmatrix} = \begin{pmatrix} w_k \ \dots \ w_0 \\ v_k \ \dots \ v_0 \\ u_k \ \dots \ u_0 \end{pmatrix}.$$

and processed from left to right using Straus' idea, see Sect. 2.3. The only points that we precompute are $[3]Q_i$, $[5]Q_i, \dots, [2^{w-1} - 1]Q_i$, for $i \in [0, 2]$.

Proposition 2. *Let n be an integer of binary length ℓ. The average complexity of the w-w-w interleaving with NAFs method to compute the scalar multiplication*

$[n]P$ *with* $w > 3$ *is*

$$((8w + 32)M + (11w + 26)S)\frac{\ell}{3(w + 1)} + 3 \times 2^{w-2}(I + 2M + S) + 2I + 24M + 7S.$$

For $w = 3$, *the complexity is simply*

$$(\tfrac{14}{3}M + \tfrac{59}{12}S)\ell + 5I + 42M + 19S.$$

Proof. The proof is similar to Proposition 1. It is clear that we need $2\frac{\ell}{3}$ successive x-doublings and $\frac{\ell}{3}$ normal doublings, plus a certain number of additions, which depends on the size of the window w. The exact number can be derived via some probabilistic analysis. Given that the density of the NAF_w is $\frac{1}{w+1}$, we may assume that the probability for a coefficient in a long expansion to be nonzero is $\frac{1}{w+1}$. It follows that the w-w-w interleaving method requires $\frac{\ell}{w+1}$ mixed additions on average. To determine the precomputations, we could compute $[2]Q_0$, $[2]Q_1$, and $[2]Q_2$ in LD coordinates, make those three points affine simultaneously, before performing $3(2^{w-2} - 1)$ LD mixed additions, and converting all the resulting points to affine simultaneously again. This approach only needs two inversions. Instead, in our implementation as well as in this analysis, we perform all the computations directly in affine coordinates for simplicity. The formula follows by adding all the different contributions.

The complexity is very low, but in practice the main drawback of this approach is the number of precomputations, which grows as $3 \times 2^{w-2}$. Another method along those lines, called $x - \mathrm{JSF}_2$, requires less storage and involves splitting n in four shares as $2^{3k}n_3 + 2^{2k}n_2 + 2^k n_1 + n_0$ with $k = \lfloor \ell/4 \rfloor$. The points $Q_3 = [2^{3k}]P$, $Q_2 = [2^{2k}]P$, $Q_1 = [2^k]P$, $Q_0 = P$ are determined after $3\frac{\ell}{4}$ straight x-doublings. Four extra bits of information are necessary to fully recover the points. Then we compute the JSF expansions of n_3 and n_2 and of n_1 and n_0, together with the precomputed affine points $Q_3 \pm Q_2$, and $Q_1 \pm Q_0$. We then need $\frac{\ell}{4}$ regular LD doublings as well as $\frac{\ell}{4}$ mixed additions. The following result follows immediately.

Proposition 3. *Let* n *be an integer of binary length* ℓ. *The average complexity of the* x-JSF_2 *method to compute the scalar multiplication* $[n]P$ *is*

$$(\tfrac{9}{2}M + \tfrac{19}{4}S)\ell + 4I + 40M + 13S.$$

Proof. We perform $3\frac{\ell}{4}$ x-doublings, then need $I + 30M + 8S$ to recover the four points Q_0, Q_1, Q_2, and Q_3 in affine coordinates. We need $2(I + 4M + 2S)$ to compute $Q_3 \pm Q_2$ and $Q_1 \pm Q_0$. Then, we perform $\frac{\ell}{4}$ regular doublings and $\frac{\ell}{4}$ mixed additions on average. Finally, we express the point in affine coordinates with $I + 2M + S$.

Tests show that the x-JSF_2 achieves a speed-up close to $18\,\%$ over the fastest known method in $\mathbb{F}_{2^{571}}$, i.e. Montgomery's method. See Sect. 5 for details.

3.3 Trading Off Even More Doublings for x-Doublings

In some sense, the x-JSF_2 relies on interleaving with JSFs. Generalizing this idea, the x-JSF_t uses 2^t shares, each of size $\ell/2^t$ bits, and needs $\frac{2^t-1}{2^t}$ x-doublings and $\frac{1}{2^t}$ regular doublings. Arranging the scalars two by two, and computing their corresponding JSF expansions, we see that $\frac{\ell}{4}$ mixed additions are necessary on average, provided that we precompute 2^{t-1} pairs of points of the form $Q_{2i+1}\pm Q_{2i}$.

To further reduce the number of regular doublings without using precomputations, we turn our attention to a method first described by de Rooij, but credited to Bos and Coster [10]. As previously, write n in base 2^k, for a well chosen k. It follows that $[n]P = [n_{t-1}]Q_{t-1} + \cdots + [n_0]Q_0$, where $Q_i = [2^{ki}]P$.

The main idea of the Bos–Coster method is to sort the shares in decreasing order according to their coefficients and to recursively apply the relation

$$[n_1]Q_1 + [n_2]Q_2 = [n_1](Q_1 + [q]Q_2) + [n_2 - qn_1]Q_2$$

where $n_2 > n_1$ and $q = \lfloor n_2/n_1 \rfloor$. The process stops when there is only one nonzero scalar remaining. Because the coefficients are roughly of the same size throughout the process, we have $q = 1$ at each step almost all the time. This implies that $[n]P$ can be computed almost exclusively with additions once the shares Q_i's are obtained via x-doublings.

Clearly, this approach requires $k(t-1)$ successive x-doublings and t point reconstructions. The precise number of additions involved is much harder to analyze but can be approximated by $\frac{\ell}{\log k}$ for reasonable values of k. So, with the Bos–Coster method, we have replaced almost all the doublings by x-doublings, but one detail plays against us. Most of the additions that we need are full additions and not mixed additions as it was the case for the x-JSF and interleaving with NAFs. Indeed, even if the different points $Q_0, \ldots, Q_{t-1}$ are initially expressed in affine coordinates, then after a few steps of the algorithm, it is no longer the case and subsequent additions need to be performed in full. Those full additions are too expensive to make this scheme competitive with Montgomery's method.

Next, we investigate Yao's method [29]. As for the previous approach, we express n in base 2^k as $(n_{t-1} \ldots n_0)_{2^k}$ and we consider the points $Q_i = [2^{ki}]P$, for $i = 0, \ldots, t-1$, obtained with x-doublings only. Note that we can rewrite the sum $[n]P = [n_{t-1}]Q_{t-1} + \cdots + [n_0]Q_0$ as

$$[n]P = \sum_{j=1}^{2^k-1} [j]\left(\sum_{n_i=j} Q_i\right).$$

We deduce the following algorithm. Starting from $T = P_\infty$, $R = P_\infty$, and $j = 2^k - 1$, we repeat $R = R + Q_i$ for each i such that $n_i = j$, followed by $T = T + R$ and $j = j - 1$ until $j = 0$.

To update R, we use mixed additions, but the statement $T = T + R$ requires a full LD addition. Therefore, the complexity of this approach is essentially $k(t-1)$ successive x-doublings, t point reconstructions, $\left(1 - \frac{1}{2^k}\right)t$ mixed additions on average, and 2^k full additions. In order to minimize the number of full additions, we need to keep k low, which means increasing t. This increases the number of mixed additions. Also it is quite expensive to retrieve a point in affine coordinates from its X, Z-coordinates and the last bit of y/x. As explained in Sect. 3.1, we need $H + 7M + 2S$ per additional point Q_i to fully recover it in affine coordinates. This proves to be too much and all the parameters k that we tried failed to introduce any improvement over Montgomery's method.

3.4 Generic Protocol Setup Compatible with x-doublings

The purpose of this article is to evaluate the relevance of x-doublings to perform a scalar multiplication, not to precisely describe how to use this operation in a specific protocol. However, it seems that the most realistic setup to use one of the schemes presented in Sects. 3.1 and 3.2 is for the owner of a point P to precompute and store the last bit b_k of y_{2^k}/x_{2^k}, for all $k \in [0, d + 1]$. This of course is done only once at the very beginning and does not affect the security of the scheme. Since P is public, anybody can perform the computations and retrieve those bits. The other party can then access x_1, the x-coordinate of P, as well as a few bits b_k. At most four bits are sufficient to deliver a significant speed-up with the x-JSF$_2$ approach, see Sect. 5. The choice of those bits does not reveal anything on the scalar n except maybe its size, which we do not see as a problem.

4 Affine Precomputations with Sole Inversion in Char 2

The other contribution of this paper is a generalization of the work of Dahmen et al. [9] to precompute all the affine points required by the NAF$_w$ method with just one inversion. Indeed, starting from the affine point P, Dahmen et al. show how to obtain $[3]P$, $[5]P, \ldots, [2t - 1]P$ also in affine coordinates with $I + (10t - 11)M + 4tS$. But their work only addresses the case of large odd characteristic.

With a generalized scheme, we can precompute all the points necessary for the w-w-w interleaving with NAFs method with just three inversions instead of $3 \times 2^{w-2}$, using affine arithmetic. We mimic their approach and follow three easy steps. First, we compute all the denominators involved. Then we apply Montgomery's inversion trick [19] that combines j inversions in $\mathbb{F}_{2^d}$ at the expense of one inversion and $3j - 3$ field multiplications. Finally, we reconstruct all the points. The total complexity to compute $[2]P$, $[3]P$, $[5]P, \ldots, [2t-1]P$ for $t > 2$ is $I + (11t - 13)M + 2tS$. See the Appendix for the actual algorithm. When we only need $[3]P$, for instance for the NAF$_3$, we compute $[3]P$ directly following the approach explained in [7]. Note however that $I + 6M + 4S$ are enough to determine $[3]P$, saving one multiplication.

5   Tests and Results

To validate the use of the x-doubling operation and the methods described in Sect. 3, we have implemented all of them in C++ using NTL 6.0.0 [22] built on top of GMP 5.1.2 [13]. The program is compiled and executed on a quad core i7-2620 at 2.70Ghz.

In the following, we test some of the techniques described in Sects. 2 and 3 to perform a scalar multiplication on a random curve defined over $\mathbb{F}_{2^d}$ for $d = 233$, 409, and 571. Namely, we compare the following methods: Montgomery (Mont.), window NAF in LD coordinates with $w \in [2,6]$ (NAF_w), x-JSF, x-JSF$_2$, and interleaving with NAFs (w-w-w). Note that $\underline{\mathrm{NAF}_w}$ and $\underline{w - w - w}$ are slightly different variants where the precomputations are obtained with the sole inversion technique, explained in Sect. 4. We generate a total of 100 curves of the form

$$E : y^2 + xy = x^3 + x^2 + a_6,$$

where a_6 is a random element of $\mathbb{F}_{2^d}^*$. For each curve, a random point P is created as well as 100 random scalars selected in the interval $[0, 2^d + 2^{d/2} - 1]$. We assume that the point P needs to be decompressed for all the methods. The different methods are then tested against the same curves, points, and scalars. The computations are timed over 10 repetitions.

Together with the average timings of the best methods in each category, we present the average number of basic operations required to compute $[n]P$. Those basic operations, i.e. inversion, half-trace computation, multiplication, and squaring in $\mathbb{F}_{2^d}$ are respectively represented by I_d, H_d, M_d, and S_d. In any case we have, $\mathrm{I}_d/\mathrm{M}_d$ between 8 and 10, and $\mathrm{S}_d/\mathrm{M}_d$ between 0.14 and 0.23.

See Table 1 for the actual figures, which features timings and operation counts of the x-JSF, the x-JSF$_2$, as well as the fastest interleaving with NAFs methods among w-w-w, for $w \in [2,5]$ and among $\underline{w - w - w}$ again for $w \in [2,5]$. Table 1 also includes the number of stored points required by each method ($\#\mathcal{P}$), and the improvement, if any, over Montgomery's method and the fastest window NAF method.

With our implementation, the x-JSF$_2$ breaks even with Montgomery's method around $d = 233$ and enjoys a much bigger speed-up for larger degrees, reflecting Proposition 3. The interleaving with NAFs method $\underline{5\text{-}5\text{-}5}$ is the fastest of all for $d = 571$, with a speed-up that is close to 20 %.

Remark 1. *A careful reader would have noticed that for $d = 233$, $\underline{3\text{-}3\text{-}3}$ is faster than $\underline{4\text{-}4\text{-}4}$. This is surprising for two reasons. First, 4-4-4 is faster than 3-3-3 Second, it is more efficient, given the value of the ratio $\mathrm{I}_{233}/\mathrm{M}_{233}$, to determine the precomputations using the single inversion approach. So $\underline{4\text{-}4\text{-}4}$ should be faster. This is confirmed by an analysis of the average numbers of multiplications and squarings required. Indeed, we need $1112\mathrm{M} + 1120\mathrm{S}$ for $\underline{4\text{-}4\text{-}4}$, against $1143\mathrm{M} + 1165\mathrm{S}$ for $\underline{3\text{-}3\text{-}3}$. We observe the same phenomenon for degrees $d = 163$ and $d = 283$, but not for $d = 409$ or $d = 571$. We explain this by the large number of variables needed to determine the precomputations when $w > 3$. See the Appendix for details. For $w = 3$, the formulas are simpler, requiring much less*

Table 1. Comparison of different methods for degrees 233, 409, and 571

Degree 233: $I_{233}/M_{233} = 8.651$ and $S_{233}/M_{233} = 0.226$						
	$\#\mathcal{P}$	I_{233}	H_{233}	M_{233}	S_{233}	Time (ms)	Speed-up (%)
Mont.	1	2	0	1402	928	1.102	0
NAF$_5$	8	10	0	1253	1360	1.221	-10.81
NAF$_5$	8	3	0	1312	1368	1.241	-12.66
x-JSF	4	3	2	1181	1229	1.118	-1.51
x-JSF$_2$	8	4	4	1094	1126	1.053	4.43
4-4-4	12	14	3	1043	1108	1.079	2.05
3-3-3	6	5	3	1143	1165	1.083	1.70
Degree 409: $I_{409}/M_{409} = 9.289$ and $S_{409}/M_{409} = 0.140$						
	$\#\mathcal{P}$	I_{409}	H_{409}	M_{409}	S_{409}	Time (ms)	Speed-up (%)
Mont.	1	2	0	2457	1631	4.289	-0.68
NAF$_5$	8	10	0	2192	2386	4.267	-0.16
NAF$_5$	8	3	0	2251	2394	4.260	0
x-JSF	4	3	2	2061	2153	3.928	7.79
x-JSF$_2$	8	4	4	1885	1962	3.650	14.33
4-4-4	12	14	3	1793	1929	3.667	13.94
4-4-4	12	5	3	1862	1941	3.752	11.94
Degree 571: $I_{571}/M_{571} = 9.212$ and $S_{571}/M_{571} = 0.153$						
	$\#\mathcal{P}$	I_{571}	H_{571}	M_{571}	S_{571}	Time (ms)	Speed-up (%)
Mont.	1	2	0	3430	2280	10.986	0
NAF$_6$	16	18	0	2961	3269	12.154	-10.64
NAF$_6$	16	3	0	3092	3285	12.464	-13.46
x-JSF	4	3	2	2871	3004	10.153	7.58
x-JSF$_2$	8	4	4	2618	2735	9.014	17.94
5-5-5	24	26	3	2355	2601	8.843	19.51
5-5-5	24	5	3	2532	2625	8.810	19.81

intermediate storage. This overhead of declaring and manipulating extra variables tends to have less impact for larger degrees because multiplications and squarings take relatively longer.

6   Conclusion and Future Work

We have shown how to make use of x-doublings to compute a scalar multiplication on a binary elliptic curve. Our main approach is to trade off regular doublings for cheaper x-doublings using classical multi-scalar multiplication techniques.

Unfortunately, it seems impossible to generalize the use of x-doublings in large characteristic, since solving quadratic equations is much slower than in characteristic 2.

A possible generalization of this work would be to investigate which endomorphisms different from doublings enjoy similar properties, i.e. have an x-coordinate that can be computed efficiently and independently from the y-coordinate. Certain endomorphisms $[k]P$ that can be split as the product of two isogenies on special families of curves are known to have this property [12]. It would be interesting to see what kind of improvements those endomorphisms could bring when it comes to computing a scalar multiplication.

Acknowledgments. We would like to thank Tanja Lange and Daniel J. Bernstein as well as the reviewers of this article for their numerous comments and suggestions, which greatly contributed to improve its contents.

Appendix: Affine Precomputations with Sole Inversion in Characteristic 2

Let $P = (x_1, y_1)$ be a point on the curve $y^2 + xy = x^3 + a_2 x^2 + a_6$. For $t > 2$, the following procedure computes the points $[2]P, [3]P, [5]P, \ldots, [2t-1]P$ with $I + (11t - 13)M + 2tS$.

```
Step 1. Computing all the denominators dᵢ's to be inverted
```
$d_1 \leftarrow x_1, \quad s_1 \leftarrow d_1^2, \quad c_1 \leftarrow s_1 \cdot d_1, \quad n_1 \leftarrow s_1 + y_1$
$A \leftarrow n_1(n_1 + d_1), \quad d_2 \leftarrow A + (d_1 + a_2)s_1$
$B \leftarrow d_1 \cdot d_2, \quad C \leftarrow B + s_1^2, \quad n_2 \leftarrow n_1 \cdot d_2 + C$
$s_2 \leftarrow d_2^2, \quad A \leftarrow A \cdot s_2, \quad c_2 \leftarrow s_2 \cdot d_2, \quad d_3 \leftarrow A + n_2(n_2 + B) + c_2$
```
for i = 3 to t − 1 do
```
$\quad B \leftarrow B \cdot d_i, \quad C \leftarrow C \cdot c_{i-1}, \quad n_i \leftarrow n_{i-1} \cdot d_i + B + C$
$\quad s_i \leftarrow d_i^2, \quad A \leftarrow A \cdot s_i, \quad c_i \leftarrow s_i \cdot d_i, \quad d_{i+1} \leftarrow A + n_i(n_i + B) + c_i$
```
end for
```


```
Step 2. Montgomery's inversion trick
```
$B \leftarrow B \cdot d_t, \quad INV \leftarrow B^{-1}, \quad e_1 \leftarrow c_1$
```
for i = 2 to t − 1 do
```
$\quad e_i \leftarrow e_{i-1} \cdot c_i$
```
end for
```


```
Step 3. Reconstructing the points
for i = t down to 2 do
```
$\quad j_i \leftarrow INV \cdot e_{i-1}, \quad INV \leftarrow INV \cdot d_i$
```
end for
```
$j_1 \leftarrow INV$
$\lambda_2 \leftarrow j_1 \cdot n_1$
$x_2 \leftarrow \lambda_2^2 + \lambda_2 + a_2$
$y_2 \leftarrow \lambda_2(x_2 + x_1) + x_2 + y_1$
$\lambda_3 \leftarrow j_2(y_2 + y_1)$
$x_3 \leftarrow \lambda_3^2 + \lambda_3 + x_2 + x_1 + a_2,$
$y_3 \leftarrow \lambda_3(x_2 + x_3) + x_3 + y_2$
```
for i = 4 to t + 1 do
```
$\quad \lambda_{2i-3} \leftarrow j_{i-1}(y_2 + y_{2i-5})$
$\quad x_{2i-3} \leftarrow \lambda_{2i-3}^2 + \lambda_{2i-3} + x_2 + x_{2i-5} + a_2$
$\quad y_{2i-3} \leftarrow \lambda_{2i-3}(x_2 + x_{2i-3}) + x_{2i-3} + y_2$
```
end for
```

References

1. Antipa, A., Brown, D., Gallant, R.P., Lambert, R., Struik, R., Vanstone, S.A.: Accelerated verification of ECDSA signatures. In: Preneel, B., Tavares, S. (eds.) SAC 2005. LNCS, vol. 3897, pp. 307–318. Springer, Heidelberg (2006)
2. Avanzi, R.M.: Another look at square roots (and other less common operations) in fields of even characteristic. In: Adams, C., Miri, A., Wiener, M. (eds.) SAC 2007. LNCS, vol. 4876, pp. 138–154. Springer, Heidelberg (2007)
3. Avanzi, R.M., Cohen, H., Doche, C., Frey, G., Lange, T., Nguyen, K., Vercauteren, F.: Handbook of elliptic and hyperelliptic curve cryptography. In: Avanzi, R.M., Cohen, H., Doche, C., Frey, G., Lange, T., Nguyen, K., Vercauteren, F. (eds.) Discrete Mathematics and its Applications. Chapman & Hall, Boca Raton (2005)
4. Bernstein, D.J., Lange, T.: Explicit-formulas database. http://www.hyperelliptic.org/EFD/
5. Blake, I.F., Seroussi, G., Smart, N.P.: Elliptic Curves in Cryptography. London Mathematical Society Lecture Note Series, vol. 265. Cambridge University Press, Cambridge (1999)
6. Blake, I.F., Seroussi, G., Smart, N.P.: Advances in Elliptic Curve Cryptography. London Mathematical Society Lecture Note Series, vol. 317. Cambridge University Press, Cambridge (2005)
7. Ciet, M., Joye, M., Lauter, K., Montgomery, P.L.: Trading inversions for multiplications in elliptic curve cryptography. Des. Codes Crypt. **39**(2), 189–206 (2006)
8. Cohen, H., Miyaji, A., Ono, T.: Efficient elliptic curve exponentiation using mixed coordinates. In: Ohta, K., Pei, D. (eds.) ASIACRYPT 1998. LNCS, vol. 1514, pp. 51–65. Springer, Heidelberg (1998)
9. Dahmen, E., Okeya, K., Schepers, D.: Affine precomputation with sole inversion in elliptic curve cryptography. In: Pieprzyk, J., Ghodosi, H., Dawson, E. (eds.) ACISP 2007. LNCS, vol. 4586, pp. 245–258. Springer, Heidelberg (2007)
10. de Rooij, P.: Efficient exponentiation using precomputation and vector addition chains. In: De Santis, A. (ed.) EUROCRYPT 1994. LNCS, vol. 950, pp. 389–399. Springer, Heidelberg (1995)
11. Doche, C.: Exponentiation. In: [3], pp. 145–168 (2005)
12. Doche, Ch., Icart, T., Kohel, D.R.: Efficient scalar multiplication by isogeny decompositions. In: Yung, M., Dodis, Y., Kiayias, A., Malkin, T. (eds.) PKC 2006. LNCS, vol. 3958, pp. 191–206. Springer, Heidelberg (2006)
13. Free Software Foundation. GNU Multiple Precision Library. http://gmplib.org/
14. Hankerson, D., Menezes, A.J., Vanstone, S.A.: Guide to Elliptic Curve Cryptography. Springer, Heidelberg (2003)
15. Knudsen, E.W.: Elliptic scalar multiplication using point halving. In: Lam, K.-Y., Okamoto, E., Xing, Ch. (eds.) ASIACRYPT 1999. LNCS, vol. 1716, pp. 135–149. Springer, Heidelberg (1999)
16. López, J., Dahab, R.: Fast Multiplication on Elliptic Curves over $GF(2_m)$ without Precomputation. In: Koç, C., Paar, C. (eds.) CHES 1999. LNCS, vol. 1717, pp. 316–327. Springer, Heidelberg (1999)
17. López, J., Dahab, R.: Improved algorithms for elliptic curve arithmetic in $GF(2_n)$. In: Tavares, S., Meijer, H. (eds.) SAC 1998. LNCS, vol. 1556, pp. 201–212. Springer, Heidelberg (1999)
18. Cohen, H., Miyaji, A., Ono, T.: Efficient elliptic curve exponentiation using mixed coordinates. In: Ohta, K., Pei, D. (eds.) ASIACRYPT 1998. LNCS, vol. 1514, pp. 51–65. Springer, Heidelberg (1998)

19. Montgomery, P.L.: Speeding the Pollard and elliptic curves methods of factorisation. Math. Comp. **48**, 243–264 (1987)
20. Morain, F., Olivos, J.: Speeding up the computations on an elliptic curve using addition-subtraction chains. Inf. Theor. Appl. **24**, 531–543 (1990)
21. Reitwiesner, G.: Binary arithmetic. Adv. Comput. **1**, 231–308 (1962)
22. Shoup, V.: NTL: A Library for doing Number Theory. http://www.shoup.net/ntl
23. Solinas, J.A.: Improved algorithms for arithmetic on anomalous binary curves. Technical Report CORR 99–46, CACR. http://cacr.uwaterloo.ca/techreports/1999/corr99-46.pdf (1999)
24. Solinas, J.A.: Low-weight binary representations for pairs of integers. Combinatorics and Optimization Research Report CORR 2001–41, University of Waterloo (2001)
25. Stam, M.: On montgomery-like representations for elliptic curves over $GF(2^k)$. In: Desmedt, Y.G. (ed.) Public Key Cryptography — PKC 2003. LNCS, vol. 2567. Springer, Heidelberg (2003)
26. Straus, E.G.: Addition chains of vectors (problem 5125). Amer. Math. Mon. **70**, 806–808 (1964)
27. Takagi, T., Yen, S.-M., Wu, B.-C.: Radix-r non-adjacent form. In: Zhang, K., Zheng, Y. (eds.) ISC 2004. LNCS, vol. 3225, pp. 99–110. Springer, Heidelberg (2004)
28. Washington, L.C.: Elliptic Curves: Number Theory and Cryptography. Discrete Mathematics and its Applications. Chapman & Hall, Boca Raton (2003)
29. Yao, A.C.C.: On the evaluation of powers. SIAM J. Comput. **5**(1), 100–103 (1976)

Montgomery Multiplication
Using Vector Instructions

Joppe W. Bos, Peter L. Montgomery, Daniel Shumow,
and Gregory M. Zaverucha[✉]

Microsoft Research, Redmond, USA
{jbos,peter.montgomery,danshu,gregz}@microsoft.com

Abstract. In this paper we present a parallel approach to compute *interleaved* Montgomery multiplication. This approach is particularly suitable to be computed on 2-way single instruction, multiple data platforms as can be found on most modern computer architectures in the form of vector instruction set extensions. We have implemented this approach for tablet devices which run the x86 architecture (Intel Atom Z2760) using SSE2 instructions as well as devices which run on the ARM platform (Qualcomm MSM8960, NVIDIA Tegra 3 and 4) using NEON instructions. When instantiating modular exponentiation with this parallel version of Montgomery multiplication we observed a performance increase of more than a factor of 1.5 compared to the sequential implementation in OpenSSL for the classical arithmetic logic unit on the Atom platform for 2048-bit moduli.

1 Introduction

Modular multiplication of large integers is a computational building block used to implement public-key cryptography. For schemes like RSA [34], ElGamal [11] or DSA [36], the most common size of the modulus for parameters in use is large; 1024 bits long [20,28]. The typical modulus size will increase to 2048 and 3072 bits over the coming years, in order to comply with the current 112- and 128-bit security standard (cf. [31]). When computing multiple modular multiplications, Montgomery multiplication [30] provides a speed up to this core arithmetic operation. As RSA-based schemes are arguably the most frequently computed asymmetric primitives today, improvements to Montgomery multiplication are of immediate practical importance.

Many modern computer architectures provide vector instruction set extensions in order to perform single instruction, multiple data (SIMD) operations. Example platforms include the popular x86 architecture as well as the ARM platform that can be found in almost all modern smartphones and tablets. The research community has studied ways to reduce the latency of Montgomery multiplication by parallelizing this computation. These approaches vary from using the SIMD paradigm [8,10,18,23] to the single instruction, multiple threads paradigm using a residue number system [14,29] as described in [4,19] (see Sect. 2.3 for a more detailed overview).

T. Lange, K. Lauter, and P. Lisoněk (Eds.): SAC 2013, LNCS 8282, pp. 471–489, 2014.
DOI: 10.1007/978-3-662-43414-7_24, © Springer-Verlag Berlin Heidelberg 2014

In this paper we present an approach to split the Montgomery multiplication into two parts which can be computed in parallel. We flip the sign of the precomputed Montgomery constant and accumulate the result in two separate intermediate values that are computed concurrently. This avoids using a redundant representation, for example suggested in the recent SIMD approach for Intel architectures [18], since the intermediate values do not overflow to an additional word. Moreover, our approach is suitable for implementation using vector instruction set extensions which support 2-way SIMD operations, i.e., a single instruction that is applied to two data segments simultaneously. We implemented the sequential Montgomery multiplication algorithm using schoolbook multiplication on the classical arithmetic logic unit (ALU) and the parallel approach on the 2-way SIMD vector instruction set of both the x86 (SSE2) and the ARM (NEON) processors. Our experimental results show that on both 32-bit x86 and ARM platforms, widely available in a broad range of mobile devices, this parallel approach manages to outperform our classical sequential implementation.

Note, that the approach and implementation used in the GNU multiple precision arithmetic library (GMP) [13], is faster than the one presented in this paper and the one used in OpenSSL [32] on some Intel platforms we tested. This approach does not use the interleaved Montgomery multiplication but first computes the multiplication, using asymptotically fast method like Karatsuba [25], followed by the Montgomery reduction. GMP uses dedicated squaring code which is not used in our implementation. Note, however, that GMP is not a cryptographic library and does not strive to provide constant-time implementations. See Sect. 3.1 for a more detailed discussion of the different approaches.

2   Preliminaries

In this section we recall some of the facts related to SIMD instructions and Montgomery multiplication. In Sect. 2.3 we summarize related work of parallel software implementations of Montgomery multiplication.

2.1   SIMD Instruction Set Extensions

Many processors include instruction set extensions. In this work we mainly focus on extensions which support vector instructions following the single instruction, multiple data (SIMD) paradigm. The two platforms we consider are the x86 and the ARM, and the instruction set extensions for these platforms are outlined below. The main vector instructions used in this work (on both processor types) are integer multiply, shift, bitwise AND, addition, and subtraction.

The x86 SIMD Instruction Set Extensions. SIMD operations on x86 and x64 processors have been supported in a number of instruction set extensions, beginning with MMX in 1997. This work uses the streaming SIMD extensions 2 (SSE2) instructions, introduced in 2001. SSE2 has been included on most Intel and AMD processors manufactured since then. We use "SSE" to refer to SSE2.

Algorithm 1. The radix-r interleaved Montgomery multiplication [30] method.

Input: $\begin{cases} A, B, M, \mu \text{ such that } A = \sum_{i=0}^{n-1} a_i r^i, 0 \le a_i < r, \ 0 \le A, B < M, \ 2 \nmid M, \\ r^{n-1} \le M < r^n, \ \gcd(r, M) = 1, \ \mu = -M^{-1} \bmod r. \end{cases}$

Output: $C \equiv A \cdot B \cdot r^{-n} \bmod M$ such that $0 \le C < M$.

1: $C \leftarrow 0$
2: **for** $i = 0$ to $n - 1$ **do**
3:      $C \leftarrow C + a_i \cdot B$
4:      $q \leftarrow \mu \cdot C \bmod r$
5:      $C \leftarrow (C + q \cdot M)/r$
6: **if** $C \ge M$ **then**
7:      $C \leftarrow C - M$
8: **return** C

SSE provides 128-bit SIMD registers (eight registers on x86 and sixteen registers on x64) which may be viewed as vectors of 1-, 8-, 16-, 32-, or 64-bit integer elements operating using 128-, 16-, 8-, 4-, or 2-way SIMD respectively. Vector operations allow multiple arithmetic operations to be performed simultaneously, for example PMULLUDQ multiplies the low 32-bits of a pair of 64-bit integers and outputs a pair of 64-bit integers. For a description of SSE instructions, see [22].

The ARM NEON SIMD Engine. Some ARM processors provide a set of additional SIMD operations, called NEON. The NEON register file can be viewed as either sixteen 128-bit registers or 32 64-bit registers. The NEON registers can contain integer vectors, as in SSE. The operations provided by NEON are comparable to those provided by SSE. For example, the vector multiply instruction vmul takes two pairs of 32-bit integers as input and produces a pair of 64-bit outputs. This is equivalent to the SSE2 instruction PMULUDQ, except the inputs are provided in 64-bit registers, rather than 128-bit registers. Another example, but without an SSE equivalent is the vmlal instruction which performs a vmull and adds the results to a 128-bit register (treated as two 64-bit integers). For a complete description of the NEON instructions, see [3].

2.2 Montgomery Arithmetic

Montgomery arithmetic [30] consists of transforming operands into a Montgomery representation, performing the desired computations on these transformed numbers, then converting the result (also in Montgomery representation) back to the regular representation. Due to the overhead of changing representations, Montgomery arithmetic is best when used to replace a sequence of modular multiplications, since the overhead is amortized.

The idea behind Montgomery multiplication is to replace the expensive division operations required when computing the modular reduction by cheap shift operations (division by powers of two). Let w denote the word size in bits. We write integers in a radix r system, for $r = 2^w$ where typical values of w are $w = 32$ or $w = 64$. Let M be an n-word odd modulus such that $r^{n-1} \le M < r^n$.

The Montgomery radix r^n is a constant such that $\gcd(r^n, M) = 1$. The Montgomery residue of an integer $A \in \mathbf{Z}/M\mathbf{Z}$ is defined as $\widetilde{A} = A \cdot r^n \bmod M$. The Montgomery product of two residues is defined as $M(\widetilde{A}, \widetilde{B}) = \widetilde{A} \cdot \widetilde{B} \cdot r^{-n} \bmod M$. Algorithm 1 outlines interleaved Montgomery multiplication, denoted as coarsely integrated operand scanning in [26], where the multiplication and reduction are interleaved. Note that residues may be added and subtracted using regular modular algorithms since $\widetilde{A} \pm \widetilde{B} \equiv (A \cdot r^n) \pm (B \cdot r^n) \equiv (A \pm B) \cdot r^n \pmod{M}$.

2.3 Related Work

There has been a considerable amount of work related to SIMD implementations of cryptography. The authors of [6,12,35] propose ways to speed up cryptography using the NEON vector instructions. Intel's SSE2 vector instruction set extension is used to compute pairings in [15] and multiply big numbers in [21]. Simultaneously, people have studied techniques to create hardware and software implementations of Montgomery multiplication. We now summarize some of the techniques to implement Montgomery multiplication concurrently in a software implementation. A parallel software approach describing systolic (a specific arrangement of processing units used in parallel computations) Montgomery multiplication is described in [10,23]. An approach using the vector instructions on the Cell microprocessor is considered in [8]. Exploiting much larger parallelism using the single instruction multiple threads paradigm, is realized by using a residue number system [14,29] as described in [4]. This approach is implemented for the massively parallel graphics processing units in [19]. An approach based on Montgomery multiplication which allows one to split the operand into two parts, which can be processed in parallel, is called bipartite modular multiplication and is introduced in [24]. More recently, the authors of [18] describe an approach using the soon to be released AVX2 SIMD instructions, for Intel's Haswell architecture, which uses 256-bit wide vector instructions. The main difference between the method proposed in this work and most of the SIMD approaches referred to here is that we do not follow the approach described in [21]. We do not use a redundant representation to accumulate multiple multiplications. We use a different approach to make sure no extra words are required for the intermediate values (see Sect. 3).

Another approach is to use the SIMD vector instructions to compute *multiple* Montgomery multiplications in parallel. This can be useful in applications where many computations need to be processed in parallel such as batch-RSA. This approach is studied in [33] using the SSE2 vector instructions on an Pentium 4 and in [7] on the Cell processor.

3   Montgomery Multiplication Using SIMD Extensions

Montgomery multiplication, as outlined in Algorithm 1, does not lend itself to parallelization directly. In this section we describe an algorithm capable of computing the Montgomery multiplication using two threads running in parallel

Algorithm 2. A parallel radix-2^{32} interleaved Montgomery multiplication algorithm. Except for the computation of q, the arithmetic steps in the outer for-loop performed by both Computation 1 and Computation 2 are identical. This approach is suitable for 32-bit 2-way SIMD vector instruction units. Note that the value of the precomputed Montgomery inverse μ is different ($\mu = M^{-1} \bmod 2^{32}$) than the one used in Algorithm 1 ($\mu = -M^{-1} \bmod 2^{32}$).

Input: $\begin{cases} A, B, M, \mu \text{ such that } A = \sum_{i=0}^{n-1} a_i 2^{32i}, B = \sum_{i=0}^{n-1} b_i 2^{32i}, \\ M = \sum_{i=0}^{n-1} m_i 2^{32i}, 0 \le a_i, b_i < 2^{32}, \ 0 \le A, B < M, \\ 2^{32(n-1)} \le M < 2^{32n}, 2 \nmid M, \ \mu = M^{-1} \bmod 2^{32}. \end{cases}$

Output: $C \equiv A \cdot B \cdot 2^{-32n} \bmod M$ such that $0 \le C < M$.

Computation 1	Computation 2
$d_i = 0$ for $0 \le i < n$	$e_i = 0$ for $0 \le i < n$
for $j = 0$ to $n - 1$ **do**	**for** $j = 0$ to $n - 1$ **do**
	$\quad q \leftarrow ((\mu \cdot b_0) \cdot a_j + \mu \cdot (d_0 - e_0)) \bmod 2^{32}$
$\quad t_0 \leftarrow a_j \cdot b_0 + d_0$	$\quad t_1 \leftarrow q \cdot m_0 + e_0$ // Note that $t_0 \equiv t_1 \pmod{2^{32}}$
$\quad t_0 \leftarrow \left\lfloor \dfrac{t_0}{2^{32}} \right\rfloor$	$\quad t_1 \leftarrow \left\lfloor \dfrac{t_1}{2^{32}} \right\rfloor$
$\quad$ **for** $i = 1$ to $n - 1$ **do**	$\quad$ **for** $i = 1$ to $n - 1$ **do**
$\qquad p_0 \leftarrow a_j \cdot b_i + t_0 + d_i$	$\qquad p_1 \leftarrow q \cdot m_i + t_1 + e_i$
$\qquad t_0 \leftarrow \left\lfloor \dfrac{p_0}{2^{32}} \right\rfloor$	$\qquad t_1 \leftarrow \left\lfloor \dfrac{p_1}{2^{32}} \right\rfloor$
$\qquad d_{i-1} \leftarrow p_0 \bmod 2^{32}$	$\qquad e_{i-1} \leftarrow p_1 \bmod 2^{32}$
$\quad d_{n-1} \leftarrow t_0$	$\quad e_{n-1} \leftarrow t_1$

$$C \leftarrow D - E \quad // \text{ where } D = \sum_{i=0}^{n-1} d_i 2^{32i}, \ E = \sum_{i=0}^{n-1} e_i 2^{32i}$$

$$\textbf{if } C < 0 \textbf{ do } \ C \leftarrow C + M$$

which perform identical arithmetic steps. Hence, this algorithm can be implemented efficiently using common 2-way SIMD vector instructions. For illustrative purposes we assume a radix-2^{32} system, but this can be adjusted accordingly to other choices of radix.

As can be seen from Algorithm 1 there are two $1 \times n \to (n+1)$ limb ($a_i B$ and qM) and a single $1 \times 1 \to 1$ limb ($\mu C \bmod r$) multiplications per iteration. These three multiplications depend on each other, preventing concurrent computation. In order to remove this dependence, note that for the computation of q only the first limb c_0 of $C = \sum_{i=0}^{n-1} c_i 2^{32i}$ is required. Hence, if one is willing to compute the updated value of c_0 twice then the two larger $1 \times n \to (n + 1)$ limb multiplications become independent of each other and can be computed in parallel. More precisely, lines 3, 4, and 5 of Algorithm 1 can be replaced with

$$q \leftarrow ((c_0 + a_i \cdot b_0)\mu) \bmod r$$
$$C \leftarrow (C + a_i \cdot B + q \cdot M)/r$$

ensuring that the two larger multiplications do not depend on each other.

The second idea is to flip the sign of the Montgomery constant μ: i.e. instead of using $-M^{-1} \bmod 2^{32}$ (as in Algorithm 1) we use $\mu = M^{-1} \bmod 2^{32}$ (the reason for this choice is outlined below). When computing the Montgomery product $C = A \cdot B \cdot 2^{-32n} \bmod M$, for an odd modulus M such that $2^{32(n-1)} \leq M < 2^{32n}$, one can compute D, which contains the sum of the products $a_i B$, and E, which contains the sum of the products qM, separately. Due to our choice of the Montgomery constant μ we have $C = D - E \equiv A \cdot B \cdot 2^{-32n} \pmod{M}$, where $0 \leq D, E < M$: the maximum values of both D and E fit in an n-limb integer, avoiding a carry that might result in an $(n + 1)$ limb long integer as in Algorithm 1. This approach is outlined in Algorithm 2.

At the start of every iteration of j the two separate computations need some communication in order to compute the new value of q. In practice, this communication requires extracting the values d_0 and e_0, the first limb of D and E respectively, from the SIMD vector. No such extracting is required in the inner-most loop over the i values in Algorithm 2. The value of q is computed as

$$q = ((\mu \cdot b_0) \cdot a_j + \mu \cdot (d_0 - e_0)) \bmod 2^{32} = \mu(a_j \cdot b_0 + c_0) \bmod 2^{32}$$

since $c_0 = d_0 - e_0$. Note that one can compute $(\mu \cdot b_0) \bmod 2^{32}$ at the beginning of the algorithm once and reuse it for every iteration of the for-loop.

Except for the computation of q, all arithmetic computations performed by Computation 1 and Computation 2 are identical but work on different data. This makes Algorithm 2 suitable for implementation using 2-way 32-bit SIMD vector instructions. This approach benefits from 2-way SIMD $32 \times 32 \rightarrow 64$-bit multiplication and matches exactly the 128-bit wide vector instructions as present in SSE and NEON. Changing the radix used in Algorithm 2 allows implementation with larger or smaller vector instructions. For example, if a $64 \times 64 \rightarrow 128$-bit vector multiply instruction is provided in a future version of AVX, implementing Algorithm 2 in a 2^{64}-radix system with 256-bit wide vector instructions could potentially speed-up modular multiplication by a factor of up to two on 64-bit systems (see Sect. 3.1).

At the end of Algorithm 2, there is a conditional addition, as opposed to a conditional subtraction in Algorithm 1, due to our choice of μ. The condition is whether $D - E$ is negative (produces a borrow), in this case the modulus must be added to make the result positive. This conditional addition can be converted into straight-line code by creating a mask depending on the borrow and selecting either $D - E$ (if there is no borrow) or $D - E + M$ (if there is a borrow) so that the code runs in constant-time (an important characteristic for side-channel resistance [27]).

3.1 Expected Performance

The question remains if Algorithm 2, implemented for a 2-way SIMD unit, outperforms Algorithm 1, implemented for the classical ALU. This mainly depends on the size of the inputs and outputs of the integer instructions, how many

Table 1. A simplified comparison, only stating *the number of arithmetic operations required*, of the expected performance of Montgomery multiplication when using a $32n$-bit modulus for a positive even integer n. The left side of the table shows arithmetic instruction counts for the sequential algorithm using the classical ALU (Algorithm 1) and when using 2-way SIMD instructions with the parallel algorithm (Algorithm 2). The right side of the table shows arithmetic instruction counts when using one level of Karatuba's method [25] for the multiplication as analyzed in [17]

Instruction	Classical		2-way SIMD	Karatsuba	Instruction
	32-bit	64-bit	32-bit	32-bit	
add	-	-	n	$\frac{13}{4}n^2 + 8n + 2$	add
sub	-	-	n	$\frac{7}{4}n^2 + n$	mul
shortmul	n	$\frac{n}{2}$	$2n$		
muladd	$2n$	n	-		
muladdadd	$2n(n-1)$	$n(\frac{n}{2}-1)$	-		
SIMD muladd	-	-	n		
SIMD muladdadd	-	-	$n(n-1)$		

instructions can be dispatched per cycle, and the number of cycles an instruction needs to complete. In order to give a (simplified) prediction of the performance we compute the expected performance of a Montgomery multiplication using a $32n$-bit modulus for a positive even integer n. Let $\texttt{muladd}_w(e, a, b, c)$ and $\texttt{muladdadd}_w(e, a, b, c, d)$ denote the computation of $e = a \times b + c$ and $e = a \times b + c + d$, respectively, for $0 \leq a, b, c, d < 2^w$ and $0 \leq e < 2^{2w}$ as a basic operation on a compute architecture which works on w-bit words. Some platforms have these operations as a single instruction (e.g., on some ARM architectures) or they must be implemented using a multiplication and addition(s) (as on the x86 platform). Furthermore, let $\texttt{shortmul}_w(e, a, b)$ denote $e = a \times b \bmod 2^w$: this only computes the lower word of the result and can be done faster (compared to a full product) on most platforms.

Table 1 summarizes the expected performance of Algorithm 1 and 2 in terms of arithmetic operations only (e.g., the data movement, shifting and masking operations are omitted). Also the operations required to compute the final conditional subtraction or addition have been omitted. When solely considering the $\texttt{muladd}$ and $\texttt{muladdadd}$ instructions it becomes clear from Table 1 that the SIMD approach uses exactly half of the number of operations compared to the 32-bit classical implementation and almost twice as many operations compared to the classical 64-bit implementations. However, the SIMD approach requires more operations to compute the value of q every iteration and has various other overhead (e.g., inserting and extracting values from the vector). Hence, when assuming that all the characteristics of the SIMD and classical (non-SIMD) instructions are identical, which will not be the case on all platforms, then we expect Algorithm 2 running on a 2-way 32-bit SIMD unit to outperform a classical 32-bit implementation using Algorithm 1 by at most a factor of two while being roughly twice as slow when compared to a classical 64-bit implementation.

Inherently, the interleaved Montgomery multiplication algorithm (as used in this work) is not compatible with asymptotically faster integer multiplication algorithms like Karatsuba multiplication [25]. We have not implemented the Montgomery multiplication by first computing the multiplication using such faster methods, and then computing the modular reduction, using SIMD vector instructions in one or both steps. In [17], instruction counts are presented when using the interleaved Montgomery multiplication, as used in our baseline implementation, as well as for an approach where the multiplication and reduction are computed separately. Separating these two steps makes it easier to use a squaring algorithm. In [17] a single level of Karatsuba on top of Comba's method [9] is considered: the arithmetic instruction counts are stated in Table 1. For 1024-bit modular multiplication (used for 2048-bit RSA decryption using the CRT), the Karatsuba approach can reduce the number of multiplication and addition instructions by a factor 1.14 and 1.18 respectively on 32-bit platforms compared to the sequential interleaved approach. When comparing the arithmetic instructions only, the SIMD approach for interleaved Montgomery multiplication is 1.70 and 1.67 times faster than the sequential Karatsuba approach for 1024-bit modular multiplication on 32-bit platforms. Obviously, the Karatsuba approach can be sped up using SIMD instructions as well.

The results in Table 1 are for Montgomery multiplication only. It is known how to optimize (sequential) Montgomery squaring [16], but as far as we are aware, not how to optimize squaring using SIMD instructions. Following the analysis from [17], the cost of a Montgomery squaring is $\frac{11n+14}{14n+8}$ and $\frac{3n+5}{4n+2}$ the cost of a Montgomery multiplication when using the Karatsuba or interleaved Montgomery approach on n-limb integers. For 1024-bit modular arithmetic (as used in RSA-2048 with $n = 32$) this results in 0.80 (for Karatsuba) and 0.78 (for interleaved). For RSA-2048, approximately 5/6 of all operations are squarings: this highlights the potential of an efficient squaring implementation.

4   Implementation Results

We have implemented interleaved Montgomery modular multiplication (Algorithm 1) as a baseline for comparison with the SIMD version (Algorithm 2). In both implementations, the final addition/subtraction was implemented using masking such that it runs in constant time, to resist certain types of side-channel attacks using timing and branch prediction. Since the cost of this operation was observed to be a small fraction of the overall cost, we chose not to write a separate optimized implementation for operations using only public values (such as signature verification).

Benchmark Hardware. Our implementations were benchmarked on recent Intel x86-32, x64 and ARM platforms. On the Intel systems, Windows 7 and Windows 8 were used, and on ARM systems Windows RT was used. The Microsoft

C/C++ Optimizing Compiler Version 16.10 was used for x86 and x64, and version 17.00 was used for ARM.[1] Our benchmark systems are the following:

Intel Xeon E31230. A quad core 3.2 GHz CPU on an HP Z210 workstation. We used SSE2 for Algorithm 2 and also benchmark x86-32 and x86-64 implementations of Algorithm 1 for comparison.

Intel Atom Z2760. A dual core 1.8 GHz system-on-a-chip (SoC), on an Asus Vivo Tab Smart Windows 8 tablet.

NVIDIA Tegra T30. A quad core 1.4 GHz ARM Cortex-A9 SoC, on an NVIDIA developer tablet.

Qualcomm MSM8960. A quad core 1.8 GHz Snapdragon S4 SoC, on a Dell XPS 10 tablet.

NVIDIA Tegra 4. A quad core 1.91 GHz ARM Cortex-A15 SoC, on an NVIDIA developer tablet.

We chose to include the Xeon processor to confirm the analysis of Sect. 3.1, that the x64 implementation should give the best performance, and to compare it with the SIMD implementation. The other processors are common in tablets and smartphones, and on these platforms, the SIMD implementation should be the best available. The performance of 32-bit code is also of interest on 64-bit systems, since 32-bit crypto libraries are included on 64-bit systems (e.g., on 64-bit Windows), to allow existing x86 applications to run on the 64-bit system without being ported and recompiled.

On the Xeon system, Intel's *Turbo Boost* feature will dynamically increase the frequency of the processor under high computational load. We found Turbo Boost had a modest impact on our timings. Since it is a potential source of variability, all times reported here were measured with Turbo Boost disabled.

Benchmarks. We chose to benchmark the cost of modular multiplication for 512-bit, 1024-bit and 2048-bit moduli, since these are currently used in deployed cryptography. The 512-bit modular multiplication results may also be interesting for usage in elliptic curve and pairing based cryptosystems. We created implementations optimized for these "special" bitlengths as well as *generic* implementations, i.e., implementations that operate with arbitrary length inputs. For comparison, we include the time for modular multiplication with 1024- and 2048-bit generic implementations. Our x64 baseline implementation has no length-specific code (we did not observe performance improvements).

We also benchmark the cost of RSA encryption and decryption using the different modular multiplication routines. We do not describe our RSA implementation in detail, because it is the same for all benchmarks, but note that: (i) decryption with an n-bit modulus is done with $n/2$-bit arithmetic using the Chinese remainder theorem approach, (ii) this is a "raw" RSA operation, taking an integer as plaintext input, no padding is performed, (iii) no specialized squaring routine is used, and (iv) the public exponent in our benchmarks is always $2^{16}+1$.

---

[1] These were the newest versions available for each architecture at the time of writing.

We compute the modular exponentiation using a windowing based approach. As mentioned in (iii), we have not considered a specialized Montgomery squaring algorithm for the sequential or the SIMD algorithms. Using squaring routines can significantly enhance the performance of our code as discussed in Sect. 3.1.

All of our benchmarks are *average* times, computed over 10^5 runs for modular multiplication, and 100 runs for RSA operations, with random inputs for each run. With these choices the standard deviation is three percent or less. Note that the performance results for RSA-1024 are stated for comparison's sake only, this 80-bit secure scheme should not be used anymore (see NIST SP 800-57 [31]).

x86/x64 Results. In the first 32-bit benchmark (Xeon x86), our implementation using SIMD instructions is 1.6 to 2.5 times faster than the serial version (see Table 2). The speed-up of the length-specific SIMD implementation over the generic implementation is on average a factor 1.4, noticeably more than the factor 1.2 for the baseline. Algorithm 2 results in faster RSA operations as well, which are roughly sped-up by a factor of two. Our second 32-bit benchmark (Atom x86) was on average 1.69 times faster than our baseline. This makes our SIMD algorithm the better option on this platform. However, the speed-up observed was not as large as our Xeon x86 benchmark. This may be because the Atom has an in-order instruction scheduler. The 64-bit implementation of Algorithm 1 is roughly four times as fast as the 32-bit implementation and the SIMD algorithm (also 32-bit) is right in the middle, roughly twice as slow as the 64-bit algorithm. This agrees with our analysis from Sect. 3.1. On all platforms the performance ratio between baseline and SIMD is slightly worse for 512-bit moduli due to the overhead of using SIMD instructions. Algorithm 2 is still faster than the baseline for 512-bit moduli on the Xeon x86, Atom and the Snapdragon S4.

ARM Results. On ARM our results are more mixed (see Table 3). First we note that on the Tegra 3 SoC, our NEON implementation of Algorithm 2 is consistently worse than the baseline, almost twice as slow. Going back to our analysis in Sect. 3.1, this would occur if the cost of a vector multiply instruction (performing two 32-bit multiplies) was about the cost of two non-vector multiply instructions. This is (almost) the case according to the Cortex-A9 instruction latencies published by ARM.[2] Our efforts to pipeline multiple vector multiply instructions did not sufficiently pay off – the length-specific implementations give a 1.27 factor speed-up over the generic implementations, roughly the same speed-up obtained when we optimize the baseline for a given bitlength (by fully unrolling the inner loop).

On the newer ARM SoCs in our experiments, the S4 and Tegra 4, the results are better. On the Snapdragon S4 the SIMD implementation is consistently better than the baseline. The NEON length-specific implementations were especially

---

[2] Results of the NEON `vmull`/`vmlal` instructions are available after 7 cycles, while the two 32-bit outputs of the ARM `umaal` instruction become ready after 4 and 5 cycles [1,2].

Table 2. Implementation timings in microseconds and cycles for x86/x64 based processors. The "ratio" column is baseline/SIMD. The 512 g, 1024 g and 2048 g rows are generic implementations that do not optimize for a specific bitlength.

Benchmark	Xeon x86			Xeon x64			Atom (x86)		
	Baseline	SIMD	Ratio	Baseline	SIMD	Ratio	Baseline	SIMD	Ratio
modmul 512	1.229	0.805	1.53	0.498	0.805	0.62	5.948	4.317	1.38
(cycles)	3933	2577	1.53	1598	2577	0.62	10706	7775	1.38
modmul 1024	3.523	1.842	1.91	1.030	1.842	0.56	21.390	12.388	1.73
(cycles)	11255	5887	1.91	3295	5887	0.56	38479	22288	1.73
RSA enc 1024	75.459	36.745	2.05	16.411	36.745	0.45	407.835	250.285	1.63
(cycles)	241014	117419	2.05	52457	117419	0.45	733224	450092	1.63
RSA dec 1024	1275.030	656.831	1.94	278.444	656.831	0.42	6770.646	4257.838	1.59
(cycles)	4070962	2097258	1.94	889103	2097258	0.42	12167933	7652178	1.59
modmul 2048	13.873	5.488	2.53	3.012	5.488	0.55	72.870	41.402	1.76
(cycles)	44302	17529	2.53	9621	17529	0.55	130975	74425	1.76
RSA enc 2048	277.719	129.876	2.14	56.813	129.876	0.44	1437.459	891.185	1.61
(cycles)	886828	414787	2.14	181412	414787	0.44	2583643	1601878	1.61
RSA dec 2048	8231.233	3824.690	2.15	1543.666	3824.690	0.40	44629.140	28935.088	1.54
(cycles)	26280725	12211700	2.15	4928633	12211700	0.40	80204317	52000367	1.54
modmul 512g	1.356	0.986	1.38	0.498	0.986	0.51	6.387	5.116	1.25
(cycles)	4336	3155	1.37	1598	3155	0.51	11496	9213	1.25
modmul 1024g	4.111	2.534	1.62	1.030	2.534	0.41	25.362	13.560	1.87
(cycles)	13132	8098	1.62	3295	8098	0.41	45631	24393	1.87
modmul 2048g	15.607	9.304	1.68	3.012	9.304	0.32	74.212	44.806	1.66
(cycles)	49838	29714	1.68	9621	29714	0.32	133387	80543	1.66

Table 3. Implementation timings in microseconds for ARM-based processors. The "ratio" column is baseline/SIMD. The 512 g, 1024 g and 2048 g rows are generic implementations that do not optimize for a specific bitlength.

Benchmark	Snapdragon S4			Tegra 4			Tegra 3		
	Baseline	SIMD	Ratio	Baseline	SIMD	Ratio	Baseline	SIMD	Ratio
modmul 512	4.097	3.384	1.21	1.976	2.212	0.89	3.553	5.265	0.67
(cycles)	6443	5372	1.20	3658	4020	0.91	4678	6861	0.68
modmul 1024	10.676	7.281	1.47	8.454	8.622	0.98	9.512	15.891	0.60
(cycles)	16382	11243	1.46	10351	10560	0.98	12314	20490	0.60
RSA enc 1024	198.187	142.956	1.38	168.617	179.227	0.94	189.420	295.110	0.64
(cycles)	302898	219244	1.38	195212	207647	0.94	245167	379736	0.65
RSA dec 1024	3424.413	2475.716	1.38	1999.211	2303.588	0.87	3306.230	5597.280	0.59
(cycles)	5179365	3746371	1.38	3288177	3332262	0.99	4233862	7166897	0.59
modmul 2048	36.260	21.531	1.68	30.465	32.064	0.95	31.912	55.070	0.58
(cycles)	55260	32978	1.68	37185	36984	1.01	41004	70655	0.58
RSA enc 2048	716.160	467.713	1.53	593.326	617.758	0.96	679.920	1060.050	0.64
(cycles)	1087318	710910	1.53	725336	712542	1.02	872468	1355955	0.64
RSA dec 2048	22992.576	14202.886	1.62	19024.405	19797.988	0.96	21519.880	36871.550	0.58
(cycles)	34769147	21478047	1.62	23177617	22812040	1.02	27547434	47205919	0.58
modmul 512 g	4.586	4.149	1.11	2.187	2.798	0.78	4.108	6.177	0.67
(cycles)	7179	6627	1.08	4045	5166	0.78	5383	8029	0.67
modmul 1024 g	12.274	9.697	1.27	8.973	12.151	0.74	12.112	19.421	0.62
(cycles)	18795	14894	1.26	10984	14870	0.74	15652	25004	0.63
modmul 2048 g	40.554	30.743	1.32	31.959	44.841	0.71	40.494	69.009	0.59
(cycles)	61621	46945	1.31	37786	51693	0.73	51993	88500	0.59

Table 4. Performance results expressed in cycles of RSA 1024-bit and 2048-bit encryption (enc) and decryption (dec). The first four performance numbers have been obtained from eBACS: ECRYPT Benchmarking of Cryptographic Systems [5] while the fifth row corresponds to running the performance benchmark suite of OpenSSL [32] on the same Atom device used to obtain the performance results in Table 2. The last two rows correspond to running GMP on our Atom and Xeon (in 32-bit mode)

Platform	RSA 1024		RSA 2048	
	Enc	Dec	Enc	Dec
ARM – Tegra 250 (1000 MHz)	261677	11684675	665195	65650103
ARM – Snapdragon S3 (1782 MHz)	276836	7373869	609593	39746105
x86 – Atom N280 (1667 MHz)	315620	13116020	871810	81628170
x64 – Xeon E3-1225 (3100 MHz)	49652	1403884	103744	6158336
x86 – Atom Z2760 (1800 MHz)	610200	10929600	2323800	75871800
x86 – Atom Z2760 (1800 MHz)	305545	5775125	2184436	37070875
x86 – Xeon E3-1230 (3200 MHz)	106035	1946434	695861	11929868

important and resulted in a speed-up by a factor of 1.30 to 1.40 over generic implementations, while optimizing the baseline implementation for a specific length was only faster by a factor slightly above 1.10. This is likely due to the inability of the processor to effectively re-order NEON instructions to minimize pipeline stalls – the main difference in our length-specific implementation was to partially unroll the inner loop and re-order instructions to use more registers and pipeline four multiply operations.

Performance of the SIMD algorithm on the Tegra 4 was essentially the same as the baseline performance. This is a solid improvement in NEON performance compared to our benchmarks on the Tegra 3, however the Tegra 4's NEON performance still lags behind the S4 (for the instructions used in our benchmarks). We suspect (based on informal experiments) that an implementation of Algorithm 2 specifically optimized for the Tegra 4 could significantly outperform the baseline, but still would not be comparable to the S4.

There is a slight difference between the cycle count measurement and the microsecond measurement for the 2048-bit ARM benchmarks on the Tegra 4. To measure cycles on ARM we read the cycle count register (PMCCNTR), and time is measured with the Windows QueryPerformanceCounter function. Since these are different time sources, a small difference is not surprising.

4.1 Comparison to Previous Work

Comparison to eBACS and OpenSSL. We have compared our SIMD implementation of the interleaved Montgomery multiplication algorithm to our baseline implementation of this method. To show that our baseline is competitive and put our results in a wider context, we compare to benchmark results from eBACS: ECRYPT Benchmarking of Cryptographic Systems [5] and to OpenSSL [32]. Table 4 summarizes the cycle counts from eBACS on platforms which are close to the ones we consider in this work, and also includes the results of running the performance benchmark of OpenSSL 1.0.1e [32] on our Atom device. As can be seen from Table 4, our baseline implementation results from Table 2 and 3 are similar (except for 1024-bit RSA decryption, which our implementation does not optimize, as mentioned above).

Comparison to GMP. The implementation in the GNU multiple precision arithmetic library (GMP) [13] is based on the non-interleaved Montgomery multiplication. This means the multiplication is computed first, possibly using a asymptotically faster algorithm than schoolbook, followed by the Montgomery reduction (see Sect. 3.1). The last two rows in Table 4 summarize performance numbers for our Atom and Xeon (in 32-bit mode) platforms. The GMP performance numbers for RSA-2048 decryption on the Atom (37.1 million) are significantly faster compared to OpenSSL (75.9 million), our baseline (80.2 million) and our SIMD (52.0 million) implementations. On the 32-bit Xeon the performance of the GMP implementation, which uses SIMD instructions for the multiplication and has support for asymptotically faster multiplication algorithms, is almost identical to our SIMD implementation which uses interleaved Montgomery multiplication. Note that both OpenSSL and our implementations are designed to resist side-channel attacks, and run in constant time, while both the GMP modular exponentiation and multiplication are not, making GMP unsuitable for use in many cryptographic applications. The multiplication and reduction routines in GMP can be adapted for cryptographic purposes but it is unclear at what performance price. From Table 2, it is clear that our SIMD implementation performs better on the 32-bit Xeon than on the Atom. The major difference between these two processors is the instruction scheduler (in-order on the Atom and out-of-order on the Xeon).

4.2 Engineering Challenges

In this section we discuss some engineering challenges we had to overcome in order to use SIMD in practice. Our goal is an implementation that is efficient and supports multiple processors, but is also maintainable. The discussion here may not be applicable in other circumstances.

ASM or Intrinsics? There are essentially two ways to access the SIMD instructions directly from a C program. One either writes assembly language (ASM), or uses compiler intrinsics. Intrinsics are macros that the compiler translates to specific instructions, e.g., on ARM, the Windows RT header file arm_neon.h defines the intrinsic vmull_u32, which the compiler implements with the vmull instruction. In addition to instructions, the header also exposes special data types corresponding to the 64 and 128-bit SIMD registers. We chose to use intrinsics for our implementation, for the following reasons. C with intrinsics is easier to debug, e.g., it is easier to detect mistakes using assertions. Furthermore, while there is a performance advantage for ASM implementations, these gains are limited in comparison to a careful C implementation with intrinsics (in our experience). In addition ASM is difficult to maintain. For example, in ASM the programmer must handle all argument passing and set up the stack frame, and this depends on the calling conventions. If calling conventions are changed, the ASM will need to be rewritten, rather than simply recompiled. Also, when writing for the Microsoft Visual Studio Compiler, the compiler automatically generates the code to perform structured exception handling (SEH), which is an exception handling mechanism at the system level for Windows and a requirement for all code running on this operating system. Incorrect implementation of SEH code may result in security bugs that are often difficult to detect until they are used in an exploit. Also, compiler features such as Whole Program Optimization and Link Time Code generation, that optimize code layout and time-memory usage tradeoffs, will not work correctly on ASM.

Despite the fact that one gets more control of the code (e.g. register usage) when writing in ASM, using instrinsics and C can still be efficient. Specifically, we reviewed the assembly code generated by the compiler to ensure that the run-time of this code remains in constant time and register usage is as we expected. In short, we have found that ASM implementations require increased engineering time and effort, both in initial development and maintenance, for a relatively small gain in performance. We have judged that this trade off is not worthwhile for our implementation.

simd.h Abstraction Layer. Both SSE2 and NEON vector instructions are accessible as intrinsics, however, the types and instructions available for each differ. To allow a single SIMD implementation to run on both architectures, we abstracted a useful subset of SSE2 and NEON in header named simd.h. Based on the architecture, this header defines inline functions wrapping a processor-specific intrinsic. simd.h also refines the vector data types, e.g., the type simd32x2p_t stores two 32-bit unsigned integers in a 64-bit register on ARM, but on x86 stores them in a 128-bit integer (in bits 0–31 and 64–95), so that they are in the correct format for the vector multiply instruction (which returns a value of type simd64x2_t on both architectures). The compiler will check that the arguments to the simd.h functions match the prototype, something that is not possible with intrinsics (which are preprocessor macros). While abstraction layers are almost always technically possible, we find it noteworthy that in this case it can be done without adding significant overhead, and code using the abstraction performs well on multiple processors. With simd.h containing all of architecture-specific code, the SIMD timings in the tables above were generated with two implementations: a generic one, and a length-specific one that requires the number of limbs in the modulus be divisible by four, to allow partial unrolling of the inner loop of Algorithm 2.

Length-Specific Routines. Given the results from Tables 2 and 3, it is clear that having specialized routines for certain bitlengths is worthwhile. In a math library used to implement multiple crypto primitives, each supporting a range of allowed keysizes, routines for arbitrary length moduli are required as well.

This raises the question of how to automatically select one of multiple implementations. We experimented with two different designs. The first design stores a function pointer to the modular multiplication routine along with the modulus. The second uses a function pointer to a length-specific exponentiation routine. On the x86 and x64 platforms, with 1024-bit (and larger) operands, the performance difference between the two approaches is small (the latter was faster by a factor around 1.10), however on ARM, using function pointers to multiplication routines is slower by a factor of up to 1.30 than when using pointers to exponentiation routines. The drawback of this latter approach is the need to maintain multiple exponentiation routines.

SoC-Specific Routines. Our experiments with multiple ARM SoCs also show that performance can vary by SoC. This is expected, however we were surprised by the range observed, compared to x86/x64 processors which are more homogeneous. We also observed that small code changes can result in simultaneous speed improvements on one SoC, and regression on another. Our current implementation performs a run-time check to identify the SoC, to decide whether to use Algorithm 1 or 2. Our results highlight that there is a great deal of variability between different implementations of the ARM architecture and that, for the time being, it is difficult to write code that performs well on multiple ARM SoCs simultaneously. This also implies that published implementation results for one ARM microprocessor core give little to no information on how it would perform on another. For more information, see the ARM technical reference manuals [3].

5 Conclusions and Future Work

In this paper we present a parallel version of the interleaved Montgomery multiplication algorithm that is amenable to implementation using widely available SIMD vector extension instructions (SSE2 and NEON). The practical implications of this approach are highlighted by our performance results on common tablet devices. When using 2048-bit moduli we are able to outperform our sequential implementation using the schoolbook multiplication method by a factor of 1.68 to 1.76 on both 32-bit x86 and ARM processors.

The performance numbers agree with our analysis that a 2-way SIMD implementation using 32-bit multipliers is not able to outperform a classical interleaved Montgomery multiplication implementation using 64-bit multiplication instructions. Hence, we also conclude that it would be beneficial for new 256-bit SIMD instruction sets to include 2-way integer multipliers. For example, our results suggest that modular multiplication could be sped-up by up to a factor of two on x64 systems if a future set of AVX instructions included a $64 \times 64 \to 128$-bit 2-way SIMD multiplier.

It remains of independent interest to study ways to use both asymptotically faster integer multiplication methods (like Karatsuba) and Montgomery reduction using SIMD instructions to reduce latency, including side-channel protections. This is left as future work. Furthermore, as pointed out by an anonymous reviewer, another possibility might be to compute the proposed parallel Montgomery multiplication routine using both the integer and floating point unit instead of using vector instructions.

Acknowledgements. The authors would like to thank: Adam Glass for discussions on ARM SoCs; Patrick Longa for comments on baseline implementations and general help; Jason Mackay for catching mistakes in early drafts; Paul Schofield for help timing on the Tegra 4; and Niels Ferguson for discussions of SIMD. Also, we thank the anonymous reviewers of SAC for their helpful feedback and thank Daniel J. Bernstein and Tanja Lange for the additional suggestions, both of which improved the quality of this paper.

References

1. ARM. Cortex-A9. Technical Reference Manual (2010). Version r2p2
2. ARM. Cortex-A9 NEON Media Processing Engine. Technical Reference Manual (2012). Version r4p1
3. ARM Limited. ARM Architechture Reference Manual ARMv7-A and ARMv7-R edition (2010)
4. Bajard, J.-C., Didier, L.-S., Kornerup, P.: An RNS Montgomery modular multiplication algorithm. IEEE Trans. Comput. **47**(7), 766–776 (1998)
5. Bernstein, D.J., Lange, T. (eds.): eBACS: ECRYPT Benchmarking of Cryptographic Systems. http://bench.cr.yp.to. Accessed 2 July 2013
6. Bernstein, D.J., Schwabe, P.: NEON crypto. In: Prouff, E., Schaumont, P. (eds.) CHES 2012. LNCS, vol. 7428, pp. 320–339. Springer, Heidelberg (2012)
7. Bos, J.W.: High-performance modular multiplication on the cell processor. In: Hasan, M.A., Helleseth, T. (eds.) WAIFI 2010. LNCS, vol. 6087, pp. 7–24. Springer, Heidelberg (2010)
8. Bos, J.W., Kaihara, M.E.: Montgomery multiplication on the cell. In: Wyrzykowski, R., Dongarra, J., Karczewski, K., Wasniewski, J. (eds.) PPAM 2009, Part I. LNCS, vol. 6067, pp. 477–485. Springer, Heidelberg (2010)
9. Comba, P.G.: Exponentiation cryptosystems on the IBM PC. IBM Syst. J. **29**(4), 526–538 (1990)
10. Dixon, B., Lenstra, A.K.: Massively parallel elliptic curve factoring. In: Rueppel, R.A. (ed.) EUROCRYPT 1992. LNCS, vol. 658, pp. 183–193. Springer, Heidelberg (1993)
11. ElGamal, T.: A public key cryptosystem and a signature scheme based on discrete logarithms. In: Blakley, G., Chaum, D. (eds.) CRYPTO 1984. LNCS, vol. 196, pp. 10–18. Springer, Heidelberg (1985)
12. Faz-Hernandez, A., Longa, P., Sanchez, A.H.: Efficient and secure algorithms for GLV-based scalar multiplication and their implementation on GLV-GLS curves. Cryptology ePrint Archive, Report 2013/158 (2013). http://eprint.iacr.org/. CT-RSA. doi:10.1007/978-3-319-04852-9_1
13. Free Software Foundation, Inc. GMP: The GNU Multiple Precision Arithmetic Library (2013). http://www.gmplib.org/
14. Garner, H.L.: The residue number system. IRE Trans. Electron. Comput. **8**, 140–147 (1959)
15. Grabher, P., Großschädl, J., Page, D.: On software parallel implementation of cryptographic pairings. In: Avanzi, R.M., Keliher, L., Sica, F. (eds.) SAC 2008. LNCS, vol. 5381, pp. 35–50. Springer, Heidelberg (2009)

16. Großschädl, J.: Architectural support for long integer modulo arithmetic on RISC-based smart cards. Int. J. High Perform. Comput. Appl. - IJHPCA **17**(2), 135–146 (2003)

17. Großschädl, J., Avanzi, R.M., Savaş, E., Tillich, S.: Energy-efficient software implementation of long integer modular arithmetic. In: Rao, J.R., Sunar, B. (eds.) CHES 2005. LNCS, vol. 3659, pp. 75–90. Springer, Heidelberg (2005)

18. Gueron, S., Krasnov, V.: Software implementation of modular exponentiation, using advanced vector instructions architectures. In: Özbudak, F., Rodríguez-Henríquez, F. (eds.) WAIFI 2012. LNCS, vol. 7369, pp. 119–135. Springer, Heidelberg (2012)

19. Harrison, O., Waldron, J.: Efficient acceleration of asymmetric cryptography on graphics hardware. In: Preneel, B. (ed.) AFRICACRYPT 2009. LNCS, vol. 5580, pp. 350–367. Springer, Heidelberg (2009)

20. Holz, R., Braun, L., Kammenhuber, N., Carle, G.: The SSL landscape: a thorough analysis of the x.509 PKI using active and passive measurements. In: Proceedings of the 2011 ACM SIGCOMM Conference on Internet Measurement Conference, IMC '11, pp. 427–444. ACM (2011)

21. Intel Corporation. Using streaming SIMD extensions (SSE2) to perform big multiplications. Whitepaper AP-941 (2000). http://software.intel.com/file/24960

22. Intel Corporation. Intel 64 and IA-32 Architectures Software Developers Manual (Combined Volumes 1, 2A, 2B, 2C, 3A, 3B and 3C) (2013). http://download.intel.com/products/processor/manual/325462.pdf

23. Iwamura, K., Matsumoto, T., Imai, H.: Systolic-arrays for modular exponentiation using montgomery method. In: Rueppel, R.A. (ed.) EUROCRYPT 1992. LNCS, vol. 658, pp. 477–481. Springer, Heidelberg (1993)

24. Kaihara, M.E., Takagi, N.: Bipartite modular multiplication method. IEEE Trans. Comput. **57**(2), 157–164 (2008)

25. Karatsuba, A.A., Ofman, Y.: Multiplication of many-digital numbers by automatic computers. Proc. USSR Acad. Sci. **145**, 293–294 (1962)

26. Koc, K., Acar, T., Kaliski Jr, B.S.: Analyzing and comparing montgomery multiplication algorithms. IEEE Micro **16**(3), 26–33 (1996)

27. Kocher, P.C.: Timing attacks on implementations of Diffie-Hellman, RSA, DSS and other systems. In: Koblitz, N. (ed.) CRYPTO 1996. LNCS, vol. 1109, pp. 104–113. Springer, Heidelberg (1996)

28. Lenstra, A.K., Hughes, J.P., Augier, M., Bos, J.W., Kleinjung, T., Wachter, C.: Public keys. In: Safavi-Naini, R., Canetti, R. (eds.) CRYPTO 2012. LNCS, vol. 7417, pp. 626–642. Springer, Heidelberg (2012)

29. Merrill, R.D.: Improving digital computer performance using residue number theory. IEEE Trans. Electron. Comput. **EC–13**(2), 93–101 (1964)

30. Montgomery, P.L.: Modular multiplication without trial division. Math. Comput. **44**(170), 519–521 (1985)

31. National Institute of Standards and Technology. Special publication 800–57: Recommendation for key management part 1: General (revision 3). http://csrc.nist.gov/publications/nistpubs/800-57/sp800-57_part1_rev3_general.pdf

32. OpenSSL. The open source toolkit for SSL/TLS (2013)

33. Page, D., Smart, N.P.: Parallel cryptographic arithmetic using a redundant Montgomery representation. IEEE Trans. Comput. **53**(11), 1474–1482 (2004)

34. Rivest, R.L., Shamir, A., Adleman, L.: A method for obtaining digital signatures and public-key cryptosystems. Commun. ACM **21**, 120–126 (1978)

35. Sánchez, A.H., Rodríguez-Henríquez, F.: NEON implementation of an attribute-based encryption scheme. In: Jacobson, M., Locasto, M., Mohassel, P., Safavi-Naini, R. (eds.) ACNS 2013. LNCS, vol. 7954, pp. 322–338. Springer, Heidelberg (2013)

36. U.S. Department of Commerce/National Institute of Standards and Technology. Digital Signature Standard (DSS). FIPS-186-3 (2009). http://csrc.nist.gov/publications/fips/fips186-3/fips_186-3.pdf

Hash Functions and MACs

Improved Single-Key Distinguisher on HMAC-MD5 and Key Recovery Attacks on Sandwich-MAC-MD5

Yu Sasaki[1][✉] and Lei Wang[2]

[1] NTT Secure Platform Laboratories, Tokyo, Japan
sasaki.yu@lab.ntt.co.jp
[2] Nanyang Technological University, Singapore, Singapore
Wang.Lei@ntu.edu.sg

Abstract. This paper presents key recovery attacks on Sandwich-MAC instantiating MD5, where Sandwich-MAC is an improved variant of HMAC and achieves the same provable security level and better performance especially for short messages. The increased interest in lightweight cryptography motivates us to analyze such a MAC scheme. We first improve a distinguishing-H attack on HMAC-MD5 proposed by Wang *et al.* We then propose key recovery attacks on Sandwich-MAC-MD5 by combining various techniques such as distinguishing-H for HMAC-MD5, IV Bridge for APOP, dBB-near-collisions for related-key NMAC-MD5, meet-in-the-middle attack *etc.* In particular, we generalize a previous key-recovery technique as a new tool exploiting a conditional key-dependent distribution. Our attack also improves the partial-key (K_1) recovery on MD5-MAC, and extends it to recover both K_1 and K_2.

Keywords: HMAC · Sandwich-MAC · MD5-MAC · MD5 · Key recovery

1 Introduction

A Message Authentication Code (MAC) is a cryptographic primitive which produces authenticity and data integrity. It takes a message M and a secret key K as input and computes a tag τ. A secure MAC must resist forgery attacks.

A MAC is often constructed from a hash function such as MD5 [1] and SHA-2 [2] for its performance and availability in software libraries. There are three hash-based MAC constructions [3]. Let $\mathcal{H}$ be a hash function. A *secret-prefix* method computes a tag of a message M by $\mathcal{H}(K\|M)$. A *secret-suffix* method computes a tag by $\mathcal{H}(M\|K)$. A *hybrid* method computes a tag by $\mathcal{H}(K\|M\|K)$.

When $\mathcal{H}$ processes M by iteratively applying a compression function h, a generic existential forgery attack with a complexity of $2^{n/2}$ exists for any of those three methods, where n is the size of the tag, τ, and the internal chaining variable [4]. Besides, each of the three types has its own features. The secret-prefix method

T. Lange, K. Lauter, and P. Lisoněk (Eds.): SAC 2013, LNCS 8282, pp. 493–512, 2014.
DOI: 10.1007/978-3-662-43414-7_25, © Springer-Verlag Berlin Heidelberg 2014

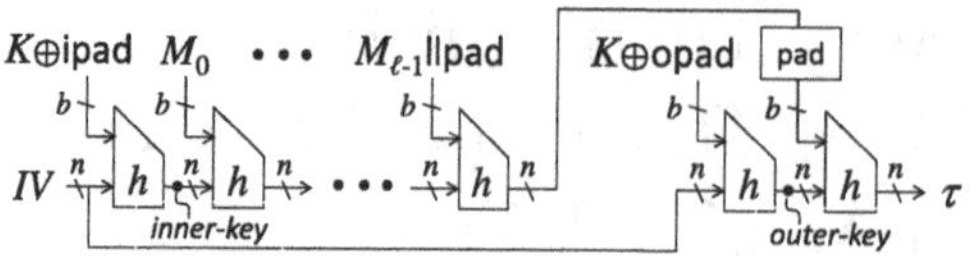

Fig. 1. Description of HMAC 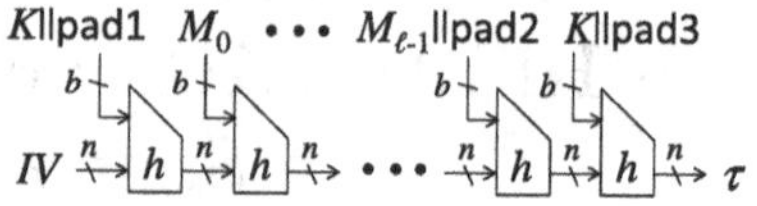   **Fig. 2.** Description of Sandwich-MAC

is vulnerable when a finalization process is not performed. This is called *length-extension attack* [5,6]. The secret-suffix method suffers from the collision attack on h. Two distinct messages (M, M') such that $h(M) = h(M')$ cause forgery attacks. The hybrid method seems to hide the weakness of two methods at a short glance. Strictly speaking, the hybrid method in [3] computes a tag by $\mathcal{H}(K\|\text{pad}\|M\|K')$ where K and K' are two independent keys and .pad denotes the padding string making the length of $K\|\text{pad}$ equal to the block length. The security of this construction can be proven by [7] up to $O(2^{n/2})$ queries. The single-key version, where $K = K'$, is well-known as *envelope MAC*, and was standardized for IPsec version 1 [8,9]. However, Preneel and van Oorschot showed that collisions of h can reveal the second key K or K' of the hybrid method [10] when the padding is not performed between M and the second key.

Currently, the most widely used hash-based MAC is HMAC [7,11] whose structure is a hybrid method with an appropriate padding before the second key. It computes a tag by $\mathcal{H}((K \oplus \text{opad})\|\mathcal{H}((K \oplus \text{ipad})\|M))$ as shown in Fig. 1. HMAC was proven to be a secure PRF up to $O(2^{n/2})$ queries [12]. Several researchers proposed improvement of HMAC from various viewpoints, e.g., security bound [13], performance [14–16], and side-channel resistance [17].

Comparison of HMAC and Sandwich-MAC. Sandwich-MAC [15] is another hybrid-type MAC with an appropriate padding before the second key. It computes a tag by $\mathcal{H}(K\|\text{pad1}\|M\|\text{pad2}\|K)$ as shown in Fig. 2. As with HMAC, it can call current hash functions without modifying the Merkle-Damgård (MD) implementations. It was proven to have the same security as HMAC, i.e., it is a PRF up to $O(2^{n/2})$ queries as long as the underlying compression function h is a PRF. Then, Sandwich-MAC has several advantages compared to HMAC.

Sandwich-MAC can be computed only with a single key K, while HMAC creates an inner-key $h(IV, K \oplus \text{ipad})$ and an outer-key $h(IV, K \oplus \text{opad})$. This reduces the number of additional blocks, where the "additional" is defined to be the number of h invocations in the scheme minus that in the usual Merkle-Damgård. HMAC requires 3 additional blocks, while Sandwich-MAC requires 1 or 2. It also avoids a related-key attack on HMAC [18] which exploits two keys with difference $\text{ipad} \oplus \text{opad}$. Another advantage is the number of hash function calls. HMAC requires 2 invocations of $\mathcal{H}$, while Sandwich-MAC requires only 1.

Table 1. Summary and comparison of results. ISR stands for internal state recovery.

Target	Model	Attack goal	Data	Time	Memory	Ref.	Remarks
HMAC-MD5	Adaptive	Dist-H/ISR	2^{97}	2^{97}	2^{89}	[32]	
	Adaptive	Dist-H/ISR	$2^{89.09}$	2^{89}	2^{89}	Ours	
	Non-adaptive	Dist-H/ISR	2^{113}	2^{113}	2^{66}	[32]	
	Non-adaptive	Dist-H/ISR	2^{113-x}	2^{113-x}	2^{66+x}	Ours	$0 \leq x \leq 6$
MD5-MAC		K_1-recovery	2^{97}	2^{97}	2^{89}	[32]	
		K_1-recovery	$2^{89.09}$	2^{89}	2^{89}	Ours	
		(K_1, K_2)-recovery	$2^{89.04}$	2^{89}	2^{89}	Ours	
Sandwich-	Basic	Key recovery	$2^{89.04}$	2^{89}	2^{89}	Ours	
MAC-MD5	Variant B	Key recovery	$2^{89.04}$	2^{89}	2^{89}	Ours	
	Extended B	Key recovery	$2^{89.04}$	2^{89}	2^{89}	Ours	

As shown in [19], these drawbacks of HMAC are critical especially for short messages. Taking these features into account, though it is not widely used at present, Sandwich-MAC is potentially a good candidate for a future MAC use.

Cryptanalysis Against Hybrid MAC. If the padding is not applied before the second key, the key is recovered with $O(2^{n/2})$ [10]. The attack was optimized when the underlying hash function is MD5 [20–23] through attacks against APOP protocol [24]. In this paper, the *IV Bridge* technique [21] will be exploited. However, these analyses basically cannot be used if an appropriate padding is applied before the second key as HMAC and Sandwich-MAC.

For HMAC/NMAC, most of attacks have been proposed with specific underlying hash functions. Kim *et al.* [25] proposed the notion of distinguishing-H attack. Contini and Yin presented how to exploit a differential characteristic of an underlying compression function to recover an inner-key of HMAC/NMAC [26]. Since then, many attacks have developed for HMAC/NMAC instantiating the MD4-family [27–31]. Regarding MD5, inner-key and outer-key recovery attacks were proposed only for NMAC only in the related-key model. Wang *et al.* presented a distinguishing-H attack on full HMAC-MD5 in the single-key model [32]. This is the only known result in the single-key model against hybrid MAC constructions with an appropriate padding instantiating full MD5.

Our Contributions. In this paper, we present key-recovery attacks against several hybrid MAC schemes with an appropriate padding when MD5 is instantiated as an underlying hash function. The summary of results is given in Table 1. The main contribution is an original-key recovery attack against Sandwich-MAC-MD5. This is the first result that recovers the original-key in the hybrid method. Even if the key-length is longer than the tag size n, the key is recovered faster than 2^n computations. Moreover, an attacker does not need to know the key length in advance. Given the specification of MD5, up to a 447-bit key is recovered with $2^{89.04}$ queries, 2^{89} table look-ups, and 2^{89} memory.

For the first step, we improve the distinguishing-H attack against HMAC-MD5 in the single-key model presented by Wang et al. [32], which can be utilized to reveal an internal state value. This reduces the number of queries from 2^{98} to $2^{89.09}$. This can be achieved by combining the attack in [32] with the message modification technique presented by Contini and Yin [26].

We then explain our original-key recovery attack against Sandwich-MAC-MD5 and its variant with combining various techniques on MD5. Specifically, we generalize the idea in [31] as a tool exploiting conditional key-dependent distributions. Note that a similar idea can be seen in [33] against Phelix. In this paper our goal is generalizing and simplifying the technique so that it can be applied to other cases. In the below, let α, κ and β be x-bit variables, and α_i, κ_i and β_i be the i-th bit of α, κ and β, respectively, where $0 \leq i \leq x - 1$.

Let us consider a modular addition $\alpha + \kappa = \beta$; α is a partially known variable where 1 bit (MSB) of α_{x-1} is known but α_i is unknown for the other i. κ is an unknown constant. β is a public variable computed by $\alpha + \kappa$, and its value is known. Intuitively, α, κ, and β correspond to the internal state, the key, and the tag, respectively. Then, the attacker can recover all bits of κ by iteratively collecting many pairs (β, α_{x-1}).

Experimental verification of this observation is shown in Appendix A.

Our attack on Sandwich-MAC-MD5 recovers the key with a complexity below 2^n, hence it also leads to a universal forgery attack on Sandwich-MAC-MD5.

MD5-MAC [4] generates three keys K_0, K_1, and K_2. The previous attack [32] only recovers K_1 with a cost of 2^{97}. Our improvement of HMAC-MD5 also reduces this complexity to $2^{89.09}$. Moreover, by applying our techniques on Sandwich-MAC-MD5, we achieve the first attack that recovers both K_1 and K_2.

2   Preliminaries

2.1   HMAC

HMAC is a hash-based MAC proposed by Bellare et al. [7]. Denote a hash function by $\mathcal{H}$. On an input message M, HMAC based on $\mathcal{H}$ is computed using a single secret key K as HMAC-$\mathcal{H}_K(M) = \mathcal{H}(\overline{K} \oplus \mathsf{opad} \| \mathcal{H}(\overline{K} \oplus \mathsf{ipad} \| M))$, where $\overline{K}$ is K padded to a full block by adding '0's, opad and ipad are two public constants, and '$\|$' denotes the concatenation.

2.2   Sandwich-MAC

Sandwich-MAC [15] is another hash-based MAC proposed by Yasuda. Besides the main scheme called *Basic*, there exist three variants called *variant A, B*, and *C*. Inside variant B, one extension is proposed, which we call *extended B*. In this paper, we analyze Basic, variant B, and extended B. We assume that the length of the key after the padding, $|K\|\mathsf{pad}|$, is shorter than the block length, b.

Sandwich-MAC Basic. Sandwich-MAC Basic computes tag values as follows.

$$\text{Sandwich-MAC-}\mathcal{H}_K(M) = \mathcal{H}(K\|\text{pad1}\|M\|\text{pad2}\|K), \tag{1}$$

where, pad1 appends $b - |K|$ bits of '0's so that $|K\|\text{pad1}|$ becomes equal to b and pad2 appends a single bit '1' and $b - ((|M| + 1) \bmod b)$ bits of '0's so that $|M\|\text{pad2}|$ becomes a multiple of b. Note that the input message for the last block always becomes $K\|\text{pad3}$, where pad3 is the padding scheme defined in a hash function $\mathcal{H}$. As long as MD5 is analyzed, pad3 is MD-strengthening.

Variant B and Extended B. Variant B is an optimized version when $|M|$ is already a multiple of the block length. The computation is described in Eq. (2).

Extended B is another optimization when the input message M ends in the middle of the block. Intuitively, the meaningless bits of '0' in pad3 in the last message block can be replaced with the message to be processed. For example, MD5 uses the MD-strengthening as pad3 and 65 bits are enough for it. Therefore, up to $b - |K| - 66$ bits in the last message block can be used to process the message. Let M consist of ℓ blocks $(M_0\| \cdots \|M_{\ell-1})$, and $|M_{\ell-1}| < b - |K| - 66$. The computation of extended B is described in Eq. (3).

$$\text{Sandwich-MAC}_B\text{-}\mathcal{H}_K(M) = \mathcal{H}(K\|\text{pad1}\|M\|K\|1). \tag{2}$$

$$\text{Sandwich-MAC}_{\text{ExtB}}\text{-}\mathcal{H}_K(M) = \mathcal{H}(K\|\text{pad1}\|M_0\| \cdots \|M_{\ell-2}\|K\|1\|M_{\ell-1}). \tag{3}$$

2.3 MD5 Specification and Free-Start Collision Attack on MD5

MD5 [1] is a Merkle-Damgård based hash function. Its block length is 512 bits and the output size is 128 bits. At first, an input message M is padded by the MD strengthening. The padded message is divided into 512-bit blocks, M_i $(i = 0, 1, \ldots, N - 1)$. First H_0 is set to IV, which is the initial value defined in the specification. Then, $H_{i+1} \leftarrow h(H_i, M_i)$ is computed for $i = 0, 1, \ldots, N - 1$, where h is a compression function and H_N is the hash value of M.

h takes a 128-bit value H_i and a 512-bit value M_i as input. M_i is divided into sixteen 32-bit values $m_0\|m_1\| \cdots \|m_{15}$, and H_i is divided into four 32-bit values $Q_{-3}\|Q_0\|Q_{-1}\|Q_{-2}$. Then, $Q_{j+1} \leftarrow R_j(Q_{j-3}\|Q_j\|Q_{j-1}\|Q_{j-2}, m_{\pi(j)})$ is computed for $j = 0, \ldots, 63$ and $(Q_{61}+Q_{-3})\|(Q_{64}+Q_0)\|(Q_{63}+Q_{-1})\|(Q_{62}+Q_{-2})$ is the output of h. R_j is the step function which computes Q_{j+1} as below.

$$Q_{j+1} \leftarrow Q_j + (Q_{j-3} + \Phi_j(Q_j, Q_{j-1}, Q_{j-2}) + m_{\pi(j)} + c_j) \lll s_j,$$

where Φ_j, c_j, and $\lll s_j$ denote Boolean function, constant, and left rotation by s_j-bits, respectively. $\pi(j)$ denotes a message expansion. Refer to [1] for details. Hereafter, we denote the B-th bit of variable X and Q_j by X_B and $Q_{j,B}$.

den Boer and Bosselaers [34] generated paired values (H_i, M_i) and (H_i', M_i) such that $h(H_i, M_i) = h(H_i', M_i)$, where H_i and H_i' have the difference: $H_i \oplus H_i' = (80000000, 80000000, 80000000, 80000000)$. Moreover, the MSB of the second, third, and fourth variables of H_i must be equal. Hereafter, we denote this difference (including two conditions of H_i) by Δ^{MSB}. To satisfy the characteristic, 46 conditions shown below must be satisfied: $Q_{j-1,31} = Q_{j-2,31}$ $(2 \leq j \leq 15)$, $Q_{j,31}$ $= Q_{j-1,31}$ $(16 \leq j \leq 31)$, $Q_{j,31} = Q_{j-2,31}$ $(48 \leq j \leq 63)$.

3   Improved Single-Key Attacks on HMAC-MD5

3.1   Previous Distinguishing-H Attack on HMAC-MD5

Wang et al. presented the distinguishing-H attack on HMAC-MD5 [32], which can also recover the internal-state value. The attack aims to detect a 2-block message where Δ^{MSB} is generated by the birthday paradox in the first block and the second block forms the dBB-collision [34]. The procedure is as follows.

1. Prepare 2^{89} distinct M_0 and a single message block M_1. Then, make queries of 2^{89} two-block messages $M_0 \| M_1$, and collect collisions of tags.
2. For each collision $(M_0 \| M_1, M_0' \| M_1)$, replace M_1 with different M_1', and query $(M_0 \| M_1', M_0' \| M_1')$. If a collision of the tag is obtained, the pair is not a dBB-collision and is erased.
3. For the remaining collisions, choose up to 2^{47} distinct values of M_1', and query $(M_0 \| M_1', M_0' \| M_1')$. If a collision is obtained, the pair is a dBB-collision.

$2^{2*89-1} = 2^{177}$ pairs are generated at step 1. We expect a pair $(M_0 \| M_1, M_0' \| M_1)$ such that the internal state after the first block denoted by H_1 and H_1' satisfy Δ^{MSB} (with probability 2^{-130}; 2^{-128} for the difference and 2^{-2} for the MSB values) and the second block follows the dBB-differential characteristic (with probability 2^{-46}). The other collisions are either collisions after the first block, i.e., $H_1 = H_1'$ (2^{49} pairs), or random collisions after the second block, i.e., $\Delta H_1 \notin \{0, \Delta^{\mathrm{MSB}}\}$ (2^{50} pairs). At step 2, collisions of $H_1 = H_1'$ are erased and at step 3, a dBB-collision can be identified. Step 1 requires 2^{89} queries, table lookups, and memory. Step 2 requires $(1 + 2^{49} + 2^{50}) \cdot 2 \approx 2^{51.58}$ queries. Step 3 requires $(1 + 2^{50}) \cdot 2^{47} \approx 2^{97}$ queries. Thus, step 3 dominates the entire cost.

Wang et al. also tweaked their attack to a chosen message attack. Firstly choose 2^{66} distinct M_0. Secondly build a structure of 2^{66} two-block messages $M_0 \| M_1$ by choosing a random message M_1. Then build 2^{47} such structures by choosing 2^{47} distinct M_1. Thirdly, query each structure and collect collisions of the tag. Finally, for each collision $(M_0 \| M_1, M_0' \| M_1)$, check the situation for the other $2^{47} - 1$ M_1. If there exists at least one M_1' such that $(M_0 \| M_1', M_0' \| M_1')$ do not collide, which implies $H_1 \neq H_1'$, and exists another M_1'' such that $(M_0 \| M_1'', M_0' \| M_1'')$ collides, then $(M_0 \| M_1, M_0' \| M_1)$ is a dBB-collision. The attack requires $2^{66+47} = 2^{113}$ queries, while the memory is reduced to 2^{66}.

Distinguishing-H Attack. Let MD5^r be a hash function where the compression function of MD5 is replaced with a random function with the same domain and range. This implies that the domain extension and the padding algorithm for MD5^r are the same as the ones of MD5. The distinguishing-H attack aims to decide whether a given oracle is HMAC-MD5 or HMAC-MD5^r. Wang et al. applied their attack to the given oracle. If a dBB-collision is found, they decide that the given oracle is HMAC-MD5. Otherwise, the oracle is HMAC-MD5^r.

Internal-State Recovery Attack. After a dBB-collision $(M_0\|M_1, M_0'\|M_1)$ is obtained, Wang *et al.* apply the technique proposed by Contini and Yin [26] to recover the chaining variables $Q_7\|Q_8\|Q_9\|Q_{10}$ of $h(H_1, M_1)$. Then H_1 will be recovered by an inverse computation. For a completed description we refer to [26]. The complexity of recovering H_1 is only 2^{44} queries and 2^{60} computations. The procedure of recovering H_1 is an adaptive chosen message attack. Thus the whole attack is an adaptive chosen message attack with a complexity of 2^{97} queries.

3.2   Improved Attacks on HMAC-MD5

We observe that the complexity of the core part i.e., finding a dBB-collision can be improved by applying the technique in [26]. In order to verify whether a collision $(M_0\|M_1, M_0'\|M_1)$ is a dBB-collision at step 3, Wang *et al.* chooses 2^{47} *completely* different values as M_1' to generate a second pair following the dBB-characteristic. Our idea is generating many M_1' by modifying M_1 only *partially* so that the differential characteristic for the first several steps remains satisfied.

We focus on the computations of $h(H_1, M_1)$ and $h(H_1', M_1)$. Recall the MD5 specification. M_1 is divided into $m_0\|m_1\|\cdots\|m_{15}$ and m_i is used at step i in the first 16 steps. Our strategy is only modifying message words that appear later. Note that one bit of m_{13} and the entire bits of m_{14} and m_{15} are fixed to the padding string and thus cannot be modified. So we modify m_{12} and 31 bits of m_{13} to generate distinct $m_{12}'\|m_{13}'$. Therefore, if $(M_0\|M_1, M_0'\|M_1)$ is a dBB-collision, the modified pair can always satisfy the conditions for the first 12 steps. Thus we only need to generate $2^{35(=47-12)}$ pairs at step 3. The complexity of step 3 is now reduced to $(1 + 2^{50}) \cdot 2^{35} \approx 2^{85}$ queries. Finally, the query complexity is improved from the previous 2^{97} to the sum of 2^{89} for step 1 and 2^{85} for step 3, which is $2^{89.09}$. Time and memory complexities remain unchanged (2^{89}). The success probability is around 0.87, following the similar evaluation in [32].

Our idea can also improve the previous non-adaptive chosen message attack. We prepare 2^{66+x} ($0 \le x \le 6$) distinct values for M_0. We can make 2^{131+2x} pairs of $M_0\|M_1$ for a fixed M_1. ΔH_1 satisfies Δ^{MSB} with probability 2^{-130}, and we need 2^{131} pairs to observe this event with a good probability. Therefore, with 2^{131+2x} pairs, one pair should satisfy Δ^{MSB} at H_1 and conditions for the first $2x$ steps in the second block. Then, M_1 is partially modified. We choose 2^{47-2x} distinct M_1 differing in the words m_{2x} and m_{2x+1}, and build 2^{47-2x} structures. Then, the above conditions are satisfied in any structure. Finally we find about two collisions $(M_0\|M_1, M_0'\|M_1)$ and $(M_0\|M_1', M_0'\|M_1')$, where $H_1 \ne H_1'$ holds, i.e., there exists at least one M_1'' such that $(M_0\|M_1'', M_0'\|M_1'')$ do not collide. The complexity is 2^{113-x} queries and the memory is 2^{66+x}, where $0 \le x \le 6$.

4   Key Recovery Attacks on Sandwich-MAC-MD5

4.1   Attacks on Sandwich-MAC-MD5 Basic

We show the attack for a key K with $|K| < 447$, which indicates that $K\|\mathrm{pad3}$ fits in one block. The attack can recover all bits of $K\|\mathrm{pad3}$ and the value of $\mathrm{pad3}$

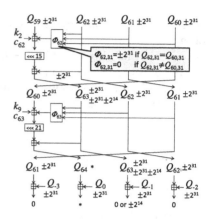

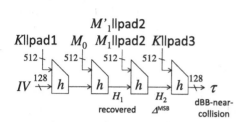

Fig. 3. Attack structure for Sandwich-MAC-MD5

Fig. 4. dBB-near-collisions

depends on $|K|$. Hence the attacker does not have to know $|K|$ in advance. Also note that the value of pad3 is determined as the MD-strengthening defined in MD5, whereas the Sandwich-MAC can principally accept any padding scheme but the same padding as pad1. Our attack can be extended for any padding scheme as long as $K\|$pad3 fits in one block. Hereafter, we denote a 512-bit value $K\|$pad3 by sixteen 32-bit values $k_0\|k_1\|\cdots\|k_{15}$, and aim to recover these values.

Overview. The attack is divided into 5 phases. The structure is shown in Fig. 3

1. Apply the internal state recovery attack in Sect. 3.2 to Sandwich-MAC to obtain the first message block M_0 and the corresponding internal state H_1.
2. For the second message block, search for 2^{77} message pairs (M_1, M_1') such that $\Delta H_2 = h(H_1, M_1\|\text{pad2}) \oplus h(H_1, M_1'\|\text{pad2}) = \Delta^{\text{MSB}}$. Because H_1 is already recovered, the computation can be done offline.
3. Query 2^{77} 2-block message pairs $(M_0\|M_1, M_0\|M_1')$, and pick the ones which produce dBB-near-collisions at the tag τ. A pair forms a dBB-near-collision with a probability 2^{-45}. Hence, we will obtain $2^{77-45} = 2^{32}$ pairs.
4. From 2^{32} pairs, recover the 32-bit subkey for the last step by exploiting a conditional key-dependent distribution.
5. As with phase 4, recover 512-bit key during the last 16 steps.

Phase 1: Internal State Recovery. The same procedure as the internal state recovery for HMAC-MD5 can be applied. Strictly speaking, the procedure can be optimized for Sandwich-MAC. Recall that our method in Sect. 3.2 could not modify m_{14} and m_{15} because they are fixed for the padding. In Sandwich-MAC, pad2 forces only 1 bit to be fixed, and thus we can modify m_{14} and 31 bits of m_{15}. This reduces the number of queries from $2^{89} + 2^{85}$ to $2^{89} + 2^{84} \approx 2^{89.04}$.

Phase 2: Generating (M_1, M_1') Producing Δ^{MSB}. This phase is offline without queries. For any underlying hash function, 2^{77} message pairs (M_1, M_1') can be found by the birthday attack with 2^{104} computations and memory. For MD5, the attack can be optimized. With the help of the collision attack techniques [35,36], Sasaki *et al.* proposed a tool called IV Bridge [21], which is a message difference producing the output difference $\Delta H_{i+1} = \Delta^{\text{MSB}}$ from the input difference $\Delta H_i = 0$ with a complexity of 2^{42}. The complexity was later improved by Xie and Feng to 2^{10} [37]. With the IV Bridge, message pairs can be found much faster than the birthday attack. Note that both characteristics in [21,37] assume that H_i is MD5's IV. Therefore, if IV is replaced with another H_1, the differential characteristic search must be performed again. Because the known automated differential characteristic search [37–39] can deal with any IV, a new characteristic will be found in the same manner. Also note that if the padding string pad2 forces many bits to be fixed, the IV Bridge search becomes harder or impossible due to the hardness of applying the message modification [36]. Because pad2 forces only 1 bit to be fixed, this is not a problem. The complexity for this phase is one execution of the differential characteristic search and $2^{10} \cdot 2^{77} = 2^{87}$ computations. The memory can be saved by running phase 3 as soon as we obtain each pair.

Phase 3: Detecting dBB-Near-Collisions. For the last message block, the probability that a pair produces the dBB-collision is 2^{-46}. We observe that producing collisions is not necessary because the attacker can observe the output values as a tag τ. Hence, the dBB-collision can be relaxed to the dBB-near-collision, and this increases the probability of the differential characteristic.

Considering the details for phase 4, the pair must follow the dBB-collision characteristic up to step 62. The differential propagation for the last 2 steps is depicted in Fig. 4. One condition in step 63 is erased, and the probability of the characteristic becomes 2^{-45}. After examining 2^{77} pairs, we obtain $2^{77-45} = 2^{32}$ pairs. This phase requires 2^{77} queries, and the memory to store 2^{32} pairs.

Note that false positives are unlikely. Our dBB-near-collisions do not produce any difference in the left most and right most words. Besides, the difference for the second right most word is limited to 2 patterns. The probability for randomly satisfying the dBB-near-collision is 2^{-95}, which is unlikely with 2^{77} trials.

Phase 4: Recovering the Last Subkey. Because both tags and H_2 are known, the attacker can compute $Q_{61}\|Q_{64}\|Q_{63}\|Q_{62}$ for each dBB-near-collision. We then analyze the last step. The equation to compute Q_{64} is $Q_{64} = Q_{63} + (Q_{60} + \Phi_{63}(Q_{63}, Q_{62}, Q_{61}) + k_9 + c_{63}) \lll 21$. The value of $(Q_{64} \ggg 21) - Q_{63} - \Phi_{63}(Q_{63}, Q_{62}, Q_{61}) - c_{63}$ can be computed with known values of $Q_{61}\|Q_{64}\|Q_{63}\|Q_{62}$. We denote this value by Z_{63}. Then, the equation becomes $Z_{63} = Q_{60} + k_9$.

We then observe that the attacker can know the MSB of Q_{60} from the difference of Q_{63}. The difference $\Delta Q_{63} = \pm 2^{31}$ indicates that $\Delta \Phi_{62} = \pm 2^{31}$. This only occurs when $Q_{62,31} = Q_{60,31}$. The difference $\Delta Q_{63} = \pm 2^{31} \pm 2^{14}$ indicates that $\Delta \Phi_{62} = 0$. This only occurs when $Q_{62,31} \neq Q_{60,31}$. Because the value of

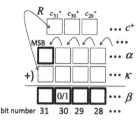

Fig. 5. Recovering κ_{31} and κ_{30}. Known bits are in bold squares.

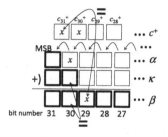

Fig. 6. Recovering κ_{29} to κ_0. Known bits are in bold squares.

Q_{62} is known, the value of $Q_{60,31}$ can be computed. In the following, we show how to recover k_9 with exploiting a conditional key-dependent distribution.

> **Conditional Key-dependent Distribution Technique:** *Let us consider a modular addition $\alpha + \kappa = \beta$; α is a variable where 1 bit (MSB) is known but the other bits are unknown. κ is an unknown constant. β is a public variable computed by $\alpha + \kappa$, and its value is known. Then, the attacker can recover all bits of κ by collecting many pairs (β, α_{x-1}).[1]*
>
> *The attacker separates the collected data into two groups depending on a condition on several bits of β. For each separated group, behavior of the other unconditioned bits is analyzed, i.e., conditional distribution is analyzed. If the conditional distribution differs depending on some bits of κ, those bits can be recovered by observing the conditional distribution.*

The details of the modular addition computation is shown in Fig. 5. We denote the carry value from bit position B to $B+1$ by c_{B+1}^+, e.g. the carry value to the MSB is c_{31}^+. Because α_{31} and β_{31} are known, the 1-bit relation of $c_{31}^+ \oplus \kappa_{31}$ denoted by R can be computed by $R = \alpha_{31} \oplus \beta_{31}$.

At first, we recover κ_{31} and κ_{30}. We separate the data into two groups by the condition $\beta_{30} = 0$ or 1, i.e., a group satisfying $\beta_{30} = 0$ and a group satisfying $\beta_{30} = 1$. For the group with $\beta_{30} = 0$, the distribution of other bits differs depending on the value of κ_{30}.

- If $\kappa_{30} = 0$, c_{31}^+ is 0 with probability $1/2$ and is 1 with probability $1/2$. This is because $\beta_{30} = \kappa_{30} = 0$ occurs only if $\alpha_{30} = c_{30}^+ = 0$ (with $c_{31}^+ = 0$) or $\alpha_{30} = c_{30}^+ = 1$ (with $c_{31}^+ = 1$).
- If $\kappa_{30} = 1$, c_{31}^+ is 1 with probability 1.

To utilize this difference, for each data in the group with $\beta_{30} = 0$, we simulate the value of κ_{31} by assuming that c_{31}^+ is 1. If $\kappa_{30} = 0$, the simulation returns the right value and wrong value of κ_{31} with a probability of $1/2$. Therefore, we will obtain 2 possibilities of κ_{31}. If $\kappa_{30} = 1$, the simulation always returns the right

---

[1] As a tool, the technique can be generalized more. If the B-th bit of α is known instead of the MSB, from the LSB to the B-th bit of κ can be recovered.

value of κ_{31}. Therefore, we can obtain the unique (right) value of κ_{31}. Due to the difference, we can recover κ_{30}, and at the same time, recover κ_{31}.

We can do the same for the group with $\beta_{30} = 1$.

- If $\kappa_{30} = 0$, c_{31}^+ is 0 with probability 1.
- If $\kappa_{30} = 1$, c_{31}^+ is 0 with probability 1/2 and is 1 with probability 1/2.

For each data in the group with $\beta_{30} = 1$, we simulate the value of κ_{31} by assuming that c_{31}^+ is 0, and check the number of returned values of the simulation.

We then recover κ_{29} to κ_0 in this order. In this time, we filter the data rather than separate it. In order to recover κ_B, where $29 \geq B \geq 0$, we set $(31 - B)$-bit conditions, and only pick the data satisfying all conditions. The conditions are $(\kappa_{30} = \beta_{30}), \ldots, (\kappa_{B+1} = \beta_{B+1})$, and $(c_{31}^+ = \beta_B)$. Note that $\kappa_{31,30,\ldots,B+1}$ are already recovered and c_{31}^+ can be easily computed by $\alpha_{31} \oplus \kappa_{31} \oplus \beta_{31}$. Let x be the value of c_{31}^+, where $x \in \{0,1\}$. Then, we can deduce that the value of κ_B is x. The proof is shown below, and is described in Fig. 6.

Proof. The value of β_B is x by the condition $c_{31}^+ = \beta_B$. From the condition $\kappa_{30} = \beta_{30}$, the values of α_{30} and c_{30}^+ are also known to be x. By iterating the same analysis from bit position 30 to $B + 1$, the values of α_{B+1} and c_{B+1}^+ are known to be x. The event $c_{B+1}^+ = \beta_B = 0$ only occurs when $\kappa_B = 0$. Similarly, the event $c_{B+1}^+ = \beta_B = 1$ only occurs when $\kappa_B = 1$.   □

The number of necessary pairs to recover all bits of κ is dominated by the recovery for κ_0, which is 2^{31} pairs. To increase the success probability, we generate 2^{32} pairs. Note that these pairs can also be used to analyze the other bits.

By replacing (α, κ, β) with (Q_{60}, k_9, Z_{63}), k_9 is recovered with 2^{32} dBB-near-collisions. If a high success probability is required, more pairs than 2^{32} should be collected. See Appendix A for more discussion.

Note that recovering κ with exhaustive search instead of the conditional key-dependent distribution is possible but inefficient. The attempt is as follows. *Guess κ, and then compute α by $\beta - \kappa$. The known 1-bit α_{31} takes a role of the filtering function.* During the computation of $\beta - \kappa$, the probability that flipping κ_0 changes the value of α_{31} (through the carry effect) is 2^{-31}. If we collect 2^{32} pairs of (β, α_{x-1}) and guess 32 bits of κ, all wrong guesses can be filtered out. However, this requires 2^{64} additions, which is worse than our attack.

Phase 5: Recovering 512-Bit Key in the Last 16 Steps. This phase is basically the iteration of phase 4. After k_9 is recovered, the tag value can be computed until step 63 in backward, and the same analysis as k_9 can be applied to the second last step to recover k_2. By iterating this for the last 16 steps, the original key K and the padding string pad3 are recovered. The number of dBB-near-collisions that we can use will increase as we recover more subkeys. This is because the probabilistic part of the differential characteristic will be shorter.

Attack Evaluation. Phase 1 requires $2^{89.04}$ queries, 2^{89} table look-ups, and a memory for 2^{89} states. Phase 2 requires $2^{10} \cdot 2^{77} = 2^{87}$ compression function computations. Phase 3 queries 2^{77} 2-block paired messages. It also requires to store 2^{32} pairs of H_2 and H_2', which requires a memory for 2^{33} states. Phase 4 requires $2^{32} \cdot 1/64 = 2^{26}$ computations. Phase 5 requires $15 \cdot 2^{32} \cdot 16/64$ which is less than 2^{34} computations. Hence, the dominant part is the internal state recovery attack for Phase 1. Our experiment in Appendix A suggests that generating more pairs at Phase 2 is better to obtain a high success probability. Then, the complexity for Phase 2 becomes 2^{88} or 2^{89} compression functions. The attack works without knowing $|K|$ as long as $|K| < 447$. The length of the queried message can always be a multiple of the block size. Hence, the attack can be extended to Sandwich-MAC variant B.

4.2   Attacks on Sandwich-MAC-MD5 Extended B

For this variant, the last message block can contain several bits chosen by the attacker. This reduces the complexity of the key recovery phase. Although the bottleneck of the attack is the internal state recovery phase, we show the attacks from two viewpoints. (1) We show the security gap between extended B and Basic. Although they have the the same provable security, the attack is easier in extended B. (2) In practice, K may be stored in a tamper-resistant device to prevent the side-channel analysis. However, the internal state value may not be protected, and the bottleneck of the attack may become the key-recovery part.

The range of $|K|$ in extended B is $|K| < 446$ because pad3 for MD5 is 65 bits minimum and one extra bit '1' is appended right after K. Although the attack strategy and the complexity depend on $|K|$, the initial part of the attack is the same. Due to the message block structure $K\|1\|M_1\|$pad3 and the MD5 message expansion $\pi(\cdot)$, the first steps of the compression function are updated by K. We call these steps *keyed steps*. The following steps are updated by the controlled message or the padding string until step 16. For example, if $|K|$ is 128, the first 4 steps are the keyed steps. The initial part of the attack is as follows.

1. Recover the internal state value H_1 by applying the internal state recovery attack in Sect. 3.2 or some side-channel analysis.
2. Searching for $\#X \cdot 2^{45}$ message pairs (M_1, M_1') such that $\Delta H_2 = \Delta^{\mathrm{MSB}}$, where $\#X$ depends on $|K|$. Query them to obtain $\#X$ dBB-near-collisions.
3. Recover the internal state value right after the keyed steps by using the freedom degrees of M_2 with the approach by Contini and Yin [26].

Phase 2 requires about $\#X \cdot 2^{45} \cdot 2^{10}$ computations and $\#X \cdot 2^{45}$ queries. Phase 3 requires about $\#X \cdot 2^{47}$ queries. We then recover K with the recovered internal state value right after the keyed steps. The attack strategy depends on $|K|$.

Case Study for $|K| = 128$. Because the tag size is 128 bits, $|K| = 128$ is a natural choice. We choose $\#X = 1$ for this case. In the last block, the value of $H_2 = Q_{-3}\|Q_0\|Q_{-1}\|Q_{-2}$ is known. After phase 3, the value of $Q_1\|Q_4\|Q_3\|Q_2$

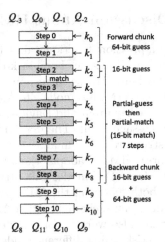

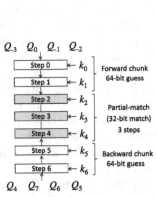

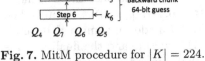

Fig. 7. MitM procedure for $|K| = 224$.   **Fig. 8.** MitM procedure for $|K| = 352$.

becomes known. Then, all of k_0, k_1, k_2, and k_3 are easily recovered by solving the equation of the step function, e.g. k_0 is recovered by $k_0 = ((Q_1 - Q_0) \ggg 7) - Q_{-3} - \Phi_0(Q_0, Q_{-1}, Q_{-2}) - c_0$. Other keys are also recovered with 1 computation.

Case Study for $|K| = 224$. K is divided into 7 words $k_0, \ldots, k_6$. In the last block, the values for $Q_{-3}\|Q_0\|Q_{-1}\|Q_{-2}$ and $Q_4\|Q_7\|Q_6\|Q_5$ are known after phase 3. To recover $k_0, \ldots, k_6$, we use the meet-in-the-middle (MitM) attack [40,41]. Particularly, *all subkey recovery attacks* [42] can be applied directly. The attack structure is depicted in Fig. 7. For each of the forward and backward chunks, the attacker guesses 64 key bits. The results from two chunks can match without computing 3 middle steps with the *partial-matching* [43]. To reduce the key space into a sufficiently small size, 4 pairs of $Q_{-3}\|Q_0\|Q_{-1}\|Q_{-2}$ and $Q_4\|Q_7\|Q_6\|Q_5$ are required. Hence, we set $\#X = 4$. The attack complexity is about $4 \cdot 2^{64} = 2^{66}$.

Case Study for $|K| = 352$. K is divided into 11 words $k_0, \ldots, k_{10}$. The attack structure is depicted in Fig. 8. For each chunk, 16 key bits are additionally guessed (all bits of k_0, k_1, k_9, k_{10} and 16 bits of k_2, k_8). This increases the number of skipped steps from 3 to 7 with the *partial-fixing* [44] or the *indirect partial-matching* [45]. To reduce the key space, we use 10 pairs of $Q_{-3}\|Q_0\|Q_{-1}\|Q_{-2}$ and $Q_8\|Q_{11}\|Q_{10}\|Q_9$, thus $\#X = 10$. The complexity for the attack is about $10 \cdot 2^{80} < 2^{84}$. After k_0, k_1, k_9, k_{10} and 16 bits of k_2, k_8 are recovered, the remaining 192 bits can be recovered by iterating the MitM attack. Note that if $|K| > 352$, the attack becomes worse than the one in Sect. 4.1.

5   Discussion About HMAC and Sandwich-MAC

The compression function takes two information as input; previous chaining variable and message. For block-cipher based compression functions including the MD4-family, these correspond to the key input and plaintext input. Matyas-Meyer-Oseas (MMO) mode [46, Algorithm 9.41] takes the previous chaining variable as the key input and Davies-Meyer (DM) mode [46, Algorithm 9.42] takes it as the message input. The main difference between HMAC and Sandwich-MAC is the structure of the finalization (computation after M is processed by the MD structure). HMAC adopts the MMO mode while Sandwich-MAC adopts the Davies-Meyer DM mode. Our attack shows that the (outer-)key can be recovered if both modes in the MD structure and the finalization are the DM-mode and a differential characteristic ($\Delta H_i \neq 0$, $\Delta M = 0$, $\Delta H_{i+1} = 0$) exists in h. The attack can also work if both modes are the MMO-mode. In summary, to minimize the risk, using different modes for the MD structure and the finalization is preferable. On the other hand, Okeya showed that, among 12 secure PGV modes [47], using the MMO-mode in the finalization is the only choice to protect the outer-key from the side-channel analysis [48, 49]. Taking into account our results, Okeya's results, and the fact that most of hash functions in practice adopt the DM-mode, we can learn that the HMAC construction is best.

The padding rule can impact the attack complexity. If the MD-strengthening is adopted as pad2 of Sandwich-MAC, the number of attacker's controlling bits decreases. This prevents the IV Bridge and makes the attack less efficient.

There are some gaps between the hardness of the attack and the provable security. From the provable security viewpoint, the choice of the padding scheme and the choice of HMAC, Sandwich-MAC Basic, variant B, and extended B are not very different. However, once the assumption for the proof (PRF of h) is broken, these choices make a significant difference. Hence, this is a trade-off between security and performance depending on how the assumption is trusted. These differences should be taken into account when a system is designed. We never conclude that Sandwich-MAC extended B is a bad idea. Reducing the amount of meaningless padding bits is very nice especially for tree hashing, where the hash value is computed with several hash function calls and thus the amount of the padding bits is bigger than the sequential hashing. Our point is that the damage of the scheme when the assumption is broken is usually not discussed, but it deserves the careful attention because industry continues using broken hash functions such as MD5 for long time.

In general, the impact of a differential attack on h for applications is unclear. Wang et al. showed the characteristic with $\Pr[h(H_i, M) = h(H_i', M)] > 2^{n/2}$ can mount the distinguishing-H attack against HMAC [32]. We extend it to the key-recovery on Sandwich-MAC. Finding such a conversion is an open problem.

6   Applications to MD5-MAC

MD5-MAC is an instantiation of the message authentication code MDx-MAC proposed by Preneel and van Oorschot [4] based on the hash function MD5.

MD5-MAC takes a single 128-bit key K as input, which is expanded to three 128-bit subkeys K_0, K_1 and K_2 as $K_i = \overline{\text{MD5}}(K\|U_i\|K), 0 \leq i \leq 2$; where $\overline{\text{MD5}}$ is the MD5 algorithm without the padding, and U_i with $0 \leq i \leq 2$ is a public constant. K_0 is used to replace the public initial value (IV) of MD5, and transforms the public function MD5(IV, M) into a keyed hash function MD5(K_0, M). K_1 is used inside the MD5 compression function. More precisely, K_1 is split into four 32-bit substrings $K_1[i]$ ($0 \leq i \leq 3$), and $K_1[i]$ is added to the constants used in round i of the MD5 compression function in modulo 2^{32}. We denote MD5 with K_1 inside the compression function and without the padding by $\overline{\text{MD5}}_{K_1}$. Then K_2 is expanded to a full block $\overline{K_2}$, namely 512-bit long, as $\overline{K_2} = K_2\|(K_2 \oplus T_0)\|(K_2 \oplus T_1)\|(K_2 \oplus T_2)$ where T_i with $0 \leq i \leq 2$ is a public constant. Let M be an input message and pad be the padding algorithm of MD5. Then, MD5-MAC is computed as below:

$$\text{MD5-MAC}_K(M) = \overline{\text{MD5}}_{K_1}(K_0, \text{pad}(M)\|\overline{K_2}).$$

Previous Attacks. Wang *et al.* proposed a partial key-recovery attack on MD5-MAC [32], which recovers a 128-bit key K_1 with about 2^{97} MAC queries and $2^{61.58}$ offline computations. Their attack [32] is divided into three phases.

1. Generate 3 dBB-collisions of the form $(M_0\|M_1)$ and $(M_0'\|M_1)$.
2. Recover 95 bits of Q_1, Q_2, Q_3, Q_4, Q_5 and 90 bits of $Q_6, Q_7, Q_8, Q_9, Q_{10}$ with the method proposed by Contini and Yin [26].
3. Recover $K_1[0]$. Then recover $K_1[1], K_1[2]$, and $K_1[3]$.

The first phase requires 2^{97} queries. The second phase requires $(95 + 90) \cdot 2^{47} \approx 2^{54.53}$ queries. To recover $K_1[0]$ in the third phase, the step function equation is solved by guessing unknown 65 bits of $(Q_1, Q_2, Q_3, Q_4, Q_5)$. For each guess, the following 5 steps are computed and check the match with already recovered 90 bits of $(Q_6, Q_7, Q_8, Q_9, Q_{10})$. Hence, this requires $2^{65} \cdot 6/64 \approx 2^{61.58}$ MD5 computations. $K_1[1], K_1[2]$, and $K_1[3]$ are recovered with the divide-and-conquer approach. Hence the cost to recover each key is several iterations of 2^{32} guesses. Overall, the dominant part of the attack is finding dBB-collisions. Note that the attack cannot recover any information about K_0 and K_2.

Improved Key Recovery for K_1. Because the dominant part of the attack is finding 3 dBB-collisions, the attack can be improved with our improved procedure on HMAC-MD5 in Sect. 3. The application is straight-forward and thus we omit the details. The attack cost becomes $2^{89.09}$ queries and 2^{89} table lookups.

Extended Key Recovery for K_2. Once K_1 is recovered, the MAC computation structure becomes essentially the same as the one for Sandwich-MAC Basic with MD5. Because our attack on Sandwich-MAC-MD5 can recover 512-bit secret information of the last message block faster than 2^{128} queries and computations, a 512-bit key $\overline{K_2}$ can be recovered with exactly the same procedure as the one for Sandwich-MAC-MD5. The bottleneck of the attack is still finding dBB-collisions, which requires $2^{89.04}$ queries and 2^{89} table lookups. We emphasize that this is the first result which can recover K_2 of MD5-MAC.

7 Concluding Remarks

In this paper, we first improved the distinguishing-H attacks on HMAC-MD5. We then proposed the key-recovery attack on Sandwich-MAC-MD5 by combining various techniques. In particular, we generalized the key-recovery technique exploiting the conditional key-dependent distributions. As a result, we achieved the first results that can recover the original-key against a hybrid MAC with an appropriate padding. Our results also improved the previous key-recovery attack on MD5-MAC, and extended the recovered key to both of K_1 and K_2. We believe our results lead to a better understanding of the MAC construction.

A Testing Conditional Key-Dependent Distributions

We implemented the key recovery procedure with the conditional key-dependent distributions. The first experiment verifies the key recovery procedure for κ_{31} and κ_{30}. The second experiment verifies the key recovery procedure for κ_{29} to κ_0.

To recover κ_{31} and κ_{30}, we first observe whether the simulated value of κ_{31} is always the same or not for the group with $\beta_{30} = 0$. We then observe the same thing for the group with $\beta_{30} = 1$. If $\kappa_{30} = 0$ (resp. $\kappa_{30} = 1$), two values are returned from the group with $\beta_{30} = 0$ (resp. $\beta_{30} = 1$) and only one value is returned from the group with $\beta_{30} = 1$ ($\beta_{30} = 0$). κ_{30} is recovered after two values are returned from one of two groups. If the number of data is small, the simulation may return only one value. This occurs probabilistically.

Let D be the number of available data. In our experiment, we first fix the value of κ. We then choose α D times from a uniformly distributed space, and compute $\beta = \kappa + \alpha$ for each α. Then, we run the key recovery algorithm and check κ_{30} is recovered or not i.e., one group returns two values. Finally, we iterate this procedure 100,000 times and count how many times κ_{30} is recovered. The results are shown in Table 2. From Table 2, collecting 2^{10} data seems enough to recover κ_{31} and κ_{30} with a high probability. Because our attack generates 2^{32} dBB-near-collisions, recovering κ_{30} and κ_{31} succeeds with probability almost 1.

To recover κ_{29} to κ_0, we search for a data satisfying all conditions. Because the recovery procedure is almost the same for different bit positions, we do the experiment only for recovering the 8 bits, κ_{29} to κ_{22}. The experiment successfully recovers the key as long as sufficient data is available. We performed the key recovery procedure 1,000 times by changing the number of data D. The number of successes is listed in Table 3. Underlined values show the data for the theoretical evaluation. We can see that the theoretical evaluation has a low success probability. In our attack, we generate 2^{32} data for recovering κ_0, which is a double of the theoretical evaluation. From Table 3, the probability that κ_0 is successfully recovered is expected to be about 55 %. Moreover, the success probability of recovering κ_1 is about 75 %, κ_2 is about 87 %, κ_3 is about 94 %,

Table 2. Experiment for the recovery procedure of κ_{31} and κ_{30}.

D	#Success	Success prob. (%)
2	8368	8.4
4	28673	28.7
8	56067	56.1
16	76510	76.5
32	87970	88.0
64	93743	93.7
128	96955	97.0
256	98465	98.5
512	99216	99.2

Table 3. Experiment for the recovery procedure of κ_{29} to κ_{22}.

Target bit	D 2	4	8	16	32	64	128	256	512	1024
κ_{29}	238	378	598	768	891	928	975	978	989	995
κ_{28}	116	202	374	559	751	886	953	973	989	987
κ_{27}	58	122	214	360	539	721	878	935	969	980
κ_{26}	15	58	101	195	361	587	731	871	952	969
κ_{25}	10	28	50	118	212	381	557	774	862	944
κ_{24}	4	20	36	70	122	208	370	566	760	875
κ_{23}	2	7	10	28	64	119	199	380	552	752
κ_{22}	4	2	8	12	31	60	104	211	373	573

and so on. If the expected value is calculated, 2.25 candidates, which is about $2^{1.18}$, candidates of κ will remain after the analysis of 2^{32} pairs. We can use the exhaustive search to reduce these space. At phase 5 of the procedure, the analysis with 2^{32} data is iterated 16 times, and thus the remaining space will be $2^{1.18*16} = 2^{18.88}$. Of course, by generating more pairs than 2^{32} at phases 2 and 3, the success probability of recovering κ can be close to 1.

References

1. Rivest, R.L.: Request for Comments 1321: The MD5 Message Digest Algorithm. The Internet Engineering Task Force (1992). http://www.ietf.org/rfc/rfc1321.txt
2. U.S. Department of Commerce, National Institute of Standards and Technology: Secure Hash Standard (SHS) (Federal Information Processing Standards Publication 180-3) (2008). http://csrc.nist.gov/publications/fips/fips180-3/fips180-3_final.pdf
3. Tsudik, G.: Message authentication with one-way hash functions. ACM SIGCOMM Comput. Commun. Rev. **22**(5), 29–38 (1992)
4. Preneel, B., van Oorschot, P.C.: MDx-MAC and building fast MACs from hash functions. In: Coppersmith, D. (ed.) CRYPTO 1995. LNCS, vol. 963, pp. 1–14. Springer, Heidelberg (1995)

5. Coron, J.-S., Dodis, Y., Malinaud, C., Puniya, P.: Merkle-Damgård revisited: how to construct a hash function. In: Shoup, V. (ed.) CRYPTO 2005. LNCS, vol. 3621, pp. 430–448. Springer, Heidelberg (2005)
6. U.S. Department of Commerce, National Institute of Standards and Technology: Federal Register, vol. 72, no. 212, November 2, 2007/Notices (2007). http://csrc. nist.gov/groups/ST/hash/documents/FR_Notice_Nov07.pdf
7. Bellare, M., Canetti, R., Krawczyk, H.: Keying hash functions for message authentication. In: Koblitz, N. (ed.) CRYPTO 1996. LNCS, vol. 1109, pp. 1–15. Springer, Heidelberg (1996)
8. Kaliski Jr., B.S., Robshaw, M.J.B.: Message authentication with MD5. Technical report, CryptoBytes (1995)
9. Metzger, P., Simpson, W.A.: Request for Comments 1852: IP Authentication using Keyed SHA. The Internet Engineering Task Force (1995). http://www.ietf.org/rfc/ rfc1852.txt
10. Preneel, B., van Oorschot, P.C.: On the security of two MAC algorithms. In: Maurer, U.M. (ed.) EUROCRYPT 1996. LNCS, vol. 1070, pp. 19–32. Springer, Heidelberg (1996)
11. U.S. Department of Commerce, National Institute of Standards and Technology: The Keyed-Hash Message Authentication Code (HMAC) (Federal Information Processing Standards Publication 198), July 2008. http://csrc.nist.gov/ publications/fips/fips198-1/FIPS-198-1_final.pdf
12. Bellare, M.: New proofs for NMAC and HMAC: security without collision-resistance. In: Dwork, C. (ed.) CRYPTO 2006. LNCS, vol. 4117, pp. 602–619. Springer, Heidelberg (2006)
13. Yasuda, K.: Multilane HMAC— security beyond the birthday limit. In: Srinathan, K., Rangan, C.P., Yung, M. (eds.) INDOCRYPT 2007. LNCS, vol. 4859, pp. 18–32. Springer, Heidelberg (2007)
14. Yasuda, K.: Boosting Merkle-Damgård hashing for message authentication. In: Kurosawa, K. (ed.) ASIACRYPT 2007. LNCS, vol. 4833, pp. 216–231. Springer, Heidelberg (2007)
15. Yasuda, K.: "Sandwich" is indeed secure: how to authenticate a message with just one hashing. In: Pieprzyk, J., Ghodosi, H., Dawson, E. (eds.) ACISP 2007. LNCS, vol. 4586, pp. 355–369. Springer, Heidelberg (2007)
16. Yasuda, K.: HMAC without the "second" key. In: Samarati, P., Yung, M., Martinelli, F., Ardagna, C.A. (eds.) ISC 2009. LNCS, vol. 5735, pp. 443–458. Springer, Heidelberg (2009)
17. Gauravaram, P., Okeya, K.: An update on the side channel cryptanalysis of MACs based on cryptographic hash functions. In: Srinathan, K., Rangan, C.P., Yung, M. (eds.) INDOCRYPT 2007. LNCS, vol. 4859, pp. 393–403. Springer, Heidelberg (2007)
18. Peyrin, T., Sasaki, Y., Wang, L.: Generic related-key attacks for HMAC. In: Wang, X., Sako, K. (eds.) ASIACRYPT 2012. LNCS, vol. 7658, pp. 580–597. Springer, Heidelberg (2012)
19. Patel, S.: An efficient MAC for short messages. In: Nyberg, K., Heys, H.M. (eds.) SAC 2002. LNCS, vol. 2595, pp. 353–368. Springer, Heidelberg (2003)
20. Leurent, G.: Message freedom in MD4 and MD5 collisions: application to APOP. In: Biryukov, A. (ed.) FSE 2007. LNCS, vol. 4593, pp. 309–328. Springer, Heidelberg (2007)
21. Sasaki, Y., Wang, L., Ohta, K., Kunihiro, N.: Security of MD5 challenge and response: extension of APOP password recovery attack. In: Malkin, T. (ed.) CT-RSA 2008. LNCS, vol. 4964, pp. 1–18. Springer, Heidelberg (2008)

22. Sasaki, Y., Yamamoto, G., Aoki, K.: Practical password recovery on an MD5 challenge and response. Cryptology ePrint Archive, Report 2007/101 (2007). http://eprint.iacr.org/2007/101

23. Wang, L., Sasaki, Y., Sakiyama, K., Ohta, K.: Bit-free collision: application to APOP attack. In: Takagi, T., Mambo, M. (eds.) IWSEC 2009. LNCS, vol. 5824, pp. 3–21. Springer, Heidelberg (2009)

24. Myers, J., Rose, M.: Post office protocol - version 3. RFC 1939 (Standard), May 1996. Updated by RFCs 1957, 2449. http://www.ietf.org/rfc/rfc1939.txt

25. Kim, J.-S., Biryukov, A., Preneel, B., Hong, S.H.: On the security of HMAC and NMAC based on HAVAL, MD4, MD5, SHA-0 and SHA-1 (extended abstract). In: De Prisco, R., Yung, M. (eds.) SCN 2006. LNCS, vol. 4116, pp. 242–256. Springer, Heidelberg (2006)

26. Contini, S., Yin, Y.L.: Forgery and partial key-recovery attacks on HMAC and NMAC using hash collisions. In: Lai, X., Chen, K. (eds.) ASIACRYPT 2006. LNCS, vol. 4284, pp. 37–53. Springer, Heidelberg (2006)

27. Fouque, P.-A., Leurent, G., Nguyen, P.Q.: Full key-recovery attacks on HMAC/NMAC-MD4 and NMAC-MD5. In: Menezes, A. (ed.) CRYPTO 2007. LNCS, vol. 4622, pp. 13–30. Springer, Heidelberg (2007)

28. Lee, E., Chang, D., Kim, J.-S., Sung, J., Hong, S.H.: Second preimage attack on 3-Pass HAVAL and partial key-recovery attacks on HMAC/NMAC-3-pass HAVAL. In: Nyberg, K. (ed.) FSE 2008. LNCS, vol. 5086, pp. 189–206. Springer, Heidelberg (2008)

29. Rechberger, C., Rijmen, V.: On authentication with HMAC and Non-random properties. In: Dietrich, S., Dhamija, R. (eds.) FC 2007 and USEC 2007. LNCS, vol. 4886, pp. 119–133. Springer, Heidelberg (2007)

30. Rechberger, C., Rijmen, V.: New results on NMAC/HMAC when instantiated with popular hash functions. J. Univ. Comput. Sci. 14(3), 347–376 (2008)

31. Wang, L., Ohta, K., Kunihiro, N.: New key-recovery attacks on HMAC/NMAC-MD4 and NMAC-MD5. In: Smart, N.P. (ed.) EUROCRYPT 2008. LNCS, vol. 4965, pp. 237–253. Springer, Heidelberg (2008)

32. Wang, X., Yu, H., Wang, W., Zhang, H., Zhan, T.: Cryptanalysis on HMAC/NMAC-MD5 and MD5-MAC. In: Joux, A. (ed.) EUROCRYPT 2009. LNCS, vol. 5479, pp. 121–133. Springer, Heidelberg (2009)

33. Wu, H., Preneel, B.: Differential-linear attacks against the stream cipher phelix. In: Biryukov, A. (ed.) FSE 2007. LNCS, vol. 4593, pp. 87–100. Springer, Heidelberg (2007)

34. den Boer, B., Bosselaers, A.: Collisions for the compression function of MD-5. In: Helleseth, T. (ed.) EUROCRYPT 1993. LNCS, vol. 765, pp. 293–304. Springer, Heidelberg (1994)

35. Klima, V.: Tunnels in hash functions: MD5 collisions within a minute. IACR Cryptology ePrint Archive: Report 2006/105 (2006). http://eprint.iacr.org/2006/105.pdf

36. Wang, X., Yu, H.: How to break MD5 and other hash functions. In: Cramer, R. (ed.) EUROCRYPT 2005. LNCS, vol. 3494, pp. 19–35. Springer, Heidelberg (2005)

37. Xie, T., Feng, D.: How to find weak input differences for MD5 collision attacks. Cryptology ePrint Archive, Report 2009/223 (2009) Version 20090530:102049. http://eprint.iacr.org/2009/223

38. De Cannière, C., Rechberger, C.: Finding SHA-1 characteristics: general results and applications. In: Lai, X., Chen, K. (eds.) ASIACRYPT 2006. LNCS, vol. 4284, pp. 1–20. Springer, Heidelberg (2006)

39. Mendel, F., Rechberger, C., Schläffer, M.: MD5 Is weaker than weak: attacks on concatenated combiners. In: Matsui, M. (ed.) ASIACRYPT 2009. LNCS, vol. 5912, pp. 144–161. Springer, Heidelberg (2009)

40. Diffie, W., Hellman, M.E.: Exhaustive cryptanalysis of the NBS data encryption standard. Computer **10**(6), 74–84 (1977)

41. Bogdanov, A., Rechberger, C.: A 3-subset meet-in-the-middle attack: cryptanalysis of the lightweight block cipher KTANTAN. In: Biryukov, A., Gong, G., Stinson, D.R. (eds.) SAC 2010. LNCS, vol. 6544, pp. 229–240. Springer, Heidelberg (2011)

42. Isobe, T., Shibutani, K.: All subkeys recovery attack on block ciphers: extending meet-in-the-middle approach. In: Knudsen, L.R., Wu, H. (eds.) SAC 2012. LNCS, vol. 7707, pp. 202–221. Springer, Heidelberg (2013)

43. Aoki, K., Sasaki, Y.: Preimage attacks on one-block MD4, 63-step MD5 and more. In: Avanzi, R.M., Keliher, L., Sica, F. (eds.) SAC 2008. LNCS, vol. 5381, pp. 103–119. Springer, Heidelberg (2009)

44. Sasaki, Y., Aoki, K.: Finding preimages in full MD5 faster than exhaustive search. In: Joux, A. (ed.) EUROCRYPT 2009. LNCS, vol. 5479, pp. 134–152. Springer, Heidelberg (2009)

45. Aoki, K., Guo, J., Matusiewicz, K., Sasaki, Y., Wang, L.: Preimages for step-reduced SHA-2. In: Matsui, M. (ed.) ASIACRYPT 2009. LNCS, vol. 5912, pp. 578–597. Springer, Heidelberg (2009)

46. Menezes, A.J., van Oorschot, P.C., Vanstone, S.A.: Handbook of Applied Cryptography. CRC Press, Boca Raton (1997)

47. Preneel, B., Govaerts, R., Vandewalle, J.: Hash functions based on block ciphers: a synthetic approach. In: Stinson, D.R. (ed.) CRYPTO 1993. LNCS, vol. 773, pp. 368–378. Springer, Heidelberg (1994)

48. Okeya, K.: Side channel attacks against HMACs based on block-cipher based hash functions. In: Batten, L.M., Safavi-Naini, R. (eds.) ACISP 2006. LNCS, vol. 4058, pp. 432–443. Springer, Heidelberg (2006)

49. Okeya, K.: Side channel attacks against hash-based MACs with PGV compression functions. IEICE Transactions **91–A**(1), 168–175 (2008)

Provable Second Preimage Resistance Revisited

Charles Bouillaguet[1]([✉]) and Bastien Vayssière[2]

[1] LIFL, Université Lille-1, Lille, France
`charles.bouillaguet@lifl.Fr`
[2] PRISM Lab, Université de Versailles/Saint-Quentin-en-Yvelines,
Versailles, France
`Bastien.Vayssiere@prism.uvsq.fr`

Abstract. Most cryptographic hash functions are iterated constructions, in which a mode of operation specifies how a compression function or a fixed permutation is applied. The Merkle-Damgård mode of operation is the simplest and more widely deployed mode of operation, yet it suffers from generic second preimage attacks, even when the compression function is ideal.

In this paper we focus on provable security against second preimage attacks. Based on the study of several existing constructions, we describe simple properties of modes of operation and show that they are sufficient to allow some form of provable security, first in the random oracle model and then in the standard model. Our security proofs are extremely simple. We show for instance that the claims of the designers of HAIFA regarding second preimage resistance are valid.

Lastly, we give arguments that proofs of second preimage resistance by a black-box reduction incur an unavoidable security loss.

Keywords: Hash function · Second preimage resistance · Security proof · Unavoidable security loss · Black-box reductions

1   Introduction

Of all major cryptographic primitives, hash functions have been continuously avoiding the theoretical nirvana other cryptographic primitives enjoy. While ciphers, encryption schemes, message authentication codes and signature schemes have well understood theoretical foundations, acknowledged security definitions, and some can be idealized using primitives which are considered natural and fair, hash functions have remained as elusive as they were. There is however a consensus to consider that a cryptographic hash function $H : \{0,1\}^* \rightarrow \{0,1\}^n$ cannot be "good" if it does not simultaneously resist:

1. Collision adversaries up to about $2^{n/2}$ queries
2. Preimage adversaries up to about 2^n queries
3. Second-Preimage adversaries up to about 2^n queries

T. Lange, K. Lauter, and P. Lisoněk (Eds.): SAC 2013, LNCS 8282, pp. 513–532, 2014.
DOI: 10.1007/978-3-662-43414-7_26, © Springer-Verlag Berlin Heidelberg 2014

Many modern hash functions are usually built by combining a *compression function*, hashing a small number of bits (typically 512) into a smaller number (typically 256), and of a *mode of operation*, describing how the compression function should be used to process arbitrarily big messages. The most popular and well-known mode of operation is the *Merkle-Damgård* construction, introduced in 1989 and named after its two independent inventors [6,14]. Besides its simplicity and elegance, the most distinctive feature of this mode of operation is that it promotes the collision-resistance of the compression function to that of the full hash function. Indeed, its inventors proved that there exist an efficient algorithm which, given two messages $M \neq M'$ such that $H^f(M) = H^f(M')$, extracts two compression-function inputs $x \neq x'$ such that $f(x) = f(x')$, where H^f denotes the Merkle-Damgård iteration of the compression function f.

The Merkle-Damgård mode of operation therefore enjoys a form of *provable security*, since the whole hash function is not less secure than the compression function with respect to collision adversaries. This allows hash function designers to focus on designing collision-resistant compression functions, arguably an easier task than designing a full-blown hash function. A comparable result holds for preimage resistance, since a preimage on the full hash function would lead to a pseudo-preimage on the compression function.

The situation is however not as good for the remaining classical security notion, namely second preimage resistance. In fact, it turned out that the Merkle-Damgård iteration of a secure compression function is not as secure as the compression function itself: in 2005, Kelsey and Schneier described an attack [12] that finds a second preimage of an ℓ-block message with $2^n/\ell$ evaluations of the compression function, even if it is ideal (i.e., a public random function).

The existence of several generic attacks [10–12] demonstrated that there was definitely a problem with the Merkle-Damgård construction, and motivated further research, and new modes of operations have emerged. It also motivated hash function designers to provide *proofs* that their mode of operation is sounds, and that it does not suffer from generic attacks.

An elegant solution, both theoretically and practically appealing, is the *wide-pipe* hash proposed by Lucks in 2005 [13]. The underlying idea is simple: make the internal state twice as big as the output. This makes the construction provably resistant to second preimage attacks in the standard model, because a second preimage on the iteration yields either an n-bit second preimage or a $2n$-bit collision on the compression function. This construction is also very practical, and it is implemented by 4 out of the 5 SHA-3 finalists. However, the memory footprint of a wide-pipe construction is as least twice as big compared to Merkle-Damgård, so in some cases where memory is restricted, it would be beneficial to have a "narrow-pipe" mode of operation.

In this paper, we focus on *narrow-pipe*[1] modes of operation, where several questions remain unanswered. For instance, the exact resistance to generic second preimage attack of the Merkle-Damgård construction is in fact unknown.

---

[1] We call "narrow-pipe" a construction where the internal state has the same length as the digest.

Existing attacks give an upper-bound above the birthday paradox, and the fact that a second preimage is also a collision give a birthday lower-bound. The generic second preimage security of Merkle-Damgård is thus known to lie somewhere between $2^{n/2}$ and $2^n/\ell$ queries, for messages of size ℓ.

Our Goal and Our Results. The objective of this paper is to describe very simple conditions that, when satisfied by a narrow-pipe mode of operations, are sufficient to provide some form of provable resistance against second preimage attacks beyond the birthday bound.

Provable security against second preimage attack comes in several flavors. One possible setting to discuss the security of a mode of operation is the *random oracle model*, i.e., assuming that the compression function is a public random function. Proofs that there cannot exist second preimage attacks under the assumption that the compression function is a random oracle show that the mode of operation is immune to *generic attacks*, i.e., attacks that target the mode of operation itself and thus work for any compression function. The second preimage attacks of Kelsey-Schneier and that of Andreeva *et al.* [2] are generic attacks.

We show that a simple tweak to the Merkle-Damgård mode is sufficient to prevent all generic second preimage attacks. This modification, namely the inclusion of a round counter, is one of the distinctive features of HAIFA. Biham and Dunkelman proposed HAIFA in 2006 [8], as a collection of tweaks to the original Merkle-Damgård mode of operation; they claimed a security level of 2^n against second preimage adversaries, without providing proofs. We thus show that their claim is valid.

The assumption that hash functions, or just components thereof, are random, is strong and unrealistic enough to make some uncomfortable, so that we would like to get rid of it. Constructions of *keyed* hash functions provably achieving a form of second preimage resistance without relying on the existence of public random functions, but instead based on the hardness of a general assumption have been known for quite a while [9,15], under the name of *Universal One-Way Hash Functions* (UOWHFs). Later on, modes of operation of keyed hash functions that promote a form of second preimage resistance from the compression function to the whole construction have been designed [4,17].

The security of the latter modes of operation is established by a *black-box reduction*, namely an algorithm that turns a successful attacker against the hash function into a (somewhat less) successful attacker against the compression function. Thus, the iteration remains secure, up to some level, as long as the compression functions are themselves secure.

Inspired by these constructions we again isolate a specific property of modes of operation which is sufficient to provide this kind of "reductionist" security, without heavy assumptions on the compression function. This feature is, again, simple: given a bit string x, it must be possible to forge a message M such that $f(x)$ is evaluated while computing $H^f(M)$. We then describe a "generic" reduction that solely requires this specific property to show that a mode of operation promotes the second preimage resistance of the compression function. This proof is, to some extent, an abstraction of the security proofs of several existing schemes.

Lastly, we observe that in all these proofs of second preimage security by reduction there is always a *security loss* proportional to the size of hashed messages (i.e., security is guaranteed up to a level of $2^n/\ell$ where ℓ denotes the size of hashed messages). We give arguments hinting that this security loss is unavoidable, and is caused by the proof technique itself.

Organisation of the Paper. In Sect. 2 we recall the security notions we are concerned with. Then in Sect. 3 we introduce a generic narrow-pipe mode of operation, and we show that all the particular constructions that we consider are instances of this generic framework. In Sect. 4 we discuss the generic attacks that apply to the known provably second-preimage resistant constructions we consider, and we show how to make them immune to these attacks. Lastly, in Sect. 5 we show our main result, namely that the security loss in the security proofs is unavoidable.

2   Definitions

We recall the definition of the usual second preimage notions. The Spr notion is folklore and applies to unkeyed hash functions, while Sec and eSec security notions have been defined in [16] and applies to families of hash functions indexed by a key.

Spr   The adversary receives a (random) challenge M and has to find a second message M' such that $H(M) = H(M')$ with $M \neq M'$. The advantage of the adversary is its success probability (taken over the random coins used by the adversary and the random choice of the challenge).

Sec   The adversary receives a random challenge message and a random key, and she has to produce a colliding message for the given key. The advantage is the success probability of the adversary (over the random coins used by the adversary and the random choice of the challenge).

eSec The adversary chooses the challenge message. Then, she receives a random key and has to find a colliding message under this key. The advantage is the maximum taken over the choice of M by the adversary of her success probability (taken over the random coins used and the random choice of the key).

Historically, eSec-secure hash function families have been called Universal One-Way Hash Functions (UOWHFs). It must be noted that a Sec-adversary can be used to win the eSec security game (just generate the challenge message randomly-first). Therefore, if $H^{(\cdot)}$ is eSec-secure, then it is also Sec-secure.

Note that the size of the challenges plays an important role in the discussion of second preimage resistance. The known generic attacks are faster when the challenges become longer. For this reason, the second preimage security notions are often parametrized by the size of the challenges. When the challenge consists of an ℓ-block long message, the notions are denoted by $\mathsf{Spr}[\ell], \mathsf{Sec}[\ell]$ and $\mathsf{eSec}[\ell]$.

We say that an adversary against a security notion (t, ε)-*breaks* the security notion if it terminates in time t and wins the game with probability ε. Let us note a fact that will have some importance later on. In all these notions, the success probability is taken over the random coins of the adversary *and over the choice of the challenge*. This means that an adversary implementing an attack against "weak messages" or "weak keys" may succeed on a small fraction of the challenge space and fail systematically on non-weak messages, while still having a non-zero advantage. A consequence is that it is not possible to increase the success probability of adversaries against a single challenge by repeating them until they succeed.

How to compare the efficiency of adversaries that have different running time and success probability? If an adversary (t, ε)-breaks a security notion, then the expected number of repetitions of the experiment defining the notion before the adversary wins is $1/\varepsilon$. This represents a total of t/ε time units, and this is a meaningful scale. Intuitively, it represents "how much time do we have to wait before the adversary shows me what she is capable of". We call the *global complexity* of an adversary the ratio between its time complexity and its success probability. As an example, notice that the global complexity of exhaustive search is 2^n (for all second preimage notions).

Following the notations in use in the existing literature, we will denote by $\mathcal{A}_H$ an adversary against an iterated hash function, and by $\mathcal{A}_f$ the adversary against the corresponding compression function. Hopefully, things will be clear by the context.

3   Abstract Narrow-Pipe Modes of Operations

Because we would like to state results that are as generic as possible, we introduce a framework of abstract modes of operation, which encompasses all the narrow-pipe modes of operation known to the authors. This framework will enable us to show that our results hold for any mode of operation satisfying a minimum set of conditions.

We will consider that a *narrow-pipe mode of operation* $H^{(\cdot)}$ is a circuit that takes as its input M (the full message), K (the key, if present), h_i (the current chaining value) and i (the block counter). This circuit is responsible for preparing the input to the compression function. The next chaining value h_{i+1} is the output of the compression function on the input prepared by the circuit. The output of the whole hash function is the output of the compression function on its last invocation. The circuit activate a special wire "last call" to indicate that the hash process is terminated. We denote by $e : \mathbb{N} \to \mathbb{N}$ the function that returns the number of calls to the compression function given the size of M. We thus implicitly assume that the number of calls to the compression function does not depend on the input of the hash function (i.e., on M and K), but only on the size of M. We are inclined to believe that this restriction is natural.

The incoming chaining value is set to a predefined value (say, zero) on the first invocation. This particular class of modes of operation imposes that the output of the full hash function comes out of the compression function without post-treatment, in particular without truncation. This, coupled with the fact that the circuit has no internal memory makes it a narrow-pipe mode of operation. Apart from that, $H^{(\cdot)}$ may include a "final transformation", or process each message block multiple times. Formally, the hash process works according to the pseudo-code shown in Algorithm 1.

Algorithm 1. Formal definition of the hash process with an abstract mode of operation

---

function ABSTRACT-MODE-OF-OPERATION(M, K)
   $h_{-1} \leftarrow 0$
   $i \leftarrow 0$
   while not finished **do**
      $x_i \leftarrow H^{(\cdot)}(M, K, i, h_{i-1})$
      $h_i \leftarrow f(x_i)$
      $i \leftarrow i + 1$
   end while
   return h_{i-1}
end function

There are constructions that are apparently not narrow-pipe, but that still fit in this framework, such as the GOST hash function (the checksum can be computed in the last invocation, and does not need to be transmitted between each invocation of the compression function). Note that this requires the full message M to be given to the mode of operation at each invocation.

Note that by choosing $H^{(\cdot)}$ to be a *circuit*, we implicitly admit the existence of an upper-bound on the size of the messages (if only because the block counter comes on a finite number of wires). In the sequel, by "mode of operation", we implicitly mean "a narrow-pipe mode of operation that fits the above framework". This does not seem to be a restriction, as we are not aware of any narrow-pipe construction using a single compression function that does not fit the above definition.

3.1   Collision-Resistance Preserving Modes of Operation

While we tried to make the definition of a mode of operation as generic as it gets, we are not interested in *really bad* modes of operation. We are not interested in non-collision resistant constructions, for instance. In this section, we characterize a few properties modes of operation should have not to be totally worthless.

We say that a mode of operation **is strengthened** if the binary encoding of the size of the processed message is contained in the input to the last invocation of the compression function. It is well-known that the Merkle-Damgård mode of operation is strengthened, which is the key in establishing its important collision-resistance preservation. However, in general, being strengthened is not completely sufficient to be collision-resistance preserving. Some further technicalities are required.

We say that a mode of operation is **message-injective** if for all functions f and all keys K, the function that maps the message M to the sequence of compression-function inputs (x_i) is injective. This implies that hashing two different messages M and M' cannot generate the same sequence of inputs (x_i). This property is necessary for collision-resistance preservation: if $H^{(\cdot)}$ is not message-injective, there exists a function f and a key K such that there exist two colliding messages M and M' generating the same hash, without causing a collision in the compression function.

We also say that a mode of operation is **chaining-value-injective** if for all f and all K, there exists a (deterministic) function that maps x_i to h_{i-1}. The combination of these three properties is sufficient to ensure collision-resistance preservation.

Lemma 1. *A mode of operation $H^{(\cdot)}$ simultaneously message-injective, chaining-value-injective and strengthened is collision-resistance preserving.*

This lemma is just a restatement of the well-known result of Merkle and Damgård, but we include its proof, because it is a good warm-up, and because it will be useful later on.

Proof. Suppose we have two messages $M \neq M'$ such that $H^f(K, M) = H^f(K, M')$, for some compression function f. Then:

- Either $|M| \neq |M'|$. In this case, because $H^{(\cdot)}$ is strengthened, the inputs of the last invocation of the compression are not the same when hashing M and M', and because M and M' collide, we have found a collision on f (on its last invocation).
- Or $|M| = |M'|$. Suppose that the compression function is invoked $r = \mathfrak{e}(|M|)$ times in both cases. In this case, there are again two possibilities. Either $x_r \neq x'_r$, and we have a collision since $h_r = h'_r$, or $x_r = x'_r$. By chaining-value-injectivity, we have $h_{r-1} = h'_{r-1}$. The argument repeats. Either we find a collision along the way, or we reach the conclusion that $x_i = x'_i$, for all i, which is impossible by message-injectivity. □

Because of this lemma, we call a mode $H^{(\cdot)}$ "collision-resistance preserving" if it satisfies these three conditions.

3.2 Some Particular Modes of Operations

We briefly describe the Merkle-Damgård mode of operation and HAIFA, as well as the three provably second-preimage resistant modes of operations mentioned in the introduction. Figure 1 shows a possible implementation of the corresponding modes of operation in our generic framework.

```
1: function MD(M, K, i, h_{i-1})
2:     let (m_0, ..., m_ℓ) ← Pad(M)
3:     return (h_{i-1}, m_i)
4: end function
```

```
1: function HAIFA(M, K, i, h_{i-1})
2:     let (m_0, ..., m_ℓ) ← Pad(M)
3:     return (h_{i-1}, m_i, i)
4: end function
```

```
1: function SHOUP(M, K, i, h_{i-1})
2:     let (k, μ_0, ..., μ_κ) ← K
3:     let (m_0, ..., m_ℓ) ← Pad(M)
4:     return (k, h_{i-1} ⊕ μ_{ν_2(i)}, m_i)
5: end function
```

```
1: function SPLIT-PADDING(M, K, i, h_{i-1})
2:     let (m_0, ..., m_ℓ) ← Special-Pad(M)
3:     return (h_{i-1}, m_i)
4: end function
```

```
1: function BCM(M, K, i, h_{i-1})
2:     let (K_1, K_2) ← K
3:     let (m_0, ..., m_ℓ) ← Pad(M)
4:     if i = 0 then return (K_0 ⊕ m_1, m_0)
5:     if 0 < i < ℓ - 1 then return (h_{i-1} ⊕ m_{i+1}, m_i)
6:     if i = ℓ - 1 then return (h_{ℓ-2} ⊕ m_ℓ ⊕ K_2, m_ℓ ⊕ K_1)
7:     if i = ℓ then return (h_{ℓ-1} ⊕ K_1, m_ℓ ⊕ K_2)
8: end function
```

Fig. 1. Pseudo-code of possible implementations of the modes of operations considered in Sect. 3.2 in the generic framework for narrow-pipe constructions.

Merkle-Damgård. The Merkle-Damgård mode of iteration was independently suggested in 1989 by Merkle [14] and Damgård [6]. It is an unkeyed mode of operation, so the circuit $H^{(\cdot)}$ just ignores the key input. In this mode, the input to the compression function is usually considered to be formed of two parts playing different roles: the chaining value input, on n bits, and the message block input, on m bit, the output of the function being n-bit wide.

The padding is done usually by appending a single '1' bit followed by as many '0' bits as needed to complete an m-bit block including the length of M in bits (the well-known Merkle-Damgård strengthening). However, for the sake of simplicity, we will consider in the sequel a *simplified* padding scheme: the last block is padded with zeroes, and the message length in bits is included in an extra block.

HAIFA. The HAsh Iterative FrAmework (HAIFA), introduced in 2006 by Biham and Dunkelman [8], is a Merkle-Damgård-like construction where a counter and salt are added to the input of the compression function. In this paper, we consider a *simplified* version of HAIFA (amongst other things, we disregard the salt). For our purposes, the definition we use is of course equivalent. In HAIFA, the compression function $f: \{0,1\}^n \times \{0,1\}^m \times \{0,1\}^{64} \to \{0,1\}^n$ takes three inputs: the chaining value, the message block, and the round counter (we arbitrarily limit the number of rounds to 2^{64}). The designers of HAIFA claimed that the round counter was sufficient to prevent all generic second preimage attacks.

Shoup's UOWHF. Shoup's Universal One-Way Hash Function works just like Merkle-Damgård by iterating an eSec-secure compression function family f : $\{0,1\}^k \times \{0,1\}^n \times \{0,1\}^m \to \{0,1\}^n$ to obtain a (keyed) eSec-secure hash function (i.e., a UOWHF).

The scheme uses a set of masks $\mu_0, \ldots, \mu_{\kappa-1}$ (where $2^\kappa - 1$ is the length of the longest possible message), each one of which is a random n-bit string. The key of the whole iterated function consists of the key k of the compression function and of these masks. The size of the key is therefore logarithmic in the maximal size of the messages that can be hashed. The order in which the masks are applied is defined by a specified sequence: in the i-th invocation of the compression function, the $\nu_2(i)$-th mask is used, where $\nu_2(i)$ denotes the largest integer ν such that 2^ν divides i. As advertised before, this construction enjoys a form of provable second-preimage security in the standard model: it promotes the eSec security of the compression function to that of the whole hash function.

Theorem 1 [17]. *Let $H^{(\cdot)}$ denote Shoup's mode of operation. If an adversary is able to break the eSec$[\ell]$ notion of H^f with probability ε in time T, then one can construct an adversary that breaks the eSec notion of f in time $T + \mathcal{O}(\ell)$, with probability ε/ℓ.*

The Backwards Chaining Mode. Andreeva and Preneel described in [3] the *Backwards Chaining Mode* (BCM) which promotes the second-preimage resistance of an unkeyed compression function to the Sec notion of the (keyed) full hash function. We will assume for the sake of simplicity that the message block and the chaining values have the same size. The iteration is keyed, and the key is formed by a triplet (K_0, K_1, K_2) of n-bit strings (note that the size of the key is independent of the size of the messages).

This construction also enjoys a form of provable second-preimage security in the standard model. It promotes the Spr security of the compression function to the Sec-security of the whole hash function.

Theorem 2 [3]. *Let $H^{(\cdot)}$ denote the BCM mode of operation. If an adversary is able to break the Sec$[\ell]$ notion of H^f with probability ε in time T, then one can construct an adversary that breaks the Spr notion of f in time $T + \mathcal{O}(\ell)$, with probability ε/ℓ.*

The Split Padding. Yasuda introduced the *Split Padding* in 2008 [18], as a minor but clever tweak to the Merkle-Damgård strengthening. For the sake of simplicity, we will assume that the message block is twice bigger than the chaining values (i.e., it is $2n$-bit wide). The tweak ensures that any message block going into the compression function contains at least n bits from the original message (this is not necessarily the case in the last block of the usual Merkle-Damgård padding scheme).

It promotes a kind of eSec-security of the compression function to the Spr-security of the (unkeyed) iteration. More precisely, the security notion required of the compression function is the following: the adversary chooses a chaining value h and the first n bits of the message block m_1, and is then challenged with the last n bits of the message block m_2. She has to find a new pair $(h', m') \neq (h, m_1 \,\|\, m_2)$ such that $f(h, m_1 \,\|\, m_2) = f(h', m')$. To some extent, this is the eSec security notion, but here the "key" of the compression function is the last n bits of the message block.

Theorem 3 [18]. *Let $H^{(\cdot)}$ denote the Split Padding mode of operation. If an adversary is able to break the $\mathsf{Spr}[\ell]$ notion of H^f with probability ε in time T, then one can construct an adversary that breaks the eSec-like notion of f in time $T + \mathcal{O}(\lambda)$, with probability ε/ℓ.*

4 How to Make Your Mode of Operation Resistant Against Second Preimage Attacks?

In this section, we describe two simple properties of modes of operation, and we show that these properties allows some kind of security results against second preimage adversaries.

4.1 Resistance Against Generic Attacks

Generic attacks are attacks against the modes of operation, i.e., attacks that do not exploit any property of the compression function, and that could therefore work regardless of its choice. Generic attacks can therefore break the hash function even if the compression function does not have any weakness, and they could work even if the compression function were a random oracle (a public, perfectly random function).

Symmetrically, an attack against a hash function where the compression is perfectly random is necessarily an attack against the mode of operation (since it is impossible to break a perfectly random function).

We will therefore follow the existing literature [1, 2, 7, 10–12] by assuming that the compression function is random. In the random oracle model, the relevant measure of efficiency of an adversary is the number of query sent to the random oracle, rather than time. Indeed, the adversaries cannot obtain any kind of advantage by computation alone without querying the random function. In this particular setting, we say that an adversary (q, ε)-breaks a security notion if she sends at most q queries to the random oracle and wins with probability at least ε.

We now show that a very simple criterion, directly inspired from HAIFA, is sufficient to obtain an optimal level of provable resistance to generic second preimage attacks.

Definition 1. *A mode of operation $H^{(\cdot)}$ has domain separation if there exist a deterministic algorithm* **idxEx** *which, given an input to the compression function x_i produced when evaluating $H^f(K, M)$, recovers i, regardless of the choice of M, K and f.*

Amongst all the modes of operation considered above, only HAIFA has domain separation: the round counter is part of the input to the compression function. The following theorem show that HAIFA is optimally resistant to generic second preimage attacks, as was claimed by its designers.

Theorem 4. *Let $H^{(\cdot)}$ be a mode of operation satisfying the conditions of Lemma 1 and also having domain separation, and let f be a public random function. Let $\mathcal{A}$ be a second-preimage adversary that (q, ε)-break the Spr$[\ell]$ notion for H^f. Then:*

$$\varepsilon \leq q/2^{n-1}.$$

Proof. Suppose that the adversary, challenged with an ℓ-block message M, succeeds and finds $M' \neq M$ such that $H^f(M) = H^f(M')$. Then:

1. Either $|M| \neq |M|$, and because $H^{(\cdot)}$ is strengthened, then the adversary has found a (second) preimage of $H^f(M)$ for the compression function f. Since f is a random oracle, each query has a probability 2^{-n} to give this preimage.
2. Or M and M' have the same size. Because $H^{(\cdot)}$ is strengthened, injective and extractable, we know (by looking at the proof of Lemma 1) that there exists a collision on f of the form:

$$f(x_i) = f(x'_i) = h_i$$

It is important to notice that the same value of i occurs in the three members of this equation. The "index extractor" **idxEx** of the domain separation mechanism can be used to partition the possible inputs to f into disjoint classes (corresponding to the preimages of integers). In the collision above, x_i and x'_i belong to the same, "i-th" class. When submitting a query x to f, the adversary implicitly chooses the index $i = \mathbf{idxEx}(x)$ of the class to which x belong. The collision above can only be found if $f(x) = h_{\mathbf{idxEx}(x)}$, meaning that for each query, there is only one target value that ensures victory. Therefore, because f is a random oracle, each query hits the single target with probability 2^{-n}.

Now, each query sent by the adversary has probability $2^{-n} + 2^{-n}$ of fulfilling a sufficient success condition, which proves the result. □

4.2   Resistance Against All Attacks

The assumption that the compression function is random is the crux of the proof of the previous result. While it is completely unrealistic, results proved under this assumption still say something meaningful: they show that the mode of operation itself does not exhibit obvious weaknesses, and that the adversaries have to look into the compression function to break the iteration.

Nevertheless, it would be more satisfying to drop this requirement. In that case, the adversary "knows" the source code of the compression function, so that she does not need an external oracle interface to evaluate it. The relevant measure of her complexity is thus her running time. We say that an adversary (t, ε)-break a hash function (or a compression function) if she runs in time at most t and succeeds with probability at least ε.

For this, we show that another simple criterion is enough to offer a non-trivial level of security. This criterion is directly inspired by the three constructions with provable security in the standard model discussed above.

Definition 2. *Given a mode of operation $H^{(\cdot)}$ and a compression function f, let $P(i, y)$ denote the set of pairs (M, K) such that when evaluating $H^f(M, K)$, then the i-th input to f is y (i.e., $x_i = y$ in Algorithm 2).*

We say that a mode of operation $H^{(\cdot)}$ allows for embedding if $P(i, y) \neq \emptyset$ for any y and if it is computationally easy to sample random elements in $P(i, y)$.

Shoup's UOWHF allows for embedding, yet proving it is not so easy. We refer the reader to [17] for the full details, but here is an intuitive version. Controlling the message block in the i-th iteration is easy, but controlling the chaining value is not so obvious. Clearly, the mask used in the i-th iteration must be chosen carefully, but the problem is that choosing it will also randomize the output of the previous iterations. The key idea is that between two arbitrary points of the iteration, there is always a mask that is used only *once* (the one with the greatest index). By choosing this particular mask *after* all the others, it is possible to control the chaining value at this particular point, regardless of the other masks. This yields a recursive procedure to control the chaining value between the first and the i-th iterations: observe that the chaining value can be set to (say) zero in the iteration where the mask with the greatest index occur before the i-th iteration, independently of what happens afterward. Suppose that this mask happens in iteration j. Then, we are left with the problem of controlling the chaining value between the j-th and the i-th iteration, a strictly smaller problem, to which the same technique can be applied recursively.

The backwards chaining mode easily allows for embedding. To embed in the first block, just set K_0 appropriately. To embed at any other index smaller than $\ell - 1$, just choose m_i and m_{i+1} with care. Finally, to embed at index $\ell - 1$ or ℓ, pick the message at random and choose K_1 and K_2 accordingly (the keys are necessary to embed in the last blocks because of the padding scheme). The split-padding does not allows for this definition of embedding, but it allows to embed n bits of message block into any compression function input.

Theorem 5. *Let $H^{(\cdot)}$ be a mode of operation satisfying the hypotheses of Lemma 1 and that additionally allows for embedding.*

If an adversary is able to break the Sec[ℓ] notion of H^f with probability ε in time T, then one can construct an adversary that breaks the Spr notion of f in time $T + \mathcal{O}\left(\mathfrak{e}(\ell)\right)$, with probability $\varepsilon / \mathfrak{e}(\ell)$.

Proof. The proof works by exhibiting a reduction $\mathcal{R}$ that turns an adversary $\mathcal{A}_H$ against the iteration into an adversary against the compression function. The reduction $\mathcal{R}$ is described by the pseudo-code of Algorithm 2.

The reduction starts by forging a random message M that "embeds" the challenge x at a random position i, and then it sends this to the adversary $\mathcal{A}_H$. If the adversary succeeds in producing a second preimage M', then M and M' collide. If the collision happen just at position i, then a second preimage of the challenge x is readily found.

The sequence of compression function inputs (the x_i in Algorithm 2) generated during the iteration of $H^f(M, K)$ is denoted by $blocks(f, M, K)$.

Algorithm 2. Formal definition of the generic reduction.

1: **function** REDUCTION$[\ell](x)$
2:     $i \xleftarrow{\$} \{0, 1, \ldots, \mathfrak{e}(\ell)\}$
3:     $(M, K) \xleftarrow{\$} P(i, x)$
4:     $M' \leftarrow \mathcal{A}_H(f, M, K)$
5:     **if** $M' = \bot$ **then return** $\bot$
6:     $x_0, \ldots, x_{\mathfrak{e}(\ell)-1} \leftarrow blocks(f, M, K)$
7:     $x'_0, \ldots, x'_{\mathfrak{e}(\ell')-1} \leftarrow blocks(f, M', K)$
8:     $j \leftarrow 1$
9:     **while** $x_{\mathfrak{e}(\ell)-j} = x'_{\mathfrak{e}(\ell')-j}$ **do**
10:         $j \leftarrow j + 1$
11:     **if** $\mathfrak{e}(\ell) - j = i$ **then return** $x'_{\mathfrak{e}(\ell')-j}$ **else** $\bot$
12: **end function**

The running time of the reduction is clearly that of $\mathcal{A}_H$ plus the time needed to hash both M and M'. Clearly, M' cannot be larger that the running time of $\mathcal{A}_H$, so that the running time of $\mathcal{R}$ is essentially that of the adversary.

It remains to determine the success probability of the reduction. First of all, the adversary succeeds with probability ε on line 3. Note that the challenge fed to $\mathcal{A}_H$ is uniformly random: the challenge x given to $\mathcal{R}$ is supposed to be chosen uniformly at random, and (M, K) is uniformly random amongst the possibilities that place the random block x at a random position i.

Next, we show that when the adversary $\mathcal{A}_H$ succeeds, the reduction itself succeeds with probability $1/\mathfrak{e}(\ell)$. First, we claim that at the beginning of line 11, we have $x_{\mathfrak{e}(\ell)-j} \neq x'_{\mathfrak{e}(\ell')-j}$ and $f\left(x_{\mathfrak{e}(\ell)-j}\right) = f\left(x'_{\mathfrak{e}(\ell')-j}\right)$. The reasoning behind this is exactly the same as that in the proof of Lemma 1. This establishes the correctness of the reduction in passing.

Finally, we see that the reduction succeeds if and only if $\mathfrak{e}(\ell) - j = i$. Because i has been chosen uniformly at random, this happens with probability $1/\mathfrak{e}(\ell)$, regardless of the value of j (which is under the control of the adversary). $\qquad \square$

Discussion. All the proof of resistance considered above (Theorems 1, 2, 3 and 5) only provide a security level of $2^n/\ell$. In some cases, this makes perfect sense, because a generic attack of this complexity is applicable. However, such generic attacks could be made impossible by including a counter in the mode of operation, and yet it seems impossible to provide better security proofs in the standard model.

It is then natural to ask whether these security proofs could be improved to reflect the effect of the patch on the security of the schemes. In other terms, we ask whether it is it possible to prove the patched schemes resistant to second preimage attacks in the standard model up to a level of roughly 2^n?

The last contribution of this paper is to show that this is in fact impossible with the "usual" proof technique.

5   Unavoidable Security Loss in Black-Box Reduction

Resistance against second preimage attacks in the standard model of a mode of operation $H^{(\cdot)}$ is often announced by theorem formulated similar to the following "typical" result.

Theorem 6 (informal and typical). *There is a black-box reduction $\mathcal{R}(\cdot, \cdot)$ such that $\mathcal{R}(f, \mathcal{A}_H)$ is a second-preimage adversary against the compression function f that $(t + t', \alpha \cdot \varepsilon + \beta)$-breaks f, for all compression functions f and all second preimage adversaries $\mathcal{A}_H$ that (t, ε)-break H^f.*

The reduction is given *black-box* access to both the adversary and the compression function f, and this is a way of formalizing that the reduction must work for any adversary and any compression function. For the sake of simplicity, in this paper we allow the reduction to issue *only one query* to the adversary. To some extent, this narrows our study a little, but all the reductions we are aware of (in [3,17,18]) fit into this category. Note also that the adversary $\mathcal{A}_H$ may fail deterministically on a given challenge, so that it is pointless to re-run it again and again to increase its success probability.

In setting of our security theorem above, there are three parties: the challenger, the reduction and the adversary. To make the discussion simpler we will focus on the Sec security notion, but our reasoning extends to other notions. In the Sec game, the challenger sends the reduction a challenge made of an input x to f, and a "key" k for f. The reduction has to find a distinct input x' such that $f_k(x) = f_k(x')$. For this purpose, the reduction may use the $\mathcal{A}_H$ adversary: the reduction sends the adversary a challenge made of a message M of at most ℓ message blocks, and a key K. The adversary may either returns a message M' such that $H^f(K, M) = H^f(K, M')$ or fail. The precise sequence of interactions is the following:

$$
\begin{array}{ll}
\text{Challenger} \xrightarrow{x,k} \text{Reduction} & \\
\qquad\qquad \text{Reduction} \xrightarrow{M,K} \text{Adversary} & \\
\qquad\qquad \text{Reduction} \xleftarrow{M'} \text{Adversary} & M \neq M' \quad H_K(M) = H_K(M') \\
\text{Challenger} \xleftarrow{x'} \text{Reduction} & x \neq x' \qquad f_k(x) = f_k(x')
\end{array}
$$

If the compression function f is secure, then the "time/success probability" ratio of any adversary against f is greater than 2^n. The interest of the reductions

---

function f-SIMULATOR(x, k)
    if $Log[x, k] = \perp$ **then** $Log[x, k] \xleftarrow{\$} \{0, 1\}^n$
    return $Log[x, k]$
end function

Fig. 2. A dummy random function simulator

is that given an adversary $\mathcal{A}_H$ against H^f, one must have: $(t+t')/(\alpha \cdot \varepsilon + \beta) \geq 2^n$, and therefore the "time/advantage" ratio of $\mathcal{A}_H$ is lower-bounded by:

$$\frac{t}{\varepsilon} \geq 2^n \alpha + \frac{2^n \beta - t'}{\varepsilon}. \tag{1}$$

The right-hand side of Eq. (1) is the *provable security level* that the reduction offers. Note that it bizarrely depends on the success probability of the adversary, but this seems unavoidable.

Reductions are generally assumed to have to simulate the legitimate input challenge distribution the adversary is normally expecting. In our case, this means that the distribution of the challenges M, K must be indistinguishable from random. Note that if M, K were biased, then the adversary could detect that it is "being used", and fail deterministically. In any case, when we mention the success probability ε of the adversary $\mathcal{A}_H$, we assume that its input distribution is uniformly random.

When considering a single run of the reduction, its success probability should depend very much on whether the adversary succeeds or not. Therefore, it makes sense to write:

$$\mathbb{P}\left[\mathcal{R} \text{ succeeds}\right] = \varepsilon \cdot \mathbb{P}\left[\mathcal{R} \text{ succeeds} \mid \mathcal{A}_H \text{ succeeds}\right] + (1-\varepsilon)\mathbb{P}\left[\mathcal{R} \text{ succeeds} \mid \mathcal{A}_H \text{ fails}\right]$$

This justifies why we assumed the success probability of the reduction to be of the form $\alpha \cdot \varepsilon + \beta$, and in fact we have:

$$\alpha = \mathbb{P}\left[\mathcal{R} \text{ succeeds} \mid \mathcal{A}_H \text{ succeeds}\right] - \mathbb{P}\left[\mathcal{R} \text{ succeeds} \mid \mathcal{A}_H \text{ fails}\right]$$
$$\beta = \mathbb{P}\left[\mathcal{R} \text{ succeeds} \mid \mathcal{A}_H \text{ fails}\right]$$

Now, while our objective is to understand what happens when $\mathcal{A}_H$ *succeeds*, it is easier to get a glimpse of what happens when $\mathcal{A}_H$ *fails*. In this setting, the reduction is just a randomized Turing machine trying to break the second preimage resistance of an arbitrary black-box function, which cannot be done faster than exhaustive search. For instance, f could be a Pseudo-Random Function with a randomly-chosen secret key. We could even use the algorithm shown in Fig. 2 to simulate a "truly" random function. In any case, it follows that $\beta \leq t'/2^n$. The provable security level offered by a reduction is thus upper-bounded by $\alpha \cdot 2^n$. We will thus say that a reduction is *useable* if $\alpha > t'/2^n$, as this implies that the reduction offers a provable security level better than that of exhaustive search (or equivalently, that the reduction actually makes use of the adversary).

5.1   How Do Reductions Use the Adversary?

In the sequel, we will make the natural assumption that the $\mathcal{A}_H$ adversary the reduction has access to has a non-zero success probability. We will also restrict our attention to useable reductions. By doing so we rule out modes of operation for which no useable reduction is known (such as the Merkle-Damgård construction), but at the same time we rule out bogus modes that would have been a problem.

Let us consider a provably secure mode of operation H also satisfying the hypotheses of Lemma 1. (i.e., injective, extractable and strengthened). We need to define yet another property to make our argument work. We say that a mode of operation is *suffix-clonable* if given an ℓ-block message M, a key K and an integer $0 < i \leq \ell$, and the sequence $h_0, \ldots, h_{\ell+1}$ of compression function outputs generated during the evaluation of $H^f(M, K)$, it is always possible to find a different ℓ-block message M' such that:

(i) $H^{(\cdot)}(K, M, i-1, h_{i-2}) \neq H^{(\cdot)}(K, M', i-1, h_{i-2})$
(ii) For all j such that $i \leq j \leq \ell$, $H^{(\cdot)}(K, M, j, h_{j-1}) = H^{(\cdot)}(K, M', j, h_{j-1})$

This is a bit technical, but is required by a part of the proof. Intuitively, it means that it is possible to find a message that would generate the same compression function inputs after the i-th iteration if a collision occurred, while generating a different input for the i-th iteration.

The Merkle-Damgård construction (and therefore HAIFA) and the split-padding are easily seen to be suffix clonable: it is sufficient to change the i-th message block while leaving all the subsequent messages blocks untouched. Shoup's construction is also easily seen to be suffix-clonable: it suffices to leave K untouched and to modify the beginning of M. Lastly, the BCM mode of operation is also suffix-clonable (and it again suffices to keep the right suffix of M).

We will thus assume that our mode of operation $H^{(\cdot)}$ is suffix-clonable. Since it is provably secure, there exists a reduction $\mathcal{R}$ with a reasonably high success probability. Our objective, and the main technical contribution of this section, is to show the following theorem:

Theorem 7. *We always have $\alpha \leq 1/\ell + t'/2^n$. It follows that the provable security level offered by $\mathcal{R}$ cannot be higher than $2^n/\ell + t'$.*

The remaining of this section is devoted to the proof of this result. The general idea of the proof is to build an environment around the reduction $\mathcal{R}$ that simulates a legitimate "world" for $\mathcal{R}$, but in which it is easy to see that $\mathcal{R}$ has a low success probability. Then because the security level offered by $\mathcal{R}$ has to hold in all legitimates environment, it follows that in general $\mathcal{R}$ cannot offer more in general than in the simulated world.

Connection Point. Before going any further, let us observe what happens when the adversary finds a second preimage. Let us denote by x_i and h_i (resp.

x_i' and h_i') the sequence of inputs and outputs of f while evaluating $H^f(M)$ (resp. $H^f(M')$). Since M and M' collide, and because H satisfies the hypotheses of Lemma 1, then a second preimage of one of the x_i input values can be readily obtained from M'. If we look closely at the proof of Lemma 1, we will see that if $|M| \neq |M'|$, then we obtain a second preimage of f on the last invocation. Otherwise, there exists an index i such that $f(x_i) = f(x_i')$ and $x_i \neq x_i'$. In the sequel, we call this particular index i the "connection point", and we note that at this particular index a second preimage of x_i for f is revealed, which we call "the second preimage at connection point".

Embedding. The strategy used by all the reductions we are aware of is to *embed* the small challenge (x, k) into the big challenge (M, K). Following our definition, we say that (x, k) is *embedded* into (M, K) at location i if and only if $f_k(x)$ is evaluated during the i-th iteration of the main loop of Algorithm 2 during the evaluation of $H^k(K, M)$. We will show that the second preimage returned by the adversary can only be used by the reduction if the second preimage at connection points directly gives a solution to the small challenge. Let us denote by ♣ the condition "the second preimage at connection point is a second preimage of the small challenge sent by the Challenger to $\mathcal{R}$". Formally, this means that:

$$\mathbb{P}\left[\clubsuit\right] = \mathbb{P}\left[(\exists i.\ x_i = (x, k) \text{ in Algorithm 2}) \land (x_i \neq x_i') \land (h_i = h_i')\right]$$

We can then write:

$$\mathbb{P}\left[\mathcal{R} \text{ succeeds} \mid \mathcal{A} \text{ succeeds}\right] = \mathbb{P}\left[\mathcal{R} \text{ succeeds} \mid \mathcal{A} \text{ succeeds} \land \clubsuit\right] \cdot \mathbb{P}\left[\clubsuit\right]$$
$$+ \mathbb{P}\left[\mathcal{R} \text{ succeeds} \mid \mathcal{A} \text{ succeeds} \land \neg \clubsuit\right] \cdot \mathbb{P}\left[\neg \clubsuit\right] \quad (2)$$

We first argue that the challenge cannot be embedded more than once. If the challenge were embedded twice or more, the input distribution of the adversary would not be random, because we would have $x_i = x_j$ for $i \neq j$ in Algorithm 2, something that is highly unlikely when M and K are drawn at random. This is not allowed in the first place, and the adversaries could straightforwardly detect it and abort.

Next, we claim that in order to be usable, a reduction *must* embed the challenge (x, k) into (M, K). This justifies *a posteriori* our observation that the three schemes of interest all allow some form of embedding. To establish this result, we first show that a legitimate world with various interesting properties can be built around the reduction. When we argued that β was small, we used the (somewhat informal) argument that f could be implemented by a Random Function simulator, and that inverting such a function faster than exhaustive search is impossible. We now make this argument more formal, with the additional feature that we will be able to choose whether the adversary succeeds or fails, and where it connects.

Simulation. The easy case is when we want $\mathcal{A}_H$ to fail, as it is sufficient to let f simulate an arbitrary random function, and let $\mathcal{A}_H$ return a random string, or fail explicitly. The more interesting case is when we want $\mathcal{A}_H$ to succeed. The difficulty comes from the fact that the view of the reduction must be consistent: after having received M' from the $\mathcal{A}_H$, the reduction must be able to check that $H_K^f(M) = H_K^f(M')$ by querying f. This is in fact quite easy to achieve, by *programming* the function f. We thus simulate a complete environment around the execution with the following procedure:

1. Before $\mathcal{R}$ sends its query (M, K) to $\mathcal{A}_H$, we simulate f by generating random answers and storing them (for consistency), "implementing" f with the random function simulator of Fig. 2.
2. When $\mathcal{R}$ sends its query (M, K) to $\mathcal{A}_H$, we choose an integer $i \in \{0, \dots, \ell\}$ (this will be the connection point), and we use the suffix-clonability property of the mode of operation to generate a different message $M' \neq M$ satisfying the conditions of the definition of suffix-clonability.
3. We evaluate $H^f(M')$ in a special way. On the first $i - 1$ iterations we use the random function simulator in place of f. On the i-th iteration we program f so that $f(x_i') = h_i$, thus "connecting" M' to M in iteration i.
4. We return M' as the answer of $\mathcal{A}_H$ to the reduction, and keep simulating f. The reduction will be able to check that $H_K^f(M) = H_K^f(M')$ by sending the appropriate queries to f.

When running inside this environment, the view of the reduction is consistent and legitimate. In this environment, we are able to choose the connection point at will. For instance, we can make sure that the ♣ event never happens. In this case, the reduction, even though it knows a collision on f, cannot find a second preimage on f faster than exhaustive search (because each new query to f returns an independent random answer, and thus each query yields a second preimage with probability 2^{-n}).

It follows if a reduction does not embed its challenge, then it cannot be usable. We conclude that a usable reduction must embed its challenge exactly once with non-zero probability. As a matter of fact, the reductions of the three schemes considered in the introduction published in the literature embed their challenge with probability one. Equation (2) then gives:

$$\mathbb{P}\big[\mathcal{R} \text{ succeeds} \mid \mathcal{A} \text{ succeeds}\big] \leq \mathbb{P}\big[\mathcal{R} \text{ succeeds} \mid \mathcal{A} \text{ succeeds} \wedge \clubsuit\big] \cdot \mathbb{P}\big[\clubsuit\big] + \frac{t'}{2^n} \quad (3)$$

Now, to prove Theorem 7, we upper-bound the probability that the ♣ condition occurs. The reduction cannot control "where" the adversary will "connect" to the big challenge M. Conversely, if the adversary could guess where the challenge is embedded, then she could systematically refuse to connect precisely there. In fact, we need not even worry about this complication, since the adversary can foil all the reduction's plan by connecting randomly. In our simulation procedure, if we choose the connection point uniformly at random between 0 and ℓ, then the ♣ event only happens with probability $1/\ell$. Combining this with

Eq. (3) yields:

$$\mathbb{P}\left[\mathcal{R}\text{ succeeds} \mid \mathcal{A}_H\text{ succeeds}\right] \leq \frac{1}{\ell} + \frac{t'}{2^n}$$

And this is exactly what we needed to complete the proof of Theorem 7. We conclude by pondering on this intriguing situation, where some narrow-pipe modes of operations are provably resistant to generic second preimage attacks, yet this cannot be shown in the standard model.

References

1. Andreeva, E., Bouillaguet, C., Dunkelman, O., Kelsey, J.: Herding, second preimage and trojan message attacks beyond Merkle-Damgård. In: Jacobson Jr, M.J., Rijmen, V., Safavi-Naini, R. (eds.) SAC 2009. LNCS, vol. 5867, pp. 393–414. Springer, Heidelberg (2009)
2. Andreeva, E., Bouillaguet, C., Fouque, P.-A., Hoch, J.J., Kelsey, J., Shamir, A., Zimmer, S.: Second preimage attacks on dithered hash functions. In: Smart, N.P. (ed.) EUROCRYPT 2008. LNCS, vol. 4965, pp. 270–288. Springer, Heidelberg (2008)
3. Andreeva, E., Preneel, B.: A three-property-secure hash function. In: Avanzi, R.M., Keliher, L., Sica, F. (eds.) SAC 2008. LNCS, vol. 5381, pp. 228–244. Springer, Heidelberg (2009)
4. Bellare, M., Rogaway, P.: Collision-resistant hashing: towards making UOWHFs practical. In: Kaliski Jr, B.S. (ed.) CRYPTO 1997. LNCS, vol. 1294, pp. 470–484. Springer, Heidelberg (1997)
5. Brassard, G. (ed.): CRYPTO 1989. LNCS, vol. 435. Springer, Heidelberg (1990)
6. Damgård, I.B.: A design principle for hash functions. In: Brassard [5], pp. 416–427
7. Dean, R.D.: Formal aspects of mobile code security. Ph.D. thesis, Princeton University, Jan 1999
8. Eli Biham, O.D.: A framework for iterative hash functions – HAIFA. Presented at the second NIST hash workshop, 24–25 Aug 2006
9. Impagliazzo, Russell, Naor, Moni: Efficient cryptographic schemes provably as secure as subset sum. J. Cryptol. 9(4), 199–216 (1996)
10. Joux, A.: Multicollisions in iterated hash functions. Application to cascaded constructions. In: Franklin, M. (ed.) CRYPTO 2004. LNCS, vol. 3152, pp. 306–316. Springer, Heidelberg (2004)
11. Kelsey, J., Kohno, T.: Herding hash functions and the Nostradamus attack. In: Vaudenay, S. (ed.) EUROCRYPT 2006. LNCS, vol. 4004, pp. 183–200. Springer, Heidelberg (2006)
12. Kelsey, J., Schneier, B.: Second preimages on n-bit hash functions for much less than 2^n work. In: Cramer, R. (ed.) EUROCRYPT 2005. LNCS, vol. 3494, pp. 474–490. Springer, Heidelberg (2005)
13. Lucks, S.: A failure-friendly design principle for hash functions. In: Roy, B. (ed.) ASIACRYPT 2005. LNCS, vol. 3788, pp. 474–494. Springer, Heidelberg (2005)
14. Merkle, R.C.: One way hash functions and DES. In: Brassard [5], pp. 428–446
15. Naor, M., Yung, M.: Universal one-way hash functions and their cryptographic applications. In: STOC, pp. 33–43. ACM (1989)
16. Rogaway, P., Shrimpton, T.: Cryptographic hash-function basics: definitions, implications, and separations for preimage resistance, second-preimage resistance, and collision resistance. In: Roy, B., Meier, W. (eds.) FSE 2004. LNCS, vol. 3017, pp. 371–388. Springer, Heidelberg (2004)

17. Shoup, V.: A composition theorem for universal one-way hash functions. In: Preneel, B. (ed.) EUROCRYPT 2000. LNCS, vol. 1807, pp. 445–452. Springer, Heidelberg (2000)

18. Yasuda, K.: How to fill up Merkle-Damgård hash functions. In: Pieprzyk, J. (ed.) ASIACRYPT 2008. LNCS, vol. 5350, pp. 272–289. Springer, Heidelberg (2008)

Multiple Limited-Birthday Distinguishers and Applications

Jérémy Jean[1], María Naya-Plasencia[2], and Thomas Peyrin[3]([✉])

[1] École Normale Supérieure, Paris, France
Jeremy.Jean@ens.fr
[2] SECRET Project-Team - INRIA Paris-Rocquencourt, Paris, France
[3] Nanyang Technological University, Singapore, Singapore
thomas.peyrin@gmail.com

Abstract. In this article, we propose a new improvement of the rebound techniques, used for cryptanalyzing AES-like permutations during the past years. Our improvement, that allows to reduce the complexity of the attacks, increases the probability of the outbound part by considering a new type of differential paths. Moreover, we propose a new type of distinguisher, the multiple limited-birthday problem, based on the limited-birthday one, but where differences on the input and on the output might have randomized positions. We also discuss the generic complexity for solving this problem and provide a lower bound of it as well as we propose an efficient and generic algorithm for solving it. Our advances lead to improved distinguishing or collision results for many AES-based functions such as AES, ECHO, Grøstl, LED, PHOTON and Whirlpool.

Keywords: AES-like permutation · Distinguishers · Limited-birthday · Rebound attack

1   Introduction

On October the 2nd of 2012, the NIST chose Keccak [4] as the winner of the SHA-3 hash function competition. This competition started on 2008, and received 64 submissions. Amongst them, 56 passed to the first round, 14 to the second and 5 to the final on December 2010. Through all these years, a large amount of cryptanalysis has been published on the different candidates and new techniques have been proposed. One of the new techniques that can be fairly considered as among the most largely applied to the different candidates is the rebound

Jérémy Jean is supported by the French Agence Nationale de la Recherche through the SAPHIR2 project under Contract ANR-08-VERS-014 and by the French *Délégation Générale pour l'Armement* (DGA).

María Naya-Plasencia is partially supported by the French Agence Nationale de la Recherche through the BLOC project under Contract ANR-11-INSE-0011.

Thomas Peyrin is supported by the Singapore National Research Foundation Fellowship 2012 (NRF-NRFF2012-06).

T. Lange, K. Lauter, and P. Lisoněk (Eds.): SAC 2013, LNCS 8282, pp. 533–550, 2014.
DOI: 10.1007/978-3-662-43414-7_27, © Springer-Verlag Berlin Heidelberg 2014

attack. Presented in [23], at first for analyzing AES-like compression functions, it has found many more applications afterwards.

Rebound attacks is a freedom degrees utilization method, and, as such, it aims at finding solutions for a differential characteristic faster than the probabilistic approach. The characteristic is divided in two parts: a middle one, called inbound, and both remaining sides, called outbound. In the inbound phase, the expensive part of the characteristic, like one fully active AES state around the non-linear transformation, is considered. The rebound technique allows to find many solutions for this part with an average cost of one. These solutions are then exhausted probabilistically forwards and backwards through the outbound part to find one out of them that conforms to the whole characteristic.

Several improvements have appeared through the new analyses, like start-from-the-middle attack [22] or Super-SBoxes [13,19], which allow to control three rounds in the middle, multinbounds [21] which extend the number of rounds analyzed by a better use of the freedom degrees (better ways of merging the inbounds were proposed in [24]), or non-fully-active states [27] that permits to reduce the complexity of the outbound part. In [17], a method for controlling four rounds in the middle with high complexity was proposed, and it allows to reach a total of 9 rounds with regards to distinguishers in the case of a large permutation size.

This class of attacks is interesting mostly for hash functions, because they require the attacker to be able to know and to control the internal state of the primitive, which is not possible if a secret is involved, for example in a block cipher. Yet, another application is the study of block ciphers in the so-called known-key or chosen-key models, where the attacker knows or even has full control of the secret key. These models were recently made popular because many SHA-3 or new hash functions are based on block ciphers or fixed-key permutations, and also one may want to be sure that a cipher has no flaw whatsoever, even in weaker security models.

Various types of attacks are possible for hash functions, such as collision and (second) preimage search, or even distinguishers. Indeed, hash functions being often utilized to mimic the behavior of random oracles [7] in security protocols, e.g. RSA-OAEP [2], it is important to ensure that no special property can be observed that allows an attacker to distinguish the primitive from a random oracle. Distinguishers on hash functions, compression functions or permutations can be very diverse, from classical differential distinguishers (limited-birthday [13] or subspace [20]) to rotational [18] or zero-sum distinguishers [6]. In any case, for the distinguisher to be valid, the cryptanalyst has to compare the cost of finding the specific property for the function analyzed and for an ideal primitive. The bounds compared in this article refer to the computational bounds, and not information-theoretic bounds.

Rebound-like techniques are well adapted for various types of distinguishers and it remains an open problem to know how far (and with what complexity) they can be pushed further to attack AES-like permutations and hash/compression functions. So far, the best results could reach 8 or 9 rounds, depending on the size of the permutation attacked.

Our Contributions. In this paper, we propose a new improvement of the previous rebound techniques, reducing the complexity of known differential distinguishers and by a lower extend, reducing some collision attack complexities. We observed that the gap between the distinguisher complexity and the generic case is often big and some conditions might be relaxed in order to minimize as much as possible the overall complexity. The main idea is to generalize the various rebound techniques and to relax some of the input and output conditions of the differential distinguishers. That is, instead of considering pre-specified active cells in the input and output (generally full columns or diagonals), we consider several possible position combinations of these cells. In some way, this idea is related to the outbound difference randomization that was proposed in [11] for a rebound attack on Keccak, a non-AES-like function. Yet, in [11], the randomization was not used to reduce the attack complexity, but to provide enough freedom degrees to perform the attack.

As this improvement affects directly the properties of the inputs and outputs, we now have to deal with a new differential property observed and we named this new problem the *multiple limited-birthday problem* (LBP), which is more general than the limited-birthday one. A very important question arising next is: what is the complexity of the best generic algorithm for obtaining such set of inputs/outputs? For previous distinguishers, where the active input and output columns were fixed, the limited-birthday algorithm [13] is yet the best one for solving the problem in the generic case. Now, the multiple limited-birthday is more complex, and in Sect. 3.3 we discuss how to bound the complexity of the best generic distinguisher. Moreover, we also propose an efficient, generic and non-trivial algorithm in order to solve the multiple limited-birthday problem, providing the best known complexity for solving this problem.

Finally, we generalize the various rebound-like techniques in Sect. 4 and we apply our findings on various AES-like primitives. Due to space constraints, Sect. 5 presents our main results, while the full results are detailed in the extended version of our paper. Our main results dealing with AES [9] and Whirlpool [1] are summarized and compared to previous works in Table 1. In the full version, we also derive results on ECHO [3], Grøstl [12], LED [15], PHOTON [14], that are reported in Appendix A.

2   AES-like Permutations

We define an AES-like permutation as a permutation that applies N_r rounds of a round function to update an internal state viewed as a square matrix of t rows and t columns, where each of the t^2 cells has a size of c bits. We denote $\mathcal{S}$ the set of all theses states: $|\mathcal{S}| = 2^{ct^2}$. This generic view captures various permutations in cryptographic primitives such as AES, ECHO, Grøstl, LED, PHOTON and Whirlpool.

The round function (Fig. 1) starts by xoring a round-dependent constant to the state in the **AddRoundConstant** operation (AC). Then, it applies a substitution layer **SubBytes** (SB) which relies on a $c \times c$ non-linear bijective S-box S. Finally, the round function performs a linear layer, composed of the

Table 1. Known and improved results for three rebound-based attacks on AES-based primitives.

Target	Subtarget	Rounds	Type	Time	Memory	Ideal	Reference
AES-128	Cipher	8	KK dist.	2^{48}	2^{32}	2^{65}	[13]
		8	KK dist.	2^{44}	2^{32}	2^{61}	Sect. 5.1
		8	CK dist.	2^{24}	2^{16}	2^{65}	[10]
		8	CK dist.	$2^{13.4}$	2^{16}	$2^{31.7}$	Sect. 5.1
AES-128	DM-mode	5	CF collision	2^{56}	2^{32}	2^{65}	[22]
		6	CF collision	2^{32}	2^{16}	2^{65}	Sect. 5.1
Whirlpool	CF	10	dist.	2^{176}	2^{8}	2^{384}	[20]
		10	dist.	$2^{115.7}$	2^{8}	2^{125}	Sect. 5.2
Whirlpool	Permutation	7.5	collision	2^{184}	2^{8}	2^{256}	[20]
		7.5	collision	2^{176}	2^{8}	2^{256}	Sect. 5.2
Whirlpool	Hash func.	5.5	collision	2^{184}	2^{8}	2^{256}	[20]
		5.5	collision	2^{176}	2^{8}	2^{256}	Sect. 5.2

ShiftRows transformation (SR), that moves each cell belonging to the x-th row by x positions to the left in its own row, and the **MixCells** operation (MC), that linearly mixes all the columns of the matrix separately by multiplying each one with a matrix **M** implementing a Maximum Distance Separable (MDS) code, which provides diffusion.

Fig. 1. One round of the AES-like permutation instantiated with $t = 4$.

Note that this description encompasses permutations that really follow the AES design strategy, but very similar designs (for example with a slightly modified **ShiftRows** function or with a **MixCells** layer not implemented with an MDS matrix) are likely to be attacked by our techniques as well. In the case of AES-like block ciphers analyzed in the known/chosen-key model, the subkeys generated by the key schedule are incorporated into the known constant addition layer **AddRoundConstant**.

3 Multiple Limited-Birthday Distinguisher

In this section, we present a new type of distinguisher: the multiple limited-birthday (Sect. 3.3). It is inspired from the limited-birthday one that we recall in Sect. 3.2, where some of the input and output conditions are relaxed. We discuss how to bound the complexity of the best generic algorithm for solving this problem, as well as we provide an efficient algorithm solving the problem with the best known complexity. Due to the keyless particularity of the primitives, we precise the relevance of distinguishers in that context.

3.1   Structural Distinguishers

We precise here what we consider to be a distinguishing algorithm for a keyless primitives. Let F be a primitive analyzed in the open-key model (either known- or chosen-key). In that context, there is no secret: F could be for instance a hash function or a block cipher where the key is placed into the public domain.

To formalize the problem, we say that the goal of the adversary is to validate a certain property P on the primitive F. For example, if F is a hash function, P could be "find two *different* inputs x, x' such that $F(x) = F(x')$" to capture the collision property. One other example, more related to our approach, would be $P = LPB$, the limited-birthday problem. In that sense, limited-birthday, collision and other similar problems are all particular kinds of distinguishers.

It is easy to see that when no random challenge is input to the adversary (like for collision definition for example) there always exists (at least) one algorithm that outputs a solution to P in constant time and without any query to F. We do not know this algorithm, but its existence can be proven. The main consequence about this argument is the lower bound on the number of queries Q of the distinguishing algorithm. Indeed, because of that algorithm, we have $0 \leq Q$. Therefore, we cannot reach any security notion in that context.

Now, we can circumvent this problem by introducing a challenge C to the problem P, that is, we *force* the distinguishing algorithm to use some value it does not know beforehand. To ease the formal description, one can think of an adversarial model where the memory is restricted to a fixed and constant amount M. That way, we get rid of the trivial (but unknown) algorithms that return a solution to P in constant time, since they do not know the parameter/challenge C. More precisely, if it does return a solution in constant time, then it is a wrong one with overwhelming probability, such that its winning advantage is nearly zero. Consequently, reasonable winning advantages are reached by getting rid of all those trivial algorithms. Then, the lower bound increases and becomes dependent of the size of C.

As an example, a challenge C could be an particular instantiation of the S-Box used in the primitive F. One could say that C selects a particular primitive F in a space of structurally-equivalent primitives, and asks the adversary to solve P on that particular instance F.

In all the published literature, the distinguishers in the open-key model do not consider any particular challenges, and they also ignore the trivial algorithms. From a structural point of view, there is no problem in doing so since we know that those distinguishers would also work if we were to introduce a challenge. But formally, these are not proper distinguishers because of the constant time algorithms that make the lower bound $0 \leq Q$. In this article, we do not claim to have strong distinguishers in the theoretical sense, but we provide structural distinguishing algorithms in the same vein as all the previously published results (q-multicollision, k-sum, limited-birthday, etc.).

3.2   Limited-Birthday

In this section, we briefly recall the limited-birthday problem and the best known algorithm for solving it. As described in Sect. 3.1, to obtain a fair comparison of algorithms solving this structural problem, we ignore the trivial algorithms mentioned. That way, we can stick to structural distinguishers and compare their time complexities to measure efficiency.

Following the notations of the previous section, the limited-birthday problem consists in obtaining a pair of inputs (x, x') (each of size n) to a permutation F with a truncated difference $x \oplus x'$ on $\log_2(IN)$ predetermined bits, that generates a pair of outputs with a truncated difference $F(x) \oplus F(x')$ on $\log_2(OUT)$ predetermined bits (therefore IN and OUT represent the set size of the admissible differences on the input and on the output respectively).

The best known cost for obtaining such a pair for an ideal permutation is denoted by $C(IN, OUT)$ and, as described in [13], can be computed the following way:

$$C(IN, OUT) = \max \left\{ \min \left\{ \sqrt{2^n/IN}, \sqrt{2^n/OUT} \right\}, \frac{2^{n+1}}{IN \cdot OUT} \right\}. \quad (1)$$

The main differences with the subspace distinguisher [20] is that in the limited-birthday distinguisher both input and output are constrained (thus limiting the ability of the attacker to perform a birthday strategy), and only a single pair is to be exhibited.

3.3   Multiple Limited-Birthday and Generic Complexity

We now consider the distinguisher represented in Fig. 2, where the conditions regarding previous distinguishers have been relaxed: the number of active diagonals (resp. anti-diagonals) in the input (resp. output) is fixed, but their positions are not. Therefore, we have $\binom{t}{n_B}$ possible different configurations in the input and $\binom{t}{n_F}$ in the output. We state the following problem.

Problem 1 (Multiple limited-birthday). Let $n_F, n_B \in \{1, \ldots, t\}$, F a permutation from the symmetric group $\mathfrak{S}_S$ of all permutations on S, and Δ_{IN} be the set of truncated patterns containing all the $\binom{t}{n_B}$ possible ways to choose n_B active diagonals among the t ones. Let Δ_{OUT} defined similarly with n_F active anti-diagonals. Given F, Δ_{IN} and Δ_{OUT}, the problem asks to find a pair $(m, m') \in S^2$ of inputs to F such that $m \oplus m' \in \Delta_{IN}$ and $F(m) \oplus F(m') \in \Delta_{OUT}$.

As for the limited-birthday distinguisher, we do not consider this problem in the theoretical sense, as there would be a trivial algorithm solving it (see Sect. 3.1). Therefore, and rather than introducing a challenge that would confuse

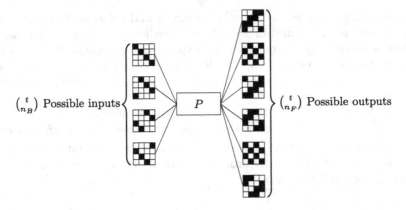

Fig. 2. Possible inputs and outputs of the relaxed generic distinguisher. The blackbox P implements a random permutation uniformly drawn from $\mathfrak{S}_S$. The figure shows the case $t = 4$, $n_B = 1$ and $n_F = 2$.

the description of our algorithm, we are interested in structural distinguishing algorithms, that ignore the constant-time trivial algorithms. Following notations of the previous section, the permutation defined in Problem 1 refer to the general primitive F of Sect. 3.1 and the particular property P the adversary is required to fulfill on P has been detailed in the problem definition.

We conjecture that the best generic algorithm for finding one solution to Problem 1 has a time complexity that is lower bounded by the limited-birthday algorithm when considering $\underline{IN} = \binom{t}{n_B}2^{t \cdot c \cdot n_B}$ and $\underline{OUT} = \binom{t}{n_F}2^{t \cdot c \cdot n_F}$. This can be reasonably argued as we can transform the multiple limited-birthday algorithm into a similar (but not equivalent) limited-birthday one, with a size of all the possible truncated input and output differences of $\underline{IN}$ and $\underline{OUT}$ respectively. Solving the similar limited-birthday problem requires a complexity of $C(\underline{IN}, \underline{OUT})$, but solving the original multiple limited-birthday problem would require an equal or higher complexity, as though having the same possible input and output difference sizes, for the same number of inputs (or outputs), the number of valid input pairs that can be built might be lower. This is directly reflected on the complexity of solving the problem, as in the limited-birthday algorithm, it is considered that for 2^n inputs queried, we can build 2^{2n-1} valid input pairs. The optimal algorithm solving Problem 1 would have a time complexity T such that: $C(\underline{IN}, \underline{OUT}) \leq T$.

We have just provided a lower bound for the complexity of solving Problem 1 in the ideal case, but an efficient generic algorithm was not known. For finding a solution, we could repeat the algorithm for solving the limited-birthday while considering sets of input or output differences that do not overlap, with a complexity of $\min\{C(\overline{IN}, \underline{OUT}), C(\underline{IN}, \overline{OUT})\}$, where $\overline{IN} = 2^{t \cdot c \cdot n_B}$, $\overline{OUT} = 2^{t \cdot c \cdot n_F}$, $\underline{IN} = \binom{t}{n_B}2^{t \cdot c \cdot n_B}$ and $\underline{OUT} = \binom{t}{n_F}2^{t \cdot c \cdot n_F}$.

We propose in the sequel a new generic algorithm to solve Problem 1 whose time complexity verifies the claimed bound and improves the complexity of the algorithm previously sketched. It allows then to find solutions faster than previous algorithms, as detailed in Table 2. Without loss of generality, because the problem is completely symmetrical, we explain the procedure in the forward direction. The same reasoning applies for the backward direction, when changing the roles between input and output of the permutation, and the complexity would then be the lowest one.

From Problem 1, we see that a random pair of inputs have a probability $P_{out} = \binom{t}{n_F} 2^{-t(t-n_F)c}$ to verify the output condition. We therefore need at least P_{out}^{-1} input pairs so that one verifying the input and output conditions can be found. The first goal of the procedure consists in constructing a structure containing enough input pairs.

Structures of Input Data. We want to generate the amount of valid input pairs previously determined, and we want do this while minimizing the numbers of queries performed to the encryption oracle, as the complexity directly depends on them. A natural way to obtain pairs of inputs consists in packing the data into structured sets. These structures contain all 2^{ct} possible values on n'_B different diagonals at the input, and make the data complexity equivalent to $2^{n'_B ct}$ encryptions. If there exists $n'_B \leq n_B$ such that the number N of possible pairs $\binom{2^{n'_B ct}}{2}$ we can construct within the structure verifies $N \geq P_{out}^{-1}$, then Problem 1 can be solved easily by using the birthday algorithm. If this does not hold, we need to consider a structure with $n'_B > n_B$. In this case, we can construct as many as $\binom{n'_B}{n_B} 2^{(n'_B - n_B)tc} \binom{2^{n_B tc}}{2}$ pairs (m, m') of inputs such that $m \oplus m'$ already belongs to Δ_{IN}. We now propose an algorithm that handles this case.

We show how to build a fixed number of pairs with the smallest structure that we could find, and we conjecture that the construction is optimal in the sense this structure is the smallest possible. The structure of input data considers n'_B

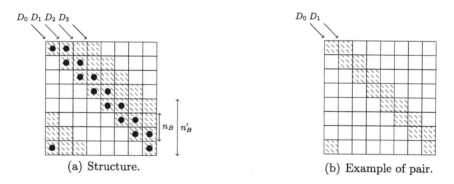

(a) Structure.   (b) Example of pair.

Fig. 3. Structure of input data: example with $n_B = 2$ and $n'_B = 4$. We construct a pair with n_B active diagonals like (b) from the structure depitected on (a). Hatched cells are active, so that the structure allows to select $\binom{n'_b}{n_B}$ different patterns to form the pairs (one is represented by the bullets •).

diagonals $D_1, \ldots, D_{n'_B}$ assuming all the 2^{ct} possible values, and an extra diagonal D_0 assuming $2^y < 2^{ct}$ values (see Fig. 3). In total, the number of queries equals $2^{y+n'_B tc}$. Within this structure, we can get[1] a number of pairs parameterized by n'_B and y:

$$N_{pairs}(n'_B, y) := \binom{n'_B}{n_B}\binom{2^{n_B ct}}{2} 2^y 2^{(n'_B - n_B)tc}$$
$$+ \binom{n'_B}{n_B - 1}\binom{2^{y+(n_B-1)ct}}{2} 2^{(n'_B - (n_B-1))ct}. \tag{2}$$

The first term of the sum considers the pairs generated from n_B diagonals among the $D_1, \ldots, D_{n'_B}$ diagonals, while the second term considers D_0 and $n_B - 1$ of the other diagonals. The problem of finding an algorithm with the smallest time complexity is therefore reduced to finding the smallest n'_B and the associated y so that $N_{pairs}(n'_B, y) = P_{out}^{-1}$. Depending on the considered scenarios, P_{out}^{-1} would have different values, but finding (n'_B, y) such that $N_{pairs}(n'_B, y) = P_{out}^{-1}$ can easily be done by an intelligent search in $\log(t) + \log(ct)$ simple operations by trying different parameters until the ones that generate the wanted amount of pairs P_{out}^{-1} are found.

Generic Algorithm. Once we have found the good parameters n'_B and y, we generate the $2^{y+n'_B ct}$ inputs as previously described, and query their corresponding outputs to the permutation F. We store the input/output pairs in a table ordered by the output values. Assuming they are uniformly distributed, there exists a pair in this table satisfying the input and output properties from Problem 1 with probability close to 1.

To find it, we first check for each output if a matching output exists in the list. When this is the case, we next check if the found pair also verifies the input conditions. The time complexity of this algorithms therefore costs about $2^{y+n'_B ct} + 2^{2y+2n'_B tc} P_{out}$ operations. The first term in the sum is the number of outputs in the table: we check for each one of them if a match exists at cost about one. The second term is the number of output matches that we expect to find, for which we also test if the input patterns conform to the wanted ones.

Finally, from the expression of P_{out}, we approximate the time complexity $2^{y+n'_B ct} + 2^{2y+2n'_B tc} P_{out}$ to $2^{y+n'_B ct}$ operations, as the second term is always smaller than the first one. The memory complexity if we store the table would be $2^{y+n'_B ct}$ as well, but we can actually perform this research without memory, as in practice what we are doing is a collision search. In Table 2, we show some examples of different complexities achieved by the bounds proposed and by our algorithm.

---

[1] When $y = 0$, we compute the number of terms as $N_{pairs}(n'_B, 0) := \binom{n'_B}{n_B}\binom{2^{n_B ct}}{2} 2^{(n'_B - n_B)tc}$.

Table 2. Examples of time complexities for several algorithms solving the multiple limited-birthday problem.

Parameters (t, c, n_B, n_F)	Bound: $C(\underline{IN}, \underline{OUT})$	Our algorithm	$C(\overline{IN}, \underline{OUT})$
(8,8,1,1)	2^{379}	$2^{379.7}$	2^{382}
(8,8,1,2)	$2^{313.2}$	$2^{314.2}$	$2^{316.2}$
(8,8,2,2)	$2^{248.4}$	$2^{250.6}$	$2^{253.2}$
(8,8,1,3)	$2^{248.19}$	$2^{249.65}$	$2^{251.19}$
(4,8,1,1)	2^{61}	$2^{62.6}$	2^{63}
(4,4,1,1)	2^{29}	$2^{30.6}$	2^{31}

4   Truncated Characteristic with Relaxed Conditions

In this section, we present a representative 9-round example of our new distinguisher.

4.1   Relaxed 9-round Distinguisher for AES-like Permutation

We show how to build a 9-round distinguisher when including the idea of relaxing the input and output conditions. In fact, this new improvement allows to reduce the complexity of the distinguisher, as the probability of verifying the outbound is higher. We point out here that we have chosen to provide an example for 9 rounds as it is the distinguisher that reaches the highest number of rounds, solving three fully-active states in the middle. We also recall that for a smaller number of rounds, the only difference with the presented distinguisher is the complexity $C_{inbound}$ for the inbound part, that can be solved using already well-known methods such as rebound attacks, Super-SBoxes or start-from-the-middle, depending on the particular situation that we have. For the sake of simplicity, in the end of this section, we provide the complexity of the distinguisher depending on the inbound complexity $C_{inbound}$.

In the end of the section, we compare our distinguisher with the previously explained best known generic algorithm to find pairs conforming to those cases. We show how the complexities of our distinguisher are still lower than the lowest bound for such a generic case.

Following the notations from [17], we parameterize the truncated differential characteristic by four variables (see Fig. 4) such that trade-offs are possible by finding the right values for each one of them. Namely, we denote c the size of the cells, $t \times t$ the size of the state matrix, n_B the number of active diagonals in the input (alternatively, the number of active cells in the second round), n_F the number of active independent diagonals in the output (alternatively, the number of active cells in the eighth round), m_B the number of active cells in the third round and m_F the number of active cells in the seventh round.

Hence, the sequence of active cells in the truncated differential characteristic becomes:

$$t\,n_B \xrightarrow{R_1} n_B \xrightarrow{R_2} m_B \xrightarrow{R_3} t\,m_B \xrightarrow{R_4} t^2 \xrightarrow{R_5} t\,m_F \xrightarrow{R_6} m_F \xrightarrow{R_7} n_F \xrightarrow{R_8} t\,n_F \xrightarrow{R_9} t^2, \quad (3)$$

with the constraints $n_F + m_F \geq t + 1$ and $n_B + m_B \geq t + 1$ that come from the MDS property, and relaxation conditions on the input and output, meaning that the positions of the n_B input active diagonals, and of the n_F active anti-diagonals generating the output can take any possible configuration, and not a fixed one. This allows to increase the probability of the outbound part and the number of solutions conforming to the characteristic. This is reflected in a reduction of the complexity of the distinguisher. The amount of solutions that we can now generate for the differential path equals to ($\log_2$):

$$\log_2\left(\binom{t}{n_B}\binom{t}{n_F}\right) + ct^2 + ctn_B$$

$$- c(t-1)n_B - c(t - m_B) - ct(t - m_F) - c(t-1)m_F - c(t - n_F) \quad (4)$$

$$= c(n_B + n_F + m_B + m_F - 2t) + \log_2\left(\binom{t}{n_B}\binom{t}{n_F}\right).$$

If follows from the MDS constraints that there are always at least $\binom{t}{n_B}\binom{t}{n_F}2^{2c}$ freedom degrees, independently of t.

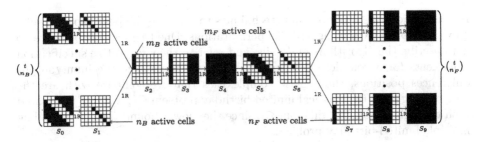

Fig. 4. The 9-round truncated differential characteristic used to distinguish an **AES**-like permutation from an ideal permutation. The figure shows some particular values: $t = 8$, $n_B = 5$, $m_B = 4$, $m_F = 4$ and $n_F = 5$.

To find a conforming pair we use the algorithm proposed in [17] for solving the inbound part and finding a solution for the middle rounds. The cost of those uncontrolled rounds is given by:

$$C_{outbound} := \frac{2^{c(t-n_B)}}{\binom{t}{n_B}} \cdot \frac{2^{c(t-n_F)}}{\binom{t}{n_F}} = \frac{2^{c(2t-n_B-n_F)}}{\binom{t}{n_B}\binom{t}{n_F}}, \quad (5)$$

since we need to pass one $n_B \leftarrow m_B$ transition in the backward direction with $\binom{t}{n_B}$ possibilities and one $m_F \rightarrow n_F$ transition in the forward direction with $\binom{t}{n_F}$ possibilities.

4.2 Comparison with Ideal Case

As we discussed in Sect. 3.3, in the ideal case, the generic complexity T is bounded by $C(\underline{IN}, \underline{OUT}) \leq T \leq \min\left\{C(\underline{IN}, \overline{OUT}), C(\overline{IN}, \underline{OUT})\right\}$, where we have $\underline{IN} = \binom{t}{n_B} 2^{t \cdot c \cdot n_B}$, $\underline{OUT} = \binom{t}{n_F} 2^{t \cdot c \cdot n_F}$, $\overline{IN} = 2^{t \cdot c \cdot n_B}$ and $\overline{OUT} = 2^{t \cdot c \cdot n_F}$.

We proposed the algorithm with the best known complexity for solving the problem in the ideal case in Sect. 3.3, for being sure that our distinguishers have smaller complexity than the best generic algorithm, we compare our complexities with the inferior bound given: $C(\underline{IN}, \underline{OUT})$, so that we are sure that our distinguisher is a valid one. We note that the algorithm we propose gives a distinguisher for 9 rounds of an AES-like permutation as soon as the state verifies $t \geq 8$.

We recall here that the complexity of the distinguishers that we build varies depending on the number of rounds solved in the middle, or the parameters chosen, and we provide some examples of improvements of previous distinguishers and their comparisons with the general bounds and algorithms in the next section.

5 Applications

In this section, we apply our new techniques to improve the best known results on various primitives using AES-like permutations. Due to a lack of space, we do not describe the algorithms in details, and refer to their respective specification documents for a complete description. When we randomize the input/output differences positions, the generic complexities that we compare with are the ones coming from the classical limited-birthday problem $C(\underline{IN}, \underline{OUT})$ (updated with the right amount of differences), since they lower bound the corresponding multiple limited-birthday problem.

5.1 AES

AES-128 [9] is an obvious target for our techniques, and it is composed of 10 rounds and has parameters $t = 4$ and $c = 8$.

Distinguisher. The current best distinguishers (except the biclique technique [5] which allows to do a speed-up search of the key by a factor of 0.27 for the full AES) can reach 8 rounds with 2^{48} computations in the known-key model (see [13]) and with 2^{24} computations in the chosen-key model (see [10]). By relaxing some input/output conditions, we are able to obtain a 8-round distinguisher with 2^{44} computations in the known-key model and with $2^{13.4}$ computations in the chosen-key model.

In the case of the known-key distinguisher, we start with the 8-round differential characteristic depicted in Fig. 5. One can see that it is possible to randomize the position of the unique active byte in both states S_1 and S_6, resulting in 4 possibles positions for both the input and output differences. We reuse the

Super-SBox technique that can find solutions from state S_2 to state S_5 with a single operation on average. Then, one has to pay $2^{24}/4 = 2^{22}$ for both transitions from state S_2 to S_1 backward and from state S_5 to S_6 forward, for a total complexity of 2^{44} computations. In the ideal case, our multiple limited-birthday problem gives us a generic complexity bounded by 2^7.

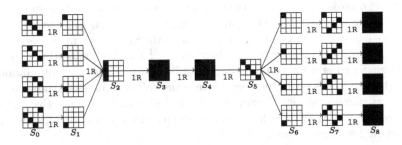

Fig. 5. Differential characteristic for the 8-round known-key distinguisher for AES-128

Concerning the chosen-key distinguisher, we start with the 8-round differential characteristic depicted in Fig. 6. Here, we use the technique introduced in [10] that can find solutions from state S_2 to state S_6 with a single operation on average. It is therefore not possible to randomize the position of the unique active byte in state S_6 since it is already specified. However, for the transition from state S_2 to S_1, we let two active bytes to be present in S_2, with random positions (6 possible choices). This happens with a probability $6 \cdot 2^{-16}$ and the total complexity to find a solution for the entire characteristic is $2^{13.4}$ computations. In the ideal case, our multiple limited-birthday problem gives us a generic complexity bounded by $2^{31.7}$.

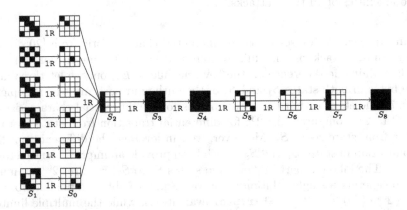

Fig. 6. Differential characteristic for the 8-round chosen-key distinguisher for AES-128

Collision. It is also interesting to check what happens if the AES cipher is plugged into a classical Davies-Meyer mode in order to get a compression function. A collision attack for this scenario was proposed in [22] for 6 rounds of AES with 2^{56} computations. By considering the characteristic from state S_1 to state S_7 state in Fig. 5 (the **MixCells** in the last round is omitted for AES, thus S_7 contains only a single active byte), and by using the technique introduced in [10] (only for chosen-key model, but in the Davies-Meyer mode the key input of the cipher is fully controlled by the attacker since it represents the message block input), we can find solutions from state S_2 to state S_6 with a single operation on average. Then, one has to pay a probability 2^{-24} for the differential transition from state S_2 to state S_1 when computing backward. One can not randomize the single active cells positions here because the collision forces us to place them at the very same position. Getting the single input and output active bytes to collide requires 2^8 tries and the total complexity of the 6-round collision search is therefore 2^{32} computations.

5.2 Whirlpool

Whirlpool [1] is a 512-bit hash function whose compression function is built upon a block cipher E in a Miyaguchi-Preneel mode: $h(H, M) = E_H(M) \oplus M \oplus H$. This block cipher E uses two 10-round AES-like permutations with parameters $t = 8$ and $c = 8$, one for the internal state transformation and one for the key schedule. The first permutation is fixed and takes as input the 512-bit incoming chaining variable, while the second permutation takes as input the 512-bit message block, and whose round keys are the successive internal states of the first permutation. The current best distinguishing attack can reach the full 10 rounds of the internal permutation and compression function (with 2^{176} computations), while the best collision attack can reach 5.5 rounds of the hash function and 7.5 rounds of the compression function [20] (with 2^{184} computations). We show how to improve the complexities of all these attacks.

Distinguisher. We reuse the same differential characteristic from [20] for the distinguishing attack on the full 10-round Whirlpool compression function (which contains no difference on the key schedule of E), but we let three more active bytes in both states S_1 and S_8 of the outbound part and this is depicted in Fig. 7. The effect is that the outbound cost of the differential characteristic is reduced to 2^{64} computations: 2^{32} for differential transition from state S_2 to S_1 and 2^{32} from state S_7 to S_8. Moreover, we can leverage the difference position randomization in states S_1 and S_8, which both provide an improvement factor of $\binom{8}{4} = 70$. The inbound part in [20] (from states S_2 to S_7) requires 2^{64} computations to generate a single solution on average, and we obtain a final complexity of $2^{64} \cdot 2^{64} \cdot (70)^{-2} = 2^{115.7}$ Whirlpool evaluations, while the multiple limited-birthday problem has a generic complexity bounded by 2^{125} computations.

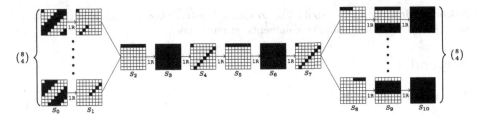

Fig. 7. 10-round truncated differential characteristic for the full `Whirlpool` compression function distinguisher.

Collision. We reuse the same differential characteristic from [20] for the 7.5-round collision attack on the `Whirlpool` compression function (which contains no difference on the key schedule of E), but we let one more active byte in both states S_0 and S_7 of the outbound part (see Fig. 8). From this, we gain an improvement factor of 2^8 in both forward and backward directions of the outbound (from state S_1 to S_0 and from state S_6 to S_7), but we have two byte positions to collide on with the feed-forward instead of one. After incorporating this 2^8 extra cost, we obtain a final improvement factor of 2^8 over the original attack (it is to be noted that this improvement will not work for 7-round reduced `Whirlpool` since the active byte position randomization would not be possible anymore). The very same method applies to the 5.5-round collision attack on the `Whirlpool` hash function.

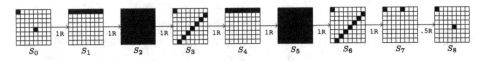

Fig. 8. 7.5-round truncated differential characteristic for the `Whirlpool` compression function collision.

6   Conclusion

In this article, we propose a new type of distinguisher for `AES`-like permutations that we call the *multiple limited-birthday* distinguisher. It generalizes the simple limited-birthday one in the sense that it allows more than just one pattern of fixed difference at both the input and the output of the permutation. We provide an algorithm to efficiently solve the problem for the ideal case, while it remains an open problem to prove its optimality, which can probably be reduced to proving the optimality of the simple limited-birthday algorithm in terms of number of queries. As applications of this work, we show how to improve almost all previously known rebound distinguishers for `AES`-based primitives.

Acknowledgments. We would like to thank Dmitry Khovratovich and the anonymous referees for their valuable comments on our paper.

Appendix

A   Other Results

Table 3. Other improvements for various rebound-based attacks on AES-based primitives. Our results marked as **New** are detailed in the extended version of this article

Target	Subtarget	Rounds	Type	Time	Memory	Ideal	Reference
ECHO	Permutation	7	dist.	2^{118}	2^{38}	2^{1025}	[27]
		7	dist.	2^{102}	2^{38}	2^{256}	**New**
		8	dist.	2^{151}	2^{67}	2^{257}	[24]
		8	dist.	2^{147}	2^{67}	2^{256}	**New**
Grøstl-256	Permutation	8	dist.	2^{16}	2^{8}	2^{33}	[27]
		8	dist.	2^{10}	2^{8}	$2^{31.5}$	**New**
		9	dist.	2^{368}	2^{64}	2^{385}	[17]
		9	dist.	2^{362}	2^{64}	2^{379}	**New**
Grøstl-256	Comp. func.	6	collision	2^{120}	2^{64}	2^{257}	[28]
		6	collision	2^{119}	2^{64}	2^{257}	**New**
Grøstl-256	Hash func.	3	collision	2^{64}	2^{64}	2^{129}	[28]
		3	collision	2^{63}	2^{64}	2^{129}	**New**
LED-64	Cipher	15	CK dist.	2^{16}	2^{16}	2^{33}	[15]
		16	CK dist.	$2^{33.5}$	2^{32}	$2^{41.4}$	[25]
		20	CK dist.	$2^{60.2}$	$2^{61.5}$	$2^{66.1}$	[25]
		19	CK dist.	2^{18}	2^{16}	2^{33}	**New**
PHOTON-80/20/16	Permutation	8	dist.	2^{8}	2^{4}	2^{11}	[14]
		8	dist.	$2^{3.4}$	2^{4}	$2^{9.8}$	**New**
PHOTON-128/16/16	Permutation	8	dist.	2^{8}	2^{4}	2^{13}	[14]
		8	dist.	$2^{2.8}$	2^{4}	$2^{11.7}$	**New**
PHOTON-160/36/36	Permutation	8	dist.	2^{8}	2^{4}	2^{15}	[14]
		8	dist.	$2^{2.4}$	2^{4}	$2^{13.6}$	**New**
PHOTON-224/32/32	Permutation	8	dist.	2^{8}	2^{4}	2^{17}	[14]
		8	dist.	2^{2}	2^{4}	$2^{15.5}$	**New**
		9	dist.	2^{184}	2^{32}	2^{193}	[17]
		9	dist.	2^{178}	2^{32}	2^{187}	**New**
PHOTON-256/32/32	Permutation	8	dist.	2^{16}	2^{8}	2^{25}	[14]
		8	dist.	$2^{10.8}$	2^{8}	$2^{23.7}$	**New**

References

1. Barreto, P.S.L.M., Rijmen, V.: Whirlpool. In: van Tilborg, H.C.A., Jajodia, S. (eds.) Encyclopedia of Cryptography and Security, 2nd edn, pp. 1384–1385. Springer, New York (2011)

2. Bellare, M., Rogaway, P.: Optimal asymmetric encryption. In: De Santis, A. (ed.) EUROCRYPT 1994. LNCS, vol. 950, pp. 92–111. Springer, Heidelberg (1995)
3. Benadjila, R., Billet, O., Gilbert, H., Macario-Rat, G., Peyrin, T., Robshaw, M., Seurin, Y.: SHA-3 proposal: ECHO. Submission to NIST (2008)
4. Bertoni, G., Daemen, J., Peeters, M., Assche, G.V.: The Keccak reference. Submission to NIST (Round 3) (2011)
5. Bogdanov, A., Khovratovich, D., Rechberger, C.: Biclique cryptanalysis of the full AES. In: Lee, D.H., Wang, X. (eds.) ASIACRYPT 2011. LNCS, vol. 7073, pp. 344–371. Springer, Heidelberg (2011)
6. Boura, C., Canteaut, A., De Cannière, C.: Higher-order differential properties of Keccak and Luffa. In: Joux, A. (ed.) FSE 2011. LNCS, vol. 6733, pp. 252–269. Springer, Heidelberg (2011)
7. Canetti, R., Goldreich, O., Halevi, S.: The random oracle methodology. Revisited J. ACM 51(4), 557–594 (2004)
8. Canteaut, A. (ed.): FSE 2012. LNCS, vol. 7549. Springer, Heidelberg (2012)
9. Daemen, J., Rijmen, V.: Rijndael for AES. In: AES Candidate Conference, pp. 343–348 (2000)
10. Derbez, P., Fouque, P.-A., Jean, J.: Faster chosen-key distinguishers on reduced-round AES. In: Galbraith, S., Nandi, M. (eds.) INDOCRYPT 2012. LNCS, vol. 7668, pp. 225–243. Springer, Heidelberg (2012)
11. Duc, A., Guo, J., Peyrin, T., Wei, L.: Unaligned rebound attack: application to Keccak. In: [8] pp. 402–421
12. Gauravaram, P., Knudsen, L.R., Matusiewicz, K., Mendel, F., Rechberger, C., Schläffer, M., Thomsen, S.S.: Grøstl - a SHA-3 candidate. Submitted to the competition, NIST (2008)
13. Gilbert, H., Peyrin, T.: Super-Sbox cryptanalysis: improved attacks for AES-like permutations. In: [26] pp. 365–383
14. Guo, J., Peyrin, T., Poschmann, A.: The PHOTON family of lightweight hash functions. In: [26] pp. 222–239
15. Guo, J., Peyrin, T., Poschmann, A., Robshaw, M.: The LED block cipher. In: Preneel, B., Takagi, T. (eds.) CHES 2011. LNCS, vol. 6917, pp. 326–341. Springer, Heidelberg (2011)
16. Hong, S., Iwata, T. (eds.): FSE 2010. LNCS, vol. 6147. Springer, Berlin (2010)
17. Jean, J., Naya-Plasencia, M., Peyrin, T.: Improved rebound attack on the finalist Grøstl. In: [8] pp. 110–126
18. Khovratovich, D., Nikolic, I.: Rotational cryptanalysis of ARX. In: [16] pp. 333–346
19. Lamberger, M., Mendel, F., Rechberger, C., Rijmen, V., Schläffer, M.: Rebound distinguishers: results on the full Whirlpool compression function. In: Matsui, M. (ed.) ASIACRYPT 2009. LNCS, vol. 5912, pp. 126–143. Springer, Heidelberg (2009)
20. Lamberger, M., Mendel, F., Rechberger, C., Rijmen, V., Schläffer, M.: The rebound attack and subspace distinguishers: application to whirlpool. Cryptology ePrint Archive, Report 2010/198 (2010)
21. Matusiewicz, K., Naya-Plasencia, M., Nikolić, I., Sasaki, Y., Schläffer, M.: Rebound attack on the full LANE compression function. In: Matsui, M. (ed.) ASIACRYPT 2009. LNCS, vol. 5912, pp. 106–125. Springer, Heidelberg (2009)
22. Mendel, F., Peyrin, T., Rechberger, C., Schläffer, M.: Improved cryptanalysis of the reduced Grøstl compression function, ECHO permutation and AES block cipher. In: Jacobson Jr, M.J., Rijmen, V., Safavi-Naini, R. (eds.) SAC 2009. LNCS, vol. 5867, pp. 16–35. Springer, Heidelberg (2009)

23. Mendel, F., Rechberger, C., Schläffer, M., Thomsen, S.S.: The rebound attack: cryptanalysis of reduced Whirlpool and Grøstl. In: Dunkelman, O. (ed.) FSE 2009. LNCS, vol. 5665, pp. 260–276. Springer, Heidelberg (2009)
24. Naya-Plasencia, M.: How to improve rebound attacks. In: [26] pp. 188–205
25. Nikolic, I., Wang, L., Wu, S.: Cryptanalysis of Round-Reduced LED. In: FSE. Lecture Notes in Computer Science (2013) (To appear)
26. Rogaway, P. (ed.): CRYPTO 2011. LNCS, vol. 6841. Springer, Heidelberg (2011)
27. Sasaki, Y., Li, Y., Wang, L., Sakiyama, K., Ohta, K.: Non-full-active Super-Sbox analysis: applications to ECHO and Grøstl. In: Abe, M. (ed.) ASIACRYPT 2010. LNCS, vol. 6477, pp. 38–55. Springer, Heidelberg (2010)
28. Schläffer, M.: Updated differential analysis of Grøstl. Grøstl website (2011)

Side-Channel Attacks

Horizontal Collision Correlation Attack
on Elliptic Curves

Aurélie Bauer[⊠], Eliane Jaulmes, Emmanuel Prouff, and Justine Wild

ANSSI, 51, Bd de la Tour-Maubourg, SP 07, 75700 Paris, France
{aurelie.bauer,eliane.jaulmes,emmanuel.prouff,justine.wild}@ssi.gouv.fr

Abstract. Elliptic curves based algorithms are nowadays widely spread among embedded systems. They indeed have the double advantage of providing efficient implementations with short certificates and of being relatively easy to secure against side-channel attacks. As a matter of fact, when an algorithm with constant execution flow is implemented together with randomization techniques, the obtained design usually thwarts classical side-channel attacks while keeping good performances. Recently, a new technique that makes some randomizations ineffective, has been successfully applied in the context of RSA implementations. This method, related to a so-called *horizontal modus operandi*, introduced by Walter in 2001, turns out to be very powerful since it only requires leakages on a single algorithm execution. In this paper, we combine such kind of techniques together with the *collision correlation* analysis, introduced at CHES 2010 by Moradi *et al.*, to propose a new attack on elliptic curves atomic implementations (or unified formulas) with input randomization. We show how it may be applied against several state-of-the art implementations, including those of Chevallier-Mames *et al.*, of Longa and of Giraud-Verneuil and also Bernstein and Lange for unified Edward's formulas. Finally, we provide simulation results for several sizes of elliptic curves on different hardware architectures. These results, which turn out to be the very first horizontal attacks on elliptic curves, open new perspectives in securing such implementations. Indeed, this paper shows that two of the main existing countermeasures for elliptic curve implementations become irrelevant when going from vertical to horizontal analysis.

1 Introduction

Elliptic Curves Cryptosystems (ECC) that have been introduced by N. Koblitz [21] and V. Miller [29], are based on the notable *discrete logarithm problem*, which has been thoroughly studied in the literature and is supposed to be a hard mathematical problem. The main benefit in elliptic curves based algorithms is the size of the keys. Indeed, for the same level of security, the schemes require keys that are far smaller than those involved in classical public-key cryptosystems. The success of ECC led to a wide variety of applications in our daily life and they are now implemented on lots of embedded devices: smart-cards, micro-controller,

T. Lange, K. Lauter, and P. Lisoněk (Eds.): SAC 2013, LNCS 8282, pp. 553–570, 2014.
DOI: 10.1007/978-3-662-43414-7_28, © Springer-Verlag Berlin Heidelberg 2014

and so on. Such devices are small, widespread and in the hands of end-users. Thus the range of threats they are confronted to is considerably wider than in the classical situation. In particular, physical attacks are taken into account when assessing the security of the application implementation (e.g. the PACE protocol in e-passports [20]) and countermeasures are implemented alongside the algorithms.

A physical attack may belong to one of the two following families: *perturbation analysis* or *observation analysis*. The first one tends to modify the cryptosystem processing with laser beams, clock jitter or voltage perturbation. Such attacks can be thwarted by monitoring the device environment with captors and by verifying the computations before returning the output. The second kind of attacks consists in measuring a physical information, such as the power consumption or the electro-magnetic emanation, during sensitive computations. Inside this latter area we can distinguish, what we call *simple attacks*, that directly deduces the value of the secret from one or a small number of observation(s) (e.g. *Simple Power Analysis* [23]) and *advanced attacks* involving a large number of observations and exploiting them through statistics (e.g. *Differential Power Analysis* [24] or *Correlation Power Analysis* [9]). Such attacks require the use of a statistical tool, also known as a *distinguisher*, together with a *leakage model* to compare hypotheses with real traces (each one related to known or chosen inputs). The latter constraint may however be relaxed thanks to the so-called *collision attacks* [32] which aim at detecting the occurrences of colliding values during a computation, that can be linked to the secret [8,14,30,31]. In order to counteract all those attacks, randomization techniques can be implemented (e.g. scalar/message blinding for ECC [16]). The recent introduction of the so-called *horizontal* side-channel technique by Clavier *et al.* in [13] seems to have set up a new deal. This method, which is inspired by Walter's work [33], takes its advantage in requiring a unique power trace, thus making classical randomization techniques ineffective. Up to now, it has been applied successfully on RSA implementations and we show in this paper that it can be combined with collision correlation analysis to provide efficient attack on elliptic curves protected implementations.

Core idea. In the context of embedded security, most ECC protocols (e.g. ECDSA [1] or ECDH [2]) use a short term secret that changes at each protocol iteration. In this particular setting, advanced side-channel attacks, which require several executions of the algorithm with the same secret, are ineffective. As a consequence, only protection against SPA is usually needed, that can be done thanks to the popular *atomicity* principle [11,18,26]. Up to now, this technique is considered as achieving the best security/efficiency trade-off to protect against side-channel analysis. In this paper, we provide a new side-channel attack, called *horizontal collision correlation analysis* that defeats such protected ECC implementations. In particular, implementations using point/scalar randomization combined with atomicity are not secure, contrary to what was thought up to now. Moreover in order to complete our study, we also investigate the case of unified formulas[1]. Indeed, we show that our horizontal collision correlation attack allows to distinguish, with a single leakage trace, a doubling operation from an addition one. This technique, which allows to eventually recover the secret scalar, is applied to three different atomic formulae on elliptic curves, namely those proposed by Chevallier-Mames *et al.* in [11], by Longa in [26], by Giraud and Verneuil in [18].

The paper is organized as follows. First, Sect. 2 recalls some basics about ECC in a side-channel attacks context. Then, under the assumption that one can distinguish common operands in modular multiplications, the outlines of our new *horizontal collision correlation* attack are presented in Sect. 3. After a theoretical analysis explaining how to practically deal with the distinguishability assumption, we provide in Sect. 4 experimental results for 160, 256 and 384-bit-size curves working with 8, 16 or 32-bit registers. These results show that the attack success rate stays high even when significant noise is added to the leakage.

2   Preliminaries

2.1   Notations and Basics on Side-Channel Attacks

Notations. A realization of a random variable X is referred to as the corresponding lower-case letter x. A *sample* of n observations of X is denoted by (x) or by $(x_i)_{1 \le i \le n}$ when a reference to the indexation is needed. In this case, the global event is summed up as $(x) \hookleftarrow X$. The jth coordinate of a variable X (resp. a realization x), viewed as a vector, is denoted by $X[j]$ (resp. $x[j]$). As usual, the notation $\mathbb{E}[X]$ refers to the mean of X. For clarity reasons we sometimes use the notation $\mathbb{E}_X[Y]$ when Y depends on X and other variables, to enlighten the fact that the mean is computed over X. Attacks presented in this paper involve the *linear correlation coefficient* which measures the linear interdependence between two variables X and Y. It is defined as $\rho(X, Y) = \frac{\text{cov}(X, Y)}{\sigma_X \sigma_Y}$, where $\text{cov}(X, Y)$, called *covariance between* X *and* Y, equals $\mathbb{E}[XY] - \mathbb{E}[X]\mathbb{E}[Y]$ and where σ_X and σ_Y respectively denotes the standard deviation of X and Y. The linear correlation coefficient can be approximated from realizations samples $(x_i)_{1 \le i \le n}$ and $(y_i)_{1 \le i \le n}$ of X and Y respectively. For this approximation, the following so-called *Pearson's coefficient* is usually involved:

$$\hat{\rho}(X, Y) = \frac{n \sum_i x_i y_i - \sum_i x_i \sum_j y_j}{\sqrt{n \sum_i x_i^2 - \left(\sum_i x_i\right)^2} \sqrt{n \sum_j y_j^2 - \left(\sum_j y_j\right)^2}} . \tag{1}$$

General Attack Context. In the subsequent descriptions of side-channel analyses, an algorithm $\mathcal{A}$ is modelled by a sequence of *elementary calculations* $(C_i)_i$ that are Turing machines augmented with a common random access

---

[1] Among the unified formulas, we especially focus on the Edward's ones in [5] introduced by Bernstein and Lange since they lead to efficient doubling and addition computations compared to the Weierstrass case [10].

memory (see [28] for more details about this model). Each elementary calculation C_i reads its input X_i in this memory and updates it with its output $O_i = C_i(X_i)$. During the processing of $\mathcal{A}$, each calculation C_i may be associated with an information *leakage* random variable L_i (a.k.a. *noisy observation*). A prerequisite for the side-channel analyses described in this paper to be applicable is that the *mutual information* between O_i and L_i is non-zero. The alternative notation $L_i(O_i)$ will sometimes be used to stress the relationship between the two variables.

A side-channel analysis aims at describing a strategy to deduce information on the algorithm secret parameter from the leakages L_i. Let us denote by s this secret parameter. In this paper, we pay particular attention to two attacks sub-classes. The first ones are called *simple* and try to exploit a dependency between the sequence of operations C_i and s (independently of the C_i inputs and outputs). A well-known example of such an attack is the simple power analysis (SPA) [16]. In this attack, the algorithm input is kept constant and the unprotected sequence of C_i is usually composed of two distinct operations (for instance a doubling and an addition in the case of ECC). It can easily be checked that the order of those operations in the sequence is a one-to-one function of the secret scalar s. Hence, if the leakages L_i enable to clearly differentiate the operations, then the adversary may recover the order of the latters, and thus the secret.

Following the framework presented in [4], we call *advanced* the attacks belonging to the second class of side-channel analyses. Among them, we find the well-known differential power analysis (DPA) [24] or the correlation power analysis (CPA) [9]. Contrary to simple attacks, the advanced ones do not only focus on the *operations* but also on the *operands*. They usually focus on a small subset I of the calculations C_i and try to exploit a statistical dependency between the results O_i of those calculations and the secret s. For such a purpose, the adversary must get a sufficiently large number N of observations $(\ell^i_j)_j \hookleftarrow L_i(O_i)$, where $i \in I$ and $1 \leq j \leq N$.

In the literature, two strategies have been specified to get the observations samples $(\ell^i_j)_j$ for a given elementary computation $O_i = C_i(X_i)$. The first method, called *vertical*, simply consists in executing the implementation several times and in defining ℓ^i_j as the observation related to the result O_i at the jth algorithm execution. Most attacks [3,9,24] enter into this category and the number of different indices i may for instance correspond to the *attack order* [27]. The second method, called *horizontal* [13,33], applies on a single algorithm execution. It starts by finding the sequence of elementary calculations $(C_{i_j})_j$ that processes the same mathematical operation than C_i (e.g. a field multiplication) and depends on the same secret sub-part. By construction, all the outputs O_{i_j} of the C_{i_j} can be viewed as a realization of $O_i = C_i(X_i)$ and the ℓ^i_j are here defined as the observations of the O_{i_j}. We can eventually notice that the vertical and horizontal strategies are perfectly analogous to each other and that they can be applied to both simple and advanced attacks.

2.2   Background on Elliptic Curves

As this paper focuses on side-channel attacks on ECC, let us recall now some basics on elliptic curves and especially on the various ways of representing points on such objects (the reader could refer to [15, 19] for more details).

Throughout this paper, we are interested in elliptic curve implementations running on platforms (ASIC, FPGA, micro-controller) embedding a hardware modular multiplier (e.g. a 16-bit, 32-bit or 64-bit multiplier). On such implementations, the considered elliptic curves are usually defined over a prime finite field $\mathbb{F}_p$. In the rest of this paper, we will assume that all curves are defined over $\mathbb{F}_p$ with $p \neq \{2, 3\}$. The algorithm used for the hardware modular multiplication is assumed to be known to the attacker. Moreover, to simplify the attack descriptions, we assume hereafter that the latter multiplication is performed in a very simple way: a schoolbook long integer multiplication followed by a reduction. Most of current devices do not implement the modular multiplications that way, but the attacks described hereafter can always be adapted by changing the definition of the elementary operations of Sect. 3.3 (see the full version of the paper for a complete discussion on that point).

Definition. An elliptic curve E over a prime finite field $\mathbb{F}_p$ with $p \neq \{2, 3\}$ can be defined as an algebraic curve of affine reduced Weierstrass equation:

$$(E) : y^2 = x^3 + ax + b , \tag{2}$$

with $(a, b) \in (\mathbb{F}_p)^2$ and $4a^3 + 27b^2 \neq 0$. Let $P = (x_1, y_1)$ and $Q = (x_2, y_2)$ be two points on (E), the sum $R = (x_3, y_3)$ of P and Q belongs to the curve under a well-known addition rule [21]. The set of pairs $(x, y) \in (\mathbb{F}_p)^2$ belonging to (E), taken with an extra point $\mathcal{O}$, called *point at infinity*, form an abelian group named $E(\mathbb{F}_p)$.

In the rest of the paper, the points will be represented using their projective coordinates. Namely, a point $P = (x, y)$ is expressed as a triplet $(X : Y : Z)$ such that $X = xZ$ and $Y = yZ$.

2.3   Points Operations in Presence of SCA

This paper focusses on elliptic curves cryptosystems which involve the scalar multiplication $[s]P$, implemented with the well-known *double and add* algorithm.

In a non-protected implementation, the sequence of point doublings and point additions can reveal the value of s with a single leakage trace. Thus to protect the scheme against SPA, the sequence of point operations must be independent from the secret value. This can be achieved in several ways. The double and add *always* algorithm [16] is the simplest solution. It consists in inserting dummy point additions each time the considered bit value of s is equal to 0. In average, this solution adds an overhead of $\frac{\log_2(s)}{2}$ point additions. Another technique consists in using unified formulae for both addition and doubling [6, 7, 25]. Finally, the scheme that is usually adopted in constrained devices such as smart cards, since it achieves the best time/memory trade-off, remains atomicity [11, 18, 26].

This principle is a refinement of the double and add always technique. It consists in writing addition and doubling operations as a sequence of a unique pattern. This pattern is itself a sequence of operations over $\mathbb{F}_p$. Since the pattern is unique, the same sequence of field operations is repeated for the addition and the doubling, the only difference being the number of times the pattern is applied for each operation. It thus becomes impossible to distinguish one operation from the other or even to identify the starting and ending of these operations.

To defeat an atomic implementation, the adversary needs to use advanced side-channel attacks (see Sect. 2.1), such as DPA, CPA and so on. These attacks focus on the operations operands instead of only focusing on the kind of operations. They usually require more observations than for SPA since they rely on statistical analyses. In the ECC literature, such attacks have only been investigated in the vertical setting, where they can be efficiently prevented by input randomization.

3   Horizontal Collision Correlation Attack on ECC

We show hereafter that implementations combining atomicity and randomization techniques are in fact vulnerable to collision attacks in the horizontal setting. This raises the need for new dedicated countermeasures.

This section starts by recalling some basics on collision attacks. Then, assuming that the adversary is able to distinguish when two field multiplications have a common (possibly unknown) operand, we show how to exhibit flaws in the atomic algorithms proposed in [11,18,26]) and also in implementations using the unified formulas for Edward's curves [5]. Eventually, we apply the collision attack presented in the first subsection to show how to efficiently deal with the previous assumption.

3.1   Collision Power Analysis in the Horizontal Setting

To recover information on a subpart s of the secret $\boldsymbol{s}$, collision side-channel analyses are usually performed on a sample of observations related to the processing, by the device, of two variables O_1 and O_2 that jointly depend on s. The advantage of those attacks, compared to the classical ones, is that the algorithm inputs can be unknown since the adversary does not need to compute predictions on the manipulated data. When performed in the horizontal setting, the observations on O_1 and O_2 are extracted from the same algorithm execution (see Sect. 2.1). Then, the correlation between the two samples of observations is estimated thanks to the Pearson's coefficient (see Eq. (1)) in order to recover information on s. We sum up hereafter the outlines of this attack, that will be applied in the following.

Remark 1. In Table 1, we use Pearson's coefficient to compare the two samples of observations but other choices are possible (e.g. mutual information).

Remark 2. In order to deduce information on s from the knowledge of $\hat{\rho}$, one may use for instance a *Maximum Likelihood* distinguisher (see a discussion on that point in Sect. 4).

Table 1. Collision power analysis

1.	Identify two elementary calculations $C_1(\cdot)$ and $C_2(\cdot)$ which are processed several times, say N, with input(s) drawn from the same distribution(s). The correlation between the random variables O_1 and O_2 corresponding to the outputs of C_1 and C_2 must depend on the same secret sub-part s.
2.	For each of the N processings of C_1 (resp. C_2) get an observation ℓ_j^1 (resp. ℓ_j^2) with $j \in [1; N]$.
3.	Compute the quantity: $\hat{\rho} = \hat{\rho}\big((\ell_j^1)_j, (\ell_j^2)_j\big)$
4.	Deduce information on s from $\hat{\rho}$.

In the next section, the attack in Table 1 is invoked as an Oracle enabling to detect whether two field multiplications share a common operand.

Assumption 1. *The adversary can detect when two field multiplications have at least one operand in common.*

In Sect. 3.3, we will come back to the latter hypothesis and will detail how it can indeed be satisfied in the particular context of ECC implementations on constrained systems.

3.2 Attacks on ECC Implementations: Core Idea

We start by presenting the principle of the attack on atomic implementations, and then on an implementation based on unified (addition and doubling) formulas over Edward's curves.

***Attack on Chevallier-Mames* et al.*'s Scheme.** In Chevallier-Mames *et al.*'s atomic scheme, historically the first one, the authors propose the three first patterns[2] given in Fig. 1 for the doubling of a point $Q = (X_1 : Y_1 : Z_1)$ and the addition of Q with a second point $P = (X_2 : Y_2 : Z_2)$.

As expected, and as a straightforward implication of the atomicity principle, the doubling and addition schemes perform exactly the same sequence of field operations if the *star* (dummy) operations are well chosen[3]. This implies that it is impossible to distinguish a doubling from an addition by just looking at the sequence of calculations (i.e. by SPA). Let us now focus on the operations' operands. In the addition scheme, the field multiplications in Patterns 1 and 3 both involve the coordinate Z_2. On the contrary, the corresponding multiplications in the doubling scheme have *a priori* independent operands (indeed the first one corresponds to the multiplication $X_1 \cdot X_1$, whereas the other one corresponds to $Z_1^2 \cdot Z_1^2$). If an adversary has a mean to detect this difference (which is actually the case under Assumption 1), then he is able to distinguish a doubling from an addition and thus to fully recover the secret scalar s. Indeed, let us

---

[2] For readability reasons we do not recall the full patterns but the interested reader can find them in [11].

[3] Guidelines are given in [11] to define the dummy operations in a pertinent way.

DOUBLING	ADDITION
$R_0 \leftarrow a,\ R_1 \leftarrow X_1,\ R_2 \leftarrow Y_1,\ R_3 \leftarrow Z_1$	$R_1 \leftarrow X_1,\ R_2 \leftarrow Y_1,\ R_3 \leftarrow Z_1,$
	$R_7 \leftarrow X_2,\ R_8 \leftarrow Y_2,\ R_9 \leftarrow Z_2$

DOUBLING

1.
$$\begin{bmatrix} \boldsymbol{R_4 \leftarrow R_1 \cdot R_1}\ (= X_1 \cdot X_1) \\ R_5 \leftarrow R_4 + R_4 \\ \star \\ R_4 \leftarrow R_4 + R_5 \end{bmatrix}$$

2.
$$\begin{bmatrix} R_5 \leftarrow R_3 \cdot R_3 \\ R_1 \leftarrow R_1 + R_1 \\ \star \\ \star \end{bmatrix}$$

3.
$$\begin{bmatrix} \boldsymbol{R_5 \leftarrow R_5 \cdot R_5}\ (= Z_1^2 \cdot Z_1^2) \\ \star \\ \star \\ \star \end{bmatrix}$$

ADDITION

1.
$$\begin{bmatrix} \boldsymbol{R_4 \leftarrow R_9 \cdot R_9}\ (= Z_2 \cdot Z_2) \\ \star \\ \star \\ \star \end{bmatrix}$$

2.
$$\begin{bmatrix} R_1 \leftarrow R_1 \cdot R_4 \\ \star \\ \star \\ \star \end{bmatrix}$$

3.
$$\begin{bmatrix} \boldsymbol{R_4 \leftarrow R_4 \cdot R_9}\ (= Z_2^2 \cdot Z_2) \\ \star \\ \star \\ \star \end{bmatrix}$$

Fig. 1. Three first atomic patterns of point doubling and addition.

focus on the processing of the second step of the double and add left-to-right algorithm, and let us denote by s the most significant bit of s. Depending on s, this sequence either corresponds to the processing of the doubling of $Q = [2]P$ (case $s = 0$) or to the addition of $Q = [2]P$ with P (case $s = 1$). Eventually, the results T_1 and T_2 of the field multiplications in respectively Patterns 1 and 3 satisfy:

$$\begin{cases} T_1 = (X_1 \cdot X_1)^{1-s} \cdot (Z_2 \cdot Z_2)^{s} \\ T_2 = (Z_1^2 \cdot Z_1^2)^{1-s} \cdot (Z_2^2 \cdot Z_2)^{s} \end{cases} \tag{3}$$

where we recall that we have $P = (X_2 : Y_2 : Z_2)$ and $Q = (X_1 : Y_1 : Z_1)$. Equation (3) and Assumption 1 enables to deduce whether s equals 0 or 1. Applying this attack $\log_2(s)$ times, all the bits of s can be recovered one after the other.

We now show that the same idea can successfully be applied to attack the other atomic implementations proposed in the literature, namely those of Longa [26] and Giraud and Verneuil [18].

Attack on Longa's Scheme. The atomic pattern introduced by Longa in [26] is more efficient than that of Chevallier-Mames *et al.*'s scheme. This improvement is got by combining affine and Jacobian coordinates in the points addition, see Fig. 2.

It can be seen that the first and third patterns of Longa's scheme contain two field multiplications that either have no operand in common (doubling case) or share the operand Z_1 (addition case). Similarly to Chevallier-Mames *et al.*'s scheme, we can hence define the two following random variables:

$$\begin{cases} T_1 = (Z_1 \cdot Z_1)^{1-s} \cdot (Z_1 \cdot Z_1)^{s} \\ T_2 = (X_1 \cdot 4Y_1^2)^{1-s} \cdot (Z_1^2 \cdot Z_1)^{s} \end{cases} \tag{4}$$

DOUBLING

$$R_1 \leftarrow X_1, \; R_2 \leftarrow Y_1, \; R_3 \leftarrow Z_1$$

$$
1. \begin{bmatrix} \boldsymbol{R_3 \leftarrow R_3^2} \quad (= Z_1 \cdot Z_1) \\ \star \\ R_5 \leftarrow R_1 + R_4 \\ R_6 \leftarrow R_2^2 \\ R_4 \leftarrow -R_4 \\ R_2 \leftarrow R_2 + R_2 \\ R_4 \leftarrow R_1 + R_4 \end{bmatrix}
\qquad
3. \begin{bmatrix} R_5 \leftarrow R_4^2 \\ \star \\ R_6 \leftarrow R_2 + R_2 \\ \boldsymbol{R_6 \leftarrow R_1 \cdot R_6} \quad (= X_1 \cdot 4Y_1^2) \\ R_1 \leftarrow -R_6 \\ R_1 \leftarrow R_1 + R_1 \\ R_1 \leftarrow R_1 + R_5 \end{bmatrix}
$$

ADDITION
(mixed coordinates)

Input: $P = (X_1 : Y_1 : Z_1)$ and $Q = (X_2, Y_2)$
Output: $P + Q = (X_3 : Y_3 : Z_3 : X_1' : Y_1')$
$$R_1 \leftarrow X_1, \; R_2 \leftarrow Y_1, \; R_3 \leftarrow Z_1, \; R_x \leftarrow X_2, \; R_y \leftarrow Y_2$$

$$
1. \begin{bmatrix} \boldsymbol{R_4 \leftarrow R_3^2} \quad (= Z_1 \cdot Z_1) \\ \star \\ \star \\ R_5 \leftarrow R_x \cdot R_4 \\ R_6 \leftarrow -R_1 \\ R_5 \leftarrow R_5 + R_6 \\ \star \end{bmatrix}
\qquad
3. \begin{bmatrix} R_9 \leftarrow R_5 \cdot R_6 \\ \star \\ R_8 \leftarrow R_8 + R_9 \\ \boldsymbol{R_4 \leftarrow R_3 \cdot R_4} \quad (= Z_1^2 \cdot Z_1) \\ \star \\ \star \\ \star \end{bmatrix}
$$

Fig. 2. The first and third patterns used in atomicity of Longa

Under Assumption 1, it leads to the recovery of s.

Attack on Giraud and Verneuil's Scheme. Giraud and Verneuil introduced in [18] a new atomic pattern which reduces the number of field additions, negations and dummy operations ($\star$) compared to the above proposals. The patterns are recalled in Fig. 3.

Once again, depending on the secret s, we observe a repetition of two multiplications with a common operand in the first pattern of the addition scheme (ADD 1.), leading to the following equations:

$$\begin{cases} T_1 = (X_1 \cdot X_1)^{1-s} \cdot (Z_2 \cdot Z_2)^s \\ T_2 = (2Y_1 \cdot Y_1)^{1-s} \cdot (Z_2^2 \cdot Z_2)^s \end{cases}, \tag{5}$$

which, under Assumption 1, leads to the recovery of s.

Remark 3. A second version of the patterns in Fig. 3 has been proposed in [18] which allows to save more field additions and negations without addition of dummy operations. This proposal share the same weakness as the previous ones and our attack still applies.

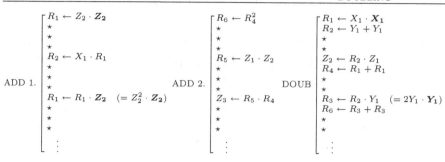

ADDITION   DOUBLING

Fig. 3. The beginning of Giraud and Verneuil's patterns

Attack on Edward's Curves. Edward's representation of elliptic curves has been introduced in [17]. In a subsequent paper [6], Bernstein and Lange homogenized the curve equation in order to avoid field inversions in Edward's addition and doubling formulas. For this homogenized representation, points addition and doubling are both computed thanks to the same formula. Let $P = (X_1 : Y_1 : Z_1)$ and $Q = (X_2 : Y_2 : Z_2)$ be two points on the curve, the sum $R = (X_3 : Y_3 : Z_3)$ of P and Q is given by the following system:

$$\begin{cases} X_3 = Z_1 Z_2 (X_1 Y_2 - Y_1 X_2)(X_1 Y_1 Z_2^2 + Z_1^2 X_2 Y_2) \\ Y_3 = Z_1 Z_2 (X_1 X_2 + Y_1 Y_2)(X_1 Y_1 Z_2^2 - Z_1^2 X_2 Y_2) \\ Z_3 = d Z_1^2 Z_2^2 (X_1 X_2 + Y_1 Y_2)(X_1 Y_2 - Y_1 X_2) \end{cases} ,$$

where d is some constant related to the Edward curve equation. These formulae correspond to the sequence of operations given by Fig. 4.

This sequence also works when $P = Q$, meaning that it applies similarly for addition and doubling. This is one of the main advantage of Edward's representation compared to the other ones (e.g. Projectives) where such a unified formula does not exist. However it is significantly more costly than the separate addition and doubling formulas.[4]

Here, we can exploit the fact that the multiplication $X_1 Z_1$ is performed twice if $P = Q$ (i.e. when the formula processed a doubling), which is not the case otherwise (see Fig. 4). We can hence define the two following random variables:

$$\begin{cases} T_1 = (X_1 \cdot Z_1)^{1-s} \cdot (X_1 \cdot Z_2)^s \\ T_2 = (X_1 \cdot Z_1)^{1-s} \cdot (X_2 \cdot Z_1)^s \end{cases} , \tag{6}$$

---

[4] Indeed, let us denote by M the cost of a field multiplication and by S the cost of a squaring. We assume $S = 0.8M$, which is usually satisfied in current implementations. For points in projective coordinates, the unified formulas for Weierstrass curves [10] require around $15.8M$ which represents a similar cost than for addition points (around $16M$) but is significantly higher than that of the doubling (around $9M$). The unified formula for Edward curves costs around $11M$ which is less than in the Weierstrass case but still higher than the classical formulas.

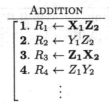

Fig. 4. First steps of algorithm for addition.

which, under Assumption 1, leads to the recovery of s.

Remark 4. This technique still applies in the case of other unified formulas (e.g. those introduced in [10]). Indeed, the sequence of operations in [10] present the same weaknesses as Edward's case. The multiplication X_1Z_1 is performed twice if the current operation is a doubling (see the first and third multiplications in [10, Sect. 3, Fig. 1]).

3.3 Distinguishing Common Operands in Multiplications

In this section we apply the collision attack principle presented in Sect. 3.1 to show how an adversary may deal with Assumption 1. This will conclude our attack description. As mentioned before, we assume that the field multiplications are implemented in an arithmetic co-processor with a *Long Integer Multiplication* (LIM) followed by a reduction. Many other multiplication methods exist but our attack can always be slightly adapted to also efficiently apply to those methods (see the full version of the paper).

Let ω denote an architecture size (e.g. ω equals 8, 16 or 32) and let us denote by $(X[t], \cdots, X[1])_{2^\omega}$ the base-2^ω representation of an integer. We recall hereafter the main steps of the LIM when applied between two integers X and Y.

Let W, X, Y and Z be four independent values of size $t\omega$ bits. We show hereafter how to distinguish by side-channel analysis the two following cases:

- Case (1) where the device processes $\text{LIM}(X, W)$ and $\text{LIM}(Y, Z)$ (all the operands are independent),
- Case (2) where $\text{LIM}(X, Z)$ and $\text{LIM}(Y, Z)$ are processed (the two LIM processings share an operand).

For such a purpose, and by analogy with our side-channel model in Sect. 2.1 and Table 1, we denote by C_1 (resp. C_2) the multiplication in the loop during the first LIM processing (resp. the second LIM processing) and by O_1 (resp. O_2) its result. The output of each multiplication during the loop may be viewed as a realization of the random variable O_1 (resp. O_2). To each of those realizations we associate a leakage $\ell_{a,b}^1$ (resp. $\ell_{a,b}^2$). To distinguish between cases (1) and (2), we directly apply the attack described in Table 1 and we compute the Pearson's correlation coefficient:

$$\hat{\rho}\left((\ell_{a,b}^1)_{a,b}, (\ell_{a,b}^2)_{a,b}\right). \tag{7}$$

Algorithm 1. Long Integer Multiplication (LIM)

Input: $X = (X[t], X[t-1], \ldots, X[1])_{2^\omega}$, $Y = (Y[t], Y[t-1], \ldots, Y[1])_{2^\omega}$.
Output: LIM(X, Y).
for a from 1 to $2t$ **do**
  $\lfloor$ $R[a] \leftarrow 0$
for a from 1 to t **do**
  $C \leftarrow 0$
  for b from 1 to t **do**
    $(U, V)_{2^\omega} \leftarrow X[a] \cdot Y[b]$ // Operation C_1 (resp. C_2)
    $(U, V)_{2^\omega} \leftarrow (U, V)_{2^\omega} + C$
    $(U, V)_{2^\omega} \leftarrow (U, V)_{2^\omega} + R[a+b-1]$
    $R[a+b-1] \leftarrow V$
    $\lfloor$ $C \leftarrow U$
  $\lfloor$ $R[a+t] \leftarrow C$
return R

In place of (7), the following correlation coefficient can be used in the attack:

$$\hat{\rho}\left(\left(\frac{1}{t}\sum_a \ell^1_{a,b}\right)_b, \left(\frac{1}{t}\sum_a \ell^2_{a,b}\right)_b\right). \tag{8}$$

In the following section we actually argue that this second correlation coefficient gives better results, which is confirmed by our attacks simulations reported in Sect. 4.

3.4   Study of the Attack Soundness

This section aims at arguing on the soundness of the approach described previously to distinguish common operands in multiplications. For such a purpose, we explicit formulae for the correlation coefficients given in (7) and (8). For simplicity, the development is made under the assumption that the device leaks the Hamming weight of the processed data but similar developments could be done for other models and would lead to other expressions. Under the Hamming weight assumption, we have $\ell^1_{a,b} \hookleftarrow \mathrm{HW}(O_1) + B_1$ and $\ell^2_{a,b} \hookleftarrow \mathrm{HW}(O_2) + B_2$ where B_1 and B_2 are two independent Gaussian random variables with zero mean and standard deviation σ.

- If O_1 and O_2 correspond to the internal multiplications during the processings of LIM(X, W) and LIM(Y, Z) respectively, then, for every $(a, b) \in [1; t]^2$, we have:

$$\ell^1_{a,b} = \mathrm{HW}(x[a] \cdot w[b]) + b_{1,a,b} \tag{9}$$

$$\ell^2_{a,b} = \mathrm{HW}(y[a] \cdot z[b]) + b_{2,a,b}. \tag{10}$$

Since W, X, Y and Z are independent, the correlation coefficients in (7) and (8) tend towards 0 when t tends towards infinity.

– If O_1 and O_2 correspond to the internal multiplications during the processings of $\mathtt{LIM}(X,\,Z)$ and $\mathtt{LIM}(Y,\,Z)$ respectively, then we have:

$$\ell_{a,b}^1 = \mathrm{HW}(x[a] \cdot z[b]) + b_{1,a,b} \tag{11}$$

$$\ell_{a,b}^2 = \mathrm{HW}(y[a] \cdot z[b]) + b_{2,a,b} \ . \tag{12}$$

Since the two multiplications share an operand, their results are dependent. In this case indeed, it can be proved that the correlation coefficients (7) and (8) satisfy:

$$\hat{\rho}\Big((\ell_{a,b}^1)_{a,b}, (\ell_{a,b}^2)_{a,b}\Big) \simeq \cfrac{1}{1 + \cfrac{2^{2\omega+2}\sigma^2+(\omega-1)2^{2\omega}+2^\omega}{2.2^{2\omega}-(2\omega+1)2^\omega-1}}$$

and

$$\hat{\rho}\left(\Big(\frac{1}{t}\sum_a \ell_{a,b}^1\Big)_b, \Big(\frac{1}{t}\sum_a \ell_{a,b}^2\Big)_b\right) \simeq \cfrac{1}{1 + \cfrac{1}{t}\cfrac{2^{2\omega+2}\sigma^2+(\omega-1)2^{2\omega}+2^\omega}{2.2^{2\omega}-(2\omega+1)2^\omega-1}} \ .$$

When t tends towards infinity, it may be noticed that the second correlation coefficient tends towards 1 (which is optimal).

4   Experiments

In order to validate the approach presented in Sect. 3.3 and thus to illustrate the practical feasibility of our attack, we performed several simulation campaigns for various sizes of elliptic curves, namely $\lceil \log_2(p) \rceil \in \{160, 256, 384\}$, implemented on different kinds of architectures, namely $\omega \in \{8, 32\}$ using the Chevallier-Mames *et al.*'s scheme. Each experiment has been performed in the same way. For each (p, ω), we computed Pearson's correlation coefficients (7) and (8) between the sample of observations coming from the leakages on operations C_1 and C_2 in the two following cases:

– when the secret bit s is equal to 1, that is when an addition is performed (which implies correlated random variables, see (3)),
– when the secret bit s is equal to 0, that is when a doubling operation is performed (which implies independent random variables, see (3)).

From the configuration (p, ω), the size t of the observations' samples used in the attack can be directly deduced: it equals $\lceil \frac{\log_2(p)}{\omega} \rceil$. The quality of the estimations of the correlation coefficient by Pearson's coefficient depends on both the observations *signal to noise ratio* (SNR) and t. When the SNR tends towards 0, the sample size t must tend towards infinity to deal with the noise. Since, in our attack the samples size cannot be increased (it indeed only depends on the implementation parameters p and ω), our correlation estimations tend towards zero when the SNR decreases. As a consequence, distinguishing the two Pearson coefficients coming from $s = 0$ and $s = 1$ becomes harder when the SNR decreases.

This observation raises the need for a powerful (and robust to noise) test to distinguish the two coefficients. To take this into account for each setting (p, ω) and several SNR, we computed the mean and the variance of Pearson's coefficient defined in (7) and (8) over 1000 different samples of size t. To build those kinds of templates, leakages have been generated in the Hamming weight model with additive Gaussian noise of mean 0 and standard deviation σ (i.e. according to (9)-(10) for $s = 0$ and to (11)-(12) for $s = 1$)[5]. When there is no noise at all, namely when $\sigma = 0$ (i.e. SNR $= +\infty$), one can observe that the mean of Pearson's coefficient is coherent with the predictions evaluated in Sect. 3.4.

Figures (5, 6, 7, 8) illustrate the spreading of the obtained Pearson's coefficient around the mean value. This variance gives us information about the amount of trust we can put into the mean values. It also shows whether a distinction between the right hypothesis and the wrong one can easily be highlighted. For each SNR value (denoted by τ) and each sample size t, let us denote by $\hat{\rho}_{0,t}(\tau)$ (resp. $\hat{\rho}_{1,t}(\tau)$) the random variable associated to the processing of (7) for $s = 0$ (resp. for $s = 1$). In Figs. (5, 6, 7, 8), we plot estimations of the mean and variance of $\hat{\rho}_{0,t}(\tau)$ and $\hat{\rho}_{1,t}(\tau)$ for several pairs (τ, t). Clearly, the efficiency of the attack described in Sect. 3 depends on the ability of the adversary to distinguish, for a fixed pair (t, τ), the distribution of $\hat{\rho}_{0,t}(\tau)$ from that of $\hat{\rho}_{1,t}(\tau)$. In other terms, once the adversary has computed a Pearson coefficient $\hat{\rho}$ he must decide between the two following hypotheses; $H_0 : \hat{\rho} \hookleftarrow \hat{\rho}_{0,t}(\tau)$ or $H_1 : \hat{\rho} \hookleftarrow \hat{\rho}_{1,t}(\tau)$. For such a purpose, we propose here to apply a *maximum likelihood* strategy and to choose the hypothesis having the highest probability to occur. This led us to approximate the distribution of the coefficients $\hat{\rho}_{0,t}(\tau)$ and $\hat{\rho}_{1,t}(\tau)$ by a Gaussian distribution with mean and variance estimated in the Hamming weight model (as given in Figs. 5, 6, 7, 8). Attacks reported in Figs. 9 and 10 are done with this strategy.

Remark 5. Since the adversary is not assumed to know the exact leakage SNR, the maximum likelihood can be computed for several SNR values τ starting from ∞ to some pre-defined threshold. This problematic occurs each time that the principle of collision attacks is applied.

Remark 6. For a curve of size $n = \lceil \log_2(p) \rceil$ and a ω-bit architecture, the adversary can have a sample of $t = \lceil \frac{n}{\omega} \rceil$ observations if he averages over the columns and $t = \lceil (\frac{n}{\omega})^2 \rceil$ without averaging. All experiments provided in this section have been performed using the "average" strategy.

This attack works for any kind of architecture, even for a 32-bit one (see Fig. 10), which is the most common case in nowadays implementations. In the presence of noise, the attack success decreases highly but stays quite successful for curves of size 160, 256 and 384 bits. In all experiments (Figs. 9, 10), we also observe that the success rate of our attack increases when the size of the curve becomes larger. This behaviour can be explained by the increasing number of observations available in this case. Paradoxically, it means that when the

---

[5] In this context, the SNR simply equals $\omega/4\sigma^2$.

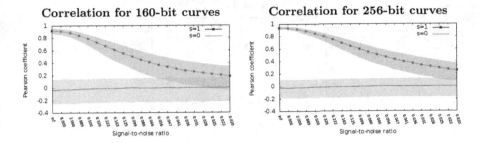

Fig. 5. Pre-computations on $w = 8$-bit registers

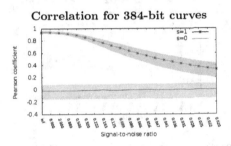

Fig. 6. Pre-computations on $w = 8$-bit registers

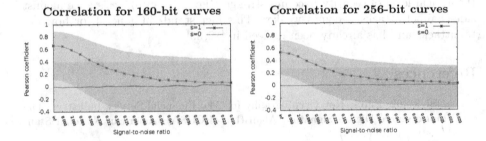

Fig. 7. Pre-computations on $w = 32$-bit registers

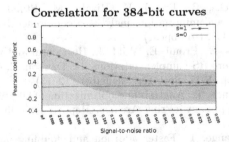

Fig. 8. Pre-computations on $w = 32$-bit registers

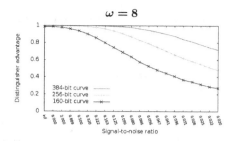

Fig. 9. Success rate of the attack on 8-bit registers

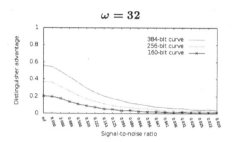

Fig. 10. Success rate of the attack on 32-bit registers

theoretical level of security becomes stronger (i.e. p is large), resistance against side-channel attacks becomes weaker. This fact stands in general for horizontal attacks and has already been noticed in [12,33].

References

1. ANSI X9.62: Public Key Cryptography for The Financial Service Industry : The Elliptic Curve Digital Signature Algorithm (ECDSA). American National Standards Institute (1998)
2. ANSI X9.63: Public Key Cryptography for The Financial Service Industry : Key Agreement and Key Transport Using Elliptic Curve Cryptography. American National Standards Institute (1998)
3. Batina, L., Gierlichs, B., Prouff, E., Rivain, M., Standaert, F.-X., Veyrat-Charvillon, N.: Mutual information analysis: a comprehensive study. J. Cryptol. **24**(2), 269–291 (2011). (to appear)
4. Bauer, A., Jaulmes, E., Prouff, E., Wild, J.: Horizontal and vertical side-channel attacks against secure RSA implementations. In: Dawson, E. (ed.) CT-RSA 2013. LNCS, vol. 7779, pp. 1–17. Springer, Heidelberg (2013)
5. Bernstein, D.J., Lange, T.: Analysis and optimization of elliptic-curve single-scalar multiplication. Cryptology ePrint Archive, Report 2007/455 http://eprint.iacr.org/ (2007)
6. Bernstein, D.J., Lange, T.: Faster addition and doubling on elliptic curves. In: Kurosawa, K. (ed.) ASIACRYPT 2007. LNCS, vol. 4833, pp. 29–50. Springer, Heidelberg (2007)

7. Billet, O., Joye, M.: The Jacobi model of an elliptic curve and side-channel analysis. Cryptology ePrint Archive, Report 2002/125 (2002)
8. Bogdanov, A., Kizhvatov, I., Pyshkin, A.: Algebraic methods in side-channel collision attacks and practical collision detection. In: Chowdhury, D.R., Rijmen, V., Das, A. (eds.) INDOCRYPT 2008. LNCS, vol. 5365, pp. 251–265. Springer, Heidelberg (2008)
9. Brier, E., Clavier, Ch., Olivier, F.: Correlation power analysis with a leakage model. In: Joye, M., Quisquater, J.-J. (eds.) CHES 2004. LNCS, vol. 3156, pp. 16–29. Springer, Heidelberg (2004)
10. Brier, E., Joye, M.: Weierstraß elliptic curves and side-channel attacks. In: Naccache, D., Paillier, P. (eds.) PKC 2002. LNCS, vol. 2274, pp. 335–345. Springer, Heidelberg (2002)
11. Chevallier-Mames, B., Ciet, M., Joye, M.: Low-cost solutions for preventing simple side-channel analysis: side-channel atomicity. IEEE Trans. Comput. 53(6), 760–768 (2004)
12. Clavier, Ch., Feix, B., Gagnerot, G., Giraud, Ch., Roussellet, M., Verneuil, V.: ROSETTA for single trace analysis. In: Galbraith, S., Nandi, M. (eds.) INDOCRYPT 2012. LNCS, vol. 7668, pp. 140–155. Springer, Heidelberg (2012)
13. Clavier, Ch., Feix, B., Gagnerot, G., Roussellet, M., Verneuil, V.: Horizontal correlation analysis on exponentiation. In: Soriano, M., Qing, S., López, J. (eds.) ICICS 2010. LNCS, vol. 6476, pp. 46–61. Springer, Heidelberg (2010)
14. Clavier, Ch., Feix, B., Gagnerot, G., Roussellet, M., Verneuil, V.: Improved collision-correlation power analysis on first order protected AES. In: Preneel, B., Takagi, T. (eds.) CHES 2011. LNCS, vol. 6917, pp. 49–62. Springer, Heidelberg (2011)
15. Cohen, H., Frey, G. (eds.): Handbook of Elliptic and Hyperelliptic Curve Cryptography. CRC Press, Baco Raton (2005)
16. Coron, J.-S.: Resistance against differential power analysis for elliptic curve cryptosystems. In: Koç, Ç.K., Paar, C. (eds.) CHES 1999. LNCS, vol. 1717, pp. 292–302. Springer, Heidelberg (1999)
17. Edwards, H.M.: A normal form for elliptic curves. Bull. Am. Math. Soc. 44, 393–422 (2007)
18. Giraud, Ch., Verneuil, V.: Atomicity improvement for elliptic curve scalar multiplication. In: Gollmann, D., Lanet, J.-L., Iguchi-Cartigny, J. (eds.) CARDIS 2010. LNCS, vol. 6035, pp. 80–101. Springer, Heidelberg (2010)
19. Hankerson, D., Menezes, A.J., Vanstone, S.: Guide to Elliptic Curve Cryptography. Springer Professional Computing Series. Springer, New York (2003)
20. ISO/IEC JTC1 SC17 WG3/TF5 for the International Civil Aviation Organization. Supplemental Access Control for Machine Readable Travel Documents. Technical Report (2010)
21. Koblitz, N.: Elliptic curve cryptosystems. Math. Comput. 48(177), 203–209 (1987)
22. Koç, Ç.K., Naccache, D., Paar, C. (eds.): CHES 2001. LNCS, vol. 2162. Springer, Heidelberg (2001)
23. Kocher, P.C.: Timing attacks on implementations of Diffie-Hellman, RSA, DSS, and other systems. In: Koblitz, N. (ed.) CRYPTO 1996. LNCS, vol. 1109, pp. 104–113. Springer, Heidelberg (1996)
24. Kocher, P.C., Jaffe, J., Jun, B.: Differential power analysis. In: Wiener, M. (ed.) CRYPTO 1999. LNCS, vol. 1666, pp. 388–397. Springer, Heidelberg (1999)
25. Liardet, P.-Y., Smart, N.P.: Preventing SPA/DPA in ECC systems using the Jacobi form. In: Koç, Ç.K., et al. (eds.) [22], pp. 401–411

26. Longa, P.: Accelerating the scalar multiplication on elliptic curve cryptosystems over prime fields. Master's thesis, School of Information Technology and Engineering, University of Ottawa, Canada (2007)

27. Messerges, T.S.: Using second-order power analysis to attack DPA resistant software. In: Paar, Ch., Koç, Ç.K. (eds.) CHES 2000. LNCS, vol. 1965, pp. 238–251. Springer, Heidelberg (2000)

28. Micali, S., Reyzin, L.: Physically observable cryptography. In: Naor, M. (ed.) TCC 2004. LNCS, vol. 2951, pp. 278–296. Springer, Heidelberg (2004)

29. Miller, V.S.: Use of elliptic curves in cryptography. In: Williams, H.C. (ed.) CRYPTO 1985. LNCS, vol. 218, pp. 417–426. Springer, Heidelberg (1986)

30. Moradi, A.: Statistical tools flavor side-channel collision attacks. In: Pointcheval, D., Johansson, T. (eds.) EUROCRYPT 2012. LNCS, vol. 7237, pp. 428–445. Springer, Heidelberg (2012)

31. Moradi, A., Mischke, O., Eisenbarth, T.: Correlation-enhanced power analysis collision attack. In: Mangard, S., Standaert, F.-X. (eds.) CHES 2010. LNCS, vol. 6225, pp. 125–139. Springer, Heidelberg (2010)

32. Schramm, K., Wollinger, T., Paar, Ch.: A new class of collision attacks and its application to des. In: Johansson, T. (ed.) FSE 2003. LNCS, vol. 2887, pp. 206–222. Springer, Heidelberg (2003)

33. Walter, C.D.: Sliding windows succumbs to big mac attack. In: Koç, Ç.K., et al. (eds.) [22], pp. 286–299

When Reverse-Engineering Meets Side-Channel Analysis – Digital Lockpicking in Practice

David Oswald[✉], Daehyun Strobel, Falk Schellenberg, Timo Kasper, and Christof Paar

Horst Görtz Institute for IT-Security, Ruhr-University Bochum, Bochum, Germany
{david.oswald,daehyun.strobel,falk.schellenberg,timo.Kasper, christof.paar}@rub.de

Abstract. In the past years, various electronic access control systems have been found to be insecure. In consequence, attacks have emerged that permit unauthorized access to secured objects. One of the few remaining, allegedly secure digital locking systems—the system 3060 manufactured and marketed by SimonsVoss—is employed in numerous objects worldwide. Following the trend to analyze the susceptibility of real-world products towards implementation attacks, we illustrate our approach to understand the unknown embedded system and its components. Detailed investigations are performed in a step-by-step process, including the analysis of the communication between transponder and lock, reverse-engineering of the hardware, bypassing the read-out protection of a microcontroller, and reverse-engineering the extracted program code. Piecing all parts together, the security mechanisms of the system can be completely circumvented by means of implementation attacks. We present an EM side-channel attack for extracting the secret system key from a door lock. This ultimately gives access to all doors of an entire installation. Our technique targets a proprietary function (used in combination with a DES for key derivation), probably originally implemented as an obscurity-based countermeasure to prevent attacks.

Keywords: Access control · Symmetric key cryptosystem · Digital lock · Wireless door openers · EM side-channel attack · Obscurity

1 Introduction

Electronic access control systems are becoming increasingly popular and are on the way to replace conventional mechanical locks and keys in many applications. Often, the security of these systems is based on keeping the proprietary protocols and cryptographic algorithms secret. Admittedly, although violating Kerckhoffs's principle, this approach often prevents both mathematical analysis and implementation attacks, as long as the details remain undisclosed. In this paper, we focus on the latest generation "G2" of the widespread digital locking and access control system 3060 manufactured by SimonsVoss Technologies AG.

T. Lange, K. Lauter, and P. Lisoněk (Eds.): SAC 2013, LNCS 8282, pp. 571–588, 2014.
DOI: 10.1007/978-3-662-43414-7_29, © Springer-Verlag Berlin Heidelberg 2014

A transponder, the digital equivalent of a mechanical key, wirelessly communicates with an electronically enhanced locking cylinder that—after successful authentication—mechanically connects the otherwise freewheeling knob to the bolt so that the door can be opened. By the example of this system, we illustrate which major problems have to be overcome in the real-world before successful (mathematical and) side-channel attacks can be mounted.

SimonsVoss is the European leader in digital locking and access control systems [18] and has sold over three million transponders for more than one million electronic locks. Despite the high price of the digital locks—compared to their mechanical counterparts—the purchase can pay out due to the flexible administration of access permissions via a wireless link, especially in buildings with a lot of doors and users.

1.1   Related Work

In the context of conventional mechanical locks exist well-known techniques to duplicate individual keys, if physical access is given. Likewise, the security of mechanical pin tumbler locks can be bypassed, e.g., by means of lockpicking with special tools. The practical threat of these attacks is usually negligible, as long as each key and each lock has to be treated individually. When it comes to the security of large installations and the corresponding master keys, even in the mechanical world the impact becomes more severe: In [3], a procedure is described that allows the creation of a master key to open all doors in an installation, if access to a single master-keyed lock and an associated key is given.

For wireless, electronic access control systems, obtaining the ingredients required for copying a transponder can be even more straightforward. They could be, e.g., eavesdropped from the Radio Frequency (RF) interface. To counteract attacks, numerous manufacturers developed and offer (often proprietary) cryptographic solutions. Most of these have in common that they turn out to be insecure from a cryptanalytical perspective once the secret protocols and algorithms have been reverse-engineered. Today most security products used for access control, such as Texas Instrument's Digital Signature Transponder (DST) [5], NXP's Mifare Classic cards [7,10], Hitag 2 transponders [21], and Legic Prime [17], have something in common: Mathematical attacks emerging from cryptographic weaknesses enable to break their protection in minutes.

For systems with a higher level of mathematical security, several examples of real-world side-channel attacks have demonstrated a huge attack potential: The 112-bit secret key of the Mifare DESfire MF3ICD40 smartcard (based on the 3DES cipher) can be extracted with Electro-Magnetic (EM)-based Side Channel Analysis (SCA) [16]. Likewise, the mathematical weaknesses found in the proprietary remote keyless entry system KeeLoq [1,4] are insufficient for a practical attack. However, a side-channel attack yielding the master key of the system allows to duplicate remote controls by one-time eavesdropping from several hundred meters [8].

The mathematical properties of the SimonsVoss digital lock and access control system 3060 "G2" are investigated in [20]. Sophisticated mathematical attacks, exploiting weaknesses of the proprietary obfuscation function (see Sect. 3) and a security vulnerability of the authentication protocol, are presented. As a consequence of the traditional cryptanalysis, transponders with a known identifier can be duplicated in seconds. The attack exploits that an internal protocol value is re-used as a "random number" in the next protocol run and thus can be obtained by an adversary. However, this flaw can be easily fixed, e. g., by a firmware update of the door lock, rendering the most severe mathematical attacks not applicable. The manufacturer SimonsVoss is currently preparing an according patch to protect existing installations against the cryptanalytical attacks.

1.2   Contribution

In contrast to the existing mathematical analyses, we illustrate how to circumvent the security mechanisms of SimonsVoss's system 3060 "G2" solely by means of physical attacks. In Sect. 2 we describe our varyingly successful attempts to bring the internals of the access control system to light and demonstrate from the perspective of an adversary how—despite the admittedly very time-consuming and demanding black-box analysis—a skilled engineer can finally succeed in extracting SimonsVoss's undisclosed secrets, detailed in Sect. 3. As the main part of our contribution in Sect. 4 we present a side-channel attack targeting the key derivation function running on a lock. Our non-invasive attack is able to extract the system key with approximately 150 EM measurements and enables access to all doors of an entire SimonsVoss installation. We finally discuss the learned lessons for SCA in the context of obscurity.

2   Reverse-Engineering: An Obstacle Course

Using the information SimonsVoss provides publicly, it is impossible to reason about the claimed level of security for the system 3060. Thus, in the following section, we present the process of reverse-engineering the inner workings of the digital locking cylinder and the corresponding transponder.

2.1   Radio Protocol

The documentation available on the Internet [19] yields only little information on the RF interface used to open a door: The transponder communicates with the counterpart in the door at 25 kHz at a specified maximum range of approx. 0.5 m. To capture the messages exchanged during an authentication, we used a simple coil made from copper wire and connected it to a USRP2 Software-Defined Radio (SDR) [9], as shown in Fig. 1b. We eavesdropped several (successful) protocol runs between a door and a transponder. An example of a monitored RF signal is depicted in Fig. 1a: The parts with the lower amplitude (marked 1, 3, 5, 7, and

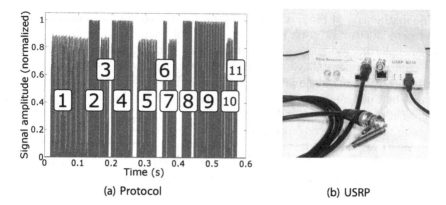

Fig. 1. A successful run of the 11-step authentication protocol between transponder and door, recorded with the USRP and a connected antenna coil.

10) are sent by the transponder, while the other parts originate from the door (marked as 2, 4, 6, 8, 9, and 11).

From studying and comparing various recorded messages, some conclusions can be drawn: The used modulation scheme is On-Off Keying (OOK), i.e., the carrier at 25 kHz is switched on and off according to the sequence of data bits. The protocol starts with the transponder transmitting a synchronization preamble consisting of approximately 110 one-zero cycles. The raw bits of each message are encoded using a differential Manchester code [23], i.e., a transition during the bit period corresponds to a logical zero and no transition to a logical one. On the packet level, the messages follow a simple format: Data bytes following an 8-bit header (0x7F) have no further format requirements. In contrast, the 16-bit header (0xFF, 0x7F) indicates that an integrity check value, computed over the data bytes, has to be appended. This check value is computed by taking the complement of the bit-wise XOR of all data bytes.

We conducted several experiments that involved replaying previously recorded signals using the USRP2. However, the module in the door did not accept replayed messages and the door could not be unlocked. During further analyses of the interchanged messages, we found that some appear to be (pseudo-)random in each protocol run and thus that a cryptographic authentication scheme might be implemented. However, after several weeks of analyzing the RF interface we were convinced that some quite sophisticated scheme had been implemented by SimonsVoss. Unfortunately, the significance of the messages remained unclear. Thus, we decided to continue with the reverse-engineering on the hardware level.

2.2 Hardware and Circuit Boards

In order to understand the interaction between the mechanical and the electrical parts, we disassembled a door lock in a destructive manner, cf. Fig. 2a. We identified a magnetic pin that mechanically interlocks the bolt when voltage

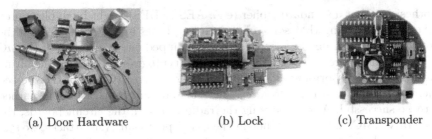

(a) Door Hardware   (b) Lock   (c) Transponder

Fig. 2. "Exploded view" of the mechanical parts of a door lock 3061 and the PCBs contained in the door knob and a transponder 3064.

is applied to its contacts. The circuitry in the door thus controls whether the otherwise free-wheeling door knob is mechanically connected to the door latch and the deadbolt in order to grant access. No additional electronic circuits were found inside the lock, thus all security functionality must be implemented on the door's Printed Circuit Board (PCB). We observed several installations in which this circuitry is installed in the publicly accessible outer knob of the door. This holds especially for "panic"-locks which can be unlocked from the inside.

The PCB depicted in Fig. 2b is located inside one of the door knobs of the lock, that can be easily opened with a commercially available tool. The IC in the bottom-left corner is a proprietary SimonsVoss ASIC. On the right, a Microchip PIC16F886 microcontroller (μC) [15] is located. One connection between the MCLR pin of the PIC and the ASIC enables the former to wake up the μC from the power save mode. The ASIC is also connected to the μC's OSC1/CLKIN, hence the μC can be clocked from the ASIC. Moreover, an external EEPROM in an SOT-8 package is connected to the μC. The plastic case of the transponder contains the PCB depicted in Fig. 2c. A comparison with the lock shows many identical parts, e.g., a PIC16F886 connected to an external EEPROM and the ASIC. A push-button triggering an authentication to the door is connected to the PIC.

The ASIC is a 16-pin IC with a custom label ("MA124D") for which we could find no information on the Internet. The pinout and the activity on the data lines did not point to any distinct manufacturer, thus, we decapsulated the silicon die of several ICs, cf. [2, p.10]. Figure 8 in Appendix B depicts a high resolution image of the silicon die. After analyzing microscopic pictures of the chip, it turned out that it contains a mask-configurable gate array IC with a rather limited amount of implementable logic. Besides, the ASIC does not feature internal memories. We figured out that the majority of the available logic cells is used (i) for a counter that periodically wakes up the μC and (ii) for functions of the RF interface. It became clear that the ASIC does not contain security-related functions and thus can be ruled out as a target for further analyses: All relevant algorithms must thus be contained in the PIC μC.

As an (almost) last resort in order to understand the "randomly" looking protocol and find a security vulnerability in the system, we proceeded with hypothesizing that a standard cipher (e.g., AES or DES) might be implemented on the PIC. Assuming that some of the varying bytes in the protocol could be input or output of a one of these ciphers, we tapped the power line of the μC and spent some more weeks trying to recover cryptographic keys, by acquiring power traces and performing a Correlation Power Analysis (CPA) for the guessed ciphers, one after another. However, none of our numerous attempts turned out to be successful. After analyzing the radio protocol, the circuit boards, the proprietary ASIC, and trying "shot-in-the-dark" power-analysis attacks, we still had no clue about the security features of the SimonsVoss system 3060 and were close to giving up with the conclusion that it was "secure enough". However, as a last attempt, we decided to try to obtain the machine code of the PIC.

2.3   The Breakthrough: Extracting and Reverse-Engineering the Firmware of the PIC

After connecting a PIC programmer to the μC and trying to read out its content it turned out that the read-out protection was enabled. Thus, following the methods proposed in [24] and [13], we tried to erase the code and data read-out protection bits: The PIC was decapsulated, and the memory cells containing the protection bits were exposed to Ultraviolet-C (UV-C) light. Even though Microchip covers the top of the respective cells of the PIC16F886 with small metal plates as a countermeasure, applying the UV-C light at an angle (so that it bounces off multiple structures around the floating gate) deactivated the read-out protection. The whole process required less than 30 min. After that, the complete content of the PIC's program memory and its internal EEPROM could be extracted. We performed the read-out process for the PICs of several transponders and door locks and started to analyze their program code.

In order to disassemble and understand the extracted program code, we utilized the reverse-engineering tool IDA Pro [12]. Analyzing the program code, we were able to recover most previously unknown details of the SimonsVoss system 3060, including the authentication protocol and the employed cryptographic primitives, cf. Sect. 3. In addition to performing a static analysis of the program code, we also inserted a debug routine debug_dump into the assembly code and re-programmed the PICs with our modified firmware. Given that the correct (matching) combination of program code and internal and external EEPROM content is written, the modified transponder or door lock operates correctly. The inserted routine allows to dump the registers and the SRAM during the execution of the original program. To this end, we utilized an unused pin of the μC to transfer the memory dump in a straightforward serial manner.

The debug routine cannot be directly inserted into the program code, as this would lead to a shift of all (absolute) jump addresses and thus render the program inoperable. To solve this problem, we had to overwrite code that was found to be not linked to the authentication protocol with the code of debug_dump. Since the PIC16F886 uses a segmented program memory (consisting of four banks with 2 K instruction words each), we furthermore had to place a small piece of wrapper code at the end of each segment (thereby overwriting a few unused instructions). Then, the call to debug_dump was inserted as follows: A target instruction (e.g., a movwf) is replaced by a call to the wrapper function. The wrapper function then selects the segment in which debug_dump resides and subsequently invokes debug_dump. Before outputting the dump, the value of the STATUS register is saved in an unused memory location to preserve the state of the actual program. Before returning, this value is restored, and the subsequent instructions (of the wrapper) do not modify the STATUS register. After debug_dump has returned to the wrapper, the segment is reset to the originally selected value. Then, the wrapper executes the replaced instruction before returning to the normal program flow.

With the capability to dump the memory contents, e.g., during the execution of a successful authentication protocol run, we are able to verify the results of the static analysis and to understand also those parts of the code that heavily depend on external input (e.g., from received data or data stored in the external memory). Obtaining and analyzing the program code was the essential step to enable a detailed scrutiny, including mathematical and side-channel analyses. Being now able to understand the exchanged messages and the used cryptographic functions, the authentication mechanism described in Sect. 3 can be attacked in several ways, including the SCA presented in Sect. 4. Without the complete reverse-engineering, the SCA of the—in this regard extremely vulnerable—PIC μC would have been impossible.

3   SimonsVoss's Proprietary Cryptography

In this section, as a mandatory prerequisite for an SCA, we summarize the relevant results of reverse-engineering the code running on the PIC of the transponder and the lock. To this end, we describe the key derivation mechanism, the cryptographic primitives, and the protocol used for mutual authentication.

The authentication protocol consists of in total eleven steps that are given in Fig. 7 in Appendix A. In the symmetric-key scheme, the transponder and the lock prove that they know a shared long-term secret K_T. On each transponder, this individual 128-bit key K_T is computed as the XOR of a 128-bit value $K_{T,\text{int}}$ stored in the internal EEPROM of the μC (not accessible from the outside) and a 128-bit value $K_{T,\text{ext}}$ stored in the (unprotected) external EEPROM, i.e., $K_T = K_{T,\text{ext}} \oplus K_{T,\text{int}}$. Each door within an entire SimonsVoss installation has an identical set of four 128-bit keys $K_{L,1}$, $K_{L,2}$, $K_{L,3}$, $K_{L,4}$, here called *system key*. Again, these keys are computed as the XOR of values contained in the internal and in the external EEPROM. However, the internally stored value is identical for all four keys, i.e., $K_{L,j} = K_{L,j,\text{ext}} \oplus K_{L,\text{int}}$. Note that when one of the four $K_{L,j}$ has been recovered, the remaining three can be determined after reading the respective values from the external EEPROM.

The system key is used to derive the key K_T of a transponder to be authenticated. After receiving the identifier I_T of a transponder, the lock computes K_T on-the-fly using a key derivation function $\mathcal{K}$ involving the system key, previously exchanged "authentication data" D, and I_T. The authentication data D

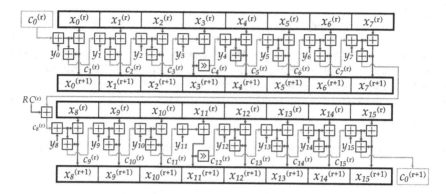

Fig. 3. One round r of the obscurity function $\mathcal{O}$: The key bytes y_i are constant, while the $x_i^{(r)}$ and the chaining values $c_i^{(r)}$ are updated in each round. The first chaining value is $c_0^{(1)} = RC^{(0)}$. The two 8-byte halves $x_0 \ldots x_7$ and $x_8 \ldots x_{15}$ are processed in an identical manner.

is a value sent by the transponder and controls certain protocol functions. D is, however, transmitted in plain and unrelated to the cryptographic security of the protocol. All valid transponder identifiers that can authenticate to a particular door lock are stored unencrypted in its external EEPROM. Note that the key derivation is always executed by the door lock, even if it does not know the received I_T.

The key derivation $\mathcal{K}$ consists of two building blocks: a modified DES denoted as $\mathcal{D}$ and a SimonsVoss-proprietary function $\mathcal{O}$ which we refer to as "obscurity function". $\mathcal{D}(K; M)$ is a slightly modified DES encrypting a 64-bit plaintext M under a 64-bit key K.

$\mathcal{O}(Y; X)$ consists of eight rounds r, with $1 \le r \le 8$. It takes a 16-byte plaintext $X = (x_0^{(1)} \ldots x_{15}^{(1)})$ and a 16-byte key $Y = (y_0 \ldots y_{15})$ to compute a 16-byte ciphertext $x_0^{(9)} \ldots x_{15}^{(9)}$. Figure 3 depicts the structure of one round of $\mathcal{O}$. The internal "chaining values" $c_1^{(r)} \ldots c_{15}^{(r)}$ are processed horizontally in each round r and the last chaining value is used as the input $c_0^{(r+1)}$ for the subsequent round $r + 1$. The round constants $RC^{(r)}$ are fixed byte values, i.e., they are identical for every execution of $\mathcal{O}$, that are added in each round after the first eight bytes have been processed. The first chaining value is initialized with $c_0^{(1)} = RC^{(0)}$. All additions and shifts are performed modulo 256.

$\mathcal{K}$ takes the system key and a 128-bit parameter P_0 as inputs, where P_0 is derived from the first three bytes of I_T and the first three bytes of the authentication data D as $P_0 = (I_{T,0}, I_{T,1}, I_{T,2} \,\&\, \mathtt{0xC7}, D_0, D_1, D_2 \,\&\, \mathtt{0x3F}, 0, \ldots, 0)$. The transponder key K_T is then computed by a series connection of $\mathcal{O}$, $\mathcal{D}$, and $\mathcal{O}$ as

$$\mathcal{K}(K_{L,j}; P_0) = \mathcal{O}\left(P_0; \mathcal{D}\left(\mathcal{O}(K_{L,j}; P_0)_{64..127}; \mathcal{O}(K_{L,j}; P_0)_{0..63}\right) \| 0 \ldots 0\right).$$

Depending on the two Most Significant Bits (MSBs) of $I_{T,2}$, one of the four $K_{L,j}$ is selected as the key for the first (innermost) instance of $\mathcal{O}$ in $\mathcal{K}$ to encrypt P_0. The result is split into two 64-bit halves, the lower 64 bit being the plaintext and the upper 64 bit being the key of $\mathcal{D}$. The 64-bit result of $\mathcal{D}$ is then padded with 64 zero bits and encrypted with $\mathcal{O}$, this time using P_0 as the key. The resulting ciphertext is the transponder key K_T used in the subsequent steps of the challenge-response protocol. A lock is opened, if K_T on the transponder and K_T derived by the door match. To this end, both transponder and door compute a 64-bit response involving the challenge C and several protocol values as

$$\mathcal{R}\left(K_T; P_1, P_2\right) = \mathcal{D}\left(\mathcal{O}\left(\mathcal{O}(K_T; P_1); P_2\right)_{64..127}; \mathcal{O}\left(\mathcal{O}\left(K_T; P_1\right); P_2\right)_{0..63}\right),$$

with

$$P_1 = (C_0, \ldots, C_{10}, D_6, \ldots, D_9, 0)$$
$$P_2 = (I_{L,2}, I_{T,2}, I_{T,3}, D_3, D_4, D_5, 0, \ldots)$$

The transponder sends the first 32-bit half R_0 of the output of $\mathcal{R}$, to which the door responds with the second half R_1, if R_0 was correct. Obviously, the key derivation function $\mathcal{K}$ is the main target for an SCA, because recovering the system key allows to derive the key of any transponder in an installation given its I_T.

4 Extraction of the System Key with SCA

In this section, we describe the steps to perform a side-channel attack on the Device-Under-Test (DUT), the SimonsVoss door lock 3061. As the main result, we show that the system key can be extracted from the employed PIC μC with a non-invasive, CPA-based attack using approximately 150 traces. Possessing the system key, an adversary is able to create functionally identical clones of *all* transponders in an entire SimonsVoss installation. Note that the SCA can in general also be applied to a transponder, e.g., in order to duplicate it, but in a practical setting it is highly unlikely that an adversary will take the efforts for the attack just for cloning a single transponder.

4.1 Side-Channel Attacks

A side-channel attack is usually performed in two steps. First, the adversary has physical access to the target device and acquires a side-channel signal (e.g., the power consumption or the EM emanation) during the cryptographic computation. This is repeated N times with different input data M_n, yielding N time-discrete waveforms $w_n(t)$ or traces. To recover the cryptographic key, the traces are then statistically processed in the evaluation phase, e.g., using the Pearson correlation coefficient when performing a CPA [6]. The adversary fixes a (small) subset $\mathcal{K}_{cand} \subseteq \mathcal{K}$ (e.g., the 256 possible 8-bit subkeys entering one S-box of the AES) and considers all key candidates $k \in \mathcal{K}_{cand}$. Then, for each $k \in \mathcal{K}_{cand}$ and for each $n \in \{0, \ldots, N-1\}$, a hypothesis $V_{k,n}$ on the value of some intermediate (e.g., the output of one 8-bit AES S-box) is computed. Using a power model f, this value is then mapped to $h_{k,n} = f(V_{k,n})$ to describe the process that causes the side-channel leakage. In practice, a Hamming weight (HW) or

Hamming distance (HD) power model is often suitable for CMOS devices like μCs [14]. In order to detect the dependency between $h_{k,n}$ and $w_n(t)$, the correlation coefficient $\rho_k(t)$ (for each point in time t and each key candidate $k \in \mathcal{K}_{cand}$) is given as

$$\rho_k(t) = \frac{cov(w(t), h_k)}{\sqrt{var(w(t)) var(h_k)}}$$

with $var(\cdot)$ indicating the sample variance and $cov(\cdot, \cdot)$ the sample covariance according to the standard definitions [22]. The key candidate $\hat{k}$ with the maximum correlation $\hat{k} = \arg\max_{k,t} \rho_k(t)$ is assumed to be the correct secret key. When for instance attacking an implementation of the AES, this process is performed for each S-box separately, yielding the full 128-bit key with a much lower complexity of $16 \cdot 2^8$ compared to 2^{128} steps for an exhaustive search. However, for the obscurity function $\mathcal{O}$ used in the key derivation step (cf. Sect. 3), performing a side-channel attack is more complex. Hence, in the following Sect. 4.2, the process for extracting the system key by means of SCA is described in detail.

4.2   Theoretical Attack: Predicting Intermediate Values in $\mathcal{O}$

The most promising target for an SCA to recover the system key is the first instance of $\mathcal{O}$ in the key derivation. In the following, we (theoretically) derive an attack to obtain the full 16-byte key $y_0 \ldots y_{15}$.

Note that only the first six bytes of the input to $\mathcal{O}$ can be chosen by the adversary, since the remaining bytes of P_0 are set to zero. Due to the carry propagation properties of $\mathcal{O}$ (which are described in detail in [20]), these input bytes do not lead to a "full" randomization of all intermediates in the first round of the obscurity function. A straightforward CPA of the first round targeting the addition operation $x_i^{(r+1)} = x_i^{(r)} + c_i^{(r)} + y_i$ hence only allows to recover the first seven key bytes $y_0 \ldots y_6$.

For the remaining key bytes, at least a part of the addition in the first round is carried out with completely constant data, ruling out a CPA: For revealing y_7, one obtains already two candidates, because the Least Significant Bit (LSB) of $c_7^{(1)}$ does not depend on the varying part of the input and hence remains constant. For $c_8^{(1)}$, two bits are not randomized, leading to four candidates for y_8 (if c_7 was known). Thus, to obtain these two bytes, two CPAs each with four additional candidates would be necessary. To recover all key bytes using this approach, an overall number of $2^{1+2+3+4+5+4+5+6+7} = 2^{37}$ key candidates would have to be tested, leading to an impractical attack. Hence, we utilize further properties of $\mathcal{O}$ to reduce the computational cost by extending the attack to initially non-recoverable key bytes in subsequent rounds of $\mathcal{O}$.

First, note that all bits in the (initially not fully randomized) update involving the key bytes $y_7 \ldots y_{15}$ are fully dependent on $x_0^{(1)} \ldots x_5^{(1)}$ after two, three, four, five, six, six, six, seven, and seven rounds, respectively. Thus, these key bytes can be recovered by means of a CPA in the respective round, if all other values preceding the update operation for a targeted key byte y_i can be simulated. Assuming that all key bytes up to y_i and all $c_0^{(r)}$ up to the respective round are known, the only unknown constant in the i-th update operation is y_i. The correct value can be determined using a CPA with 256 candidates for y_i.

The remaining problem with this attack is how to determine $c_0^{(r)}$. For this, note that in the second round, $c_0^{(2)}$ is independent of $x_0^{(1)} \ldots x_5^{(1)}$, i.e., a constant only depending on the (constant) key bytes y_i. Hence, $c_0^{(2)}$ can be found using a CPA, because y_0 was already determined in the first round, so $x_0^{(2)}$ can be computed. The CPA for obtaining $c_0^{(2)}$ is performed with 256 candidates. Having found $c_0^{(2)}$, all values up to the update of $x_7^{(2)}$ can be computed. This update, in turn, only depends on known values $(x_7^{(1)}, c_7^{(1)}, \text{and } c_7^{(2)})$ and the unknown key byte y_7. Hence, with 256 candidates, y_7 can be determined with a CPA.

In the third, fourth, and fifth round, only the MSBs of $c_0^{(3,4,5)}$ vary. The remaining bits are constant and can be recovered. In addition, due to the multiplication by two (i.e., a binary left-shift) in the propagation of c_i, the unknown MSB only affects (the MSB of) $x_0^{(4)}$, $x_0^{(5)}$, $x_1^{(5)}$, $x_0^{(6)}$, $x_1^{(6)}$, and $x_2^{(6)}$. Subsequent bytes do not depend on the unknown MSB and can be fully predicted. Hence, it is possible to recover y_8, y_9, and y_{10} in rounds three to five. Finally, in the sixth, seventh, and eighth round, the three MSBs of $c_0^{(6)}$ and the five MSBs of $c_0^{(7)}$ and $c_0^{(8)}$ vary. Again, the constant part of $c_0^{(6,7,8)}$ can still be recovered. For the varying three MSBs, only $x_0^{(7)} \ldots x_2^{(7)}$ are affected. This recoverable part is sufficient to fully predict the state update for the targeted key bytes y_{11}, y_{12}, and y_{13}. Finally, for round seven, the change in the five MSBs of $c_0^{(7)}$ only affects $x_0^{(8)} \ldots x_6^{(8)}$, posing no problem to the recovery of the remaining bytes y_{14} and y_{15}.

In short, the attack can be summarized as follows: First, one recovers the first seven key bytes in round one. Then, the constant part of c_0 at the beginning of each round has to be found. Finally, all key bytes for which the update operation is fully randomized in the respective round can be obtained.

4.3   Practical Results

In the following, we first describe the measurement setup used to acquire side-channel traces for the SimonsVoss door part 3061. Using techniques and results of the reverse-engineering described in Sect. 2, we profile the DUT and determine the point in time where the leakage occurs in the power trace. Finally, applying the attack described in Sect. 4.2 to real-world power traces, we recover the system key using a limited number of power traces in a non-invasive manner.

To trigger the key derivation on the DUT, we directly connect to the data lines between the ASIC and the PIC. The respective pins (marked with a red rectangle in Fig. 4a) are accessible without removing the PCB from the door. Equivalently, the communication with the DUT could also be performed sending data over the RF interface, e.g., using the USRP2 as described in Sect. 2.1. We primarily decided not to use the RF interface to increase the (mechanical) stability of the measurement setup.

We non-invasively measured the power consumption during the execution of the key derivation function for randomly chosen ID I_T and authentication data

(a) PCB in the door part   (b) EM probe on PIC

Fig. 4. Setup and EM trace for SCA of the door part

D (apart from a few bits that are required to be set by the protocol). To this end, we placed an EM probe on the package close to the power supply pins of the PIC, cf. Fig. 4b. Initial experiments to measure the power consumption by inserting a shunt resistor into the battery connection yielded heavily smoothed power traces, presumably due to several bypass/voltage stabilization capacitors on the PCB. Moreover, the ASIC is also connected to the main battery supply, resulting in wide-band, high-amplitude noise that could not be filtered out.

In contrast, the EM probe at the given position mainly picked up the power consumption of the PIC. Using the described setup, we recorded 1,000 power traces using a Digital Storage Oscilloscope (DSO) at a sample rate of 500 MHz. With the current measurement setup, due to delays caused by the protocol, about 10 traces can be acquired per minute. Note that the PIC runs on the internal RC oscillator at a frequency of approximately 8 MHz. Hence, we further (digitally) bandpass-filtered the recorded traces. Experimentally varying the lower and upper frequency of the passband, we found that a passband from 6 MHz to 9 MHz yields the best result.

To determine the relevant part of the power trace belonging to the key derivation, we initially inserted a small function into the (otherwise unmodified) code of the PIC using the method described in Sect. 2.3. This function generates a rising edge on an unused pin of the PIC, serving as a trigger signal for profiling purposes. Figure 5 exemplarily depicts the part of a trace belonging to the initial execution of $\mathcal{O}$ in the key derivation. The eight rounds of the function can be recognized as eight distinct "humps". Furthermore, a unique pattern occurs at the beginning of the relevant part (and each round). This pattern can serve for alignment purposes: Having profiled the DUT, we removed the artificial trigger signal and recorded traces for the original, unmodified code. We then used the pattern to align the traces for the actual CPA attack.

Having determined the relevant part of the trace and the appropriate preprocessing steps, we practically performed the (theoretical) attack described in Sect. 4.2. We use the HD between a byte $x_i^{(\mathrm{r})}$ and its updated value $x_i^{(\mathrm{r}+1)}$ as the power model, i.e., $h = \mathrm{HD}\left(x_i^{(\mathrm{r})}, x_i^{(\mathrm{r}+1)}\right)$ (dropping the indices n for the trace and k for the key candidate for better readability). This model was derived based on the analysis of the assembly code implementing $\mathcal{O}$ and the leakage model

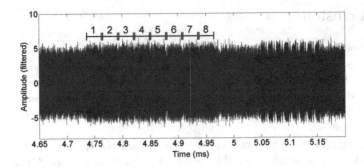

Fig. 5. Filtered EM trace during the execution of the first obscurity function in the key derivation

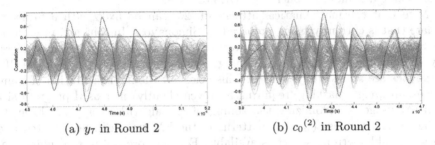

(a) y_7 in Round 2   (b) $c_0^{(2)}$ in Round 2

Fig. 6. Correlation for key byte y_7 after 100 traces and $c_0^{(2)}$ after 150 traces. Correct candidate: red, dashed

for the PIC series described in [11]. Using this model, we obtained correlation values of approximately 0.75 for the correct candidate, while all other (wrong) candidates exhibit a lower value. This allows to unambiguously determine the key with approximately 100 traces, as exemplarily depicted in Fig. 6a.

The CPA for $c_0^{(r)}$ exhibit a similar behavior, cf. for instance Fig. 6b for $c_0^{(2)}$. However, for determining the partial $c_0^{(r)}$ in later rounds, a (slightly) higher number of traces is needed (especially for round six and seven), since only the LSBs of the respective intermediate values are predicted correctly. Still, approximately 150 traces are sufficient to obtain the maximum correlation at the correct point in time for the correct candidate.

Note that—at a higher computational cost—the CPA on $c_0^{(6)}$ and $c_0^{(7)}$ could be left out altogether: The attack on the actual key bytes in round six and seven could be carried out for all 2^5 or 2^3 candidates for $c_0^{(6)}$ or $c_0^{(7)}$, respectively. This would increase the number of candidates to $2^5 \cdot 2^8 = 2^{13}$ and $2^3 \cdot 2^8 = 2^{11}$. For this amount of candidates, a CPA can still be executed efficiently.

5 Conclusion

In this paper, we presented a practical, non-invasive side-channel attack on the SimonsVoss 3060 system, allowing to extract the system key from a door lock in an installation. The attack requires approximately 150 EM traces which can be recorded in approximately 15 min using our current measurement setup. An adversary possessing the system key ultimately gains access to all doors of the entire installation.

Reverse-engineering the embedded code of the PIC μC enabled the profiling and the development of a suitable prediction function for the CPA. Surprisingly, the cryptanalytical weakness of the employed obscurity function (highly linear structure, slow avalanche effect) together with its specific usage in the key derivation (input largely constant) require a more complicated SCA compared to attacking a standard cipher, e.g., DES or AES.

Note that the mathematical attacks of [20] can be fixed with a firmware update that is currently being prepared by SimonsVoss. In contrast, preventing the SCA without replacing all hardware components (locks and transponders) is very difficult in our opinion. The program memory and the RAM of the PIC of the lock are almost fully utilized. This rules out the implementation of countermeasures, e.g., masking, requiring an (even slightly) increased program size or RAM usage. Randomizing the timing of the algorithms appears likely to be ineffective, because (i) clear patterns in the EM trace can be detected and (ii) no suitable entropy source is available. Furthermore, software countermeasures could again be reverse-engineered and closely inspected on a program-code level.

The most important lesson to be learned from the demonstrated attack is that the overall security of a system depends on the weakest link in the chain: The cryptographic algorithm used by SimonsVoss, i.e., a DES core combined with an obscurity function that obfuscates the input and output bytes of the DES and enlarges the key length to 128 bit, provided a reasonable level of security: As long as the proprietary scheme remained undisclosed, neither a brute-force attack nor mathematical cryptanalysis of the unknown cipher were a practical option. Likewise, an analysis of the protocol and SCA attacks targeting a hypothesized cipher were fruitless.

One single factor, however, overthrew the security of the SimonsVoss system: a vulnerability of the PIC microcontroller that enables to bypass the code read-out protection. Without this weakest link of the chain and the respective central step of the analysis—reverse-engineering the program code—probably no feasible (mathematical and implementation) attacks would have been found.

A   SimonsVoss Authentication Protocol

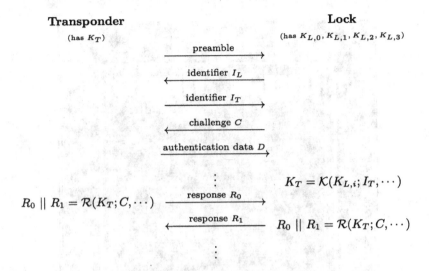

Fig. 7. Protocol for the mutual authentication between a transponder and a lock

B   SimonsVoss Proprietary ASIC

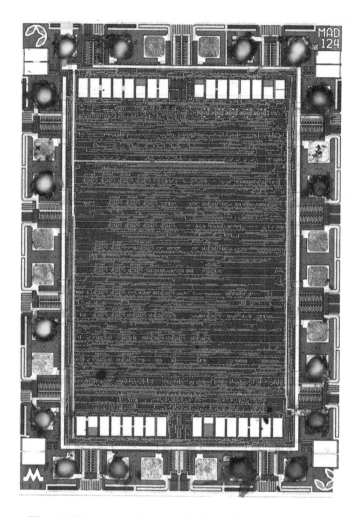

Fig. 8. Microscope photograph of the SimonsVoss ASIC

References

1. Aerts, W., Biham, E., De Moitié, D., De Mulder, E., Dunkelman, O., Indesteege, S., Keller, N., Preneel, B., Vandenbosch, G., Verbauwhede, I.: A Practical Attack on KeeLoq, pp. 1–22. Springer, New York (2010)
2. Beck, F.: Präparationstechniken Für Die Fehleranalyse an Integrierten Halbleiterschaltungen. VCH Verlagsgesellschaft, Weinheim (1988)

3. Blaze, M.: Rights amplification in master-keyed mechanical locks. IEEE Secur. Priv. **1**(2), 24–32 (2003). http://www.crypto.com/papers/mk.pdf

4. Bogdanov, A.: Attacks on the keeloq block cipher and authentication systems. In Workshop on RFID Security (RFIDSec'08) (2007). http://rfidsec07.etsit.uma.es/slides/papers/paper-22.pdf

5. Bono, S.C., Green, M., Stubblefield, A., Juels, A., Rubin, A.D., Szydlo, M.: Security analysis of a cryptographically-enabled RFID device. In: Proceedings of the 14th Conference on USENIX Security Symposium, vol. 14. USENIX Association (2005) http://www.usenix.org/events/sec05/tech/bono/bono.pdf

6. Brier, E., Clavier, C., Olivier, F.: Correlation power analysis with a leakage model. In: Joye, M., Quisquater, J.-J. (eds.) CHES 2004. LNCS, vol. 3156, pp. 16–29. Springer, Heidelberg (2004)

7. Courtois, N.: The dark side of security by obscurity - and cloning mifare classic rail and building passes, anywhere, anytime. In SECRYPT, pp. 331–338. INSTICC (2009)

8. Eisenbarth, T., Kasper, T., Moradi, A., Paar, C., Salmasizadeh, M., Shalmani, M.T.M.: On the power of power analysis in the real world: a complete break of the KEELOQ code hopping scheme. In: Wagner, D. (ed.) CRYPTO 2008. LNCS, vol. 5157, pp. 203–220. Springer, Heidelberg (2008)

9. Ettus Research. USRP N200/210 Networked Series (2012). https://www.ettus.com/content/files/07495_Ettus_N200-210_DS_Flyer_HR_1.pdf

10. Garcia, F.D., van Rossum, P., Verdult, R., Schreur, R.W.: Wirelessly pickpocketing a mifare classic card. In: IEEE Symposium on Security and Privacy, pp. 3–15. IEEE (2009)

11. Goldack, M.: Side-Channel Based Reverse Engineering for Microcontrollers. Diploma thesis, Ruhr-University Bochum (2008). https://www.emsec.rub.de/media/attachments/files/2012/10/da_goldack.pdf

12. Hex-Rays. IDA Starter Edition. http://www.hex-rays.com/products/ida/processors.shtml as of 24 July 2013

13. Huang, A.: Hacking the PIC 18F1320 (2005). http://www.bunniestudios.com/blog/?page_id=40 as of 24 July 2013

14. Mangard, S., Oswald, E., Popp, T.: Power Analysis Attacks: Revealing the Secrets of Smart Cards. Springer (2007). http://www.dpabook.org

15. Microchip Technology Inc. PIC16F882/883/884/886/887 Data Sheet (2009). http://ww1.microchip.com/downloads/en/devicedoc/41291f.pdf

16. Oswald, D., Paar, C.: Breaking mifare DESfire MF3ICD40: power analysis and templates in the real world. In: Preneel, B., Takagi, T. (eds.) CHES 2011. LNCS, vol. 6917, pp. 207–222. Springer, Heidelberg (2011)

17. Plötz, H., Nohl, K.: Legic Prime: Obscurity in Depth (2009). http://events.ccc.de/congress/2009/Fahrplan/attachments/1506_legic-slides.pdf

18. SimonsVoss Technologies AG. SimonsVoss posts record sales yet again in (2011). http://www.simons-voss.us/Record-sales-in-2011.1112.0.html?&L=6 as of 24 July 2013

19. SimonsVoss Technologies AG. Infocenter - Downloads (2006). http://www.simons-voss.com/Downloads.45.0.html?&L=1 as of 24 July 2013

20. Strobel, D., Driessen, B., Kasper, T., Leander, G., Oswald, D., Schellenberg, F., Paar, Ch.: Fuming acid and cryptanalysis: handy tools for overcoming a digital locking and access control system. In: Canetti, R., Garay, J.A. (eds.) CRYPTO 2013, Part I. LNCS, vol. 8042, pp. 147–164. Springer, Heidelberg (2013)

21. Verdult, R., Garcia, F.D., Balasch, J.: Gone in 360 seconds: Hijacking with Hitag2. In USENIX Security Symposium, pp. 237–252. USENIX Association, August 2012. https://www.usenix.org/system/files/conference/usenixsecurity12/sec12-final95.pdf
22. Eric W. Weisstein. Variance. Mathworld - A Wolfram Web Resource, December 2010. http://mathworld.wolfram.com/Variance.html
23. Wikipedia. Differential Manchester Encoding – Wikipedia, The Free Encyclopedia (2012). Accessed 12 November 2012
24. Zonenberg, A.: Microchip PIC12F683 teardown (2011). http://siliconexposed.blogspot.de/2011/03/microchip-pic12f683-teardown.html

Author Index

Aranha, Diego F. 3

Barreto, Paulo S.L.M. 3
Bauer, Aurélie 553
Benadjila, Ryad 324
Berger, Thierry P. 289
Bogdanov, Andrey 306
Bos, Joppe W. 438, 471
Bouillaguet, Charles 205, 513
Buchmann, Johannes 48, 402

Cabarcas, Daniel 402
Cheng, Chen-Mou 205
Cheon, Jung Hee 121
Chou, Tung 205
Collard, Baudoin 306
Costello, Craig 438

De Mulder, Yoni 265
Delerablée, Cécile 247
Doche, Christophe 456

Eisenbarth, Thomas 223
El Bansarkhani, Rachid 48

Geng, Huizheng 306
Göloğlu, Faruk 136
Göptert, Flurian 402
Granger, Robert 136
Güneysu, Tim 68
Guo, Jian 324

Henry, Kevin 89
Hu, Gengran 29
Hülsing, Andreas 402

Isobe, Takanori 155

Jaulmes, Eliane 553
Jean, Jérémy 533
Jing, Jiwu 421
Joux, Antoine 355

Kasper, Timo 571
Khovratovich, Dmitry 174
Kim, Taechan 121

Lepoint, Tancrède 247, 265
Liu, Zongbin 421
Lomné, Victor 324
Longa, Patrick 3

Ma, Yuan 421
McGuire, Gary 136
Minier, Marine 289
Montgomery, Peter L. 471
Morii, Masakatu 155

Naehrig, Michael 438
Naya-Plasencia, María 533
Niederhagen, Ruben 205

Ohigashi, Toshihiro 155
Oswald, David 571

Paar, Christof 571
Paillier, Pascal 247
Pan, Wuqiong 421
Pan, Yanbin 29
Paterson, Maura B. 89
Peyrin, Thomas 324, 533
Pöppelmann, Thomas 68
Preneel, Bart 185, 265
Prouff, Emmanuel 553

Rechberger, Christian 174
Ricardini, Jefferson E. 3
Rivain, Matthieu 247, 265
Roelse, Peter 265

Sasaki, Yu 493
Schellenberg, Falk 571
Shumow, Daniel 471
Sinha Roy, Sujoy 383
Song, Yong Soo 121
Stinson, Douglas R. 89
Strobel, Daehyun 571
Sutantyo, Daniel 456

Thomas, Gaël 289

Vayssière, Bastien 513
Verbauwhede, Ingrid 383

Vercauteren, Frederik   383
von Maurich, Ingo   223

Wang, Lei   493
Wang, Meiqin   306
Watanabe, Yuhei   155
Weiden, Patrick   402
Wen, Long   306

Wild, Justine   553
Wu, Hongjun   185

Yang, Bo-Yin   205
Ye, Xin   223

Zaverucha, Gregory M.   471
Zhang, Feng   29
Zumbrägel, Jens   136

Printed in the United States
By Bookmasters